BPP College

Library & Information Service

Cases and Materials on UK and EC
Competition Law

D1337928

Cases and Materials on UK and EC Competition Law

Second edition

Kirsty Middleton
Formerly Senior Lecturer in Law, University of Strathclyde

Barry Rodger
Professor of Law, University of Strathclyde

Angus MacCulloch
Senior Lecturer in Law, Lancaster University

Jonathan Galloway
Lecturer in Law, Newcastle University

OXFORD
UNIVERSITY PRESS

OXFORD
UNIVERSITY PRESS

Great Clarendon Street, Oxford OX2 6DP

Oxford University Press is a department of the University of Oxford.
It furthers the University's objective of excellence in research, scholarship,
and education by publishing worldwide in

Oxford New York

Auckland Cape Town Dar es Salaam Hong Kong Karachi
Kuala Lumpur Madrid Melbourne Mexico City Nairobi
New Delhi Shanghai Taipei Toronto

With offices in

Argentina Austria Brazil Chile Czech Republic France Greece
Guatemala Hungary Italy Japan Poland Portugal Singapore
South Korea Switzerland Thailand Turkey Ukraine Vietnam

Oxford is a registered trade mark of Oxford University Press
in the UK and in certain other countries

Published in the United States
by Oxford University Press Inc., New York

© K. Middleton, B. Rodger, A. MacCulloch, and J. Galloway 2009

The moral rights of the author have been asserted

Crown copyright material is reproduced under Class Licence
Number C01P0000148 with the permission of OPSI
and the Queen's Printer for Scotland

Database right Oxford University Press (maker)

First published 2003
Second edition 2009

British Library Cataloguing in Publication Data

Data available

Library of Congress Cataloging-in-Publication Data

Data available Typeset by Newgen

Printed in Great Britain
on acid-free paper by
Ashford Colour Press Ltd. Gosport, Hants

ISBN 978–0–19–929039–0

1 3 5 7 9 10 8 6 4 2

OUTLINE CONTENTS

DETAILED CONTENTS

PREFACE TO THE SECOND EDITION

Competition law remains a popular subject for undergraduate law students who are often introduced to the subject while studying EU law, and who quickly realise it is a fast moving and complex area of law in itself. A study of competition law today requires an understanding of basic economic theory and its role in competition law policy and analysis, it also demands an understanding of the complex jurisdictional issues and procedural powers as well as an appreciation of how the substantive provisions operate. The intention of this text is to equip students with a broad range of materials – case extracts, statutory extracts, policy statements and relevant academic writings – to enable them to study and make sense of this area of law while appreciating its place within the wider legal system. Our goal was to provide students with extracts from a diverse range of US, European and domestic UK sources in the one location in order to facilitate a better awareness and clear understanding of the issues involved. This text should therefore complement most student texts on the subject of UK and EC competition law and will appeal to undergraduate law students studying competition law as part of their LL.B. or B.A. degree.

One of the striking changes since the first edition was published six years ago is the decentralisation of EC competition law, thereby placing greater emphasis on national competition authorities and national courts in competition law enforcement. The first edition was published at a time of great change in EC and UK competition law with Regulation 1/2003 adopted but not yet in force and with many parts of the Enterprise Act 2002 still to enter into force. Materials and commentary in this edition highlight how the new EC framework is operating and covers recent UK activity marking the nascent use of key powers under the Enterprise Act 2002, such as the criminal cartel offence. The authors have also sought to establish a narrative through the selection of materials to follow the increasing influence of economic theory and analysis in all aspects of competition law. The changing policy focus of EC competition law in particular can be seen from the revised Block Exemption Regulations with respect to the applicability of Article 81(3) EC, the revised ECMR, Regulation 139/2004, and other aspects of the December 2002 reform package, and also the recent review of Exclusionary Practices under Article 82 EC culminating with the December 2008 European Commission guidance. Several other developments required significant change from the first edition, including the efforts aimed at facilitating private enforcement of competition law, to which we have devoted a new chapter, and there is also a new chapter on cartels and leniency. The recent financial crisis, which has re-opened the debate on the objectives of competition policy and its role within society, also merits coverage in Chapter 13 on UK merger control and Chapter 14 on State aid. This new edition should allow students to understand the key institutions, laws and processes involved in EC and UK competition law in a simple and accessible way.

We owe a great deal of thanks to Alex Clabburn and his colleagues at OUP for their patience and efficiency in seeing the second edition through to publication. We would also like to thank our colleagues, past and present for their understanding, encouragement and support in the course of this project.

Barry J Rodger
Angus MacCulloch
Jonathan Galloway
June 2009

The second edition has seen a change in the author team with Jonathan Galloway working alongside Barry Rodger and Angus MacCulloch, while Kirsty Middleton was not an active contributor in light of commitments elsewhere.

ACKNOWLEDGMENTS

The authors and publishers would like to thank the following for permission to reproduce copyright material:

Sweet & Maxwell Ltd: extract from European Law Review: Arnull, "Competition, the Commission and Some Constitutional Questions of More than Minor Importance" [1998] 23 ELR 1; extracts from European Competition Law Review: Willimsky, 'The Concept(s) of Competition' [1997] 1 ECLR 54; Ahdar, R., 'Consumers' Redistribution of Income and the Purpose of Competition Law', [2002] ECLR 34; Galloway, J., 'The Pursuit of National Champions: the Intersection of Competition Law and Industrial Policy', [2007] ECLR 272; Majumdar, A., 'Whither Dominance?' [2006] ECLR 161; Paterson, L., 'The Power Of The Puppy – Does Advertising Deter Entry' [1997] ECLR 337; Ridyard, D., 'Essential facilities and the Obligation to Supply Competitors Under the UK and EC Competition Law' [1996] 17(8) ECLR 438; Bergman, M.A., 'The Bronner Case - A Turning Point for the Essential Facilities Doctrine' [2000] 21(2) ECLR 59;Rodger, B.J., 'Reinforcing the Scottish "Ring-fence": A Critique of UK Mergers Policy vis-à-vis the Scottish Economy' [1996] ECLR 104; Rodger, B.J., 'UK Merger Control: Politics, the Public Interest and Reform' [2000] ECLR 24; Rodger, B.J., 'State Aid – A Fully Level Playing Field?' [1999] ECLR 251; Abbamonte, G.B., 'Market Economy Investor Principles: A Legal Analysis of an Economic Problem' [1996] ECLR 258

Oxford University Press: extracts from Faul & Nikpay (eds): EC Law of Competition (second edition, Oxford, 2007); extracts from Oxford Yearbook of European Law Vol 7 Whish, R., and Sufrin, B., 'Article 85 and the Rule of Reason' [1987] 7 YEL 1; extracts from Gerber, D: Law and Competition in Twentieth Century Europe: Protecting Prometheus, (Oxford, 1998)

Hart Publishing: Extracts from Amato, G., Antitrust and the Bounds of Power, (Hart, 1997); Extracts from Rodger, B.J., and MacCulloch, A. (eds): The UK Competition Act: A New Era for UK Competition Law, Hart, 2000

Columbia Journal of European Law: extracts from Columbia Journal of European Law: Rodger, B.J., 'The Oligopoly Problem and the Concept of Collective Dominance: EC Developments in the Light of US Trends in Antitrust Law and Policy' Vol. 2, No 1, 1995/96; Rodger, B.J., 'Competition Policy, Liberalism and Globalization: A European Perspective, Columbia Journal of European Law, 6/3, Fall 2000

Kluwer: Extracts from World Competition: Andreangeli, A: 'Toward an EU Competition Court: "Article-6-Proofing" antitrust proceedings before the Commission?' (2007) 30 World Comp 595. Extracts from Common market Law Review: Hawk, B.E., 'System Failure: Vertical Restraints and EC Competition Law' (1995) 32 CML Rev, p. 973

Tony Mason: Extracts from Wilks, S., In the Public Interest, Competition Policy and the Monopolies and Mergers Commission, Manchester, MUP, 1999

American Society of International Law: Extract from American Journal of International Law: Lowenfield, A.F., 'Conflict, Balancing of Interests, and the Exercise of Jurisdiction to Prescribe: Reflections on the Insurance Antitrust Case' (1995) 89 AJIL 42

Every effort has been made to trace and contact copyright holders prior to publication but this has not been possible in every case. If notified the publisher will undertake to rectify any omissions or errors at the earliest opportunity.

DEDICATION

For Susan, Kirsty and Euan

B.J.R.

For Lucy, Coll and Connor

A.M.

For Lisa

J.G.

TABLE OF CASES

*Page numbers in **bold** indicate that the text is reproduced in full.*

Numerical Table European Court of Justice

Court of First Instance

TABLE OF STATUTES

*Page numbers in **bold** indicate that the text is reproduced in full.*

TABLE OF STATUTORY INSTRUMENTS

*Page numbers in **bold** indicate that the text is reproduced in full.*

TABLE OF UNITED STATES STATUTES

*Page numbers in **bold** indicate that the text is reproduced in full.*

National Legislation

Statutes of the Courts of Justice

TABLE OF EUROPEAN MATERIAL

*Page numbers in **bold** indicate that the text is reproduced in full.*

Treaties and Conventions

Decisions

Guidelines

Notices

1

Competition law and policy

SECTION 1: **INTRODUCTION**

What is meant by competition? *The Oxford English Dictionary* defines competition as the 'striving of two or more for the same object'. In a commercial context, competition is defined as 'rivalry in the market'.

Willimsky, S., 'The Concept(s) of Competition'
[1997] 1 ECLR 54 [footnotes omitted]

Competition is the principal regulator of commercial forces in a capitalist market, presuming that individual competitors' motivating force derives from the pursuit of self-interest. The struggle for superiority in the marketplace is defined by the objective to persuade consumers on grounds of quality and value to make a particular purchase.

...

Competition policy is deeply embedded in the way one views human nature and the role of society and the state. The liberal view of the state and man, driven by self-interest as the supreme motivating force, favoured a more classical model of competition. Posner, for example, clearly favoured the view of individuals as rational maximisers of wealth. To advocate a more regulatory and interventionist model would, according to this view, unnecessarily interfere with the proper quasi-Darwinist pursuit for superiority and the natural selection of the most efficient market participants. It is believed that only selection as expressed through consumer choice, would lead to an equilibrium of demand and supply and hence further the interests of society as a whole. Adam Smith's 'invisible hand' as opposed to the very visible hand of the state would, according to this view, lead to the best overall solution.

Marxist social theory and the way human nature is perceived leads to the diametrically opposed view of competition. It would necessarily lead to a system whereby political and economic strands of thought would inevitably be closely intertwined with the perception of man as only one part of a greater web of society. Of course, it has to be remembered that even the crudest capitalist systems present a framework with a number of highly complex social, economic and political strata. However, the underlying value base is freedom as opposed to actual social equality and social justice and this general principle forms the foundations of commercial activity, assuming that the commercial and political ends are not separable.

Is there a difference between competition and competition policy?

Doern, G.B., Chapter 2, 'Comparative Competition Policy: Boundaries and Levels of Political Analysis', in Doern, G.B., and Wilks, S. (eds), *Comparative Competition Policy: National Institutions in a Global Market*
OUP, 1996, p. 7 [footnote omitted]

Competition policy consists of those policies and actions of the state intended to prevent certain restraints of trade by private firms. Stated more positively, it is policy intended to promote rivalry among firms, buyers, and sellers through actions in areas of activity such as mergers, abuse of dominance, cartels, conspiracies in restraints of trade, misleading advertising, and related criminal and economic offences that are held to be anti-competitive.

...

Competition and competition policy are not the same thing. However, understanding the former is crucial, and it starts with economics and economists. Understanding the latter means one has to deal with politics, because it is states that make public policies, and political interests and institutions that determine their implementation in practice.

NOTE: Whish notes that 'the competitive process contains an inevitable paradox. Some competitors win. By being the most innovative, the most responsive to customers' wishes, and by producing goods or services in the most efficient way possible, one firm may succeed in seeing off its rivals. It would be strange, and indeed harmful, if that firm could then be condemned for being a monopolist'. Whish, R., *Competition Law*, 6th edn, Oxford, OUP, 2008, p. 15. The paradox explained by Whish therefore requires a balance to be achieved between providing incentives for efficiency and innovation in the market whilst also ensuring competitive constraints exist so as to secure the longer-term success of the market. Jenny offers his view on the appropriate balance to be achieved.

Jenny, F., Chapter 16, 'Globalization, competition and trade policy: convergence, divergence and cooperation', in Jones, C.A., and Matsushita, M., *Competition policy in the global trading system: perspectives from the EU, Japan and the USA*
Kluwer, 2002, at pp. 300–1 [footnotes omitted]

The actual functioning of markets for goods and services depends on various considerations. Entrepreneurship, endowment in natural resources and level of technological development are all important. Equally important is the fact that trade liberalization allows foreign firms to challenge domestic firms. Beyond this, and as we just mentioned, there is the recognition that because firms do not operate in a vacuum, the legal environment of business in any country will be an important determinant of actual competition. Finally, there is the fact that business strategies will shape the intensity of competition.

The market process is a decentralized process based on the notion that individual strategic behavior by myriads of firms and consumers will be consistent with general welfare only to the extent that firms face competitive pressure. In other words, whereas the natural inclination of each firm would be to eliminate competition, they must be prevented from doing this so as to keep them under the pressure of having to produce at the lowest possible cost and sell at the lowest possible price to consumers. In the absence of such a mechanism, the expected overall benefits of decentralized decision making will be partly lost and transformed into rents by monopolistic firms.

The major goal of competition law is thus to allow firms to take advantage of business opportunities and to make sure that through the competitive process the actual working of decentralized markets will foster static and dynamic economic efficiency to the fullest possible extent given the regulatory environment of these markets.

NOTE: One very important aspect of competition law and policy is the ongoing policy debate, often played out within the context of individual cases, as to whether the balance described above has been correctly achieved. US antitrust will generally place greater weight on providing incentives for innovation than protecting competitive constraints. A different tone from Jenny's argument is discernable from the US Supreme Court.

Verizon Communications v *Law Offices of Curtis V Trinko*
540 US 398, 407 (2004)

The mere possession of monopoly power, and the concomitant charging of monopoly prices, is not only not unlawful; it is an important element of the free-market system. The opportunity to charge monopoly prices—at least for a short period—is what attracts "business acumen" in the first place; it induces risk taking that produces innovation and economic growth. To safeguard the incentive to innovate, the possession of monopoly power will not be found unlawful unless it is accompanied by an element of anticompetitive *conduct*.

NOTE: It is clear from *Trinko* that US antitrust seeks to ensure clear incentives are in place to encourage efficiency and innovation, and by demonstrating a willingness to accept monopoly power, albeit with limitations, the existence of competitors in the market place is not an objective in itself. Bishop and Walker also warn against intervention to simply secure the presence of competitors in the market.

Bishop, S., and Walker, M., *The Economics of EC Competition Law, Concepts, Application and Measurement*
Sweet & Maxwell, 2002, Chapter 1, pp. 13–15 [footnotes omitted]

On an intuitive level, effective competition might be equated with the process of rivalry. Such a definition is intuitively appealing since rivalry is the means by which a competitively structured industry creates and confers its benefits. Moreover, competition law investigations often arise in those situations in which rivalry is eliminated, e.g. by merger or through a cartel agreement. But this definition of effective competition provides no benchmarks for how much rivalry is required for competition to be effective and invites the erroneous conclusion that the elimination of rivalry must always be deemed to be anti-competitive or restrictive of competition.

. . .

Rather than always being anti-competitive, reductions in rivalry may be pro-competitive in the sense that they increase consumer welfare.

Hence, such a definition of effective competition is entirely inappropriate for the purposes of competition law. It would make rivalry an end in itself, regardless of whether the elimination of some rivalry had any substantive negative effect on consumer welfare. One must recognise that all market economies require there to be some elimination of rivalry, since this is necessary to every integration or co-ordination of productive economic efforts and to the specialisation of effort. As Bork notes:

No firm, no partnership, no corporation, no economic unit containing more than a single person could exist without the elimination of some kinds of rivalry between persons.

■ QUESTION

Is the intent to eliminate rivals an inherent part of a free market, and when should competition law intervene to protect competition in the market?

SECTION 2: **PERFECT COMPETITION**

Competition law seeks to address anti-competitive behaviour and instances of market failure. In order to correctly identify when these problems exist, and consider how best to remedy them, it is necessary to have an economic model of how a market could operate in ideal conditions, while recognizing that 'real life' markets will have many imperfections.

Willimsky, S., 'The Concept(s) of Competition'
[1997] 1 ECLR 54 [footnotes omitted]

The basic ideological premise about human nature also has to be viewed in context with the objectives of competition. 'Perfect competition' is a goal in which economic resources are allocated between different goods and services in exactly those quantities which reflect consumer demand, reflected in the price consumers are prepared to pay for goods. This basic utopian ideal is, of course, very difficult to attain and some would even question whether it would be desirable to pursue in any case.

There are, for example, sectors which ought to be 'inefficient', be it for economic reasons (for example agriculture) or for reasons of safety, such as transport. Sometimes, for R&D purposes, for instance, experts in a particular field have to be granted 'time out' from the competitive race in order to develop new drugs, etc., in situations where the drive for efficiency would not allow for such an investment in terms of time and money.

Allocative efficiency is also a term which denotes the state of a market in which resources are allocated precisely in accordance with consumer demand. Pursuant to the neo-classical theory, it is presumed that under allocative efficiency, where competition is perfect, a producer will increase output to the point at which marginal cost and marginal revenue, the net addition to revenue of selling the last unit, coincide. Consequently, a reduction in his own output cannot affect the market price and so there would be no reason to limit it.

Productive efficiency is achieved when a producer is unable to sell above cost: if he did, he would lose customers. He would of course not sell below it, presuming that each producer wishes to maximise profits. If a producer were to charge above cost, other competitors would enter the market in the hope of undercutting the other competitors, charging below price and therefore acquiring a large market share. Eventually, the point will be reached where price and average cost of producing goods coincide, i.e. price would not rise above cost. The combined effect of allocative and productive efficiency is that society's wealth is maximised.

NOTE: Consumer welfare is furthered in a theoretical model when the market is in a state of 'perfect competition' due to the presence of allocative and productive efficiency, i.e. static efficiency, but this involves an incomplete discussion of the benefits that may accrue from the operation of an ideal market.

Peeperkorn, K., and Verouden, V., Chapter 1, 'The Economics of Competition', in Faull, J., and Nikpay, A. (eds), *The EC law of Competition*
2nd edn, Oxford, OUP, 2007, at paras 1.117–1.118 [footnotes omitted] by permission of Oxford University Press

1.117 The static welfare analysis…does not take dynamic aspects of competition, most notably innovation, into account. Technological developments are abstracted away, by assuming the level of technology as constant. This of course is at best reflective of reality in the short term and certainly not in the longer term. In the real world product markets develop and change over time because of innovation; improved or new products and production processes are introduced. New or improved products will in general lead to greater consumer satisfaction and improved or new production processes will lead to lower production costs. In other words, these dynamic efficiencies lead to welfare gains. A proper welfare analysis of market power should thus not only take the static but also the dynamic efficiencies into account and in case the rate of innovation is affected by the market structure or the level of competition it may be necessary to assess any trade-off between static and dynamic efficiencies.

1.118 There is agreement that competition is the driving force for static allocative efficiency. Competition forces companies in a market with a given technology to offer the best quality products at the lowest prices. However, it is also a generally accepted and well-substantiated point of view that innovation is the main source of increases in economic welfare. The literature shows that technological innovation together with an increased ability on the part of the labour force are the main driving forces behind productivity gains and welfare growth. This explains why societies in general try to spur the creation and dissemination of innovation. In case of a choice between dynamic and static efficiencies, the former will quickly outweigh the latter.

NOTE: While Peeperkorn and Verouden do not suggest that static and dynamic efficiency are mutually exclusive it is clear that competition policy may have to prioritize one over the other in certain cases, a particularly live issue in 'new economy' markets. See discussion in Peeperkorn, L., 'IP licences and competition rules: striking the right balance' (2003) World Comp 527.

Recognizing that perfect competition is a 'basic utopian idea' as suggested by Willimsky, some economists have advanced the theory of 'workable competition' which is regarded as a compromise approach. The theory of workable competition rests on the assumption that firms should strive to attain the most competitive structure possible and has been invoked on a number of occasions by the Commission and the European Court. The concept could be seen as allowing for the pursuit of policy objectives, other than maximization of consumer welfare, through the application of competition law.

In Case 26/76 *Metro-SB-Grossmarkte GmbH & Co KG* v *Commission* [1977] ECR 1875 the European Court held that:

> The requirement contained in Articles 3 and 85 of the EEC Treaty that competition shall not be distorted implies the existence on the market of workable competition, that is to say the degree of competition necessary to ensure the observance of the basic requirements and attainment of the objectives of the Treaty, in particular the creation of a single market achieving conditions similar to those of a domestic market.

■ **QUESTION**

Should competition law prioritize price competition (resulting from static efficiencies) over innovation (resulting from dynamic efficiency)?

SECTION 3: GOALS OF COMPETITION

What are the policy objectives of competition? Should competition serve non-political goals? Should the state intervene to re-create a competitive structure? If so, to what extent? Giuliano Amato discusses some of these issues and the ideological tensions inherent in the competition process in his book, *Antitrust and the Bounds of Power*.

Amato, G., ***Antitrust and the Bounds of Power***
Oxford, Hart Publishing, 1997, pp. 2–3

Antitrust law was, as we know, invented neither by the technicians of commercial law (though they became its first specialists) nor by economists themselves (though they supplied its most solid cultural background). It was instead desired by politicians and (in Europe) by scholars attentive to the pillars of the democratic systems, who saw it as an answer (if not indeed 'the' answer) to a crucial problem for democracy: the emergence from the company or firm, as an expression of the fundamental freedom of individuals, of the opposite phenomenon of private power; a power devoid of legitimation and dangerously capable of infringing not just economic freedom of other private individuals, but also the balance of public decisions exposed to its domineering strength.

On the basis of the principles of liberal democracy, the problem was twofold and constituted a real dilemma. Citizens have the right to have their freedoms acknowledged and to exercise them; but just because they are freedoms they must never become coercion, an imposition on others. Power in liberal democratic societies is, in the public sphere, recognized only in those who hold it legitimately on the basis of law, while, in the private sphere, it does not go beyond the limited prerogatives allotted within the firm to its owner. Beyond those limits, private power in a liberal democracy (by contrast with what has occurred, and continues to occur, in societies of other inspirations) is in principle seen to be abusive, and must be limited so that no-one can take decisions that produce effects on others without their assent being given. On the basis of the same principles, the power of government exists specifically to guarantee against the emergence of phenomena of that sort; that is, it exists to protect the freedoms of each against attacks and abuses of others. But this, which is its task, is also its limitation: abuses forbidden for individuals are not allowed for rulers either. Here, then, is the dilemma. How can private power be prevented from becoming a threat to the freedoms of others? But at the same time, how can power conferred on institutions for this purpose be prevented from itself enlarging to the point of destroying the very freedoms it ought to protect.

...

What is coming out again is, then, the crucial issue of the boundary and hence the risk to be run depending where it is set, the risk of 'too much' public power or, contrawise, 'too much' private power.

The dilemma, as we said at the outset, has its roots in the very principles of liberal democracy, affecting first and foremost the interpretations and translations they are given. It is however wrong to think that antitrust law, now free of the initial, improper burden of democratic efficiency, guided by events and the refined doctrines of economists to pay attention to economic efficiency alone, is now immunized against the dilemma and consequently running along such well-defined tracks as to be sheltered from the choices it requires. The error lies not so much in the intervening awareness of the separation between democratic efficiency, which is actually beyond the direct antitrust horizon, and economic efficiency. The error lies in accepting as the truth the one dimensional economic efficiency mentioned earlier. Why should only the restriction of output of a given product, such as to shift demand to second-choice products (to do which society is constrained to higher costs with poorer results), be economically inefficient? This certainly is inefficient, and an agreement or concentration leading to such a result should certainly be prohibited by antitrust law. But who says that 'consumer welfare', the pillar of this notion of efficiency, amounts solely to not having to shift to second choice goods, and is hence satisfied where one or a few satisfy the demand for existing products, without output restrictions? Someone has rightly noted that 'there is a strong tendency among economists to define welfare in terms of efficiency in doing accustomed things in an accustomed way'. But might not consumers regard as serving their welfare the diversity of sources of goods and services, the existence of diversified potential for innovation, as much room as possible for market dynamics that favour the new products not yet designed and ways of producing them not yet designed? Can it be said that all this has nothing to do with economic efficiency just because it shakes up the antitrust views of those economists who feel safer with one-dimensional efficiency? The truth is that there is no one single concept of economic efficiency: there are at least two, and their antitrust implications are in the main different.

NOTE: There are two dominant schools of antitrust thought, the Harvard and Chicago schools. The Chicago scholars believe that the fundamental goal of antitrust is, or ought to be, the pursuit of efficiency, or rather the maximization of allocative efficiency. Certainly, this is a view which Robert Bork, an influential American economist and former Federal Court of Appeals judge associated with the Chicago school, supports.

Bork, R.H., *The Antitrust Paradox: A Policy at War with Itself*

Basic Books, 1978 (reprinted with a new Introduction and Epilogue, 1993), pp. 90–1
[footnotes omitted]

Antitrust is about the effects of business behavior on consumers. An understanding of the relationship of that behavior to consumer well-being can be gained only through basic economic theory. The economic models involved are essential to all antitrust analysis, but they are simple and require no previous acquaintance with economics to be comprehended. Indeed, since we can hardly expect legislators, judges, and lawyers to be sophisticated economists as well, it is only the fact that the simple ideas of economics are powerful and entirely adequate to this field that makes it conceivable for the law to frame and implement useful policy.

Consumer welfare is greatest when society's economic resources are allocated so that consumers are able to satisfy their wants as fully as technological constraints permit. Consumer welfare, in this sense, is merely another term for the wealth of the nation. Antitrust thus has a built-in preference for material prosperity, but it has nothing to say about the ways prosperity is distributed or used. Those are matters for other laws. Consumer welfare, as the term is used in antitrust, has no sumptuary or ethical component, but permits consumers to define by their expression of wants in the marketplace what things they regard as wealth. Antitrust litigation is not a process for deciding who should be rich or poor, nor can it decide how much wealth should be expended to reduce pollution or undertake to mitigate the anguish of the cross-country skier at the desecration wrought by snowmobiles. It can only increase collective wealth by requiring that any lawful products, whether skis or snowmobiles, be produced and sold under conditions most favorable to consumers.

The role of the antitrust laws, then, lies at that stage of the economic process in which production and distribution of goods and services are organized in accordance with the scale of values that consumers choose by their relative willingness to purchase. The law's mission is to preserve, improve, and reinforce the powerful economic mechanisms that compel businesses to respond to consumers. 'From a social point of view,' as Frank H. Knight puts it, 'this process may be viewed under two aspects, (a) the assignment or *allocation* of the available productive forces and materials among the various lines of industry, and (b) the effective *coordination* of the various means of production in each industry into such groupings as will produce the greatest result.'

These two factors may conveniently be called *allocative efficiency* and *productive efficiency*. (When, for convenience, the word 'efficiency' alone is used, productive efficiency is meant.) These two types of efficiency make up the overall efficiency that determines the level of our society's wealth, or consumer welfare. The whole task of antitrust can be summed up as the effort to improve allocative efficiency without impairing productive efficiency so greatly as to produce either no gain or a net loss in consumer welfare. That task must be guided by basic economic analysis, otherwise the law acts blindly upon forces it does not understand and produces results it does not intend.

NOTE: The Chicago school of economists believe that in free markets consumer welfare is optimized, rendering state intervention unnecessary. Even monopolistic markets are acceptable to the Chicago economists and intervention is only required in extreme cases where new entrants are prohibited from the market. However, Bork's thesis, that economic efficiency is the sole pursuit of antitrust, has been criticized. See, e.g. Fox, E.M., and Sullivan, L.A., 'Antitrust-Retrospective and Prospective: Where are we coming from? Where are we going?' (1987) 62 New York Univ Law Rev 936.

Rodger, B.J., 'The Oligopoly Problem and the Concept of Collective Dominance: EC Developments in the Light of US Trends in Antitrust Law and Policy'

Columbia Journal of European Law, Vol. 2, No 1, 1995/96, pp. 28–30 [footnotes omitted]

The 'Harvard School' of analysis had its origins in the 1930s and its work developed into the structure-conduct-performance paradigm within economics: 'Before anyone starts prescribing structural changes to improve performance he had better have some clear and convincing notions about the way oligopolistic structure affects conduct'. Proponents of this paradigm sought to provide the link between the three elements. The economists would justify structurally de-concentrative remedies on an empirical basis, by analyzing each of the three aspects within an industry. The empirical associations thus discovered would reveal the appropriate ramifications for public policy. Though the paradigm has been fiercely criticized, it is still enlightening to view oligopoly antitrust policy through the perspective of the Harvard School: the history and traditions of US antitrust law form an essential backdrop to the continuing debate about its role and purposes. As Sullivan commented, 'American antitrust law is not only about "law" but also a socio-political statement about our society'.

During much of the early development of antitrust law, the political consensus reflected in the law was that high concentration lessened competition—a notion derived from a basically liberal vision of society. This mainstream antitrust tradition was eclectic and its political input was embraced and encapsulated by industrial organization economic theorists, the main link between the economic and the socio-political liberal goals being the skepticism that markets adequately control market power. This is one of Sullivan's main contentions, namely that 'behind the theorizing, a political ideology can often be identified'.

The Harvard, or Structuralist, School of industrial economics placed great emphasis on market structure as the root of market failure. In particular, it stressed that excessive concentration of market power resulted in undeservedly high profits. Parallel to the academic prominence the theory achieved in the 1960s and 1970s, the Warren Court appeared to adopt a similar broad-based appeal to social and political objections with concern for increasing concentration, particularly in dealing with horizontal mergers. An essential element in this mainstream tradition was its more open acknowledgment of political objectives, though in practice, as Sullivan highlights, this skeptical tradition is both pragmatic and seldom doctrinaire.

The basic features of the Chicago School of antitrust law and economic analysis were formulated by the work of Aaron Director in the 1950s, and developed by his students—Bowman, Bork, McGee and Telsen, among others. This tradition approaches antitrust problems through the 'lens of price theory': 'In their intellectual universe, antitrust is embodied in a reductionist paradigm; antitrust concerns the functioning of markets; microeconomics is the study of the functioning of markets; therefore antitrust is microeconomics'.

The Chicago School tends to focus on two 'truths'. The first is the advocacy of the efficient allocation of resources by the market: antitrust ought only to intervene in cases where not to do so would result in the inefficient allocation of resources. A preliminary criticism of this approach is that the Chicago School adopts static models as the basis of its efficiency principle. The main problem, however, lies in the second 'truth,' derived from the first: that 'Chicago beliefs are only compatible with the most minimal law'. Consequently the role of antitrust law and government intervention in the functioning of markets is greatly reduced. This is, perhaps, a logical consequence of the Chicago School's presumption of the efficiency of firms and the functioning of markets, but, as Fox observes, the latter is not a 'descriptive observation … [but] … simply argument supporting the normative claim that people (including firms) should be left free to act and that there is almost never a higher social interest.' Thus the aim of the Chicago School seems to be 'keeping government out' and always seeking the least disruptive way to correct market failures. Flynn concludes that behind the Chicago School lies 'a simplistic form of deductive reasoning reaffirming the theological postulates underlying the model without regard for the reality under investigation or the moral ends of the law in question and the moral consequences those ends dictate'. In any event, the instalment of President Reagan in 1980 (who promised to curtail government's role in business), resulted in the administration's adoption of the Chicago School approach, and as a result, government enforcement of antitrust came to an ebb. However, even during that period, the Supreme Court never fully embraced the concept that only efficiency mattered.

As observed above, the two starting points of specific analysis—structure and conduct—are inextricably linked. Though the theoretical differences in approach are important, it is largely a matter of emphasis, linked to wider perceptions of the kind of 'important social judgements that should be made'.

The rapprochement between the two approaches has been particularly noted by Larner and Meehan. They comment on the recent rise of a new school of industrial economics in response to the Chicago School, seeking to analyze the effect of strategic behavior on competition under certain circumstances. Although wary of overemphasizing the importance of concentration, they recognize the need for further research. The identification of market power is crucial, but it is no substitute for in-depth analysis of the market. Larner and Meehan find that the structural concept of competition is analytically and practically admirable as a policy norm because of its essential simplicity. But although structural analysis is an essential element, it is inadequate: they conclude that 'while behavior is now subject to closer scrutiny and analysis than in the structural view, concentration is still an early and important component in any competitive analysis'.

Ahdar, R., 'Consumers' Redistribution of Income and the Purpose of Competition Law'
[2002] ECLR, 341–353

No one would deny that competition law is, broadly speaking, designed to advance the lot of consumers. Even Bork agrees: '[a]ntitrust is about the effects of business behaviour on consumers'. But, as we shall see, Bork's conception of consumers is strikingly at odds with the normal understanding. To understand the issues more fully it is helpful to invoke Oliver Williamson's trade-off model. This depicts the economic effects of a merger that results in both an increase in market power and cost savings

Based on certain strict assumptions (the merging firms are duopolists, the product is homogeneous, etc. Williamson's model sought to show that society may still be better off despite the monopoly enhancement that transpires. Following the merger, the firm's market power has increased: the firm reduces its output from Q1 to Q2 and price rises from P1 to P2. The loss in allocative efficiency is represented by triangle A1 (the deadweight loss). This is the bad news. The good news is that the acquisition generates cost savings represented by the firm's level of average costs dropping, postmerger, from AC1 to AC2. The net allocative effect is ascertained by comparing the triangle (A1) with the rectangle (A2). Williamson demonstrated that a merger promising 'nontrivial economies—say greater than 2 per cent—will generally yield a net-efficiency gain'. Now there have been all sorts of qualifications and criticisms levied at this model which need not detain us here. What is of present concern is another effect of the increased market power. This is the income distribution effect (or wealth transfer).

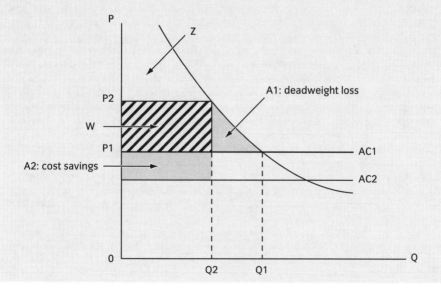

The striped rectangle, W, immediately above rectangle A2, 'represents a loss of consumers' surplus (gain in monopoly profits) that the merger produces'. Income (or wealth) is transferred from consumers to producers, from the purchasers of the product to the owners of the company. Is this redistribution a concern of competition law? This issue has generated much debate, but before revisiting it, it is important to note that, generally speaking, vigorous competition policy operates to advance both efficiency and distributive goals simultaneously. Curtailing monopolies, oligopolies and cartels will generally enhance both aggregate social wealth and the consumers' share of that wealth. Kenneth Elzinga explains:

> Antitrust enforcement generally serves to help those at the low end of the income distribution range without decreasing efficiency. Antitrust achieves this double benefit when it promotes efficiency in resource allocation by preventing the cartelization or monopolization of a market shopped in by low-income buyers. The reason is straightforward: prices will be lower in the market so that for any given income, however low, a larger basket of goods and services can be purchased. Antitrust policy, therefore, need not concern itself directly with increasing the purchasing power of the poor because it accomplishes this indirectly when it prohibits cartels and monopolies in the single-minded pursuit of efficiency.

Actually, it is probably more accurate to say antitrust policy achieves the goals of superior economic performance (growth, innovation, efficiency) and 'equity' goals (greater income equality, dispersion of concentrated economic and political power, fostering business opportunity and so on) through the single-minded pursuit of competition.

Competition policy generally harmonises the goals of efficiency and egalitarian income distribution. There are occasions however, when, as Williamson's model demonstrates, an anti-competitive arrangement or merger may be beneficial in terms of net efficiency and yet result in a transfer of income from consumers to producers. There are two major responses to this phenomenon: first, ignore the redistribution, or, secondly, address it.

Ignore redistribution

The stance of Chicagoans, amongst others, is to ignore the transfer of wealth. If it is a concern at all, it is not a matter for competition law. Other arms of public policy are better suited to deal with the phenomenon. But what about consumers? Was not antitrust, according to Bork, 'about the effects of business behaviour on consumers'? Bork maintains that the sole goal of antitrust law is to forward 'consumer welfare'. How is consumer welfare advanced by customers paying higher prices in the form of monopoly profits that enrich the pockets of the corporate owners? The Chicagoan answer is that consumer welfare is really another name for allocative efficiency or total welfare:

> Consumer welfare is greatest when society's economic resources are allocated so that consumers are able to satisfy their wants as fully as technological constraints permit. Consumer welfare, in this sense, is merely another term for the wealth of the nation. Antitrust thus has a built-in preference for material prosperity, but it has nothing to say about the ways prosperity is distributed or used.

To backtrack a little: total welfare comprises both consumer surplus (or welfare) and producer surplus. Defining consumer welfare as total welfare enables consumer welfare to be 'advanced' so long as producers gain—and even though consumers' lot is worsened. When monopoly occurs, a consumer surplus is expunged and becomes a producer surplus (monopoly profits) but this is fine since total welfare is still enhanced. Thus, the redistribution should be ignored.

In conventional neoclassical welfare economics the redistribution of income is, as Williamson puts it, 'a matter of indifference' and 'is treated as a wash'. Scherer affirms: '[i]n the standard analysis of efficiency, the redistribution is of no concern. It merely reflects a robbing of Peter (the consumer) to pay Paul (the producer), and since Paul may be more deserving than Peter, who knows whether society is worse off as a consequence?' This stance is sometimes reinforced by invoking Hume's law, 'that a dollar is a dollar'.

Hume's law means that if two persons are bidding at an auction for a seaside cottage and a poor homeless family is outbid by a wealthy family wishing to own a seaside weekender, the result is efficient. The house has been placed in the hands of those who offer the more dollar votes. The effect of Hume's law is to divorce consideration of the allocation of resources from consideration of the distribution of wealth (or income).

A sort of conjuring trick is involved here. Producers (the minority) are defined to be consumers whose welfare interests count equally, dollar for dollar, with those of consumers who are not producers (the majority). Bork brazenly glides over this.

Those who continue to buy after a monopoly is formed pay more for the same output, and that shifts income from them to the monopoly and its owners, who are also consumers. This is not a deadweight loss due to the restriction in output but merely a shift in income between two classes of consumers.

Consumers still benefit because producers are consumers too. Two supporting defences are sometimes advanced. First, submits Bork, some consumers are richer and more deserving than producers. Elzinga's example of artists who make handcraft porcelain might be what Bork had in mind. Would this justify price fixing by poorly renumerated producers? Antitrust law tradition-ally says 'no', indeed, a New Zealand decision refused to countenance price fixing by rural grape growers whose product would eventually be consumed by affluent, urban wine drinkers. Yet while there are some products manufactured by struggling producers and acquired by the rich, the vast majority of goods and services (electricity, bread, milk, petrol, dentistry) are not in this category. A second defence is similarly unconvincing. Some producers, being companies, are composed of numerous shareholders. In other words, some consumers may be producers. Again that is true but only for a minority of the population, and the more affluent section at that.

When the substantive merits of the wealth transfer are difficult to defend, the Chicagoan gam-bit is to stress the inappropriateness of entertaining the distributional question at all. Williamson acknowledged that the redistribution of income under monopoly produces 'social discontent'. Bork grudgingly conceded it may cause some but this was a matter for the legislature, not the courts, to address. The latter are simply the wrong institution to make 'these unstructured inter-personal comparisons'. The decision whether, to use Scherer's parlance, Peter is more deserving than Paul (or vice versa) is simply too subjective: '[t]here is no common denominator between these values, and there is no economics, no social science, no systematized knowledge of any sort that can provide criteria for making the trade-off decision'. Attempts to evaluate distributional matters is simply 'distracting' and to do it thoroughly would 'introduce horrendous complexities in which it is surely undesirable to mire the processes of antitrust'. Antitrust is better suited to the advance-ment of allocative efficiency leaving income distribution objectives to 'the province of taxation, expenditure, and transfer payment activities'. Dealing with distributional concerns in competition law is tantamount to 'tinkering and is apt to be unrewarding, because a massive reshaping of the system is really needed'.

Address redistribution

Let us return to the Chicagoan definition of consumer welfare as total welfare (or allocative efficiency). This is plainly wrong. Consumer welfare means 'consumer surplus'. Returning to Williamson's diagram, the consumer surplus prior to the merger was the entire area above AC1, (the triangle A1, the rectangle W, and Z, the white area above W). Following the merger, the con-sumer surplus has shrunk to Z alone—A1 is totally expunged, a deadweight social loss, and W redounds to the producer. Consumer surplus captures the notion that consumers receive more value from consuming a good than the money value they must pay to the seller. In less technical language it represents 'the direct and explicit economic benefits received by consumers of a par-ticular product as measured by its price and quality'. It 'embraces what individual consumers are entitled to expect from a competitive economy'. Bork's redefinition of consumer welfare was counterintuitive and disingenuous, 'an Orwellian term of art that has little or nothing to do with the welfare of true consumers'!

The redistribution of income is said to be 'neutral'. This is a strange concept of neutrality for it means countenancing the betterment of a small, generally richer, collection of 'consumers' (corpor-ate owners) at the expense of the multitude of less affluent consumers. How can a phenomenon (mon-opoly) which 'tends to tilt the income and wealth distributions toward greater inequality' be regarded with benign indifference? This link between monopoly and maldistribution of wealth and income is not pure speculation. There is some empirical evidence that indicates that monopoly power, past and present, has contributed significantly to the above average wealth of the most wealthy families.

The fact that antitrust law operates to advance a more equal distribution of income in society does not mean that competition law is the principal vehicle to secure some fair overall distribution of wealth. No one is arguing competition law is the major or a sufficient redistributive tool. Its contribution here is modest yet, nonetheless, it is still a contribution. Equitable redistribution is another of the many significant indirect benefits or by-products of a policy promoting effective competition.

Economists seem squeamish about the prospect of making value judgments. This seems to be part of a larger project to fashion their discipline into a value-free science. The futility of this venture has been well-exposed by others. Suffice to say economics has ineradicable normative premises that are necessarily political, ideological, and subjective. Fortunately, economists are spared the task of making decisions of a distributional nature as legislatures, including New Zealand's, are quite prepared to say one sector of society is more deserving than another. As Brodley comments: 'to hold that producers perform a civic duty when they systematically take from buyers the entire economic surplus is an Orwellian result that no democratic government could long sustain'. And so history has shown.

Robert Lande has argued convincingly that Congress's main goal in passing the Sherman Act was to protect ordinary consumers from the evils of monopoly:

> Congress's primary aim was to enable consumers to purchase products at competitive prices. Artificially high prices were condemned not for causing allocative inefficiency but for 'unfairly' transforming consumers' wealth into monopoly profits. All purchasers, whether consumers or businesses, were given the right to purchase competitively priced goods.

The political reality is that when it comes to deciding whether consumers are more deserving than producers, the verdict is clear cut. Hume's law is nowhere to be found.

Chicagoans and other efficiency-only advocates seek to avoid subjectivity and awkward value judgments by excluding distributional questions from decision-making. Yet the notion of economic efficiency they posit as the sole objective of antitrust is itself a subjective, ideological choice imbued with an implicit value judgment.

If efficiency is judged under the Kaldor-Hicks or wealth maximisation criterion, the costs and benefits of a rule are valued according to the affected persons' willingness to pay (a hypothetical 'one-dollar, one-vote' referendum). If the beneficiaries of the rule could in theory compensate the losers for their losses and still came out ahead—in other words, if the total benefits exceed the total costs—the rule is efficiency-enhancing, even though the theoretical compensation sums are not paid to the losers. The last point is crucial, for it represents the losses incurred by ordinary consumers. Brian Easton explains: '[b]ut the compensation need not occur, so efficiency may increase but some consumers may be worse off, and there is no obvious, value free reason why this situation should be described as an improvement, without consideration of the distributional implications'. A notion of economic efficiency which ignores distributional effects (and the initial distribution of wealth) is hardly neutral in practice for it appears to encourage inequality in the distribution of income throughout society. It is neutral only if you believe helping the wealthy get wealthier is neutral.

NOTE: The harsh reality of the Chicago school of thought, within which consumer welfare has a narrow meaning, is highlighted by Ahdar who advocates a broader, albeit less predictable, policy approach to antitrust.

■ QUESTION

What other concerns should competition law protect?

Rodger, B.J., 'Competition Policy, Liberalism and Globalization: A European Perspective'
Columbia Journal of European Law, Vol. 6, No 3, Fall 2000, pp. 303–4

In practice there are a number of different economic, social and political objectives which may form part of any particular competition policy. It is often the extent to which these other policies do and should play a role that causes the greatest debate, particularly on the basis that they cause tensions with the standards of the liberal rule of law. Some of these other policies have been termed 'extra-competition' policies or 'non-competition law proper' policies and it has often been suggested that competition law should not be concerned with them. This relates to the concern over the legal/political format of the rules and has consequences upon the method of enforcement of the competition rules. Competition law or policy has no fixed content and is dependent to a great extent upon the particular political and social emphases of the legal system in which it operates. It can therefore be justifiably stated that in applying the core economic thesis which informs competition law, any set of appropriate principles and policies may play a part in a coherent competition law system. Indeed, it has been recognized that the fundamental rationale for the introduction of a set of competition policies has been to promote the economy of a given country.

There are a variety of political objectives which may form part of competition policy, of which the following are examples. The prevention of the concentration of economic power is based on the idea that economic corporations should not become more powerful and influential than elected democratic governments. The dual objectives of the regulation of excessive profits and the more fair distribution of wealth are essentially derived from the neo-classical theory's concern with monopolies. The general idea has been fairly topical recently in the UK despite the advanced debate on incentives to new market entrants created by such excessive profits and the ongoing criticism that the redistribution of wealth should not be a concern of competition law. The protection of consumers is a key feature of most competition laws and is of particular and direct interest in the UK, where the link between consumer policy and competition policy is also highlighted in the UK by the existence of one official, the Director General of Fair Trading, who supervises both areas. [now both areas are within the remit of the Office of Fair Trading]

Regional policy may seem to be a strange component of competition policy but it can be understood given that competition law is part of an overall policy to promote and enhance a national, or other, economy. Thus, regional policy formed a clear part of UK competition policy under the Fair Trading Act 1973. Further, it constituted an overriding consideration in the analysis of a series of mergers which may have proven specifically detrimental to the Scottish economy and which were prohibited under this regional policy criterion. Regional policy is also important under Community law, specifically in relation to state aid, where financial assistance may be allowed for a deprived region of the Community.

The creation of unified markets is a political objective which is related to Community competition policy in particular. This is referred to as a policy of 'market integration' and is crucial to European competition policy. It is derived from the overall aim of integrating the markets of Member States to create a more united Europe. The concept of 'small is beautiful' seeks to foster smaller companies' ability to compete more directly with established powerful companies. One way that it can achieve this is by responding more leniently to forms of cooperation between smaller firms, which might involve the sharing of technology. The promotion of SMEs (Small and Medium-sized Enterprises) is a particular goal of the Community authorities as it is believed that such companies may start to compete across national frontiers and hence indirectly support the market integration policy.

NOTE: US antitrust scholars and authorities have traditionally been the most critical of so-called 'extra-competition' policies, which has led to tension at times in relations with the European Commission given that the latter must consider other policy objectives due to the EC legislative and institutional framework.

Galloway, J., 'The Pursuit of National Champions: The Intersection of Competition Law and Industrial Policy'
[2007] ECLR 172 at 173–5

The question as to what are appropriate objectives for competition law has always been a source of vigorous debate within the field, and highlights disparities between competition authorities from many different jurisdictions. There remains no definitive answer to this question, although it is clear that objectives have changed over time, and have converged upon greater weight being given to economic rather than political objectives. Since the Chicago School of thought took hold in

US antitrust during the Reagan administration, the US authorities have consistently been of the opinion that the economic concept of maximisation of consumer welfare is the only legitimate goal of competition/antitrust policy, and while there are different models of consumer welfare, the field of debate has narrowed somewhat. The emphasis on consumer welfare is not a view that every jurisdiction shares however, which is problematic given that there are now in excess of 100 jurisdictions with competition laws of some description.

The European Commission, one of the leading competition authorities in international affairs along with the Antitrust Division of the US Department of Justice, certainly cannot subscribe to such a view, for while it endorses consumer welfare as the predominant objective of modern competition law, there have been clear instances of additional policy goals being furthered through the application of EC competition law. This should not be surprising as EC competition policy is set within the legislative framework of the EC Treaty which sets out a number of other objectives. Thus it is perhaps clear that EC competition policy will always have to contribute towards the overriding political objective of the day, whether that is market integration or increasing competitiveness to secure growth and jobs. Confirmation of the multiple objectives approach of EC competition law and policy can be seen from Regulation 139/2004 on the control of concentrations (the ECMR). Recital 23 of the ECMR places the system providing for merger control within its wider context by stating:

> "the Commission must place its appraisal within the general framework of the achievement of the fundamental objectives referred to in Article 2 of the Treaty establishing the European Community and Article 2 of the Treaty on European Union."

Furthermore, non-competition factors have strongly influenced the Commission's approach to other areas of competition law aside from merger control, notably the early approach to enforcing Art.81(1) EC, and the exercise of its powers under Art.83 EC to adopt block exemption Regulations. However, the adoption of the Block Exemption Regulation on vertical agreements in 1999 does appear to have marked a significant shift in policy and has brought economic rationale firmly to the fore. The shift in emphasis has continued with the revised Technology Transfer Block Exemption Regulation in 2004. The OECD's peer review report of competition law and policy in the EU acknowledged the multiple objective approach of EC competition law but also commented on the increasing importance of consumer welfare:

> "With progress toward realisation of the internal market, the relative importance of the market integration goal has declined. Policy statements now stress efficiency, consumer welfare and competitiveness. The mission statement of DG Competition sets out a number of possible goals, including in the same sentence both the welfare of consumers and the competitiveness of the European economy."

NOTE: The EC Treaty and the operation of the College of Commissioners serves to ensure that EC competition law and policy cannot exist in a vacuum independent from the other policy objectives of the European Union or the priorities of the European Commission. Nonetheless legislative reforms in the approach to agreements (see Chapters 6, 8, and 9) and merger control (see Chapter 12), as well as a shift in policy with regards to unilateral conduct (see Chapter 10) all further a more economic analysis and effects-based approach to EC competition law enforcement. The gradual trend towards excluding 'extra-competition' policies from competition law is, however, controversial in difficult economic conditions when public pressure for protectionist measures increases, and the necessity of protecting vital national infrastructure (such as the banking sector) takes priority over competition policy. The impact of the financial crisis originating in late 2008 is highlighted in Chapters 13 and 14 on UK merger control and State aid respectively.

Section 4: COMPETITION PROBLEMS

Vigorous debate continues in relation to two issues that have only recently arisen as serious considerations for competition law in Europe: private enforcement and criminal sanctions. Both issues are a significant part of the dynamic along with investigatory powers, fines, and leniency programmes which seeks to maximize deterrence, detection, and availability of damages in competition law.

Komninos, A.P., *EC Private Antitrust Enforcement: Decentralised Application of EC Competition Law by National Courts*
Oxford, Hart Publishing, 2008, at xiii

Private antitrust enforcement has been a very familiar subject in the United States. This was not the case in Europe until recently. If a book on private enforcement of EC competition law had been published 15 years ago, few in Europe would have understood its title, and perhaps fewer would have read it. There are many reasons for the current interest in such a subject. These may be seen from two angles: from the Community law angle and from the competition law angle. From the first angle, one can mention as explanations the development of the decentralised application of Community law, the maturity of the relationship between Community and national law, the increased inroads made by the Community into private law and, as always, the Court of Justice's determination to safeguard the effectiveness of Community law and ever increase Community citizens' effective judicial protection and their access to a court, in particular to the juges communautaire de droit commun. From the competition law angle, we can mention the steady establishment in Europe of a competition culture, the acquisition of a sufficient degree of confidence by the European Commission as antitrust enforcer, the realisation of the need to enforce the competition rules effectively and to punish competition law infringements severely, the will to bring in more agents for the enforcement of the Treaty competition rules, such as national competition authorities and courts, and ultimately the inevitable decentralisation of competition law enforcement in today's Europe of 27 Member States.

Whish, R., *Competition Law*
6th edn, Oxford, OUP, 2008, p. 498 [footnotes omitted]

There is a very real sense today among the world's competition authorities that, if competition law is about one thing above all, it is the detection and punishment of hard-core cartels. In the European Union Mario Monti, the former Commissioner for Competition, once described cartels as 'cancers on the open market economy', and the Supreme Court in the US has referred to cartels as 'the supreme evil of antitrust'. At both a moral and a practical level there is not a great deal of difference between price fixing and theft. US law has for many decades treated hard-core cartels as *per se* infringements of the Sherman Act and as criminal offences, punishable not only by fines but also by the imprisonment of individuals. In 2008 the House of Lords, the highest appeal court in the UK, reached the conclusion that some forms of price fixing amount to the crime of conspiracy to defraud at common law: in other words some cartels could lead to the imprisonment of individuals even without the specific criminal cartel offence established by section 188 of the Enterprise Act 2002. A significant consequence of this judgment is that price-fixing agreements may therefore be criminal offences in many countries throughout the world whose legal systems are based on the common law of the UK, irrespective of whether they have adopted their own domestic competition laws or, where they have adopted such laws, of whether they contain specific criminal sanctions.

NOTE: Efforts aimed at stimulating private enforcement of competition law and the hardening of the EC and UK authorities' approach to hard-core cartels in recent years are discussed in Chapters 4 and 9 respectively.

SECTION 5: US ANTITRUST

The starting point for competition laws may be traced to US antitrust. The Sherman Act 1890 is the earliest example of a competition law system and remains in force today. The Supreme Court in *US* v *Topco* (1972) described the antitrust laws as the 'Magna Carta of free enterprise' and compared them to the Bill of Rights. Section 1 of the Sherman Act states:

> Every contract, combination in the form of trust or otherwise, or conspiracy, in restraint of trade or commerce among the several States, or with foreign nations, is hereby declared to be illegal. Every person who shall make any contract or engage in any combination or conspiracy hereby declared to be illegal shall be declared to be guilty of a felony.

Section 2 states:

> Every person who shall monopolize, or attempt to monopolize, or combine or conspire with any other person or persons, to monopolize any part of the trade or commerce among several States, or with foreign nations, shall be deemed guilty of a felony.

The influence of US antitrust scholars on the development of competition laws throughout the world has been profound. See, e.g. Bork above.

■ **QUESTION**

In 1970 Neale commented that 'There is evidence that the aims and scope of antitrust have changed a good deal since the passage of the Sherman Act, and may easily change some more in the future'. What are the goals of US antitrust? How have they changed since 1890? See, e.g. the Harvard v Chicago debate outlined in excerpts from Ahdar, Bork, and Rodger above.

SECTION 6: EC COMPETITION LAW

The creation of a single market has been the overriding aim of the Community since its inception and the commitment to free market principles is evident throughout the treaties. The main objectives of the Community are articulated as follows:
   Article 2 (as amended) states that:

> The Community shall have as its task, by establishing a common market and an economic and monetary union and by implementing common policies or activities referred to in Articles 3 and 4, to promote throughout the Community a harmonious, balanced and sustainable development of economic activities, a high level of employment and of social protection, equality between men and women, sustainable and non-inflationary growth, a high degree of competitiveness and convergence of economic performance, a high level of protection and improvement of the quality of the environment, the raising of the standard of living and quality of life, and economic and social cohesion and solidarity among Member States.

Article 3 (as amended) lists the means necessary to achieve the goals in Article 2 and requires in para. (g) the institution of:

> a system ensuring that competition in the common market is not distorted.

The Ninth Report on Competition Policy presents an authoritative view of the policy objectives of Community competition policy almost three decades ago.

Commission Ninth Report on Competition Policy
(1980) pp. 9–12

The first fundamental objective is to keep the common market open and unified... There is... a continuing need—and this is the primary task of the Community's competition policy—to forestall and suppress restrictive or abusive practices of firms attempting to divide up the market again so as to apply artificial price differences or impose unfair terms on their consumers...

It is an established fact that competition carries within it the seeds of its own destruction. An excessive concentration of economic, financial and commercial power can produce such far-reaching structural changes that free competition is no longer able to fulfil its role as an effective regulator of economic activity. Consequently, the second fundamental objective of the Community's competition policy must be to ensure that at all stages of the common market's development there exists the right amount of competition in order for the Treaty's requirements to be met and its aims attained. The desire to maintain a competitive structure dictates the Commission's constant vigilance over abuses by dominant firms...

Thirdly, the competition system instituted by the Treaty requires that the conditions under which competition takes place remain subject to the principle of fairness in the market place [these principles are]...

First, equality of opportunity must be preserved for all commercial operators in the common market. A second aspect of the principle of fairness in the market place is the need to have regard to the great variety of situations in which firms carry on business... this factor makes it necessary to adapt the Community competition rules so as to pay special regard in particular to small and medium [size] firms that lack strength.

Finally, equity demands that the Commission's competition policy takes account of the legitimate interests of workers, users and consumers.

NOTE: A comparison with a more recent Commission Annual Report demonstrates the clear shift in emphasis away from the operation of the Common Market towards the efficiencies generated by the *relevant* market and the overall impact on consumer welfare.

Commission 2006 Report on Competition Policy
Foreword by Commissioner Neelie Kroes, p. 3

The experience of the past fifty years of European integration shows that fair and undistorted competition in a single market works to the benefit of everyone in terms of prosperity, consumer choice, and sustainable employment.

'Free competition' is not an end in itself—it is a means to an end. When we strive to get markets working better, it is because competitive markets provide citizens with better goods and better services, at better prices. Competitive markets provide the right conditions for companies to innovate and prosper, and so to increase overall European wealth. More wealth means more money for governments to use to sustain the fabric of our societies and to guarantee social justice and a high-quality environment for generations to come.

When companies fix prices in markets like beer or elevators, customers pay higher prices and the economy at large picks up the bill. When companies abuse a dominant position, they not only exclude competitors but also dampen innovation since other companies know that however good their products are, they cannot compete on the merits. So our European anti-trust rules outlaw such behaviour throughout the Union, to the benefit of consumers.

European companies need to be able to take advantage of an open internal market, by creating efficiencies of scale and diversifying. Our merger control rules allow European champions to grow on their merits, developing into global players, provided that consumers are not harmed through reduced competition.

Our properly balanced state aids discipline prevents undue state intervention which would distort competition on the merits, but also increasingly helps Member States to target support where it is most effective in filling genuine gaps in the overall public interest, and so get real added value for tax-payers' money.

The spirit and objectives underlying the European competition rules, and the need to enforce them effectively, remain as pertinent today as ever before. But of course the environment in which competition policy functions changes and develops over time. European companies, employees and consumers are increasingly part of a global economy, and are having to adjust to reap the benefits globalisation has to offer.

■ QUESTION

Korah has previously suggested that 'integration has been elevated by the Commission and the Court to a goal in itself, more important than efficiency'. To what extent does this remain true today?

Gerber, D., *Law and Competition in Twentieth Century Europe: Protecting Prometheus*
OUP, 1998, pp. 347–8 by permission of Oxford University Press

2. Integration and the goals of competition law

The goal of a unified market dominated the process of constructing the competition law system, because it was *the* central impetus for the 'new Europe'. As Barry Hawk has put it, 'Single market integration, and the elimination of restrictive practices which interfere with that integration, is the first principle of EEC antitrust law . . .' This 'unification imperative' has shaped institutional structures and competences within the system, supplied much of its legitimacy, and generated the conceptual framework for the development and application of its substantive norms.

To begin to appreciate the centrality and force of this idea, one need only recall that economic co-operation was the last remaining hope for a co-operative Europe that would banish the specter of that continent's nationalist past. Attempts to move toward political union had been rejected, and the plans for a European Defense Community had been defeated. If there was to be a new Europe, it would have to be built on economic co-operation and integration.

In addition to this political goal of replacing conflict with co-operation, the Common Market was seen as serving a variety of economic goals. Above all, many viewed it as necessary for further economic improvement. European national markets were seen as too small to support significant economic growth. Moreover, an integrated market would allow European firms to acquire sufficient size to compete effectively on world markets, and consumers would benefit from a Europe-sized market with its concomitant economies of scale.

Many Europeans also saw economic integration as the only means of dealing with the combined economic and political power of the United States. These were the years of the Jean-Jacques Servan-Schreiber's famous *Défi Américain*, the 'American Challenge' to Europe, and an integrated market represented a means of regaining independence, power, and status *vis-à-vis* the country that had assumed world leadership in the wake of two world wars.

This does not mean that there was no interest in obtaining the generic benefits of competition. There was. Both the Commission and the Court referred at times to the potential benefits—lower prices, more rapid technological progress, etc.—anticipated as a result of improved competition. These references were imbedded, however, in a discourse and practice that was focused on economic integration. In particular, it is important to remember that socialist thought was still highly influential in many parts of Europe at this time, and thus there were political disincentives to associating competition law too closely with the protection of the competitive process as such.

Furthermore, there was little reason to distinguish between the two goals. They were related, and they reinforced each other. To the extent that competition law eliminated obstacles to the flow of goods, services, and capital across European borders, for example, it served the cause of unifying the market while simultaneously benefiting consumers by increasing the number of actual and potential competitors on European markets.

In the next extract Gerber asserts that market integration will not be the dominant concern in future years.

Gerber, D., *Law and Competition in Twentieth Century Europe:*
Protecting Prometheus
OUP, 1998, pp. 388–9

This uncertainty is exacerbated by increasing demands for accommodation between competition law goals and other goals of the Community. Trade policy, social concerns and environmental claims, *inter alia*, demand to be reconciled with the objectives of competition law. Consequently, just as the keystone of the existing goal structure is being removed—and in part because of the imminence of that removal—lateral pressure on that structure from other values and policies is increasing, generating even further uncertainty about the roles of competition law.

One response has been to turn toward more 'generic' competition law goals—that is, generic benefits associated with protecting the process of competition. Such goals have lived in the shadow of the integration imperative since the foundational period, but they have been little explored in their own right, primarily because integrationist and generic goals have been intermingled, and there has been little reason to distinguish between them. This has led to the assumption that 'unbundling' these goals will change little, and to a lack of concern about the potential impact of eliminating integrationist goals. The assumption remains unexamined, however, shielded from examination not only by the natural resistance to changing one's conceptual framework, but also by the political risks of doing so.

Yet removal of the integration imperative necessarily alters competition law goal structures and the discourse associated with them. Without it, there will be increased pressure on DG IV's decision-makers to articulate other goals with far more care than in the past. Should market efficiency be the sole goal? If not, which other values should be served and how should they relate to each other—that is, what should be the new goal structure?

NOTE: Gerber was prescient in predicting a move away from the 'integration imperative' and the debate as to whether market efficiency should be the sole goal of competition policy remains as relevant today as it was two decades ago.

A: Treaty provisions

The Community's rules on competition can be found in Articles 81–6 EC which apply to undertakings, private and public. Articles 81 and 82 EC in particular, are the cornerstones of Community competition policy. Articles 87–9 EC apply to State aid. Article 81 EC prohibits agreements, decisions, or concerted practices, which have an anti-competitive object or effect, whereas Article 82 EC prohibits an abuse of a dominant position. These articles are not mutually exclusive and complement the free movement of goods provisions, Articles 18–25 EC and 28–30 EC.

As previously explained, the theory and practice of competition law is inextricably tied to economics. See, e.g. the Chicago versus Harvard debate above. The following extracts explain the important role of economics in EC competition law although the authors' comments are not limited to EC law.

Peeperkorn, K., and Verouden, V., Chapter 1, 'The Economics of Competition', in Faull, J., and Nikpay, A. (eds), *The EC law of Competition*

2nd edn, OUP, 2007, at paras 1.01–1.04 [footnotes omitted] by permission of Oxford University Press

1.01 Nowadays, there is a clear awareness among competition policy makers, competition lawyers and judges of the importance of economics for their daily work. In the EU and in the US it is normal practice to discuss competition cases in terms of economic concepts such as market power, entry barriers, and sunk costs, and to evaluate cases according to their effects on the market. Competition policy is economic policy concerned with economic structures, economic conduct, and economic effects. It is for this reason that in a book on competition law an introduction to the economics of competition is of importance.

1.02 The growing acceptance and importance of economics in competition policy raises questions regarding the usefulness of economics, both for devising competition rules and for deciding on competition cases. A word of caution is appropriate in this respect. Economic thinking and economic models have proved not to be perfect guides.

1.03 Economic theories and models are built on and around assumptions. This approach has the benefit of making explicit the various elements relied upon in arriving at a particular conclusion or insight. At the same time, these assumptions by definition do not cover (all) real world situations. In addition, when the assumptions are changed the outcomes of the models may look very different. It is for these reasons that the application of economic theories may not always be able to give a clear and definite answer, for example as to what will happen in a market when companies merge, or when companies try to collude or engage in specific types of conduct.

1.04 The best that the application of economic principles can do in general is to provide a coherent framework of analysis, to provide relevant lines of reasoning, to identify the main issues to be checked in the context of certain theories of competitive harm, and possibly to exclude certain outcomes. In other words, it helps to tell the most plausible story. In individual cases it will be necessary first to find the concepts and the model that best fit the actual market conditions of the case and then to proceed with the analysis of the actual or possible competition consequences. Economic insights can also be useful in the formulation of policy rules, indicating under what conditions anti-competitive outcomes are very unlikely, very likely, or rather likely, and helping to devise safe harbours.

SECTION 7: UK COMPETITION LAW

The objectives of UK competition law have evolved considerably since the 1970s leading towards a relatively depoliticized and effects-based approach to enforcement, but the most prominent objective is that deriving from the Competition Act 1998, to harmonize the substantive provisions of UK competition law with EC competition law and to ensure consistent interpretation.

COMPETITION ACT 1998 [S. 60]

Principles to be applied in determining questions

60.—(1) The purpose of this section is to ensure that so far as is possible (having regard to any relevant differences between the provisions concerned), questions arising under this Part in relation to competition within the United Kingdom are dealt with in a manner which is consistent with the treatment of corresponding questions arising in Community law in relation to competition within the Community.

(2) At any time when the court determines a question arising under this Part, it must act (so far as is compatible with the provisions of this Part and whether or not it would otherwise be required to do so) with a view to securing that there is no inconsistency between—

    (a) the principles applied, and decision reached, by the court in determining that question; and

    (b) the principles laid down by the Treaty and the European Court, and any relevant decision of that Court, as applicable at that time in determining any corresponding question arising in Community law.

(3) The court must, in addition, have regard to any relevant decision or statement of the Commission.

(4) Subsections (2) and (3) also apply to—

    (a) the [OFT]; and

    (b) any person acting on behalf of the [OFT], in connection with any matter arising under this Part.

(5) In subsections (2) and (3), "court" means any court or tribunal.

(6) In subsections (2)(b) and (3), "decision" includes a decision as to—

    (a) the interpretation of any provision of Community law;

    (b) the civil liability of an undertaking for harm caused by its infringement of Community law.

NOTE: The consistent and harmonious application of UK and EC competition law is essential given that the laws are not mutually exclusive and that the UK national competition authority, the Office of Fair Trading('OFT'), has an obligation to enforce EC competition law under certain conditions as a result of Regulation 1/2003 (OJ L1/1, 2003). Nonetheless the UK has also prioritized the objective of further enhancing the deterrent effect of its competition laws, as can be seen from the introduction of the criminal cartel offence and possibility of director disqualification: see Chapters 3 and 9.

FURTHER READING:

Foer, A.A., Chapter 21, 'The goals of antitrust: thoughts on consumer welfare in the US', in Marsden, P. (ed), *Handbook of Research in Trans-Atlantic Antitrust* (Cheltenham, Edward Elgar, 2006).

Fox, E.M., and Sullivan, L.A., 'Antitrust-retrospective and prospective: Where are we coming from? Where are we going?' (1987) 62 New York Univ Law Rev 936.

Frazer, T., 'Competition Policy after 1992: The Next Step' (1990) 53 MLR 609.

Furse, M., 'The role of competition policy: a survey' [1996] ECLR 250.

Niels, N., 'Collective Dominance: More than Just Oligopolistic Interdependence' [2001] ECLR 168.

Pera, A., 'Changing Views of Competition, Economic Analysis and EC Antitrust Law' (2008) 4 Euro CJ 127.

Rodger, B.J., 'Competition Policy, Liberalism and Globalization: A European Perspective', Columbia Journal of European Law, Vol. 6, No 3, Fall 2000.

Wood, D.P., 'The Role of Economics and Economists in Competition Cases' [1999] OECD Journal of Competition Law and Policy, Vol. 1/1.

2

EC enforcement

When examining the current enforcement regime for the Community competition rules, it is important to start with some indication of the administrative structure which instigated EC competition law enforcement in the 1960s. The current structure was adopted in Regulation 1/2003/EC and came into force in 2004. It was described as the most important change in competition law since the introduction of the original enforcement mechanism. The first system was set out in Regulation 17/62. The enforcement regime is used to enforce both Article 81 and 82 EC, but much of the debate on enforcement powers occurs in relation to the peculiarities of Article 81 EC. There are separate enforcement arrangements for merger control, discussed in Chapter 12.

Regulation No 17: First Regulation Implementing Articles 81 and 82 of the Treaty

OJ, Spec Ed 1962, No 204/62, p. 87, as amended by Regulation 1216/1999/EC, OJ, 1999, L148/5

Article 1 Basic provision

Without prejudice to Articles 6, 7 and 23 of this Regulation, agreements, decisions and concerted practices of the kind described in Article 85(1) of the Treaty and the abuse of a dominant position in the market, within the meaning of Article 86 of the Treaty, shall be prohibited, no prior decision to that effect being required.

Article 2 Negative clearance

Upon application by the undertakings or associations of undertakings concerned, the Commission may certify that, on the basis of the facts in its possession, there are no grounds under Article 85(1) or Article 86 of the Treaty for action on its part in respect of an agreement, decision or practice.

Article 3 Termination of infringements

1. Where the Commission, upon application or upon its own initiative, finds that there is infringement of Article 85 or Article 86 of the Treaty, it may by decision require the undertakings or associations of undertakings concerned to bring such infringement to an end.

2. Those entitled to make application are:
   (a) Member States;
   (b) natural or legal persons who claim a legitimate interest.

3. Without prejudice to the other provisions of this Regulation, the Commission may, before taking a decision under paragraph 1, address to the undertakings or associations of undertakings concerned recommendations for termination of the infringement.

Article 4 Notification of new agreements, decisions and practices

1. Agreements, decisions and concerted practices of the kind described in Article 85(1) of the Treaty which come into existence after the entry into force of this Regulation and in respect of which the parties seek application of Article 85(3) must be notified to the Commission. Until they have been notified, no decision in application of Article 85(3) may be taken.

2. Paragraph 1 shall not apply to agreements, decisions or concerted practices where:

(1) the only parties thereto are undertakings from one Member State and the agreements, decisions or practices do not relate either to imports or to exports between Member States;

[2.(a) the agreements or concerted practices are entered into by two or more undertakings, each operating, for the purposes of the agreement, at a different level of the production or distribution chain, and relate to the conditions under which the parties may purchase, sell or resell certain goods or services;

(b) not more than two undertakings are party thereto, and the agreements only impose restrictions on the exercise of the rights of the assignee or user of industrial property rights, in particular patents, utility models, designs or trade marks, or of the person entitled under a contract to the assignment, or grant, of the right to use a method of manufacture or knowledge relating to the use and to the application of industrial processes.]

(3) they have as their sole object:

(a) the development or uniform application of standards or types; or

[(b) joint research and development;

(c) specialisation in the manufacture of products, including agreements necessary for the achievement thereof;

— where the products which are the subject of specialisation do not, in a substantial part of the common market, represent more than 15 per cent of the volume of business done in identical products or those considered by consumers to be similar by reason of their characteristics, price and use, and

— where the total annual turnover of the participating undertakings does not exceed 200 million units of account.

These agreements, decisions and concerted practices may be notified to the Commission.]

Article 6 Decisions pursuant to Article 85(3)

1. Whenever the Commission takes a decision pursuant to Article 85(3) of the Treaty, it shall specify therein the date from which the decision shall take effect. Such date shall not be earlier than the date of notification.

2. The second sentence of paragraph 1 shall not apply to agreements, decisions or concerted practices falling within Article 4(2) and Article 5(2), nor to those falling within Article 5(1) which have been notified within the time limit specified in Article 5(1).

Article 9 Powers

1. Subject to review of its decision by the Court of Justice, the Commission shall have sole power to declare Article 85(1) inapplicable pursuant to Article 85(3) of the Treaty.

2. The Commission shall have power to apply Article 85(1) and Article 86 of the Treaty; this power may be exercised notwithstanding that the time limits specified in Article 5(1) and in Article 7(2) relating to notification have not expired.

3. As long as the Commission has not initiated any procedure under Article 2, 3 or 6, the authorities of the Member States shall remain competent to apply Article 85(1) and Article 86 in accordance with Article 88 of the Treaty; they shall remain competent in this respect notwithstanding that the time limits specified in Article 5(1) and in Article 7(2) relating to notification have not expired.

NOTE: The adoption of Regulation 17 set the tone for the early development of the EC Competition rules, by securing the vital importance of the Commission within the enforcement system. Regulation 17 secured the Commission's position in two ways. First, it gave the Commission the authority and investigatory powers to enforce Articles 81 and 82 EC. Second, it secured the Commission's central role within Article 81 EC by reserving it the sole power to grant exemptions under Article 81(3) EC. This system served the Community well until the 1980s when the Commission began to struggle to deal with its increasing workload. A modernization process began in the 1990s where the Commission consulted on various schemes to reshape the way it worked (see White Paper on modernisation of the rules implementing Article 85 and 86 of the EC Treaty, Commission Programme No 99/027, OJ, 1999, C132/01). The role of the Commission in Article 81(3) was central to that discussion. Eventually the Community adopted a Regulation, Regulation 1/2003/EC which revolutionized the enforcement of competition law. One of the most revolutionary aspects was the direct applicability of Article 81(3) EC. The Commission no longer has sole authority over the application of Article 81(3); it can be applied by the National Competition Authorities or the domestic courts. This allowed for the decentralization of competition enforcement, although the Commission retained a central role.

Regulation 1/2003/EC on the implementation of the rules on competition laid down in Articles 81 and 82 of the Treaty
OJ, 2003, L1/1

CHAPTER I PRINCIPLES

Article 1 Application of Articles 81 and 82 of the Treaty

1. Agreements, decisions and concerted practices caught by Article 81(1) of the Treaty which do not satisfy the conditions of Article 81(3) of the Treaty shall be prohibited, no prior decision to that effect being required.

2. Agreements, decisions and concerted practices caught by Article 81(1) of the Treaty which satisfy the conditions of Article 81(3) of the Treaty shall not be prohibited, no prior decision to that effect being required.

3. The abuse of a dominant position referred to in Article 82 of the Treaty shall be prohibited, no prior decision to that effect being required.

Article 2 Burden of proof

In any national or Community proceedings for the application of Articles 81 and 82 of the Treaty, the burden of proving an infringement of Article 81(1) or of Article 82 of the Treaty shall rest on the party or the authority alleging the infringement. The undertaking or association of undertakings claiming the benefit of Article 81(3) of the Treaty shall bear the burden of proving that the conditions of that paragraph are fulfilled.

Article 3 Relationship between Articles 81 and 82 of the Treaty and national competition laws

1. Where the competition authorities of the Member States or national courts apply national competition law to agreements, decisions by associations of undertakings or concerted practices within the meaning of Article 81(1) of the Treaty which may affect trade between Member States within the meaning of that provision, they shall also apply Article 81 of the Treaty to such agreements, decisions or concerted practices. Where the competition authorities of the Member States or national courts apply national competition law to any abuse prohibited by Article 82 of the Treaty, they shall also apply Article 82 of the Treaty.

2. The application of national competition law may not lead to the prohibition of agreements, decisions by associations of undertakings or concerted practices which may affect trade between Member States but which do not restrict competition within the meaning of Article 81(1) of the Treaty, or which fulfil the conditions of Article 81(3) of the Treaty or which are covered by a Regulation for the application of Article 81(3) of the Treaty. Member States shall not under this Regulation be precluded from adopting and applying on their territory stricter national laws which prohibit or sanction unilateral conduct engaged in by undertakings.

3. Without prejudice to general principles and other provisions of Community law, paragraphs 1 and 2 do not apply when the competition authorities and the courts of the Member States apply

national merger control laws nor do they preclude the application of provisions of national law that predominantly pursue an objective different from that pursued by Articles 81 and 82 of the Treaty.

CHAPTER II POWERS

Article 4 Powers of the Commission

For the purpose of applying Articles 81 and 82 of the Treaty, the Commission shall have the powers provided for by this Regulation.

Article 5 Powers of the competition authorities of the Member States

The competition authorities of the Member States shall have the power to apply Articles 81 and 82 of the Treaty in individual cases. For this purpose, acting on their own initiative or on a complaint, they may take the following decisions:

— requiring that an infringement be brought to an end,
— ordering interim measures,
— accepting commitments,
— imposing fines, periodic penalty payments or any other penalty provided for in their national law.

Where on the basis of the information in their possession the conditions for prohibition are not met they may likewise decide that there are no grounds for action on their part.

Article 6 Powers of the national courts

National courts shall have the power to apply Articles 81 and 82 of the Treaty.

CHAPTER III COMMISSION DECISIONS

Article 7 Finding and termination of infringement

1. Where the Commission, acting on a complaint or on its own initiative, finds that there is an infringement of Article 81 or of Article 82 of the Treaty, it may by decision require the undertakings and associations of undertakings concerned to bring such infringement to an end. For this purpose, it may impose on them any behavioural or structural remedies which are proportionate to the infringement committed and necessary to bring the infringement effectively to an end. Structural remedies can only be imposed either where there is no equally effective behavioural remedy or where any equally effective behavioural remedy would be more burdensome for the undertaking concerned than the structural remedy. If the Commission has a legitimate interest in doing so, it may also find that an infringement has been committed in the past.

2. Those entitled to lodge a complaint for the purposes of paragraph 1 are natural or legal persons who can show a legitimate interest and Member States.

Article 8 Interim measures

1. In cases of urgency due to the risk of serious and irreparable damage to competition, the Commission, acting on its own initiative may by decision, on the basis of a prima facie finding of infringement, order interim measures.

2. A decision under paragraph 1 shall apply for a specified period of time and may be renewed in so far this is necessary and appropriate.

Article 9 Commitments

1. Where the Commission intends to adopt a decision requiring that an infringement be brought to an end and the undertakings concerned offer commitments to meet the concerns expressed to them by the Commission in its preliminary assessment, the Commission may by decision make those commitments binding on the undertakings. Such a decision may be adopted for a specified period and shall conclude that there are no longer grounds for action by the Commission.

2. The Commission may, upon request or on its own initiative, reopen the proceedings:
   (a) where there has been a material change in any of the facts on which the decision was based;

(b) where the undertakings concerned act contrary to their commitments; or

(c) where the decision was based on incomplete, incorrect or misleading information provided by the parties.

Article 10 Finding of inapplicability

Where the Community public interest relating to the application of Articles 81 and 82 of the Treaty so requires, the Commission, acting on its own initiative, may by decision find that Article 81 of the Treaty is not applicable to an agreement, a decision by an association of undertakings or a concerted practice, either because the conditions of Article 81(1) of the Treaty are not fulfilled, or because the conditions of Article 81(3) of the Treaty are satisfied.

The Commission may likewise make such a finding with reference to Article 82 of the Treaty.

CHAPTER IV COOPERATION

Article 11 Cooperation between the Commission and the competition authorities of the Member States

1. The Commission and the competition authorities of the Member States shall apply the Community competition rules in close cooperation.

2. The Commission shall transmit to the competition authorities of the Member States copies of the most important documents it has collected with a view to applying Articles 7, 8, 9, 10 and Article 29(1). At the request of the competition authority of a Member State, the Commission shall provide it with a copy of other existing documents necessary for the assessment of the case.

3. The competition authorities of the Member States shall, when acting under Article 81 or Article 82 of the Treaty, inform the Commission in writing before or without delay after commencing the first formal investigative measure. This information may also be made available to the competition authorities of the other Member States.

4. No later than 30 days before the adoption of a decision requiring that an infringement be brought to an end, accepting commitments or withdrawing the benefit of a block exemption Regulation, the competition authorities of the Member States shall inform the Commission. To that effect, they shall provide the Commission with a summary of the case, the envisaged decision or, in the absence thereof, any other document indicating the proposed course of action. This information may also be made available to the competition authorities of the other Member States. At the request of the Commission, the acting competition authority shall make available to the Commission other documents it holds which are necessary for the assessment of the case. The information supplied to the Commission may be made available to the competition authorities of the other Member States. National competition authorities may also exchange between themselves information necessary for the assessment of a case that they are dealing with under Article 81 or Article 82 of the Treaty.

5. The competition authorities of the Member States may consult the Commission on any case involving the application of Community law.

6. The initiation by the Commission of proceedings for the adoption of a decision under Chapter III shall relieve the competition authorities of the Member States of their competence to apply Articles 81 and 82 of the Treaty. If a competition authority of a Member State is already acting on a case, the Commission shall only initiate proceedings after consulting with that national competition authority.

Article 12 Exchange of information

1. For the purpose of applying Articles 81 and 82 of the Treaty the Commission and the competition authorities of the Member States shall have the power to provide one another with and use in evidence any matter of fact or of law, including confidential information.

2. Information exchanged shall only be used in evidence for the purpose of applying Article 81 or Article 82 of the Treaty and in respect of the subject-matter for which it was collected by the transmitting authority. However, where national competition law is applied in the same case and in parallel to Community competition law and does not lead to a different outcome, information exchanged under this Article may also be used for the application of national competition law.

3. Information exchanged pursuant to paragraph 1 can only be used in evidence to impose sanctions on natural persons where:
— the law of the transmitting authority foresees sanctions of a similar kind in relation to an infringement of Article 81 or Article 82 of the Treaty or, in the absence thereof,
— the information has been collected in a way which respects the same level of protection of the rights of defence of natural persons as provided for under the national rules of the receiving authority. However, in this case, the information exchanged cannot be used by the receiving authority to impose custodial sanctions.

Article 13 Suspension or termination of proceedings

1. Where competition authorities of two or more Member States have received a complaint or are acting on their own initiative under Article 81 or Article 82 of the Treaty against the same agreement, decision of an association or practice, the fact that one authority is dealing with the case shall be sufficient grounds for the others to suspend the proceedings before them or to reject the complaint. The Commission may likewise reject a complaint on the ground that a competition authority of a Member State is dealing with the case.

2. Where a competition authority of a Member State or the Commission has received a complaint against an agreement, decision of an association or practice which has already been dealt with by another competition authority, it may reject it.

Article 14 Advisory Committee

1. The Commission shall consult an Advisory Committee on Restrictive Practices and Dominant Positions prior to the taking of any decision under Articles 7, 8, 9, 10, 23, Article 24(2) and Article 29(1).

2. For the discussion of individual cases, the Advisory Committee shall be composed of representatives of the competition authorities of the Member States. For meetings in which issues other than individual cases are being discussed, an additional Member State representative competent in competition matters may be appointed. Representatives may, if unable to attend, be replaced by other representatives.

3. The consultation may take place at a meeting convened and chaired by the Commission, held not earlier than 14 days after dispatch of the notice convening it, together with a summary of the case, an indication of the most important documents and a preliminary draft decision. In respect of decisions pursuant to Article 8, the meeting may be held seven days after the dispatch of the operative part of a draft decision. Where the Commission dispatches a notice convening the meeting which gives a shorter period of notice than those specified above, the meeting may take place on the proposed date in the absence of an objection by any Member State. The Advisory Committee shall deliver a written opinion on the Commission's preliminary draft decision. It may deliver an opinion even if some members are absent and are not represented. At the request of one or several members, the positions stated in the opinion shall be reasoned.

4. Consultation may also take place by written procedure. However, if any Member State so requests, the Commission shall convene a meeting. In case of written procedure, the Commission shall determine a time-limit of not less than 14 days within which the Member States are to put forward their observations for circulation to all other Member States. In case of decisions to be taken pursuant to Article 8, the time-limit of 14 days is replaced by seven days. Where the Commission determines a time-limit for the written procedure which is shorter than those specified above, the proposed time-limit shall be applicable in the absence of an objection by any Member State.

5. The Commission shall take the utmost account of the opinion delivered by the Advisory Committee. It shall inform the Committee of the manner in which its opinion has been taken into account.

6. Where the Advisory Committee delivers a written opinion, this opinion shall be appended to the draft decision. If the Advisory Committee recommends publication of the opinion, the Commission shall carry out such publication taking into account the legitimate interest of undertakings in the protection of their business secrets.

7. At the request of a competition authority of a Member State, the Commission shall include on the agenda of the Advisory Committee cases that are being dealt with by a competition authority

of a Member State under Article 81 or Article 82 of the Treaty. The Commission may also do so on its own initiative. In either case, the Commission shall inform the competition authority concerned.

A request may in particular be made by a competition authority of a Member State in respect of a case where the Commission intends to initiate proceedings with the effect of Article 11(6).

The Advisory Committee shall not issue opinions on cases dealt with by competition authorities of the Member States. The Advisory Committee may also discuss general issues of Community competition law.

Article 15 Cooperation with national courts

1. In proceedings for the application of Article 81 or Article 82 of the Treaty, courts of the Member States may ask the Commission to transmit to them information in its possession or its opinion on questions concerning the application of the Community competition rules.

2. Member States shall forward to the Commission a copy of any written judgment of national courts deciding on the application of Article 81 or Article 82 of the Treaty. Such copy shall be forwarded without delay after the full written judgment is notified to the parties.

3. Competition authorities of the Member States, acting on their own initiative, may submit written observations to the national courts of their Member State on issues relating to the application of Article 81 or Article 82 of the Treaty. With the permission of the court in question, they may also submit oral observations to the national courts of their Member State. Where the coherent application of Article 81 or Article 82 of the Treaty so requires, the Commission, acting on its own initiative, may submit written observations to courts of the Member States. With the permission of the court in question, it may also make oral observations.

For the purpose of the preparation of their observations only, the competition authorities of the Member States and the Commission may request the relevant court of the Member State to transmit or ensure the transmission to them of any documents necessary for the assessment of the case.

4. This Article is without prejudice to wider powers to make observations before courts conferred on competition authorities of the Member States under the law of their Member State.

Article 16 Uniform application of Community competition law

1. When national courts rule on agreements, decisions or practices under Article 81 or Article 82 of the Treaty which are already the subject of a Commission decision, they cannot take decisions running counter to the decision adopted by the Commission. They must also avoid giving decisions which would conflict with a decision contemplated by the Commission in proceedings it has initiated. To that effect, the national court may assess whether it is necessary to stay its proceedings. This obligation is without prejudice to the rights and obligations under Article 234 of the Treaty.

2. When competition authorities of the Member States rule on agreements, decisions or practices under Article 81 or Article 82 of the Treaty which are already the subject of a Commission decision, they cannot take decisions which would run counter to the decision adopted by the Commission.

CHAPTER V POWERS OF INVESTIGATION

Article 17 Investigations into sectors of the economy and into types of agreements

1. Where the trend of trade between Member States, the rigidity of prices or other circumstances suggest that competition may be restricted or distorted within the common market, the Commission may conduct its inquiry into a particular sector of the economy or into a particular type of agreements across various sectors. In the course of that inquiry, the Commission may request the undertakings or associations of undertakings concerned to supply the information necessary for giving effect to Articles 81 and 82 of the Treaty and may carry out any inspections necessary for that purpose.

The Commission may in particular request the undertakings or associations of undertakings concerned to communicate to it all agreements, decisions and concerted practices.

The Commission may publish a report on the results of its inquiry into particular sectors of the economy or particular types of agreements across various sectors and invite comments from interested parties.

2. Articles 14, 18, 19, 20, 22, 23 and 24 shall apply mutatis mutandis.

Article 18 Requests for information

1. In order to carry out the duties assigned to it by this Regulation, the Commission may, by simple request or by decision, require undertakings and associations of undertakings to provide all necessary information.

2. When sending a simple request for information to an undertaking or association of undertakings, the Commission shall state the legal basis and the purpose of the request, specify what information is required and fix the time-limit within which the information is to be provided, and the penalties provided for in Article 23 for supplying incorrect or misleading information.

3. Where the Commission requires undertakings and associations of undertakings to supply information by decision, it shall state the legal basis and the purpose of the request, specify what information is required and fix the time-limit within which it is to be provided. It shall also indicate the penalties provided for in Article 23 and indicate or impose the penalties provided for in Article 24. It shall further indicate the right to have the decision reviewed by the Court of Justice.

4. The owners of the undertakings or their representatives and, in the case of legal persons, companies or firms, or associations having no legal personality, the persons authorised to represent them by law or by their constitution shall supply the information requested on behalf of the undertaking or the association of undertakings concerned. Lawyers duly authorised to act may supply the information on behalf of their clients. The latter shall remain fully responsible if the information supplied is incomplete, incorrect or misleading.

5. The Commission shall without delay forward a copy of the simple request or of the decision to the competition authority of the Member State in whose territory the seat of the undertaking or association of undertakings is situated and the competition authority of the Member State whose territory is affected.

6. At the request of the Commission the governments and competition authorities of the Member States shall provide the Commission with all necessary information to carry out the duties assigned to it by this Regulation.

Article 19 Power to take statements

1. In order to carry out the duties assigned to it by this Regulation, the Commission may interview any natural or legal person who consents to be interviewed for the purpose of collecting information relating to the subject-matter of an investigation.

2. Where an interview pursuant to paragraph 1 is conducted in the premises of an undertaking, the Commission shall inform the competition authority of the Member State in whose territory the interview takes place. If so requested by the competition authority of that Member State, its officials may assist the officials and other accompanying persons authorised by the Commission to conduct the interview.

Article 20 The Commission's powers of inspection

1. In order to carry out the duties assigned to it by this Regulation, the Commission may conduct all necessary inspections of undertakings and associations of undertakings.

2. The officials and other accompanying persons authorised by the Commission to conduct an inspection are empowered:
   - (a) to enter any premises, land and means of transport of undertakings and associations of undertakings;
   - (b) to examine the books and other records related to the business, irrespective of the medium on which they are stored;
   - (c) to take or obtain in any form copies of or extracts from such books or records;
   - (d) to seal any business premises and books or records for the period and to the extent necessary for the inspection;
   - (e) to ask any representative or member of staff of the undertaking or association of undertakings for explanations on facts or documents relating to the subject-matter and purpose of the inspection and to record the answers.

3. The officials and other accompanying persons authorised by the Commission to conduct an inspection shall exercise their powers upon production of a written authorisation specifying the subject matter and purpose of the inspection and the penalties provided for in Article 23 in case the production of the required books or other records related to the business is incomplete or where the answers to questions asked under paragraph 2 of the present Article are incorrect or misleading. In good time before the inspection, the Commission shall give notice of the inspection to the competition authority of the Member State in whose territory it is to be conducted.

4. Undertakings and associations of undertakings are required to submit to inspections ordered by decision of the Commission. The decision shall specify the subject matter and purpose of the inspection, appoint the date on which it is to begin and indicate the penalties provided for in Articles 23 and 24 and the right to have the decision reviewed by the Court of Justice. The Commission shall take such decisions after consulting the competition authority of the Member State in whose territory the inspection is to be conducted.

5. Officials of as well as those authorised or appointed by the competition authority of the Member State in whose territory the inspection is to be conducted shall, at the request of that authority or of the Commission, actively assist the officials and other accompanying persons authorised by the Commission. To this end, they shall enjoy the powers specified in paragraph 2.

6. Where the officials and other accompanying persons authorised by the Commission find that an undertaking opposes an inspection ordered pursuant to this Article, the Member State concerned shall afford them the necessary assistance, requesting where appropriate the assistance of the police or of an equivalent enforcement authority, so as to enable them to conduct their inspection.

7. If the assistance provided for in paragraph 6 requires authorisation from a judicial authority according to national rules, such authorisation shall be applied for. Such authorisation may also be applied for as a precautionary measure.

8. Where authorisation as referred to in paragraph 7 is applied for, the national judicial authority shall control that the Commission decision is authentic and that the coercive measures envisaged are neither arbitrary nor excessive having regard to the subject matter of the inspection. In its control of the proportionality of the coercive measures, the national judicial authority may ask the Commission, directly or through the Member State competition authority, for detailed explanations in particular on the grounds the Commission has for suspecting infringement of Articles 81 and 82 of the Treaty, as well as on the seriousness of the suspected infringement and on the nature of the involvement of the undertaking concerned. However, the national judicial authority may not call into question the necessity for the inspection nor demand that it be provided with the information in the Commission's file. The lawfulness of the Commission decision shall be subject to review only by the Court of Justice.

Article 21 Inspection of other premises

1. If a reasonable suspicion exists that books or other records related to the business and to the subject-matter of the inspection, which may be relevant to prove a serious violation of Article 81 or Article 82 of the Treaty, are being kept in any other premises, land and means of transport, including the homes of directors, managers and other members of staff of the undertakings and associations of undertakings concerned, the Commission can by decision order an inspection to be conducted in such other premises, land and means of transport.

2. The decision shall specify the subject matter and purpose of the inspection, appoint the date on which it is to begin and indicate the right to have the decision reviewed by the Court of Justice. It shall in particular state the reasons that have led the Commission to conclude that a suspicion in the sense of paragraph 1 exists. The Commission shall take such decisions after consulting the competition authority of the Member State in whose territory the inspection is to be conducted.

3. A decision adopted pursuant to paragraph 1 cannot be executed without prior authorisation from the national judicial authority of the Member State concerned. The national judicial authority shall control that the Commission decision is authentic and that the coercive measures envisaged are neither arbitrary nor excessive having regard in particular to the seriousness of the suspected infringement, to the importance of the evidence sought, to the involvement of the

undertakingconcernedandtothereasonablelikelihoodthatbusinessbooksandrecordsrelatingtothe subject matter of the inspection are kept in the premises for which the authorisation is requested. The national judicial authority may ask the Commission, directly or through the Member State competition authority, for detailed explanations on those elements which are necessary to allow its control of the proportionality of the coercive measures envisaged.

However, the national judicial authority may not call into question the necessity for the inspection nor demand that it be provided with information in the Commission's file. The lawfulness of the Commission decision shall be subject to review only by the Court of Justice.

4. The officials and other accompanying persons authorised by the Commission to conduct an inspection ordered in accordance with paragraph 1 of this Article shall have the powers set out in Article 20(2)(a), (b) and (c). Article 20(5) and (6) shall apply mutatis mutandis.

Article 22 Investigations by competition authorities of Member States

1. The competition authority of a Member State may in its own territory carry out any inspection or other fact-finding measure under its national law on behalf and for the account of the competition authority of another Member State in order to establish whether there has been an infringement of Article 81 or Article 82 of the Treaty. Any exchange and use of the information collected shall be carried out in accordance with Article 12.

2. At the request of the Commission, the competition authorities of the Member States shall undertake the inspections which the Commission considers to be necessary under Article 20(1) or which it has ordered by decision pursuant to Article 20(4). The officials of the competition authorities of the Member States who are responsible for conducting these inspections as well as those authorised or appointed by them shall exercise their powers in accordance with their national law.

If so requested by the Commission or by the competition authority of the Member State in whose territory the inspection is to be conducted, officials and other accompanying persons authorised by the Commission may assist the officials of the authority concerned.

CHAPTER VI PENALTIES

Article 23 Fines

1. The Commission may by decision impose on undertakings and associations of undertakings fines not exceeding 1% of the total turnover in the preceding business year where, intentionally or negligently:

    (a) they supply incorrect or misleading information in response to a request made pursuant to Article 17 or Article 18(2);

    (b) in response to a request made by decision adopted pursuant to Article 17 or Article 18(3), they supply incorrect, incomplete or misleading information or do not supply information within the required time-limit;

    (c) they produce the required books or other records related to the business in incomplete form during inspections under Article 20 or refuse to submit to inspections ordered by a decision adopted pursuant to Article 20(4);

    (d) in response to a question asked in accordance with Article 20(2)(e),

        — they give an incorrect or misleading answer,

        — they fail to rectify within a time-limit set by the Commission an incorrect, incomplete or misleading answer given by a member of staff, or

        — they fail or refuse to provide a complete answer on facts relating to the subject-matter and purpose of an inspection ordered by a decision adopted pursuant to Article 20(4);

    (e) seals affixed in accordance with Article 20(2)(d) by officials or other accompanying persons authorised by the Commission have been broken.

2. The Commission may by decision impose fines on undertakings and associations of undertakings where, either intentionally or negligently:

    (a) they infringe Article 81 or Article 82 of the Treaty; or

    (b) they contravene a decision ordering interim measures under Article 8; or

    (c) they fail to comply with a commitment made binding by a decision pursuant to Article 9.

For each undertaking and association of undertakings participating in the infringement, the fine shall not exceed 10% of its total turnover in the preceding business year.

Where the infringement of an association relates to the activities of its members, the fine shall not exceed 10% of the sum of the total turnover of each member active on the market affected by the infringement of the association.

3. In fixing the amount of the fine, regard shall be had both to the gravity and to the duration of the infringement.

4. When a fine is imposed on an association of undertakings taking account of the turnover of its members and the association is not solvent, the association is obliged to call for contributions from its members to cover the amount of the fine.

Where such contributions have not been made to the association within a time-limit fixed by the Commission, the Commission may require payment of the fine directly by any of the undertakings whose representatives were members of the decision-making bodies concerned of the association.

After the Commission has required payment under the second subparagraph, where necessary to ensure full payment of the fine, the Commission may require payment of the balance by any of the members of the association which were active on the market on which the infringement occurred.

However, the Commission shall not require payment under the second or the third subparagraph from undertakings which show that they have not implemented the infringing decision of the association and either were not aware of its existence or have actively distanced themselves from it before the Commission started investigating the case.

The financial liability of each undertaking in respect of the payment of the fine shall not exceed 10% of its total turnover in the preceding business year.

5. Decisions taken pursuant to paragraphs 1 and 2 shall not be of a criminal law nature.

Article 24 Periodic penalty payments

1. The Commission may, by decision, impose on undertakings or associations of undertakings periodic penalty payments not exceeding 5% of the average daily turnover in the preceding business year per day and calculated from the date appointed by the decision, in order to compel them:

    (a) to put an end to an infringement of Article 81 or Article 82 of the Treaty, in accordance with a decision taken pursuant to Article 7;

    (b) to comply with a decision ordering interim measures taken pursuant to Article 8;

    (c) to comply with a commitment made binding by a decision pursuant to Article 9;

    (d) to supply complete and correct information which it has requested by decision taken pursuant to Article 17 or Article 18(3);

    (e) to submit to an inspection which it has ordered by decision taken pursuant to Article 20(4).

2. Where the undertakings or associations of undertakings have satisfied the obligation which the periodic penalty payment was intended to enforce, the Commission may fix the definitive amount of the periodic penalty payment at a figure lower than that which would arise under the original decision. Article 23(4) shall apply correspondingly.

Riley, A., 'EC Antitrust Modernisation: The Commission Does Very Nicely—Thank You! Part 2: Between the Idea and the Reality: Decentralisation under Regulation 1'

[2003] ECLR 657, pp. 671–2 [footnotes omitted]

Regulation 1/2003: who benefits?

Undertakings do not benefit much from the abolition of the notification procedure, nor does the Commission. It is also clear that the NCAs do not benefit much from the decentralisation aspects of Regulation 1. In many national cases EC competition law may be applied instead of national competition law, but the cases will still be intrinsically national cases although "badged" as European. Given the lack of effective cross-border procedures and the potential impact on the rights of defence of such procedures, the NCAs are unlikely to be participating in many more cross-border cases than they are now. At the margin national cases with a slight crossborder element may result in an NCA requesting assistance, such as inspection at the premises of an undertaking in another Member State, or a minor file may be transferred to another NCA. Equally, given the weakness of national civil procedures and the powerful streak of independence to executive interference amongst the judiciary of the Member States, Art.15 is likely to prove as equally unused as the National Courts Notice.

However, on closer examination, the "who benefits" analysis of Regulation 1, it is submitted, reveals that it is the Commission who is the principal if not sole beneficiary of the new regulation. Article 3 ensures uniform application of EC competition law over national competition law in respect of Art.81 in almost all major cases in all Member States. As a result therefore, the Commission obtains significant supervisory powers over the NCAs, including rights to be informed of proceedings; copies of draft decisions and crucially the right to takeover NCA proceedings. In addition to which the Commission has had its major decisional powers updated and rendered more legally secure. In particular, the power to obtain information contained in Art.18 is strengthened; it has acquired an interview power in Art.19 and the power to carry out inspections has been extended to private premises. Furthermore, it has had its powers to impose procedural fines refurbished.

NOTE: The 'Communitarization' of competition law enforcement in the Member States through Regulation 1/2003 is one of the key aspects of system. The vast majority of competition infringement actions brought in the EU will be based on the Treaty prohibitions, although most of those actions will go through the domestic enforcement regimes administered by the National Competition Authorities, such as the OFT in the UK and the Bundeskartellamt in Germany. Competition law enforcement in Europe is now coordinated through a network of Competition Authorities ('NCAs') know as the European Competition Network. The ECN works on the basis of formal methods of cooperation, but is also an important source of informal cooperation and education whereby the various authorities, which have very different levels of expertise and experience, can learn from each other and share information and experience. While the majority of cases will be handled by the NCAs, the Commission, through the Directorate General for Competition ('DG Comp'), retains an important role at the centre of the system. Its main role is now to ensure consistency across the ECN and develop European competition policy. The Commission will continue to handle some cases; these will be the large pan-European investigations that cannot be dealt with effectively by the NCAs and cases which deal with important policy issues. The direct applicability of Article 81(3) EC also means that the domestic courts can now play a greater role in competition law enforcement. The complexity surrounding the relationship between the private and public enforcement is discussed in Chapter 4.

SECTION 2: COOPERATION AND CASE HANDLING WITHIN THE ECN

Commission Notice on the handling of complaints by the Commission under Articles 81 and 82 of the EC Treaty
OJ, 2004, C101/65

II. DIFFERENT POSSIBILITIES FOR LODGING COMPLAINTS ABOUT SUSPECTED INFRINGEMENTS OF ARTICLES 81 OR 82

A. COMPLAINTS IN THE NEW ENFORCEMENT SYSTEM ESTABLISHED BY REGULATION 1/2003

7. Depending on the nature of the complaint, a complainant may bring his complaint either to a national court or to a competition authority that acts as public enforcer. The present chapter of this Notice intends to help potential complainants to make an informed choice about whether to address themselves to the Commission, to one of the Member States' competition authorities or to a national court.

8. While national courts are called upon to safeguard the rights of individuals and are thus bound to rule on cases brought before them, public enforcers cannot investigate all complaints, but must set priorities in their treatment of cases. The Court of Justice has held that the Commission, entrusted by Article 85(1) of the EC Treaty with the task of ensuring application of the principles laid down in Articles 81 and 82 of the Treaty, is responsible for defining and implementing the orientation of Community competition policy and that, in order to perform that task effectively, it is entitled to give differing degrees of priority to the complaints brought before it.

9. Regulation 1/2003 empowers Member States' courts and Member States' competition authorities to apply Articles 81 and 82 in their entirety alongside the Commission. Regulation 1/2003 pursues as one principal objective that Member States' courts and competition authorities should participate effectively in the enforcement of Articles 81 and 82.

10. Moreover, Article 3 of Regulation 1/2003 provides that Member States' courts and competition authorities have to apply Articles 81 and 82 to all cases of agreements or conduct that are capable of affecting trade between Member States to which they apply their national competition laws. In addition, Articles 11 and 15 of the Regulation create a range of mechanisms by which Member States' courts and competition authorities cooperate with the Commission in the enforcement of Articles 81 and 82.

11. In this new legislative framework, the Commission intends to refocus its enforcement resources along the following lines:

— enforce the EC competition rules in cases for which it is well placed to act, concentrating its resources on the most serious infringements;
— handle cases in relation to which the Commission should act with a view to define Community competition policy and/or to ensure coherent application of Articles 81 or 82.

B. THE COMPLEMENTARY ROLES OF PRIVATE AND PUBLIC ENFORCEMENT

12. It has been consistently held by the Community Courts that national courts are called upon to safeguard the rights of individuals created by the direct effect of Articles 81(1) and 82.

13. National courts can decide upon the nullity or validity of contracts and only national courts can grant damages to an individual in case of an infringement of Articles 81 and 82. Under the case law of the Court of Justice, any individual can claim damages for loss caused to him by a contract or by conduct which restricts or distorts competition, in order to ensure the full effectiveness of the Community competition rules. Such actions for damages before the national courts can make a significant contribution to the maintenance of effective competition in the Community as they discourage undertakings from concluding or applying restrictive agreements or practices.

14. Regulation 1/2003 takes express account of the fact that national courts have an essential part to play in applying the EC competition rules. By extending the power to apply Article 81(3) to national courts it removes the possibility for undertakings to delay national court proceedings by a notification to the Commission and thus eliminates an obstacle for private litigation that existed under Regulation No 17.

15. Without prejudice to the right or obligation of national courts to address a preliminary question to the Court of Justice in accordance with Article 234 EC, Article 15(1) of Regulation 1/2003 provides expressly that national courts may ask for opinions or information from the Commission. This provision aims at facilitating the application of Articles 81 and 82 by national courts.

16. Action before national courts has the following advantages for complainants:
— National courts may award damages for loss suffered as a result of an infringement of Article 81 or 82.
— National courts may rule on claims for payment or contractual obligations based on an agreement that they examine under Article 81.
— It is for the national courts to apply the civil sanction of nullity of Article 81(2) in contractual relationships between individuals. They can in particular assess, in the light of the applicable national law, the scope and consequences of the nullity of certain contractual provisions under Article 81(2), with particular regard to all the other matters covered by the agreement.

— National courts are usually better placed than the Commission to adopt interim measures(18).

— Before national courts, it is possible to combine a claim under Community competition law with other claims under national law.

— Courts normally have the power to award legal costs to the successful applicant. This is never possible in an administrative procedure before the Commission.

17. The fact that a complainant can secure the protection of his rights by an action before a national court, is an important element that the Commission may take into account in its examination of the Community interest for investigating a complaint.

18. The Commission holds the view that the new enforcement system established by Regulation 1/2003 strengthens the possibilities for complainants to seek and obtain effective relief before national courts.

. . .

III. THE COMMISSION'S HANDLING OF COMPLAINTS PURSUANT TO ARTICLE 7(2) OF REGULATION 1/2003

A. GENERAL

26. According to Article 7(2) of Regulation 1/2003 natural or legal persons that can show a legitimate interest are entitled to lodge a complaint to ask the Commission to find an infringement of Articles 81 and 82 EC and to require that the infringement be brought to an end in accordance with Article 7(1) of Regulation 1/2003. The present part of this Notice explains the requirements applicable to complaints based on Article 7(2) of Regulation 1/2003, their assessment and the procedure followed by the Commission.

27. The Commission, unlike civil courts, whose task is to safeguard the individual rights of private persons, is an administrative authority that must act in the public interest. It is an inherent feature of the Commission's task as public enforcer that it has a margin of discretion to set priorities in its enforcement activity.

28. The Commission is entitled to give different degrees of priority to complaints made to it and may refer to the Community interest presented by a case as a criterion of priority. The Commission may reject a complaint when it considers that the case does not display a sufficient Community interest to justify further investigation. Where the Commission rejects a complaint, the complainant is entitled to a decision of the Commission without prejudice to Article 7(3) of Regulation 773/2004.

Commission Notice on cooperation within the Network of Competition Authorities
OJ, 2004, C101/43

1. INTRODUCTION

1. Council Regulation (EC) No 1/2003 of 16 December 2002 on the implementation of the rules on competition laid down in Articles 81 and 82 of the Treaty(1) (hereafter the "Council Regulation") creates a system of parallel competences in which the Commission and the Member States' competition authorities (hereafter the "NCAs")(2) can apply Article 81 and Article 82 of the EC Treaty (hereafter the "Treaty"). Together the NCAs and the Commission form a network of public authorities: they act in the public interest and cooperate closely in order to protect competition. The network is a forum for discussion and cooperation in the application and enforcement of EC competition policy. It provides a framework for the cooperation of European competition authorities in cases where Articles 81 and 82 of the Treaty are applied and is the basis for the creation and maintenance of a common competition culture in Europe. The network is called "European Competition Network" (ECN).

2. The structure of the NCAs varies between Member States. In some Member States, one body investigates cases and takes all types of decisions. In other Member States, the functions are divided between two bodies, one which is in charge of the investigation of the case and another, often a college, which is responsible for deciding the case. Finally, in certain Member States,

prohibition decisions and/or decisions imposing a fine can only be taken by a court: another competition authority acts as a prosecutor bringing the case before that court. Subject to the general principle of effectiveness, Article 35 of the Council Regulation allows Member States to choose the body or bodies which will be designated as national competition authorities and to allocate functions between them. Under general principles of Community law, Member States are under an obligation to set up a sanctioning system providing for sanctions which are effective, proportionate and dissuasive for infringements of EC law(3). The enforcement systems of the Member States differ but they have recognised the standards of each other's systems as a basis for cooperation(4).

3. The network formed by the competition authorities should ensure both an efficient division of work and an effective and consistent application of EC competition rules. The Council Regulation together with the joint statement of the Council and the Commission on the functioning of the European Competition Network sets out the main principles of the functioning of the network. This notice presents the details of the system.

4. Consultations and exchanges within the network are matters between public enforcers and do not alter any rights or obligations arising from Community or national law for companies. Each competition authority remains fully responsible for ensuring due process in the cases it deals with.

2. DIVISION OF WORK

2.1. Principles of allocation

5. The Council Regulation is based on a system of parallel competences in which all competition authorities have the power to apply Articles 81 or 82 of the Treaty and are responsible for an efficient division of work with respect to those cases where an investigation is deemed to be necessary. At the same time each network member retains full discretion in deciding whether or not to investigate a case. Under this system of parallel competences, cases will be dealt with by:
— a single NCA, possibly with the assistance of NCAs of other Member States; or
— several NCAs acting in parallel; or
— the Commission.

6. In most instances the authority that receives a complaint or starts an ex-officio procedure(5) will remain in charge of the case. Re-allocation of a case would only be envisaged at the outset of a procedure (see paragraph 18 below) where either that authority considered that it was not well placed to act or where other authorities also considered themselves well placed to act (see paragraphs 8 to 15 below).

7. Where re-allocation is found to be necessary for an effective protection of competition and of the Community interest, network members will endeavour to re-allocate cases to a single well placed competition authority as often as possible(6). In any event, re-allocation should be a quick and efficient process and not hold up ongoing investigations.

8. An authority can be considered to be well placed to deal with a case if the following three cumulative conditions are met:
1. the agreement or practice has substantial direct actual or foreseeable effects on competition within its territory, is implemented within or originates from its territory;
2. the authority is able to effectively bring to an end the entire infringement, i.e. it can adopt a cease-and-desist order the effect of which will be sufficient to bring an end to the infringement and it can, where appropriate, sanction the infringement adequately;
3. it can gather, possibly with the assistance of other authorities, the evidence required to prove the infringement.

9. The above criteria indicate that a material link between the infringement and the territory of a Member State must exist in order for that Member State's competition authority to be considered well placed. It can be expected that in most cases the authorities of those Member States where competition is substantially affected by an infringement will be well placed provided they are capable of effectively bringing the infringement to an end through either single or parallel action unless the Commission is better placed to act (see below paragraphs 14 and 15).

10. It follows that a single NCA is usually well placed to deal with agreements or practices that substantially affect competition mainly within its territory.

Example 1: Undertakings situated in Member State A are involved in a price fixing cartel on products that are mainly sold in Member State A.

The NCA in A is well placed to deal with the case.

11. Furthermore single action of an NCA might also be appropriate where, although more than one NCA can be regarded as well placed, the action of a single NCA is sufficient to bring the entire infringement to an end.

Example 2: Two undertakings have set up a joint venture in Member State A. The joint venture provides services in Member States A and B and gives rise to a competition problem. A cease-and-desist order is considered to be sufficient to deal with the case effectively because it can bring an end to the entire infringement. Evidence is located mainly at the offices of the joint venture in Member State A.

The NCAs in A and B are both well placed to deal with the case but single action by the NCA in A would be sufficient and more efficient than single action by NCA in B or parallel action by both NCAs.

12. Parallel action by two or three NCAs may be appropriate where an agreement or practice has substantial effects on competition mainly in their respective territories and the action of only one NCA would not be sufficient to bring the entire infringement to an end and/or to sanction it adequately.

Example 3: Two undertakings agree on a market sharing agreement, restricting the activity of the company located in Member State A to Member State A and the activity of the company located in Member State B to Member State B.

The NCAs in A and B are well placed to deal with the case in parallel, each one for its respective territory.

13. The authorities dealing with a case in parallel action will endeavour to coordinate their action to the extent possible. To that effect, they may find it useful to designate one of them as a lead authority and to delegate tasks to the lead authority such as for example the coordination of investigative measures, while each authority remains responsible for conducting its own proceedings.

14. The Commission is particularly well placed if one or several agreement(s) or practice(s), including networks of similar agreements or practices, have effects on competition in more than three Member States (cross-border markets covering more than three Member States or several national markets).

Example 4: Two undertakings agree to share markets or fix prices for the whole territory of the Community. The Commission is well placed to deal with the case.

Example 5: An undertaking, dominant in four different national markets, abuses its position by imposing fidelity rebates on its distributors in all these markets. The Commission is well placed to deal with the case. It could also deal with one national market so as to create a "leading" case and other national markets could be dealt with by NCAs, particularly if each national market requires a separate assessment.

15. Moreover, the Commission is particularly well placed to deal with a case if it is closely linked to other Community provisions which may be exclusively or more effectively applied by the Commission, if the Community interest requires the adoption of a Commission decision to develop Community competition policy when a new competition issue arises or to ensure effective enforcement.

2.2. Mechanisms of cooperation for the purpose of case allocation and assistance

2.2.1. Information at the beginning of the procedure (Article 11 of the Council Regulation)

16. In order to detect multiple procedures and to ensure that cases are dealt with by a well placed competition authority, the members of the network have to be informed at an early stage of the cases pending before the various competition authorities(7). If a case is to be re-allocated, it is indeed in the best interest both of the network and of the undertakings concerned that the re-allocation takes place quickly.

17. The Council Regulation creates a mechanism for the competition authorities to inform each other in order to ensure an efficient and quick re-allocation of cases. Article 11(3) of the Council Regulation lays down an obligation for NCAs to inform the Commission when acting under Article 81 or 82 of the Treaty before or without delay after commencing the first formal investigative measure. It also states that the information may be made available to other NCAs(8). The rationale of Article 11(3) of the Council Regulation is to allow the network to detect multiple procedures and address possible case re-allocation issues as soon as an authority starts investigating a case. Information should therefore be provided to NCAs and the Commission before or just after any step similar to the measures of investigation that can be undertaken by the Commission under Articles 18 to 21 of the Council Regulation. The Commission has accepted an equivalent obligation to inform NCAs under Article 11(2) of the Council Regulation. Network members will inform each other of pending cases by means of a standard form containing limited details of the case, such as the authority dealing with the case, the product, territories and parties concerned, the alleged infringement, the suspected duration of the infringement and the origin of the case. They will also provide each other with updates when a relevant change occurs.

18. Where case re-allocation issues arise, they should be resolved swiftly, normally within a period of two months, starting from the date of the first information sent to the network pursuant to Article 11 of the Council Regulation. During this period, competition authorities will endeavour to reach an agreement on a possible re-allocation and, where relevant, on the modalities for parallel action.

19. In general, the competition authority or authorities that is/are dealing with a case at the end of the re-allocation period should continue to deal with the case until the completion of the proceedings. Re-allocation of a case after the initial allocation period of two months should only occur where the facts known about the case change materially during the course of the proceedings.

2.2.2. Suspension or termination of proceedings (Article 13 of the Council Regulation)

20. If the same agreement or practice is brought before several competition authorities, be it because they have received a complaint or have opened a procedure on their own initiative, Article 13 of the Council Regulation provides a legal basis for suspending proceedings or rejecting a complaint on the grounds that another authority is dealing with the case or has dealt with the case. In Article 13 of the Council Regulation, "dealing with the case" does not merely mean that a complaint has been lodged with another authority. It means that the other authority is investigating or has investigated the case on its own behalf.

21. Article 13 of the Council Regulation applies when another authority has dealt or is dealing with the competition issue raised by the complainant, even if the authority in question has acted or acts on the basis of a complaint lodged by a different complainant or as a result of an ex-officio procedure. This implies that Article 13 of the Council Regulation can be invoked when the agreement or practice involves the same infringement(s) on the same relevant geographic and product markets.

22. An NCA may suspend or close its proceedings but it has no obligation to do so. Article 13 of the Council Regulation leaves scope for appreciation of the peculiarities of each individual case. This flexibility is important: if a complaint was rejected by an authority following an investigation of the substance of the case, another authority may not want to re-examine the case. On the other hand, if a complaint was rejected for other reasons (e.g. the authority was unable to collect the evidence necessary to prove the infringement), another authority may wish to carry out its own investigation and deal with the case. This flexibility is also reflected, for pending cases, in the choice open to each NCA as to whether it closes or suspends its proceedings. An authority may be unwilling to close a case before the outcome of another authority's proceedings is clear. The ability to suspend its proceedings allows the authority to retain its ability to decide at a later point whether or not to terminate its proceedings. Such flexibility also facilitates consistent application of the rules.

23. Where an authority closes or suspends proceedings because another authority is dealing with the case, it may transfer—in accordance with Article 12 of the Council Regulation—the information provided by the complainant to the authority which is to deal with the case.

24. Article 13 of the Council Regulation can also be applied to part of a complaint or to part of the proceedings in a case. It may be that only part of a complaint or of an ex-officio procedure overlaps with a case already dealt or being dealt with by another competition authority. In that case, the

competition authority to which the complaint is brought is entitled to reject part of the complaint on the basis of Article 13 of the Council Regulation and to deal with the rest of the complaint in an appropriate manner. The same principle applies to the termination of proceedings.

25. Article 13 of the Council Regulation is not the only legal basis for suspending or closing ex-officio proceedings or rejecting complaints. NCAs may also be able to do so according to their national procedural law. The Commission may also reject a complaint for lack of Community interest or other reasons pertaining to the nature of the complaint(9).

...

3. CONSISTENT APPLICATION OF EC COMPETITION RULES(18)

3.1. Mechanism of cooperation (Article 11(4) and 11(5) of the Council Regulation)

43. The Council Regulation pursues the objective that Articles 81 and 82 of the Treaty are applied in a consistent manner throughout the Community. In this respect NCAs will respect the convergence rule contained in Article 3(2) of the Council Regulation. In line with Article 16(2) they cannot—when ruling on agreements, decisions and practices under Article 81 or Article 82 of the Treaty which are already the subject of a Commission decision—take decisions, which would run counter to the decisions adopted by the Commission. Within the network of competition authorities the Commission, as the guardian of the Treaty, has the ultimate but not the sole responsibility for developing policy and safeguarding consistency when it comes to the application of EC competition law.

44. According to Article 11(4) of the Council Regulation, no later than 30 days before the adoption of a decision applying Articles 81 or 82 of the Treaty and requiring that an infringement be brought to an end, accepting commitments or withdrawing the benefit of a block-exemption regulation, NCAs shall inform the Commission. They have to send to the Commission, at the latest 30 days before the adoption of the decision, a summary of the case, the envisaged decision or, in the absence thereof, any other document indicating the proposed course of action.

45. As under Article 11(3) of the Council Regulation, the obligation is to inform the Commission, but the information may be shared by the NCA informing the Commission with the other members of the network.

46. Where an NCA has informed the Commission pursuant to Article 11(4) of the Council Regulation and the 30 days deadline has expired, the decision can be adopted as long as the Commission has not initiated proceedings. The Commission may make written observations on the case before the adoption of the decision by the NCA. The NCA and the Commission will make the appropriate efforts to ensure the consistent application of Community law (cf. paragraph 3 above).

47. If special circumstances require that a national decision is taken in less than 30 days following the transmission of information pursuant to Article 11(4) of the Council Regulation, the NCA concerned may ask the Commission for a swifter reaction. The Commission will endeavour to react as quickly as possible.

48. Other types of decisions, i.e. decisions rejecting complaints, decisions closing an ex-officio procedure or decisions ordering interim measures, can also be important from a competition policy point of view, and the network members may have an interest in informing each other about them and possibly discussing them. NCAs can therefore on the basis of Article 11(5) of the Council Regulation inform the Commission and thereby inform the network of any other case in which EC competition law is applied.

49. All members of the network should inform each other about the closure of their procedures which have been notified to the network pursuant to Article 11(2) and (3) of the Council Regulation(19).

3.2. The initiation of proceedings by the Commission under Article 11(6) of the Council Regulation

50. According to the case law of the Court of Justice, the Commission, entrusted by Article 85(1) of the Treaty with the task of ensuring the application of the principles laid down in Articles 81 and 82 of the Treaty, is responsible for defining and implementing the orientation of Community competition policy(20). It can adopt individual decisions under Articles 81 and 82 of the Treaty at any time.

51. Article 11(6) of the Council Regulation states that the initiation by the Commission of proceedings for the adoption of a decision under the Council Regulation shall relieve all NCAs of their competence to apply Articles 81 and 82 of the Treaty. This means that once the Commission has opened proceedings, NCAs cannot act under the same legal basis against the same agreement(s) or practice(s) by the same undertaking(s) on the same relevant geographic and product market.

52. The initiation of proceedings by the Commission is a formal act(21) by which the Commission indicates its intention to adopt a decision under Chapter III of the Council Regulation. It can occur at any stage of the investigation of the case by the Commission. The mere fact that the Commission has received a complaint is not in itself sufficient to relieve NCAs of their competence.

53. Two situations can arise. First, where the Commission is the first competition authority to initiate proceedings in a case for the adoption of a decision under the Council Regulation, national competition authorities may no longer deal with the case. Article 11(6) of the Council Regulation provides that once the Commission has initiated proceedings, the NCAs can no longer start their own procedure with a view to applying Articles 81 and 82 of the Treaty to the same agreement(s) or practice(s) by the same undertaking(s) on the same relevant geographic and product market.

54. The second situation is where one or more NCAs have informed the network pursuant to Article 11(3) of the Council Regulation that they are acting on a given case. During the initial allocation period (indicative time period of two months, see paragraph 18 above), the Commission can initiate proceedings with the effects of Article 11(6) of the Council Regulation after having consulted the authorities concerned. After the allocation phase, the Commission will in principle only apply Article 11(6) of the Council Regulation if one of the following situations arises:

   (a) Network members envisage conflicting decisions in the same case.

   (b) Network members envisage a decision which is obviously in conflict with consolidated case law; the standards defined in the judgements of the Community courts and in previous decisions and regulations of the Commission should serve as a yardstick; concerning the assessment of the facts (e.g. market definition), only a significant divergence will trigger an intervention of the Commission;

   (c) Network member(s) is (are) unduly drawing out proceedings in the case;

   (d) There is a need to adopt a Commission decision to develop Community competition policy in particular when a similar competition issue arises in several Member States or to ensure effective enforcement;

   (e) The NCA(s) concerned do not object.

55. If an NCA is already acting on a case, the Commission will explain the reasons for the application of Article 11(6) of the Council Regulation in writing to the NCA concerned and to the other members of the Network(22).

56. The Commission will announce to the network its intention of applying Article 11(6) of the Council Regulation in due time, so that Network members will have the possibility of asking for a meeting of the Advisory Committee on the matter before the Commission initiates proceedings.

57. The Commission will normally not—and to the extent that Community interest is not at stake—adopt a decision which is in conflict with a decision of an NCA after proper information pursuant to both Article 11(3) and (4) of the Council Regulation has taken place and the Commission has not made use of Article 11(6) of the Council Regulation.

NOTE: The provisions in Article 11(6) are designed to ensure that the Commission continues to play the central role in the ECN; it can 'call in' important cases to ensure consistent application of the rules and allow it to develop competition policy.

Dekeyser, K., and Jaspers, M., 'A New Era of ECN Cooperation. Achievements and Challenges with Special Focus on Work in the Leniency Field'
(2007) 30 World Competition 3, pp. 7–8 [footnotes omitted]

The first experiences of the work-sharing within the Network have confirmed that the flexible and pragmatic approach which has been introduced by the Regulation and the Network Notice functions very well in practice. There are relatively few cases where case-allocation discussions have at all been needed and even fewer occasions where a case has changed hands. The situations where work-sharing has played a role to date, is typically where a complainant or a leniency applicant have chosen to contact both the Commission and one or more national competition authorities. The experiences have shown that the ECN is well equipped to identify attempts of forum-shopping and likewise equipped to avoid unnecessary duplication of work. It has also manifested the ECN members' readiness to solve case-allocations issues in a manner that ensures the most efficient work-sharing arrangement for a particular case. There have been no examples so far where the allocation of an individual case has not been solved through bilateral discussions.

...

The first experiences with mutual assistance and exchange of information within the Network are likewise positive. The possibility to exchange and use information in evidence has proven to be valuable, not only in re-allocation scenarios, but also as a source to detect competition infringements. Some of the investigations currently pending are the result of leads and indications of market failures that have been mutually shared within the Network. This shows that the exchange of information mechanism and the willingness to share information and knowledge within the ECN can strengthen the individual ECN members' ability to detect and to end competition law infringements. There have also already been examples where NCAs have successfully assisted each other in different fact-finding measures; including carrying out unannounced inspections. It is to be expected that ECN members will make even further use of these possibilities in the future.

SECTION 3: COMMISSION INVESTIGATIONS

The investigatory powers of the DG Comp under Articles 18–20 of Regulation 1/2003 are broad, allowing it to seek wide categories of information from undertakings and take supporting statements. Most of the Commission's investigations are carried out using the Article 18 powers, requests for information, but it does use Article 20, powers of inspection, where it is concerned that a suspect undertaking may take steps to dispose of evidence if the Article 18 procedure was used. Article 19 statements are usually taken when an undertaking is cooperating with a Commission investigation; usually following a leniency application or negotiating a direct settlement. Where the Commission wishes to undertake an investigation it should do so with the cooperation of the relevant Member State via the NCA. Where, during an investigation, the Commission is concerned that it is necessary, it can adopt interim measures under Article 3 (see *Camera Care* v *Commission* (Case 792/79R) [1980] ECR 119, [1980] 1 CMLR 334). During an investigation two types of information are protected and need not be disclosed: information protected by professional legal privilege, and that protected by the privilege against self incrimination.

AM & S Europe Ltd v Commission
(Case 155/79) [1982] ECR 1575, [1982] 2 CMLR 264

The Commission sought to gather certain documents from AM & S relating to an alleged zinc cartel through an Article 14 procedure. AM & S refused to disclose certain documents, claiming that correspondence between an undertaking and its lawyers was subject to legal professional privilege ('LPP').

[18] However, the above rules do not exclude the possibility of recognising, subject to certain conditions, that certain business records are of a confidential nature. Community law, which derives from not only the economic but also the legal interpenetration of the Member States, must take into account the principles and concepts common to the laws of those States concerning the

observance of confidentiality, in particular, as regards certain communications between lawyer and client. That confidentiality serves the requirement, the importance of which is recognised in all of the Member States, that any person must be able, without constraint, to consult a lawyer whose profession entails the giving of independent legal advice to all those in need of it.

[19] As far as the protection of written communications between lawyer and client is concerned, it is apparent from the legal systems of the Member States that, although the principle of such protection is generally recognised, its scope and the criteria for applying it vary, as has, indeed, been conceded both by the applicant and by the parties who have intervened in support of its conclusions.

[20] Whilst in some of the Member States the protection against disclosure afforded to written communications between lawyer and client is based principally on a recognition of the very nature of the legal profession, inasmuch as it contributes towards the maintenance of the rule of law, in other Member States the same protection is justified by the more specific requirement (which, moreover, is also recognised in the first-mentioned States) that the rights of the defence must be respected.

[21] Apart from these differences, however, there are to be found in the national laws of the Member States common criteria inasmuch as those laws protect, in similar circumstances, the confidentiality of written communications between lawyer and client provided that, on the one hand, such communications are made for the purposes and in the interests of the client's rights of defence and, on the other hand, they emanate from independent lawyers, that is to say, lawyers who are not bound to the client by a relationship of employment.

[22] Viewed in that context Regulation 17 must be interpreted as protecting, in its turn, the confidentiality of written communications between lawyer and client subject to those two conditions, and thus incorporating such elements of that protection as are common to the laws of the Member States.

[23] As far as the first of those two conditions is concerned, in Regulation 17 itself, in particular in the eleventh recital in its preamble and in the provisions contained in Article 19, care is taken to ensure that the rights of the defence may be exercised to the full, and the protection of the confidentiality of written communications between lawyer and client is an essential corollary to those rights. In those circumstances, such protection must, if it is to be effective, be recognised as covering all written communications exchanged after the initiation of the administrative procedure under Regulation 17 which may lead to a decision on the application of Articles 85 and 86 of the Treaty or to a decision imposing a pecuniary sanction on the undertaking. It must also be possible to extend it to earlier written communications which have a relationship to the subject-matter of that procedure.

[24] As regards the second condition, it should be stated that the requirement as to the position and status as an independent lawyer, which must be fulfilled by the legal adviser from whom the written communications which may be protected emanate, is based on a conception of the lawyer's role as collaborating in the administration of justice by the courts and as being required to provide, in full independence, and in the overriding interests of that cause, such legal assistance as the client needs. The counterpart of that protection lies in the rules of professional ethics and discipline which are laid down and enforced in the general interest by institutions endowed with the requisite powers for that purpose. Such a concept reflects the legal traditions common to the Member States and is also to be found in the legal order of the Community, as is demonstrated by Article 17 of the Protocols on the Statutes of the Court of Justice of the EEC and the EAEC, and also by Article 20 of the Protocol on the Statute of the Court of Justice of the ECSC.

Akzo Nobel Chemicals Ltd and Akcros Chemicals Ltd v *Commission*
(Joined Cases T-125 and 253/03) [2007] ECR II-3523

Commission officials, assisted by the OFT, carried out an investigation at the applicants' premises in Manchester. During that investigation the applicants claimed professional legal privilege in relation to certain documents. The Commission sought to 'briefly examine' the documents to establish if they were privileged. One of the documents concerned was a communication between a general manager and a competition law 'coordinator', who was a member of Akzo Nobel's in-house legal department and an Advocaat of the Netherlands Bar.

[79] As regards the procedure to be followed when applying that protection, the Court held that if an undertaking which is the subject of an investigation under Article 14 of Regulation No 17 refuses, by claiming protection under LPP, to produce, as part of the business records demanded by the Commission, written communications between itself and its lawyer, it must nevertheless provide the Commission officials with relevant material which demonstrates that the communications fulfil the conditions for the grant of legal protection, while not being bound to disclose their contents. The Court went on to state that, where the Commission considers that such evidence has not been provided, it must, pursuant to Article 14(3) of Regulation No 17, order production of the communications in question and, if necessary, impose on the undertaking fines or periodic penalty payments under that regulation as a penalty for the undertaking's refusal either to supply such additional evidence as the Commission considers necessary or to produce the documents whose confidentiality, in the Commission's view, is not protected in law (AM & S, paragraphs 29 to 31). The undertaking under investigation may subsequently bring an action for the annulment of such a Commission decision, where appropriate, coupled with a request for interim relief pursuant to Articles 242 EC and 243 EC (see, to that effect, AM & S, paragraph 32).

[80] It is apparent, therefore, that the mere fact that an undertaking claims that a document is protected by legal professional privilege is not sufficient to prevent the Commission from reading that document if the undertaking produces no relevant material of such a kind as to prove that it is actually protected by LPP. The undertaking concerned may, in particular, inform the Commission of the author of the document and for whom it was intended, explain the respective duties and responsibilities of each, and refer to the objective and the context in which the document was drawn up. Similarly, it may also mention the context in which the document was found, the way in which it was filed and any related documents.

[81] In a significant number of cases, a mere cursory look by the Commission officials at the general layout, heading, title or other superficial features of the document will enable them to confirm the accuracy of the reasons invoked by the undertaking and to determine whether the document at issue was confidential, when deciding whether to put it aside. Nevertheless, on certain occasions, there would be a risk that, even with a cursory look at the document, in spite of the superficial nature of their examination, the Commission officials would gain access to information covered by legal professional privilege. That may be so, in particular, if the confidentiality of the document in question is not clear from external indications.

[82] As stated in paragraph 79 above, it is clear from AM & S that the undertaking concerned is not bound to reveal their contents when presenting the Commission officials with relevant material of such a nature as to demonstrate that the documents fulfil the conditions for being granted legal protection (paragraph 29 of the judgment). Accordingly, the Court concludes that an undertaking subject to an investigation under Article 14(3) of Regulation No 17 is entitled to refuse to allow the Commission officials to take even a cursory look at one or more specific documents which it claims to be covered by LPP, provided that the undertaking considers that such a cursory look is impossible without revealing the content of those documents and that it gives the Commission officials appropriate reasons for its view.

[83] Where, in the course of an investigation under Article 14(3) of Regulation No 17, the Commission considers that the material presented by the undertaking is not of such a nature as to prove that the documents in question are confidential, in particular where that undertaking refuses to give the Commission officials a cursory look at a document, the Commission officials may place a copy of the document or documents in question in a sealed envelope and then remove it with a view to a subsequent resolution of the dispute. This procedure enables risks of a breach of legal professional privilege to be avoided while at the same time enabling the Commission to retain a certain control over the documents forming the subject-matter of the investigation and avoiding the risk that the documents will subsequently disappear or be manipulated.

[84] Use of the sealed envelope procedure cannot, moreover, be considered to be at odds with the requirement set out in paragraph 31 of AM & S that, in the case of a dispute with the undertaking

concerned as to whether a particular document is confidential, the Commission must adopt a decision ordering that document to be produced. The reason for such a requirement lies in the specific context of the judgment in *AM & S*, in particular the fact that the initial decision ordering an inspection at the premises of the undertaking in question was not a formal decision under Article 14(3) of Regulation No 17 (Opinion of Advocate General Warner in *AM & S*, p. 1624) and the undertaking in question was therefore entitled, as it in fact did, to refuse to produce the documents requested by the Commission.

[85] In any event, the Court would point out that where the Commission is not satisfied with the material and explanations provided by the representatives of the undertaking for the purposes of proving that the document concerned is covered by LPP, the Commission must not read the contents of the document before it has adopted a decision allowing the undertaking concerned to refer the matter to the Court of First Instance, and, if appropriate, to make an application for interim relief (see, to that effect, *AM & S*, paragraph 32).

[86] Having regard to the particular nature of the principle of LPP, the purpose of which is both to guarantee the full exercise of individuals' rights of defence and to safeguard the requirement that any person must be able, without constraint, to consult his lawyer (see paragraph 77 above), the Court considers that the fact that the Commission reads the content of a confidential document is in itself a breach of this principle. Contrary to what the Commission seems to submit, the protection of LPP therefore goes beyond the requirement that information provided by an undertaking to its lawyer or the content of the advice given by that lawyer cannot be used against it in a decision which penalises a breach of the competition rules.

[87] First, that protection seeks to safeguard the public interest in the proper administration of justice in ensuring that a client is free to consult his lawyer without fear that any confidences which he imparts may subsequently be disclosed. Secondly, its purpose is to avoid the harm which may be caused to the undertaking's rights of the defence as a result of the Commission reading the contents of a confidential document and improperly adding it to the investigation file. Therefore, even if that document is not used as evidence in a decision imposing a penalty under the competition rules, the undertaking may suffer harm which cannot be made good or can only be made good with great difficulty. Information covered by LPP might be used by the Commission, directly or indirectly, in order to obtain new information or new evidence without the undertaking in question always being able to identify or prevent such information or evidence from being used against it. Moreover, harm which the undertaking concerned would suffer as a result of disclosure to third parties of information covered by LPP could not be made good, for example if that information were used in a statement of objections in the course of the Commission's administrative procedure. The mere fact that the Commission cannot use privileged documents as evidence in a decision imposing a penalty is thus not sufficient to make good or eliminate the harm which resulted from the Commission's reading the content of the documents.

[88] Protection under LPP also requires the Commission, once it has adopted its decision rejecting a request under that head, not to read the content of the documents in question until it has given the undertaking concerned the opportunity to refer the matter to the Court of First Instance. In that regard, the Commission is bound to wait until the time-limit for bringing an action against the rejection decision has expired before reading the contents of those documents. In any event, to the extent that such an action does not have suspensory effect, it is for the undertaking concerned to bring an application for interim relief seeking suspension of operation of the decision rejecting the request for LPP (see, to that effect, *AM & S*, paragraph 32).

...

[123]...preparatory documents, even if they were not exchanged with a lawyer or were not created for the purpose of being sent physically to a lawyer, may none the less be covered by LPP, provided that they were drawn up exclusively for the purpose of seeking legal advice from a lawyer in exercise of the rights of the defence. On the other hand, the mere fact that a document has been discussed with a lawyer is not sufficient to give it such protection.

[124] It must be borne in mind that protection under LPP is an exception to the Commission's powers of investigation, which are essential to enable it to discover, bring to an end and penalise infringements of the competition rules. Such infringements are often carefully concealed and

usually very harmful to the proper functioning of the common market. For this reason, the possibility of treating a preparatory document as covered by LPP must be construed restrictively. It is for the undertaking relying on this protection to prove that the documents in question were drawn up with the sole aim of seeking legal advice from a lawyer. This should be unambiguously clear from the content of the documents themselves or the context in which those documents were prepared and found.

. . .

[165] The Set B documents contain, in addition to the manuscript notes already examined, e-mail correspondence of May and June 2000 exchanged between the General Manager of Akcros Chemicals and Mr S., an Advocaat on the roll of the Netherlands Bar, who at the material time was a member of the legal department of Akzo Nobel, in which capacity he coordinated competition-law matters.

[166] As regards, first of all, the applicants' principal argument, it must be pointed out that in its judgment in *AM & S*, the Court of Justice expressly held that the protection accorded to LPP under Community law, in the application of Regulation No 17, only applies to the extent that the lawyer is independent, that is to say, not bound to his client by a relationship of employment (paragraphs 21, 22 and 27 of the judgment). The requirement as to the position and status as an independent lawyer, which must be met by the legal adviser from whom the written communications which may be protected emanate, is based on a concept of the lawyer's role as collaborating in the administration of justice by the courts and as being required to provide, in full independence, and in the overriding interests of the administration of justice, such legal assistance as the client needs (*AM & S*, paragraph 24).

[167] It follows that the Court expressly excluded communications with in-house lawyers, that is, legal advisers bound to their clients by a relationship of employment, from protection under LPP. It must also be pointed out that the Court reached a conscious decision on that exception, given that the issue had been debated at length during the proceeding and that Advocate General Sir Gordon Slynn had expressly proposed in his Opinion for that judgment that where a lawyer bound by an employment contract remains a member of the profession and subject to its discipline and ethics, he should be treated in the same way as independent lawyers (Opinion of Advocate General Sir Gordon Slynn in *AM & S*, p. 1655).

[168] The Court therefore concludes that, contrary to what the applicants and certain interveners submit, the Court in its judgment in *AM & S* defined the concept of independent lawyer in negative terms in that it stipulated that such a lawyer should not be bound to his client by a relationship of employment (see paragraph 166 above), rather than positively, on the basis of membership of a Bar or Law Society or being subject to professional discipline and ethics. The Court thus laid down the test of legal advice provided 'in full independence' (*AM & S*, paragraph 24), which it identifies as that provided by a lawyer who, structurally, hierarchically and functionally, is a third party in relation to the undertaking receiving that advice.

[169] Accordingly, this Court rejects the applicants' principal argument and holds that the correspondence exchanged between a lawyer bound to Akzo Nobel by a relationship of employment and a manager of a company belonging to that group is not covered by LPP, as defined in *AM & S*.

NOTE: The privilege extends only to lawyers that are independent of the undertaking. Communications between an undertaking and its in-house lawyers are therefore not protected. This is somewhat unusual as employed lawyers, in many Member States, have the same rights as those who operate independently. An appeal has been lodged in *Akzo Nobel* (Case C-550/07 P), in which a number of organizations of legal professionals, including the Law Society of England & Wales, have intervened.

Mannesmannröhren-Werke AG v *Commission*
(Case T-112/98) [2001] ECR II-729, [2001] 5 CMLR 1

The Commission undertook an investigation into producers of steel tubes in which it made various requests for information. The applicant refused to answer a number of questions as they were self-incriminatory. They claimed the Commission could not require them to answer such questions as it would be contrary to Article 6 of the ECHR.

[61] Next, it must be borne in mind that the purpose of the powers conferred on the Commission by Regulation 17 is to enable that institution to fulfil its duty under the Treaty to ensure that the rules on competition within the Common Market are observed.

[62] During the preliminary investigation procedure, Regulation 17 does not give an undertaking that is subjected to an investigative measure any right to avoid the application of that measure on the ground that the results thereof might provide evidence of an infringement by it of the competition rules. On the contrary, it places the undertaking under a duty of active co-operation, which means that it must be prepared to make available to the Commission any information relating to the subject-matter of the investigation (*Orkem*, para. [27] and *Societe Generale*, para. [72]).

[63] In the absence of any right to silence expressly provided for in Regulation 17, it is necessary to consider whether certain limitations on the Commission's powers of investigation during a preliminary investigation are, however, implied by the need to safeguard the rights of defence (*Orkem*, para. [32]).

[64] In this respect, it is necessary to prevent the rights of defence from being irremediably impaired during preliminary investigation procedures which may be decisive in providing evidence of the unlawful nature of conduct engaged in by undertakings (*Orkem*, para. [33] and *Societe Generale*, para. [73]).

[65] However, it is settled case law that, in order to ensure the effectiveness of Article 11(2) and (5) of Regulation 17, the Commission is entitled to compel an undertaking to provide all necessary information concerning such facts as may be known to it and to disclose to the Commission, if necessary, such documents relating thereto as are in its possession, even if the latter may be used to establish, against it or another undertaking, the existence of anti-competitive conduct (*Orkem*, para. [34] and Case 27/88, *Solvay* v *EC Commission*, [[1989] ECR 3355; [1991] 4 CMLR 502] and *Societe Generale*, para. [74]).

[66] To acknowledge the existence of an absolute right to silence, as claimed by the applicant, would go beyond what is necessary in order to preserve the rights of defence of undertakings, and would constitute an unjustified hindrance to the Commission's performance of its duty under Article 89 of the EC Treaty (now, after amendment, Article 85 EC) to ensure that the rules on competition within the Common Market are observed.

[67] It follows that an undertaking in receipt of a request for information pursuant to Article 11(5) of Regulation 17 can be recognised as having a right to silence only to the extent that it would be compelled to provide answers which might involve an admission on its part of the existence of an infringement which it is incumbent upon the Commission to prove (*Orkem*, para. [35]).

NOTE: The Court of First Instance approved the ruling of the Court in cases such as *Orkem* (Case 374/87, [1989] ECR 3283) and *Solvay* (Case 27/88, [1989] ECR 3355), which gave an undertaking under investigation relatively limited protection from self-incrimination. They can be required to produce all documentation demanded by the Commission, even if it may be considered incriminating, and the privilege as recognized in relation to competition cases only extends to material which would in effect constitute an admission of some sort. Several commentators have questioned the compatibility of this decision with judgments of the European Court of Human Rights, particularly *Funke* v *France* [1993] 1 CMLR 897, (1993) 16 EHRR 297. See Willis, P.R., ' "You have the right to remain silent…", or do you? The privilege against self-incrimination following *Mannesmannröhren-Werke* and other recent decisions' [2001] ECLR 313 and Wils, W., 'Self-incrimination in EC antitrust enforcement: a legal and economic analysis' (2003) 26 World Comp. 567. There is a also a wider debate regarding the extent of human rights protection that can be claimed by corporations, see MacCulloch, A., 'The Privilege against Self-Incrimination in Competition Investigations: Theoretical Foundations and Practical Implications' (2006) 26(2) Legal Studies 211, and Emberland, M., *The Human Rights of Companies*, Oxford, OUP, 2006.

The detailed rules on the conduct of infringement actions by the Commission are not found in Regulation 1/2003. The detailed rules are set out in the Regulation 773/2004. It contains the rules which govern how the Commission should proceed. It also contains many of the rules which seek to protect the 'rights of the defence' during an investigation.

Commission Regulation 773/2004/EC relating to the conduct of proceedings by the Commission pursuant to Articles 81 and 82 of the EC Treaty
OJ, 2004, L123/18

CHAPTER I SCOPE

Article 1 Subject-matter and scope

This regulation applies to proceedings conducted by the Commission for the application of Articles 81 and 82 of the Treaty.

CHAPTER II INITIATION OF PROCEEDINGS

Article 2 Initiation of proceedings

1. The Commission may decide to initiate proceedings with a view to adopting a decision pursuant to Chapter III of Regulation (EC) No 1/2003 at any point in time, but no later than the date on which it issues a preliminary assessment as referred to in Article 9(1) of that Regulation or a statement of objections or the date on which a notice pursuant to Article 27(4) of that Regulation is published, whichever is the earlier.

2. The Commission may make public the initiation of proceedings, in any appropriate way. Before doing so, it shall inform the parties concerned.

3. The Commission may exercise its powers of investigation pursuant to Chapter V of Regulation (EC) No 1/2003 before initiating proceedings.

4. The Commission may reject a complaint pursuant to Article 7 of Regulation (EC) No 1/2003 without initiating proceedings.

CHAPTER III INVESTIGATIONS BY THE COMMISSION

Article 3 Power to take statements

1. Where the Commission interviews a person with his consent in accordance with Article 19 of Regulation (EC) No 1/2003, it shall, at the beginning of the interview, state the legal basis and the purpose of the interview, and recall its voluntary nature. It shall also inform the person interviewed of its intention to make a record of the interview.

2. The interview may be conducted by any means including by telephone or electronic means.

3. The Commission may record the statements made by the persons interviewed in any form. A copy of any recording shall be made available to the person interviewed for approval. Where necessary, the Commission shall set a time-limit within which the person interviewed may communicate to it any correction to be made to the statement.

Article 4 Oral questions during inspections

1. When, pursuant to Article 20(2)(e) of Regulation (EC) No 1/2003, officials or other accompanying persons authorised by the Commission ask representatives or members of staff of an undertaking or of an association of undertakings for explanations, the explanations given may be recorded in any form.

2. A copy of any recording made pursuant to paragraph 1 shall be made available to the undertaking or association of undertakings concerned after the inspection.

3. In cases where a member of staff of an undertaking or of an association of undertakings who is not or was not authorised by the undertaking or by the association of undertakings to provide explanations on behalf of the undertaking or association of undertakings has been asked for explanations, the Commission shall set a time-limit within which the undertaking or the association of undertakings may communicate to the Commission any rectification, amendment or supplement to the explanations given by such member of staff. The rectification, amendment or supplement shall be added to the explanations as recorded pursuant to paragraph 1.

CHAPTER IV HANDLING OF COMPLAINTS

Article 5 Admissibility of complaints

1. Natural and legal persons shall show a legitimate interest in order to be entitled to lodge a complaint for the purposes of Article 7 of Regulation (EC) No 1/2003.

Such complaints shall contain the information required by Form C, as set out in the Annex. The Commission may dispense with this obligation as regards part of the information, including documents, required by Form C.

2. Three paper copies as well as, if possible, an electronic copy of the complaint shall be submitted to the Commission. The complainant shall also submit a non-confidential version of the complaint, if confidentiality is claimed for any part of the complaint.

3. Complaints shall be submitted in one of the official languages of the Community.

Article 6 Participation of complainants in proceedings

1. Where the Commission issues a statement of objections relating to a matter in respect of which it has received a complaint, it shall provide the complainant with a copy of the non-confidential version of the statement of objections and set a time-limit within which the complainant may make known its views in writing.

2. The Commission may, where appropriate, afford complainants the opportunity of expressing their views at the oral hearing of the parties to which a statement of objections has been issued, if complainants so request in their written comments.

Article 7 Rejection of complaints

1. Where the Commission considers that on the basis of the information in its possession there are insufficient grounds for acting on a complaint, it shall inform the complainant of its reasons and set a time-limit within which the complainant may make known its views in writing. The Commission shall not be obliged to take into account any further written submission received after the expiry of that time-limit.

2. If the complainant makes known its views within the time-limit set by the Commission and the written submissions made by the complainant do not lead to a different assessment of the complaint, the Commission shall reject the complaint by decision.

3. If the complainant fails to make known its views within the time-limit set by the Commission, the complaint shall be deemed to have been withdrawn.

Article 8 Access to information

1. Where the Commission has informed the complainant of its intention to reject a complaint pursuant to Article 7(1) the complainant may request access to the documents on which the Commission bases its provisional assessment. For this purpose, the complainant may however not have access to business secrets and other confidential information belonging to other parties involved in the proceedings.

2. The documents to which the complainant has had access in the context of proceedings conducted by the Commission under Articles 81 and 82 of the Treaty may only be used by the complainant for the purposes of judicial or administrative proceedings for the application of those Treaty provisions.

Article 9 Rejections of complaints pursuant to Article 13 of Regulation (EC) No 1/2003

Where the Commission rejects a complaint pursuant to Article 13 of Regulation (EC) No 1/2003, it shall inform the complainant without delay of the national competition authority which is dealing or has already dealt with the case.

CHAPTER V EXERCISE OF THE RIGHT TO BE HEARD

Article 10 Statement of objections and reply

1. The Commission shall inform the parties concerned in writing of the objections raised against them. The statement of objections shall be notified to each of them.

2. The Commission shall, when notifying the statement of objections to the parties concerned, set a time-limit within which these parties may inform it in writing of their views. The Commission shall not be obliged to take into account written submissions received after the expiry of that time-limit.

3. The parties may, in their written submissions, set out all facts known to them which are relevant to their defence against the objections raised by the Commission. They shall attach any relevant documents as proof of the facts set out. They shall provide a paper original as well as an electronic copy or, where they do not provide an electronic copy, 28 paper copies of their submission and of the documents attached to it. They may propose that the Commission hear persons who may corroborate the facts set out in their submission.

Article 11 Right to be heard

1. The Commission shall give the parties to whom it has addressed a statement of objections the opportunity to be heard before consulting the Advisory Committee referred to in Article 14(1) of Regulation (EC) No 1/2003.

2. The Commission shall, in its decisions, deal only with objections in respect of which the parties referred to in paragraph 1 have been able to comment.

Article 12 Right to an oral hearing

The Commission shall give the parties to whom it has addressed a statement of objections the opportunity to develop their arguments at an oral hearing, if they so request in their written submissions.

Article 13 Hearing of other persons

1. If natural or legal persons other than those referred to in Articles 5 and 11 apply to be heard and show a sufficient interest, the Commission shall inform them in writing of the nature and subject matter of the procedure and shall set a time-limit within which they may make known their views in writing.

2. The Commission may, where appropriate, invite persons referred to in paragraph 1 to develop their arguments at the oral hearing of the parties to whom a statement of objections has been addressed, if the persons referred to in paragraph 1 so request in their written comments.

3. The Commission may invite any other person to express its views in writing and to attend the oral hearing of the parties to whom a statement of objections has been addressed. The Commission may also invite such persons to express their views at that oral hearing.

Article 14 Conduct of oral hearings

1. Hearings shall be conducted by a Hearing Officer in full independence.

2. The Commission shall invite the persons to be heard to attend the oral hearing on such date as it shall determine.

3. The Commission shall invite the competition authorities of the Member States to take part in the oral hearing. It may likewise invite officials and civil servants of other authorities of the Member States.

4. Persons invited to attend shall either appear in person or be represented by legal representatives or by representatives authorised by their constitution as appropriate. Undertakings and associations of undertakings may also be represented by a duly authorised agent appointed from among their permanent staff.

5. Persons heard by the Commission may be assisted by their lawyers or other qualified persons admitted by the Hearing Officer.

6. Oral hearings shall not be public. Each person may be heard separately or in the presence of other persons invited to attend, having regard to the legitimate interest of the undertakings in the protection of their business secrets and other confidential information.

7. The Hearing Officer may allow the parties to whom a statement of objections has been addressed, the complainants, other persons invited to the hearing, the Commission services and the authorities of the Member States to ask questions during the hearing.

8. The statements made by each person heard shall be recorded. Upon request, the recording of the hearing shall be made available to the persons who attended the hearing. Regard shall be had to the legitimate interest of the parties in the protection of their business secrets and other confidential information.

CHAPTER VI ACCESS TO THE FILE AND TREATMENT OF CONFIDENTIAL INFORMATION

Article 15 Access to the file and use of documents

1. If so requested, the Commission shall grant access to the file to the parties to whom it has addressed a statement of objections. Access shall be granted after the notification of the statement of objections.

2. The right of access to the file shall not extend to business secrets, other confidential information and internal documents of the Commission or of the competition authorities of the Member States. The right of access to the file shall also not extend to correspondence between the Commission and the competition authorities of the Member States or between the latter where such correspondence is contained in the file of the Commission.

3. Nothing in this Regulation prevents the Commission from disclosing and using information necessary to prove an infringement of Articles 81 or 82 of the Treaty.

4. Documents obtained through access to the file pursuant to this Article shall only be used for the purposes of judicial or administrative proceedings for the application of Articles 81 and 82 of the Treaty.

Article 16 Identification and protection of confidential information

1. Information, including documents, shall not be communicated or made accessible by the Commission in so far as it contains business secrets or other confidential information of any person.

2. Any person which makes known its views pursuant to Article 6(1), Article 7(1), Article 10(2) and Article 13(1) and (3) or subsequently submits further information to the Commission in the course of the same procedure, shall clearly identify any material which it considers to be confidential, giving reasons, and provide a separate non-confidential version by the date set by the Commission for making its views known.

3. Without prejudice to paragraph 2 of this Article, the Commission may require undertakings and associations of undertakings which produce documents or statements pursuant to Regulation (EC) No 1/2003 to identify the documents or parts of documents which they consider to contain business secrets or other confidential information belonging to them and to identify the undertakings with regard to which such documents are to be considered confidential. The Commission may likewise require undertakings or associations of undertakings to identify any part of a statement of objections, a case summary drawn up pursuant to Article 27(4) of Regulation (EC) No 1/2003 or a decision adopted by the Commission which in their view contains business secrets.

The Commission may set a time-limit within which the undertakings and associations of undertakings are to:
    (a) substantiate their claim for confidentiality with regard to each individual document or part of document, statement or part of statement;
    (b) provide the Commission with a non-confidential version of the documents or statements, in which the confidential passages are deleted;
    (c) provide a concise description of each piece of deleted information.

4. If undertakings or associations of undertakings fail to comply with paragraphs 2 and 3, the Commission may assume that the documents or statements concerned do not contain confidential information.

CHAPTER VII GENERAL AND FINAL PROVISIONS

Article 17 Time-limits

1. In setting the time-limits provided for in Article 3(3), Article 4(3), Article 6(1), Article 7(1), Article 10(2) and Article 16(3), the Commission shall have regard both to the time required for preparation of the submission and to the urgency of the case.

2. The time-limits referred to in Article 6(1), Article 7(1) and Article 10(2) shall be at least four weeks. However, for proceedings initiated with a view to adopting interim measures pursuant to Article 8 of Regulation (EC) No 1/2003, the time-limit may be shortened to one week.

3. The time-limits referred to in Article 3(3), Article 4(3) and Article 16(3) shall be at least two weeks.

4. Where appropriate and upon reasoned request made before the expiry of the original time-limit, time-limits may be extended.

NOTE: The role of the Hearing Officer was introduced to the administrative procedure to ensure the rights of the defence in competition proceedings. Before the introduction of this procedure, the Commission was in effect acting as investigator, prosecutor, and judge. The Hearing Officer is an independent officer, who ensures that the accused undertaking can properly defend themselves before an impartial body.

SECTION 4: POWER TO FINE

For the procedure in Regulation 1 to be effective, an adverse finding must be supported by a proper deterrent. The Regulation sets out the importance of the Commission through its considerable power to fine undertakings that breach the competition rules. With a maximum fine of up to 10 per cent of global turnover, the Commission has the opportunity to impose significant fines with real deterrent power. In 1998, the Commission produced Guidelines that first indicated the manner in which the Commission will determine a fine appropriate to the circumstances of the case. The Guidelines were amended in 2006, increasing the potential for the imposition of higher fines.

Commission Guidelines on the method of setting fines imposed pursuant to Article 23(2)(a) of Regulation No 1/2003

OJ, 2006, C210/2

INTRODUCTION

1. Pursuant to Article 23(2)(a) of Regulation No 1/2003 [1], the Commission may, by decision, impose fines on undertakings or associations of undertakings where, either intentionally or negligently, they infringe Article 81 or 82 of the Treaty.

2. In exercising its power to impose such fines, the Commission enjoys a wide margin of discretion [2] within the limits set by Regulation No 1/2003. First, the Commission must have regard both to the gravity and to the duration of the infringement. Second, the fine imposed may not exceed the limits specified in Article 23(2), second and third subparagraphs, of Regulation No 1/2003.

3. In order to ensure the transparency and impartiality of its decisions, the Commission published on 14 January 1998 guidelines on the method of setting fines. After more than eight years of implementation, the Commission has acquired sufficient experience to develop further and refine its policy on fines.

4. The Commission's power to impose fines on undertakings or associations of undertakings which, intentionally or negligently, infringe Article 81 or 82 of the Treaty is one of the means conferred on it in order for it to carry out the task of supervision entrusted to it by the Treaty. That task not only includes the duty to investigate and sanction individual infringements, but it also encompasses the duty to pursue a general policy designed to apply, in competition matters, the principles laid down by the Treaty and to steer the conduct of undertakings in the light of those principles. For this purpose, the Commission must ensure that its action has the necessary deterrent effect.

Accordingly, when the Commission discovers that Article 81 or 82 of the Treaty has been infringed, it may be necessary to impose a fine on those who have acted in breach of the law. Fines should have a sufficiently deterrent effect, not only in order to sanction the undertakings concerned (specific deterrence) but also in order to deter other undertakings from engaging in, or continuing, behaviour that is contrary to Articles 81 and 82 of the EC Treaty (general deterrence).

5. In order to achieve these objectives, it is appropriate for the Commission to refer to the value of the sales of goods or services to which the infringement relates as a basis for setting the fine. The duration of the infringement should also play a significant role in the setting of the appropriate amount of the fine. It necessarily has an impact on the potential consequences of the infringement on the market. It is therefore considered important that the fine should also reflect the number of years during which an undertaking participated in the infringement.

6. The combination of the value of sales to which the infringement relates and of the duration of the infringement is regarded as providing an appropriate proxy to reflect the economic importance of the infringement as well as the relative weight of each undertaking in the infringement. Reference to these factors provides a good indication of the order of magnitude of the fine and should not be regarded as the basis for an automatic and arithmetical calculation method.

7. It is also considered appropriate to include in the fine a specific amount irrespective of the duration of the infringement, in order to deter companies from even entering into illegal practices.

8. The sections below set out the principles which will guide the Commission when it sets fines imposed pursuant to Article 23(2)(a) of Regulation No 1/2003.

METHOD FOR THE SETTING OF FINES

9. Without prejudice to point 37 below, the Commission will use the following two-step methodology when setting the fine to be imposed on undertakings or associations of undertakings.

10. First, the Commission will determine a basic amount for each undertaking or association of undertakings (see Section 1 below).

11. Second, it may adjust that basic amount upwards or downwards (see Section 2 below).

1. Basic amount of the fine

12. The basic amount will be set by reference to the value of sales and applying the following methodology.

A. Calculation of the value of sales

13. In determining the basic amount of the fine to be imposed, the Commission will take the value of the undertaking's sales of goods or services to which the infringement directly or indirectly [6] relates in the relevant geographic area within the EEA. It will normally take the sales made by the undertaking during the last full business year of its participation in the infringement (hereafter "value of sales").

14. Where the infringement by an association of undertakings relates to the activities of its members, the value of sales will generally correspond to the sum of the value of sales by its members.

15. In determining the value of sales by an undertaking, the Commission will take that undertaking's best available figures.

16. Where the figures made available by an undertaking are incomplete or not reliable, the Commission may determine the value of its sales on the basis of the partial figures it has obtained and/or any other information which it regards as relevant and appropriate.

17. The value of sales will be determined before VAT and other taxes directly related to the sales.

18. Where the geographic scope of an infringement extends beyond the EEA (e.g. worldwide cartels), the relevant sales of the undertakings within the EEA may not properly reflect the weight of each undertaking in the infringement. This may be the case in particular with worldwide market-sharing arrangements.

In such circumstances, in order to reflect both the aggregate size of the relevant sales within the EEA and the relative weight of each undertaking in the infringement, the Commission may assess the total value of the sales of goods or services to which the infringement relates in the relevant geographic area (wider than the EEA), may determine the share of the sales of each undertaking party to the infringement on that market and may apply this share to the aggregate sales within the EEA of the undertakings concerned. The result will be taken as the value of sales for the purpose of setting the basic amount of the fine.

B. Determination of the basic amount of the fine

19. The basic amount of the fine will be related to a proportion of the value of sales, depending on the degree of gravity of the infringement, multiplied by the number of years of infringement.

20. The assessment of gravity will be made on a case-by-case basis for all types of infringement, taking account of all the relevant circumstances of the case.

21. As a general rule, the proportion of the value of sales taken into account will be set at a level of up to 30% of the value of sales.

22. In order to decide whether the proportion of the value of sales to be considered in a given case should be at the lower end or at the higher end of that scale, the Commission will have regard to a number of factors, such as the nature of the infringement, the combined market share of all the undertakings concerned, the geographic scope of the infringement and whether or not the infringement has been implemented.

23. Horizontal price-fixing, market-sharing and output-limitation agreements, which are usually secret, are, by their very nature, among the most harmful restrictions of competition. As a matter of policy, they will be heavily fined. Therefore, the proportion of the value of sales taken into account for such infringements will generally be set at the higher end of the scale.

24. In order to take fully into account the duration of the participation of each undertaking in the infringement, the amount determined on the basis of the value of sales (see points 20 to 23 above) will be multiplied by the number of years of participation in the infringement. Periods of less than six months will be counted as half a year; periods longer than six months but shorter than one year will be counted as a full year.

25. In addition, irrespective of the duration of the undertaking's participation in the infringement, the Commission will include in the basic amount a sum of between 15% and 25% of the value of sales as defined in Section A above in order to deter undertakings from even entering into horizontal price-fixing, market-sharing and output-limitation agreements. The Commission may also apply such an additional amount in the case of other infringements. For the purpose of deciding the proportion of the value of sales to be considered in a given case, the Commission will have regard to a number of factors, in particular those referred in point 22.

26. Where the value of sales by undertakings participating in the infringement is similar but not identical, the Commission may set for each of them an identical basic amount. Moreover, in determining the basic amount of the fine, the Commission will use rounded figures.

2. Adjustments to the basic amount

27. In setting the fine, the Commission may take into account circumstances that result in an increase or decrease in the basic amount as determined in Section 1 above. It will do so on the basis of an overall assessment which takes account of all the relevant circumstances.

A. Aggravating circumstances

28. The basic amount may be increased where the Commission finds that there are aggravating circumstances, such as:
   — where an undertaking continues or repeats the same or a similar infringement after the Commission or a national competition authority has made a finding that the undertaking infringed Article 81 or 82: the basic amount will be increased by up to 100% for each such infringement established;
   — refusal to cooperate with or obstruction of the Commission in carrying out its investigations;
   — role of leader in, or instigator of, the infringement; the Commission will also pay particular attention to any steps taken to coerce other undertakings to participate in the infringement

and/or any retaliatory measures taken against other undertakings with a view to enforcing the practices constituting the infringement.

B. Mitigating circumstances

29. The basic amount may be reduced where the Commission finds that mitigating circumstances exist, such as:
    — where the undertaking concerned provides evidence that it terminated the infringement as soon as the Commission intervened: this will not apply to secret agreements or practices (in particular, cartels);
    — where the undertaking provides evidence that the infringement has been committed as a result of negligence;
    — where the undertaking provides evidence that its involvement in the infringement is substantially limited and thus demonstrates that, during the period in which it was party to the offending agreement, it actually avoided applying it by adopting competitive conduct in the market: the mere fact that an undertaking participated in an infringement for a shorter duration than others will not be regarded as a mitigating circumstance since this will already be reflected in the basic amount;
    — where the undertaking concerned has effectively cooperated with the Commission outside the scope of the Leniency Notice and beyond its legal obligation to do so;
    — where the anti-competitive conduct of the undertaking has been authorized or encouraged by public authorities or by legislation.

C. Specific increase for deterrence

30. The Commission will pay particular attention to the need to ensure that fines have a sufficiently deterrent effect; to that end, it may increase the fine to be imposed on undertakings which have a particularly large turnover beyond the sales of goods or services to which the infringement relates.

31. The Commission will also take into account the need to increase the fine in order to exceed the amount of gains improperly made as a result of the infringement where it is possible to estimate that amount.

D. Legal maximum

32. The final amount of the fine shall not, in any event, exceed 10% of the total turnover in the preceding business year of the undertaking or association of undertakings participating in the infringement, as laid down in Article 23(2) of Regulation No 1/2003.

33. Where an infringement by an association of undertakings relates to the activities of its members, the fine shall not exceed 10% of the sum of the total turnover of each member active on the market affected by that infringement.

E. Leniency Notice

34. The Commission will apply the leniency rules in line with the conditions set out in the applicable notice.

F. Ability to pay

35. In exceptional cases, the Commission may, upon request, take account of the undertaking's inability to pay in a specific social and economic context. It will not base any reduction granted for this reason in the fine on the mere finding of an adverse or loss-making financial situation. A reduction could be granted solely on the basis of objective evidence that imposition of the fine as provided for in these Guidelines would irretrievably jeopardise the economic viability of the undertaking concerned and cause its assets to lose all their value.

FINAL CONSIDERATIONS

36. The Commission may, in certain cases, impose a symbolic fine. The justification for imposing such a fine should be given in its decision.

37. Although these Guidelines present the general methodology for the setting of fines, the particularities of a given case or the need to achieve deterrence in a particular case may justify departing from such methodology or from the limits specified in point 21.

38. These Guidelines will be applied in all cases where a statement of objections is notified after their date of publication in the Official Journal, regardless of whether the fine is imposed pursuant to Article 23(2) of Regulation No 1/2003 or Article 15(2) of Regulation 17/62.

Völker, S.B., 'Rough justice? An analysis of the European Commission's new fining guidelines'
(2007) 44 CML Rev 1285, pp. 1317–18 [footnotes omitted]

the Commission's own statements suggest that the 2006 Guidelines are designed to lead to higher fines in many if not most cases, at least for long-lasting infringements in large markets, and certainly for recidivists. One may question whether such an increase is necessary and whether new guidelines were required to achieve it. It is generally recognized that complete deterrence is impossible and that continuing discovery of new infringements does not in itself justify the conclusion that the level of fines imposed in the past was insufficient. Even under the 1998 Guidelines, the Commission has been able to impose extremely large fines approaching euro 1 billion for all cartel members and euro 500 million for a single company. It is debatable whether still higher fines will be more effective in preventing cartels or whether they will simply lead to a wealth transfer from shareholders to the Community budget. The ceiling of Article 23(2) of Regulation 1/2003 effectively means that fines of several hundred million Euros or more can only be imposed on large multinational, multi-product companies. Such companies are typically characterized by a separation of ownership and control, and their complex organizational structure will often mean little alignment between a local manager's incentives to enter into a cartel and central management's interest in maintaining full compliance with the competition rules. Given its inability to impose fines on individuals, the Commission apparently expects companies to use all means at their disposal to prevent anticompetitive conduct by their employees. But at the same time the Commission—with the courts' blessing—has given no credit to large companies that have argued that the infringements were committed by lower-level managers despite a strict corporate compliance policy, and that the company took immediate action to punish the individuals involved after it discovered the infringements. It is submitted that without evidence of senior management involvement, there can be no assumption that a large company weighed the gains of a possible infringement against the risk that it might be subject to a fine that it could easily pay given its overall financial resources. Consequently, it would seem appropriate for the Commission to reserve the highest fines for cases in which a multi-product company's top management had direct involvement in the cartel.

NOTE: The introduction of the 2006 Notice does appear to have had an impact on fines. The impact of the Notice has taken some time to filter through the system, but the total fines imposed in cartel cases gives an example of the increase. The total fines in cartel cases from 2006–2008 were as follows: 2006–€1.846bn; 2007–€3.334bn; and, 2008–€2.271bn. The average fine per undertaking (excluding the effect of leniency reductions) in 2008 was €82.3m.

SECTION 5: REVIEW OF COMMISSION DECISIONS

As a Commission Decision can have very serious consequences for an undertaking, or undertakings in the case of anti-competitive agreements and mergers, they are often controversial. In many cases it is very common to see the Commission's Decision challenged by the affected parties, or interested third parties such as complainants. The process for review is to challenge the Decision, as the act of a Community institution, under Article 230 EC, which sets out four grounds for review: lack of competence; infringement of essential procedural requirements; infringement of the Treaty or any rule of law relating to its application; and, misuse of power. The review of Commission Decisions initially goes before the Court of First Instance. There is appeal from the Court of First Instance on points of law to the Court of Justice. The task of the Commission, in adopting Decisions, and the role of the Court, in reviewing Commission Decisions, has been discussed in a number of cases before the Court. The majority of recent examples have come in the field of merger control, but it is likely that the Court would adopt the same principles, notwithstanding the peculiar issues to be found in merger cases, in all competition cases.

Commission v Tetra Laval BV
(Case C-12/03 P) [2005] ECR I-987

The Commission reviewed a merger between Tetra Laval and Sidel. Both companies were involved in the production of different types of liquid packaging. The Commission initially prohibited the merger, but that Decision was overturned by the CFI in Case T-5/02. It was suggested that the CFI required a higher standard of proof for a Commission Decision under the Merger Regulation and the Commission lodged an appeal.

[37] By its first ground of appeal, the Commission contests the judgment under appeal in so far as the Court of First Instance required it, when adopting a decision declaring a concentration incompatible with the common market, to satisfy a standard of proof and to provide a quality of evidence in support of its line of argument which are incompatible with the wide discretion which it enjoys in assessing economic matters. It thus complains that the Court of First Instance infringed Article 230 EC by exceeding the limits of its power of review established by case-law and, as a result, misapplied Article 2(2) and (3) of the Regulation by creating a presumption of legality in respect of certain concentrations.

[38] It should be observed that, in paragraph 119 of the judgment under appeal, the Court of First Instance correctly set out the tests to be applied when carrying out judicial review of a Commission decision on a concentration as laid down in the judgment in *Kali & Salz*. In paragraphs 223 and 224 of that judgment, the Court stated that the basic provisions of the Regulation, in particular Article 2, confer on the Commission a certain discretion, especially with respect to assessments of an economic nature, and that, consequently, review by the Community Courts of the exercise of that discretion, which is essential for defining the rules on concentrations, must take account of the margin of discretion implicit in the provisions of an economic nature which form part of the rules on concentrations.

[39] Whilst the Court recognises that the Commission has a margin of discretion with regard to economic matters, that does not mean that the Community Courts must refrain from reviewing the Commission's interpretation of information of an economic nature. Not only must the Community Courts, inter alia, establish whether the evidence relied on is factually accurate, reliable and consistent but also whether that evidence contains all the information which must be taken into account in order to assess a complex situation and whether it is capable of substantiating the conclusions drawn from it. Such a review is all the more necessary in the case of a prospective analysis required when examining a planned merger with conglomerate effect.

[40] Thus, the Court of First Instance was right to find, in paragraph 155 of the judgment under appeal, in reliance on, in particular, the judgment in *Kali & Salz*, that the Commission's analysis of a merger producing a conglomerate effect is subject to requirements similar to those defined by the Court with regard to the creation of a situation of collective dominance and that it calls for a close examination of the circumstances which are relevant for an assessment of that effect on the conditions of competition on the reference market.

[41] Although the Court of First Instance stated, in paragraph 155, that proof of anti-competitive conglomerate effects of a merger of the kind notified calls for a precise examination, supported by convincing evidence, of the circumstances which allegedly produce those effects, it by no means added a condition relating to the requisite standard of proof but merely drew attention to the essential function of evidence, which is to establish convincingly the merits of an argument or, as in the present case, of a decision on a merger.

[42] A prospective analysis of the kind necessary in merger control must be carried out with great care since it does not entail the examination of past events—for which often many items of evidence are available which make it possible to understand the causes—or of current events, but rather a prediction of events which are more or less likely to occur in future if a decision prohibiting the planned concentration or laying down the conditions for it is not adopted.

[43] Thus, the prospective analysis consists of an examination of how a concentration might alter the factors determining the state of competition on a given market in order to establish whether it would give rise to a serious impediment to effective competition. Such an analysis makes it necessary to envisage various chains of cause and effect with a view to ascertaining which of them are the most likely.

Bertelsmann AG and Sony Corp of America v *Independent Music Publishers and Labels Association (Impala)*
(Case C-413/06 P) [2008] 5 CMLR 17

The Commission reviewed a merger between two major music companies, Sony & BMG. The Commission had opened a Stage II investigation, but on receipt of new evidence cleared the merger unconditionally. The Independent Music Publishers and Labels Association (Impala) challenged that clearance, and the CFI annulled the Decision in Case T-464/04. One of the issues in both the CFI and ECJ was the standard of proof required for a clearance, as opposed to the standard required for a prohibition.

[45] As regards the substance, as Impala points out, at the heart of the second part of the third ground of appeal is the premise that the standard of proof will differ according to whether a decision approving a concentration or a decision prohibiting a concentration is involved. In this connection, it is common ground between the parties that in the judgment under appeal the Court of First Instance applied the same standard of proof to the contested decision—an approval decision—as that which it would have applied to a prohibition decision.

[46] In that regard, it should be noted at the outset that there is nothing in Article 2(2) or (3) of the Regulation which states that it imposes different standards of proof in relation to decisions approving a concentration, on the one hand, and decisions prohibiting a concentration, on the other.

[47] Thus, as the Court has, in substance, already held, the prospective analysis called for in relation to the control of concentrations, which consists of an examination of how a concentration might alter the factors determining the state of competition on a given market in order to establish whether it would give rise to a significant impediment to effective competition, makes it necessary to envisage various chains of cause and effect with a view to ascertaining which of them is the most likely (see, to that effect, Case C-12/03 P *Commission v Tetra Laval* [2005] ECR I-987, paragraph 43).

[48] Contrary to what the appellants submit, it cannot therefore be inferred from the Regulation that there is a general presumption that a notified concentration is compatible with, or incompatible with, the common market.

[49] That interpretation of the Regulation is not invalidated by Article 10(6), which provides that a notified concentration is to be deemed compatible with the common market where the Commission has not taken a decision on the compatibility of that concentration within the prescribed period. That provision is a specific expression of the need for speed, which characterises the general

scheme of the Regulation and which requires the Commission to comply with strict time-limits for the adoption of the final decision (see, in that regard, Case C-202/06 P *Cementbouw Handel & Industrie v Commission* [2007] ECR I-0000, paragraph 39). It is, however, an exception to the general scheme of the Regulation, which is laid down in particular in Articles 6(1) and 8(1), according to which the Commission is to rule expressly on the concentrations which are notified to it.

[50] Furthermore, it is true that, as is apparent from the Court's case-law, the decisions of the Commission as to the compatibility of concentrations with the common market must be supported by a sufficiently cogent and consistent body of evidence (see, to that effect, Joined Cases C-68/94 and C-30/95 *France and Others v Commission* [1998] ECR I-1375, '*Kali & Salz*', paragraph 228) and that in the context of the analysis of a 'conglomerate-type' concentration the quality of the evidence produced by the Commission in order to establish that it is necessary to adopt a decision declaring the concentration incompatible with the common market is particularly important (see *Commission v Tetra Laval*, paragraph 44).

[51] However, it cannot be deduced from that that the Commission must, particularly where it pursues a theory of collective dominance, comply with a higher standard of proof in relation to decisions prohibiting concentrations than in relation to decisions approving them. That case-law merely reflects the essential function of evidence, which is to establish convincingly the merits of an argument or, as in the case of the control of concentrations, to support the conclusions underpinning the Commission's decisions (see, to that effect, *Commission v Tetra Laval*, paragraphs 41 and 44). Furthermore, the fact that an issue of collective dominance does, or does not, arise, cannot of itself have an impact on the standard of proof which applies. In that regard, the inherent complexity of a theory of competitive harm put forward in relation to a notified concentration is a factor which must be taken into account when assessing the plausibility of the various consequences such a concentration may have, in order to identify those which are most likely to arise, but such complexity does not, of itself, have an impact on the standard of proof which is required.

[52] It follows that, where it has been notified of a proposed concentration pursuant to the Regulation, the Commission is, in principle, required to adopt a position, either in the sense of approving or of prohibiting the concentration, in accordance with its assessment of the economic outcome attributable to the concentration which is most likely to ensue.

[53] The appellants are accordingly incorrect in maintaining that, since it was a decision approving a concentration that was at issue, the Court of First Instance should have considered only whether the Commission could, by applying a particularly high standard of proof, have prohibited that concentration. Consequently, without it being necessary to adopt a position on the admissibility of the specific criticisms relating to the paragraphs of the judgment under appeal listed in paragraph 41 of this judgment, it must be held that since the premise underlying those criticisms is groundless, they cannot, in any event, be accepted.

NOTE: See also Bailey, D., 'Scope of Judicial Review under Article 81 EC' (2004) 41(5) CML Rev 1327. With the large sums of money involved in most competition cases it is not surprising that a great many eventually come before the European courts. The recourse to the courts is almost automatic when a fine is imposed in relation to the antitrust prohibitions. Most prohibition Decisions in the merger regime are also challenged. In recent years many of the steps taken to reform the substance of competition law can be seen as being part of the process whereby the Commission are reforming their practices to make Decisions 'review proof'; largely by setting out the factors they will take into account and their methodology more clearly. The discretion of the Commission not only relates to the finding of an infringement. The Commission discretion also relates to the amount of any fine imposed. Many challenges to Commission Decisions relate to the fine alone, with no effective challenge to the infringement itself. There is a fuller discussion of the Commission's fining practice in Chapter 9 on cartels, but an example of a significant fine reduction can be seen in cases such as, Joined cases T-236, 239, 244–6, 251, and 252/01 *Tokai Carbon* v *Commission* [2004] ECR II-1181.

When adopting a decision under Regulation 1 the Commission acts as investigator, prosecutor, and judge. There are therefore many questions regarding the protection of the rights of the defence, 'due process', and the 'human rights' of undertakings under investigation in competition cases. As the protection of human rights and fundamental freedoms have become more entrenched as part of EC law, arguments of that nature have become more important in the competition field.

Reproduced with permission of Kluwer Law International from Andreangeli, A., 'Toward an EU Competition Court: "Article-6-Proofing" antitrust proceedings before the Commission?'
(2007) 30 World Competition 595, pp. 609–610 [footnotes omitted]

the Strasbourg Court has adopted a "composite approach" according to which it is necessary that every administrative decision affecting the determination of civil rights and obligations or of a criminal charge be "subject to subsequent control by a judicial body that has full jurisdiction and does provide the guarantees of Article 6(1)". Consequently, the assessment of the compliance of competition proceedings with the level of protection enshrined in Article 6(1) of the Convention requires the consideration of the extent to which the judicial scrutiny exercised on the final decision complies with the standards of judicial review provided by the ECHR.

With respect to decisions concerning the "determination of civil rights and obligations", the case law of the European Court of Human Rights supports the view that "judicial review-type" appeals will be sufficient to satisfy the requirements of the Convention. As was held in *Bryan* v *United Kingdom*, the circumstance that the impugned decision could have been annulled by the High Court if it had been adopted "by reference to irrelevant factors or without regard to relevant factors", or on the basis of insufficient evidence, or if it had been "based on an inference from facts which was perverse or irrational" was considered consistent with the standards enshrined in Article 6(1) ECHR.

A more stringent type of review is instead applicable to the scrutiny of "administrative" decisions that are "criminal" in nature. In the *Schmautzer* decision, concerning the compatibility of administrative decision concerning motoring offences with the Convention, a violation of Article 6(1) was found in the lack on the part of the competent administrative court of the power to annul the final decision "in all respects, on questions of fact and law": unlike decisions concerning merely "civil" matters, there should be "no room for limitation on the scope of review required of the decisions of administrative authorities".

It may therefore be argued that, despite their legislative classification as "administrative" in nature, the proceedings for the application of articles 81 and 82 of the Treaty and the Merger Regulation may in fact be, respectively, "criminal" and "civil" in nature, and therefore within the scope of the application of the standards of procedural "fairness" dictated by Article 6(1) of the ECHR. This finding may have far reaching consequences for the rules of "due process" applicable to them both at administrative and at judicial level, in consideration of the "composite approach" adopted by the Strasbourg Court in assessing the compliance of administrative action to Article 6(1) ECHR.

NOTE: Legal challenges relating to Commission Decisions have an increasing propensity to invoke 'due process' or human rights arguments. It is likely that this trend will continue; notwithstanding the uncertain status of the EU's Charter of Fundamental Rights.

■ QUESTIONS

Given that the normal subjects of competition law are very well resourced companies, can they be said to deserve 'human rights' protections?

In the previous section we examined the review of Commission Decisions. It is clear that the Commission, on occasion, have their Decisions overturned. What remedies are available for the parties who have been affected by a Commission Decision which was eventually overturned?

FURTHER READING

Brammer, S., 'Concurrent jurisdiction under Regulation 1/2003 and the issue of case allocation' (2005) 42(5) CML Rev 1383.

Dekeyser, K., and Jaspers, M., 'A New Era of ECN Co-operation' (2007) 30(1) World Competition 3.

Gilliams, H.M., 'Modernisation: from policy to practice' (2003) 28 EL Rev 451.

Riley, A., 'EC Antitrust Modernisation: The Commission Does Very Nicely—Thank You! Part 1: Regulation 1 and the Notification Burden' [2003] ECLR 604; 'Part 2: Between the Idea and the Reality; Decentralisation under Regulation 1' [2003] ECLR 687.

Völker, S.B., 'Rough justice? An analysis of the European Commission's new fining guidelines' (2007) 44(5) CML Rev 1285.

3

UK enforcement

The framework for the enforcement of UK competition law has undergone a dramatic overhaul in recent years; largely through the introduction of the Competition Act 1998 ('CA 1998') and the Enterprise Act 2002 ('EA 2002'). Until the enactment of the CA 1998, the enforcement structure under the principal legislation, the Fair Trading Act 1973 ('FTA 1973'), was essentially tripartite, involving the Director General of Fair Trading ('DGFT'), the Competition Commission (previously the MMC), and the Secretary of State. UK competition law was essentially administrative in nature, lacking redress for private parties (with the exception of s. 35(2) of the Restrictive Trade Practices Act 1976 ('RTPA 1976'), and the possibility of judicial review of the administrative decision-making process), and ultimate decision making rested with a politician, the Secretary of State. The CA 1998 signalled the end of the tripartite structure of competition law enforcement in the UK.

Wilks, S., *In the Public Interest, Competition Policy and the Monopolies and Mergers Commission*
Manchester, MUP, 1999

> Compared with the MMC the OFT is a mere stripling but, even so, it has survived rather successfully and was able to celebrate its twenty-fifth birthday in 1998, along with that of the tripartite structure of British competition authorities. In 1995 the DTI affirmed that 'the tripartite structure is designed to provide for effective action against damaging monopolies, and at the same time to provide checks and balances to the exercise of power by the authorities...The Government are content with this broad structure, which they believe has shown its worth over a period of more than 20 years'. The tripartite structure, with its checks and balances, has proved attractive enough to be retained for merger control and for some aspects of monopoly control. Under the 1998 Competition Act, however, the 'operational' aspects of the tripartite structure have been abolished. The prohibition will be operated by the DGFT who will become a more important, and a more controversial, figure. The 'structural' aspects of the tripartite system are, however, being retained and the system will continue to rely on co-operative relations between the OFT, the new Competition Commission and the DTI.

NOTE: There was debate during the 1990s, particularly following the influential House of Commons Trade and Industry Committee Report, *UK Policy on Monopolies*, 1995, suggesting the creation of a unitary authority by merging the OFT and MMC. See Wilks, above, particularly Chapter 9. This was ultimately rejected, but the tripartite scheme is effectively extinct. The Secretary of State has no real enforcement role under the CA 1998, and the Enterprise Act significantly curtailed ministerial involvement in mergers and 'market investigations'.

A further key development in the enforcement of UK competition law has been the shift from a purely administrative system of enforcement to a 'hybrid' system, which also involves rights of redress to private parties through normal court processes. Mechanisms to facilitate private actions in competition disputes were introduced in the CA 1998 and further enhanced under the EA 2002. The role of private actions in the UK is still underdeveloped and subject to an ongoing process of reform, both at the domestic and European levels. For further discussion of these issues see Chapter 4.

This chapter will look at the enforcement structures under the 1998 Act in relation to the prohibitions and 2002 Act in relation to mergers and market investigations. Detailed examination of the substantive provisions can be seen in later chapters. At this stage we are interested in outlining the institutional structure and the role of the different institutions.

SECTION 2: COMPETITION ACT 1998

The CA 1998 reformed UK substantive competition law but it also instituted a new enforcement framework in respect of the two prohibitions, based largely on the European model.

Wilks, S., *In the Public Interest, Competition Policy and the Monopolies and Mergers Commission*
Manchester, MUP, 1999

The Competition Act 1998

With an elegant accident of symmetry the Act comes exactly fifty years after the Monopolies and Restrictive Practices Act 1948. It is potentially a revolutionary piece of legislation which has considerable implications for the institutions of British capitalism. As explored in the concluding chapter, the 1948 Act catered to the voluntarism, the self-regulation and the accommodative arm's-length relationship between government and industry which permeated the political economy of the 1940s. The 1998 Act creates a more formal and legally objective framework for industry. It provides didactic guidance rather than the co-operative exploration which underlay its 1948 predecessor. The formal provisions of the Act are briefly reviewed in chapter 10.

Despite its European provenance, the new Act is a piece of British legislation although it builds in novel provisions to employ European jurisprudence. It is designed to dovetail with the European regime and doubtless many hope that this new, more effective, Act will increase the element of real subsidiarity. It represents something of a compromise, as can be seen if it is considered in the context of the debates reviewed above. In respect of the first debate it almost certainly represents a more active British competition policy, and one that stresses 'competition' as a principle rather than 'the public interest'. In respect of the second debate it adopts the European stance of prohibition and an effects doctrine, and does so for monopolies as well as restrictive practices. But the monopolies element is enacted with due caution and the mergers regime remains unaltered. In respect of the third debate the institutions have changed in their relationships with one another and in the abolition of one court and the creation of a new tribunal. These changes have been the product of wide consultation. The Government has pursued a neo-pluralist path of involvement of the policy network through a proliferation of Green and White Papers and by giving every indication of listening to the responses. There is nothing impetuous or dogmatic about this legislation. Government has sought advice, built consensus and moved with judicious caution. This is indicative of a neo-pluralist policy stance which seeks to build consensus but which also requires technical support. The Government was genuinely uncertain about the potential effects of new legislation and in true civil service style (and very unlike the sweeping Thatcherite policy initiatives) it enrolled the views and the advice of business, lawyers and other specialists. It is indicative of this caution that the new model has perhaps embraced the European certainties too emphatically. After years of being reproached as not being European enough, some lawyers are now suggesting that the Government has become too European. The European blueprint does indeed involve some major shifts in the regime of monopoly control. In order to evaluate the extent of change consider the following:

- the shift from agnostic investigation to prohibition
- the replacement of the 'public interest' test by an 'effect on competition' test
- the exclusion of the Secretary of State from the administrative process as regards actions and remedies
- the incorporation of the principles of European competition law jurisprudence into British administration
- hence the likely growth of legal involvement through defence, appeal and third-party action
- the empowerment of third parties through rights of appeal and the potential to pursue damages in the courts
- the imposition of substantial penalties.

NOTE: Along with the creation of a hybrid system of private and public enforcement, the OFT adopted the central enforcement role, similar to the European Commission in relation to Articles 81 and 82 EC. Section 54, together with Sch. 10, provides for the concurrent exercise of the powers under the CA 1998 by the sectoral regulators, for instance, OFCOM has undertaken a number of investigations already under the Act. See, for instance, OFT, *Concurrent application to regulated industries*, OFT405; Prosser, T., 'Competition, Regulators and Public Services', Chapter 10 in Rodger, B.J., and MacCulloch, A. (eds), *The UK Competition Act: A New Era for UK Competition Law*, Oxford, Hart Publishing, 2000; and Whiddington, C., 'The New Emperor's New Clothes: Ofcom's Competition Powers' (2004) 9(3) Comms L 87.

A: OFT

The CA 1998, in Chapter III, amended the previous role of the DGFT in two major respects: in relation to investigation and sanctions. Sanctions were bolstered following criticisms in earlier reform proposals, see, e.g. DTI Green Paper, *Abuse of Market Power*, Cm 2100, 1992, Chapter 2, and the DGFT's powers of investigation were strengthened. It should be noted that following the entry into force of the EA 2002 the DGFT's functions were assumed by the OFT and references in this section to the DGFT are revised accordingly.

McNeil, I., 'Investigations under the Competition Act 1998', in Rodger, B.J., and MacCulloch, A. (eds), *The UK Competition Act: A New Era for UK Competition Law*
Oxford, Hart Publishing, 2000

Prior to the introduction of the Competition Act 1998 the framework of competition law in the United Kingdom did not give the competition authorities the extensive powers of investigation available to the European Commission and those national authorities whose competition law is based on the Community model. It is difficult to attribute this directly to the nature of the substantive provisions of competition law which have developed in the United Kingdom, but there were nevertheless several aspects of the framework which influenced the manner in which investigations were undertaken. First, the fragmentation of the substantive provisions of competition law between different statutes has resulted in separate provisions governing different types of investigation: the Fair Trading Act 1973, the Restrictive Trade Practices Act 1976 (RTPA 1976), and the Competition Act 1980 all have their own provisions relating to investigations. Secondly, the division of investigative functions between the Office of Fair Trading and the Monopolies and Mergers Commission resulted in an additional layer of complexity in the framing of powers of investigation. Thirdly, the use of the 'public interest' test, in section 84 of the 1973 Act, as the main criterion for distinguishing legitimate business conduct from anti-competitive behaviour, in the broad sense, has meant that the focus of an investigation differed from investigations under Community law which relate to prohibited behaviour. Fourthly, the absence of financial sanctions within the regime can arguably be seen to have limited the development of powers of investigation. Competition authorities in the United Kingdom, in contrast to most other national authorities in the Community, have not had to establish a link between an infringement and a financial penalty.

The absence of effective powers of investigation in the United Kingdom has generally been seen as a serious restriction on the ability of the competition authorities to enforce the law. Referring to cartels in the concrete industry, John Bridgeman, the Director General of Fair Trading, remarked in 1995:

> I feel that greater investigative powers would make our handling of such cases far easier. For that reason, I welcome the DTI's renewed commitment to reform, especially reform of the Restrictive Trade Practices Act. I look forward particularly to improvements such as an extension of my investigatory powers, both in pursuing secret cartels (where it is crucial) and in probing other possible abuses of market power (where our enquiries could be more focused and expeditious).

The 1998 Act aims to remedy these deficiencies and will bring UK competition law much closer to the Community model in terms of the process of investigation and the decision-making procedure which follows. The 1998 Act provides for more extensive powers of investigation for the Director General both in relation to the two new prohibitions contained in the 1998 Act and in relation to complex and scale monopoly investigations under the provisions of the 1973 Act.

The significance of the extension of investigatory powers is increased, as the extent to which the substantive rules of domestic competition law are being changed is not entirely clear. The nature and formulation of the rules has changed but, as recognised by the Trade and Industry Secretary, the identification of the particular conduct prohibited by the new rules, which was permitted under the old rules, is problematic. Viewed in this context, the primary purpose of the Act is arguably to allow for more effective enforcement action to be taken against obvious infringements. In other words, the real objective of the Act may not be to fine-tune the substantive rules of competition law but to provide effective means of taking action against those breaches of competition law which have in the past escaped enforcement action because of a lack of evidence and enforcement powers available to the competition authorities.

The key powers of investigation are contained in ss. 25 to 9 of the Act.

COMPETITION ACT 1998, [SS. 25–9], AS AMENDED

Investigations

25. **Power of the OFT to investigate**

(1) In any of the following cases, the OFT may conduct an investigation.

(2) The first case is where there are reasonable grounds for suspecting that there is an agreement which—

   (a) may affect trade within the United Kingdom; and

   (b) has as its object or effect the prevention, restriction or distortion of competition within the United Kingdom.

(3) The second case is where there are reasonable grounds for suspecting that there is an agreement which—

   (a) may affect trade between Member States; and

   (b) has as its object or effect the prevention, restriction or distortion of competition within the Community.

(4) The third case is where there are reasonable grounds for suspecting that the Chapter II prohibition has been infringed.

(5) The fourth case is where there are reasonable grounds for suspecting that the prohibition in Article 82 has been infringed.

(6) The fifth case is where there are reasonable grounds for suspecting that, at some time in the past, there was an agreement which at that time—
    (a) may have affected trade within the United Kingdom; and
    (b) had as its object or effect the prevention, restriction or distortion of competition within the United Kingdom.

(7) The sixth case is where there are reasonable grounds for suspecting that, at some time in the past, there was an agreement which at that time—
    (a) may have affected trade between Member States; and
    (b) had as its object or effect the prevention, restriction or distortion of competition within the Community.

(8) Subsection (2) does not permit an investigation to be conducted in relation to an agreement if the OFT—
    (a) considers that the agreement is exempt from the Chapter I prohibition as a result of a block exemption or a parallel exemption; and
    (b) does not have reasonable grounds for suspecting that the circumstances may be such that it could exercise its power to cancel the exemption.

(9) Subsection (3) does not permit an investigation to be conducted if the OFT—
    (a) considers that the agreement is an agreement to which the prohibition in Article 81(1) is inapplicable by virtue of a regulation of the Commission ("the relevant regulation"); and
    (b) does not have reasonable grounds for suspecting that the conditions set out in Article 29(2) of the EC Competition Regulation for the withdrawal of the benefit of the relevant regulation may be satisfied in respect of that agreement.

(10) Subsection (6) does not permit an investigation to be conducted in relation to any agreement if the OFT considers that, at the time in question, the agreement was exempt from the Chapter I prohibition as a result of a block exemption or a parallel exemption.

(11) Subsection (7) does not permit an investigation to be conducted in relation to any agreement if the OFT considers that, at the time in question, the agreement was an agreement to which the prohibition in Article 81(1) was inapplicable by virtue of a regulation of the Commission.

(12) It is immaterial for the purposes of subsection (6) or (7) whether the agreement in question remains in existence.

26. Powers when conducting investigations

(1) For the purposes of an investigation, the OFT may require any person to produce to it a specified document, or to provide it with specified information, which he considers relates to any matter relevant to the investigation.

(2) The power conferred by subsection (1) is to be exercised by a notice in writing.

(3) A notice under subsection (2) must indicate—
    (a) the subject matter and purpose of the investigation; and
    (b) the nature of the offences created by sections 42 to 44.

(4) In subsection (1) "specified" means —
    (a) specified, or described, in the notice; or
    (b) falling within a category which is specified, or described, in the notice.

(5) The OFT may also specify in the notice—
    (a) the time and place at which any document is to be produced or any information is to be provided;
    (b) the manner and form in which it is to be produced or provided.

(6) The power under this section to require a person to produce a document includes power—
    (a) if the document is produced—

     (i) to take copies of it or extracts from it;

     (ii) to require him, or any person who is a present or past officer of his, or is or was at any time employed by him, to provide an explanation of the document;

  (b) if the document is not produced, to require him to state, to the best of his knowledge and belief, where it is.

27. Power to enter business premises without a warrant

(1) Any officer of the OFT who is authorised in writing by the OFT to do so ("an investigating officer") may enter any business premises in connection with an investigation.

(2) No investigating officer is to enter any premises in the exercise of his powers under this section unless he has given to the occupier of the premises a written notice which—

  (a) gives at least two working days' notice of the intended entry;

  (b) indicates the subject matter and purpose of the investigation; and

  (c) indicates the nature of the offences created by sections 42 to 44.

(3) Subsection (2) does not apply—

  (a) if the [OFT] has a reasonable suspicion that the premises are, or have been, occupied by—

     (i) a party to an agreement which it is investigating under section 25; or

     (ii) an undertaking the conduct of which it is investigating under section 25; or

  (b) if the investigating officer has taken all such steps as are reasonably practicable to give notice but has not been able to do so.

(4) In a case falling within subsection (3), the power of entry conferred by subsection (1) is to be exercised by the investigating officer on production of—

  (a) evidence of his authorisation; and

  (b) a document containing the information referred to in subsection (2)(b) and (c).

(5) An investigating officer entering any premises under this section may—

  (a) take with him such equipment as appears to him to be necessary;

  (b) require any person on the premises—

     (i) to produce any document which he considers relates to any matter relevant to the investigation; and

     (ii) if the document is produced, to provide an explanation of it;

  (c) require any person to state, to the best of his knowledge and belief, where any such document is to be found;

  (d) take copies of, or extracts from, any document which is produced;

  (e) require any information which is stored in any electronic form and is accessible from the premises and which the investigating officer considers relates to any matter relevant to the investigation, to be produced in a form—

     (i) in which it can be taken away, and

     (ii) in which it is visible and legible or from which it can readily be produced in a visible and legible form;

  (f) take any steps which appear to be necessary for the purpose of preserving or preventing interference with any document which he considers relates to any matter relevant to the investigation.

(6) In this section "business premises" means premises (or any part of premises) not used as a dwelling.

28. Power to enter business premises under a warrant

(1) On an application made by the OFT to the court in accordance with rules of court, a judge may issue a warrant if he is satisfied that—

  (a) there are reasonable grounds for suspecting that there are on any business premises documents—

     (i) the production of which has been required under section 26 or 27; and

     (ii) which have not been produced as required;

  (b) there are reasonable grounds for suspecting that—

(i) there are on any business premises documents which the OFT has power under section 26 to require to be produced; and

(ii) if the documents were required to be produced, they would not be produced but would be concealed, removed, tampered with or destroyed; or

(c) an investigating officer has attempted to enter premises in the exercise of his powers under section 27 but has been unable to do so and that there are reasonable grounds for suspecting that there are on the premises documents the production of which could have been required under that section.

(2) A warrant under this section shall authorise a named officer of the OFT, and any other of the OFT's officers whom the OFT has authorised in writing to accompany the named officer—

(a) to enter the premises specified in the warrant, using such force as is reasonably necessary for the purpose;

(b) to search the premises and take copies of, or extracts from, any document appearing to be of a kind in respect of which the application under subsection (1) was granted ("the relevant kind");

(c) to take possession of any documents appearing to be of the relevant kind if—

(i) such action appears to be necessary for preserving the documents or preventing interference with them; or

(ii) it is not reasonably practicable to take copies of the documents on the premises;

(d) to take any other steps which appear to be necessary for the purpose mentioned in paragraph (c)(i);

(e) to require any person to provide an explanation of any document appearing to be of the relevant kind or to state, to the best of his knowledge and belief, where it may be found;

(f) to require any information which is stored in any electronic form and is accessible from the premises and which the named officer considers relates to any matter relevant to the investigation, to be produced in a form—

(i) in which it can be taken away, and

(ii) in which it is visible and legible or from which it can readily be produced in a visible and legible form.

(3) If, in the case of a warrant under subsection (1)(b), the judge is satisfied that it is reasonable to suspect that there are also on the premises other documents relating to the investigation concerned, the warrant shall also authorise action mentioned in subsection (2) to be taken in relation to any such document.

(3A) A warrant under this section may authorise persons specified in the warrant to accompany the named officer who is executing it.

(4) Any person entering premises by virtue of a warrant under this section may take with him such equipment as appears to him to be necessary.

(5) On leaving any premises which he has entered by virtue of a warrant under this section, the named officer must, if the premises are unoccupied or the occupier is temporarily absent, leave them as effectively secured as he found them.

(6) A warrant under this section continues in force until the end of the period of one month beginning with the day on which it is issued.

(7) Any document of which possession is taken under subsection (2)(c) may be retained for a period of three months.

(8) In this section "business premises" has the same meaning as in section 27.

28A. Power to enter domestic premises under a warrant

(1) On an application made by the OFT to the court in accordance with rules of court, a judge may issue a warrant if he is satisfied that—

(a) there are reasonable grounds for suspecting that there are on any domestic premises documents—

(i) the production of which has been required under section 26; and

(ii) which have not been produced as required; or

(b) there are reasonable grounds for suspecting that—
    (i) there are on any domestic premises documents which the OFT has power under section 26 to require to be produced; and
    (ii) if the documents were required to be produced, they would not be produced but would be concealed, removed, tampered with or destroyed.

(2) A warrant under this section shall authorise a named officer of the OFT, and any other of its officers whom the OFT has authorised in writing to accompany the named officer—

(a) to enter the premises specified in the warrant, using such force as is reasonably necessary for the purpose;

(b) to search the premises and take copies of, or extracts from, any document appearing to be of a kind in respect of which the application under subsection (1) was granted ("the relevant kind");

(c) to take possession of any documents appearing to be of the relevant kind if—
    (i) such action appears to be necessary for preserving the documents or preventing interference with them; or
    (ii) it is not reasonably practicable to take copies of the documents on the premises;

(d) to take any other steps which appear to be necessary for the purpose mentioned in paragraph (c)(i);

(e) to require any person to provide an explanation of any document appearing to be of the relevant kind or to state, to the best of his knowledge and belief, where it may be found;

(f) to require any information which is stored in any electronic form and is accessible from the premises and which the named officer considers relates to any matter relevant to the investigation, to be produced in a form—
    (i) in which it can be taken away, and
    (ii) in which it is visible and legible or from which it can readily be produced in a visible and legible form.

(3) If, in the case of a warrant under subsection (1)(b), the judge is satisfied that it is reasonable to suspect that there are also on the premises other documents relating to the investigation concerned, the warrant shall also authorise action mentioned in subsection (2) to be taken in relation to any such document.

(4) A warrant under this section may authorise persons specified in the warrant to accompany the named officer who is executing it.

(5) Any person entering premises by virtue of a warrant under this section may take with him such equipment as appears to him to be necessary.

(6) On leaving any premises which he has entered by virtue of a warrant under this section, the named officer must, if the premises are unoccupied or the occupier is temporarily absent, leave them as effectively secured as he found them.

(7) A warrant under this section continues in force until the end of the period of one month beginning with the day on which it is issued.

(8) Any document of which possession is taken under subsection (2)(c) may be retained for a period of three months.

(9) In this section, "domestic premises" means premises (or any part of premises) that are used as a dwelling and are—

(a) premises also used in connection with the affairs of an undertaking or association of undertakings; or

(b) premises where documents relating to the affairs of an undertaking or association of undertakings are kept.

29. Entry of premises under warrant: supplementary

(1) A warrant issued under section 28 or 28A must indicate—

(a) the subject matter and purpose of the investigation;

(b) the nature of the offences created by sections 42 to 44.

(2) The powers conferred by section 28 or 28A are to be exercised on production of a warrant issued under that section.

(3) If there is no one at the premises when the named officer proposes to execute such a warrant he must, before executing it—

(a) take such steps as are reasonable in all the circumstances to inform the occupier of the intended entry; and

(b) if the occupier is informed, afford him or his legal or other representative a reasonable opportunity to be present when the warrant is executed.

(4) If the named officer is unable to inform the occupier of the intended entry he must, when executing the warrant, leave a copy of it in a prominent place on the premises.

(5) In this section—

"named officer" means the officer named in the warrant; and

"occupier", in relation to any premises, means a person whom the named officer reasonably believes is the occupier of those premises.

NOTE: Section 26 allows the OFT to require the production of a document or other specified relevant information, and ss. 27–9 extend to the OFT the power to enter premises with or without a warrant.

McNeil, I., 'Investigations under the Competition Act 1998', in Rodger, B.J., and MacCulloch, A. (eds), *The UK Competition Act: A New Era for UK Competition Law* Oxford, Hart Publishing, 2000

Entry to premises

The provisions of the 1998 Act providing for entry to premises by the Director General represent a significant expansion of the powers of investigation available under the previous regime, which made no provision for entry to premises. The 1998 Act provides for entry with a warrant issued by a court and in other circumstances without a warrant. The powers available to the investigator are more extensive where entry is with a warrant, but the powers available on entry without a warrant will be adequate in many cases to secure sufficient evidence of an infringement. The definition of premises in section 59 of the 1998 Act excludes domestic premises unless they are also used in connection with the affairs of an undertaking or documents relating to the affairs of an undertaking are kept there. This definition goes some way towards taking account of the provisions of Article 8 of the European Convention on Human Rights 1950 which provides for the right to respect for private and family life. However, the case law of the European Court of Human Rights does not provide quite such a categorical split between the private sphere in which Article 8 rights apply and the business or professional sphere in which they do not. For example in *Niemetz* v *Germany* the Court said that:

> to interpret the words 'private life' and 'home' as including certain professional or business activities or premises would be consonant with the essential objective and purpose of Article 8, namely to protect the individual against arbitrary interference by the public authorities.

In *Chappell* v *United Kingdom*, a case involving an Anton Pillar order directed against material in breach of copyright held by the applicant in premises used both for business and domestic purposes, the Court did not rely on the fact that the search was directed solely at business activities as a ground for excluding the application of Article 8 under the head of 'private life'. It may well therefore be the case that the category of premises defined by the 1998 Act as being open to inspection by the Director General may be too wide to comply with the European Convention and the Human Rights Act 1998.

Entry with a warrant

This power is designed to deal with three different situations. The first is where there are reasonable grounds for suspecting that there are on the premises documents which have been required to be produced which have not been produced. The second is where there is a suspicion that documents which could be required to be produced will be concealed, removed, tampered with or destroyed. The third is where an investigating officer has been unable to secure entry to premises without a warrant, where this is authorised by the 1998 Act. A warrant authorises the investigating officer to enter the premises using such force as is necessary, to search the premises and, if necessary for their preservation, to remove relevant documents. The investigator is also empowered to remove equipment, to require explanations of documents and to require the location of documents to be disclosed. The formulation of these powers is more specific than the parallel provision of Article 14 of Regulation 17/62 which does not expressly provide for a right to search for documents, although the European Court has interpreted it in such a manner. There is no wider power to ask questions not directly related to documents on the premises, such as questions relating to broader aspects of the investigation. As pointed out by the European Court, in dealing with this issue in the context of Community investigations, allowing investigators to compel answers to such questions would confuse the general power to require information with the more specific powers associated with on-site inspections.

Entry without a warrant

Where premises are occupied by a party to an agreement prohibited by Chapter I or an undertaking being investigated in relation to an infringement of the Chapter II prohibition, the Director General can enter premises without a warrant and without giving notice. This allows the Director General to engage in what are referred to in Community parlance as 'dawn raids'. In other circumstances, for instance, where the premises are occupied by a third party who has relevant information, the Director General can enter premises without a warrant provided that two days' notice, and the other requirements of the Act, are observed. In this respect the Director General's powers are more limited than those of the European Commission which is able to subject third parties to dawn raids as well as undertakings suspected of being a party to a contravention. Once on the premises, the investigating officer cannot undertake a search but has the right to require the production of relevant documents, take copies and require explanations of the documents. A similar power of entry without a warrant is available in the case of monopoly investigations under the 1973 Act.

The power to enter premises without a warrant puts the Director General in a privileged position by comparison with other public agencies undertaking investigations. No such power is granted to the Financial Services Authority under the Financial Services and Markets Act: such a power was proposed in the first draft of the Bill but was withdrawn following opposition during parliamentary scrutiny. Entry to premises without a warrant is not available to the Department of Trade and Industry when undertaking a company investigation, nor to the Serious Fraud Office when undertaking an investigation into serious fraud. All these agencies may be involved in the investigation of activity which constitutes a criminal offence, but none has powers as extensive as the Director General. The privileged position of the Director General can to some extent be rationalised on the basis that the collection of information relating to the contravention of competition law is particularly difficult and therefore an element of surprise is sometimes necessary to capture the necessary evidence. Nonetheless, it is clear from the extensive powers given to the Director General to investigate breaches of the 1998 Act that the operation of competitive markets has assumed a much greater significance not merely by comparison with the old framework of competition law but also in relation to other areas of business regulation.

NOTE: These powers are subject to limitations in relation to privileged communications (s. 30) and the right to self-incrimination. See Case 347/87 *Orkem* v *Commission* [1989] ECR 3283 and Case T-112/98 *Mannesmannröhren-Werke AG* v *Commission* [2001] ECR II-729. See generally, OFT guideline, *Powers of investigation*, OFT 404 and OFT guideline, *Under investigation?*, OFT 426. The OFT has made good use of the powers of investigation available under the Act. The first example of an investigation leading to the discovery of a breach of the prohibition and the imposition of fines was in *Arriva/First Group*, DGFT Decision No CA98/9/2002, 30 January 2002.

Arriva/FirstGroup
DGFT Decision No CA98/9/2002, 30 January 2002, para. 7

> 7. Enquiries into the complaint began on 31 July 2000. They led to an investigation under the Competition Act 1998 Act ('the Act'). The Director General of Fair Trading ('the Director') applied to the High Court and the Court of Session for warrants to enter premises of the two undertakings in England and Scotland, and exercise powers under section 28 of the Act. Warrants were issued on 4 and 6 October 2000. Unannounced visits to the premises took place on 10 and 11 October 2000 and copies of documents were taken. On 16 March 2001, a Notice under section 26 of the Act was issued to the TAS Partnership Limited ('TAS'), specialist consultants in public transport, and specified documents and information were received by the Director as required in the Notice. The Director also received documents from the Traffic Commissioner of the North Eastern Traffic Area in Leeds.

NOTE: This was the first decision imposing a fine under the Chapter I prohibition and applying the leniency programme under the Act, see further below. Section 203 of the EA 2002 amended the CA 1998 to allow people who are not employees of the OFT to accompany and assist OFT officers on raids conducted under warrant; this is helpful where they have, for instance, specialist IT expertise. Other notable examples of investigations leading to fines can also be seen in cases, such as *Replica Kits*, OFT Decision No CA98/06/2003, 1 August 2003 and *Genzyme*, DGFT Decision No CA98/3/03, 27 March 2003.

B: Enforcement

Breach of the prohibitions is to be enforced directly by the OFT, utilizing a range of effective sanctions. See OFT guideline, *Enforcement*, OFT 407. The procedure for decision-making procedures following an investigation are outlined in the Competition Act 1998 (Office of Fair Trading's Rules) Order 2004 (SI 2004/2751). The OFT issues a Statement of Objections ('SO'), under Rule 4, outlining the basis of any suspected infringement. The parties concerned are then given the opportunity to submit written and oral submissions in relation to the SO. If the OFT proceeds to find a breach, there are a range of possible sanctions available. The first is to issue a direction relating to the agreement or conduct under ss. 32 and 33 respectively. The following is an excerpt from Directions issued in the *Napp* case:

Napp Pharmaceutical Holdings Ltd and Subsidiaries
DGFT Directions No CA98/2D/2001, 4 May 2001, pp. 1–2

Direction to bring the infringement to an end

1. Save as provided in paragraph 4 below, Napp shall bring the Infringement to an end and shall refrain from any conduct having the same or equivalent effect.

Pricing

2. Without prejudice to the generality of paragraph 1 above and save as provided in paragraph 4 below, Napp shall in respect of each strength of MST Tablet which it supplies or offers for supply in the United Kingdom:
   (a) within fifteen Working Days from the date of these directions replace its Current NHS List Price with a revised NHS List Price which is equal to or lower than 85 per cent of the Current NHS List Price;
   (b) not without the prior written consent of the Director increase its NHS List Price to a level which is higher than 85 per cent of the Current NHS List Price;

(c) where it offers supplies of MST Tablets in the United Kingdom, offer such supplies at a price which is equal to or lower than 87.5 per cent of the NHS List Price;

(d) not without the prior written consent of the Director supply or offer to supply MST Tablets to a Hospital at a price which is lower than 20 per cent of the NHS List Price; and

(e) where the effect of such supply would be to circumvent the object of paragraph (d) above, not without the prior written consent of the Director, either:

(i) supply or offer to supply MST Tablets to a Hospital on terms which make the supply or the terms of supply, including the price, conditional on the supply of any other product or service to the Hospital or to any other person; or

(ii) supply or offer to supply any other product or service to any person, including a Hospital, on terms which make the supply or the terms of supply, including the price, conditional on the supply of MST Tablets to a Hospital.

Existing contracts

3. (1) Napp shall within four months from the date of these directions cease to supply MST Tablets to Hospitals on the terms of its Existing Contracts.

(2) Napp shall in all good faith enter into negotiations with the other parties to its Existing Contracts with a view to agreeing revised terms for the supply of MST Tablets to the Hospitals covered by those contracts following the expiry of the period of four months from the date of these directions.

(3) Any agreements or arrangements made by Napp following the negotiations referred to in subparagraph (2) above shall be fully compliant with paragraphs 1 and 2 above.

NOTE: These directions, issued five weeks after the initial decision, required Napp to institute a revised list price and allowed it four months to renegotiate in good faith its existing contracts. A substantial fine was also imposed and both issues were considered by the CCAT (now the CAT): see further below. Napp applied for the directions to be suspended, and ultimately a consent order was agreed as the CCAT was satisfied that the Act provided for directions to be varied by the tribunal and for these to be enforceable by the OFT, paras 3(2), 3(3), and 10 of Sch. 8. The OFT also has powers to impose interim measures under s. 35.

C: Penalties

The most important sanction in practice is the OFT's power to impose penalties under s. 36. Section 36(8) provides that no penalty may be imposed that exceeds 10 per cent of the turnover of an undertaking in the business year preceding the date of the decision. This is to be determined in accordance with the CA 1998 (Determination of Turnover for Penalties) Order 2000 (SI 2000/309), as amended by the CA 1998 (Determination of Turnover for Penalties) (Amendment) Order 2004 (SI 2004/1259). The OFT has issued guidance on their practice in the imposition of penalties.

OFT's guidance as to the appropriate amount of a penalty
OFT 423, paras 1.4–1.5, 2.1–2.20

1.4 The twin objectives of the OFT's policy on financial penalties are:
- to impose penalties on infringing undertakings which reflect the seriousness of the infringement, and
- to ensure that the threat of penalties will deter undertakings from engaging in anti-competitive practices.

The OFT has a discretion to impose financial penalties and intends, where appropriate, to impose financial penalties which are severe, in particular in respect of agreements between undertakings which fix prices or share markets and other cartel activities, and serious abuses of a dominant position. The OFT considers that these are among the most serious infringements of competition law. The deterrent is aimed at other undertakings which might be considering activities contrary to Article 81, Article 82, the Chapter I and/or Chapter II prohibition, as well as at the undertakings which are subject to the decision.

1.5 The OFT also wishes to encourage undertakings to come forward with information relating to any cartel activities in which they are involved. The OFT therefore sets out in part 3 of this guidance when lenient treatment will be given to such undertakings.

2 Steps for determining the level of a penalty

Method of calculation

2.1 A financial penalty imposed by the OFT under section 36 of the Act will be calculated following a five step approach:
- calculation of the starting point having regard to the seriousness of the infringement and the relevant turnover of the undertaking
- adjustment for duration
- adjustment for other factors
- adjustment for further aggravating or mitigating factors, and
- adjustment if the maximum penalty of 10 per cent of the worldwide turnover of the undertaking is exceeded and to avoid double jeopardy.

Details on each of these steps are set out in paragraphs 2.3 to 2.20 below.

2.2 An undertaking participating in cartel activity may benefit from total immunity from, or a significant reduction in the level of, a financial penalty, if the requirements for lenient treatment set out in part 3 of this guidance are satisfied.

Step 1—Starting point

2.3 The starting point for determining the level of financial penalty which will be imposed on an undertaking is calculated having regard to:
- the seriousness of the infringement, and
- the relevant turnover of the undertaking.

2.4 The starting point will depend in particular upon the nature of the infringement. The more serious and widespread the infringement, the higher the starting point is likely to be. Price-fixing or market-sharing agreements and other cartel activities are among the most serious infringements of Article 81 and/or the Chapter I prohibition. Conduct which infringes Article 82 and/or the Chapter II prohibition and which by virtue of the undertaking's dominant position and the nature of the conduct has, or is likely to have a particularly serious effect on competition, for example, predatory pricing, is also one of the most serious infringements.

2.5 It is the OFT's assessment of the seriousness of the infringement which will be taken into account in determining the starting point for the financial penalty. When making its assessment, the OFT will consider a number of factors, including the nature of the product, the structure of the market, the market share(s) of the undertaking(s) involved in the infringement, entry conditions and the effect on competitors and third parties. The damage caused to consumers whether directly or indirectly will also be an important consideration. The assessment will be made on a case by case basis for all types of infringement, taking account of all the circumstances of the case.

2.6 In cases concerning infringements of Article 81 and/or Article 82, the OFT may, in determining the starting point, take into account effects in another Member State of the agreement or conduct concerned. The OFT will take into account effects in another Member State through its assessment of relevant turnover; the OFT may consider turnover generated in another Member State if the relevant geographic market for the relevant product is wider than the United Kingdom and the express consent of the relevant Member State or NCA, as appropriate, is given in each particular case.

2.7 The relevant turnover is the turnover of the undertaking in the relevant product market and relevant geographic market affected by the infringement in the undertaking's last business year.

2.8 The starting point may not in any event exceed 10 per cent of the relevant turnover of the undertaking.

2.9 Where an infringement involves several undertakings, an assessment of the appropriate starting point will be carried out for each of the undertakings concerned, in order to take account of the real impact of the infringing activity of each undertaking on competition.

Step 2—Adjustment for duration

2.10 The starting point may be increased or, in exceptional circumstances, decreased to take into account the duration of the infringement. Penalties for infringements which last for more than one year may be multiplied by not more than the number of years of the infringement. Part years may be treated as full years for the purpose of calculating the number of years of the infringement.

Step 3—Adjustment for other factors

2.11 The penalty figure reached after the calculations in steps 1 and 2 may be adjusted as appropriate to achieve the policy objectives outlined in paragraph 1.4 above, in particular, of imposing penalties on infringing undertakings in order to deter undertakings from engaging in anticompetitive practices. The deterrent is not aimed solely at the undertakings which are subject to the decision, but also at other undertakings which might be considering activities which are contrary to Article 81, Article 82, the Chapter I and/or Chapter II prohibition. Considerations at this stage may include, for example, the OFT's objective estimate of any economic or financial benefit made or likely to be made by the infringing undertaking from the infringement and the special characteristics, including the size and financial position of the undertaking in question. Where relevant, the OFT's estimate would account for any gains which might accrue to the undertaking in other product or geographic markets as well as the 'relevant' market under consideration.

2.12 The assessment of the need to adjust the penalty will be made on a case by case basis for each individual infringing undertaking. This step may result in either an increase or reduction of the financial penalty calculated at the earlier step.

2.13 In exceptional circumstances, where the relevant turnover of an undertaking is zero (for example, in the case of buying cartels) and the penalty figure reached after the calculation in Steps 1 and 2 is therefore zero, the OFT may adjust the amount of this penalty at this step.

Step 4—Adjustment for aggravating and mitigating factors

2.14 The basic amount of the financial penalty, adjusted as appropriate at steps 2 and 3, may be increased where there are other aggravating factors, or decreased where there are mitigating factors.

2.15 Aggravating factors include:
- role of the undertaking as a leader in, or an instigator of, the infringement
- involvement of directors or senior management (notwithstanding paragraph 1.14 above)
- retaliatory or other coercive measures taken against other undertakings aimed at ensuring the continuation of the infringement
- continuing the infringement after the start of the OFT's investigation
- repeated infringements by the same undertaking or other undertakings in the same group
- infringements which are committed intentionally rather than negligently, and
- retaliatory measures taken or commercial reprisal sought by the undertaking against a leniency applicant.

2.16 Mitigating factors include:
- role of the undertaking, for example, where the undertaking is acting under severe duress or pressure
- genuine uncertainty on the part of the undertaking as to whether the agreement or conduct constituted an infringement

- adequate steps having been taken with a view to ensuring compliance with Articles 81 and 82 and the Chapter I and Chapter II prohibitions
- termination of the infringement as soon as the OFT intervenes, and
- co-operation which enables the enforcement process to be concluded more effectively and/or speedily.

Note that in cases of cartel activity an undertaking which co-operates fully with the investigation may benefit from total immunity from, or a significant reduction in the level of, a financial penalty, if it satisfies the requirements for lenient treatment set out in part 3 of this guidance.

Step 5—Adjustment to prevent the maximum penalty being exceeded and to avoid double jeopardy

2.17 The final amount of the penalty calculated according to the method set out above may not in any event exceed 10 per cent of the worldwide turnover of the undertaking in its last business year. The business year on the basis of which worldwide turnover is determined will be the one preceding the date on which the decision of the OFT is taken or, if figures are not available for that business year, the one immediately preceding it. The penalty will be adjusted if necessary to ensure that it does not exceed this maximum.

2.18 In addition, where an infringement ended prior to 1 May 2004 any penalty imposed in respect of an infringement of the Chapter I prohibition or the Chapter II prohibition (but not any penalty imposed in respect of an infringement of Article 81 or Article 82) will, if necessary, be adjusted further to ensure that it does not exceed the maximum penalty applicable in respect of an infringement of the Chapter I prohibition or the Chapter II prohibition prior to 1 May 2004, i.e. 10 per cent of turnover in the United Kingdom of the undertaking in the financial year preceding the date when the infringement ended (multiplied pro rata by the length of the infringement where the length of the infringement was in excess of one year, up to a maximum of three years). The adjustments referred to in paragraphs 2.17 and 2.18 will be made after all the relevant adjustments have been made in steps 2 to 4 above and also, in cases of cartel activity, before any adjustments are made on account of leniency under part 3 of this guidance.

2.19 Where any infringement by an association of undertakings (e.g. a trade association) relates to the activities of its members, the penalty shall not exceed 10 per cent of the sum of the worldwide turnover of each member of the association of undertakings active on the market affected by the infringement. See the competition law guideline *Trade associations, professions and self-regulating bodies* (OFT408) for further details on the imposition and enforcement of penalties on associations of undertakings.

2.20 If a penalty or fine has been imposed by the European Commission, or by a court or other body in another Member State in respect of an agreement or conduct, the OFT must take that penalty or fine into account when setting the amount of a penalty in relation to that agreement or conduct. This is to ensure that where an anticompetitive agreement or conduct is subject to proceedings resulting in a penalty or fine in another Member State, an undertaking will not be penalised again in the United Kingdom for the same anticompetitive effects.

NOTE: Deterrence is a central plank of the fining policy and this was made clear in the *Aberdeen Journals* decision by the DGFT.

Aberdeen Journals Ltd
DGFT Decision No CA98/5/2001, paras 130–2

Step 3: Adjustment for other factors

130. Aberdeen Journals, which had a turnover of £33.9 million is owned by Northcliffe, which publishes over 50 separate regional titles and achieved turnover of £59.3m (not including the turnovers of the subsidiaries it controls, including Aberdeen Journals), and is in turn owned by Daily Mail & General Trust plc, with a turnover of £1,620 million for the year ended 3 October 1999. The management of Northcliffe was intimately involved

in Aberdeen Journals' conduct with regard to the *Herald & Post*, authorising, directing, and financing the losses the predatory conduct incurred. Further, the acquisition
of a reputation for predation by Northcliffe could have far-reaching adverse effects on
competition in several markets served by the newspaper publishing industry across
the UK.[67]

131. To ensure that the penalty acts as an adequate deterrent to predation to this undertaking, to the broader newspaper publishing industry, and more generally, the Director has
increased the proposed penalty by a factor of four, i.e., to £1,897,200. While this increase
is significant, the Director considers that any lesser increase would fail to act as a fully
effective deterrent to predation.

Step 4: Adjustment for mitigating factors

132. The Director accepts first that Aberdeen Journals has cooperated fully throughout the
investigation, and second, that it took rapid steps to cease its infringement (albeit in the
face of an active investigation, and an explicit warning that it was at risk of infringing the
Chapter II prohibition). He therefore has reduced the amount of the penalty by 10 per cent
and 20 per cent respectively for each of these mitigating factors, and therefore imposes a
penalty of £1,328,040.

NOTE: Fines can only be imposed if the infringement was intentional or negligent (s. 36(3)).
The CCAT (now the CAT) in *Napp* confirmed that these tests were alternatives. It should also
be noted at this stage that the CCAT in *Napp* considered that it is not bound by the Guidelines
when reviewing the amount of any penalty imposed. The limit imposed by Order (SI 2000/309)
is binding and ss. 39 and 40 also provide for immunity from fines in relation to the Chapter I and
II prohibitions in respect of small agreements and conduct of minor significance respectively.
See the Competition Act (Small Agreements and Conduct of Minor Significance) Regulations
2000 (SI 2000/262).

In the US and the Community (see Chapters 2 and 9) there exists the possibility for members
of a cartel to be granted partial or total immunity from competition law penalties in exchange
for providing information about the cartel. The existence of a leniency programme can encourage members of cartels to 'whistleblow' and undermines the stability of the cartel. The
OFT decided to adopt a leniency programme as part of its enforcement armoury under the CA
1998. Key elements of the programme, contained in the *OFT's guidance as to the appropriate
amount of a penalty*, OFT 423. Details of the scheme are discussed in Chapter 9, Cartels and
Leniency. The scheme provides for partial or total immunity dependent on the fulfilment of
the requisite conditions. Immunity can be granted even *after* an investigation has been started
by the OFT. The additional reductions available in paras 3.16–3.17 are known as 'Amnesty
Plus'. History has shown that where an undertaking is involved in a successful cartel it may
be tempted to enter into cartel arrangements in other markets. If this is the case the Amnesty
Plus policy encourages an undertaking to inform regarding all of its cartel activities as soon as
one cartel comes to the OFT's attention. The application of the leniency programme was first
demonstrated in the *Arriva/FirstGroup* decision.

Market Sharing by Arriva plc and FirstGroup plc
DGFT Decision No CA98/9/2002, 30 January 2002, paras 70–1
[footnotes omitted]

This was the first infringement decision by the DGFT under the Chapter I prohibition, and concerned a blatant market-sharing agreement involving bus routes in
the Leeds area. The factual background demonstrates a flagrant disregard for the
new Act, as the executives involved had each received training for the Act and were
aware of their companies' compliance programmes. Dawn raids had taken place

---

[67] See para. 2.4, footnote 9 of OFT423.

following the issue of warrants by the High Court yet the DGFT agreed to grant leniency as follows:

Leniency

70. Under the terms of the Director's leniency scheme, FirstGroup, as the first party to the cartel to approach the Director, after he had started his investigation, and provide evidence thereof, was granted 100 per cent immunity from any financial penalty. The granting of leniency in a letter dated 2 November 2000, and signed on behalf of FirstGroup and the Director, was conditional on FirstGroup providing evidence of the cartel, co-operating with the Director throughout his investigation and complying with the other conditions set out in paragraph 3.4 of the Guidance on Penalties. The Director is satisfied that FirstGroup complied with those conditions and accordingly, the penalty calculated for it is reduced to nil.

71. Arriva approached the Director with a request for leniency second and was granted leniency in a letter dated 8 December 2000, on the same conditions as FirstGroup but only to the extent that any penalty would be reduced by 36 per cent. The Director is also satisfied that Arriva has complied with the conditions for its leniency and, as a result, the penalty for Arriva is reduced to £203,632.

NOTE: It is unclear why the figure of 36 per cent in respect of Arriva was selected in this case. The OFT hoped that awareness of the leniency programme, and the creation of a 'race to the competition authority', would act as a deterrent to the formation of cartels and encourage members of existing cartels to come forward for leniency. Experience in the US has demonstrated the importance of an effective leniency, or 'corporate amnesty', policy to antitrust enforcement. See Riley, A., 'Cartel Whistleblowing: Toward an American Model?' (2002) 9 MJ 1. Further discussion of the policy behind leniency programmes can be found in the discussion of the role of leniency policy in relation to cartels in Chapter 9.

The OFT's leniency policy has proved to be instrumental in the discovery of a large number of high profile cartels. The following cases indicate a range of situations in which leniency has been sought. It is also interesting to note in these cases the way in which the OFT often uses leniency information, gained from one or more parties in a case, to quickly resolve cases through a negotiated 'early resolution' settlement. Even where an undertaking has not been awarded leniency it may be wise to settle a case by agreeing to pay a fine in the face of damning leniency evidence. This is functionally similar to 'plea bargaining' seen in US cases.

British Airways to pay record £121.5m penalty in price fixing investigation
OFT Press Release 113/07, 1 August 2007

British Airways has admitted collusion over the price of 'long-haul passenger fuel surcharges' (surcharges) and will pay a penalty of £121.5m to be imposed by the OFT, thus enabling the OFT to close its civil investigation and resolve this case. The penalty will be the highest ever imposed by the OFT for infringements of competition law, and demonstrates the determination of the OFT to deal vigorously with anti-competitive behaviour.

British Airways has admitted that between August 2004 and January 2006, it colluded with Virgin Atlantic over the surcharges which were added to ticket prices in response to rising oil prices. Over that period, the surcharges rose from £5 to £60 per ticket for a typical BA or Virgin Atlantic long-haul return flight.

Virgin Atlantic is not expected to pay any penalty as it qualifies in principle for full immunity under the OFT's leniency policy. Under this policy, a company which has been involved in cartel conduct and which is the first to give full details about it to the OFT will qualify for immunity from penalties in relation to that conduct. In addition, any company staff involved in the price fixing disclosed will qualify for immunity from criminal prosecution in relation to that conduct. The OFT's investigation was prompted after Virgin Atlantic came forward with information about price fixing with BA over the surcharges. British Airways has also provided full co-operation with the OFT's investigation under the leniency programme and this is reflected in the penalty announced today.

British Airways accepts the OFT's finding that on at least six occasions the two companies discussed and/or informed each other about proposed changes to the level of the surcharges, rather than setting levels independently as required under clear and well-established competition law principles.

The OFT's investigation was conducted in parallel with a similar case brought by the United States Department of Justice (DoJ). The investigations by the OFT and DoJ were separate but the two agencies have consulted each other closely throughout.

OFT welcomes early resolution agreements and agrees over £116m penalties

Investigations continue against other supermarkets and a dairy processor

OFT Press Release 170/07, 7 December 2007

Following the OFT's Statement of Objections (SO) of 20 September 2007 which provisionally found evidence of collusion between certain large supermarkets (Asda, Morrisons, Safeway, Sainsbury's and Tesco) and dairy processors (Arla, Dairy Crest, Lactalis McLelland, The Cheese Company (formerly Glanbia Foods Limited) and Wiseman) on the retail prices of some dairy products, certain of these parties have now admitted involvement in anti-competitive practices and have agreed to pay individual penalties which, combined, come to a maximum of over £116 million.

With a view to maintaining strong and effective competition law, the OFT will continue with its case against the remaining parties.

The SO set out the OFT's provisional findings that certain large supermarkets and dairy processors have colluded to increase the retail prices of one or more of liquid milk, value butter and UK produced cheese. The OFT's provisional findings were that the collusion took place through the sharing of commercially sensitive information in 2002 and, in some cases, in 2003. Details on the scope of the OFT's infringement allegations are set out below.

The OFT has now concluded early resolution agreements with Asda, Dairy Crest, Safeway (in relation to conduct prior to its acquisition by Morrisons), Sainsbury's, The Cheese Company and Wiseman based upon the provisional findings made in the SO. These parties have all admitted involvement in certain of the anti-competitive practices identified by the OFT in the SO and have undertaken to co-operate fully with the OFT in its investigation, including providing further evidence as far as reasonably possible.

These parties have accepted a liability in principle, and will pay penalties which amount to a maximum of over £116 million. However each party will receive a significant reduction in the financial penalty that would otherwise have been imposed on it, on condition that it continues to provide full co-operation.

The OFT has also taken into account information provided by the parties involved in the early resolution discussions which demonstrated the pressures they were under at this time to support dairy farmers.

The OFT is very pleased that the early and constructive cooperation of Asda, Dairy Crest, Safeway, Sainsbury's, The Cheese Company and Wiseman, has enabled some of this case to be resolved effectively and swiftly, which will significantly reduce the costs of pursuing the investigation to the OFT and to the businesses concerned. This case demonstrates the flexible approach the OFT is prepared to take to reduce the burden of investigations, while maintaining strong and effective competition law enforcement.

Arla had previously applied to the OFT for leniency and will receive complete immunity from financial penalty if it continues to fully co-operate.

The OFT will continue with its case against Lactalis McLelland, Morrisons and Tesco. These parties have an opportunity to make representations on the OFT's provisional findings. The OFT will carefully consider any representations, and the evidence in the case as a whole before reaching any final decision.

OFT issues statement of objections against 112 construction companies
OFT Press Release 52/08, 17 April 2008

Following one of the largest ever Competition Act investigations, the OFT has today issued a Statement of Objections (SO) against 112 firms in the construction sector in England.

The OFT formally alleges that the construction companies named in the SO have engaged in bid rigging activities, and in particular cover pricing. Cover pricing describes a situation where one or more bidders collude with a competitor during a tender process to obtain a price or prices which are intended to be too high to win the contract. The tendering authority, for example a local council or other customer, is not made aware of the contacts between bidders, leaving it with a false impression of the level of competition and this may result in it paying inflated prices.

Cover pricing arrangements have previously been found by the OFT and the Competition Appeal Tribunal to be illegal and in breach of the Competition Act 1998 due to the restrictions on competition that arise.

In addition, the SO formally alleges that a minority of the construction companies have variously entered into one or more arrangements whereby it was agreed that the successful tenderer would pay an agreed sum of money to the unsuccessful tenderer (known as a 'compensation payment'). These more serious forms of bid rigging are usually facilitated by false invoices.

The construction companies under investigation carry out general building work including construction of housing, as well as commercial and industrial construction both in the public and private sector. The SO allegations cover a diverse range of projects, including tenders for schools, universities and hospitals.

The OFT's investigation originated from a specific complaint in the East Midlands in 2004, but it quickly became clear from the evidence that the practice of cover pricing was widespread. The SO's formal allegations therefore cover neighbouring areas including Yorkshire and Humberside and also elsewhere in England. The OFT has also received evidence of cover pricing implicating many more companies on thousands of tender processes, but has focused its investigation on approximately 240 alleged infringements which are being pursued in the SO.

During the course of the investigation, the OFT carried out site visits at the premises of 57 firms. The OFT received 37 leniency applications in the investigation leading to this SO, and all other parties received an offer of a reduced financial penalty (see press notices 49/07 and 50/07), which led to over 40 further companies subsequently admitting participation in some bid rigging activities.

No assumption should be made at this stage that there has been an infringement of competition law by any of the companies named in the SO. The 112 parties concerned now have the opportunity to make written and oral representations which the OFT will take into account before making a final decision as to whether competition law has been infringed, and as to the appropriate amount of any penalties the OFT may decide to impose on each of the firms concerned.

OFT reaches early resolution agreements in tobacco case
OFT Pres Release 82/08, 11 July 2008

Six companies have today reached early resolution agreements with the OFT in which they have admitted engaging in unlawful practices in relation to retail prices for tobacco products in the UK, and have agreed to pay individual penalties which come to a combined maximum of £173.3m before discounts.

The companies are Asda, First Quench, Gallaher, One Stop Stores (formerly named T&S Stores), Somerfield, and TM Retail.

Today's agreements result from a process following the OFT's Statement of Objections issued in April 2008. This set out the OFT's proposed findings that two tobacco manufacturers and eleven retailers had variously engaged in one or more unlawful practices in relation to the retail prices of a number of tobacco products in breach of the Competition Act 1998. More details of the allegations are set out in the OFT's press statement dated 25 April 2008.

The OFT has now concluded early resolution agreements with these six parties, each of which has admitted liability in respect of all of the infringements alleged against it, and each of these parties will receive a significant reduction in the financial penalty that might have otherwise been imposed on condition that it continues to provide full co-operation with the OFT.

A number of the six parties had previously applied to the OFT for leniency, and the total penalties the parties have agreed to pay if all leniency and early resolution discounts are given is £132.3m, rather than the pre-discount penalties total of £173.3m.

The negotiation of settlements by the OFT also raises the possibility of complementing fines with other, more innovative, forms of penalty.

OFT issues final decision and imposes penalties in independent schools investigation
OFT Press Release 166/06, 23 November 2006

The findings are set out in a formal decision confirming the OFT's earlier provisional finding that the schools infringed the Competition Act and marks the end of a case which is one of the largest OFT investigations carried out. The decision also imposes penalties totalling just under £500,000 on the schools.

The schools concerned exchanged confidential information relating to their intended fee levels for boarding and day pupils through a survey known as the 'Sevenoaks Survey'. Surveys were compiled for the academic years 2001–02 to 2003–04.

The OFT's decision follows the announcement in May that the schools concerned had admitted exchanging information regarding their intended fee levels in breach of competition law. The admission was made as part of an agreed resolution of an OFT investigation between the OFT and the schools. The schools do not, however, make any admission that the agreement had any effect upon fees, and the OFT's decision does not make any such finding.

With one exception, each school must pay a penalty of £10,000, reduced in the case of six of the schools by up to 50 per cent for leniency. The relatively low fine for each school reflects the exceptional circumstances of the case, including the fact that all the schools will make payments totalling £3 million into an educational charitable trust designed to benefit the pupils who attended the schools during the relevant academic years, and the schools' charitable status. It is the first time the OFT has imposed penalties on charities and sends out a message that competition law applies to all businesses enjoying charitable status, who should not assume the OFT will in future accept the payment of a relatively low penalty as appropriate.

John Fingleton, OFT Chief Executive, said:

'The penalties imposed on the schools and the contributions that they will make to the charitable trust, represent a fair and proportionate outcome to this case, given the parties' charitable status and their acceptance that there has been a competition law infringement. This is the first case where the OFT has imposed penalties as part of an agreed resolution and demonstrates our willingness to consider innovative solutions in appropriate cases.'

NOTE: The setting up of an education trust in this case is appropriate on its unique facts, but it is unlikely to be suitable in many other instances. Details on the operation of the trust can be found at: www.scast.org.uk. The OFT's willingness to explore such potential solutions demonstrates that, given the potential scope of competition law, the use of ever increasing fines will not be suitable for all cases.

■ QUESTION

A great many undertakings, who have clearly been in breach of the competition rules, manage to escape or reduce their penalties; through leniency or 'early resolution' settlements. Are these reductions fair when compared to the fines paid by other undertakings similarly responsible for the breach?

SECTION 3: THE COMPETITION APPEAL TRIBUNAL ('CAT')

The CAT acts as an appeal tribunal under the CA 1998. Part 2 of the EA 2002 (ss. 11–15 and Schs 2, 4, and 5) makes provision on the constitution of the CAT and for its rules. Appointments are to be made by the Lord Chancellor and the Tribunal consists of a President, panel of chairmen, and ordinary members. Section 46(1) and (2) sets out what types of decision may be appealed to the CAT.

The CAT was originally called the Competition Commission Appeal Tribunal ('CCAT') and was part of the Competition Commission, but was given its independence and renamed following the entry into force of Part 2 of the EA 2002. In this section we shall treat the practice of both the CAT and CCAT together.

A: What can be appealed?

Section 46(3) details the type of decisions which can be appealed against:

COMPETITION ACT 1998

46. Appealable decisions

(1) Any party to an agreement in respect of which the OFT has made a decision may appeal to the Tribunal against, or with respect to, the decision.

(2) Any person in respect of whose conduct the OFT has made a decision may appeal to the Tribunal against, or with respect to, the decision.

(3) In this section "decision" means a decision of the OFT–
    (a) as to whether the Chapter I prohibition has been infringed,
    (b) as to whether the prohibition in Article 81(1) has been infringed,
    (c) as to whether the Chapter II prohibition has been infringed,
    (d) as to whether the prohibition in Article 82 has been infringed,
    (e) cancelling a block or parallel exemption,
    (f) withdrawing the benefit of a regulation of the Commission pursuant to Article 29(2) of the EC Competition Regulation,
    (g) not releasing commitments pursuant to a request made under section 31A(4)(b)(i),
    (h) releasing commitments under section 31A(4)(b)(ii),
    (i) as to the imposition of any penalty under section 36 or as to the amount of any such penalty, and includes a direction under section 32, 33 or 35 and such other decisions under this Part as may be prescribed.

(4) Except in the case of an appeal against the imposition, or the amount, of a penalty, the making of an appeal under this section does not suspend the effect of the decision to which the appeal relates.

(5) Part I of Schedule 8 makes further provision about appeals.

NOTE: This gives the term 'decision' a fairly wide coverage. However, in one early case, the DGFT argued that no formal decision had been taken at all. Could an aggrieved complainant appeal on the basis of the rejection of a complaint?

Bettercare Group Ltd v *DGFT*
[2002] CAT 6, 26 March 2002

Bettercare is engaged in the provision of nursing homes and residential care services in Northern Ireland and complained to the DGFT that a local health and social services trust had abused its position as the sole purchaser of care services from Bettercare by offering unreasonably low contract prices and unfair terms. The complaint was 'rejected' on the basis of the view that the trust did not constitute an undertaking. Bettercare appealed under s. 46. The key issue was whether the communications between the DGFT and Bettercare, without the DGFT instituting the full administrative procedure, constituted a decision.

82. That takes us on to the main question, which is how the Director's decision to reject Bettercare's complaint in this case is to be analysed. Is it, as the Director submits, to be analysed merely as the exercise of the Director's discretion not to conduct an investigation under section 25 for lack of reasonable grounds to suspect an infringement? Or is it, as Bettercare submits, a decision that the Chapter II prohibition is not infringed because North & West is not acting as an undertaking when purchasing social care?

83. In addressing this central issue, it is not in our view helpful to use the concept of a 'decision to reject a complaint' because such a term is ambiguous. The Director may decide to 'reject a complaint' for many reasons. For example, he may have other cases that he wishes to pursue in priority (compare Case T-24 and 28/90 *Automec* v *Commission* [1992] ECR II-2223); he may have insufficient information to decide whether there is an infringement or not; he may suspect that there may be an infringement, but the case does not appear sufficiently promising, or the economic activity concerned sufficiently important, to warrant the commitment of further resources. None of these cases necessarily gives rise to a decision by the Director as to whether a relevant prohibition is infringed.

84. On the other hand, the Director may, in fact, decide to reject a complaint on the ground that there is no infringement. Nothing in the Act prevents the Director from taking a decision, following a complaint, that there has been no infringement. The Director has already done so in a number of decisions which seem to be plainly decisions, within the meaning of section 46(3)(a) or (b), to the effect that the Chapter I or Chapter II prohibitions has not been infringed, for example because there is no dominant position: (see e.g. *Dixon Stores Group Limited/Compaq Computer Limited/Packard Bell NEC Limited* UKCLR [2001] 670; *Consignia plc and Postal Preference Service Limited* UKCLR [2001] 846; *ICL/Synstar* UKCLR [2001] 902.

85. It is true that the decisions of this kind so far taken have a more formal appearance, have apparently been more fully investigated and are more fully reasoned than in the present case. However, we see nothing in the Act to exclude the possibility that the Director may legitimately decide that there is no infringement without conducting a formal investigation, and giving only brief reasons, because in his view the matter is sufficiently clear to enable him to reach a decision without further ado.

86. In our view that is the reality of the situation in this case. As already indicated, in our opinion the correspondence viewed objectively does disclose a decision by or on behalf of the Director to the effect that North & West is not an undertaking within the meaning of section 18 of the Act when acting as a purchaser of social care. As Bettercare submits, the question whether the conduct in question is that of 'an undertaking' within the meaning of section 18 is one of the essential ingredients in establishing an infringement of the Chapter II prohibition. We therefore accept Bettercare's submission that, in deciding that North & West is not acting as an undertaking in the relevant respect, the Director has necessarily decided that the Chapter II prohibition is not infringed as regards the subject matter of Bettercare's complaint. It follows that, in our respectful view, the Director, in this case, has taken a decision as to whether or not the Chapter II prohibition has been infringed, within the meaning of section 46(3)(b) of the Act.

87. It is true that, on the contested view of the facts and the law he takes, the Director's decision that North & West is not an undertaking also precludes him from launching an investigation under section 25 of the Act since, on the Director's view, it necessarily follows that he has 'no reasonable grounds for suspecting' an infringement. However, in our view, one cannot convert what is in substance an appealable decision into an unappealable decision by the simple device of describing it as the exercise of the Director's administrative discretion not to proceed further on the basis of lack of reasonable grounds for suspecting an infringement. It all depends on the substance. In our view, if, as a matter of substance, the Director's statement that he has no reasonable grounds for suspecting an infringement in fact masks a decision by the Director that the Chapter II prohibition is not infringed, there is still a 'relevant decision' for the purposes of section 47(1). In the present case, in our view, the Director has, in effect, decided that the conduct in question does not infringe the Chapter II prohibition, *with the consequence* that he cannot proceed under section 25. But that consequence, in our view, is merely the secondary result of the primary decision that there has been no infringement.

88. We thus reject the Director's submission that the decision in this case should be characterised merely as an unappealable exercise of his discretion not to proceed further on the ground that the Director 'has no reasonable grounds for suspecting an infringement' under section 25. There may well be cases where the Director feels he has insufficient material in his possession to conduct an investigation under section 25, without being in a position to decide whether or not there is, in fact, an infringement. But in this case, it seems to us, the statements in the letters of 25 September and 2 November 2001, that the Director has 'no reasonable grounds for suspecting an infringement', while correct as far as they go, should not be allowed to conceal the fact that the Director has, in reality, decided that there is no infringement.

NOTE: Bettercare were appealing as a third party, under s. 47 of the Act: see further below. The CCAT stressed that whether the DGFT had taken a relevant decision was a question of fact. Appeal will not be available in all instances whereby the OFT does not proceed to investigate a complaint fully, for instance on the basis of the prioritizing of resources. In that event, a third party has the alternative of seeking judicial review in the courts. In *Bettercare*, the next phase was the determination of the appeal on the substantive issue upon which the DGFT's decision was based.

B: Who can appeal?

Obviously a party to an agreement or a person in respect of whose conduct the OFT has taken a decision can appeal, under s. 46(1) and (2) respectively. In addition, s. 47 makes provision for third-party appeals. The original provisions regarding third party appeals were very complicated, and have been substantially amended. The amended s. 47 now allows a party with 'sufficient interest' to appeal. Criticism of the original provisions can be seen in *The Institute of Independent Insurance Brokers* v *DGFT* [2001] CAT 4.

■ QUESTION

Are individual end-product consumers 'interested' third parties for the purposes of an appeal under the Act in respect of, for example, a producers' cartel?

C: Determination of an appeal

The CAT has a wide range of decision-making powers in respect of appeals, as set out, in particular in Sch. 8, para. 3(2) to the CA 1998.

COMPETITION ACT 1998
SCH. 8, PARA. 3(2)

(2) The Tribunal may confirm or set aside the decision which is the subject of the appeal, or any part of it, and may—

(a) remit the matter to the OFT,

(b) impose or revoke, or vary the amount of, a penalty,

...

(d) give such directions, or take such other steps, as the OFT could itself have given or taken, or

(e) make any other decision which the OFT could itself have made.

NOTE: The CAT has already utilized a number of these powers. In *Napp Pharamaceticals* [2001] CAT 1 and *Replica Kit* [2005] CAT 22 fines were reduced. In *Aberdeen Journals* [2002] CAT 6 and *Bettercare* [2002] CAT 7 the cases were remitted to the DGFT. In *Racehorse Association* [2005] CAT 29 the decision of the OFT was set aside.

Napp Pharmaceutical Holdings Limited and Subsidiaries v *DGFT*
(Case 1000/1/1/01) (final judgment), 15 January 2002

Findings
General observations

497. We observe first, that the Tribunal is not bound by the *Director's Guidance*. The Act contains no provision which requires the Tribunal to even have regard to that *Guidance*.

498. Schedule 8, paragraph 3(2) of the Act, provides that 'the tribunal may confirm or set aside the decision which is the subject to the appeal, or any part of it, and may ... (b) impose, or revoke, or vary the amount of, a penalty ... or (e) make any other decision which the Director could have made.'

499. It follows, in our judgment, that the Tribunal has a full jurisdiction itself to assess the penalty to be imposed, if necessary regardless of the way the Director has approached the matter in application of the *Director's Guidance*. Indeed, it seems to us that, in view of Article 6(1) of the ECHR, an undertaking penalised by the Director is entitled to have that penalty reviewed *ab initio* by an impartial and independent tribunal able to take its own decision unconstrained by the *Guidance*. Moreover, it seems to us that, in fixing a penalty, this Tribunal is bound to base itself on its own assessment of the infringement in the light of the facts and matters before the Tribunal at the stage of its judgment.

500. That said, it does not seem to us appropriate to disregard the *Director's Guidance*, or the Director's own approach in the Decision under challenge, when reaching our own conclusion as to what the penalty should be. The *Director's Guidance* will no doubt over time take account of the various indications given by this Tribunal in appeals against penalties.

501. We emphasise, however, that the only constraint on the amount of the penalty binding on this Tribunal is that which flows from the Maximum Penalties Order. In the present case the maximum penalty under that Order is £5.56 million, for an infringement by Napp lasting from 1 March 2000 to 31 March 2001. It is clear from that Order that Parliament intended that it is the overall turnover of the undertaking concerned, rather than its turnover in the products affected by the infringement, which is the final determinant for the amount of the penalty. As the Director points out in the *Guidance*, any other approach would mean that abuses by powerful companies in small relevant markets might not be appropriately sanctioned.

502. We agree with the thrust of the *Director's Guidance* that while the turnover in the products affected by the infringement may be an indicative starting point for the assessment of the penalty, the sum imposed must be such as to constitute a serious and effective deterrent,

both to the undertaking concerned and to other undertakings tempted to engage in similar conduct. The policy objectives of the Act will not be achieved unless this Tribunal is prepared to uphold severe penalties for serious infringements. As the *Guidance* makes clear, the achievement of the necessary deterrent may well involve penalties above, often well above, 10 per cent of turnover in the products directly concerned by the infringement, subject only to the overall 'cap' imposed by the Maximum Penalties Order. The position in this respect is no different in principle under Article 15(2) of Council Regulation No 17, albeit that the applicable maximum penalty under that provision is differently calculated.

503. We observe in parenthesis that since 1998 the European Commission has published *Guidelines on the Method of Setting Fines* OJ 1998 C9/3 ('the *Commission's Guidelines*') which have some similarities with, and some differences from, the *Director's Guidance*. The essential approach of the *Commission's Guidelines* is to indicate that the penalty will be made up of a fixed 'basic amount' depending on whether the infringement is categorised as 'minor', 'serious' or 'very serious'. The basic amount is then liable to be increased by reference to whether the infringement has lasted more than a year, and then further adjusted, upwards or downwards, according to whether there are aggravating or mitigating circumstances. Where there are differences between the *Director's Guidance* and the *Commission's Guidelines*, it seems to us that the differences are probably 'relevant differences' for the purposes of section 60 of the Act, so that we are not required, at present, to take account of the *Commission's Guidelines*. Neither party has suggested that we should do so. However the principle of starting with a certain amount (either a percentage figure, as under the *Director's Guidance*, or a fixed sum, as under the *Commission's Guidelines*) and then adjusting that starting figure to meet the circumstances of the case, is common to both approaches.

...

The Tribunal's assessment of the penalty

535. This is the first occasion on which the Tribunal has considered the amount of a penalty under the Act. We propose to adopt a 'broad brush' approach. Each case will depend on its own circumstances.

536. In this case the Director considered an appropriate penalty to be some £3.2 million. Omitting the 'aggravating circumstance' that we are minded to exclude (paragraph 516 above) the Director's figure is £2.92 million.

537. We begin by taking the case as a whole. This is a serious case of predatory and selective pricing, lasting for thirteen months up to the date of the Decision, committed by a 'super-dominant' undertaking in one segment of the market (the hospital segment) and tending to protect high prices and margins in another segment of the market where that undertaking is also a virtual monopolist (the community segment). In addition, Napp's prices in the community segment have been maintained well above the competitive level. If the objectives of the Act are to be achieved such conduct calls, in our judgment, for severe penalties. In those circumstances, absent any significant mitigating factors, we do not think that a penalty of £3 million, as a global figure, is outside the range of penalties that could reasonably be imposed, in a case such as the present, having regard to the permitted maximum of £5.56 million.

538. However, in view of the mitigating factors we have mentioned in paragraph 533 above, and to a slight extent those mentioned at paragraph 523 above, we have come to the conclusion that the overall penalty in this case should be fixed at the sum of £2.2 million.

539. If, as a 'cross-check', we were to apply the methodology of the *Director's Guidance*, the same result would be reached by taking the Director's starting percentage under Step 1, applying to that percentage a multiplier of slightly over three to reach £2.92 million under Step 3, and then reducing that figure by some 25 per cent for mitigating factors under Step 4. That in our view would equally have been a reasonable approach.

540. For the reasons already indicated, in paragraphs 507 et seq above, we do not use the calculations of gain presented to us as the basis for our decision. However, we are satisfied that

> Napp's calculations of the gain do not adequately capture the full commercial advantage of the policy it has followed, for the reasons already given.
>
> 541. We consider that a penalty of £2.2 million is the lowest amount that can reasonably be arrived at to penalise Napp's conduct and to send an appropriate signal to the business community of the seriousness of infringements of the Competition Act 1998.

NOTE: As *Napp* was one of the first cases it raised a number of points of interest. The Tribunal indicated that the Guidelines were not binding on them, thereby leaving the practice of determining the level of fines potentially difficult to predict. Hopefully that difficulty will reduce as the body of caselaw increases. Similar issues were canvassed in *Umbro* v *OFT* [2005] CAT 22 and *Argos Ltd and Littlewoods Ltd* v *OFT* [2005] CAT 13. Another theme which recurs in cases where fines are imposed are the 'due process' rights of target undertakings in competition cases.

Napp Pharmaceutical Holdings Limited and Subsidiaries v *DGFT*
(Case 1000/1/1/01) (final judgment), 15 January 2002

> 98. As we have already stated in our interim judgment of 8 August 2001, we agree that the Director's concession that these proceedings are 'criminal', for the purposes of Article 6 of the ECHR, is properly made: see Case C-235/92P *Montecatini* v *Commission* [1999] ECR I-4575, paragraphs 175 and 176. That is particularly so since penalties under the Act are intended to be severe and to have a deterrent effect: see the Director's statutory *Guidance as to the appropriate amount of the Penalty*, (OFT 423, March 2000) issued under section 38(1) of the Act.
>
> 99. The fact that these proceedings may be classified as 'criminal' for the purposes of the ECHR gives Napp the protection of Article 6, and in particular the right to 'a fair and public hearing within a reasonable time by an independent and impartial tribunal established by law' (Article 6(1)), to the presumption of innocence (Article 6(2)), and to the minimum rights envisaged by Article 6(3) including the right 'to examine or have examined witnesses against him and to obtain the attendance and examination of witnesses on his behalf under the same conditions as witnesses against him' (Article 6(3)(d)).
>
> 100. In our view it follows from Article 6(2) that the burden of proof rests throughout on the Director to prove the infringements alleged.
>
> 101. However, as the Court of Appeal held in *Han*, cited above, to which we referred in our judgment of 8 August 2001, the fact that Article 6 applies does not of itself lead to the conclusion that these proceedings must be subject to the procedures and rules that apply to the investigation and trial of offences classified as criminal offences for the purposes of domestic law: see Potter LJ at paragraph 84, and Mance LJ at paragraph 88 of that judgment.
>
> 102. Neither the ECHR itself nor the European Court of Human Rights has laid down a particular standard of proof that must be applied in proceedings to which Article 6(2) or (3) apply, and still less that the standard should be that of 'proof beyond reasonable doubt', which is not a concept to be found in the domestic systems of many of the signatory States (see Sir Richard Buxton, cited above, at pp. 338 and 339).
>
> 103. In our view it follows that neither Article 6, nor the Human Rights Act 1998, in themselves oblige us to apply the criminal standard of proof as established in domestic law in cases where the Director seeks to impose a financial penalty in respect of alleged infringements of the Chapter I or Chapter II prohibitions under the Act.
>
> 104. In our view the standard of proof to be applied under the Act is to be decided in accordance with the normal rules of the United Kingdom domestic legal systems. Neither party has cited to us any decided domestic cases which suggest that, in circumstances such as these, the criminal standard should be applied, nor invited us to apply by analogy certain civil situations where traditionally the criminal standard of proof is required (e.g. committal proceedings).

105. Infringements of the Chapter I and Chapter II prohibitions imposed by sections 2 and 18 of the Act are not classified as criminal offences in domestic law, in contrast, for example, to the criminal offences created under sections 42 to 44. Under section 38(8), penalties are recoverable by the Director as a civil debt. Directions are enforceable by civil proceedings under section 34. In our view the structure of the Act points to the conclusion that under domestic law the standard of proof we must apply in deciding whether infringements of the Chapter I or Chapter II prohibitions are proved is the civil standard, commonly known as the preponderance or balance of probabilities, notwithstanding that the civil penalties imposed may be intended by the Director to have a deterrent effect.

106. We add that in many cases under the Act the factual issues before this Tribunal will often relate to such matters as determining the relevant market, whether dominance exists, and assessing whether conduct characterised as an 'abuse' is economically justified. Issues of that kind involve a more or less complex assessment of mainly economic data and perhaps conflicting expert evidence. It seems to us more likely that Parliament would have intended us to apply the civil standard of proof to issues of this kind, rather than the time-honoured criminal standard of 'proof beyond reasonable doubt'.

107. In our view it follows from the speech of Lord Nicholls (with whom Lord Goff and Lord Mustill agreed) in *Re H*, cited above, at pp. 586 to 587, that under the law of England and Wales there are only two standards of proof, the criminal standard and the civil standard; there is no 'intermediate' standard. The position is the same in the law of Scotland and Northern Ireland. Within the civil standard, however, the more serious the allegation, the more cogent should be the evidence before the court concludes that the allegation is established on the preponderance of probability: see Lord Nicholls' speech in *Re H*, citing notably *In re Dellow's Will Trusts* [1964] 1 WLR 451, 455 and *Hornal v Neuberger Products Ltd* [1957] 1 QB 247, 266.

108. Since cases under the Act involving penalties are serious matters, it follows from *Re H* that strong and convincing evidence will be required before infringements of the Chapter I and Chapter II prohibitions can be found to be proved, even to the civil standard. Indeed, whether we are, in technical terms, applying a civil standard on the basis of strong and convincing evidence, or a criminal standard of beyond reasonable doubt, we think in practice the result is likely to be the same. We find it difficult to imagine, for example, this Tribunal upholding a penalty if there were a reasonable doubt in our minds, or if we were anything less than sure that the Decision was soundly based.

109. In those circumstances the conclusion we reach is that, formally speaking, the standard of proof in proceedings under the Act involving penalties is the civil standard of proof, but that standard is to be applied bearing in mind that infringements of the Act are serious matters attracting severe financial penalties. It is for the Director to satisfy us in each case, on the basis of strong and compelling evidence, taking account of the seriousness of what is alleged, that the infringement is duly proved, the undertaking being entitled to the presumption of innocence, and to any reasonable doubt there may be.

■ QUESTION

If the sanctions under the CA 1998 are penal in nature, should it not follow that the authorities should adhere fully to the protections afforded to the defence under criminal proceedings?

Under s. 49 of the Act a further appeal lies from decisions of an appeal tribunal either on a point of law or as to the amount of any penalty, or as to an award under s. 47A or B of the CA 1998. Any such appeal is to: the Court of Appeal in England and Wales in relation to proceedings before a tribunal in England and Wales; to the Court of Session in Scotland for proceedings before a tribunal in Scotland; and to the Court of Appeal in Northern Ireland for proceedings before a tribunal in Northern Ireland. Following the *Napp* judgment, Napp sought leave to appeal to the Court of Appeal and the CCAT adopted a very restricted definition of what constitutes a 'point of law'.

Napp Pharmaceutical Holdings Limited and Subsidiaries v DGFT
(Case 1000/1/1/01) (re reasons for refusing permission to appeal), 26 March 2002

Appeal on a point of law

25. In determining this request for permission to appeal, we have addressed, at least provisionally, what is meant by 'a point of law arising from a decision of an appeal tribunal' under section 49(1)(a) of the Act. This point is not addressed in Napp's application or skeleton argument, albeit it is briefly mentioned in Napp's further observations.

26. It is trite to say that a point of law is to be distinguished from a point of fact. As is well known, it may be difficult to say, in any given case, where the border lies between the two. In the present case, the issue is whether Napp has committed an 'abuse' within the meaning of the Chapter II prohibition. At one end of the spectrum, the Court of Justice and the Court of First Instance have laid down certain legal principles which apply when determining whether the Chapter II prohibition has been infringed. Whether we had, for example, ignored a relevant decision of the Court of Justice, would, we would have thought, be a point of law. At the other end of the spectrum, there will plainly be points of primary fact. For example, whether in this case Napp's prices to hospitals were or were not below the cost of raw materials is a point of fact. However, between these opposite ends of the spectrum there will, so it seems to us, often be questions arising under the Act which are essentially questions of appreciation or economic assessment of a more or less complex kind, depending on the circumstances, in which the Tribunal will be called upon to assess a range of factors, bringing to bear such expertise as it has, in order to determine such matters as the boundaries of the 'relevant market', the existence of 'barriers to entry', whether 'dominance' is established, whether a response by the dominant undertaking is 'proportionate' and so on.

27. In the present application, for example, a substantial part of Napp's argument on the hospital pricing abuse is that its pricing policy constituted 'normal competition' (grounds 1 (i), (ii), (iii) and (vi) of the request), this being, apparently, a reference to a dictum by the Court of Justice in Case 85/76 *Hoffman-La Roche* v *Commission* [1979] ECR 461, paragraph 91, which refers to a dominant undertaking committing an abuse 'through recourse to methods different from those which condition normal competition' (see paragraph 207 of the Tribunal's judgment). The issues surrounding this argument, from the many different angles it has been presented, are dealt with at paragraphs 231 to 352 of the Tribunal's judgment, Napp's contentions being rejected on every point. Whether, on the facts of this case what Napp did can be defended on the ground that it constituted 'normal competition' does not seem to us to be a 'point of law' as such, but rather a question of appreciation of the various interrelated facts and considerations discussed in paragraphs 231 to 352 of the judgment.

...

35. These cases, notably *Bairstow* v *Edwards* read with *South Yorkshire Transport*, cited above, seem to point to the conclusion that there is a 'point of law' under section 49(1)(a) where the issue is whether (i) there is a misdirection on a point of law; (ii) there is no evidence to support a relevant finding of fact; or (iii) the tribunal's appreciation of the facts and issues before it is one that no reasonable tribunal could reach, that is to say the appreciation in question is outside 'the permissible field of judgment'. In the light of *Nipa Begum*, it may well be that the principles to be applied are not signficantly different from those applicable in judicial review proceedings. We bear these cases in mind in deciding whether Napp's arguments do involve 'a point of law' under section 49(1)(a), and if so whether any such point of law has a real prospect of success.

NOTE: This is a rather restrictive interpretation of what constitutes a 'point of law', limited to 'judicial review' type issues. The Tribunal concluded that there were no real points of law raised in the appeal and no compelling reason to allow an appeal to proceed merely because this case involved the first infringement and penalty imposed under the Act. The Court of Appeal subsequently supported the refusal to allow permission to appeal as the appeal did not involve points of law (*Napp Pharmaceutical Holdings Ltd* v *DGFT* [2002] EWCA Civ 796, 8 May 2002). Interestingly, Buxton LJ, at para. 34, stated that even if the court had authority to review the CCAT's findings, it would be very reluctant to interfere with the conclusions of an expert and specialist tribunal. For another example of the issues surrounding appeals see the combined case of *JJB Sports Plc* v *Office of Fair Trading* [2005] CAT 27 and *Argos Ltd* v *Office of Fair Trading* [2006] EWCA Civ 1318.

SECTION 4: THE ENTERPRISE ACT 2002: OTHER MAIN ISSUES

The main competition law provisions in the EA 2002 deal with merger control and market investigations. The detail of those procedures is discussed in Chapters 11 and 13. In this section we shall outline the respective institutions and their main roles.

A: An independent competition authority

The EA 2002 continued the trend towards the depoliticization of UK competition law by reducing the role and influence of the Secretary of State and by the creation of the OFT as an independent authority.

DTI White Paper, *World Class Competition Regime*
Cm 5233, London, HMSO, July 2001

Strong, proactive and independent competition authorities

- The Government wishes to see truly independent competition authorities which work proactively to root out instances of anti-competitive behaviour.
- There will be clear legal duties for the OFT to promote competition.
- Government invites our competition authorities to advise on the impact of laws and regulations on competition. The Government is committed to responding publicly within 90 days.
- Government welcomes the OFT's move to introduce 'super-complaints' from consumer groups. This new power will be enshrined in legislation.
- Only those with expertise relevant to competition will be appointed to the Competition Commission. Only those with expertise relevant to competition or consumer affairs will be appointed to the Board of the OFT.
- Both the Competition Commission and the OFT will improve their staffing—with recruitment on the basis of expertise relevant to competition becoming the norm for those working in competition.
- The Government, the OFT and the Competition Commission, all share a common understanding of the aims of our competition regime—to increase the level of competition in the economy, to improve the UK's productivity performance and to make markets work well for consumers.
- The Government invites Parliament to actively scrutinise our competition regime. The mission statements of the Competition Commission, the OFT and Government will help it to do so.

4.1 While the Government can set a strong framework for competition, it is our competition authorities which carry responsibility for implementing it. For an effective competition regime, UK consumers and businesses rely on the OFT and the Competition Commission to detect instances where markets are not working well, and to take the necessary action to remedy the problems.

NOTE: Part 1 of the EA 2002 established the Office of Fair Trading and set out its general functions. Previously, the OFT was an administrative support body to assist the DGFT in the exercise of his/her functions. Section 1 established the OFT as a new corporate authority, a non-Ministerial Government Department, and all the DGFT's tasks and functions were transferred to it by s. 2. Schedule 1 made detailed provision for the appointment of the Chairman, by the Chief Executive, and of the other members. The remainder of Part 1 of the Act sets out more detail on the OFT's functions, including the publication of an annual plan (s. 3), information gathering (s. 5), and the provision of information and advice to Ministers (s. 7).

Notwithstanding the new found independence of the UK competition authorities, following the events surrounding the Lloyds TSB/HBOS merger in late 2008, it is clear that the Secretary of State still has the power to intervene in high-profile cases. See 'OFT report to the Secretary of State on Lloyds/HBOS merger', ME/3862/08, 31 October 2008.

■ QUESTION

To what extent has the creation of an independent authority weakened the accountability of the UK competition regime?

B: Super-complaints to the OFT

The EA 2002 contains provisions on competition law, insolvency law, and consumer law. The protection of the consumer is a cornerstone of the Act. The DTI White Paper, *World Class Competition Regime*, proposed the creation of a fast-track procedure for complaints by consumer bodies. Section 11 of the Act introduces a super-complaint procedure for recognized consumer bodies.

ENTERPRISE ACT [S. 11(1)]

11 Super-complaints to OFT

(1) This section applies where a designated consumer body makes a complaint to the OFT that any feature, or combination of features, of a market in the United Kingdom for goods or services is or appears to be significantly harming the interests of consumers.

NOTE: This procedure is designed to encourage consumer representative groups to make collective complaints on their behalf. The benefit is that the OFT will be required to respond and make a considered response, in most cases, within 90 days (sub-ss. (2) and (3)). Subsection (6) makes provision as to how consumer bodies can be designated as entitled to make super-complaints.

Super-Complaints: Guidance for designated consumer bodies
July 2003, OFT 514

Paragraphs 2.4–2.5, 2.11–2.16, 2.25–2.26

2.4 The super-complaint process is intended to be a fast-track system for designated consumer bodies to bring to the attention of the OFT and the Regulators, market features that appear to be significantly harming the interests of consumers. When deciding whether or not to make a super-complaint, careful thought should be given as to whether the super-complaint process is the most effective route. It may be that specific competition or consumer legislation would provide a more immediate and/or effective means of satisfying and addressing the issue. For example when the feature of a market that is, or appears to be, significantly harming the interests of consumers relates to single firm conduct. Given the definition of consumer outlined at 2.2, super-complainants assessing the impact of a market feature should focus on the effect on end consumers and not business intermediaries.

Who can make a super-complaint?

2.5 Only designated consumer bodies can make a super-complaint. Under section 11(5) of the Act it is specified that a consumer body has to be designated by the Secretary of State for Trade and Industry by order. The Secretary of State can make any organisation a designated consumer body provided it appears to her to represent the interests of consumers of any description and also meets any other criteria published by the Secretary of State which are applied when determining whether to make or revoke a designation. It is expected that those designated will be informed bodies who are in a strong position to represent the interests of groups of consumers and able to provide solid analysis and evidence in support of any super-complaint they may make.

What needs to be in a super-complaint?

2.11 When making a complaint the super-complainant should provide a paper setting out the reasons why in its view a UK market for goods or services has a feature or combination of features which is or appears to be significantly harming the interests of consumers and should therefore be investigated. This paper should be supported, wherever possible, by documented facts and evidence.

2.12 The objective of presenting the case is to help the receiving authority undertake a full appraisal of whether any feature or combination of features of a UK market is or appears to be significantly harming consumer interests and what action, if any, should be taken. Super-complainants are not expected to provide the level of evidence necessary for the OFT or a Regulator to decide that immediate action is appropriate. However, they should present a reasoned case for further investigation. Complaints that are, or that appear to be, frivolous or vexatious will be rejected.

2.13 The annexe sets out the kind of evidence that designated consumer bodies should consider providing when deciding whether to make a super-complaint.

2.14 Complaints raised by individuals or bodies about specific instances of anti-competitive behaviour or infringements of consumer protection legislation will continue to be considered under other legislation as at present. Procedural safeguards that ensure fairness for those who may be the subject of enforcement action are unaffected by super-complaints.

How will super-complaints be handled?

2.15 Super-complaints will be given fast-track consideration. Those with the duty to respond to super-complaints are required to publish a reasoned response within 90 calendar days from the day after a complaint is received.

2.16 On receipt of a complaint the super-complainant will be contacted within five working days to acknowledge receipt and let them know who within the OFT or relevant Regulator will be the main contact during the 90 day period.

What action will result from a super-complaint?

2.25 The possible outcomes of a super-complaint include:
- enforcement action by the OFT's competition or consumer regulation divisions
- finding that another authority with concurrent duties is better placed to deal with the complaint
- launching a market study into the issue
- making a market investigation reference to the Competition Commission (CC) if there is a competition problem
- action by a sectoral regulator with concurrent duties
- referring the complaint to a sectoral regulator without concurrent duties

- referring the complaint to the OFT for action (if the complaint was sent to a regulator with concurrent duties)
- referring the complaint to another consumer enforcement body
- finding the complaint requires no action
- finding the complaint to be unfounded
- dismissing the complaint as frivolous or vexatious.

2.26 The above list is not exhaustive. It should also be noted that a super-complaint could generate more than one outcome depending on the issues raised.

Response to Which?'s super-complaint: 'Restrictions on business structures and direct access in the Scottish legal profession'
31 July 2007, OFT 946, paras 1.1–1.4, 7.1–7.3, and 9.1–9.3

1.1 Which? submitted a super-complaint to the OFT on 8 May 2007 asserting that the following restrictions imposed on providers of legal services in Scotland significantly harm the interests of consumers by stifling choice, inhibiting innovation, and excluding potential entrants from the legal services market:
- the restrictions on advocates' business structures
- the restrictions on solicitors and advocates providing services jointly
- the restrictions on third party entry, and
- the restrictions on direct access to advocates.

1.2 Which? further submitted that the regulatory structure for legal services in Scotland should be reformed in order to accommodate the lifting of these restrictions.

1.3 The right to submit a super-complaint was created by section 11 of the Enterprise Act 2002 (the Act). A super-complaint is defined under section 11(1) of the Act as a complaint made by a designated consumer body that 'any feature, or combination of features, of a market in the United Kingdom for goods or services is or appears to be significantly harming the interests of consumers'. The OFT is satisfied that the super-complaint meets the criteria set out in section 11(1) of the Act.

1.4 Section 11(2) of the Act requires the OFT, within 90 days after the day on which it receives a super-complaint, to publish a response stating whether it has decided to take any action in respect of the complaint, or to take no action, in response to the complaint, and if it has decided to take action, what action it proposes to take. Under section 11(3) of the Act, the response must state the OFT's reasons for its proposals. This document represents the OFT's response to the super-complaint submitted by Which?.

...

7.1 It is important to note that lifting the restrictions on ABSs will not compel legal services providers to adopt such structures. The current business models will still be available to solicitors and advocates should they feel that the current structure is best for their business. Legal services providers should, however, be free to choose the model that best suits their clients' needs. Enabling providers to choose from a number of business models will allow them to respond to the different needs of different consumers more effectively.

7.2 Concerns have been raised regarding the regulation of ABSs. One possible option is that lawyers in ABSs should be regulated by their respective professional bodies. There may be instances where the rules of the respective professional bodies would need to be amended in order to reflect new responsibilities that might fall to a legal services provider operating in an ABS (for example advocates may be responsible for handling clients' funds in an ABS). Another possible option is that a single regulator should take charge of regulating ABSs. While these issues are important and should be considered carefully before allowing ABSs, the OFT does not believe that the difficulties are insurmountable, nor that they form a valid argument for maintaining the current restrictions.

7.3 For the reasons outlined, the OFT agrees with Which? that it would be in the interests of consumers for the restrictions on ABSs and on direct access to advocates to be removed. In these circumstances we believe that the potential benefits of lifting the restrictions would outweigh the costs to the SE and the profession of conducting policy work to consider how to take the issues forward. The SE should, we believe, also consider with the professions how these restrictions might best be lifted, and the appropriate safeguards that would need to be put in place in order to protect the interests of consumers and the integrity of the profession.

...

9.1 There is little evidence that progress has been made on these issues since the publication of the SE Research Working Group Report in April 2006. It would be helpful if the SE would set out its own views on how it proposes to take the issues forward, with particular regard to how it believes legal services in Scotland should be regulated. These views might reflect, in particular, whether and how the SE foresees that the restrictions identified in the super-complaint could be lifted and when the issues will be resolved. The SE may wish to consider whether it would be appropriate to discuss the way forward with all interested parties. The OFT would, of course, be content to participate in that process.

9.2 The OFT believes that Scottish consumers are disadvantaged by these restrictions on Scottish legal services providers. Given that similar restrictions will be lifted on legal services providers in England and Wales it is timely to ensure that due consideration is given to, and action taken to set in hand, the process that will ensure that consumers and legal services providers in Scotland are not unnecessarily disadvantaged. Both the FoA and the LSS should carry out wide-ranging reviews of their respective rules and make significant and transparent progress towards lifting the restrictions discussed in this response. The OFT notes that the LSS is already looking at the available options and urges it to continue this work.

NOTE: The Scottish Executive responded, rather negatively, to the OFT's suggestions. See 'Scottish Government Policy Statement on OFT Response to Which? Super-Complaint', 18 December 2007.

C: Mergers

The OFT is under a duty to refer a merger if it satisfies the requirements set out in Chapter 1 of Part 3. The EA 2002 retains a two-stage approach to merger control, with the Competition Commission carrying out the second-stage in-depth investigation if necessary: see Chapter 13. The Act introduces strict statutory timetables for the completion of each investigation stage (ss. 39 and 40). There is a new procedure for information to be obtained by the OFT in relation to mergers under s. 30. The Commission's role, set out in ss. 35–41, is broadly similar as under the FTA 1973 but with the crucial change in status to that of being the determinative body in respect of all merger investigations, other than those involving public interest considerations. It has the investigative powers afforded to it under ss. 109–117, in order to complete its investigation and report. Section 109 gives the Competition Commission a power to serve notices requiring any person to attend to give evidence to the Competition Commission or to provide it with specified documents or information by specified dates. If it reports that there is a substantial lessening of competition, it is required to decide on appropriate remedial action to achieve as comprehensive a solution as is reasonable and practicable. Section 41 sets out the duty incumbent upon the Competition Commission:

ENTERPRISE ACT 2002 [S. 41]

41 Duty to remedy effects of completed or anticipated mergers

(1) Subsection (2) applies where a report of the Commission has been prepared and published under section 37 within the period permitted by section 38 and contains the decision that there is an anti-competitive outcome.

(2) The Commission shall take such action under section 79 or 81 as it considers to be reasonable and practicable—

  (a) to remedy, mitigate or prevent the substantial lessening of competition concerned; and

  (b) to remedy, mitigate or prevent any adverse effects which have resulted from, or may be expected to result from, the substantial lessening of competition.

(3) The decision of the Commission under subsection (2) shall be consistent with its decisions as included in its report by virtue of section 34(3) or (as the case may be) 35(2) unless there has been a material change of circumstances since the preparation of the report or the Commission otherwise has a special reason for deciding differently.

(4) In making a decision under subsection (2), the Commission shall, in particular, have regard to the need to achieve as comprehensive a solution as is reasonable and practicable to the substantial lessening of competition and any adverse effects resulting from it.

(5) In making a decision under subsection (2), the Commission may, in particular, have regard to the effect of any action on any relevant customer benefits in relation to the creation of the relevant merger situation concerned.

NOTE: There is a specialized regime in respect of mergers involving 'public interest' considerations in relation to which the Secretary of State has retained an important role, and this is detailed in Chapter 2 of Part 3 of the Act. The use of this power in the relation to the Lloyds TSB/HBOS merger in 2008 is of particular note (see OFT, 'OFT report to the Secretary of State on Lloyds/HBOS merger', No ME/3862/08, 31 October 2008 and BERR, 'Peter Mandelson gives regulatory clearance to Lloyds TSB merger with HBOS', 31 October 2008). There are also provisions in Chapter 3 for other special cases including mergers involving Government defence contractors and the protection of legitimate interests in the mergers falling within the scope of the Community Merger Regulation.

Chapter 4 of Part 3 deals with enforcement (ss. 71–94 and Schs. 7 and 8). The regime under the 2002 Act is similar to the FTA 1973 scheme except that the Competition Commission can accept final undertakings (s. 82), and make an order (s. 84 and Sch. 8) to remedy competition problems identified in its final report. The OFT has a duty to monitor undertakings and Orders (ss. 92–3).

Section 120 introduces a new level of review of the merger control process, whereby decisions taken in connection with a merger reference may be reviewed by the CAT on the same grounds as a court on an application for judicial review. See, for instance, the *Merger Action Group* v *Secretary of State for BERR* [2008] CAT 34, as discussed in Chapter 13.

D: Market investigations

Many of the changes, set out in Part 4 of the EA 2002, to the FTA 1973 system of investigation and enforcement are of a similar nature to those outlined above on mergers, and Part 4 should be consulted in detail. An initial difference is that OFT has a power and not a duty to make references in Part 4. However, the remainder is similar, including the separate public interest regime and the possibility of review of decisions under Part 4 by the CAT: see Chapter 11.

E: The new cartel offence

Part 6 of the EA 2002 introduces a new cartel offence, discussed at greater length in Chapter 9. The OFT are to play a key role in the investigation and prosecution of the new offence.

ENTERPRISE ACT 2002 [S. 190]

190 Cartel offence: penalty and prosecution

(1) A person guilty of an offence under section 188 is liable—
   (a) on conviction on indictment, to imprisonment for a term not exceeding five years or to a fine, or to both;
   (b) on summary conviction, to imprisonment for a term not exceeding six months or to a fine not exceeding the statutory maximum, or to both.

(2) In England and Wales and Northern Ireland, proceedings for an offence under section 183 may be instituted only—
   (a) by the Director of the Serious Fraud Office, or
   (b) by or with the consent of the OFT.

(3) No proceedings may be brought for an offence under section 188 in respect of an agreement outside the United Kingdom, unless it has been implemented in whole or in part in the United Kingdom.

(4) Where, for the purpose of the investigation or prosecution of offences under section 188, the OFT gives a person written notice under this subsection, no proceedings for an offence under section 188 that falls within a description specified in the notice may be brought against that person in England and Wales or Northern Ireland except in circumstances specified in the notice.

NOTE: The lead prosecutor in England and Wales will be the Serious Fraud Office, and in Scotland the Lord Advocate. There is provision for leniency in sub-s. (4) and the OFT have issued guidance in, *The cartel offence*, April 2003, OFT 513. Sections 192–202 make detailed provision on the investigatory powers, including surveillance powers (s. 199 and Sch. 26), afforded the OFT in relation to the criminal investigations. Guidance on the OFT's investigation powers can be found in, *Powers for investigating criminal cartels*, January 2004, OFT 515.

Powers for investigating criminal cartels

January 2004, OFT 515, Chapter 2, paras 3.1–3.17, 5.1–5.6, and 6.1–6.5 [footnotes omitted]

2 Trigger for the use of the powers of investigation

2.1 The OFT can conduct a formal investigation under the Enterprise Act if there are reasonable grounds for suspecting that a criminal cartel offence has been committed.

2.2 Whether there are reasonable grounds for suspecting is an objective test and will depend upon the information available to the OFT. Examples of sources of information that may lead to reasonable grounds for suspecting that the criminal offence has been committed include statements provided by employees or ex-employees or former members of a cartel, correspondence evidencing the existence of a secret cartel agreement or information provided in an application made by an undertaking or an individual under the OFT's leniency programmes.

2.3 The OFT may obtain information about individuals, undertakings, agreements and markets at any time through informal enquiries. Such enquiries, which may be made at a meeting, by correspondence, in a telephone conversation or during the course of a voluntary interview may be made in addition to, or instead of, using the formal investigation powers set out in the Enterprise Act. The OFT will make it clear to individuals and undertakings that they are not compelled to respond to an informal enquiry. Undertakings and individuals are however encouraged to co-operate with the OFT enquiries.

3 Powers of investigation

3.1 The Enterprise Act gives the OFT the power:
   • to require persons to answer questions, provide information or produce documents
   • to enter and search premises under a warrant.

These powers of investigation are only exerciseable for the purposes of an investigation where it appears to the OFT that there is good reason to exercise them for the purpose of investigating the affairs, or any aspect of the affairs, of any person.

Powers to require information and documents

3.2 For the purposes of an investigation, the OFT has the power to require a person under investigation or any other person who it has reason to believe has relevant information to answer questions, or provide information, and to produce specified documents which appear to the OFT to relate to any matter relevant to the investigation. This power must be exercised by serving a written notice. The notice must indicate the subject matter and purpose of the investigation and the nature of the offences which may be committed by failing to co-operate with an investigation, which are set out in paragraph 7.1 below. The notice will state the time and place at which information or documents must be produced. The notice may also require a person to attend an interview to answer questions with respect to any matter relevant to the investigation. This is referred to as a compulsory interview (paragraph 4.3).

3.3 Where documents are produced, the OFT may take copies or extracts from them and require the person producing the documents to provide an explanation of any of them. Where documents are not produced, the OFT may require the person who was required to produce them to state, to the best of his knowledge and belief, where they are.

3.4 The powers to require information to be provided and specified documents to be produced may be used at any time during the investigation of a suspected criminal offence, including during the execution of a search warrant. A person may also receive more than one notice during the course of an investigation. The OFT is not limited to using the powers against persons under investigation. In setting an appropriate time limit for complying with a written notice, the OFT will consider the amount and complexity of the information required. However, the OFT can require information and documents to be provided immediately if appropriate.

3.5 The 'specified documents' which the OFT can require to be produced in a written notice (subject to the limitations outlined in section 6 below) include both specified individual documents, for example a particular agreement, or documents of a specified description, such as price lists or sales invoices over a certain period. The term 'documents' includes information recorded in any form and includes information that may be held electronically.

Power to enter premises under a warrant

3.6 For the purposes of a criminal investigation and on specified grounds, the OFT may apply to the High Court or, in Scotland, the procurator fiscal may apply to the sheriff, for a warrant authorising a named officer of the OFT, and any other OFT officers and specified persons authorised to accompany the named officer, to enter and search premises and to take possession of relevant documents, or to take necessary steps for preserving them or preventing interference with them.

3.7 The Enterprise Act sets out the circumstances in which a judge in the High Court or the sheriff may issue a warrant to enter and search premises specified in the warrant. The judge or the sheriff must be satisfied that there are reasonable grounds for believing that there are on the premises documents which the OFT has the power to require to be produced in a written notice (paragraph 3.2) and that:
- a person has failed to comply with the requirement to produce them, or
- it is not practicable to serve a written notice, or
- the service of such a notice might seriously prejudice the investigation (for example, relevant documents are likely to be destroyed or tampered with).

3.8 A warrant issued by a judge in the High Court or by the sheriff shall authorise the named officer and OFT officers authorised in writing to accompany him to:
- enter the premises, using such force as is reasonably necessary for the purpose of gaining entry
- search the premises and take possession of documents appearing to be of the kind in respect of which the warrant was granted (subject to the limitations outlined in section 6

below). Original documents will be taken, as is the usual practice under search warrants issued in respect of suspected criminal offences although the person who had custody or control of a document before it was taken by the OFT will, on request, be provided with a copy as soon as is reasonably practicable after the execution of the warrant

- require any person to provide an explanation of any document appearing to be of a kind in respect of which the warrant was granted or to state to the best of his knowledge and belief where it may be found
- require information which is held electronically and is accessible from the premises and which the named officer considers relates to any matter relevant to the investigation to be produced in a visible and legible form (or in a form from which it can be readily produced in a visible and legible form) and taken away.

3.9 A warrant can authorise persons who are not employees of the OFT to accompany and assist the named officer in the search. Such persons may be needed, for example, to provide expertise which is not available within the OFT but is necessary to utilise fully the terms of the warrant. For example, an IT expert who could assist OFT officers to retrieve information from computers located on premises for which the warrant was issued.

3.10 A warrant will indicate the subject matter and purpose of the investigation and the nature of the offences which may be committed by failing to co-operate with an investigation, which are set out in paragraph 7.1 below. Upon entry to the premises the named officer will produce the warrant and all officers will also produce evidence of their identity. If the occupier is present, a copy of the warrant shall, if practicable, be given to the occupier before the search begins along with a copy of a notice that summarises the extent of the powers being used and explains the rights of the occupier unless the named officer believes this would frustrate the object of the search or endanger officers or other people. Where possible, the person in charge at the premises should designate an appropriate person to be a point of contact for the officer during his investigation.

3.11 The named officer shall first attempt to communicate with the occupier, or any other person entitled to grant access to the premises, explain the authority under which entry is sought to the premises and ask the occupier to allow entry unless:

- the premises to be searched are unoccupied, or
- the occupier and any other person entitled to grant access are absent, or
- there are reasonable grounds for believing that alerting the occupier or any other person entitled to grant access would frustrate the object of the search or endanger officers or other people.

3.12 If any of the above circumstances apply, reasonable and proportionate force may be used if necessary to enter premises if the named officer is satisfied that the premises are those specified in the warrant. Reasonable and proportionate force may also be used where the occupier or any other person entitled to grant access has refused entry to the premises or it is impossible to communicate with the occupier or any other person entitled to grant access. If the occupier is not present, a copy of the warrant and of the notice of powers and rights shall be left in a prominent place on the premises and endorsed with the date and time of the search and the name of the named officer. On leaving premises which have been entered by force, the named officer must make sure that they are secure either by arranging for the occupier or the occupier's representative to be present or by any other appropriate means. If the occupier is informed, he, or one of his representatives, must be given a reasonable opportunity to be present when the warrant is executed.

3.13 In addition, OFT officers also have the power to seize material where it is not reasonably practicable, while on the premises, to determine the extent to which it may be seized, if at all, or for the seizable material to be separated from the non-seizable material in which it is comprised. This may be the case, for example, where there is a large bulk of material or where special technical equipment is needed to separate out material the OFT would be entitled to take from material which it is not (for example, material held on a computer). The factors that the OFT must take into account in deciding whether to exercise these seize and sift powers are the length of time and the number of persons required to carry out the determination or separation on the premises; whether the determination or separation would (or would if carried out on the premises) involve damage to property; the need for any special apparatus or equipment to carry out the determination or separation; and whether the separation (either in itself or if carried out on the premises by the only practicable means) would be likely to prejudice the use of some or all of the material to be taken. OFT officers must always give careful consideration to whether removing copies or images of relevant material or data would be a satisfactory alternative to removing the originals.

3.14 The exercise of seize and sift powers is subject to strict safeguards and the OFT will fully comply with Home Office guidance on operating these powers and the revised version of PACE Code B.

Access to legal advice during criminal investigations

3.15 When executing a warrant obtained under the Enterprise Act in respect of a suspected criminal offence the OFT officers will not wait for an individual's or undertaking's legal advisers to arrive before commencing the search. However, a friend, neighbour or other person will be allowed to witness the search unless the named officer in charge of the search has reasonable grounds for believing that the presence of the person asked for would seriously hinder the investigation or endanger officers or other people. A search need not be unreasonably delayed for this purpose. A record of the action taken, including the grounds for refusing a request from the occupier, should be made on the premises search record. During the course of a search under a warrant, the OFT officers may be prepared to wait a reasonable amount of time for an undertaking's or an individual's legal advisers to arrive if it is the OFT's intention to remove material from the premises where it is not reasonably practicable to examine it properly on the premises (paragraphs 3.13 and 3.14 above), although the rest of the search will proceed without delay.

3.16 A person suspected of having committed a criminal cartel offence will be advised that he is free to seek legal advice before being interviewed under caution (paragraph 4.2 below). A person being interviewed under the powers of investigation in the Enterprise Act (paragraph 3.2 above) will also be entitled to seek legal advice. OFT officers will not generally conduct interviews under caution or using the compulsory powers of investigation in the Enterprise Act during the course of a search under warrant. An interview under caution may be conducted during the course of a search under warrant if a person voluntarily decides to provide information to OFT officers in which case he will be cautioned and advised that he is free to seek legal advice. A person is not required to be cautioned prior to being asked questions that are solely necessary for the purpose of furthering the proper and effective conduct of a search, such as to obtain computer passwords or safe combinations.

3.17 PACE does not apply in Scotland nor do PACE Codes of Practice. Accordingly, the procedures set out in paragraphs 3.10 to 3.12 inclusive and 3.14 to 3.16 inclusive insofar as these relate to PACE Codes of Practice, do not constitute legal requirements for the execution of search warrants in Scotland. Nevertheless, the OFT officers may follow these procedures in Scotland, if appropriate.

...

5 Intrusive surveillance and action in respect of property

5.1 The Enterprise Act introduces new powers of intrusive surveillance for the OFT for the sole purpose of investigating the criminal cartel offence. The Enterprise Act amends the Regulation of Investigatory Powers Act 2000 ('RIPA') and the Police Act 1997 to grant the OFT the power of intrusive surveillance and the related power of property interference.

5.2 Intrusive Surveillance is defined as covert surveillance carried out in relation to anything taking place on any residential premises (including hotel accommodation) or in any private vehicle and involves the presence of an individual on the premises or in a vehicle or by means of a surveillance device(s) to either hear or see what is happening within the premises or vehicle. Property Interference allows for the covert installation of such a device(s) in property which would otherwise involve some element of trespass.

5.3 These forms of surveillance, which will only be used by the OFT in its investigations under the Enterprise Act, require the personal authority of the Chairman of the OFT and the prior approval of the Office of Surveillance Commissioners before deployment can take place. In cases of urgency, which are likely to be rare, if prior approval from a Surveillance Commissioner cannot be sought and granted in time, the Chairman of the OFT (or a designated officer of the OFT) will authorise the deployment of intrusive surveillance and give notice to a Surveillance Commissioner as soon as is reasonably practicable, explaining why it was necessary to use the urgency provisions. If the Surveillance Commissioner is at any time satisfied that there were no reasonable grounds for believing the case was urgent, he may quash the authorisation and the surveillance must cease immediately. The use of intrusive surveillance must be necessary to prevent or detect the cartel offence and must be proportionate to what is sought to be achieved by carrying it out.

5.4 Beyond the scope of the Enterprise Act, the OFT has been added to the list of public authorities which can authorise the use of other methods of surveillance in accordance with RIPA. The OFT is allowed to authorise directed surveillance (for example, watching a person's office) and covert human intelligence sources (i.e. informants) in its cartel investigations under both the Enterprise Act and the CA98.

5.5 The OFT is also authorised to obtain access to communications data (for example, obtaining records of telephone numbers called). The OFT can only use the facility to access communications data in its investigations under the Enterprise Act.

5.6 The OFT intends to publish Codes of Practice in relation to its procedures for exercising the various powers outlined in paragraphs 5.2 to 5.5 above in its investigations.

6 Limitations on the use of the powers of investigation

Privileged communications

6.1 The power of the OFT to obtain documents under the Enterprise Act, whether by written notice or during the execution of a search warrant, does not extend to communications benefiting from legal professional privilege ("LPP"). A person may not be required to produce or disclose any information or document which he would be entitled to refuse to produce or disclose on grounds of LPP in proceedings in the High Court or in Scottish Courts on grounds of confidentiality of communications. However, a lawyer may be obliged to provide the name and address of his client as part of an investigation being conducted under the powers in the Enterprise Act. LPP does not apply to communications made with the intention of furthering a criminal purpose (whether the lawyer is acting unwittingly or culpably). The OFT will adopt suitable procedures to determine the proper status of disputed LPP material.

6.2 The Enterprise Act also provides a safeguard in respect of confidential banking information, i.e. confidential communication between a bank and its client. A person may not be required under the powers of investigation in the Enterprise Act to disclose any information or produce any document if the information or document is protected by a banking obligation of confidence, unless the person to whom the obligation of confidence is owed consents to the disclosure or the OFT has authorised the disclosure.

Self-incrimination

6.3 The Enterprise Act provides safeguards in relation to the use of information gained by the OFT using its compulsory powers of investigation under the Enterprise Act. Statements made by a person in response to a requirement imposed by the OFT using its powers of investigation under the Enterprise Act, may only be used as evidence in criminal proceedings against that person in two circumstances:

- where that person has knowingly or recklessly made a false or misleading statement in response to that requirement and is then prosecuted for an offence of knowingly or recklessly making a false or misleading statement (part 7 below)
- where that person is being prosecuted for some other offence and he makes a statement that is inconsistent with it and if evidence relating to it is adduced or a question relating to it is asked by him or on his behalf.

6.4 Statements made by a person in response to a requirement imposed by the OFT using its compulsory powers of investigation under the CA98 may only be used as evidence in a cartel prosecution against the person who made it if, in giving evidence during a prosecution of the cartel offence under the Enterprise Act, he makes a statement inconsistent with it and if evidence relating to it is adduced or a question relating to it is asked by him or on his behalf.

6.5 A person's answers to questions required under section 2 of the CJA 1987 (paragraph 3.20 above) may only be used in evidence in criminal proceedings against the person under the same two circumstances outlined in paragraph 6.3 above. Similar restrictions apply to the use in evidence of answers given to questions required under section 28 of the Criminal Law (Consolidation) (Scotland) Act 1995.

Finally, the OFT also has a role in relation to the new provisions in Part 7 of the Act on directors' disqualification in relation to competition law breaches (s. 204). The OFT (or sectoral regulator) has investigatory powers for this purpose, and can accept a disqualification undertaking or seek a court disqualification. See the OFT guidance in *Competition disqualification orders*, May 2003, OFT 510.

FURTHER READING

Rodger, B.J., and MacCulloch, A. (eds), *The UK Competition Act: A New Era for UK Competition Law*, Oxford, Hart Publishing, 2000.

DTI White Paper, *World Class Competition Regime*, July 2001, Cm 5233.

Lawrence, J., and Moffat, J., 'A dangerous new world—practical implications of the Enterprise Act 2002' [2004] ECLR 1.

4

Private enforcement

SECTION 1: **INTRODUCTION**

In the European Community, and the UK in particular, competition law enforcement has traditionally been the virtually exclusive dominion of administrative authorities, the European Commission ('DG Competition') and the Office of Fair Trading, respectively, as discussed in Chapters 2 and 3. However, there have been a number of developments over the last 20 years in the European Community generally, and UK specifically, to encourage and facilitate private enforcement of the competition rules in litigation before the civil courts. This chapter will address the ongoing developments in relation to private enforcement of EC and UK competition law. This introduction will consider the US system where private antitrust enforcement is a well-developed and mature system of litigation. Section 2 will consider the background developments under EC law and the obstacles to private enforcement. Section 3 will consider the debate regarding whether private enforcement should be promoted and its relationship to the traditional public enforcement model. Section 4 will outline the more recent important EC case law developments, notably in *Crehan* and *Manfredi*, and policy developments culminating in the White Paper of April 2008. Section 5 will assess private enforcement under the Competition Act 1998, later statutory developments and proposals to further facilitate private damages actions under UK law. Section 6 will focus on a range of key themes in relation to private litigation: collective redress, funding competition litigation, the passing-on defence/indirect purchasers, and damages.

A: US private antitrust enforcement

Historically, a range of factors have combined to ensure that private enforcement is effectively the default setting for antitrust enforcement in general, namely the wider litigation culture, the significant period of development of antitrust law and economics, and the specific characteristics of US civil procedure: the rules on discovery, funding of actions, the availability of class actions, and the existence of treble damages actions, together with clarification (and modification) of the legal position in relation to issues such as the passing-on defence and standing for indirect purchasers. The system was reviewed recently by the US Antitrust Modernization Commission ('AMC').

Antitrust Modernization Commission Report and Recommendations, 2007

http://govinfo.library.unt.edu/amc/report_recommendation/toc.htm

Chapter 3: Civil and Criminal Remedies at pp 241–2 [footnotes omitted]

Private parties injured by an alleged antitrust violation can sue to recover three times their actual damages, plus costs and attorneys' fees, and for equitable relief similar to what the government can obtain. Private antitrust enforcement has been more vigorous in the United States than anywhere else in the world. The vitality of private antitrust enforcement in the United States is largely attributed to two factors: (1) the availability of treble damages plus costs and attorneys' fees, and (2) the U.S. class action mechanism, which allows plaintiffs to sue on behalf of both themselves and similarly situated, absent plaintiffs. An aggressive and capable antitrust plaintiffs' bar has developed to pursue class actions following on to government criminal prosecutions and in situations where individual plaintiffs might not have the ability or incentive to sue. Congress, state legislatures, and the courts have developed rules governing who can recover for injuries that are "passed on" to various levels of consumers, the availability of attorneys' fees and prejudgment interest on damages, and how liability is allocated among alleged participants in an antitrust conspiracy. Over the years, observers have debated the effectiveness of this public-private enforcement framework in achieving optimal levels of deterrence and compensation to victims. With respect to private civil actions, for example, the availability of treble damages has been both lauded as the key to an effective enforcement system and blamed for burdening business with litigation of questionable merit. Some observers contend that treble damages are insufficient to deter and compensate at optimal levels and should be increased to some higher multiplier; others take the opposite view.

2. TREBLE DAMAGE

A. Background

Section 4 of the Clayton Act allows "any person...injured in his business or property by reason of anything forbidden in the antitrust laws" to "recover threefold the damages by him sustained." This provision directly descends from the original Sherman Act, passed in 1890, which included the same treble damages provision. At the time of the Sherman Act's passage, congressional debate centered on whether to provide for double or treble damages; single damages were not seriously considered as an alternative. Senator Sherman and others argued that multiple damages should be "commensurate with the difficulty of maintaining a private action," punitive, and provide incentives to plaintiffs to act as private attorneys general. Treble damages have remained the rule in antitrust cases, despite periodic efforts to eliminate or limit their availability.

NOTE: Treble damages are the most notable characteristic of the US antitrust system and the AMC outlined the five related and important goals which they serve: (1) Deterring anticompetitive conduct; (2) Punishing violators of the antitrust laws;(3) Forcing disgorgement of the benefits of anticompetitive conduct from those violators; (4) Providing full compensation to victims of anticompetitive conduct; and (5) Providing an incentive to victims to act as 'private attorneys general'. The AMC recommended retention of treble damages. Nonetheless, there have been criticisms of the excessive litigation and compensation culture in the US system, as noted by Lande and Davis.

Lande, R. H., and Davis, J. P., 'Benefits from Private Antitrust Enforcement: An Analysis of Forty Cases'

(2008) 42 USFLR 879 at 883–7 [footnotes omitted]

While government criminal and civil actions are essential in deterring future antitrust violations, virtually the only way to secure redress for the victims of antitrust violations is through private litigation. And, as we explore below, private enforcement also plays a significant role in deterring antitrust violations. This Study attempts to provide an empirical basis for assessing these benefits. Before doing so, however, it is worthwhile to canvass some of the criticisms of private enforcement of the antitrust laws. Indeed, detractors of private enforcement seem to greatly outnumber its supporters, even if those detractors rarely provide any empirical basis for their position.

Many commentators have criticized the existing system of private antitrust litigation. Some assert that private actions too often result in remedies that provide lucrative attorney's fees but secure no real benefits for overcharged purchasers. Others suggest that private class actions often follow an easy trail blazed by government enforcers and that, as a result, private actions add much less than they should to government enforcement. Still others contend that private antitrust damages lead to excessive deterrence in light of government sanctions. Indeed, one common criticism of private actions in general—and of class actions in particular—is that they are a form of blackmail or extortion, one in which plaintiffs' attorneys, with little risk to themselves, coerce defendants into settlements based not on meritorious claims, but rather on the cost of litigation or fear of an erroneous and catastrophic judgment. These actions also serve to discourage legitimate competitive behavior. For these and related reasons many prominent members of the antitrust community, even those not a part of the Chicago School on antitrust matters, have called for the curtailment of private enforcement in significant ways. Some even call for the complete abolition of private rights of action. While these criticisms are longstanding and widespread, they have been made without any systematic substantive or empirical basis. FTC Chair William Kovacic succinctly summarized the prevailing view of the antitrust profession as follows: "[P]rivate rights of action U.S.-style are poison. They over-reached dramatically. And we have to use substantive liability standards to push back on what we think are hard-wired elements of the private rights of action mechanism."

NOTE: Lande and Davis are sceptical regarding the varied criticisms of private antitrust enforcement. They undertook a study of 40 major cases that resulted in damages awards of $50 million or greater. Despite considerable unease about the lawyers' incentives to bring antitrust class actions, partly due to the availability of contingency fees whereby the winning lawyer earns a percentage of the damages award, their research indicated that the courts were generally satisfied with the levels of damages settlements and the appropriateness of the contingency fees, given the considerable work undertaken in preparing for antitrust litigation. The US system of private antitrust enforcement has developed over a considerable period of time and in the context of a particular legal system and culture. Although private enforcement ensures that there is greater compensation for victims of antitrust breaches and greater deterrence of potential anti-competitive activity, it would be difficult to transpose all elements of the US system into a different legal context and competition culture, in the legal systems of the Member States, even if it were considered to be desirable from a policy perspective.

■ QUESTION

To what extent is private enforcement of US antitrust law an attractive and suitable model for the EC and UK to follow?

SECTION 2: EC LAW BACKGROUND AND OBSTACLES TO PRIVATE ENFORCEMENT

Regulation 17/62 introduced a very centralized system of competition law enforcement, with the Commission effectively acting as the sole enforcer of Community competition law. This was necessary in the early years of the development of Community competition law, but it was recognized that the doctrine of direct effect ensured that parties could rely on Community law in private litigation.

Van Gend en Loos
[1963] ECR 1 at 12

Community law ... not only imposes obligations on individuals but is also intended to confer upon them rights which become part of their legal heritage. These rights arise not only where they are expressly granted by the Treaty, but also by reason of obligations which the Treaty imposes in a clearly defined way upon individuals as well as upon the Member States and upon the institutions of the Community.

NOTE: The app lication of the direct effect doctrine in a competition law context was subsequently confirmed by the European Court in *BRT* v *SABAM* (Case 127/73) [1974] 1 ECR 51. Community competition law could potentially be relied on by private litigants in court procedures as a shield, by a defendant for instance in an IPR infringement action, or as a sword, by a claimant for instance seeking damages in a cartel or abuse case. An early and important example of the latter, in the UK, arose in the case of *Garden Cottage Foods Ltd* v *Milk Marketing Board* [1984] AC 130.

Garden Cottage Foods Ltd v Milk Marketing Board
[1984] AC 130, per Lord Wilberforce at pp. 144–5

The Milk Marketing Board reduced its number of butter distributors, excluding Garden Cottage Foods from the revised list. Garden Cottage Foods claimed this infringed Article 82 (ex Article 86) and sought an interlocutory injunction to stop the revocation of the contract.

My Lords, in the light (a) of the uniform jurisprudence of the European Court of Justice, of which it is sufficient to mention Belgische Radio en Televisie v. S.V. S.A.B.A.M. (Case 127/73) [1974] 1 E.C.R. 51 (which I have already cited) and the subsequent case of Rewe-Zentralfinanz e.G. v. Landwirtschaftskammer für das Saarland (Case 33/76) [1976] 3 E.C.R. 1989, which was to the same effect as respects the duty of national courts to protect rights conferred on individual citizens by directly applicable provisions of the Treaty; and (b) of sections 2(1) and 3(1) of the European Communities Act 1972, I, for my own part, find it difficult to see how it can ultimately be successfully argued, as M.M.B. will seek to do, that a contravention of article 86 which causes damage to an individual citizen does not give rise to a cause of action in English law of the nature of a cause of action for breach of statutory duty; but since it cannot be regarded as unarguable that is not a matter for final decision by your Lordships at the interlocutory stage that the instant case has reached. What, with great respect to those who think otherwise, I do regard as quite unarguable is the proposition, advanced by the Court of Appeal itself but disclaimed by both parties to the action: that if such a contravention of article 86 gives rise to any cause of action at all, it gives rise to a cause of action for which there is no remedy in damages to compensate for loss already caused by that contravention but only a remedy by way of injunction to prevent future loss being caused. A cause of action to which an unlawful act by the defendant causing pecuniary loss to the plaintiff gives rise, if it possessed those characteristics as respects the remedies available, would be one which, so far as my understanding goes, is unknown in English private law, at any rate since 1875 when the jurisdiction conferred upon the Court of Chancery by Lord Cairns' Act passed to the High Court. I leave aside as irrelevant for present purposes injunctions granted in matrimonial causes or wardship proceedings which may have no connection with pecuniary loss. I likewise leave out of account injunctions obtainable as remedies in public law whether upon application for judicial review or in an action brought by the Attorney-General ex officio or ex relatione some private individual. It is private law, not public law, to which the company has had recourse. In its action it claims damages as well as an injunction. No reasons are to be found in any of the judgments of the Court of Appeal and none has been advanced at the hearing before your Lordships, why in law, in logic or in justice, if contravention of article 86 of the Treaty of Rome is capable of giving rise to a cause of action in English private law at all, there is any need to invent a cause of action with characteristics that are wholly novel as respects the remedies that it attracts, in order to deal with breaches of articles of the Treaty of Rome which have in the United Kingdom the same effect as statutes.

The notion that it is seriously arguable that a contravention of article 86 may give rise to a cause of action possessing such unique characteristics appears to have been based upon a misunderstanding by the Court of Appeal of a cautionary obiter dictum of my noble and learned friend, Lord Roskill (then Roskill L.J.) in *Valor International Ltd. v. Application des Gaz S.A.* [1978] 3 C.M.L.R. 87. In a previous decision of the Court of Appeal, *Application des Gaz S.A. v. Falks Veritas Ltd.* [1974] Ch. 381, 396, Lord Denning M.R. had stated that "articles 85 and 86 are part of our law. They create new torts or wrongs." The issue in that case, however, which was one for breach of copyright in a drawing of a tin for holding liquid gas, was whether a defendant could plead breaches by the plaintiff of article 85 or 86 as a defence to the plaintiff's claim. The court was unanimous in holding that the defendant could so plead but only the Master of the Rolls expressed any view as to whether those articles created new torts or wrongs in English law. It was unnecessary for the purposes of that case to do more than to decide that it was arguable that those articles could be used as a shield, whether or not they could also be used as a sword; and in the *Valor International case* [1978] 3 C.M.L.R. 87, Roskill L.J., who had been a member of the court in the *Falks Veritas* case, pointed this out and said, at p. 100, that there were "many questions which will have to be argued in this court or elsewhere in this country or at Luxembourg, before it can be stated categorically ... that articles 85 and 86 create new torts or wrongs ... "

NOTE: The House of Lords refused to grant an interlocutory injunction, on the basis that damages would be an adequate remedy for infringement of the competition rules. Nonetheless, the case is an important landmark, with the House of Lords confirming the right to bring an action in the courts for alleged competition law infringements, as noted by Hoskins.

Hoskins, M., 'Garden Cottage revisited: the availability of damages in the national courts for breaches of the EEC competition rules'
[1992] ECLR 257 at 265 [footnotes omitted]

it appears that although the majority decision of the House of Lords in the *Garden Cottage Foods* case gives strong indications that damages should be available in English law for a breach of the EEC competition rules, this issue has not yet been settled definitively. However, on an analysis of Community law, it appears that the English courts may well be under an obligation to recognise such a right. The most appropriate means for the English courts to do so would be to allow a claim for damages to be based on the economic tort of unlawful interference with the business of another.

It may well be that the type of debate which has been considered here will become increasingly common as Community law enters a new phase heralded by the *Francovich* judgment. Having defined the nature of Community rights, the Court of Justice is now seeking to ensure that those rights are properly protected in the Member States by means of available national remedies. The focus may well be switching from the nature of rights to the nature of remedies under Community law.

NOTE: Hoskins accurately predicted that the key debate would relate to remedies to ensure the effectiveness of the EC competition rules, particularly in the light of the *Francovich* ruling. In the early 1990s the Commission developed a decentralization policy in which it sought to stimulate and raise awareness of the possibilities of litigation before the national courts. Following the *Automec (No. 2)* ruling ([1992] 2 ECR-2223) in which the Court indirectly encouraged private enforcement by confirming that the Commission could reject complaints from private parties on the basis of its prioritization of resources, in 1993 the Commission issued a Notice on cooperation between the Commission and the national courts.

Commission notice on cooperation between national courts and the Commission

OJ, 1993, C39/6, paras 1–3, 13–16 [footnotes omitted]

I. Introduction

1. The abolition of internal frontiers enables firms in the Community to embark on new activities and Community consumers to benefit from increased competition. The Commission considers that these advantages must not be jeopardized by restrictive or abusive practices of undertakings and that the completion of the internal market thus reaffirms the importance of the Community's competition policy and competition law.

2. A number of national and Community institutions have contributed to the formulation of Community competition law and are responsible for its day-to-day application. For this purpose, the national competition authorities, national and Community courts and the Commission each assume their own tasks and responsibilities, in line with the principles developed by the case-law of the Court of Justice of the European Communities.

3. If the competition process is to work well in the internal market, effective cooperation between these institutions must be ensured. The purpose of this Notice is to achieve this in relations between national courts and the Commission. It spells out how the Commission intends to assist national courts by closer cooperation in the application of Articles 85 and 86 of the EEC Treaty in individual cases.

   ...

III. The exercise of powers by the Commission

13. As the administrative authority responsible for the Community's competition policy, the Commission must serve the Community's general interest. The administrative resources at the Commission's disposal to perform its task are necessarily limited and cannot be used to deal with all the cases brought to its attention. The Commission is therefore obliged, in general, to take all organizational measures necessary for the performance of its task and, in particular, to establish priorities.

14. The Commission intends, in implementing its decision-making powers, to concentrate on notifications, complaints and own-initiative proceedings having particular political, economic or legal significance for the Community. Where these features are absent in a particular case, notifications will normally be dealt with by means of a comfort letter and complaints should, as a rule, be handled by national courts or authorities.

15. The Commission considers that there is not normally a sufficient Community interest in examining a case when the plaintiff is able to secure adequate protection of his rights before the national court. In these circumstances the complaint will normally be filed.

16. In this respect the Commission would like to make it clear that the application of Community competition law by the national courts has considerable advantages for individuals and companies:
    — the Commission cannot award compensation for loss suffered as a result of an infringement of Article 85 or Article 86. Such claims may be brought only before the national courts. Companies are more likely to avoid infringements of the Community competition rules if they risk having to pay damages or interest in such an event,
    — national courts can usually adopt interim measures and order the ending of infringements more quickly than the Commission is able to do,
    — before national courts, it is possible to combine a claim under Community law with a claim under national law. This is not possible in a procedure before the Commission,
    — in some Member States, the courts have the power to award legal costs to the successful applicant. This is never possible in the administrative procedure before the Commission.

IV. Application of Articles 85 and 86 by national courts

17. The national court may have to reach a decision on the application of Articles 85 and 86 in several procedural situations. In the case of civil law proceedings, two types of action are particularly frequent: actions relating to contracts and actions for damages. Under the former, the defendant usually relies on Article 85(2) to dispute the contractual obligations invoked by the plaintiff. Under the latter, the prohibitions contained in Articles 85 and 86 are generally relevant in determining whether the conduct which has given rise to the alleged injury is illegal.

18. In such situations, the direct effect of Article 85(1) and Article 86 gives national courts sufficient powers to comply with their obligation to hand down judgment. Nevertheless, when exercising these powers, they must take account of the Commission's powers in order to avoid decisions which could conflict with those taken or envisaged by the Commission in applying Article 85(1) and Article 86, and also Article 85(3).

19. In its case-law the Court of Justice has developed a number of principles which make it possible for such contradictory decisions to be avoided. The Commission feels that national courts could take account of these principles in the following manner.

NOTE: This Notice set out the difficulties that the Commission and the national courts could face when trying to apply their concurrent jurisdiction under the competition rules. It suggested a number of procedural measures to help national courts, and emphasized the benefits to private parties who could seek damages and other remedies from a court that would not be available if they simply complained to the Commission. The Notice acknowledged the superior investigative powers of the Commission and the Notice did not prove to be enormously useful in practice partly due to the centralized structure of Regulation 17 at that stage. (See Waller, S.W., 'Decentralization of the Enforcement Process of EC Competition Law—the Greater Role of National Courts' [1996] 2 LIEI 1). A new Notice was adopted in 2004, as discussed below, to coincide with the new enforcement regime introduced by Regulation 1/2003.

The failure of the 1993 Notice to result in great practical change put further pressure on the Commission to take much more significant steps to allow the national courts to play a greater role in the enforcement of Community competition law. Nonetheless, this would not be a straightforward task, as stressed by Kon and Maxwell.

Kon, S., and Maxwell, A., 'Enforcement in the National Courts of the EC and New UK Competition Rules: Obstacles to Private Enforcement'
[1998] ECLR 443 at 443 [footnotes omitted]

The superficial attraction of the principle of decentralised enforcement of Articles 85 and 86 of the E.C. Treaty via the forum of the national court obscures the numerous and significant obstacles to effective enforcement which in practice confront the potential litigant.

The starting point for any analysis is the fact that the Commission enjoys certain inherent advantages in its own centralised administrative jurisdiction in enforcement of the E.C. competition rules which simply cannot be replicated by national courts and which will therefore always tend to show up limitations in decentralised enforcement by national courts of Member States. It is these inherent disadvantages, together with numerous obstacles created by national rules of domestic civil procedure, which has led many to question whether national courts can, in fact, provide effective protection to victims of alleged infringement of the E.C. competition rules.

...

In many senses, in seeking to consolidate these legal principles and administrative practice on decentralised enforcement, the Notice in fact lays bare the limited advantages and numerous obstacles for undertakings seeking to enforce the competition rules before national courts.

At paragraph 16 of the Notice, the Commission advances four primary advantages of domestic court proceedings, notably:

— the Commission cannot award compensation for the loss caused by infringements;

— national courts can act more speedily in interim proceedings;

— national courts offer the possibility of combining claims based on national laws and Community law; and

— national courts can award applicants costs in respect of the proceedings.

However, against these advantages of proceeding before national courts (which are relatively modest, other than in the case of damages) should be weighed the inherent advantages which the Commission enjoys in exercise of its centralised administrative competence in enforcement of the E.C. competition rules and the corresponding disadvantages and obstacles which exist in domestic rules of civil procedure for judicial enforcement of the E.C. competition rules. Neither the Notice itself nor the subsequent operation of the Notice by the Commission go to alleviate these obstacles; on the contrary, in certain respects they go to emphasise that a radical new approach is needed if domestic enforcement is to be effective.

NOTE: Kon and Maxwell noted the advantages to private party litigants as detailed in the Notice, but emphasized the existence of a considerable number of obstacles in terms of national procedural law if private enforcement was to be a viable complement to public enforcement of the competition laws. This was also highlighted in the subsequent Ashurst Report commissioned by the European Commission.

Ashurst Study on the conditions of claims for damages in case of infringement of EC competition rules

31 August 2004, http://ec.europa.eu/competition/antitrust/actionsdamages/study.html

Executive summary

I Introduction

The picture that emerges from the present study on damages actions for breach of competition law in the enlarged EU is one of astonishing diversity and total underdevelopment. As regards the latter point, the study has revealed only around 60 judged cases for damages actions (12 on the basis of EC law, around 32 on the basis of national law and 6 on both). Of these judgments 28 have so far resulted in an award being made (8 on the basis of EC competition law, 16 on national law and 4 on both).

On the basis of answers by national reporters from each of the 25 Member States to a set of questions prepared by the European Commission, the comparative report sets out to give a comparative analysis of the different legal systems in the Member States of the enlarged EU and, on this basis, tentatively to identify what the real obstacles are to private enforcement and how damages actions might be facilitated.

NOTE: The Ashurst Report focused only on private damages actions and considered the position across the Member States. A wide range of national procedural issues was considered including access to evidence, rules of proof, whether specialist competition courts were available, rules in relation to damages, and the passing-on defence. Very few damages claims had been raised and the noteworthy comment is that private damages actions across the EU were in a state of 'astonishing diversity and total underdevelopment' particularly in comparison with the US, where it is recognized that over 90 per cent of antitrust enforcement proceedings are raised by private litigants. We will return to the case law and policy developments since the bleak picture painted by the Ashurst Report, but the next section will consider the debate concerning the promotion of private enforcement in Europe and its relationship with the traditional system of public enforcement.

SECTION 3: **PROMOTING PRIVATE ENFORCEMENT AND COMPLEMENTARITY WITH PUBLIC ENFORCEMENT**

As discussed earlier, there is considerably more antitrust litigation in the US, with class actions, treble damages, and contingency fees notable features of the system in which private enforcement predominates and relatively few antitrust cases are undertaken by the Department of Justice and Federal Trade Commission. Nonetheless, as indicated by Davis and Lande, there has been a backlash, with attempts to curtail the scope of private enforcement, sometimes by the Supreme Court limiting the substantive rules in the context of private litigation. The following passages reveal a similar debate at the European level.

Wils, W.P.J., 'Should Private Antitrust Enforcement be Encouraged in Europe?'
(2003) 26 World Competition 473 at 488 [footnotes omitted]

The EC antitrust prohibitions are regularly invoked in private litigation as a shield. Private parties also play an important role in public antitrust enforcement through complaints to the competition authorities. In marked contrast with the situation in the US, private actions for damages or injunctive relief are rare.

In this article I have argued that this situation is a desirable one. Indeed from the perspective of ensuring that the antitrust prohibitions are not violated, public antitrust enforcement is inherently superior to private enforcement, because of more investigative and sanctioning powers, because private antitrust enforcement is driven by private profit motives which fundamentally diverge from the general interest in this area, and because of the high cost of private antitrust enforcement. There is not even a case for a supplementary role for private enforcement, as the adequate level of sanctions and the adequate number and variety of prosecutions can be ensured more effectively and at a lower cost through public enforcement.

It also seems difficult to justify an increased role for private enforcement in Europe by the pursuit of corrective justice, as there does not appear to be a clear social need for such action, and because truly achieving corrective justice in the antitrust context is in practice a very difficult task. Any attempts to do so are likely to be very costly or to lead to results which do not really serve corrective justice.

Jones, C.A., 'Private Antitrust Enforcement in Europe: A Policy Analysis and Reality Check'
(2004) 27 World Competition 13, 13 and 24

The position asserted in Wils (2003) is that private actions for damages are to be discouraged as undesirable. Wils even asserts that private damages claims should not be available to supplement public enforcement of the competition rules, although his argument *prima facie* is inadequate to carry this point. What is troublesome here is that Wils proffers a private damages policy analysis which inexplicably runs counter to both Commission policy and the fundamental legal structure of the Community without the substantial justification necessary to support such a conclusion.

In short, most of the undesirable aspects Wils finds in private damages are present in nearly equal measure in cases of which he does approve: voidness proceedings and, apparently, injunctions. All require additional proceedings beyond the public ones, additional sanctions beyond the public ones, private selection based in private interests, settlements based on private interests, court proceedings beyond the administrative proceedings, and so on. The fact that private damages claims can be asserted in the same proceedings simply demonstrates that there is no principled policy reason to discourage private enforcement in the Community. The policy advocated by Wils flies in the face of the Community legal order, the principle of direct effect, the judgments of the ECJ, the experience and policy formulations of the Commission, much of the rationale underlying the new Regulation 1/2003, and ultimately, sensible judgments about policy over economic theory diverted from reality.

NOTE: Although a legal official with the European Commission, and prominent and respected academic commentator on Community competition law developments, Wils is very much a lone voice in rejecting proposals to enhance and develop private enforcement. Jones, an American antitrust academic, suggested that Wils' views were akin to advocating that the antitrust laws should be repealed, and that such views were discredited even in the US. This debate is related to the issue regarding the complementary roles of public and private enforcement of the competition law rules. A starting point here is to consider the ruling of the ECJ in the Masterfoods dispute.

Masterfoods v HB Ice Cream

(Case C-344/98) [2000] ECR I-11369, [2001] 4 CMLR 14

HB, the leading manufacturer of ice-cream in Ireland supplied retail outlets with freezer cabinets free of charge, while retaining ownership of the cabinets, provided they were used exclusively for HB products. Masterfoods, a subsidiary of Mars Inc., entered the ice-cream market in 1989. A number of retailers subsequently began to stock Masterfoods products in cabinets supplied by HB, but HB demanded that the retailers comply with the 'exclusivity clause'. Masterfoods brought an action before the Irish courts seeking a declaration that the exclusivity clause was null and void under Articles 81 and 82 EC. HB brought a separate action seeking an injunction to restrain Masterfoods from inducing retailers to breach the exclusivity clause. Masterfoods' action was dismissed and HB were granted the injunction they sought. Masterfoods appealed to the Irish Supreme Court.

In parallel with those proceedings, Masterfoods lodged a complaint against HB with the European Commission. In 1998, by Decision 98/531/EC, the Commission ruled that the exclusivity clause constituted an infringement of Articles 81 and 82 EC. HB lodged an appeal against that decision under Article 230 EC and applied, under Article 242 EC, for the Decision to be suspended. In view of the proceedings in the European Courts, the Irish Supreme Court decided to stay proceedings and refer a number of questions to the Court of Justice for preliminary ruling under Article 234 EC.

[45] First of all, the principles governing the division of powers between the Commission and the national courts in the application of the Community competition rules should be borne in mind.

[46] The Commission, entrusted by Article 89(1) of the EC Treaty (now, after amendment, Article 85(1) EC) with the task of ensuring application of the principles laid down in Articles 85 and 86 of the Treaty, is responsible for defining and implementing the orientation of Community competition policy. It is for the Commission to adopt, subject to review by the Court of First Instance and the Court of Justice, individual decisions in accordance with the procedural rules in force and to adopt exemption regulations. In order effectively to perform that task, which necessarily entails complex economic assessments, it is entitled to give differing degrees of priority to the complaints brought before it (*Delimitis*, para. [44]; and Case C-119/97 P, *Ufex and Others v EC Commission* [[1999] ECR I-1341, [2000] 4 CMLR 266, para. [88]]).

[47] The Commission has exclusive competence to adopt decisions in implementation of Article 85(3) of the Treaty, pursuant to Article 9(1) of Regulation 17 (*Delimitis*, para. [44]). However, it shares competence to apply Articles 85(1) and 86 of the Treaty with the national courts (*Delimitis*, para. [45]). The latter provisions produce direct effects in relations between individuals and create direct rights in respect of the individuals concerned which national courts must safeguard (*BRT I*, cited at fn. 114 above, para. [16]). The national courts thus continue to have jurisdiction to apply the provisions of Articles 85(1) and 86 of the Treaty even after the Commission has initiated a procedure in application of Articles 2, 3 or 6 of Regulation 17 (*BRT I*, paras [17] to [20]).

[48] Despite that division of powers, and in order to fulfil the role assigned to it by the Treaty, the Commission cannot be bound by a decision given by a national court in application of Articles 85(1) and 86 of the Treaty. The Commission is therefore entitled to adopt at any time individual decisions under Articles 85 and 86 of the Treaty, even where an agreement or practice has already been the subject of a decision by a national court and the decision contemplated by the Commission conflicts with that national court's decision.

[49] It is also clear from the case law of the Court that the Member States' duty under Article 5 of the EC Treaty to take all appropriate measures, whether general or particular, to ensure fulfilment of the obligations arising from Community law and to abstain from any measure which could jeopardise the attainment of the objectives of the Treaty is binding on all the authorities of Member States including, for matters within their jurisdiction, the courts (see, to that effect, Case C-2/97, *IP* v *Borsana* [1998] ECR I-8597, para. [26]).

[50] Under the fourth paragraph of Article 189 of the Treaty, a decision adopted by the Commission implementing Article 85(1), 85(3) or 86 of the Treaty is to be binding in its entirety upon those to whom it is addressed.

[51] The Court has held, in paragraph [47] of *Delimitis*, that in order not to breach the general principle of legal certainty, national courts must, when ruling on agreements or practices which may subsequently be the subject of a decision by the Commission, avoid giving decisions which would conflict with a decision contemplated by the Commission in the implementation of Articles 85(1) and 86 and Article 85(3) of the Treaty.

[52] It is even more important that when national courts rule on agreements or practices which are already the subject of a Commission decision they cannot take decisions running counter to that of the Commission, even if the latter's decision conflicts with a decision given by a national court of first instance.

[53] In that connection, the fact that the President of the Court of First Instance suspended the application of Decision 98/531 until the Court of First Instance had given judgment terminating the proceedings before it is irrelevant. Acts of the Community institutions are in principle presumed to be lawful until such time as they are annulled or withdrawn (Case C-137/92 P, *EC Commission* v *BASF and Others* [1994] ECR I-2555, para. [48]). The decision of the judge hearing an application to order the suspension of the operation of the contested act, pursuant to Article 185 of the Treaty, has only provisional effect. It must not prejudge the points of law or fact in issue or neutralise in advance the effects of the decision subsequently to be given in the main action (order in Case C-149/95 P(R) *EC Commission* v *Atlantic Container Line and Others* [[1995] ECR I-2165, [1997] 5 CMLR 167, para. [22]]).

[54] Moreover, if a national court has doubts as to the validity or interpretation of an act of a Community institution it may, or must, in accordance with the second and third paragraphs of Article 177 of the Treaty, refer a question to the Court of Justice for a preliminary ruling.

[55] If, as here in the main proceedings, the addressee of a Commission decision has, within the period prescribed in the fifth paragraph of Article 173 of the Treaty, brought an action for annulment of that decision pursuant to that article, it is for the national court to decide whether to stay proceedings until a definitive decision has been given in the action for annulment or in order to refer a question to the Court for a preliminary ruling.

[56] It should be borne in mind in that connection that application of the Community competition rules is based on an obligation of sincere cooperation between the national courts, on the one hand, and the Commission and the Community Courts, on the other, in the context of which each acts on the basis of the role assigned to it by the Treaty.

[57] When the outcome of the dispute before the national court depends on the validity of the Commission decision, it follows from the obligation of sincere cooperation that the national court should, in order to avoid reaching a decision that runs counter to that of the Commission, stay its proceedings pending final judgment in the action for annulment by the Community Courts, unless it considers that, in the circumstances of the case, a reference to the Court of Justice for a preliminary ruling on the validity of the Commission decision is warranted.

[58] If a national court stays proceedings, it is incumbent on it to examine whether it is necessary to order interim measures in order to safeguard the interests of the parties pending final judgment.

NOTE: The *Masterfoods* judgment reaffirmed the central importance of the Commission within the competition system and the subservient position of the national courts, which must wait for Community proceedings to be completed before they can deal effectively with a case. The only option which appeared to be open to a national court is to stay proceedings, and await the finalization of the Community proceedings, or to make a reference to the Court of Justice under Article 234 EC. Both of these may be unsatisfactory in many cases because of their inherent delay. The position is less clear if the Commission has not yet adopted its initial decision. It seems that the national court is not required to stay proceedings or refer, but it may decide that it is the appropriate course of action. The outcome in *Masterfoods* was given a legislative basis in Article 16 of Regulation 1/2003, and in 2004 a revised Notice on cooperation between the Commission and the national courts was adopted.

COUNCIL REGULATION (EC) NO 1/2003 OF 16 DECEMBER 2002 ON THE IMPLEMENTATION OF THE RULES ON COMPETITION LAID DOWN IN ARTICLES 81 AND 82 OF THE TREATY (TEXT WITH EEA RELEVANCE)

OJ, 2003, L1/1

Article 16
Uniform application of Community competition law

1. When national courts rule on agreements, decisions or practices under Article 81 or Article 82 of the Treaty which are already the subject of a Commission decision, they cannot take decisions running counter to the decision adopted by the Commission. They must also avoid giving decisions which would conflict with a decision contemplated by the Commission in proceedings it has initiated. To that effect, the national court may assess whether it is necessary to stay its proceedings. This obligation is without prejudice to the rights and obligations under Article 234 of the Treaty.

2. When competition authorities of the Member States rule on agreements, decisions or practices under Article 81 or Article 82 of the Treaty which are already the subject of a Commission decision, they cannot take decisions which would run counter to the decision adopted by the Commission.

Commission Notice on the co-operation between the Commission and the courts of the EU Member States in the application of Articles 81 and 82 EC
OJ, 2004, C101/54 [footnotes omitted]

I. THE SCOPE OF THE NOTICE

1. The present notice addresses the co-operation between the Commission and the courts of the EU Member States, when the latter apply Articles 81 and 82 EC. For the purpose of this notice, the "courts of the EU Member States" (hereinafter "national courts") are those courts and tribunals within an EU Member State that can apply Articles 81 and 82 EC and that are authorised to ask a preliminary question to the Court of Justice of the European Communities pursuant to Article 234 EC.

2. The national courts may be called upon to apply Articles 81 or 82 EC in lawsuits between private parties, such as actions relating to contracts or actions for damages. They may also act as public enforcer or as review court. A national court may indeed be designated as a competition authority of a Member State (hereinafter "the national competition authority") pursuant to Article 35(1) of Regulation (EC) No 1/2003 (hereinafter "the regulation"). In that case, the co-operation between the national courts and the Commission is not only covered by the present notice, but also by the notice on the co-operation within the network of competition authorities.

II. THE APPLICATION OF EC COMPETITION RULES BY NATIONAL COURTS

A. THE COMPETENCE OF NATIONAL COURTS TO APPLY EC COMPETITION RULES

3. To the extent that national courts have jurisdiction to deal with a case, they have the power to apply Articles 81 and 82 EC. Moreover, it should be remembered that Articles 81 and 82 EC are a matter of public policy and are essential to the accomplishment of the tasks entrusted to the Community, and, in particular, for the functioning of the internal market. According to the Court of Justice, where, by virtue of domestic law, national courts must raise of their own motion points of

law based on binding domestic rules which have not been raised by the parties, such an obligation also exists where binding Community rules, such as the EC competition rules, are concerned. The position is the same if domestic law confers on national courts a discretion to apply of their own motion binding rules of law: national courts must apply the EC competition rules, even when the party with an interest in application of those provisions has not relied on them, where domestic law allows such application by the national court. However, Community law does not require national courts to raise of their own motion an issue concerning the breach of provisions of Community law where examination of that issue would oblige them to abandon the passive role assigned to them by going beyond the ambit of the dispute defined by the parties themselves and relying on facts and circumstances other than those on which the party with an interest in application of those provisions bases his claim.

4. Depending on the functions attributed to them under national law, national courts may be called upon to apply Articles 81 and 82 EC in administrative, civil or criminal proceedings. In particular, where a natural or legal person asks the national court to safeguard his individual rights, national courts play a specific role in the enforcement of Articles 81 and 82 EC, which is different from the enforcement in the public interest by the Commission or by national competition authorities. Indeed, national courts can give effect to Articles 81 and 82 EC by finding contracts to be void or by awards of damages.

5. National courts can apply Articles 81 and 82 EC, without it being necessary to apply national competition law in parallel. However, where a national court applies national competition law to agreements, decisions by associations of undertakings or concerted practices which may affect trade between Member States within the meaning of Article 81(1) EC or to any abuse prohibited by Article 82 EC, they also have to apply EC competition rules to those agreements, decisions or practices.

6. The regulation does not only empower the national courts to apply EC competition law. The parallel application of national competition law to agreements, decisions of associations of undertakings and concerted practices which affect trade between Member States may not lead to a different outcome from that of EC competition law. Article 3(2) of the regulation provides that agreements, decisions or concerted practices which do not infringe Article 81(1) EC or which fulfil the conditions of Article 81(3) EC cannot be prohibited either under national competition law. On the other hand, the Court of Justice has ruled that agreements, decisions or concerted practices that violate Article 81(1) and do not fulfil the conditions of Article 81(3) EC cannot be upheld under national law. As to the parallel application of national competition law and Article 82 EC in the case of unilateral conduct, Article 3 of the regulation does not provide for a similar convergence obligation. However, in case of conflicting provisions, the general principle of primacy of Community law requires national courts to disapply any provision of national law which contravenes a Community rule, regardless of whether that national law provision was adopted before or after the Community rule.

7. Apart from the application of Articles 81 and 82 EC, national courts are also competent to apply acts adopted by EU institutions in accordance with the EC Treaty or in accordance with the measures adopted to give the Treaty effect, to the extent that these acts have direct effect. National courts may thus have to enforce Commission decisions or regulations applying Article 81(3) EC to certain categories of agreements, decisions or concerted practices. When applying these EC competition rules, national courts act within the framework of Community law and are consequently bound to observe the general principles of Community law.

8. The application of Articles 81 and 82 EC by national courts often depends on complex economic and legal assessments. When applying EC competition rules, national courts are bound by the case law of the Community courts as well as by Commission regulations applying Article 81(3) EC to certain categories of agreements, decisions or concerted practices. Furthermore, the application of Articles 81 and 82 EC by the Commission in a specific case binds the national courts when they apply EC competition rules in the same case in parallel with or subsequent to the Commission. Finally, and without prejudice to the ultimate interpretation of the EC Treaty by the Court of Justice, national courts may find guidance in Commission regulations and decisions which present elements

of analogy with the case they are dealing with, as well as in Commission notices and guidelines relating to the application of Articles 81 and 82 EC and in the annual report on competition policy.

B. PROCEDURAL ASPECTS OF THE APPLICATION OF EC COMPETITION RULES BY NATIONAL COURTS

9. The procedural conditions for the enforcement of EC competition rules by national courts and the sanctions they can impose in case of an infringement of those rules, are largely covered by national law. However, to some extent, Community law also determines the conditions in which EC competition rules are enforced. Those Community law provisions may provide for the faculty of national courts to avail themselves of certain instruments, e.g. to ask for the Commission's opinion on questions concerning the application of EC competition rules or they may create rules that have an obligatory impact on proceedings before them, e.g. allowing the Commission and national competition authorities to submit written observations. These Community law provisions prevail over national rules. Therefore, national courts have to set aside national rules which, if applied, would conflict with these Community law provisions. Where such Community law provisions are directly applicable, they are a direct source of rights and duties for all those affected, and must be fully and uniformly applied in all the Member States from the date of their entry into force.

10. In the absence of Community law provisions on procedures and sanctions related to the enforcement of EC competition rules by national courts, the latter apply national procedural law and—to the extent that they are competent to do so—impose sanctions provided for under national law. However, the application of these national provisions must be compatible with the general principles of Community law. In this regard, it is useful to recall the case law of the Court of Justice, according to which:

(a) where there is an infringement of Community law, national law must provide for sanctions which are effective, proportionate and dissuasive;

(b) where the infringement of Community law causes harm to an individual, the latter should under certain conditions be able to ask the national court for damages;

(c) the rules on procedures and sanctions which national courts apply to enforce Community law
— must not make such enforcement excessively difficult or practically impossible (the principle of effectiveness) and they
— must not be less favourable than the rules applicable to the enforcement of equivalent national law (the principle of equivalence).

On the basis of the principle of primacy of Community law, a national court may not apply national rules that are incompatible with these principles.

C. PARALLEL OR CONSECUTIVE APPLICATION OF EC COMPETITION RULES BY THE COMMISSION AND BY NATIONAL COURTS

11. A national court may be applying EC competition law to an agreement, decision, concerted practice or unilateral behaviour affecting trade between Member States at the same time as the Commission or subsequent to the Commission. The following points outline some of the obligations national courts have to respect in those circumstances.

12. Where a national court comes to a decision before the Commission does, it must avoid adopting a decision that would conflict with a decision contemplated by the Commission. To that effect, the national court may ask the Commission whether it has initiated proceedings regarding the same agreements, decisions or practices and if so, about the progress of proceedings and the likelihood of a decision in that case. The national court may, for reasons of legal certainty, also consider staying its proceedings until the Commission has reached a decision. The Commission, for its part, will endeavour to give priority to cases for which it has decided to initiate proceedings within the meaning of Article 2(1) of Commission Regulation (EC) No 773/2004 and that are the subject of national proceedings stayed in this way, in particular when the outcome of a civil dispute depends on them. However, where the national court cannot reasonably doubt the Commission's contemplated decision or where the Commission has already decided on a similar case, the national court may decide on the case pending before it in accordance with that contemplated or earlier decision

without it being necessary to ask the Commission for the information mentioned above or to await the Commission's decision.

13. Where the Commission reaches a decision in a particular case before the national court, the latter cannot take a decision running counter to that of the Commission. The binding effect of the Commission's decision is of course without prejudice to the interpretation of Community law by the Court of Justice. Therefore, if the national court doubts the legality of the Commission's decision, it cannot avoid the binding effects of that decision without a ruling to the contrary by the Court of Justice. Consequently, if a national court intends to take a decision that runs counter to that of the Commission, it must refer a question to the Court of Justice for a preliminary ruling (Article 234 EC). The latter will then decide on the compatibility of the Commission's decision with Community law. However, if the Commission's decision is challenged before the Community courts pursuant to Article 230 EC and the outcome of the dispute before the national court depends on the validity of the Commission's decision, the national court should stay its proceedings pending final judgment in the action for annulment by the Community courts unless it considers that, in the circumstances of the case, a reference to the Court of Justice for a preliminary ruling on the validity of the Commission decision is warranted.

14. When a national court stays proceedings, e.g. awaiting the Commission's decision (situation described in point 12 of this notice) or pending final judgement by the Community courts in an action for annulment or in a preliminary ruling procedure (situation described in point 13), it is incumbent on it to examine whether it is necessary to order interim measures in order to safeguard the interests of the parties.

NOTE: The potential for increased private enforcement of EC competition law was a major feature of the new regime following the introduction of Regulation 1/2003, and the 2004 Notice seeks to clarify aspects of the national courts' role in this context.

The relationship between private and public enforcement is clearly important, and also potentially problematic, and the following passages indicate two alternative viewpoints regarding the primacy of public enforcement and the complementary role for private litigation.

Komninos, A.P., 'Public and Private Antitrust Enforcement in Europe: Complement? Overlap?'
(2006) 3(1) Comp L Rev 5 at 5 (Abstract)

The European discovery of the merits of private antitrust enforcement, and the objective to enhance private actions both at the Community and at the national level, has raised the question of the relationship between public and private enforcement. There is a common misconception that public enforcement serves the public interest while private enforcement is only driven by the private interest of litigants. Yet private actions enhance the effectiveness of the competition law prohibitions and do not vary from the basic aim of the competition rules; the protection of competition. Thus, any private interest is subsumed within the public interest in protecting effective competition. A related misconception is that public enforcement is hierarchically superior and that decisions by competition authorities should always bind civil courts. Yet public and private enforcement are two separate limbs of antitrust enforcement independent of each other. The fact that certain recent national legislation or the proposals of the Commission Green Paper on Damages Actions convey or favour a binding effect of such authorities' decisions over civil proceedings, does not bring into question the principle of independence since such measures are only intended to function as incentives for follow-on civil actions. At the same time, the current Community principle that national courts must not contradict decisions by the Commission is not indicative of a primacy of public over private antitrust enforcement but rather of Community over national measures, always under the final control of the Court of Justice.

NOTE: Komninos emphasizes that Article 16 does not introduce a principle of primacy of public over private enforcement, that private enforcement incentives should be increased, and that it should not be subjugated to public enforcement, nor should the courts simply become damages calculators. Wils does not argue directly with Komninos but indicates the different objectives of public and private competition enforcement, the former more appropriate to achieve deterrence and the latter to achieve compensation.

Wils, W.P.J., 'The Relationship Between Public Antitrust Enforcement and Private Actions for Damages'
(2009) 32 World Competition 3 [footnotes omitted]

If, as argued above, public antitrust enforcement is the superior instrument to pursue the object-ives of clarification and development of the law and of deterrence and punishment, whereas private actions for damages are superior for the pursuit of corrective justice through compensation, then the optimal antitrust enforcement system would appear to be a system in which public antitrust enforcement aims at clarification and development of the law and at deterrence and punishment, while private actions for damages aim at compensation. Such a separate-tasks approach, under which public antitrust enforcement and private actions for damages are each assigned the tasks they are best at, appears to be the approach adopted by the European Commission in its 2008 White Paper on Damages actions for breach of the EC antitrust rules. Indeed, the 2008 White Paper states that its 'primary objective … is to improve the legal conditions for victims to exercise their right under the Treaty to reparation of all damage suffered as a result of a breach of the EC antitrust rules. Full compensation is, therefore, the first and foremost guiding principle. …Another important guiding principle of the Commission's policy is to preserve strong public enforcement of Articles 81 and 82 by the Commission and the competition authorities of the Member States. Accordingly, the measures put forward in this White Paper are designed to create an effective system of private enforcement by means of damages actions that complements, but does not replace or jeopardise, public enforcement'.

The separate-tasks approach corresponds to the classic, time-honoured conception of the dif-ferent roles of public enforcement and private actions for damages, not just in the area of antitrust but in the law more generally […]

The separate-tasks approach also appears best in line with the provisions of the EC Treaty and the case law of the EC Court of Justice and Court of First Instance. Indeed, according to the *Musique Diffusion Française* and *Masterfoods* case law, the European Commission has been entrusted […] with a supervisory task that includes the task of 'defining and implementing the orientation of Community competition policy', as well as 'the duty to investigate and penalise indi-vidual infringements'. A careful reading of *Courage* v *Crehan*, in the light of the wider case law of the Court of Justice, also shows that the rationale behind the right to damages of victims of antitrust infringements is compensation, rather than deterrence.

NOTE: A particular aspect of the relationship which remains problematic concerns leniency applicants. It is believed that potential leniency applicants may be discouraged from confess-ing because of the possibility of damages awards in subsequent private litigation. This issue has been considered in the Commission's White Paper, which will be considered further *infra*.

■ QUESTION

To what extent should private enforcement be promoted in Europe and should it be encouraged to achieve deterrence, compensation, or a combination of the two?

SECTION 4: **RECENT EC CASE LAW AND POLICY DEVELOPMENTS**

This area of law and policy has been evolving dramatically in recent years with a number of case law developments and policy proposals by the European Commission to facilitate and encourage private litigation. This section will commence with consideration of the crucial *Crehan* ECJ ruling and subsequent process in the English courts.

Courage Ltd v *Crehan*

(Case C-453/99) [2001] ECR I-6297, [2001] 5 CMLR 28

Mr Crehan concluded two 20-year leases for public houses which imposed an obligation to purchase products from Courage. The tenant had to purchase a fixed minimum quantity of specified beers at the prices shown in the price list. Courage, the claimant in the main proceedings, brought an action for the recovery from Mr Crehan of the sums due for unpaid deliveries of beer. Mr Crehan contested the action on its merits, contending that the beer tie was contrary to Article 81 EC. He also counter-claimed for damages. Questions were raised before the Court of Justice under the Article 234 EC procedure concerning the compatibility of English law on damages with Community law.

[25.] As regards the possibility of seeking compensation for loss caused by a contract or by conduct liable to restrict or distort competition, it should be remembered from the outset that, in accordance with settled case-law, the national courts whose task it is to apply the provisions of Community law in areas within their jurisdiction must ensure that those rules take full effect and must protect the rights which they confer on individuals (see *inter alia* the judgments in Case 106/77 *Simmenthal* [1978] ECR 629, paragraph 16, and in Case C-213/89 *Factortame* [1990] ECR I-2433, paragraph 19).

[26.] The full effectiveness of Article 85 of the Treaty and, in particular, the practical effect of the prohibition laid down in Article 85(1) would be put at risk if it were not open to any individual to claim damages for loss caused to him by a contract or by conduct liable to restrict or distort competition.

[27.] Indeed, the existence of such a right strengthens the working of the Community competition rules and discourages agreements or practices, which are frequently covert, which are liable to restrict or distort competition. From that point of view, actions for damages before the national courts can make a significant contribution to the maintenance of effective competition in the Community.

[28.] There should not therefore be any absolute bar to such an action being brought by a party to a contract which would be held to violate the competition rules.

[29.] However, in the absence of Community rules governing the matter, it is for the domestic legal system of each Member State to designate the courts and tribunals having jurisdiction and to lay down the detailed procedural rules governing actions for safeguarding rights which individuals derive directly from Community law, provided that such rules are not less favourable than those governing similar domestic actions (principle of equivalence) and that they do not render practically impossible or excessively difficult the exercise of rights conferred by Community law (principle of effectiveness) (see Case C-261/95 *Palmisani* [1997] ECR I-4025, paragraph 27).

[30.] In that regard, the Court has held that Community law does not prevent national courts from taking steps to ensure that the protection of the rights guaranteed by Community law does not entail the unjust enrichment of those who enjoy them (see, in particular, Case 238/78 *Ireks-Arkady* v *Council and Commission* [1979] ECR 2955, paragraph 14, Case 68/79 *Just* [1980] ECR 501, paragraph 26, and Joined Cases C-441/98 and C-442/98 *Michaïlidis* [2000] ECR I-7145, paragraph 31).

[31.] Similarly, provided that the principles of equivalence and effectiveness are respected (see *Palmisani*, cited above, paragraph 27), Community law does not preclude national law from denying a party who is found to bear significant responsibility for the distortion of competition the right to obtain damages from the other contracting party. Under a principle which is recognised in most of the legal systems of the Member States and which the Court has applied in the past (see Case 39/72 *Commission* v *Italy* [1973] ECR 101, paragraph 10), a litigant should not profit from his own unlawful conduct, where this is proven.

[32.] In that regard, the matters to be taken into account by the competent national court include the economic and legal context in which the parties find themselves and, as the United Kingdom

Government rightly points out, the respective bargaining power and conduct of the two parties to the contract.

[33.] In particular, it is for the national court to ascertain whether the party who claims to have suffered loss through concluding a contract that is liable to restrict or distort competition found himself in a markedly weaker position than the other party, such as seriously to compromise or even eliminate his freedom to negotiate the terms of the contract and his capacity to avoid the loss or reduce its extent, in particular by availing himself in good time of all the legal remedies available to him.

[34.] Referring to the judgments in Case 23/67 *Brasserie de Haecht* [1967] ECR 127 and Case C-234/89 *Delimitis* [1991] ECR I-935, paragraphs 14 to 26, the Commission and the United Kingdom Government also rightly point out that a contract might prove to be contrary to Article 85(1) of the Treaty for the sole reason that it is part of a network of similar contracts which have a cumulative effect on competition. In such a case, the party contracting with the person controlling the network cannot bear significant responsibility for the breach of Article 85, particularly where in practice the terms of the contract were imposed on him by the party controlling the network.

[35.] Contrary to the submission of Courage, making a distinction as to the extent of the parties' liability does not conflict with the case-law of the Court to the effect that it does not matter, for the purposes of the application of Article 85 of the Treaty, whether the parties to an agreement are on an equal footing as regards their economic position and function (see *inter alia* Joined Cases 56/64 and 58/64 *Consten and Grundig* v *Commission* [1966] ECR 382). That case-law concerns the conditions for application of Article 85 of the Treaty while the questions put before the Court in the present case concern certain consequences in civil law of a breach of that provision.

NOTE: The Court's ruling in *Crehan* was very important as it clarified the availability of damages in Article 81 EC cases. The Court clearly indicated that the English common law rules which prevented recovery were contrary to EC law as they curtailed the effectiveness of Article 81 EC. The Court did make it clear that such a rule would be compatible with EC law in situations where one party would be unjustly enriched, or where that party bore responsibility for the creation of the agreement. That would not be applicable in Mr Crehan's situation where the brewery effectively dictated the terms of the contract through the use of their standard lease. Mr Crehan had no real responsibility for the anti-competitive restriction. (See, for instance, Komninos, A., 'New Prospects for private enforcement of EC Competition Law: Courage v Crehan and the Community right to damages' (2002) 39 CML Rev 447; Rodger, B., 'The Interface Between Competition Law and Private Law: Article 81, Illegality and Unjustified Enrichment' (2002) 6 Edin LR 217, particularly at 217–26 and 232–43.)

The case returned to the High Court, Chancery Division where Park J rejected the claim against the first defendant, Inntrepreneur Pub Company CPC, (*Crehan* v *Inntrepreneur CPC* [2003] EWHC 1510(Ch) on the basis that the *Delimitis* conditions were not satisfied. Nonetheless, Park J proceeded to consider the specific issue dealt with by the ECJ, and concluded that if the *Delimitis* conditions had been satisfied, Crehan would have succeeded. Park J assessed damages at £361,500. The case was appealed to the Court of Appeal, which in a unanimous single judgment, allowed the appeal and awarded Crehan damages.

Crehan v *Inntrepreneur CPC*
[2004] EWCA Civ 637, [2004] ECC 28, CA, paras 163–7

163. So the essential question we have to decide under issue (6) is the second question which was referred to the ECJ in 1999 (see para. 44 above), but as applied to the particular claim of Mr. Crehan. The second question proceeded on the footing that the first question would be answered (as indeed it was) in the sense that a party to a prohibited tied house agreement might rely on Art.81 to seek relief from the other contracting party. The second question asked:

"Is the party claiming relief entitled to recover damages alleged to arise as a result of his adherence to the clause in the [tied house] agreement which is prohibited under Art.81?"

A specific answer to that question was not given. Instead, it was elided with the third question (illegality) and the following composite answer given (see para. 49 above):

> "Article 85 of the Treaty precludes a rule of national law under which a party to a contract liable to restrict or distort competition within the meaning of that provision is barred from claiming damages for loss caused by performance of that contract on the sole ground that the claimant is a party to that contract."

164. Shortly stated, Mr. Crehan's basic submission (we express it in our own words) is, first, that the ECJ effectively answered the second question in the affirmative and, secondly, that in giving that general answer it intended, or should be taken to have intended, that it should apply to the particular claim of Mr. Crehan. The first part of that submission is undoubtedly correct. The second part has been the subject of acute controversy in this court.

165. The starting-point for a consideration of the question whether the ECJ had, or should be taken to have had, the intention attributed to it by Mr. Crehan is the judgment of this court in *Courage v Crehan* [1999] EuLR 834 (see para. 43 above), pursuant to which the reference was made. At the conclusion of the argument before us, we gave leave for the written observations of the parties on the reference to the ECJ to be put in, which they subsequently were, together with short written submissions on behalf of Mr. Crehan and Inntrepreneur respectively. On behalf of Mr. Crehan it is submitted that these materials show that Courage's case to the ECJ was not restricted to the illegality issue and, further, that the statutory duty argument was advanced to and rejected by the ECJ. Mr. Crehan submits that the ECJ was well aware of the type of loss claimed by him, namely loss flowing from his inability as a result of the tie to "shop around for best buys", and that the ECJ ruled on that basis. On the other side, Inntrepreneur submits that Courage's case to the ECJ was restricted to the illegality issue and, further, that the statutory duty argument was neither advanced to nor considered by the ECJ.

166. Having carefully considered the earlier judgment of this court and the written observations of the parties on the reference to the ECJ, we are of the opinion that it cannot fairly be said that the statutory duty argument was advanced to or considered by the ECJ in any significant way. The whole point of the reference was to determine whether the rule of English law on illegality was a bar to the recovery of damages in Community law. Thus far we accept the submissions of Inntrepreneur. That, however, is not an end of the matter. It is still necessary to decide whether the decision of the ECJ is consistent only with the view that it intended, or should be taken to have intended, that its answer to the second question should apply to the particular claim of Mr. Crehan.

167. The ECJ's understanding of the nature of Mr. Crehan's claim was set out in para. 7 of the judgment in *Courage Ltd. v Crehan* [2002] QB 507 at p. 519:

> "[Mr. Crehan] contended that [Courage] sold its beers to independent tenants of pubs at substantially lower prices than those in the price list imposed on [Inntrepreneur] tenants subject to a beer tie. He contended that that price difference reduced the profitability of tied tenants, driving them out of business."

It is submitted on behalf of Inntrepreneur that that was a misunderstanding of Mr. Crehan's claim. While it may be that the extent of the claim was not fully stated, we cannot accept that the ECJ was under any misunderstanding as to what Mr. Crehan's case was all about. Moreover, the ECJ was well aware that it was only distortion at the distribution level that constituted a breach of Art.81 and, further, that Mr. Crehan had neither claimed, nor could he have claimed, a loss at that level. Nevertheless, it gave, or effectively gave, an affirmative answer to two questions which specifically referred to the parties to "a prohibited tied house agreement". We think it must follow that the effect of the ECJ decision was to put its imprimatur on the particular claim of Mr. Crehan, holding that a right to the type of damages he claimed was conferred on him by Community law.

NOTE: It should be noted that the Court of Appeal and the High Court disagreed on the issue of the quantification of damages, the latter awarding a higher sum based on assessment of damages up to the date of judgment, whereas the Court of Appeal awarded the lower figure of £131,336 by assessing damages at the earlier date in 1993 when Mr Crehan gave up possession of the pubs involved in the dispute. Given the paucity of final damages awards in the UK and across Europe, resolution *inter alia* of this crucial issue by the House of Lords would have been an important factor in clarifying the scope of the remedies available under English law for competition law breaches. Disappointingly, on appeal, the House of Lords did not rule on the key remedy issue or on the appropriate quantification of damages, but focused on the issue of the national court's duty of sincere cooperation (*Crehan* v *Inntrepreneur Pub Co (CPC)*, 19 July 2006, [2007] 1 AC 333, HL). In overruling the Court of Appeal on the issue, the judgment of Park J in the High Court was restored, on the basis that where there was no 'real conflict' between a Commission decision and a national court ruling, the national court was not required to follow the Commission decision but was only required to give such weight to the Commission's assessment as the evidence merited. (See Petch, T., 'Relying on Commission Decisions' (2007) 123 LQR 186; Andreangeli, A., 'The Enforcement of Article 81 EC Treaty before National Courts after the House of Lords' decision in Inntrepreneur Pub Co Ltd v Crehan' (2007) 32 EL Rev. 260.) Accordingly, as determined earlier by Park J, Crehan was not entitled to damages and there have still been no final judgments in the UK courts awarding damages on the basis of the EC competition law rules.

The European Court reaffirmed its earlier ruling in *Crehan* in the Italian case of *Manfredi*, re-emphasising the importance of the need for Community rules to be effective and of the right of individuals to sue for compensation for losses.

Manfredi v *Lloyd Adriatico Assicurazioni SpA*
(Joined Cases C-295/04, C-296/04, C-297/04, and C-298/04) [2006] 5 CMLR 17, paras 89–99

This was a follow-on damages action in the Italian courts in relation to a cartel in the car insurance market that had fixed premium levels.

89 In accordance with settled case law, the national courts whose task it is to apply the provisions of Community law in areas within their jurisdiction must ensure that those rules take full effect and must protect the rights which they confer on individuals (see, inter alia, *Simmenthal* (106/77): [1978] E.C.R. 629; [1978] 3 C.M.L.R. 263 at [16], *Factortame and Others* (C-213/89): [1990] E.C.R. I-2433; [1990] 3 C.M.L.R. 1 at [19], and *Courage v Crehan*, cited above, at [25]).

90 As was pointed out in para.[60] of this judgment, the full effectiveness of Art.81 EC and, in particular, the practical effect of the prohibition laid down in Art.81(1) EC would be put at risk if it were not open to any individual to claim damages for loss caused to him by a contract or by conduct liable to restrict or distort competition.

91 Indeed, the existence of such a right strengthens the working of the Community competition rules and discourages agreements or practices, frequently covert, which are liable to restrict or distort competition. From that point of view, actions for damages before the national courts can make a significant contribution to the maintenance of effective competition in the Community (*Courage v Crehan*, cited above, at [27]).

92 As to the award of damages and the possibility of an award of punitive damages, in the absence of Community rules governing the matter, it is for the domestic legal system of each Member State to set the criteria for determining the extent of the damages, provided that the principles of equivalence and effectiveness are observed.

93 In that respect, first, in accordance with the principle of equivalence, it must be possible to award particular damages, such as exemplary or punitive damages, pursuant to actions founded on the Community competition rules, if such damages may be awarded pursuant to similar actions founded on domestic law (see, to that effect, *Brasserie du Pêcheur and Factortame*, cited above, at [90]).

94 However, it is settled case law that Community law does not prevent national courts from taking steps to ensure that the protection of the rights guaranteed by Community law does not entail the unjust enrichment of those who enjoy them (see, in particular, *Ireks-Arkady v Council and Commission* (238/78): [1979] E.C.R. 2955 at [14], *Michaïlidis* (C-441 & 442/98): [2000] E.C.R. I-7145; [2001] 1 C.M.L.R. 13 at [31], and *Courage v Crehan*, cited above, at [30]).

95 Secondly, it follows from the principle of effectiveness and the right of any individual to seek compensation for loss caused by a contract or by conduct liable to restrict or distort competition that injured persons must be able to seek compensation not only for actual loss (*damnum emergens*) but also for loss of profit (*lucrum cessans*) plus interest.

96 Total exclusion of loss of profit as a head of damage for which compensation may be awarded cannot be accepted in the case of a breach of Community law since, especially in the context of economic or commercial litigation, such a total exclusion of loss of profit would be such as to make reparation of damage practically impossible (see *Brasserie du Pêcheur and Factortame*, cited above, at [87], and *Metallgesellschaft and Others* (C-397 & 410/98): [2001] E.C.R. I-1727; [2001] 2 C.M.L.R. 32 at [91]).

97 As to the payment of interest, the Court pointed out in para.[31] of *Marshall* (C-271/91): [1993] E.C.R. I-4367; [1993] 3 C.M.L.R. 293 that an award made in accordance with the applicable national rules constitutes an essential component of compensation.

98 It follows that the answer to the fourth question in Cases C-295–297/04 and the fifth question in Case C-298/04 must be that, in the absence of Community rules governing that field, it is for the domestic legal system of each Member State to set the criteria for determining the extent of the damages for harm caused by an agreement or practice prohibited under Art.81 EC, provided that the principles of equivalence and effectiveness are observed.

99 Therefore, first, in accordance with the principle of equivalence, if it is possible to award specific damages, such as exemplary or punitive damages, in domestic actions similar to actions founded on the Community competition rules, it must also be possible to award such damages in actions founded on Community rules. However, Community law does not prevent national courts from taking steps to ensure that the protection of the rights guaranteed by Community law does not entail the unjust enrichment of those who enjoy them.

NOTE: The Court followed its earlier case law in re-stating the importance of the principle of effectiveness, but recognizing that in the absence of Community rules in the area, it was for national law to determine the various issues relating to the damages action. In particular, although exemplary (or multiple) damages may be awarded (and were not precluded by Community Law), they were not required by Community law. (For a fuller discussion, see Carpagnano, M., 'Private Enforcement of Competition law Arrives in Italy: Analysis of the Judgment of the European Court of Justice in Joined Cases C-295–289/04 Manfredi' (2006) 3(1) Comp L Rev 47.)

In the meantime, between the *Crehan* and the *Manfredi* rulings, the Ashurst Report had been published, as outlined above, and subsequently the Commission issued a Green Paper on Antitrust damages, outlining a range of possible options for reform of this area.

Green Paper, *Damages actions for breach of the EC antitrust rules*

http://ec.europa.eu/competition/antitrust/actionsdamages/documents.html#greenpaper

(SEC(2005) 1732) COM/2005/0672 final, paras 1.1–1.3 [footnotes omitted]

Vigorous competition on an open internal market provides the best guarantee that European companies will increase their productivity and innovative potential. Competition law enforcement is therefore a key element of the "Lisbon strategy", which aims at making the economy of the European Union grow and create employment for Europe's citizens.

As part of an effort to improve the enforcement of competition law after the modernisation of the procedural law on the application of Articles 81 and 82 of the EC Treaty, this Green Paper and the Commission Staff Working Paper attached to it address the conditions for bringing damages claims for infringement of EC antitrust law. They identify obstacles to a more efficient system for bringing such claims and propose options for solving these problems. Facilitating damages claims for breach of antitrust law will not only make it easier for consumers and firms who have suffered damages arising from an infringement of antitrust rules to recover their losses from the infringer but also strengthen the enforcement of antitrust law.

1 Background and Objectives of the Green Paper

1.1 Damages claims as part of the enforcement system of Community antitrust law

The antitrust rules in Articles 81 and 82 of the Treaty are enforced both by public and private enforcement. Both forms are part of a common enforcement system and serve the same aims: to deter anti-competitive practices forbidden by antitrust law and to protect firms and consumers from these practices and any damages caused by them. Private as well as public enforcement of antitrust law is an important tool to create and sustain a competitive economy.

With regard to public enforcement, both the Commission and the competition authorities of the Member States (NCAs) apply Community competition law in individual cases. Under Regulation 1/2003, the Commission and NCAs constitute a network of competition authorities responsible for public enforcement of the applicable Community antitrust rules. As part of their enforcement activities, these authorities adopt, among other things, decisions finding that an undertaking has infringed antitrust law as well as decisions imposing fines. Public enforcement is indispensable for effective protection of the rights conferred and effective enforcement of the obligations imposed by the Treaty.

All parts of Articles 81 and 82 of the Treaty are directly applicable. From the outset private enforcement has also played a role in the enforcement of Articles 81 and 82 of the Treaty. Private enforcement in this context means application of antitrust law in civil disputes before national courts. Such application can take different forms. Article 81(2) of the Treaty states that agreements or decisions prohibited by Article 81 are void. The Treaty rules can also be used in actions for injunctive relief. Also, damages awards can be awarded to those who have suffered a loss caused by an infringement of the antitrust rules.

This Green Paper focuses on damages actions alone. Damages actions for infringement of antitrust law serve several purposes, namely to compensate those who have suffered a loss as a consequence of anti-competitive behaviour and to ensure the full effectiveness of the antitrust rules of the Treaty by discouraging anti-competitive behaviour, thus contributing significantly to the maintenance of effective competition in the Community (deterrence). By being able effectively to bring a damages claim, individual firms or consumers in Europe are brought closer to competition rules and will be more actively involved in enforcement of the rules. The Court of Justice of the European Communities (ECJ) has ruled that effective protection of the rights granted by the Treaty requires that individuals who have suffered a loss arising from an infringement of Articles 81 or 82 have the right to claim damages.

1.2 Outline of the problem

While Community law therefore demands an effective system for damages claims for infringements of antitrust rules, this area of the law in the 25 Member States presents a picture of "total underdevelopment".

The ECJ has ruled that, in the absence of Community rules on the matter, it is for the legal systems of the Member States to provide for detailed rules for bringing damages actions. As the Community courts have no jurisdiction in the matter (outside the procedure for preliminary rulings), the courts of the Member States will generally hear these cases. Significant obstacles exist in the different Member States to the effective operation of damages actions for infringement of Community antitrust law.

1.3 Objectives

The purpose of this Green Paper and of the Commission Staff Working Paper is to identify the main obstacles to a more efficient system of damages claims and to set out different options for further reflection and possible action to improve damages actions both for follow-on actions (e.g. cases in which the civil action is brought after a competition authority has found an infringement) and for stand-alone actions (that is to say actions which do not follow on from a prior finding by a competition authority of an infringement of competition law).

NOTE: Following the Ashurst Report, the Green Paper identified the obstacles to effective private enforcement and set out a range of options in relation to a number of issues. For instance, in relation to damages the range of options included the introduction of double damages for cartel cases, with a further possibility of double damages being reduced to single damages in the case of a successful leniency applicant, in order to address the risk that follow-on litigation may undermine the incentives necessary for a successful leniency programme. Jones considered the adoption of the Green Paper to represent the third devolution in Community competition law.

Jones, C.A., 'After the Green Paper: The Third Devolution in European Competition Law and Private Enforcement'

(2006) 3(1) Comp L Rev 1 at pp. 1–2 [footnotes omitted]

Following *BRT v SABAM* in 1974 and *Delimitis v Henninger Bräu* in 1991, the Commission's first *Cooperation Notice* ushered in what I have called the 'First Devolution' of Community competition law, in which the Commission relied on exhortation to encourage undertakings to resort to national courts (self-help, if you will), and later NCAs with their competition complaints. After this generally failed to have the desired effect, it was clear that stronger measures were in order. The impending enlargement to 25 and now 27 Member States no doubt raised the spectre of another avalanche of notifications, not to mention the enforcement problems likely to be generated in the several new Member States for which the free market was still a voyage of discovery and in which formerly state-owned undertakings were likely to be dominant. The 'Second Devolution' was of course the 'modernised' Regulation 1/2003 which transformed the bully pulpit of the Notices into a directly applicable Regulation, abolished notifications, almost all individual exemptions, and devolved many cases to the NCAs, while simultaneously both freeing the national courts to fully apply Art 81 EC in its entirety and ensuring the Commission had a place at the table in both the national courts (as amicus curiae) and in the NCAs through the European Competition Network. Armed with *Courage*, and Regulation 1/2003, national courts could finally begin to seriously entertain private actions without some of the discouraging obstacles of the past forty years.

However, other obstacles and uncertainties remain which hinder the development of private enforcement in the European Union. Recognition of this led to the Green Paper and has Europe poised on the brink of a Third Devolution, in which private enforcement may become a substantial factor in EU competition law enforcement. Comments on the Green Paper have closed, and we await the outcome, which may be EU legislation designed to facilitate private actions. It is unclear at this point whether there will be a Directive, notwithstanding the Commission's clear interest. The politics of such legislation are complex, and undertakings across Europe were not too keen on the multiplying of antitrust enforcers that occurred in Regulation 1/2003; they are sure to be even less keen on turning loose a veritable army of what Americans call the 'private attorney general'. Even Member States may be hesitant to do anything to disadvantage potential national champions, which may be strong argument for EC level action.

NOTE: Jones considered that the Third Devolution was already taking place in some Member States. There has been, as we shall note shortly, some statutory developments in the UK, and in Germany private litigation has been facilitated and is taking place more regularly than in any other Member State. Nonetheless, the Commission would prefer a minimal harmonized approach across the Community, and there was an extensive period of consultation following the Green Paper. Eventually, the White Paper on Antitrust Damages was published in April 2008.

White Paper, *Damages actions for breach of the EC antitrust rules*

http://ec.europa.eu/competition/antitrust/actionsdamages/files_white_paper/ whitepaper_en.pdf

COM(2008) 165 final, Brussels, 2 April 2008, paras 1.2–2.1 [footnotes omitted]

1.2. Objectives, guiding principles and scope of the White Paper

This White Paper considers and puts forward proposals for policy choices and specific measures that would ensure, more than is the case today, that **all victims** of infringements of EC competition law have access to effective redress mechanisms so that they can be fully compensated for the harm they suffered.

This White Paper is to be read in conjunction with two Commission staff working documents: (a) a Commission staff working paper on EC antitrust damages actions ("the SWP") which explains in greater detail the considerations underlying the White Paper and also provides a concise overview of the already existing *acquis communautaire*; and (b) an Impact Assessment Report (the "IAR") analysing the potential benefits and costs of various policy options, and an executive summary of this report.

The **primary objective** of this White Paper is to improve the legal conditions for victims to exercise their right under the Treaty to reparation of all damage suffered as a result of a breach of the EC antitrust rules. **Full compensation** is, therefore, the first and foremost guiding principle.

More effective compensation mechanisms mean that the costs of antitrust infringements would be borne by the infringers, and not by the victims and law-abiding businesses. Effective remedies for private parties also increase the likelihood that a greater number of illegal restrictions of competition will be detected and that the infringers will be held liable. Improving compensatory justice would therefore **inherently** also produce beneficial effects in terms of **deterrence** of future infringements and greater compliance with EC antitrust rules. Safeguarding undistorted competition is an integral part of the internal market and important for implementing the Lisbon strategy. A competition culture contributes to better allocation of resources, greater economic efficiency, increased innovation and lower prices.

The Commission followed the further guiding principle that the legal framework for more effective antitrust damages actions should be based on a genuinely European approach. The policy choices proposed in this White Paper therefore consist of **balanced measures** that are rooted in **European legal culture** and **traditions**.

Another important guiding principle of the Commission's policy is to **preserve strong public enforcement** of Articles 81 and 82 by the Commission and the competition authorities of the Member States. Accordingly, the measures put forward in this White Paper are designed to create an effective system of private enforcement by means of damages actions that complements, but does not replace or jeopardise, public enforcement.

In view of the foregoing and in line with the requirement set out by the Court of Justice that *any* victim of antitrust infringements must be able to exercise his right to compensation effectively, the issues addressed in the White Paper concern, in principle, **all categories of victim**, **all types of breach** of Articles 81 and 82 and **all sectors of the economy**. The Commission also considers it appropriate that the policy should cover both actions for damages which do, and actions which do not, rely on a prior finding of an infringement by a competition authority.

2. THE PROPOSED MEASURES AND POLICY CHOICES

2.1. Standing: indirect purchasers and collective redress

In the context of legal standing to bring an action, the Commission welcomes the confirmation by the Court of Justice that **"any individual"** who has suffered harm caused by an antitrust infringement must be allowed to claim damages before national courts. This principle also applies to **indirect purchasers**, i.e. purchasers who had no direct dealings with the infringer, but who nonetheless may have suffered considerable harm because an illegal overcharge was passed on to them along the distribution chain.

With respect to **collective redress**, the Commission considers that there is a clear need for mechanisms allowing aggregation of the individual claims of victims of antitrust infringements. Individual consumers, but also small businesses, especially those who have suffered **scattered and relatively low-value damage**, are often deterred from bringing an individual action for damages by the costs, delays, uncertainties, risks and burdens involved. As a result, many of these victims currently **remain uncompensated**. At the rare occasions where a multitude of individual actions are brought in relation to the same infringement, **procedural inefficiencies** arise, for claimants, defendants and the judicial system alike.

The Commission therefore suggests a combination of two complementary mechanisms of collective redress to address effectively those issues in the field of antitrust:

- **representative actions**, which are brought **by qualified entities**, such as consumer associations, state bodies or trade associations, on behalf of identified or, in rather restricted cases, identifiable victims. These entities are either (i) officially designated in advance or (ii) certified on an *ad hoc* basis by a Member State for a particular antitrust infringement to bring an action on behalf of some or all of their members; and

- **opt-in collective actions**, in which victims **expressly decide** to combine their individual claims for harm they suffered into one single action.

Considering that qualified entities will not be able or willing to pursue every claim, it is necessary that these two types of action **complement** each other to ensure effective collective redress for victims of antitrust infringements. In addition, it is important that victims are not deprived of their right to bring an individual action for damages if they so wish. However, safeguards should be put in place to avoid that the same harm is compensated more than once.

These suggestions on damages actions in the field of antitrust are part of the Commission's wider initiative to strengthen collective redress mechanisms in the EU and may develop further within this context.

NOTE: In addition to standing of indirect purchasers and collective redress, the White Paper proposes the introduction of minimum Community rules in relation to discovery procedures across the legal systems of the Community, for the binding effect of all NCA decisions and for measures to address the problem in relation to evidence provided by leniency applicants becoming available to litigants in damages actions. In addition, the Commission will provide guidance in relation to quantification of damages. The White Paper has been criticized as failing to create sufficient incentives to stimulate private litigation, as suggested in the following excerpt.

'A little more action please!—The White paper on damages actions for breach of the EC antitrust rules'
Editorial [2008] CML Rev 609–615

Bearing in mind the range of options presented in the Green Paper and pondered in the debate surrounding it, readers of the White Paper will get the impression that the current proposals are not really revolutionary, but aim at a rather modest reform. In summary:...

As far as the notoriously difficult handling of "passing-on" problems is concerned, the Commission does not want to follow American suit, either. The infringer's defence that his customers (the direct purchasers) were able to pass on the illegal overcharge (the difference between the cartel price and the hypothetical price in a competitive market) to their own customers in the downstream market (the indirect purchasers) should not be excluded. Vice versa, in accordance with the Court's holding that any individual harmed by antitrust infringements must be able to claim damages, indirect purchasers should be entitled to invoke the passing-on of overcharges as a basis for their damages actions. Because there is a risk that infringers can successfully raise the passing-on defence against direct purchasers while indirect purchasers as claimants remain unable to produce evidence for the harm they suffered due to passing-on, the Commission suggests helping indirect purchasers with a rebuttable presumption that the overcharge was passed on to them.

This answer to the passing-on question leads to an enforcement problem. If the overcharge is passed on along the distribution chain, the damage will most likely be scattered among large groups of customers. If it finally stops with consumers (but not only then), the individual harm will often be so small that an individual action will not make any sense. The Commission intends to solve this problem by introducing mechanisms of collective redress, i.e. by allowing representative actions brought by consumer associations and other qualified entities and opt-in collective actions, in which victims expressly decide to combine their individual claims into one single action. Again, this proposal steers clear of any radicalism as it does not include the adoption of a US style opt-out group action that would force group members to declare they will not participate if they do not want the action to have any legal effect for them.

NOTE: This demonstrates scepticism that the Commission proposals will lead to more effective private enforcement and suggested more radical action was required by the Commission.

Nonetheless, it should be recognized that the Commission faced a dilemma in preparing the White Paper. There were concerns in many Member States about the excessive competition litigation culture prevalent in the US and that the various characteristics of US private enforcement, for instance contingency fees, broad discovery rules, treble damages, and class actions, were inimical to Continental civil legal traditions. Therefore, the Commission has adopted a gradualist approach, and the White Paper proposals are currently being considered by the European Parliament. Some of the key themes will be examined in the final section, but it should be noted that the Community developments have focused on damages actions, although competition law, as noted earlier, may be raised by claimants and defendants in a range of different contexts before the courts.

■ QUESTION

What are the key proposals set out in the White Paper? Should the Commission have been more radical?

SECTION 5: PRIVATE ENFORCEMENT UNDER THE CA 1998

Proposals to reform UK competition law during the late 1980s and early 1990s identified the absence of private rights of redress, particularly under the FTA 1973 regime, as an area of weakness. As discussed earlier in the chapter, in the US antitrust damages actions by claimants have played a significant role in the enforcement regime. (See Jones, C., *Private Enforcement of Antitrust Law in the EU, UK, and USA*, Oxford: OUP, 1999) Accordingly, it was recognized by the UK authorities that private enforcement of the competition rules, in tandem with administrative enforcement, could enhance their deterrent impact.

A: Competition Act 1998

As MacCulloch explains, the CA 1998 was introduced with the intention, albeit implied, of instituting a hybrid system of enforcement of the new prohibitions:

MacCulloch, A., Chapter 5, 'Private Enforcement of the Competition Act Prohibitions', in Rodger, B.J., and MacCulloch, A. (eds), *The UK Competition Act: A New Era for UK Competition Law*
Oxford, Hart Publishing, 2000

The possibility of compensation actions following the breach of one of the prohibitions was heralded by the, then, President of the Board of Trade, Margaret Beckett, in the Draft Bill and explanatory document published in August 1997.[8] The change was undoubtedly to be welcomed, as it will give those who are directly affected by infringements an important new weapon. However, the exact manner in which such an action stems from the Act is uncertain. The main difficulty flows from the absence of a specific provision in the Act that states that private parties can bring an action based on an infringement of the Act's prohibitions. The lack of a specific provision leaves many important questions unanswered.

[8] *A Prohibition Approach to Anti-Competitive Agreements and Abuse of a Dominant Position: Draft Bill* (London, DTI, 1997) ch 7.23.

The failure to provide directly for private actions received scant attention during debate in the Lords.[9] The only relevant provisions in the Act appear to be sections 55 and 58. Section 55(3)(b) provides that the Director General may disclose information to third parties if the disclosure is made for the purposes of civil proceedings. Section 58(1) provides that a finding of fact by the Director General in Part I proceedings is binding on the parties if the time for bringing an appeal has expired or an appeal tribunal has confirmed the decision. The reference to 'Part I proceedings' is defined in section 58(2) to include actions brought under Chapter I or II prohibitions by parties other than the Director General. The proceedings referred to in sections 55 and 58 must be actions brought by private individuals under the prohibitions, presumably for compensation, after administrative enforcement procedures have been completed.[10] This would be of obvious assistance to private claimants, as they would no longer need to prove the existence of an infringement to succeed in such an action, but could simply rely on any findings in the administrative action. This would enact a rule similar to that developed by the courts in *Iberian UK Ltd* v *BPB Industries*[11] for findings made by the European Commission during Community competition procedures or the rules developed in the USA under section 5(a) of the Clayton Act 1914.

It is submitted that the 1998 Act provides for a right of private action, but on what basis should a claimant proceed? The most obvious cause of action where a person seeks a remedy based on a statutory prohibition is that of breach of statutory duty. The common law rules surrounding the availability of such an action in the competition field were discussed recently in relation to sections 93 and 93A of the Fair Trading Act 1973 in *Mid Kent Holdings plc* v *General Utilities plc*.[12] The court came to the conclusion that there was no private right of action, even though section 93(2) and section 93A(2) appear, on their face, to give a right of action to a third party who apprehends the breach of an order, under section 93(2), or an undertaking, under section 93A(2). Without delving too deeply into the logic that led to that particular outcome, the reasons given by Knox J were based on the application of the general law governing the availability of civil remedies for the breach of a statutory provision.[13] The same principles will be used to establish if the prohibitions in the 1998 Act are enforceable by private parties. The fact that an ostensibly enabling provision was interpreted in that case in such a restrictive manner gives cause for concern.

The first general principle is that stated by Lord Simmons in *Cutler* v *Wandsworth Stadium Ltd*:[14]

> The only rule which in all the circumstances is valid is that the answer must depend on a consideration of the whole Act and the circumstances, including the pre-existing law, in which it was enacted.

As far as this principle is concerned, it appears that the Chapter I and II prohibitions of the 1998 Act may be amenable to a civil remedy. The arguments for the availability of civil remedies come from two main sources. The first potential argument rests upon the interpretation of the prohibitions themselves. Under the terms of section 60, the 1998 Act is designed to ensure that questions arising in the Act are 'dealt with in a manner which is consistent with the treatment of corresponding questions arising in Community law'. Concerns have been raised about the potential scope of this provision with regard to the particular needs of Community law, on one hand, and UK law, on the other.[15] Here we have an example of a potential difficulty. How far can the jurisprudence of the European Court go in assisting a national court to discover Parliament's intention? The argument could run as follows.

[9] Hansard, HL, 17 November 1997, col 956.

[10] A private action could seek injunctive relief, but as administrative action would have been completed it can be assumed that the infringing practices would have been discontinued.

[11] [1996] 2 CMLR 601.

[12] [1997] 1 WLR 14, [1996] 3 All ER 132.

[13] The court's reasoning is explained fully in Rodger, B.J., 'Mid Kent Holdings plc v General Utilities plc: Remedies under the Fair Trading Act 1973' [1997] ECLR 273.

[14] [1949] 1 All ER 544 at 548.

[15] See Scholes, J., and others, 'The UK Draft Competition Bill: Based on the Observations of the Competition Law Association' [1998] ECLR 32.

- Parliament had the intention of making the UK provisions as consistent as possible with the corresponding Community provisions. Accordingly it copied the wording of Articles 81 and 82 of the EC Treaty, as far as possible in the UK context, in the Chapter I and II provisions; and added the interpretation provisions in section 60.

- The European Court in *BRT* v *SABAM*[16] held that, 'as the prohibitions in Articles 85(1) and 86 tend by their very nature to produce direct effects in relations between individuals, these Articles create direct rights in respect of the individuals concerned which the national courts must safeguard'.

- Therefore, Parliament must have intended that the Chapter I and II prohibitions in the 1998 Act create rights directly enforceable by individuals.

The Director General, in its Guideline on enforcement, is of the view that third party rights exist by implication in the Act.[17] In paragraph 5.1 the Guidance refers to section 60(6)(b) and states:

Section 60, which sets out certain principles to provide for the UK authorities to handle cases in such a way as to ensure consistency with EC law, expressly refers to decisions of the European Court and the European Commission as to the civil liability of an undertaking for harm caused by its infringement of Community law.

The express reference in the Act to expansive Community jurisprudence in the area of civil liability would be missed on all but the closest reading of the legislation. Section 60 appears to be a very general provision. The OFT's desire to give section 60 a broad inclusive interpretation does it credit but raises questions as to the scope of the wholesale adoption of Community competition law and policy. It also remains to be seen whether the UK courts will be as receptive to such an expansive interpretation. It is possible to view the interpretation provision as referring only to the application of the prohibitions themselves.[18]

While that argument is interesting, a second, more 'traditional', way of discovering Parliament's intention is also available to the courts. Since the decision of the House of Lords in *Pepper* v *Hart*[19] the courts may look back at parliamentary debates to assist them in their interpretation of statutes. There is sufficient evidence in the debates to come to the conclusion that private actions were envisaged. In response to a question on private remedies tabled by Lord Lucas in the Lords the government spokesman stated that there was 'no need to make explicit provision in the bill'.[20] While this may be evidence of their intention it certainly shows limited understanding of the canons of statutory interpretation.

It may therefore be possible to show that the general principle has been satisfied but there are also several more specific rules, one of which may cause problems with regard to the 1998 Act. Lord Simmons was of the opinion, in *Cutler* v *Wandsworth Stadium*,[21] that a court was not bound by the general principle. He went on to approve the statement by Lord Tenterden CJ in *Doe d. Rochester* v *Bridges*[22] that 'where an Act creates an obligation, and enforces the performance in a specified manner, we take it to be a general rule that performance cannot be enforced in any other manner'. Obviously the 1998 Act gives the Director General broad powers to enforce the prohibitions; including the power to levy fines of up to 10 per cent of the UK turnover of the undertakings concerned. If one follows the 'general rule' in *Rochester* it would appear to be the case that private remedies would not be available in addition to the sweeping enforcement powers set out in the Act.

---

[16] [1974] ECR 51, para 16.

[17] *Enforcement* (OFT 407), para 5.1.

[18] In other parts of the guidance the OFT stress that textual differences between the UK and EC provisions result in different interpretations. See *The Major Provisions* (OFT 400), para 6.3.

[19] [1993] AC 593, [1992] 3 WLR 1032, [1993] All ER 42.

[20] Hansard, HL, 17 November 1997, col 956. The Government's reasoning behind the lack of provision will be discussed in more detail *infra*.

[21] [1949] AC 398.

[22] (1831) 1 B & Ad 847 at 859, [1824–34] All ER Rep 167 at 170.

There is, of course, an exception to this rule. It is found in *Butler v Fife Coal Co Ltd*,[23] where it was held that 'when a duty of this kind is imposed for the benefit of particular persons, there arises at common law a correlative right in those persons who may be injured by its contravention'. Again, in this situation it could be valuable to return to the jurisprudence of the European Court. In *BRT v SABAM* it set out that Articles 81(1) and 82 EC, upon which the Chapter I and II prohibitions are based, 'produce direct effects in relations between individuals' and 'create direct rights in respect of the individuals concerned which the national courts must safeguard'. It may therefore be possible that the 1998 Act, with assistance from section 60, is to be interpreted as creating the same rights for individuals as a protected class, and therefore the general rule is to be displaced.

NOTE: It remains unclear why the Government did not insert an express provision in the Act although the purported rationale was to retain harmony with the Community system. There have been a number of private actions raised in relation to the prohibitions. See, for discussion of some of the earlier cases, Rodger, B, 'Competition Law Litigation in the UK Courts: A study of All Cases to 2004', Parts I-III, [2006] ECLR 241, 279, and 341, and more recently Rodger, B, 'Competition Law litigation in the UK Courts: A Study of All cases 2005–2008', Part I, [2009] Global Competition Litigation Review 92. To a great extent, the earlier debate on the availability of private actions (see, for instance, Turner, J., 'The UK Competition Act 1998 and Private Rights' [1999] ECLR 62), has now been superseded. The Enterprise Act 2002 ('EA 2002') introduced provisions to further facilitate private competition litigation in the UK, notably by the creation of the Competition Appeal Tribunal which was afforded a key role in relation to private enforcement.

B: EA 2002 provisions on private enforcement

A principal aim of the EA 2002 competition reforms was to enhance the rights of redress available to parties allegedly harmed by competition law infringements and thereby to enhance the deterrent effect of the competition rules.

Section 18 of the EA 2002 inserted a new s. 47A into the CA 1998 and allows claims for damages or any other sum of money to be brought before the Competition Appeal Tribunal ('CAT'):

COMPETITION ACT 1998 [S. 47A]

Monetary claims before Tribunal

47A.—(1) This section applies to—
  (a) any claim for damages, or
  (b) any other claim for a sum of money,
  which a person who has suffered loss or damage as a result of the infringement of a relevant prohibition may make in civil proceedings brought in any part of the United Kingdom.

(2) In this section 'relevant prohibition' means any of the following—
  (a) the Chapter I prohibition;
  (b) the Chapter II prohibition;
  (c) the prohibition in Article 81(1) of the Treaty;
  (d) the prohibition in Article 82 of the Treaty;
  (e) the prohibition in Article 65(1) of the Treaty establishing the European Coal and Steel Community;
  (f) the prohibition in Article 66(7) of that Treaty.

(3) For the purpose of identifying claims which may be made in civil proceedings, any limitation rules that would apply in such proceedings are to be disregarded.

---

[23] [1912] AC 149 at 165.

(4) A claim to which this section applies may (subject to the provisions of this Act and Tribunal rules) be made in proceedings brought before the Tribunal.

(5) But no claim may be made in such proceedings—
   (a) until a decision mentioned in subsection (6) has established that the relevant prohibition in question has been infringed; and
   (b) otherwise than with the permission of the Tribunal, during any period specified in subsection (7) or (8) which relates to that decision.

(6) The decisions which may be relied on for the purposes of proceedings under this section are—
   (a) a decision of the OFT that the Chapter I prohibition or the Chapter II prohibition has been infringed;
   (b) a decision of the OFT that the prohibition in Article 81(1) or Article 82 of the Treaty has been infringed;
   (c) a decision of the Tribunal on an appeal from a decision of the OFT that the Chapter I prohibition, the Chapter II prohibition or the prohibition in Article 81(1) or Article 82 of the Treaty has been infringed;
   (d) a decision of the European Commission that the prohibition in Article 81(1) or Article 82 of the Treaty has been infringed; or
   (e) a decision of the European Commission that the prohibition in Article 65(1) of the Treaty establishing the European Coal and Steel Community has been infringed, or a finding made by the European Commission under Article 66(7) of that Treaty.

(7) The periods during which proceedings in respect of a claim made in reliance on a decision mentioned in subsection (6)(a), (b) or (c) may not be brought without permission are—
   (a) in the case of a decision of the OFT, the period during which an appeal may be made to the Tribunal under section 46, section 47 or the EC Competition Law (Articles 84 and 85) Enforcement Regulations 2001 (SI 2001/2916);
   (b) in the case of a decision of the OFT which is the subject of an appeal mentioned in paragraph (a), the period following the decision of the Tribunal on the appeal during which a further appeal may be made under section 49 or under those Regulations;
   (c) in the case of a decision of the Tribunal mentioned in subsection (5)(c), the period during which a further appeal may be made under section 49 or under those Regulations;
   (d) in the case of any decision which is the subject of a further appeal, the period during which an appeal may be made to the House of Lords from a decision on the further appeal;

   and, where any appeal mentioned in paragraph (a), (b), (c) or (d) is made, the period specified in that paragraph includes the period before the appeal is determined.

(8) The periods during which proceedings in respect of a claim made in reliance on a decision or finding of the European Commission may not be brought without permission are—
   (a) the period during which proceedings against the decision or finding may be instituted in the European Court; and
   (b) if any such proceedings are instituted, the period before those proceedings are determined.

(9) In determining a claim to which this section applies the Tribunal is bound by any decision mentioned in subsection (6) which establishes that the prohibition in question has been infringed.

(10) The right to make a claim to which this section applies in proceedings before the Tribunal does not affect the right to bring any other proceedings in respect of the claim.

NOTE: The tribunal can make monetary awards for breaches of both UK and EC competition law, but only if the relevant UK or EC authorities have made infringement decisions. These are called follow-on actions, as opposed to stand-alone actions, which may be raised in the normal civil courts where there has been no prior decision by a competition authority. Section 47A(10) makes it clear that a unitary system for dealing with damages claims under UK or EC law has not been instituted, by providing that this section does not affect the right to commence ordinary civil proceedings in respect of any of the infringements.

Section 19 inserted a new s. 47(B) to allow representative actions on behalf of consumers to be brought before the Tribunal:

COMPETITION ACT 1998 [S. 47B]

47B Claims brought on behalf of consumers

(1) A specified body may (subject to the provisions of this Act and Tribunal rules) bring proceedings before the Tribunal which comprise consumer claims made or continued on behalf of at least two individuals.

(2) In this section 'consumer claim' means a claim to which section 47A applies which an individual has in respect of an infringement affecting (directly or indirectly) goods or services to which subsection (7) applies.

(3) A consumer claim may be included in proceedings under this section if it is—
   (a) a claim made in the proceedings on behalf of the individual concerned by the specified body; or
   (b) a claim made by the individual concerned under section 47A which is continued in the proceedings on his behalf by the specified body;
   and such a claim may only be made or continued in the proceedings with the consent of the individual concerned.

(4) The consumer claims included in proceedings under this section must all relate to the same infringement.

(5) The provisions of section 47A(5) to (10) apply to a consumer claim included in proceedings under this section as they apply to a claim made in proceedings under that section.

(6) Any damages or other sum (not being costs or expenses) awarded in respect of a consumer claim included in proceedings under this section must be awarded to the individual concerned; but the Tribunal may, with the consent of the specified body and the individual, order that the sum awarded must be paid to the specified body (acting on behalf of the individual).

(7) This subsection applies to goods or services which—
   (a) the individual received, or sought to receive, otherwise than in the course of a business carried on by him (notwithstanding that he received or sought to receive them with a view to carrying on a business); and
   (b) were, or would have been, supplied to the individual (in the case of goods whether by way of sale or otherwise) in the course of a business carried on by the person who supplied or would have supplied them.

(8) A business includes—
   (a) a professional practice;
   (b) any other undertaking carried on for gain or reward;
   (c) any undertaking in the course of which goods or services are supplied otherwise than free of charge.

(9) 'Specified' means specified in an order made by the Secretary of State, in accordance with criteria to be published by the Secretary of State for the purposes of this section.

(10) An application by a body to be specified in an order under this section is to be made in a form approved by the Secretary of State for the purpose.

NOTE: There is provision in s. 47B for specifying appropriate consumer representative bodies for this purpose. The only specified body is Which? (The Consumers' Association), pursuant to Specified Body (Consumer Claims) Order 2005, SI 2005/2365. This section contains a fairly wide definition of consumer for these purposes and reading subsections (2) and (7) together indicates that this procedure may be utilized in respect of indirect purchasers, in contrast with the current position in the US set out in *Illinois Brick* v *State of Illinois* 431 US 720 (1977). See Petrucci, and Van Dijk and Niels, below.

Rodger, B., 'Private enforcement and the Enterprise Act: an exemplary system of awarding damages?'
[2003] ECLR 103 at 106 and 108 [footnotes omitted]

During the passage of the 1998 Act, the issue of a possible role for the CAT in damages actions was debated but ultimately rejected. The new proposal, four years after that debate, will allow monetary claims to be raised before the CAT, where there has been a finding of an infringement of the Ch.I or II prohibitions or Arts 81 and 82. The original version of the Enterprise Bill provided only for damages awards but this was revised to recognise the possibility of other forms of claims consequent upon competition law infringements. In addition, the Bill originally contained a provision in s.47A(3) stating that the CAT was to apply the same principles as a court would apply in awarding damages in respect of a claim in delict or tort, and although this was ultimately removed, the CAT will effectively operate as a court would in determining such claims in either principal legal system. This is reinforced by the amendment of s.49 of the 1998 Act to allow appeals to the appropriate court in respect of a CAT award under either s.47A or s.47B....

Consumer claims—the "Erin Brockovitch" provision

Section 19 adds s.47B to the 1998 Act and allows damages claims to be brought before the CAT by a specified body on behalf of two or more consumers who have claims in respect of the same infringement. The representative body requires the consent of the individuals to pursue their claims. Section 47B(6) sets out who constitute consumers for these purposes, and states that a consumer is an individual who received goods or services, or sought to receive them, otherwise than in the course of a business, notwithstanding that this was with a view to carrying on a business. In addition, the goods or services must be supplied to the individual in the course of a business. This is a fairly wide definition of consumer for these purposes and reading s.47B(2) and (7) together makes clear that this procedure may be utilised in respect of indirect purchasers. This provision is likely to facilitate "class actions" in relation to UK and EC competition law before the CAT and prima facie this is a welcome development which will enhance the deterrent effect of the law.

NOTE: There have been a number of follow-on claims raised before the CAT. There have been no final damages awards as yet, as many cases have settled, although the CAT awarded £2 million as an interim payment in *Healthcare at Home Ltd* v *Genzyme Ltd* [2006] CAT 29 before that case also settled. However, there has been one high-profile s. 47B claim, in the *Consumers' Association* v *JJB Sports plc*. The OFT, upheld by the CAT and Court of Appeal, decided that there had been an infringement of the Chapter I prohibition involving illegal resale price maintenance in relation to Manchester United and England shirts during 2000 and 2001. The price increase per replica shirt was approximately £15 and JJB and others were fined a considerable sum by the OFT. Ultimately, this action, with only 144 consumers party to the action, was settled on the basis of compensation of £20 for each replica kit purchase if receipts had been retained. The paucity of s. 47B claims is disappointing.

C: UK reform proposals

Despite the introduction of the Competition Act 1998, the specific facilitative provisions to encourage and facilitate follow-on damages actions be fore the CAT in the EA 2002, and evidence of a limited increase in the level of competition litigation in the UK, there are still a number of limitations and difficulties (See Kon, S., and Maxwell, A.J., 'Enforcement in National Courts of the EC and New UK Competition Rules: Obstacles to Effective Enforcement' [1998] ECLR 443), for instance in relation to the opt-in representative procedure in s. 47B. In particular, there has been no final award of damages by a UK court under the Act and questions relating to the range of potential claimants, remoteness of damages, and the quantification of damages remain unanswered. The OFT has been considering further steps to enhance levels of private enforcement in the UK.

Private actions in competition law: effective redress for
consumers and business
www.oft.gov.uk/shared_oft/reports/comp_policy/oft916resp.pdf

OFT, November 2007, at para. 1.2 [footnotes omitted]

1.2 The Paper recommends that Government consult on the following measures to make private actions in competition law as effective as *A World Class Competition Regime* (the 'White Paper') intended them to be. The measures should be designed and implemented in such a way as to comply with the principles outlined in the OFT's discussion paper, *Private actions in competition law: effective redress for consumers and business* (the 'Discussion Paper'), as supplemented in Chapter 4 below:

- Modifying existing procedures, or introducing new procedures, so as to allow representative bodies to bring standalone and follow-on representative actions for damages and applications for injunctions on behalf of consumers (named consumers or consumers at large)
- Modifying existing procedures, or introducing new procedures, so as to allow representative bodies to bring standalone and follow-on representative actions for damages and applications for injunctions on behalf of businesses (named businesses or businesses at large)
- Introducing CFAs in representative actions which allow for an increase of greater than 100 per cent on lawyers' fees
- Codifying courts' discretion to cap parties' costs liabilities and to provide for the courts' discretion to give the claimant cost protection in appropriate cases
- Establishing a merits-based litigation fund
- Requiring UK courts and tribunals to 'have regard' to UK NCAs' decisions and guidance
- Conferring a power on the Secretary of State to exclude leniency documents, appropriately defined, from use in litigation without the consent of the leniency applicant, and
- Conferring a power on the Secretary of State to remove joint and several liability for immunity recipients in private actions in competition law so that they are only liable for the harm they caused (or not liable at all in exceptional circumstances).

NOTE: The OFT proposals, published a few months before the Commission White Paper of April 2008, tackle a range of potential disincentives to potential litigants in relation to funding, costs, and representative actions, and are being considered by the Department for Business, Enterprise and Regulatory Reform ('BERR').

■ QUESTION

Why have there been so few follow-on actions raised before the CAT, particularly under the consumer representative action provision? To what extent would the OFT recommendations overcome the current limitations?

SECTION 6: **KEY THEMES**

This final section will outline aspects of the debate relating to certain themes which are key to incentivizing and facilitating private enforcement of Community and UK competition law: collective redress; funding litigation; passing-on and the indirect purchaser; and damages. Obviously there are other aspects of US litigation culture that are also important, but which will not be considered here, notably the liberal pre-trial discovery process providing claimants with access to swathes of documentation kept by the other party.

A: Collective redress

The Commission has made the following proposals in the White Paper:

White Paper, *Damages actions for breach of the EC antitrust rules*

http://ec.europa.eu/competition/antitrust/actionsdamages/files_white_paper/
whitepaper_en.pdf

COM(2008) 165 final, Brussels, 2 April 2008, at para. 2.1

With respect to **collective redress**, the Commission considers that there is a clear need for mechanisms allowing aggregation of the individual claims of victims of antitrust infringements. Individual consumers, but also small businesses, especially those who have suffered **scattered and relatively low-value damage**, are often deterred from bringing an individual action for damages by the costs, delays, uncertainties, risks and burdens involved. As a result, many of these victims currently **remain uncompensated**. At the rare occasions where a multitude of individual actions are brought in relation to the same infringement, **procedural inefficiencies** arise, for claimants, defendants and the judicial system alike.

The Commission therefore suggests a combination of two complementary mechanisms of collective redress to address effectively those issues in the field of antitrust:

- **representative actions**, which are brought **by qualified entities**, such as consumer associations, state bodies or trade associations, on behalf of identified or, in rather restricted cases, identifiable victims. These entities are either (i) officially designated in advance or (ii) certified on an *ad hoc* basis by a Member State for a particular antitrust infringement to bring an action on behalf of some or all of their members; and

- **opt-in collective actions**, in which victims **expressly decide** to combine their individual claims for harm they suffered into one single action. Considering that qualified entities will not be able or willing to pursue every claim, it is necessary that these two types of action **complement** each other to ensure effective collective redress for victims of antitrust infringements. In addition, it is important that victims are not deprived of their right to bring an individual action for damages if they so wish. However, safeguards should be put in place to avoid that the same harm is compensated more than once.

These suggestions on damages actions in the field of antitrust are part of the Commission's wider initiative to strengthen collective redress mechanisms in the EU and may develop further within this context.

NOTE: The proposals, if implemented, would introduce an opt-in procedure similar to that instituted by the EA 2002 in the UK. The experience of this procedure, as demonstrated by the JJB action, indicates its clear limitations, which the OFT has sought to overcome by its 2007 proposals which would extend the procedure to stand-alone actions and actions involving businesses. Most importantly, the OFT also recommended a mixed opt-in/opt-out procedure, which the UK Civil Justice Council has also recently advocated. (' "Improving Access to Justice Through Collective Actions" Developing a More Efficient and Effective Procedure for Collective Actions', Final Report, Nov 2008, Civil Justice Council.) Adoption of the US class action procedure has been considered to be inappropriate by both the EU and UK authorities.

Schnell, G., 'Class Action Madness in Europe—a Call for a More Balanced Debate'
[2007] ECLR 617 at pp. 618–619 [footnotes omitted]

A lopsided debate

The problem is that an unbridled fear of greedy lawyers and the class action abuse they can foster appears to be dominating the discussion in Europe. To most, it seems to be a foregone conclusion that the US class action model is broken, and that a so-called "litigation culture" runs rampant. The US system has thus become the poster-child for the anti-class action movement abroad. And, almost everyone appears to be signing on. They are doing so, however, without fully appreciating the vital role class actions play in US antitrust enforcement...

Even more troubling is that absent from the dialogue appears to be any recognition of the numerous antitrust class actions that have actually succeeded in remedying serious market deficiencies and bringing about wide-scale consumer relief. One such case, for example, is the action brought on behalf of five million merchants against Visa and MasterCard, challenging their exclusionary conduct in the debit card market. Over the six year life of the case, the plaintiffs spent roughly $18 million in costs and 250,000 hours of attorney time. Obviously, it was not a case brought lightly. The results were staggering—$3.4 billion in monetary damages and tens of billions of dollars more in reduced pricing. ....

There have been many other cases just like it. And there are surely many more to come.

Yet, not many are willing to include these important class action triumphs as part of the debate. They are either brushed aside as aberrations, or ignored altogether. This does not permit a fair assessment of the US system. Nor does it provide reliable direction to those in Europe looking to learn from the American experience (both the good and the bad).

If all of the recent talk in Europe about promoting private antitrust enforcement is for real, then there has to be a more balanced study of the US system. There has to be an understanding of the important role class actions play in American antitrust enforcement. There has to be an appreciation of the significant difficulty, risk and expense involved in bringing these kinds of cases—natural deterrents to frivolous filings. .... Only then can there be a truly meaningful discussion of what needs to be done in Europe to advance private antirust enforcement beyond the mere recovery of a few quid and a coffee mug for some overpriced football shirts.

NOTE: Schnell's critique is accurate, but it should be noted that the (opt-out) class action procedure would be inimical to the legal traditions, cultures, and procedures in the vast majority of Community Member States.

B: Funding litigation

The available funding mechanisms and costs rules can clearly act as a major incentive or disincentive to claimants and/or lawyers in relation to competition law claims. (See Riley, A., and Peysner, J., 'Damages in EC Antitrust actions: who pays the piper?' [2006] EL Rev 748; Peysner, J., 'Costs and Funding in private Third Party Competition Damages Actions' [2006] Comp L Rev 97) The English rule of cost-shifting, the likelihood of paying up-front costs and other side's costs if unsuccessful are major disincentives, compounded by the complexity and heavy costs involved in competition cases due to the economic and considerable documentary evidence required to advance a claim.

Riley, A., and Peysner, J., 'Damages in EC Antitrust actions: who pays the piper?'
[2006] EL Rev 748 [footnotes omitted]

There are two fundamental advantages of any contingency fee system. First, it provides significant access to justice for potential plaintiffs without the means to bring cases themselves and without calling on state resources. Secondly, by obtaining a slice of the damages lawyers are both incentivised to bring cases and can afford to take on costly time consuming and complex cases. Clearly lack of means and the complex nature of competition cases affects plaintiffs willingness to seek remedies and lawyers willingness to run such cases. A reformed contingency fee system could provide part of the solution to funding competition cases in Europe. It also has to be recognised that the principal criticisms of the contingency fee system in the USA, such as the overpayment of lawyers and the abusive use of non-cash payment systems are not central features of contingency fee systems per se. For example, it would be possible to limit contingency fee systems in the European Union to no more than 10 per cent of the value of the award (substantially less than up to 30 per cent in the USA); it would also be possible to restrict contingency fee awards to direct purchaser actions, which would have the effect of barring abusive non-cash awards. Again recognising the egregious nature of price fixing, contingency fees could again be limited to damages actions brought by victims of cartels where the cartel members have been subject to a Commission or NCA prohibition decision that has been subsequently judicially upheld.

While their political toxicity is acknowledged, contingency fees are definitively worth greater consideration even though they have not been included in the Green Paper, when the Commission is considering legislative options and recommendations to the Member States. Without a discussion of the major funding options there is a real question as to how far any other litigation reforms can work effectively. Even if all the most optimal reforms are adopted plaintiffs will still be facing paying out for heavy initial costs, and very severe fiscal sanctions if they lose. This will undoubtedly remain a major disincentive whatever other reforms are implemented. An alternative approach to contingency fees, which may not generate the same hostility, which works with the grain of European conceptions of solidarity and which is already operating in several jurisdictions worldwide, is the contingency legal aid fund, ("CLAF") which is discussed further below.

NOTE: Although conditional fee agreements involving a reward (success fee) to the winning lawyer recoverable from the loser, are available in England and Wales, and the potential costs of the other party can be insured against using ATE insurance, Peysner has suggested that 'there is no sign that they are being routinely offered by lawyers or litigation insurers in competition cases' (Peysner, J., 'Costs and Funding in private Third Party Competition Damages Actions' [2006] Comp L Rev 97). In the article above Riley and Peysner advocated the introduction of a Contingency Legal Aid Fund, and Peysner has also recognized that contingency fees would create greater incentives for lawyers than CFAs ([2006] Comp L Rev 97 at 100). Contingency fees have also recently been advocated by a research paper for the Civil Justice Council (Civil Justice Council, '"Improving Access to Justice" Contingency Fees, A Study of their operation in the United States of America: A research paper informing the Review of Costs', November 2008, Moorhead, R, Hurst, P). The OFT 2007 Recommendations include the introduction of CFAs in representative actions to allow for increases of greater than 100 per cent on lawyer's fees, codifying courts' discretion to cap cost liabilities, in addition to establishing a merits-based litigation fund.

C: Passing-on and indirect purchasers

These are two (related) issues relating to the broader question of who can sue for damages following alleged anti-competitive behaviour. Many cartels relate to homogenous raw materials that are incorporated in final products sold to consumers. The direct purchaser from a cartel member may have passed on the initial overcharge to subsequent purchasers by incorporating it in the price of the final product. Who should be able to sue the cartel members?

Petrucci, C., 'The Issues of the Passing-on Defence and Indirect Purchasers' Standing in European Competition Law'
[2008] ECLR 33 at p. 35 [footnotes omitted]

The US experience on the passing-on defence and the indirect purchasers' standing illuminates certain issues that the EU should take into account. In this regard, US federal law consists of three judgments. In Hanover Shoe Co v United Shoe Machinery Corp, the Supreme Court held that price-fixers cannot invoke the passing-on defence when sued by a direct purchaser.

In Illinois Brick Co v Illinois, the Supreme Court ruled that indirect purchasers are denied standing against price-fixers. Finally, with respect to the relationship between federal and state law, in California v ARC America Corp, the Supreme Court held that single states may enact statutes allowing indirect purchasers to recover damages. Illinois Brick sparked criticisms, since consumers, to whom the overcharge has been passed on, are injured, but they cannot sue price-fixers. Conversely, direct purchasers may sue price-fixers and be compensated even though they neutralised or mitigated the loss by passing on the overcharge (this is the so-called "windfall" to direct buyers).

In Illinois Brick, three main arguments justified denial of standing to indirect purchasers. First, allowing the offensive use of the passing-on—but not defensive passing-on—creates the risk of multiple liability. Secondly, allowing the passing-on defence requires the need to prove whether and how much an overcharged input has affected the price of a product incorporating that input. In most circumstances, this task is extremely difficult. Indeed, this argument justified denial of the passing-on defence in Hanover Shoe, and a fortiori, it justified denial of the offensive use of the passing-on in Illinois Brick. Thirdly, direct purchasers are better enforcers than indirect ones, i.e. concentrating the claim on the former is more effective than allowing both to bring proceedings.

NOTE: US federal antitrust law prevents defendants from alleging that claimants have passed on the overcharges to subsequent purchasers of their products and the corollary is that indirect purchasers may not sue for antitrust damages. The rationale is that the direct purchasers are more likely to sue for damages and this enhances the effectiveness and deterrent impact of the antitrust rules.

The Commission White Paper suggests a distinctive Community approach to these issues.

White Paper, *Damages actions for breach of the EC antitrust rules*
http://ec.europa.eu/competition/antitrust/actionsdamages/files_white_paper/whitepaper_en.pdf

COM(2008) 165 final, Brussels, 2 April 2008, para. 2.6 [footnotes omitted]

2.6. Passing-on overcharges
If the direct customer of the infringer fully or partially passed on the illegal overcharge to his own customers (the indirect purchasers), several legal issues can arise. At present, these create a great degree of legal uncertainty and difficulties in antitrust damages actions.

Problems arise, on the one hand, if the **infringer** invokes the passing-on of overcharges as a **defence** against a damages claimant, arguing that the claimant suffered no loss because he passed on the price increase to his customers.

The Commission recalls the Court's emphasis on the **compensatory principle** and its premise that **damages** should be **available to any injured person** who can show a sufficient causal link with the infringement. Against this background, infringers should be allowed to invoke the possibility that the overcharge might have been passed on. Indeed, to deny this defence could result in **unjust enrichment** of purchasers who passed on the overcharge and in undue **multiple compensation** for the illegal overcharge by the defendant. The Commission therefore suggests that:

- **defendants** should be **entitled to invoke the passing-on defence** against a claim for compensation of the overcharge. The standard of proof for this defence should be not lower than the standard imposed on the claimant to prove the damage.

Difficulties also arise, on the other hand, if an **indirect purchaser** invokes the passing-on of over-charges as a basis **to show the harm suffered**. Purchasers at, or near the end of the distribution chain are often those most harmed by antitrust infringements, but given their **distance from the infringement** they find it particularly difficult to produce sufficient proof of the existence and extent of passing-on of the illegal overcharge along the distribution chain. If such claimants are unable to produce this proof, they will **not be compensated** and the infringer, who may have successfully used the passing-on defence against another claimant upstream, would retain an **unjust enrichment**.

To avoid such scenario, the Commission therefore proposes to lighten the victim's burden and suggests that:

- indirect purchasers should be able to rely on the rebuttable presumption that the illegal overcharge was passed on to them in its entirety.

NOTE: The Commission's approach was inevitable, given the Court case law in *Crehan* and *Manfredi*, and the emphasis on the availability of effective remedies in relation to Community rights.

Van Dijk, R., and Niels, G., 'The Economics of Quantifying Damages'
[2002] 1 Comp LJ 69 [footnotes omitted]

Who should be allowed to claim damages?

Arguably, only a party that suffers an injury that competition law was designed to prevent should be allowed to claim damages. This principle might mean that not only the direct purchasers of the cartel's products should be able to claim damages, but also the indirect purchasers—ie the customers of the customers of the cartel—if the direct purchasers' increased costs have been passed on to them.

However, in the US, a Supreme Court decision of 1977 generally denied indirect buyers such rights. Thus, in a cartel case involving an input into a final consumer good, only the immediate down-stream producers of that final good are entitled to damages. End consumers are not allowed standing, even if the downstream producers fully pass on the cartel price increase to consumer prices.

The main economic rationale behind this decision is that direct buyers have greater incentives to sue.

...

End consumers might be able to sue as a class, but this has the potential disadvantage that, in the end, the damages awarded must be divided among a large number of parties. This reduces the incentives for individuals to take active part in the class action, and may induce free riding. Direct buyers are normally fewer in numbers, so there is less of a free-rider problem.

The above may reflect a difference in the design of the legal framework for damages ...in the EU damages are mainly intended to compensate victims, while the US Supreme Court's decision referred to above attached relatively more weight to the deterrence effect.

...

Conclusion

The number of private competition law litigation cases in the national courts in Europe is still small, especially when contrasted with the situation in the USA. However, awareness and understanding of competition law are growing among European businesses and consumers, and policy initiatives are being taken to further facilitate private actions.

Quantifying damages is therefore becoming increasingly important. Courts are required to scrutinise damages claims. They have to judge whether claims are based on sound counterfactual analysis—and no doubt a few affected parties will tend to exaggerate the profits they would have made absent the anti-competitive behaviour. In US antitrust law, the principles and methodologies behind damages claims are now reasonably established. The challenge is to further develop such expertise and case-law in the national courts of Europe.

NOTE: This demonstrates the close link between these two related issues and the final key theme: the type of damages which should be available for competition law breaches. US experience in quantifying damages will be instructive although it will be of less assistance in determining the types of remedies and range of potential claimants.

D: Damages

Probably the most notable feature of US antitrust litigation is the availability of treble damages: the claimant's loss is quantified and they are awarded three times that amount as damages. There was considerable debate about the possible introduction of rules providing for multiple damages following the Commission's Green Paper, but the Commission opted for a light-touch approach in the White Paper, with the promised publication of guidelines on quantification of damages.

White Paper, *Damages actions for breach of the EC antitrust rules*

http://ec.europa.eu/competition/antitrust/actionsdamages/files_white_paper/whitepaper_en.pdf

COM(2008) 165 final, Brussels, 2 April 2008, para. 2.6 [footnotes omitted]

To facilitate the calculation of damages, the Commission therefore intends:

- to draw up a framework with pragmatic, non-binding guidance for quantification of damages in antitrust cases, e.g. by means of approximate methods of calculation or simplified rules on estimating the loss.

The ECJ considered in *Manfredi* that national systems could provide for exemplary damages, an issue considered in the *Devenish* case.

Devenish Nutrition Ltd v *Sanofi Aventis SA (France)*

[2008] EWCA Civ 1086 (CA), paras 130–5

This was a post-*Vitamins* follow-on action in the High Court and concerned the preliminary issue of whether the claimant would be entitled to restitution of unjust enrichment and exemplary damages, although only the former issue was considered on appeal.

130. In my judgment, Community law does not prevent the making of a restitutionary award. I have already indicated that, if it were open to the Court to make such an award, it would be awarded only in exceptional circumstances that would not include the case such as this where a claimant in the position of Devenish (on the assumed facts) would in an appropriate case be able to prove its loss on conventional principles. There is no relevantly exceptional difficulty in this case in doing so. It is, therefore, unnecessary to go further into this Community law question for the purposes of this case. Provisionally, however, it seems to me that, if the award were permitted by domestic law to enable Devenish to recover profits made by the respondents where it had failed to show any harm, it would in my judgment be no more extensive a remedy than the punitive damages considered in *Manfredi*. If the award were in those circumstances available in domestic law, the principle of equivalence would apply. Since, if *Blake* applies, a restitutionary award could only be made in exceptional circumstances where the justice of the case required it, I do not consider that there is likely to arise any question of such an award offending the Community law principle that the claimant should not receive unjust enrichment.

131. In my judgment, Mr de la Mare's argument proceeds on the mistaken basis that a restitutionary award would require the respondents to account for profits on transactions where the overcharge was passed on. If the passing-on defence is available, then the profits to be accounted for would be adjusted accordingly (see above). If the passing-on defence is not available, but the subsequent purchasers have separate claims, issues of multiple liability arise in any event.

132. I do not need to deal with the further argument (based on *Van Colson*, referred to below, at [133]) that in considering the adequacy of remedies it uses to implement art 81 the court must have regard to the combined effect of both the civil remedy and the fine. I have already accepted above that the court needs to consider the impact of the fine. I do not read the jurisprudence cited to us as establishing that this court must refuse to grant a restitutionary remedy simply because the breach of regulatory rules is capable of resulting in a fine.

133. Mr de la Mare further submits that a remedy by way of a restitutionary award is impliedly excluded by the scheme of remedies provided by domestic law. He relies for this submission by analogy on cases such as *Deutsche Morgan Grenfell Group plc v IRC* [2007] 1 AC 558. This submission requires a detailed analysis of the domestic legislation. We were not taken to that legislation, as the submission was not fully pursued. In the circumstances, I do not consider that I need to deal with this submission.

134. The second question is whether the availability of a restitutionary award is necessary for the purposes of the effectiveness principle of Community law. Mr Vajda relies on Case 14/83 *Von Colson v Land Nordrhein-Westfalen* [1984] ECR 1891. This case concerned an application for damages pursuant to rights conferred by Directive 76/207/EEC for discrimination on the grounds of sex by a female applicant turned down for employment which was awarded to less qualified men. The Court of Justice held that, although the directive left member states free to choose between the different solutions suitable for achieving its objective if compensation for this kind of breach was awarded it must be "adequate in relation to the damage sustained". This compensation, therefore, had to be more than purely nominal compensation such as, for example, the reimbursement only of the expenses incurred in connection with the application.

135. *Van Colson* was decided in a completely different context. Even so, it is clear that the remedy under national law need be no more than "adequate in relation to the damage sustained". (Mr Hoskins cited Case 271/91 *Marshall* [1993] ECR 1-4367, but that decision does not take the matter materially further for this purpose). It is also clear from cases such as *Manfredi* that purely compensatory damages are sufficient for the purposes of safeguarding the rights of private persons under art 81. The doctrine of effectiveness is therefore directed to ensuring sufficient remedies rather than the fullest possible remedies. An action for compensatory damages fulfils the requirements of sufficiency. Accordingly I would dismiss the appeal on this ground.

136. As to the question of a reference for a preliminary ruling to the Court of Justice, I consider that there is no doubt about the answer to the last question and moreover I do not consider that it is appropriate to make a reference while the question of domestic law remains subject to a further appeal. If Devenish were to appeal and to be successful on appeal, a reference on the basis sought would have been unnecessary.

NOTE: The *Devenish* rulings at first instance and on appeal have emphasized that the UK courts will adopt a strictly compensatory approach and that there will be little scope for restitutionary, exemplary, or other forms of multiple damages awards. There has been an interim damages award by the CAT in *Healthcare at Home* v *Genzyme Ltd* [2006] CAT 29, but different approaches adopted at first instance and the Court of Appeal in *Crehan* to quantification and the trickier issue of the passing-on defence raised in some of the post-*Vitamins* CAT litigation remains unresolved, where the cases have ultimately settled.

■ **QUESTION**

What key changes should be made to facilitate and incentivize competition litigation? To what extent would these be feasible and likely to be adopted by the EU or UK authorities?

FURTHER READING

Bulst, F., 'Of Arms and Armour—The European Commission's White Paper on Damages Actions for Breach of EC Antitrust Law' [2008] Bucerius Law Journal 81.

Eilmansberger, T., 'The Green Paper on Damages for Breach of the EC Antitrust Rules and Beyond: Reflections on the Utility and Feasibility of Stimulating Private Enforcement Through Legislative Action' [2007] CML Rev 431.

Hodges, C., 'Competition Enforcement, Regulation and Civil Justice: What is the Case? [2006] CML Rev 1381.

Komninos, A., 'New Prospects for private enforcement of EC Competition Law: Courage v Crehan and the Community right to damages' [2002] CML Rev 447.

Komninos, A., 'Public and Private Antitrust Enforcement in Europe: Complement? Overlap?' [2006] 3 Comp Law Rev 5–26.

Kon, S., and Maxwell, A., 'Enforcement in National Courts of the EC and New UK Competition Rules: Obstacles to Effective Enforcement' [1998] ECLR 443.

Lande, R.H., and Davis, J.P., 'Benefits from Private Antitrust Enforcement: An Analysis of Forty Cases' (2008) 42 USFLR 879.

Nebbia, P., 'Damages Actions for the infringement of EC competition law: compensation or deterrence?' [2008] EL Rev 23.

Petrucci, C., 'The issues of the Passing-on Defence and Indirect Purchasers' Standing in European Competition Law' [2008] ECLR 33.

Riley, A., and Peysner, J., 'Damages in EC Antitrust actions: who pays the piper?' (2006) 31 EL Rev 748.

Wils, W.P.J., 'Should Private Antitrust Enforcement be Encouraged in Europe' (2003) 26(3) World Competition 473–488.

5

Competition law and policy in global markets

SECTION 1: **INTRODUCTION**

As competition law is concerned with the functioning of markets, the process of trade liberalization and globalization creates certain tension in cases with an international dimension because there is no international competition law, as yet. The lack of a developed system of international competition law has been countered by a combination of three approaches:

1. jurisdictions unilaterally applying domestic competition laws to the conduct of foreign undertakings (extraterritoriality);
2. bilateral cooperation between jurisdictions, for example between the US and the European Community, making it possible to investigate cases jointly, or at least to exchange information and provide investigatory assistance; and
3. multilateral engagement on key issues tending to give rise to conflict.

Traditionally, jurisdictions with 'developed' or mature competition authorities tend to rely more heavily on extraterritoriality than on the latter two, more cooperative approaches, yet the increasing number of competition law jurisdictions globally, and the growing expertise and experience of 'developing' regimes makes the unilateral approach to enforcement more difficult to sustain.

The 1990s marked a period of considerable growth in the number of jurisdictions with some form of competition law: many were former Soviet states in the process of implementing free market principles, and the continued enlargement of the European Union has also furthered this trend. Since 2000 there has been steady growth in both the number of jurisdictions with competition law, which now exceeds 100, and also the modernization of existing laws by enacting more stringent competition regimes. Countries including Brazil, South Africa, and South Korea now have respected competition regimes in place, and others such as China and India have passed significant competition laws. Within the context of more national enforcers and market globalization there is an obvious risk of substantial disharmony between legal systems. The position is aptly described by the US First Circuit Court of Appeals as follows: 'We live in an age of international commerce, where decisions reached in one corner of the world can reverberate around the globe in less time than it takes to tell the tale' (*United States* v *Nippon Paper Industries Co* 109 F 3d (1st Cir, 1997)). Competition law is no exception to this trend.

Noonan, C., *The Emerging Principles of International Competition Law*
Oxford, Oxford University Press, 2008, at pp. 8–10

Markets are becoming increasingly international through lower transportation costs, new information and communication technologies, reduced trade and investment barriers, and less state direction and ownership of the means of production and distribution of services. The increasingly internationalization of business activity is measurable in terms of trade and investment flows, trade and investment treaties, state-owned enterprises privatized, and industries deregulated.

...

Since the 1980s, internationalization has gone beyond exporting and foreign investment. Corporations now interact on a global scale through a wide range of external alliances, including joint ventures, subcontracting and licensing agreements, and looser strategic alliances.

...

Globalization has also changed the structure of national and international markets. When one firm seeks to achieve a competitive advantage through a cross-border acquisition or alliance, its competitors often feel compelled to do likewise. Industries may then become globally concerned in relatively short time periods. The high global concentration of many important industries suggest that trade and investment liberalization, as well as increased market size and lower barriers to entry, has not eliminated the possibility of harmful anticompetitive conduct.

International business activity has increased in importance relative to domestic business activity and is taking an increasingly wide range of forms. The growth in international business activity means than an increasing number of competition law cases will have an international element. The business practices that will be the subject of international competition law cases will include virtually all the types of conduct that could be the subject of a domestic competition law case. International competition law problems have already arisen in a wide variety of cases, ranging from international cartels that raise prices to consumers in many countries to exclusionary conduct and distribution agreements that deny access to foreign markets to international mergers and acquisitions subject to approval by many competition authorities.

NOTE: The 'increasingly internationalization of business activity', alongside the growth of competition regimes presents considerable challenges for all competition authorities and the business community. Competition authorities attempt to address these challenges by a combination of the three approaches outlined above, and this chapter will consider each of these in turn.

SECTION 2: EXTRATERRITORIALITY

A: Position in the United States

Extraterritoriality is controversial because it implies an infringement of a state's territorial sovereignty. The US developed the notion of extraterritorial application of antitrust at a period in time when few countries had competition rules. The discussion begins with Judge Learned Hand's famous exposition of the 'effects doctrine' in *Alcoa*.

United States v Aluminium Co of America
148 F 2d 416 (2nd Cir, 1945)

The US Department of Justice brought an action against a Canadian corporation that allegedly conspired with Alcoa in 1931 and 1936 to restrain commerce in the manufacture and sale of virgin aluminium ingot. The alleged conspiracy was effected entirely outside the United States. The court had to consider whether the conduct complained of violated s. 1 of the Sherman Act. The key passages are highlighted in italic.

The answer does not depend upon whether we shall recognize as a source of liability a liability imposed by another state. On the contrary we are concerned only with whether Congress chose to attach liability to the conduct outside the United States of persons not in allegiance to it. That being so, the only question open is whether Congress intended to impose the liability, and whether our own Constitution permitted it to do so: as a court of the United States, we cannot look beyond our own law. Nevertheless, it is quite true that we are not to read general words, such as those in this Act, without regard to the limitations customarily observed by nations upon the exercise of their powers; limitations which generally correspond to those fixed by the 'Conflict of Laws'. We should not impute to Congress an intent to punish all whom its courts can catch, for conduct which has no consequences within the United States. *American Banana Co.* v *United Fruit Co.*, 213 US 347, 357, 29 S. Ct. 511, 53 L. Ed. 826, 16 Ann. Cas. 1047; *United States* v *Bowman*, 260 US 94, 98, 43 S. Ct. 39, 67 L. Ed. 149; *Blackmer* v *United States*, 284 US 421, 437, 52 S. Ct. 252, 76 L. Ed. 375. *On the other hand, it is settled law ... that any state may impose liabilities, even upon persons not within its allegiance, for conduct outside its borders that has consequences within its borders which the state reprehends; and these liabilities other states will ordinarily recognize.* Strassheim v Daily, 221 US 280, 284, 285, 31 S. Ct. 558, 55 L. Ed. 735; *Lamar* v *United States*, 240 US 60, 65, 66, 36 S. Ct. 255, 60 L. Ed. 526, *Ford* v *United States*, 273 US 593, 620, 621, 47 S. Ct. 531, 71 L. Ed. 793; Restatement of Conflict of Laws Sec. 65. It may be argued that this Act extends further. Two situations are possible. There may be agreements made beyond our borders not intended to affect imports, which do affect them, or which affect exports. Almost any limitation of the supply of goods in Europe, for example, or in South America, may have repercussions in the United States if there is trade between the two. Yet when one considers the international complications likely to arise from an effort in this country to treat such agreements as unlawful, it is safe to assume that Congress certainly did not intend the Act to cover them. Such agreements may on the other hand intend to include imports into the United States, and yet it may appear that they had no effect upon them. That situation might be thought to fall within the doctrine that intent may be a substitute for performance in the case of a contract made within the United States; or it might be thought to fall within the doctrine that a statute should not be interpreted to cover acts abroad which have no consequence here. We shall not choose between these alternatives; but for argument we shall assume that the Act does not cover agreements, even though intended to affect imports or exports, unless its performance is shown actually to have had some effect upon them. Where both conditions are satisfied, the situation certainly falls within such decisions as *United States* v *Pacific & Artic R. & Navigation Co.*, 228 US 87, 33 S. Ct. 443, 57 L. Ed. 742; *Thomsen* v *Cayser*, 243 US 66, 37 S. Ct. 353, 61 L. Ed. 597, Ann. Cas. 1917D, 322 and *United States* v *Sisal Sales Corporation*, 274 US, 268, 47 S. Ct. 592, 71 L. Ed. 1042. (*United States* v *Nord Deutcher Lloyd*, 223 US, 512, 32 S. Ct. 244, 56 L. Ed. 531, illustrates the same conception in another field.) It is true that in those cases the persons held liable had sent agents into the United States to perform part of the agreement; but an agent is merely an animate means of executing his principal's purposes, and, for the purposes of this case, he does not differ from an inanimate means; besides, only human agents can import and sell ingot.

Both agreements would clearly have been unlawful, had they been made within the United States; and it follows from what we have just said that both were unlawful, though made abroad, if they were intended to affect imports and did affect them. Since the shareholders almost at once agreed that the agreement of 1931 should not cover imports, we may ignore it and confine our discussion to that of 1936: indeed that we should have to do anyway, since it superseded the earlier agreement. The judge found that it was not the purpose of the agreement to 'suppress or restrain the exportation of aluminum to the United States for sale in competition with '*Alcoa*'. By that we understand that he meant that the agreement was not specifically directed to '*Alcoa*', because it only applied generally to the production of the shareholders. If he meant that it was not expected that the general restriction upon production would have an effect upon imports, we cannot agree, for the change made in 1936 was deliberate and was expressly made to accomplish just that. It would have been an idle gesture, unless the shareholders had supposed that it would, or at least might, have that effect. The first of the conditions which we mentioned was therefore satisfied; the intent was to set up a quota system for imports.

NOTE: Not surprisingly, the legal basis for this doctrine is contentious and traditional public international law principles of jurisdiction based on nationality or territorial grounds have limited value.

Timberlane Lumber Co v *Bank of America*
549 F 2d 597 (9th Cir, 1976)

The effects doctrine was subject to ongoing refinement in the US courts following *Alcoa*, although inconsistent views were held on the weight to attach to the interests of foreign jurisdictions. The Ninth Circuit Court of Appeals considered these issues in the context of a private action brought by US firm Timberlane against firms it alleged were conspiring to foreclose the Honduran timber market, one of its target export markets.

that American law covers some conduct beyond this nation's borders does not mean that it embraces all, however. Extraterritorial application is understandably a matter of concern for the other countries involved. Those nations have sometimes resented and protested, as excessive intrusions into their own spheres, broad assertions of authority by American courts...Our courts have recognized this concern and have, at times, responded to it, even if not always enough to satisfy all the foreign critics...In any event, it is evident that at some point the interests of the United States are too weak and the foreign harmony incentive for restraint too strong to justify an extraterritorial assertion of jurisdiction.

NOTE: This so-called 'jurisdictional rule of reason' rests on the premise that the US has jurisdiction but should choose not to exercise it in certain circumstances. This approach gained support in other US courts, but not all. The Third, Fifth, and Tenth Circuits' Court of Appeals appeared to endorse the *Timberlane* rule of reason, yet the D.C. and Seventh Circuits followed an approach comparable with Alcoa.

Hawk, B.E., 'The Sherman Act: The Second Century: The International Application of The Sherman Act in its Second Century'
(1990) 59 Antitrust LJ 161

Three distinct periods mark the expansion of Sherman Act international jurisdiction during the first century. First, from 1909 to 1945, there was a gradual erosion of *American Banana's* narrow interpretation of the Sherman Act as limited to the territory of the United States. The second period began in 1945 when Learned Hand announced the effects doctrine in *Alcoa*, which evolved into the standard under which the Sherman Act applies to foreign conduct having a direct and substantial effect on U.S. import, export, or domestic commerce. There was considerable foreign reaction in the form of diplomatic protests and blocking statutes to application of the Sherman Act to reach essentially foreign conduct and parties based on the effects doctrine. Partly in response to that foreign reaction, Judge Choy ushered in the third period in 1976 when he announced in *Timberlane* that effect on U.S. commerce is a necessary but not sufficient condition for antitrust jurisdiction, and that, in addition, comity requires a balancing of foreign and U.S. interests before a court can exercise antitrust jurisdiction. That is the period we are now in. However, all courts have not followed *Timberlane*, and the jury is still out on the question whether *Timberlane* and its balancing of interests in addition to effects will survive.

NOTE: Hawk also suggested that the 'purported balancing of US and foreign interests à la conflict of laws analysis and *Timberlane* will eventually be rejected'. This prediction was borne out when the matter arose before the US Supreme Court in 1993 in *Hartford Fire*, but not before the US Congress intervened in the ongoing judicial debate with the Foreign Trade Antitrust Improvement Act ('FTAIA') of 1982. The FTAIA provided that the Sherman Act would only apply if the foreign conduct 'has a direct, substantial, and reasonably foreseeable effect on domestic trade or commerce' (§ 402 of the FTAIA, 15 USC §6a).

Hartford Fire Ins Co v *California*
509 US 764 (1993)

Nineteen states and numerous private plaintiffs brought actions under s. 1 of the Sherman Act 1890 against domestic insurers and domestic and foreign reinsurers of general commercial liability. The plaintiffs alleged that the insurance companies, acting in the UK, had collaborated in refusing commercial liability reinsurance coverage for US lawyers except on terms agreed amongst themselves. The London defendants denied they had entered into any anti-competitive agreements and further that they acted in accordance with UK law and moved to dismiss. Lowenfield discusses the Court's ruling:

Lowenfield, A.F., 'Conflict, Balancing of Interests, and the Exercise of Jurisdiction to Prescribe: Reflections on the *Insurance Antitrust* Case'
(1995) 89 AJIL 42

The English defendants did not deny that their actions had effects in the United States—indeed, direct and substantial effects. They argued, however, that their conduct was legal in the state where it took place; that they had operated in full compliance with a regime of regulation and self-regulation as prescribed by the British Parliament; and that under principles of international law and comity, as spelled out particularly in two major decisions of US courts of appeals—*Timberlane Lumber Co* v *Bank of America* and *Mannington Mills, Inc* v *Congoleum Corp*—as well as two generations of the Restatement of the Foreign Relations Law of the United States, jurisdiction to apply US law should not be exercised in this case.

In the much-discussed *Timberlane* case, it will be recalled, Judge Choy had written that the 'effects doctrine' as formulated by Judge Learned Hand in *Alcoa* is incomplete, because it fails to consider the interests of other nations in the application or non-application of United States law. Judge Choy had proposed a three-part test: first, to see if the challenged conduct had had some effect on the commerce of the United States—the mininum contact to support application of US law; second, to see if a greater showing could be made that the conduct in question imposed a burden or restraint on US commerce—i.e. whether the complaint stated a claim under the anti-trust laws; and third, to consider 'the additional question which is unique to the international setting of whether the interests of, and links to, the United States . . . are sufficiently strong, vis-à-vis those of other nations, to justify an assertion of extraterritorial authority.

Judge Choy then proceeded to set out seven factors by which to judge the third or 'ought to' question, based on a list of factors proposed some years earlier by Professor Kingman Brewster. Other courts and the Restatement (Third) modified the criteria somewhat, but for the most part adopted the approach of the *Timberlane* case.

In *Insurance Antitrust*, the federal district court in San Francisco and the US Court of Appeals for the Ninth Circuit both considered the international aspect of the case in the light of *Timberlane*, and in particular in the light of the list of factors set out in that case by Judge Choy. Judge Schwarzer in the district court dismissed the action, on the basis that the conflict with English law and policy which would result from the extra-territorial application of the [US] antitrust laws in this case is not outweighed by other factors'. Judge Noonan, for the court of appeals, going through the same factors, acknowledged the 'significant conflict' with English law and policy, but held that the conflict was outweighed by the 'significance of the effects on American commerce, their foreseeability and their purposefulness'. Accordingly, the Court of Appeals reinstated the action. Thus, when the Supreme Court granted review, much of the argument on the international aspect of the case focused on the relative importance under *Timberlane* of conduct—clearly in England, versus effect—largely in the United States. Since both lower courts had accepted that there was a conflict between US and English law, not much argument focused on defining the conflict. In the Supreme Court, however, it was precisely the existence or nonexistence of conflict that divided the majority and the dissent…

Justice David Souter, for the majority of five, wrote: 'The only substantial question in this case is whether there is in fact a true conflict between domestic and foreign law'.

Justice Souter went on to acknowledge the argument of the London reinsurers, supported by the British Government, that applying the Sherman Act to their conduct would conflict significantly with British law. But British law did not require the agreements that were the basis of the challenge under the Sherman Act. All that British law did was to establish a regulatory—and largely self-regulatory—regime with which the challenged conduct was consistent. '[T]his,' said Justice Souter, citing the Restatement, 'is not to state a conflict…No conflict exists, for these purposes, where a person subject to regulation by two states can comply with the laws of both'.

…For the moment, I want to point out only that Justice Souter's opinion seems to equate 'conflict' with 'foreign compulsion'. For conflict, that is for inconsistent interests of states, *Timberlane* taught that one should evaluate or balance; for foreign compulsion, in contrast, we had understood since the *Nylon* and *Light Bulb* cartel cases of the early 1950s that no person would be required to do an act in another state that is prohibited by the law of that state or would be prohibited from doing an act in another state that is required by the law of that state; in other words, that the territorial preference would make balancing unnecessary. But Justice Souter said nothing about the controversial subject of balancing—either for or against—and barely mentioned *Timberlane*. 'We have no need in this case,' he concluded, 'to address other considerations that might inform a decision to refrain from the exercise of jurisdiction on grounds of international comity'.

To Justice Scalia and the four-person minority, the case looked entirely different. Justice Scalia started with two presumptions: first, that legislation of Congress, unless a contrary intent appears, 'is meant to apply only within the territorial jurisdiction of the United States'; and second, that 'an act of congress ought never to be construed to violate the law of nations if any other possible construction remains', a quotation going back to Chief Justice Marshall, and that customary international law includes limitations on a nation's exercise of its jurisdiction to prescribe. The first point, of course, begs the question about whether one looks at conduct—here in London—or effect— here in the United States. If one looks at effect, then application of the Sherman Act would not be extraterritorial. In any event, Justice Scalia conceded that there were numerous precedents for application of the Sherman Act to conduct outside the United States. The second point, about customary international law, led Justice Scalia right to the series of court of appeals decisions from *Alcoa* to *Timberlane* and *Mannington Mills*, plus decisions by the US Supreme Court in a series of seamen's cases cited to the Court by the English defendants, as well as the Restatement. 'Whether the Restatement precisely reflects international law in every detail matters little here,' he wrote, 'as I believe this case would be resolved the same way under virtually any conceivable test that takes account of foreign regulatory interests'. Justice Scalia went through the approach of the Restatement, including the factors set out in section 403(2). 'Rarely,' he concluded, perhaps exaggerating in order to emphasize his difference from the majority, 'would these factors point more clearly against application of United States law'.

Further, on the conclusion by the majority that a true conflict would exist only if compliance with US law would constitute violation of the other state's law, Justice Scalia wrote: 'That breathtakingly broad proposition, which contradicts the many cases discussed earlier, will bring the Sherman Act and other laws into sharp and unnecessary conflict with the legitimate interests of other countries—particularly our closest trading partners'.

NOTE: *Hartford Fire* helps to highlight distinct views regarding the concept of comity. The first approach is to consider comity as an element in determining jurisdiction: i.e. if a court should decline to hear a particular case on the grounds of comity, then the court would lack subject matter jurisdiction. The balancing of interests test in *Timberlane* reflects this approach, and was endorsed by Scalia J's dissent in *Hartford Fire*. The second basic approach is to contend that comity is a matter of discretion, normally in the hands of the judge and thus only a consideration once subject matter jurisdiction has been seized. This latter approach was adopted by the Seventh Circuit Court of Appeals in *Re: Uranium Antitrust Litigation* 617 F 2d 1248 and was endorsed by Souter J writing for the majority in *Hartford Fire*, when he concluded that a court should only be forced to decline to exercise jurisdiction on the grounds of international comity when compliance with both sets of laws is impossible.

United States v *Nippon Paper Industries Co*
109 F 3d (1st Cir, 1997)

An indictment served on Nippon Paper alleged that its predecessor met with various co-conspirators on a number of occasions in 1990 to discuss increasing prices of jumbo roll thermal fax paper to be sold in the US and Canada. Although the meetings took place in Japan, the effects of the agreement to increase prices had a substantial adverse effect on commerce in the United States and unreasonably restrained trade in violation of s. 1 of the Sherman Act. Nippon Paper argued in its defence that 'if the alleged conduct occurred at all, it took place entirely in Japan, and thus the indictment failed to limit an offense under Section One of the Sherman Act'. The Court concluded that s. 1 of the Sherman Act used precisely the same language to identify criminal conduct as it used to delineate conduct violative of civil law, provided the conduct produced substantial and intended effects within the United States. The Court then rejected arguments that it should refrain from exercising jurisdiction on the basis of international comity on the basis that a nation's decision to prosecute wholly foreign conduct is discretionary.

> we see no tenable reason why principles of comity should shield [the defendant] from prosecution. We live in an age of international commerce, where decisions reached in one corner of the world can reverberate around the globe in less time than it takes to tell the tale. Thus, a ruling in [the defendant's] favor would create perverse incentives for those who would use nefarious means to influence markets in the United States, rewarding them for enacting as many territorial firewalls as possible between cause and effect.

NOTE: The Supreme Court established that antitrust actions predicated on foreign conduct, which has an intended and substantial effect in the US, fall within the jurisdictional ambit of the Sherman Act, thereby exposing foreign nationals and companies to significant fines and imprisonment. In 1995, the Department of Justice and Federal Trade Commission (the Agencies) jointly issued Antitrust Enforcement Guidelines for International Operations. The Guidelines indicate that the Agencies will evaluate the laws and policies of foreign nations before they take any action, but where the United States antitrust enforcement mechanism is in a 'better position' to address the 'competitive problem', the DOJ and FTC will handle the situation (s. 3.2). The Guidelines clearly reflect the expansionist approach adopted by Congress and the Supreme Court in *Hartford Fire*. See Brockbank, D., 'The 1995 International Antitrust Guidelines: The Reach of US Antitrust Law Continues to Expand' 2 Journal of Intl Legal Studies 1.

Hoffmann-La Roche Ltd v *Empagran SA*
542 US (2004), 124 S Ct 2359, 159 L Ed 2d 226.

In litigation associated with the worldwide vitamins cartel, the claimants (Empagran and other non-US distributors who had purchased vitamins from the cartel) sought to bring a private damages action in US courts against vitamins manufacturers for losses sustained as a result of the cartel's conduct outside the United States. The only US connection was that Hoffmann-La Roche and other manufacturers had reached a settlement with the Department of Justice and US purchasers for Sherman Act liability arising out of the cartel's effect on US commerce. The Supreme Court reviewed a ruling by the D.C. Court of Appeals that granted jurisdiction. The case required the Court to consider the interpretation of the FTAIA, and several countries submitted amicus curiae briefs arguing against the expansive interpretation of jurisdiction.

Brief of the UK, Ireland and the Netherlands as Amici Curiae in support of Petitioners

The decision below would permit United States courts to hear private claims by foreign plaintiffs seeking redress for antitrust injuries allegedly suffered by them in Australia, Ecuador, Panama and Ukraine from sales of vitamins there and in other foreign countries by foreign sellers. These injuries do not arise from any contacts or relationships with plaintiffs in the United States. The argument that treble damages for foreign injuries can be recovered in a United States court because the conduct at issue also resulted in injuries to *other* parties who made purchases in the United States is a complete *non sequitur*. These unrelated injuries were the basis for other private actions in United States courts and have been fully compensated. In addition, such a rule potentially would permit virtually any significant commercial transaction to be the basis for private United States treble damage claims, usurping the enforcement systems of other countries to United States private actions.

This decision would provide substantial encouragement for widespread forum shopping, might impede competition law enforcement programs in the United Kingdom, Ireland and the Netherlands as well as the European Community, and would undermine respect for national sovereignty. The court of appeals' ruling has the potential for generating needless friction between foreign and United States legal systems and could lead to less, not more, cooperation and coordination of competition laws by all nations. It would wrongly expand the extraterritorial reach of the United States antitrust laws beyond this Court's or, to our knowledge, any foreign court's exercise of jurisdiction. International law principles recognize that a nation may prescribe laws and adjudicate claims beyond its own territory only where its assertion of jurisdiction does not infringe the rights of other nations to determine the law applicable to conduct within their own territories.

NOTE: The US Department of Justice also submitted an amicus curiae brief to the Supreme Court, arguing that permitting foreign claimants to seek redress for foreign injuries in US courts would significantly harm the relationships with key trading partners and hamper international antitrust enforcement activities. In a unanimous ruling written by Breyer J the Supreme Court reversed the Court of Appeals' decision.

First, this Court ordinarily construes ambiguous statutes to avoid unreasonable interference with the sovereign authority of other nations … This rule of construction reflects principles of customary international law—law that (we must assume) Congress ordinarily seeks to follow …

This rule of statutory construction cautions courts to assume that legislators take account of the legitimate sovereign interests of other nations when they write American laws. It thereby helps the potentially conflicting laws of different nations work together in harmony—a harmony particularly needed in today's highly interdependent commercial world.

No one denies that America's antitrust laws, when applied to foreign conduct, can interfere with a foreign nation's ability independently to regulate its own commercial affairs. But our courts have long held that application of our antitrust laws to foreign anticompetitive conduct is nonetheless reasonable, and hence consistent with principles of prescriptive comity, insofar as they reflect a legislative effort to redress domestic antitrust injury that foreign anticompetitive conduct has caused. See *United States* v. *Aluminum Co. of America*, 148 F.2d 416, 443—444 (CA2 1945) (L. Hand, J.); 1 P. Areeda & D. Turner, Antitrust Law 236 (1978).

But why is it reasonable to apply those laws to foreign conduct insofar as that conduct causes independent foreign harm and that foreign harm alone gives rise to the plaintiff's claim? Like the former case, application of those laws creates a serious risk of interference with a foreign nation's ability independently to regulate its own commercial affairs. But, unlike the former case, the justification for that interference seems insubstantial. See Restatement §403(2) (determining reasonableness on basis of such factors as connections with regulating nation, harm to that nation's interests, extent to which other nations regulate, and the potential for conflict). Why should American law supplant, for example, Canada's or Great Britain's or Japan's own determination about how best to protect Canadian or British or Japanese customers from anticompetitive conduct engaged in significant part by Canadian or British or Japanese or other foreign companies?

We recognize that principles of comity provide Congress greater leeway when it seeks to control through legislation the actions of American companies, see Restatement §402; and some of the anticompetitive price-fixing conduct alleged here took place in America. But the higher foreign prices of which the foreign plaintiffs here complain are not the consequence of any domestic anticompetitive conduct that Congress sought to forbid, for Congress did not seek to forbid any such conduct insofar as it is here relevant, i.e., insofar as it is intertwined with foreign conduct that causes independent foreign harm. Rather Congress sought to release domestic (and foreign) anticompetitive conduct from Sherman Act constraints when that conduct causes foreign harm. Congress, of course, did make an exception where that conduct also causes domestic harm. See House Report 13 (concerns about American firms' participation in international cartels addressed through "domestic injury" exception). But any independent domestic harm the foreign conduct causes here has, by definition, little or nothing to do with the matter.

We thus repeat the basic question: Why is it reasonable to apply this law to conduct that is significantly foreign insofar as that conduct causes independent foreign harm and that foreign harm alone gives rise to the plaintiff's claim? We can find no good answer to the question.

The Areeda and Hovenkamp treatise notes that under the Court of Appeals' interpretation of the statute

"a Malaysian customer could...maintain an action under United States law in a United States court against its own Malaysian supplier, another cartel member, simply by noting that unnamed third parties injured [in the United States] by the American [cartel member's] conduct would also have a cause of action. Effectively, the United States courts would provide worldwide subject matter jurisdiction to any foreign suitor wishing to sue its own local supplier, but unhappy with its own sovereign's provisions for private antitrust enforcement, provided that a different plaintiff had a cause of action against a different firm for injuries that were within U.S. [other-than-import] commerce. It does not seem excessively rigid to infer that Congress would not have intended that result." P. Areeda & H. Hovenkamp, Antitrust Law ¶273, pp. 51—52 (Supp. 2003).

We agree with the comment. We can find no convincing justification for the extension of the Sherman Act's scope that it describes.

Respondents reply that many nations have adopted antitrust laws similar to our own, to the point where the practical likelihood of interference with the relevant interests of other nations is minimal. Leaving price fixing to the side, however, this Court has found to the contrary. See, e.g., Hartford Fire, 509 U.S. at 797—799 (noting that the alleged conduct in the London reinsurance market, while illegal under United States antitrust laws, was assumed to be perfectly consistent with British law and policy); see also, e.g., 2 W. Fugate, Foreign Commerce and the Antitrust Laws §16.6 (5th ed. 1996) (noting differences between European Union and United States law on vertical restraints).

Regardless, even where nations agree about primary conduct, say price fixing, they disagree dramatically about appropriate remedies. The application, for example, of American private treble-damages remedies to anticompetitive conduct taking place abroad has generated considerable controversy. See, e.g., 2 ABA Section of Antitrust Law, Antitrust Law Developments 1208—1209 (5th ed. 2002). And several foreign nations have filed briefs here arguing that to apply our remedies would unjustifiably permit their citizens to bypass their own less generous remedial schemes, thereby upsetting a balance of competing considerations that their own domestic antitrust laws embody....

These briefs add that a decision permitting independently injured foreign plaintiffs to pursue private treble-damages remedies would undermine foreign nations' own antitrust enforcement policies by diminishing foreign firms' incentive to cooperate with antitrust authorities in return for prosecutorial amnesty. Brief for Federal Republic of Germany et al. as *Amici Curiae* 28—30; Brief for Government of Canada as *Amicus Curiae* 11—14. See also Brief for United States as *Amicus Curiae* 19—21 (arguing the same in respect to American antitrust enforcement).

Respondents alternatively argue that comity does not demand an interpretation of the FTAIA that would exclude independent foreign injury cases *across the board*. Rather, courts can take (and sometimes have taken) account of comity considerations case by case, abstaining where comity considerations so dictate. Cf., e.g., *Hartford Fire*, supra, at 797, n. 24; *United States* v. *Nippon Paper Industries Co.*, 109 F.3d 1, 8 (CA1 1997); *Mannington Mills, Inc.* v. *Congoleum Corp.*, 595 F.2d 1287, 1294—1295 (CA3 1979).

In our view, however, this approach is too complex to prove workable. The Sherman Act covers many different kinds of anticompetitive agreements. Courts would have to examine how foreign law, compared with American law, treats not only price fixing but also, say, information-sharing agreements, patent-licensing price conditions, territorial product resale limitations, and various forms of joint venture, in respect to both primary conduct and remedy. The legally and economically technical nature of that enterprise means lengthier proceedings, appeals, and more proceedings—to the point where procedural costs and delays could themselves threaten interference with a foreign nation's ability to maintain the integrity of its own antitrust enforcement system. Even in this relatively simple price-fixing case, for example, competing briefs tell us (1) that potential treble-damage liability would help enforce widespread anti-price-fixing norms (through added deterrence) and (2) the opposite, namely that such liability would hinder antitrust enforcement (by reducing incentives to enter amnesty programs). Compare, e.g., Brief for Certain Professors of Economics as *Amici Curiae* 2—4 with Brief for United States as *Amicus Curiae* 19—21. How could a court seriously interested in resolving so empirical a matter—a matter potentially related to impact on foreign interests—do so simply and expeditiously?

We conclude that principles of prescriptive comity counsel against the Court of Appeals' interpretation of the FTAIA. Where foreign anticompetitive conduct plays a significant role and where foreign injury is independent of domestic effects, Congress might have hoped that America's antitrust laws, so fundamental a component of our own economic system, would commend themselves to other nations as well. But, if America's antitrust policies could not win their own way in the international marketplace for such ideas, Congress, we must assume, would not have tried to impose them, in an act of legal imperialism, through legislative fiat.

NOTE: The decision is significant as the issue of where damages can be sought in an era of globalization was at stake, and permitting Empagran's claim would encourage other foreign litigants who suffer harm outside the US to seek damages in US courts. Foreign litigants are attracted to the US by the prospect of treble damages awards, broad rules of discovery, and contingency fees, and this type of forum shopping would have renewed tension as a result of the further extraterritorial application of US antitrust law. The US Supreme Court left open the possibility that Empagran could bring its claim if the harm it suffered outside the US was inseparable from the harm suffered by US purchasers, but the D.C. Court of Appeals rejected Empagran's argument on this point in a subsequent case, *Empagran SA* v *F Hoffmann-La Roche Ltd* 417 F 3d 1267 (DC Cir, 2005).

Not surprisingly, foreign governments have protested strongly against US assertions of extraterritorial jurisdiction, although the importance of this issue has significantly diminished as more jurisdictions adopt competition laws and/or more effective regimes are put in place. For an account see, e.g. Griffin, J.P., 'Foreign Governmental Reactions to US Assertions of Extraterritorial Jurisdiction' [1998] ECLR 64. Besides the usual diplomatic exchanges, some countries also enacted 'blocking' statutes to impede discovery outside the US or render certain types of US antitrust judgment unenforceable in foreign courts. The British Secretary of State for Trade, in introducing the Protection of Trading Interests Bill in 1979, stated that the objective of the law was 'to reassert and reinforce the defences of the United Kingdom against attempts by other countries to enforce their economic and commercial policies unilaterally on us'. Thus, the legislation applies to any activity that may harm the commercial interests of the UK and is not confined to competition matters.

PROTECTION OF TRADING INTERESTS ACT 1980

Overseas measures affecting United Kingdom trading interests

1.—(1) If it appears to the Secretary of State—

    (a) that measures have been or are proposed to be taken by or under the law of any overseas country for regulating or controlling international trade; and

    (b) that those measures, in so far as they apply or would apply to things done or to be done outside the territorial jurisdiction of that country by persons carrying on business in the United Kingdom, are damaging or threaten to damage the trading interests of the United Kingdom,

    the Secretary of State may by order direct that this section shall apply to those measures either generally or in their application to such cases as may be specified in the order.

  (2) The Secretary of State may by order make provision for requiring, or enabling the Secretary of State to require, a person in the United Kingdom who carries on business there to give notice to the Secretary of State of any requirement or prohibition imposed or threatened to be imposed on that person pursuant to any measures in so far as this section applies to them by virtue of an order under subsection (1) above.

  (3) The Secretary of State may give to any person in the United Kingdom who carries on business there such directions for prohibiting compliance with any such requirement or prohibition as aforesaid as he considers appropriate for avoiding damage to the trading interests of the United Kingdom.

  (4) The power of the Secretary of State to make orders under subsection (1) or (2) above shall be exercisable by statutory instrument subject to annulment in pursuance of a resolution of either House of Parliament.

  (5) Directions under subsection (3) above may be either general or special and may prohibit compliance with any requirement or prohibition either absolutely or in such cases or subject to such conditions as to consent or otherwise as may be specified in the directions; and general directions under that subsection shall be published in such manner as appears to the Secretary of State to be appropriate.

  (6) In this section 'trade' includes any activity carried on in the course of a business of any description and 'trading interests' shall be construed accordingly.

Documents and information required by overseas courts and authorities

2.—(1) If it appears to the Secretary of State—

    (a) that a requirement has been or may be imposed on a person or persons in the United Kingdom to produce to any court, tribunal or authority of an overseas country any commercial document which is not within the territorial jurisdiction of that country or to furnish any commercial information to any such court, tribunal or authority; or

    (b) that any such authority has imposed or may impose a requirement on a person or persons in the United Kingdom to publish any such document or information,

    the Secretary of State may, if it appears to him that the requirement is inadmissible by virtue of subsection (2) or (3) below, give directions for prohibiting compliance with the requirement.

  (2) A requirement such as is mentioned in subsection (1)(a) or (b) above is inadmissible—

    (a) if it infringes the jurisdiction of the United Kingdom or is otherwise prejudicial to the sovereignty of the United Kingdom; or

    (b) if compliance with the requirement would be prejudicial to the security of the United Kingdom or to the relations of the government of the United Kingdom with the government of any other country.

  (3) A requirement such as is mentioned in subsection (1)(a) above is also inadmissible—

    (a) if it is made otherwise than for the purposes of civil or criminal proceedings which have been instituted in the overseas country; or

    (b) if it requires a person to state what documents relevant to any such proceedings are or have been in his possession, custody or power or to produce for the purposes of any such proceedings any documents other than particular documents specified in the requirement.

(4) Directions under subsection (1) above may be either general or special and may prohibit compliance with any requirement either absolutely or in such cases or subject to such conditions as to consent or otherwise as may be specified in the directions; and general directions under that subsection shall be published in such manner as appears to the Secretary of State to be appropriate.

(5) For the purposes of this section the making of a request or demand shall be treated as the imposition of a requirement if it is made in circumstances in which a requirement to the same effect could be or could have been imposed; and

    (a) any request or demand for the supply of a document or information which, pursuant to the requirement of any court, tribunal or authority of an overseas country, is addressed to a person in the United Kingdom; or

    (b) any requirement imposed by such a court, tribunal or authority to produce or furnish any document or information to a person specified in the requirement,

shall be treated as a requirement to produce or furnish that document or information to that court, tribunal or authority.

(6) In this section 'commercial document' and 'commercial information' mean respectively a document or information relating to a business of any description and 'document' includes any record or device by means of which material is recorded or stored.

Offences under ss. 1 and 2

3.—(1) Subject to subsection (2) below, any person who without reasonable excuse fails to comply with any requirement imposed under subsection (2) of section 1 above or knowingly contravenes any directions given under subsection (3) of that section or section 2(1) above shall be guilty of an offence and liable—

    (a) on conviction on indictment, to a fine;

    (b) on summary conviction, to a fine not exceeding the statutory maximum.

(2) A person who is neither a citizen of the United Kingdom and Colonies nor a body corporate incorporated in the United Kingdom shall not be guilty of an offence under subsection (1) above by reason of anything done or omitted outside the United Kingdom in contravention of directions under section 1(3) or 2(1) above.

(3) No proceedings for an offence under subsection (1) above shall be instituted in England, Wales or Northern Ireland except by the Secretary of State or with the consent of the Attorney General or, as the case may be, the Attorney General for Northern Ireland.

(4) Proceedings against any person for an offence under this section may be taken before the appropriate court in the United Kingdom having jurisdiction in the place where that person is for the time being.

Restriction of Evidence (Proceedings in Other Jurisdictions) Act 1975

4.—A court in the United Kingdom shall not make an order under section 2 of the Evidence (Proceedings in Other Jurisdictions) Act 1975 for giving effect to a request issued by or on behalf of a court or tribunal of an overseas country if it is shown that the request infringes the jurisdiction of the United Kingdom or is otherwise prejudicial to the sovereignty of the United Kingdom; and a certificate signed by or on behalf of the Secretary of State to the effect that it infringes that jurisdiction or is so prejudicial shall be conclusive evidence of that fact.

Restriction on enforcement of certain overseas judgments

5.—(1) A judgment to which this section applies shall not be registered under Part II of the Administration of Justice Act 1920 or Part I of the Foreign Judgments (Reciprocal Enforcement) Act 1933 and no court in the United Kingdom shall entertain proceedings at common law for the recovery of any sum payable under such a judgment.

(2) This section applies to any judgment given by a court of an overseas country, being—

    (a) a judgment for multiple damages within the meaning of subsection (3) below;

    (b) a judgment based on a provision or rule of law specified or described in an order under subsection (4) below and given after the coming into force of the order; or

    (c) a judgment on a claim for contribution in respect of damages awarded by a judgment falling within paragraph (a) or (b) above.

(3) In subsection (2)(a) above a judgment for multiple damages means a judgment for an amount arrived at by doubling, trebling or otherwise multiplying a sum assessed as compensation for the loss or damage sustained by the person in whose favour the judgment is given.

(4) The Secretary of State may for the purposes of subsection (2)(b) above make an order in respect of any provision or rule of law which appears to him to be concerned with the prohibition or regulation of agreements, arrangements or practices designed to restrain, distort or restrict competition in the carrying on of business of any description or to be otherwise concerned with the promotion of such competition as aforesaid.

(5) The power of the Secretary of State to make orders under subsection (4) above shall be exercisable by statutory instrument subject to annulment in pursuance of a resolution of either House of Parliament.

(6) Subsection (2)(a) above applies to a judgment given before the date of the passing of this Act as well as to a judgment given on or after that date but this section does not affect any judgment which has been registered before that date under the provisions mentioned in subsection (1) above or in respect of which such proceedings as are there mentioned have been finally determined before that date.

Recovery of awards of multiple damages

6.—(1) This section applies where a court of an overseas country has given a judgment for multiple damages within the meaning of section 5(3) above against—

    (a) a citizen of the United Kingdom and Colonies; or

    (b) a body corporate incorporated in the United Kingdom or in a territory outside the United Kingdom for whose international relations Her Majesty's Government in the United Kingdom are responsible; or

    (c) a person carrying on business in the United Kingdom, (in this section referred to as a 'qualifying defendant') and an amount on account of the damages has been paid by the qualifying defendant either to the party in whose favour the judgment was given or to another party who is entitled as against the qualifying defendant to contribution in respect of the damages.

(2) Subject to subsections (3) and (4) below, the qualifying defendant shall be entitled to recover from the party in whose favour the judgment was given so much of the amount referred to in subsection (1) above as exceeds the part attributable to compensation; and that part shall be taken to be such part of the amount as bears to the whole of it the same proportion as the sum assessed by the court that gave the judgment as compensation for the loss or damage sustained by that party bears to the whole of the damages awarded to that party.

(3) Subsection (2) above does not apply where the qualifying defendant is an individual who was ordinarily resident in the overseas country at the time when the proceedings in which the judgment was given were instituted or a body corporate which had its principal place of business there at that time.

(4) Subsection (2) above does not apply where the qualifying defendant carried on business in the overseas country and the proceedings in which the judgment was given were concerned with activities exclusively carried on in that country.

(5) A court in the United Kingdom may entertain proceedings on a claim under this section notwithstanding that the person against whom the proceedings are brought is not within the jurisdiction of the court.

(6) The reference in subsection (1) above to an amount paid by the qualifying defendant includes a reference to an amount obtained by execution against his property or against

the property of a company which (directly or indirectly) is wholly owned by him; and references in that subsection and subsection (2) above to the party in whose favour the judgment was given or to a party entitled to contribution include references to any person in whom the rights of any such party have become vested by succession or assignment or otherwise.

(7) This section shall, with the necessary modifications, apply also in relation to any order which is made by a tribunal or authority of an overseas country and would, if that tribunal or authority were a court, be a judgment for multiple damages within the meaning of section 5(3) above.

(8) This section does not apply to any judgment given or order made before the passing of this Act.

■ QUESTIONS

Why has the effects doctrine proven controversial with so many jurisdictions outside the US?

Is extraterritoriality a prerequisite for successful competition law enforcement?

B: Position in the United Kingdom

The stance of the UK towards extraterritoriality has undergone subtle shifts over time to the extent that conflict with the US as a result of reasonable extraterritorial application of US antitrust is now very unlikely. Granting the foreign claimants jurisdiction in *Empagran* would have been an example where unreasonable extraterritoriality would have likely resulted in conflict. The following materials chart the shift in the UK position, starting with an aide-mémoire submitted by the UK in the *Dyestuffs* case (discussed below) which set out the Government's objections to the jurisdiction claimed by the Commission. In spite of the shifts in tone, UK Government policy remains hostile to extraterritoriality on the basis of the effects doctrine.

Aide-mémoire submitted by the UK Government to the European Court in the
Dyestuffs case [1972] ECR 619, in Lowe, A.V., *Extraterritorial Jurisdiction:*
An Annotated Collection of Legal Materials
(Grotius Publications Ltd, 1983) pp. 144–6

Aide-mémoire

The United Kingdom Government have noted, in the *Journal Officiel* of the European Communities dated 7 August 1969, the publication of a decision of the Commission of 24 July 1969 (No IV/26267) concerning proceedings pursuant to Article 85 of the Treaty establishing the European Economic Community in the matter of dyestuffs. Article 1 of this decision declares that 'the concerted practices of fixing the rate of price increases and the conditions of application of these increases in the dye-stuffs sector...constitute violations of the provisions of Article 85 of the EEC Treaty'. Article 2 of the decision inflicts or purports to inflict certain fines upon the commercial undertakings who are alleged to have participated in these concerted practices. Among the undertakings specified in Articles 1 and 2 of the decision are Imperial Chemical Industries Limited (hereinafter referred to as 'I.C.I.'), which is a company incorporated and carrying on business in the United Kingdom. Article 4 of the decision declares that the present decision is directed to the undertakings mentioned in Article 1; it then goes on to state that as far as I.C.I. and certain Swiss undertakings are concerned, '[the decision] may like-wise be notified to them at the seat of one of their subsidiaries established in the Common Market'.

The United Kingdom Government neither wish nor intend to take issue with the Commission about the merits of this particular case. They accept that it is for the undertakings to whom the decision is directed to pursue whatever remedies are available to them under the EEC Treaty if they desire for their part to challenge the legality or correctness of this measure taken by the Commission. It is in any event their understanding that certain of the undertakings to whom the decision is directed have already indicated their intention to institute proceedings before the European Court of Justice challenging the decision on various grounds.

The concern of the United Kingdom Government in this matter is rather directed towards the more fundamental point concerning the reach and extent of the jurisdiction exercisable by the Commission *vis-à-vis* undertakings which are neither incorporated in the territory of a Member-State of the European Economic Community, nor carrying on business nor resident therein.

The Commission will be aware that certain claims to exercise extra-territorial jurisdiction in anti-trust proceedings have given rise to serious and continuing disputes between Western European Governments (including the Governments of some EEC Member-States) and the United States Government, inasmuch as these claims have been based on grounds which the Western European Governments consider to be unsupported by public international law.

In particular, the United Kingdom Government have for their part consistently objected to the assumption of extra-territorial jurisdiction in antitrust matters by the courts or authorities of a foreign state when that jurisdiction is based upon what is termed the 'effects doctrine'—that is to say, the doctrine that territorial jurisdiction over conduct which has occurred wholly outside the territory of the State claiming jurisdiction may be justified because of the resulting economic 'effects' of such conduct within the territory of that State. This doctrine becomes even more open to objection when, on the basis of the alleged 'effects' within the State claiming jurisdiction of the conduct of foreign corporations abroad (that is to say, conduct pursued outside the territory of that State), such corporations are actually made subject to penal sanctions.

The United Kingdom Government are of the view that certain of the 'considerations' advanced in the decision of the Commission of 24 July 1969 conflict with the principles of public international law concerning the basis upon which personal and substantive jurisdiction may be exercised over foreign corporations in antitrust matters. A summary statement of these principles as seen by the United Kingdom Government, is annexed to this *aide-mémoire* for ease of reference.

In particular, it will be noted that the method by which the decision of the Commission was purportedly notified to I.C.I. (Article 4 of the decision) ignores the clear legal distinction between a parent company and its subsidiaries and the separate legal personalities of the latter. The United Kingdom Government consider that this attempted 'notification' of a parent company through its subsidiary is designed to support a doctrine of substantive jurisdiction which is itself open to objection as going beyond the limits imposed by the accepted principles of international law.

So far as substantive jurisdiction is concerned, the United Kingdom Government are of the view that the decision of the Commission incorporates an interpretation of the relevant provisions of the EEC Treaty which is not justified by the accepted principles of international law governing the exercise of extra-territorial jurisdiction over foreigners in respect of acts committed abroad.

The United Kingdom Government deem it necessary to bring these considerations to the attention of the Commission lest there be any misunderstanding as to their position in the matter.

Statement of Principles According to which in the view of the UK government jurisdiction may be exercised over foreign corporations in antitrust matters, in Lowe, A.V., *Extraterritorial Jurisdiction: An Annotated Collection of Legal Materials*
Cambridge, Grotius Publications Ltd, 1983, pp. 146–7

The basis on which personal jurisdiction may be exercised over foreign corporations

(1) Personal jurisdiction should be assumed only if the foreign company 'carries on business' or 'resides' within the territorial jurisdiction.

(2) A foreign company may be considered to 'carry on business' within the jurisdiction by an agent only if the agent has legal power to enter into contracts on behalf of the principal.

(3) A foreign parent company may not be considered to 'carry on business' within the jurisdiction by a subsidiary company, unless it can be shown that the subsidiary is the agent for the parent in the sense of carrying on the parent's business within the jurisdiction.

(4) The separate legal personalities of a parent company and its subsidiary should be respected. Such concepts as 'enterprise entity' and 'reciprocating partnership' when applied for the purpose of asserting personal jurisdiction over a foreign parent company by reason of the presence within the jurisdiction of a subsidiary (and a foreign subsidiary by reason of the presence of its parent company) are contrary to sound legal principle in that they disregard the distinction of personality between parent and subsidiary.

(5) The normal rules governing the exercise of personal jurisdiction should not be extended in such a manner as to extend beyond proper limits the exercise of substantive jurisdiction in respect of the activities of foreigners abroad. Nor can the assertion of extended personal jurisdiction be justified on the basis that it is necessary for the enforcement of legislation which in itself exceeds the proper limits of substantive jurisdiction.

(6) There is no justification for applying a looser test to methods of personal service in antitrust matters than is permissible in relation to other matters.

The basis on which substantive jurisdiction may be exercised in antitrust matters

(1) On general principles, substantive jurisdiction in antitrust matters should only be taken on the basis of either
   (a) the territorial principle, or
   (b) the nationality principle.

There is nothing in the nature of antitrust proceedings which justifies a wider application of these principles than is generally accepted in other matters: on the contrary there is much which calls for a narrower application.

(2) The territorial principle justifies proceedings against foreigners and foreign companies only in respect of conduct which consists in whole or in part of some activity by them in the territory of the State claiming jurisdiction. A State should not exercise jurisdiction against a foreigner who or a foreign company which has committed no act within its territory. In the case of conspiracies the assumption of jurisdiction is justified:
   (a) if the entire conspiracy takes place within the territory of the State claiming jurisdiction; or
   (b) if the formation of the conspiracy takes place within the territory of the State claiming jurisdiction even if things are done in pursuance of it outside its territory; or
   (c) if the formation of the conspiracy takes place outside the territory of the State claiming jurisdiction, but the person against whom the proceedings are brought has done things within its territory in pursuance of the conspiracy.

(3) The nationality principle justifies proceedings against nationals of the State claiming jurisdiction in respect of their activities abroad only provided that this does not involve interference with the legitimate affairs of other States or cause such nationals to act in a manner which is contrary to the laws of the State in which the activities in question are conducted.

NOTE: The UK opposed the economic entity doctrine in the aide-mémoire, but this policy stance has likely changed since UK accession to the EU and due to obligations arising out of Regulation 1/2003. The English High Court has used the economic entity doctrine to dismiss a jurisdictional challenge in *Provimi Ltd* v *Aventis Animal Nutrition SA* [2003] EWHC 961 (Comm), [2003] 2 All ER 683 (Comm). The case concerned litigation as a result of the international vitamins cartel where many parties and the conduct involved lacked a clear connection with the UK, but the case was allowed to proceed against foreign parent companies due to the existence of UK subsidiaries. The UK position on extraterritoriality is more recently articulated in the CA 1998. Section 2(3) provides that the prohibition set out in sub-s. (1) shall only apply 'if the agreement, decision or practice is, or intended to be, *implemented* in the United Kingdom'. The italicised phrase is an explicit reference to the ECJ's decision in *Wood Pulp*. Following the reasoning of the Court in that case, it is possible that the Chapter I prohibition could be applied extraterritorially, where the agreement, having its origins outside the UK is implemented within it. Although this is a much wider view of jurisdiction than UK practice has followed, the Government made it clear that it does not wish to follow any development of the Community position on the 'effects' doctrine. Lord Simon explained:

> by copying out the test in *Wood Pulp* on the face of the Bill, we are also ensuring that in the event that EC jurisprudence develops and creates a pure effects-doctrine, the application of the UK prohibitions will not follow suit. (Hansard, HL, 13 November 1997, col. 261)

Section 190(3) of the Enterprise Act 2002 ('EA 2002') adopts the same standard for the criminal cartel offence, which is committed by individuals where the agreement has been 'implemented in whole or in part in the United Kingdom', irrespective of the place of agreement and nationality and domicile of the individual. The criminal prosecution in the marine hose cartel (*R v Whittle, Allison & Brammar* [2008] EWCA Crim 2560) involving several international undertakings conspiring to fix prices and rig bids via telephone conversations and occasional meetings in venues such as Houston, Texas, amply demonstrates the international nature of such cartels, although jurisdiction was never in doubt as the agreement was clearly implemented within the UK, and the defendants pleaded guilty. The Extradition Act 2003 also allows for the possibility of extradition of individuals to and from the UK to face charges so long as there is 'double criminality'. A requesting state would have to show that the conduct involved would constitute an offence under the cartel offence and vice versa if the UK made an extradition request. The issue of extradition in a cartel case was considered by the House of Lords in *Norris v Government of the USA* [2008] UKHL 16, [2008] 1 AC 920, although the case involved conduct before the coming into force of the EA 2002 and was therefore concerned with whether the common law criminal offence of conspiracy to defraud satisfied the requirements of 'double criminality'.

C: Position in the Community

The European Court has exercised a cautionary approach to the extraterritorial application of Articles 81 and 82 EC and cases have been resolved without reference to the controversial 'effects' doctrine. Instead the Court has relied on the 'single economic entity' doctrine and the theory of implementation.

ICI v *Commission (Dyestuffs)*
(Case 48/69) [1972] ECR 619, [1972] CMLR 557, paras 130–142

The Commission found that 10 undertakings, including ICI, were guilty of concerted practices, which infringed Article 81(1) EC, on the grounds that they had participated in illegal price-fixing agreements through subsidiaries which were under their control and which were located within the then EEC. ICI appealed on the basis that, as it was outside the territory of the EEC, the Commission lacked jurisdiction and could not impose fines on it merely on the basis of effects produced in the territory of the EEC by actions alleged to have taken place outside the EEC. Note the UK was not in the EEC at the time the alleged conduct was meant to have occurred.

[130] By making use of its power to control its subsidiaries established in the Community, the applicant was able to ensure that its decision was implemented on that market.

[131] The applicant objects that this conduct is to be imputed to its subsidiaries and not to itself.

[132] The fact that a subsidiary has separate legal personality is not sufficient to exclude the possibility of imputing its conduct to the parent company.

[133] Such may be the case in particular where the subsidiary, although having separate legal personality, does not decide independently upon its own conduct on the market, but carries out, in all material respects, the instructions given to it by the parent company.

[134] Where a subsidiary does not enjoy real autonomy in determining its course of action in the market, the prohibitions set out in Article 85(1) may be considered inapplicable in the relationship between it and the parent company with which it forms one economic unit.

[135] In view of the unity of the group thus formed, the actions of the subsidiaries may in certain circumstances be attributed to the parent company.

[136] It is well-known that at the time the applicant held all or at any rate the majority of the shares in those subsidiaries.

[137] The applicant was able to exercise decisive influence over the policy of the subsidiaries as regards selling prices in the Common Market and in fact used this power upon the occasion of the three price increases in question.

[138] In effect the Telex messages relating to the 1964 increase, which the applicant sent to its subsidiaries in the Common Market, gave the addressees orders as to the prices which they were to charge and the other conditions of sale which they were to apply in dealing with their customers.

[139] In the absence of evidence to the contrary, it must be assumed that on the occasion of the increases of 1965 and 1967 the applicant acted in a similar fashion in its relations with its subsidiaries established in the Common Market.

[140] In the circumstances the formal separation between these companies, resulting from their separate legal personality, cannot outweigh the unity of their conduct on the market for the purposes of applying the rules on competition.

[141] It was in fact the applicant undertaking which brought the concerted practice into being within the Common Market.

[142] The submission as to lack of jurisdiction raised by the applicant must therefore be declared to be unfounded.

The Commission's application of the effects doctrine was supported by Advocate General Mayras.

C—I have stated, in reviewing national legislation, that the principal criterion for the applicability of laws on competition is the territorial effect. But I do not myself believe that this criterion should be accepted unless its *conditions* and *limits* are specified in relation to international law.

1. The conditions for the application of the criterion of territorial effect

   (a) I think that the first condition lies in the fact that the agreement or the concerted practice must create a *direct and immediate* restriction on competition on the national market or, as here, on the Community market. In other words, an agreement only having effects at one stage removed by way of economic mechanisms themselves taking place abroad could not justify jurisdiction over participating undertakings whose registered offices are also situated abroad.
I would suggest that the American Restatement of Foreign Relations Law should be interpreted in this way in so far as it states that jurisdiction over conduct occurring abroad may be admitted when the effect occurs as a *direct result of that conduct*.

   (b) Secondly, the effect of the conduct must be *reasonably foreseeable*, although there is no need to show that the effect was intended.

   (c) Thirdly and lastly, the effect produced on the territory must be *substantial*.

It should also be noted that the main intention of the counter-legislation adopted in France, as in the Netherlands and in other countries, is to forbid their own nationals to submit to inquiries, supervision and orders emanating from foreign authorities. These facts lead me to adopt the distinction made in international law by the Commission and by academic writers between 'prescriptive jurisdiction' and 'enforcement jurisdiction', or between *jurisdictio* and *imperium*.

Whether it be criminal law or, as in the present cases, administrative proceedings that are involved, the courts or administrative authorities of a State—and, *mutatis mutandis*, of the Community—are certainly not justified under international law in taking coercive measures or indeed any measure of inquiry, investigation or supervision outside their territorial jurisdiction where execution would inevitably infringe the internal sovereignty of the State on the territory of which they claimed to act.

On the other hand, it must be recognized that those same authorities are competent to prohibit an agreement or practice which produces direct, foreseeable and substantial effects inimical to competition on their own territory and thus, in this case, in the Common Market, and that they are even competent to impose sanctions, even pecuniary ones, by judicial or administrative decisions.

NOTE: Although the Court did not support the Advocate General's endorsement of the effects doctrine it upheld the Commission's decision on the basis of the single economic entity doctrine. The decision has been criticized because it disregarded the separate legal personality of the companies. See the UK Government's aide-mémoire discussed above. Griffin explains the US practice:

Griffin, J.P., 'Foreign Governmental Reactions to US Assertions of Extraterritorial Jurisdiction'
[1998] ECLR, pp. 69–70 [footnotes omitted]

Jurisdiction based on nationality

Nearly all nations agree that nationality can be a valid basis for asserting extraterritorial jurisdiction. However, US assertions of jurisdiction based upon the control exercised by an American parent over a subsidiary incorporated and operating abroad are not accepted as valid under international law by a number of nations. These nations contend that despite the American parent's majority ownership or its possession of effective working control, under international law nationality is properly determined by the place of incorporation. Moreover, according to one knowledgeable British official, 'even where nationality is a legitimate basis for extraterritorial jurisdiction it must remain subject to the primacy of the laws and policies of the territorial state'. US officials typically respond to these contentions with the assertion that they cannot permit 'technicalities' such as the place of incorporation and inconsistent policies of host states to be used by American companies to evade their obligations under US law.

A Ahlström Oy v Commission
(Cases 89, 104, 11, 116, 117, and 125–9/85) **(Re Wood Pulp)** [1988] 5 ECR 5193, [1988] 4 CMLR 901

In *Wood Pulp* the Commission decided that there was a concerted practice between undertakings situated in non-EC countries and that jurisdiction could be based on the *effects* of that concerted practice on competition in the Community (OJ, 1985, L85/1). Although the Court did not endorse the effects doctrine, it confirmed that jurisdiction could be exercised extraterritorially where the agreement or concerted practice was *implemented* in the Community.

[11] In so far as the submission concerning the infringement of Article 85 of the Treaty itself is concerned, it should be recalled that that provision prohibits all agreements between undertakings and concerted practices which may affect trade between Member States and which have as their object or effect the restriction of competition within the common market.

[12] It should be noted that the main sources of supply of wood pulp are outside the Community, in Canada, the United States, Sweden and Finland and that the market therefore has global

dimensions. Where wood pulp producers established in those countries sell directly to purchasers established in the Community and engage in price competition in order to win orders from those customers, that constitutes competition within the common market.

[13] It follows that where those producers concert on the prices to be charged to their customers in the Community and put that concertation into effect by selling at prices which are actually coordinated, they are taking part in concertation which has the object and effect of restricting competition within the common market within the meaning of Article 85 of the Treaty.

[14] Accordingly, it must be concluded that by applying the competition rules in the Treaty in the circumstances of this case to undertakings whose registered offices are situated outside the Community, the Commission has not made an incorrect assessment of the territorial scope of Article 85.

[15] The applicants have submitted that the decision is incompatible with public international law on the grounds that the application of the competition rules in this case was founded exclusively on the economic repercussions within the common market of conduct restricting competition which was adopted outside the Community.

[16] It should be observed that an infringement of Article 85, such as the conclusion of an agreement which has had the effect of restricting competition within the common market, consists of conduct made up of two elements, the formation of the agreement, decision or concerted practice and the implementation thereof. If the applicability of prohibitions laid down under competition law were made to depend on the place where the agreement, decision or concerted practice was formed, the result would obviously be to give undertakings an easy means of evading those prohibitions. The decisive factor is therefore the place where it is implemented.

[17] The producers in this case implemented their pricing agreement within the common market. It is immaterial in that respect whether or not they had recourse to subsidiaries, agents, sub-agents, or branches within the Community in order to make their contacts with purchasers within the Community.

[18] Accordingly the Community's jurisdiction to apply its competition rules to such conduct is covered by the territoriality principle as universally recognized in public international law.

[19] As regards the argument based on the infringement of the principle of non-interference, it should be pointed out that the applicants who are members of KEA have referred to a rule according to which where two States have jurisdiction to lay down and enforce rules and the effect of those rules is that a person finds himself subject to contradictory orders as to the conduct he must adopt, each State is obliged to exercise its jurisdiction with moderation. The applicants have concluded that by disregarding that rule in applying its competition rules the Community has infringed the principle of non-interference.

[20] There is no need to enquire into the existence in international law of such a rule since it suffices to observe that the conditions for its application are in any event not satisfied. There is not, in this case, any contradiction between the conduct required by the United States and that required by the Community since the Webb Pomerene Act merely exempts the conclusion of export cartels from the application of United States anti-trust laws but does not require such cartels to be concluded.

[21] It should further be pointed out that the United States authorities raised no objections regarding any conflict of jurisdiction when consulted by the Commission pursuant to the OECD Council Recommendation of 25 October 1979 concerning cooperation between member countries on restrictive business practices affecting international trade (*Acts of the organization*, Vol. 19, p. 376).

[22] As regards the argument relating to disregard of international comity, it suffices to observe that it amounts to calling in question the Community's jurisdiction to apply its competition rules to conduct such as that found to exist in this case and that, as such, that argument has already been rejected.

[23] Accordingly it must be concluded that the Commission's decision is not contrary to Article 85 of the Treaty or to the rules of public international law relied on by the applicants.

NOTE: Compare the practice followed by some Member States, e.g. Germany. The German Act Against Restraints of Competition, explicitly states that 'this act shall apply to all restrictions of competition occurring in the territory of the application of the act itself, even if they result from restraints conducted outside such territory' (s. 130(2)).

Note also that the distinction between effects and implementation remains unclear although Griffin suggests that in practice the EC and US tests often produce similar outcomes, with the exception of a narrow, but significant group of cases.

Griffin, J.P., 'Foreign Governmental Reactions to US Assertions of Extraterritorial Jurisdiction'
[1998] ECLR 64, p. 68

For example, if a cartel of American purchasers declined to purchase goods from European sellers, it is doubtful that the purchasers would be deemed to have 'implemented' their conduct within the European Union. Similarly, an agreement by a group of American companies who refuse to sell to firms in the European Union would not likely be viewed as 'implemented' in the Union. Thus, in a narrow class of cases, i.e. situations where the United States would assert jurisdiction over wholly foreign conduct that satisfies the jurisdictional test of the FTAIA, the ECJ has not yet asserted jurisdiction.

In an implicit acceptance of the ABA's criticism, the footnote in the International Guidelines was changed to read, 'in the context of import trade, the "implementation" test adopted in the European Court of Justice usually produces the same outcome as the "effects" test employed in the United States'.

NOTE: Extraterritoriality has particular relevance in the context of mergers which often transcend international borders. The Merger Regulation 139/2004 applies to all mergers with a Community dimension.

Gencor Ltd v *Commission*
(Case T-102/96) [1999] ECR II-753, [1999] 4 CMLR 971

Gencor Ltd was a metals company incorporated under South African law and whose platinum group metals activities were performed by Implats, a company controlled by Gencor and also incorporated under South African law. Lonhro plc was a metals company incorporated under English law. Gencor and Lonrho sought to acquire joint control of Implats which would then acquire sole control of LPD and combine their platinum group metals business. The South African Competition Board approved the proposed concentration, but the Commission prohibited the merger on the basis that it would lead to a situation of oligopolistic dominance. On appeal, Gencor contended that the then Merger Regulation 4064/89 did not give the Commission jurisdiction to assess whether the proposed concentration was compatible with the Common Market as the activities forming the subject matter of the concentration were conducted outside the Community. The CFI responded as follows.

[78] The Regulation, in accordance with Article I thereof, applies to all concentrations with a Community dimension, that is to say to all concentrations between undertakings which do not each achieve more than two-thirds of their aggregate Community-wide turnover within one and the same Member State, where the combined aggregate worldwide turnover of those undertakings is more than ECU 5,000 million and the aggregate Community-wide turnover of at least two of them is more than ECU 250 million.

[79] Article I does not require that, in order for a concentration to be regarded as having a Community dimension, the undertakings in question must be established in the Community or that the production activities covered by the concentration must be carried out within Community territory.

[80] With regard to the criterion of turnover, it must be stated that, as set out in paragraph 13 of the contested decision, the concentration at issue has a Community dimension within the meaning of Article 1(2) of the Regulation. The undertakings concerned have an aggregate worldwide turnover of more than ECU 10,000 million, above the ECU 5,000 million threshold laid down by the Regulation. Gencor and Lonrho each had a Community-wide turnover of more than ECU 250 million in the latest financial year. Finally, they do not each achieve more than two-thirds of their aggregate Community-wide turnover within one and the same Member State.

[81] The applicant's arguments to the effect that the legal bases for the Regulation and the wording of its preamble and substantive provisions preclude its application to the concentration at issue cannot be accepted.

[82] The legal bases for the Regulation, namely Articles 87 and 235 of the Treaty, and more particularly the provisions to which they are intended to give effect, that is to say Articles 3(g) and 85 and 86 of the Treaty, as well as the first to fifth, ninth and eleventh recitals in the preamble to the Regulation, merely point to the need to ensure that competition is not distorted in the common market, in particular by concentrations which result in the creation or strengthening of a dominant position. They in no way exclude from the Regulation's field of application concentrations which, while relating to mining and/or production activities outside the Community, have the effect of creating or strengthening a dominant position as a result of which effective competition in the common market is significantly impeded.

[83] In particular, the applicant's view cannot be founded on the closing words of the 11th recital in the preamble to the Regulation.

[84] That recital states that 'a concentration with a Community dimension exists... where the concentrations are effected by undertakings which do not have their principal fields of activities in the Community but which have substantial operations there'.

[85] By that reference, in general terms, to the concept of substantial operations, the Regulation does not, for the purpose of defining its territorial scope, ascribe greater importance to production operations than to sales operations. On the contrary, by setting quantitative thresholds in Article 1 which are based on the worldwide and Community turnover of the undertakings concerned, it rather ascribes greater importance to sales operations within the common market as a factor linking the concentration to the Community. It is common ground that Gencor and Lonrho each carry out significant sales in the Community (valued in excess of ECU 250 million).

[86] Nor is it borne out by either the 30th recital in the preamble to the Regulation or Article 24 thereof that the criterion based on the location of production activities is well founded. Far from laying down a criterion for defining the territorial scope of the Regulation, Article 24 merely regulates the procedures to be followed in order to deal with situations in which non-member countries do not grant Community undertakings treatment comparable to that accorded by the Community to undertakings from those non-member countries in relation to the control of concentrations.

[87] The applicant cannot, by reference to the judgment in *Wood Pulp*, rely on the criterion as to the implementation of an agreement to support its interpretation of the territorial scope of the Regulation. Far from supporting the applicant's view, that criterion for assessing the link between an agreement and Community territory in fact precludes it. According to *Wood Pulp*, the criterion as to the implementation of an agreement is satisfied by mere sale within the Community, irrespective of the location of the sources of supply and the production plant. It is not disputed that Gencor and Lonrho carried out sales in the Community before the concentration and would have continued to do so thereafter.

[88] Accordingly, the Commission did not err in its assessment of the territorial scope of the Regulation by applying it in this case to a proposed concentration notified by undertakings whose registered offices and mining and production operations are outside the Community.

2. Compatibility of the contested decision with public international law

[89] Following the concentration agreement, the previously existing competitive relationship between Implats and LPD, in particular so far as concerns their sales in the Community, would have

come to an end. That would have altered the competitive structure within the common market since, instead of three South African PGM suppliers, there would have remained only two. The implementation of the proposed concentration would have led to the merger not only of the parties' PGM mining and production operations in South Africa but also of their marketing operations throughout the world, particularly in the Community where Implats and LPD achieved significant sales.

[90] Application of the Regulation is justified under public international law when it is foreseeable that a proposed concentration will have an immediate and substantial effect in the Community.

[91] In that regard, the concentration would, according to the contested decision, have led to the creation of a dominant duopoly on the part of Amplats and Implats/LPD in the platinum and rhodium markets, as a result of which effective competition would have been significantly impeded in the common market within the meaning of Article 2(3) of the Regulation.

[92] It is therefore necessary to verify whether the three criteria of immediate, substantial and foreseeable effect are satisfied in this case.

[93] With regard, specifically, to the criterion of immediate effect, the words 'medium term' used in paragraphs 206 and 210 of the contested decision in relation to the creation of a dominant duopoly position are, contrary to the applicant's assertion, entirely unambiguous. They clearly refer to the time when it is envisaged that Russian stocks will be exhausted, enabling a dominant duopoly on the part of Amplats and Implats/LPD to be created on the world platinum and rhodium markets and, by the same token, in the Community as a substantial part of those world markets.

[94] That dominant position would not be dependent, as the applicant asserts, on the future conduct of the undertaking arising from the concentration and of Amplats but would result, in particular, from the very characteristics of the market and the alteration of its structure. In referring to the future conduct of the parties to the duopoly, the applicant fails to distinguish between abuses of dominant position which those parties might commit in the near or more distant future, which might or might not be controlled by means of Articles 85 and/or 86 of the Treaty, and the alteration to the structure of the undertakings and of the market to which the concentration would give rise. It is true that the concentration would not necessarily lead to abuses immediately, since that depends on decisions which the parties to the duopoly may or may not take in the future. However, the concentration would have had the direct and immediate effect of creating the conditions in which abuses were not only possible but economically rational, given that the concentration would have significantly impeded effective competition in the market by giving rise to a lasting alteration to the structure of the markets concerned.

[95] Accordingly, the concentration would have had an immediate effect in the Community.

[96] So far as concerns the criterion of substantial effect, it should be noted that, as held in paragraph 297 below, the Commission established to the requisite legal standard that the concentration would have created a lasting dominant duopoly position in the world platinum and rhodium markets.

[97] The applicant cannot maintain that the concentration would not have a substantial effect in the Community in view of the low sales and small market share of the parties to the concentration in the EEA. While the level of sales in western Europe (20 per cent of world demand) and the Community market share of the entity arising from the concentration ((...) per cent in respect of platinum) were already sufficient grounds for the Community to have jurisdiction in respect of the concentration, the potential impact of the concentration proved even higher than those figures suggested. Given that the concentration would have had the effect of creating a dominant duopoly position in the world platinum and rhodium markets, it is clear that the sales in the Community potentially affected by the concentration would have included not only those of the Implats/LPD undertaking but also those of Amplats (approximately 35 per cent to 50 per cent), which would have represented a more than substantial proportion of platinum and rhodium sales in western Europe and a much higher combined market share held by Implats/LPD and Amplats (approximately (...) per cent to 65 per cent).

[98] Finally, it is not possible to accept the applicant's argument that the creation of the dominant position referred to by the Commission in the contested decision is not of greater concern to

the Community than to any other competent body and is even of less concern to it than to others. The fact that, in a world market, other parts of the world are affected by the concentration cannot prevent the Community from exercising its control over a concentration which substantially affects competition within the common market by creating a dominant position.

[99] The arguments by which the applicant denies that the concentration would have a substantial effect in the Community must therefore be rejected.

[100] As for the criterion of foreseeable effect, it follows from all of the foregoing that it was in fact foreseeable that the effect of creating a dominant duopoly position in a world market would also be to impede competition significantly in the Community, an integral part of that market.

[101] It follows that the application of the Regulation to the proposed concentration was consistent with public international law.

[102] It is necessary to examine next whether the Community violated a principle of non-interference or the principle of proportionality in exercising that jurisdiction.

[103] The applicant's argument that, by virtue of a principle of non-interference, the Commission should have refrained from prohibiting the concentration in order to avoid a conflict of jurisdiction with the South African authorities must be rejected, without it being necessary to consider whether such a rule exists in international law. Suffice it to note that there was no conflict between the course of action required by the South African Government and that required by the Community given that, in their letter of 22 August 1995, the South African competition authorities simply concluded that the concentration agreement did not give rise to any competition policy concerns, without requiring that such an agreement be entered into (see, to that effect, *Wood Pulp*, paragraph 20).

[104] In its letter of 19 April 1996 the South African Government, far from calling into question the Community's jurisdiction to rule on the concentration at issue, first simply expressed a general preference, having regard to the strategic importance of mineral exploitation in South Africa, for intervention in specific cases of collusion when they arose and did not specifically comment on the industrial or other merits of the concentration proposed by Gencor and Lonrho. It then merely expressed the view that the proposed concentration might not impede competition, having regard to the economic power of Amplats, the existence of other sources of supply of PGMs and the opportunities for other producers to enter the South African market through the grant of new mining concessions.

[105] Finally, neither the applicant nor, indeed, the South African Government in its letter of 19 April 1996 have shown, beyond making mere statements of principle, in what way the proposed concentration would affect the vital economic and/or commercial interests of the Republic of South Africa.

[106] As regards the argument that the Community cannot claim to have jurisdiction in respect of a concentration on the basis of future and hypothetical behaviour, namely parallel conduct on the part of the undertakings operating in the relevant market where that conduct might or might not fall within the competence of the Community under the Treaty, it must be stated, as pointed out above in connection with the question whether the concentration has an immediate effect, that, while the elimination of the risk of future abuses may be a legitimate concern of any competent competition authority, the main objective in exercising control over concentrations at Community level is to ensure that the restructuring of undertakings does not result in the creation of positions of economic power which may significantly impede effective competition in the common market. Community jurisdiction is therefore founded, first and foremost, on the need to avoid the establishment of market structures which may create or strengthen a dominant position, and not on the need to control directly possible abuses of a dominant position.

[107] Consequently, it is unnecessary to rule on the question whether the letter of 22 August 1995 from the South African Competition Board constituted a definitive position on the concentration, on whether or not the South African Government was an authority responsible for competition matters and, finally, on the scope of South African competition law. There is accordingly no need to grant the application for measures of organisation of procedure or of inquiry made by the applicant in its letter of 3 December 1996.

[108] In those circumstances, the contested decision is not inconsistent with either the Regulation or the rules of public international law relied on by the applicant.

[109] For the same reasons, the objection, based on Article 184 of the Treaty, that the Regulation is unlawful because it confers upon the Commission competence in respect of the concentration between Gencor and Lonrho must be rejected.

[110] As regards the reasoning in the contested decision justifying Community jurisdiction to apply the Regulation to the concentration, it must be held that the explanations contained in paragraphs 4, 13 to 18, 204 to 206, 210 and 213 of the contested decision satisfy the obligations incumbent on the Commission under Article 190 of the Treaty to give reasons for its decisions so as to enable the Community judicature to exercise its power of review, the parties to defend their rights and any interested party to ascertain the conditions in which the Commission applied the Treaty and its implementing legislation.

[111] Accordingly, both pleas of annulment which have been examined must be rejected, without it being necessary to grant the application for measures of organisation of procedure or of inquiry made by the applicant in its letter of 3 December 1996.

NOTE: The parallels with the US effects doctrine are obvious. Given the European Court's reluctance to embrace the effects doctrine, the judgment in *Gencor* is significant, particularly since the Court did not consider the fact that LPD's parent company, Lonrho, was established in the UK as an alternative ground for jurisdiction. It is not yet clear whether the judgment will be restricted to merger control. Fox has suggested that 'in matters of antitrust, the most prohibitory nation wins', Fox, E.M., 'National Law, Global Matters, and *Hartford*. Eyes Wide Shut' (2000) 68(1) Antitrust LJ 81. For example, what would have happened if the South African competition authorities had taken a more proactive stance in favour of their 'national champion'?

■ QUESTION

To what extent has EC competition law followed US antitrust in endorsing extraterritoriality?

SECTION 3: **COOPERATION**

Multijurisdictional competition law enforcement is clearly a complex issue and presents national competition authorities with many challenges. However, as Karl Van Miert explains:

Commission's 28th Report on Competition Policy
1998, p. 8

National or regional competition authorities are ill-equipped to grapple with the problems posed by commercial behaviour occurring beyond their borders. Information may be difficult to obtain, and decisions—once taken—may be impossible to enforce. Although new competition legislation has been introduced in many countries in recent years, some behaviour might not be unlawful in the country where it is being carried out, or the authorities there may be unwilling to condemn it. Alternatively, incoherent or even directly contradictory conclusions might be reached by different enforcement authorities, both of which may claim jurisdiction over the same subject-matter. Such divergent treatment not only entails the risk of precipitating a dispute between countries or trading blocks, as was illustrated by the initial disagreement between the US and the EU over the proposed Boeing/MDD merger last year, but is also a source of considerable uncertainty and cost for companies engaging in global transactions.

Cooperation among the national competition authorities is vital to deal with anti-competitive practices with transnational characteristics. Cooperation among the Member States' national competition authorities is common and enhanced by Regulation 1/2003 and the creation of the European Competition Network ('ECN'): see Chapter 2. However, cooperation in the global arena is only a recent phenomenon. Faull makes some suggestions as to why this is the case:

Faull, J., 'Why Do We Need More Cooperation in the Field of Competition Policy?'
Speech delivered in Tokyo, Japan Competition Policy Seminar, 22 November 1995

One reason may be that countries do not always agree on the purposes of competition policy. Even if the details of tax law differ from one country to another, most countries would agree that tax fraud is an offence. More generally, democratic countries share basically the same approach on the scope of the criminal law, although rules differ from jurisdiction to jurisdiction. Perhaps this sort of broad consensus has not yet been achieved in some areas of competition policy.

Within the same country, policy emphasis may vary over time. Competition policy is influenced by political change and our developing understanding of economics. Above all, policy must change and adapt to the rapid evolution of the industries and markets which are its focus of attention. I am sure that no-one pretends that our policies in the EU and in Japan must remain static and impervious to changes in the world around us. Our friends in the USA have lived through such changes recently: US competition policy today is somewhat different from the one conducted by the Reagan administration, which was itself different from the policy implemented by previous administrations.

We must also acknowledge that competition policies focus on domestic markets. A good illustration of this approach is the fact that export cartels, which have harmful effects on foreign markets, are, in most instances, not subjected to competition rules. However, in Europe I think it is fair to recognize that our active competition policy in support of the completion of the Single Market has helped third country firms establish themselves on an equal footing.

A second obstacle to cooperation among competition authorities stems from the very nature of competition policy. This can be better understood if we compare competition policy with trade policy.

Trade policy deals with measures adopted by countries, which in most cases, are publicly known and easily identifiable. It has therefore been possible under the GATT (and now under the WTO) to set up dispute settlement mechanisms in order to ensure that measures adopted by national authorities are consistent with internationally agreed principles and rules. Assuming that comparable sets of common rules could be negotiated among competition authorities, we would still have a specific difficulty with fact-finding, which is after all an essential part of competition policy. Restrictive practices are often concealed and are certainly not readily identifiable. Even if all the contracting parties to a possible international agreement on competition rules undertook to put an end to certain restrictive practices, it would be far from easy to make sure that these commitments were fully complied with.

NOTE: Despite these difficulties the competition authorities of the world have devised a number of ways to cooperate on competition matters. The former EC Competition Commissioner outlines the merits of cooperation in the next extract.

Commission's 30th Report on Competition Policy
2000, Foreword extract, Mario Monti

The rapid globalisation of the world economy brings major limitations—both legal and practical—to our ability to apply our own rules extraterritorially. Even when this possibility is not prevented, there are many drawbacks in doing so: it can give rise to conflicts, or to incoherence, with the rulings of foreign agencies or courts, and even to conflicts with foreign laws. As a result, undertakings operating on a global environment may be able to escape those rules that are essential to govern economic and social processes.

The main policy response available to competition authorities is one that calls upon them to establish networks and instruments of global governance ensuring that the international integration of markets leads to maintained competitive outcomes, thus making the globalisation process both economically more efficient and socially more acceptable. In this context, competition policy—and specifically international cooperation on competition policy—has an important role to play, if we are to avoid resentment against globalisation and a protectionist backlash.

A: Bilateral cooperation

Primitive bilateral cooperation agreements were entered into by the United States with key trading partners such as Germany and Canada in the 1970s and 1980s but the agreement with the European Community in 1991 has become an exemplar to other jurisdictions and has been closely followed in format and substance since. Several jurisdictions including the EC, its Member States, the US, Canada, Australia, Japan, and South Korea have specific competition cooperation agreements in place. The 1991 EC–US Agreement provides for notification, consultation, information sharing, and cooperation and coordination on enforcement matters and its success provided the basis for a subsequent, complementary agreement on positive comity in 1998 ([1998] OJ L173/117). The latter agreement allows one jurisdiction to request the other to investigate and if necessary, remedy anti-competitive behaviour.

Agreement between the European Communities and the United States
23 September 1991 [1991] 30 ILM 1487, OJ, 1995, L95/47

THE GOVERNMENT OF THE UNITED STATES OF AMERICA AND THE COMMISSION OF THE EUROPEAN COMMUNITIES,

Recognizing that the world's economies are becoming increasingly interrelated, and in particular that this is true of the economies of the United States of America and the European Communities;

Noting that the Government of the United States of America and the Commission of the European Communities share the view that the sound and effective enforcement of competition law is a matter of importance to the efficient operation of their respective markets and to trade between them;

Noting that the sound and effective enforcement of the Parties' competition laws would be enhanced by cooperation and, in appropriate cases, coordination between them in the application of those laws;

Noting further that from time to time differences may arise between the Parties concerning the application of their competition laws to conduct or transactions that implicate significant interests of both Parties;

Having regard to the Recommendation of the Council of the Organization for Economic Cooperation and Development Concerning Cooperation Between Member Countries on Restrictive Business Practices Affecting International Trade, adopted on June 5, 1986; and

Having regard to the Declaration on US–EC Relations adopted on November 23, 1990,

HAVE AGREED AS FOLLOWS:

Article I: Purpose and definitions

1. The purpose of this Agreement is to promote cooperation and coordination and lessen the possibility or impact of differences between the Parties in the application of their competition laws.

2. For the purpose of this Agreement, the following terms shall have the following definitions:
   A. 'competition law(s)' shall mean
      (i) for the European Communities, Articles 85, 86, 89 and 90 of the Treaty establishing the European Economic Community, Regulation (EEC) No 4064/89 on the control of concentrations between undertakings, Articles 65 and 66 of the Treaty establishing the European Coal and Steel Community (ECSC), and their implementing Regulations including High Authority Decision No 24–54, and
      (ii) for the United States of America, the Sherman Act (15 USC paras 1–7), the Clayton Act (15 USC paras 12–27), the Wilson Tariff Act (15 USC paras 8–11), and the Federal Trade Commission Act (15 USC paras 41–68, except as these sections relate to consumer protection functions),
      as well as such other laws or regulations as the Parties shall jointly agree in writing to be a 'competition law' for purposes of this Agreement;
   B. 'competition authorities' shall mean (i) for the European Communities, the Commission of the European Communities, as to its responsibilities pursuant to the competition laws of the European Communities, and (ii) for the United States, the Antitrust Division of the United States Department of Justice and the Federal Trade Commission;
   C. 'enforcement activities' shall mean any application of competition law by way of investigation or proceeding conducted by the competition authorities of a Party; and
   D. 'anticompetitive activities' shall mean any conduct or transaction that is impermissible under the competition laws of a Party.

Article II: Notification

1. Each Party shall notify the other whenever its competition authorities become aware that their enforcement activities may affect important interests of the other Party.

2. Enforcement activities as to which notification ordinarily will be appropriate include those that:
   (a) are relevant to enforcement activities of the other Party;
   (b) involve anticompetitive activities (other than a merger or acquisition) carried out in significant part in the other Party's territory;
   (c) involve a merger or acquisition in which one or more of the parties to the transaction, or a company controlling one or more of the Parties to the transaction, is a company incorporated or organized under the laws of the other Party or one of its States or Member States;
   (d) involve conduct believed to have been required, encouraged or approved by the other Party; or
   (e) involve remedies that would, in significant respects, require or prohibit conduct in the other Party's territory.

3. With respect to mergers or acquisitions required by law to be reported to the competition authorities, notification under this Article shall be made:
   (a) in the case of the Government of the United States of America,
      (i) not later than the time its competition authorities request, pursuant to 15 USC para 18 a(e), additional information or documentary material concerning the proposed transaction,
      (ii) when its competition authorities decide to file a complaint challenging the transaction, and
      (iii) where this is possible, far enough in advance of the entry of a consent decree to enable the other Party's views to be taken into account; and
   (b) in the case of the Commission of the European Communities,
      (i) when notice of the transaction is published in the Official Journal, pursuant to Article 4 (3) of Council Regulation No 4064/89, or when notice of the transaction is received under Article 66 of the ECSC Treaty and a prior authorization from the Commission is required under that provision,

      (ii) when its competition authorities decide to initiate proceedings with respect to the proposed transaction, pursuant to Article 6(1)(c) of Council Regulation (EEC) No 4064/89, and

      (iii) far enough in advance of the adoption of a decision in the case to enable the other Party's views to be taken into account.

4. With respect to other matters, notification shall ordinarily be provided at the stage in an investigation when it becomes evident that notifiable circumstances are present, and in any event far enough in advance of:

    (a) the issuance of a statement of objections in the case of the Commission of the European Communities, or a complaint or indictment in the case of the Government of the United States of America; and

    (b) the adoption of a decision or settlement in the case of the Commission of the European Communities, or the entry of a consent decree in the case of the Government of the United States of America;

to enable the other Party's views to be taken into account.

5. Each Party shall also notify the other whenever its competition authorities intervene or otherwise participate in a regulatory or judicial proceeding that does not arise from its enforcement activities, if the issues addressed in the intervention or participation may affect the other Party's important interests. Notification under this paragraph shall apply only to:

    (a) regulatory or judicial proceedings that are public;

    (b) intervention or participation that is public and pursuant to formal procedures; and

    (c) in the case of regulatory proceedings in the United States, only proceedings before federal agencies.

Notification shall be made at the time of the intervention or participation or as soon thereafter as possible.

6. Notifications under this Article shall include sufficient information to permit an initial evaluation by the recipient Party of any effects on its interests.

Article III: Exchange of information

1. The Parties agree that it is in their common interest to share information that will (a) facilitate effective application of their respective competition laws, or (b) promote better understanding by them of economic conditions and theories relevant to their competition authorities' enforcement activities and interventions or participation of the kind described in Article 11(5).

2. In furtherance of this common interest, appropriate officials from the competition authorities of each Party shall meet at least twice each year, unless otherwise agreed, to (a) exchange information on their current enforcement activities and priorities, (b) exchange information on economic sectors of common interest, (c) discuss policy changes which they are considering, and (d) discuss other matters of mutual interest relating to the application of competition laws.

3. Each Party will provide the other Party with any significant information that comes to the attention of its competition authorities about anti-competitive activities that its competition authorities believe is relevant to, or may warrant, enforcement activity by the other Party's competition authorities.

4. Upon receiving a request from the other Party, and within the limits of Articles VIII and IX, a Party will provide to the requesting Party such information within its possession as the requesting Party may describe that is relevant to an enforcement activity being considered or conducted by the requesting Party's competition authorities.

Article IV: Cooperation and coordination in enforcement activities

1. The competition authorities of each Party will render assistance to the competition authorities of the other Party in their enforcement activities, to the extent compatible with the assisting Party's laws and important interests, and within its reasonably available resources.

2. In cases where both Parties have an interest in pursuing enforcement activities with regard to related situations, they may agree that it is in their mutual interest to coordinate their

enforcement activities. In considering whether particular enforcement activities should be coordinated, the Parties shall take account of the following factors, among others:

(a) the opportunity to make more efficient use of their resources devoted to the enforcement activities;

(b) the relative abilities of the Parties' competition authorities to obtain information necessary to conduct the enforcement activities;

(c) the effect of such coordination on the ability of both Parties to achieve the objectives of their enforcement activities; and

(d) the possibility of reducing costs incurred by persons subject to the enforcement activities.

3. In any coordination arrangement, each Party shall conduct its enforcement activities expeditiously and, insofar as possible, consistently with the enforcement objectives of the other Party.

4. Subject to appropriate notice to the other Party, the competition authorities of either Party may limit or terminate their participation in a coordination arrangement and pursue their enforcement activities independently.

Article V: Cooperation regarding anti-competitive activities in the territory of one Party that adversely affect the interests of the other Party

1. The Parties note that anti-competitive activities may occur within the territory of one Party that, in addition to violating that Party's competition laws, adversely affect important interests of the other Party. The Parties agree that it is in both their interests to address anti-competitive activities of this nature.

2. If a Party believes that anti-competitive activities carried out on the territory of the other Party are adversely affecting its important interests, the first Party may notify the other Party and may request that the other Party's competition authorities initiate appropriate enforcement activities. The notification shall be as specific as possible about the nature of the anti-competitive activities and their effects on the interests of the notifying Party, and shall include an offer of such further information and other cooperation as the notifying Party is able to provide.

3. Upon receipt of a notification under paragraph 2, and after such other discussion between the Parties as may be appropriate and useful in the circumstances, the competition authorities of the notified Party will consider whether or not to initiate enforcement activities, or to expand ongoing enforcement activities, with respect to the anti-competitive activities identified in the notification. The notified Party will advise the notifying Party of its decision. If enforcement activities are initiated, the notified Party will advise the notifying Party of their outcome and, to the extent possible, of significant interim developments.

4. Nothing in this Article limits the discretion of the notified Party under its competition laws and enforcement policies as to whether or not to undertake enforcement activities with respect to the notified anti-competitive activities, or precludes the notifying Party from undertaking enforcement activities with respect to such anti-competitive activities.

Article VI: Avoidance of conflicts over enforcement activities

Within the framework of its own laws and to the extent compatible with its important interests, each Party will seek, at all stages in its enforcement activities, to take into account the important interests of the other Party. Each Party shall consider important interests of the other Party in decisions as to whether or not to initiate an investigation or proceeding, the scope of an investigation or proceeding, the nature of the remedies or penalties sought, and in other ways, as appropriate. In considering one another's important interests in the course of their enforcement activities, the Parties will take account of, but will not be limited to, the following principles:

1. While an important interest of a Party may exist in the absence of official involvement by the Party with the activity in question, it is recognized that such interests would normally be reflected in antecedent laws, decisions or statements of policy by its competent authorities.

2. A Party's important interests may be affected at any stage of enforcement activity by the other Party. The Parties recognize, however, that as a general matter the potential for adverse

impact on one Party's important interests arising from enforcement activity by the other Party is less at the investigative stage and greater at the stage at which conduct is prohibited or penalized, or at which other forms of remedial orders are imposed.

3. Where it appears that one Party's enforcement activities may adversely affect important interests of the other Party, the Parties will consider the following factors, in addition to any other factors that appear relevant in the circumstances, in seeking an appropriate accommodation of the competing interests:

   (a) the relative significance to the anti-competitive activities involved of conduct within the enforcing Party's territory as compared to conduct within the other Party's territory;

   (b) the presence or absence of a purpose on the part of those engaged in the anti-competitive activities to affect consumers, suppliers or competitors within the enforcing Party's territory;

   (c) the relative significance of the effects of the anti-competitive activities on the enforcing Party's interests as compared to the effects on the other Party's interests;

   (d) the existence or absence of reasonable expectations that would be furthered or defeated by the enforcement activities;

   (e) the degree of conflict or consistency between the enforcement activities and the other Party's laws or articulated economic policies; and

   (f) the extent to which enforcement activities of the other Party with respect to the same persons, including judgments or undertakings resulting from such activities, may be affected.

Article VII: Consultation

1. Each Party agrees to consult promptly with the other Party in response to a request by the other Party for consultations regarding any matter related to this Agreement and to attempt to conclude consultations expeditiously with a view to reaching mutually satisfactory conclusions. Any request for consultations shall include the reasons therefor and shall state whether procedural time limits or other considerations require the consultations to be expedited.

   These consultations shall take place at the appropriate level, which may include consultations between the heads of the competition authorities concerned.

2. In each consultation under paragraph 1, each Party shall take into account the principles of cooperation set forth in this Agreement and shall be prepared to explain to the other Party the specific results of its application of those principles to the issue that is the subject of consultation.

Article VIII: Confidentiality of information

1. Notwithstanding any other provision of this Agreement, neither Party is required to provide information to the other Party if disclosure of that information to the requesting Party (a) is prohibited by the law of the Party possessing the information, or (b) would be incompatible with important interests of the Party possessing the information.

2. Each Party agrees to maintain, to the fullest extent possible, the confidentiality of any information provided to it in confidence by the other Party under this Agreement and to oppose, to the fullest extent possible, any application for disclosure of such information by a third party that is not authorized by the Party that supplied the information.

Article IX: Existing law

Nothing in this Agreement shall be interpreted in a manner inconsistent with the existing laws, or as requiring any change in the laws, of the United States of America or the European Communities or of their respective States or Member States.

Article X: Communications under this Agreement

Communications under this Agreement, including notifications under Articles II and V, may be carried out by direct oral, telephonic, written or facsimile communication from one Party's competition authority to the other Party's authority. Notifications under Articles II, V and XI, and requests under Article VII, shall be confirmed promptly in writing through diplomatic channels.

Article XI: Entry into force, termination and review

1. This Agreement shall enter into force upon signature.

2. This Agreement shall remain in force until 60 days after the date on which either Party notifies the other Party in writing that it wishes to terminate the Agreement.

3. The Parties shall review the operation of this Agreement not more than 24 months from the date of its entry into force, with a view to assessing their cooperative activities, identifying additional areas in which they could usefully cooperate and identifying any other ways in which the Agreement could be improved.

    The Parties agree that this review will include, among other things, an analysis of actual or potential cases to determine whether their interests could be better served through closer cooperation.

The second cooperation agreement in 1998 reinforces the principle of positive comity in Article V of the first Agreement.

Article III Positive comity

The competition authorities of a Requesting Party may request the competition authorities of a Requested Party to investigate and, if warranted, to remedy anti-competitive activities in accordance with the Requested Party's competition laws. Such a request may be made regardless of whether the activities also violate the Requesting Party's competition laws, and regardless of whether the competition authorities of the Requesting Party have commenced or contemplate taking enforcement activities under their own competition laws.

Article IV Deferral or suspension of investigations in reliance on enforcement activity by the Requested Party

1. The competition authorities of the Parties may agree that the competition authorities of the Requesting Party will defer or suspend pending or contemplated enforcement activities during the pendency of enforcement activities of the Requested Party.

2. The competition authorities of a Requesting Party will normally defer or suspend their own enforcement activities in favor of enforcement activities by the competition authorities of the Requested Party when the following conditions are satisfied:

    (a) The anti-competitive activities at issue:
      (i)   do not have a direct, substantial and reasonably foreseeable impact on consumers in the Requesting Party's territory, or
      (ii) where the anti-competitive activities do have such an impact on the Requesting Party's consumers, they occur principally in and are directed principally towards the other Party's territory;

    (b) The adverse effects on the interests of the Requesting Party can be and are likely to be fully and adequately investigated and, as appropriate, eliminated or adequately remedied pursuant to the laws, procedures, and available remedies of the Requested Party. The Parties recognize that it may be appropriate to pursue separate enforcement activities where anti-competitive activities affecting both territories justify the imposition of penalties within both jurisdictions; and

    (c) The competition authorities of the Requested Party agree that in conducting their own enforcement activities, they will:
      (i)   devote adequate resources to investigate the anti-competitive activities and, where appropriate, promptly pursue adequate enforcement activities;
      (ii) use their best efforts to pursue all reasonably available sources of information, including such sources of information as may be suggested by the competition authorities of the Requesting Party;
      (iii) inform the competition authorities of the Requesting Party, on request or at reasonable intervals, of the status of their enforcement activities and intentions, and where appropriate provide to the competition authorities of the Requesting Party relevant confidential information if consent has been obtained from the source concerned. The use and disclosure of such information shall be governed by Article V;

> (iv) promptly notify the competition authorities of the Requesting Party of any change in their intentions with respect to investigation or enforcement;
> (v) use their best efforts to complete their investigation and to obtain a remedy or initiate proceedings within six months, or such other time as agreed to by the competition authorities of the Parties, of the deferral or suspension of enforcement activities by the competition authorities of the Requesting Party;
> (vi) fully inform the competition authorities of the Requesting Party of the results of their investigation, and take into account the views of the competition authorities of the Requesting Party, prior to any settlement, initiation of proceedings, adoption of remedies, or termination of the investigation; and
> (vii) comply with any reasonable request that may be made by the competition authorities of the Requesting Party.
>
> When the above conditions are satisfied, a Requesting Party which chooses not to defer or suspend its enforcement activities shall inform the competition authorities of the Requested Party of its reasons.
>
> 3. The competition authorities of the Requesting Party may defer or suspend their own enforcement activities if fewer than all of the conditions set out in paragraph 2 are satisfied.
> 4. Nothing in this Agreement precludes the competition authorities of a Requesting Party that choose to defer or suspend independent enforcement activities from later initiating or reinstituting such activities. In such circumstances, the competition authorities of the Requesting Party will promptly inform the competition authorities of the Requested Party of their intentions and reasons. If the competition authorities of the Requested Party continue with their own investigation, the competition authorities of the two Parties shall, where appropriate, coordinate their respective investigations under the criteria and procedures of Article IV of the 1991 Agreement.

NOTE: Mergers do not fall within the scope of the Agreements as both EC and US merger legislation provides for a deferral or suspension of action as envisaged by the Agreement, but the EC and US authorities regularly cooperate closely in such cases following an agreed set of best practices on cooperation in merger investigations There is no doubting that such cooperation can be highly effective and substantially reduce the risk of a protectionist backlash or resentment between counterpart authorities. Bilateral cooperation between the EC and the US has proved highly effective over the years, and has facilitated a convergent approach towards the analysis of markets and appropriate sanctions, as well as leading to coordinated remedies and even joint monitoring trustees in merger cases. However, the limitations of this case-specific cooperation were exposed in the *Boeing/McDonnell Douglas* case.

Boeing and McDonnell Douglas ('MDC') notified the US and EC competition authorities of a decision to merge in February 1997. In July the US Federal Trade Commission concluded that the transaction would not substantially lessen competition.

In the Matter of The Boeing Company/McDonnell Douglas Corporation
File No 971–0051

Statement of Chairman Robert Pitofsky and Commissioners Janet D. Steiger, Roscoe B. Starek III and Christine A. Varney

After an extensive and exhaustive investigation, the Federal Trade Commission has decided to close the investigation of The Boeing Company's proposed acquisition of McDonnell Douglas Corporation. For reasons discussed below, we have concluded that the acquisition would not substantially lessen competition or tend to create a monopoly in either defense or commercial aircraft markets.

There has been speculation in the press and elsewhere that the United States antitrust authorities might allow this transaction to go forward—particularly the portion of the transaction dealing with the manufacture of commercial aircraft—because aircraft manufacturing occurs in a global market, and the United States, in order to compete in that market, needs a single powerful firm to serve as its 'national champion'. A powerful United States firm is all the more important, the argument proceeds, because that firm's success contributes much to improving the United States' balance of trade and to providing jobs for US workers.

The national champion argument does not explain today's decision. Our task as enforcers, conferred in clear terms by Congress in enacting the antitrust statutes, is to ensure the vitality of the free market by preventing private actions that may substantially lessen competition or tend to create a monopoly. In the Boeing-McDonnell Douglas matter, the Commission's task was to review a merger between two direct competitors.

We do not have the discretion to authorize competitive but 'good' mergers because they may be thought to advance the United States' trade interests. If that were thought to be a wise approach, only Congress could implement it. In any event, the 'national champion' argument is almost certainly a delusion. In reality, the best way to boost the United States' exports, address concerns about the balance of trade, and create jobs is to require United States' firms to compete vigorously at home and abroad. Judge Learned Hand put the matter well a half century ago in describing the reasons for the commitment in the United States to the protection of the free market:

> Many people believe that possession of unchallenged economic power deadens initiative, discourages thrift and depresses energy; that immunity from competition is a narcotic, and rivalry is a stimulant, to industrial progress; that the spur of constant stress is necessary to counteract inevitable disposition to let well enough alone.[1]

On its face, the proposed merger appears to raise serious antitrust concerns. The transaction involves the acquisition by Boeing, a company that accounts for roughly 60 per cent of the sales of large commercial aircraft, of a non-failing direct competitor in a market in which there is only one other significant rival, Airbus Industrie, and extremely high barriers to entry. The merger would also combine two firms in the US defense industry that develop fighter aircraft and other defense products. Nevertheless, for reasons we will now discuss, we do not find that this merger will substantially lessen competition in any relevant market.

The Commission reached its decision not to oppose the merger following a lengthy and detailed investigation into the acquisition's potential effects on competition by a large team of FTC attorneys, economists and accountants. The Commission staff interviewed over 40 airlines (including almost every US carrier, large and small, and many foreign carriers), as well as other industry participants, such as regional aircraft producers and foreign aerospace companies. Staff deposed McDonnell Douglas and Boeing officials responsible for marketing commercial aircraft, assessing their firms' financial conditions, and negotiating the proposed acquisition. Finally, the Commission staff reviewed hundreds of boxes of documents submitted by the merging companies and third parties, such as airlines and aircraft manufacturers.

With respect to the commercial aircraft sector, our decision not to challenge the proposed merger was a result of evidence that (1) McDonnell Douglas, looking to the future, no longer constitutes a meaningful competitive force in the commercial aircraft market and (2) there is no economically plausible strategy that McDonnell Douglas could follow, either as a standalone concern or as part of another concern, that would change that grim prospect.

The evidence collected during the staff investigation, including the virtually unanimous testimony of 40 airlines that staff interviewed, revealed that McDonnell Douglas's commercial aircraft division, Douglas Aircraft Company, can no longer exert a competitive influence in the worldwide market for commercial aircraft. Over the past several decades, McDonnell Douglas has not invested at nearly the rate of its competitors in new product lines, production facilities, company infrastructure, or research and development. As a result, Douglas Aircraft's product line is not only very limited, but lacks the state of the art technology and performance characteristics that Boeing and Airbus have developed.[2] Moreover, Douglas Aircraft's line of aircraft do not have common features

---

[1] *United States* v *Aluminum Company of America,* 148 F.2d 416, 427 (2d Cir. 1945).

[2] Our colleague Commissioner Azcuenaga seems to speculate that these problems may be the result of 'strategic behavior' to avoid government challenge, and that others in

such as cockpit design or engine type, and thus cannot generate valuable efficiencies in interchangeable spare parts and pilot training that an airline may obtain from a family of aircraft, such as Boeing's 737 family or Airbus's A-320 family.

In short, the staff investigation revealed that the failure to improve the technology and efficiency of its commercial aircraft products has led to a deterioration of Douglas Aircraft's product line to the point that the vast majority of airlines will no longer consider purchasing Douglas aircraft and that the company is no longer in a position to influence significantly the competitive dynamics of the commercial aircraft market.

Our decision not to challenge the proposed merger does not reflect a conclusion that McDonnell Douglas is a failing company or that Douglas Aircraft is a failing division. Nor does our decision not to challenge the proposed merger reflect a conclusion that Douglas Aircraft could maintain competitively significant sales, but has simply decided to redeploy or retire its assets. While McDonnell Douglas's prospects for future commercial aircraft sales are virtually non-existent, its commercial aircraft production assets are likely to remain in the market for the near future as a result of a modest backlog of aircraft orders. As a result, it is unlikely that the aircraft division would have been liquidated quickly. Moreover, the failing company defense comes into play only where the Commission first finds that the transaction is likely to be anti-competitive. Here, the absence of any prospect of significant commercial sales, combined with a dismal financial forecast, indicate that Douglas Aircraft is no longer an effective competitor, and there is no prospect that position could be reversed.

The merger also does not threaten competition in military programs. Though both Boeing and McDonnell Douglas develop fighter aircraft, there are no current or future procurements of fighter aircraft by the Department of Defense in which the two firms would likely compete. Finally, there are no other domestic military markets in which the products offered by the companies are substitutes for each other. The Department of Defense, in a letter to the Commission dated July 1, 1997, indicated that competition would remain in the defense industry post-merger.

While the merger seems to pose no threat to the competitive landscape in either the commercial aircraft or in various defense markets, we find the 20 year exclusive contracts Boeing recently entered with three major airlines potentially troubling. Boeing is the largest player in the global commercial aircraft market and though the contracts now foreclose only about 11 per cent of that market, the airlines involved are prestigious. They represent a sizeable portion of airlines that can serve as 'launch' customers for aircraft manufacturers, that is, airlines that can place orders large enough and have sufficient market prestige to serve as the first customer for a new airplane. We intend to monitor the potential anti-competitive effects of these, and any future, long term exclusive contracts.

Federal Trade Commissioner Mary Azcuenaga dissented

Statement of Commissioner Mary L. Azcuenaga

The Commission today announces that it will not challenge the proposed merger of The Boeing Company and McDonnell Douglas Corporation. I agree that no action is warranted against the combination of assets in the defense and space lines of business, which constitutes the greater portion of the proposed transaction, although I do not join the discussion of the other commissioners[1] on this point.

I also agree with my colleagues that no action is warranted concerning the 20-year exclusive arrangements for commercial aircraft that Boeing recently reached with three major US airlines. The arrangements account for an estimated 11 per cent of the market, well below any level that should be of concern under the laws enforced by the Commission. Given the state of the law and the

the future may pursue a similar strategy. Speculation is easy, but there is absolutely no evidence that any such behavior occurred here.

[1] See Statement of Chairman Robert Pitofsky and Commissioners Janet D. Steiger, Roscoe B. Starek, III, and Christine A. Varney in The Boeing Company, File No. 971–0051 (1 July, 1997).

fact that the exclusive arrangements apparently are unrelated to the proposed transaction, what is curious is that my colleagues choose to mention them at all.

Another aspect of the proposed transaction is the combination of two of the three remaining manufacturers of commercial aircraft in the world. Boeing is the largest commercial aircraft firm in the world; McDonnell Douglas, through Douglas Aircraft Company ('Douglas'), is number three in the industry. This horizontal combination of two of the three firms in the market appears to present a rather straightforward case for a challenge by the Commission. Absent action by the Commission, the merger will eliminate one of three firms in a highly concentrated market in which entry is difficult and unlikely.

My colleagues conclude that most airlines will not buy planes from Douglas, a factual conclusion with a surprising reach for a simple announcement of failure to prosecute and a conclusion and implication of competitive insignificance with which I disagree after having reviewed the available information. It is true that Douglas has a small share of the commercial aircraft market, but that does not mean that it exercises no competitive constraint.[2] The evidence shows that Douglas has added an element of competition at the stage at which commercial aircraft producers bid for the business of airlines, and it has continued to win some business.

My colleagues rely in their statement on the so-called *General Dynamics*[3] defense, that is, that market shares based on past performance may overstate a firm's future competitive significance. In *General Dynamics*, the government's statistical case based on historical production of coal was deemed an inadequate predictor of anti-competitive effects in light of the acquired firm's inability to obtain additional coal reserves. The company could not compete for future sales, because its coal reserves already were committed and it could not acquire additional reserves. No such definitive impediment is present here. Douglas may need more customers for its products, but having won fewer customers than it might want does not make Douglas unable to compete for future sales.[4] One problem with accepting a 'flailing firm' or 'exiting assets' claim is that it creates an incentive for strategic action to avoid competitive overlaps and government challenge under s. 7 of the Clayton Act.[5] This is a dangerous precedent when we move from the realm of finite reserves of natural resources to the more indeterminate realm of managerial discretion, because of the susceptibility of the defense to self-serving statements, manipulation and strategic behavior.[6]

After reviewing the available information, I conclude that the combination in the commercial aircraft market creates a classic case for challenge in accordance with the merger guidelines, and I find reason to believe that it would violate s. 7 of the Clayton Act. What is less clear on the existing information is the availability of an adequate remedy. On that issue, it seems to me that reasonable people can disagree but, on balance, I would pursue the matter further.

[2] In 1996, Douglas obtained orders amounting to '4 per cent of the total narrow-body and wide-body orders received in the commercial aircraft industry', and its backlog of commercial aircraft orders was $7 billion at the end of 1996, down from $7.2 billion at the end of 1995. 1996 McDonnell Douglas Corporation Annual Report 30 and 34 (Jan. 1977). Although the six months since the December 1996 announcement of the merger with Boeing may not be representative (because one would expect customers to be chary of placing orders for future delivery given the uncertainty about the business), Douglas has continued to seek aircraft business. See, e.g., 'Customer Interest Is Renewed as First MD-95 Takes Shape', *Flight International*, 18 June, 1997; 'Jet Leasing Takes Off in Taiwan; McDonnell To Hold 20% Stake in Venture', *Int'l Herald Tribune*, 20 June, 1997.

[3] *United States* v *General Dynamics Corp.*, 415 U.S. 486 (1974).

[4] The stringent requirements of the failing firm defense apply to test whether a firm's imminent failure would, absent the proposed transaction, cause the firm to exit the relevant market. See 1992 Horizontal Merger Guidelines 5. As I understand it, the parties to the transaction do not claim that the failing firm defense applies to this proposed transaction.

[5] 15 USC 18 (barring acquisitions the effect of which 'may be substantially to lessen competition, or to tend to create a monopoly').

[6] See Azcuenaga, 'New Directions in Antitrust Enforcement', remarks before NERA 12th Annual Antitrust & Trade Regulation Seminar 11–15 (4 July, 1991).

NOTE: By contrast the European Commission concluded that the transaction would significantly strengthen an already dominant position in the global market for large commercial jet aircraft and should be prohibited unless significant remedies were agreed.

Commission press release IP/97/729

The Commission clears the merger between Boeing and McDonnell Douglas under conditions and obligations

Brussels, 30th July 1997

The European Commission has decided to declare the acquisition by The Boeing Company (Boeing) of the McDonnell Douglas Corporation (MDC) compatible with the common market subject to full compliance by Boeing with commitments submitted to the Commission. The Commission has found that the proposed merger leads to a significant strengthening of Boeing's already existing dominant position in the worldwide market for large commercial jet aircraft. The Commission considers that this strengthening arises from MDC's own competitive potential in large commercial jet aircraft, from the enhanced opportunity for Boeing to enter into long-term exclusive supply deals with airlines (already exemplified by those with American, Continental and Delta), and from the acquisition of MDC's defence and space activities, which latter confer advantages in the commercial aircraft sector through 'spill-over' effects in the form of R&D benefits and technology transfer.

Boeing, in the course of intensive negotiations with the Commission, has offered commitments to resolve the competition problems identified by the Commission.

These include:

— the cessation of existing and future exclusive supply deals,
— the 'ring-fencing' of MDC's commercial aircraft activities,
— the licensing of patents to other jet aircraft manufacturers,
— commitments not to abuse relationships with customers and suppliers and—a commitment to report annually to the Commission on military and civil aeronautics R&D projects benefiting from public funding.

These commitments are considered adequate to resolve the identified competition problems, and the Commission has therefore decided to declare the operation compatible with the common market subject to conditions and obligations. The Commission has reached its decision after a rigorous analysis based on EU merger control law, and in accordance with its own past practice and the jurisprudence of the European Court. The Commission expects Boeing to comply fully with its decision, in particular as regards the commitments made by Boeing to resolve the competition problems identified by the Commission. The Commission will strictly monitor Boeing's compliance with these commitments. The EU Merger Regulation allows for appropriate measures to be taken by the Commission in the event of non-compliance by Boeing.

The market for large commercial jet aircraft is world-wide and the EU is an integral and important part of this world market, with a similar competitive structure. European airlines are forecast to account for almost a third of future demand over the next ten years, and Boeing and MDC's combined market share is about two thirds of the EU market.

In arriving at this decision the Commission has taken into account concerns expressed by the US Government relating to important US defence interests. The Commission took the US Government's concerns into consideration to the extent consistent with EU law, and has limited the scope of its action to the civil side of the operation, including the effects of the merger on the commercial jet aircraft market resulting from the combination of Boeing's and MDC's large defence and space interests.

After an intensive five-month investigation, the Commission has found that Boeing, a fully integrated civil and military aerospace company, already has a dominant position in the world-wide market for large commercial jet aircraft. Boeing's existing dominance stems from its very high market share (64 per cent world-wide), the size of its fleet in service (60 per cent world-wide), and the fact that it is the only manufacturer that offers a complete family of aircraft. This position cannot be challenged by potential new entrants, given the extremely high barriers to entry in this hugely capital intensive market. Boeing's dominance is further demonstrated by the recent conclusion of long-term exclusive supply deals with three of the world's leading carriers, American, Delta and Continental Airlines, who would have been unlikely to lock themselves into twenty year agreements with a supplier who did not already dominate, and seem likely to continue to dominate, the large jet aircraft market.

The most immediate reinforcement of Boeing's dominance in large commercial jet aircraft would arise through Boeing's increase in overall market share (in terms of current order backlog) from 64 per cent to 70 per cent. Moreover, Boeing could add to its already existing monopoly in the largest wide-body aircraft segment (the segment of the Boeing 747) a further monopoly in the smallest narrow-body segment.

The Commission recognises that Douglas Aircraft Company (DAC, the commercial aircraft division of MDC) has suffered a decline in its business performance in recent years (although the potential success of the MD95 has not yet been tested). This decline has been due to a level of investment which has been low relative to that of Boeing and Airbus, and seems likely to have been exacerbated by a fall in customer and investor confidence following MDC's abandonment of the MDXX program, and indeed the announcement of the proposed Boeing take-over. Nevertheless, Boeing itself has declared since that announcement that it would be able to benefit from DAC's remaining competitive potential. The acquisition of such an advantage constitutes a strengthening of a dominant position under EU law.

Another vital element in the strengthening of Boeing's dominance would result from the large increase of Boeing's customer base, from 60 per cent to 84 per cent of the current world-wide fleet in service. By ensuring preferential access to this customer base, Boeing would increase opportunities for future sales through significant leverage over existing MDC aircraft users (through customer support services for example). Closer ties with those airlines that currently use MDC aircraft would give Boeing the opportunity to better identify and influence customer needs, or to induce them to change their current MDC aircraft for Boeing models. In particular, Boeing could use this leverage to induce airlines to enter into long term exclusive deals. Boeing has already entered into exclusive agreements with airlines which are currently the first, third and fourth largest operators of MDC aircraft. Prior to these agreements, exclusivity deals of this kind had never been used in this industry. The proposed merger would further enhance Boeing's capability to enter into similar exclusive agreements in the future, and could create a knock-on effect on other large airlines which could be induced to enter into similar deals.

Although the Commission's investigation did not lead it to conclude that the proposed merger would create or strengthen dominance in the defence or space sectors, the Commission considers that Boeing's dominant position on the civil aircraft market would be significantly strengthened as a result of the addition of MDC's defence and space business. The acquisition of the world's number two defence manufacturer and leading manufacturer of military aircraft would considerably enhance Boeing's access to publicly-funded R&D and intellectual property. The large increase in Boeing's defence-related R&D would confer an increase in know-how and other general advantages as well as an increase in the benefits obtained from the transfer of military technology to commercial aircraft. The combination of Boeing's and MDC's know-how and patent portfolio would be a further element for the strengthening of Boeing's dominance. Moreover, the overall combination of both the civil and defence and space activities of the two companies would increase Boeing's bargaining power vis-à-vis suppliers, enabling Boeing to leverage its relationships with suppliers to the detriment of its competitors.

Boeing has proposed remedies, with a view to resolving the reinforcement of the dominant position resulting from the combination of the competitive potential of DAC with Boeing's dominant position, from the increased opportunity for exclusive contracts, which have a foreclosure effect on the market, and from the overall effects ('spillover') arising from military operations, in particular research and development, on large commercial jet aircraft activities. As far as the first point is concerned, the Commission's investigations revealed that no existing aircraft manufacturer was interested in acquiring DAC from Boeing, nor was it possible to find a potential entrant to the commercial jet aircraft market who might achieve entry through the acquisition of DAC. In view of the impossibility of a divestment of DAC, Boeing commits itself to maintain DAC as a separate legal

entity for a period of ten years and to supply to the Commission reports, publicly available and certified by an independent auditor, on DAC's results. Moreover, Boeing proposes to limit the leverage
effect created by MDC's existing fleet, by committing itself not to link the sale of Boeing aircraft to
its access to the DAC fleet in service. As far as exclusive deals are concerned, Boeing commits itself
to refrain from further such deals until 2007, and not to enforce the exclusivity rights in the existing
contracts.

On the overall effects, Boeing has offered to concede to competitors non-exclusive licenses for
patents, together with underlying know-how, held by Boeing arising from publicly-financed R&D.
Moreover, Boeing commits itself to provide to the Commission, for a period of 10 years, an annual
report on 'non-classified' aeronautical projects in which it participates, and which benefit from
public financing. These commitments will increase transparency of links between civil and military
activities. Finally Boeing commits itself not to profit from its relationships with suppliers in order to
obtain preferential treatment. This package of remedies, taken as a whole, addresses the competition problems identified by the Commission, and the Commission has therefore decided to declare
the operation compatible with the common market.

In accordance with the Agreement between the European Communities and the Government
of the United States of America regarding the application of their competition laws, the European
Commission and the Federal Trade Commission have carried out consultations. The Commission
has taken into account concerns expressed by the US Government relating to important US defence
interests. The Commission took the US Government's concerns into consideration to the extent
consistent with EU law, and has limited the scope of its action to the civil side of the operation,
including the effects of the merger on the commercial jet aircraft market resulting from the
combination of Boeing's and MDC's large defence and space interests.

NOTE: Although the parties had mechanisms in place for close cooperation, Schaub,
writing in the Competition Policy Newsletter after the affair, noted that '[p]rocedures of notification and consultation and the principles of traditional and positive comity allow us to bring
our respective approaches closer in cases of common interest but there exist no mechanisms
for resolving conflicts in cases of substantial divergence of analysis' (1998, Issue 1, February).
Indeed the general impression in the US was that 'naked economic nationalism' predicated
the EC's decision to prohibit the merger. Certainly Boeing's European rival, Airbus, enjoyed
a prominent role in proceedings courtesy of the Commission—the company was allowed to
question Boeing's witnesses and was even permitted to review Boeing's proposed remedial
obligations before the Commission accepted them. The FTC's tolerance of the merger suggested
to Commission officials that political motivations were the main concern. However, Kovacic
cautions against assuming that national champion considerations shaped the decisions of the
competition officials on both sides of the Atlantic and suggests that competition policy scrutiny formed the substance of the final outcome.

Kovacic, W.E., 'Transatlantic Turbulence: The Boeing-McDonnell Douglas Merger and International Competition Policy'
(2001) Vol. 68, Issue 3 Antitrust Law Journal 805 at p. 842 [footnotes omitted]

The author advised McDonnell Douglas on the merger, which offers us a unique
insight into the transaction and the issues at stake.

The competition agency leaders know that if they accept the national champion argument in
one case, they will invite similar pleas in other matters and will lose their ability to resist them.
Competition agencies also make a number of contentious, high-stakes enforcement decisions that
contradict the interests of home country champions.

Without more revelations by insiders, we cannot confidently say why the policy officials acted
as they did. Perhaps the best we can do is to evaluate the decisions by their consistency with
past enforcement practice. A decision severely at odds with previous decisions of the tribunal or
reviewing courts might provide a rough, initial basis for suspecting that the competition officials

have embraced new decision-making criteria. An abrupt departure from a mainstream of analysis, undertaken in a politically charged environment, could suggest that the competition body bent its judgment to account for factors alien to routine antitrust analysis.

Even this is admittedly a modest test of political influence. Applying 'mainstream' antitrust principles often involves the exercise of discretion. Deciding, for example, whether a firm lacks capability to compete for future sales under the *General Dynamics* standard can require problematic assessments of the acquired firm's business prospects. In close cases, a host of unexpressed or inexpressible motives or intuitions could shape the exercise of discretion. Nevertheless, if we use obvious departures from analytical orthodoxy as a measure of motive, it is hard to find evidence of economic nationalism in the FTC or EC decisions in the *Boeing-MDC* case.

NOTE: This view is not widely shared, e.g. Bishop argues that 'the actual result was a compromise making little economic sense since customers were not protected by it at all' and 'by the light of international politics it was all too easy to understand the result', Editorial [1997] ECLR 417. Another controversial EC/US dispute in the context of international mergers was GE/Honeywell. On 31 July 2001, the Commission declared the proposed merger between the US companies General Electric ('GE') and Honeywell incompatible with the common market (see [2001] OJ CO74/06), despite receiving clearance from the US authorities. The decision followed a lengthy investigation, which found that the combination of the leading aircraft make with the leading avionics/engine manufacturer would create a dominant position in the relevant markets in which the companies were active. The Commission could not agree remedies with the parties and the merger was abandoned. The decision was received with horror in US political circles, including President Bush. See Burnside, A., 'Gee, Honey, I Sunk the Merger' [2002] ECLR 107 and Pflanz, M., and Caffarra, C., 'The Economics of GE/Honeywell' [2002] ECLR 115. What lessons can we draw from *Boeing/MDC* and *GE/Honeywell*? More recent tension was evident in the transatlantic relationship involving Microsoft where the Department of Justice made negative comments about the significant behavioural remedies imposed by the European Commission in March 2004, and upheld by the Court of First Instance in September 2007 (in Case T-201/04 *Microsoft* v *Commission* [2007] ECR II-3601). The former Assistant Attorney General for Antitrust Thomas Barnett stated

> In light of the United States' own antitrust case and judgment against Microsoft, and the importance of the computer industry to consumers and to the global economy, the United States has a particular interest in today's CFI decision...We are, however, concerned that the standard applied to unilateral conduct by the CFI, rather than helping consumers, may have the unfortunate consequence of harming consumers by chilling innovation and discouraging competition. (DOJ Press Release, 17 September 2007)

If there is no mechanism for resolving conflicts in cases of substantial divergence of analysis as noted by Schaub, what purpose do the 1991/1998 cooperation agreements serve?

■ **QUESTIONS**

With reference to terms within the agreements, and cases, discuss whether bilateral cooperation agreements minimize the risk of conflicting decisions between competition authorities?

Should developed competition law jurisdictions enter into cooperation agreements with jurisdictions that have recently enacted competition laws?

B: Multilateral cooperation

Although the promotion of deeper bilateral cooperation is widely supported, bilateral agreements are limited both in scope and effect—relatively few countries have concluded such agreements and those that have lack substantive rules or principles. The existence of a bilateral cooperation agreement does not guarantee an avoidance of conflicting decisions, and certainly does not remove the burdens experienced by the business community as a result of multijurisdictional scrutiny (particularly acute in merger control). Moreover, *Boeing/MDC* demonstrates the limitations of bilateral cooperation where key political or economic interests are at stake. Many commentators have long believed that the agreement of a multilateral code is required, although several initiatives since the 1940s have failed to bring about an international competition law. See, e.g. Fox, E.M., 'Toward World Antitrust and Market Access' (1997) 91 AJIL 1. The EC has been at the forefront of efforts to advance that cause of an international agreement:

Communication submitted by Sir Leon Brittan and Karel Van Miert, 'Towards an international framework of competition rules', Communication to the Council COM (96) 284

There are four alternative fora to house an international framework: the OECD, UNCTAD, the negotiation of a separate, standalone agreement, or the WTO.

The OECD has been involved in the area of international competition rules for a long time and is serviced by an independent Secretariat. It has the organisational capacity to cater for the negotiation of an agreement on international competition rules. However the OECD has three disadvantages: it does not have a track record of dealing with binding commitments and dispute settlement, it does not provide the disciplines on competition-related trade measures (which are dealt with in the WTO), and, importantly, it has a limited membership.

UNCTAD developed a full Competition Code in the 1970s which has been regularly revised. However, many of the same objections that apply to the OECD also apply to UNCTAD, i.e. the absence of a tradition of dealing with binding commitments and the lack of an overlap with competition-related trade disciplines (which are dealt with in WTO).

It may be difficult to gather the necessary political momentum in different countries for an independent, standalone agreement, and its functioning would likely have higher overhead costs.

The WTO is the prime candidate for a framework of competition rules: it has a near universal membership. The WTO can provide a balanced response sensitive to the varying interests and concerns of both developed and developing countries.

The WTO is the recognised institution for trade-related international economic rules. Many of its present rules are closely related to competition issues (especially those on subsidies, state enterprises and intellectual property). Some of its Agreements already have a number of specific provisions to address anticompetitive practices.

The institutional infrastructure of the WTO includes a system of transparency and surveillance through notification requirements and monitoring provisions. These are common to many WTO/ GATT Agreements. The WTO also provides a forum for continuous negotiation and consultation, where its Members could bring their trade-related competition concerns. Furthermore, the Organisation has a reinforced and legalised dispute settlement system between governments. This can back-up agreed rules and provide means for conflict resolution.

The WTO also caters for the possibility of negotiating an Agreement with specific disciplines between a limited number of signatories (thereby creating a so-called Plurilateral Agreement under Annex IV of the WTO Agreement).

III. An international framework of rules on competition—issues for consideration

A premise of this Communication is that the creation of an International Competition Authority, with its own powers of investigation and enforcement, is not a feasible option for the medium term. Countries would at this stage be unwilling to accept the constraints on national sovereignty and policies that such a structure would impose. The proposals set out below and in the annex therefore reflect a more modest approach, built on commitments binding governments and providing intergovernmental procedures. This is also the model on which the international trading system has been built since the Second World War.

Work on a framework of international competition rules is most likely to make headway if a progressive approach is adopted.

The objective would be to strengthen competition policy coordination in steps (building-blocks approach). This could be achieved through the creation of a working group in WTO, whereby initial work might be limited to those areas where consensus can be mustered at an early stage, and more ambitious objectives would be tackled later. The main steps can be identified as follows:

(a) Adoption of domestic competition structures

A first step could be taken by WTO Members committing themselves individually to assuring the existence of domestic competition structures. The core elements of such a structure would be:

— having basic competition rules in domestic laws to address anti-competitive practices, covering restrictive agreements of companies, abuse of dominant position, and mergers;
— having or creating domestic enforcement structures to guarantee an effective implementation of those rules, including proper investigatory instruments and appropriate sanctions;
— ensuring access for private parties to the domestic enforcement authorities, including national courts, on equitable, transparent and non-discriminatory terms.

(b) Adoption of common rules

In parallel WTO Members could seek to identify a core of common principles, and work towards their adoption at international level. This would:

— promote equal conditions of competition world-wide;
— facilitate closer cooperation between competition authorities and pave the way for the coordination of international enforcement activity;
— promote a gradual convergence of competition laws.

Common principles or rules can be developed progressively and step by step. It may be opportune, in a first stage, to concentrate on horizontal restraints (price or output fixing or market sharing cartels, bid-rigging, group boycotts, export cartels). Work on other practices (abuse of a dominant position, certain vertical restraints such as exclusive distribution or supply agreements) could start in parallel, but may take more time.

(c) Establishment of an instrument of cooperation between competition authorities

Transparency is an essential element of a framework of competition. Provisions could be developed on notification, information exchange and cooperation between competition authorities. These could include provisions regarding cooperation procedures, for example when agencies are launching parallel investigations into the same practice. Negative and positive comity instruments could also be developed further.

(d) Dispute settlement

Apart from its natural role as a permanent forum for negotiation adapting or strengthening agreed rules and obligations, the WTO also provides a compliance mechanism to help settle disputes between governments when a country claims that agreed WTO rules have been breached. Private parties do not have access to the WTO's dispute settlement system. The WTO mechanisms could be applied if a country for example fails to set up a domestic competition structure or if it fails to react in a specific case to a request for enforcement action lodged by another WTO Member. The relevant rules could be adapted, if necessary, to the specificities of competition law and policy, and could be applied in a progressive way.

IV. Related issues

(a) Who should participate?

An international agreement on competition rules would bring benefits to all nations of the trading community. All countries could participate in an agreement to incorporate competition law provisions in their domestic laws.

At the same time the application of the cooperation and enforcement provisions would require, of participating countries, that they have a sophisticated administration capable of handling sensitive information and of assessing commercial practices in a dynamic context. Many developing countries do not yet have this administrative machinery.

It is therefore realistic to expect that, if adopted, cooperation provisions of a competition agreement would, in a first stage, apply only between a limited number of signatories with mature antitrust agencies. Provisions could group together developed and advanced developing countries to start with, and gradually come to include more countries. Any country able to shoulder the obligations of the agreement could be eligible to participate. A different intensity of cooperation, for example in the field of information exchange, could apply between different countries.

(b) The interest of developing countries

Private anticompetitive practices have long been a concern for developing countries. As the turnover of many multinationals has come to surpass the GDP of middle size developing countries, developing countries have seen a growing need for a minimum of discipline on private conduct in their markets. It was in response to this that UNCTAD developed its competition Code in 1980. It would certainly be consistent with this stance for developing countries to support a further strengthening of international rules, certainly if these would come to cover practices, such as export cartels, that today escape effective control.

Even if developing countries might not, in a first stage, participate in the provisions on cooperation between competition authorities (see under IIIa, above), they would be beneficiaries of enhanced control over anticompetitive practices with an international dimension. They would also, like other WTO Members, have access to the dispute settlement provisions if agreed basic rules and enforcement structures had not been properly implemented by other countries. Moreover, they would benefit from the acceptance by developed or newly industrialised countries of MFN obligations in the competition field, even if their own obligations were lighter (e.g. in respect of transitional periods). Finally, all WTO Members, including developing countries, would benefit from possible dispute settlement judgments which might create new market access opportunities.

Insofar as competition rules can ensure that investments are made under sound and fair conditions, effective competition structures can support liberal investment regimes.

The establishment of appropriate competition structures is a complex task and requires substantial resources and training. A framework on competition should include provisions on technical assistance for those countries requesting it.

(c) The relation to trade defence instruments

The relation between the elaboration of a competition framework and the functioning of existing trade instruments is a key issue in the trade-competition debate. It is true that the incorporation of competition provisions into trade law and/or more comprehensive and effective enforcement of competition policies through increased international cooperation, would lessen the need to have recourse to instruments of commercial defence. However, competition instruments cannot be seen as substitutes for trade instruments. The latter only lose their raison d'être in the context of fully integrated markets. A framework of competition rules would, therefore, complement present trade law and create a new instrument to tackle anticompetitive behaviour in markets which are not integrated. Thus the development of new instruments would complement, not supplant, present instruments.

NOTE: The reference to trade and competition policy in the last paragraph. There is a plethora of literature that discusses the interaction between trade and competition norms and the issue is worthy of a book in its own right. See, e.g. Tarullo, D.K., 'Norms and Institutions in Global Competition Policy' (2000) 94 AJIL 478. In an earlier article Tarullo discusses the merits of a competition code housed under the auspices of the WTO.

Tarullo, D., 'Competition Policy for Global Markets'
(1999) Vol. 2, No 3 Journal of International Economic Law, 445

In deciding how to proceed, two questions are key: first, to what degree will international competition be treated as a trade policy issue and negotiated within the WTO? Second, should international competition issues be addressed through creation of a new code or arrangement, as opposed to through successive initiatives that build on existing arrangements?

The importance of the first question arises from the fact that trade and competition authorities have different, often very different, perspectives on the same economic activities. Trade negotiators tend to pursue the interests of companies from their countries, rather than the competitive markets and consumer interests generally pursued by competition enforcers. While these goals are frequently complementary, they can sometimes conflict. Moreover, the trade policy approach tends to pit nation against nation, with one complaining on behalf of its producers and the other defending on behalf of its own producers. There is, of course, nothing wrong with this approach in and of itself. But the trade agreements approach that has evolved in the WTO does not create frameworks for governments to achieve their shared interest in regulating private international economic activities.

An alternative approach, already pursued by competition authorities to some degree, is for nations to undertake collective efforts to protect their consumers from private anti-competitive conduct that crosses national boundaries. Rather than acting as surrogates for private market actors, national regulatory officials organize themselves to achieve the shared end of controlling anti-competitive activities by private market actors. This strategy of regulatory coordination has its own limitations, including inaction on market access problems whose competition implications are not agreed among national antitrust authorities. An instinct to preserve cooperation with their counterparts on key enforcement issues may lead national authorities to avoid pushing too hard on what they regard as peripheral market access concerns.

An important consideration in answering this question is that conflict between trade and competition aims and processes may be inevitable in practice, even if it can be avoided in theory. As a result, governments and their constituencies may need to choose between these priorities in fashioning international responses to competition problems.

NOTE: Proposals to create an international competition regime are politically unrealistic in the short-to-medium term as several key jurisdictions, notably the US, are unwilling to cede any sovereign decision-making powers to an international regime. The protection of confidential information and experience and expertise of staff are also issues that hamper significant progress on this issue. In the absence of an international regime, leading competition law jurisdictions are keen to foster greater international convergence on common issues and encourage wider debate among developed and developing competition regimes. Multilateral engagement fostering convergence takes place within several fora, including the Organisation for Economic Co-operation and Development ('OECD'), the United Nations Conference on Trade and Development ('UNCTAD'), the WTO and the International Competition Network ('ICN'). Non-governmental stakeholder groups, such as the International Bar Association, have also been actively involved in promoting best practices in international competition law. Discourse on this topic has gradually shifted towards more politically feasible initiatives to address the problems encountered when competition authorities encounter cases with an international dimension, Von Meibom and Geiger highlight the potential benefits of focusing on procedural issues instead of substantive harmonization:

Von Meibom, W., and Geiger, A., 'A World Competition Law as an Ultima Ratio'
(2002) 23 ECLR 445 at 450–1 [footnotes excluded]

Multilateral agreements below the level of a World Competition Law are an alternative to bilateral agreements.

Procedural law
It would be possible, for instance, to forego the harmonisation of substantive law and to make do with an international procedural law on a multilateral level. The aim of introducing such an international procedural law would be to establish procedures for the application and enforcement of national law. In this context procedures in parallel proceedings could be standardised, rules established for co-operation on procedures and responsibilities clarified. This would mean, for instance,

that all signatory states would standardise their filing procedures and review periods in competition proceedings. Decisions made on this basis could be enforced without supranational authorities. The participating states could, for instance, agree to deny civil legal protection to proposed mergers that infringe a multilateral agreement. The related degree of legal uncertainty would, in all likelihood, stop companies from going ahead with transactions prohibited by competition law.

Another approach would be to treat the effects of mergers and cartel agreements on foreign markets in the same manner as the effects on domestic markets. This would put an end to the domestic common practice of exempting exports from competition law with each competition authority only considering its own area of responsibility. This point is crucial if even just a minimum of harmonisation is to be achieved, and has been rightly termed the "crunch question of international competition law". It is still the case that national states only make use of competition law to protect their domestic markets. If a benefit is seen for domestic companies which only restricts competition outwith the domestic markets, the national state does not subject such companies to any competition law restrictions. In this respect, competition law also follows the "not-in-my-backyard" principle. Competition should, however, be recognised as a fundamental principal of a globalised market economy. In practice, a filing procedure standardised by multilateral agreements would mean considerable relief for companies. The standardisation of review periods would make the time-frame required to consummate a merger simpler to calculate. It would be much easier to obtain international consensus on procedural issues than on questions of substantive law as the loss of sovereignty would not be so great. In addition, the scope of material that would have to be included in a contractual set of rules would be smaller.

NOTE: Von Meibom and Geiger's view of advancing procedural harmonization has been furthered by the efforts of the ICN. A global competition initiative was proposed by the US-based International Competition Policy Advisory Committee ('ICPAC') in 2000, and the ICN was subsequently created in October 2001 on the basis of a consensus between leading competition jurisdictions on the need to have a forum that was 'all antitrust all the time'. EC Competition Commissioner Neelie Kroes discusses the strengths of the ICN since its creation:

Kroes, N., 'The International Competition Network—Achievements and Goals'
Speech delivered to the ICN Annual Conference in Moscow, May 2007 (SPEECH/07/345)

The global market place is a reality. Right around the world, more competition is driving more economic growth. Never have there been more opportunities open to businesses of all sizes and all backgrounds to spread their wings and fly.

That of course brings both benefits and challenges. But international competition is no zero sum game. The benefits of competitiveness, growth and lasting social and environmental development are mutually reinforcing. A properly-managed environment for business sustains and promotes competitiveness, productivity and growth, at global, regional and national levels. Delivering this environment is the common challenge all competition authorities face.

Yet the increasing integration of the world economy is reflected by the rise in multi-jurisdictional mergers and anti-competitive conduct across borders. These trends mean international cooperation is vitally important for modern competition authorities. If we want to play our full part as promoters of sustainable growth in our national, regional and global markets, we, the competition authorities, need to do more to coordinate our actions and policies.

Active bilateral co-operation between competition authorities is of unquestionable value. It promotes effective joint responses to anti-competitive practices, amongst other things by avoiding conflicting conclusions in cross-border cases...

But with the growing number of competition authorities world-wide, bilateral cooperation is clearly not enough. A global market requires a multilateral response. That is why the ICN is so crucial. The ICN gives us the opportunity to learn from each others' experiences, successes and failures. Competition authorities are growing around the world, developing new ways of thinking and doing things. In a rapidly changing world, we all need to stay very much on our toes...

If competition authorities are to remain effective in an ever-changing world, we all have to keep our policy and tools under continuous monitoring and review. There is no exception to that. And sharing experiences between ourselves can help us all design ever-better systems.

That is where the ICN really comes to the fore. The Network was set up in the year 2000 to promote a competition culture in a joint effort, through better competition enforcement and better competition advocacy.

Has the ICN lived up to these ambitions? Let me give you my personal view. Mozart had already composed his first Andantes and Allegros by the age of six. The ICN is also a bit of a precocious child! Not only does it have a number of Guiding Principles and Recommended Practices under its belt, but also numerous reports, manuals and workshops. In particular, its two annual workshops, on cartels and mergers, are a valuable source of information and training for all ICN members. And I hope that in the future, these will be complemented by an annual ICN unilateral conduct workshop.

NOTE: The ICN has made significant progress in promoting best practices in relation to procedural rules relevant to competition law investigations, which have had some success in influencing jurisdictions when new or revised competition laws are being drafted. The work model of the ICN is limited to 'soft convergence', preferring to bring about convergence via a process of open dialogue between very diverse competition authorities, and incremental changes in law and policy towards a common approach that minimizes conflict. Soft convergence is likely an inadequate solution for proponents of an international competition regime and the calls for more substantive convergence, as well as enhanced cooperation and coordination between competition authorities continue. Nonetheless, since the WTO's failure to agree the basis for a competition agreement at its Fifth Ministerial Conference in Cancún in 2003, it is likely that the ICN represents the best opportunity for convergence towards harmonization in this area. The US Antitrust Modernization Commission ('AMC') was established in 2004 to review US antitrust laws including the relationship with international counterparts, and suggested a mixture of modest and ambitious reforms for the operation of competition law involving global markets.

Antitrust Modernization Commission Final Report
April 2007, Chapter II.D International Antitrust Enforcement

Although the United States and other countries have reached a substantial degree of convergence, improved by cooperation and coordination, further steps are appropriate. Divergence can create problems of at least three types. First, companies may be subject to conflicting and inconsistent laws, creating uncertainty as to the legal standards applicable to their business arrangements. Second, companies must comply with the procedural requirements of multiple jurisdictions, potentially increasing their costs significantly, particularly with respect to notification requirements for mergers. Third, different countries may ultimately impose different, and inconsistent, remedies with respect to the same conduct or transaction. U.S. companies that have been subject to differing remedies from different enforcers, which resulted from the lack of greater convergence, include some of the largest U.S. companies, such as Boeing, General Electric, and Microsoft. Based on its study, the Commission makes several recommendations intended to further convergence on appropriate standards, encourage cooperation, and minimize conflict in the future, as follows.

The Federal Trade Commission and the Antitrust Division of the Department of Justice should, to the extent possible, pursue procedural and substantive convergence on sound principles of competition law.

As a matter of priority, the Federal Trade Commission and the Antitrust Division of the Department of Justice should study and report to Congress promptly on the possibility of developing a centralized international pre-merger notification system that would ease the burden on companies engaged in cross-border transactions...

The United States should pursue bilateral and multilateral antitrust cooperation agreements that incorporate comity principles with more of its trading partners and make greater use of the comity provisions in existing cooperation agreements.

Cooperation agreements should explicitly recognize the importance of promoting global trade, investment, and consumer welfare, and the impediment that inconsistent or conflicting antitrust enforcement poses. Existing agreements should be amended to add appropriate language.

Cooperation agreements should incorporate several principles of negative and positive comity relating to circumstances when deference is appropriate, the harmonization of remedies, consultation and cooperation, and "benchmarking reviews."...

The FTC and the DOJ should evaluate, in consultation with other jurisdictions, how to implement some kind of common premerger notification system across countries that would reduce the burden associated with multiple filings—for example, by providing an opportunity for companies to provide a single, simple initial submission for use by all affected jurisdictions. Recent efforts to harmonize filing requirements have been a useful first step, but further progress is needed. For example, one Commission witness noted that Germany, France, and Britain attempted to implement a joint filing form, but that it is not frequently used because "it really didn't serve anybody's interest." The Commission believes that further steps toward a common system would be valuable and should be feasible. The antitrust agencies should report to Congress promptly as to whether a more uniform and less burdensome notification system is feasible.

NOTE: In spite of the status of the AMC and its final report, it seems unlikely that the more ambitious proposals regarding international merger control will be pursued in the near future.

■ QUESTIONS

Is cooperation between competition authorities and soft convergence sufficient to address the risk of conflict in competition cases involving global markets?

Should competition authorities defer to international counterparts that are better placed to conduct an investigation?

FURTHER READING

Amato, F., 'International Antitrust: What Future?' (2001) 24 World competition 451.

Canenbley, C., and Rosenthal, M., 'Co-operation Between Antitrust Authorities In—and Outside the EU: What Does It Mean for Multinational Corporations?: Part 1' (2005) 26 ECLR 106.

Canenbley, C., and Rosenthal, M., 'Co-operation Between Antitrust Authorities In—and Outside the EU: What Does It Mean for Multinational Corporations?: Part 2' (2005) 26 ECLR 178.

Fiebig, A., 'International Law Limits on the Extraterritorial Application of the European Merger Control Regulation and Suggestions for Reform' [1998] 19 ECLR 323.

Fox, E.M., 'The Merger Regulation and its Territorial Reach: *Gencor Ltd* v *Commission*' (1999) 20 ECLR 334.

Lowe, A.V., 'Blocking Extraterritorial Jurisdiction' (1980) 75 AJIL 257.

Maher, I., 'Competition Law in the International Domain: Networks as a New Form of Governance' [2002] Journal of Law and Society 111.

Piilola, A., 'Assessing Theories of Global Governance: A Case Study of International Antitrust Regulation' (2003) 39 Stanford Journal of International Law 207.

Ryngaert, C., 'Case Comment: Foreign-to-foreign claims: the US Supreme Court's decision (2004) v the English High Court's decision (2003) in the Vitamins case' (2004) 24 ECLR 611.

Von Meibom, W., and Geiger, A., 'A World Competition Law as an Ultima Ratio' (2002) 23 ECLR 445.

6

Article 81 EC

SECTION 1: **INTRODUCTION, ARTICLE 81 EC**

Article 81 EC is concerned with collaborative behaviour between independent undertakings, the aim of which is to prevent, distort, or restrict competition within the common market. An agreement that is caught by the prohibition in Article 81(1) EC is automatically null and void under Article 81(2) EC unless it fulfils the criteria set out in Article 81(3) EC. The Commission and the Court have applied Article 81 EC broadly in order to catch as much anti-competitive behaviour as possible. Article 81 EC is directly effective.

ARTICLE 81 EC

1. The following shall be prohibited as incompatible with the common market: all agreements between undertakings, decisions by associations of undertakings and concerted practices which may affect trade between Member States and which have as their object or effect the prevention, restriction or distortion of competition within the common market, and in particular those which:
   (a) directly or indirectly fix purchase or selling prices or any other trading conditions;
   (b) limit or control production, markets, technical development, or investment;
   (c) share markets or sources of supply;
   (d) apply dissimilar conditions to equivalent transactions with other trading parties, thereby placing them at a competitive disadvantage;
   (e) make the conclusion of contracts subject to acceptance by the other parties of supplementary obligations which, by their nature or according to commercial usage, have no connection with the subject of such contracts.

2. Any agreements or decisions prohibited pursuant to this Article shall be automatically void.

3. The provisions of paragraph 1 may, however, be declared inapplicable in the case of:
   — any agreement or category of agreements between undertakings;
   — any decision or category of decisions by associations of undertakings;
   — any concerted practice or category of concerted practices;
   which contributes to improving the production or distribution of goods or to promoting technical or economic progress, while allowing consumers a fair share of the resulting benefit, and which does not:
   (a) impose on the undertakings concerned restrictions which are not indispensable to the attainment of these objectives;
   (b) afford such undertakings the possibility of eliminating competition in respect of a substantial part of the products in question.

NOTE: The Community rules concerning the control of anti-competitive agreements have been inimical to the achievement of market integration. The drafters of the EC Treaty recognized that undertakings might erect their own barriers to trade and seek to maintain their position in a market by concluding agreements with actual or potential competitors situated in other Member States. According to the Court, Article 81 EC is 'a fundamental provision which is essential for the accomplishment of the tasks entrusted to the Community and, in particular, the functioning of the internal market': see Case C-126/97 *Eco Swiss China Time* v *Benetton International* [1999] ECR I-3055 at 3092. Single market concerns have played a crucial part in the development of the Court's jurisprudence and sometimes this formalistic approach has been to the detriment of economic efficiency considerations. An appreciation of the tension between market integration and economic efficiency, and the close relationship between the Community competition rules and the free movement of goods, begins with the Court's seminal judgment in the following case:

Etablissements Consten SA and Grundig GmbH v Commission
(Joined Cases 56 and 58/64) [1966] ECR 299, [1966] CMLR 418

Consten, a French distributor, entered into an agreement with Grundig, a major manufacturer in West Germany of electrical and electronic products. Grundig agreed to supply only Consten in France and to ensure that its customers outside France were restrained from delivering the contract goods into France. Grundig granted exclusive rights to Grundig's trade mark GINT in France. In return, Consten agreed not to re-export Grundig products into any of the other Member States. This was an exclusive dealing agreement that conferred absolute territorial protection in France on Consten. Later, Consten discovered that UNEF, another French firm, had obtained Grundig's products from sources in another Member State and was selling them in France at a lower price than Consten. Consten sought to stop the resale of these goods and brought an action in the French courts against UNEF, the parallel importer, for unfair competition and infringement of its trade mark. UNEF complained to the Commission that the exclusive dealing agreement between Consten and Grundig breached Article 81(1) EC. The Commission decided that the agreement was unlawful under Article 81(1) EC because it segregated national markets, and refused to grant an exemption as the absolute territorial protection granted was not indispensable. Both parties appealed to the Court for an annulment of the Commission's decision under Article 230(4) (ex 173(2) EEC). Note that the case refers to Article 85 EC, now Article 81.

The Court ruled, in part, as follows:

The complaints concerning the applicability of Article 85(1) to sole distributorship contracts

The applicants submit that the prohibition in Article 85(1) applies only to so-called horizontal agreements. The Italian Government submits furthermore that sole distributorship contracts do not constitute 'agreements between undertakings' within the meaning of that provision, since the parties are not on a footing of equality. With regard to these contracts, freedom of competition may only be protected by virtue of Article 86 of the Treaty.

Neither the wording of Article 85 nor that of Article 86 gives any ground for holding that distinct areas of application are to be assigned to each of the two Articles according to the level in the economy at which the contracting parties operate. Article 85 refers in a general way to all agreements which distort competition within the Common Market and does not lay down any distinction between those agreements based on whether they are made between competitors operating at the same level in the economic process or between non-competing persons operating at different levels. In principle, no distinction can be made where the Treaty does not make any distinction.

Furthermore, the possible application of Article 85 to a sole distributorship contract cannot be excluded merely because the grantor and the concessionnaire are not competitors *inter se* and not on a footing of equality. Competition may be distorted within the meaning of Article 85(1) not only by agreements which limit it as between the parties, but also by agreements which prevent or restrict the competition which might take place between one of them and third parties. For this purpose, it is irrelevant whether the parties to the agreement are or are not on a footing of equal-ity as regards their position and function in the economy. This applies all the more, since, by such an agreement, the parties might seek, by preventing or limiting the competition of third parties in respect of the products, to create or guarantee for their benefit an unjustified advantage at the expense of the consumer or user, contrary to the general aims of Article 85.

It is thus possible that, without involving an abuse of a dominant position, an agreement between economic operators at different levels may affect trade between Member States and at the same time have as its object or effect the prevention, restriction or distortion of competition, thus falling under the prohibition of Article 85(1).

In addition, it is pointless to compare on the one hand the situation, to which Article 85 applies, of a producer bound by a sole distributorship agreement to the distributor of his products with on the other hand that of a producer who includes within his undertaking the distribution of his own products by some means, for example, by commercial representatives, to which Article 85 does not apply. These situations are distinct in law and, moreover, need to be assessed differently, since two marketing organizations, one of which is integrated into the manufacturer's undertaking whilst the other is not, may not necessarily have the same efficiency. The wording of Article 85 causes the prohibition to apply, provided that the other conditions are met, to an agreement between several undertakings. Thus it does not apply where a sole undertaking integrates its own distribution network into its business organization. It does not thereby follow, however, that the contractual situation based on an agreement between a manufacturing and a distributing undertaking is rendered legally acceptable by a simple process of economic analogy—which is in any case incom-plete and in contradiction with the said Article. Furthermore, although in the first case the Treaty intended in Article 85 to leave untouched the internal organization of an undertaking and to render it liable to be called in question, by means of Article 86, only in cases where it reaches such a degree of seriousness as to amount to an abuse of a dominant position, the same reservation could not apply when the impediments to competition result from agreement between two different under-takings which then as a general rule simply require to be prohibited.

Finally, an agreement between producer and distributor which might tend to restore the national divisions in trade between Member States might be such as to frustrate the most fundamental objections of the Community. The Treaty, whose preamble and content aim at abolishing the barri-ers between States, and which in several provisions gives evidence of a stern attitude with regard to their reappearance, could not allow undertakings to reconstruct such barriers. Article 85(1) is designed to pursue this aim, even in the case of agreements between undertakings placed at different levels in the economic process.

The submissions set out above are consequently unfounded.

The complaints relating to the concept of 'agreements ... which may affect trade between Member States'

The applicants and the German Government maintain that the Commission has relied on a mistaken interpretation of the concept of an agreement which may affect trade between Member States and has not shown that such trade would have been greater without the agreement in dispute.

The defendant replies that this requirement in Article 85(1) is fulfilled once trade between Member States develops, as a result of the agreement, differently from the way in which it would have done without the restriction resulting from the agreement, and once the influence of the agreement on market conditions reaches a certain degree. Such is the case here, according to the defendant, particularly in view of the impediments resulting within the Common Market from the disputed agreement as regards the exporting and importing of Grundig products to and from France.

The concept of an agreement 'which may affect trade between Member States' is intended to define, in the law governing cartels, the boundary between the areas respectively covered by

Community law and national law. It is only to the extent to which the agreement may affect trade between Member States that the deterioration in competition caused by the agreement falls under the prohibition of Community law contained in Article 85; otherwise it escapes the prohibition.

In this connexion, what is particularly important is whether the agreement is capable of constituting a threat, either direct or indirect, actual or potential, to freedom of trade between Member States in a manner which might harm the attainment of the objectives of a single market between States. Thus the fact that an agreement encourages an increase, even a large one, in the volume of trade between States is not sufficient to exclude the possibility that the agreement may 'affect' such trade in the abovementioned manner. In the present case, the contract between Grundig and Consten, on the one hand by preventing undertakings other than Consten from importing Grundig products into France, and on the other hand by prohibiting Consten from re-exporting those products to other countries of the Common Market, indisputably affects trade between Member States. These limitations on the freedom of trade, as well as those which might ensue for third parties from the registration in France by Consten of the GINT trade mark, which Grundig places on all its products, are enough to satisfy the requirement in question.

Consequently, the complaints raised in this respect must be dismissed.

The complaints concerning the criterion of restriction on competition

The applicants and the German Government maintain that since the Commission restricted its examination solely to Grundig products the decision was based upon a false concept of competition and of the rules on prohibition contained in Article 85(1), since this concept applies particularly to competition between similar products of different makes; the Commission, before declaring Article 85(1) to be applicable, should, by basing itself upon the 'rule of reason', have considered the economic effects of the disputed contrast upon competition between the different makes. There is a presumption that vertical sole distributorship agreements are not harmful to competition and in the present case there is nothing to invalidate that presumption. On the contrary, the contract in question has increased the competition between similar products of different makes.

The principle of freedom of competition concerns the various stages and manifestations of competition. Although competition between producers is generally more noticeable than that between distributors of products of the same make, it does not thereby follow that an agreement tending to restrict the latter kind of competition should escape the prohibition of Article 85(1) merely because it might increase the former.

Besides, for the purpose of applying Article 85(1), there is no need to take account of the concrete effects of an agreement once it appears that it has as its object the prevention, restriction or distortion of competition.

Therefore the absence in the contested decision of any analysis of the effects of the agreement on competition between similar products of different makes does not, of itself, constitute a defect in the decision.

It thus remains to consider whether the contested decision was right in founding the prohibition of the disputed agreement under Article 85(1) on the restriction on competition created by the agreement in the sphere of the distribution of Grundig products alone. The infringement which was found to exist by the contested decision results from the absolute territorial protection created by the said contract in favour of Consten on the basis of French law. The applicants thus wished to eliminate any possibility of competition at the wholesale level in Grundig products in the territory specified in the contract essentially by two methods.

First, Grundig undertook not to deliver even indirectly to third parties products intended for the area covered by the contract. The restrictive nature of that undertaking is obvious if it is considered in the light of the prohibition on exporting which was imposed not only on Consten but also on all the other sole concessionnaires of Grundig, as well as the German wholesalers. Secondly, the registration in France by Consten of the GINT trade mark, which Grundig affixes to all its products, is intended to increase the protection inherent in the disputed agreement, against the risk of parallel imports into France of Grundig products, by adding the protection deriving from the law on industrial property rights. Thus no third party could import Grundig products from other Member States of the Community for resale in France without running serious risks.

The defendant properly took into account the whole distribution system thus set up by Grundig. In order to arrive at a true representation of the contractual position the contract must be placed in the economic and legal context in the light of which it was concluded by the parties. Such a procedure is not to be regarded as an unwarrantable interference in legal transactions or circumstances which were not the subject of the proceedings before the Commission.

The situation as ascertained above results in the isolation of the French market and makes it possible to charge for the products in question prices which are sheltered from all effective competition. In addition, the more producers succeed in their efforts to render their own makes of product individually distinct in the eyes of the consumer, the more the effectiveness of competition between producers tends to diminish. Because of the considerable impact of distribution costs on the aggregate cost price, it seems important that competition between dealers should also be stimulated. The efforts of the dealer are stimulated by competition between distributors of products of the same make. Since the agreement thus aims at isolating the French market for Grundig products and maintaining artificially, for products of a very well-known brand, separate national markets within the Community, it is therefore such as to distort competition in the Common Market.

It was therefore proper for the contested decision to hold that the agreement constitutes an infringement of Article 85(1). No further considerations, whether of economic data (price differences between France and Germany, representative character of the type of appliance considered, level of overheads borne by Consten) or of the corrections of the criteria upon which the Commission relied in its comparisons between the situations of the French and German markets, and no possible favourable effects of the agreement in other respects, can in any way lead, in the face of abovementioned restrictions, to a different solution under Article 85(1).

NOTE: The Court's judgment confirmed that, in this period of development, market integration lay at the heart of Article 81 EC. According to the Court, the object and effect of the agreement was to compartmentalize the French market '[making] it possible to charge for the products in question prices which are sheltered from all effective competition' (paras 342–3). That view must now be placed in its historical context. In the post-1992 environment a highly integrated market exists and the Commission and the Court are no longer so concerned about promoting market integration in the same way.

The Court also emphatically rejected claims that Article 81(1) EC only applies to horizontal agreements between parties operating at the same level of the economy and confirmed that vertical agreements between parties operating at different levels and not in direct competition with each other constitute an 'agreement between undertakings'. This part of the judgment attracted particular criticism. Although the exclusivity restrictions had the effect of tying Consten to Grundig in an exclusive dealing agreement and, in turn, isolating the French market for the contract goods, French consumers were previously unable to obtain Grundig products in France. The arrangement enabled penetration of a new market that had been previously closed to German products and, therefore, contrary to the Court's conclusions, it was arguable that the agreement in fact encouraged competition and market integration. Furthermore, critics of the Court's judgment consider that the existence of market power is the real issue in these circumstances and point to the fact that inter-brand competition would prevent Grundig's products from being sold at a high price. In a subsequent case, Case 56/65 *Société Technique Minière* ('*STM*'), the Court confirmed that market analysis is not necessary where the object of the agreement is clearly to restrict competition. It seems the Court will not countenance *absolute* territorial protection but may accept partial exclusivity where this is necessary to penetrate a new market. The issues raised in these cases, and subsequent developments, are considered more generally in Chapter 8.

SECTION 2: THE ELEMENTS OF ARTICLE 81 EC

The simplest way to understand how Article 81 EC operates is to consider each element in turn.

A: Undertakings

The term used in Community competition law to describe commercial enterprises is 'undertakings'. The same term is also used in Article 82 EC and the Court has consistently held that the term has the same meaning in both contexts. The Court has, as in many other areas, given the term a broad meaning to maximize the scope of competition law. It will include any natural or legal person carrying on a commercial activity in the goods and services sector.

Polypropylene
OJ, 1986, L230/1, [1998] 4 CMLR 347, Commission decision

The subjects of [EC] competition rules are undertakings, a concept which is not identical with the question of legal personality for the purposes of company law or fiscal law. The term 'undertaking' is not defined in the Treaty. It may however refer to any entity engaged in commercial activities...

NOTE: Clearly this is a broad interpretation and has been confirmed by the Court in Case C-41/90 *Höfner and Elser* v *Macroton* [1991] ECR I-1979 to include 'every entity engaged in an economic activity regardless of the legal status of the entity and the way in which it is financed' (para. 21). The absence of a profit motive is irrelevant provided there is evidence of a commercial or economic activity being pursued. Does the definition extend to public authorities? The case law has focused on whether the entity concerned carries out functions of an economic nature or performs an essential function of the state. In *Höfner*, the Court classified the German federal public employment agency as an undertaking because it deemed employment procurement to be an economic activity. See also Case C-364/92 *SAT Fluggesellschaft* v *Eurocontrol* [1994] ECR I-43, [1994] 5 CMLR 208, paras 19–32 and Case C-343/95 *Diego Cali* v *SEPG* [1997] ECR I-1547, [1997] 5 CMLR 484, paras 22–3 in which the Court considered whether a private limited company entrusted with anti-pollution surveillance by the Genoese national port authority could constitute an undertaking for the purposes of Article 81 EC. The term 'undertaking' also embraces entities concerned with the supply of goods or the provision of services, for example individuals (opera singers, *RAI* v *UNITEL* OJ 1978, L157/39), professional bodies (Case C-221/99 *Conte* v *Rossi* [2001] ECR I-9359) and even football associations, e.g. *FIFA* (distribution of package tours during the 1990 World Cup, OJ, 1992, L326/31). Can employees be regarded as undertakings? It appears from the Court's jurisprudence that the term 'undertaking' does not include employees acting in their capacity as employees. However, trade unions and employees carrying on a business independently of their employer but in connection with that business have been held to be undertakings—see, e.g. Case C-22/98 *Jean Claude Becu* [1999] ECR I-5665, paras 26 and 27.

FENIN v Commission
(Case T-319/99) [2003] ECR II-357

FENIN is an association of the majority of the undertakings that market medical goods and equipment used in Spanish hospitals run by the Spanish public health service, the SNS. FENIN had complained that the SNS were in breach of competition law as they often failed to pay invoices for up to 300 days. The Commission dismissed the complaint on the basis that the SNS, being funded by direct taxation, was not an undertaking for the purposes of competition law.

[35] It is appropriate to begin by observing that, according to settled case-law, in Community competition law the concept of an undertaking covers any entity engaged in an economic activity, regardless of its legal status and the way in which it is financed (*Höfner and Elser*, cited in paragraph

17 above, paragraph 21, *Poucet and Pistre*, cited in paragraph 14 above, paragraph 17, *Fédération française des sociétés d'assurances and Others*, cited in paragraph 26 above, paragraph 14, Case C-55/96 *Job Centre* [1997] ECR I-7119, paragraph 21, *Albany*, cited in paragraph 27 above, paragraph 77, Case T-61/89 *Dansk Pelsdyravlerforening v Commission* [1992] ECR II-1931, paragraph 50, and Case T-513/93 *Consiglio Nazionale degli Spdizionieri Doganali v Commission* [2000] ECR II-1807, paragraph 36).

[36] In this connection, it is the activity consisting in offering goods and services on a given market that is the characteristic feature of an economic activity (see, to that effect, Case C-35/96 *Commission v Italy* [1998] ECR I-3851, paragraph 36, and *Consiglio Nazionale degli Spedizionieri Doganali v Commission*, cited in the preceding paragraph, paragraph 36), not the business of purchasing, as such. Thus, as the Commission has argued, it would be incorrect, when determining the nature of that subsequent activity, to dissociate the activity of purchasing goods from the subsequent use to which they are put. The nature of the purchasing activity must therefore be determined according to whether or not the subsequent use of the purchased goods amounts to an economic activity.

[37] Consequently, an organisation which purchases goods—even in great quantity—not for the purpose of offering goods and services as part of an economic activity, but in order to use them in the context of a different activity, such as one of a purely social nature, does not act as an undertaking simply because it is a purchaser in a given market. Whilst an entity may wield very considerable economic power, even giving rise to a monopsony, it nevertheless remains the case that, if the activity for which that entity purchases goods is not an economic activity, it is not acting as an undertaking for the purposes of Community competition law and is therefore not subject to the prohibitions laid down in Articles 81(1) EC and 82 EC.

[38] Next, it is appropriate to point out that, in *Poucet and Pistre*, cited in paragraph 14 above (paragraphs 18 and 19), in reaching the conclusion that the organisations managing the health funds in question in that case were not carrying on an economic activity and were not, therefore, undertakings for the purposes of Articles 81 EC and 82 EC, the Court relied on the fact that they were fulfilling an exclusively social function, that their activity was based on the principle of national solidarity and, lastly, that they were non-profit-making, the benefits paid out being statutory benefits that bore no relation to the level of contributions. As regards the judgments in *Fédération française des sociétés d'assurance* and *Others* and *Albany*, cited in paragraphs 26 and 27 above respectively, it should be observed that, in those judgments, the Court confirmed the approach adopted in *Poucet and Pistre* (*Fédération française des sociétés d'assurance and Others*, paragraphs 15 and 16, and *Albany*, paragraph 78), albeit that a lesser degree of solidarity in the operation of those schemes persuaded it that the organisations concerned were in fact undertakings. Those cases thus leave the principle posited in *Poucet and Pistre* intact.

[39] It is not disputed in the present case that the SNS, managed by the ministries and other organisations cited in the applicant's complaint, operates according to the principle of solidarity in that it is funded from social security contributions and other State funding and in that it provides services free of charge to its members on the basis of universal cover. In managing the SNS, these organisations do not, therefore, act as undertakings.

[40] It follows that, in accordance with the rule set out in paragraphs 37 and 38 above, the organisations in question also do not act as undertakings when purchasing from the members of the applicant association the medical goods and equipment which they require in order to provide free services to SNS members.

[41] However, the applicant submitted in its reply that SNS hospitals in Spain do, at least on occasion, provide private care for which patients not covered by the SNS, such as foreign visitors, are charged. According to the applicant, the organisations in question therefore necessarily act as undertakings at least in so far as they provide such services and in so far as they purchase medical goods and equipment in connection therewith.

NOTE: The Court of First Instance's judgment on this matter was upheld on appeal before the Court of Justice in Case C-205/03 P *FENIN* v *Commission* [2006] ECR I-6295. The position of state-backed institutions, particularly those associated with healthcare and social security, are increasingly controversial. Historically they have not been subject to competition law, but as Governments become more willing to use 'market' methodology in social provision, and state bodies have increasing economic influence, they may come within competition law's control. See also Case C-264/01 *AOK-Bundesverband* [2004] ECR I-2493; van de Gronden, J.W., 'Purchasing Care: Economic Activity of Service of General (Economic) Interest' [2004] ECLR 87; and Boeger, N., 'Solidarity and EC Competition Law' (2007) 32 EL Rev 319.

B: Economic entity principle

Generally, Article 81(1) EC will only apply to the activities of two or more independent undertakings. The question of independence becomes an issue when companies belonging to the same group and having the status of parent and subsidiary are involved. In these circumstances the traditional definition of legal personality is irrelevant.

Béguelin Import v GL Import-Export
(Case 22/71) [1971] ECR 949, [1972] CMLR 81

Béguelin was the exclusive importer for WIN pocket lighters in Belgium and France. In 1967 a French subsidiary of Béguelin took over the concession for France. GL Import-Export imported a quantity of WIN lighters into France and were challenged by Béguelin. In defence, GL Import-Export claimed that the agreement between Béguelin and its French subsidiary was void under Article 81 EC. That argument was dependent upon whether Béguelin and its subsidiary were separate undertakings.

[5] A—The first question first seeks to establish whether, when a parent company established in a Member State and holder of an exclusive concession granted to it in respect of two Member States, grants to its subsidiary or allows it to acquire the exclusive concession in the second Member State, the prohibition in Article 85(1) applies in so far as the exclusive concession covers the territory of the said State.

[6] If the answer is in the affirmative, the question then seeks to establish what would be the consequences of infringement of the Treaty on the validity of the concession granted to the said subsidiary.

[7] Article 85(1) prohibits agreements which have as their object or effect an impediment to competition.

[8] This is not the position in the case of an exclusive sales agreement when in fact the concession granted under that agreement is in part transferred from the parent company to a subsidiary which, although having separate legal personality, enjoys no economic independence.

[9] Accordingly the relationship between the companies cannot be taken into account in determining the validity of an exclusive dealing agreement entered into between the subsidiary and a third party.

NOTE: This doctrine has become known as the 'economic entity' doctrine and makes clear that legally separate entities can be considered to be the same undertaking if they operate as a single entity on a market.

Viho Europe BV v Commission
(Case T-102/92) [1995] ECR II-17, [1997] 4 CMLR 469

Viho lodged complaints with the Commission about Parker Pen's distribution system, which heavily utilised its subsidiary companies. Again the independence of the subsidiary companies was the key to Viho's complaint.

[47] As regards the appraisal under Article 85(1) of the Treaty of agreements concluded within a group of companies, the Court of Justice has held that 'where a subsidiary does not enjoy real autonomy in determining its course of action in the market, the prohibitions set out in Article 85(1) may be considered inapplicable in the relationship between it and the parent company with which it forms one economic unit' (judgment in Case 48/69 *ICI* v *Commission* [1972] ECR 619, paragraph 134). Similarly, in its judgment in *Ahmed Saeed Flugreisen and Others*, cited above, paragraph 35, the Court of Justice held that 'Article 85 does not apply where the concerted practice in question is between undertakings belonging to a single group as parent company and subsidiary if those undertakings form an economic unit within which the subsidiary has no real freedom to determine its course of action on the market' and added that '[h]owever, the conduct of such a unit on the market is liable to come within the ambit of Article 86'. It also follows from the case-law of the Court of First Instance that Article 85(1) of the Treaty refers only to relations between economic entities which are capable of competing with one another and does not cover agreements or concerted practices between undertakings belonging to the same group if the undertakings form an economic unit (judgment in Joined Cases T-68/89, T-77/89 and T-78/89 *SIV and Others* v *Commission* [1992] ECR II-1403, paragraph 357).

[48] It is not disputed in this case that Parker owns 100 per cent of the capital of its subsidiaries established in Germany, France, Belgium and the Netherlands. It is also apparent from the description given by Parker of the operation of its subsidiary companies, which the applicant has not disputed, that the sales and marketing activities of the subsidiaries are directed by an area team which is appointed by the parent company and which controls, in particular, sales targets, gross margins, sales costs, cash flow and stocks. That area team also lays down the range of products to be sold, monitors advertising and issues directives concerning prices and discounts.

[49] Consequently, the Court concludes that, in point 2 of its decision, the Commission correctly classifies the Parker group as 'one economic unit within which the subsidiaries do not enjoy real autonomy in determining their course of action in the market'.

[50] The Court of Justice has also held that 'in competition law, the term "undertaking" must be understood as designating an economic unit for the purpose of the subject-matter of the agreement in question even if in law that economic unit consists of several persons, natural or legal' (judgment in Case 170/83 *Hydrotherm* v *Compact* [1984] ECR 2999, paragraph 11). Similarly, the Court of First Instance has held that 'Article 85(1) of the EEC Treaty is aimed at economic units which consist of a unitary organization of personal, tangible and intangible elements which pursues a specific economic aim on a long-term basis and can contribute to the commission of an infringement of the kind referred to in that provision' (judgment in Case T-11/89 *Shell* v *Commission* [1992] ECR II-757, paragraph 311). Therefore, for the purposes of the application of the competition rules, the unified conduct on the market of the parent company and its subsidiaries takes precedence over the formal separation between those companies as a result of their separate legal personalities.

[51] It follows that, where there is no agreement between economically independent entities, relations within an economic unit cannot amount to an agreement or concerted practice between undertakings which restricts competition within the meaning of Article 85(1) of the Treaty. Where, as in this case, the subsidiary, although having a separate legal personality, does not freely determine its conduct on the market but carries out the instructions given to it directly or indirectly by the parent company by which it is wholly controlled, Article 85(1) does not apply to the relationship between the subsidiary and the parent company with which it forms an economic unit.

NOTE: In deciding whether one undertaking is truly autonomous from another, it is necessary to examine its different aspects of independence including its financial and managerial independence. Wils suggests that the determinative factor is the degree of control.

Wils, W.P.J., 'The Undertaking as a Subject of EC Competition Law and the Imputation of Infringements to Natural or Legal Persons'
(2000) 25 EL Rev 99, p 103

The distinctive characteristic of the firm is thus the existence of authority or the power to exercise control over people and physical assets. Employment relationships and ownership of physical assets usually provide the legal basis for such power, as they allow the employer-owner to direct human and physical assets. To some extent direction of inputs also takes place in the marketplace. An agreement for the provision of services by one firm to another may give the latter some specific control rights over some of the former's assets. A firm, however, is characterised by the more general, residual control over physical assets and over the actions of employees.

Given that the use of authority and the price system are alternative coordination mechanisms, firms have a choice as to how much they rely on the one or the other. The choice is in fact a double one. First, firms can choose whether to produce certain goods or services in-house or rather to purchase them from other firms across a market. This choice will be made on the basis of a comparison of the respective costs of both options. Secondly, firms may decide to make some use of the market mechanism in their internal organization. Separate departments or divisions may supply one another as a result either of instructions from a higher authority or of what resemble market transactions between them. Some kinds of market may thus exist within firms, in that some transactions within the firm are coordinated by the price mechanism. However, as long as there is a higher authority which has the power to direct the departments' or divisions' operations, such markets within the firm can only exist by the grace of that higher authority, which wants this form of internal organization to exist and which could always interfere with it. The situation is thus quite different from market transactions between independent firms.

■ QUESTION

Wils concludes that 'for the purposes of competition law undertakings are to be identified with "economic units" rather than legal units'. Do you agree?

C: Agreements, decisions of associations, and concerted practices

These terms essentially overlap with each other. Provided some form of collusion is identifiable, the Commission has not expressed any concern with categorizing the 'arrangement' as an agreement, decision, or concerted practice; the Court tends to agree. For example, the term 'agreement' encapsulates a broad range of behaviour and is not restricted to legally binding and enforceable agreements, as this would make it straightforward for undertakings to evade the prohibition. In the following case the Court held that so-called gentlemen's agreements fell within Article 81(1) EC. The case is commonly known as *Quinine*.

ACF Chemiefarma NV v Commission
(Case 41/69) [1970] ECR 661

I—The status and duration of the gentlemen's agreement

[106] The applicant complains that the Commission considered that the export agreement relating to trade with third countries and the gentlemen's agreement governing the conduct of its members in the Common Market constituted an indivisible entity as far as Article 85 was concerned.

[107] The applicant states that the gentlemen's agreement, unlike the export agreement, did not constitute an agreement within the meaning of Article 85(1) and in any event it definitively ceased to exist from the end of October 1962.

[108] The conduct of the parties to the export agreement does not in the applicant's view indicate that they continued the restrictions on competition which were originally provided for in the gentlemen's agreement.

[109] The opposite conclusions reached by the contested decision are therefore alleged to be vitiated because they are based on incorrect findings.

[110] The gentlemen's agreement, which the applicant admits existed until the end of October 1962, had as its object the restriction of competition within the Common Market.

[111] The parties to the export agreement mutually declared themselves willing to abide by the gentlemen's agreement and concede that they did so until the end of October 1962.

[112] This document thus amounted to the faithful expression of the joint intention of the parties to the agreement with regard to their conduct in the Common Market.

[113] Furthermore it contained a provision to the effect that infringement of the gentlemen's agreement would *ipso facto* constitute an infringement of the export agreement.

[114] In those circumstances account must be taken of this connexion in assessing the effects of the gentlemen's agreement with regard to the categories of acts prohibited by Article 85(1).

[115] The defendant bases its view that the gentlemen's agreement was continued until February 1965 on documents and declarations emanating from the parties to the agreement the tenor of which is indistinct and indeed contradictory so that it is impossible to conclude whether those undertakings intended to terminate the gentlemen's agreement at their meeting on 29 October 1962.

[116] The conduct of the undertakings in the Common Market after 29 October 1962 must therefore be considered in relation to the following four points: sharing out of domestic markets, fixing of common prices, determination of sales quotas and prohibition against manufacturing synthetic quinidine.

II—Protection of the producers' domestic markets

[117] The gentlemen's agreement guaranteed protection of each domestic market for the producers in the various Member States.

[118] After October 1962 when significant supplies were delivered on one of those markets by producers who were not nationals, as for example in the case of sales of quinine and quinidine in France, there was a substantial alignment of prices conforming to French domestic prices which were higher than the export prices to third countries.

[119] It does not appear that there were alterations in the insignificant volume of trade between the other Member States referred to by the clause relating to domestic protection in spite of considerable differences in the prices prevailing in each of those States.

[120] The divergences between the domestic legislation of those States cannot by itself explain those differences in price or the substantial absence of trade.

[121] Obstacles which might arise in the trade in quinine and quinidine from differences between national legislation governing pharmaceutical products under trademark cannot relevantly be invoked to explain those facts.

[122] The correspondence exchanged in October and November 1963 between the parties to the export agreement with regard to the protection of domestic markets merely confirmed the intention of those undertakings to allow this state of affairs to remain unchanged.

[123] This intention was subsequently confirmed by Nedchem during the meeting of the undertakings concerned in Brussels on 14 March 1964.

[124] From those circumstances it is clear that with regard to the restriction on competition arising from the protection of the producers' domestic markets the producers continued after the meeting on 29 October 1962 to abide by the gentlemen's agreement of 1960 and confirmed their common intention to do so.

[125] The applicant maintains that owing in particular to the shortage of raw materials the sharing out of domestic markets, as emerges from the exchange of letters of October and November 1963, had no effect on competition in the Common Market.

[126] Despite the scarcity of raw materials and an increase in the demand for the products in question, as the contested decision finds, a serious threat of shortage nevertheless emerged only in 1964 as a result of the interruption of Nedchem's supplies from the American General Service Administration.

[127] On the other hand such a situation cannot render lawful an agreement the object of which is to restrict competition in the Common Market and which affects trade between the Member States.

[128] The sharing out of domestic markets has as its object the restriction of competition and trade within the Common Market.

[129] The fact that, if there were a threatened shortage of raw materials, such an agreement might in practice have had less influence on competition and on international trade than in a normal period in no way alters the fact that the parties did not terminate their activities.

[130] Furthermore the applicant has furnished no conclusive evidence capable of proving that it had ceased to act in accordance with the agreement before the date of expiry of the export agreement.

[131] Consequently, the submissions concerning that part of the decision relating to the continuation of the agreement on the protection of the producers' domestic markets until the beginning of February 1965 are unfounded.

NOTE: Whish suggested that 'in a particular case, linguistically it is more natural to use one term than the other, but legally nothing turns on the distinction: the important distinction is between collusive and non-collusive behaviour', *Competition Law*, 4th edn, p. 78. See also Case T-305/94 *LVM v Commission* [1999] ECR I-931 in which the CFI stated that in 'the context of a complex infringement which involves many producers seeking over a number of years to regulate the market between them, the Commission cannot be expected to classify the infringement precisely'.

Rhone-Poulenc SA v Commission (Polypropylene)
(Case T-1/89) [1991] ECR II-867

The Commission had carried out an investigation of a complex cartel in the petrochemicals sector involving 15 undertakings. The agreement was not in writing and instead comprised a series of oral, non-binding arrangements with no enforceable sanctions. Not all of the undertakings attended each meeting and those that did, did not always fully participate in discussions.

(c) Assessment by the Court

[118] It must be stated first of all that the question whether the Commission was obliged to characterize each factual element found against the applicant either as an agreement or a concerted practice within the meaning of Article 85(1) of the EEC Treaty is irrelevant. It is apparent from the second paragraph of point 80, the third paragraph of point 81 and the first paragraph of point 82 of the Decision, read together, that the Commission characterized each of those different elements primarily as an 'agreement'.

[119] It is likewise apparent from the second and third paragraphs of point 86, the third paragraph of point 87 and point 88 of the Decision, read together, that the Commission in the alternative characterized the elements of the infringement as 'concerted practices' where those elements either did not enable the conclusion to be drawn that the parties had reached agreement in advance on a common plan defining their action on the market but had adopted or adhered to collusive devices which facilitated the coordination of their commercial behaviour, or did not, owing to the complexity of the cartel, make it possible to establish that some producers had expressed their definite assent to a particular course of action agreed by the others, although they had indicated their general support for the scheme in question and conducted themselves accordingly. The Decision thus concludes that in certain respects the continuing cooperation and collusion of the producers in the implementation of an overall agreement may display the characteristics of a concerted practice.

[120] Since it is clear from the case-law of the Court of Justice that in order for there to be an agreement within the meaning of Article 85(1) of the EEC Treaty it is sufficient that the undertakings

in question should have expressed their joint intention to conduct themselves on the market in a specific way (see the judgment in Case 41/69 *ACF Chemiefarma NV* v *Commission* [1970] ECR 661, paragraph 112, and the judgment in Joined Cases 209 to 215 and 218/78 *Heintz van Landewyck Sàrl* v *Commission* [1980] ECR 3125, paragraph 86), this Court holds that the Commission was entitled to treat the common intentions existing between the applicant and other polypropylene producers, which the Commission has proved to the requisite legal standard and which related to target prices for the period from July to December 1979 and sales volume targets for 1979 and 1980, as agreements within the meaning of Article 85(1) of the EEC Treaty.

[121] For a definition of the concept of concerted practice, reference must be made to the case-law of the Court of Justice, which shows that the criteria of coordination and cooperation previously laid down by that Court must be understood in the light of the concept inherent in the competition provisions of the EEC Treaty according to which each economic operator must determine independently the policy which he intends to adopt on the common market. Although this requirement of independence does not deprive economic operators of the right to adapt themselves intelligently to the existing and anticipated conduct of their competitors, it does, however, strictly preclude any direct or indirect contact between such operators the object or effect whereof is either to influence the conduct on the market of an actual or potential competitor or to disclose to such a competitor the course of conduct which they themselves have decided to adopt or contemplate adopting on the market (judgment in Joined Cases 40 to 48, 50, 54 to 56, 111, 113 and 114/73 *Suiker Unie and Others* v *Commission*, cited above, paragraphs 173 and 174).

[122] In the present case, the applicant participated in meetings concerning the fixing of price and sales volume targets during which information was exchanged between competitors about the prices they wished to see charged on the market, the prices they intended to charge, their profitability thresholds, the sales volume restrictions they judged to be necessary, their sales figures or the identity of their customers. Through its participation in those meetings, it took part, together with its competitors, in concerted action the purpose of which was to influence their conduct on the market and to disclose to each other the course of conduct which each of the producers itself contemplated adopting on the market.

[123] Accordingly, not only did the applicant pursue the aim of eliminating in advance uncertainty about the future conduct of its competitors but also, in determining the policy which it intended to follow on the market, it could not fail to take account, directly or indirectly, of the information obtained during the course of those meetings. Similarly, in determining the policy which they intended to follow, its competitors were bound to take into account, directly or indirectly, the information disclosed to them by the applicant about the course of conduct which the applicant itself had decided upon or which it contemplated adopting on the market.

[124] The Commission was therefore justified, in the alternative, having regard to their purpose, in categorizing the EATP meeting of 22 November 1977 in which the applicant participated and the regular meetings of polypropylene producers in which the applicant participated between the end of 1978 or the beginning of 1979 and the end of 1980 as concerted practices within the meaning of Article 85(1) of the EEC Treaty.

NOTE: Moreover, it seems that the Commission and the Court are not prepared to absolve certain members of a cartel who express reservations about whether or not to participate in the agreed course of action. The Court of First Instance confirmed that an undertaking may be held responsible for a cartel even though it only participated in one or some of its constituent parts if it can be shown that it was aware of an overall plan to distort competition. See Joined Cases T-305/94 etc. *Limburgse Vinyl Maatschappij NV* v *Commission* [1999] ECR II-931, [1999] 5 CMLR 303, para 773.

BASF AG and UCB SA v Commission
(Joined Cases T-101 and 111/05) [2007] ECR II-4949

The Commission found that a number of undertakings had infringed Article 81 EC by participating in a complex set of agreements and concerted practices consisting of price fixing, market sharing, and agreed actions against competitors in the choline chloride sector. A global level cartel operated from 1992 to 1994, which was followed by a European level cartel from 1994 to 1998. The Commission found both levels to be part of a global plan which determined the conduct of the members of the cartel and restricted their individual commercial conduct in order to pursue a single anti-competitive economic objective. This was contested by the cartel members.

[160] The concept of single infringement can also be applied to the personal nature of liability for the infringements of the competition rules. An undertaking which has participated in an infringement by virtue of its own conduct, which met the definition of an agreement or a concerted practice within the meaning of Article 81(1) EC and which was intended to help to bring about the infringement as a whole, may also be responsible for the conduct of other undertakings followed in the context of the same infringement throughout the period of its participation in the infringement. That is the case where it is proved that the undertaking in question was aware of the unlawful conduct of the other participants, or that it could reasonably have foreseen that conduct, and that it was prepared to accept the risk. That conclusion has its origin in a widespread conception in the legal orders of the Member States concerning the attribution of responsibility for infringements committed by several perpetrators according to their participation in the infringement as a whole. It is not therefore contrary to the principle that responsibility for such infringements is personal in nature, it does not ignore the individual analysis of the incriminating evidence and it does not breach the rights of defence of the undertakings involved (*Commission v Anic Partecipazioni*, paragraph 150 above, paragraphs 83, 84 and 203, and *HFB and Others v Commission*, paragraph 150 above, paragraph 231).

[161] Thus, it has been held that a case of infringement of Article 81(1) EC could result from a series of acts or from continuous conduct which formed part of an 'overall plan' because they had the same object of distorting competition within the common market. In such a case, the Commission is entitled to attribute liability for those actions on the basis of participation in the infringement considered as a whole (*Aalborg Portland and Others v Commission*, paragraph 66 above, paragraph 258), even if it is established that the undertaking concerned directly participated in only one or some of the constituent elements of the infringement (*PVC II*, paragraph 159 above, paragraph 773). Likewise, the fact that different undertakings played different roles in the pursuit of a common objective does not mean that there was no identity of anti-competitive object and, accordingly, of infringement, provided that each undertaking contributed, at its own level, to the pursuit of the common objective (*Cement*, paragraph 157 above, paragraph 4123, and *JFE Engineering and Others v Commission*, paragraph 139 above, paragraph 370).

[162] In the present case, the characterisation by the Commission of the global and European parts of the cartel as a single and continuous infringement had the consequence that a single cartel was found to have lasted from 13 October 1992 until 30 September 1998. On the other hand, should the Court consider that those two parts constitute separate infringements, it must be held, in consequence, that the global cartel, which lasted from 13 October 1992 until 20 April 1994, is time-barred (see paragraph 9 above). In addition to the partial annulment of the Decision, that finding would have consequences for the calculation of both BASF's and UCB's fines.

...

[177] In accordance with the case-law cited at paragraph 159 above, the anti-competitive activities at the global level described at recital 69 to the Decision constitute in themselves a single infringement. That infringement consists of agreements (on fixing and increasing worldwide prices, on the withdrawal of the North American producers from the European market and on the control of distributors and converters) and concerted practices (the exchange of sensitive information with a view to mutually influencing the business conduct of the participants).

[178] The same applies to the anti-competitive activities at the European level which in themselves constitute a single and continuous infringement consisting of agreements (on fixing and

increasing prices for the EEA, for home markets and also for individual customers, on the allocation of customers, on the allocation of market shares and on the control of distributors and converters) and also of concerted practices (the exchange of sensitive information for the purpose of mutually influencing the participants' business conduct).

[179] However, it does not automatically follow from the application of that case-law to the present case that the arrangements at the global and European levels, taken together, form a single and continuous infringement. It appears that, in the cases which the case-law envisages, the existence of a common objective consisting in distorting the normal development of prices provides a ground for characterising the various agreements and concerted practices as the constituent elements of a single infringement. In that regard, it cannot be overlooked that those actions were complementary in nature, since each of them was intended to deal with one or more consequences of the normal pattern of competition and, by interacting, contributed to the realisation of the set of anti-competitive effects intended by those responsible, within the framework of a global plan having a single objective.

[180] In that connection, it must be made clear that the concept of single objective cannot be determined by a general reference to the distortion of competition in the choline chloride market, since an impact on competition, whether it is the object or the effect of the conduct in question, constitutes a consubstantial element of any conduct covered by Article 81(1) EC. Such a definition of the concept of a single objective is likely to deprive the concept of a single and continuous infringement of a part of its meaning, since it would have the consequence that different types of conduct which relate to a particular economic sector and are prohibited by Article 81(1) EC would have to be systematically characterised as constituent elements of a single infringement.

[181] The Court must therefore ascertain whether the two sets of agreements and concerted practices penalised by the Commission in the Decision as a single and continuous infringement are complementary in the way described at paragraph 179 above. The Commission itself bases its theory on the fact that the global and European arrangements were 'closely linked' (see paragraphs 4, 142 and 169 above). In that regard, it will be necessary to take into account any circumstance capable of establishing or casting doubt on that link, such as the period of application, the content (including the methods used) and, correlatively, the objective of the various agreements and concerted practices in question.

NOTE: The CFI eventually found that there was not a sufficient link between the global and European agreements to characterize them as a single infringement. This judgment indicates the extent of the 'single agreement' concept and the level of 'complementarity' that the Commission will have to prove to bring a series of events together and characterize them as a unitary whole. See Seifert, K., 'The Single Complex and Continuous Infringement—"Effet" Utilitarism?' [2008] ECLR 546.

D: Decisions by associations of undertakings

At first glance, it is difficult to appreciate why decisions by associations of undertakings where they restrict competition are prohibited given the wide interpretation of agreement. However, the difficulties faced by the Commission in proving an agreement often makes it easier to establish the existence of a decision by an association of undertakings. Undertakings often participate through the auspices of either a trade or professional association set up to represent their interests. The actual form of the decision is not important; what is crucial is the potential limit placed on the freedom of action of an association's members. A good example of how the decision of a trade association might affect competition in a market is *COAPI*.

COAPI

Commission Decision 95/188/EC, OJ, 1995, L122/37, [1995] 5 CMLR 468

[33] The Coapi, which incorporates all industrial property agents in Spain, therefore constitutes an association of undertakings within the meaning of Article 85(1) of the EC Treaty. The fact that it forms a professional association to which the public authorities have entrusted certain functions for the regulation of the profession and that in Spanish law it forms a legal person governed by public law, does not prevent Coapi from being regarded as an association of undertakings.

[34] The Coapi Regulations (which are concerned with both the establishment of the Coapi and its rules of procedure) form in their origins an agreement between undertakings. They were adopted by a meeting of industrial property agents. Subsequently, the general meeting of the Coapi has modified these regulations several times. Therefore, it follows from this that the Coapi Regulations also consti-tute a decision by an association of undertakings within the meaning of Article 85(1) of the EC Treaty.

[35] Likewise, the acts of the Coapi's general meeting and of its administrative board in fixing prices, which were adopted under the Coapi Regulations, constitute decisions by associations of undertakings within the meaning of Article 85(1). These acts are binding on all members and the Coapi ensures that they are applied, employing its power to impose penalties (fines and other sanctions extending to expulsion from the Coapi).

NOTE: Often, the trade association itself can act as a cloak, shielding the anti-competitive practices of its members. Thus, the Court has held that the constitution of a trade association in itself can amount to a decision for the purposes of Article 81 EC: see, e.g. *National Sulphuric Acid Association* OJ, 1980, L 260/24.

E: Concerted practices

The inclusion in Article 81 EC (1) of the term 'concerted practice' was designed to catch more informal means of cooperation. Although the Court refuses to differen-tiate an agreement from a concerted practice, since both are caught by Article 81(1) EC, it is nevertheless crucial to distinguish collusion from genuine (and legitimate) parallel behaviour, particularly in an oligopolistic market. However, as we shall see, distinguishing parallel behaviour that is genuine from that which is not, is not always an easy task; the essential difficulty being one of proof. The Court expounded its famous definition of a concerted practice in the following case. The case is better known as the *Dyestuffs* case.

ICI v Commission

(Case 48/69) [1972] ECR 619, [1972] CMLR 557

On a number of occasions between 1964 and 1967 ten major producers of dyestuffs, who held 80 per cent of the market for dyes sold in the Community, announced price rises of about 10 per cent. Telexed messages were sent from parent compan-ies to their subsidiaries all within the space of an hour, and all containing similar wording. The Commission held that there was a concerted practice that contra-vened Article 81(1) EC and imposed heavy fines.

The concept of a concerted practice

[64] Article 85 draws a distinction between the concept of 'concerted practices' and that of 'agreements between undertakings' or of 'decisions by associations of undertakings'; the object is

to bring within the prohibition of that article a form of coordination between undertakings which, without having reached the stage where an agreement properly so-called has been concluded, knowingly substitutes practical cooperation between them for the risks of competition.

[65] By its very nature, then, a concerted practice does not have all the elements of a contract but may *inter alia* arise out of coordination which becomes apparent from the behaviour of the participants.

[66] Although parallel behaviour may not by itself be identified with a concerted practice, it may however amount to strong evidence of such a practice if it leads to conditions of competition which do not correspond to the normal conditions of the market, having regard to the nature of the products, the size and number of the undertakings, and the volume of the said market.

[67] This is especially the case if the parallel conduct is such as to enable those concerned to attempt to stabilize prices at a level different from that to which competition would have led, and to consolidate established positions to the detriment of effective freedom of movement of the products in the Common Market and of the freedom of consumers to choose their suppliers.

[68] Therefore the question whether there was a concerted action in this case can only be correctly determined if the evidence upon which the contested decision is based is considered, not in isolation, but as a whole, account being taken of the specific features of the market in the products in question.

The characteristic features of the market in dyestuffs

[69] The market in dyestuffs is characterized by the fact that 80 per cent of the market is supplied by about ten producers, very large ones in the main, which often manufacture these products together with other chemical products or pharmaceutical specialities.

[70] The production patterns and therefore the cost structures of these manufacturers are very different, and this makes it difficult to ascertain competing manufacturers' costs.

[71] The total number of dyestuffs is very high, each undertaking producing more than a thousand.

[72] The average extent to which these products can be replaced by others is considered relatively good for standard dyes, but it can be very low or even non-existent for speciality dyes.

[73] As regards speciality products, the market tends in certain cases towards an oligopolistic situation.

[74] Since the price of dyestuffs forms a relatively small part of the price of the final product of the user undertaking, there is little elasticity of demand for dyestuffs on the market as a whole and this encourages price increases in the short term.

[75] Another factor is that the total demand for dyestuffs is constantly increasing, and this tends to induce producers to adopt a policy enabling them to take advantage of this increase.

[76] In the territory of the Community, the market in dyestuffs in fact consists of five separate national markets with different price levels which cannot be explained by differences in costs and charges affecting producers in those countries.

[77] Thus the establishment of the Common Market would not appear to have had any effect on this situation, since the differences between national price levels have scarcely decreased.

[78] On the contrary, it is clear that each of the national markets has the characteristics of an oligopoly and that in most of them price levels are established under the influence of a 'price-leader', who in some cases is the largest producer in the country concerned, and in other cases is a producer in another Member State or a third State, acting through a subsidiary.

[79] According to the experts this dividing-up of the market is due to the need to supply local technical assistance to users and to ensure immediate delivery, generally in small quantities, since, apart from exceptional cases, producers supply their subsidiaries established in the different Member States and maintain a network of agents and depots to ensure that user undertakings receive specific assistance and supplies.

[80] It appears from the data produced during the course of the proceedings that even in cases where a producer establishes direct contact with an important user in another Member State,

prices are usually fixed in relation to the place where the user is established and tend to follow the level of prices on the national market.

[81] Although the foremost reason why producers have acted in this way is in order to adapt themselves to the special features of the market in dyestuffs and to the needs of their customers, the fact remains that the dividing-up of the market which results tends, by fragmenting the effects of competition, to isolate users in their national market, and to prevent a general confrontation between producers throughout the Common Market.

[82] It is in this context, which is peculiar to the way in which the dyestuffs market works, that the facts of the case should be considered.

[83] The increases of 1964, 1965 and 1967 covered by the contested decision are interconnected.

[84] The increase of 15 per cent in the prices of most aniline dyes in Germany on 1 January 1965 was in reality nothing more than the extension to another national market of the increase applied in January 1964 in Italy, the Netherlands, Belgium and Luxembourg.

[85] The increase in the prices of certain dyes and pigments introduced on 1 January 1965 in all the Member States, except France, applied to all the products which had been excluded from the first increase.

[86] The reason why the price increase of 8 per cent introduced in the autumn of 1967 was raised to 12 per cent for France was that there was a wish to make up for the increases of 1964 and 1965 in which that market had not taken part because of the price control system.

[87] Therefore the three increases cannot be isolated one from another, even though they did not take place under identical conditions.

[88] In 1964 all the undertakings in question announced their increases and immediately put them into effect, the initiative coming from Ciba-Italy which, on 7 January 1964, following instructions from Ciba-Switzerland, announced and immediately introduced an increase of 15 per cent. This initiative was followed by the other producers on the Italian market within two or three days.

[89] On 9 January ICI Holland took the initiative in introducing the same increase in the Netherlands, whilst on the same day Bayer took the same initiative on the Belgo-Luxembourg market.

[90] With minor differences, particularly between the price increases by the German undertakings on the one hand and the Swiss and United Kingdom undertakings on the other, these increases concerned the same range of products for the various producers and markets, namely, most aniline dyes other than pigments, food colourings and cosmetics.

[91] As regards the increase of 1965 certain undertakings announced in advance price increases amounting, for the German market, to an increase of 15 per cent for products whose prices had already been similarly increased on the other markets, and to 10 per cent for products whose prices had not yet been increased. These announcements were spread over the period between 14 October and 28 December 1964.

[92] The first announcement was made by BASF, on 14 October 1964, followed by an announcement by Bayer on 30 October and by Casella on 5 November.

[93] These increases were simultaneously applied on 1 January 1965 on all the markets except for the French market because of the price freeze in that State, and the Italian market where, as a result of the refusal by the principal Italian producer, ACNA, to increase its prices on the said market, the other producers also decided not to increase theirs.

[94] ACNA also refrained from putting its prices up by 10 per cent on the German market.

[95] Otherwise the increase was general, was simultaneously introduced by all the producers mentioned in the contested decision, and was applied without any differences concerning the range of products.

[96] As regards the increase of 1967, during a meeting held at Basel on 19 August 1967, which was attended by all the producers mentioned in the contested decision except ACNA, the Geigy undertaking announced its intention to increase its selling prices by 8 per cent with effect from 16 October 1967.

[97] On that same occasion the representatives of Bayer and Francolor stated that their undertakings were also considering an increase.

[98] From mid-September all the undertakings mentioned in the contested decision announced a price increase of 8 per cent raised to 12 per cent for France, to take effect on 16 October in all the countries except Italy, where ACNA again refused to increase its prices, although it was willing to follow the movement in prices on two other markets, albeit on dates other than 16 October.

[99] Viewed as a whole, the three consecutive increases reveal progressive cooperation between the undertakings concerned.

[100] In fact, after the experience of 1964, when the announcement of the increases and their application coincided, although with minor differences as regards the range of products affected, the increases of 1965 and 1967 indicate a different mode of operation. Here, the undertakings taking the initiative, BASF and Geigy respectively, announced their intentions of making an increase some time in advance, which allowed the undertakings to observe each other's reactions on the different markets, and to adapt themselves accordingly.

[101] By means of these advance announcements the various undertakings eliminated all uncertainty between them as to their future conduct and, in doing so, also eliminated a large part of the risk usually inherent in any independent change of conduct on one or several markets.

[102] This was all the more the case since these announcements, which led to the fixing of general and equal increases in prices for the markets in dyestuffs, rendered the market transparent as regard the precentage rates of increase.

[103] Therefore, by the way in which they acted, the undertakings in question temporarily eliminated with respect to prices some of the preconditions for competition on the market which stood in the way of the achievement of parallel uniformity of conduct.

[104] The fact that this conduct was not spontaneous is corroborated by an examination of other aspects of the market.

[105] In fact, from the number of producers concerned it is not possible to say that the European market in dyestuffs is, in the strict sense, an oligopoly in which price competition could no longer play a substantial role.

[106] These producers are sufficiently powerful and numerous to create a considerable risk that in times of rising prices some of them might not follow the general movement but might instead try to increase their share of the market by behaving in an individual way.

[107] Furthermore, the dividing-up of the Common Market into five national markets with different price levels and structures makes it improbable that a spontaneous and equal price increase would occur on all the national markets.

[108] Although a general, spontaneous increase on each of the national markets is just conceivable, these increases might be expected to differ according to the particular characteristics of the different national markets.

[109] Therefore, although parallel conduct in respect of prices may well have been an attractive and risk-free objective for the undertakings concerned, it is hardly conceivable that the same action could be taken spontaneously at the same time, on the same national markets and for the same range of products.

[110] Nor is it any more plausible that the increases of January 1964, introduced on the Italian market and copied on the Netherlands and Belgo-Luxembourg markets, which have little in common with each other either as regards the level of prices or the pattern of competition, could have been brought into effect within a period of two to three days without prior concertation.

[111] As regards the increases of 1965 and 1967 concertation took place openly, since all the announcements of the intention to increase prices with effect from a certain date and for a certain range of products made it possible for producers to decide on their conduct regarding the special cases of France and Italy.

[112] In proceeding in this way, the undertakings mutually eliminated in advance any uncertainties concerning their reciprocal behaviour on the different markets and thereby also eliminated a large part of the risk inherent in any independent change of conduct on those markets.

[113] The general and uniform increase on those different markets can only be explained by a common intention on the part of those undertakings, first, to adjust the level of prices and the situation resulting from competition in the form of discounts, and secondly, to avoid the risk, which is inherent in any price increase, of changing the conditions of competition.

NOTE: The coverage of Article 81 EC to the forms of practical cooperation discussed in *Dyestuffs* was expanded in the *Sugar Cartel* case. Various sugar producers argued that they had not participated in a concerted practice, contrary to Article 81 EC, as there was no plan to do so. The Court concluded that the absence of a plan was not detrimental to a finding of concertation, provided there was some form of mental consensus between the parties.

Cooperative Vereniging 'Suiker Unie' v Commission
(Joined Cases 40–48, 50, 54–56, 111, and 113–14/73) [1975] ECR 663, [1976] 1 CMLR 295

[173] The criteria of coordination and cooperation laid down by the case-law of the Court, which in no way require the working out of an actual plan, must be understood in the light of the concept inherent in the provisions of the Treaty relating to competition that each economic operator must determine independently the policy which he intends to adopt on the common market including the choice of the persons and undertakings to which he makes offers or sells.

[174] Although it is correct to say that this requirement of independence does not deprive economic operators of the right to adapt themselves intelligently to the existing and anticipated conduct of their competitors, it does however strictly preclude any direct or indirect contact between such operators, the object or effect whereof is either to influence the conduct on the market of an actual or potential competitor or to disclose to such a competitor the course of conduct which they themselves have decided to adopt or contemplate adopting on the market.

NOTE: The Commission and the Court have been criticized for relying on seemingly circumstantial evidence, for example contemporaneous price rises. In *Dyestuffs*, the Court was persuaded by the discovery of telexed instructions by different undertakings to subsidiary companies on the same evening. Is this circumstantial evidence? Was there any other evidence that the Commission relied upon? The extract from the following case illustrates how the Court considers faxes, internal memoranda, and telephone calls to prove the existence of a concerted practice.

Van Megen Sports v Commission
(Case T-49/95) [1996] ECR II-1799

Findings of the Court

[34] The applicant does not deny that Tretorn operated a system of exclusive distribution coupled with a prohibition of exports and with mechanisms intended to ensure that that prohibition was applied as effectively as possible. It acknowledges that it has been Tretorn's exclusive distributor in the Netherlands since 1985. It denies, on the other hand, that Tretorn imposed an export ban on *it* and that *it* participated in the reporting and investigating of parallel imports. Until the Commission initiated the infringement procedure, it had not even been aware of the ban on parallel exports.

[35] According to the case-law of the Court of Justice and the Court of First Instance, the provisions of Article 85(1) of the Treaty may not be declared inapplicable to an exclusive distribution contract which does not in itself include a prohibition of re-exports of the products which are the subject of the contract, where the contracting parties are engaged in a concerted practice aimed

at restricting parallel imports intended for an unauthorized dealer (see Case 86/82 *Hasselblad* v *Commission* [1984] ECR 883 and Case T-43/92 *Dunlop Slazenger* v *Commission* [1994] ECR II-441, paragraph 88).

[36] In the present case, the Commission had relied on the following two documents, described in points 24 and 25 of the Decision, as proof that the applicant had taken part in the Netherlands in the reporting and investigating of parallel imports:

— a fax of 16 July 1987 from Mr M of Tretorn to Mr A of Tretorn AB:

I just had a phone call from Will Van Megen to advise that XL boxes of 4 again turning up in a major shoe chain in Holland.

I have asked Will to forward the Code No to [Mr O] so that he can advise which country has shipped.

While I of course suspect our friends, we must wait for the proof.

If it is the UK, then obviously the shipment has been made to Holland in the past few weeks.

— a Tretorn internal memorandum of 20 June 1988 from Mr M to Mr O:

Please ring Will Van Megen. He has parallel from two different sources.

1 Box of 4, made in Ireland, no date code yet.

2 Box of 4, USTA approved, no date code yet.

He hopes to have date codes in a few days.

[37] Those two documents from Tretorn have probative force. As the Commission rightly observed, they were written by a well-informed third party who had no reason to give false information. Moreover, they were written outside the context of any procedure for defence or justification before the Commission or this Court.

[38] Those two pieces of evidence clearly establish that the applicant participated in the reporting and investigating of parallel imports of tennis balls, for the purposes of applying Tretorn's policy. It is clear from the fax of 16 July 1987 that the applicant informed Tretorn of the existence of parallel imports of Tretorn tennis balls in the Netherlands, that it was not the first time that it gave Tretorn such information, and that it had been asked to provide the date codes which might enable Tretorn to determine the country from which the balls came. As to the internal memorandum of 20 June 1988, that document shows that the applicant again informed Tretorn of the existence of parallel imports of Tretorn tennis balls in the Netherlands, that it had identified two different sources of those imports, and that it was investigating to obtain the date codes.

[39] With respect to the Tretorn internal memorandum of 23 August 1988, mentioned at point 46 of the Decision, recommending the stopping of deliveries to the American market because tennis balls delivered there were reappearing in the Netherlands via parallel imports, it is sufficient to observe that the Commission did not rely on that document with regard to the applicant. Point 46 of the Decision comes under the heading 'Suspension of supplies to prevent parallel imports', under which the Commission mentions the measures adopted by Tretorn to deal with those imports. That document is thus relied on as against Tretorn, and not the applicant, in whose case the Commission rightly considered that it had sufficient evidence.

[40] As to the date codes, the fax of 16 July 1987, the internal memorandum of 20 June 1988 and the other evidence relied on by the Commission in the Decision (see points 36 to 38 and 40) show beyond doubt that Tretorn could identify the origin of parallel imports from the date codes. That can be seen in particular from a fax of 17 April 1987 from Tretorn to Formula Sport International Ltd (see point 37), in which Mr M of Tretorn stated: 'The date codes are all from the shipment to Formula.' It can also be seen from a fax of 15 May 1987, also from Tretorn to Formula Sport International Ltd, in which Mr M states: 'We are sure of our facts/date codes and the balls shipped to Formula ended up in Switzerland. . . . Formula is guilty so let's not have any more discussion'.

[41] As for the letter from Scapino, that document does not in any way contradict the Commission's evidence. The applicant could not itself prevent the parallel imports by Scapino. Had it wished to prevent them, it would have had to contact Tretorn, so that that company might take the necessary measures for that purpose. Moreover, it was naturally in the applicant's interest to

sell as many Tretorn tennis balls as possible, to Scapino amongst others. It should also be noted that Tretorn's policy was to prohibit exports. There is nothing before the Court to suggest that Scapino would have exported the Tretorn tennis balls supplied by the applicant. The applicant therefore did not infringe Tretorn's policy by selling the balls to Scapino, which, like the applicant, is a Netherlands undertaking. Tretorn thus had no interest either in asking the applicant to refuse to supply Scapino, even assuming that it had been informed of those sales.

[42] The reasons given by the applicant to explain why it made reports to Tretorn cannot be accepted. If the applicant had wished to make those reports solely in order to find out whether Tretorn was making direct supplies to customers in the Netherlands and to strengthen its position in negotiations with Tretorn and thereby obtain a better price, it would not have needed to try to obtain the date codes of the tennis balls imported in parallel. It is thus apparent that it was in fact aware of Tretorn's policy of prohibiting parallel imports. It follows that the Commission was correct in finding, in point 70 of the Decision, that even if the interpretation given by the applicant was correct, 'the fact remains that the information was given in the context of a ban on parallel exports of which Van Megen was well aware and it actively participated in identifying the source of the parallel imports'.

[43] The applicant cannot, finally, argue that its two telephone conversations with Tretorn cannot be described as active participation, since it was the applicant which took the initiative in contacting Tretorn, not vice versa. Moreover, it can be seen from paragraph 38 above that the applicant made inquiries to obtain the date codes of the parallel imports. It follows that the applicant actively participated in Tretorn's policy.

[44] It follows from the foregoing that the pleas in law alleging that the Commission did not adduce sufficient evidence and did not give an adequate statement of reasons for its decision must be rejected.

Harding, C., and Joshua, J., *Regulating Cartels in Europe—A Study of Legal Control of Corporate Delinquency*
Oxford, OUP, 2003, pp. 164–5

There are of course a number of types of 'plus' evidence which may be used to establish participation in a cartel, even when the behaviour in question is clandestine. Most importantly, such evidence will relate to meetings and other communications and will record the working out and consummation of planned collusion. In the nature of things, such communications and their outcomes cannot remain wholly unrecorded, simply kept in the heads of a number of people working in different places and not wanting to be observed together. Material evidence of some kind, in hard copy or electronic form, perhaps later substantiated by oral evidence, therefore has to be the basis of the case.

As in the analogous domain of criminal investigation, the practical difficulty is one of locating and retrieving such evidence. In its role as a competition regulator, the Commission has called in aid two particular techniques of evidence detection, which have in turn accounted for much of its actual 'cartel-busting' success. The first was a technique of stealth: the surprise inspection of company premises, or so called 'dawn raid'. The second and latter technique was one of cunning, emulating the success of the US Department of Justice: the offer of leniency. The dawn raid relied upon an element of surprise and exploited a certain unavoidable level of human carelessness. The leniency programme relies upon an element of uncertainty and exploits the natural nervousness inherent in cartel conspiracy. Both, in different ways, can trigger a flow of evidence and 'bust' the cartel.

NOTE: The difficult issues surrounding the discovery of proof in cartel cases will be highlighted more fully in Chapter 9. What Harding and Joshua make clear is that the legal niceties of what constitutes an agreement is in many cases subordinate to the more real problems of gaining good evidence of the true relationship between the parties to the supposed agreement.

F: The oligopoly defence

Another issue to arise from the Court's jurisprudence concerns behaviour that may in fact be a normal consequence of an oligopolistic market. There is clearly a very fine line between innocent parallel behaviour, which is acceptable and indeed commercially prudent, and the 'knowing substitution of practical cooperation for the risks of competition'. This was exactly the difficulty faced by the Commission in the next case, better known as *Wood Pulp*. This important case confirms the importance of using economic analysis, where other means of proof may be impracticable or impossible, and the merits of obtaining expert economic advice.

A Ahlström Oy v Commission
(Joined Cases C-89, 104, 114, 116, 117, and 125–9/85) [1993] ECR I-1307, [1993] 4 CMLR 407

The Commission concluded that 43 undertakings producing bleached sulphate pulp, used in the manufacture of fine quality paper, had participated in a concerted practice. The Commission based its findings partly on evidence of direct and indirect exchanges of information amongst the producers which had led to a situation whereby prices were announced in advance and followed quickly by similar announcements from competitors. The Commission concluded that 'the parallel conduct following a proper economic analysis, cannot be explained as independently chosen parallel conduct in a narrow oligopolistic situation'. On appeal, the Court emphatically rejected the main thrust of the Commission's argument. The importance of the Court's judgment necessitates a lengthy extract.

A. The system of quarterly price announcements constitutes in itself the infringement of Article 85 of the Treaty

2. The other evidence adduced by the Commission

[70] Since the Commission has no documents which directly establish the existence of concertation between the producers concerned, it is necessary to ascertain whether the system of quarterly price announcements, the simultaneity or near-simultaneity of the price announcements and the parallelism of price announcements as found during the period from 1975 to 1981 constitute a firm, precise and consistent body of evidence of prior concertation.

[71] In determining the probative value of those different factors, it must be noted that parallel conduct cannot be regarded as furnishing proof of concertation unless concertation constitutes the only plausible explanation for such conduct. It is necessary to bear in mind that, although Article 85 of the Treaty prohibits any form of collusion which distorts competition, it does not deprive economic operators of the right to adapt themselves intelligently to the existing and anticipated conduct of their competitors (see the judgment in *Suiker Unie*, cited above, paragraph 174).

[72] Accordingly, it is necessary in this case to ascertain whether the parallel conduct alleged by the Commission cannot, taking account of the nature of the products, the size and the number of the undertakings and the volume of the market in question, be explained otherwise than by concertation.

(a) The system of price announcements

[73] As stated above, the Commission regards the system of quarterly price announcements as evidence of concertation at an earlier stage.

[74] In their pleadings, on the other hand, the applicants maintain that the system is ascribable to the particular commercial requirements of the pulp market.

[75] By orders of 25 October 1990 and 14 March 1991, the Court requested two experts to examine the characteristics of the market for bleached sulphate pulp during the period covered by the contested decision. Their report sets out the following considerations.

[76] The experts observe first that the system of announcements at issue must be viewed in the context of the long-term relationships which existed between producers and their customers and which were a result both of the method of manufacturing the pulp and of the cyclical nature of the market. In view of the fact that each type of paper was the result of a particular mixture of pulps having their own characteristics and that the mixture was difficult to change, a relationship based on close cooperation was established between the pulp producers and the paper manufacturers. Such relations were all the closer since they also had the advantage of protecting both sides against the uncertainties inherent in the cyclical nature of the market: they guaranteed security of supply to buyers and at the same time security of demand to producers.

[77] The experts point out that it is in the context of those long-term relationships that, after the Second World War, purchasers demanded the introduction of that system of announcements. Since pulp accounts for between 50 per cent and 75 per cent of the cost of paper, those purchasers wished to ascertain as soon as possible the prices which they might be charged in order to estimate their costs and to fix the prices of their own products. However, as those purchasers did not wish to be bound by a high fixed price in the event of the market weakening, the announced price was regarded as a ceiling price below which the transaction price could always be renegotiated.

[78] The explanation given for the use of a quarterly cycle is that it is the result of a compromise between the paper manufacturers' desire for a degree of foreseeability as regards the price of pulp and the producers' desire not to miss any opportunities to make a profit in the event of a strengthening of the market.

[79] The US dollar was, according to the experts, introduced on the market by the North American producers during the 1960s. That development was generally welcomed by purchasers who regarded it as a means of ensuring that they did not pay a higher price than their competitors.

(b) The simultaneity or near-simultaneity of announcements

[80] In paragraph 107 of its decision, the Commission claims that the close succession or even simultaneity of price announcements would not have been possible without a constant flow of information between the undertakings concerned.

[81] According to the applicants, the simultaneity or near-simultaneity of the announcements—even if it were established—must instead be regarded as a direct result of the very high degree of transparency of the market. Such transparency, far from being artificial, can be explained by the extremely well-developed network of relations which, in view of the nature and the structure of the market, have been established between the various traders.

[82] The experts have confirmed that analysis in their report and at the hearing which followed.

[83] First, they pointed out, a buyer was always in contact with several pulp producers. One reason for that was connected with the paper-making process, but another was that, in order to avoid becoming overdependent on one producer, pulp buyers took the precaution of diversifying their sources of supply. With a view to obtaining the lowest possible prices, they were in the habit, especially in times of falling prices, of disclosing to their suppliers the prices announced by their competitors.

[84] Secondly, it should be noted that most of the pulp was sold to a relatively small number of large paper manufacturers. Those few buyers maintained very close links with each other and exchanged information on changes in prices of which they were aware.

[85] Thirdly, several producers who made paper themselves purchased pulp from other producers and were thus informed, in times of both rising prices and falling prices, of the prices charged by their competitors. That information was also accessible to producers who did not themselves manufacture paper but were linked to groups that did.

[86] Fourthly, that high degree of transparency in the pulp market resulting from the links between traders or groups of traders was further reinforced by the existence of agents established

in the Community who worked for several producers and by the existence of a very dynamic trade press.

[87] In connection with the latter point, it should be noted that most of the applicants deny having communicated to the trade press any information on their prices and that the few producers who acknowledged having done so point out that such communications were sporadic and were made at the request of the press itself.

[88] Finally, it is necessary to add that the use of rapid means of communication, such as the telephone and telex, and the very frequent recourse by the paper manufacturers to very well-informed trade buyers meant that, notwithstanding the number of stages involved—producer, agent, buyer, agent, producer—information on the level of the announced prices spreads within a matter of days, if not within a matter of hours on the pulp market.

(c) Parallelism of announced prices

[89] The parallelism of announced prices on which the Commission relies as evidence of concertation is described in paragraph 22 of its decision. In that paragraph, the Commission, relying on Table 6 annexed to the decision, finds that the prices announced by the Canadian and United States producers were the same from the first quarter of 1975 to the third quarter of 1977 and from the first quarter of 1978 to the third quarter of 1981, that the prices announced by the Swedish and Finnish producers were the same from the first quarter of 1975 to the second quarter of 1977 and from the third quarter of 1978 to the third quarter of 1981 and, finally, that the prices of all the producers were the same from the first quarter of 1976 to the second quarter of 1977 and from the third quarter of 1979 to the third quarter of 1981.

[90] According to the Commission, the only explanation for such parallelism of prices is concertation between the producers. That contention is essentially based on the considerations that follow.

[91] In the first place, the single price charged by the producers during the period at issue cannot be regarded as an equilibrium price, that is to say a price resulting from the natural operation of the law of supply and demand. The Commission emphasizes that there was no testing of the market 'by trial and error', as evidenced by the stability of prices established between the first quarter of 1975 and the fourth quarter of 1976, and the fact that, generally in the case of softwood from the third quarter of 1979 to the second quarter of 1980, the first higher price demanded was always followed by the other producers.

[92] Nor can the argument concerning 'price leadership' be accepted: the similarity of announced prices, and that of transaction prices moreover, cannot be explained by the existence of a market leader whose prices were adopted by its competitors. The order in which the announcements were made continued to change from quarter to quarter and no one producer held a strong enough position to act as leader.

[93] Secondly, the Commission considers that, since economic conditions varied from one producer to another or from one group of producers to another, they should have charged different prices. Pulp manufacturers with low costs should have lowered their prices in order to increase their market shares to the detriment of their least efficient competitors. According to the Commission, the divergences in question related to production and transport costs, the relationship between those costs (determined in the national currencies: Canadian dollar, Swedish krona or Finnish mark) and selling prices (fixed in US dollars), size of orders, variations in demand for pulp in the various importing countries, the relative importance of the European market, which was greater for Scandinavian producers than for United States and Canadian producers, and the production capacity utilization ratios which, generally speaking, were higher in the United States and Canada than in Sweden and Finland.

[94] So far as the size of orders is concerned, the Commission considers that since the sale of large quantities enabled producers to cut their costs substantially, the price records should have shown significant price differences between purchasers of large quantities and purchasers of small quantities. In practice, those differences rarely amounted to more than 3 per cent.

[95] Thirdly, the Commission claims that, at any rate for a time in 1976, 1977 and 1981, announced prices for pulp stood at an artificially high level which differed widely from that which might have

been expected under normal competitive conditions. For example, it is inconceivable, without concertation, for a single unchanged price of US$ 415 to have been announced for northern softwood from the first quarter of 1975 to the third quarter of 1977 and, especially during the second and third quarters of 1977, for the announced price to have stood at US$ 100 above the selling price actually obtainable on the market. The contention that prices stood at an abnormally high level is borne out by the fact that in 1977 and 1982 the fall in prices was particularly abrupt.

[96] Finally, the Commission relies on the grant of secret rebates and on changes in market shares.

[97] So far as concerns the grant of secret rebates, it should be noted that there is a contradiction between the decision and what has been said subsequently. In paragraph 112 of its decision, the Commission refers to the exclusion of secret competition but then states in its pleadings that, if the rebates were secret, it was because they undermined concertation and therefore had to remain concealed from the other producers.

[98] So far as concerns the shifts in market shares established between 1975 and 1981, the Commission considers that they do not justify the finding that there was no concertation. Those shifts were much less marked between 1975 and 1976 and between 1980 and 1981 than the shifts between 1978 and 1979 and between 1979 and 1980.

[99] The applicants disputed the view that parallelism of prices was attributable to concertation.

[100] In commissioning the second expert's report, the Court requested the experts to specify whether, in their opinion, the natural operation of the wood pulp market should lead to a differential price structure or to a uniform price structure.

[101] It is apparent from the expert's report, together with the ensuing discussion, that the experts regard the normal operation of the market as a more plausible explanation for the uniformity of prices than concertation. The main thrust of their analysis may be summarized as follows:

(i) Description of the market

[102] The experts describe the market as a group of oligopolies-oligopsonies consisting of certain producers and of certain buyers and each corresponding to a given kind of pulp. That market structure results largely from the method of manufacturing paper pulp: since paper is the result of a characteristic mixture of pulps, each paper manufacturer can deal only with a limited number of pulp producers and, conversely, each pulp producer can supply only a limited number of customers. Within the groupings so constituted, cooperation was further consolidated by the finding that it offered both buyers and sellers of pulp security against the uncertainties of the market.

[103] That organization of the market, in conjunction with its very high degree of transparency, leads in the short-term to a situation where prices are slow to react. The producers know that, if they were to increase their prices, their competitors would no doubt refrain from following suit and thus lure their customers away. Similarly, they would be reluctant to reduce their prices in the knowledge that, if they did so, the other producers would follow suit, assuming that they had spare production capacity. Such a fall in prices would be all the less desirable in that it would be detrimental to the sector as a whole: since overall demand for pulp is inelastic, the loss of revenue resulting from the reduction in prices could not be offset by the profits made as a result of the increased sales and there would be a decline in the producers' overall profits.

[104] In the long-term, the possibility for buyers to turn, at the price of some investment, to other types of pulp and the existence of substitute products, such as Brazilian pulp or pulp from recycled paper, have the effect of mitigating oligopolistic trends on the market. That explains why, over a period of several years, fluctuations in prices have been relatively contained.

[105] Finally, the transparency of the market could be responsible for certain overall price increases recorded in the short-term: when demand exceeds supply, producers who are aware—as was the case on the pulp market—that the level of their competitors' stocks is low and that their production capacity utilization rate is high would not be afraid to increase their prices. There would then be a serious likelihood of their being followed by their competitors.

...

3. Conclusions

[126] Following that analysis, it must be stated that, in this case, concertation is not the only plausible explanation for the parallel conduct. To begin with, the system of price announcements may be regarded as constituting a rational response to the fact that the pulp market constituted a long-term market and to the need felt by both buyers and sellers to limit commercial risks. Further, the similarity in the dates of price announcements may be regarded as a direct result of the high degree of market transparency, which does not have to be described as artificial. Finally, the parallelism of prices and the price trends may be satisfactorily explained by the oligopolistic tendencies of the market and by the specific circumstances prevailing in certain periods. Accordingly, the parallel conduct established by the Commission does not constitute evidence of concertation.

[127] In the absence of a firm, precise and consistent body of evidence, it must be held that concertation regarding announced prices has not been established by the Commission. Article 1(1) of the contested decision must therefore be annulled.

NOTE: Following the *Wood Pulp* judgment the Commission has used Article 82 EC and the Merger Regulation to challenge oligopolistic behaviour on the basis of collective dominance of the relevant market. See the landmark decisions of the CFI regarding the concept of 'collective dominance' in Joined Cases T-68, 77–8/89 *Re Italian Flat Glass: Societa Italiano Vetio SpA v Commission* [1992] ECR II-1403, [1992] 5 CMLR 302 and Case T-342/99 *Airtours v Commission* [2002] ECR II-2585.

■ QUESTIONS

Following the Court's rejection of the Commission's 'circumstantial' evidence in *Wood Pulp* the Commission must produce much more to prove the existence of an agreement in Article 81 EC; what sort of evidence will now be required for the Commission to prove an infringement?

'It is difficult to define in legal language the precise line between lawful and unlawful combinations. This must be left for the courts to determine in each particular case. All that we, as lawmakers, can do is to declare general principles, and we can be assured that the courts will apply them as to carry out the meaning of the law... This bill is only an honest effort to declare a rule of action.'

(Senator John Sherman on introducing the Bill to the US Senate, 1889)

Discuss.

G: Unilateral conduct

The general principle is that Article 81 EC applies to the activities of two or more undertakings and is thereby to be distinguished from Article 82 EC. However, the Commission has held that unilateral conduct can, in certain contexts, for example within a distribution system, amount to an agreement or concerted practice for the purposes of Article 81 EC. This is a view shared by the Court in a series of decisions.

AEG-Telefunken v Commission
(Case 107/82) [1983] ECR 3151, [1984] 3 CMLR 325

The Court accepted the Commission's findings that admission to a selective distribution system was based upon an acceptance, tacit or express, of the policies pursued by the manufacturer. It followed that a refusal by AEG to supply certain distributors that met the criteria set by AEG formed an integral part of the operation of the distribution network and thus constituted an agreement for the purposes of Article 81 EC.

[31] AEG contends that the acts complained of in the contested decision, namely the failure to admit certain traders and steps taken to exert an influence on prices, are unilateral acts and do not therefore, as such, fall within Article 85(1), which relates only to agreements between undertakings, decisions by associations of undertakings and concerted practices.

[32] In order properly to appreciate that argument it is appropriate to consider the legal significance of selective distribution systems.

[33] It is common ground that agreements constituting a selective system necessarily affect competition in the common market. However, it has always been recognized in the case-law of the Court that there are legitimate requirements, such as the maintenance of a specialist trade capable of providing specific services as regards high-quality and high-technology products, which may justify a reduction of price competition in favour of competition relating to factors other than price. Systems of selective distribution, in so far as they aim at the attainment of a legitimate goal capable of improving competition in relation to factors other than price, therefore constitute an element of competition which is in conformity with Article 85(1).

[34] The limitations inherent in a selective distribution system are however acceptable only on condition that their aim is in fact an improvement in competition in the sense above mentioned. Otherwise they would have no justification inasmuch as their sole effect would be to reduce price competition.

[35] So as to guarantee that selective distribution systems may be based on that aim alone and cannot be set up and used with a view to the attainment of objectives which are not in conformity with Community law, the Court specified in its judgment of 25 October 1977 (*Metro* v *Commission*, [1977] ECR 1875) that such systems are permissible, provided that resellers are chosen on the basis of objective criteria of a qualitative nature relating to the technical qualifications of the reseller and his staff and the suitability of his trading premises and that such conditions are laid down uniformly for all potential resellers and are not applied in a discriminatory fashion.

[36] It follows that the operation of a selective distribution system based on criteria other than those mentioned above constitutes an infringement of Article 85(1). The position is the same where a system which is in principle in conformity with Community law is applied in practice in a manner incompatible therewith.

[37] Such a practice must be considered unlawful where the manufacturer, with a view to maintaining a high level of prices or to excluding certain modern channels of distribution, refuses to approve distributors who satisfy the qualitative criteria of the system.

[38] Such an attitude on the part of the manufacturer does not constitute, on the part of the undertaking, unilateral conduct which, as AEG claims, would be exempt from the prohibition contained in Article 85(1) of the Treaty. On the contrary, it forms part of the contractual relations between the undertaking and resellers. Indeed, in the case of the admission of a distributor, approval is based on the acceptance, tacit or express, by the contracting parties of the policy pursued by AEG which requires inter alia the exclusion from the network of all distributors who are qualified for admission but are not prepared to adhere to that policy.

[39] The view must therefore be taken that even refusals of approval are acts performed in the context of the contractual relations with authorized distributors inasmuch as their purpose is to guarantee observance of the agreements in restraint of competition which form the basis of contracts between manufacturers and approved distributors. Refusals to approve distributors who satisfy the qualitative criteria mentioned above therefore supply proof of an unlawful application of the system if their number is sufficient to preclude the possibility that they are isolated cases not forming part of systematic conduct.

NOTE: In Joined Cases 25 and 26/84 *Ford Werke AG* v *Commission* [1985] ECR 2725 the Court accepted the Commission's reasoning that a circular sent by a car manufacturer to its German dealers in which it suggested that it would not meet orders from them for right-hand-drive motor cars, thus isolating markets in the UK and Ireland, formed part of the contractual relations between manufacturer and dealer as an implied term. Similarly, in Case C-277/87 *Sandoz* [1990] ECR I-45 the Court concluded that:

> the Commission was justified in considering that the set of continuous commercial relations, of which the 'export prohibited' clause formed an integral part, established between Sandoz PF and its customers was governed by a pre-established general agreement applicable to innumerable individual orders for Sandoz products. Such an agreement is covered by the provisions of Article 85(1) of the EEC Treaty.

However, the Commission and Court adopted a different approach in the more recent case, commonly known as the *Adalat*. It is likely that this approach will be carried forward.

Bayer v Commission
(Case T-41/96) [2000] ECR II-3383, [2001] 4 CMLR 4

Bayer, a large German pharmaceutical manufacturer, through its wholly owned subsidiaries in France and Spain, enjoyed long-standing sales to wholesalers in those markets. The Commission concluded that, through these subsidiaries, Bayer had withheld from the wholesalers supplies of a broad range of medicinal products used in the treatment of cardiovascular diseases. Furthermore, the Commission held that the wholesalers 'complied' with this ban, despite evidence that they actually resisted attempts to limit supplies. The Commission formed the view that the export ban became an integral part of their commercial relations and that this amounted to an agreement for the purposes of Article 81(1) EC. However, the Commission's decision was overturned by the Court of First Instance.

[65] In this case, it is found in the Decision that there is an agreement between undertakings within the meaning of that article. The applicant maintains, however, that the Decision penalises unilateral conduct on its part that falls outside the scope of the article. It claims that the Commission has given the concept of an agreement within the meaning of Article 85(1) of the Treaty an interpretation which goes beyond the precedents in the case-law and that its application to the present case infringes that provision of the Treaty. The Commission contends that it has fully followed the case-law in its evaluation of that concept and has applied it in a wholly appropriate manner to the facts of this case. It therefore needs to be determined whether, having regard to the definition of that concept in the case-law, the Commission was entitled to perceive in the conduct established in the Decision the factors constituting an agreement between undertakings within the meaning of Article 85(1) of the Treaty.

B. The concept of an agreement within the meaning of Article 85(1) of the Treaty

[66] The case-law shows that, where a decision on the part of a manufacturer constitutes unilateral conduct of the undertaking, that decision escapes the prohibition in Article 85(1) of the Treaty (Case 107/82 *AEG* v *Commission* [1983] ECR 3151, paragraph 38; Joined Cases 25/84 and 26/84 *Ford and Ford Europe* v *Commission* [1985] ECR 2725, paragraph 21; Case T-43/92 *Dunlop Slazenger* v *Commission* [1994] ECR II-441, paragraph 56).

[67] It is also clear from the case-law in that in order for there to be an agreement within the meaning of Article 85(1) of the Treaty it is sufficient that the undertakings in question should have expressed their joint intention to conduct themselves on the market in a specific way (Case 41/69 *ACF Chemiefarma* v *Commission* [1970] ECR 661, paragraph 112; Joined Cases 209/78 to 215/78 and 218/78 *Van Landewyck and Others* v *Commission* [1980] ECR 3125, paragraph 86; Case T-7/89 *Hercules Chemicals* v *Commission* [1991] ECR II-1711, paragraph 256).

[68] As regards the form in which that common intention is expressed, it is sufficient for a stipulation to be the expression of the parties' intention to behave on the market in

accordance with its terms (see, in particular, *ACF Chemiefarma*, paragraph 112, and *Van Landewyck*, paragraph 86), without its having to constitute a valid and binding contract under national law (*Sandoz*, paragraph 13).

[69] It follows that the concept of an agreement within the meaning of Article 85(1) of the Treaty, as interpreted by the case-law, centres around the existence of a concurrence of wills between at least two parties, the form in which it is manifested being unimportant so long as it constitutes the faithful expression of the parties' intention.

[70] In certain circumstances, measures adopted or imposed in an apparently unilateral manner by a manufacturer in the context of his continuing relations with his distributors have been regarded as constituting an agreement within the meaning of Article 85(1) of the Treaty (Joined Cases 32/78, 36/78 to 82/78 *BMW Belgium and Others* v *Commission* [1979] ECR 2435, paragraphs 28 to 30; *AEG*, paragraph 38; *Ford and Ford Europe*, paragraph 21; Case 75/84 *Metro* v *Commission* ('*Metro II*' [1986] ECR 3021, paragraphs 72 and 73; *Sandoz*, paragraphs 7 to 12; Case C-70/93 *BMW* v *ALD* [1995] ECR I-3439, paragraphs 16 and 17).

[71] That case-law shows that a distinction should be drawn between cases in which an undertaking has adopted a genuinely unilateral measure, and thus without the express or implied participation of another undertaking, and those in which the unilateral character of the measure is merely apparent. Whilst the former do not fall within Article 85(1) of the Treaty, the latter must be regarded as revealing an agreement between undertakings and may therefore fall within the scope of that article. That is the case, in particular, with practices and measures in restraint of competition which, though apparently adopted unilaterally by the manufacturer in the context of its contractual relations with its dealers, nevertheless receive at least the tacit acquiescence of those dealers.

NOTE: The Commission's reasoning had serious implications for the principle of freedom of contract that underpins Article 81 EC and the Court's insistence at para. 69 on the existence of a 'concurrence of wills' is welcome. Lidgard suggests that:

> where a non-dominant company is unilaterally carrying out a strategy without seeking the assistance of others, there is simply no legal base for condemning the activity. From a general industry perspective it appears important to allow non-dominant companies to design their strategy to take products to the European market. Refusals to supply do not endanger the competitive climate. If Bayer is operating through wholesalers rather than integrating forwards, it should be entitled to require that these wholesalers perform their task, which is to provide Adalat on optimal terms to the French/Spanish market. If the wholesaler is more interested in performing a parallel trade function—in conflict with Bayer's interests—it should purchase freely available Adalat and sell it to the United Kingdom. Bayer is under this theory not only fully entitled to reduce requested quantities, but also to refuse supplies entirely. (See Lidgard, H.H., 'Unilateral Refusal to Supply: An agreement in disguise?' [1997] ECLR 354 at 360)

Do you support this assertion?

H: Effect on trade between Member States

This part of the prohibition sets out the jurisdictional line between Community law and domestic competition law. If behaviour has an 'effect on trade between Member States' then Community law will apply to that behaviour. That does not mean that domestic law cannot apply, but the Member States, including the national courts, should not, through the operation of Article 10 EC, act in a manner that is inconsistent with Community law. The requirement of an 'effect on trade' has enjoyed a broad construction under Article 81 EC and the case law demonstrates a firm focus on the promotion of the market integration paradigm. The classic definition is enunciated in *STM*, which sets out the extent of behaviour that is required to trigger Community competition law.

Société Technique Minière v *Maschinenbau Ulm GmbH*
(Case 56/65) [1966] ECR 337, [1966] CMLR 357

On the relations with trade between Member-States

The agreement should further be 'capable of affecting trade between Member-States'. This provision, clarified by the introductory clause of Article 85 which applies to agreements in so far as they are 'incompatible with the Common Market,' aims to fix the field of application of the prohibition by the requirement of a prior condition consisting in the possibility of hindering the realisation of a sole market among the Member-States. It is in fact to the extent that the agreement may effect trade between Member-States that the distortion of competition, induced by the agreement, involves the prohibitions of Community law in Article 85, whereas in the contrary case it escapes. To fulfil this condition, the agreement in question should, on the basis of a collection of objective legal or factual elements, allow one to expect, with a sufficient degree of probability, that it would exercise a direct or indirect, actual or potential, effect on the eddies of trade between Member-States.

NOTE: The Court decided in Joined Cases 56 and 58/64 *Consten and Grundig* that 'the fact that an agreement encourages an increase, even a large one, in the volume of trade between states is not sufficient to exclude the possibility that the agreement may affect such trade' (p. 341). There is much greater focus on the structure of markets within the Article 82 EC jurisprudence whereas Article 81 EC is more concerned with attempts to partition markets on national lines. For example, an agreement between undertakings based in the same Member State may still have an effect on interstate trade: see, e.g. Case C-193/83 *Windsurfing International Inc* v *European Commission* [1986] ECR 611, [1986] 3 CMLR 489. In these circumstances the Court will consider the agreement in its proper economic context and in particular the so-called bundling effect of complex trade distribution systems. For instance, a particular market may become compartmentalized from the rest of the common market. This issue arose in *Almelo*.

Municipality of Almelo v *IJM*
(Case C-393/92) [1994] ECR I-1477

The Court decided *inter alia*:

[34] Article 85 of the Treaty applies, in its own terms, to agreements between undertakings which restrict competition and affect trade between Member States.

[35] As regards the existence of an agreement between undertakings, it is to be observed, as the Commission found in the 1991 Decision, that the electricity distribution system in the Netherlands is based on a network of contractual legal relationships between generators, between generators and regional distributors, between regional distributors and local distributors and, finally, between local distributors and end-users. The exclusive purchasing clause in issue before the national court is contained in the general conditions for the supply of electric power by a regional distributor to local distributors and therefore constitutes a clause contained in an agreement as referred to in Article 85 of the Treaty.

[36] An agreement containing such a clause has a restrictive effect on competition, inasmuch as the clause prohibits the local distributors from obtaining electricity supplies from other suppliers.

[37] In order to determine whether such an agreement has an appreciable effect on trade between Member States, it is necessary, as the Court observed in its judgments in Case 23/67 *Brasserie de Haecht* [1967] ECR 525 and Case C-234/89 *Delimitis* [1991] ECR I-935, to assess it in its economic and legal context and to take account of any cumulative effect resulting from the existence of other exclusivity agreements.

[38] In that regard, it appears from the documents before the Court that the general conditions governing the relations between the parties to the main proceedings, which contain the exclusivity clause, follow the model General Terms and Conditions for the supply of electricity drawn up by the Association of Operators of Electricity Undertakings in the Netherlands.

[39] Those contractual relationships have the cumulative effect of compartmentalizing the national market, inasmuch as they have the effect of prohibiting local distributors established in the Netherlands from obtaining supplies of electricity from distributors or producers in other Member States.

NOTE: The importance of 'affect on interstate trade' has assumed even greater importance in the context of the Regulation 1/2003. Article 3 of the Regulation states that:

1. Where the competition authorities of the Member States or national courts apply national competition law to agreements, decisions of associations of undertakings or concerted practices within the meaning of Article 81(1) of the Treaty which may affect trade between Member States within the meaning of that provision, they shall also apply Article 81 of the Treaty to such agreements, decisions or concerted practices.

To assist in the understanding of the effect on interstate trade criteria the Commission have published a Guidance Notice.

Commission Notice—Guidelines on the effect on trade concept contained in Articles 81 and 82 of the Treaty
OJ, 2004, C101/81 [footnotes omitted]

[18] It follows from the wording of Articles 81 and 82 and the case law of the Community Courts that in the application of the effect on trade criterion three elements in particular must be addressed:
   (a) The concept of 'trade between Member States',
   (b) The notion of 'may affect', and
   (c) The concept of 'appreciability'.

2.2. The concept of 'trade between Member States'

[19] The concept of 'trade' is not limited to traditional exchanges of goods and services across borders (10). It is a wider concept, covering all cross-border economic activity including establishment. This interpretation is consistent with the fundamental objective of the Treaty to promote free movement of goods, services, persons and capital.

[20] According to settled case law the concept of 'trade' also encompasses cases where agreements or practices affect the competitive structure of the market. Agreements and practices that affect the competitive structure inside the Community by eliminating or threatening to eliminate a competitor operating within the Community may be subject to the Community competition rules. When an undertaking is or risks being eliminated the competitive structure within the Community is affected and so are the economic activities in which the undertaking is engaged.

[21] The requirement that there must be an effect on trade 'between Member States' implies that there must be an impact on cross-border economic activity involving at least two Member States. It is not required that the agreement or practice affect trade between the whole of one Member State and the whole of another Member State. Articles 81 and 82 may be applicable also in cases involving part of a Member State, provided that the effect on trade is appreciable.

[22] The application of the effect on trade criterion is independent of the definition of relevant geographic markets. Trade between Member States may be affected also in cases where the relevant market is national or sub-national.

2.3. The notion 'may affect'

[23] The function of the notion 'may affect' is to define the nature of the required impact on trade between Member States. According to the standard test developed by the Court of Justice, the notion 'may affect' implies that it must be possible to foresee with a sufficient degree of probability on the basis of a set of objective factors of law or fact that the agreement or practice may have an influence, direct or indirect, actual or potential, on the pattern of trade between Member

States. As mentioned in paragraph 20 above the Court of Justice has in addition developed a test based on whether or not the agreement or practice affects the competitive structure. In cases where the agreement or practice is liable to affect the competitive structure inside the Community, Community law jurisdiction is established.

[24]   The 'pattern of trade'-test developed by the Court of Justice contains the following main elements, which are dealt with in the following sections:

   (a) 'A sufficient degree of probability on the basis of a set of objective factors of law or fact',
   (b) An influence on the 'pattern of trade between Member States',
   (c) 'A direct or indirect, actual or potential influence' on the pattern of trade.

2.3.1. *A sufficient degree of probability on the basis of a set of objective factors of law or fact*

[25]   The assessment of effect on trade is based on objective factors. Subjective intent on the part of the undertakings concerned is not required. If, however, there is evidence that undertakings have intended to affect trade between Member States, for example because they have sought to hinder exports to or imports from other Member States, this is a relevant factor to be taken into account.

[26]   The words 'may affect' and the reference by the Court of Justice to 'a sufficient degree of probability' imply that, in order for Community law jurisdiction to be established, it is not required that the agreement or practice will actually have or has had an effect on trade between Member States. It is sufficient that the agreement or practice is 'capable' of having such an effect.

[27]   There is no obligation or need to calculate the actual volume of trade between Member States affected by the agreement or practice. For example, in the case of agreements prohibiting exports to other Member States there is no need to estimate what would have been the level of parallel trade between the Member States concerned, in the absence of the agreement. This interpretation is consistent with the jurisdictional nature of the effect on trade criterion. Community law jurisdiction extends to categories of agreements and practices that are capable of having cross-border effects, irrespective of whether a particular agreement or practice actually has such effects.

[28]   The assessment under the effect on trade criterion depends on a number of factors that individually may not be decisive. The relevant factors include the nature of the agreement and practice, the nature of the products covered by the agreement or practice and the position and importance of the undertakings concerned.

[29]   The nature of the agreement and practice provides an indication from a qualitative point of view of the ability of the agreement or practice to affect trade between Member States. Some agreements and practices are by their very nature capable of affecting trade between Member States, whereas others require more detailed analysis in this respect. Cross-border cartels are an example of the former, whereas joint ventures confined to the territory of a single Member State are an example of the latter. This aspect is further examined in section 3 below, which deals with various categories of agreements and practices.

[30]   The nature of the products covered by the agreements or practices also provides an indication of whether trade between Member States is capable of being affected. When by their nature products are easily traded across borders or are important for undertakings that want to enter or expand their activities in other Member States, Community jurisdiction is more readily established than in cases where due to their nature there is limited demand for products offered by suppliers from other Member States or where the products are of limited interest from the point of view of cross-border establishment or the expansion of the economic activity carried out from such place of establishment. Establishment includes the setting-up by undertakings in one Member State of agencies, branches or subsidiaries in another Member State.

[31]   The market position of the undertakings concerned and their sales volumes are indicative from a quantitative point of view of the ability of the agreement or practice concerned to affect trade between Member States. This aspect, which forms an integral part of the assessment of appreciability, is addressed in section 2.4 below.

[32] In addition to the factors already mentioned, it is necessary to take account of the legal and factual environment in which the agreement or practice operates. The relevant economic and legal context provides insight into the potential for an effect on trade between Member States. If there are absolute barriers to cross-border trade between Member States, which are external to the agreement or practice, trade is only capable of being affected if those barriers are likely to disappear in the foreseeable future. In cases where the barriers are not absolute but merely render cross-border activities more difficult, it is of the utmost importance to ensure that agreements and practices do not further hinder such activities. Agreements and practices that do so are capable of affecting trade between Member States.

2.3.2. An influence on the 'pattern of trade between Member States'

[33] For Articles 81 and 82 to be applicable there must be an influence on the 'pattern of trade between Member States'.

[34] The term 'pattern of trade' is neutral. It is not a condition that trade be restricted or reduced. Patterns of trade can also be affected when an agreement or practice causes an increase in trade. Indeed, Community law jurisdiction is established if trade between Member States is likely to develop differently with the agreement or practice compared to the way in which it would probably have developed in the absence of the agreement or practice.

[35] This interpretation reflects the fact that the effect on trade criterion is a jurisdictional one, which serves to distinguish those agreements and practices which are capable of having cross-border effects, so as to warrant an examination under the Community competition rules, from those agreements and practices which do not.

2.3.3. A 'direct or indirect, actual or potential influence' on the pattern of trade

[36] The influence of agreements and practices on patterns of trade between Member States can be 'direct or indirect, actual or potential'.

[37] Direct effects on trade between Member States normally occur in relation to the products covered by an agreement or practice. When, for example, producers of a particular product in different Member States agree to share markets, direct effects are produced on trade between Member States on the market for the products in question. Another example of direct effects being produced is when a supplier limits distributor rebates to products sold within the Member State in which the distributors are established. Such practices increase the relative price of products destined for exports, rendering export sales less attractive and less competitive.

[38] Indirect effects often occur in relation to products that are related to those covered by an agreement or practice. Indirect effects may, for example, occur where an agreement or practice has an impact on cross-border economic activities of undertakings that use or otherwise rely on the products covered by the agreement or practice. Such effects can, for instance, arise where the agreement or practice relates to an intermediate product, which is not traded, but which is used in the supply of a final product, which is traded. The Court of Justice has held that trade between Member States was capable of being affected in the case of an agreement involving the fixing of prices of spirits used in the production of cognac. Whereas the raw material was not exported, the final product—cognac—was exported. In such cases Community competition law is thus applicable, if trade in the final product is capable of being appreciably affected.

[39] Indirect effects on trade between Member States may also occur in relation to the products covered by the agreement or practice. For instance, agreements whereby a manufacturer limits warranties to products sold by distributors within their Member State of establishment create disincentives for consumers from other Member States to buy the products because they would not be able to invoke the warranty. Export by official distributors and parallel traders is made more difficult because in the eyes of consumers the products are less attractive without the manufacturer's warranty.

[40] Actual effects on trade between Member States are those that are produced by the agreement or practice once it is implemented. An agreement between a supplier and a distributor within the same Member State, for instance one that prohibits exports to other Member States, is likely to

produce actual effects on trade between Member States. Without the agreement the distributor would have been free to engage in export sales. It should be recalled, however, that it is not required that actual effects are demonstrated. It is sufficient that the agreement or practice be capable of having such effects.

[41] Potential effects are those that may occur in the future with a sufficient degree of probability. In other words, foreseeable market developments must be taken into account. Even if trade is not capable of being affected at the time the agreement is concluded or the practice is implemented, Articles 81 and 82 remain applicable if the factors which led to that conclusion are likely to change in the foreseeable future. In this respect it is relevant to consider the impact of liberalisation measures adopted by the Community or by the Member State in question and other foreseeable measures aiming at eliminating legal barriers to trade.

[42] Moreover, even if at a given point in time market conditions are unfavourable to cross-border trade, for example because prices are similar in the Member States in question, trade may still be capable of being affected if the situation may change as a result of changing market conditions. What matters is the ability of the agreement or practice to affect trade between Member States and not whether at any given point in time it actually does so.

[43] The inclusion of indirect or potential effects in the analysis of effects on trade between Member States does not mean that the analysis can be based on remote or hypothetical effects. The likelihood of a particular agreement to produce indirect or potential effects must be explained by the authority or party claiming that trade between Member States is capable of being appreciably affected. Hypothetical or speculative effects are not sufficient for establishing Community law jurisdiction. For instance, an agreement that raises the price of a product which is not tradable reduces the disposable income of consumers. As consumers have less money to spend they may purchase fewer products imported from other Member States. However, the link between such income effects and trade between Member States is generally in itself too remote to establish Community law jurisdiction.

I: *De minimis*

Article 81 EC requires that any effect on competition or trade must be to an 'appreciable extent'; hence the *de minimis* doctrine can operate to limit the application of Article 81 EC. Where an agreement does not have an appreciable effect it will escape the prohibition in Article 81(1) EC. This principle emerged from the Court's judgment in an early case, Case 5/69 *Völk* v *Ets Vervaecke Sprl* [1969] ECR 295, [1969] CMLR 273. Here a German producer of washing machines, Völk, and a Belgian-based distributor, Vervaecke, entered into an exclusive distribution agreement that guaranteed absolute territorial protection for the distributor. The Court held that 'an agreement escapes the prohibition of Article [81(1)] where it has only an insignificant effect on the market, taking into account the weak position which the persons concerned have on the market of the product in question'. Völk's share of the market represented 0.6 per cent. The *de minimis* doctrine has since found expression in a Commission Notice, most recently revised in late 2001 to ensure coherence with the Commission's revised rules for vertical and horizontal agreements. The Notice attempts to give undertakings important practical guidance as to whether an agreement falls within the scope of the *de minimis* doctrine. The 2001 Notice replaces the 1997 Notice, OJ, 1997, C372/13, which introduced market share thresholds. The 2001 Notice confirms this economic approach and the emphasis on a quantitative assessment. Note that the 2001 Notice is not concerned with the effect on trade between Member States.

Commission Notice on agreements of minor importance which do not appreciably restrict competition under Article 81(1) (de minimis)[1]

I

1. Article 81(1) prohibits agreements between undertakings which may affect trade between Member States and which have as their object or effect the prevention, restriction or distortion of competition within the common market. The Court of Justice of the European Communities has clarified that this provision is not applicable where the impact of the agreement on intra-Community trade or on competition is not appreciable.

2. In this notice the Commission quantifies, with the help of market share thresholds, what is not an appreciable restriction of competition under Article 81 of the EC Treaty. This negative definition of appreciability does not imply that agreements between undertakings which exceed the thresholds set out in this notice appreciably restrict competition. Such agreements may still have only a negligible effect on competition and may therefore not be prohibited by Article 81(1)[1].

3. Agreements may in addition not fall under Article 81(1) because they are not capable of appreciably affecting trade between Member States. This notice does not deal with this issue. It does not quantify what does not constitute an appreciable effect on trade. It is however acknowledged that agreements between small and medium-sized undertakings, as defined in the Annex to Commission Recommendation 96/280/EC[2], are rarely capable of appreciably affecting trade between Member States. Small and medium-sized undertakings are currently defined in that recommendation as undertakings which have fewer than 250 employees and have either an annual turnover not exceeding EUR 40 million or an annual balance-sheet total not exceeding EUR 27 million.

4. In cases covered by this notice the Commission will not institute proceedings either upon application or on its own initiative. Where undertakings assume in good faith that an agreement is covered by this notice, the Commission will not impose fines. Although not binding on them, this notice also intends to give guidance to the courts and authorities of the Member States in their application of Article 81.

5. This notice also applies to decisions by associations of undertakings and to concerted practices.

6. This notice is without prejudice to any interpretation of Article 81 which may be given by the Court of Justice or the Court of First Instance of the European Communities.

II

7. The Commission holds the view that agreements between undertakings which affect trade between Member States do not appreciably restrict competition within the meaning of Article 81(1):

(a) if the aggregate market share held by the parties to the agreement does not exceed 10 per cent on any of the relevant markets affected by the agreement, where the agreement is made between undertakings which are actual or potential competitors on any of these markets (agreements between competitors)[3]; or

---

[1] This notice replaces the notice on agreements of minor importance published in OJ C 372, 9.12.1997.

[1] See also the Commission notice 'Guidelines on vertical restraints', OJ C 291, 13.10.2000, in particular paragraphs 73, 142, 143 and 189. While in the guidelines on vertical restraints in relation to certain restrictions reference is made not only to the total but also to the tied market share of a particular supplier or buyer, in this notice all market share thresholds refer to total market shares.

[2] OJ C 372, 9.12.1997, p. 5.

[3] Without prejudice to situations of joint production with or without joint distribution as defined in Article 5, paragraph 2, of Commission Regulation (EC) No 2658/2000 and Article 5, paragraph 2, of Commission Regulation (EC) No 2659/2000, OJ L 304, 5.12.2000, pp. 3 and 7 respectively.

(b) if the market share held by each of the parties to the agreement does not exceed 15 per cent on any of the relevant markets affected by the agreement, where the agreement is made between undertakings which are not actual or potential competitors on any of these markets (agreements between non-competitors).

In cases where it is difficult to classify the agreement as either an agreement between competitors or an agreement between non-competitors the 10 per cent threshold is applicable.

8. Where in a relevant market competition is restricted by the cumulative effect of agreements for the sale of goods or services entered into by different suppliers or distributors (cumulative foreclosure effect of parallel networks of agreements having similar effects on the market), the market share thresholds under point 7 are reduced to 5 per cent, both for agreements between competitors and for agreements between non-competitors. Individual suppliers or distributors with a market share not exceeding 5 per cent are in general not considered to contribute significantly to a cumulative foreclosure effect. A cumulative foreclosure effect is unlikely to exist if less than 30 per cent of the relevant market is covered by parallel (networks of) agreements having similar effects.

9. The Commission also holds the view that agreements are not restrictive of competition if the market shares do not exceed the thresholds of respectively 10 per cent, 15 per cent and 5 per cent set out in points 7 and 8 during two successive calendar years by more than 2 percentage points.

10. In order to calculate the market share, it is necessary to determine the relevant market. This consists of the relevant product market and the relevant geographic market. When defining the relevant market, reference should be had to the notice on the definition of the relevant market for the purposes of Community competition law. The market shares are to be calculated on the basis of sales value data or, where appropriate, purchase value data. If value data are not available, estimates based on other reliable market information, including volume data, may be used.

11. Points 7, 8 and 9 do not apply to agreements containing any of the following hardcore restrictions:

(1) as regards agreements between competitors as defined in point 7, restrictions which, directly or indirectly, in isolation or in combination with other factors under the control of the parties, have as their object:
  (a) the fixing of prices when selling the products to third parties;
  (b) the limitation of output or sales;
  (c) the allocation of markets or customers;

(2) as regards agreements between non-competitors as defined in point 7, restrictions which, directly or indirectly, in isolation or in combination with other factors under the control of the parties, have as their object:
  (a) the restriction of the buyer's ability to determine its sale price, without prejudice to the possibility of the supplier imposing a maximum sale price or recommending a sale price, provided that they do not amount to a fixed or minimum sale price as a result of pressure from, or incentives offered by, any of the parties;
  (b) the restriction of the territory into which, or of the customers to whom, the buyer may sell the contract goods or services, except the following restrictions which are not hardcore:
    — the restriction of active sales into the exclusive territory or to an exclusive customer group reserved to the supplier or allocated by the supplier to another buyer, where such a restriction does not limit sales by the customers of the buyer,
    — the restriction of sales to end users by a buyer operating at the wholesale level of trade,
    — the restriction of sales to unauthorised distributors by the members of a selective distribution system, and
    — the restriction of the buyer's ability to sell components, supplied for the purposes of incorporation, to customers who would use them to manufacture the same type of goods as those produced by the supplier;

(c) the restriction of active or passive sales to end users by members of a selective distribution system operating at the retail level of trade, without prejudice to the possibility of prohibiting a member of the system from operating out of an unauthorised place of establishment;

(d) the restriction of cross-supplies between distributors within a selective distribution system, including between distributors operating at different levels of trade;

(e) the restriction agreed between a supplier of components and a buyer who incorporates those components, which limits the supplier's ability to sell the components as spare parts to end users or to repairers or other service providers not entrusted by the buyer with the repair or servicing of its goods;

(3) as regards agreements between competitors as defined in point 7, where the competitors operate, for the purposes of the agreement, at a different level of the production or distribution chain, any of the hardcore restrictions listed in paragraphs (1) and (2) above.

12. (1) For the purposes of this notice, the terms 'undertaking', 'party to the agreement', 'distributor', 'supplier' and 'buyer' shall include their respective connected undertakings.

(2) 'Connected undertakings' are:

(a) undertakings in which a party to the agreement, directly or indirectly:
— has the power to exercise more than half the voting rights, or
— has the power to appoint more than half the members of the supervisory board, board of management or bodies legally representing the undertaking, or
— has the right to manage the undertaking's affairs;

(b) undertakings which directly or indirectly have, over a party to the agreement, the rights or powers listed in (a);

(c) undertakings in which an undertaking referred to in (b) has, directly or indirectly, the rights or powers listed in (a);

(d) undertakings in which a party to the agreement together with one or more of the undertakings referred to in (a), (b) or (c), or in which two or more of the latter undertakings, jointly have the rights or powers listed in (a);

(e) undertakings in which the rights or the powers listed in (a) are jointly held by:
— parties to the agreement or their respective connected undertakings referred to in (a) to (d), or
— one or more of the parties to the agreement or one or more of their connected undertakings referred to in (a) to (d) and one or more third parties.

(3) For the purposes of paragraph 2(e), the market share held by these jointly held undertakings shall be apportioned equally to each undertaking having the rights or the powers listed in paragraph 2(a).

NOTE: The *de minimis* thresholds have been increased for agreements between competitors from 5 per cent under the previous Notice to 10 per cent and for agreements between non-competitors from 10 per cent to 15 per cent. Furthermore, the Notice introduces a market share threshold for networks of agreements producing a cumulative anti-competitive effect. It contains the same list of hard-core restrictions, which cannot benefit from the *de minimis* Notice, as the vertical block exemption regulations: see Chapter 8. The Notice also confirms that agreements between small and medium-sized enterprises are in general *de minimis*.

A Commission Notice is not binding although it is unusual for the Commission to depart from its terms later. However, in several cases, the Court has departed from a quantitative *de minimis* approach and instead adopted a qualitative assessment: see, e.g. Case 30/78 *Distillers Co Ltd* v *Commission* [1980] ECR 2229 in which the Court held at paras 27 and 28 that 'although an agreement may escape the prohibition in Article 85(1) when it affects the market only to an insignificant extent, having regard to the weak position which those concerned have in the market in the products in question, the same considerations do not apply in the case of a product of a large undertaking responsible for the entire production.'

J: Within the Common Market

This element concerns the territorial extent of Article 81 EC and suggests that only agreements that restrict competition within the Community are caught by the Community competition rules. Notwithstanding this territorial requirement, Article 81 EC may be applied to agreements concluded *outside* the territory of the Community that produce *effects within* the Community (the Commission's approach) or are *implemented* through a subsidiary situated within it (the Court's preferred approach). The extent to which Articles 81 and 82 EC can be applied to agreements between undertakings established outside the Community, known as extraterritoriality, is considered in Chapter 5.

K: Object or effect the prevention, restriction, or distortion of competition

An agreement will not infringe Article 81 EC unless it has as its 'object or effect the prevention, restriction or distortion of competition'. Although Article 81 EC provides some indication of the types of agreement prohibited, the list is not exhaustive, and, as we shall see, the Commission and Court have given the term, 'object or effect' an expansive interpretation. The 'object or effect' requirement has caused the Commission and the Court significant interpretative difficulties. The key problem concerns the drafting of the provision: is the phrase to be read disjunctively, or are the conditions cumulative? In *STM* the Court held that 'object or effect' was to be read disjunctively.

Société Technique Minière v Maschinenbau Ulm GmbH
(Case 56/65) [1966] ECR 235, [1966] CMLR 357

On the relations of the agreement with competition

Finally, to be hit by the prohibition of Article 85(1), the agreement in the proceedings should 'be designed to prevent, restrict or distort competition within the Common Market or have that effect'. The fact that these are not cumulative but alternative conditions, indicated by the conjunction 'or', suggests first the need to consider the very object of the agreement, in the light of the economic context in which it is to be applied. The alterations in the play of competition envisaged by Article 85(1) should result from all or part of the clauses of the agreement itself. Where, however, an analysis of the said clauses does not reveal a sufficient degree of harmfulness with regard to competition, examination should then be made of the effects of the agreement and, if it is to be subjected to the prohibition, the presence of those elements which establish that competition has in fact been prevented, restricted or distorted to a noticeable extent should be required. The competition in question should be understood within the actual context in which it would occur in the absence of the agreement in question. In particular, the alteration of the conditions of competition may be thrown in doubt if the said agreement appears precisely necessary for the penetration of an undertaking into an area in which it was not operating. Therefore, to judge whether a contract containing a clause 'granting an exclusive right of sale' should be regarded as prohibited by reason of its object or its effect, it is necessary to take into account, in particular, the nature and the quantity, whether limited or not, of the products which are the object of the agreement, the position and size of the grantor and concessionaire on the market for the products concerned, the isolated nature of the agreement in question or, on the contrary, its position in a series of agreements, the severity of the clauses aiming at protecting the exclusive right or, on the contrary, the possibilities left for other commercial currents upon the same products by means of re-exports and parallel imports.

NOTE: Article 81 EC includes a non-exhaustive list of the types of agreement that will 'prevent, restrict or distort' competition. The Court has confirmed, in a number of cases, that price-fixing agreements (*Dyestuffs*), agreements to share markets (*Quinine*), information exchanges (*Italian Flat Glass*) and export restrictions (*Consten and Grundig*) have the object of restricting competition. In these circumstances there is no need to assess the effect of the agreement on competition. Such restrictions may be weighed against any pro-competitive effects only in the context of Article 81(3) EC with a view to obtaining an exemption. In Case C-209/07 *Competition Authority* v *Beef Industry Development Society Ltd*, judgment of 20 November 2008, the Court reaffirmed that view saying (at para 21):

> to determine whether an agreement comes within the prohibition laid down in Article 81(1) EC, close regard must be paid to the wording of its provisions and to the objectives which it is intended to attain. In that regard, even supposing it to be established that the parties to an agreement acted without any subjective intention of restricting competition, but with the object of remedying the effects of a crisis in their sector, such considerations are irrelevant for the purposes of applying that provision. Indeed, an agreement may be regarded as having a restrictive object even if it does not have the restriction of competition as its sole aim but also pursues other legitimate objectives (*General Motors* v *Commission*, paragraph 64 and the case-law cited). It is only in connection with Article 81(3) EC that matters such as those relied upon by BIDS may, if appropriate, be taken into consideration for the purposes of obtaining an exemption from the prohibition laid down in Article 81(1) EC.

Anti-competitive behaviour does not exist in the abstract and, where the 'object' element is not satisfied, the Court has emphasized the importance of conducting a full market analysis to ascertain whether the agreement has prevented, restricted, or distorted competition within the meaning of Article 81(1) EC.

Brasserie de Haecht SA v *Wilkin*
(Case 23/67) [1967] ECR 407, [1968] CMLR 26

A brewer and a café owner, both situated in Belgium, had entered into an exclusive purchasing agreement. The Court held that it was necessary to consider the whole economic context in which the agreement operated, in particular the existence of a network of such agreements that could have the effect of foreclosing competition.

Article 85(1) mentions agreements, decisions and practices. By referring in the same sentence to agreements between undertakings, decisions by associations of undertakings and concerted practices, which may involve many parties, Article [85(1)] implies that the constituent elements of those agreements, decisions and practices may be considered together as a whole.

Furthermore, by basing its application to agreements, decisions or practices, not only their subject-matter but also on their effects in relation to competition, Article [85(1)] implies that regard must be had to such effects in the context in which they occur, that is to say, in the economic and legal context of such agreements, decisions or practices and where they might combine with others to have a cumulative effect on competition. In fact, it would be pointless to consider an agreement, decision or concerted practice by reason of its effects if those effects were to be taken distinct from the body of effects, whether convergent or not, surrounding their implementation. Thus in order to examine whether it is caught by Article [85(1)] an agreement cannot be examined in isolation from the above context, that is from the factual or legal circumstances causing it to prevent, restrict or distort competition. The existence of similar contracts may be taken into consideration for this objective to the extent to which the general body of contracts of this type is capable of restricting the freedom of trade.

Lastly, it is only to the extent to which agreements, decisions or practices are capable of affecting trade between Member States that the alteration of competition comes under Community prohibitions. In order to satisfy this condition, it must be possible for the agreement, decision or practice, when viewed in the light of a combination of the objective, factual or legal circumstances, to appear to be capable of having some influence, direct or indirect, on trade between Member States, of being conducive to a partitioning of the market and of hampering the economic interpenetration sought by the Treaty. When this point is considered the agreement, decision or practice cannot therefore be isolated from all the others of which it is one.

The existence of similar contracts is a circumstance which, together with others, is capable of being a factor in the economic and legal context within which the contract must be judged. Accordingly, whilst such a situation must be taken into account it should not be considered as decisive by itself, but merely as one among others in judging whether trade between Member States is capable of being affected through any alteration in competition.

In a further case involving beer supply agreements, the Court confirmed that where the object of an agreement is not to restrict competition, the agreement will only be caught by Article 81(1) EC if it produces anti-competitive effects.

Delimitis v Henninger Bräu
(Case C-234/89) [1991] ECR I-935, [1992] 5 CMLR 210

The compatibility of beer supply agreements with Article 85(1) of the Treaty

[10] Under the terms of beer supply agreements, the supplier generally affords the reseller certain economic and financial benefits, such as the grant of loans on favourable terms, the letting of premises for the operation of a public house and the provision of technical installations, furniture and other equipment necessary for its operation. In consideration for those benefits, the reseller normally undertakes, for a predetermined period, to obtain supplies of the products covered by the contract only from the supplier. That exclusive purchasing obligation is generally backed by a prohibition on selling competing products in the public house let by the supplier.

[11] Such contracts entail for the supplier the advantage of guaranteed outlets, since, as a result of his exclusive purchasing obligation and the prohibition on competition, the reseller concentrates his sales efforts on the distribution of the contract goods. The supply agreements, moreover, lead to cooperation with the reseller, allowing the supplier to plan his sales over the duration of the agreement and to organize production and distribution effectively.

[12] Beer supply agreements also have advantages for the reseller, inasmuch as they enable him to gain access under favourable conditions and with the guarantee of supplies to the beer distribution market. The reseller's and supplier's shared interest in promoting sales of the contract goods likewise secures for the reseller the benefit of the supplier's assistance in guaranteeing product quality and customer service.

[13] If such agreements do not have the object of restricting competition within the meaning of Article 85(1), it is nevertheless necessary to ascertain whether they have the effect of preventing, restricting or distorting competition.

[14] In its judgment in Case 23/67 Brassèrie De Haecht v Wilkin [1967] ECR 407, the Court held that the effects of such an agreement had to be assessed in the context in which they occur and where they might combine with others to have a cumulative effect on competition. It also follows from that judgment that the cumulative effect of several similar agreements constitutes one factor amongst others in ascertaining whether, by way of a possible alteration of competition, trade between Member States is capable of being affected.

[15] Consequently, in the present case it is necessary to analyse the effects of a beer supply agreement, taken together with other contracts of the same type, on the opportunities of national competitors or those from other Member States, to gain access to the market for beer consumption or to increase their market share and, accordingly, the effects on the range of products offered to consumers.

[16] In making that analysis, the relevant market must first be determined. The relevant market is primarily defined on the basis of the nature of the economic activity in question, in this case the sale of beer. Beer is sold through both retail channels and premises for the sale and consumption of drinks. From the consumer's point of view, the latter sector, comprising in particular public houses and restaurants, may be distinguished from the retail sector on the grounds that the sale of beer in public houses does not solely consist of the purchase of a product but is also linked with the provision of services, and that beer consumption in public houses is not essentially dependent on economic considerations. The specific nature of the public house trade is borne out by the fact that the breweries organize specific distribution systems for this sector which require special installations, and that the prices charged in that sector are generally higher than retail prices.

[17] It follows that in the present case the reference market is that for the distribution of beer in premises for the sale and consumption of drinks. That finding is not affected by the fact that there is a certain overlap between the two distribution networks, namely inasmuch as retail sales allow new competitors to make their brands known and to use their reputation in order to gain access to the market constituted by premises for the sale and consumption of drinks.

[18] Secondly, the relevant market is delimited from a geographical point of view. It should be noted that most beer supply agreements are still entered into at a national level. It follows that, in applying the Community competition rules, account is to be taken of the national market for beer distribution in premises for the sale and consumption of drinks.

[19] In order to assess whether the existence of several beer supply agreements impedes access to the market as so defined, it is further necessary to examine the nature and extent of those agreements in their totality, comprising all similar contracts tying a large number of points of sale to several national producers (judgment in Case 43/69 *Bilger* v *Jehle* [1970] ECR 127). The effect of those networks of contracts on access to the market depends specifically on the number of outlets thus tied to national producers in relation to the number of public houses which are not so tied, the duration of the commitments entered into, the quantities of beer to which those commitments relate, and on the proportion between those quantities and the quantities sold by free distributors.

[20] The existence of a bundle of similar contracts, even if it has a considerable effect on the opportunities for gaining access to the market, is not, however, sufficient in itself to support a finding that the relevant market is inaccessible, inasmuch as it is only one factor, amongst others, pertaining to the economic and legal context in which an agreement must be appraised (Case 23/67 *Brasserie De Haecht*, cited above). The other factors to be taken into account are, in the first instance, those also relating to opportunities for access.

[21] In that connection it is necessary to examine whether there are real concrete possibilities for a new competitor to penetrate the bundle of contracts by acquiring a brewery already established on the market together with its network of sales outlets, or to circumvent the bundle of contracts by opening new public houses. For that purpose it is necessary to have regard to the legal rules and agreements on the acquisition of companies and the establishment of outlets, and to the minimum number of outlets necessary for the economic operation of a distribution system. The presence of beer wholesalers not tied to producers who are active on the market is also a factor capable of facilitating a new producer's access to that market since he can make use of those wholesalers' sales networks to distribute his own beer.

[22] Secondly, account must be taken of the conditions under which competitive forces operate on the relevant market. In that connection it is necessary to know not only the number and the size of producers present on the market, but also the degree of saturation of that market and customer fidelity to existing brands, for it is generally more difficult to penetrate a saturated market in which customers are loyal to a small number of large producers than a market in full expansion in which a large number of small producers are operating without any strong brand names. The trend in beer sales in the retail trade provides useful information on the development of demand and thus an indication of the degree of saturation of the beer market as a whole. The analysis of that trend is, moreover, of interest in evaluating brand loyalty. A steady increase in sales of beer under new brand names may confer on the owners of those brand names a reputation which they may turn to account in gaining access to the public-house market.

[23] If an examination of all similar contracts entered into on the relevant market and the other factors relevant to the economic and legal context in which the contract must be examined shows that those agreements do not have the cumulative effect of denying access to that market to new national and foreign competitors, the individual agreements comprising the bundle of agreements cannot be held to restrict competition within the meaning of Article 85(1) of the Treaty. They do not, therefore, fall under the prohibition laid down in that provision.

[24] If, on the other hand, such examination reveals that it is difficult to gain access to the relevant market, it is necessary to assess the extent to which the agreements entered into by the brewery in question contribute to the cumulative effect produced in that respect by the totality of the similar contracts found on that market. Under the Community rules on competition, responsibility for such an effect of closing off the market must be attributed to the breweries which make an appreciable contribution thereto. Beer supply agreements entered into by breweries whose contribution to the cumulative effect is insignificant do not therefore fall under the prohibition under Article 85(1).

[25] In order to assess the extent of the contribution of the beer supply agreements entered into by a brewery to the cumulative sealing-off effect mentioned above, the market position of the contracting parties must be taken into consideration. That position is not determined solely by the market share held by the brewery and any group to which it may belong, but also by the number of outlets tied to it or to its group, in relation to the total number of premises for the sale and consumption of drinks found in the relevant market.

[26] The contribution of the individual contracts entered into by a brewery to the sealing-off of that market also depends on their duration. If the duration is manifestly excessive in relation to the average duration of beer supply agreements generally entered into on the relevant market, the individual contract falls under the prohibition under Article 85(1). A brewery with a relatively small market share which ties its sales outlets for many years may make as significant a contribution to a sealing-off of the market as a brewery in a relatively strong market position which regularly releases sales outlets at shorter intervals.

[27] The reply to be given to the first three questions is therefore that a beer supply agreement is prohibited by Article 85(1) of the EEC Treaty, if two cumulative conditions are met. The first is that, having regard to the economic and legal context of the agreement at issue, it is difficult for competitors who could enter the market or increase their market share to gain access to the national market for the distribution of beer in premises for the sale and consumption of drinks. The fact that, in that market, the agreement in issue is one of a number of similar agreements having a cumulative effect on competition constitutes only one factor amongst others in assessing whether access to that market is indeed difficult. The second condition is that the agreement in question must make a significant contribution to the sealing-off effect brought about by the totality of those agreements in their economic and legal context. The extent of the contribution made by the individual agreement depends on the position of the contracting parties in the relevant market and on the duration of the agreement.

NOTE: In the context of horizontal agreements, see the decision of the CFI in Joined Cases T-374, 375, 384, and 388/94 *European Night Services* v *Commission* [1998] ECR II-3141 [1998], 5 CMLR 718 in which the CFI stressed at para. 137 'that the examination of conditions of competition is based not only on existing competition between undertakings already present on the relevant market but also on potential competition, in order to ascertain whether, in the light of the structure of the market and the economic and legal context within which it functions, there are either concrete possibilities both for the undertakings concerned to compete among themselves, or for a new competitor to penetrate the relevant market and compete with the undertakings already established'.

Over the years the Court has developed a limited rule of reason approach, partially borrowed from US antitrust law in an attempt to deal with the 'object or effect' issue. The Court tends to view many agreements containing restraints on the parties' conduct, with the exception of significant territorial or price restraints, as falling outside the scope of Article 81(1) altogether. For example, it has held that restraints in an agreement do not restrict competition within the meaning of Article 81(1) if they are necessary or ancillary to a pro-competitive agreement (*Remia*); are essential to induce a distributor to make a substantial investment necessary to ensure the commercial viability of the venture (*STM, Nungesser*); or are generally essential to the proper working of a selective distribution system (*Metro*).

Advocate General Leger's opinion in Case C-309/99 *Wouters* provided an excellent appraisal of 'object or effect' in the context of competition and the professions; in this case the impact of the rules of the Dutch Bar which prohibited Dutch lawyers from forming partnerships with other professionals, notably accountants. Note in particular the discussion of the rule of reason at para. 99 where AG Leger explains the difficulty in drawing a dividing line between purely ethical rules that lie outside the scope of the competition provisions and rules or practices whose object or effect is contrary to Article 81 EC. The Court itself was less forthcoming.

Wouters v Netherlands Bar Council
(Case C-309/99) [2002] ECR I-1577

[87] As regards the adverse effect on competition, the areas of expertise of members of the Bar and of accountants may be complementary. Since legal services, especially in business law, more and more frequently require recourse to an accountant, a multi-disciplinary partnership of members of the Bar and accountants would make it possible to offer a wider range of services, and indeed to propose new ones. Clients would thus be able to turn to a single structure for a large part of the services necessary for the organisation, management and operation of their business (the 'one-stop shop' advantage).

[88] Furthermore, a multi-disciplinary partnership of members of the Bar and accountants would be capable of satisfying the needs created by the increasing interpenetration of national markets and the consequent necessity for continuous adaptation to national and international legislation.

[89] Nor, finally, is it inconceivable that the economies of scale resulting from such multi-disciplinary partnerships might have positive effects on the cost of services.

[90] A prohibition of multi-disciplinary partnerships of members of the Bar and accountants, such as that laid down in the 1993 Regulation, is therefore liable to limit production and technical development within the meaning of Article 85(1)(b) of the Treaty.

[91] It is true that the accountancy market is highly concentrated, to the extent that the firms dominating it are at present known as 'the big five' and the proposed merger between two of them, Price Waterhouse and Coopers & Lybrand, gave rise to Commission Decision 1999/152/EC of 20 May 1998 declaring a concentration to be compatible with the common market and the functioning of the EEA Agreement (Case IV/M.1016—*Price Waterhouse/Coopers & Lybrand*) (OJ 1999 L 50, p. 27), adopted pursuant to Council Regulation (EEC) No 4064/89 of 21 December 1989 on the control of concentrations between undertakings (OJ 1989 L 395, p. 1), as amended by Council Regulation (EC) No 1310/97 of 30 June 1997 (OJ 1997 L 180, p. 1).

[92] On the other hand, the prohibition of conflicts of interest with which members of the Bar in all Member States are required to comply may constitute a structural limit to extensive concentration of law-firms and so reduce their opportunities of benefiting from economies of scale or of entering into structural associations with practitioners of highly concentrated professions.

[93] In those circumstances, unreserved and unlimited authorisation of multi-disciplinary partnerships between the legal profession, the generally decentralised nature of which is closely linked to some of its fundamental features, and a profession as concentrated as accountancy, could lead to an overall decrease in the degree of competition prevailing on the market in legal services, as a result of the substantial reduction in the number of undertakings present on that market.

[94] Nevertheless, in so far as the preservation of a sufficient degree of competition on the market in legal services could be guaranteed by less extreme measures than national rules such as the 1993 Regulation, which prohibits absolutely any form of multi-disciplinary partnership, whatever the respective sizes of the firms of lawyers and accountants concerned, those rules restrict competition.

[95] As regards the question whether intra-Community trade is affected, it is sufficient to observe that an agreement, decision or concerted practice extending over the whole of the territory of

a Member State has, by its very nature, the effect of reinforcing the partitioning of markets on a national basis, thereby holding up the economic interpenetration which the Treaty is designed to bring about (Case 8/72 *Vereeniging van Cementhandelaren* v *Commission* [1972] ECR 977, paragraph 29; Case 42/84 *Remia and Others* v *Commission* [1985] ECR 2545, paragraph 22; and CNSD, paragraph 48).

[96] That effect is all the more appreciable in the present case because the 1993 Regulation applies equally to visiting lawyers who are registered members of the Bar of another Member State, because economic and commercial law more and more frequently regulates transnational transactions and, lastly, because the firms of accountants looking for lawyers as partners are generally international groups present in several Member States.

[97] However, not every agreement between undertakings or every decision of an association of undertakings which restricts the freedom of action of the parties or of one of them necessarily falls within the prohibition laid down in Article 85(1) of the Treaty. For the purposes of application of that provision to a particular case, account must first of all be taken of the overall context in which the decision of the association of undertakings was taken or produces its effects. More particularly, account must be taken of its objectives, which are here connected with the need to make rules relating to organisation, qualifications, professional ethics, supervision and liability, in order to ensure that the ultimate consumers of legal services and the sound administration of justice are provided with the necessary guarantees in relation to integrity and experience (see, to that effect, Case C-3/95 *Reisebüro Broede* [1996] ECR I-6511, paragraph 38). It has then to be considered whether the consequential effects restrictive of competition are inherent in the pursuit of those objectives.

[98] Account must be taken of the legal framework applicable in the Netherlands, on the one hand, to members of the Bar and to the Bar of the Netherlands, which comprises all the registered members of the Bar in that Member State, and on the other hand, to accountants.

[99] As regards members of the Bar, it has consistently been held that, in the absence of specific Community rules in the field, each Member State is in principle free to regulate the exercise of the legal profession in its territory (Case 107/83 *Klopp* [1984] ECR 2971, paragraph 17, and *Reisebüro*, paragraph 37). For that reason, the rules applicable to that profession may differ greatly from one Member State to another.

[100] The current approach of the Netherlands, where Article 28 of the Advocatenwet entrusts the Bar of the Netherlands with responsibility for adopting regulations designed to ensure the proper practice of the profession, is that the essential rules adopted for that purpose are, in particular, the duty to act for clients in complete independence and in their sole interest, the duty, mentioned above, to avoid all risk of conflict of interest and the duty to observe strict professional secrecy.

[101] Those obligations of professional conduct have not inconsiderable implications for the structure of the market in legal services, and more particularly for the possibilities for the practice of law jointly with other liberal professions which are active on that market.

[102] Thus, they require of members of the Bar that they should be in a situation of independence vis-à-vis the public authorities, other operators and third parties, by whom they must never be influenced. They must furnish, in that respect, guarantees that all steps taken in a case are taken in the sole interest of the client.

[103] By contrast, the profession of accountant is not subject, in general, and more particularly, in the Netherlands, to comparable requirements of professional conduct.

[104] As the Advocate General has rightly pointed out in paragraphs 185 and 186 of his Opinion, there may be a degree of incompatibility between the 'advisory' activities carried out by a member of the Bar and the 'supervisory' activities carried out by an accountant. The written observations submitted by the respondent in the main proceedings show that accountants in the Netherlands perform a task of certification of accounts. They undertake an objective examination and audit of their clients' accounts, so as to be able to impart to interested third parties their personal opinion concerning the reliability of those accounts. It follows that in the Member State concerned

accountants are not bound by a rule of professional secrecy comparable to that of members of the Bar, unlike the position under German law, for example.

[105] The aim of the 1993 Regulation is therefore to ensure that, in the Member State concerned, the rules of professional conduct for members of the Bar are complied with, having regard to the prevailing perceptions of the profession in that State. The Bar of the Netherlands was entitled to consider that members of the Bar might no longer be in a position to advise and represent their clients independently and in the observance of strict professional secrecy if they belonged to an organisation which is also responsible for producing an account of the financial results of the transactions in respect of which their services were called upon and for certifying those accounts.

[106] Moreover, the concurrent pursuit of the activities of statutory auditor and of adviser, in particular legal adviser, also raises questions within the accountancy profession itself, as may be seen from the Commission Green Paper 96/C/321/01 'The role, the position and the liability of the statutory auditor within the European Union' (OJ 1996 C 321, p. 1; see, in particular, paragraphs 4.12 to 4.14).

[107] A regulation such as the 1993 Regulation could therefore reasonably be considered to be necessary in order to ensure the proper practice of the legal profession, as it is organised in the Member State concerned.

NOTE: The assertion by the Court that the 'overall context' of the agreement should be taken into account has been read by some as the introduction of some form of 'rule of reason' into EC competition law. The rule of reason has particular resonance in US antitrust law in the context of vertical restraints and was much discussed in the reform of vertical restraints policy following the Commission's Green Paper on *Vertical Restraints in EC Competition Policy* (COM C96) 721 (final) and subsequent. For further discussion of the particular problems of vertical restraints see Chapter 8.

SECTION 3: CONSEQUENCES OF INFRINGEMENT: ARTICLE 81(2) EC

Parties face severe consequences for infringement of Article 81(1) EC. First, there are important civil consequences. Article 81(2) EC provides that 'any agreements or decisions prohibited pursuant to this Article shall be automatically void' unless the provisions that infringe Article 81(1) EC are severable and are not sufficiently serious to render the whole agreement void. The prohibited clauses are unenforceable although the parties may be required to implement the remainder of the agreement, subject to the possibility of severance. Reference however must be made to the important judgment of the English Court of Appeal in *Passmore* v *Morland* in which the Court of Appeal determined that the automatic nullity of Article 81(2) is of a 'temporaneous or transient character' (*Passmore* v *Morland* [1999] Eu LR, [1999] 1 CMLR 1129 (*per* Chadwick LJ)). Accordingly, the agreement may move 'in and out' of the prohibition in Article 81(1). It should be noted that the, peculiarly English, idea of 'transient voidness' has been doubted in Assimakis Komninos, *EC Private Antitrust Enforcement*, Oxford, Hart 2008, at p 152.

The landmark decision of the Court in Case C-453/99 *Courage* v *Crehan* [2001] ECR I-6297, [2001] 5 CMLR 28 (see the Opinion of Advocate General Mischo in particular, 22 March 2001) highlights the tension between the application of Community law in the national courts and national procedural autonomy. The Court confirmed that Community law precludes a rule of national law which prevents the recovery of damages merely by reason of being a party to an illegal contract. This decision is of great potential significance and is discussed more fully in Chapter 4.

SECTION 4: EXCEPTIONS AND EXEMPTIONS: ARTICLE 81(3) EC

A: Exceptions

Article 81(3) EC has had an important role given the large number of agreements that are potentially caught by Article 81(1) EC. To recap: an agreement caught by the prohibition contained in Article 81(1) EC is null and void under Article 81(2) EC unless it fulfils the criteria set out in Article 81(3) EC. Before 2004 there was a system based on exemptions, where parties who wished to benefit from Article 81(3) EC had to apply for an individual exemption, from DG Comp, or fulfil the conditions set out in a block exemption Regulation. Regulation 17/62 gave the Commission exclusive power to grant exemptions under Article 81(3) EC. That system was drastically reformed by Regulation 1/2003. The Commission is no longer solely responsible for Article 81(3) EC; under Article 1 of Regulation 1/2003 the whole of Article 81 EC is now directly applicable and Article 81(3) operates as an 'exception rule'. Article 81(3) EC can now be directly relied upon by interested parties who are seeking to defend their agreements before the Commission, the NCAs, or the courts. It is no longer possible to seek an individual exemption to 'clear' an agreement in advance. The parties are expected to consider the potential application of Article 81 EC when they are putting together an agreement. In order to assist the parties the Commission has published guidance and the previous block exemption Regulations continue to operate to offer certainty for certain popular categories of agreement.

Commission Notice—Guidelines on the application of Article 81(3) of the Treaty
OJ, 2004, C101/97 [footnotes omitted]

2.3. The exception rule of Article 81(3)

32. The assessment of restrictions by object and effect under Article 81(1) is only one side of the analysis. The other side, which is reflected in Article 81(3), is the assessment of the positive economic effects of restrictive agreements.

33. The aim of the Community competition rules is to protect competition on the market as a means of enhancing consumer welfare and of ensuring an efficient allocation of resources. Agreements that restrict competition may at the same time have pro-competitive effects by way of efficiency gains. Efficiencies may create additional value by lowering the cost of producing an output, improving the quality of the product or creating a new product. When the pro-competitive effects of an agreement outweigh its anti-competitive effects the agreement is on balance pro-competitive and compatible with the objectives of the Community competition rules. The net effect of such agreements is to promote the very essence of the competitive process, namely to win customers by offering better products or better prices than those offered by rivals. This analytical framework is reflected in Article 81(1) and Article 81(3). The latter provision expressly

acknowledges that restrictive agreements may generate objective economic benefits so as to outweigh the negative effects of the restriction of competition.

34. The application of the exception rule of Article 81(3) is subject to four cumulative conditions, two positive and two negative:

  (a) The agreement must contribute to improving the production or distribution of goods or contribute to promoting technical or economic progress,
  (b) Consumers must receive a fair share of the resulting benefits,
  (c) The restrictions must be indispensable to the attainment of these objectives, and finally
  (d) The agreement must not afford the parties the possibility of eliminating competition in respect of a substantial part of the products in question.

When these four conditions are fulfilled the agreement enhances competition within the relevant market, because it leads the undertakings concerned to offer cheaper or better products to consumers, compensating the latter for the adverse effects of the restrictions of competition.

35. Article 81(3) can be applied either to individual agreements or to categories of agreements by way of a block exemption regulation. When an agreement is covered by a block exemption the parties to the restrictive agreement are relieved of their burden under Article 2 of Regulation 1/2003 of showing that their individual agreement satisfies each of the conditions of Article 81(3). They only have to prove that the restrictive agreement benefits from a block exemption. The application of Article 81(3) to categories of agreements by way of block exemption regulation is based on the presumption that restrictive agreements that fall within their scope fulfil each of the four conditions laid down in Article 81(3).

36. If in an individual case the agreement is caught by Article 81(1) and the conditions of Article 81(3) are not fulfilled the block exemption may be withdrawn. According to Article 29(1) of Regulation 1/2003 the Commission is empowered to withdraw the benefit of a block exemption when it finds that in a particular case an agreement covered by a block exemption regulation has certain effects which are incompatible with Article 81(3) of the Treaty. Pursuant to Article 29(2) of Regulation 1/2003 a competition authority of a Member State may also withdraw the benefit of a Commission block exemption regulation in respect of its territory (or part of its territory), if this territory has all the characteristics of a distinct geographic market. In the case of withdrawal it is for the competition authorities concerned to demonstrate that the agreement infringes Article 81(1) and that it does not fulfil the conditions of Article 81(3).

37. The courts of the Member States have no power to withdraw the benefit of block exemption regulations. Moreover, in their application of block exemption regulations Member State courts may not modify their scope by extending their sphere of application to agreements not covered by the block exemption regulation in question. Outside the scope of block exemption regulations Member State courts have the power to apply Article 81 in full (cf. Article 6 of Regulation 1/2003).

3. THE APPLICATION OF THE FOUR CONDITIONS OF ARTICLE 81(3)

38. The remainder of these guidelines will consider each of the four conditions of Article 81(3). Given that these four conditions are cumulative it is unnecessary to examine any remaining conditions once it is found that one of the conditions of Article 81(3) is not fulfilled. In individual cases it may therefore be appropriate to consider the four conditions in a different order.

39. For the purposes of these guidelines it is considered appropriate to invert the order of the second and the third condition and thus deal with the issue of indispensability before the issue of pass-on to consumers. The analysis of pass-on requires a balancing of the negative and positive effects of an agreement on consumers. This analysis should not include the effects of any restrictions, which already fail the indispensability test and which for that reason are prohibited by Article 81.

3.1. General principles

40. Article 81(3) of the Treaty only becomes relevant when an agreement between undertakings restricts competition within the meaning of Article 81(1). In the case of non-restrictive agreements there is no need to examine any benefits generated by the agreement.

41. Where in an individual case a restriction of competition within the meaning of Article 81(1) has been proven, Article 81(3) can be invoked as a defence. According to Article 2 of Regulation 1/2003 the burden of proof under Article 81(3) rests on the undertaking(s) invoking the benefit of the exception rule. Where the conditions of Article 81(3) are not satisfied the agreement is null and void, cf. Article 81(2). However, such automatic nullity only applies to those parts of the agreement that are incompatible with Article 81, provided that such parts are severable from the agreement as a whole. If only part of the agreement is null and void, it is for the applicable national law to determine the consequences thereof for the remaining part of the agreement.

42. According to settled case law the four conditions of Article 81(3) are cumulative, i.e. they must all be fulfilled for the exception rule to be applicable. If they are not, the application of the exception rule of Article 81(3) must be refused. The four conditions of Article 81(3) are also exhaustive. When they are met the exception is applicable and may not be made dependant on any other condition. Goals pursued by other Treaty provisions can be taken into account to the extent that they can be subsumed under the four conditions of Article 81(3).

43. The assessment under Article 81(3) of benefits flowing from restrictive agreements is in principle made within the confines of each relevant market to which the agreement relates. The Community competition rules have as their objective the protection of competition on the market and cannot be detached from this objective. Moreover, the condition that consumers must receive a fair share of the benefits implies in general that efficiencies generated by the restrictive agreement within a relevant market must be sufficient to outweigh the anti-competitive effects produced by the agreement within that same relevant market. Negative effects on consumers in one geographic market or product market cannot normally be balanced against and compensated by positive effects for consumers in another unrelated geographic market or product market. However, where two markets are related, efficiencies achieved on separate markets can be taken into account provided that the group of consumers affected by the restriction and benefiting from the efficiency gains are substantially the same. Indeed, in some cases only consumers in a downstream market are affected by the agreement in which case the impact of the agreement on such consumers must be assessed. This is for instance so in the case of purchasing agreements.

44. The assessment of restrictive agreements under Article 81(3) is made within the actual context in which they occur and on the basis of the facts existing at any given point in time. The assessment is sensitive to material changes in the facts. The exception rule of Article 81(3) applies as long as the four conditions are fulfilled and ceases to apply when that is no longer the case. When applying Article 81(3) in accordance with these principles it is necessary to take into account the initial sunk investments made by any of the parties and the time needed and the restraints required to commit and recoup an efficiency enhancing investment. Article 81 cannot be applied without taking due account of such *ex ante* investment. The risk facing the parties and the sunk investment that must be committed to implement the agreement can thus lead to the agreement falling outside Article 81(1) or fulfilling the conditions of Article 81(3), as the case may be, for the period of time required to recoup the investment.

45. In some cases the restrictive agreement is an irreversible event. Once the restrictive agreement has been implemented the *ex ante* situation cannot be re-established. In such cases the assessment must be made exclusively on the basis of the facts pertaining at the time of implementation. For instance, in the case of a research and development agreement whereby each party agrees to abandon its respective research project and pool its capabilities with those of another party, it may from an objective point of view be technically and economically impossible to revive a project once it has been abandoned. The assessment of the anti-competitive and pro-competitive effects of the agreement to abandon the individual research projects must therefore be made as of the time of the completion of its implementation. If at that point in time the agreement is compatible with Article 81, for instance because a sufficient number of third parties have competing research and development projects, the parties' agreement to abandon their individual projects remains compatible with Article 81, even if at a later point in time the third party projects fail. However, the prohibition of Article 81 may apply to other parts of the agreement in respect of which the issue of irreversibility does not arise. If for example in addition to joint research and development,

the agreement provides for joint exploitation, Article 81 may apply to this part of the agreement if due to subsequent market developments the agreement becomes restrictive of competition and does not (any longer) satisfy the conditions of Article 81(3) taking due account of *ex ante* sunk investments, cf. the previous paragraph.

46. Article 81(3) does not exclude *a priori* certain types of agreements from its scope. As a matter of principle all restrictive agreements that fulfil the four conditions of Article 81(3) are covered by the exception rule. However, severe restrictions of competition are unlikely to fulfil the conditions of Article 81(3). Such restrictions are usually black-listed in block exemption regulations or identified as hardcore restrictions in Commission guidelines and notices. Agreements of this nature generally fail (at least) the two first conditions of Article 81(3). They neither create objective economic benefits nor do they benefit consumers. For example, a horizontal agreement to fix prices limits output leading to misallocation of resources. It also transfers value from consumers to producers, since it leads to higher prices without producing any countervailing value to consumers within the relevant market. Moreover, these types of agreements generally also fail the indispensability test under the third condition.

47. Any claim that restrictive agreements are justified because they aim at ensuring fair conditions of competition on the market is by nature unfounded and must be discarded. The purpose of Article 81 is to protect effective competition by ensuring that markets remain open and competitive. The protection of fair conditions of competition is a task for the legislator in compliance with Community law obligations and not for undertakings to regulate themselves.

3.2. First condition of Article 81(3): Efficiency gains

3.2.1. General remarks

48. According to the first condition of Article 81(3) the restrictive agreement must contribute to improving the production or distribution of goods or to promoting technical or economic progress. The provision refers expressly only to goods, but applies by analogy to services.

49. It follows from the case law of the Court of Justice that only objective benefits can be taken into account. This means that efficiencies are not assessed from the subjective point of view of the parties. Cost savings that arise from the mere exercise of market power by the parties cannot be taken into account. For instance, when companies agree to fix prices or share markets they reduce output and thereby production costs. Reduced competition may also lead to lower sales and marketing expenditures. Such cost reductions are a direct consequence of a reduction in output and value. The cost reductions in question do not produce any pro-competitive effects on the market. In particular, they do not lead to the creation of value through an integration of assets and activities. They merely allow the undertakings concerned to increase their profits and are therefore irrelevant from the point of view of Article 81(3).

50. The purpose of the first condition of Article 81(3) is to define the types of efficiency gains that can be taken into account and be subject to the further tests of the second and third conditions of Article 81(3). The aim of the analysis is to ascertain what are the objective benefits created by the agreement and what is the economic importance of such efficiencies. Given that for Article 81(3) to apply the pro-competitive effects flowing from the agreement must outweigh its anti-competitive effects, it is necessary to verify what is the link between the agreement and the claimed efficiencies and what is the value of these efficiencies.

51. All efficiency claims must therefore be substantiated so that the following can be verified:
   (a) The *nature* of the claimed efficiencies;
   (b) The *link* between the agreement and the efficiencies;
   (c) The *likelihood* and *magnitude* of each claimed efficiency; and
   (d) *How* and *when* each claimed efficiency would be achieved.

52. Letter (a) allows the decision-maker to verify whether the claimed efficiencies are objective in nature, cf. paragraph 49 above.

53. Letter (b) allows the decision-maker to verify whether there is a sufficient causal link between the restrictive agreement and the claimed efficiencies. This condition normally requires that the efficiencies result from the economic activity that forms the object of the agreement. Such

activities may, for example, take the form of distribution, licensing of technology, joint production or joint research and development. To the extent, however, that an agreement has wider efficiency enhancing effects within the relevant market, for example because it leads to a reduction in industry wide costs, these additional benefits are also taken into account.

54. The causal link between the agreement and the claimed efficiencies must normally also be direct. Claims based on indirect effects are as a general rule too uncertain and too remote to be taken into account. A direct causal link exists for instance where a technology transfer agreement allows the licensees to produce new or improved products or a distribution agreement allows products to be distributed at lower cost or valuable services to be produced. An example of indirect effect would be a case where it is claimed that a restrictive agreement allows the undertakings concerned to increase their profits, enabling them to invest more in research and development to the ultimate benefit of consumers. While there may be a link between profitability and research and development, this link is generally not sufficiently direct to be taken into account in the context of Article 81(3).

55. Letters (c) and (d) allow the decision-maker to verify the value of the claimed efficiencies, which in the context of the third condition of Article 81(3) must be balanced against the anticompetitive effects of the agreement, see paragraph 101 below. Given that Article 81(1) only applies in cases where the agreement has likely negative effects on competition and consumers (in the case of hardcore restrictions such effects are presumed) efficiency claims must be substantiated so that they can be verified. Unsubstantiated claims are rejected.

56. In the case of claimed cost efficiencies the undertakings invoking the benefit of Article 81(3) must as accurately as reasonably possible calculate or estimate the value of the efficiencies and describe in detail how the amount has been computed. They must also describe the method(s) by which the efficiencies have been or will be achieved. The data submitted must be verifiable so that there can be a sufficient degree of certainty that the efficiencies have materialised or are likely to materialise.

57. In the case of claimed efficiencies in the form of new or improved products and other non-cost based efficiencies, the undertakings claiming the benefit of Article 81(3) must describe and explain in detail what is the nature of the efficiencies and how and why they constitute an objective economic benefit.

58. In cases where the agreement has yet to be fully implemented the parties must substantiate any projections as to the date from which the efficiencies will become operational so as to have a significant positive impact in the market.

3.2.2. The different categories of efficiencies

59. The types of efficiencies listed in Article 81(3) are broad categories which are intended to cover all objective economic efficiencies. There is considerable overlap between the various categories mentioned in Article 81(3) and the same agreement may give rise to several kinds of efficiencies. It is therefore not appropriate to draw clear and firm distinctions between the various categories. For the purpose of these guidelines, a distinction is made between cost efficiencies and efficiencies of a qualitative nature whereby value is created in the form of new or improved products, greater product variety etc.

60. In general, efficiencies stem from an integration of economic activities whereby undertakings combine their assets to achieve what they could not achieve as efficiently on their own or whereby they entrust another undertaking with tasks that can be performed more efficiently by that other undertaking.

61. The research and development, production and distribution process may be viewed as a value chain that can be divided into a number of stages. At each stage of this chain an undertaking must make a choice between performing the activity itself, performing it together with (an)other undertaking(s) or outsourcing the activity entirely to (an)other undertaking(s).

62. In each case where the choice made involves cooperation on the market with another undertaking, an agreement within the meaning of Article 81(1) normally needs to be concluded. These agreements can be vertical, as is the case where the parties operate at different levels of the value

chain or horizontal, as is the case where the firms operate at the same level of the value chain. Both categories of agreements may create efficiencies by allowing the undertakings in question to perform a particular task at lower cost or with higher added value for consumers. Such agreements may also contain or lead to restrictions of competition in which case the prohibition rule of Article 81(1) and the exception rule of Article 81(3) may become relevant.

63. The types of efficiencies mentioned in the following are only examples and are not intended to be exhaustive.

3.2.2.1. Cost efficiencies

64. Cost efficiencies flowing from agreements between undertakings can originate from a number of different sources. One very important source of cost savings is the development of new production technologies and methods. In general, it is when technological leaps are made that the greatest potential for cost savings is achieved. For instance, the introduction of the assembly line led to a very substantial reduction in the cost of producing motor vehicles.

65. Another very important source of efficiency is synergies resulting from an integration of existing assets. When the parties to an agreement combine their respective assets they may be able to attain a cost/output configuration that would not otherwise be possible. The combination of two existing technologies that have complementary strengths may reduce production costs or lead to the production of a higher quality product. For instance, it may be that the production assets of firm A generate a high output per hour but require a relatively high input of raw materials per unit of output, whereas the production assets of firm B generate lower output per hour but require a relatively lower input of raw materials per unit of output. Synergies are created if by establishing a production joint venture combining the production assets of A and B the parties can attain a high(er) level of output per hour with a low(er) input of raw materials per unit of output. Similarly, if one undertaking has optimised one part of the value chain and another undertaking has optimised another part of the value chain, the combination of their operations may lead to lower costs. Firm A may for instance have a highly automated production facility resulting in low production costs per unit whereas B has developed an efficient order processing system. The system allows production to be tailored to customer demand, ensuring timely delivery and reducing warehousing and obsolescence costs. By combining their assets A and B may be able to obtain cost reductions.

66. Cost efficiencies may also result from economies of scale, i.e. declining cost per unit of output as output increases. To give an example: investment in equipment and other assets often has to be made in indivisible blocks. If an undertaking cannot fully utilise a block, its average costs will be higher than if it could do so. For instance, the cost of operating a truck is virtually the same regardless of whether it is almost empty, half-full or full. Agreements whereby undertakings combine their logistics operations may allow them to increase the load factors and reduce the number of vehicles employed. Larger scale may also allow for better division of labour leading to lower unit costs. Firms may achieve economies of scale in respect of all parts of the value chain, including research and development, production, distribution and marketing. Learning economies constitute a related type of efficiency. As experience is gained in using a particular production process or in performing particular tasks, productivity may increase because the process is made to run more efficiently or because the task is performed more quickly.

67. Economies of scope are another source of cost efficiency, which occur when firms achieve cost savings by producing different products on the basis of the same input. Such efficiencies may arise from the fact that it is possible to use the same components and the same facilities and personnel to produce a variety of products. Similarly, economies of scope may arise in distribution when several types of goods are distributed in the same vehicles. For instance, a producer of frozen pizzas and a producer of frozen vegetables may obtain economies of scope by jointly distributing their products. Both groups of products must be distributed in refrigerated vehicles and it is likely that there are significant overlaps in terms of customers. By combining their operations the two producers may obtain lower distribution costs per distributed unit.

68. Efficiencies in the form of cost reductions can also follow from agreements that allow for better planning of production, reducing the need to hold expensive inventory and allowing for better capacity utilisation. Efficiencies of this nature may for example stem from the use of 'just in

time' purchasing, i.e. an obligation on a supplier of components to continuously supply the buyer according to its needs thereby avoiding the need for the buyer to maintain a significant stock of components which risks becoming obsolete. Cost savings may also result from agreements that allow the parties to rationalise production across their facilities.

3.2.2.2. Qualitative efficiencies

69. Agreements between undertakings may generate various efficiencies of a qualitative nature which are relevant to the application of Article 81(3). In a number of cases the main efficiency enhancing potential of the agreement is not cost reduction; it is quality improvements and other efficiencies of a qualitative nature. Depending on the individual case such efficiencies may therefore be of equal or greater importance than cost efficiencies.

70. Technical and technological advances form an essential and dynamic part of the economy, generating significant benefits in the form of new or improved goods and services. By cooperating undertakings may be able to create efficiencies that would not have been possible without the restrictive agreement or would have been possible only with substantial delay or at higher cost. Such efficiencies constitute an important source of economic benefits covered by the first condition of Article 81(3). Agreements capable of producing efficiencies of this nature include, in particular, research and development agreements. An example would be A and B creating a joint venture for the development and, if successful, joint production of a cell-based tyre. The puncture of one cell does not affect other cells, which means that there is no risk of collapse of the tyre in the event of a puncture. The tyre is thus safer than traditional tyres. It also means that there is no immediate need to change the tyre and thus to carry a spare. Both types of efficiencies constitute objective benefits within the meaning of the first condition of Article 81(3).

71. In the same way that the combination of complementary assets can give rise to cost savings, combinations of assets may also create synergies that create efficiencies of a qualitative nature. The combination of production assets may for instance lead to the production of higher quality products or products with novel features. This may for instance be the case for licence agreements, and agreements providing for joint production of new or improved goods or services. Licence agreements may, in particular, ensure more rapid dissemination of new technology in the Community and enable the licensee(s) to make available new products or to employ new production techniques that lead to quality improvements. Joint production agreements may, in particular, allow new or improved products or services to be introduced on the market more quickly or at lower cost. In the telecommunications sector, for example, cooperation agreements have been held to create efficiencies by making available more quickly new global services. In the banking sector cooperation agreements that made available improved facilities for making crossborder payments have also been held to create efficiencies falling within the scope of the first condition of Article 81(3).

72. Distribution agreements may also give rise to qualitative efficiencies. Specialised distributors, for example, may be able to provide services that are better tailored to customer needs or to provide quicker delivery or better quality assurance throughout the distribution chain.

3.3. Third condition of Article 81(3): Indispensability of the restrictions

73. According to the third condition of Article 81(3) the restrictive agreement must not impose restrictions, which are not indispensable to the attainment of the efficiencies created by the agreement in question. This condition implies a two-fold test. First, the restrictive agreement as such must be reasonably necessary in order to achieve the efficiencies. Secondly, the individual restrictions of competition that flow from the agreement must also be reasonably necessary for the attainment of the efficiencies.

74. In the context of the third condition of Article 81(3) the decisive factor is whether or not the restrictive agreement and individual restrictions make it possible to perform the activity in question more efficiently than would likely have been the case in the absence of the agreement or the restriction concerned. The question is not whether in the absence of the restriction the agreement would not have been concluded, but whether more efficiencies are produced with the agreement or restriction than in the absence of the agreement or restriction.

75. The first test contained in the third condition of Article 81(3) requires that the efficiencies be specific to the agreement in question in the sense that there are no other economically practicable and less restrictive means of achieving the efficiencies. In making this latter assessment the market conditions and business realities facing the parties to the agreement must be taken into account. Undertakings invoking the benefit of Article 81(3) are not required to consider hypothetical or theoretical alternatives. The Commission will not second guess the business judgment of the parties. It will only intervene where it is reasonably clear that there are realistic and attainable alternatives. The parties must only explain and demonstrate why such seemingly realistic and significantly less restrictive alternatives to the agreement would be significantly less efficient.

76. It is particularly relevant to examine whether, having due regard to the circumstances of the individual case, the parties could have achieved the efficiencies by means of another less restrictive type of agreement and, if so, when they would likely be able to obtain the efficiencies. It may also be necessary to examine whether the parties could have achieved the efficiencies on their own. For instance, where the claimed efficiencies take the form of cost reductions resulting from economies of scale or scope the undertakings concerned must explain and substantiate why the same efficiencies would not be likely to be attained through internal growth and price competition. In making this assessment it is relevant to consider, *inter alia*, what is the minimum efficient scale on the market concerned. The minimum efficient scale is the level of output required to minimise average cost and exhaust economies of scale. The larger the minimum efficient scale compared to the current size of either of the parties to the agreement, the more likely it is that the efficiencies will be deemed to be specific to the agreement. In the case of agreements that produce substantial synergies through the combination of complementary assets and capabilities the very nature of the efficiencies give rise to a presumption that the agreement is necessary to attain them.

77. These principles can be illustrated by the following hypothetical example:

A and B combine within a joint venture their respective production technologies to achieve higher output and lower raw material consumption. The joint venture is granted an exclusive licence to their respective production technologies. The parties transfer their existing production facilities to the joint venture. They also transfer key staff in order to ensure that existing learning economies can be exploited and further developed. It is estimated that these economies will reduce production costs by a further 5%. The output of the joint venture is sold independently by A and B. In this case the indispensability condition necessitates an assessment of whether or not the benefits could be substantially achieved by means of a licence agreement, which would be likely to be less restrictive because A and B would continue to produce independently. In the circumstances described this is unlikely to be the case since under a licence agreement the parties would not be able to benefit in the same seamless and continued way from their respective experience in operating the two technologies, resulting in significant learning economies.

78. Once it is found that the agreement in question is necessary in order to produce the efficiencies, the indispensability of each restriction of competition flowing from the agreement must be assessed. In this context it must be assessed whether individual restrictions are reasonably necessary in order to produce the efficiencies. The parties to the agreement must substantiate their claim with regard to both the nature of the restriction and its intensity.

79. A restriction is indispensable if its absence would eliminate or significantly reduce the efficiencies that follow from the agreement or make it significantly less likely that they will materialise. The assessment of alternative solutions must take into account the actual and potential improvement in the field of competition by the elimination of a particular restriction or the application of a less restrictive alternative. The more restrictive the restraint the stricter the test under the third condition. Restrictions that are black listed in block exemption regulations or identified as hardcore restrictions in Commission guidelines and notices are unlikely to be considered indispensable.

80. The assessment of indispensability is made within the actual context in which the agreement operates and must in particular take account of the structure of the market, the economic risks related to the agreement, and the incentives facing the parties. The more uncertain the success of the product covered by the agreement, the more a restriction may be required to ensure that the efficiencies will materialise. Restrictions may also be indispensable in order to align the incentives of the

parties and ensure that they concentrate their efforts on the implementation of the agreement. A restriction may for instance be necessary in order to avoid hold-up problems once a substantial sunk investment has been made by one of the parties. Once for instance a supplier has made a substantial relationship-specific investment with a view to supplying a customer with an input, the supplier is locked into the customer. In order to avoid that *ex post* the customer exploits this dependence to obtain more favourable terms, it may be necessary to impose an obligation not to purchase the component from third parties or to purchase minimum quantities of the component from the supplier.

81. In some cases a restriction may be indispensable only for a certain period of time, in which case the exception of Article 81(3) only applies during that period. In making this assessment it is necessary to take due account of the period of time required for the parties to achieve the efficiencies justifying the application of the exception rule. In cases where the benefits cannot be achieved without considerable investment, account must, in particular, be taken of the period of time required to ensure an adequate return on such investment, see also paragraph 44 above.

82. These principles can be illustrated by the following hypothetical examples:

P produces and distributes frozen pizzas, holding 15% of the market in Member State X. Deliveries are made directly to retailers. Since most retailers have limited storage capacity, relatively frequent deliveries are required, leading to low capacity utilisation and use of relatively small vehicles. T is a wholesaler of frozen pizzas and other frozen products, delivering to most of the same customers as P. The pizza products distributed by T hold 30% of the market. T has a fleet of larger vehicles and has excess capacity. P concludes an exclusive distribution agreement with T for Member State X and undertakes to ensure that distributors in other Member States will not sell into T's territory either actively or passively. T undertakes to advertise the products, survey consumer tastes and satisfaction rates and ensure delivery to retailers of all products within 24 hours. The agreement leads to a reduction in total distribution costs of 30% as capacity is better utilised and duplication of routes is eliminated. The agreement also leads to the provision of additional services to consumers. Restrictions on passive sales are hardcore restrictions under the block exemption regulation on vertical restraints and can only be considered indispensable in exceptional circumstances. The established market position of T and the nature of the obligations imposed on it indicate this is not an exceptional case. The ban on active selling, on the other hand, is likely to be indispensable. T is likely to have less incentive to sell and advertise the P brand, if distributors in other Member States could sell actively in Member State X and thus get a free ride on the efforts of T. This is particularly so, as T also distributes competing brands and thus has the possibility of pushing more of the brands that are the least exposed to free riding.

S is a producer of carbonated soft drinks, holding 40% of the market. The nearest competitor holds 20%. S concludes supply agreements with customers accounting for 25% of demand, whereby they undertake to purchase exclusively from S for 5 years. S concludes agreements with other customers accounting for 15% of demand whereby they are granted quarterly target rebates, if their purchases exceed certain individually fixed targets. S claims that the agreements allow it to predict demand more accurately and thus to better plan production, reducing raw material storage and warehousing costs and avoiding supply shortages. Given the market position of S and the combined coverage of the restrictions, the restrictions are very unlikely to be considered indispensable. The exclusive purchasing obligation exceeds what is required to plan production and the same is true of the target rebate scheme. Predictability of demand can be achieved by less restrictive means. S could, for example, provide incentives for customers to order large quantities at a time by offering quantity rebates or by offering a rebate to customers that place firm orders in advance for delivery on specified dates.

3.4. Second condition of Article 81(3): Fair share for consumers

3.4.1. General remarks

83. According to the second condition of Article 81(3) consumers must receive a fair share of the efficiencies generated by the restrictive agreement.

84. The concept of *'consumers'* encompasses all direct or indirect users of the products covered by the agreement, including producers that use the products as an input, wholesalers, retailers and

final consumers, i.e. natural persons who are acting for purposes which can be regarded as outside their trade or profession. In other words, consumers within the meaning of Article 81(3) are the customers of the parties to the agreement and subsequent purchasers. These customers can be undertakings as in the case of buyers of industrial machinery or an input for further processing or final consumers as for instance in the case of buyers of impulse ice-cream or bicycles.

85. The concept of *'fair share'* implies that the pass-on of benefits must at least compensate consumers for any actual or likely negative impact caused to them by the restriction of competition found under Article 81(1). In line with the overall objective of Article 81 to prevent anti-competitive agreements, the net effect of the agreement must at least be neutral from the point of view of those consumers directly or likely affected by the agreement. If such consumers are worse off following the agreement, the second condition of Article 81(3) is not fulfilled. The positive effects of an agreement must be balanced against and compensate for its negative effects on consumers. When that is the case consumers are not harmed by the agreement. Moreover, society as a whole benefits where the efficiencies lead either to fewer resources being used to produce the output consumed or to the production of more valuable products and thus to a more efficient allocation of resources.

86. It is not required that consumers receive a share of each and every efficiency gain identified under the first condition. It suffices that sufficient benefits are passed on to compensate for the negative effects of the restrictive agreement. In that case consumers obtain a fair share of the overall benefits. If a restrictive agreement is likely to lead to higher prices, consumers must be fully compensated through increased quality or other benefits. If not, the second condition of Article 81(3) is not fulfilled.

87. The decisive factor is the overall impact on consumers of the products within the relevant market and not the impact on individual members of this group of consumers. In some cases a certain period of time may be required before the efficiencies materialise. Until such time the agreement may have only negative effects. The fact that pass-on to the consumer occurs with a certain time lag does not in itself exclude the application of Article 81(3). However, the greater the time lag, the greater must be the efficiencies to compensate also for the loss to consumers during the period preceding the pass-on.

88. In making this assessment it must be taken into account that the value of a gain for consumers in the future is not the same as a present gain for consumers. The value of saving 100 euro today is greater than the value of saving the same amount a year later. A gain for consumers in the future therefore does not fully compensate for a present loss to consumers of equal nominal size. In order to allow for an appropriate comparison of a present loss to consumers with a future gain to consumers, the value of future gains must be discounted. The discount rate applied must reflect the rate of inflation, if any, and lost interest as an indication of the lower value of future gains.

89. In other cases the agreement may enable the parties to obtain the efficiencies earlier than would otherwise be possible. In such circumstances it is necessary to take account of the likely negative impact on consumers within the relevant market once this lead-time has lapsed. If through the restrictive agreement the parties obtain a strong position on the market, they may be able to charge a significantly higher price than would otherwise have been the case. For the second condition of Article 81(3) to be satisfied the benefit to consumers of having earlier access to the products must be equally significant. This may for instance be the case where an agreement allows two tyre manufacturers to bring to market three years earlier a new substantially safer tyre but at the same time, by increasing their market power, allows them to raise prices by 5%. In such a case it is likely that having early access to a substantially improved product outweighs the price increase.

90. The second condition of Article 81(3) incorporates a sliding scale. The greater the restriction of competition found under Article 81(1) the greater must be the efficiencies and the pass-on to consumers. This sliding scale approach implies that if the restrictive effects of an agreement are relatively limited and the efficiencies are substantial it is likely that a fair share of the cost savings will be passed on to consumers. In such cases it is therefore normally not necessary to engage in a detailed analysis of the second condition of Article 81(3), provided that the three other conditions for the application of this provision are fulfilled.

91. If, on the other hand, the restrictive effects of the agreement are substantial and the cost savings are relatively insignificant, it is very unlikely that the second condition of Article 81(3) will be fulfilled. The impact of the restriction of competition depends on the intensity of the restriction and the degree of competition that remains following the agreement.

92. If the agreement has both substantial anti-competitive effects and substantial pro-competitive effects a careful analysis is required. In the application of the balancing test in such cases it must be taken into account that competition is an important long-term driver of efficiency and innovation. Undertakings that are not subject to effective competitive constraints—such as for instance dominant firms—have less incentive to maintain or build on the efficiencies. The more substantial the impact of the agreement on competition, the more likely it is that consumers will suffer in the long run.

93. The following two sections describe in more detail the analytical framework for assessing consumer pass-on of efficiency gains. The first section deals with cost efficiencies, whereas the section that follows covers other types of efficiencies such as new or improved products (qualitative efficiencies). The framework, which is developed in these two sections, is particularly important in cases where it is not immediately obvious that the competitive harms exceed the benefits to consumers or *vice versa*.

94. In the application of the principles set out below the Commission will have regard to the fact that in many cases it is difficult to accurately calculate the consumer pass-on rate and other types of consumer pass-on. Undertakings are only required to substantiate their claims by providing estimates and other data to the extent reasonably possible, taking account of the circumstances of the individual case.

3.4.2. Pass-on and balancing of cost efficiencies

95. When markets, as is normally the case, are not perfectly competitive, undertakings are able to influence the market price to a greater or lesser extent by altering their output. They may also be able to price discriminate amongst customers.

96. Cost efficiencies may in some circumstances lead to increased output and lower prices for the affected consumers. If due to cost efficiencies the undertakings in question can increase profits by expanding output, consumer pass-on may occur. In assessing the extent to which cost efficiencies are likely to be passed on to consumers and the outcome of the balancing test contained in Article 81(3) the following factors are in particular taken into account:

  (a) The characteristics and structure of the market,
  (b) The nature and magnitude of the efficiency gains,
  (c) The elasticity of demand, and
  (d) The magnitude of the restriction of competition.

All factors must normally be considered. Since Article 81(3) only applies in cases where competition on the market is being appreciably restricted, see paragraph 24 above, there can be no presumption that residual competition will ensure that consumers receive a fair share of the benefits. However, the degree of competition remaining on the market and the nature of this competition influences the likelihood of pass-on.

97. The greater the degree of residual competition the more likely it is that individual undertakings will try to increase their sales by passing on cost efficiencies. If undertakings compete mainly on price and are not subject to significant capacity constraints, pass-on may occur relatively quickly. If competition is mainly on capacity and capacity adaptations occur with a certain time lag, pass-on will be slower. Pass-on is also likely to be slower when the market structure is conducive to tacit collusion. If competitors are likely to retaliate against an increase in output by one or more parties to the agreement, the incentive to increase output may be tempered, unless the competitive advantage conferred by the efficiencies is such that the undertakings concerned have an incentive to break away from the common policy adopted on the market by the members of the oligopoly. In other words, the efficiencies generated by the agreement may turn the undertakings concerned into so-called 'mavericks'.

98. The nature of the efficiency gains also plays an important role. According to economic theory undertakings maximise their profits by selling units of output until marginal revenue equals

marginal cost. Marginal revenue is the change in total revenue resulting from selling an additional unit of output and marginal cost is the change in total cost resulting from producing that additional unit of output. It follows from this principle that as a general rule output and pricing decisions of a profit maximising undertaking are not determined by its fixed costs (i.e. costs that do not vary with the rate of production) but by its variable costs (i.e. costs that vary with the rate of production). After fixed costs are incurred and capacity is set, pricing and output decisions are determined by variable cost and demand conditions. Take for instance a situation in which two companies each produce two products on two production lines operating only at half their capacities. A specialisation agreement may allow the two undertakings to specialise in producing one of the two products and scrap their second production line for the other product. At the same time the specialisation may allow the companies to reduce variable input and stocking costs. Only the latter savings will have a direct effect on the pricing and output decisions of the undertakings, as they will influence the marginal costs of production. The scrapping by each undertaking of one of their production lines will not reduce their variable costs and will not have an impact on their production costs. It follows that undertakings may have a direct incentive to pass on to consumers in the form of higher output and lower prices efficiencies that reduce marginal costs, whereas they have no such direct incentive with regard to efficiencies that reduce fixed costs. Consumers are therefore more likely to receive a fair share of the cost efficiencies in the case of reductions in variable costs than they are in the case of reductions in fixed costs.

99. The fact that undertakings may have an incentive to pass on certain types of cost efficiencies does not imply that the pass-on rate will necessarily be 100%. The actual pass-on rate depends on the extent to which consumers respond to changes in price, i.e. the elasticity of demand. The greater the increase in demand caused by a decrease in price, the greater the pass-on rate. This follows from the fact that the greater the additional sales caused by a price reduction due to an increase in output the more likely it is that these sales will offset the loss of revenue caused by the lower price resulting from the increase in output. In the absence of price discrimination the lowering of prices affects all units sold by the undertaking, in which case marginal revenue is less than the price obtained for the marginal product. If the undertakings concerned are able to charge different prices to different customers, i.e. price discriminate, pass-on will normally only benefit price-sensitive consumers.

100. It must also be taken into account that efficiency gains often do not affect the whole cost structure of the undertakings concerned. In such event the impact on the price to consumers is reduced. If for example an agreement allows the parties to reduce production costs by 6%, but production costs only make up one third of the costs on the basis of which prices are determined, the impact on the product price is 2%, assuming that the full amount is passed-on.

101. Finally, and very importantly, it is necessary to balance the two opposing forces resulting from the restriction of competition and the cost efficiencies. On the one hand, any increase in market power caused by the restrictive agreement gives the undertakings concerned the ability and incentive to raise price. On the other hand, the types of cost efficiencies that are taken into account may give the undertakings concerned an incentive to reduce price, see paragraph 98 above. The effects of these two opposing forces must be balanced against each other. It is recalled in this regard that the consumer pass-on condition incorporates a sliding scale. When the agreement causes a substantial reduction in the competitive constraint facing the parties, extraordinarily large cost efficiencies are normally required for sufficient pass-on to occur.

3.4.3. Pass-on and balancing of other types of efficiencies

102. Consumer pass-on can also take the form of qualitative efficiencies such as new and improved products, creating sufficient value for consumers to compensate for the anticompetitive effects of the agreement, including a price increase.

103. Any such assessment necessarily requires value judgment. It is difficult to assign precise values to dynamic efficiencies of this nature. However, the fundamental objective of the assessment remains the same, namely to ascertain the overall impact of the agreement on the consumers within the relevant market. Undertakings claiming the benefit of Article 81(3) must substantiate that consumers obtain countervailing benefits (see in this respect paragraphs 57 and 86 above).

104. The availability of new and improved products constitutes an important source of consumer welfare. As long as the increase in value stemming from such improvements exceeds any harm from a maintenance or an increase in price caused by the restrictive agreement, consumers are better off than without the agreement and the consumer pass-on requirement of Article 81(3) is normally fulfilled. In cases where the likely effect of the agreement is to increase prices for consumers within the relevant market it must be carefully assessed whether the claimed efficiencies create real value for consumers in that market so as to compensate for the adverse effects of the restriction of competition.

3.5. Fourth condition of Article 81(3): No elimination of competition

105. According to the fourth condition of Article 81(3) the agreement must not afford the undertakings concerned the possibility of eliminating competition in respect of a substantial part of the products concerned. Ultimately the protection of rivalry and the competitive process is given priority over potentially pro-competitive efficiency gains which could result from restrictive agreements. The last condition of Article 81(3) recognises the fact that rivalry between undertakings is an essential driver of economic efficiency, including dynamic efficiencies in the shape of innovation. In other words, the ultimate aim of Article 81 is to protect the competitive process. When competition is eliminated the competitive process is brought to an end and short-term efficiency gains are outweighed by longer-term losses stemming *inter alia* from expenditures incurred by the incumbent to maintain its position (rent seeking), misallocation of resources, reduced innovation and higher prices.

106. The concept in Article 81(3) of elimination of competition in respect of a substantial part of the products concerned is an autonomous Community law concept specific to Article 81(3). However, in the application of this concept it is necessary to take account of the relationship between Article 81 and Article 82. According to settled case law the application of Article 81(3) cannot prevent the application of Article 82 of the Treaty. Moreover, since Articles 81 and 82 both pursue the aim of maintaining effective competition on the market, consistency requires that Article 81(3) be interpreted as precluding any application of this provision to restrictive agreements that constitute an abuse of a dominant position. However, not all restrictive agreements concluded by a dominant undertaking constitute an abuse of a dominant position. This is for instance the case where a dominant undertaking is party to a non-full function joint venture, which is found to be restrictive of competition but at the same time involves a substantial integration of assets.

107. Whether competition is being eliminated within the meaning of the last condition of Article 81(3) depends on the degree of competition existing prior to the agreement and on the impact of the restrictive agreement on competition, i.e. the reduction in competition that the agreement brings about. The more competition is already weakened in the market concerned, the slighter the further reduction required for competition to be eliminated within the meaning of Article 81(3). Moreover, the greater the reduction of competition caused by the agreement, the greater the likelihood that competition in respect of a substantial part of the products concerned risks being eliminated.

108. The application of the last condition of Article 81(3) requires a realistic analysis of the various sources of competition in the market, the level of competitive constraint that they impose on the parties to the agreement and the impact of the agreement on this competitive constraint. Both actual and potential competition must be considered.

109. While market shares are relevant, the magnitude of remaining sources of actual competition cannot be assessed exclusively on the basis of market share. More extensive qualitative and quantitative analysis is normally called for. The capacity of actual competitors to compete and their incentive to do so must be examined. If, for example, competitors face capacity constraints or have relatively higher costs of production their competitive response will necessarily be limited.

110. In the assessment of the impact of the agreement on competition it is also relevant to examine its influence on the various parameters of competition. The last condition for exception under Article 81(3) is not fulfilled, if the agreement eliminates competition in one of its most important expressions. This is particularly the case when an agreement eliminates price competition or competition in respect of innovation and development of new products.

111. The actual market conduct of the parties can provide insight into the impact of the agreement. If following the conclusion of the agreement the parties have implemented and maintained substantial price increases or engaged in other conduct indicative of the existence of a considerable degree of market power, it is an indication that the parties are not subject to any real competitive pressure and that competition has been eliminated with regard to a substantial part of the products concerned.

112. Past competitive interaction may also provide an indication of the impact of the agreement on future competitive interaction. An undertaking may be able to eliminate competition within the meaning of Article 81(3) by concluding an agreement with a competitor that in the past has been a 'maverick'. Such an agreement may change the competitive incentives and capabilities of the competitor and thereby remove an important source of competition in the market.

113. In cases involving differentiated products, i.e. products that differ in the eyes of consumers, the impact of the agreement may depend on the competitive relationship between the products sold by the parties to the agreement. When undertakings offer differentiated products the competitive constraint that individual products impose on each other differs according to the degree of substitutability between them. It must therefore be considered what is the degree of substitutability between the products offered by the parties, i.e. what is the competitive constraint that they impose on each other. The more the products of the parties to the agreement are close substitutes the greater the likely restrictive effect of the agreement. In other words, the more substitutable the products the greater the likely change brought about by the agreement in terms of restriction of competition on the market and the more likely it is that competition in respect of a substantial part of the products concerned risks being eliminated.

114. While sources of actual competition are usually the most important, as they are most easily verified, sources of potential competition must also be taken into account. The assessment of potential competition requires an analysis of barriers to entry facing undertakings that are not already competing within the relevant market. Any assertions by the parties that there are low barriers to market entry must be supported by information identifying the sources of potential competition and the parties must also substantiate why these sources constitute a real competitive pressure on the parties.

115. In the assessment of entry barriers and the real possibility for new entry on a significant scale, it is relevant to examine, *inter alia*, the following:

(i) The regulatory framework with a view to determining its impact on new entry.

(ii) The cost of entry including sunk costs. Sunk costs are those that cannot be recovered if the entrant subsequently exits the market. The higher the sunk costs the higher the commercial risk for potential entrants.

(iii) The minimum efficient scale within the industry, i.e. the rate of output where average costs are minimised. If the minimum efficient scale is large compared to the size of the market, efficient entry is likely to be more costly and risky.

(iv) The competitive strengths of potential entrants. Effective entry is particularly likely where potential entrants have access to at least as cost efficient technologies as the incumbents or other competitive advantages that allow them to compete effectively. When potential entrants are on the same or an inferior technological trajectory compared to the incumbents and possess no other significant competitive advantage entry is more risky and less effective.

(v) The position of buyers and their ability to bring onto the market new sources of competition. It is irrelevant that certain strong buyers may be able to extract more favourable conditions from the parties to the agreement than their weaker competitors. The presence of strong buyers can only serve to counter a prima facie finding of elimination of competition if it is likely that the buyers in question will pave the way for effective new entry.

(vi) The likely response of incumbents to attempted new entry. Incumbents may for example through past conduct have acquired a reputation of aggressive behaviour, having an impact on future entry.

(vii) The economic outlook for the industry may be an indicator of its longer-term attractiveness. Industries that are stagnating or in decline are less attractive candidates for entry than industries characterised by growth.

(viii) Past entry on a significant scale or the absence thereof.

116. The above principles can be illustrated by the following hypothetical examples, which are not intended to establish thresholds:

Firm A is brewer, holding 70% of the relevant market, comprising the sale of beer through cafés and other on-trade premises. Over the past 5 years A has increased its market share from 60%. There are four other competitors in the market, B, C, D and E with market shares of 10%, 10%, 5% and 5%. No new entry has occurred in the recent past and price changes implemented by A have generally been followed by competitors. A concludes agreements with 20% of the on-trade premises representing 40% of sales volumes whereby the contracting parties undertake to purchase beer only from A for a period of 5 years. The agreements raise the costs and reduce the revenues of rivals, which are foreclosed from the most attractive outlets. Given the market position of A, which has been strengthened in recent years, the absence of new entry and the already weak position of competitors it is likely that competition in the market is eliminated within the meaning of Article 81(3).

Shipping firms A, B, C, and D, holding collectively more than 70% of the relevant market, conclude an agreement whereby they agree to coordinate their schedules and their tariffs. Following the implementation of the agreement prices rise between 30% and 100%. There are four other suppliers, the largest holding about 14% of the relevant market. There has been no new entry in recent years and the parties to the agreement did not lose significant market share following the price increases. The existing competitors brought no significant new capacity to the market and no new entry occurred. In light of the market position of the parties and the absence of competitive response to their joint conduct it can reasonably be concluded that the parties to the agreement are not subject to real competitive pressures and that the agreement affords them the possibility of eliminating competition within the meaning of Article 81(3).

A is a producer of electric appliances for professional users with a market share of 65% of a relevant national market. B is a competing manufacturer with 5% market share which has developed a new type of motor that is more powerful while consuming less electricity. A and B conclude an agreement whereby they establish a production joint venture for the production of the new motor. B undertakes to grant an exclusive licence to the joint venture. The joint venture combines the new technology of B with the efficient manufacturing and quality control process of A. There is one other main competitor with 15% of the market. Another competitor with 5% market share has recently been acquired by C, a major international producer of competing electric appliances, which itself owns efficient technologies. C has thus far not been active on the market mainly due to the fact that local presence and servicing is desired by customers. Through the acquisition C gains access to the service organisation required to penetrate the market. The entry of C is likely to ensure that competition is not being eliminated.

NOTE: The Commission Notice is a very full description of the Commission's policy in this area giving a clear view of how the NCAs and the courts should deal with Article 81(3) EC. It is interesting to note that the policy set out in the Notice is clearly focused on the economic impact of agreements. The gains discussed in the Notice are very much efficiency and innovation, rather than wider social goals. This is somewhat at odds with the Commission's previous practice, where they appeared to be willing to look at wider 'benefits' from agreements. It is, perhaps, not surprising that the Commission has been reticent to suggest that the NCAs and, particularly, the domestic courts, should operate the wide discretion it allowed itself when it had sole power to grant exemptions under Regulation 17/62. It will be interesting to see whether the NCAs or the courts attempt to use a wider view of Article 81(3) EC than that suggested in the Notice. A number of examples of this wider discretion can be seen below.

Metro-SB-Grossmärkte GmbH v Commission (No 1)
(Case 26/76) [1977] ECR 1875, [1978] 2 CMLR 1

[43] With regard to the first condition set out above, the conclusion of supply contracts for six months taking account of the probable growth of the market should make it possible to ensure both a certain stability in the supply of the relevant products, which should allow the requirements of persons obtaining supplies from the wholesaler to be more fully satisfied, and, since such supply

contracts are of relatively short duration, a certain flexibility, enabling production to be adapted to the changing requirements of the market. Thus a more regular distribution is ensured, to the benefit both of the producer, who takes his share of the planned expansion of the market in the relevant product, of the wholesaler, whose supplies are secured, and, finally, of the undertakings which obtain supplies from the wholesaler, in that the variety of available products is increased. Another improvement in distribution is provided under the clause in the cooperation agreement obliging SABA to compensate wholesalers for service performed under guarantee and to supply spare parts necessary for repairs under guarantee. Furthermore, the establishment of supply forecasts for a reasonable period constitutes a stabilising factor with regard to the provision of employment which, since it improves the general conditions of production, especially when the market conditions are unfavourable, comes within the framework of the objectives to which reference may be had pursuant to Article 85(3).

CECED

Commission Decision 2000/475/EC, OJ, 2000, L187/47 [footnotes omitted]

(47) The agreement is designed to reduce the potential energy consumption of new washing machines by at least 15 to 20% (relative to 1994 data on models of washing machines). According to CECED, were models of phased-out machines to be replaced by an equivalent number of machines in categories A, B and C, currently available on the market, 7,5 TWh would be saved in 2015 out of the estimated 38 TWh consumed by the operation of washing machines in the Community in 1995.

(48) Washing machines which, other factors being constant, consume less electricity are objectively more technically efficient. Reduced electricity consumption indirectly leads to reduced pollution from electricity generation. The future operation of the total of installed machines providing the same service with less indirect pollution is more economically efficient than without the agreement.

(49) Such potential improvement in four years of implementation of the agreement is remarkable, compared to improvements in the past. Were energy efficiency to improve at the same rate as it did between 1978 and 1994 without any agreement, the attainment of a 20% improvement would require eight years, instead of four. In addition to faster and more certain results, there is no evidence that changes in behaviour may nullify the improvement of the efficiency ratio.

(50) The agreement is also likely to focus future research and development on furthering energy efficiency beyond the current technological limits of category A, thereby allowing for increased product differentiation amongst producers in the long run.

(51) CECED estimates the pollution avoided at 3,5 million tons of carbon dioxide, 17 000 tons of sulphur dioxide and 6 000 tons of nitrous oxide per year in 2010, working on the basis of average emission values. Although such emissions are more efficiently tackled at the stage of electricity generation, the agreement is likely to deliver both individual and collective benefits for users and consumers.

(a) Individual economic benefits

(52) The level at which the minimum performance standard is set provides a fair return within reasonable pay-back periods to a typical consumer for higher initial purchase costs derived from the more stringent standard in fact set out by CECED. Savings on electricity bills allow recouping of increased costs of upgraded, more expensive machines within nine to 40 months, depending mainly on frequency of use and electricity prices.

(53) While the agreement will eliminate certain models which are in category D and below, it is not possible to determine in advance its effect on the average selling price of those models of washing machines which are not directly affected. Indeed, the restriction in one product dimension, energy consumption, may increase competition on other product characteristics, including price. Therefore, while the minimum price of washing machines is likely to increase, it cannot be ruled out that products in categories A and B may become available at a lower price.

In a market characterised by strong competition amongst manufacturers and bargaining power from distributors, these benefits are likely to accrue to consumers.

(54) Were these competition-enhancing effects to take place, the narrowing of the price range and the increase in average selling prices would be less pronounced than would otherwise be foreseeable.

(b) *Collective environmental benefits*

(55) According to Article 174 of the EC Treaty, environmental damage should be rectified at source. The Community pursues the objective of a rational utilisation of natural resources, taking into account the potential benefits and costs of action. Agreements like CECED's must yield economic benefits outweighing their costs and be compatible with competition rules. Although electricity is not a scarce resource and consumption reductions do not tackle emissions at source, account can also be taken of the costs of pollution.

(56) The Commission reasonably estimates the saving in marginal damage from (avoided) carbon dioxide emissions (the so-called 'external costs') at EUR 41 to 61 per ton of carbon dioxide. On a European scale, avoided damage from sulphur dioxide amounts to EUR 4 000 to 7 000 per ton and EUR 3 000 to 5 000 per ton of nitrous oxide. On the basis of reasonable assumptions, the benefits to society brought about by the CECED agreement appear to be more than seven times greater than the increased purchase costs of more energy-efficient washing machines. Such environmental results for society would adequately allow consumers a fair share of the benefits even if no benefits accrued to individual purchasers of machines.

(57) The expected contribution to furthering energy efficiency both within the current technological limits of categories A to C and beyond the limits of category A, the cost-benefit ratio of the standard and the return on investment for individual users point to the conclusion that the agreement is likely to contribute significantly to technical and economic progress whilst allowing users a fair share of the benefits.

B: Block exemptions

Block exemptions offer practical benefits for undertakings since they guarantee the exemption of 'categories of agreements' without requiring detailed analysis of an agreement's effects. The four criteria articulated in Article 81(3) EC equally apply to block exemption Regulations. Block exemptions offer the business world greater certainty and, provided an agreement conforms with the terms of the Regulation, it is deemed compatible with the Community competition rules. The Commission has adopted block exemptions for a number of different types of agreement: research and development (Regulation 2659/2000/EC); specialization agreements (Regulation 2658/2000/EC); motor vehicle distribution (Regulation 1400/2002/EC); technology transfer (Regulation 772/2004/EC); and the so-called single umbrella regulation for vertical agreements (Regulation 2790/1999/EC).

In practice the most important block exemptions are those that deal with vertical restraints; these are dealt with more fully in Chapter 8. In this chapter we shall look at a block exemption dealing with horizontal agreements. Collusion in a market is generally prohibited under Article 81(1); however, there may be occasions when cooperation between independent undertakings is desirable, for instance research and development projects ('R & D'). The Commission has tended to adopt a strict approach to horizontal cooperation agreements; any efficiency gains are only considered under Article 81(3). In keeping with its new economic-oriented approach to verticals implemented in 2000 (Regulation 2790/1999), the Commission adopted two new block exemptions, Regulation 2658/2000 for specialization agreements (OJ, 2000, L304/3) and Regulation 2659/2000 for R & D agreements, (OJ, 2000, L304/7). They both introduce market share thresholds and are accompanied by detailed Guidelines on Horizontal Cooperation Agreements (OJ, 2001, C3/2). The Guidelines articulate the Commission's new economic-oriented approach in relation to horizontal cooperation agreements and establish an analytical framework for the most common types of agreements.

Guidelines on the applicability of Article 81 of the EC Treaty to horizontal cooperation agreements
OJ, 2001 C3/2

2. Horizontal cooperation may lead to competition problems. This is for example the case if the parties to a cooperation agree to fix prices or output, to share markets, or if the cooperation enables the parties to maintain, gain or increase market power and thereby causes negative market effects with respect to prices, output, innovation or the variety and quality of products.

3. On the other hand, horizontal cooperation can lead to substantial economic benefits. Companies need to respond to increasing competitive pressure and a changing market place driven by globalisation, the speed of technological progress and the generally more dynamic nature of markets. Cooperation can be a means to share risk, save costs, pool know-how and launch innovation faster. In particular for small and medium-sized enterprises cooperation is an important means to adapt to the changing market place.

...

6. Changing markets have generated an increasing variety and use of horizontal cooperation. More complete and updated guidance is needed to improve clarity and transparency regarding the applicability of Article 81 in this area. Within the assessment greater emphasis has to be put on economic criteria to better reflect recent developments in enforcement practice and the case law of the Court of Justice and Court of First Instance of the European Communities.

7. The purpose of these guidelines is to provide an analytical framework for the most common types of horizontal cooperation. This framework is primarily based on criteria that help to analyse the economic context of a cooperation agreement. Economic criteria such as the market power of the parties and other factors relating to the market structure, form a key element of the assessment of the market impact likely to be caused by a cooperation and therefore for the assessment under Article 81. Given the enormous variety in types and combinations of horizontal cooperation and market circumstances in which they operate, it is impossible to provide specific answers for every possible scenario. The present analytical framework based on economic criteria will nevertheless assist businesses in assessing the compatibility of an individual cooperation agreement with Article 81.

...

Market power and market structure

27. The starting point for the analysis is the position of the parties in the markets affected by the cooperation. This determines whether or not they are likely to maintain, gain or increase market power through the cooperation, i.e. have the ability to cause negative market effects as to prices, output, innovation or the variety or quality of goods and services. To carry out this analysis the relevant market(s) have to be defined by using the methodology of the Commission's market definition notice. Where specific types of markets are concerned such as purchasing or technology markets, these guidelines will provide additional guidance.

...

29. In addition to the market position of the parties and the addition of market shares, the market concentration, i.e. the position and number of competitors, may have to be taken into

account as an additional factor to assess the impact of the cooperation on market competition. As an indicator the Herfindahl-Hirshman Index ('HHI'), which sums up the squares of the individual market shares of all competitors, can be used: With an HHI below 1,000 the market concentration can be characterised as low, between 1,000 and 1,800 as moderate and above 1,800 as high. Another possible indicator would be the leading firm concentration ratio, which sums up the individual market shares of the leading competitors.

30. Depending on the market position of the parties and the concentration in the market, other factors such as the stability of market shares over time, entry barriers and the likelihood of market entry, the countervailing power of buyers/suppliers or the nature of the products (e.g. homogeneity, maturity) have to be considered as well. Where an impact on competition in innovation is likely and cannot be assessed adequately on the basis of existing markets, specific factors to analyse these impacts may have to be taken into account.

NOTE: The Commission have begun a process of consultation in late 2008/early 2009 into the reform of this area.

FURTHER READING

Burnley, R., 'Interstate Trade Revisited—The Jurisdictional Criterion for Articles 81 and 82 EC' [2002] ECLR 217.

Ehlermann, C.D., 'The modernisation of EC Antitrust Policy: a legal and cultural revolution' (2000) 37 CML Rev 537.

Jakobsen, P.S., and Broberg, M., 'The Concept of Agreement in Article 81 EC: In the Manufacturers' Right to Prevent Parallel Trade Within the European Community' [2002] ECLR 127.

Joshua, J., 'Proof in Contested EEC Competition Cases' [1987] EL Rev 315.

Odudu, O., *The Boundaries of EC Competition Law: The Scope of Article 81*, Oxford, OUP, 2006.

Odudu, O., 'Interpreting Article 81(1): object as subjective intention', (2001) EL Rev 60.

Van Gerven, G., and Varona, E.N., 'The Wood Pulp Case and the Future of Concerted Practices' (1994) 31 CML Rev 575.

7

Control of anti-competitive agreements in the UK

Prior to the UK Competition Act 1998 ('CA 1998') the domestic competition law applicable to anti-competitive agreements could be found in the Restrictive Trade Practices Act 1976 ('RTPA') which consolidated earlier restrictive trade practices legislation. By the late 1980s it became clear that reform of the legislative framework was necessary. Once an integral part of the commercial landscape in the UK, the RTPA lacked adequate investigative powers and effective sanctions and failed to catch certain significant agreements, particularly vertical agreements. The domestic regime was also out of step with Community competition law. The CA 1998, s. 1 repealed the RTPA 1976 and 1977, the Resale Prices Act 1976, and much of the Competition Act 1980. The overriding objective of the CA 1998 was to align domestic competition law with the Community rules for the sake of consistency and to reduce the burden on business. The Enterprise Act 2002 ('EA 2002') strengthened this regime even further with the introduction of US-style criminal sanctions for individuals involved in cartels, and disqualification of company directors.

A: Reform of the Restrictive Trade Practices Legislation

Reform of domestic competition law was a laborious process. The decade prior to enactment of the CA 1998 saw the publication of Green and White Papers, which both suggested that reform of the law on restrictive trade practices was necessary: see Department of Trade and Industry Consultation Documents: *Review of Restrictive Trade Practices Policy* (March 1988, Cm 331); and *Opening Markets: New Policy on Restrictive Trade Practices* (July 1989, Cm 727). In 1992, a Green Paper on Monopoly Control proposed the introduction of an Article 82 prohibition, *Abuse of Market Power* (November 1992, Cm 2100). However, instead of the sweeping reforms desired, the Government made minor amendments to the Fair Trading Act 1973 and the Competition Act 1980. In 1996, the Government took heed of mounting criticism following a Select Committee investigation and published a further consultation document, *Tackling Cartels and the Abuse of Market Power* (March 1996, London, DTI, URN 96/905), this time accompanied by a draft Bill. The explanatory document observed that 'our present system is inflexible and slow, too often concerned with cases which are obviously harmless and not directed sufficiently at anti-competitive agreements' (Cm 727 at para. 2.8.).

Despite widespread recognition that systematic reform was overdue, legislation was not enacted. For an excellent exposition of the prior debate and reasons for the delay see Wilks, S., 'The Prolonged Reform of UK Competition Policy', in Doern, B., and Wilks, S. (eds), *Comparative Competition Policy: National Institutions in a Global Market* (Oxford, Clarendon Press, 1996).

As Wilks explains at p. 174:

> The 'San Andreas' fault line within the Conservative Party was over attitudes to Europe. The proposed RTP reforms could have been presented as 'pro-European', adapting UK law to the Brussels model. This might in itself have been enough to make Ministers shy away from it.

Shortly after the general election in May 1997, the new Labour Government made clear its intention to fulfil a manifesto commitment to reform domestic competition law and a second draft Bill was laid before Parliament in October 1997. Margaret Beckett, the former President of the Board of the Trade, stated in her foreword to the 1997 draft Bill that 'Present competition law is not working well...Consumers need a better deal. We need to prevent and remedy anti-competitive behaviour more effectively. We also need to do so efficiently, avoiding placing any unnecessary burden on business'.

SECTION 2: COMPETITION ACT 1998: HARMONIZATION AND CONSISTENCY WITH EC LAW

The CA 1998 heralded a new era in domestic competition law. The Act, which entered into force on 1 March 2000, repealed the RTPA legislation and replaced it with a radically different prohibition system, modelled closely on the competition provisions of the EC Treaty. The primary objective was harmonization of domestic law with the Community model, namely Articles 81 and 82 EC.

Middleton comments on the factors that prompted harmonization.

Middleton, K., Chapter 2, 'Harmonisation with Community Law—The Euro-clause', in Rodger, B. J., and MacCulloch, A. (eds), *The UK Competition Act: A New Era for UK Competition Law*
Oxford, Hart Publishing, 2000, pp. 22–4 [footnotes omitted]

> One of the driving forces behind harmonisation is a recognition that commerce is no longer contained on a purely national or even European level, but one which is increasingly global. As companies expand their commercial activities, geographic and political boundaries become increasingly blurred. It is therefore appropriate that businesses operating in the single market should be subject to a uniform set of rules and principles. The primary objective behind reform of UK competition law is a desire to 'level the playing field' and make it easier for British business to compete effectively in global markets. Since the majority of the larger companies in the United Kingdom already have some exposure to the Community competition rules, it made sense to align domestic competition law with an established benchmark, namely Articles 81 and 82 EC.
>
> The Minister responsible for the passage of the Competition Bill through the House of Lords, Lord Simon of Highbury, outlined the practical benefits of convergence:

Such consistency would be of great benefit to so many of our businesses that currently have to worry about two different approaches to competition policy. It delivers a level playing field for our business community in the UK as firms become more and more engaged in European home markets.

Further, national competition authorities are able to cooperate more efficiently in cases with cross-border implications if the laws and procedures of the countries concerned are broadly similar. This is of particular importance in an enlarged Community where transactions with a cross-border aspect are likely to increase. Certainly, in recent years, there has been a discernible trend amongst the Member States to harmonise domestic competition law with Articles 81 and 82, despite the absence of any legal compulsion to do so. In the past few years, Member States such as Sweden, Denmark, Ireland, and The Netherlands, have introduced national competition legislation based on the Community rules, thereby reducing the risk of conflict between Community law and domestic law and encouraging competitiveness in international markets. A number of Central and Eastern European countries such as Romania and Hungary have done likewise. This trend towards harmonisation undoubtedly influenced the decision of the new Labour Government to choose Articles 81 and 82 EC as the appropriate model for new domestic laws.

NOTE: Maher also suggested that the 'current debates about international harmonisation of competition law and policy [make] it almost inevitable that the EC model be considered in the context of competition law reform'. Moreover, 'the considerable experience of the OFT of the EC rules also operates in favour of that model and on a more practical level, by harmonising the domestic and EC rules, reduces the regulatory demands on the OFT'. See Maher, I., 'Juridification, Codification and Sanction in UK Competition Law' (2000) 63 MLR 544–69 and an earlier article by the same author, 'Alignment of Competition Laws in the EC' (1996) YBEL 223.

The overriding purpose of the CA 1998 was to harmonize domestic competition law with the Community model. This objective is articulated in s. 60(1) of the Act, the so-called 'Euro-clause', which seeks to:

ensure that so far as is possible (having regard to any relevant differences between the provisions concerned), questions arising under this Part in relation to competition within the United Kingdom are dealt with in a manner which is consistent with the treatment of corresponding questions arising in Community law in relation to competition within the Community.

Where a question arises under Part I of the CA 1998, the competition authorities and the courts will be obliged to consider the Community position on the matter to ensure consistency; hence, the Act is deliberately silent on key terms and reference is to be made to the jurisprudence of the European Court and decisional practice of the Commission. The phrase 'in so far as is possible (having regard to any relevant differences between the relevant provisions concerned)' is clearly intended to permit departures from Community law. Lord Borrie explained the purpose of this phrase in Parliamentary debate: 'We have a structure, system and procedures which are not precisely the same as in the EU. Therefore, it is inevitable that one has to use words like "as far as possible" and others of that kind' (Hansard, HL, 23 February 1998, col 515). There are clear instances in which the Act intentionally departs from the Community model as Middleton explained:

Middleton, K., 'Harmonisation with Community Law—The Euro-clause', in Rodger, B.J., and MacCulloch, A. (eds), *The UK Competition Act: A New Era for UK Competition Law*
Oxford, Hart Publishing, 2000, pp. 26–9 [footnotes omitted]

The Act is also silent regarding the availability of third party rights. Once again, the operation of the consistency principle will import the same right to sue that is available to parties under Articles 81 and 82 EC. Lord Haskel confirmed the Government's:

clear intention in framing this [Bill] is that third parties may seek injunctions or damages in the courts if they have been adversely affected by the action of undertakings in breach of the prohibitions.

He went on to say: 'There is no need to make explicit provision in the Bill to achieve that result. Third party rights of action are to be the same as those under Articles 85 and 86'.

Section 60(6)(b) of the Act is also relevant in this context as it provides that decisions of the European Court and Commission on the question of the remedies available under Articles 81 and 82 EC will guide the UK courts in making a similar decision.

Further, section 30 of the Act confers a greater degree of legal professional privilege against production of documentation than exists under Community law. In contrast to the anomalous position in Community law, the Government has made it clear that legal privilege will extend to privileged communications between an in-house lawyer and the company. Privileged communications is defined in section 30 as being a communication 'between a professional legal adviser and his client' or 'made in connection with, or in contemplation of legal proceedings'. Any material that falls within this definition will not require to be produced to officials authorised by the Director General during an investigation.

An example of a 'relevant difference' that is intended to depart from Community law, is to be found in section 2(3), which provides that the prohibition set out in subsection (1) shall only apply 'if the agreement, decision or practice is, or intended to be, *implemented* in the United Kingdom'. The italicised phrase is an explicit reference to the European Court's decision in *Woodpulp*. Following the reasoning of the European Court in that case, it is possible that the Chapter I prohibition could be applied extra-territorially, where the agreement, having its origins outside the United Kingdom, is implemented within it. Although this is a much wider view of jurisdiction than UK practice currently follows the Government has made it clear that it does not wish to follow the Community position on the 'effects' doctrine.

COMPETITION ACT 1998 [S. 60]

60.—(2) At any time when the court determines a question arising under this Part, it must act (so far as is compatible with the provisions of this Part and whether or not it would otherwise be required to do so with a view to securing that there is no inconsistency between—

(a) the principles applied, and decision reached, by the court in determining that question; and

(b) the principles laid down by the Treaty and the European Court, and any relevant decision of that Court, as applicable at that time in determining any corresponding question arising in Community law.'

(3) The court must, in addition, have regard to any relevant decision or statement of the Commission.

NOTE: It is not obvious from s. 60(2) whether the obligation to ensure consistency with Community jurisprudence applies to general principles of Community law such as objectivity and proportionality. Reference to Hansard debates however confirms that the Government's intention to import fundamental principles of Community law into the domestic regime extended beyond the substantive law, to include general procedural safeguards developed under Community law; for example, the right against self-incrimination, the right to be heard and access to the file. Section 60(2) would not, however, appear to require consistency with the procedural practices of the Commission.

Section 60(3) does not impose a binding obligation on national courts to follow Commission decisions. Instead, the UK courts are merely to 'have regard' to statements, such as press releases, Policy Reports, Notices, and decisions. Finally, there are risks in importing concepts from a supra-national system without proper consideration of the domestic context. Will Community case law, which raises single market concerns, be regarded as 'corresponding', to any issues likely to arise under the domestic prohibitions? The next extract from Middleton noted the potential importance of the preliminary ruling procedure for national courts in discharging their obligation under s. 60(2).

Middleton, K., 'Harmonisation with Community Law—The Euro-clause', in
The UK Competition Act: A New Era for UK Competition Law
pp. 33–7 [footnotes omitted]

Since the 1998 Act is a domestic statute, which does not fall within the European Court's jurisdiction, the competency of an Article 234 reference is, however, uncertain and merits detailed consideration.

First, it is clear from the text of Article 234 that the national courts may refer to the European Court any question of Community law, if clarification of that matter is essential to the determination of the case. Thus, in cases involving the application of Articles 81 and 82 EC before the national courts a request for a preliminary ruling would be competent. As a general rule, the European Court has no competence to interpret a provision of domestic law, or decide on the compatibility of domestic law with Community law. However, recent Community jurisprudence casts doubt on this position; particularly where a provision of national law is based on, or makes reference to, Community law.

The European Court, for instance, has recently held that it does have jurisdiction in appropriate circumstances to rule on the interpretation of provisions of national law. In *Bernd Giloy* v *Hauptzollamt Frankfurt am Main-Ost* the European Court stated:

> neither the wording of Article 177 nor the aim of the procedure established by that article indicates that the Treaty makers intended to exclude from the jurisdiction of the Court requests for a preliminary ruling on a Community provision where the domestic law of the Member State refers to [a] Community provision in order to determine the rules applicable to a situation which is purely internal to that State.

The Court went on to state:

> [it] has repeatedly held that it has jurisdiction to give preliminary rulings on questions concerning Community provisions in situations where the facts of the cases being considered by the national courts were outside the scope of Community law but where *those provisions had been rendered applicable either by domestic law* or merely by virtue of terms in a contract.

The European Court distinguished *Bernd Giloy* from its earlier judgment in *Kleinwort Benson Ltd* v *Glasgow City Council*. In that case the European Court declined a request from the English Court of Appeal for a preliminary ruling regarding the interpretation of Article 5(1) and (3) in Schedule 4 to the Civil Jurisdiction and Judgments Act 1982, which implemented the Brussels Convention on Jurisdiction and Judgments 1968. The Court noted:

> [while] certain provisions of the 1982 Act are taken almost word for word from the Convention, others depart from the wording of the corresponding Convention provision. That is true in particular of Article 5(3).

Thus, unlike the position in *Giloy*, and the *Dzodzi* cases, the provision of the Convention which the Court was asked to interpret in *Kleinwort Benson* had not been incorporated into domestic law. In addition, the Court noted:

> express provision was made in the Act for the authorities of the contracting State concerned to adopt modifications 'designed to produce divergence' between provisions of the Act and the corresponding provisions of the Convention.

Finally, the European Court observed that although the Civil Jurisdiction and Judgments Act 1982 provided in section 3(1) for questions of interpretation arising under the Brussels Convention to be decided consistently with Community case law, it was not a binding obligation and UK courts were merely to 'have regard' to Community principles when interpreting Schedule 4 provisions. Thus, the Court held that it could not give a preliminary ruling in *Kleinwort Benson* as its ruling would be advisory and not mandatory for UK courts.

Although the European Court has indicated that an *absolute* transposition of the relevant Community provision is necessary to ensure the competence of an Article 234 reference on matters wholly internal, the Court recently confirmed in *Oscar Bronner* v *Mediaprint* that:

it is for the national courts alone which are seised of the case and are responsible for the judgment to be delivered to determine, in view of the special features of each case, both the need for a preliminary ruling in order to enable them to give their judgment and the relevance of the questions which they put to the Court. Consequently where the questions put by national courts concern the interpretation of a provision of Community law, the Court is, in principle, bound to give a ruling.

The Court then added that:

Article 177 [234] of the Treaty, which is based on a clear separation of functions between a national court and this Court, does not allow this Court to review the reasons for which a reference is made.

In the key paragraph of its judgment the European Court states:

the fact that a national court is dealing with a restrictive practices dispute by applying national competition law should not prevent it from making reference to the Court on the interpretation of Community law on the matter, and in particular on the interpretation of Article 86 of the Treaty in relation to that same situation, when it considers that a conflict between Community law and national law is capable of arising.

It is clear from its decisions in *Giloy* and *Oscar Bronner* that the European Court considers it is in the Community interest to ensure that Community provisions or concepts which have been transposed into domestic law are interpreted uniformly. Accordingly, the European Court seems favourably disposed to giving preliminary rulings on matters perceived to be wholly internal to a Member State. Further, unlike the case of *Kleinwort Benson* where the courts were merely to 'have regard' to Community jurisprudence under section 16(3) of the Civil Jurisdiction and Judgments Act 1982, section 60(2) of the 1998 Act obliges national courts to ensure consistency with Community law. On this basis, it is likely that the European Court will allow a request for a preliminary ruling where the national court requires clarification of a term directly transposed from Community law, for example, 'undertaking' or 'concerted practice'. Indeed, since the primary objective of section 60 is to ensure consistency with Community law, a preliminary ruling on 'corresponding' issues would be vital 'to ensure compliance with the rule of primacy of Community law and consequently, not to tolerate a situation in national law contrary to Community law'. Thus section 60 and Article 234 EC are complementary and will ensure Community law and UK law develop in parallel. It is only where the 1998 Act departs from Community law, for example, the requirement that trade is affected within the United Kingdom, and the matter would not be 'corresponding', that a preliminary ruling would not be competent.

None the less, the recent trend among Member States towards harmonisation with the Community rules may require the European Court to restrict the numbers of Article 234 references on grounds of expediency. The implications for the European Court's workload, should it be required to give preliminary rulings on provisions of national law in an enlarged Community, are obvious. Despite a dramatic upturn in its workload in recent years, the European Court has infrequently declined to exercise jurisdiction under Article 234. However, the UK courts have demonstrated a reluctance in the past to refer cases to Luxembourg and there is no indication that this will necessarily change when the 1998 Act comes into force. There is a concern that a reference merely results in unnecessary delay. Moreover, as judges gain expertise in competition matters, and confidence in their ability within the new regime, there may be a reduced need for national courts to refer questions to the European Court. It is doubtful in any case whether the potential overburdening of the European Court is a legitimate concern of the national courts.

NOTE: Section 60 acts as the cornerstone of the CA 1998 and heralded the beginning of a new process of judicial interpretation in domestic law. The courts, and the OFT and Competition Appeal Tribunal in particular, have consistently applied EC competition law principles, and relied on Court case law, in relation to both prohibitions, without controversy, or, as yet, the need to make a reference to the Court for a preliminary ruling. For a fuller discussion of preliminary rulings in competition law cases, see Rodger, B. (ed.), *Article 234 and Competition Law: An Analysis*, The Hague, Kluwer Law International, 2008.

SECTION 3: **THE CHAPTER I PROHIBITION**

The 'Chapter I prohibition' is modelled closely on Article 81 EC. Section 2 contains the general prohibition and operates subject to s. 3 which provides for excluded agreements and ss. 6 and 8–11 which deal with exemptions.

COMPETITION ACT 1998 [S. 2]

Agreements etc. preventing, restricting or distorting competition

2.—(1) Subject to section 3, agreements between undertakings, decisions by associations of undertakings or concerted practices which—

    (a) may affect trade within the United Kingdom, and

    (b) have as their object or effect the prevention, restriction or distortion of competition within the United Kingdom, are prohibited unless they are exempt in accordance with the provisions of this Part.

(2) Subsection (1) applies, in particular, to agreements, decisions or practices which—

    (a) directly or indirectly fix purchase or selling prices or any other trading conditions;

    (b) limit or control production, markets, technical development or investment;

    (c) share markets or sources of supply;

    (d) apply dissimilar conditions to equivalent transactions with other trading parties, thereby placing them at a competitive disadvantage;

    (e) make the conclusion of contracts subject to acceptance by the other parties of supplementary obligations which, by their nature or according to commercial usage, have no connection with the subject of such contracts.

(3) Subsection (1) applies only if the agreement, decision or practice is, or is intended to be, implemented in the United Kingdom.

(4) Any agreement or decision which is prohibited by subsection (1) is void.

(5) A provision of this Part which is expressed to apply to, or in relation to, an agreement is to be read as applying equally to, or in relation to, a decision by an association of undertakings or a concerted practice (but with any necessary modifications).

(6) Subsection (5) does not apply where the context otherwise requires.

(7) In this section 'the United Kingdom' means, in relation to an agreement which operates or is intended to operate only in a part of the United Kingdom, that part.

(8) The prohibition imposed by subsection (1) is referred to in this Act as 'the Chapter I prohibition'.

■ **QUESTION**

Compare the wording of s. 2 with Article 81(1) EC. What differences, if any, do you notice?

As required by s 52 of the Act, the OFT has published a number of guidelines in relation to the new regime, available from the OFT's website at www.oft.gov. uk/advice_and_resources/publications/guidance/competiton-act/. Although the guidelines do not enjoy the status of legally binding rules they are equivalent to Commission Notices.

Following the introduction of Regulation 1/2003, the OFT can apply both the Chapter I prohibition and Article 81 where appropriate, and accordingly, its guidance was revised to deal with the application of both provisions within the same guideline, *Agreements and concerted practices*, OFT 401.

OFT, *Agreements and concerted practices*
www.oft.gov.uk/advice_and_resources/publications/guidance/competiton-act/

OFT 401, paras 2.1–2.3

2.1 There are two substantive provisions which may be applied by the OFT to anti-competitive agreements: Article 81 and the Chapter I prohibition. The key difference between the two is their geographic scope. Both these provisions apply to agreements between undertakings which have as their object or effect the prevention, restriction or distortion of competition:

- within the common market and which may affect trade between Member States in the case of Article 81, and
- within the United Kingdom and which may affect trade within the United Kingdom in the case of the Chapter I prohibition.

2.2 Article 81(1) and section 2(2) of the Act provide an identical list of agreements to which the provisions apply, namely those which:

(a) directly or indirectly fix purchase or selling prices or any other trading conditions
(b) limit or control production, markets, technical development or investment
(c) share markets or sources of supply
(d) apply dissimilar conditions to equivalent transactions with other trading parties, thereby placing them at a competitive disadvantage
(e) make the conclusion of contracts subject to acceptance by the other parties of supplementary obligations which, by their nature or according to commercial usage, have no connection with the subject of such contracts.

2.3 This is a non-exhaustive, illustrative list and does not set a limit on the investigation and enforcement activities of the OFT under Article 81 or the Chapter I prohibition. Discussion of the OFT's approach to these types of agreement, and other potentially anti-competitive agreements can be found in Part 3 of this guideline. It should be noted, however, that any agreement that has an appreciable adverse effect on competition is likely to fall within Article 81(1) and/or the Chapter I prohibition irrespective of whether or not it is of a type described in the illustrative list in Article 81(1) and section 2(2) of the Act (or is considered in Part 3 of this guideline). Such an agreement may nevertheless be enforceable without prior approval if it meets the conditions set out in Article 81(3) and/or section 9(1) of the Act.

This section shall review briefly the key issues in determining a breach of Article 81(1), and consequently the Chapter I prohibition, discussed in Chapter 6, and outline any particular UK developments or case law.

A: Undertakings

The competition rules only apply to undertakings, or an association of undertakings.

OFT, *Agreements and concerted practices*
www.oft.gov.uk/advice_and_resources/publications/guidance/competiton-act/

OFT 401, paras 2.5–2.6 [footnotes omitted]

Undertakings

2.5 The term undertaking is not defined in the EC Treaty or the Act but its meaning has been set out under Community law. It covers any natural or legal person engaged in economic activity, regardless of its legal status and the way in which it is financed. It includes companies, firms, businesses, partnerships, individuals operating as sole traders, agricultural co-operatives, trade associations and non profit-making organisations. The key consideration in assessing whether an entity is an undertaking for the application of Article 81 and/or the Chapter I prohibition is whether it is engaged in economic activity. An entity may engage in economic activity in relation to some of its functions but not others.

2.6 Article 81 and the Chapter I prohibition do not apply to agreements where there is only one undertaking: that is, between undertakings which form a single economic unit. In particular, an agreement between a parent and its subsidiary company or between two companies which are under the control of a third will not be agreements between undertakings if the subsidiary has no real freedom to determine its course of action on the market and, although having a separate legal personality, enjoys no economic independence. Whether or not the entities form a single economic unit will depend on the facts of each case.

NOTE: The definition of the term 'undertaking' follows earlier Community case law on its interpretation, notably in case C-41/90 *Höfner and Elser* v *Macrotron* [1991] ECR I-1979 and case T-319/99 *Fenin* v *Commission* [2003] ECR II-357.

The question of an entity's status as an 'undertaking' arose in the first 'substantive' judgment handed down by the Competition Commission Appeal Tribunal, which set aside key aspects of the DGFT's earlier decision of 24 January 2001. The case concerned the application of the Chapter I prohibition to self-regulation in the insurance industry.

Institute of Independent Insurance Brokers, The v Director General of Fair Trading supported by the General Insurance Standards Council; Association of British Travel Agents Limited v The Director General of Fair Trading supported by the General Insurance Standards Council
(Case Nos 1002/2/1/01 (Ir), 1003/2/1/01, 1004/2/1/01) [2001] CAT 4, paras 252–8

252. It is common ground that Article 81 of the Treaty applies to the carrying on of 'economic activities' by 'undertakings'. As appears from the opinion of Advocate General Jacobs of 17 May 2001 in Case C-475/99 *Ambulanz Glöckner*, the concept of undertaking encompasses every entity engaged in an economic activity regardless of the legal status of the entity and the way it is financed. The basic test is whether the entity in question is engaged in an activity which consists in offering goods and services on a given market and which could, at least in principle, be carried out by a private actor in order to make a profit (paragraph 67). By contrast, while public bodies carrying on economic activities may be regarded as undertakings, 'activities in the exercise of official authority' are sheltered from the application of the competition rules (paragraph 72 of that opinion). The test is whether the activity in question is to be analysed as 'the exercise of public powers' or as 'economic activities': Case 118/85 *Commission* v *Italy* [1987] ECR 2599, paragraph 7. One test for whether the activity in question constitutes the exercise of public powers, or of official authority, is whether the activity in question 'is connected by its nature, its aim and the rules to which it is subject with the exercise of powers which are typically those of a public authority' (see paragraph 76 of the opinion of Advocate General Jacobs in *Ambulanz Glöckner*, citing Case 364/92 *Eurocontrol* [1994] ECR I-43, paragraph 30).

253. To illustrate the difference between the exercise of 'public powers' or 'official authority' on the one hand and 'economic activity' on the other hand, in *Ambulanz Glöckner* itself Advocate General Jacobs concluded that the provision of ambulance services, including emergency services, was an 'economic activity' and thus within the rules on competition, since those were not services that must *necessarily* be carried out by public entities (paragraph 68 of his opinion). On the other hand, the grant or refusal by a public authority under statute of an authorisation to provide ambulance services fell outside the rules on competition, since it was 'a typical administrative decision taken in the exercise of prerogatives conferred by law which are usually reserved for public authorities' (paragraph 76). Other illustrative examples of the exercise of public authority falling outside Articles 81 and 82 of the Treaty include the arrangements for international air traffic control made by

the European Organisation for the Safety of Air Navigation, an international organisation set up and run by 14 Contracting States in pursuance of an international Convention (see *Eurocontrol*, cited above); the fixing by public authorities under statute of tariffs for the use of German waterways (Case C-153/93 *Germany* v *Delta Schiffahrts* [1994] ECR I-2517); and anti-pollution surveillance carried out by virtue of a public authorisation which was held to be 'a task in the public interest which forms part of the essential functions of the State as regards protection of the environment in sensitive areas' and thus 'connected by its nature, its aim and the rules to which it is subject with the exercise of powers... which are typically those of a public authority...' (Case 343/95 *Cali & Figli* v *SEPG* [1997] ECR I-1547, at paragraphs 22 to 23).

254. Applying those principles to the present case, we note first that GISC is a private company that has been set up by the industry itself without any statutory basis. It exists solely by contract. GISC is not accountable to Parliament, nor to Ministers, nor indeed to anyone other than those in the industry who belong to GISC. As far as the constitution of GISC is concerned, GISC is run by a Board of Directors most of whom are, or have been, active in the industry. At present only two out of the Board of some 16 members are 'public interest' directors recruited, so we are told, through head-hunters and not appointed by a public authority. It is true that it is currently proposed that there should be five 'public interest directors', but that still leaves the 'outside' directors in a substantial minority vis-à-vis the ten 'industry' directors (see paragraphs 53 to 55 above). There is no independent chairman (without industry connections). It is also proposed that in future the directors will be elected by the Members of GISC, who will become shareholders in the company, six directors being elected by intermediaries and four directors elected by insurers. This change is proposed, notably, in order that 'the Board would be directly accountable to regulated businesses' and in order to give 'the regulated businesses a greater say in the running of the company'. There is to be weighted voting, on the basis that 'a large business in the industry should, in principle, have a greater number of votes than a small business'. A number of these changes are proposed on the basis of the principles of the Combined Code, which is a publicly available document dealing with the principles of corporate governance relevant to listed public companies in the United Kingdom (see paragraphs 55 to 58 above).

255. On this basis GISC appears to us to have the features normally to be found in a private sector organisation or company accountable to its members, rather than a publicly constituted body exercising 'public powers'. We note also that, in the cases cited to us where the exercise of official or public authority was held to fall outside the competition rules, the activity in question had been exercised on some statutory basis of one kind or another. In the present case, GISC lacks any such statutory foundation.

256. We doubt whether, as a matter of Community law, the notion of the exercise of 'official authority' or 'public powers' can extend to cases where the legal basis of the activity in question is not to be found in the public law of the Member State but relies entirely on contract between private parties. Even if the Government is supportive of the principle of self regulation in the general insurance sector—which may not be quite the same thing as supporting a monopoly regulator for the whole sector, as shown by the Treasury paper of April 1998 cited at paragraph 38 above—the Government is not, constitutionally speaking, the legislature. Statements by Government ministers are not the same thing as a legal basis founded in public law. Again, as a matter of statutory interpretation, we would not expect to find that an activity could be taken outside section 2 of the Act on the basis of ministerial statements made in Parliament rather than on the basis of the various exclusions and order making powers to be found in section 3 and schedules 1 to 4 of the Act.

257. Lastly, while it is true that the assumption of regulatory powers in respect of general insurance could properly be an activity of the State, for example under the FSMA, the setting up of a framework for promoting professional standards and consumer protection in general insurance is not an activity which, by reason of its intrinsic nature, can *necessarily* only be carried out by public authorities, as the case law appears to require. Self evidently GISC, the

IIB and ABTA are all private sector bodies who have sought to establish self-regulatory or quality assurance schemes of one kind or another in the industries in which they operate. While we do not doubt the good intentions of those concerned, it seems to us clear that each of those bodies is acting not solely in the public interest but also in the commercial interests of their members in promoting the various schemes in question. In the case of GISC, emphasis has been placed on developing the GISC brand, creating what GISC sees as a 'level playing field', and avoiding the threat of statutory intervention. Although GISC itself is not run for profit, the particular structure set up under the GISC Rules would hardly have been adopted if the industry did not see real commercial advantages in proceeding in the way it has. It seems to us that Advocate General Léger, at paragraphs 144 to 154 of his opinion in *Wouters*, was considering a different factual situation, namely regulatory powers conferred by statute (see paragraphs 154 and 258(3) of that opinion). Similarly, the two domestic cases cited to us, *Institute of Chartered Accountants* v *Customs & Excise* [1999] 1 WLR 701 and *R* v *Panel on Takeovers and Mergers ex p Datafin* [1987] 1 QB 815, were each decided in a different factual and legal context.

258. In all those circumstances we can see no compelling reason why GISC should not be regarded as itself an undertaking although, as we have said, we do not need to decide that point for the purposes of this judgment, nor make any reference to the Court of Justice under Article 234 of the Treaty.

NOTE: In accordance with the s. 60 requirement to interpret the prohibition consistently with EC law, the Tribunal ruled that a regulator like the General Insurance Standards Council ('GISC') pursued an economic activity in accordance with the definition of undertaking in Community law.

B: Agreements and concerted practices

The Chapter I prohibition, like Article 81, prohibits agreements, concerted practices, and decisions of associations, and the next extract from OFT guideline 401 again demonstrates that the domestic competition regime is aligned with the EC rules.

OFT, *Agreements and concerted practices*
www.oft.gov.uk/advice_and_resources/publications/guidance/competiton-act/.
OFT 401, paras 2.7–2.13 [footnotes omitted]

Agreement

2.7 Agreement has a wide meaning and covers agreements whether legally enforceable or not, written or oral; it includes so-called *gentlemen's agreements*. There does not have to be a physical meeting of the parties for an agreement to be reached: an exchange of letters or telephone calls may suffice.

2.8 The fact that a party may have played only a limited part in the setting up of the agreement, or may not be fully committed to its implementation, or may have participated only under pressure from other parties does not mean that it is not party to the agreement (although these facts may be taken into account in deciding the level of any financial penalty: for further details see the *OFT's guidance as to the appropriate amount of a penalty* (OFT423)).

Decisions by associations of undertakings

2.9 Article 81 and the Chapter I prohibition also cover decisions by associations of undertakings. Trade associations are the most common form of associations of undertakings but the provisions are not limited to any particular type of association. A decision by a trade association may include, for example, the constitution or rules of an association or its recommendations or other activities. In the day to day conduct of the business of an association, resolutions of the management committee or of the full membership in general meeting, binding decisions of the management or executive committee of the association, or rulings of its chief executive may all be 'decisions' of the association. The key consideration is whether the object or effect of the decision, whatever form it takes, is to influence the conduct or coordinate the activity of the members. A trade association's co-ordination of its members' conduct in accordance with its constitution may also be a decision even if its recommendations are not binding on its members, and may not have been fully complied with. It will be a question of fact in each case whether an association of undertakings is itself a party to an agreement.

2.10 The competition law guideline *Trade associations, professions and self-regulating bodies* (OFT408) elaborates on the application and enforcement of Article 81 and the Chapter I prohibition in respect of both trade associations and the rules of self-regulating bodies.

Concerted practices

2.11 Article 81 and the Chapter I prohibition apply to concerted practices as well as to agreements. The boundary between the two concepts is imprecise. The key difference is that a concerted practice may exist where there is informal cooperation without any formal agreement or decision.

2.12 In considering if a concerted practice exists, the OFT will follow relevant Community precedents established under Article 81. The OFT will need to establish that the parties, even if they did not enter into an agreement, knowingly substituted cooperation between them for the risks of competition.

2.13 The following are examples of factors which the OFT may consider in establishing if a concerted practice exists:
- whether the parties knowingly enter into practical cooperation;
- whether behaviour in the market is influenced as a result of direct or indirect contact between undertakings;
- whether parallel behaviour is a result of contact between undertakings which leads to conditions of competition which do not correspond to normal conditions of the market;
- the structure of the relevant market and the nature of the product involved;
- the number of undertakings in the market, and where there are only a few undertakings whether they have similar cost structures and outputs.

NOTE: The EC case law on ascertaining what constitutes an agreement and the degree of understanding or collaboration required to establish a concerted practice, is considered in Chapter 6. The CAT have had to grapple with the application of the concerted practice concept, for instance in *Apex Asphalt and Paving Co Ltd* v *OFT* [2005] CAT 4. This case related to the making of tender bids for flat roofing contracts in the West Midlands. The CAT undertook a thorough review of EC law at paras 92–7 and thereafter applied the legal principles to the facts of the case to uphold the OFT's finding of a concerted practice in the tendering process.

Determining what constitutes a concerted practice also arose in two very prominent and related cases, known as *Replica Kits* and *Toys and Games* respectively. The two separate cases and appeals were joined for the purpose of an appeal to the Court of Appeal.

Argos, Littlewoods and JJB Ltd v *OFT*
[2006] EWCA Civ 1318, on appeal from [2004] CAT 24, [2005] CAT 13, [2004] CAT 17, [2005] CAT 22, paras 92–104 and 138–43

These were two cases involving resale price maintenance, first in relation to Replica Kits, involving JJB and various other parties, and second in relation to Toys and

Games, involving Hasbro, Littlewoods, and Argos. The OFT fined various parties in relation to each case, and following unsuccessful appeals to the CAT (where the fines were reduced in certain cases), three of the parties appealed on issues of liability and penalty to the Court of Appeal.

The communications between JJB, Umbro and Sports Soccer

92 Thus, the starting point for an analysis of the communications between Mr Ronnie and Mr Sharpe is not that Mr Ronnie, unprompted, called Mr Sharpe to ask about JJB's pricing intentions as regards England replica kit during Euro 2000. Rather the starting point is that JJB had been badgering Umbro for some time to do something about the fact that Sports Soccer was already selling England replica kit at a discount, and that a crucial selling period was approaching during which it would be particularly important for JJB that it should not have to face or engage in a price war, such as it had been engaged in with Sports Soccer for some 6 months until April 2000, and that JJB's commercial strength as against Umbro was such that Umbro had to try to do something to satisfy JJB's concerns. Furthermore, Mr Ronnie knew, from speaking to Mr Ashley of Sports Soccer, that if he was to have any chance of persuading Sports Soccer to agree to raise its prices, he would have to be able to assure Mr Ashley that other retailers, including JJB, would not discount themselves. That was the context in which Mr Ronnie spoke to Mr Sharpe and was told that JJB would not discount.

93 At that time JJB was selling the England shirt at the High Street price, and had made it clear to Umbro that it wanted to be able to go on doing so. Sports Soccer, on the other hand, was selling at a discount. There had been a price war between JJB and Sports Soccer although it had come to an end in April when JJB stopped discounting as a general policy as against Sports Soccer. JJB's detailed pricing policy, certainly as regards the launch of a new product, was confidential and was decided only a few days in advance (see paragraph 628), so that other parties could not safely assume that they knew what JJB would do in terms of pricing.

94 Mr Ronnie spoke to Mr Sharpe about JJB's pricing intentions, in response to which Mr Sharpe told him that JJB would sell at High Street prices unless others discounted. Mr Lasok submitted that there was no finding, and no basis for a finding, that Mr Sharpe knew that this information would go any further than Umbro, and certainly not that it would be passed to Sports Soccer. We disagree. It seems to us that it must have been apparent to Mr Sharpe, even if there was no express reference to Sports Soccer, that Mr Ronnie wanted the information in the context of taking steps to guard against discounting. Mr Sharpe was among those who had spoke to Umbro staff about the Sports Soccer discounting policy. It would be extraordinary to suppose that, when Mr Ronnie asked him about JJB's own attitude to pricing England replica kit during Euro 2000, it did not occur to Mr Sharpe that this was connected with the question of discounting by Sports Soccer and attempts to prevent it occurring, which Mr Sharpe and others at JJB had been asking for over some time past.

95 Mr Lasok took up a sentence in paragraph 661 of the Tribunal's judgment, as follows:

> "In the present case there is no evidence that JJB disclosed its future pricing intentions to Umbro for some legitimate purpose."

He said that this revealed a wrong approach to the burden of proof; it was not for JJB to prove that its purpose was legitimate, but for the OFT to prove the opposite. On the face of that sentence alone, that criticism could be justified. However, in the context of the other material which was before the Tribunal, the matter is to be seen quite differently. There was ample evidence, especially from the pressure brought to bear by JJB on Umbro, that the purpose of the disclosure was anti-competitive. Absent any basis for a suggestion that there was some different and legitimate purpose to the disclosure, the OFT's burden of proof had been discharged. The Tribunal's reference is therefore to the absence of any such material.

96 In those circumstances it seems to us to be more than somewhat artificial to suggest that Mr Sharpe did not envisage that the information would be passed on to Sports Soccer, or that he did not expect to receive a later call from Mr Ronnie after the latter had spoken to Sports Soccer.

97 The second stage in the process was Mr Ronnie's call to Mr Ashley, to persuade him that he should raise Sports Soccer's prices for the England shirt. It is evident that Mr Ashley was very

reluctant to do so. It required pressure from Umbro by way of veiled or not so veiled threats as regards supplies. It also required an assurance that other retailers would not be discounting the shirts. Mr Ronnie gave him that assurance. He did not mention any retailer by name, but because JJB was so dominant in the field, any assurance as to retailers must have been taken, and intended to be taken, as including JJB. Mr Ashley agreed to raise Sports Soccer's prices on that basis, conditionally on the others also raising or maintaining their prices to or at the same level. It seems to us that, in turn, he must have recognised that others concerned would be told of his agreement. He knew, from what Mr Ronnie told him about other retailers, that Umbro had been in touch with the other retailers about their pricing intentions, and that these had been passed on to him. He must have realised that what he told Mr Ronnie about Sports Soccer's intentions would, correspondingly, be passed back to the others, including, necessarily, JJB.

98 Then at the third stage, Mr Ronnie telephoned Mr Sharpe again and told him that Sports Soccer had agreed to raise their prices and to sell at High Street prices. He did so in order to make it known to JJB that Umbro had, as asked, "done something" about Sports Soccer's discounting, by securing an agreement that it would come to an end as regards this product. He also needed to make sure that JJB knew of this because of Mr Sharpe having mentioned that JJB might discount if others did, so that JJB should be aware that, at any rate if Sports Soccer kept to their agreement, JJB would not need to discount. Because Sports Soccer was still selling at a discount at that time, JJB could not be sure what Sports Soccer's intentions were unless informed of them by Umbro. But for being told that Sports Soccer had agreed to raise its prices, it might not have been willing to wait until 3 June to see whether Sports Soccer did in fact come into line. There may therefore have been a risk that, if the information as to Sports Soccer's intentions was not passed on to JJB, the latter would respond to Sports Soccer's still discounted price by discounting itself, which would certainly have led to Sports Soccer not raising its prices. It does not seem to us that, in this context, Mr Sharpe could have been surprised to receive this telephone call. Mr Lasok in his written material described the call as coming "out of the blue". We do not think that can be right.

99 Mr Lasok submitted that, when Mr Sharpe told Mr Ronnie of JJB's pricing intentions at the first stage, he was doing nothing which could be regarded as anti-competitive, and he referred to the second sentence of paragraph 49 of the Commission's decision in *Hasselblad*, quoted above. It does not seem to us that this is correct. It is one thing for a manufacturer to ask its distributors, as a matter of routine, to inform it of the prices at which and the terms on which they sell its products, which it may wish or need to be aware of for its own commercial purposes and in the context of the ongoing relationship with each distributor separately. It is quite another (as it was found to be in the *Hasselblad* case itself) where the information is obtained in order to be shared with other customers of the same manufacturer. It is all the more another thing if the information is given to the manufacturer in the context of pressure by the party supplying the information, brought to bear on the manufacturer, in order to get another customer into line as regards prices, expecting that the information may be used by the manufacturer in relation to the other customer to persuade it to raise its prices.

100 Another submission by Mr Lasok on this point was that Mr Ronnie's call to Mr Sharpe did not affect JJB's conduct on the market, because JJB was already selling at High Street prices, and this did not change. That ignores the fact that, if Sports Soccer had not raised its prices, JJB might itself have discounted. On being told by Mr Ronnie of Sports Soccer's agreement, JJB knew that, assuming that Sports Soccer complied with their agreement and that no other major retailer broke ranks and discounted, JJB would be able to maintain its prices at their current level. A decision not to discount, in such circumstances, is just as much conduct on the market as a decision to discount would be.

101 Putting his same point in different terms, Mr Lasok borrowed from the words of the ECJ in *Bayer* (see paragraph [26] above) and submitted that Mr Ronnie did not, by his call back to Mr Sharpe, "invite" JJB to fulfil an anti-competitive goal jointly with Umbro and Sports Soccer. We disagree, though we can see that this is not the language that the parties would have used at the time. The context was that JJB had started the process by issuing what could, in a sense, be called an "invitation" to Umbro, by way of its pressure to do something about Sports Soccer's discounting. That invitation involved bringing Sports Soccer in as well, in order to achieve the anti-competitive aim of stabilising prices at the High Street price level and avoiding a price-cutting war. In that context,

when Mr Ronnie spoke again to Mr Sharpe, it was not only to tell him that Sports Soccer had agreed, but also to make sure that JJB was aware that Sports Soccer would be raising its prices, and JJB need not consider discounting on its own part. Of course, it was known that JJB wanted prices raised and it was therefore easy to see that JJB would accede to Mr Ronnie's "invitation" to maintain JJB's prices. If it seems unnatural to speak, in these circumstances, of Umbro inviting JJB to fulfil an anti-competitive goal jointly with Umbro and Sports Soccer, the main reason is that JJB had taken the original initiative towards the anti-competitive arrangement, by putting pressure on Umbro in the first place. Umbro would not have regarded JJB's pressure on it as an "invitation", but in terms of the language of the ECJ, it could be regarded as such.

The Football Shirts appeal on liability—conclusion

102 In these circumstances it seems to us that the Tribunal was entitled to find that (1) JJB provided confidential price information to Umbro in circumstances in which it was obvious that it would or might be passed on to Sports Soccer in support of Umbro's attempt to persuade Sports Soccer to raise its prices (thereby adopting the pricing policy which JJB explicitly wanted adopted by all significant retailers), (2) Umbro did use the information in relation to Sports Soccer in that way, (3) Sports Soccer did agree to raise its prices in reliance on this information, and foreseeing that others including JJB would be told of its agreement, and later did raise its prices as it had agreed to do, and (4) Umbro did tell JJB of this, thereby making it clear to JJB that it would be able to maintain its prices at their current level, as it did.

103 It also seems to us that the Tribunal was right to hold that this sequence of events amounted to a concerted practice to which JJB was a party, as well as Umbro and Sports Soccer, whereby the two retailers coordinated their conduct on the market in such as way as, knowingly, to substitute practical co-operation between them for the risks of competition (see *Dyestuffs*, referred to at paragraph [21(i)] above), which had the object or effect of preventing, restricting or distorting competition and in particular of fixing the retail sale price of England replica football shirts in the period before and during Euro 2000, and therefore constituted a breach of the Chapter I prohibition.

104 Mr Lasok analysed paragraphs 654 and 655 of the judgment in his submissions and criticised the Tribunal's language in those paragraphs. He questioned the use of the word "knowingly" in the part of paragraph 654 annotated in the quotation set out above (at paragraph [63]) as (2). Each of JJB and Sports Soccer knew that it was giving Umbro an intimation of its intended pricing. He submitted that the use of the word meant no more than that. But that cannot be right. It is not a case of an unconscious disclosure of pricing intentions, for example by someone talking in his sleep. It seems to us plain that "knowingly" must, in context, refer to the knowledge of JJB and Sports Soccer respectively that their pricing intentions would be passed on by Umbro to the other. For the reasons already given, it seems to us that this finding was justified.

. . .

138 We turn, therefore, to the challenge to the Tribunal's finding that there was a trilateral agreement or concerted practice. The challenge (advanced by both Argos and Littlewoods) is, perhaps, most clearly articulated at paragraph 37 of the skeleton argument filed on behalf of Littlewoods:

> "[The Tribunal's] failure to appreciate that the *Bayer* judgments qualified or clarified earlier case law on the meaning of agreement and concerted practice tainted the CAT's entire approach to the evidence and led it wrongly to conclude that there was a tripartite agreement or concerted practice between Hasbro, Argos and Littlewoods. In cases such as the present where there is no direct contact between two undertakings (viz Littlewoods and Argos), it is particularly important to analyse the evidence carefully in order to establish whether…the subjective consensus requirement has been met. The CAT failed to do this and did not make any sufficient findings of fact on this point. The judgment is therefore defective as a matter of law as it did not deal with the essential element of the infringement i.e. the subjective consensus between the parties."

139 We have set out the relevant passages in the judgments of the CFI and the ECJ in *Bayer v Commission* (Joined Cases C-2/01 and C-3/01) [2000] ECR II-3383 earlier in this judgment, at

paragraphs [23] to [26]. We draw attention, in the present context, to the observation, at paragraph 102 in the judgment of the Court of Justice, that "it is necessary that the manifestation of the wish of one of the contracting parties to achieve an anti-competitive goal constitute an invitation to the other party, whether express or implied, to fulfil that goal jointly".

140 We have expressed our view, in paragraph [91], when discussing the Tribunal's judgment on liability in the Football Shirts appeal, that the Tribunal may have gone too far in paragraph 659 of that judgment, with its suggestion that if a retailer (A) privately discloses to a supplier (B) its future pricing intentions "in circumstances where it is reasonably foreseeable that B might make use of that information to influence market conditions" and B then passes that pricing information on to a competing retailer (C), that is sufficient basis for concluding, even if A did not in fact foresee what was reasonably foreseeable or C did not appreciate the basis on which A had provided the information, that A, B and C are all to be regarded as parties to a concerted practice having as its object or effect the prevention, restriction or distortion of competition. But it is not necessary to decide whether a proposition in such wide terms could be supported in order to determine the appeal in Toys and Games any more than it is for the other appeal.

141 The proposition which, in our view, falls squarely within the Bayer judgment in the ECJ and which is sufficient to dispose of the point in the present appeal can be stated in more restricted terms: if (i) retailer A discloses to supplier B its future pricing intentions in circumstances where A may be taken to intend that B will make use of that information to influence market conditions by passing that information to other retailers (of whom C is or may be one), (ii) B does, in fact, pass that information to C in circumstances where C may be taken to know the circumstances in which the information was disclosed by A to B and (iii) C does, in fact, use the information in determining its own future pricing intentions, then A, B and C are all to be regarded as parties to a concerted practice having as its object the restriction or distortion of competition. The case is all the stronger where there is reciprocity: in the sense that C discloses to supplier B its future pricing intentions in circumstances where C may be taken to intend that B will make use of that information to influence market conditions by passing that information to (amongst others) A, and B does so.

142 The findings of fact made by the Tribunal bring the case within the proposition which we have just set out, whichever of Argos or Littlewoods is cast as retailer A.

(1) Taking Argos as retailer A and Littlewoods as retailer C, the relevant findings were these. Argos (through Mr Needham) disclosed to Hasbro (through Mr Wilson) its future pricing intentions for the autumn/winter 1999 and spring/summer 2000 catalogues in respect of Core Games and Action Man—paragraph 512(i)–(iii). It did so in circumstances in which (as Mr Needham accepted "as a statement of the obvious") Hasbro was "communicating with other retailers with a view to increasing margins towards RRPs"—paragraph 512(vi). Mr Needham "must have known" that his conversations with Mr Wilson were taking place in a context where Hasbro was talking to Argos and its principal competitors "with a view to achieving a situation in which Argos, Littlewoods and other retailers were all pricing at Hasbro's RRPs"—paragraph 512(viii). Mr Needham "must have been aware" that the disclosure that he was making to Mr Wilson "would support or at least facili-tate Hasbro's efforts to persuade other retailers to price at RRPs"—(*ibid*). Hasbro (through Mr Thomson) did in fact disclose to Littlewoods (through Mr Burgess) Argos' pricing intentions as to Core Games and Action Man: "Mr Thomson gave Mr Burgess assurances that Argos would stick to RRPs" in relation to those products—paragraph 530(iv). Mr Burgess knew that Hasbro had been in discussion with Argos (*ibid*). Littlewoods did rely upon the information in determining its own future pricing intentions—paragraph 530(vii). "Hasbro had aroused in Littlewoods an expect-ation that Littlewoods would not be undercut by Argos if they priced at RRPs, and Littlewoods had indicated to Hasbro that it was willing to sell at Hasbro's RRPs in the next relevant catalogue"—paragraph 531.

(2) Taking Littlewoods as retailer A and Argos as retailer C, the relevant findings are these. Littlewoods (through Mr Burgess) disclosed to Hasbro (through Mr Thomson) its future pricing intentions for the autumn/winter 1999 and spring/summer 2000 catalogues in respect of Core Games and Action Man—paragraph 530(iv). It did so in circumstances in which Mr Burgess knew that Mr Thomson would "go back and talk to people" to ensure that competitors also priced at

Hasbro's RRPs—paragraph 530(vii). Hasbro (through Mr Wilson) did, in fact, disclose to Argos (through Mr Needham) Littlewoods' future pricing intentions as to Core Games and Action Man—paragraph 512(vi) and (vii). Mr Needham "must have been aware" that the information had come from Littlewoods—(*ibid*). Argos did rely upon the information in determining its own pricing intentions: "The indications from Mr Wilson about other retailers' pricing intentions assisted Argos in achieving [its objectives of a better margin on toys while avoiding being undercut]"—paragraph 515.

The conduct to which we have referred occurred before the Act came into force on 1 March 2000, but the Tribunal proceeded on the basis that the agreements or concerted practices which had been reached before that date continued, and were extended, after that date. This conduct is therefore a relevant illustration of the point.

143 On the facts found by the Tribunal it seems to us impossible to avoid the conclusion that Hasbro's pricing initiative was acceptable to both Argos and Littlewoods. To adopt and adapt the observation of the Court of Justice in Bayer : "the manifestation of the wish of one of the contracting parties [Argos or Littlewoods] to achieve an anti-competitive goal—[when made known to the other, through the initiative of Hasbro]—constitute[d] an invitation to the other party, whether express or implied, to fulfil that goal jointly".

NOTE: This was the first case to be considered by the Court of Appeal in relation to the public enforcement process under the Competition Act 1998. Paras 92–104 relate to *Replica Kits* and paras 138–43 relate to *Toys and Games*. The Court of Appeal relied on European Court jurisprudence in relation to the determination of what constitutes a concerted practice in confirming the earlier rulings of the CAT.

C: Effect on Competition and appreciability

Section 2 of the CA 1998 mirrors Article 81(1) EC by prohibiting agreements etc., which 'have as their object or effect the prevention, restriction or distortion of competition'. This seemingly simple phrase has caused the Commission and the European Court great difficulties, as discussed in Chapter 6, involving a clear distinction between agreements which have the object of restricting competition and those which have the effect of doing so.

Section 2(2) of the CA 1998 provides a list of agreements to which, in particular, the prohibition is to apply, namely those which:

(a) directly or indirectly fix purchase or selling prices or any other trading conditions;
(b) limit or control production, markets, technical development, or investment;
(c) share markets or sources of supply;
(d) apply dissimilar conditions to equivalent transactions with other trading parties, thereby placing them at a competitive disadvantage;
(e) make the conclusion of contracts subject to acceptance by the other parties of supplementary obligations which, by their nature or according to commercial usage, have no connection with the subject of such contracts.

The list mirrors Article 81 EC; it is non-exhaustive and illustrates the types of behaviour that will infringe Chapter I. Further guidance may be sought from the OFT's guideline, OFT 401 at paras 3.1–3.27. There has been some limited consideration as to the types of agreement which may produce an anti-competitive effect.

Institute of Independent Insurance Brokers, The* v *Director General of Fair Trading supported by the General Insurance Standards Council; Association of British Travel Agents Limited* v *The Director General of Fair Trading supported by the General Insurance Standards Council

(Case Nos 1002/2/1/01 (Ir), 1003/2/1/01, 1004/2/1/01) [2001] CAT 4, paras 229–43

The GISC notified its Rules, which established a system of self-regulation for insurance sellers and brokers, to the DGFT in June 2000. Rule F42 prevented members of the GISC from dealing with intermediaries engaged in selling and broking insurance, unless the intermediaries were members of the GISC or their agents.

The main issue in the appeal was whether the GISC rules, and in particular Rule F42, had 'as their object or effect the prevention, restriction or distortion of competition within the United Kingdom' within the meaning of s. 2(1)(b) of the Act.

229. We next address the question whether the de facto exclusion, by GISC, of an alternative scheme of regulation for the independent broking sector gives rise, at first sight, to restrictions or distortions of competition which merited investigation by the Director.

230. In their article Kay & Vickers express the view that self regulatory organisations tend to act in the interests of their members, and may be inefficient in enforcing or promoting higher standards if they are under no competitive pressure to do so. For these reasons, Kay & Vickers suggest that competition between self regulatory organisations may be desirable (see pp. 239 to 241). In particular, situations in which persons cannot trade unless they are members of a particular self regulatory body 'should normally be resisted except where the service provided is a public rather than a private one' (see p. 238).

231. The GISC Rules give rise to a situation very close to that which Kay & Vickers suggest, at p. 238 of their article, 'should normally be resisted', in that intermediaries in the general insurance sector cannot in practice trade unless they are members of GISC. However, it is unnecessary for us in this case to enter into a theoretical debate. We are confronted by a specific factual situation, which is that the setting up of GISC has caused the collapse of a proposed alternative regulatory or certification scheme, namely IBRC Mk II, which was supported by some 1,000 broker firms, representing, we are told, half the independent broking sector, who did not wish to be regulated or certified by GISC. It seems to us, at first sight, that that situation in itself gives rise to a restriction or distortion of competition within the meaning of section 2(1)(b) of the Act.

232. In effect the evidence before us suggests that one way in which independent brokers are able to compete with insurers' direct selling operations and other intermediaries is by promoting themselves as offering higher 'quality' standards of professional competence and consumer protection. One potentially important means of competing in this way is for independent brokers to establish their own regulatory or 'quality assurance' scheme (such as IBRC Mk II) by means of which they may collectively promote themselves as meeting the quality standards of their own scheme. The evidence of the IIB with regards to its attempts to launch IBRC Mk II indicates the importance which a substantial part of the independent broking sector attaches to the establishment of its own regulatory or certification scheme as a means of competing with insurers and other intermediaries. We conclude that there is plainly a market for the provision of regulatory or certification services to independent brokers as an alternative to, and in competition with, GISC. To the extent that the Director found to the contrary at paragraph 18 of the IIB Decision, we reject that finding on the basis of the evidence before us.

233. It seems to us, therefore, at first sight, that the position of GISC as 'sole regulator' restricts or distorts competition in the provision of competing regulatory or certification services for which there is a demand from independent brokers in the general insurance sector. That, on the evidence before us, is potentially a restriction or distortion of competition in

the market for regulatory or certification services in the general insurance sector which merited investigation by the Director.

234. We are reinforced in that view by the fact, already mentioned, that once compelled to join, an intermediary faces practical difficulties in leaving GISC, except by discontinuing its business altogether or ceding its business to another member (Rule F34). It follows that, however high the GISC fees were to become, however inappropriate were to be the standards it develops, or however inefficiently it were to conduct its business, the option of leaving to join an alternative regulatory scheme is not in practice open. Even if GISC does not misconduct itself, the option of belonging to an alternative regulatory scheme, for example one that does not exclude its own liability, as GISC does, or which promotes higher standards or, for example, offers a compensation fund, is not in practical terms an option for any intermediary in the general insurance industry. In preventing, apparently in perpetuity, the emergence of an alternative to GISC, it does seem to us that competition from alternative regulatory schemes is potentially eliminated altogether.

235. Moreover, in our view, at first sight, the elimination of an alternative regulatory or quality assurance scheme for the independent broking sector also tends to restrict or distort competition in the separate market in which independent brokers are competing against the direct sales organisations of insurance companies, and other intermediaries, in selling or advising on general insurance products.

236. As we have already indicated, a potentially important element of competition in this, as in most other markets, is the ability to differentiate the product offered, notably by establishing a particular brand or image. GISC itself places considerable emphasis on establishing the GISC logo as a brand (paragraphs 68 and 165 above). The evidence before us is, however, that the inability to launch schemes such as IBRC Mk II is likely to make it more difficult for the independent broking sector to differentiate itself from the generality of suppliers of insurance by promoting its own distinctive image, based (as the IIB sees it) on higher regulatory standards, through the medium of an alternative regulatory scheme. In the absence of GISC, the members of the IIB would have the competitive freedom to promote themselves distinctively on the basis of their membership of such an independent scheme. The effective exclusion of that possibility, by the establishment of GISC seems to us, at first sight, to be a potential restriction or distortion of competition in the market for the selling, advising or broking of general insurance services.

237. It seems to us that that potential restriction or distortion of competition is reinforced in the present case by the fact that GISC itself comprises of a number of constituencies with different and opposing interests. It is a particular (and unusual) feature of this case that GISC, a body partly composed of suppliers (the insurers), seeks to exercise regulatory and disciplinary powers over the customers of those suppliers (the intermediaries). In addition, the insurer members of GISC sell insurance direct, in competition with intermediaries. In some sectors, particularly the consumer sector, insurers may have a substantial interest at gaining market share at the expense of independent intermediaries, or in promoting sales through tied outlets through agency agreements. Independent brokers, for their part, have an overriding interest in preserving their independence from insurers, since the essence of the service they provide is that of offering impartial advice in the best interests of the client.

238. In such circumstances it seems to us, at first sight, that the independent broking sector has a particular competitive need to differentiate, even to distance, itself from other Members of GISC. That sector depends very largely on the public perception that there are advantages in seeking impartial advice from a broker, whose duty it is to act in the client's best interest independently of the insurers, whether it is in placing the business or in handling any subsequent claims. It seems to us possible that that perception could be weakened if independent intermediaries are forced to belong to, and be disciplined by, a body in which insurers' interests are very strong.

239. The IIB also submits that GISC will have the effect of preventing higher standards emerging in the general insurance sector and has already had the effect of lowering standards. In this regard, there is some evidence before us that the GISC regime contemplates lower standards as compared with those of the previous IBRC regime or IBRC Mk II. For example, under the GISC Rules the liability of GISC is excluded, only firms rather than individuals are regulated, audit requirements may be waived by a procedure of 'self-certification', breach of the Commercial Code does not appear in itself to be a disciplinary matter and no compensation fund is provided. Since GISC seeks to bring within its net all kinds of inter-mediaries, it seems to us not implausible that the general standard of regulation may set-tle at a lower level than that desirable for certain specific sectors such as independent brokers. Again, without expressing any view on the relative advantages and disadvantages of the GISC Rules and IBRC Mk II, it seems to us that the question whether the establish-ment of GISC would tend to militate against the independent broking sector maintaining higher standards, and thus restrict or distort competition, was a question meriting inves-tigation by the Director.

240. In the IIB Decision, the Director takes the view that it was unnecessary for him to take into account the possibility of the lowering of regulatory standards, and in particular, that 'it was not necessary and would not have been appropriate for the Director to carry out a comparative analysis of the different types of regulation that may currently or in the future exist in the industry' (paragraph 23).

241. We find ourselves unable to agree with that approach. It seems to us that, once it was appreciated that the GISC Rules created a monopoly, in this instance a monopoly in the regulation of the general insurance industry, it was incumbent on the Director to examine potential effects on competition of the creation of that regulatory monopoly. It having been submitted to him on credible evidence that one of the effects of that monopoly was to make more difficult the maintenance of higher regulatory standards, and thus to diminish competition on product quality, which is one of the essential aspects of competition, the Director should, in our view, have investigated whether that evidence did in fact support the conclusion that GISC's regulatory monopoly did tend to restrict or distort competition in the respect alleged.

242. We are unpersuaded that the restrictions of competition identified above are materially affected by GISC's submission that the threat of statutory regulation under the FSMA will suffice to ensure that GISC acts solely in the public interest. That is a quite different issue. In any event, the possibility that the present or any future Government might, at some unknown future date, wish to replace GISC with statutory regulation under the FSMA, and if so in what circumstances, is far too uncertain a consideration for us to take into account when analysing restrictions or distortions of competition under section 2(1)(b) of the Act.

243. We also observe that a number of the possible consequences of the exclusion of alternative regulatory or certification regimes would be avoided if there were a realistic possibility for a waiver of the GISC Rules where such an alternative scheme was in place. Any such waivers would have to be granted on the basis of objective and transparent criteria, and any refus-als of waiver would have to be open to challenge by some appropriate and independent procedure. Since, however, that is not the case at present, it does not seem to us that the waiver provisions of the GISC Rules, as presently applied, affect the analysis set out above.

NOTE: In light of this judgment, Rodger noted: 'Although some professional rules may encourage competition and fall outside the prohibition due to the rule of reason, this robust judgment by the tribunal will have implications in many areas of self-regulation in the economy.' (Rodger, B.J., 'Early Steps to a Mature Competition Law System' [2002] ECLR 61–7, at p. 64.) Certainly, this case highlighted that certain rules associated with *inter alia* member-ship of the liberal professions may be potentially anti-competitive. Following the case, GISC removed the particular rule F42 and accordingly the OFT subsequently concluded that their rules did not infringe the Chapter I prohibition.

The CAT was required to consider the impact of the ECJ's ruling in case C-309/99 *Wouters* [2002] ECR I-1577, in the subsequent case of the *Racecourse Association and BHRB v OFT*.

Racecourse Association and BHRB v OFT
[2005] CAT 29, paras 167–75

This case involved two appeals against an OFT decision in April 2004 that the sale of certain media rights infringed the Chapter I prohibition. In 2001, a 'Media Rights Agreement' ('the MRA'), was made between various parties including Attheraces Holdings Limited, AttheRaces plc ('ATR'), and 49 of the 59 racecourses ('the Courses'). ATR was a joint venture company formed by various broadcasting organisations, and was used to acquire various media rights from the Courses under the MRA, in particular 'the Non-LBO bookmaking rights', and it was their sale which the OFT held to infringe the prohibition. These were picture rights which, in combination with betting rights and data, could be used to allow interactive betting using television or the internet. The OFT decided that the MRA involved a collective sale of the Non-LBO bookmaking rights which had the effect of appreciably preventing, restricting, or distorting competition by increasing the price for the supply in the UK of these rights.

167. We confess to some difficulty in reconciling the approach of the ECJ in *Gøttrup-Klim* and *Wouters* with that of the CFI in *Métropole*, but find it unnecessary to dwell on the explanation in *Métropole* as to the rationale that the CFI perceived as underlying cases such as *Gøttrup-Klim* and *Wouters* (the latter of course being decided after *Métropole*). We consider that these two decisions of the ECJ show that the assessment of whether or not a particular arrangement constitutes an infringement of Article 85(1) (now Article 81(1)), or therefore of the Chapter I prohibition, is a rather more flexible exercise than the CFI was perhaps willing to appreciate. It is not enough that the arrangement is apparently anti-competitive, as in *Gøttrup-Klim* and *Wouters*. What those cases show is that ostensibly restrictive arrangements which are *necessary* to achieve a proper commercial objective will not, or may not, constitute an anti-competitive infringement at all. Whether or not they will do so requires an objective analysis of the particular arrangement entered into by the parties, assessed by reference to their subjective "wants" and against the evidence of the particular market in which they made their arrangement. The task then is to consider whether the restrictive arrangement of which complaint is made is "necessary" to achieve the objective. The RCA appellants also submitted that the concept of "necessity" in this context is not an absolute one, but has an element of flexibility about it, for which they referred us to paragraph 109 in the *Métropole* case in which the court observed that "If, without the restriction, the main operation is difficult or even impossible to implement, the restriction may be regarded as objectively necessary for its implementation." We also accept this last submission: competition law is not an area of law in which there is much scope for absolute concepts or sharp edges.

168. The RCA appellants said that the present case falls squarely within this concept of "necessity". ATR entered into the MRA in order to create a wholly untried and innovative product— the channel and linked interactive website. The Courses entered into the MRA in order to sell ATR the rights which would enable ATR to create and exploit that new product and so in turn to generate a new source of much needed income for the Courses with a view to replacing the income drought with which they were faced by the proposed abolition of the levy. The creation of that new product was a legitimate commercial objective from everyone's point of view: horseracing generally, the punters and the parties to the MRA. The new channel was to be financed principally from betting income and so ATR needed, so far as possible, to have uninterrupted race coverage on each day of each week of each

year in order to maximise its betting income. That need required it in turn to seek to acquire the interactive rights from as many racecourses as possible. It did not need (albeit that it would have liked) to acquire the interactive rights of *all* 59 courses, but it did at least need to acquire a "critical mass" of such rights in order for the new venture to be viable. There is no agreement between the parties as to what ATR's critical mass was, but the OFT now accepts that ATR (or any other bidder) required at least a majority of the rights of the 59 courses by reference to betting turnover and that therefore there could only be one successful bidder for the rights.

169. Save for the quantum of the necessary critical mass, all this was common ground. The point of difference was the next step. Whereas the RCA and the Courses claimed that, from a practical point of view, collective selling, or negotiation, was the only realistic way to achieve a sale and purchase of the rights (being rights which had never been dealt with in the market before), the OFT found that the buyers could have assembled the rights themselves by individual negotiation with the course owners or with small groups of courses. In practice, they would have had to negotiate with up to about 37 separate course owners. It made the point that any such separate contracts so negotiated could have been made conditional on obtaining sufficient rights from other courses "(as in fact occurred in the Notified Arrangement, itself a conditional agreement)". It also said that BSkyB and Channel 4 had considerable experience of assembling packages of rights necessary to launch channels.

170. The suggestion that the acquisition of the necessary critical mass by individual negotiation with up to 37 course owners either could have been done, might have been done, or was ever even contemplated as something which could or might have been done, appears to us to represent a triumph of theory over commercial reality and to ignore the evidence of the events leading up to the MRA. We have summarised the course of the negotiations fairly fully and do not refer to those details again here. We regard it as apparent from the totality of the negotiations that Channel 4, Arena and ATR (whom we lump together for this purpose, since ATR simply continued the negotiations earlier started by Channel 4 and Arena)—and also Carlton—had one major objective in mind. That was to acquire the rights of as many courses as they could and, with a view to achieving that end, to deal with the courses as a whole. There is no evidence that, at the time of the negotiations, any of the bidders ever had it in mind to pick off the courses individually or in small groups and the notion that they might have tried to do so appears to be unrealistic. We do not overlook the staged acquisition operation that Arena proposed in its discussion document in January 2000, but record that it then took no steps towards carrying it out. Since there could and would be no deal with any courses until the necessary critical mass had been tied up, each individual deal would have had to be made conditional upon the signing of other courses until such time as the critical mass had been achieved. This could have been done in theory. In practice, the bidders never sought to do it, for the obvious reason that so to have proceeded would, in practice, have been extremely difficult if not impossible. The OFT's point that the availability of this route was in part illustrated by the fact that the MRA was itself a conditional agreement was, in our view, a false one. The MRA reflected the fruit of the centrally negotiated agreement and its stated conditions were in substance no more than a public statement by ATR to all 59 courses to the effect that the MRA would only bite as a matter of contract if enough courses signed up to it. A conditional agreement of that sort was quite different from that which would have been required if ATR had sought to negotiate separate deals with up to 37 different owners. We do not know what conditions the OFT had in mind as those to which the contracts might have been subject: but if they were, for example, equivalent to those in clause 2.2 in the MRA, then that would appear to present a good many courses further down the queue with an obvious veto on the self-assembly exercise ever being consummated except at prices dictated by them. We also consider that the OFT's point that the ATR consortium had experience in assembling rights from different suppliers ignored the fact that the courses' interactive rights were being sought for the creation of a wholly new product: we are unaware that there was any evidence that such earlier self-assembly experience involved the self-assembly of a particular critical mass of rights.

171. In our view, therefore, an acquisition via a central negotiation was the only realistic way forward both from the viewpoint of both bidder and sellers and we regard it as probable that any initial attempt at a self-assembly exercise via individual negotiations would have led quickly to a centrally negotiated one. This is illustrated by the failure of Channel 4's attempt first to sign up with the Super 12 and then with the 47. Put another way, we consider that the weight of the evidence before the OFT, being evidence as to what actually happened, showed that collective negotiation was the *necessary* way forward, and that is the way that was in fact adopted.

172. In so concluding, we are saying nothing new. That always was, and remains, the view of the Courses, the RCA and the BHB. Once upon a time it was also the view of ATR, which expressly agreed in the notification that: "It was necessary for the Rights to be sold pursuant to a centrally negotiated agreement in order to put together a package of rights sufficient to be attractive to purchasers and to allow the radical move away from the current method of funding British Racing (i.e. the Levy plus limited commercial revenues). The involvement of a significant number of courses was necessary in order to achieve an efficient sale of the Rights and the necessary 'critical mass to make [ATR's] product offering feasible." The point that ATR was there acknowledging—and asserting—was that it *needed* a critical mass of rights and therefore engaged in the one commercially obvious—and necessary—way to achieve it, which was by a central negotiation. Of course, ATR much later decided that its own commercial interests lay in a repudiation of the MRA and the OFT chose to prefer ATR's later evidence produced in August 2003 to the effect that what they had there said in the notification was (in effect) a mistake and that in reality, contrary to that assertion, central negotiation had not been necessary at all. That self-serving evidence was a self-contradiction and was unsupported by ATR's actions at the time of the negotiations. It is also contrary to what was said in a briefing paper submitted by the RCA to the OFT in March 2003, one which was first endorsed by ATR and paragraph 3.9 of which confirmed that ATR was only prepared to negotiate through a central entity and would not have been willing to deal separately with up to 38 sellers: had ATR been faced with a need to do so, "it is likely that they would not have proceeded". ATR made an express reference to paragraph 3.9, with apparent approval of its contents, in its letter of 25 July 2003 to the OFT. It is also of note that Arena (an ATR company), in response to section 26 notices served by the OFT, made the point that whilst certain of the larger courses would have had the resources to sell their interactive rights individually, the typical course would not, since as it would hold few, if any, fixtures of any intrinsic value to a broadcaster, it could not make a commercially attractive offer to a broadcaster. Arena's view was that (the largest courses apart), a typical course might not therefore be able to sell any interactive rights at all unless it were to do so as part of some wider negotiating process under which the buyer requires a larger package of rights of interest to both parties. Its evidence was that for most courses the sale of rights individually was simply not a viable option for either buyer or seller. The OFT appears to have ignored this evidence in its Decision.

173. No bidder went down the self-assembly route in this case, although there was, in practice, nothing to stop them doing so. They were free at any time to approach any racecourse and make it an offer. We presume that the reason for the adopted method of acquisition is because no bidder regarded anything other than central negotiation as offering a practicable way forward.

174. We record that the OFT placed reliance upon the decision of the Commission in the *UEFA Champions League* OJ [2003] L291/25 as providing a pointer against our conclusion on the necessity argument. We consider that counsel for the RCA appellants was correct in his response that in that case the argument failed on the facts identified in paragraph 131 of the decision.

175. We conclude, therefore, that the central negotiation in which the Courses engaged was necessary for the achievement both by them and by ATR of the legitimate commercial

> objective of creating the new product that ATR proposed to exploit for the benefit of itself, the punters, the racecourses and racing generally. In our view, the evidence pointed to that conclusion and there was no reliable evidence supporting the different view that the OFT preferred, which appears to us to have been founded in theory rather than reality. We conclude that the MRA involved no infringement of the Chapter I prohibition.

NOTE: The CAT emphasized the extent to which the collective selling or negotiation of the rights was necessary, relying in particular upon the *Wouters* ruling. In any event, the CAT considered that the OFT had not proved that the MRA resulted in an appreciable increase in price.

■ QUESTION

Why was the existence of the collective agreement in this case not sufficient alone to satisfy the requirements for an infringement of the Chapter I prohibition?

The concept of appreciability has an important part to play in terms of delineating the scope of the Chapter I prohibition. Note the term 'appreciable' does not actually appear in the text of the Act. This was deemed unnecessary since the Court's jurisprudence on appreciability applies through s. 60, as indicated by Lord Simons in the House of Lords:

> an explicit appreciability test does not fit well with our approach of reliance on European case law except in areas where it is clear a different approach is required. Worse, there is a risk that in apparently departing from established European principles, we might inadvertently create so high a threshold for action that we could impede the effective tackling of anti-competitive agreements. [Hansard, HL, 13 November 1997, col 259]

OFT, *Agreements and concerted practices*
www.oft.gov.uk/advice_and_resources/publications/guidance/competiton-act

OFT 401, paras 2.15–2.21 [footnotes omitted]

The appreciable effect on competition test

2.15 An agreement will fall within Article 81 and/or the Chapter I prohibition only if it has as its object or effect an appreciable prevention, restriction or distortion of competition within:
- the common market in the case of Article 81, or
- the United Kingdom in the case of the Chapter I prohibition.

2.16 The European Commission's *Notice on Agreements of Minor Importance* (the *Notice on Agreements of Minor Importance*) sets out, using market share thresholds, what is **not** an appreciable restriction of competition under Article 81. The European Commission considers that agreements between undertakings which affect trade between Member States do not appreciably restrict competition within the meaning of Article 81 if:
- the aggregate market share of the parties to the agreement does not exceed 10 per cent on any of the relevant markets affected by the agreement where the agreement is made between competing undertakings (i.e. undertakings which are actual or potential competitors on any of the markets concerned), or
- the market share of each of the parties to the agreement does not exceed 15 per cent on any of the relevant markets affected by the agreement where the agreement is made between non-competing undertakings, (i.e. undertakings which are neither actual nor potential competitors on any of the markets concerned).

In both cases, these thresholds are reduced to five per cent where competition on the relevant market is restricted by the cumulative foreclosure effect of parallel networks of agreements having similar effects on the market.

2.17 The above approach does **not** apply to an agreement containing any of the restrictions set out in paragraph 11 of the *Notice on Agreements of Minor Importance*. These include:
- in the case of an agreement between competing undertakings a provision which:
  — directly or indirectly fixes prices, shares markets or limits production, or
- in the case of an agreement between non-competing undertakings a provision which:
  — limits a buyer's ability to determine its resale price, or
  — restricts a buyer operating at a retail level from selling to any end user in response to an unsolicited order (passive selling), or
  — restricts active or passive selling by the authorised distributors to end-users or other authorised distributors in a selective distribution network, or
  — restricts, by agreement between a supplier of components and a buyer who incorporates those components in its products, the supplier's ability to sell the components as spare parts to end users or independent repairers not entrusted by the buyer with the repair or servicing of its products.

For the full list of restrictions please see paragraph 11 of the Notice. Agreements containing any of the restrictions set out in paragraph 11 of the *Notice on Agreements of Minor Importance* are regarded as being capable of having an appreciable effect even where the market shares fall below the thresholds explained in paragraph 2.16.

2.18 In determining whether an agreement has an appreciable effect on competition for the purposes of Article 81 and/or the Chapter I prohibition, the OFT will have regard to the European Commission's approach as set out in the *Notice on Agreements of Minor Importance*.

2.19 As a matter of practice the OFT is likely to consider that an agreement will not fall within either Article 81 or the Chapter I prohibition when it is covered by the *Notice on Agreements of Minor Importance*. Where the OFT considers that undertakings have in good faith relied on the terms of the *Notice on Agreements of Minor Importance*, the OFT will not impose financial penalties for an infringement of Article 81 and/or the Chapter I prohibition. A review of the types of agreements which would generally fall within Article 81 and/or the Chapter I prohibition are covered in Part 3 of this guideline.

2.20 The mere fact that the parties' market shares exceed the thresholds set out in paragraph 2.16, does **not** mean that the effect of an agreement on competition **is** appreciable. Other factors will be considered in determining whether the agreement has an appreciable effect. Relevant factors may include for example, the content of the agreement and the structure of the market or markets affected by the agreement, such as entry conditions or the characteristics of buyers and the structure of the buyers' side of the market (see the competition law guideline *Assessment of market power* (OFT415)).

2.21 When applying the market share thresholds discussed above, the relevant market share will be the combined market share not only of the parties to the agreement but also of other undertakings belonging to the same group of undertakings as the parties to the agreement. These will include, in the case of each party to the agreement: (i) undertakings over which it exercises control; and (ii) undertakings which exercise control over it as well as any other undertakings which are controlled by those undertakings. Further details on defining the relevant market are given in the competition law guideline *Market definition* (OFT403).

NOTE: The guideline confirms that the concept of appreciability follows established Community jurisprudence and Commission practice as set out in the Notice on Agreements of Minor Importance. It should be noted that the OFT's policy on appreciability was revised considerably in 2004 to coincide with the introduction of Regulation 1 and the concurrent application of Article 81 and the Chapter 1 prohibition by the OFT. The earlier guideline provided for a higher appreciability threshold of 25 per cent market share. Guideline 401 must be read in conjunction with the OFT's *Enforcement* guideline, OFT 407, which provides limited immunity for 'small agreements' and 'conduct of minor significance'.

Enforcement
www.oft.gov.uk/advice_and_resources/publications/guidance/competiton-act/

OFT 407, paras 5.16–5.20 [footnotes omitted]

Limited immunity for 'small agreements' and 'conduct of minor significance'

5.16 In order to avoid the prohibition regime being unduly burdensome on small businesses, the Act provides limited immunity from financial penalties for **small agreements** in relation to infringements of the Chapter I prohibition and for **conduct of minor significance** in relation to infringements of the Chapter II prohibition. This immunity does not apply to any infringements of Article 81 or Article 82, so small businesses whose activities may have an effect on trade between Member States may be subject to penalties even in respect of small agreements or conduct of minor significance. Neither does the immunity apply to infringements of the Chapter I prohibition which are price-fixing agreements.

5.17 The term **small agreements** relates to agreements, other than price fixing agreements, between undertakings whose combined annual turnover does not exceed £20 million. Conduct will be considered to be of minor significance if the annual turnover of the undertaking concerned does not exceed £50 million.

5.18 Undertakings will benefit from immunity from financial penalties for infringement of the Chapter I prohibition or Chapter II prohibition, as appropriate, if the OFT is satisfied that they acted on the reasonable assumption that on the facts they qualified for the limited immunity for **small agreements** or **conduct of minor significance**.

5.19 The immunity applies only to financial penalties: an anti-competitive agreement or abusive conduct by such undertakings is still an infringement, and consequently the OFT may take other enforcement action, and the immunity does not prevent third parties from claiming damages for the loss caused by such an agreement or conduct (see further paragraph 6.1 below).

5.20 The OFT may still investigate small agreements or conduct of minor significance and can decide to withdraw the immunity from financial penalties if, having investigated the agreement or conduct, it considers that it is likely to infringe the Chapter I and/or Chapter II prohibition.

D: Extra-territoriality

Section 2(1)(a) of the 1998 Act provides that the Chapter I prohibition will only apply where 'trade is affected *within* the United Kingdom' and s. 2(3) states that it will only apply 'if the agreement, decision or practice is, or is intended to be, implemented, in the United Kingdom.' There is no similar provision within Article 81.

OFT, *Agreements and concerted practices*
www.oft.gov.uk/advice_and_resources/publications/guidance/competiton-act/

OFT 401, paras 2.24–2.27

2.24 The Chapter I prohibition only applies to agreements that may affect trade within the United Kingdom.

2.25 In practice it is very unlikely that an agreement which appreciably restricts competition within the United Kingdom does not also affect trade within the United Kingdom. So, in applying the Chapter I prohibition the OFT's focus will be on the effect that an agreement has on competition, discussed in paragraph 2.20 above.

2.26 The Chapter I prohibition applies only if an agreement is, or is intended to be, implemented in the United Kingdom.

2.27 The United Kingdom means Great Britain (England, Wales and Scotland and the subsidiary islands, excluding the Isle of Man and the Channel Islands) and Northern Ireland. For the purposes of the Chapter I prohibition, the United Kingdom includes any part of the United Kingdom where an agreement operates or is intended to operate.

NOTE: If an agreement affects both trade between Member States and trade within the UK, it will be subject to UK and EC competition rules (see Article 3 of Regulation 1/2003, Chapter 2).

The 1998 Act catches agreements that are *implemented* within the UK or any part of the UK. Does this mean the Chapter I prohibition has extraterritorial application? Extraterritoriality remains controversial in both UK and Community law; the UK government preferring a more traditional view of jurisdiction based on the territorial and nationality principles of public international law. As Lord Simon explained during debate:

> by copying out the test in *Wood Pulp* on the fact of the Bill, we are also ensuring that in the event that EC jurisprudence develops and creates a pure effects-doctrine, the application of the UK prohibitions will not follow suit. (Hansard, HL, 13 November, col 261)

For a fuller discussion of EC case law in relation to extraterritorial application, see Chapter 5.

SECTION 4: EXEMPTIONS AND EXCLUSIONS

A: Exemptions

When the 1998 Act was introduced, it copied the existing Community regime by including provision for individual and block exemption, with a system of notification of agreements for individual exemption. When Regulation 1/2003 was introduced, abolishing the system of notifications and individual exemptions under EC law, the 1998 Act was also amended. As of 1 May 2004, as under the EC system, an agreement may only be exempted from the Chapter I prohibition by a block exemption Regulation.

COMPETITION ACT 1998 [SS. 6 AND 8–11]

Block exemptions

6.—(1) If agreements which fall within a particular category of agreement are, in the opinion of the OFT, likely to be exempt agreements, the OFT may recommend that the Secretary of State make an order specifying that category for the purposes of this section.

(2) The Secretary of State may make an order ('a block exemption order') giving effect to such a recommendation—
   (a) in the form in which the recommendation is made; or
   (b) subject to such modifications as he considers appropriate.

(3) An agreement which falls within a category specified in a block exemption order is exempt from the Chapter I prohibition.

(4) An exemption under this section is referred to in this Part as a block exemption.

(5) A block exemption order may impose conditions or obligations subject to which a block exemption is to have effect.

(6) A block exemption order may provide—
   (a) that breach of a condition imposed by the order has the effect of cancelling the block exemption in respect of an agreement;
   (b) that if there is a failure to comply with an obligation imposed by the order, the OFT may, by notice in writing, cancel the block exemption in respect of the agreement;

    (c) that if the OFT considers that a particular agreement is not an exempt agreement, it may cancel the block exemption in respect of that agreement.

(7) A block exemption order may provide that the order is to cease to have effect at the end of a specified period.

(8) In this section "exempt agreement" means an agreement which is exempt from the Chapter I prohibition as a result of section 9; and "specified" means specified in a block exemption order.

Block exemptions: procedure

8.—(1) Before making a recommendation under section 6(1), the OFT must—
    (a) publish details of its proposed recommendation in such a way as it thinks most suitable for bringing it to the attention of those likely to be affected; and
    (b) consider any representations about it which are made to it.

(2) If the Secretary of State proposes to give effect to such a recommendation subject to modifications, he must inform the OFT of the proposed modifications and take into account any comments made by the OFT.

(3) If, in the opinion of the OFT, it is appropriate to vary or revoke a block exemption order it may make a recommendation to that effect to the Secretary of State.

(4) Subsection (1) also applies to any proposed recommendation under subsection (3).

(5) Before exercising his power to vary or revoke a block exemption order (in a case where there has been no recommendation under subsection (3)), the Secretary of State must—
    (a) inform the OFT of the proposed variation or revocation; and
    (b) take into account any comments made by the OFT.

(6) A block exemption order may provide for a block exemption to have effect from a date earlier than that on which the order is made.

Exempt Agreements

9.—(1) An agreement is exempt from the Chapter I prohibition if it
    (a) contributes to—
        (i) improving production or distribution, or
        (ii) promoting technical or economic progress, while allowing consumers a fair share of the resulting benefit; but
    (b) does not—
        (i) impose on the undertakings concerned restrictions which are not indispensable to the attainment of those objectives; or
        (ii) afford the undertakings concerned the possibility of eliminating competition in respect of a substantial part of the products in question.

(2) In any proceedings in which it is alleged that the Chapter I prohibition is being or has been infringed by an agreement, any undertaking or association of undertakings claiming the benefit of subsection (1) shall bear the burden of proving that the conditions of that subsection are satisfied.

Parallel exemptions

10.—(1) An agreement is exempt from the Chapter I prohibition if it is exempt from the Community prohibition—
    (a) by virtue of a Regulation,
    (b) because of a decision by the Commission under Article 10 of the EC Competition Regulation.

(2) An agreement is exempt from the Chapter I prohibition if it does not affect trade between Member States but otherwise falls within a category of agreement which is exempt from the Community prohibition by virtue of a Regulation.

(3) An exemption from the Chapter I prohibition under this section is referred to in this Part as a parallel exemption.

  (4) A parallel exemption—

    (a) takes effect on the date on which the relevant exemption from the Community prohibition takes effect or, in the case of a parallel exemption under subsection (2), would take effect if the agreement in question affected trade between Member States; and

    (b) ceases to have effect—

      (i) if the relevant exemption from the Community prohibition ceases to have effect; or

      (ii) on being cancelled by virtue of subsection (5) or (7).

  (5) In such circumstances and manner as may be specified in rules made under section 51, the Director may—

    (a) impose conditions or obligations subject to which a parallel exemption is to have effect;

    (b) vary or remove any such condition or obligation;

    (c) impose one or more additional conditions or obligations;

    (d) cancel the exemption.

  (6) In such circumstances as may be specified in rules made under section 51, the date from which cancellation of an exemption is to take effect may be earlier than the date on which notice of cancellation is given.

  (7) Breach of a condition imposed by the OFT has the effect of cancelling the exemption.

  (8) In exercising his powers under this section, the OFT may require any person who is a party to the agreement in question to give him such information as he may require.

  (9) For the purpose of this section references to an agreement being exempt from the Community prohibition are to be read as including references to the prohibition being inapplicable to the agreement by virtue of a Regulation other than the EC Competition Regulation or a decision by the Commission.

  (10) In this section—'the Community prohibition' means the prohibition contained in—

    (a) Article 81(1);

    (b) any corresponding provision replacing, or otherwise derived from, that provision;

    (c) such other Regulation as the Secretary of State may by order specify; and 'Regulation' means a Regulation adopted by the Commission or by the Council.

  (11) This section has effect in relation to the prohibition contained in paragraph 1 of Article 53 of the EEA Agreement (and the EFTA Surveillance Authority) as it has effect in relation to the Community prohibition (and the Commission) subject to any modifications which the Secretary of State may by order prescribe.

Exemption for certain other agreements

  11.—(1) The fact that a ruling may be given by virtue of Article 84 of the Treaty on the question whether or not agreements of a particular kind are prohibited by Article 81(1) does not prevent such agreements from being subject to the Chapter I prohibition.

    (2) But the Secretary of State may by regulations make such provision as he considers appropriate for the purpose of granting an exemption from the Chapter I prohibition, in prescribed circumstances, in respect of such agreements.

    (3) An exemption from the Chapter I prohibition by virtue of regulations under this section is referred to in this Part as a section 11 exemption.

OFT guideline 401, *Agreements and concerted practices,* explains the two types of exemption in more detail.

OFT, *Agreements and concerted practices*

www.oft.gov.uk/advice_and_resources/publications/guidance/competiton-act/

OFT 401, paras 5.13–5.16 [footnotes omitted]

  5.13 Under the Act the Secretary of State may, acting on the OFT's recommendation, make domestic block exemptions that specify particular categories of agreement which the OFT considers are likely to be exempt from the Chapter I prohibition as a result of section 9(1). An agreement which falls within a category specified in the block exemption will not be prohibited under the Chapter I prohibition. Any such block exemption may impose conditions or obligations subject to which the block exemption will have effect.

5.14 Breach of a condition imposed by the block exemption cancels the block exemption in respect of an agreement. The failure to comply with an obligation imposed by the block exemption enables the OFT to cancel the block exemption in respect of an agreement. Furthermore if the OFT thinks that an agreement is not exempt from the Chapter I prohibition as a result of section 9(1) of the Act, the OFT may cancel the block exemption in respect of that agreement.

Parallel exemption under the Act

5.15 An agreement is exempt from the Chapter I prohibition if it is covered by a finding of inapplicability by the European Commission or an EC block exemption regulation, or would be covered by an EC block exemption regulation if the agreement had an effect on trade between Member States. These types of agreement are not prohibited under the Chapter I prohibition, no prior decision to that effect being required.

5.16 Where an agreement has no effect on trade between Member States but it would be covered by an EC block exemption regulation if the agreement had an effect on trade between Member States and therefore benefits from a parallel exemption, the OFT may nevertheless impose conditions on the parallel exemption or cancel the exemption following procedures specified in the OFT's Rules if the agreement has effects in the United Kingdom, or a part of it, which are incompatible with the conditions in section 9(1).

NOTE: In practice, given the Commission's experience in issuing block exemptions, as discussed in Chapter 2, the parallel exemption provisions are very important in practice in ensuring that a number of important commercial agreements, including vertical agreements, are automatically exempted from the scope of both Article 81 EC and the domestic Chapter I prohibition. To date one block exemption order has been adopted, backdated to 1 March 2000 in relation to travel cards, following a recommendation that public transport ticketing schemes should be exempted.

COMPETITION ACT 1998 (PUBLIC TRANSPORT TICKETING SCHEMES BLOCK EXEMPTION) ORDER 2001

(SI 2001/319 as amended by the Competition Act 1998 (Public Transport Ticketing Schemes Block Exemption) (Amendment) Order 2005, SI 2005/3347)

Citation, commencement, duration and interpretation

1. This Order may be cited as the Competition Act 1998 (Public Transport Ticketing Schemes Block Exemption) Order 2001 and shall come into force on 1st March 2001.

2. This Order shall have effect from the beginning of 1st March 2000 and shall cease to have effect at the end of the period of ten years commencing on 1st March 2001.

3. In this Order—

'the Act' means the Competition Act 1998;

'block exemption' means the exemption from the Chapter I prohibition arising by virtue of this Order for the category of agreements specified in this Order;

'bus service' has the meaning given in section 159(1) of the Transport Act 1968 but excludes a bus service which is a tourist service;

'chartered service' means a public transport service:
   (a) for which the whole capacity of the vehicle, vessel or craft supplying that service has been purchased by one or more charterers for his or their own use or for resale;
   (b) which is a journey or trip organised privately by any person acting independently of the person operating the vehicle, vessel or craft supplying that service; or

(c) on which the passengers travel together on a journey, with or without breaks, from one or more places to one or more places and back;

'complementary services' means local public transport services which are not in competition with each other over a substantial part of the route covered by the ticket in question;

'connecting service' means a service (other than a bus service, a chartered service or a tourist service) for the carriage of passengers by road, tramway, railway, inland waterway or air which is a long distance service and which runs between—

(a) a station or stopping place at or in the vicinity of which the relevant local public transport service stops; and

(b) any other place;

'inland waterway' includes both natural and artificial waterways, and waterways within parts of the sea that are in the United Kingdom;

'journey' means any journey made by an individual passenger and includes a return journey;

'local public transport service' means:

(a) a bus service; or

(b) a scheduled public transport service (other than a bus service) using one or more vehicles or vessels for the carriage of passengers by road, railway, tramway or inland waterway at separate fares other than a long distance service, a chartered service or a tourist service;

'long distance add-on' means:

(a) a ticket (or tickets) entitling the holder to make a journey solely on the local public transport services of any one operator;

(b) a multi-operator travelcard; or

(c) a through ticket,

each being purchased as an add-on to a ticket (or tickets) entitling the holder to make a particular journey on one or more connecting services;

'long distance operator' means an undertaking (other than an operator) supplying a scheduled long distance service using one or more vehicles, vessels or craft for the carriage of passengers by road, railway, tramway, inland waterway or air at separate fares other than a chartered service or a tourist service;

'long distance service' means a public transport service in relation to which (except in an emergency) one or both of the following conditions are met with respect to every passenger using the service:

(a) the place where he is set down is fifteen miles or more, measured in a straight line, from the place where he was taken up;

(b) some point on the route between those places is fifteen miles or more, measured in a straight line, from either of those places,

and where a public transport service consists of one or more parts with respect to which one or both of these conditions are met, and one or more parts with respect to which neither of them is met, each of those parts shall be treated as a separate public transport service;

'members of the public' means any person other than an operator, potential operator, long distance operator or potential long distance operator;

'multi-operator individual ticket' means a ticket (or tickets) entitling the holder, where a particular journey could be made on local public transport services provided by any of two or more operators, to make that journey or any part of it on whichever service the holder chooses;

'multi-operator travel card' means a ticket (or tickets) entitling the holder to make three or more journeys on three or more specified local public transport services operating on three or more routes provided that:

(a) these routes are not substantially the same;

(b) these local public transport services are not substantially the same; and

(c) for each of these routes and local public transport services, the passenger usage and revenue received from the ticket and other such tickets purchased as a result of the relevant agreement, demonstrate that the ticket is not, in practice, a multi-operator individual ticket or a through ticket;

'operator' means an undertaking supplying local public transport services;

'posted price' means, where a ticket is purchased from one undertaking (the seller), a wholesale price set independently by another undertaking ('the creditor') for the carriage of passengers bearing that ticket on the public transport services of the creditor;

'public transport ticketing scheme' has the meaning given in Article 4(2);

'the register' means the register maintained by the Office of Fair Trading under rule 20 of the Office of Fair Trading's Rules set out in the Schedule to the Competition Act 1998 (Office of Fair Trading's Rules) Order 2004;

'short distance add-on' means a multi-operator travelcard purchased as an add-on to a ticket (or tickets) entitling the holder to make a particular journey on a local public transport service pursuant to an agreement which provides for onward travel connections for passengers on complementary services;

'stopping place' means a point at which passengers are taken up or set down in the course of a public transport service;

'through ticket' means a ticket (or tickets) entitling the holder to make a particular journey on two or more local public transport services provided that such a journey is made on complementary services;

'ticket' means evidence of a contractual right to travel;

'tourist service' means a public transport service where the price charged for that service includes payment for a live or recorded commentary about the locality being a service primarily for the benefit of tourists;

'vehicle' includes vehicles constructed or adapted to run on flanged wheels but excludes hackney carriages, taxis, cabs, hire cars and any vehicle propelled by an animal; and

'working day' means a day which is not a Saturday, Sunday or any other day on which the Office of Fair Trading is closed for business.

Block exemption

4.—(1) The category of agreements identified in paragraph (2) as public transport ticketing schemes is hereby specified for the purposes of section 6 of the Act.

   (2) For the purpose of this Order a public transport ticketing scheme is one or more of the following:

     (a) a written agreement between operators to the extent that it provides for members of the public to purchase, in a single transaction, a multi-operator travelcard;

     (b) a written agreement between operators to the extent that it provides for members of the public to purchase, in a single transaction, a through ticket;

     (c) a written agreement between operators to the extent that it provides for members of the public to purchase, in a single transaction, a multi-operator individual ticket;

     (d) a written agreement between operators to the extent that it provides for members of the public to purchase, in a single transaction, a short distance add-on;

     (e) a written agreement between one or more operators and one or more long distance operators to the extent that it provides for members of the public to purchase, in a single transaction, a long distance add-on;

5.   This block exemption has effect subject to the conditions and the obligation specified in Articles 6 to 17.

Conditions and consequences of breach of conditions

6.   Unless there is an objective, transparent and non-discriminatory reason, a public transport ticketing scheme shall not, directly or indirectly, in isolation or in combination with other factors under the control of the parties:

     (a) have the object or effect of preventing any operator or potential operator from participating in that public transport ticketing scheme; or

   (b) to the extent that the scheme provides for members of the public to purchase a long distance add-on, have the object or effect of preventing any operator, potential operator, long distance operator or potential long distance operator from participating in that public transport ticketing scheme.

7. A public transport ticketing scheme shall not, directly or indirectly, in isolation or in combination with other factors under the control of the parties, have the object or effect of limiting:

   (a) the variety or number of routes on which any operator or long distance operator provides or may provide public transport services; or

   (b) the freedom of operators or long distance operators to set the price or availability of, the fare structure relating to, or the zones or geographical validity applicable for, any ticket entitling the holder to make a journey solely on the public transport services of any one operator or any one long distance operator.

8. A public transport ticketing scheme shall not, directly or indirectly, in isolation or in combination with other factors under the control of the parties, have the object or effect or limiting the frequency or timing of any public transport services operated by any operator or long distance operator, unless such restriction is indispensable to the effective operation of that scheme, pursuant to an agreement which provides for onward travel connections for passengers.

9.—(1) Subject to paragraph (2), a public transport ticketing scheme shall not, directly or indirectly, in isolation or in combination with other factors under the control of the parties, have the object or effect of facilitating an exchange of information between the parties to that public transport ticketing scheme.

(2) Paragraph (1) shall not prevent an exchange of information between the parties to a public transport ticketing scheme which is directly related and indispensable to the effective operation of that scheme, provided that the relevant provision under which the information is exchanged is objective, transparent and non-discriminatory and that it does not breach any of the other conditions imposed by this Order.

10. Breach of any of the conditions imposed by any of Articles 6, 7, 8 or 9 shall have the effect of cancelling the block exemption in respect of that public transport ticketing scheme.

11. The parties to a public transport ticketing scheme, which provides for members of the public to purchase a multi-operator travelcard, shall not distribute between themselves the revenue received by virtue of the operation of that scheme in a way that provides the parties with an incentive to set their own fares higher than they would have been set in the absence of the multi-operator travelcard, or significantly reduces the incentive for each of the parties to compete for passengers.

12. Breach of the condition imposed by Article 11 shall have the effect of cancelling the block exemption in respect of the relevant public transport ticketing scheme to the extent that such scheme provides for members of the public to purchase a multi-operator travelcard.

13. (1) Subject to paragraph (2), a public transport ticketing scheme which provides for members of the public to purchase a through ticket, multi-operator individual ticket, short distance add-on or long distance add-on, shall not directly or indirectly, in isolation or in combination with other factors under the control of the parties have the object or effect of fixing a price at which the respective through ticket, multi-operator individual ticket, short distance add-on or long distance add-on is offered for sale.

(2) Paragraph (1) shall not prevent:

   (a) the parties to a public transport ticketing scheme from agreeing to charge each other non-discriminatory posted prices for sales of the respective through ticket, short distance add-on or long distance add-on; or

   (b) operators from fixing the price of a multi-operator travelcard which may be purchased as a short distance add-on or long distance add-on provided that such action does not breach any of the other conditions imposed by this Order.

14. Breach of the condition imposed by Article 13 shall have the effect of cancelling the block exemption in respect of the relevant public transport ticketing scheme to the extent that such scheme provides for members of the public to purchase the relevant through ticket, multi-operator individual ticket, short distance add-on or long distance add-on.

15. The parties to a public transport ticketing scheme which provides for members of the public to purchase a multi-operator individual ticket, shall not:

    (b) distribute between themselves the revenue received by virtue of the operation of that scheme other than pursuant to terms contained in that scheme whereby the operator which sells any particular multi-operator individual ticket retains exclusively all the revenue received from that sale.

16. Breach of the condition imposed by Article 15 shall have the effect of cancelling the block exemption in respect of the relevant public transport ticketing scheme to the extent that such scheme provides for members of the public to purchase a multi-operator individual ticket.

Obligation

17. A person shall, within ten working days from the date on which it receives notice in writing under this Article, supply to the Director such information in connection with those public transport ticketing schemes to which it is a party as the Director may require.

Cancellation by notice

18. If there is a failure to comply with the obligation imposed by Article 17 without reasonable excuse, the Director may, subject to Article 20, by notice in writing cancel this block exemption in respect of any public transport ticketing scheme to which the relevant request for information under Article 17 relates.

19. If the Director considers that a particular public transport ticketing scheme is not one to which section 9 of the Act applies, he may, subject to Article 20, by notice in writing cancel this block exemption in respect of that scheme.

20. If the Director proposes to cancel the block exemption in accordance with Article 18 or Article 19, he shall first give notice in writing of his proposal and shall consider any representations made to him.

21. For the purpose of Articles 18, 19 and 20, notice in writing is given by:

    (a) the Director giving notice in writing of his decision or proposal to those persons whom he can reasonably identify as being parties to the relevant public transport ticketing scheme; or

    (b) where it is not reasonably practicable for the Office of Fair Trading to comply with paragraph (a), the Office of Fair Trading publishing a summary of its decision or proposal in the register and causing a reference to that summary to be published in—

    (i) the London, Edinburgh and Belfast Gazettes;

    (ii) at least one national daily newspaper; and

    (iii) if there is in circulation an appropriate trade journal which is published at intervals not exceeding one month, in such trade journal,

    stating the facts on which he bases it and his reasons for making it.

EXPLANATORY NOTE

(This note is not part of the Order)

This Order is a block exemption Order under section 6 of the Competition Act 1998 ('the Act'). It gives effect to the Director General of Fair Trading's recommendation that public transport ticketing schemes (as defined in the Order) for local public transport services constitute a category of agreements which are likely to be agreements to which section 9 of the Act applies. Agreements which fall within the category specified in the block exemption Order are exempt from the prohibition in Chapter I of the Act.

The recommendation was made by the Director following consultation in accordance with section 8(1) of the Act.

The block exemption has effect subject to certain conditions and obligations and concerns particularly agreements between local public transport operators (and in one case, together with long distance public transport operators) which provide for the purchase, in a single transaction, of:

(a) multi-operator travelcards (MTCs)

(b) through tickets (TTs)

(c) multi-operator individual tickets (MITs)

(d) short distance add-ons

(e) long distance add-ons

as defined in the Order.

B: Exclusions

One aspect of the new regime, which has no express counterpart in Community competition law, is excluded agreements. Schedules 1–3 to the CA 1998 lists certain types of agreements to which the Chapter I prohibition does not apply; the details are expanded in the OFT guideline:

Agreements and concerted practices

www.oft.gov.uk/advice_and_resources/publications/guidance/competiton-act/

OFT 401, paras 6.2–6.3 [footnotes omitted]

6.2 Schedules 1–3 of the Act specifically exclude from the Chapter I prohibition certain categories of agreement:

- an agreement to the extent to which it would result in a merger or joint venture within the merger provisions of the Enterprise Act 2002 (see the Enterprise Act publication *Mergers: substantive assessment guidance* (OFT506) for further detail)
- an agreement which would result in a concentration with a Community dimension and thereby be subject to the EC Merger Regulation
- an agreement which is subject to competition scrutiny under the Financial Services and Markets Act 2000, the Broadcasting Act 1990 or the Communications Act 2003
- an agreement which is required in order to comply with, and to the extent that it is, a planning obligation
- (until 1 May 2005) an agreement to the extent that it is a land agreement, as defined in the Competition (Land and Vertical Agreements) Exclusion Order 2000 (see the competition law guideline *Land agreements* (OFT420) for further detail)
- (from 1 May 2005) an agreement to the extent that it is a land agreement, as defined in the Competition Act 1998 (Land Agreements Exclusion and Revocation) Order 2004 (see the competition law guideline *Land agreements* (OFT 420) for further detail)
- (until 1 May 2005) an agreement to the extent that it is a vertical agreement, as defined in the Competition Act 1998 (Land and Vertical Agreements) Exclusion Order 2000, and does not have the object or effect of fixing resale prices (see the competition law guideline *Vertical agreements* (OFT419) for further detail)
- (until 1 May 2007) an agreement which is the subject of a direction under section 21(2) of the Restrictive Trade Practices Act 1976
- an agreement for the constitution of a European Economic Area regulated market, to the extent that it relates to the rules made or guidance issued by that market
- an agreement made by an undertaking entrusted with the operation of services of general economic interest or having the character of a revenue-producing monopoly, insofar as the prohibition would obstruct the performance of the particular tasks assigned to the undertaking (see the competition law guideline *Services of general economic interest* (OFT421))

- an agreement to the extent to which it is made to comply with a legal requirement
- an agreement which is necessary to avoid conflict with international obligations and which is also the subject of an order by the Secretary of State
- an agreement which is necessary for compelling reasons of public policy and which is also the subject of an order by the Secretary of State
- an agreement where it relates to production of, or trade in, 'agricultural products' as defined in the EC Treaty and in Council Regulation (EEC) No 26/62, or to farmers' co-operatives.

The Secretary of State has the power to add, amend or remove exclusions in certain circumstances.

6.3 A domestic exclusion does not exclude agreements or conduct from applicable EC law: any agreements or conduct affecting trade between Member States that are excluded under the Act remain subject to Article 81. Accordingly, should conduct or agreements affecting trade between Member States infringe Article 81, all the usual consequences will follow, irrespective of any domestic exclusion.

NOTE: As the guideline notes, at para. 6.1, effectively some agreements are excluded from the ambit of Article 81, including agreements which fall within the EC Merger Regulation, as discussed in Chapter 12. Schedule 4 originally provided for the exclusion of a range of designated professional services from the scope of the prohibition, but it was repealed by the Enterprise Act 2002.

The guidance makes specific reference to land agreements and vertical agreements. Land agreements do not generally give rise to competition concerns and the OFT's guideline on *Land agreements*, OFT 420, explains that the purpose of the Exclusion Order is to provide certainty for business concerning the scope of the Chapter I prohibition. What is meant by a land agreement?

Land agreements

OFT 420, paras 2.2–2.4

2.2 The Exclusion Order defines a **land agreement** in terms of:
- the creation, alteration, transfer or termination of an interest in land; and
- certain obligations and restrictions.

These elements are considered below.

Interest in land

2.3 A land agreement is defined in the Exclusion Order as an agreement which creates, alters, transfers or terminates an interest in land. Only those parts of an agreement which have such results benefit from the exclusion (see further paragraph 3.3 below). A land agreement includes, for example, transfers of freeholds, leases or assignments of leasehold interests and easements. The term **interest in land** is defined in the Exclusion Order. This covers what is usually understood to be an interest in land and includes licences, and, in Scotland, interests under a lease and other heritable rights in or over land including heritable securities. The exclusion also covers agreements to enter into land agreements.

2.4 The exclusion does not cover agreements which relate to land but which do not create, alter, transfer or terminate an interest in land. An agreement, for example, between landowners in a particular area to fix levels of rent to be charged to tenants or an agreement between tenants as to the nature of goods they will each sell in a particular area, are not land agreements as defined in the Exclusion Order because they do not create, alter, transfer or terminate an interest in land. Therefore, they do not benefit from the exclusion.

NOTE: There is no equivalent exclusion from the prohibition contained in Article 81. The most controversial issue in relation to exclusions from the prohibition concerns vertical agreements, a topic discussed in greater detail in Chapter 8. When the CA 1998 was introduced, it was considered that with the exception of a limited number of agreements such as those involving resale price maintenance, vertical agreements were generally benign and raised limited competition concerns. Accordingly, the vast majority of vertical agreements were excluded from the prohibition by the Competition Act 1998 (Land and Vertical Agreements Exclusion Order 2000 (SI 2000/310). Subsequently, following the introduction of Regulation 1/2003, given that the OFT would be required to apply both prohibition regimes in tandem, the Order excluding vertical agreements from the Chapter I prohibition was repealed. Therefore, the Vertical Agreements Regulation 1999, as discussed in Chapter 8, requires to be considered in relation to all vertical agreements, either directly or by parallel application (see above) even where inter-state trade is not affected.

SECTION 5: CONSEQUENCES OF INFRINGEMENT

A: Voidness

Section 2(4) CA 1998 provides, 'Any agreement or decision which is prohibited by subsection (1) is void.'

As under EC law, only those elements of an agreement which are prohibited under s. 2 will be void, provided of course it is possible, as a matter of the general law of contract, to sever the offending clauses from the main body of the agreement. See, for instance, *Calor Gas Ltd* v *Express Fuels (Scotland) Ltd* [2008] CSOH 13, where an action for damages was raised by Calor Gas Ltd against a dealer which had terminated their principal dealer agreement and subsequently entered a dealership with a rival supplier. Relying upon the *Delimitis* principles, the defence that the exclusivity arrangement for a minimum period of five years rendered the agreement void under Article 81(1) was successful.

B: Sanctions

Financial penalties may be imposed for an infringement of Chapter I and these may be up to 10 per cent of annual turnover. The *OFT's guidance as to the appropriate amount of a penalty*, OFT 423, sets out how the amount is calculated and any mitigating circumstances to be considered. Penalties for infringement of either the Chapter I or Chapter II prohibition are discussed in Chapter 3 and the broader issue of deterring cartels and the range of sanctions that may be employed by the authorities, including criminal prosecutions and Director Disqualification Orders, both introduced under the EA 2002, are discussed in greater detail in Chapter 9.

■ QUESTION

To what extent has the introduction of the Chapter I prohibition in the CA 1998 effected a dramatic reform in UK competition law on anti-competitive agreements?

FURTHER READING

Rodger, B.J., and MacCulloch, A. (eds), *The UK Competition Act: A New Era for UK Competition Law*, Oxford, Hart, 2000; in particular:

Chapter 1, Whish, R., 'The Competition Act 1998 and the prior debate on reform';

Chapter 4, MacNeil, I., 'Investigations under the Competition Act 1998';

Chapter 8, Rodger, B.J., and MacCulloch, A., 'The Chapter I prohibition: prohibiting cartels? Or permitting vertical? Or both?'

8

Vertical restraints

What are vertical restraints? Vertical agreements are agreements concluded between undertakings operating at different levels of a market, for example between the producer of a product and a retailer. Vertical restraints are the contractual restrictions employed in such agreements. Vertical restraints deserve special mention because of the vital role that vertical agreements have in the distribution chain and because they are often essential to the proper workings of a market. Vertical agreements are therefore correctly subject to differential treatment from that of horizontal agreements. Nonetheless vertical restraints can legitimately give rise to anti-competitive concerns, and hence a careful balancing exercise is required.

The application of the Community competition rules to vertical restraints has been considerably stricter than, for instance, those in the US, with the exception of price-fixing, which had been per se illegal in both the US and the EU, until the US Supreme Court ruling in *Leegin Creative Leather Products, Inc* v *PSKS, Inc* 551 US 551 (2007). The Community's strict approach can be partly explained by the threat that vertical restraints pose for the underlying objective of market integration. The appointment of exclusive distributors on a Member State basis contributes to the partitioning of the single market, as well as creating barriers to entry for a new producer to enter the market and has been firmly challenged by the Commission, see, e.g. Joined Cases 56 and 58/64 *Consten and Grundig* [1966] ECR 299, [1966] CMLR 418. The Court of Justice has however demonstrated a readiness to consider economic justifications for vertical restriction, see, e.g. Case 258/78 *Nungesser (LC) KG and Kurt Eisele* v *Commission* [1982] ECR 2015, [1983] 1 CMLR 278 and Case 42/84 *Remia BV* v *Commission* [1985] ECR 2545, [1987] 1 CMLR 1. The Commission's traditionally hostile attitude towards vertical restraints was subject to severe criticism by industry, economists, and legal practitioners and academics, but has been tempered by the adoption of Block Exemption Regulation 2790/1999, which introduced a more effects-based approach to the scrutiny of vertical restraints under Article 81 EC. As will be seen, Regulation 2790/1999 replaced a form-based approach to determining the legality of particular clauses within vertical agreements, but this Regulation is due to expire in May 2010 and the Commission has already begun the process of reviewing how it operates and whether it should be renewed.

Our discussion of the legality of vertical restraints begins with an analysis of the economic debate.

SECTION 2: THE ECONOMIC DEBATE

Vertical restraints can produce either positive or negative effects. They can, for instance, restrict intra-brand competition (competition between market operators at the same level of market and in relation to the same brand). This is a particular concern in selective and exclusive distribution systems where such restraints can lead to a reduction in consumer choice and higher prices. For example, the nature of selective and exclusive distribution in the European car industry is widely believed to be the reason for the disparity in car prices across the EU and the lack of intra-brand competition in the market (see Block Exemption Regulation 1400/2002, and the Commission's 2009 'Issues Paper on the Motor Vehicle Block Exemption Regulation'). It is clear, however, that vertical agreements can also work to stimulate inter-brand competition (competition between different brands of competing products), encouraging the entry of new products on the market and enhancing consumer welfare. Note for example, the US Supreme Court's attitude towards inter-brand competition: 'Interbrand competition...is the primary concern of antitrust law....When interbrand competition exists...it provides a significant check on the exploitation of intrabrand market power because of the ability of consumers to substitute a different brand of the same product', *Continental TV Inc* v *GTE Sylvania Inc* 433 US 36 (1977) p. 581.

Given the importance of vertical restraints in competition policy, it is not surprising that there has been considerable academic debate on this issue. There are essentially two schools of thought. Proponents of the powerful Chicago school, notably Bork and Posner, advocate a non-interventionist approach towards vertical restraints and have based their favourable approach on the free rider rationale as explained by Gyselen.

Gyselen, L., 'Vertical Restraints in the Distribution Process: Strength and Weakness of the Free Rider Rationale under EEC Competition Law'
21 CML Rev (1984) 647

The free rider argument is above all a dealer service argument and is most powerful with respect to luxury or technically complex products. Restraints upon intrabrand competition can be designed to prevent 'parasite' dealers from taking a free ride on the promotional or servicing efforts of other dealers offering the same brand. Insofar as the restraints prevent the former from reaping where they have not sown, they induce the latter to continue their presale promotion (advertising, display, demonstration) and post sale servce (maintenance, repair). They will therefore enhance the brand's competitive position in a market governed *arguendo* by substantial non-price competition. Hence, restraints upon intrabrand competition have the redeeming virtue of promoting interbrand competition.

Bork's contribution to the economic debate has been particularly important.

Bork, R.H., *The Antitrust Paradox: A Policy at War with Itself*
Oxford, Maxwell Macmillan, 1993, pp. 297–8

We have seen that vertical price fixing (resale price maintenance), vertical market division (closed dealer territories), and, indeed, all vertical restraints are beneficial to consumers and should for that reason be completely lawful. Basic economic theory tells us that the manufacturer who imposes such restraints cannot intend to restrict and must (except in the rare case of price discrimination, which the law should regard as neutral) intend to create efficiency. The most common efficiency is the inducement or purchase by the manufacturer of extra reseller sales, service or promotional effort.

The proposal to legalize all truly vertical restraints is so much at variance with conventional thought on the topic that it will doubtless strike many readers as troublesome, if not bizarre. But I have never seen any economic analysis that shows how manufacturer-imposed resale price maintenance, closed dealer territories, customer allocation clauses, or the like can have the net effect of restricting output. We have too quickly assumed something that appears untrue.

Perhaps the ambiguity of the word 'restraint' accounts for some of our confusion on this topic. When the Supreme Court speaks of a restraint it often, or even usually, refers to the manufacturer's control of certain activities of his resellers or to the elimination by the manufacturer of some forms of rivalry among his resellers. There is, of course, nothing sinister or unusual about using 'restraint' in that sense. It is merely a form of vertical integration by contract, a less complete integration than that which would obtain if the manufacturer owned his outlets and directed their activities. It is merely one instance of the coordination of economic activities which is ubiquitous in the economic world and upon which our wealth depends. The important point is that such vertical control never creates 'restraint' in that other common meaning, restriction of output. Perhaps, if we are more careful about the ambiguity of the word and make it clear in which sense we use it, our reasoning about antitrust problems, including the problem of vertical restraints, will improve.

NOTE: Bork's thesis that all vertical agreements should be lawful on the grounds of efficiency is significantly out of step with legal and economic debate in the US and Europe, which tends to focus on whether particular vertical restraints should be per se illegal or subject to a 'rule of reason' analysis. Comanor suggests that the key consideration is whether vertical restraints are in the consumer interest.

Comanor, W.S., 'Vertical Price-fixing, Vertical Market Restrictions and the New Antitrust Policy'

98 Harvard L Rev 983 (1984–85) at pp. 1000–2

When vertical restraints are used to promote the provision of distribution services, the critical issue for antitrust purposes remains whether consumers are better served by lower prices and fewer services or by higher prices and more services. In its *Spray-Rite* brief, the Department of Justice suggested that pure vertical restraints always lead to increased consumer welfare. This position is unfounded, and a more hostile treatment of vertical restraints is appropriate.

Because vertical restraints can either enhance or diminish consumer welfare, depending upon the situation; it is tempting to apply the rule of reason on a case-by-case basis. After all, restraints that augment consumer welfare should be deemed 'reasonable' under existing antitrust standards. Yet it is no easy task to determine whether particular restraints increase or decrease efficiency: the answer in each case depends largely on the relative preferences of different groups of consumers. In the interests of judicial economy, therefore, it may be more expeditious to set general policy standards, even though they will sometimes lead to improper results.

Vertical restraints that concern established products are more likely to reduce consumer welfare. Large numbers of consumers are already familiar with such products and are therefore unlikely to place much value on acquiring further information about them. In this context, stringent antitrust standards should be applied to vertical price and non-price restraints alike. This approach could take the form either of a direct per se prohibition, or of a modified rule of reason analysis under which the defendant would be required to demonstrate that the restraints have benefited consumers generally. By contrast, in the case of new products or products of new entrants into the market, vertical restraints are less likely to lessen consumer welfare, because their novelty should create greater demand for information. In these circumstances, the restraints should be permissible, or at least should be treated more leniently in any modified rule of reason analysis.

NOTE: The 'battle for the soul of antitrust' continues. In the context of vertical agreements, however, a consensus has emerged among economists that vertical agreements do not generally give rise to competition concerns unless one of the parties to the agreement has significant market power, or there exists a large network of similar agreements with the possibility of foreclosure. See for example, Case 234/89 *Delimitis* v *Henninger Bräu* [1991] ECR I-935, [1992] 5 CMLR 210. This approach has been adopted by the European Commission since the late 1990s, as reflected in its Green Paper on Vertical Restraints (COM (96) 721 final) and the Block Exemption Regulation on vertical agreements, discussed below.

SECTION 3: VERTICAL RESTRAINTS AND ARTICLE 81(1) EC

A: Community case law

Article 81(1) EC provides the basic framework for the treatment of vertical restraints in Community law. Article 82 EC has a limited role in Community policy on vertical restraints.

The broad scope of Article 81(1) EC, catching all agreements that prevent, restrict, or distort competition means that most vertical agreements fall within the general prohibition, but may benefit from the application of a block exemption or individual exception under Article 81(3) EC. The operation of Article 81(3) was significantly revised by Regulation 1/2003, which abolished the previous centralized system of notification and authorization. Article 81(3) EC is now directly effective and applied by national competition authorities and national courts, as well as the Commission. See Chapter 2.

The application of Article 81(1) EC to vertical agreements has proved controversial, particularly the approach to territorial restraints, which the Commission has tended to regard as restrictions of competition regardless of their market effects. This strict approach is largely attributable to the Commission's objective of furthering market integration. The seminal decision of the Court in Joined Cases 56 and 58/64 *Consten and Grundig* illustrates the Community's concern to preserve parallel trade at the expense of economic and pro-competitive considerations. The background to this case is discussed in Chapter 6. The Court accepted the Commission's findings that absolute territorial protection, which sought to prevent any parallel imports of the contract goods, is prohibited under Article 81(1) EC, but stressed that the Commission should not have prohibited the whole agreement. Thus, the provision of territorial exclusivity does not in itself infringe Article 81(1) EC.

Amato explains the Community position.

Amato, G., *Antitrust and the Bounds of Power: The Dilemma of Liberal Democracy in the History of the Market*
Oxford, Hart Publishing, 1997, pp. 48–9

The parties maintained, first before the Commission itself and then before the Court of Justice, that Article 85 referred primarily to inter-brand competition, and that as far as intra-brand restrictions went, one had to presume efficiency in promoting inter-brand competition failing proof of the contrary. This argument copied word-for-word approaches of the Chicago School, which in fact at the time the American courts themselves had rejected, in the name of protection (dropped later in the *Sylvania* case) for the right of each distributor or retailer to exercise freedom of trade without restraint.

Our Court did not accept the arguments either, but for very different reasons. It accepted that inter-brand competition was the most relevant for the purposes of prohibition under Article 85, but added that this did not *a priori* exempt intra-brand restrictions, with the consequence— inconceivable today (and perhaps in earlier times too) for an American court—that the fact that the Commission was not concerned to ascertain the size of inter-brand competition was irrelevant. On this basis, the absolute territorial protection by which the exclusivity for France was guaranteed was illegitimate. It is indeed true, said the Court, that imports have an effect on the supply planning that Consten may engage in and on the organization of services it may offer customers. But a margin of risk is inherent in commercial activity, and in any case 'the more manufacturers isolate themselves from each other in consumers' eyes, the more competition among them is reduced. Moreover, competition among wholesale distributors of products of one and the same brand enlivens the downstream market of sales to final consumers'.

As we can see, these are very important assertions of principle that bring the decision close to the American ones of the 1960s. But there are two important differences, one explicit and the other implicit. The explicit one is that the need for intra-brand competition is based on protection not of an individual right (freedom of trade) but of a general and objective principle (competitiveness of the market in all its segments). The implicit one is that such a pervasive and rigorous principle is asserted to the extent that it serves to protect another principle, a higher one in 1966, that of market integration. For the territory protected by Consten's rigid exclusivity coincided with that of the French State, and both the Commission and the Court saw this protection as persistence of the segmentation of economic activities along national frontiers, violating the 'Grundnorm' of the whole Community system.

NOTE: Certainly the goal of full market integration must have seemed a distant dream in 1962 and the Court's strict approach is perhaps understandable. There was a notable relaxation of Community policy on vertical restraints following the Court's decision in *Consten and Grundig*. Although the Commission continued to outlaw any restriction conferring exclusivity or absolute territorial protection, it introduced a series of block exemption Regulations, which enabled legal advisers to draft distribution agreements according to established Commission policy. Thus distribution agreements continued to be prohibited in terms of Article 81(1) EC, but benefited from a block exemption under Article 81(3) EC. The Commission finally issued a block exemption for exclusive distribution agreements in 1967, Regulation 67/67, which offered companies some legal certainty, avoiding the need for notification. Exclusive distribution agreements now fall under the umbrella of block exemption Regulation 2790/1999.

In contrast to the Commission's approach, the Court indicated that it would countenance some restrictions based on an economic analysis of the effects of an agreement, provided the restrictions did not go beyond what was necessary to secure the commercial viability of the arrangement. This became known as the '*ancillary restraints*' doctrine. There have been a number of cases on this issue, mostly in the context of selective distribution. In Case 258/78 *Nungesser* v *Commission* the Court quashed the Commission's finding that an exclusive licence of plant breeders' rights infringed Article 81(1) as the Commission had failed to take into account that 'open exclusivity' might be reasonable in the circumstances to secure the considerable financial investment which was required to develop the product.

Nungesser v *Commission*
(Case 258/78) [1982] ECR 2015, [1983] 1 CMLR 278

The Court was asked to annul the Commission's decision relating to the lawfulness of an exclusive licence agreement.

B—The application of Article 85 of the EEC Treaty to exclusive licences

44 By this submission the applicants criticize the Commission for wrongly taking the view that an exclusive licence of breeders' rights must by its very nature be treated as an agreement prohibited by Article 85(1) of the Treaty. They submit that the Commission's opinion in that respect

is unfounded in so far as the exclusive licence constitutes the sole means, as regards seeds which have been recently developed in a Member State and which have not yet penetrated the market of another Member State, of promoting competition between the new product and comparable products in that other Member State; indeed, no grower or trader would take the risk of launching the new product on a new market if he were not protected against direct competition from the holder of the breeders' rights and from his other licensees.

45 This contention is supported by the German and British Governments and by the *Caisse de Gestion des Licences Végétales*. In particular, the two governments claim that the general character of the reasons given for the contested decision is incompatible with the terms of Article 85 of the Treaty and conflicts with a sensible competition policy. The reasons given for the decision are said to be based on the ill-conceived premise that every exclusive licence of an industrial or commercial property right, whatever its nature, must be regarded as an agreement prohibited by Article 85(1) and that it is therefore for the Commission to judge whether, in a given case, the conditions for the grant of an exemption under Article 85 (3) are satisfied.

...

53 It should be observed that those two sets of considerations relate to two legal situations which are not necessarily identical. The first case concerns a so-called open exclusive licence or assignment and the exclusivity of the licence relates solely to the contractual relationship between the owner of the right and the licensee, whereby the owner merely undertakes not to grant other licences in respect of the same territory and not to compete himself with the licensee on that territory. On the other hand, the second case involves an exclusive licence or assignment with absolute territorial protection, under which the parties to the contract propose, as regards the products and the territory in question, to eliminate all competition from third parties, such as parallel importers or licensees for other territories.

54 That point having been clarified, it is necessary to examine whether, in the present case, the exclusive nature of the licence, in so far as it is an open licence, has the effect of preventing or distorting competition within the meaning of Article 85(1) of the Treaty.

55 In that respect the Government of the Federal Republic of Germany emphasized that the protection of agricultural innovations by means of breeders' rights constitutes a means of encouraging such innovations and the grant of exclusive rights for a limited period, is capable of providing a further incentive to innovative efforts.

From that it infers that a total prohibition of every exclusive licence, even an open one, would cause the interest of undertakings in licences to fall away, which would be prejudicial to the dissemination of knowledge and techniques in the Community.

56 The exclusive licence which forms the subject-matter of the contested decision concerns the cultivation and marketing of hybrid maize seeds which were developed by INRA after years of research and experimentation and were unknown to German farmers at the time when the cooperation between INRA and the applicants was taking shape. For that reason the concern shown by the interveners as regards the protection of new technology is justified.

57 In fact, in the case of a licence of breeders' rights over hybrid maize seeds newly developed in one Member State, an undertaking established in another Member State which was not certain that it would not encounter competition from other licensees for the territory granted to it, or from the owner of the right himself, might be deterred from accepting the risk of cultivating and marketing that product; such a result would be damaging to the dissemination of a new technology and would prejudice competition in the Community between the new product and similar existing products.

58 Having regard to the specific nature of the products in question, the Court concludes that, in a case such as the present, the grant of an open exclusive licence, that is to say a licence which does not affect the position of third parties such as parallel importers and licensees for other territories, is not in itself incompatible with Article 85(1) of the Treaty.

59 Part B of the third submission is thus justified to the extent to which it concerns that aspect of the exclusive nature of the licence.

60 As regard to the position of third parties, the Commission in essence criticizes the parties to the contract for having extended the definition of exclusivity to importers who are not bound

> to the contract, in particular parallel importers. Parallel importers or exporters, such as Louis David KG in Germany and Robert Bomberault in France who offered INRA seed for sale to German buyers, had found themselves subjected to pressure and legal proceedings by INRA, Frasema and the applicants, the purpose of which was to maintain the exclusive position of the applicants on the German market.
>
> 61 The Court has consistently held (cf. Joined Cases 56 and 58/64 *Consten and Grundig* v *Commission* [1966] ECR 299) that absolute territorial protection granted to a licensee in order to enable parallel imports to be controlled and prevented results in the artificial maintenance of separate national markets, contrary to the Treaty.

NOTE: It should be clear by now that the Court will condone an open exclusive licence where the exclusivity can be justified on commercial grounds, but will not tolerate absolute territorial protection. For further discussion of absolute territorial restrictions in distribution contracts, see Lidgard, H.H., 'Territorial Restrictions in Vertical Relations' (1997) 21 World Competition 71.

Clearly the application of the ancillary restraints doctrine established in *Nungesser* depends on the circumstances in each case and in particular the nature of the product. In Case 42/84 *Remia* [1985] ECR 2545, [1987] 1 CMLR 1, the Court held that a restriction on a seller not to compete with a business sold with its goodwill does not infringe Article 81(1) provided it is reasonably limited in time and geographical extent. In Case 161/84 *Pronuptia* the Court adopted the '*Nungesser* principle' in respect of certain restrictions, this time in the context of a franchising agreement, and accepted that sometimes such restrictions are necessary to maintain the identity and reputation of a franchising network.

Pronuptia de Paris GmbH v *Pronuptia de Paris Irmgaard Schillgalis*
(Case 161/84) [1986] ECR 353, [1986] 1 CMLR 414

In an Article 234 EC reference the question put to the Court of Justice by the German court was 'Is Article [81(1)] (ex 85(1)) of the Treaty applicable to franchise agreements such as the contracts between the parties, which have as their object the establishment of a special distribution system whereby the franchisor provides to the franchisee, in addition to goods, certain trade names, trademarks, merchandising material and services?'

> 27 In view of the foregoing, the answer to the first question must be that:
> (1) The compatibility of franchise agreements for the distribution of goods with Article 85 (1) depends on the provisions contained therein and on their economic context.
> (2) Provisions which are strictly necessary in order to ensure that the know-how and assistance provided by the franchisor do not benefit competitors do not constitute restrictions of competition for the purposes of Article 85(1).
> (3) Provisions which establish the control strictly necessary for maintaining the identity and reputation of the network identified by the common name or symbol do not constitute restrictions of competition for the purposes of Article 85(1).
> (4) Provisions which share markets between the franchisor and the franchisees or between franchisees constitute restrictions of competition for the purposes of Article 85(1).
> (5) The fact that the franchisor makes price recommendations to the franchisee does not constitute a restriction of competition, so long as there is no concerted practice between the franchisor and the franchisees or between the franchisees themselves for the actual application of such prices.
> (6) Franchise agreements for the distribution of goods which contain provisions sharing markets between the franchisor and the franchisees or between franchisees are capable of affecting trade between Member States.

NOTE: Shortly after this decision the Commission published a block exemption Regulation on franchise agreements, Regulation 4087/88 (Commission Regulation (EEC) No 4087/88 of 30

November 1988 on the application of Article 85(3) of the Treaty to categories of franchise agreements [OJ, 1988, No L359/46]). This has now been superseded by block exemption Regulation 2790/1999.

Another form of distribution commonly used throughout the Community is selective distribution whereby (a) a producer limits the sale of his products to appointed distributors chosen according to certain qualitative and quantitative criteria; and (b) appointed distributors are not permitted to resell to anyone other than the other appointed distributors, end users, or consumers. Selective distribution tends to be limited to branded products which are either highly technical and require qualified staff to advise customers, e.g. computers, or are luxury goods, e.g. perfume or cosmetics, which demand protection. The legal framework applicable to selective distribution was established in *Metro (No 1)*.

Metro-SB-Grossmärkte GmbH v *Commission (No 1)*

(Case 26/76) [1977] ECR 1875, [1978] 2 CMLR 1

SABA manufactured televisions, radios, and tape-recorders, which it distributed through a selective distribution network. Only specialist dealers who could meet SABA's selection criteria could sell the products. Metro was refused admission to the network on the basis that it failed to meet SABA's criteria. The Commission held that Article 81(1) EC did not apply to certain aspects of the selective distribution network and granted an exemption in respect of the other provisions caught by Article 81(1) EC. Metro appealed to the Court against the Commission's decision to grant an exemption to SABA under Article 230 EC.

19 The applicant maintains that Article 2 of the contested Decision is vitiated by misuse of powers inasmuch as the Commission has failed to recognize 'what is protected under Article 85 (namely) freedom of competition for the benefit of the consumer, not the coincident interests of a manufacturer and a given group of traders who wish to secure selling prices which are considered to be satisfactory by the latter'.

Furthermore, if it were to be considered that an exemption from the prohibition might be granted in respect of the distribution system in dispute pursuant to Article 85(3), the applicant maintains that the Commission has misapplied that provision by granting an exemption in respect of restrictions on competition which are not indispensable to the attainment of the objectives of improving production or distribution or promoting technical or economic progress and which lead to the elimination of competition from self-service wholesale traders.

A—misuse of powers

20 The requirement contained in Articles 3 and 85 of the EEC Treaty that competition shall not be distorted implies the existence on the market of workable competition, that is to say the degree of competition necessary to ensure the observance of the basic requirements and the attainment of the objectives of the Treaty, in particular the creation of a single market achieving conditions similar to those of a domestic market.

In accordance with this requirement the nature and intensiveness of competition may vary to an extent dictated by the products or services in question and the economic structure of the relevant market sectors.

In the sector covering the production of high quality and technically advanced consumer durables, where a relatively small number of large—and medium-scale producers offer a varied range of items which, or so consumers may consider, are readily interchangeable, the structure of the market does not preclude the existence of a variety of channels of distribution adapted to the peculiar characteristics of the various producers and to the requirements of the various categories of consumers.

On this view the Commission was justified in recognizing that selective distribution systems constituted, together with others, an aspect of competition which accords with Article 85(1), provided that resellers are chosen on the basis of objective criteria of a qualitative nature relating to the technical qualifications of the reseller and his staff and the suitability of his trading premises and that such conditions are laid down uniformly for all potential resellers and are not applied in a discriminatory fashion.

21 It is true that in such systems of distribution price competition is not generally emphasized either as an exclusive or indeed as a principal factor.

This is particularly so when, as in the present case, access to the distribution network is subject to conditions exceeding the requirements of an appropriate distribution of the products.

However, although price competition is so important that it can never be eliminated it does not constitute the only effective form of competition or that to which absolute priority must in all circumstances be accorded.

The powers conferred upon the Commission under Article 85(3) show that the requirements for the maintenance of workable competition may be reconciled with the safeguarding of objectives of a different nature and that to this end certain restrictions on competition are permissible, provided that they are essential to the attainment of those objectives and that they do not result in the elimination of competition for a substantial part of the common market.

For specialist wholesalers and retailers the desire to maintain a certain price level, which corresponds to the desire to preserve, in the interests of consumers, the possibility of the continued existence of this channel of distribution in conjunction with new methods of distribution based on a different type of competition policy, forms one of the objectives which may be pursued without necessarily falling under the prohibition contained in Article 85(1), and, if it does fall thereunder, either wholly or in part, coming within the framework of Article 85(3).

This argument is strengthened if, in addition, such conditions promote improved competition inasmuch as it relates to factors other than prices.

NOTE: As with the other vertical restraints already discussed, selective distribution clauses are also covered by Regulation 2790/1999, although preceding jurisprudence from the Community courts continues to have relevance.

B: Comparison with the US rule of reason

The development of the '*Nungesser* principle' led some commentators to call for the formal adoption of a US-style rule of reason into Community competition law. Protagonists of the rule of reason argue that there are certain restrictions, for example in exclusive dealing, exclusive purchasing, and franchise agreements that do not actually prevent or restrict competition within the meaning of Article 81(1) EC. They argue that the balancing of the pro- and anti-competitive effects of these agreements should take place under Article 81(1), rather than under the exemption criteria in Article 81(3) EC. There are difficulties, however, in adopting a rule of reason approach into Community competition law and analogies with US anti-trust are not always helpful. The rule of reason was developed by the US courts to resolve the intellectual burden created by the early legislation. Section 1 of the Sherman Act 1890 provides that 'Every contract, combination in the form of trust or otherwise, or conspiracy, in restraint of trade or commerce is declared illegal.' Clearly every contract is prima facie in restraint of trade and the US courts set about distinguishing between those restraints that were illegal per se, and those that required further analysis to determine their status under s. 1. Horizontal price fixing and market-sharing agreements, for example, are treated as per se restrictions of competition by the US courts. Greater divergence between the EC and US approaches to vertical restraints has likely resulted from the US Supreme Court ruling in *Leegin Creative Leather Products, Inc.* v *PSKS, Inc.* 551 US 551 (2007), which overturned the 96-year-old precedent that resale price maintenance ('RPM') was also a per se restriction of competition.

Leegin Creative Leather Products, Inc v PSKS, Inc
551 US 551 (2007)

Leegin suggested minimum resale prices for its range of clothing accessories with retailers and had a policy of ceasing supplies to retailers who discounted below the suggested minimum. Leegin stopped supplying PSKS after seven years when it discovered the retailer was discounting its products below the suggested minimum price, and the retailer refused Leegin's request to stop discounting. PSKS filed a private suit for breach of §1 Sherman Act in the US District Court for the Eastern District of Texas and a jury found in the retailer's favour and awarded $1.2 million in damages. Leegin had argued that there were procompetitive justifications for its pricing policy and appealed to the Fifth Circuit Court of Appeals, which affirmed the District Court's ruling due to the long-standing precedent in *Dr Miles Medical Co* v *John D Park & Sons Co* 220 US 373 (1911) that RPM was a per se restriction of competition. The US Supreme Court accepted the case and reconsidered whether RPM should be considered a per se restriction.

Though each side of the debate can find sources to support its position, it suffices to say here that economics literature is replete with procompetitive justifications for a manufacturer's use of resale price maintenance. See, e.g., Brief for Economists as *Amici Curiae* 16 ("In the theoretical literature, it is essentially undisputed that minimum[resale price maintenance] can have procompetitive effects and that under a variety of market conditions it is unlikely to have anticompetitive effects"); Brief for United States as *Amicus Curiae* 9 ("[T]here is a widespread consensus that permitting a manufacturer to control the price at which its goods are sold may promote interbrand competition and consumer welfare in a variety of ways") . . .

. . .

The justifications for vertical price restraints are similar to those for other vertical restraints. See *GTE Sylvania*, 433 U. S., at 54–57. Minimum resale price maintenance can stimulate interbrand competition—the competition among manufacturers selling different brands of the same type of product—by reducing intrabrand competition—the competition among retailers selling the same brand. See *id.*, at 51–52. The promotion of interbrand competition is important because "the primary purpose of the antitrust laws is to protect [this type of] competition." Khan, 522 U. S., at 15. A single manufacturer's use of vertical price restraints tends to eliminate intrabrand price competition; this in turn encourages retailers to invest in tangible or intangible services or promotional efforts that aid the manufacturer's position as against rival manufacturers. Resale price maintenance also has the potential to give consumers more options so that they can choose among low-price, low-service brands; high-price, high-service brands; and brands that fall in between.

Absent vertical price restraints, the retail services that enhance interbrand competition might be underprovided. This is because discounting retailers can free ride on retailers who furnish services and then capture some of the increased demand those services generate. *GTE Sylvania*, *supra*, at 55. Consumers might learn, for example, about the benefits of a manufacturer's product from a retailer that invests in fine showrooms, offers product demonstrations, or hires and trains knowledgeable employees. R. Posner, Antitrust Law 172–173 (2d ed. 2001) (hereinafter Posner). Or consumers might decide to buy the product because they see it in a retail establishment that has a reputation for selling high-quality merchandise. Marvel & McCafferty, Resale Price Maintenance and Quality Certification, 15 Rand J. Econ. 346, 347–349 (1984) (hereinafter Marvel & McCafferty). If the consumer can then buy the product from a retailer that discounts because it has not spent capital providing services or developing a quality reputation, the high-service retailer will lose sales to the discounter, forcing it to cut back its services to a level lower than consumers would otherwise prefer. Minimum resale price maintenance alleviates the problem because it prevents the discounter from undercutting the service provider. With price competition decreased, the manufacturer's retailers compete among themselves over services.

...

While vertical agreements setting minimum resale prices can have procompetitive justifications, they may have anticompetitive effects in other cases; and unlawful price fixing, designed solely to obtain monopoly profits, is an ever present temptation. Resale price maintenance may, for example, facilitate a manufacturer cartel.

...

Notwithstanding the risks of unlawful conduct, it cannot be stated with any degree of confidence that resale price maintenance "always or almost always tend[s] to restrict competition and decrease output." *Business Electronics*, *supra*, at 723 (internal quotation marks omitted). Vertical agreements establishing minimum resale prices can have either procompetitive or anticompetitive effects, depending upon the circumstances in which they are formed. And although the empirical evidence on the topic is limited, it does not suggest efficient uses of the agreements are infrequent or hypothetical....As the rule would proscribe a significant amount of procompetitive conduct, these agreements appear ill suited for per se condemnation.

NOTE: *Leegin* is a highly significant ruling from the US Supreme Court and may have implications for the operation of Article 81 EC, as highlighted by Professor Vickers in a lecture before the Supreme Court delivered its opinion in the case.

Vickers, J., 'Competition law and economics: a mid-Atlantic viewpoint: The Burrell lecture of the Competition Law Association'
(2007) European Competition Journal 1, pp. 8 and 10–11

As to vertical agreements on price, US and EC law have until now been broadly consistent with each other. Each has, however, been less consistent with economic analysis, which in post-Chicago spirit does not support absolute hostility to resale price maintenance (RPM) agreements. But the US Supreme Court recently granted *certiorari* in the *Leegin* case, where the question is whether to overturn a precedent on RPM that has stood for nearly a century.

...

US law is not EC law and even Supreme Court decisions have no direct impact on this side of the Atlantic. However, it may be time for a European reappraisal of the hardcore categorisation of vertical price agreements, especially if *Dr Miles* is reversed.

Recall that Commission Regulation No 2790/1999...on the application of Article 81(3) of the Treaty to categories of vertical agreements and concerted practices states in Article 4 that the block exemption

"shall not apply to vertical agreements which, directly or indirectly, in isolation or in combination with other factors under the control of the parties, have as their object:
(a) the restriction of the buyer's ability to determine its sale price, without prejudice to the possibility of the supplier's imposing a maximum sale price or recommending a sale price, provided that they do not amount to a fixed or minimum sale price as a result of pressure from, or incentives offered by, any of the parties; ..."

This does not quite amount to per se illegality, because in theory exemption under Article 81(3) is still possible. However, as the Commission guidelines make clear, individual exemption of agreements containing such "hardcore" restrictions is unlikely. Likewise and furthermore, the Commission's 2001 *de minimis* notice on agreements of minor importance expressly excludes RPM, as a "hardcore" restriction, from the kinds of agreement between non-competitors that the Commission considers not to have an appreciably restrictive effect on competition.

There is a natural attraction to this approach, notwithstanding economic logic, while the US—the most mature competition law jurisdiction—condemns minimum RPM per se. If something is per se illegal "even" in the US, there may be felt to be automatic comfort with adopting a similar stance here. But what if the Supreme Court reverses *Dr Miles*? The transatlantic automatic comfort would then fall away. At least in those circumstances, reconsideration of the degree of hostility to RPM in EC competition law would seem appropriate.

NOTE: Given that the US Supreme Court subsequently overturned the *Dr Miles* precedent in *Leegin*, so that RPM falls to be considered under the rule of reason in US antitrust, Professor Vickers presents a powerful argument in favour of reconsidering the approach to RPM in Europe. This is perhaps more timely given the movement away from a form-based analysis to an effects-based analysis in other aspects of EC competition law, notably Article 82 EC. Nonetheless it is also clear that there are differences between the US *per se* approach, which prevented any analysis of the efficiencies generated by RPM for close to a century, and the EC 'hardcore' restriction approach, which makes it unlikely but not impossible for RPM to benefit from the application of Article 81(3). These differences have been explored by Peeperkorn who offers his view on whether *Leegin* creates further divergence between the EC and US.

Peeperkorn, L., 'Resale Price Maintenance and its Alleged Efficiencies'
(2008) European Competition Journal 201, p. 212

Current case law and practice in the EU towards RPM can only be understood from the application of the hardcore approach contained in the BER and Guidelines. This hardcore approach is not the same as the US per se approach and allows more flexibility, although circumscribed by a number of strong but rebuttable presumptions. One could conclude that the *Leegin* judgment provides the US authorities and courts with the possibility of applying the same policy towards RPM as is currently applied in the EU, though it remains to be seen how US policy will develop. Before giving up or changing these rebuttable presumptions in the EU, it is important to critically assess the likely positive and negative effects of RPM. It is not sufficient to rely on general statements and studies on vertical restraints. On the basis of the (possibly incomplete) analysis described above, it seems that in particular the efficiency arguments mentioned in support of RPM are not very strong and that RPM is not an efficient instrument for bringing about these efficiencies. This and possible further analyses should help to achieve a balanced and focused opinion, useful for policy formulation towards the various types of vertical restraints.

Such analyses and debates, to which the *Leegin* judgment has made a timely contribution, will help the Commission and Member States, working together in the European Competition Network, in their review of the BER and Guidelines. This review, necessitated by the expiry of the BER on 31 May 2010, has only just started. It will be an open process, with ample opportunity for all parties to comment on the current rules and practice, including the treatment of RPM.

NOTE: RPM therefore now falls to be considered under the rule of reason in US antitrust, whereby the restraint is viewed in its market context to assess its pro- and anti-competitive effects. There are different views as to whether this marks a clear divergence from EC competition law and policy, and Peeperkorn argues that the operation of Article 81(3) is closer to the US rule of reason approach than the per se approach, even if dealing with designated 'hardcore' restrictions such as RPM. It is useful to consider the rule of reason in US antitrust and whether the EC approach is comparable.

■ QUESTION

Should the US Supreme Court decision in *Leegin* influence the development of EC competition law in relation to RPM?

The following extract is from the Supreme Court decision in *Continental TV Inc* v *GTE Sylvania* 433 US 36 (1977) demonstrating the Court's willingness to accept a rule of reason approach.

Continental TV Inc v GTE Sylvania Inc
433 US 36 (1977)

Vertical restrictions promote interbrand competition by allowing the manufacturer to achieve certain efficiencies in the distribution of his products. These 'redeeming virtues' are implicit in every decision sustaining vertical restrictions under the rule of reason. Economists have identified a number of ways in which manufacturers can use such restrictions to compete more effectively against other manufacturers. See, e.g., Preston, Restrictive Distribution Arrangements: Economic Analysis and Public Policy Standards, 30 Law & Contemp Prob 506, 511 (1965).[23] For example, new manufacturers and manufacturers entering new markets can use the restrictions in order to induce competent and aggressive retailers to make the kind of investment of capital and labor that is often required in the distribution of products unknown to the consumer. Established manufacturers can use them to induce retailers to engage in promotional activities or to provide service and repair facilities necessary to the efficient marketing of their products. Service and repair are vital for many products, such as automobiles and major household appliances. The availability and quality of such services affect a manufacturer's goodwill and the competitiveness of his product. Because of market imperfections such as the so-called 'free rider' effect, these services might not be provided by retailers in a purely competitive situation, despite the fact that each retailer's benefit would be greater if all provided the services than if none did. Posner, *supra*, n 13, at 285; cf. P. Samuelson, Economics 506–507 (10th ed 1976).

NOTE: In an important early contribution to the debate, Whish and Sufrin argued against the transposition of a US-style rule of reason into the Community competition law framework.

Whish, R., and Sufrin, B., 'Article 85 and the Rule of Reason'
(1987) 7 YEL 1, pp. 36–8 By permission of Oxford University Press

In the light of the foregoing considerations, the call for the adoption of a US-style rule of reason should be resisted and, indeed, there is much to be said for dropping this term (and the terms 'ancillary restraint' and 'per se illegality') from EEC antitrust law altogether, on the basis that they do more to confuse than to clarify. EEC competition law requires its own vocabulary, carefully honed to express its own particular tensions.

Quite apart from the issue of terminology, the writers have other doubts about the wisdom of analysing Article 85(1) in a way that relies on an approach similar to that in the Sherman Act. It would not help the cause of certainty. As Joliet himself said:

> Generally business groups in Europe, just as in America, complain about the lack of certainty in Antitrust law. At the same time, they are inclined to demand more flexibility. Such demands are irreconcilable. *A rule of reason under Article 85(1) would bring about more uncertainty for business men.* [Emphasis added.]

The matter of certainty is, of course, important. It is in no one's interest to retard beneficial collaboration between firms striving to compete in a competitive international market. However, the best

---

[23] Marketing efficiency is not the only legitimate reason for a manufacturer's desire to exert control over the manner in which his products are sold and serviced. As a result of statutory and common-law developments, society increasingly demands that manufacturers assume direct responsibility for the safety and quality of their products. For example, at the federal level, apart from more specialized requirements, manufacturers of consumer products have safety responsibilities under the Consumer Product Safety Act, 15 USC § 2051 *et seq.* (1970 ed Supp V), and obligations for warranties under the Consumer Product Warranties Act, 15 USC § 2301 *et seq.* (1970 ed Supp V). Similar obligations are imposed by state law. See, e.g., Cal Civ Code Ann § 1790 *et seq.* (West 1973). The legitimacy of these concerns has been recognized in cases involving vertical restrictions. See, e.g., *Tripoli Co.* v *Wella Corp.* 425 F2d 932 (CA3 1970).

answer to this problem is for the Commission to continue to improve its procedures, to publish block exemptions where this is possible, and to develop such notions as objective necessity and potential competition. We also expect its sophistication in dealing with economics to continue to improve, but do not consider that this goes hand in hand with rule-of-reason analysis. This would stifle the proper application of Article 85 which, precisely because of its more ample wording, does not bear the same intellectual burden that the words 'restraint of trade' do in the Sherman Act. We doubt, too, that it would be helpful to draw the national courts further into the application of Article 85 by asking them to undertake extensive economic analysis under Article 85(1). We are happy for them to enforce the competition rules against blatant cartels and abuses of a dominant position. We do not consider them to be appropriate fora for deciding upon complex economic issues.

We are also of the opinion that protagonists of the rule of reason fail to give due consideration to the significance of single market integration. Even if this is not a goal approved by all observers, to call for the application of the competition rules in a way which ignores it is fundamentally to misconstrue the context in which EEC law is applied. Also, there is a certain disingenuousness in complaining about EEC competition law when it (with other provisions of the Treaty) has done so much to open up markets which until relatively recently were difficult to penetrate. Competition law in one sense benefits everyone on the market—even those who object to some of the particular ways in which it is applied.

Our conclusion, therefore, is that there are sound reasons for resisting the call for a rule of reason under Article 85(1).

■ **QUESTION**

What opportunities are there for justifying 'hardcore' restrictions on account of efficiencies under EC competition law, compared with the opportunities for justification of agreements classed as per se restrictions under US antitrust?

C: Block exemption debate

The block exemption Regulations were introduced with the principal aim of increasing legal certainty and thereby reducing the Commission's workload. The difficulties with block exemptions quickly became clear. The absence of any market-share criteria meant companies without significant market power incurred unnecessary regulation, whereas companies with significant market power could escape regulation altogether. Criticism also centred on the so-called *straitjacket* effect, which obliged advisers to structure a commercial agreement to meet certain form-based requirements, in the process compromising the commercial benefits. An agreement that did not meet these strict requirements did not qualify for exemption. Although the Commission argued that such formalism (as opposed to economic or commercial criteria) provided undertakings with legal certainty, it was argued that 'these formalistic categories have nothing to do with competition policy'.

Professor Hawk was particularly critical of the Commission's early approach in his seminal article on vertical restraints in EC Competition Law.

Reproduced with permission from Kluwer Law International from
Hawk, B.E., 'System Failure: Vertical Restraints and EC Competition Law'
(1995) 32 CML Rev, p. 973 [footnotes omitted]

It was evident as early as the 1960s that DG IV lacked the resources to deal with notifications seeking individual exemptions. This should not be surprising. No competition authority in the world has the resources to examine the vast number of vertical agreements (and licenses) whose enforceability has been called into question by the overbroad application of 85(1). The Emperor wears no clothes. The notification system set up in Regulation 17 has never worked and will never work. Like the 1976 Restrictive Practices Act in the UK, the notification system serves mostly to increase transaction costs and transfer income from firms to outside antitrust lawyers. It has no redeeming enforcement virtues and should be scrapped.

But rather than abandon an obviously deficient and inoperable notification system, the Commission has resorted to block exemptions. These vary considerably in their provision of legal certainty. One extreme is Regulation 83/83 covering exclusive distributorships, which does provide a fair degree of legal certainty for simple stand-alone exclusive distributor agreements. At the other extreme is probably the joint R & D block exemption that appears, on the basis of anecdotal evidence, rarely ever to cover a real-world arrangement.

2.4 Step D—Legal formalisms and 'analysis' by pigeonholing

The Commission largely applies Article 85(1) to distribution arrangements according to formal legal categories. One set of rules applies to exclusive distribution, another to selective distribution, another to franchising, and a chaotic array of considerations apply to distribution arrangements that are not neatly pigeonholed. Paradoxically, these rules have become enshrined by the very block exemptions that were issued to relieve the harsher aspects of the Commission's rigid application of Article 85(1).

The Commission's treatment of specific provisions in *selective distribution* and *franchises* illustrates the formalistic approach.

Commission decisions on *selective distribution* frequently are marked by conclusory reasoning and neglect of economic analysis. Some restraints are placed under 85(1) (e.g. minimum sales and stocking obligations) with no apparent economic analysis at all; the restriction on economic freedom notion apparently supports this result. However, other provisions that clearly 'restrain the economic freedom' of the dealer are placed outside 85(1) (e.g. a restriction on wholesalers not to supply end-users and restrictions on dealers supplying certain classes of customers). The result is intellectual incoherence and a substitution of formal categories for analysis.

Franchise agreements provide a second example. The Commission (and the Court) generally accord more favourable treatment to restrictive clauses in franchising agreements as compared to distribution agreements. For example, dealer location clauses, minimum purchasing obligations and stocking requirements in franchise agreements do not even fall within Article 85(1), while in selective distribution agreements the same clauses not only fall within Article 85(1) but might also be denied an exemption under Article 85(3). This is problematic: many distribution agreements have elements that are characteristic of franchises, i.e. the transfer of commercial knowhow to independent parties operating under the supplier's trademark and not dealing in certain competing goods.

2.5 Step E—Lack of substantive analysis

The legal formalisms described above ultimately eliminate what should be the heart of the matter: an antitrust (i.e. economics/law) substantive analysis of a particular agreement or practice, i.e. its competitive harms and benefits. Competition law is economic law, and economics must play a predominant (if not exclusive) role in the examination of particular agreements. That is why the Commission's frequent inattention to market power and effects on price and output is so sorely criticized.

The legal formalisms under Article 85 contrast starkly with US antitrust counselling practice. When dealing with non-territorial vertical restraints under EC law, lawyers spend the great majority of their time in pigeonholing exercises and in textual exegesis of block exemptions and interpretative guidelines. It is shocking how little time is devoted to assessing the competitive risks and benefits of the vertical restraints at issue. The practice under the Sherman Act is exactly the opposite. It is difficult to believe that EC competition policy is furthered where there is far more attention and intellectual resources devoted to doctrinal formalisms than to substantive analysis.

NOTE: With the revision of block exemption Regulations in the late 1990s and 2000s towards a more effects-based approach and the introduction of Regulation 1/2003, which abolished the notification system for Article 81(3), the Commission appears to have satisfied Hawk's criticism.

The revision of the block exemptions dealing with vertical restraints will be explored in more detail below.

■ QUESTION

Should resale price maintenance be subjected to harsher treatment than non-price vertical restraints?

It is clear the Commission applied Article 81(1) EC broadly to vertical agreements and restraints because of their threat to market integration and their potential anti-competitive effects. Criticism of the Community's strict approach and the expiry of three block exemption Regulations at the end of 1999 covering exclusive buying, selling, and franchising (later extended to 31 December 1999 and finally 31 May 2000) presented the Commission with an obvious opportunity to revise its treatment of vertical restraints. Consequently, the Commission published a *Green Paper on Vertical Restraints in EC Competition Policy*, in January 1997, (COM (96) 721 final). The Green Paper represented a radical change in Community policy towards vertical restraints, not least the realization of the importance of market structure and effects rather than legal form in determining whether an agreement is anti-competitive or not.

The Commission proposed a number of possible options for change in the Green Paper, some more radical than others, and invited comments on the direction of future reform.

Green Paper on Vertical Restraints in EC Competition Policy
COM (96) 721

II. Economic analysis of vertical restraints and the single market

10. The heated debate among economists concerning vertical restraints has calmed somewhat and a consensus is emerging. Vertical restraints are no longer regarded as per se suspicious or per se pro-competitive. Economists are less willing to make sweeping statements. Rather, they rely more on the analysis of the facts of a case in question. However, one element stands out: the importance of market structure in determining the impact of vertical restraints. The fiercer is interbrand competition, the more likely are the pro-competitive and efficiency effects to outweigh any anti-competitive effects of vertical restraints. Anti-competitive effects are only likely where interbrand competition is weak and there are barriers to entry at either producer or distributor level. In addition it is recognised that contracts in the distribution chain reduce transaction costs, and can allow the potential efficiencies in distribution to be realised. In contrast, there are cases where vertical restraints raise barriers to entry or further dampen horizontal competition in oligopolistic markets.

Option I—Maintain current system

281. Option I consists of maintaining the current system (including the special arrangements for beer and petrol).

Option II—Wider block exemptions

282. It is sometimes suggested that current block exemptions are too limited. Option II would maintain the current system, with some changes in the provisions of the block exemption

Regulations. There would be no significant procedural changes. The block exemptions would apply more widely than hitherto by an extension of their coverage to different clauses set out below thus broadening legal certainty. Fewer individual cases would require notification. Some of these changes may be made by the Commission acting under the powers already granted to it under Council Regulation 19/65. Others would require amendment of that Council Regulation. Some suggested changes are listed below and comments on their appropriateness and on other possible changes are welcome.

283. Measures to increase flexibility in general could include one or more of the following:
    — the block exemptions would cover not only the precise clauses listed, but also clauses which are similar or less restrictive;
    — the inclusion of prohibited clauses might not deny the benefit of the exemption for the rest of the agreement;
    — the block exemption could apply to agreements involving more than two parties;
    — a block exemption or a Commission notice for selective distribution could be enacted.

284. Specific measures to increase flexibility could include one or more of the following:
    — the block exemptions for exclusive distribution and exclusive purchasing could be extended to cover services or to permit the distributor to transform or process the contract goods. Distributors could be allowed to add significant value by changing the economic identity of the goods without losing the benefit of the block exemption;
    — the block exemption for exclusive purchasing agreements could be extended to cover partial as well as exclusive supply;
    — the block exemption for franchising agreements could be extended to cover maximum resale price maintenance as an exception to the general principle that resale price maintenance will not be exempted;
    — associations of independent retailers could be permitted to benefit from block exemption regulations, provided that the independent retailers are small and medium-sized enterprises[77] and that the market share of the association remains below a certain threshold;
    — an arbitration procedure could be set up for distributors denied admission to a selective distribution network.

285. Under this option the special provisions in Regulation No 1984/83 for beer and petrol would remain in force with certain changes to increase the flexibility of the application of the Regulation. One possibility could be to limit the requirement to specify the 'tied' beers to the type of beer concerned, instead of identifying the individual brands as required under the current Regulation. This gives the brewer the possibility of adding or replacing brands of a type of beer for which the tenant is already tied, instead of requiring an additional agreement with the tenant for such changes, as required by the Regulation. As regards petrol one could consider how to deal with forms of distribution other than exclusive purchase in relation to goods sold in convenience stores that form part of the service station business. Additionally, one could consider whether it is justified to maintain the requirement that the supplier should make available or finance lubrication equipment in order to benefit from an exemption for exclusivity of supply of lubricants.

Option III—More focused block exemptions

286. This option stresses Community competition policy's market integration objectives. Territorial protection and vertical restraints are seen as a significant contributory factor to the maintenance of considerable price differentials between Member States. It is certainly the case that many markets are becoming more concentrated at the production and distribution level, while vertical restraints can foreclose markets and raise barriers to entry. The value added by distribution is an important element in its own right. Intrabrand competition can play an important role in promoting competition in markets where interbrand competition is not fierce.

---

[77] In the sense of the Commission recommendation of 3 April 1996 concerning the definition of small and medium-sized enterprises, O.J. no L107 of 30.4.1996.

287. The current block exemptions apply without any market share limits. They could be amended so as to apply only where each party has less than, for instance, 40 per cent market share of the relevant market in the contract territory. There would be no block exemption above that threshold, at least in respect of the following restrictions:
    — protection against active sales from outside the territory
    — protection for exclusive dealing (prohibition to sell competing products/services).

288. Within the framework of the present option, comments are also welcome about the appropriateness to adopt a block exemption regulation in respect of selective distribution agreements, to the extent that these agreements fall within Article 85(1). In case such a regulation would be adopted, it would apply only where the producer or distributor does not hold more than for instance, 40 per cent share of the relevant market or a lower figure in an oligopolistic market.

289. The suggestions made in Option II could be applied to agreements below the market share threshold.

290. Parties may have doubts about the correct definition of a market and calculation of their share thereof, which could lead them to notify agreements to the Commission in a search for legal certainty. There would also be notifications of agreements where the parties have market shares in excess of the threshold.

291. The Commission would appreciate estimates of the number and type of cases likely to be notified, and views on whether guidelines explaining the circumstances in which the Commission would grant exemptions under Article 85(3) could solve this problem. Possible grounds for exemption could include the condition that there be no significant price discrimination to the detriment of customers.

292. In line with the general rule above, no protection would be given to exclusive beer-supply agreements in favour of a brewer with a share above e.g. 40 per cent on a given national on-trade market. However, a sector specific alternative could be to limit the extent of the exclusivity either to a given percentage of the total beer throughput of a particular pub (e.g. 3/4 tied, 1/4 free) or to certain containers (e.g. draught tied, bottles and cans free). A further alternative could be to limit the scope of the exclusivity to beer only. In the context of filling stations, it should be considered whether, in cases where the supplier has a market share in excess of a certain percentage, e.g. 40 per cent, the maximum contract term permitted by the exemption should be reduced.

Option IV—Block exemptions with measure to specify the economic circumstances in which Article 85(1) applies

293. The idea underlying this option is that economic analysis of vertical restraints should be implemented by legal instruments which give undertakings a considerable degree of legal certainty. The economic criteria designed to determine the market conditions in which Article 85(1) would apply could be developed, in the first place, within the framework of a new Commission notice and subsequently, in the light of the experience acquired, within the framework of a negative clearance regulation.

294. This option would provide for more flexible treatment of vertical arrangements for agreements between parties with no significant market power. The alleged limiting effect of block exemptions and emphasis on the legal classification of different forms of distribution would be reduced.

295. For parties with less than, for instance, 20 per cent market share in the contract territory, there would be a rebuttable presumption of compatibility with Article 85(1) ('*the negative clearance presumption*'). In other words, vertical restraints in such circumstances would not normally be caught by Article 85(1). This presumption would cover all vertical restraints except those relating to minimum resale prices, impediments to parallel trade or passive sales, or those contained in distribution agreements between competitors.

296. This negative clearance presumption could be rebutted by the Commission on the basis of a market analysis which would take account of factors such as:
    — market structure (e.g. oligopoly)

— barriers to entry
— the degree of integration of the single market, evaluated on the basis of indicators such as the price differential existing between Member States and the level of market penetration in each Member State of products imported from other Member States, or
— the cumulative impact of parallel networks.

297. Agreements which, as a result of this market analysis, were shown to fall within Article 85(1) could benefit from a block exemption if they fulfilled the necessary conditions (see below variants I and II). The negative clearance presumption could be implemented by a Commission Notice and subsequently in the light of the experience acquired, within the framework of a negative clearance regulation which would require a new Council enabling Regulation under Article 87 of the Treaty.

298. For cases with market share above for instance 20 per cent and for those below 20 per cent which fall within Article 85(1), there could be two possibilities, as follows:

Variant I

299. All cases over 20 per cent could be covered by the block exemption described in Option II (wider block exemption).

Variant II

300. All cases over 20 per cent would be covered by the block exemption described in Option III (i.e. inapplicability of block exemption to certain restrictions above 40 per cent market share).

NOTE: Despite marked opposition to the use of market share tests in response to the Green Paper, the European Commission favoured Option 4, Variant 2—i.e. automatic exemption for agreements below a market share threshold and individual examination for agreements above that threshold. Most commentators supported a shift towards a more economic approach, although not all were in support of the introduction of market shares. The level at which the market share threshold was to be fixed and whether there would be any variation according to the seriousness of the restraint, was hotly debated following publication of the follow-up communication. See for example, Schroeder, D., 'The Green Paper on Vertical Restraints: Beware of Market Share Thresholds' [1997] ECLR 430 and Kellaway, R., 'Vertical Restraints: Which Option' [1997] ECLR 387.

SECTION 5: REGULATION 2790/1999

As explained above, following the Green Paper and the consultation process, the Commission proposed replacing the existing system of sector-specific block exemptions with a single broad 'umbrella' exemption Regulation. The principal aim was to move away from a form-based system to a system which allows for greater economic analysis. In order to remove the so-called '*straitjacket* effect', the Regulation was to be based mainly on a black-clause approach. Thus, instead of defining what *is* exempted, by reference to a positive list of provisions, the current Regulation represents a shift in emphasis towards a black-list. The purpose of this approach is to reduce the regulatory burden on companies and make it easier for legal advisers to draft more flexible commercial agreements. The black-list approach abandons the differentiation in policy between types of sectors and agreements.

The current block exemption, Regulation 2790/1999 (Commission Regulation No 2790/1999 of 22 December 1999 on the application of Article 81(3) to categories of vertical agreements and concerted practices, OJ, 1999, L336/21) (hereinafter referred to as 'BER') came into force on 1 June 2000, and will operate until May 2010.

COMMISSION REGULATION (EC) NO 2790/1999 OF 22 DECEMBER 1999 ON THE APPLICATION OF ARTICLE 81(3) OF THE TREATY TO CATEGORIES OF VERTICAL AGREEMENTS AND CONCERTED PRACTICES
(Text with EEA relevance)

THE COMMISSION OF THE EUROPEAN COMMUNITIES,

Having regard to the Treaty establishing the European Community,

Having regard to Council Regulation No 19/65/EEC of 2 March 1965 on the application of Article 85(3) of the Treaty to certain categories of agreements and concerted practices, as last amended by Regulation (EC) No 1215/1999, and in particular Article 1 thereof,

Having published a draft of this Regulation,

Having consulted the Advisory Committee on Restrictive Practices and Dominant Positions,

Whereas:

(1) Regulation No 19/65/EEC empowers the Commission to apply Article 81(3) of the Treaty (formerly Article 85(3)) by regulation to certain categories of vertical agreements and corresponding concerted practices falling within Article 81(1).

(2) Experience acquired to date makes it possible to define a category of vertical agreements which can be regarded as normally satisfying the conditions laid down in Article 81(3).

(3) This category includes vertical agreements for the purchase or sale of goods or services where these agreements are concluded between non-competing undertakings, between certain competitors or by certain associations of retailers of goods; it also includes vertical agreements containing ancillary provisions on the assignment or use of intellectual property rights; for the purposes of this Regulation, the term 'vertical agreements' includes the corresponding concerted practices.

(4) For the application of Article 81(3) by regulation, it is not necessary to define those vertical agreements which are capable of falling within Article 81(1); in the individual assessment of agreements under Article 81(1), account has to be taken of several factors, and in particular the market structure on the supply and purchase side.

(5) The benefit of the block exemption should be limited to vertical agreements for which it can be assumed with sufficient certainty that they satisfy the conditions of Article 81(3).

(6) Vertical agreements of the category defined in this Regulation can improve economic efficiency within a chain of production or distribution by facilitating better coordination between the participating undertakings; in particular, they can lead to a reduction in the transaction and distribution costs of the parties and to an optimisation of their sales and investment levels.

(7) The likelihood that such efficiency-enhancing effects will outweigh any anti-competitive effects due to restrictions contained in vertical agreements depends on the degree of market power of the undertakings concerned and, therefore, on the extent to which those undertakings face competition from other suppliers of goods or services regarded by the buyer as interchangeable or substitutable for one another, by reason of the products' characteristics, their prices and their intended use.

(8) It can be presumed that, where the share of the relevant market accounted for by the supplier does not exceed 30 per cent, vertical agreements which do not contain certain types of severely anti-competitive restraints generally lead to an improvement in production or distribution and allow consumers a fair share of the resulting benefits; in the case of vertical agreements containing exclusive supply obligations, it is the market share of the buyer which is relevant in determining the overall effects of such vertical agreements on the market.

(9) Above the market share threshold of 30 per cent, there can be no presumption that vertical agreements falling within the scope of Article 81(1) will usually give rise to objective advantages of such a character and size as to compensate for the disadvantages which they create for competition.

(10) This Regulation should not exempt vertical agreements containing restrictions which are not indispensable to the attainment of the positive effects mentioned above; in particular, vertical agreements containing certain types of severely anti-competitive restraints such as

minimum and fixed resale-prices, as well as certain types of territorial protection, should be excluded from the benefit of the block exemption established by this Regulation irrespective of the market share of the undertakings concerned.

(11) In order to ensure access to or to prevent collusion on the relevant market, certain conditions are to be attached to the block exemption; to this end, the exemption of non-compete obligations should be limited to obligations which do not exceed a definite duration; for the same reasons, any direct or indirect obligation causing the members of a selective distribution system not to sell the brands of particular competing suppliers should be excluded from the benefit of this Regulation.

12) The market-share limitation, the non-exemption of certain vertical agreements and the conditions provided for in this Regulation normally ensure that the agreements to which the block exemption applies do not enable the participating undertakings to eliminate competition in respect of a substantial part of the products in question.

(13) In particular cases in which the agreements falling under this Regulation nevertheless have effects incompatible with Article 81(3), the Commission may withdraw the benefit of the block exemption; this may occur in particular where the buyer has significant market power in the relevant market in which it resells the goods or provides the services or where parallel networks of vertical agreements have similar effects which significantly restrict access to a relevant market or competition therein; such cumulative effects may for example arise in the case of selective distribution or non-compete obligations.

(14) Regulation No 19/65/EEC empowers the competent authorities of Member States to withdraw the benefit of the block exemption in respect of vertical agreements having effects incompatible with the conditions laid down in Article 81(3), where such effects are felt in their respective territory, or in a part thereof, and where such territory has the characteristics of a distinct geographic market; Member States should ensure that the exercise of this power of withdrawal does not prejudice the uniform application throughout the common market of the Community competition rules or the full effect of the measures adopted in implementation of those rules.

(15) In order to strengthen supervision of parallel networks of vertical agreements which have similar restrictive effects and which cover more than 50 per cent of a given market, the Commission may declare this Regulation inapplicable to vertical agreements containing specific restraints relating to the market concerned, thereby restoring the full application of Article 81 to such agreements.

(16) This Regulation is without prejudice to the application of Article 82.

(17) In accordance with the principle of the primacy of Community law, no measure taken pursuant to national laws on competition should prejudice the uniform application throughout the common market of the Community competition rules or the full effect of any measures adopted in implementation of those rules, including this Regulation,

HAS ADOPTED THIS REGULATION:

Article 1

For the purposes of this Regulation:

    (a) 'competing undertakings' means actual or potential suppliers in the same product market; the product market includes goods or services which are regarded by the buyer as interchangeable with or substitutable for the contract goods or services, by reason of the products' characteristics, their prices and their intended use;

    (b) 'non-compete obligation' means any direct or indirect obligation causing the buyer not to manufacture, purchase, sell or resell goods or services which compete with the contract goods or services, or any direct or indirect obligation on the buyer to purchase from the supplier or from another undertaking designated by the supplier more than 80 per cent of the buyer's total purchases of the contract goods or services and their substitutes on the relevant market, calculated on the basis of the value of its purchases in the preceding calendar year;

(c) 'exclusive supply obligation' means any direct or indirect obligation causing the supplier to sell the goods or services specified in the agreement only to one buyer inside the Community for the purposes of a specific use or for resale;

(d) 'selective distribution system' means a distribution system where the supplier undertakes to sell the contract goods or services, either directly or indirectly, only to distributors selected on the basis of specified criteria and where these distributors undertake not to sell such goods or services to unauthorised distributors;

(e) 'intellectual property rights' includes industrial property rights, copyright and neighbouring rights;

(f) 'know-how' means a package of non-patented practical information, resulting from experience and testing by the supplier, which is secret, substantial and identified: in this context, 'secret' means that the know-how, as a body or in the precise configuration and assembly of its components, is not generally known or easily accessible; 'substantial' means that the know-how includes information which is indispensable to the buyer for the use, sale or resale of the contract goods or services; 'identified' means that the know-how must be described in a sufficiently comprehensive manner so as to make it possible to verify that it fulfils the criteria of secrecy and substantiality;

(g) 'buyer' includes an undertaking which, under an agreement falling within Article 81(1) of the Treaty, sells goods or services on behalf of another undertaking.

Article 2

1. Pursuant to Article 81(3) of the Treaty and subject to the provisions of this Regulation, it is hereby declared that Article 81(1) shall not apply to agreements or concerted practices entered into between two or more undertakings each of which operates, for the purposes of the agreement, at a different level of the production or distribution chain, and relating to the conditions under which the parties may purchase, sell or resell certain goods or services ('vertical agreements').

   This exemption shall apply to the extent that such agreements contain restrictions of competition falling within the scope of Article 81(1) ('vertical restraints').

2. The exemption provided for in paragraph 1 shall apply to vertical agreements entered into between an association of undertakings and its members, or between such an association and its suppliers, only if all its members are retailers of goods and if no individual member of the association, together with its connected undertakings, has a total annual turnover exceeding EUR 50 million; vertical agreements entered into by such associations shall be covered by this Regulation without prejudice to the application of Article 81 to horizontal agreements concluded between the members of the association or decisions adopted by the association.

3. The exemption provided for in paragraph 1 shall apply to vertical agreements containing provisions which relate to the assignment to the buyer or use by the buyer of intellectual property rights, provided that those provisions do not constitute the primary object of such agreements and are directly related to the use, sale or resale of goods or services by the buyer or its customers. The exemption applies on condition that, in relation to the contract goods or services, those provisions do not contain restrictions of competition having the same object or effect as vertical restraints which are not exempted under this Regulation.

4. The exemption provided for in paragraph 1 shall not apply to vertical agreements entered into between competing undertakings; however, it shall apply where competing undertakings enter into a non-reciprocal vertical agreement and:
   (a) the buyer has a total annual turnover not exceeding EUR 100 million, or
   (b) the supplier is a manufacturer and a distributor of goods, while the buyer is a distributor not manufacturing goods competing with the contract goods, or
   (c) the supplier is a provider of services at several levels of trade, while the buyer does not provide competing services at the level of trade where it purchases the contract services.

5. This Regulation shall not apply to vertical agreements the subject matter of which falls within the scope of any other block exemption regulation.

Article 3

1. Subject to paragraph 2 of this Article, the exemption provided for in Article 2 shall apply on condition that the market share held by the supplier does not exceed 30 per cent of the relevant market on which it sells the contract goods or services.

2. In the case of vertical agreements containing exclusive supply obligations, the exemption provided for in Article 2 shall apply on condition that the market share held by the buyer does not exceed 30 per cent of the relevant market on which it purchases the contract goods or services.

Article 4

The exemption provided for in Article 2 shall not apply to vertical agreements which, directly or indirectly, in isolation or in combination with other factors under the control of the parties, have as their object:

   (a) the restriction of the buyer's ability to determine its sale price, without prejudice to the possibility of the supplier's imposing a maximum sale price or recommending a sale price, provided that they do not amount to a fixed or minimum sale price as a result of pressure from, or incentives offered by, any of the parties;

   (b) the restriction of the territory into which, or of the customers to whom, the buyer may sell the contract goods or services, except:
   — the restriction of active sales into the exclusive territory or to an exclusive customer group reserved to the supplier or allocated by the supplier to another buyer, where such a restriction does not limit sales by the customers of the buyer,
   — the restriction of sales to end users by a buyer operating at the wholesale level of trade,
   — the restriction of sales to unauthorised distributors by the members of a selective distribution system, and
   — the restriction of the buyer's ability to sell components, supplied for the purposes of incorporation, to customers who would use them to manufacture the same type of goods as those produced by the supplier;

   (c) the restriction of active or passive sales to end users by members of a selective distribution system operating at the retail level of trade, without prejudice to the possibility of prohibiting a member of the system from operating out of an unauthorised place of establishment;

   (d) the restriction of cross-supplies between distributors within a selective distribution system, including between distributors operating at different levels of trade;

   (e) the restriction agreed between a supplier of components and a buyer who incorporates those components, which limits the supplier to selling the components as spare parts to end-users or to repairers or other service providers not entrusted by the buyer with the repair or servicing of its goods.

Article 5

The exemption provided for in Article 2 shall not apply to any of the following obligations contained in vertical agreements:

   (a) any direct or indirect non-compete obligation, the duration of which is indefinite or exceeds five years. A non-compete obligation which is tacitly renewable beyond a period of five years is to be deemed to have been concluded for an indefinite duration. However, the time limitation of five years shall not apply where the contract goods or services are sold by the buyer from premises and land owned by the supplier or leased by the supplier from third parties not connected with the buyer, provided that the duration of the non-compete obligation does not exceed the period of occupancy of the premises and land by the buyer;

   (b) any direct or indirect obligation causing the buyer, after termination of the agreement, not to manufacture, purchase, sell or resell goods or services, unless such obligation:
   — relates to goods or services which compete with the contract goods or services, and
   — is limited to the premises and land from which the buyer has operated during the contract period, and

— is indispensable to protect know-how transferred by the supplier to the buyer, and provided that the duration of such non-compete obligation is limited to a period of one year after termination of the agreement; this obligation is without prejudice to the possibility of imposing a restriction which is unlimited in time on the use and disclosure of know-how which has not entered the public domain;

(c) any direct or indirect obligation causing the members of a selective distribution system not to sell the brands of particular competing suppliers.

Article 6

The Commission may withdraw the benefit of this Regulation, pursuant to Article 7(1) of Regulation No 19/65/EEC, where it finds in any particular case that vertical agreements to which this Regulation applies nevertheless have effects which are incompatible with the conditions laid down in Article 81(3) of the Treaty, and in particular where access to the relevant market or competition therein is significantly restricted by the cumulative effect of parallel networks of similar vertical restraints implemented by competing suppliers or buyers.

Article 7

Where in any particular case vertical agreements to which the exemption provided for in Article 2 applies have effects incompatible with the conditions laid down in Article 81(3) of the Treaty in the territory of a Member State, or in a part thereof, which has all the characteristics of a distinct geographic market, the competent authority of that Member State may withdraw the benefit of application of this Regulation in respect of that territory, under the same conditions as provided in Article 6.

Article 8

1. Pursuant to Article 1 a of Regulation No 19/65/EEC, the Commission may by regulation declare that, where parallel networks of similar vertical restraints cover more than 50 per cent of a relevant market, this Regulation shall not apply to vertical agreements containing specific restraints relating to that market.

2. A regulation pursuant to paragraph 1 shall not become applicable earlier than six months following its adoption.

Article 9

1. The market share of 30 per cent provided for in Article 3(1) shall be calculated on the basis of the market sales value of the contract goods or services and other goods or services sold by the supplier, which are regarded as interchangeable or substitutable by the buyer, by reason of the products' characteristics, their prices and their intended use; if market sales value data are not available, estimates based on other reliable market information, including market sales volumes, may be used to establish the market share of the undertaking concerned. For the purposes of Article 3(2), it is either the market purchase value or estimates thereof which shall be used to calculate the market share.

2. For the purposes of applying the market share threshold provided for in Article 3 the following rules shall apply:

(a) the market share shall be calculated on the basis of data relating to the preceding calendar year;

(b) the market share shall include any goods or services supplied to integrated distributors for the purposes of sale;

(c) if the market share is initially not more than 30 per cent but subsequently rises above that level without exceeding 35 per cent the exemption provided for in Article 2 shall continue to apply for a period of two consecutive calendar years following the year in which the 30 per cent market share threshold was first exceeded;

(d) if the market share is initially not more than 30 per cent but subsequently rises above 35 per cent, the exemption provided for in Article 2 shall continue to apply for one calendar year following the year in which the level of 35 per cent was first exceeded;

(e) the benefit of points (c) and (d) may not be combined so as to exceed a period of two calendar years.

Article 10

1. For the purpose of calculating total annual turnover within the meaning of Article 2(2) and (4), the turnover achieved during the previous financial year by the relevant party to the vertical agreement and the turnover achieved by its connected undertakings in respect of all goods and services, excluding all taxes and other duties, shall be added together. For this purpose, no account shall be taken of dealings between the party to the vertical agreement and its connected undertakings or between its connected undertakings.

2. The exemption provided for in Article 2 shall remain applicable where, for any period of two consecutive financial years, the total annual turnover threshold is exceeded by no more than 10 per cent.

Article 11

1. For the purposes of this Regulation, the terms 'undertaking', 'supplier' and 'buyer' shall include their respective connected undertakings.

2. Connected undertakings are:
   (a) undertakings in which a party to the agreement, directly or indirectly:
      — has the power to exercise more than half the voting rights, or
      — has the power to appoint more than half the members of the supervisory board, board of management or bodies legally representing the undertaking, or
      — has the right to manage the undertaking's affairs;
   (b) undertakings which directly or indirectly have, over a party to the agreement, the rights or powers listed in (a);
   (c) undertakings in which an undertaking referred to in (b) has, directly or indirectly, the rights or powers listed in (a);
   (d) undertakings in which a party to the agreement together with one or more of the undertakings referred to in (a), (b) or (c), or in which two or more of the latter undertakings, jointly have the rights or powers listed in (a);
   (e) undertakings in which the rights or the powers listed in (a) are jointly held by:
      — parties to the agreement or their respective connected undertakings referred to in (a) to (d), or
      — one or more of the parties to the agreement or one or more of their connected undertakings referred to in (a) to (d) and one or more third parties.

3. For the purposes of Article 3, the market share held by the undertakings referred to in paragraph 2(e) of this Article shall be apportioned equally to each undertaking having the rights or the powers listed in paragraph 2(a).

Article 12

1. The exemptions provided for in Commission Regulations (EEC) No 1983/83, (EEC) No 1984/83 and (EEC) No 4087/88 shall continue to apply until 31 May 2000.

2. The prohibition laid down in Article 81(1) of the EC Treaty shall not apply during the period from 1 June 2000 to 31 December 2001 in respect of agreements already in force on 31 May 2000 which do not satisfy the conditions for exemption provided for in this Regulation but which satisfy the conditions for exemption provided for in Regulations (EEC) No 1983/83, (EEC) No 1984/83 or (EEC) No 4087/88.

Article 13

This Regulation shall enter into force on 1 January 2000.
   It shall apply from 1 June 2000, except for Article 12(1) which shall apply from 1 January 2000. This Regulation shall expire on 31 May 2010.

NOTE: The BER is accompanied by detailed Guidelines which set out the Commission's policy on agreements above the thresholds and the circumstances which would warrant the withdrawal of the block exemption. These Guidelines were published in draft form in December 1999 and were adopted by the Commission on 24 May 2000, OJ, 2000, C291/1. A key aspect of the BER is the use of market share thresholds. This was the first time a Community block exemption contained market share criteria, a now common feature of block exemption Regulations, and the Guidelines must be consulted regarding specific issues that arise in the context of vertical restraints. The Commission's Notice on the definition of the relevant market for the purposes of Community competition law should also be consulted when considering market definition issues (OJ, 1997, C372/5). Although the Guidelines are rather technical they set out in great detail how the 30 per cent market share threshold should be calculated.

Guidelines on Vertical Restraints
OJ, 2000, C291/1

---

2 The relevant market for calculating the 30 per cent market share threshold under the BER

(89). Under Article 3 of the BER, it is in general the market share of the supplier that is decisive for the application of the BER. In the case of vertical agreements concluded between an association of retailers and individual members, the association is the supplier and needs to take into account its market share as a supplier. Only in the case of exclusive supply as defined in Article 1(c) of the BER is it the market share of the buyer, and only that market share, which is decisive for the application of the BER.

(90). In order to calculate the market share, it is necessary to determine the relevant market. For this the relevant product market and the relevant geographic market must be defined. The relevant product market comprises any goods or services which are regarded by the buyer as interchangeable, by reason of their characteristics, prices and intended use. The relevant geographic market comprises the area in which the undertakings concerned are involved in the supply and demand of relevant goods or services, in which the conditions of competition are sufficiently homogeneous, and which can be distinguished from neighbouring geographic areas because, in particular, conditions of competition are appreciably different in those areas.

(91). For the application of the BER, the market share of the supplier is its share on the relevant product and geographic market on which it sells to its buyers.[31] In the example below, this is market A. The product market depends in the first place on substitutability from the buyers' perspective. When the supplied product is used as an input to produce other products and is generally not recognisable in the final product, the product market is normally defined by the direct buyers' preferences. The customers of the buyers will normally not have a strong preference concerning the inputs used by the buyers. Usually the vertical restraints agreed between the supplier and buyer of the input only relate to the sale and purchase of the intermediate product and not to the sale of the resulting product. In the case of distribution of final goods, what are substitutes for the direct buyers will normally be influenced or determined by the preferences of the final consumers. A distributor, as reseller, cannot ignore the preferences of final consumers when it purchases final goods. In addition, at the distribution level the vertical restraints more often do not only concern the sale of products between supplier and buyer, but also their resale. As different distribution formats usually compete, markets are in general not defined by the form of distribution that is applied. Where suppliers generally sell a portfolio of products, the entire portfolio may determine the product market when the portfolios and not the individual products are regarded as substitutes by the buyers. As the buyers on market A are professional buyers, the geographic market is usually wider than the market where the product is resold to final consumers. Often, this will lead to the definition of national markets or wider geographic markets.

---

[31] For example, the Dutch market for new replacement truck and bus tyres in the *Michelin* case (Case 322/81, *Nederlandsche Banden-Industrie Michelin NV v Commission*, [1983] ECR 3461), the various meat markets in the Danish slaughter-house case: Commission Decision 2000/42/EC (*Danish Crown/Vestjyske Slagterier*, IV/M. 1313) OJ L20, 25.01.2000, p. 1.

(92). In the case of exclusive supply, the buyer's market share is its share of all purchases on the relevant purchase market.[32] In the example below, this is also market A.

(93). Where a vertical agreement involves three parties, each operating at a different level of trade, their market shares will have to be below the market share threshold of 30 per cent at both levels in order to benefit from the BER. If for instance, in an agreement between a manufacturer, a wholesaler (or association of retailers) and a retailer, a non-compete obligation is agreed, then the market share of both the manufacturer and the wholesaler (or association of retailers) must not exceed 30 per cent in order to benefit from the BER.

(94). Where a supplier produces both original equipment and the repair or replacement parts for this equipment, the supplier will often be the only or the major supplier on the after-market for the repair and replacement parts. This may also arise where the supplier (OEM supplier) subcontracts the manufacturing of the repair or replacement parts. The relevant market for application of the BER may be the original equipment market including the spare parts or a separate original equipment market and after-market depending on the circumstances of the case, such as the effects of the restrictions involved, the lifetime of the equipment and importance of the repair or replacement costs.

NOTE: In addition to the introduction of market share criteria, the Guidelines make it clear that 'the Commission will adopt an economic approach which is based on the effects on the market; vertical agreements have to be analysed in their legal and economic context' (para. 7) (with the exception of hard-core restrictions).

■ QUESTION

Why did the Commission introduce a market share criteria in the BER, and what are the strengths and weaknesses of such an approach?

SECTION 6: *DE MINIMIS*

The relationship between the BER and the Commission's *'de minimis'* Notice is complex. The Commission revised its Notice on Agreements of Minor Importance in 1997 (OJ, 1997, C29/3) to coincide with the Green Paper proposals. The most recent *de minimis* Notice was issued in 2001 (OJ, 2001, C368/7), see Chapter 6. The Notice provides that agreements between non-competitors with a market share of less than 15 per cent fall outside the scope of Article 81(1) EC altogether. However, Article 81(1) EC may still apply below the 15 per cent threshold with respect to hard-core restrictions provided that there is an appreciable effect on trade between Member States and on competition. Where this is the case, the relevant case law of the European Court will be applicable, see, e.g. Case 5/69 *Völk* v *Vervaecke* [1969] ECR 295.

SECTION 7: WITHDRAWAL OF BLOCK EXEMPTION

Article 7 of the BER provides for the benefit of the block exemption to be withdrawn if a vertical agreement, considered either in isolation or alongside similar agreements enforced by competing suppliers or buyers, falls within the scope of

[32] For an example of purchase markets see Commission Decision 1999/674/EC (*Rewe/Meinl* case, IV/M.1221), OJ L274, 23.10.1999, p. 1.

Article 81(1) EC. The Guidelines explain the circumstances in which this might happen.

Guidelines on Vertical Restraints
OJ, 2000, C291/1

(71) This may occur when a supplier, or a buyer in the case of exclusive supply agreements, holding a market share not exceeding 30 per cent, enters into a vertical agreement which does not give rise to objective advantages such as to compensate for the damage which it causes to competition. This may particularly be the case with respect to the distribution of goods to final consumers, who are often in a much weaker position than professional buyers of intermediate goods. In the case of sales to final consumers, the disadvantages caused by a vertical agreement may have a stronger impact than in a case concerning the sale and purchase of intermediate goods. When the conditions of Article 81(3) are not fulfilled, the Commission may withdraw the benefit of the Block Exemption Regulation under Article 6 and establish an infringement of Article 81(1).

(72) Where the withdrawal procedure is applied, the Commission bears the burden of proof that the agreement falls within the scope of Article 81(1) and that the agreement does not fulfil all four conditions of Article 81(3).

(73) The conditions for an exemption under Article 81(3) may in particular not be fulfilled when access to the relevant market or competition therein is significantly restricted by the cumulative effect of parallel networks of similar vertical agreements practised by competing suppliers or buyers. Parallel networks of vertical agreements are to be regarded as similar if they contain restraints producing similar effects on the market. Similar effects will normally occur when vertical restraints practised by competing suppliers or buyers come within one of the four groups listed in paragraphs 104 to 114. Such a situation may arise for example when, on a given market, certain suppliers practise purely qualitative selective distribution while other suppliers practise quantitative selective distribution. In such circumstances, the assessment must take account of the anti-competitive effects attributable to each individual network of agreements. Where appropriate, withdrawal may concern only the quantitative limitations imposed on the number of authorised distributors. Other cases in which a withdrawal decision may be taken include situations where the buyer, for example in the context of exclusive supply or exclusive distribution, has significant market power in the relevant downstream market where he resells the goods or provides the services.

(74) Responsibility for an anti-competitive cumulative effect can only be attributed to those undertakings which make an appreciable contribution to it. Agreements entered into by undertakings whose contribution to the cumulative effect is insignificant do not fall under the prohibition provided for in Article 81(1)[1] and are therefore not subject to the withdrawal mechanism. The assessment of such a contribution will be made in accordance with the criteria set out in paragraphs 137 to 229.

(75) A withdrawal decision can only have ex nunc effect, which means that the exempted status of the agreements concerned will not be affected until the date at which the withdrawal becomes effective.

(76) Under Article 7 of the Block Exemption Regulation, the competent authority of a Member State may withdraw the benefit of the Block Exemption Regulation in respect of vertical agreements whose anti-competitive effects are felt in the territory of the Member State concerned or a part thereof, which has all the characteristics of a distinct geographic market. Where a Member State has not enacted legislation enabling the national competition authority to apply Community competition law or at least to withdraw the benefit of the Block Exemption Regulation, the Member State may ask the Commission to initiate proceedings to this effect.

---

[1] Judgment in the *Delimitis* Case.

(77) Often, such cases lend themselves to decentralised enforcement by national competition authorities. However, the Commission reserves the right to take on certain cases displaying a particular Community interest, such as cases raising a new point of law.

(78) National decisions of withdrawal must be taken in accordance with the procedures laid down under national law and will only have effect within the territory of the Member State concerned. Such national decisions must not prejudice the uniform application of the Community competition rules and the full effect of the measures adopted in implementation of those rules[1]. Compliance with this principle implies that national competition authorities must carry out their assessment under Article 81 in the light of the relevant criteria developed by the Court of Justice and the Court of First Instance and in the light of notices and previous decisions adopted by the Commission.

(79) The Commission considers that the consultation mechanisms provided for in the Notice on cooperation between national competition authorities and the Commission[2] should be used to avert the risk of conflicting decisions and duplication of procedures.

NOTE: Moreover, Article 8 of the BER enables the Commission to exclude, by Regulation, from the block exemption parallel networks of similar vertical restraints where these cover more than 50 per cent of a relevant market.

(81) Whereas the withdrawal of the benefit of the Block Exemption Regulation under Article 6 implies the adoption of a decision establishing an infringement of Article 81 by an individual company, the effect of a regulation under Article 8 is merely to remove, in respect of the restraints and the markets concerned, the benefit of the application of the Block Exemption Regulation and to restore the full application of Article 81(1) and (3). Following the adoption of a regulation declaring the Block Exemption inapplicable in respect of certain vertical restraints on a particular market, the criteria developed by the relevant case-law of the Court of Justice and the Court of First Instance and by notices and previous decisions adopted by the Commission will guide the application of Article 81 to individual agreements. Where appropriate, the Commission will take a decision in an individual case, which can provide guidance to all the undertakings operating on the market concerned.

(82) For the purpose of calculating the 50 per cent market coverage ratio, account must be taken of each individual network of vertical agreements containing restraints, or combinations of restraints, producing similar effects on the market. Similar effects normally result when the restraints come within one of the four groups listed in paragraphs 104 to 114.

(83) Article 8 does not entail an obligation on the part of the Commission to act where the 50 per cent market-coverage ratio is exceeded. In general, disapplication is appropriate when it is likely that access to the relevant market or competition therein is appreciably restricted. This may occur in particular when parallel networks of selective distribution covering more than 50 per cent of a market make use of selection criteria which are not required by the nature of the relevant goods or discriminate against certain forms of distribution capable of selling such goods.

(84) In assessing the need to apply Article 8, the Commission will consider whether individual withdrawal would be a more appropriate remedy. This may depend, in particular, on the number of competing undertakings contributing to a cumulative effect on a market or the number of affected geographic markets within the Community.

(85) Any regulation adopted under Article 8 must clearly set out its scope. This means, first, that the Commission must define the relevant product and geographic market(s) and, secondly, that it must identify the type of vertical restraint in respect of which the Block Exemption Regulation will no longer apply. As regards the latter aspect, the Commission may modulate the scope of its regulation according to the competition concern which it intends to address.

[1] Judgment of the Court of Justice in Case 14/68 *Walt Wilhelm and Others* v *Bundeskartellamt* [1969] ECR 1, paragraph 4, and judgment in *Delimitis*.
[2] OJ C 313, 15.10.1997, p. 3, points 49 to 53.

For instance, while all parallel networks of single-branding type arrangements shall be taken into account in view of establishing the 50 per cent market coverage ratio, the Commission may nevertheless restrict the scope of the disapplication regulation only to non-compete obligations exceeding a certain duration. Thus, agreements of a shorter duration or of a less restrictive nature might be left unaffected, in consideration of the lesser degree of foreclosure attributable to such restraints. Similarly, when on a particular market selective distribution is practised in combination with additional restraints such as non-compete or quantity-forcing on the buyer, the disapplication regulation may concern only such additional restraints. Where appropriate, the Commission may also provide guidance by specifying the market share level which, in the specific market context, may be regarded as insufficient to bring about a significant contribution by an individual undertaking to the cumulative effect.

(86) The transitional period of not less than six months that the Commission will have to set under Article 8(2) should allow the undertakings concerned to adapt their agreements to take account of the regulation disapplying the Block Exemption Regulation.

(87) A regulation disapplying the Block Exemption Regulation will not affect the exempted status of the agreements concerned for the period preceding its entry into force.

NOTE: Regulation 2790/1999 only applies to exclusive dealing, purchasing, and franchise agreements. Discussion has centred on whether it could be extended to other sectors which have previously benefited from their own block exemption, for example the motor industry. The block exemption applicable to the car industry, Regulation 1475/95, expired on 30 September 2002 and was replaced by a new block exemption Regulation, 1400/2002 on 1 October 2002. Pressure to remove block exemption Regulation 1475/95 was intense and its demise seemed inevitable. Regulation 1400/2002 is due to expire at the same time as the BER in May 2010, and the Commission has commenced a consultation exercise on whether to replace the block exemption. See the Commission's 2009 'Issues Paper on the Motor Vehicle Block Exemption Regulation', and the press release on 9 February 2009: 'Antitrust: Commissioner Kroes hosts roundtable to discuss future of the Car Block Exemption Regulation' (MEMO/09/57). A review of the BER has already begun and is likely to gain a higher public profile in 2009.

SECTION 8: UK COMPETITION LAW AND VERTICAL RESTRAINTS

Immediately after the coming into force of the Competition Act 1998 ('CA 1998'), UK competition law adopted a far more lenient approach to vertical restraints than EC competition law. The UK Government was reluctant to follow the strict approach of the Commission and Community courts. There were also concerns as to how to cope with the anticipated large number of notifications from business seeking individual exemptions for mostly benign vertical agreements. In the passage of the Competition Bill through Parliament, Lord Simon confirmed that:

There remains a case therefore for special treatment of vertical agreements under the [Act] to avoid the burden of unnecessary notification and to ease the so-called 'straitjacket' which existing European block exemptions impose. (Hansard, HL Report Stage, 9 February 1998, col. 901).

Section 50(1) of the CA 1998 provides the Secretary of State with power to make an Order modifying the application of the Chapter I prohibition to vertical agreements. The Competition Act 1998 (Land and Vertical Agreements Exclusion Order 2000 (SI 2000/310) entered into force on 1 March 2000, and excluded vertical agreements, aside from resale price maintenance, from the application of the Chapter I prohibition of anti-competitive agreements until 30 April 2005, when it was repealed. The adoption of Regulation 2790/1999 and particularly Regulation 1/2003 persuaded the UK Government of the importance in ensuring a consistent approach to vertical restraints under UK and EC competition law. In its White Paper prior to the introduction and passage of the Enterprise Act 2002, the UK Government considered the rationale for repealing the vertical agreements exclusion order.

Productivity and Enterprise: A World Class Competition Regime
Department of Trade and Industry White Paper, Cm 5233, 31 July 2001, paras 8.14–8.16

Vertical agreements

8.14 In 1997, the Government decided that vertical agreements should be excluded from the Competition Act in order to guard against the risk of large numbers of notifications of benign agreements. Along with the decision to allow the OFT to charge for notifications, and the OFT's campaign to discourage notifications, this policy has been successful with only 12 notifications in the first year of operation of the new legislation.

8.15 In June 2000, the European Commission brought into force a block exemption which covers vertical agreements. The Commission's block exemption is more narrowly drawn than our domestic exclusion in particular, it does not cover agreements where one of the parties has a market share exceeding 30%.

8.16 The Government believes that there is a risk that the more permissive domestic exclusion may have the effect of discouraging some private actions. Now that a European-level block exemption is in place (with parallel effect in the UK), there is no strong case for retaining the domestic exclusion. Therefore, the Government intends to repeal the domestic exclusion of vertical agreements.

NOTE: The UK Government subsequently repealed the UK exclusion order with the Competition Act 1998 (Land Agreements Exclusion and Revocation) Order 2004 (SI 2004/1260) with effect from 1 May 2005, and the OFT provides guidance on the approach to vertical restraints under UK competition law in light of its obligations arising from Regulation 1/2003.

OFT guideline, *Vertical Agreements*
OFT 419, December 2004, paras 3.1–3.2, 3.30–3.33 [footnotes omitted]

3.1 The Block Exemption creates a 'safe harbour' for large numbers of vertical agreements under Article 81(3), so that agreements falling within the terms of the Block Exemption are automatically exempt from the application of Article 81(1). The Block Exemption also has the parallel effect of creating a 'safe harbour' exempting agreements from the application of the Chapter I prohibition, by virtue of section 10 of the Act. Thus agreements falling within the terms of the Block Exemption will be exempt from the application of both Article 81 and the Chapter I prohibition. The Block Exemption does not apply to agreements whose subject matter falls within the scope of any other EC block exemption regulation.

3.2 The European Commission's Notice *Guidelines on Vertical Restraints* sets out the principles for the assessment of vertical agreements under Article 81, including the application of the Block Exemption to vertical agreements. The OFT will have regard to this Notice in its assessment of vertical agreements, in relation to both Article 81 and the Chapter I prohibition. This guideline should be read together with the Block Exemption and the Notice.

NOTE: the parallel exemption of the BER under s. 10 of the CA 1998 is significant. Section 10(2) provides that 'an agreement is exempt from the Chapter I prohibition if it does not affect trade between Member States but otherwise falls within a category of agreement which is exempt from the Community prohibition by virtue of a Regulation' and thereby helps to ensure the consistent treatment of vertical restraints under EC and UK competition law. The OFT guidelines also explain the circumstances whereby the benefit of the BER could be withdrawn.

Withdrawal of the Block Exemption

3.30 As mentioned above, the Block Exemption exempts vertical agreements because they do not generally give rise to competition concerns. The OFT may, under Article 29(2) of the Modernisation Regulation, withdraw the benefit of the Block Exemption from any agreement if the following conditions are met:

- the agreement in question has effects that are incompatible with Article 81(3) in the territory of the United Kingdom, or a part of the United Kingdom, and
- the relevant territory has all the characteristics of a distinct geographical market.

In the case of withdrawal of the Block Exemption by the OFT, it will be for the OFT to demonstrate that the agreement infringes Article 81(1) and that it does not satisfy the conditions of Article 81(3) of the United Kingdom (or part of the United Kingdom) that is a distinct geographic market. In practice the OFT is likely to exercise this power only rarely. The United Kingdom courts have no power to withdraw the benefit of the Block Exemption.

3.31 Where the OFT proposes to exercise its powers to withdraw the benefit of the Block Exemption from an agreement it must, following the procedures specified in the *OFT's Rules*, give written notice to the parties to that agreement and give them the opportunity to make representations. It may also consult the public. If the OFT has decided to withdraw the benefit of the Block Exemption it will notify the parties to that agreement of its decision and will publish the decision on a public register on the OFT's website.

Consequences of withdrawal

3.32 Where the OFT decides to withdraw the benefit of the Block Exemption from a particular agreement it at the same time establishes that the agreement infringes Article 81. Such an infringement finding can have effect only from the date of the withdrawal. The agreement will be void only from the date of withdrawal and any financial penalties imposed in respect of that agreement can relate only to the period after the withdrawal of the Block Exemption.

3.33 Withdrawal of the Block Exemption in a particular case will result in any parallel exemption also ceasing to have effect, by virtue of section 10(4)(b) of the Act.

NOTE: The impact of Regulation 1/2003 can be seen from para. 3.30 above and helps to delineate the respective areas of competence between EC competition law and that of each Member State. Notably the legal certainty generated by block exemption Regulations is protected by the inability to find an infringement until after the date of withdrawal of the block exemption. The OFT guidelines also highlight that vertical restraints may be caught by other aspects of UK competition law in certain circumstances.

Article 82 and the Chapter II prohibition

6.1 A vertical agreement entered into by an undertaking which holds a dominant position in a market may be subject to Article 82 and/or the Chapter II prohibition. There is no exemption or exclusion for vertical agreements from Article 82 or the Chapter II prohibition. The OFT's application of these prohibitions is described in the competition law guideline *Abuse of a dominant position* (OFT402).

6.2 The economic analysis of vertical restraints is often similar whether a vertical restraint is assessed under Article 81 and/or the Chapter I prohibition or Article 82 and/or the Chapter II prohibition. The factors described in Part 7 of this guideline (below) therefore also apply to the analysis of a vertical restraint when it is assessed in the context of Article 82 or the Chapter II prohibition.

The Enterprise Act 2002

6.3 The market investigation provisions in the Enterprise Act 2002 (see the Enterprise Act guidance *Market investigation references* (OFT511)) may, in certain circumstances, be relevant for dealing with possible competition problems in relation to vertical agreements. A market investigation may, for example, be appropriate where vertical agreements are prevalent in a market and have the effect of preventing the entry of new competitors into the market, but there is no evidence of collusion between the firms involved which might have caused this situation to arise.

NOTE: The treatment of vertical restraints under UK competition law was initially one of the few areas of significant divergence with EC competition law after the coming into force of the CA 1998. The revised EC approach to block exemptions in this area as well as decentralization and abolishing the notification procedure under Regulation 1/2003 facilitated the repeal of the vertical agreements exclusion order in the UK. UK competition law is now consistent with the Community approach to vertical restraints.

■ QUESTION

Was the UK Government correct to repeal the vertical agreements exclusion order?

FURTHER READING

Biro, Z., and Fletcher, A., 'The EC Green Paper on Vertical Restraints: An Economic Comment', Editorial [1998] ECLR 129.

Forrester, I., and Norall, C., 'The Laicisation of Community Law: Self-help and the Rule of Reason—How Competition Law Is and Could Be Applied' (1984) 21 CML Rev 11.

Peeters, J., 'The Rule of Reason revisited: Prohibition on Restraints of Competition in the Sherman Act and the EEC Treaty' (1989) 37 AJ of Comparative Law, p. 521.

Peeperkorn, L., 'Resale Price Maintenance and its Alleged Efficiencies' (2008) European Competition Journal 201.

Posner, R.A., 'The Next Step in the Antitrust Treatment of Restricted Distribution: *per se* legality' (1981) 48 U Chi L Rev 6.

Rodger, B.J., and MacCulloch, A., Chapter 6, 'The Chapter I prohibition—prohibiting cartels or permitting verticals? Or both?', in *The UK Competition Act: A New Era for UK Competition Law*, Oxford, Hart Publishing, 2000.

Subiotto, R., and Amato, F., 'Preliminary Analysis of the Commission's Reform Concerning Vertical Restraints' (2000) 23(2) Journal of World Competition 5–26.

Whish, R., 'Regulation 2790/99: The Commission's "New Style" Block Exemption for Vertical Agreements' (2000) 37 CML Rev 887.

9

Cartels and leniency

Cartels were described as the 'supreme evil of antitrust' by the US Supreme Court in *Verizon Communications* v *Law Offices of Curtis V Trinko* 540 US 398, 408 (2004). They are generally seen as the most heinous competition violation, and one of the most damaging to the economy. It is therefore no surprise that most competition authorities are keen to target cartel activity as an enforcement priority. There is no real debate as to whether cartels should be challenged, they are the most universally accepted form of anti-competitive conduct; the main debate surrounds the best methods to catch and punish cartels that exist in order to deter others from forming. The debate is largely one surrounding enforcement mechanisms, but before considering that debate some background issues can be addressed. Cartel activity clearly falls within the definition of an anti-competitive agreement in Article 81 EC and s. 2 of the Competition Act 1998, but what is a cartel?

European Commission, 'Antitrust: Commission action against cartels—Questions and answers'
MEMO/09/32, 28 January 2009

What is a cartel?

It is an illegal secret agreement concluded between competitors to fix prices, restrict supply and/or divide up markets. The agreement may take a wide variety of forms but often relates to sales prices or increases in such prices, restrictions on sales or production capacities, sharing out of product or geographic markets or customers, and collusion on the other commercial conditions for the sale of products or services.

Why are cartels harmful to consumers, businesses and to the economy in general?

Cartels shield participants from competition allowing them to charge higher prices and removing the pressure on them to improve the products they sell or find more efficient ways in which to produce them. It is the customers (companies and consumers) who foot the bill in terms of paying higher prices for lower quality and narrower choice. This not only makes consumers and businesses suffer but also adversely affects the competitiveness of the economy as a whole.

What legal basis underpins the Commission's action to combat cartels?

Article 81 of the Treaty establishing the European Community prohibits agreements and concerted practices between firms that distort competition within the Single Market. Fines of up to 10% of their worldwide turnover may be imposed on the guilty parties.

What happens to the proceeds from fines?

The amount of the fines is paid into the Community budget. The fines therefore help to finance the European Union and reduce the tax burden on individuals.

OFT, *Cartels and the Competition Act 1998*
OFT 435, **March** 2005

What is a cartel?

At its most simple, a cartel is an agreement between businesses not to compete with each other. The agreement can often be verbal. Typically, cartel members may agree on:

- **price fixing**—the price they will charge or the discounts/credit terms they will offer their customers for goods or services
- **bid rigging**—deciding who should win a contract in a competitive tender process
- **output quotas/restrictions**—limiting the levels of products or services supplied to a market in order to increase the price, and
- **market sharing**—choosing which customers or geographic areas they will supply, or preventing competitors (eg, foreign competitors) from entering the market.

In some cartels several of these elements may be present.

Why should cartels be broken up?

Cartels allow businesses to achieve greater profits for less effort to the detriment of consumers and the economy as a whole. For the purchasers of their goods or services this means:

- higher prices
- poorer quality, and
- less or no choice.

How can you spot a cartel?

You are generally well placed to notice when your suppliers are deviating from normal competitive practices. There are a number of signs that may indicate that a cartel is operating. Some examples are where suppliers:

- raise prices by the same amount and at around the same time
- offer the same discounts or have identical discount structures
- quote or charge identical or very similar prices
- refuse to supply a customer because of their location, and
- use give-away terms or phrases, such as
  - 'the industry has decided that margins should be increased'
  - 'we have agreed not to supply in that area', and
  - 'our competitors will not quote you a different price.'

The presence of these signs does not necessarily mean that a cartel is operating. Some, such as simultaneous price changes or similar prices, can be perfectly consistent with normal competitive responses in the market place. However, you should be particularly suspicious where several of the signs are present.

Where are cartels found?

Cartels can occur in almost any industry and can involve goods or services at the manufacturing, distribution or retail level. Some sectors may be more susceptible to cartels than others because of their structure or the way in which they operate. For example, a cartel may be more likely to exist in an industry where:

- there are few competitors

- the products have similar characteristics (which leaves little scope for competition on quality or service)
- communication channels between competitors are already established (eg, trade associations), and
- the industry is suffering from excess capacity or there is general recession.

The fact that these conditions are not present does not rule out the possibility that a cartel is operating. Conversely, the fact that an industry shows some or all of these characteristics does not automatically mean that some form of cartel is operating, but you should at least be alert to that possibility.

This view of cartels was not always prevalent in the UK. For many years they were tolerated, if not encouraged. Much of the British Empire was built on the back of arrangements that would not be tolerated today.

Norris v Government of the United States of America
[2008] UKHL 16, [2008] 1 AC 920

9. In the field of restrictive trade agreements more generally, the law was developed in a series of decisions of which five in particular were relied on in argument. It was pointed out, quite correctly, that some of these cases arose on facts different from those of the present case.

10. In the first of the cases, *Jones v North* (1875) LR 19 Eq 426, four parties were invited to tender for the supply of stone to a public authority. They made a collusive agreement by which one party was to buy stone from the other three and submit the lowest tender, two parties were to submit a higher tender and the fourth party was to submit no tender. There is nothing in the report to suggest that the public authority knew of this agreement, and every reason to suppose that it did not. The matter came before the court when the defendants, in breach of the agreement, submitted a tender, which was accepted, and the party which was to supply under the agreement brought proceedings to restrain performance by the party which had broken ranks. The action succeeded. Bacon V-C considered the plaintiff's case (p 429) as "very honest". It was submitted (p 428) that the plaintiff could not obtain equitable relief since the arrangement was a device to compel the authority, under the fiction of a public competition, to accept tenders not representing the real market price of the commodity, but this submission the vice-chancellor rejected, finding the agreement (p 430) to be "perfectly lawful", to contain "nothing illegal", and not deserving to be characterised as a conspiracy.

11. The case of *Mogul Steamship Co Ltd v McGregor, Gow & Co* (1888) 21 QBD 544 was tried at first instance by Lord Coleridge CJ without a jury. The plaintiff company claimed damages for a conspiracy to prevent it carrying on its trade between China and Europe. Its complaint was made against a group of shipowners who banded together in order to keep the trade between China and London in their own hands for their own commercial benefit and to that end offered a very low rate and an agreed rebate to shippers who shipped tea on their vessels but not, in the relevant year, on the plaintiff's, the object being to exclude the plaintiff from the trade. The efficacy of the defendants' agreement depended on its being known in the market, so there was no element of secrecy or non-disclosure, but the plaintiff attacked the agreement as wrongful and malicious, supported by bribery, coercion and inducement. The chief justice (pp 552–553) found no evidence of bribery, coercion or (in the relevant sense) inducement, and held (p 554) that the agreement was not unlawful, wrongful or malicious.

12. In the Court of Appeal ((1889) 23 QBD 598) Lord Esher MR, dissenting, held the agreement to be an indictable conspiracy (p 610). But a majority of the court agreed with Lord Coleridge. Bowen LJ, in a justly-celebrated judgment, held that in the absence of aggravating features such as (pp 614, 615, 618) fraud, intimidation obstruction, violence or interference with contractual or other rights, there was nothing in the defendants' agreement or conduct to make it unlawful or actionable, and even if it were held to be a restraint of trade (pp 619–620) the agreement would be void

and unenforceable, not actionable or criminal. Fry LJ gave a reasoned judgment, upholding the judgment of the chief justice (p 632).

13. A further appeal to the House was unanimously dismissed by a seven-member bench: [1892] AC 25. It was accepted that the defendants had acted to advance their own commercial interests, and with no malicious or wrongful object of injuring the plaintiff company, although their gain was inevitably its loss. In the absence of any aggravating feature such as misrepresentation, compulsion, intimidation, violence, molestation or inducement of breach of contract, the defendants' conduct would not have been unlawful if done by a single independent party and was not rendered unlawful by their combination. Even if a restraint of trade, the defendants' agreement was at most void and unenforceable, not actionable or indictable.

14. The decision of the Privy Council in *Attorney General of the Commonwealth of Australia v Adelaide Steamship Co Ltd* [1913] AC 781 concerned an agreement between a group of colliery owners and a group of shipowners which was ancillary to an agreement between the colliery owners themselves. No more need be said of these agreements than that, as the Board held (pp 806, 808), both were very obviously in restraint of trade. The appeal turned on the Australian Industries Preservation Act 1906 which, analogously with the Sherman Act which featured in the argument and the judgment, criminalised certain anti-competitive acts done with (sections 4 and 7) the intention or (section 10) the effect that such act should be to the detriment of the public. The judgment of the Board was given by Lord Parker of Waddington, who took the opportunity to conduct a detailed review of the relevant common law principles. He summarised their effect at p 797:

> "It is only necessary to add that no contract was ever an offence at common law merely because it was in restraint of trade. The parties to such a contract, even if unenforceable, were always at liberty to act on it in the manner agreed. Similarly combinations, not amounting to contracts, in restraint of trade were never unlawful at common law. To make any such contract or combination unlawful it must amount to a criminal conspiracy, and the essence of a criminal conspiracy is a contract or combination to do something unlawful, or something lawful by unlawful means. The right of the individual to carry on his trade or business in the manner he considers best in his own interests involves the right of combining with others in a common course of action, provided such common course of action is undertaken with a single view to the interests of the combining parties and not with a view to injure others (the *Mogul Steamship Case* 23 QBD 598; [1892] AC 25)."

The attorney-general's appeal failed because the Board found (p 816) no satisfactory evidence of an intention to act to the detriment of the public and no sufficient evidence of injury to the public.

15. In *North Western Salt Co Ltd v Electrolytic Alkali Co Ltd* [1913] 3 KB 422 an obviously restrictive agreement came before the Court of Appeal and Farwell LJ said ([1914] AC 461, 465, although this does not appear in the incomplete Court of Appeal report):

> "In the present case, no circumstances in my opinion could justify such a contract made for the mere purpose of raising prices, with the inseparable incident of depriving the members of the public of the choice of manufacturers, while hoodwinking them into the belief that such choice is open to them ..."

The Court of Appeal accordingly held, by a majority, that the agreement was in restraint of trade, and so unenforceable, despite the defendants' failure to plead this defence. An appeal to the House succeeded. Clearly the combination in question was one the purpose of which was to regulate supply and keep up prices (p 469) but the public interest had not necessarily or even probably been damaged (p 471) and the Court of Appeal had no material before it to decide whether it had been damaged or not (pp 469, 470). The agreement had not been shown to be in unreasonable restraint of trade and was therefore enforceable.

16. *Rawlings v General Trading Co* [1921] 1 KB 635 concerned an agreement made between prospective bidders at an auction of military surplus stores. They agreed that in order to avoid competition only one of them should bid. Thus the defendant was to bid on their joint account, and the goods purchased were to be shared equally, each paying half the purchase price. The goods were duly knocked down to the defendant, but he reneged on the agreement, which the plaintiff

then sued to enforce. At first instance ([1920] 3 KB 30, 35) the judge held that, at any rate where goods were the property of the public, it was against public policy that people should combine at an auction to procure that goods were sold at a price considerably below their fair value, with the necessary result that the public were defrauded. It was the equivalent (p 34) of secretly using a puffer to drive the price up. He dismissed the action. In the Court of Appeal ([1921] 1 KB 635), Scrutton LJ agreed with the judge. He thought it clear that the agreement was neither criminal nor actionable at the suit of the vendors (p 643), but considered that the restrictions accepted in the agreement, although reasonable in the plaintiff's interest, were contrary to the interest of the public and thus an unjustified and unenforceable restraint of trade (pp 643, 644, 647). A majority of the court held otherwise. Bankes LJ regarded the judge's conclusion as contrary to settled authority (pp 640–641). Atkin LJ shared that view (p 652), but also held that the agreement was one the parties were free, in the absence of express or implied misrepresentations intended to deceive, to make and enforce (p 648), and there was nothing in this agreement which was ex facie illegal (p 652).

17. The effect of these authorities may be succinctly summarised. The common law recognised that an agreement in restraint of trade might be unreasonable in the public interest, and in such cases the agreement would be held to be void and unenforceable. But unless there were aggravating features such as fraud, misrepresentation, violence, intimidation or inducement of a breach of contract, such agreements were not actionable or indictable. In the course of the authorities a number of different reasons were given for this conclusion. They included the following:

(1) While commercial parties could not lawfully act with the wrongful and malicious object of injuring another party, they were free to promote their own business as they thought fit, "however severe and egotistical" such means might be, even though this might inflict loss on others. See *Mogul*: Lord Coleridge CJ (pp 552–553); Bowen LJ, p 614, 620; Fry LJ, pp 622, 624, 625; Lord Halsbury, pp 36, 40; Lord Hannen, pp 58–59.

(2) While agreements in restraint of trade might be injurious to the public interest, they might also confer benefits on the public, as by preventing cut-throat competition, loss of supplies or services or production facilities, lowering of wages or unemployment. See *Mogul*: Lord Coleridge CJ, p 548; Bowen LJ, p 619; Fry LJ, pp 626–627; Lord Bramwell, p 46; *Adelaide Steamship*, Lord Parker, pp 809–810; 813, 816; *North Western Salt*, Lord Haldane LC, pp 469–471; Lord Parker, p 480; Lord Sumner, p 481.

(3) Other than in very clear cases the courts were not well-fitted to assess whether restraints of trade were injurious to the public or not, and it was not "the province of judges to mould and stretch the law of conspiracy in order to keep pace with the calculations of political economy". See *Mogul*: Bowen LJ, pp 615, 620; Fry LJ, pp 625–626; Lord Watson, p 43; Lord Bramwell, pp 45, 49; Lord Morris, pp 50–51.

(4) To limit the bounds of competition would be contrary to what modern legislation had shown to be the present policy of the state. See *Mogul*: Fry LJ, p 626.

(5) The victim of an anti-competitive practice could show no legal right which had been infringed. See *Mogul*: Lord Halsbury LC, p 38.

(6) There was no authority for the proposition that it was actionable for one party to compete against another for the purpose of gain and not out of actual malice, even though the object was to drive that party away from his place of business and did so. See *Mogul*: Fry LJ, pp 630–632; Lord Bramwell, p 46; Lord Field, p 57.

NOTE: In this extradition case Mr Ian Norris was seeking to escape extradition to the US where he would be liable to prosecution for his role in a carbon products cartel. Extradition is only possible where the act is considered to be criminal in both the UK and US. As the events in question were before the Enterprise Act 2002 ('EA 2002') came into force it was necessary for the House of Lords to address the nature of a cartel arrangement under the English common law. It was only in the post-war era when cartels were re-appraised and steps were taken to address the way in which much of European industry was cartelized. This process has now culminated in a very hostile regulatory climate in which all cartels are clearly unlawful and a number of authorities are using whatever tools they can to bring cartels out into the open and take action against their participants.

Harding, C., and Joshua, J., *Regulating Cartels in Europe—A Study of Legal Control of Corporate Delinquency*
Oxford, OUP, 2003, p 6 [footnotes omitted]

After some 30 years of EC case law on the subject, there is now a line of historical development which may be traced: 'exploratory cases during the 1970s; more full-blooded investigations during the early 1980s; significant legal challenges to and testing of the Commission's competence and powers during the later 1980s and 1990s; and a more recent judicial 'recovery' of the Commission's position as a cartel regulator. The control of cartels at a European level has in effect become a significant legal laboratory for testing the limits of regulation and commercial activity. As a former Director-General of DG IV (Ehlermann) commented, 'in no other field of law are the limits of judicial protection and due process so frequently tested as in competition cases'. Thus while the general textbook discussion of competition law continues to emphasize the 'market analysis' approach, the more specific area of cartel law has become increasingly dominated by formal and procedural legal argument, to the extent of taking on board the language of human rights violation. It provides an instructive study of the way in which powerful commercial interests can promote a line of legal development.

SECTION 2: DETERRENCE

The contemporary debate surrounding cartels is essentially one of regulation: how to employ regulatory tools in order to best catch and punish cartelists. In that regulatory debate one of the key ideas is that of deterrence. It is better to use the law to punish those that are caught, not simply to extract retribution, but also to discourage, or deter, others from contemplating similar action in the future. The link between punishment and deterrence is vital.

Wils, W.P.J., 'Optimal Antitrust Fines: Theory and Practice'
(2006) 29 World Competition 183, pp. 187 and 190 [footnotes omitted]

[O]ne can try to prevent antitrust violations by altering the balance of expected benefits and expected costs of violations. This can be done by prosecuting and punishing violations, creating a credible threat of penalties which weighs sufficiently in the balance of expected costs and benefits so as to deter calculating companies from committing antitrust violations. Apart from such deterrence, other methods could also be used to alter the balance of expected costs and benefits. To be successful from the cartelists' perspective, price-fixing or similar cartel agreements require effort to determine the agreed price or other factors, to allocate the joint profit through quotas or otherwise, and to monitor and punish cheating by the cartel members. Antitrust enforcement can increase the cost of setting up and running cartels in different ways. One very important measure is to make cartel agreements legally unenforceable, as Article 81(2) EC does.

    ...

    The idea of deterrence is to create a credible threat of penalties which weighs sufficiently in the balance of expected costs and benefits to deter calculating companies from committing antitrust violations. Deterrence through the use of fines will work if, and only if, from the perspective of the company contemplating whether or not to commit a violation, the expected fine exceeds the expected gain from the violation. The expected fine equals the nominal amount of the fine discounted by the probability that a fine is effectively imposed. Certain types of violations are more easily detectable than others. Some companies may also be better in avoiding apprehension than others, possibly because they are more experienced. The probability of actually being fined obviously also depends on the competition authorities' enforcement priorities and their available resources. If, for instance, the probability of detection and punishment is one out of five, the expected fine is only one fifth of the nominal amount. In order to deter, the nominal amount of the fine must then be at least five times larger than the expected gain. The minimum fine for deterrence to work thus equals the expected gain from the violation multiplied by the inverse of the probability of a fine being effectively imposed.

NOTE: Through the operation of this principle it is clear that for competition regulation to be effective the authorities, such as the European Commission and the OFT, should have two main tasks: (i) to uncover and punish as many cartels as possible, and (ii) to ensure that when punishments are determined they are sufficiently high to deter potential future cartelists from entering into cartel arrangements. If levels of enforcement and punishment are too low there will not be sufficient deterrence and it is likely that cartels will still form; as the rewards, through increased profitability, outweigh the penalties imposed in the (more or less) unlikely event you are caught. This model of deterrence is usually seen as being particularly apt for economic regulation as it is seen to be most likely to be effective when the entities involved in the potentially unlawful behaviour are rational profit-maximizers; sometimes described as 'amoral calculators'. Undertakings that are driven by profit should be able to calculate which course of conduct gives the best chance of maximizing their profitability and therefore deterrence should be effective.

SECTION 3: CARTEL PENALTIES

A: Corporate fines

The main penalty for cartels in the EC and UK is corporate fines imposed by the competition authorities. Before one can analyse the deterrent effect of fines in the EC or UK it is important to have an estimation of the impact of cartel activity on the economy. Only then can the relevant authority hope to set a deterrent fine.

Connor, J.M., and Lande, R.H., 'How High Do Cartels Raise Prices? Implications for Optimal Cartel Fines'
(2005) 80 Tul L Rev 513, pp 559–60 [footnotes omitted]

Our survey identified about 200 serious social-science studies of cartels which contained 674 observations of "average" overcharges. Our primary finding is that the median cartel overcharge for all types of cartels over all time periods has been 25%: 17–19% for domestic cartels and 30–33% for international cartels. Thus, in general, international cartels have been about 75% more effective in raising prices than domestic cartels. Because the United States has historically had by far the toughest system of anticartel sanctions, this could imply that these sanctions have been having significant effects. These cartel overcharges are skewed to the high side, pushing the mean overcharge for all types of cartels over all time periods to 49%. These results are generally consistent with the few, more limited, previously published works that survey cartel overcharges. The six studies we thought exhibited the highest standards of scholarship (Table 1) report samples with simple average median overcharges of 28% and simple average mean overcharges of 31% of affected sales.

. . .

For most types of cartels there have been modest downtrends in cartel markups over time. In particular, it should be noted that since 1990, the average overcharges of discovered cartels fell to 25% for international cartels. Moreover, the thirty post-1990 domestic observations had a mean overcharge of 26% and a median overcharge of 24%. Because the post-1990 era has been the period with by far the highest level of fines imposed, these decreases are consistent with the theory of optimal deterrence discussed in Part II. They also suggest that the recent worldwide trend toward the intensification of cartel penalties has been desirable. If the worldwide system of criminal fines can be made to correspond more closely to the actual levels of cartel overcharges, sanctions against price-fixing will more closely provide optimal deterrence.

NOTE: This estimation indicates the potential harm that cartels cause, in the sense that they directly overcharge their customers, and therefore the benefits that are gained by the cartel members. What these figures cannot take into account is the 'dead-weight' loss to the economy that is not reflected in direct overcharge to customers. While this loss to the economy is important in the reasons that the law deems such agreements to be unlawful, it is not important in the terms of deterrence as the 'rational profit-maximizing' cartel member will only take their costs/benefits into account in deciding on their future course of action.

Commission Notice, 'Guidelines on the method of setting fines imposed pursuant to Article 23(2)(a) of Regulation No 1/2003'
OJ, 2006, C210/2

Method for the setting of fines

9. Without prejudice to point 37 below, the Commission will use the following two-step methodology when setting the fine to be imposed on undertakings or associations of undertakings.

10. First, the Commission will determine a basic amount for each undertaking or association of undertakings (see Section 1 below).

11. Second, it may adjust that basic amount upwards or downwards (see Section 2 below).

1. Basic amount of the fine

12. The basic amount will be set by reference to the value of sales and applying the following methodology.

A. Calculation of the value of sales

13. In determining the basic amount of the fine to be imposed, the Commission will take the value of the undertaking's sales of goods or services to which the infringement directly or indirectly relates in the relevant geographic area within the EEA. It will normally take the sales made by the undertaking during the last full business year of its participation in the infringement (hereafter "value of sales").

14. Where the infringement by an association of undertakings relates to the activities of its members, the value of sales will generally correspond to the sum of the value of sales by its members.

15. In determining the value of sales by an undertaking, the Commission will take that undertaking's best available figures.

16. Where the figures made available by an undertaking are incomplete or not reliable, the Commission may determine the value of its sales on the basis of the partial figures it has obtained and/or any other information which it regards as relevant and appropriate.

17. The value of sales will be determined before VAT and other taxes directly related to the sales.

18. Where the geographic scope of an infringement extends beyond the EEA (e.g. worldwide cartels), the relevant sales of the undertakings within the EEA may not properly reflect the weight of each undertaking in the infringement. This may be the case in particular with worldwide market-sharing arrangements.

In such circumstances, in order to reflect both the aggregate size of the relevant sales within the EEA and the relative weight of each undertaking in the infringement, the Commission may assess the total value of the sales of goods or services to which the infringement relates in the relevant geographic area (wider than the EEA), may determine the share of the sales of each undertaking party to the infringement on that market and may apply this share to the aggregate sales within the EEA of the undertakings concerned. The result will be taken as the value of sales for the purpose of setting the basic amount of the fine.

B. Determination of the basic amount of the fine

19. The basic amount of the fine will be related to a proportion of the value of sales, depending on the degree of gravity of the infringement, multiplied by the number of years of infringement.

20. The assessment of gravity will be made on a case-by-case basis for all types of infringement, taking account of all the relevant circumstances of the case.

21. As a general rule, the proportion of the value of sales taken into account will be set at a level of up to 30% of the value of sales.

22. In order to decide whether the proportion of the value of sales to be considered in a given case should be at the lower end or at the higher end of that scale, the Commission will have regard to a number of factors, such as the nature of the infringement, the combined market share of all the undertakings concerned, the geographic scope of the infringement and whether or not the infringement has been implemented.

23. Horizontal price-fixing, market-sharing and output-limitation agreements, which are usually secret, are, by their very nature, among the most harmful restrictions of competition. As a matter of policy, they will be heavily fined. Therefore, the proportion of the value of sales taken into account for such infringements will generally be set at the higher end of the scale.

24. In order to take fully into account the duration of the participation of each undertaking in the infringement, the amount determined on the basis of the value of sales (see points 20 to 23 above) will be multiplied by the number of years of participation in the infringement. Periods of less than six months will be counted as half a year; periods longer than six months but shorter than one year will be counted as a full year.

25. In addition, irrespective of the duration of the undertaking's participation in the infringement, the Commission will include in the basic amount a sum of between 15% and 25% of the value of sales as defined in Section A above in order to deter undertakings from even entering into horizontal price-fixing, market-sharing and output-limitation agreements. The Commission may also apply such an additional amount in the case of other infringements. For the purpose of deciding the proportion of the value of sales to be considered in a given case, the Commission will have regard to a number of factors, in particular those referred in point 22.

26. Where the value of sales by undertakings participating in the infringement is similar but not identical, the Commission may set for each of them an identical basic amount. Moreover, in determining the basic amount of the fine, the Commission will use rounded figures.

2. Adjustments to the basic amount

27. In setting the fine, the Commission may take into account circumstances that result in an increase or decrease in the basic amount as determined in Section 1 above. It will do so on the basis of an overall assessment which takes account of all the relevant circumstances.

A. Aggravating circumstances

28. The basic amount may be increased where the Commission finds that there are aggravating circumstances, such as:

— where an undertaking continues or repeats the same or a similar infringement after the Commission or a national competition authority has made a finding that the undertaking infringed Article 81 or 82: the basic amount will be increased by up to 100% for each such infringement established;

— refusal to cooperate with or obstruction of the Commission in carrying out its investigations;

— role of leader in, or instigator of, the infringement; the Commission will also pay particular attention to any steps taken to coerce other undertakings to participate in the infringement and/or any retaliatory measures taken against other undertakings with a view to enforcing the practices constituting the infringement.

B. Mitigating circumstances

29. The basic amount may be reduced where the Commission finds that mitigating circumstances exist, such as:
    — where the undertaking concerned provides evidence that it terminated the infringement as soon as the Commission intervened: this will not apply to secret agreements or practices (in particular, cartels);
    — where the undertaking provides evidence that the infringement has been committed as a result of negligence;
    — where the undertaking provides evidence that its involvement in the infringement is substantially limited and thus demonstrates that, during the period in which it was party to the offending agreement, it actually avoided applying it by adopting competitive conduct in the market: the mere fact that an undertaking participated in an infringement for a shorter duration than others will not be regarded as a mitigating circumstance since this will already be reflected in the basic amount;
    — where the undertaking concerned has effectively cooperated with the Commission outside the scope of the Leniency Notice and beyond its legal obligation to do so;
    — where the anti-competitive conduct of the undertaking has been authorized or encouraged by public authorities or by legislation.

C. Specific increase for deterrence

30. The Commission will pay particular attention to the need to ensure that fines have a sufficiently deterrent effect; to that end, it may increase the fine to be imposed on undertakings which have a particularly large turnover beyond the sales of goods or services to which the infringement relates.

31. The Commission will also take into account the need to increase the fine in order to exceed the amount of gains improperly made as a result of the infringement where it is possible to estimate that amount.

D. Legal maximum

32. The final amount of the fine shall not, in any event, exceed 10% of the total turnover in the preceding business year of the undertaking or association of undertakings participating in the infringement, as laid down in Article 23(2) of Regulation No 1/2003.

OFT's guidance as to the appropriate amount of a penalty
OFT 423, **December** 2004 [footnotes omitted]

2 Steps for determining the level of a penalty

Method of calculation

2.1 A financial penalty imposed by the OFT under section 36 of the Act will be calculated following a five step approach:
  • calculation of the starting point having regard to the seriousness of the infringement and the relevant turnover of the undertaking
  • adjustment for duration
  • adjustment for other factors
  • adjustment for further aggravating or mitigating factors, and
  • adjustment if the maximum penalty of 10 per cent of the worldwide turnover of the undertaking is exceeded and to avoid double jeopardy.

Details on each of these steps are set out in paragraphs 2.3 to 2.20 below.

2.2 An undertaking participating in cartel activity may benefit from total immunity from, or a significant reduction in the level of, a financial penalty, if the requirements for lenient treatment set out in part 3 of this guidance are satisfied.

Step 1—Starting point

2.3 The starting point for determining the level of financial penalty which will be imposed on an undertaking is calculated having regard to:
- the seriousness of the infringement, and
- the relevant turnover of the undertaking.

2.4 The starting point will depend in particular upon the nature of the infringement. The more serious and widespread the infringement, the higher the starting point is likely to be. Price-fixing or market-sharing agreements and other cartel activities are among the most serious infringements of Article 81 and/or the Chapter I prohibition. Conduct which infringes Article 82 and/or the Chapter II prohibition and which by virtue of the undertaking's dominant position and the nature of the conduct has, or is likely to have a particularly serious effect on competition, for example, predatory pricing, is also one of the most serious infringements.

2.5 It is the OFT's assessment of the seriousness of the infringement which will be taken into account in determining the starting point for the financial penalty. When making its assessment, the OFT will consider a number of factors, including the nature of the product, the structure of the market, the market share(s) of the undertaking(s) involved in the infringement, entry conditions and the effect on competitors and third parties. The damage caused to consumers whether directly or indirectly will also be an important consideration. The assessment will be made on a case by case basis for all types of infringement, taking account of all the circumstances of the case.

2.6 In cases concerning infringements of Article 81 and/or Article 82, the OFT may, in determining the starting point, take into account effects in another Member State of the agreement or conduct concerned. The OFT will take into account effects in another Member State through its assessment of relevant turnover; the OFT may consider turnover generated in another Member State if the relevant geographic market for the relevant product is wider than the United Kingdom and the express consent of the relevant Member State or NCA, as appropriate, is given in each particular case.

2.7 The relevant turnover is the turnover of the undertaking in the relevant product market and relevant geographic market affected by the infringement in the undertaking's last business year.

2.8 The starting point may not in any event exceed 10 per cent of the relevant turnover of the undertaking.

2.9 Where an infringement involves several undertakings, an assessment of the appropriate starting point will be carried out for each of the undertakings concerned, in order to take account of the real impact of the infringing activity of each undertaking on competition.

Step 2—Adjustment for duration

2.10 The starting point may be increased or, in exceptional circumstances, decreased to take into account the duration of the infringement. Penalties for infringements which last for more than one year may be multiplied by not more than the number of years of the infringement. Part years may be treated as full years for the purpose of calculating the number of years of the infringement.

Step 3—Adjustment for other factors

2.11 The penalty figure reached after the calculations in steps 1 and 2 may be adjusted as appropriate to achieve the policy objectives outlined in paragraph 1.4 above, in particular, of imposing penalties on infringing undertakings in order to deter undertakings from engaging in anticompetitive practices. The deterrent is not aimed solely at the undertakings which are subject to the decision, but also at other undertakings which might be considering activities which are contrary to Article 81, Article 82, the Chapter I and/or Chapter II prohibition. Considerations at this stage may include, for example, the OFT's objective estimate of any economic or financial benefit made or likely to be made by the infringing undertaking from the infringement and the special characteristics, including the size and financial position of the undertaking in question. Where relevant, the

OFT's estimate would account for any gains which might accrue to the undertaking in other product or geographic markets as well as the 'relevant' market under consideration.

2.12 The assessment of the need to adjust the penalty will be made on a case by case basis for each individual infringing undertaking. This step may result in either an increase or reduction of the financial penalty calculated at the earlier step.

2.13 In exceptional circumstances, where the relevant turnover of an undertaking is zero (for example, in the case of buying cartels) and the penalty figure reached after the calculation in Steps 1 and 2 is therefore zero, the OFT may adjust the amount of this penalty at this step.

Step 4—Adjustment for aggravating and mitigating factors

2.14 The basic amount of the financial penalty, adjusted as appropriate at steps 2 and 3, may be increased where there are other aggravating factors, or decreased where there are mitigating factors.

2.15 Aggravating factors include:
- role of the undertaking as a leader in, or an instigator of, the infringement
- involvement of directors or senior management (notwithstanding paragraph 1.14 above)
- retaliatory or other coercive measures taken against other undertakings aimed at ensuring the continuation of the infringement
- continuing the infringement after the start of the OFT's investigation
- repeated infringements by the same undertaking or other undertakings in the same group
- infringements which are committed intentionally rather than negligently, and
- retaliatory measures taken or commercial reprisal sought by the undertaking against a leniency applicant.

2.16 Mitigating factors include:
- role of the undertaking, for example, where the undertaking is acting under severe duress or pressure
- genuine uncertainty on the part of the undertaking as to whether the agreement or conduct constituted an infringement
- adequate steps having been taken with a view to ensuring compliance with Articles 81 and 82 and the Chapter I and Chapter II prohibitions
- termination of the infringement as soon as the OFT intervenes, and
- co-operation which enables the enforcement process to be concluded more effectively and/or speedily.

Note that in cases of cartel activity an undertaking which co-operates fully with the investigation may benefit from total immunity from, or a significant reduction in the level of, a financial penalty, if it satisfies the requirements for lenient treatment set out in part 3 of this guidance.

Step 5—Adjustment to prevent the maximum penalty being exceeded and to avoid double jeopardy

2.17 The final amount of the penalty calculated according to the method set out above may not in any event exceed 10 per cent of the worldwide turnover of the undertaking in its last business year. The business year on the basis of which worldwide turnover is determined will be the one preceding the date on which the decision of the OFT is taken or, if figures are not available for that business year, the one immediately preceding it. The penalty will be adjusted if necessary to ensure that it does not exceed this maximum.

2.18 In addition, where an infringement ended prior to 1 May 2004 any penalty imposed in respect of an infringement of the Chapter I prohibition or the Chapter II prohibition (but not any penalty imposed in respect of an infringement of Article 81 or Article 82) will, if necessary, be adjusted further to ensure that it does not exceed the maximum penalty applicable in respect of an infringement of the Chapter I prohibition or the Chapter II prohibition prior to 1 May 2004, i.e. 10 per cent of turnover in the United Kingdom of the undertaking in the financial year preceding the date when the infringement ended (multiplied pro rata by the length of the infringement where the length of the infringement was in excess of one year, up to a maximum of three years). The adjustments referred to in paragraphs 2.17 and 2.18 will be made after all the relevant adjustments have been made in steps 2 to 4 above and also, in cases of cartel activity, before any adjustments are made on account of leniency under part 3 of this guidance.

2.19 Where any infringement by an association of undertakings (e.g. a trade association) relates to the activities of its members, the penalty shall not exceed 10 per cent of the sum of the worldwide turnover of each member of the association of undertakings active on the market affected by the infringement. See the competition law guideline *Trade associations, professions and self-regulating bodies* (OFT408) for further details on the imposition and enforcement of penalties on associations of undertakings.

2.20 If a penalty or fine has been imposed by the European Commission, or by a court or other body in another Member State in respect of an agreement or conduct, the OFT must take that penalty or fine into account when setting the amount of a penalty in relation to that agreement or conduct. This is to ensure that where an anticompetitive agreement or conduct is subject to proceedings resulting in a penalty or fine in another Member State, an undertaking will not be penalised again in the United Kingdom for the same anticompetitive effects.

NOTE: When compared with Connor and Lande's findings it is clear that the Commission's fining powers appear to be of the right magnitude; in that they are likely to be able to strip away the benefits generated from cartel membership. The OFT policy, issued in 2004, is, however, more problematic. Its policy more closely accords with that adopted by the US authorities in the US Sentencing Guidelines (§ 2R1.1 (2006)), which presume that the level of overcharge generated by a cartel is approximately 10 per cent. The Sentencing Guidelines then set the penalty at double that overcharge at 20 per cent of 'affected sales' (see Connor, J.M., and Lande, R.H., 'The size of cartel overcharges: Implications for U.S. and EU fining policies' (2006) 51(4) Antitrust Bulletin 983). That estimate, first made in the 1980s, is now increasingly outdated and appears very low. Another issue stems from the OFT's guidance in para. 1.16, that 'In most cases the penalty imposed in respect of an infringement of an EC prohibition will be the same as the penalty imposed in respect of an infringement of a UK prohibition, because the OFT will calculate the penalty for each infringement according to the same steps as set out in part 2 of this guidance.' Given the dramatic uplift in fines following the Commission's 2006 Fining Notice, the OFT's policy needs to be reconsidered. If the OFT were to revisit their fining policy the academic evidence would therefore appear to suggest a significant increase in possible cartel fines.

While current European fining policy can result in apparently massive fines, for example the €1.38 billion fine in *Car Glass* (Commission Press Release IP/08/1685, 12 Nov 2008), it still appears that there is a real risk of under-deterrence. While large fines may strip away the benefits of cartel membership they do not account for the fact that not all cartels will be caught. Deterrence theory suggests that a multiplier should be applied to deal with situations were cartels go undetected and unpunished. One suggestion in 1995 was that the probability of being caught in Europe was very low; approximately 1 in 6 (see Wils, W.P.J., 'EC Competition Fines: To Deter or Not to Deter' in Wils, W.P.J., *The Optimal Enforcement of EC Antitrust Law: Essays in Law and Economics*, Hague, Kluwer Law International, 2002, p. 39). While detection rates are probably higher under the current regulatory regime it is highly unlikely that a fine multiplier will be introduced in Europe. It must also be remembered that, notwithstanding the 2006 Fining Notice, Regulation 1/2003 still contains a formal cap on fines set at 10 per cent of an undertaking's global turnover.

■ QUESTION

Fines in cartel cases are increasingly large to accord with the idea of deterrence, but can most undertakings truly be seen as 'amoral calculators', or are they as prone to poor decision-making and irrational behaviour as individuals?

B: Other corporate penalties

One way of increasing the level of corporate penalties for cartel membership is to seek to co-opt other actors to punish cartel members. One suggestion is to encourage private litigant actions against cartel members for compensation. Although such compensation claims are not fines, in the proper sense, they can act as a form of punishment and the likelihood of such claims would act as a deterrent to potential cartelists. Any cost that a cartel member incurs through their unlawful act can be seen as a form of punishment and a deterrent. For further detail on the complex technical questions surrounding the private enforcement of competition law see Chapter 4.

Nebbia, P., 'Damages actions for the infringement of EC competition law: compensation or deterrence?'
(2008) 33 EL Rev 23, pp. 24–5 [footnotes omitted]

In general, enforcement of competition law aims to prevent and sanction violations of prohibitions imposed by antitrust law and therefore seeks to avoid the occurrence of anti-competitive conduct and effects. This is achieved by creating and applying a set of criminal and/or administrative and/or civil sanctions. With respect to this objective:

> "[P]rivate enforcement can play an important role in enhancing compliance with antitrust legislation, since it potentially increases deterrence. This is true simply because infringements of antitrust law may not exclusively result in public proceedings and ultimately in administrative or criminal penalties, if there is also room for private enforcement. Court actions leading to damages awards can have a similar effect as sanctions imposed by the competition authorities."

The prospect of being taken to court for damages adds to the deterrent effect and therefore "strengthens the working of the Community competition rules".

...

Private enforcement is also an expression of the principle of co-operation laid down in Art.10 EC, which imposes on national courts the obligation to facilitate the achievement of the Community objectives (including the Commission's task of monitoring compliance with the Treaty).

In this sense, public and private enforcement "can work to complement each other", so as to ensure that "the private interest contributes to the safeguarding of the public interest". It is nevertheless clear that public enforcement is more suitable than private enforcement to address certain public interest concerns, such as determining the optimal amount of fines and pursuing the most meritorious claims; and that public enforcement, in pursuing the public interest of protecting competition law through administrative or criminal sanctions, is distinct from private enforcement, which pursues the private interest of protecting competitors and consumers through civil sanctions.

Accordingly, when discussing private enforcement one needs to take into account that this, as opposed to public enforcement, has a two-fold purpose:

> "[N]amely to compensate those who have suffered loss as a consequence of anticompetitive behaviour and to ensure the full effectiveness of the antitrust rules of the Treaty by discouraging anti-competitive behaviour."

While increasing corporate financial penalties will increase the deterrent effect of the law it is not possible to reach optimal deterrence through such penalties alone. Ever increasing penalties can bring problems of their own.

Stephan, A., 'The Bankruptcy Wildcard in Cartel Cases'
CCP Working Paper 06–5, March 2006

The imposition of fines that risk driving companies out of business is not acceptable to competition authorities for four main reasons. First, anything that increases the risk of bankruptcy imposes a social cost (see for example, Branch 2002). According to Posner (1998 p405), this consists mainly of the transfer of wealth away from shareholders, managers, employees and some creditors; the resulting necessary use of lawyers and bankers; reductions in efficiency of asset use; cost to those creditors who will not be paid, and the cost to other firms who relied on the bankrupt firm as a customer. The fees of professionals 'needed' for bankruptcy proceedings alone can run into hundreds of millions of dollars (Bower 2003).

Secondly, if a company is forced out of business, the industry in which it operates becomes more concentrated and so the risk of collusion in the future may actually increase as a result. There may also be the coordinated effect of fewer companies causing prices in the industry to rise (that is, by virtue of the fact that the market is more concentrated, firms can enjoy benefits from their collective market power through parallel behaviour that does not necessitate an explicit cartel agreement).

Thirdly, the imposition of fines causing bankruptcy would be politically unpopular. Management, shareholders and individuals made unemployed as a result of a firm being fined out of business could all be expected to lobby government to legislate against such high fines. There is a particular injustice in employees suffering as a result of decisions made by senior management when they are unlikely to have directly benefited from collusion, unlike their employers and shareholders (Cheffins 1997 ch14). . . .

Lastly, if a firm is allowed to go bankrupt, then parties injured by the collusion will not be able to recover damages. In the US the sentencing guidelines (s.8.C.3.3) specifically allow for a discount in fines where there is a danger that the full fine will jeopardise a firm's ability to pay restitution to injured parties. After bankruptcy the firm is liable first and foremost to its corporate creditors, and—as outlined above by reference to the SGL case—firms may try to use Chapter 11 bankruptcy in the US as a shield against civil antitrust action.

NOTE: In past cases there have been relatively few situations in which bankruptcy has been an issue in Europe. Stephan discusses those cases in his Working Paper, but as fines increase the risk of 'costs' associated with driving companies out of business increase. It is therefore vital that the competition authorities seek other ways to increase deterrence without simply increasing financial penalties.

■ QUESTION

Can competition fines be too large? Should an undertaking's (in)ability to pay be available as a defence to seek the reduction of fines?

C: Individual penalties

The majority of penalties imposed on cartels through competition law are aimed at corporate entities. But, as we discussed above, it is not always possible to deter potential cartelists sufficiently through corporate penalties alone. There has therefore been a drive to find ways of imposing penalties on the individual decision-makers within companies who take an undertaking into an unlawful arrangement. Criminal sanctions targeted at individuals are one such penalty.

Whelan, P., 'A Principled Argument for Personal Criminal Sanctions as Punishment under EC Cartel Law'

(2007) 4 Comp L Rev 7, pp. 30–1 and 35 [footnotes omitted]

Individual and Corporate Punishment

It was detailed above how EC cartel enforcement is not an effective deterrent as it is concerned solely with undertakings and not individuals. Problems included the inability of firms to effectively discipline employees, the existence of perverse incentives directly occasioned by excessive use of corporate sanctions, and a deficiency in individual condemnation. The use of personal criminal punishment avoids these problems: the state can discipline cartelists through coercive measures, including imprisonment; perverse incentives are avoided as those actually responsible for cartels will be held accountable; and criminal sanctions involve by definition a significant degree of moral condemnation. Further, individuals may be compelled by a normative (moral) commitment to obey the law that is not felt by undertakings. None of this is to say, however, that corporate sanctions are not required; in fact, such sanctions are also necessary under deterrence theory. If this were not so, firms would have the incentive to encourage cartel activity among their employees, to reduce or eliminate any monitoring activities and/or to deal lightly with any employee transgressions. Other reasons for including corporate sanctions include economies in enforcement costs and the increased potential for plea bargaining.

Threat of Custodial Sentences

It was detailed above how EC cartel enforcement practice is deficient in that fines are usually lower than their effective level, due to, amongst other things, the legal limitation of Regulation 1/2003. It is tempting to reply that fines should be increased and that this limitation should be removed. But this approach would not solve the fundamental problems associated with antitrust fines. Indeed, one of the main reasons why criminal, as opposed to administrative, individual sanctions should be imposed for cartel activity is that imprisonment—a reserve of the criminal process—helps, inter alia, to overcome the significant problems associated with optimally deterrent fines, in particular inability to pay, difficulty with individual (financial) responsibility, and proportional justice. Such punishment also negatives the criticism that current cartel enforcement lacks adequate condemnation of offenders.

...

Criminalisation of cartel activity should ideally occur without violation of certain fundamental principles, all of which affect the criminalisation process in a number of different ways. With the exception of efficiency, these principles—as employed in the criminalisation framework—do not shape the argument on the existence of criminal liability; rather, they are used to limit that liability and to develop rules concerning, inter alia, the subject and/or severity of criminal sanctions. The responsibility principle would, for example, ensure that only those actually in 'control' of the cartel would be convicted of a criminal offence. Proportionality, on the other hand, will guarantee that the maximum sentence imposed does not exceed an outer limit commensurate with the gravity and the seriousness of cartel activity. The operation of these two principles facilitates the application of the principle of autonomy to cartelists: it ensures that they are not held as mere pawns in the pursuit of the maximisation of consumer welfare. Values such as respect for human rights, fairness, or humanity can also be acknowledged under the criminalisation framework and are thus afforded the possibility of influencing the treatment of cartelists accused of criminal behaviour.

The UK introduced individual criminal penalties for cartel activity in the EA 2002. As the provisions came into force in June 2003 they only apply to behaviour after that date.

ENTERPRISE ACT 2002 [CH. 40]

Cartel offence

188.—(1) An individual is guilty of an offence if he dishonestly agrees with one or more other persons to make or implement, or to cause to be made or implemented, arrangements of the following kind relating to at least two undertakings (A and B).

(2) The arrangements must be ones which, if operating as the parties to the agreement intend, would—

(a) directly or indirectly fix a price for the supply by A in the United Kingdom (otherwise than to B) of a product or service,

(b) limit or prevent supply by A in the United Kingdom of a product or service,

(c) limit or prevent production by A in the United Kingdom of a product,

(d) divide between A and B the supply in the United Kingdom of a product or service to a customer or customers,

(e) divide between A and B customers for the supply in the United Kingdom of a product or service, or

(f) be bid-rigging arrangements.

(3) Unless subsection (2)(d), (e) or (f) applies, the arrangements must also be ones which, if operating as the parties to the agreement intend, would—

(a) directly or indirectly fix a price for the supply by B in the United Kingdom (otherwise than to A) of a product or service,

(b) limit or prevent supply by B in the United Kingdom of a product or service, or

(c) limit or prevent production by B in the United Kingdom of a product.

(4) In subsections (2)(a) to (d) and (3), references to supply or production are to supply or production in the appropriate circumstances (for which see section 189).

(5) "Bid-rigging arrangements" are arrangements under which, in response to a request for bids for the supply of a product or service in the United Kingdom, or for the production of a product in the United Kingdom—

(a) A but not B may make a bid, or

(b) A and B may each make a bid but, in one case or both, only a bid arrived at in accordance with the arrangements.

(6) But arrangements are not bid-rigging arrangements if, under them, the person requesting bids would be informed of them at or before the time when a bid is made.

(7) "Undertaking" has the same meaning as in Part 1 of the 1998 Act.

Cartel offence: supplementary

189.—(1) For section 188(2)(a), the appropriate circumstances are that A's supply of the product or service would be at a level in the supply chain at which the product or service would at the same time be supplied by B in the United Kingdom.

(2) For section 188(2)(b), the appropriate circumstances are that A's supply of the product or service would be at a level in the supply chain—

(a) at which the product or service would at the same time be supplied by B in the United Kingdom, or

(b) at which supply by B in the United Kingdom of the product or service would be limited or prevented by the arrangements.

(3) For section 188(2)(c), the appropriate circumstances are that A's production of the product would be at a level in the production chain—

(a) at which the product would at the same time be produced by B in the United Kingdom, or

(b) at which production by B in the United Kingdom of the product would be limited or prevented by the arrangements.

(4) For section 188(2)(d), the appropriate circumstances are that A's supply of the product or service would be at the same level in the supply chain as B's.

(5) For section 188(3)(a), the appropriate circumstances are that B's supply of the product or service would be at a level in the supply chain at which the product or service would at the same time be supplied by A in the United Kingdom.

(6) For section 188(3)(b), the appropriate circumstances are that B's supply of the product or service would be at a level in the supply chain—

    (a) at which the product or service would at the same time be supplied by A in the United Kingdom, or

    (b) at which supply by A in the United Kingdom of the product or service would be limited or prevented by the arrangements.

(7) For section 188(3)(c), the appropriate circumstances are that B's production of the product would be at a level in the production chain—

    (a) at which the product would at the same time be produced by A in the United Kingdom, or

    (b) at which production by A in the United Kingdom of the product would be limited or prevented by the arrangements.

Cartel offence: penalty and prosecution

190.—(1) A person guilty of an offence under section 188 is liable—

    (a) on conviction on indictment, to imprisonment for a term not exceeding five years or to a fine, or to both;

    (b) on summary conviction, to imprisonment for a term not exceeding six months or to a fine not exceeding the statutory maximum, or to both.

(2) In England and Wales and Northern Ireland, proceedings for an offence under section 188 may be instituted only—

    (a) by the Director of the Serious Fraud Office, or

    (b) by or with the consent of the OFT.

(3) No proceedings may be brought for an offence under section 188 in respect of an agreement outside the United Kingdom, unless it has been implemented in whole or in part in the United Kingdom.

(4) Where, for the purpose of the investigation or prosecution of offences under section 188, the OFT gives a person written notice under this subsection, no proceedings for an offence under section 188 that falls within a description specified in the notice may be brought against that person in England and Wales or Northern Ireland except in circumstances specified in the notice.

One key concept that differentiates the cartel offence from traditional corporate liability is the concept of dishonesty. It is a well known concept in English criminal law, but its introduction to competition law raises a number of concerns.

MacCulloch, A., 'Honesty, Morality and the Cartel Offence'
[2007] ECLR 355, p. 358 [footnotes omitted]

If there are to be successful prosecutions under the cartel offence it means that the OFT and SFO must be able to convince a jury that the behaviour of the accused individuals not only fell within the technical scope of the offence, but that they were also contrary to standards of "ordinary and honest people"; and that the accused knew that their actions were such. Many competition lawyers have tended to recoil when they see cartel activities, like price fixing, compared to theft in the media; but such comparisons are important if we are to re-construct the cartel within a new "moral" space.

The importance of morality in the criminalisation of antitrust is not only a factor in the United Kingdom. In discussing the criminal sanctions in the Sherman Act 1890 in the United States, Posner suggested:

"The rule against price fixing had become part of the law of conspiracy instead of part of the law of monopoly."

Harding and Joshua also argued:

> "The sense of moral certainty underlying the prohibition has been reinforced in the subsequent jurisprudence of the US Supreme Court, working towards a presumption of collusion from certain market behaviour, and showing an unwillingness to allow economic justification (e.g. market recession) in defence. In shorthand there is a per se condemnation."

As this is a question of morality it is near impossible to define with a high level of certainty. As Ormerod has stated:

> "it might prove difficult to produce a satisfactory legal definition of dishonesty for the simple reason that there is such plurality of opinion on the underlying moral contours and limits of dishonesty."

One key element in the move towards the cartelist as a moral actor is a shift away from the laws previous focus on the economic effect of conduct on markets; the focus under Art.81 EC and s.2 of the Competition Act. During a cartel offence prosecution the focus will not be on the position of the offence within the overall competition regime, or why the behaviour was criminalised. The focus must be on the individual behaviour of the accused and whether they knew they were wrong to act as they did. The focus of a criminal prosecution is not the market; rather the suspect.

Fisse, B., 'The Australian Cartel Criminalisation Proposals: An Overview and Critique'

(2007) 4 Comp L Rev 51 [footnotes omitted]

I have argued in a recent paper at some length that the concept of dishonesty is problematic and unnecessary as an element of the Australian Cartel Offence, for these main reasons:

(1) the Criminalisation Proposals fall short of adequately reflecting the elusive notion of 'serious cartel conduct' largely because the requirement of an 'intention to dishonestly obtain a gain' is not a touchstone of serious harm or serious culpability;

(2) the idea of making dishonesty an element of a cartel offence reflects the approach taken by the Enterprise Act 2002, but the explanatory materials on dishonesty as an element of the Enterprise Act cartel offence are seriously flawed and incapable of withstanding critical scrutiny;

(3) the 'standards of ordinary people' limb of the element of dishonesty is an undefined and undefinable populist notion the practical application of which will create real difficulties for judges and juries as well as for people in business and their advisers;

(4) the requirement for dishonesty of 'knowledge that the conduct was dishonest according to the standards of ordinary people' is a subjective test that will allow large and sophisticated corporations to deny liability and quite possibly obtain an acquittal on the basis of mistake of law and self-preferring subjectivised beliefs about the morality of their conduct; and

(5) the element of dishonesty is unnecessary given that there are several possible alternative ways of limiting a cartel offence to serious cartel conduct, including:

    (a) requiring, as a jurisdictional element of the cartel offence and as a guideline for the exercise of prosecutorial discretion, that the specific line of commerce affected by the cartel is likely to represent a minimum percentage (say 20%) or more of the value of sales by all competitors who competed in that specific line of commerce in the relevant geographic market during the period when that specific line of commerce was affected by the cartel or a specified period linked to the time of the alleged offence;

    (b) requiring, as the core mental element for the offence, a common intention: (i) to fix prices or restrict supply; and (ii) to increase bargaining power at the expense of those with whom the cartel deals; and

    (c) narrowing the definition of price fixing, restricting output, bid rigging or market sharing (as by excluding the fixing of a maximum price and indirect price fixing in a downstream market).

NOTE: The introduction of a criminal offence, and the intrinsic concept of dishonesty, to competition law, while well supported, has been controversial. There was some doubt as to whether prosecutions would be likely and the impact that the criminalization of competition law would have on the public enforcement, by either the OFT or DG Comp. The offence is still in its infancy, with only one, rather unique, prosecution. We have yet to see a full-scale criminal trial in relation to the offence.

■ QUESTIONS

Is it necessary for the cartel offence in the EA 2002 to have dishonesty at its core? Does it play an important role or does it threaten the usefulness of the offence in challenging cartel activity?

The first successful prosecutions under the cartel offence were seen in 2008. The *Marine Hose* case was highly unusual and will not be a model for a typical prosecution under the Act. However it does highlight that the UK courts are willing to countenance jail terms for individuals.

Regina v *Peter Whittle, Bryan Allison, David Brammar*
[2008] EWCA Crim 2560

[1] Section 188 of the Enterprise Act 2002 came into force on 20 June 2003 and made it a criminal offence for an individual dishonestly to agree with one or more other persons to make or implement, or to cause to be made or implemented, arrangements between at least two undertakings that are anti-competitive within the UK in one of a number of ways. The arrangement can relate to price-fixing of a product or service, limiting or preventing the supply of a product or service, limiting or preventing the production of a product, dividing between two undertakings the supply of a product or service to a customer or customers, dividing between two undertakings customers for the supply of a product or service, or it may constitute bid-rigging. An offence of this nature is termed a "cartel offence" and the activities set out in the statute are, we understand, frequently called "hard core activities."

[2] The essence of the offence is the *personal responsibility of an individual* in arrangements that have been part of the national and international commercial framework for many years: see, eg., Ramage, *The Criminal Lawyer*, 2008, 5–6. See also *Norris v. United States* [2008] 2 WLR 673, HL.

[3] The prosecution in this case was the first prosecution to be brought under the 2002 Act. Against that background and given the nature of the issue that we have been required to address, we invited the Crown to assist us with some background to the legislation and certain wider issues. We are grateful to Mr Mark Lucraft QC for producing a note about this at short notice. We have drawn on it for the purposes of some parts of this judgment.

Background to the Enterprise Act

[4] The Enterprise Act was the result of a consultative White Paper, published in July 2001, entitled "A World Class Competition Regime". The White Paper followed on from a joint Treasury and Department of Trade and Industry investigation into the effectiveness of existing competition legislation. It acknowledged that the Competition Act 1998 had made changes that deterred anti-competitive behaviour, but argued that there was a strong case for the introduction of criminal penalties.

[5] The 'executive summary' of the White Paper highlighted a number of features of the proposed criminal sanctions:

- the new criminal offence would need to catch price-fixing, market-sharing, and bid-rigging cartels;
- it should target individuals who set up and maintained cartels and senior executives or directors who either condoned or encouraged the arrangement;

- the Government intended that the Office of Fair Trading ('OFT') should be able to pursue a criminal case against an individual whenever a cartel is implemented or intended to be implemented in the UK and this would include cases where a case against the undertaking with which the individual is associated is pursued by the European Commission.

[6] A formal review of the proposed criminalisation of cartel activity was initiated by the Director General of Fair Trading. The review was undertaken by Sir Anthony Hammond QC and Roy Penrose OBE QPM. Their report was published in November 2001 and recommended that the maximum penalty for individuals convicted of a cartel offence should be five years' imprisonment and/or unlimited fines. They considered a number of factors to be of relevance to this recommendation:

- The level of maximum sentences for comparable offences, for example 'insider dealing' and 'obtaining property by deception';
- Comparable offences in Canada and Japan carry a maximum sentence of five years and the Republic of Ireland [was] proposing to increase the maximum for its cartel offence from two to five years;
- The need to have available the powers associated with an arrestable offence as defined in PACE, which requires a maximum sentence of at least five years; and
- The desirability of sending a strong signal to the courts that hard core cartels are very serious offences, which can have important and deleterious economic consequences.

[7] An expression that occurs frequently in this context is 'bid-rigging'. Bid-rigging is, in a nutshell, an agreement or arrangement between two or more undertakings that would generally be seen to be in competition with each other as to which of their number bidding for a contract will win the bid. This will be done by fixing between them the prices to be quoted in the bidding process. It is not difficult to see the anti-competitive nature of such an agreement or arrangement.

The penalty provided for by the Enterprise Act and elsewhere

[8] Parliament implemented the recommendation of the Hammond/Penrose report and section 190(1) of the Act provides that a person guilty of an offence under section 188 is liable—

a) on conviction on indictment, to imprisonment for a term not exceeding five years or to a fine, or to both;
b) on summary conviction, to imprisonment for a term not exceeding six months or to a fine not exceeding the statutory maximum, or to both.

[9] We have been told that number of European states also provide for individual criminal liability for cartel behaviour with potential penalties of between 3 and 6 years imprisonment and/or financial penalties.

[10] It is also of relevance to note the penalty for such an offence in the USA. The US Sherman Antitrust Act offence carries a maximum penalty of ten years' imprisonment and certain financial penalties.

This case and its context

[11] The three applicants in this case were the first three individuals to be convicted of offences under the Act and in respect of whom the UK Courts have been required to pass sentence. Each was of previous good character and each pleaded guilty at the first opportunity. Indeed their co-operation with the authorities, particularly in Whittle's case, has gone much further than a mere acknowledgement of guilt.

[12] It is against that background that the Registrar has referred their applications for leave to appeal against sentence direct to the Full Court.

[13] In certain of the Skeleton Arguments submitted in support of these applications, it was suggested that the Court might take the opportunity to offer some general guidance on sentencing levels in cases of this nature. That would have been difficult in any event because the Court would have had little, if any, knowledge of where to place this case in the scale of seriousness: no sufficient body of cases exists as yet to be able to make that assessment. However, there is another significant factor in this case that prevents us from doing so to which we will refer later.

The facts

[14] On 10 June 2008 at Southwark Crown Court the applicants pleaded guilty to a cartel offence under section 188 and the following day were sentenced by His Honour Judge Geoffrey Rivlin QC, Honorary Recorder of Westminster, to terms of imprisonment of, in the cases of Whittle and Allison, 3 years and, in the case of Brammar, 30 months. Whittle and Allison were each disqualified under s.2 Company Directors Disqualification Act 1986 from acting as a director of a limited company for 7 years and Brammar was similarly disqualified for 5 years. They each seek to challenge the terms of imprisonment, though not the periods of disqualification.

[15] The relevant particulars of the count to which they each pleaded guilty were as follows:

Between 20 June 2003 and 2 May 2007 they dishonestly agreed together and with others to implement arrangements relating to at least two undertakings, including Dunlop (Oil and Marine) Limited and other named companies worldwide, which:
i) directly or indirectly fixed the price for the supply by Dunlop (Oil and Marine) Limited in the United Kingdom of marine hose and ancillary equipment to others including the Ministry of Defence and the Azzawiya Oil Refining Company; and
ii) were bid-rigging arrangements.

[16] There were four other counts on the indictment relating to particular agreements embraced within that overall allegation and they have remained on the file on the usual terms.

[17] It is necessary to say a little more about the background to the offence of which the three applicants have been convicted. It will be appreciated from the particulars to which we have referred that the industry that lies behind the cartel in this case is the industry that manufactures and supplies marine hose and ancillary equipment. Marine hose is a rubber-based product used in the oil industry to facilitate the movement of oil between various offshore and onshore installations and, of course, is used in connection with the movement of oil to and from oil tankers. It is a commodity that is used worldwide.

[18] Dunlop (Oil and Marine) is a company based in Grimsby and a specialist manufacturer of marine hose. Each applicant has had a close association with that company. Whittle joined the company in 1976 and was employed by it until in 1998 he established his own consultancy. The consultancy effectively involved his being the co-ordinator of the cartel for which he was paid an annual fee of $50,000 by each participating company. Brammar joined Dunlop in 1987 and in July 1993 he was promoted to sales and marketing manager. He held that position until his employment was terminated as a result of the matters that underlie this case. He was Whittle's main point of contact within the company. Allison joined Dunlop in 1977 and moved through various positions until in February 2001 he became Managing Director. He was Brammar's supervisor at material times.

[19] The company for very many years prior to the implementation of the Enterprise Act had been part of an international cartel that operated within that specialised marine hose market. The cartel consisted of all the principal manufacturers of marine hose worldwide which, in addition to the company, consisted of two Japanese companies, two Italian companies and a French company each of which were party to a long-standing agreement or understanding to share the market for marine hose supply between them. This involved price-fixing and bid-rigging. The cartel members met from time to time and communicated regularly by telephone, fax and e-mail, doubtless in as secretive a fashion as the circumstances demanded. By its very nature the objective of the cartel was to ensure that market shares and prices were maintained. Bids for contracts were co-ordinated in order to ensure that the available business was distributed according to the agreed market share and at prices acceptable to the cartel.

[20] Whatever position may have obtained prior to the coming in to force of section 188, the position thereafter for any individual engaged in activities encompassed by that section, on behalf of the companies for whom they acted, would require such activities to be carried out clandestinely. The cartel continued to operate until 1 May 2007, when United States authorities covertly recorded a meeting of members of the cartel during the annual Offshore Technology Conference in Houston, Texas and arrested those present. The applicants were included amongst those

who were present and arrested. That the meeting was intended to be clandestine is evidenced by the comment of one of those present just before the meeting commenced when he asked whether anyone had checked for listening devices. The covert recording indicated that there was agreement that the cartel should continue so that prices were maintained internationally. The participants left the meeting in ones and twos so as not to draw attention to the meeting.

[21] It is said that the worldwide market in marine hose and ancillary equipment is worth in the region of £60 million. In order to put the criminal activities of the three applicants into its proper context it should be noted that the total value of UK contracts affected during the period from June 2003 to May 2007 was in the order of £17.5 million. It should further be noted that over that period the activities of the cartel caused an uplift of about 15% over what would otherwise have been the market price under fair and open competition—in other words, an additional profit of up to £2.5 million was made for the company over that period. That money did not, of course, go directly into the pockets of any of the applicants. Their involvement meant that the viability of the company was sustained and as a result those who were working for it benefited indirectly and Whittle, who received fees as a consultant, also benefited indirectly.

[22] As we have indicated, the applicants were arrested in the USA. What they did was an offence against the US anti-competition laws and they faced prosecution there. They made full and detailed admissions on their arrest and agreed to give full co-operation to the US Department of Justice from shortly after their arrests. They volunteered the full detail of their confessions to the OFT before an investigation began and indicated that they would, if prosecuted, plead guilty to a UK cartel offence. In July 2007, representatives of the OFT travelled to the United States and confirmed with the applicants their detailed admissions in formal interviews.

[23] Each applicant entered into a formal plea agreement with the US authorities, which included their agreement to plead guilty in the US and to a cartel offence in the UK in the event that they were prosecuted here. We will return to those agreements below.

[24] Having spent short periods in custody in Texas, the applicants were then required to remain in the United States for seven and a half months under strict curfew conditions (including tagging) until they entered guilty pleas. They were then allowed to return to the UK to face prosecution here. On their return they were seen immediately by OFT officials, charged and in due course brought before the Southwark Crown Court.

The plea agreements

[25] We have referred to the plea agreements entered into by each applicant with the US authorities. Each was a detailed document running to many pages and, as we understand it, approved by the relevant District Court. In essence what each applicant did, doubtless on the advice of his legal advisers, was to agree jointly with the US authorities to recommend to the US court a disposition of the case against him which included a term of imprisonment. That term would be reduced "by one day for each day of the total term of the sentence of imprisonment imposed upon [him] following his conviction for the UK cartel offence". Part of the agreement was that each applicant would plead guilty to such an offence and further that he would not "seek from the UK court a sentence of imprisonment less than that" provided for in the agreement. The agreements, it should be noted, incorporated a concession by each applicant that the relevant course of criminal conduct in the USA was "from at least as early as 1999 and continuing until as late as May 2007". In the UK, of course, the criminal behaviour could only begin after 20 June 2003.

[26] The sentences provided for in the respective agreements were 2½ years for Whittle, 2 years for Allison and 20 months for Brammar.

[27] The net effect of these agreements was that provided each was sentenced in the UK to not less than the terms we have indicated, they would not be expected to return to the USA to serve any period in custody there. (For the avoidance of doubt, the early release provisions of the UK are disregarded: the periods referred to in the agreements are the periods actually imposed by the UK court.) As UK nationals with families here, the incentive not to be returned for any period of incarceration in the USA can be well understood. This has resulted in the submissions to us in these applications being constrained by the terms of the agreements reached. Whilst each applicant

through Counsel has invited us to reduce the terms imposed by the judge, none has invited us to reduce the terms below the period specified in the agreement into which he entered.

[28] It follows that this court has not had the benefit of the kind of argument from counsel to which it is accustomed; we emphasise this is through no fault of theirs. They were acting upon their instructions and their instructions were imposed upon them by the terms of the plea agreements. We have our doubts as to the propriety of a US prosecutor seeking to inhibit the way in which counsel represent their clients in a UK court, but having heard no argument on the subject we shall express no concluded view.

The mitigation for each applicant

[29] Because of the way we feel obliged to dispose of the applications, we do not think that there is much purpose to be served by detailing the personal mitigation of each applicant other than in a fairly general way. As we have already indicated, each was of good character, each admitted his involvement readily, each has offered to assist the authorities further (and in Whittle's case he has gone to the USA to give evidence in proceedings arising from these matters), each has pleaded guilty at the first opportunity, each has lost a livelihood and there will be significant financial consequences for him and his family. On any view, whatever starting point was adopted had there been a trial, there would have been significant discounts from that sentence to reflect the matters to which we have referred.

[30] We were much pressed with the argument that this case could not conceivably be one of the worst cases of its kind. Yet, in Whittle and Allison's cases (where each was sentenced to 3 years imprisonment), the judge must have taken the starting point as at or near the statutory maximum given the significant discounts that ought to have been applied. Brammar's case was not far behind on this analysis. Given the normal and well-established principle that the maximum sentence for an offence is to be reserved for the most serious offence of that kind to come before the courts, it was submitted that the judge adopted too high a starting point.

[31] As we have already indicated, we are not in a position to judge the full strength of that argument and its consequences in this case because of the way the submissions have been constrained by the considerations to which we have referred. All we can say is that had the submissions not been so constrained, we may well have been persuaded to reduce the sentences further than we have been invited to do.

[32] We have considerable misgivings about disposing of these applications in the way we intend, but, if we are to avoid injustice, we feel we have no alternative. We consider it appropriate, on the facts of this case, to give leave to appeal in each case and substitute for the sentences imposed by the judge sentences equivalent to those reflected in each agreement namely 2½ years for Whittle, 2 years for Allison and 20 months for Brammar.

Guidance for the future

[33] As we have already made clear, we do not intend to lay down any guidance in this case for the disposal of other cases because of the way we have felt obliged to deal with the case. The sentences passed by the judge and those substituted by us are not to be treated as guideline sentences.

[34] By way of general guidance, we have noted the terms of the Hammond/Penrose report which suggested the following factors as being relevant to any sentence passed:

- the gravity and nature of the offence;
- the duration of the offence;
- the degree of culpability of the defendant in implementing the cartel agreement;
- the degree of culpability of the defendant in enforcing the cartel agreement;
- whether the defendant's conduct was contrary to guidelines laid down in a company compliance manual;
- mitigating factors e.g. any co-operation the defendant may have provided in respect of the enquiry; whether or not the defendant was compelled to participate in the cartel under duress; whether the offence was a first offence; and any personal circumstances of the defendant which the courts may regard as a factor suggesting leniency.

[35] Whilst we would not suggest that those factors are exhaustive, they are each plainly relevant.

NOTE: The imposition of jail time in the UK for cartel activity is a momentous step—particularly given the UK's historical toleration of cartels, as demonstrated in *Norris*. The fact that the original sentences were in the upper range of those available was to be welcomed. It is, perhaps, disappointing that the Court of Appeal reduced the sentences on appeal; notwithstanding the fact that the peculiar nature of this case made it very much stand on its own facts. As significant periods of imprisonment were retained the court's findings do not appear to question the usefulness of imprisonment as a sanction per se, but it certainly indicates that those who co-operate with the authorities can expect a significant discount on any sentence imposed. One interesting facet was that the imposition of competition disqualification orders as part of the punishment was not challenged. It therefore appears that the 'livelihood' sanction of disqualification is more palatable to the accused when compared to imprisonment; that would suggest that imprisonment is the more effective deterrent.

OFT, *Competition disqualification orders*
OFT 510, May 2003 [footnotes omitted]

4 Applications for competition disqualification orders

4.1 The OFT or Regulator has the power to apply to the court for a CDO against a person. Since, before a CDO can be made, a court must be persuaded that a person's conduct makes him or her unfit to be a director, the OFT or Regulator will only apply to the court for a CDO against a person whose relevant conduct it considers to be such as to make them unfit to be concerned in the management of a company.

Factors for consideration

4.2 The OFT or Regulator will follow a five-step process when deciding to apply for a CDO. It will:
   (1) consider whether an undertaking which is a company of which the person is a director has committed a breach of competition law
   (2) consider whether a financial penalty has been imposed for the breach
   (3) consider whether the company in question benefited from leniency (see paragraph 4.11 below for the definition of 'leniency' in this context)
   (4) consider the extent of the director's responsibility for the breach of competition law, either through action or omission
   (5) have regard to any aggravating and mitigating factors.

4.3 To help it consider these questions, the OFT or Regulator may use any or all of the information gathering powers in sections 26 to 28 of CA98.

Directors and officers of parent and subsidiary companies

4.4 As noted at paragraph 2.2 above, an undertaking may in some cases constitute a group of companies (treated for the purposes of competition law as a 'single economic entity'). In certain circumstances, such as where a subsidiary has no real independence from its parent, a parent company may be held responsible for a breach by one or more of its subsidiaries on the basis that they form a single economic entity. In such cases, for the purposes of CDOs, the OFT or Regulator will first consider which company or companies in the corporate group directly committed the breach of competition law. Applications for CDOs will then be considered against the directors of those companies using the five-step process discussed above at paragraph 4.2.

4.5 In respect of the parent company, the directors or officers of the parent company may not have been formally appointed as directors of the subsidiary company pursuant to the subsidiary's articles of association. Where this is the case, the OFT or Regulator will consider whether any of the directors or officers of the parent company are de facto or shadow directors of the subsidiary.

Where such persons are de facto or shadow directors of the subsidiary, the OFT or Regulator will consider whether to apply for a CDO against these persons, using the five-step process discussed above at paragraph 4.2.

Step 1   Breach of competition law

4.6 The first question the OFT or Regulator will consider is whether a company which is an undertaking of which the person is a director has committed a breach of competition law. The OFT or Regulator only intends to apply for CDOs in respect of breaches of competition law that have been proven in decisions or judgments (as the case may be) of the:

- OFT or a Regulator
- European Commission
- Competition Appeal Tribunal, or
- European Court.

4.7 In respect of breaches proven in a European Commission decision or a judgment of the European Court, it is not the intention of the OFT or Regulator to apply for CDOs where the breach to which the decision or judgment relates does or did not have an actual or potential effect on trade in the United Kingdom.

4.8 The OFT or Regulator will not apply for CDOs in respect of breaches of competition law which ended before the commencement of sections 9A to 9E CDDA. Breaches which started before the commencement of sections 9A to 9E CDDA, but which continued onto or after the date for commencement of those sections may be susceptible to CDO applications.

Appeals

4.9 An application for a CDO will not be made where the decision or judgment relating to the breach remains subject to appeal. 'Remains subject to appeal' for these purposes means either that the deadline for appeal against the decision or judgment has not yet passed, or that an appeal has been made, but not yet determined.

Step 2   Whether a financial penalty has been imposed for the breach

4.10 The next matter which the OFT or Regulator will take into account is whether a financial penalty has been imposed for the breach of competition law. The OFT or Regulator will not consider CDO applications to be appropriate in cases other than those in which a financial penalty has been imposed and, in the event of an appeal, upheld in whole or part.

Step 3   Leniency

4.11 The next question which the OFT or Regulator will consider is whether the company of which a person is a director benefited from leniency. 'Leniency' for these purposes means the immunity from, or any reduction in, financial penalty in the manner described in the *'Director General of Fair Trading's Guidance as to the Appropriate Amount of a Penalty'* (the penalties guidance), or that described in the European Commission *'Notice on Immunity from Fines and Reduction of Fines in Cartel Cases'* (the fining notice) or any publication replacing them. 'Reduction' for these purposes does not mean any reduction in the amount of financial penalty imposed for a breach owing to the application of any mitigating factors discussed in the penalties guidance or the fining notice. (See also paragraph 4.27 below with respect to no-action letters in cartel cases.)

4.12 The OFT or Regulator will not apply for a CDO against any current director of a company whose company benefited from leniency in respect of the activities to which the grant of leniency relates. Companies benefiting from leniency will receive confirmation of this policy.

4.13 However, where a director has at any time been removed as a director of a company owing to his or her role in the breach of competition law in question and/or for opposing the relevant application for leniency, then the OFT or Regulator may still consider applying for a CDO against that person, irrespective of whether his or her former company has been granted leniency by the OFT or Regulator or European Commission.

4.14 In order to minimise the risk of a CDO application being made against them, company directors whose companies have been involved in cartel activity should therefore ensure that their companies approach the OFT or Regulator or the European Commission for leniency.

Step 4 Extent of the director's responsibility for the breach

4.15 The next step in the OFT or Regulator's assessment will be for the OFT or Regulator to consider the extent of the director's responsibility for or involvement in the breach, whether by action or omission.

4.16 The greater the degree of the director's responsibility for or involvement in a breach, the greater the likelihood that the OFT or Regulator will consider that person to be unfit to be concerned in the management of a company and hence, of a CDO application being made against that person. The OFT or Regulator:

- is likely to apply for a CDO against a director who has been directly involved in the breach
- is quite likely to apply for a CDO against a director whom it considers improperly failed to take corrective action against the breach
- does not rule out applying for a CDO against a director whom it considers, taking into account that director's role and responsibilities, to have failed to keep himself or herself sufficiently informed of the company's activities which constituted the breach of competition law—whether an application is made in these circumstances will depend upon the OFT or Regulator's priorities.

Direct involvement—likely to apply for CDO

4.17 The OFT or Regulator will consider whether there is evidence indicating that a director was directly involved in the breach. The OFT or Regulators are of the view that this is evidence of the director, either alone or with other persons, having:

- actively taken steps to carry out the infringement (e.g. by drawing up a list of the company's prices and sending them to a competitor so as to enable them to align their prices)
- planned, devised, approved or encouraged the activity of the undertaking which caused the breach
- ordered or pressured those identified as having a direct or indirect role in the breach to engage in the activity causing the breach
- attended meetings (internal or external) in which the activity constituting the breach either occurred or was discussed, or both
- directed, ordered or pressured staff of the undertaking to attend meetings (internal or external) for the purpose of participating in or discussing the activity constituting the breach, or
- ordered, encouraged or advocated retaliation against other undertakings who were reluctant to or refused to participate in the activity constituting the breach of competition law.

Mitigating factors

4.24 Mitigating factors include evidence indicating that:

- the undertaking committed the breach as a result of coercion by another undertaking (for example, where the breach was committed as the only perceived way to avoid threatened retaliation by a dominant undertaking)
- there was genuine uncertainty prior to the breach as to whether the infringing activity constituted a breach
- the director contributed to the company taking quick remedial steps when the breach was brought to his or her attention, including the implementation or revision of a competition law compliance programme
- the director took disciplinary action against the employees responsible for the breach
- the director was himself or herself under severe internal pressure (such as from controlling shareholders of the company or directors of a parent company, for example) either to be involved in the breach or to allow it to occur.

Cartel offence: conviction/no-action letters

4.25 Any court by or before which an individual is convicted of an indictable offence (whether tried on indictment or summarily) committed in connection with the management of a company may make a disqualification order against that individual.

4.26 Where an individual company director has been convicted of the cartel offence under section 188 Enterprise Act 2002, and that offence has been committed in connection with the management of a company, the convicting court has the power to make a disqualification order against that individual director. The OFT and Regulators take the view that the court by or before which the individual director is convicted of the cartel offence is the most appropriate venue for consideration of a disqualification order, so they would not expect to have to use their powers under section 9A CDDA in these circumstances.

4.27 The OFT or Regulator will not apply for a CDO against any beneficiary of a no-action letter in respect of the cartel activities specified in that letter. Recipients of no-action letters will receive individual confirmation of this policy.

D: Increasing the chances of detection

While the competition authorities are keen to increase the deterrent effect of penalties, they have not forgotten the other side of the deterrence equation. They are also seeking to develop their enforcement regimes to increase the chance that unlawful cartels will be detected, and sanctioned. The main tool to detect cartels available to DG Comp and the OFT is their leniency programmes.

Commission Notice on Immunity from fines and reduction of fines in cartel cases
OJ, 2006, C298/17 [footnotes omitted]

II. IMMUNITY FROM FINES

A. Requirements to qualify for immunity from fines

(8) The Commission will grant immunity from any fine which would otherwise have been imposed to an undertaking disclosing its participation in an alleged cartel affecting the Community if that undertaking is the first to submit information and evidence which in the Commission's view will enable it to:

(a) carry out a targeted inspection in connection with the alleged cartel; or

(b) find an infringement of Article 81 EC in connection with the alleged cartel.

(9) For the Commission to be able to carry out a targeted inspection within the meaning of point (8)(a), the undertaking must provide the Commission with the information and evidence listed below, to the extent that this, in the Commission's view, would not jeopardize the inspections:

(a) A corporate statement which includes, in so far as it is known to the applicant at the time of the submission:

— A detailed description of the alleged cartel arrangement, including for instance its aims, activities and functioning; the product or service concerned, the geographic scope, the duration of and the estimated market volumes affected by the alleged cartel; the specific dates, locations, content of and participants in alleged cartel contacts, and all relevant explanations in connection with the pieces of evidence provided in support of the application.

— The name and address of the legal entity submitting the immunity application as well as the names and addresses of all the other undertakings that participate(d) in the alleged cartel;

— The names, positions, office locations and, where necessary, home addresses of all individuals who, to the applicant's knowledge, are or have been involved in the alleged cartel, including those individuals which have been involved on the applicant's behalf;

— Information on which other competition authorities, inside or outside the EU, have been approached or are intended to be approached in relation to the alleged cartel; and

(b) Other evidence relating to the alleged cartel in possession of the applicant or available to it at the time of the submission, including in particular any evidence contemporaneous to the infringement.

(10) Immunity pursuant to point (8)(a) will not be granted if, at the time of the submission, the Commission had already sufficient evidence to adopt a decision to carry out an inspection in connection with the alleged cartel or had already carried out such an inspection.

(11) Immunity pursuant to point (8)(b) will only be granted on the cumulative conditions that the Commission did not have, at the time of the submission, sufficient evidence to find an infringement of Article 81 EC in connection with the alleged cartel and that no undertaking had been granted conditional immunity from fines under point (8)(a) in connection with the alleged cartel. In order to qualify, an undertaking must be the first to provide contemporaneous, incriminating evidence of the alleged cartel as well as a corporate statement containing the kind of information specified in point (9)(a), which would enable the Commission to find an infringement of Article 81 EC,.

(12) In addition to the conditions set out in points (8)(a), (9) and (10) or in points (8)(b) and 11, all the following conditions must be met in any case to qualify for any immunity from a fine:

(a) The undertaking cooperates genuinely, fully, on a continuous basis and expeditiously from the time it submits its application throughout the Commission's administrative procedure. This includes:

— providing the Commission promptly with all relevant information and evidence relating to the alleged cartel that comes into its possession or is available to it;

— remaining at the Commission's disposal to answer promptly to any request that may contribute to the establishment of the facts;

— making current (and, if possible, former) employees and directors available for interviews with the Commission;

— not destroying, falsifying or concealing relevant information or evidence relating to the alleged cartel; and

— not disclosing the fact or any of the content of its application before the Commission has issued a statement of objections in the case, unless otherwise agreed;

(b) The undertaking ended its involvement in the alleged cartel immediately following its application, except for what would, in the Commission's view, be reasonably necessary to preserve the integrity of the inspections;

(c) When contemplating making its application to the Commission, the undertaking must not have destroyed, falsified or concealed evidence of the alleged cartel nor disclosed the fact or any of the content of its contemplated application, except to other competition authorities.

(13) An undertaking which took steps to coerce other undertakings to join the cartel or to remain in it is not eligible for immunity from fines. It may still qualify for a reduction of fines if it fulfils the relevant requirements and meets all the conditions therefor.

B. Procedure

(14) An undertaking wishing to apply for immunity from fines should contact the Commission's Directorate General for Competition. The undertaking may either initially apply for a marker or immediately proceed to make a formal application to the Commission for immunity from fines in order to meet the conditions in points (8)(a) or (8)(b), as appropriate. The Commission may disregard any application for immunity from fines on the ground that it has been submitted after the statement of objections has been issued.

(15) The Commission services may grant a marker protecting an immunity applicant's place in the queue for a period to be specified on a case-by-case basis in order to allow for the gathering of

the necessary information and evidence. To be eligible to secure a marker, the applicant must provide the Commission with information concerning its name and address, the parties to the alleged cartel, the affected product(s) and territory(-ies), the estimated duration of the alleged cartel and the nature of the alleged cartel conduct. The applicant should also inform the Commission on other past or possible future leniency applications to other authorities in relation to the alleged cartel and justify its request for a marker. Where a marker is granted, the Commission services determine the period within which the applicant has to perfect the marker by submitting the information and evidence required to meet the relevant threshold for immunity. Undertakings which have been granted a marker cannot perfect it by making a formal application in hypothetical terms. If the applicant perfects the marker within the period set by the Commission services, the information and evidence provided will be deemed to have been submitted on the date when the marker was granted.

(16) An undertaking making a formal immunity application to the Commission must:

   (a) provide the Commission with all information and evidence relating to the alleged cartel available to it, as specified in points (8) and (9), including corporate statements; or

   (b) initially present this information and evidence in hypothetical terms, in which case the undertaking must present a detailed descriptive list of the evidence it proposes to disclose at a later agreed date. This list should accurately reflect the nature and content of the evidence, whilst safeguarding the hypothetical nature of its disclosure. Copies of documents, from which sensitive parts have been removed, may be used to illustrate the nature and content of the evidence. The name of the applying undertaking and of other undertakings involved in the alleged cartel need not be disclosed until the evidence described in its application is submitted. However, the product or service concerned by the alleged cartel, the geographic scope of the alleged cartel and the estimated duration must be clearly identified.

(17) If requested, the Directorate General for Competition will provide an acknowledgement of receipt of the undertaking's application for immunity from fines, confirming the date and, where appropriate, time of the application.

(18) Once the Commission has received the information and evidence submitted by the undertaking under point (16)(a) and has verified that it meets the conditions set out in points (8)(a) or (8)(b), as appropriate, it will grant the undertaking conditional immunity from fines in writing.

(19) If the undertaking has presented information and evidence in hypothetical terms, the Commission will verify that the nature and content of the evidence described in the detailed list referred to in point (16)(b) will meet the conditions set out in points (8)(a) or (8)(b), as appropriate, and inform the undertaking accordingly. Following the disclosure of the evidence no later than on the date agreed and having verified that it corresponds to the description made in the list, the Commission will grant the undertaking conditional immunity from fines in writing.

(20) If it becomes apparent that immunity is not available or that the undertaking failed to meet the conditions set out in points (8)(a) or (8)(b), as appropriate, the Commission will inform the undertaking in writing. In such case, the undertaking may withdraw the evidence disclosed for the purposes of its immunity application or request the Commission to consider it under section III of this notice. This does not prevent the Commission from using its normal powers of investigation in order to obtain the information.

(21) The Commission will not consider other applications for immunity from fines before it has taken a position on an existing application in relation to the same alleged infringement, irrespective of whether the immunity application is presented formally or by requesting a marker.

(22) If at the end of the administrative procedure, the undertaking has met the conditions set out in point (12), the Commission will grant it immunity from fines in the relevant decision. If at the end of the administrative procedure, the undertaking has not met the conditions set out in point (12), the undertaking will not benefit from any favorable treatment under this Notice. If the Commission, after having granted conditional immunity ultimately finds that the immunity applicant has acted as a coercer, it will withhold immunity.

III. REDUCTION OF A FINE

A. *Requirements to qualify for reduction of a fine*

(23) Undertakings disclosing their participation in an alleged cartel affecting the Community that do not meet the conditions under section II above may be eligible to benefit from a reduction of any fine that would otherwise have been imposed.

(24) In order to qualify, an undertaking must provide the Commission with evidence of the alleged infringement which represents significant added value with respect to the evidence already in the Commission's possession and must meet the cumulative conditions set out in points (12)(a) to (12)(c) above.

(25) The concept of "added value" refers to the extent to which the evidence provided strengthens, by its very nature and/or its level of detail, the Commission's ability to prove the alleged cartel. In this assessment, the Commission will generally consider written evidence originating from the period of time to which the facts pertain to have a greater value than evidence subsequently established. Incriminating evidence directly relevant to the facts in question will generally be considered to have a greater value than that with only indirect relevance. Similarly, the degree of corroboration from other sources required for the evidence submitted to be relied upon against other undertakings involved in the case will have an impact on the value of that evidence, so that compelling evidence will be attributed a greater value than evidence such as statements which require corroboration if contested.

(26) The Commission will determine in any final decision adopted at the end of the administrative procedure the level of reduction an undertaking will benefit from, relative to the fine which would otherwise be imposed. For the:

— first undertaking to provide significant added value: a reduction of 30–50%,
— second undertaking to provide significant added value: a reduction of 20–30%,
— subsequent undertakings that provide significant added value: a reduction of up to 20%.

In order to determine the level of reduction within each of these bands, the Commission will take into account the time at which the evidence fulfilling the condition in point (24) was submitted and the extent to which it represents added value.

If the applicant for a reduction of a fine is the first to submit compelling evidence in the sense of point (25) which the Commission uses to establish additional facts increasing the gravity or the duration of the infringement, the Commission will not take such additional facts into account when setting any fine to be imposed on the undertaking which provided this evidence.

B. *Procedure*

(27) An undertaking wishing to benefit from a reduction of a fine must make a formal application to the Commission and it must present it with sufficient evidence of the alleged cartel to qualify for a reduction of a fine in accordance with point (24) of this Notice. Any voluntary submission of evidence to the Commission which the undertaking that submits it wishes to be considered for the beneficial treatment of section III of this Notice must be clearly identified at the time of its submission as being part of a formal application for a reduction of a fine.

(28) If requested, the Directorate General for Competition will provide an acknowledgement of receipt of the undertaking's application for a reduction of a fine and of any subsequent submissions of evidence, confirming the date and, where appropriate, time of each submission. The Commission will not take any position on an application for a reduction of a fine before it has taken a position on any existing applications for conditional immunity from fines in relation to the same alleged cartel.

(29) If the Commission comes to the preliminary conclusion that the evidence submitted by the undertaking constitutes significant added value within the meaning of points (24) and (25), and that the undertaking has met the conditions of points (12) and (27), it will inform the undertaking in writing, no later than the date on which a statement of objections is notified, of its intention to apply a reduction of a fine within a specified band as provided in point (26). The Commission will also, within the same time frame, inform the undertaking in writing if it comes to the preliminary conclusion that the undertaking does not qualify for a reduction of a fine. The Commission may disregard any

application for a reduction of fines on the grounds that it has been submitted after the statement of objections has been issued.

(30) The Commission will evaluate the final position of each undertaking which filed an application for a reduction of a fine at the end of the administrative procedure in any decision adopted. The Commission will determine in any such final decision:

(a) whether the evidence provided by an undertaking represented significant added value with respect to the evidence in the Commission's possession at that same time;

(b) whether the conditions set out in points (12)(a) to (12)(c) above have been met;

(c) the exact level of reduction an undertaking will benefit from within the bands specified in point (26).

If the Commission finds that the undertaking has not met the conditions set out in point (12), the undertaking will not benefit from any favourable treatment under this Notice.

OFT's guidance as to the appropriate amount of a penalty
OFT 423, **December** 2004 [footnotes omitted]

Immunity from or reduction in financial penalty for undertakings coming forward with information in cartel activity cases

3.1 Undertakings participating in cartel activities might wish to terminate their involvement and inform the OFT of the existence of the cartel activity, but be deterred from doing so by the risk of incurring large financial penalties. To encourage such undertakings to come forward, the OFT will grant total immunity from financial penalties for an infringement of Article 81 and/or the Chapter I prohibition to a participant in cartel activity who is the first to come forward and who satisfies the requirements set out in paragraph 3.9. Alternatively, the OFT may offer a reduction of up to 100 per cent from financial penalties to a participant who is the first to come forward and who satisfies the requirements set out in paragraphs 3.11 and 3.12. An undertaking which is not the first to come forward, or does not satisfy these requirements may benefit from a reduction of up to 50 per cent in the amount of the financial penalty imposed if it satisfies the requirements set out in paragraphs 3.13 to 3.15.

3.2 The OFT considers that it is in the interest of the economy of the United Kingdom, and the European Community more generally, to have a policy of granting lenient treatment to undertakings which inform it of cartel activities and which then co-operate with it in the circumstances set out below. It is the often secret nature of cartel activities which justifies such a policy. The interests of customers and consumers in ensuring that such activities are detected and prohibited outweigh the policy objectives of imposing financial penalties on those undertakings which participate in cartel activities but which co-operate to a significant degree with the OFT as set out below.

Procedure for requesting immunity or a reduction in the level of penalties

3.3 An undertaking which wishes to take advantage of the lenient treatment set out in this part must contact the Director of Cartel Investigations (the Director) at the OFT, or his/her equivalent at the appropriate Regulator. This step has to be taken by a person who has the power to represent the undertaking for that purpose.

3.4 Initial contact can be made by telephone. Prospective applications may be discussed with the Director on an anonymous basis if preferred, perhaps with the prospective applicant's legal adviser. However, before an application can then be taken forward, the applicant's name must be given to the Director.

Leniency applications and the ECN

3.5 The European Commission and a number of NCAs also have leniency programmes that facilitate the detection of infringements.

3.6 As set out at paragraph 1.2 above, the Modernisation Regulation creates a system in which NCAs and the European Commission will apply Articles 81 and 82. The European Competition

Network (the ECN) has been set up to facilitate close co-operation between NCAs and the European Commission and to ensure an effective and consistent application of EC competition rules. An NCA will be considered well placed to deal with a case where the cumulative case allocation criteria are met. Details of these criteria are provided in the European Commission's *Notice on Co-operation within the Network of Competition Authorities* (the Notice).

3.7 An application for leniency to the OFT will not be considered as an application for leniency to another NCA within the ECN, even where that other NCA deals with the case in parallel with or in place of the OFT. It is therefore in the interest of the applicant to apply for leniency to all the NCAs which have the power to apply Article 81 in the territory affected by the infringement and which may be considered well placed to deal with the infringement in question. In view of the importance of timing in most existing leniency programmes, applicants will also need to consider whether it would be appropriate to make leniency applications to the relevant NCAs simultaneously. A list of NCAs which offer a leniency programme can be found on the European Commission's website. Individual applications may be discussed with the Director.

3.8 Details on how information may be exchanged within the ECN, and the safeguards in place to protect the position of a leniency applicant with regard to such information exchange, can be found in the Notice (see paragraphs 39–42).

Total immunity for the first to come forward BEFORE an investigation has commenced in cartel activity cases

3.9 An undertaking will benefit from total immunity from financial penalties if the undertaking is the first to provide the OFT with evidence of cartel activity in a market before the OFT has commenced an investigation of the cartel activity, provided that the OFT does not already have sufficient information to establish the existence of the alleged cartel activity, and conditions (a) to (d) below are satisfied.

The undertaking must:
   a) provide the OFT with all the information, documents and evidence available to it regarding the cartel activity
   b) maintain continuous and complete co-operation throughout the investigation and until the conclusion of any action by the OFT arising as a result of the investigation
   c) refrain from further participation in the cartel activity from the time of disclosure of the cartel activity to the OFT (except as may be directed by the OFT), and
   d) not have taken steps to coerce another undertaking to take part in the cartel activity.

3.10 If an undertaking does not qualify for total immunity under paragraph 3.9 above, it may still benefit from a reduction of financial penalties of up to 100 per cent under paragraphs 3.11 and 3.12 below.

Reduction in the level of financial penalties of up to 100 per cent for the first to come forward AFTER an investigation has commenced in cartel activity cases

3.11 An undertaking may benefit from a reduction in the level of the financial penalty of up to 100 per cent if the following conditions are satisfied:
   • the undertaking seeking immunity under this paragraph is the first to provide the OFT with evidence of cartel activity in a market before the OFT has issued a statement of objections, and
   • conditions (a) to (d) in paragraph 3.9 above are satisfied.

3.12 The reduction in the level of the financial penalty of up to 100 per cent by the OFT in these circumstances is discretionary. In order for the OFT to exercise this discretion it must be satisfied that the undertaking should benefit from a reduction in the level of the financial penalty taking into account the stage at which the undertaking comes forward, the evidence in the OFT's possession and the evidence provided by the undertaking.

Reduction in the level of financial penalties of up to 50 per cent in cartel activity cases

3.13 Undertakings which provide evidence of cartel activity before a statement of objections is issued, but are not the first to come forward, or do not qualify for total immunity under paragraphs 3.9 or 3.11 and 3.12 above, may be granted a reduction of up to 50 per cent in the amount of a financial penalty which would otherwise be imposed, if conditions (a) to (c) in paragraph 3.9 above are met.

3.14 Any reduction in financial penalty will be calculated taking into account the stage at which the undertaking comes forward, the evidence in the OFT's possession and the evidence provided by the undertaking.

3.15 The grant of a reduction by the OFT in these circumstances is, however, discretionary. In order for the OFT to exercise this discretion it must be satisfied that the undertaking should benefit from a reduction, taking into account the factors described in paragraph 3.14 above.

Additional reduction in financial penalties

3.16 An undertaking co-operating with an investigation by the OFT under the Act in relation to cartel activity in one market (the first market) may also be involved in a completely separate cartel activity in another market (the second market) which also infringes Article 81 and/or the Chapter I prohibition.

3.17 If the undertaking obtains total immunity from financial penalties under paragraph 3.9 or a reduction of up to 100 per cent in the amount of the financial penalty under paragraphs 3.11 and 3.12 above in relation to its activities in the second market, it will also receive a reduction in the financial penalties imposed on it which is additional to the reduction which it would have received for its co-operation in the first market alone. For example, as a result of an investigation by the OFT of producers, including ABC Ltd, in the widgets market, ABC Ltd carries out an internal investigation and discovers that, as well as having participated in cartel activity in the widgets market, one of its divisions has participated in separate cartel activity in the sprockets market. ABC Ltd has been co-operating with the OFT's widgets investigation and is interested in seeking lenient treatment by disclosing its participation in the sprockets cartel activity. Assuming ABC Ltd qualifies for total immunity in relation to the sprockets market, it can also obtain a reduction in financial penalty in relation to the widgets market in addition to the reduction it would have received for co-operation in the widgets investigation alone, i.e. an additional reduction in respect of the widgets market (the first market) as a result of its co-operation in the investigation into the sprockets market (the second market).

Confidentiality

3.18 An undertaking coming forward with evidence of cartel activity may be concerned about the disclosure of its identity as an undertaking which has volunteered information. The OFT will therefore endeavour, to the extent that it is consistent with its statutory obligations to disclose information, and allowing for the exchange of information as required within the ECN, to keep the identity of such undertakings confidential throughout the course of its investigation until the issue of a statement of objections.

NOTE: Both the OFT and DG Comp leniency programmes offer similar incentives to encourage cartel members to approach the authorities to confess their involvement in return for immunity from fines or a fine reduction. This makes it much more likely that the authorities will become aware of a cartel, but it also has the result that the authority will have much better evidence to prove the infringement against the leniency applicant, and all the other members of the cartel. This evidence-gathering process is the reason that there is value in reducing fine discounts for subsequent leniency applicants. If the authority can gather information in this way it will not have to expend considerable time and effort using more labour-intensive methods. That means they can process more cases with the resources they have available.

Sandhu, J.S., 'The European Commission's Leniency Policy: A Success'
[2007] ECLR 148, pp 148–9 [footnotes omitted]

The European Commission's 2002 leniency policy in cartel cases has been relatively successful. In just under four years since the adoption of the 2002 Leniency Notice to the end of 2005, the

Commission had received 167 applications for full immunity and a reduction of fine. Notably, over half of those applications were made before an unannounced inspection by the Commission and, in most of these cases, the Commission granted upfront full immunity from fines. In contrast, under the previous policy, the 1996 Leniency Notice, which was in place for almost twice as long as the 2002 policy, the Commission received just over 80 leniency applications. And significantly, the majority of these applications were made only after the European Commission carried out unannounced inspections. Based on these statistics alone, it appears that the 2002 revisions to the leniency policy significantly assisted the Commission to uncover cartel activity.

In several respects, however, the 2002 policy may not have been as effective as it could have been. It did not fully take into account the importance of transparency and predictability of outcome to companies considering seeking leniency. In this regard, the recent revisions by the European Commission to the leniency programme, which increase transparency and predictability, are welcomed. As discussed in this article, transparency and predictability ensure consistency, and these are necessary prerequisites for a leniency programme seeking to induce companies to report cartels in a full and forthcoming manner. This article discusses these issues and comments on the recent revisions by the European Commission to its leniency policy that increase transparency and predictability for leniency applicants.

NOTE: To ensure the incentives of leniency are always available across Europe the Commission has developed a Model Leniency Programme to help all EC Members States to ensure they have an appropriate leniency structure (see Commission Press Release IP/06/1288, 'Competition: Commission and other ECN members co-operate in use of leniency to fight cross border cartels' 29 September 2006).

Following the UK's introduction of individual penalties for cartel involvement an individual leniency programme was also introduced. While it shares some features with the corporate leniency programme it is notable that there is no 'second place' in individual leniency; immunity from prosecution is the only reward.

OFT, *The cartel offence: Guidance on the issue of*
no-action letters for individuals
OFT 513, April 2003 [footnotes omitted]

No-action letters

3.1 The OFT considers that it is in the interest of the economic well-being of the United Kingdom to grant immunity from prosecution to individuals who inform competition authorities of cartels and who then cooperate fully in the circumstances set out below. The secret nature of cartels and their damaging effects justifies such a policy. The interests of customers and end-consumers in ensuring that such practices are detected and brought to an end outweigh the policy objectives of imposing penalties on those individuals who have committed an offence but who cooperate fully with the OFT and, where appropriate, any other competition authorities.

3.2 In the context of the cartel offence, immunity from prosecution will be granted in the form of a 'no-action letter', issued by the OFT under section 190(4) of the Enterprise Act. A no-action letter will prevent a prosecution being brought against an individual in England and Wales or Northern Ireland for the cartel offence except in circumstances specified in the letter. Whilst guarantees of immunity from prosecution cannot be given in relation to Scotland, cooperation by an individual will be reported to the Lord Advocate who will take such cooperation into account. In suitable cases this may include an early decision as to whether or not a particular individual remains liable to be prosecuted. A draft no-action letter is annexed to this guidance for information. This letter may be amended to take into account any special circumstances of an application.

Conditions for the issue of a no-action letter

3.3 In order to benefit from a no-action letter, and subject to paragraph 3.4 and 3.9 below, an individual must:

- admit participation in the criminal offence
- provide the OFT with all information available to them regarding the existence and activities of the cartel
- maintain continuous and complete cooperation throughout the investigation and until the conclusion of any criminal proceedings arising as a result of the investigation
- not have taken steps to coerce another undertaking to take part in the cartel, and
- refrain from further participation in the cartel from the time of its disclosure to the OFT (except as may be directed by the investigating authority).

3.4 However, the fact that these conditions are satisfied in any particular case is not in itself sufficient for the issue of a no-action letter. Where the OFT believes that it already has, or is in the course of gathering, sufficient information to bring a successful prosecution of an individual, it will not issue a no-action letter to that individual.

Procedure

3.5 When an individual believes that they may require a no-action letter, or an early determination as to whether they are liable to be prosecuted in Scotland, an approach should be made to the Director of Cartel Investigations at the OFT. The approach may be made:

- directly by the individual
- by a lawyer representing the individual, or
- on behalf of named employees, directors, ex-employees or exdirectors, by an undertaking (or by a lawyer representing such undertaking) seeking leniency from the OFT in accordance with the OFT's 'Guidance as to the Appropriate Amount of a Penalty' (the OFT's Guidance) or in conjunction with an application for leniency from the European Commission in accordance with the Commission Notice on immunity from fines or reduction of fines in cartel cases (the Commission Notice on Immunity).

Initially, approaches by lawyers may be made on an anonymous basis.

3.6 When an approach is made, the Director of Cartel Investigations will give an initial indication as to whether the OFT may be prepared to issue a no-action letter. In cases where an undertaking has been granted 100 per cent leniency in accordance with the OFT's Guidance or the Commission Notice on Immunity, the OFT will normally be prepared to issue no-action letters to those named employees, directors, ex-employees or ex-directors on whose behalf an approach is made, subject to the conditions set out at paragraph 3.3 above being met and subject to paragraph 3.9.

3.7 If the OFT is prepared to issue a no-action letter the individual applying for immunity from prosecution will be interviewed. Any information they provide in such interviews will not be used against them in criminal proceedings except in the following circumstances:

- where a no-action letter is not issued, if the individual applying for immunity from prosecution has knowingly or recklessly provided information that is false or misleading in a material particular, or
- where a no-action letter is issued, if it is subsequently revoked (see further paragraphs 3.11 to 3.13 below).

3.8 On completion of the interview (which may extend over several sessions), the OFT will advise the applicant in writing whether it is prepared to issue a no-action letter.

3.9 In cases where the OFT concludes that, on the basis of the information that has been given, the applicant is not at risk of criminal prosecution for the cartel offence, it will not issue a no-action letter for this reason and will confirm this in writing.

3.10 If, following discussions:

- the OFT considers that, without a no-action letter, there is a likelihood of prosecution, and
- the applicant confirms that they will meet the conditions for the issue of a no-action letter a no-action letter will be issued. Alternatively, in a case where prosecution would be brought in Scotland, the cooperation given by the applicant will be reported to the Lord Advocate with a request for an early decision as to whether the individual remains liable to prosecution.

Revocation

3.11 A no-action letter may be revoked if:
- the recipient of a letter ceases to satisfy in whole or in part any of the relevant conditions (set out at paragraph 3.3 above), or
- the recipient of a letter has knowingly or recklessly provided information that is false or misleading in a material particular.

3.12 On revocation any immunity granted by the no-action letter will cease to exist as if it had never been granted and the OFT may rely on any information given by the applicant in a prosecution against them for the cartel offence.

3.13 If a no-action letter is to be revoked the recipient of the letter will be notified in writing and given a reasonable opportunity to make representations.

Competition Disqualification Orders

3.14 Section 204 of the Enterprise Act empowers the OFT to ask the relevant court to make a Competition Disqualification Order (CDO). This is an order disqualifying a director of a company which commits a breach of competition law. For these purposes, a breach of competition law includes an infringement of the Chapter I prohibition or Article 81 EC Treaty.

3.15 The OFT has issued guidance on CDOs, in which it states that it will not seek CDOs against individuals who benefit from no-action letters or who are directors of companies that benefit from leniency from either the OFT in accordance with the OFT's guidance or the European Commission in accordance with the Commission Notice on Immunity. Individuals who apply for no-action letters and undertakings benefiting from leniency will receive individual confirmation of this policy.

NOTE: Individual leniency creates the same incentives for decision-makers inside cartels to leave the arrangement and reveal their activities to the authorities. When competition law sought to increase personal penalties they also needed to give personal incentives to leave the cartel. Corporate leniency would not be an effective incentive if the individuals who had taken the undertaking into the cartel still faced personal sanctions. Both forms of leniency must be available together. It is interesting to note that there is no 'second place' in the OFT's individual leniency programme. While there is no formalized second place with sentence reductions, we saw in *R v Whittle* that the courts will take cooperating into account in sentencing; there is still an incentive to cooperate with an investigation.

Leniency programmes are not only successful in giving incentives to leave the cartel. They also produce other very useful effects. A branch of economics known as game theory is very useful in explaining the interaction between the unique nature of a secret cartel organization and the presence of an effective leniency programme.

Leslie, C.R., 'Trust, Distrust and Antitrust'

(2004) 82(3) Texas L Rev 515, pp. 640–2 [footnotes omitted]

The rewards structure of the government's program creates a race to confess. Given the rewards for being first, "the [Antitrust] Division frequently encounters situations where a company approaches the government within days, and in some cases less than one business day, after one of its co-conspirators has secured its position as first in line for amnesty. Of course, only the first company to qualify receives amnesty." Knowing this, each cartel member may distrust the other cartel members since each has a strong incentive to confess first. While the government's amnesty program creates a race structure, the trigger that starts the race is distrust. Once the trust breaks down, whoever gets to the government first and confesses gets amnesty. This can create an unbearable pressure to race to confess. Distrust is key.

Without distrust, the program will not have its intended effect. If cartel members trust each other, then none will confess. Each firm maximizes its expected profits by belonging to a stable cartel. Although being the first to confess eliminates criminal penalties, it is still preferable to continue to participate in a stable cartel so long as the firm rationally believes that the cartel will not be discovered and no criminal penalties will be imposed anyway. Thus, confession is not a dominant strategy. The government has no leverage. However, distrust supplies the leverage because confession becomes the dominant strategy once a cartel member suspects that one of her cartel partners is considering confession.

The distrust need not be widespread. If only one cartel member distrusts his partners and believes that one or more of them is about to seek amnesty from the government, then he should race to confess the cartel's activities to antitrust authorities. It only takes one cartel member to distrust, to confess, and to subject the remaining cartel members to antitrust penalties. It is this mutual fear of defection that can lead to distrust. In the context of leniency guidelines, this fear of defection can lead a cartel member to preempt the other cartel members by confessing first.

In addition to relying on distrust to start the confession race, the Leniency Guidelines also create distrust. Leniency creates a direct incentive to confess, but it also creates an indirect incentive that both creates distrust and feeds upon it. If authorities offer one suspect a reward to defect, she may accept the offer simply in order to receive the reward. However, if in addition to offering her the reward, the authorities also inform her that they are offering the same reward to her partner, that is going to increase the probability of her accepting the offer to defect. Now, not only does she have the direct incentive of receiving something valuable (whether money or immunity), but she has to worry that if she does not accept the government's offer, the alternative is not the status quo ante. If her partner accepts the offer while she does not, she is put in a much worse position. If she trusts that her partner will not defect, then she is less likely to defect. However, if she distrusts her partner and believes that he will defect, then the potential cost of not accepting the government's offer increases significantly and she is much more likely to confess.

...

In sum, the Leniency Guidelines have two effects: providing a direct incentive to confess and creating distrust among cartel partners, which provides an additional incentive to confess. The two effects work in tandem to make quick confession the rational decision for cartelists. Merely offering a cartelist a reward—some benefit—to confess does not harness the power of distrust. Informing each cartel member that every member of the cartel has been offered the same deal sows the seeds of distrust. Seen in this light, the Leniency Guidelines are part of a long trajectory of antitrust policies creating distrust among actual and potential cartel members.

NOTE: The importance of 'distrust' is vital in understanding the incredible effectiveness of leniency in uncovering cartels. The vast majority of cartels are now discovered with the assistance of a leniency application. A corporate leniency programme ensures that the separate undertakings in the cartel have reason to distrust one another, and make it difficult to maintain the cartel. Individual leniency has an additional impact; not only does it increase distrust between undertakings, but it also increases distrust within undertakings. For leniency to uncover a cartel it is only necessary that one person seeks leniency. Individual sanctions mean that every individual who is involved in the cartel has reason to be distrustful of all the other individuals who could seek leniency to save themselves. The more difficult it becomes to keep everyone together the more likely it is that the arrangement will break down. Leniency also helps ensure that when an arrangement breaks down it is highly likely there will be a race to the authorities to seek the protection of immunity. To create even greater incentives to inform on cartels the OFT has developed a new policy whereby they are willing to pay cash rewards of up to £100,000 to individuals who can provide information on cartel activity (see OFT Press Release 31/08 'OFT offers financial incentives for information regarding cartel activity', 29 February 2008). Financial incentives are designed to incentivize those who are not central to the operation of the cartel, and who would therefore not be incentivized by leniency alone, but who have enough 'inside' information to be of real use to the OFT. For further discussion of the importance of 'faithless agents' see, Leslie, C.R., 'Cartels, Agency Costs, and Finding Virtue in Faithless Agents' (2008) 49 William and Mary Law Review 1621.

For an undertaking or individual to feel confident enough to make a leniency application they must be confident that they understand what they have to do in order to be successful. If they fear that speaking to the authorities will simply worsen their position the incentives to make the initial approach are stripped away. It is therefore key that the systems are as clear, transparent, and as predictable as possible. Many of the changes in the 2006 Leniency Notice were designed to make the system more predictable, but Sandhu, see above, argues that yet more can be done.

A threat to the success of leniency may come from an unlikely source: private actions seeking compensation. As discussed above, and in Chapters 3 and 4, private actions can increase deterrence by increasing the effective penalty for unlawful activity. But there is no leniency protection from compensation claims. If private actions become very costly their existence may mask the benefits of leniency. In designing an effective regime it is important the correct balance is struck. See Wils, W.P.J., 'The Relationship between Public Antitrust Enforcement and Private Actions for Damages' (2009) 32(1) World Comp 3, and Walsh, D.J., 'Carrots and sticks—leniency and fines in EC cartel cases' [2009] ECLR 30.

■ QUESTION

If the introduction of leniency has been such a success, to what extent will its future be threatened by the encouragement of private compensation actions in Europe?

The final development in the authorities' new approach to catching cartels is direct settlement. Following the success of leniency there are many more cartel cases going through infringement proceedings. It is now important that the competition authorities develop way to handle those cases as effectively as possible, and to free up as much administrative time as possible to ensure they can deal appropriately with all the cases they discover.

Commission Notice on the conduct of settlement procedures in view of the adoption of Decisions pursuant to Article 7 and Article 23 of Council Regulation (EC) No 1/2003 in cartel cases
OJ, 2008, C167/1, paras 5–33

2. PROCEDURE

5. The Commission retains a broad margin of discretion to determine which cases may be suitable to explore the parties' interest to engage in settlement discussions, as well as to decide to engage in them or discontinue them or to definitely settle. In this regard, account may be taken of the probability of reaching a common understanding regarding the scope of the potential objections with the parties involved within a reasonable timeframe, in view of factors such as number of parties involved, foreseeable conflicting positions on the attribution of liability, extent of contestation of the facts. The prospect of achieving procedural efficiencies in view of the progress made overall in the settlement procedure, including the scale of burden involved in providing access to non-confidential versions of documents from the file, will be considered. Other concerns such as the possibility of setting a precedent might apply. The Commission may also decide to discontinue settlement discussions if the parties to the proceedings coordinate to distort or destroy any evidence relevant to the establishment of the infringement or any part thereof or to the calculation of the applicable fine. Distortion or destruction of evidence relevant to the establishment of the infringement or any part thereof may also constitute an aggravating circumstance within the meaning of point 28 of the Commission Guidelines on the method of setting fines imposed pursuant to Article 23(2)(a) of Regulation (EC) No 1/2003 (the Guidelines on fines), and may be regarded as lack of cooperation within the meaning of points 12 and 27 of the Leniency Notice. The Commission may only engage in settlement discussions upon the written request of the parties concerned.

6. While parties to the proceedings do not have a right to settle, should the Commission consider that a case may, in principle, be suitable for settlement, it will explore the interest in settlement of all parties to the same proceedings.

7. The parties to the proceedings may not disclose to any third party in any jurisdiction the contents of the discussions or of the documents which they have had access to in view of settlement, unless they have a prior explicit authorization by the Commission. Any breach in this regard may lead the Commission to disregard the undertaking's request to follow the settlement procedure. Such disclosure may also constitute an aggravating circumstance, within the meaning of point 28 of the Guidelines on fines and may be regarded as lack of cooperation within the meaning of points 12 and 27 of the Leniency Notice.

2.1. Initiation of proceedings and exploratory steps regarding settlement

8. Where the Commission contemplates the adoptionn of a decision pursuant to Article 7 and/or Article 23 of Regulation (EC) No 1/2003, it is required in advance to identify and recognize as parties to the proceedings the legal persons on whom a penalty may be imposed for an infringement of Article 81 of the Treaty.

9. To this end, the initiation of proceedings pursuant to Article 11(6) of Regulation (EC) No 1/2003 in view of adopting such a decision can take place at any point in time, but no later than the date on which the Commission issues a statement of objections against the parties concerned. Article 2(1) of Regulation (EC) No 773/2004 further specifies that, should the Commission consider it suitable to explore the parties' interest in engaging in settlement discussions, it will initiate proceedings no later than the date on which it either issues a statement of objections or requests the parties to express in writing their interest to engage in settlement discussions, whichever is the earlier.

10. After the initiation of proceedings pursuant to Article 11(6) of Regulation (EC) No 1/2003, the Commission becomes the only competition authority competent to apply Article 81 of the Treaty to the case in point.

11. Should the Commission consider it suitable to explore the parties' interest to engage in settlement discussions, it will set a time-limit of no less than two weeks pursuant to Articles 10a(1) and 17(3) of Regulation (EC) No 773/2004 within which parties to the same proceedings should declare in writing whether they envisage engaging in settlement discussions in view of possibly introducing settlement submissions at a later stage. This written declaration does not imply an admission by the parties of having participated in an infringement or of being liable for it.

12. Whenever the Commission initiates proceedings against two or more parties within the same undertaking, the Commission will inform each of them of the other legal entities which it identifies within the same undertaking and which are also concerned by the proceedings. In such a case, should the concerned parties wish to engage in settlement discussions, they must appoint joint representatives duly empowered to act on their behalf by the end of the time-limit referred to in point 11. The appointment of joint representatives aims solely to facilitate the settlement discussions and it does not prejudge in any way the attribution of liability for the infringement amongst the different parties.

13. The Commission may disregard any application for immunity from fines or reduction of fines on the ground that it has been submitted after the expiry of the time-limit referred to in point 11.

2.2. Commencing the settlement procedure: settlement discussions

14. Should some of the parties to the proceedings request settlement discussions and comply with the requirements referred to in points 11 and 12, the Commission may decide to pursue the settlement procedure by means of bilateral contacts between the Commission Directorate-General for Competition and the settlement candidates.

15. The Commission retains discretion to determine the appropriateness and the pace of the bilateral settlement discussions with each undertaking. In line with Article 10a(2) of Regulation (EC) No 773/2004, this includes determining, in view of the progress made overall in the settlement procedure, the order and sequence of the bilateral settlement discussions as well as the timing of the disclosure of information, including the evidence in the Commission file used to establish the envisaged objections and the potential fine. Information will be disclosed in a timely manner as settlement discussions progress.

16. Such an early disclosure in the context of settlement discussions pursuant to Article 10a(2) and Article 15(1a) of Regulation (EC) No 773/2004 will allow the parties to be informed of the essential elements taken into consideration so far, such as the facts alleged, the classification of those facts, the gravity and duration of the alleged cartel, the attribution of liability, an estimation of the range of likely fines, as well as the evidence used to establish the potential objections. This will enable the parties effectively to assert their views on the potential objections against them and will allow them to make an informed decision on whether or not to settle. Upon request by a party, the Commission services will also grant it access to non-confidential versions of any specified accessible document listed in the case file at that point in time, in so far as this is justified for the purpose of enabling the party to ascertain its position regarding a time period or any other aspect of the cartel.

17. When the progress made during the settlement discussions leads to a common understanding regarding the scope of the potential objections and the estimation of the range of likely fines to be imposed by the Commission, and the Commission takes the preliminary view that procedural efficiencies are likely to be achieved in view of the progress made overall, the Commission may grant a final time-limit of at least 15 working days for an undertaking to introduce a final settlement submission pursuant to Articles 10a(2) and 17(3) of Regulation (EC) No 773/2004. The time-limit can be extended following a reasoned request. Before granting such time-limit, the parties will be entitled to have the information specified in point 16 disclosed to them upon request.

18. The parties may call upon the Hearing Officer at any time during the settlement procedure in relation to issues that might arise relating to due process. The Hearing Officer's duty is to ensure that the effective exercise of the rights of defence is respected.

19. Should the parties concerned fail to introduce a settlement submission, the procedure leading to the final decision in their regard will follow the general provisions, in particular Articles 10(2), 12(1) and 15(1) of Regulation (EC) No 773/2004, instead of those regulating the settlement procedure.

20. Parties opting for a settlement procedure must introduce a formal request to settle in the form of a settlement submission. The settlement submission provided for in Article 10a(2) of Regulation (EC) No 773/2004 should contain:

  (a) an acknowledgement in clear and unequivocal terms of the parties' liability for the infringement summarily described as regards its object, its possible implementation, the main facts, their legal qualification, including the party's role and the duration of their participation in the infringement in accordance with the results of the settlement discussions;

  (b) an indication (3) of the maximum amount of the fine the parties foresee to be imposed by the Commission and which the parties would accept in the framework of a settlement procedure;

  (c) the parties' confirmation that, they have been sufficiently informed of the objections the Commission envisages raising against them and that they have been given sufficient opportunity to make their views known to the Commission;

  (d) the parties' confirmation that, in view of the above, they do not envisage requesting access to the file or requesting to be heard again in an oral hearing, unless the Commission does not reflect their settlement submissions in the statement of objections and the decision;

  (e) the parties' agreement to receive the statement of objections and the final decision pursuant to Articles 7 and 23 of Regulation (EC) No 1/2003 in an agreed official language of the European Community.

21. The acknowledgments and confirmations provided by the parties in view of settlement constitute the expression of their commitment to cooperate in the expeditious handling of the case following the settlement procedure. However, those acknowledgments and confirmations are conditional upon the Commission meeting their settlement request, including the anticipated maximum amount of the fine.

22. Settlement requests cannot be revoked unilaterally by the parties which have provided them unless the Commission does not meet the settlement requests by reflecting the settlement submissions first in a statement of objections and ultimately, in a final decision (see in this regard points 27 and 29). The statement of objections would be deemed to have endorsed the settlement submissions if it reflects their contents on the issues mentioned in point 20(a). Additionally, for a final decision to be deemed to have reflected the settlement submissions, it should also impose a fine which does not exceed the maximum amount indicated therein.

2.4. Statement of objections and reply

23. Pursuant to Article 10(1) of Regulation (EC) No 773/2004, the notification of a written state-ment of objections to each of the parties against whom objections are raised is a mandatory preparatory step before adopting any final decision. Therefore, the Commission will issue a state-ment of objections also in a settlement procedure.

24. For the parties' rights of defence to be exercised effectively, the Commission should hear their views on the objections against them and supporting evidence before adopting a final decision and take them into account by amending its preliminary analysis, where appropriate. The Commission must be able not only to accept or reject the parties' relevant arguments expressed during the administrative procedure, but also to make its own analysis of the matters put forward by them in order to either abandon such objections because they have been shown to be unfounded or to supplement and reassess its arguments both in fact and in law, in support of the objections which it maintains.

25. By introducing a formal settlement request in the form of a settlement submission prior to the notification of the statement of objections, the parties concerned enable the Commission to effectively take their views into account already when drafting the statement of objections, rather than only before the consultation of the Advisory Committee on Restrictive Practices and Dominant Positions (hereinafter the 'Advisory Committee') or before the adoption of the final decision.

26. Should the statement of objections reflect the parties' settlement submissions, the parties concerned should within a time-limit of at least two weeks set by the Commission in accordance with Articles 10a(3) and 17(3) of Regulation (EC) No 773/2004, reply to it by simply confirming (in unequivocal terms) that the statement of objections corresponds to the contents of their settlement submissions and that they therefore remain committed to follow the settlement procedure. In the absence of such a reply, the Commission will take note of the party's breach of its commitment and may also disregard the party's request to follow the settlement procedure.

27. The Commission retains the right to adopt a statement of objections which does not reflect the parties' settlement submission. If so, the general provisions in Articles 10(2), 12(1) and 15(1) of Regulation (EC) No 773/2004 will apply. The acknowledgements provided by the parties in the settle-ment submission would be deemed to be withdrawn and could not be used in evidence against any of the parties to the proceedings. Hence, the parties concerned would no longer be bound by their settlement submissions and would be granted a time-limit allowing them, upon request, to present their defence anew, including the possibility to access the file and to request an oral hearing.

2.5. Commission decision and settlement reward

28. Upon the parties' replies to the statement of objections confirming their commitment to set-tle, Regulation (EC) No 773/2004 allows the Commission to proceed, without any other procedural step, to the adoption of the subsequent final decision pursuant to Articles 7 and/or 23 of Regulation (EC) No 1/2003, after consultation of the Advisory Committee pursuant to Article 14 of Regulation (EC) No 1/2003. In particular, this implies that no oral hearing or access to the file may be requested by those parties once their settlement submissions have been reflected by the statement of objections, in line with Articles 12(2) and 15(1a) of Regulation (EC) No 773/2004.

29. The Commission retains the right to adopt a final position which departs from its preliminary position expressed in a statement of objections endorsing the parties' settlement submissions, either in view of the opinion provided by the Advisory Committee or for other appropriate consid-erations in view of the ultimate decisional autonomy of the Commission to this effect. However,

should the Commission opt to follow that course, it will inform the parties and notify to them a new statement of objections in order to allow for the exercise of their rights of defence in accordance with the applicable general rules of procedure. It follows that the parties would then be entitled to have access to the file, to request an oral hearing and to reply to the statement of objections. The acknowledgments provided by the parties in the settlement submissions would be deemed to have been withdrawn and could not be used in evidence against any of the parties to the proceedings.

30. The final amount of the fine in a particular case is determined in the decision finding an infringement pursuant to Article 7 and imposing a fine pursuant to Article 23 of Regulation (EC) No 1/2003.

31. In line with the Commission's practice, the fact that an undertaking cooperated with the Commission under this Notice during the administrative procedure will be indicated in the final decision, so as to explain the reason for the level of the fine.

32. Should the Commission decide to reward a party for settlement in the framework of this Notice, it will reduce by 10% the amount of the fine to be imposed after the 10% cap has been applied having regard to the Guidelines on the method of setting fines imposed pursuant to Article 23(2)(a) of Regulation (EC) No 1/2003. Any specific increase for deterrence used in their regard will not exceed a multiplication by two.

33. When settled cases involve also leniency applicants, the reduction of the fine granted to them for settlement will be added to their leniency reward.

NOTE: To encourage parties to enter into settlement discussions the Commission offers a reward to the parties, a 10 per cent fine reduction. In offering such a reward the Commission has to balance a number of interests. Any fine reduction reduces the deterrent effect of fines, but if settlement frees up Commission time and streamlines the enforcement process the reduction in deterrence through fines may well be more than compensated for through an increase in enforcement activity. The greatest administrative savings would probably be made if the settlement procedure could limit the number of 'appeals' the Commission has to defend before the CFI. It, however, appears that the settlement procedure adopted may do little to reduce the incentive to seek a judicial review of Commission fining Decisions. The Commission has made it very clear it will not 'negotiate' the final fine. If there are still a large number of review cases the administrative savings made by the Commission may be small. The Commission's position can be contrasted with plea bargains in the US which settle the final fine and ensure that the parties waive their right to appeal.

The UK also operates an 'early resolution' procedure, which appears to operate more like a US-style plea bargain. It is more informal in nature and there is no formal guidance. Its operation can been seen in cases such as *Dairy Products*, 'OFT welcomes early resolution agreements and agrees over £116m penalties', OFT Press Release 170/07, 7 December 2007, and *Tobacco*, 'OFT reaches early resolution agreements in tobacco case', OFT Press Release 82/08, 11 July 2008.

FURTHER READING

Connor, J.M., and Lande, R., 'The Size of Cartel Overcharges: Implications for US and EU Fining Policies' (2006) 51(4) Antitrust Bulletin 983.

Harding, C., and Joshua, J., *Regulating Cartels in Europe—A Study of Legal Control of Corporate Delinquency*, Oxford, OUP, 2003.

Joshua, J., 'The UK's new cartel offence and its implications for EC competition law: a tangled web' (2003) 28 EL Rev 620.

Leslie, C.R., 'Trust, Distrust, and Antitrust' (2004) 82(3) Texas L Rev 515.

Leslie, C.R., 'Cartels, Agency Costs, and Finding Virtue in Faithless Agents' (2008) 49 William & Mary L Rev 1621.

MacCulloch, A., 'The cartel offence and the criminalisation of United Kingdom competition law' [2003] JBL 616.

MacCulloch, A., 'Honesty Morality and the Cartel Offence' [2007] ECLR 355.

Volcker, S.B., 'Rough justice? An analysis of the European Commission's new fining guidelines' (2007) 44 CML Rev 1285.

10

Article 82 EC

SECTION 1: **INTRODUCTION**

Article 82 EC is focused on the way that undertakings with a dominant market position exercise their economic power. While Articles 81 and 82 EC are not mutually exclusive, they primarily address distinct types of conduct; Article 81 EC addresses explicit or tacitly coordinated conduct and Article 82 EC focuses on unilateral behaviour. Another key distinction is that Article 81(3) EC explicitly allows for a balancing of the anti-competitive and beneficial effects stemming from the agreement, whereas Article 82 EC appears to summarily prohibit conduct deemed to be an abuse of the economic power of dominant undertakings. EC competition law can be seen as supporting the four freedoms within the Internal Market most vividly through the language and interpretation of Article 82, which has sought to protect the Internal Market project from the damaging effects that may be caused by the use, and abuse, of market power within the Community. Enforcement of Article 82 EC has been criticized as lacking coherence and a clear objective consistent with policy and legislative developments in other areas of EC competition law. In December 2008, at the end of a three-year review, the European Commission produced guidance and set out how it plans to prioritize and investigate Article 82 cases in future. The guidance represents an attempt to 'modernize' Article 82 EC and further the same economic and effects-based approach that can be seen through the application of Article 81 EC and the European Community Merger Control Regulation ('ECMR'). The prohibition of 'abuse' of a dominant market position is set out in Article 82 EC.

ARTICLE 82 EC

Any abuse by one or more undertakings of a dominant position within the common market or in a substantial part of it shall be prohibited as incompatible with the common market insofar as it may affect trade between Member States.

Such abuse may, in particular, consist in:

(a) directly or indirectly imposing unfair purchase or selling prices or other unfair trading conditions;

(b) limiting production, markets or technical development to the prejudice of consumers;

(c) applying dissimilar conditions to equivalent transactions with other trading parties, thereby placing them at a competitive disadvantage;

(d) making the conclusion of contracts subject to acceptance by the other parties of supplementary obligations which, by their nature or according to commercial usage, have no connection with the subject of such contracts.

NOTE: The indicative list of abusive behaviour in paras (a)–(d) is simply that, an indicative list. The prohibition contained in the first paragraph has been interpreted widely by the Commission and the Community Courts.

A: Undertakings

The term used in Community competition law to describe commercial enterprises is 'undertakings'. The same term is also used in Article 81 EC and the Court has consistently held that the term has the same meaning in both contexts. See Chapter 6.

B: Effect on trade between Member States

Because of the particular features of Article 82 EC, there is much greater focus on the structure of markets within the jurisprudence in this area.

Commercial Solvents v Commission
(Joined Cases 6 and 7/73) [1974] ECR 223, [1974] 1 CMLR 309

Istituto/Commercial Solvents were the dominant producers of a number of intermediate chemical products, including 'nitropropane' and 'aminobutanol'. Those chemicals were used for the manufacture of 'ethambutol', used as an anti-tuberculosis drug. A customer of Commercial Solvents, Zoja SpA, used the intermediary products to produce ethambutol. At the end of 1970, Zoja attempted to source further supplies of the intermediary but Commercial Solvents made it clear that none would be available. The refusal to supply Zoja would result in its removal from the market for anti-tuberculosis drugs.

[30] The applicants argue that in this case it is principally the world market which is affected, since Zoja sells 90 per cent of its production outside the Common Market and in particular in the developing countries, and that constitutes a much more important market for anti-tuberculosis drugs than the countries of the Community, where tuberculosis has largely disappeared. The sales outlets of Zoja in the Common Market are further reduced by the fact that in many member-States Zoja was blocked by the patents of other companies, in particular American Cyanamid, which prevented it from selling its specialities based on ethambutol. Therefore abuse of the dominant position, even if it were established, would not come within the ambit of Article 86, which prohibits such an abuse only 'in so far as it may effect trade between member-States'.

[31] This expression is intended to define the sphere of application of Community rules in relation to national laws. It cannot therefore be interpreted as limiting the field of application of the prohibition which it contains to industrial and commercial activities supplying the member-States.

[32] The prohibitions of Articles 85 and 86 must in fact be interpreted and applied in the light of Article 3(f) of the Treaty, which provides that the activities of the Community shall include the institution of a system ensuring that competition in the Common Market is not distorted, and Article 2 of the Treaty, which gives the Community the task of promoting 'throughout the Community harmonious development of economic activities'. By prohibiting the abuse of a dominant position within the market in so far as it may affect trade between member-States Article 86 therefore covers

abuse which may directly prejudice consumers as well as abuse which indirectly prejudices them by impairing the effective competitive structure as envisaged by Article 3(f) of the Treaty.

[33] The Community authorities must therefore consider all the consequences of the conduct complained of for the competitive structure in the Common Market without distinguishing between production intended for sale within the market and that intended for export. When an undertaking in a dominant position within the Common Market abusively exploits its position in such a way that a competitor in the Common Market is likely to be eliminated, it does not matter whether the conduct relates to the latter's exports or its trade within the Common Market, once it has been established that this elimination will have repercussions on the competitive structure within the Common Market.

[34] Moreover the contrary argument would in practice mean that the control of Zoja's production and outlets would be in the hands of Commercial Solvents Corp. and Istituto. Finally its cost prices would have been so affected that the ethambutol produced by it would possibly become unmarketable.

[35] Moreover it emerged at the hearing that Zoja is at present able to export and does indeed export the products in question to at least two member-States. These exports are endangered by the difficulties caused to this company and, by reason of this, trade between member-States may be affected.

NOTE: The existence of a large market participant may, in itself, hamper the proper operation of the Internal Market.

Soda-ash—Solvay

(Commission Decision, 91/299/EEC) OJ, 1991, L152/21

Soda-ash is a substance used in glass production and the chemical industry. Most glass producers needed a continuous and secure supply of soda-ash, which they tended to secure from a supplier in their own Member State. The Commission took action as it was concerned that suppliers were not competing outside their traditional 'spheres of influence'.

4. Effect on trade between Member States

[65] Article 86 covers not only abuse which may directly prejudice consumers but also abuse which indirectly prejudices them by impairing the effective competitive structure in the common market as envisaged by Article 3(f) of the EEC Treaty.

The fidelity rebates and other inducements to exclusivity applied by Solvay affect trade between Member States by reinforcing the links between the customers and the dominant supplier. The opportunities for competing suppliers to enter new markets or obtain new customers are effectively removed since the customer's marginal tonnage requirements for which they would be competing are currently being supplied by Solvay at prices which they would be unable to meet. The various devices employed by Solvay to tie customers had the result of reinforcing the structural rigidity and the division of the soda-ash market on national lines, and thus harmed or threatened to harm the attainment of the objective of a single market between Member States.

[66] The fact that Solvay's measures were aimed principally at imports from the United States does not affect the application of Article 86. Imports of natural ash from the United States were seen as the main threat to Solvay's domination of the soda-ash market in continental western Europe. The arrival in substantial quantities of natural ash would also have had a considerable effect upon the agreed division of the market between ICI and Solvay. The activities therefore affected the basic competitive structure of the soda-ash industry within the Community.

It should also be noted that were the major glass producers to import soda-ash from the United States in substantial quantities, they would probably do so in order to supply their works in several Member States. Furthermore, Solvay's exclusionary measures were aimed not only at the United States producers but also at smaller producers of synthetic ash located inside the Community.

All of these producers have since 1982 made deliveries from their own national market to other Community Member States although their opportunities were severely constrained by Solvay's pricing policies.

NOTE: The protection of the development of the Internal Market means that Article 82 may apply to conduct that only occurs within one Member State, if that conduct has the potential effect of retarding the development of intra-Community trade by denying potential sales to producers in other Member States.

Commission Notice—Guidelines on the effect on trade concept contained in Articles 81 and 82 of the Treaty
OJ, 2004, C101/81 [footnotes omitted]

17. In the case of Article 82 it is the abuse that must affect trade between Member States. This does not imply, however, that each element of the behaviour must be assessed in isolation. Conduct that forms part of an overall strategy pursued by the dominant undertaking must be assessed in terms of its overall impact. Where a dominant undertaking adopts various practices in pursuit of the same aim, for instance practices that aim at eliminating or foreclosing competitors, in order for Article 82 to be applicable to all the practices forming part of this overall strategy, it is sufficient that at least one of these practices is capable of affecting trade between Member States.

...

Abuses of dominant positions covering several Member States

73. In the case of abuse of a dominant position it is useful to distinguish between abuses that raise barriers to entry or eliminate competitors (exclusionary abuses) and abuses whereby the dominant undertaking exploits its economic power for instance by charging excessive or discriminatory prices (exploitative abuses). Both kinds of abuse may be carried out either through agreements, which are equally subject to Article 81(1), or through unilateral conduct, which as far as Community competition law is concerned is subject only to Article 82.

74. In the case of exploitative abuses such as discriminatory rebates, the impact is on downstream trading partners, which either benefit or suffer, altering their competitive position and affecting patterns of trade between Member States.

75. When a dominant undertaking engages in exclusionary conduct in more than one Member State, such abuse is normally by its very nature capable of affecting trade between Member States. Such conduct has a negative impact on competition in an area extending beyond a single Member State, being likely to divert trade from the course it would have followed in the absence of the abuse. For example, patterns of trade are capable of being affected where the dominant undertaking grants loyalty rebates. Customers covered by the exclusionary rebate system are likely to purchase less from competitors of the dominant firm than they would otherwise have done. Exclusionary conduct that aims directly at eliminating a competitor such as predatory pricing is also capable of affecting trade between Member States because of its impact on the competitive market structure inside the Community. When a dominant firm engages in behaviour with a view to eliminating a competitor operating in more than one Member State, trade is capable of being affected in several ways. First, there is a risk that the affected competitor will cease to be a source of supply inside the Community. Even if the targeted undertaking is not eliminated, its future competitive conduct is likely to be affected, which may also have an impact on trade between Member States. Secondly, the abuse may have an impact on other competitors. Through its abusive behaviour the dominant undertaking can signal to its competitors that it will discipline attempts to engage in real competition. Thirdly, the very fact of eliminating a competitor may be sufficient for trade between Member States to be capable of being affected. This may be the case even where the undertaking that risks being eliminated mainly engages in exports to third countries. Once the effective competitive market structure inside the Community risks being further impaired, there is Community law jurisdiction.

76. Where a dominant undertaking engages in exploitative or exclusionary abuse in more than one Member State, the capacity of the abuse to affect trade between Member States will normally

also by its very nature be appreciable. Given the market position of the dominant undertaking concerned, and the fact that the abuse is implemented in several Member States, the scale of the abuse and its likely impact on patterns of trade is normally such that trade between Member States is capable of being appreciably affected. In the case of an exploitative abuse such as price discrimination, the abuse alters the competitive position of trading partners in several Member States. In the case of exclusionary abuses, including abuses that aim at eliminating a competitor, the economic activity engaged in by competitors in several Member States is affected. The very existence of a dominant position in several Member States implies that competition in a substantial part of the common market is already weakened. When a dominant undertaking further weakens competition through recourse to abusive conduct, for example by eliminating a competitor, the ability of the abuse to affect trade between Member States is normally appreciable.

...

Abuses of dominant positions covering a single Member State

93. Where an undertaking, which holds a dominant position covering the whole of a Member State, engages in exclusionary abuses, trade between Member States is normally capable of being affected. Such abusive conduct will generally make it more difficult for competitors from other Member States to penetrate the market, in which case patterns of trade are capable of being affected. In Michelin, for example, the Court of Justice held that a system of loyalty rebates foreclosed competitors from other Member States and therefore affected trade within the meaning of Article 82. In Rennet the Court similarly held that an abuse in the form of an exclusive purchasing obligation on customers foreclosed products from other Member States.

94. Exclusionary abuses that affect the competitive market structure inside a Member State, for instance by eliminating or threatening to eliminate a competitor, may also be capable of affecting trade between Member States. Where the undertaking that risks being eliminated only operates in a single Member State, the abuse will normally not affect trade between Member States. However, trade between Member States is capable of being affected where the targeted undertaking exports to or imports from other Member States and where it also operates in other Member States. An effect on trade may arise from the dissuasive impact of the abuse on other competitors. If through repeated conduct the dominant undertaking has acquired a reputation for adopting exclusionary practices towards competitors that attempt to engage in direct competition, competitors from other Member States are likely to compete less aggressively, in which case trade may be affected, even if the victim in the case at hand is not from another Member State.

95. In the case of exploitative abuses such as price discrimination and excessive pricing, the situation may be more complex. Price discrimination between domestic customers will normally not affect trade between Member States. However, it may do so if the buyers are engaged in export activities and are disadvantaged by the discriminatory pricing or if this practice is used to prevent imports. Practices consisting of offering lower prices to customers that are the most likely to import products from other Member States may make it more difficult for competitors from other Member States to enter the market. In such cases trade between Member States is capable of being affected.

96. As long as an undertaking has a dominant position which covers the whole of a Member State it is normally immaterial whether the specific abuse engaged in by the dominant undertaking only covers part of its territory or affects certain buyers within the national territory. A dominant firm can significantly impede trade by engaging in abusive conduct in the areas or vis-à-vis the customers that are the most likely to be targeted by competitors from other Member States. For example, it may be the case that a particular channel of distribution constitutes a particularly important means of gaining access to broad categories of consumers. Hindering access to such channels can have a substantial impact on trade between Member States. In the assessment of appreciability it must also be taken into account that the very presence of the dominant undertaking covering the whole of a Member State is likely to make market penetration more difficult. Any abuse which makes it more difficult to enter the national market should therefore be considered to appreciably affect trade. The combination of the market position of the dominant undertaking and the anti-competitive nature of its conduct implies that such abuses have normally by their very

nature an appreciable effect on trade. However, if the abuse is purely local in nature or involves only an insignificant share of the sales of the dominant undertaking within the Member State in question, trade may not be capable of being appreciably affected.

Abuse of a dominant position covering only part of a Member State

97. Where a dominant position covers only part of a Member State some guidance may, as in the case of agreements, be derived from the condition in Article 82 that the dominant position must cover a substantial part of the common market. If the dominant position covers part of a Member State that constitutes a substantial part of the common market and the abuse makes it more difficult for competitors from other Member States to gain access to the market where the undertaking is dominant, trade between Member States must normally be considered capable of being appreciably affected.

98. In the application of this criterion regard must be had in particular to the size of the market in question in terms of volume. Regions and even a port or an airport situated in a Member State may, depending on their importance, constitute a substantial part of the common market. In the latter cases it must be taken into account whether the infrastructure in question is used to provide crossborder services and, if so, to what extent. When infrastructures such as airports and ports are important in providing cross-border services, trade between Member States is capable of being affected.

99. As in the case of dominant positions covering the whole of a Member State (cf. paragraph 95 above), trade may not be capable of being appreciably affected if the abuse is purely local in nature or involves only an insignificant share of the sales of the dominant undertaking.

NOTE: The Commission's Guidelines on circumstances whereby abusive behaviour might have an effect on trade between Member States is particularly important in light of Regulation 1/2003, which imposed obligations on national competition authorities and national courts to enforce Article 82 EC (see Chapter 2). Article 3(1) of the Regulation states:

> Where the competition authorities of the Member States or national courts apply national competition law to any abuse prohibited by Article 82 of the Treaty, they shall also apply Article 82 of the Treaty.

Notably, Article 3(2) does not prevent Member States from applying stricter national laws than Article 82 EC against unilateral conduct of undertakings, in contrast to the position regarding conduct caught under Article 81 EC.

C: Relevant product market

It is vital to ensure that the undertaking suspected of abusing its power does indeed have a sufficient degree of market power—a dominant position in EC terminology. Without dominance, an undertaking will be constrained by its competitors and competition law will not need to intervene. To establish whether an undertaking has such power it is necessary first to establish in which market they operate, taking into account the relevant product, geographic, and temporal aspects of the market. The question of dominance is considered second; once the parameters of the relevant market and market sales figures are known and other data can be accurately assessed. The importance of the relevant market was explained by the Court in *Continental Can*:

Continental Can v Commission
(Case 6/72) [1973] ECR 215

[14] The definition of the relevant market is of essential significance, for the possibilities of competition can only be judged in relation to those characteristics of the products in question

by virtue of which those products are particularly apt to satisfy an inelastic need and are only to a limited extent interchangeable with other products. In order to be regarded as constituting a distinct market, the products in question must be individualized not only by the mere fact that they are used for packing certain products, but by particular characteristics of production that make them specifically suitable for this purpose.

NOTE: Deciding whether a product is interchangeable with another is not always an easy task. To assist in that task, the Commission has published detailed guidance explaining its view of the process. The Commission's practice is not legally binding—merely of persuasive authority.

Commission Notice on Market Definition
OJ, 1997, C372/5, paras 7–27, 33–4

II. Definition of relevant market
Definition of relevant product market and relevant geographic market

[7] The Regulations based on Articles 85 and 86 of the Treaty, in particular in section 6 of Form A/B with respect to Regulation No 17, as well as in section 6 of Form CO with respect to Regulation (EEC) No 4064/89 on the control of concentrations having a Community dimension have laid down the following definitions, 'Relevant product markets' are defined as follows:

> 'A relevant product market comprises all those products and/or services which are regarded as interchangeable or substitutable by the consumer, by reason of the products' character-istics, their prices and their intended use'.

[8] 'Relevant geographic markets' are defined as follows:

> 'The relevant geographic market comprises the area in which the undertakings concerned are involved in the supply and demand of products or services, in which the conditions of competition are sufficiently homogeneous and which can be distinguished from neighbour-ing areas because the conditions of competition are appreciably different in those areas'.

[9] The relevant market within which to assess a given competition issue is therefore estab-lished by the combination of the product and geographic markets. The Commission interprets the definitions in paragraphs 7 and 8 (which reflect the case-law of the Court of Justice and the Court of First Instance as well as its own decision-making practice) according to the orientations defined in this notice.

Concept of relevant market and objectives of Community competition policy

[10] The concept of relevant market is closely related to the objectives pursued under Community competition policy. For example, under the Community's merger control, the objective in control-ling structural changes in the supply of a product/service is to prevent the creation or reinforcement of a dominant position as a result of which effective competition would be significantly impeded in a substantial part of the common market. Under the Community's competition rules, a dominant position is such that a firm or group of firms would be in a position to behave to an appreciable ex-tent independently of its competitors, customers and ultimately of its consumers. Such a position would usually arise when a firm or group of firms accounted for a large share of the supply in any given market, provided that other factors analysed in the assessment (such as entry barriers, cus-tomers' capacity to react, etc.) point in the same direction.

[11] The same approach is followed by the Commission in its application of Article 86 of the Treaty to firms that enjoy a single or collective dominant position. Within the meaning of Regulation No 17, the Commission has the power to investigate and bring to an end abuses of such a dominant pos-ition, which must also be defined by reference to the relevant market. Markets may also need to be defined in the application of Article 85 of the Treaty, in particular, in determining whether an appre-ciable restriction of competition exists or in establishing if the condition pursuant to Article 85(3)(b) for an exemption from the application of Article 85(1) is met.

[12] The criteria for defining the relevant market are applied generally for the analysis of certain types of behaviour in the market and for the analysis of structural changes in the supply of products. This methodology, though, might lead to different results depending on the nature

of the competition issue being examined. For instance, the scope of the geographic market might be different when analysing a concentration, where the analysis is essentially prospective, from an analysis of past behaviour. The different time horizon considered in each case might lead to the result that different geographic markets are defined for the same products depending on whether the Commission is examining a change in the structure of supply, such as a concentration or a cooperative joint venture, or examining issues relating to certain past behaviour.

Basic principles for market definition

Competitive constraints

[13] Firms are subject to three main sources or competitive constraints: demand substitutability, supply substitutability and potential competition. From an economic point of view, for the definition of the relevant market, demand substitution constitutes the most immediate and effective disciplinary force on the suppliers of a given product, in particular in relation to their pricing decisions. A firm or a group of firms cannot have a significant impact on the prevailing conditions of sale, such as prices, if its customers are in a position to switch easily to available substitute products or to suppliers located elsewhere. Basically, the exercise of market definition consists in identifying the effective alternative sources of supply for the customers of the undertakings involved, in terms both of products/services and of geographic location of suppliers.

[14] The competitive constraints arising from supply side substitutability other then those described in paragraphs 20 to 23 and from potential competition are in general less immediate and in any case require an analysis of additional factors. As a result such constraints are taken into account at the assessment stage of competition analysis.

Demand substitution

[15] The assessment of demand substitution entails a determination of the range of products which are viewed as substitutes by the consumer. One way of making this determination can be viewed as a speculative experiment, postulating a hypothetical small, lasting change in relative prices and evaluating the likely reactions of customers to that increase. The exercise of market definition focuses on prices for operational and practical purposes, and more precisely on demand substitution arising from small, permanent changes in relative prices. This concept can provide clear indications as to the evidence that is relevant in defining markets.

[16] Conceptually, this approach means that, starting from the type of products that the undertakings involved sell and the area in which they sell them, additional products and areas will be included in, or excluded from, the market definition depending on whether competition from these other products and areas affect or restrain sufficiently the pricing of the parties' products in the short term.

[17] The question to be answered is whether the parties' customers would switch to readily available substitutes or to suppliers located elsewhere in response to a hypothetical small (in the range 5 per cent to 10 per cent) but permanent relative price increase in the products and areas being considered. If substitution were enough to make the price increase unprofitable because of the resulting loss of sales, additional substitutes and areas are included in the relevant market. This would be done until the set of products and geographical areas is such that small, permanent increases in relative prices would be profitable. The equivalent analysis is applicable in cases concerning the concentration of buying power, where the starting point would then be the supplier and the price test serves to identify the alternative distribution channels or outlets for the supplier's products. In the application of these principles, careful account should be taken of certain particular situations as described within paragraphs 56 and 58.

[18] A practical example of this test can be provided by its application to a merger of, for instance, soft-drink bottlers. An issue to examine in such a case would be to decide whether different flavours of soft drinks belong to the same market. In practice, the question to address would be whether consumers of flavour A would switch to other flavours when confronted with a permanent price increase of 5 per cent to 10 per cent for flavour A. If a sufficient number of consumers would

switch to, say, flavour B, to such an extent that the price increase for flavour A would not be profitable owing to the resulting loss of sales, then the market would comprise at least flavours A and B. The process would have to be extended in addition to other available flavours until a set of products is identified for which a price rise would not induce a sufficient substitution in demand.

[19] Generally, and in particular for the analysis of merger cases, the price to take into account will be the prevailing market price. This may not be the case where the prevailing price has been determined in the absence of sufficient competition. In particular for the investigation of abuses of dominant positions, the fact that the prevailing price might already have been substantially increased will be taken into account.

Supply substitution

[20] Supply-side substitutability may also be taken into account when defining markets in those situatons in which its effects are equivalent to those of demand substitution in terms of effectiveness and immediacy. This means that suppliers are able to switch production to the relevant products and market them in the short term without incurring significant additional costs or risks in response to small and permanent changes in relative prices. When these conditions are met, the additional production that is put on the market will have a disciplinary effect on the competitive behaviour of the companies involved. Such an impact in terms of effectiveness and immediacy is equivalent to the demand substitution effect.

[21] These situations typically arise when companies market a wide range of qualities or grades of one product; even if, for a given final customer or group of consumers, the different qualities are not substitutable, the different qualities will be grouped into one product market, provided that most of the suppliers are able to offer and sell the various qualities immediately and without the significant increases in costs described above. In such cases, the relevant product market will encompass all products that are substitutable in demand and supply, and the current sales of those products will be aggregated so as to give the total value or volume of the market. The same reasoning may lead to group different geographic areas.

[22] A practical example of the approach to supply-side substitutability when defining product markets is to be found in the case of paper. Paper is usually supplied in a range of different qualities, from standard writing paper to high quality papers to be used, for instance, to publish art books. From a demand point of view, different qualities of paper cannot be used for any given use, i.e. an art book or a high quality publication cannot be based on lower quality papers. However, paper plants are prepared to manufacture the different qualities, and production can be adjusted with negligible costs and in a short time-frame. In the absence of particular difficulties in distribution, paper manufacturers are able therefore, to compete for orders of the various qualities, in particular if orders are placed with sufficient lead time to allow for modification of production plans. Under such circumstances, the Commission would not define a separate market for each quality of paper and its respective use. The various qualities of paper are included in the relevant market, and their sales added up to estimate total market value and volume.

[23] When supply-side substitutability would entail the need to adjust significantly existing tangible and intangible assets, additional investments, strategic decisions or time delays, it will not be considered at the stage of market definition. Examples where supply-side substitution did not induce the Commission to enlarge the market are offered in the area of consumer products, in particular for branded beverages. Although bottling plants may in principle bottle different beverages, there are costs and lead times involved (in terms of advertising, product testing and distribution) before the products can actually be sold. In these cases, the effects of supply-side substitutability and other forms of potential competition would then be examined at a later stage.

Potential competition

[24] The third source of competitive constraint, potential competition, is not taken into account when defining markets, since the conditions under which potential competition will actually represent an effective competitive constraint depend on the analysis of specific factors and circumstances related to the conditions of entry. If required, this analysis is only carried out at a subsequent

stage, in general once the position of the companies involved in the relevant market has already been ascertained, and when such position gives rise to concerns from a competition point of view.

III. Evidence relied on to define relevant markets

The process of defining the relevant market in practice

Product dimension

[25] There is a range of evidence permitting an assessment of the extent to which substitution would take place. In individual cases, certain types of evidence will be determinant, depending very much on the characteristics and specificity of the industry and products or services that are being examined. The same type of evidence may be of no importance in other cases. In most cases, a decision will have to be based on the consideration of a number of criteria and different items of evidence. The Commission follows an open approach to empirical evidence, aimed at making an effective use of all available information which may be relevant in individual cases. The Commission does not follow a rigid hierarchy of different sources of information or types of evidence.

[26] The process of defining relevant markets may be summarized as follows: on the basis of the preliminary information available or information submitted by the undertakings involved, the Commission will usually be in a position to broadly establish the possible relevant markets within which, for instance, a concentration or a restriction of competition has to be assessed. In general, and for all practical purposes when handling individual cases, the question will usually be to decide on a few alternative possible relevant markets. For instance, with respect to the product market, the issue will often be to establish whether product A and product B belong or do not belong to the same product market, it is often the case that the inclusion of product B would be enough to remove any competition concerns.

[27] In such situations it is not necessary to consider whether the market includes additional products, or to reach a definitive conclusion on the precise product market. If under the conceivable alternative market definitions the operation in question does not raise competition concerns, the question of market definition will be left open, reducing thereby the burden on companies to supply information.

...

The process of gathering evidence

[33] When a precise market definition is deemed necessary, the Commission will often contact the main customers and the main companies in the industry to enquire into their views about the boundaries of product and geographic markets and to obtain the necessary factual evidence to reach a conclusion. The Commission might also contact the relevant professional associations, and companies active in upstream markets, so as to be able to define, in so far as necessary, separate product and geographic markets, for different levels of production or distribution of the products/services in question. It might also request additional information to the undertakings involved.

[34] Where appropriate, the Commission will address written requests for information to the market players mentioned above. These requests will usually include questions relating to the perceptions of companies about reactions to hypothetical price increases and their views of the boundaries of the relevant market. They will also ask for provision of the factual information the Commission deems necessary to reach a conclusion on the extent of the relevant market. The Commission might also discuss with marketing directors or other officers of those companies to gain a better understanding on how negotiations between suppliers and customers take place and better understand issues relating to the definition of the relevant market. Where appropriate, they might also carry out visits or inspections to the premises of the parties, their customers and/or their competitors, in order to better understand how products are manufactured and sold.

NOTE: The Commission's practice has largely been welcomed: see, e.g. Baker, S., and Wu, L., 'Applying the Market Definition Guidelines of the European Commission' [1998] ECLR 273. However, Arnull questions the merits of the Commission's Notice.

Arnull, A, 'Competition, the Commission and Some Constitutional Questions of More than Minor Importance'
(1998) 23 EL Rev 1 [footnotes omitted]

On the vexed question of defining the relevant market, the Commission refers to a Notice devoted to that issue published in the same edition of the Official Journal. That Notice breaks new ground by adopting the so-called SSNIP test developed in the United States in the early 1980s and now applied around the world. SSNIP stands for 'small but significant non-transitory increase in prices' and the test is used to assess demand substitution. As the Commission explains: 'The question to be answered in whether the parties' customers would switch to readily available substitutes or to suppliers located elsewhere in response to a hypothetical small (in the range 5 per cent–10 per cent) but permanent relative price increase in the products and areas being considered'. The Notice goes on to explain the techniques used by the Commission in applying the SSNIP test. Importance is attached to a method known as 'shock analysis', which involves analysing recent events or shocks in the market that offer concrete examples of substitution between two products. The Commission states that this sort of information, when available, 'will normally be fundamental for market definition'. A striking aspect of the Notice is the apparent rejection by the Commission of factors which have traditionally been thought relevant to the definition of the relevant market. The Notice declares: '. . . product characteristics and intended use are insufficient to show whether two products are demand substitutes. Functional interchangeability or similarity in characteristics may not, in themselves, provide sufficient criteria, because the responsiveness of customers to relative price changes may be determined by other considerations as well'.

There are two constitutional difficulties with the burgeoning use by the Commission of instruments such as these. One is that, because such instruments do not in themselves produce any legal effects, their validity cannot be challenged before the Community Courts. Of course, decisions taken pursuant to the policies set out in them are susceptible to review, but by the time a challenge is brought, large numbers of cases may already have been resolved in accordance with the contested policy, even if it is ultimately found to be unlawful. The second difficulty is that the Commission is not required to comply with any external procedural requirements before issuing these instruments. Although it often invites comments before doing so, neither the other institutions nor the authorities of the Member States nor the Advisory Committee on Restrictive Practices and Monopolies have any formal right to be consulted. It seems undesirable for initiatives of such importance taken by a Community institution to lie beyond proper political and judicial scrutiny.

Even the objective of legal certainty may prove elusive. Whatever the theoretical merits of the Commission's new approach to defining the relevant product market, it is not easy to reconcile with the Court's case law on Article 86 EC. Until it is sanctioned by the Community Courts, national judges are likely to find decisions of those Courts more persuasive than a mere notice issued by the Commission. There even appear to be some in the Commission who have yet to be converted to the merits of the new approach. Although the 1997 version of the Notice on agreements of minor importance contains a reference to the Notice on defining the relevant market, it also states that '[t]he relevant product market comprises any products or services which are regarded as interchangeable or substitutable by the consumer, by reason of their characteristics, prices and intended use'. Old habits evidently die hard.

NOTE: While the Commission's views are expressed in the Notice, the jurisprudence of the Court is still invaluable in properly understanding this area.

United Brands v *Commission*
(Case 27/76) [1978] ECR 207, [1978] 1 CMLR 429

United Brands was the largest producer on the world's banana market. Its European subsidiary was responsible for coordinating banana sales across the EC, except in the UK and Italy. It was important to decide if the banana market was a market in its own right, or merely a part of the market for fresh fruit.

[12] As far as the product market is concerned it is first of all necessary to ascertain whether, as the applicant maintains, bananas are an integral part of the fresh fruit market, because they are reasonably interchangeable by consumers with other kinds of fresh fruit such as apples, oranges, grapes, peaches, strawberries, etc. Or whether the relevant market consists solely of the banana market which includes both branded bananas and unlabelled bananas and is a market sufficiently homogeneous and distinct from the market of other fresh fruit.

[13] The applicant submits in support of its argument that bananas compete with other fresh fruit in the same shops, on the same shelves, at prices which can be compared, satisfying the same needs: consumption as a dessert or between meals.

[14] The statistics produced show that consumer expenditure on the purchase of bananas is at its lowest between June and December when there is a plentiful supply of domestic fresh fruit on the market.

[15] Studies carried out by the food and agriculture organization (FAO) (especially in 1975) confirm that banana prices are relatively weak during the summer months and that the price of apples for example has a statistically appreciable impact on the consumption of bananas in the Federal Republic of Germany.

[16] Again according to these studies some easing of prices is noticeable at the end of the year during the 'orange season'.

[17] The seasonal peak periods when there is a plentiful supply of other fresh fruit exert an influence not only on the prices but also on the volume of sales of bananas and consequently on the volume of imports thereof.

[18] The applicant concludes from these findings that bananas and other fresh fruit form only one market and that UBC's operations should have been examined in this context for the purpose of any application of Article 86 of the Treaty.

[19] The Commission maintains that there is a demand for bananas which is distinct from the demand for other fresh fruit especially as the banana is a very important part of the diet of certain sections of the Community.

[20] The specific qualities of the banana influence customer preference and induce him not to readily accept other fruits as a substitute.

[21] The Commission draws the conclusion from the studies quoted by the applicant that the influence of the prices and availabilities of other types of fruit on the prices and availabilities of bananas on the relevant market is very ineffective and that these effects are too brief and too spasmodic for such other fruit to be regarded as forming part of the same market as bananas or as a substitute therefor.

[22] For the banana to be regarded as forming a market which is sufficiently differentiated from other fruit markets it must be possible for it to be singled out by such special features distinguishing it from other fruits that it is only to a limited extent interchangeable with them and is only exposed to their competition in a way that is hardly perceptible.

[23] The ripening of bananas takes place the whole year round without any season having to be taken into account.

[24] Throughout the year production exceeds demand and can satisfy it at any time.

[25] Owing to this particular feature the banana is a privileged fruit and its production and marketing can be adapted to the seasonal fluctuations of other fresh fruit which are known and can be computed.

[26] There is no unavoidable seasonal substitution since the consumer can obtain this fruit all the year round.

[27] Since the banana is a fruit which is always available in sufficient quantities the question whether it can be replaced by other fruits must be determined over the whole of the year for the purpose of ascertaining the degree of competition between it and other fresh fruit.

[28] The studies of the banana market on the court's file show that on the latter market there is no significant long term cross-elasticity any more than—as has been mentioned—there is any

seasonal substitutability in general between the banana and all the seasonal fruits, as this only exists between the banana and two fruits (peaches and table grapes) in one of the countries (West Germany) of the relevant geographic market.

[29] As far as concerns the two fruits available throughout the year (oranges and apples) the first are not interchangeable and in the case of the second there is only a relative degree of substitutability.

[30] This small degree of substitutability is accounted for by the specific features of the banana and all the factors which influence consumer choice.

[31] The banana has certain characteristics, appearance, taste, softness, seedlessness, easy handling, a constant level of production which enable it to satisfy the constant needs of an important section of the population consisting of the very young, the old and the sick.

[32] As far as prices are concerned two FAO studies show that the banana is only affected by the prices—falling prices—of other fruits (and only of peaches and table grapes) during the summer months and mainly in July and then by an amount not exceeding 20 per cent.

[33] Although it cannot be denied that during these months and some weeks at the end of the year this product is exposed to competition from other fruits, the flexible way in which the volume of imports and their marketing on the relevant geographic market is adjusted means that the conditions of competition are extremely limited and that its price adapts without any serious difficulties to this situation where supplies of fruit are plentiful.

[34] It follows from all these considerations that a very large number of consumers having a constant need for bananas are not noticeably or even appreciably enticed away from the consumption of this product by the arrival of other fresh fruit on the market and that even the personal peak periods only affect it for a limited period of time and to a very limited extent from the point of view of substitutability.

[35] Consequently the banana market is a market which is sufficiently distinct from the other fresh fruit markets.

NOTE: As can be seen from the discussion in *United Brands*, the key factor in deciding whether bananas were on the same market as other fruit was its interchangeability, sometimes also expressed as substitutability, with other fruit. To analyze that interchangeability, the Court examined the cross-elasticity of demand between fruits, a less technical version of the later SSNIP test, and other factors such as the particular characteristics of the banana to distinguish it from the rest of the fruit market.

Hilti AG v Commission
(Case T-30/89) [1991] ECR II-1439, [1992] 4 CMLR 16

Hilti was the largest European producer of PAF nail guns, nails, and cartridge strips ('PAF' stands for 'powder-actuated fastening'). Following complaints from undertakings supplying Hilti compatible nails, that they were being excluded from the market by Hilti's behaviour, the Commission instigated an investigation. The Commission found Hilti to be dominant on the nail gun, cartridge strip, and nail markets. Hilti appealed to the Court of First Instance.

Legal appraisal

[64] It should be observed at the outset that in order to assess Hilti's market position it is first necessary to define the relevant market, since the possibilities of competition can only be judged in relation to those characteristics of the products in question by virtue of which those products are particularly apt to satisfy an inelastic need and are only to a limited extent interchangeable with other products (judgment of the Court of Justice of 21 February 1973 in Case 6/72 *Continental Can*, paragraph 32).

[65] In order to determine, therefore, whether Hilti, as a supplier of nail guns and of consumables designed for them, enjoys such power over the relevant product market as to give it a dominant position within the meaning of Article 86, the first question to be answered is whether the relevant market is the market for all construction fastening systems or whether the relevant markets are those for PAF tools and the consumables designed for them, namely cartridge strips and nails.

[66] The Court takes the view that nail guns, cartridge strips and nails constitute three specific markets. Since cartridge strips and nails are specifically manufactured, and purchased by users, for a single brand of gun, it must be concluded that there are separate markets for Hilti-compatible cartridge strips and nails, as the Commission found in its decision (paragraph 55).

[67] With particular regard to the nails whose use in Hilti tools is an essential element of the dispute, it is common ground that since the 1960s there have been independent producers, including the interveners, making nails intended for use in nail guns. Some of those producers are specialized and produce only nails, and indeed some make only nails specifically designed for Hilti tools. That fact in itself is sound evidence that there is a specific market for Hilti-compatible nails.

[68] Hilti's contention that guns, cartridge strips and nails should be regarded as forming an indivisible whole, 'a powder-actuated fastening system' is in practice tantamount to permitting producers of nail guns to exclude the use of consumables other than their own branded products in their tools. However, in the absence of general and binding standards or rules, any independent producer is quite free, as far as Community competition law is concerned, to manufacture consumables intended for use in equipment manufactured by others, unless in doing so it infringes a patent or some other industrial or intellectual property right. Even on the assumption that, as the applicant has argued, components of different makes cannot be interchanged without the system characteristics being influenced, the solution should lie in the adoption of appropriate laws and regulations, not in unilateral measures taken by nail gun producers which have the effect of preventing independent producers from pursuing the bulk of their business.

[69] Hilti's argument that PAF tools and consumables form part of the market in PAF systems for the construction industry generally cannot be accepted either. The Court finds that PAF systems differ from other fastening systems in several important respects. The specific features of PAF systems, set out in paragraph 62 of the Decision, are such as to make them the obvious choice in a number of cases. It is evident from the documents before the Court that in many cases there is no realistic alternative either for a qualified operator carrying out a job on site or for a technician instructed to select the fastening methods to be used in a given situation.

[70] The Court considers that the Commission's description of those features in its decision is sufficiently clear and convincing to provide sound legal justification for the conclusions drawn from it.

[71] Those findings leave no real doubt as to the existence, in practice, of a variety of situations, some of which inherently favour the use of a PAF system whilst others favour one or more other fastening systems. As the Commission notes, the fact that several different fastening methods have each continued for long periods to account for an important share of total demand for fastening systems shows that there is only a relatively low degree of substitutability between them.

[72] In such circumstances the Commission was entitled to base its conclusions on arguments which took account of the qualitative characteristics of the products at issue.

[73] Its conclusions are, moreover, corroborated by the opinion prepared by Mr Yarrow and the survey conducted by Rosslyn Research Ltd, mentioned above, inasmuch as they disclose the existence of a large number of nail gun users who could see no realistic alternative to the PAF system in circumstances corresponding to most of those in which nail guns have in fact been used.

[74] Moreover, the evidence produced by the applicant is not such as to weaken the findings made by the Commission.

[75] In the first place it must be observed that the opinion of Mr Yarrow and the survey by Rosslyn Research Ltd do not demonstrate—as their authors claim—a high degree of economic substitutability between the relevant products. The questions put to construction undertakings are not apt to provide an answer to the fundamental question in this case, namely whether slight but significant

differences in the price of nails are likely to shift demand to a significant extent. In a market in which, as here, very large discounts on catalogue prices are common, the mere fact that a number of those questioned referred first to price as a decisive factor, without elaborating on the impact which a change in price would have on the choice of method to be used, cannot prove that there is a high degree of cross-price-elasticity.

[76] In the second place, it may be noted that Professor Albach's econometric analyses take account of only one factor—price—when it is clear from the documents before the Court, in particular the survey conducted by Rosslyn Research Ltd, that the choice of the consumer depends to a large extent on unquantifiable circumstances.

[77] The conclusion must be that the relevant product market in relation to which Hilti's market position must be appraised is the market for nails designed for Hilti nail guns.

[78] That finding is corroborated by the above mentioned letter of 23 March 1983 from Hilti to the Commission, in which the opinion was expressed that there were separate markets for guns, cartridge strips and nails. Although that did not, at the time, represent an interpretation of the term 'relevant market' for the purposes of Article 86 of the Treaty, the content of the letter is nevertheless quite revealing as to Hilti's own commercial view of the markets in which it operated at the time. Hilti has explained that the letter was prepared by an in-house lawyer, in conjunction with an outside legal adviser and the product manager concerned. The letter was therefore drafted by persons who may be assumed to have had a sound knowledge of the undertaking and its business.

NOTE: In *Hilti* the Court had to decide two questions. First, whether PAFs, such as nail guns, were interchangeable with other fastening systems, such as drilling and screwing. And, second, whether there were separate markets for nail guns and its consumables, cartridge strips and nails, or if they were to be considered as a single product market for the whole PAF system. The Court decided there was insufficient interchangeability with other fastening systems on the basis of the particular characteristics of the nail gun and its suitability for particular uses over other systems. The second argument was more controversial: the Court decided that there were three separate markets for nail guns, Hilti cartridge strips, and Hilti compatible nails. The evidence upon which they based their decision was largely that there were several competing producers of Hilti compatible nails, whose complaints brought about the Commission investigation. This finding has been challenged by a number of commentators. See, e.g. Price, D.R., 'Abuse of a Dominant Position—The Tale of Nails, Milk Cartons and TV Guides' [1990] ECLR 80. Many would argue that any attempt to exploit Hilti customers by raising the price of Hilti consumables would quickly result in customers switching to use other brands of nail gun. This is particularly the case where the cost of consumables is relatively high compared to the cost of the original product. Similar arguments may also arise with other related products such as photocopiers and their related toner cartridges.

Nederlandsche Banden-Industrie Michelin NV v Commission
(Case 322/81) [1983] ECR 3461, [1985] 1 CMLR 282

Complaints were made regarding Michelin's policies towards tyre dealers, especially regarding the discounts and bonuses granted to them. As Michelin produced tyres for a wide range of vehicles and sold to manufacturers and retailers, it was important to correctly define the relevant market.

[37] As the court has repeatedly emphasized, most recently in its judgment of 11 December 1980 in Case 31/80 *NV l'Oreal and SA l'Oreal v PVBA de Nieuwe Amck* (1980) ECR 3775, for the purposes of investigating the possibly dominant position of an undertaking on a given market, the possibilities of competition must be judged in the context of the market comprising the totality of the products which, with respect to their characteristics, are particularly suitable for satisfying constant needs and are only to a limited extent interchangeable with other products. However, it must be noted that the determination of the relevant market is useful in assessing whether the

undertaking concerned is in a position to prevent effective competition from being maintained and behave to an appreciable extent independently of its competitors and customers and consumers. For this purpose, therefore, an examination limited to the objective characteristics only of the relevant products cannot be sufficient: the competitive conditions and the structure of supply and demand on the market must also be taken into consideration.

[38] Moreover, it was for that reason that the Commission and Michelin NV agreed that new, original-equipment tyres should not be taken into consideration in the assessment of market shares. Owing to the particular structure of demand for such tyres characterized by direct orders from car manufacturers, competition in this sphere is in fact governed by completely different factors and rules.

[39] As far as replacement tyres are concerned, the first point which must be made is that at the user level there is no interchangeability between car and van tyres on the one hand and heavy-vehicle tyres on the other. Car and van tyres therefore have no influence at all on competition on the market in heavy-vehicle tyres.

[40] Furthermore, the structure of demand for each of those groups of products is different. Most buyers of heavy-vehicle tyres are trade users, particularly haulage undertakings, for whom, as the Commission explained, the purchase of replacement tyres represents an item of considerable expenditure and who constantly ask their tyre dealers for advice and long-term specialized services adapted to their specific needs. On the other hand, for the average buyer of car or van tyres the purchase of tyres is an occasional event and even if the buyer operates a business he does not expect such specialized advice and service adapted to specific needs. Hence the sale of heavy-vehicle tyres requires a particularly specialized distribution network which is not the case with the distribution of car and van tyres.

[41] The final point which must be made is that there is no elasticity of supply between tyres for heavy vehicles and car tyres owing to significant differences in production techniques and in the plant and tools needed for their manufacture. The fact that time and considerable investment are required in order to modify production plant for the manufacture of light-vehicle tyres instead of heavy-vehicle tyres or vice versa means that there is no discernible relationship between the two categories of tyre enabling production to be adapted to demand on the market. Moreover, that was why in 1977, when the supply of tyres for heavy vehicles was insufficient, Michelin NV decided to grant an extra bonus instead of using surplus production capacity for car tyres to meet demand.

[42] The Commission rightly examined the structure of the market and demand primarily at the level of dealers to whom Michelin NV applied the practice in question. Michelin NV has itself stated, although in another context, that it was compelled to change its discount system to take account of the tendency towards specialization amongst its dealers, some of whom, such as garage owners, no longer sold tyres for heavy vehicles and vans. This confirms the differences existing in the structure of demand between different groups of dealers. Nor has Michelin NV disputed that the distinction drawn between tyres for heavy vehicles, vans and cars is also applied by all its competitors, especially as regards discount terms, even if in the case of certain types of tyre the distinctions drawn by different manufacturers may vary in detail.

[43] Nevertheless, it cannot be deduced from the fact that the conduct to which exception is taken in this case affects dealers that Michelin NV's position ought to be assessed on the basis of the proportion of Michelin heavy-vehicle tyres in the dealers' total turnover. Since it is a question of investigating whether Michelin NV holds a dominant position in the case of certain products, it is unimportant that the dealers also deal in other products if there is no competition between those products and the products in question.

[44] On the other hand, in deciding whether a dominant position exists, neither the absence of elasticity of supply between different types and dimensions of tyres for heavy vehicles, which is due to differences in the conditions of production, nor the absence of interchangeability and elasticity of demand between those types and dimensions of tyre from the point of view of the specific needs of the user allow a number of smaller markets, reflecting those types and dimensions, to be distinguished, as Michelin NV suggests. Those differences between different types and dimensions

of tyre are not vitally important for dealers, who must meet demand from customers for the whole range of heavy-vehicle tyres. Furthermore, in the absence of any specialization on the part of the undertakings concerned, such differences in the type and dimensions of a product are not a crucial factor in the assessment of an undertaking's market position because in view of their similarity and the manner in which they complement one another at the technical level, the conditions of competition on the market are the same for all the types and dimensions of the product.

[45] In establishing that Michelin NV has a dominant position the Commission was therefore right to assess its market share with reference to replacement tyres for lorries, buses and similar vehicles and to exclude consideration of car and van tyres.

NOTE: In this decision the Court focused on the structure of supply and demand to assist it in the proper delineation of the market. Interchangeability of supply is also important to the market, as if other suppliers could easily enter the market, they must be considered as being potential competitors within the product market. In this case, suppliers of car and van tyres could not easily switch production to heavy-vehicle tyres and therefore they could be discounted from that market. The structure of demand was also important, as the Court was able to differentiate between original equipment tyres, which are fitted to cars as they are manufactured, and replacement cars, fitted by car owners once the original tyres are worn. Although the products are identical, the way in which demand operates, between individual purchases and manufacturer bulk purchases, is very different allowing the markets to be treated separately.

Europemballage Corpn and Continental Can Co Inc v Commission
(Case 6/72) [1973] ECR 215, [1973] CMLR 199

Continental Can acquired majority shares in a German company and a Dutch company. The Commission challenged these acquisitions as an abuse of a dominant position.

[31] The applicant contests the exactitude of the data on which the Commission bases its Decision. It cannot be concluded from SLW's market share, amounting to 70 to 80 per cent in meat cans, 80 to 90 per cent in cans for fish and crustacea and 50 to 55 per cent in metal closures with the exception of crown corks—percentages which moreover are too high and could not be proved by the defendant—that this undertaking dominates the market for light metal containers. The Decision, moreover, excluded the possibility of competition arising from substitute products (glass and plastic containers) relying on reasons which do not stand up to examination. The statements about possibilities of real and potential competition as well as about the allegedly weak position of the consumers are therefore, in the applicants' view, irrelevant.

[32] For the appraisal of SLW's dominant position and the consequences of the disputed merger, the definition of the relevant market is of essential significance, for the possibilities of competition can only be judged in relation to those characteristics of the products in question by virtue of which those products are particularly apt to satisfy an inelastic need and are only to a limited extent interchangeable with other products.

[33] In this context recitals Nos 5 to 7 of the second part of the Decision deal in turn with a 'market for light containers for canned meat products', a 'market for light containers for canned seafood', and a 'market for metal closures for the food packing industry, other than crown corks', all allegedly dominated by SLW and in which the disputed merger threatens to eliminate competition. The Decision does not, however, give any details of how these three markets differ from each other, and must therefore be considered separately. Similarly, nothing is said about how these three markets differ from the general market for light metal containers, namely the market for metal containers for fruit and vegetables, condensed milk, olive oil, fruit juices and chemico-technical products. In order to be regarded as constituting a distinct market, the products in question must be individualized, not only by the mere fact that they are used for packing certain products, but by particular characteristics of production which make them specificialy suitable for this purpose. Consequently, a dominant position on the market for light metal containers for meat and fish cannot be decisive,

as long as it has not been proved that competitors from other sectors of the market for light metal containers are not in a position to enter this market, by a simple adaptation, with sufficient strength to create a serious counterweight.

NOTE: This judgment shows the vital importance of correctly defining the market in respect of both supply and demand sides. Because the Commission had failed satisfactorily to adduce evidence to support its findings the Court quashed its Decision.

■ QUESTION

What are the key indicators a competition authority should look to when assessing interchangeability in order to determine the relevant product market?

D: Relevant geographic market

Once the product market is correctly defined it is necessary to define the geographical extent of the market. Some markets will be necessarily localized, while others may be global. Such a decision will have an obvious impact on the level of competition on a market.

United Brands **v** *Commission*
(Case 27/76) [1978] ECR 207, [1978] 1 CMLR 429

As United Brands was inactive in certain EC markets the inclusion of those markets would have weakened the argument that they were in a dominant position.

[44] The conditions for the application of Article 86 to an undertaking in a dominant position presuppose the clear delimitation of the substantial part of the common market in which it may be able to engage in abuses which hinder effective competition and this is an area where the objective conditions of competition applying to the product in question must be the same for all traders.

[45] The Community has not established a common organization of the agricultural market in bananas.

[46] Consequently import arrangements vary considerably from one Member State to another and reflect a specific commercial policy peculiar to the states concerned.

[47] This explains why for example the French market owing to its national organization is restricted upstream by a particular import arrangement and obstructed downstream by a retail price monitored by the administration.

[48] This market, in addition to adopting certain measures relating to a 'target price' (*'prix objectif'*) fixed each year and to packaging and grading standards and the minimum qualities required, reserves about two thirds of the market for the production of the overseas departments and one third to that of certain countries enjoying preferential relations with France (Ivory Coast, Madagascar, Cameroon) the bananas whereof are imported duty-free, and it includes a system the running of which is entrusted to the '*comite interprofessionnel bananier*' ('c.i.b.').

[49] The United Kingdom market enjoys 'commonwealth preferences', a system of which the main feature is the maintenance of a level of production favouring the developing countries of the commonwealth and of a price paid to the associations of producers directly linked to the selling price of the green banana charged in the United Kingdom.

[50] On the Italian market, since the abolition in 1965 of the state monopoly responsible for marketing bananas, a national system of quota restrictions has been introduced, the ministry for shipping and the exchange control office supervising the imports and the charter parties relating to the foreign ships which carry the bananas.

[51] The effect of the national organization of these three markets is that the applicant's bananas do not compete on equal terms with the other bananas sold in these states which benefit from a preferential system and the Commission was right to exclude these three national markets from the geographic market under consideration.

[52] On the other hand the six other states are markets which are completely free, although the applicable tariff provisions and transport costs are of necessity different but not discriminatory, and in which the conditions of competition are the same for all.

[53] From the standpoint of being able to engage in free competition these six states form an area which is sufficiently homogeneous to be considered in its entirety.

[54] UBC has arranged for its subsidiary in Rotterdam—UBCBV—to market its products. UBCBV is for this purpose a single centre for the whole of this part of the Community.

[55] Transport costs do not in fact stand in the way of the distribution policy chosen by UBC which consists in selling f.o.r. Rotterdam and Bremerhaven, the two ports where the bananas are unloaded.

[56] These are factors which go to make relevant market a single market.

[57] It follows from all these considerations that the geographic market as determined by the Commission which constitutes a substantial part of the common market must be regarded as the relevant market for the purpose of determining whether the applicant may be in a dominant position.

NOTE: The Court confirmed that the special characteristics of the markets in France, Italy, and the UK meant that those markets operated in very different ways to the rest of the Community. As Community markets become increasingly integrated, it is likely that many markets will be Community wide, but in a number of cases, because of the particular nature of some products, markets will still be locally defined: see, e.g. *Sealink/B&I-Holyhead: Interim Measures* [1992] 5 CMLR 255. The Commission guidance also addresses the relevant geographic market, and the explanation of its approach is informative.

Commission Notice on Market Definition
OJ, 1997, C372/5, paras 28–32

Geographic dimension

[28] The Commission's approach to geographic market definition might be summarized as follows: it will take a preliminary view of the scope of the geographic market on the basis of broad indications as to the distribution of market shares between the parties and their competitors, as well as a preliminary analysis of pricing and price differences at national and Community or EEA level. This initial view is used basically as a working hypothesis to focus the Commission's enquiries for the purposes of arriving at a precise geographic market definition.

[29] The reasons behind any particular configuration of prices and market shares need to be explored. Companies might enjoy high market shares in their domestic markets just because of the weight of the past, and conversely, a homogeneous presence of companies throughout the EEA might be consistent with national or regional geographic markets. The initial working hypothesis will therefore be checked against an analysis of demand characteristics (importance of national or local preferences, current patterns of purchases of customers, product differentiation/brands, other) in order to establish whether companies in different areas do indeed constitute a real alternative source of supply for consumers. The theoretical experiment is again based on substitution arising from changes in relative prices, and the question to answer is again whether the customers of the parties would switch their orders to companies located elsewhere in the short term and at a negligible cost.

[30] If necessary, a further check on supply factors will be carried out to ensure that those companies located in differing areas do not face impediments in developing their sales on competitive

terms throughout the whole geographic market. This analysis will include an examination of require-ments for a local presence in order to sell in that area the conditions of access to distribution channels, costs associated with setting up a distribution network, and the presence or absence of regulatory barriers arising from public procurement, price regulations, quotas and tariffs limiting trade or production, technical standards, monopolies, freedom of establishment, requirements for administrative authorizations, packaging regulations, etc. In short, the Commission will identify possible obstacles and barriers isolating companies located in a given area from the competitive pressure of companies located outside that area, so as to determine the precise degree of market interpenetration at national, European or global level.

[31] The actual pattern and evolution of trade flows offers useful supplementary indications as to the economic importance of each demand or supply factor mentioned above, and the extent to which they may or may not constitute actual barriers creating different geographic markets. The analysis of trade flows will generally address the question of transport costs and the extent to which these may hinder trade between different areas, having regard to plant location, costs of production and relative price levels.

Market integration in the Community

[32] Finally, the Commission also takes into account the continuing process of market integra-tion, in particular in the Community, when defining geographic markets, especially in the area of concentrations and structural joint ventures. The measures adopted and implemented in the internal market programme to remove barriers to trade and further integrate the Community mar-kets cannot be ignored when assessing the effects on competition of a concentration or a struc-tural joint venture. A situation where national markets have been artificially isolated from each other because of the existence of legislative barriers that have now been removed will generally lead to a cautious assessment of past evidence regarding prices, market shares or trade patterns. A process of market integration that would, in the short term, lead to wider geographic markets may therefore be taken into consideration when defining the geographic market for the purposes of assessing concentrations and joint ventures.

E: Relevant temporal market

Markets may also need to be defined in terms of time. It may be the case that the market conditions considered were limited in time or operate on a seasonal basis.

ABG
(Commission Decision, 77/327/EEC) OJ, 1977, L117/1, [1977] 2 CMLR D1

Firms hold a dominant position where they are able to act fully independently—in other words where they may conduct their business without regard for the reactions of competitors and cus-tomers. This can happen when general economic circumstances and particular market conditions combine so that firms with an established market position, access to raw materials and adequate industrial capacity and capital resources find themselves in a position to control production and distribution in a substantial proportion of the market.

The market under consideration is that of motor spirit.

The general economic scene was set towards 1 November 1973 with the outbreak of the oil cri-sis, which was caused by a simultaneous reduction in the supply of oil offered on the world market combined with a substantial increase in the price demanded for it.

In this situation, the only people who still had access to oil supplies at economically viable prices were the large international oil companies refining or having oil refined in the Netherlands. This was because of their special relationships with the oil-producing countries of the Middle East, their integrated structures and the multinational nature of their installations and organizations.

Such a sudden shortage, especially one that was not brought about by economic considerations, led to a restriction of both actual and potential competition among the small group of companies concerned, a restriction that was particularly marked at the level of distribution.

The general fear of shortage, the sudden reduction in supplies of oil offered and the fact that the maximum prices for motor spirit fixed by the Dutch government were below international prices meant that the independent firms in the Netherlands could only obtain supplies from the world market at prices giving rise to losses; hence they could no longer import petroleum products in large quantities without endangering their longer-term survival. Imports were no longer available on the Dutch market and the independent buyers could only obtain their supplies from companies with refineries in the Netherlands. Thus, the relevant market for this case is the Netherlands, which constitutes a substantial part of the common market.

Economic restrictions such as existed in the Netherlands during the oil crisis can substantially alter existing commercial relations between suppliers who have a substantial share of the market and quantities available and their customers. For reasons completely outside the control of the normal suppliers, their customers can become completely dependent on them for the supply of scarce products. Thus, while the situation continues, the suppliers are placed in a dominant position in respect of their normal customers.

With the general shortage of supplies, all the oil companies were faced with the same problem— that of maintaining supplies to their regular customers. Thus, they were not able to make up the deficiencies of the other companies with substantial market shares and they were in no way in competition with each other to supply each other's customers.

In the prevailing circumstances each of these companies found itself in a dominant position relative to its customers.

NOTE: The Commission made it clear that the Decision was limited to the time during the 1970s oil crisis when petrol supplies could only be acquired in the Netherlands from the limited number of refineries within that Member State. The dramatic change from the normal conditions of the market meant that it was only proper that the market be differentiated from 'normal market conditions' that existed before and after the crisis. Another discussion of a possible temporal limit to the market can be seen in *United Brands*, discussed above, where the Court eventually rejected a claim that the banana market was affected by the seasonal nature of competitor fruit such as oranges or apples.

F: Dominance

Once the relevant market has been established it is then possible to examine that market to see if the undertaking under investigation is in a dominant position. The classic definition of dominance was expounded by the Court in:

United Brands v Commission
(Case 27/76) [1978] ECR 207, [1978] 1 CMLR 429

[63] Article 86 is an application of the general objective of the activities of the Commission laid down by Article 3(f) of the Treaty: the institution of a system ensuring that competition in the Common Market is not distorted.

[64] This Article prohibits any abuse by an undertaking of a dominant position in a substantial part of the Common Market in so far as it may affect trade between member-States.

[65] The dominant position referred to in this Article relates to a position of economic strength enjoyed by an undertaking which enables it to prevent effective competition being maintained on the relevant market by giving it the power to behave to an appreciable extent independently of its competitors, customers and ultimately of its consumers.

> [66] In general a dominant position derives from a combination of several factors which, taken separately, are not necessarily determinative.

NOTE: This definition loosely corresponds with the economic understanding of a 'price-maker', an undertaking that no longer takes its price from the market but can independently set its own price. But the definition itself gives little indication of the correct manner in which to establish the existence of dominance. The Court has developed a number of important factors that should be taken into account when examining the position of an undertaking, but as it notes in para. 66, none of those factors is necessarily determinative.

Hoffmann-La Roche v *Commission*

(Case 85/76) [1979] ECR 461, [1979] 3 CMLR 211

La Roche was the largest producer of vitamins within the Community and was challenged by the Commission for a number of allegedly abusive discounting practices within a number of vitamin markets.

> [38] Article 86 is an application of the general objective of the activities of the Community laid down by Article 3(f) of the Treaty, namely, the institution of a system ensuring that competition in the Common Market is not distorted. Article 86 prohibits any abuse by an undertaking of a dominant position in a substantial part of the Common Market in so far as it may affect trade between Member States. The dominant position thus referred to relates to a position of economic strength enjoyed by an undertaking which enables it to prevent effective competition being maintained on the relevant market by affording it the power to behave to an appreciable extent independently of its competitors, its customers and ultimately of the consumers.
>
> [39] Such a position does not preclude some competition, which it does where there is a monopoly or a quasi-monopoly, but enables the undertaking which profits by it, if not to determine, at least to have an appreciable influence on the conditions under which that competition will develop, and in any case to act largely in disregard of it so long as such conduct does not operate to its detriment. A dominant position must also be distinguished from parallel courses of conduct which are peculiar to oligopolies in that in an oligopoly the courses of conduct interact, while in the case of an undertaking occupying a dominant position the conduct of the undertaking which derives profits from that position is to a great extent determined unilaterally. The existence of a dominant position may derive from several factors which, taken separately, are not necessarily determinative but among these factors a highly important one is the existence of very large market shares.
>
> [40] A substantial market share as evidence of the existence of a dominant position is not a constant factor and its importance varies from market to market according to the structure of those markets, especially as far as production, supply and demand are concerned. Even though each group of vitamins constitutes a separate market, these different markets, as has emerged from the examination of their structure, nevertheless have a sufficient number of features in common to make it possible for the same criteria to be applied to them as far as concerns the importance of the market shares for the purpose of determining whether there is a dominant position or not.
>
> [41] Furthermore although the importance of the market shares may vary from one market to another the view may legitimately be taken that very large shares are in themselves, and save in exceptional circumstances, evidence of the existence of a dominant position. An undertaking which has a very large market share and holds it for some time, by means of the volume of production and the scale of the supply which it stands for—without those having much smaller market shares being able to meet rapidly the demand from those who would like to break away from the undertaking which has the largest market share—is by virtue of that share in a position of strength which makes it an unavoidable trading partner and which already because of this secures for it, at the very least during relatively long periods, that freedom of action which is the special feature of a dominant position.

NOTE: As can be seen from this judgment, the Court puts great store in market shares as an indication of market strength. The larger the market share, the stronger an undertaking must be in comparison to its competitors in that market, but it is also clear from this judgment and *France Télécom* that competition within the market does not prevent a finding of dominance.

France Télécom v Commission
(Case T-340/03) [2007] ECR II-107, [2007] 4 CMLR 21

France Télécom (formerly Wanadoo Interactive) was fined by the Commission for engaging in predatory pricing in the French high-speed internet access market, and the Court of First Instance considered the significance of market competition to the determination of dominance.

[101] Even the existence of lively competition on a particular market does not rule out the possibility that there is a dominant position on that market, since the predominant feature of such a position is the ability of the undertaking concerned to act without having to take account of this competition in its market strategy and without for that reason suffering detrimental effects from such behaviour (*Hoffmann-La Roche* v *Commission*, paragraph 80 above, paragraph 70; see also, to that effect, Case 27/76 *United Brands* v *Commission* [1978] ECR 207, paragraphs 108 to 129). Thus, the fact that there may be competition on the market is a relevant factor for the purposes of ascertaining whether a dominant position exists, but it is not in itself a decisive factor in that regard.

NOTE: The concept of dominance has been the subject of much debate before and in the course of the Commission's review of Article 82 EC. There are particular concerns that too much weight is attached to a finding of dominance in the course of investigating potential infringements of Article 82 EC. The correct weight to attach to a position of dominance is discussed by the Court of Justice in *Michelin* and Advocate General Fennelly in *Compagnie Maritime Belge*, both noted below.

Nederlandsche Banden-Industrie Michelin NV v Commission
(Case 322/81) [1983] ECR 3461, [1985] 1 CMLR 282

[56] That situation ensures that on the Dutch market a large number of users of heavy-vehicle tyres have a strong preference for Michelin tyres. As the purchase of tyres represents a considerable investment for a transport undertaking and since much time is required in order to ascertain in practice the cost-effectiveness of a type or brand of tyre, Michelin NV therefore enjoys a position which renders it largely immune to competition. As a result, a dealer established in the Netherlands normally cannot afford not to sell Michelin tyres.

[57] It is not possible to uphold the objections made against those arguments by Michelin NV, supported on this point by the French Government, that Michelin NV is thus penalised for the quality of its products and services. A finding that an undertaking has a dominant position is not in itself a recrimination but simply means that, irrespective of the reasons for which it has such a dominant position, the undertaking concerned has a special responsibility not to allow its conduct to impair genuine undistorted competition on the Common Market.

Compagnie Maritime Belge Transports v Commission
(Joined Cases C-395 and 396/96 P) [2000] ECR I-1365, [2000] 4 CMLR 1076

Compagnie Maritime Belge ('CMB') was a member of a shipping conference ('Cewal'), whose members had been fined by the Commission for engaging in market sharing in breach of Article 81 EC, as well as for abuse of a collectively dominant position. The CFI upheld the Commission decision, and CMB appealed the ruling with regards to Article 82 EC to the Court of Justice.

Advocate General Fennelly's Opinion

[137] In all these circumstances, the Court of First Instance committed no error of law in finding that the response of Cewal members to the entrance of G & C was not "reasonable and proportionate". To my mind, Article 86 cannot be interpreted as permitting monopolists or quasi-monopolists to exploit the very significant market power which their superdominance confers so as to preclude the emergence either of a new or additional competitor. Where an undertaking, or group of undertakings whose conduct must be assessed collectively, enjoys a position of such overwhelming dominance verging on monopoly, comparable to that which existed in the present case at the moment when G & C entered the relevant market, it would not be consonant with the particularly onerous special obligation affecting such a dominant undertaking not to impair further the structure of the feeble existing competition for them to react, even to aggressive price competition from a new entrant, with a policy of targeted, selective price cuts designed to eliminate that competitor. Contrary to the assertion of the appellants, the mere fact that such prices are not pitched at a level that it actually (or can be shown to be) below total average (or long-run marginal) costs does not, to my mind, render legitimate the application of such a pricing policy.

NOTE: Discussion of the special responsibility upon dominant undertakings and the 'particularly onerous special obligation' upon super-dominant undertakings suggests a sliding scale of responsibility. The point at which this responsibility attaches is highlighted by the discussion of market shares below. Also note that the concept of collective dominance is discussed in Chapter 12.

AKZO Chemie BV v Commission
(Case C-62/86) [1991] ECR I-3359, [1993] 5 CMLR 215

AKZO was a large Dutch chemicals group active on the market for flour additives. It was accused of abusing its position on the market to exclude a competitor, ECS.

[59] It should be further observed that according to its own internal documents AKZO had a stable market share of about 50 per cent from 1979 to 1982 (Annexes 2 and 4 to the statement of objections and Table A annexed to that statement). Furthermore, AKZO has not adduced any evidence to show that its share decreased during subsequent years.

[60] With regard to market shares the Court has held that very large shares are in themselves, and save in exceptional circumstances, evidence of the existence of a dominant position: Case 85/76, *Hoffmann-La Roche* v *EC Commission* ([1979] ECR 461, [1979] 3 CMLR 211, at para. [41]). That is the situation where there is a market share of 50 per cent such as that found to exist in this case.

NOTE: The *AKZO* judgment sets out an important 'rule of thumb' which is still used in many instances. A market share of 50 per cent gives rise to a presumption of dominance. Such a presumption could, of course, be rebutted if the undertaking could present evidence indicating that its apparent strength shown by its market share does not in reality give rise to dominance and true independence. Market share is usually established by calculating the undertaking's share of total sales in the relevant market. See also Articles 9 and 10 of Commission Regulation 2790/1999/EC, OJ, 1999, L336/21. This rather formalistic approach to determining dominance has formed one of the key areas of review by the Commission. There are a number of reasons why apparent market strength may not lead to dominance, several of which are discussed later in this chapter. See discussion of barriers to entry and objective justification.

United Brands v *Commission*
(Case 27/76) [1978] ECR 207, [1978] 1 CMLR 429

During the Court's discussion of United Brands' dominance on the banana market it considered market shares to be important, but other factors were also considered.

[105] In the second place the Commission states that it estimates UBC's market share at 45 per cent.

[106] However UBC points out that this share dropped to 41 per cent in 1975.

[107] A trader can only be in a dominant position on the market for a product if he has succeeded in winning a large part of this market.

[108] Without going into a discussion about percentages, which when fixed are bound to be to some extent approximations, it can be considered to be an established fact that UBC's share of the relevant market is always more than 40 per cent and nearly 45 per cent.

[109] This percentage does not however permit the conclusion that UBC automatically controls the market.

[110] It must be determined having regard to the strength and number of the competitors.

[111] It is necessary first of all to establish that on the whole of the relevant market the said percentage represents *grosso modo* a share several times greater than that of its competitor Castle and Cooke which is the best placed of all the competitors, the others coming far behind.

[112] This fact together with the others to which attention has already been drawn may be regarded as a factor which affords evidence of UBC's preponderant strength.

[113] However an undertaking does not have to have eliminated all opportunity for competition in order to be in a dominant position.

[114] In this case there was in fact a very lively competitive struggle on several occasions in 1973 as Castle and Cooke had mounted a large-scale advertising and promotion campaign with price rebates on the Danish and German markets.

[115] At the same time Alba cut prices and offered promotional material.

[116] Recently the competition of the Villeman et Tas firm on the Netherlands market has been so lively that prices have dropped below those on the German market which are traditionally the lowest.

[117] It must however be recorded that in spite of their exertions these firms have not succeeded in increasing their market share on the national markets where they launched their attacks.

[118] It must be noted that these periods of competition limited in time and space did not cover the whole of the relevant market.

[119] Even if the local attacks of some competitors can be described as 'fierce' it can only be placed on record that UBC held out against them successfully either by adapting its prices for the time being (in the Netherlands in answer to the challenge from Villeman et Tas) or by bringing indirect pressure to bear on the intermediaries.

[120] Furthermore if UBC's position on each of the national markets concerned is considered it emerges that, except in Ireland, it sells direct and also, as far as concerns Germany, indirectly through Scipio, almost twice as many bananas as the best placed competitor and that there is no appreciable fall in its sales figures even when new competitors appear on these markets.

[121] UBC's economic strength has thus enabled it to adopt a flexible overall strategy directed against new competitors establishing themselves on the whole of the relevant market.

NOTE: Although United Brands' market share fell below the 50 per cent threshold discussed in *AKZO*, the Court had no problem establishing that a market share between 40 and 45 per cent could indicate dominance. By examining the market shares of all undertakings operating on the banana market it became clear that United Brands had a significant advantage compared to its nearest rival, which had a market share of 16 per cent, and its other competitors were in a much weaker position. Even with a market share of only 40 per cent, that meant that United Brands could exert considerable strength over the market. The judgment in *United Brands* has led to the adoption of another rule of thumb, that undertakings with market shares over 40 per cent should be very careful as to their position as they may well be considered dominant. But such a finding could be easily challenged if another competitive undertaking had a market share approaching 30 per cent to counterbalance the strength of the suspect undertaking.

Several other rules of thumb appear to be developing. If an undertaking has a very strong position with a market share reaching very high levels, perhaps as high as 80 per cent, it may be approaching a position of 'super-dominance', as discussed above. The Court has suggested that undertakings with very high market shares may be treated differently from those that are in a less strong position. If an undertaking has a very low market share, below 20 per cent, it is highly likely that they will not be considered dominant, even if the nearest competitor is considerably weaker. Furthermore, as can be seen from the following guidance, it is 'not likely' that an undertaking will be dominant with a market share below 40 per cent.

Commission Communication: Guidance on the Commission's enforcement priorities in applying Article 82 EC Treaty to abusive exclusionary conduct by dominant undertakings
OJ, 2009, C45/7, paras 9–15 [footnotes omitted]

A. Market power

9. The assessment of whether an undertaking is in a dominant position and of the degree of market power it holds is a first step in the application of Article 82. According to the case-law, holding a dominant position confers a special responsibility on the undertaking concerned, the scope of which must be considered in the light of the specific circumstances of each case.

10. Dominance has been defined under Community law as a position of economic strength enjoyed by an undertaking, which enables it to prevent effective competition being maintained on a relevant market, by affording it the power to behave to an appreciable extent independently of its competitors, its customers and ultimately of consumers. This notion of independence is related to the degree of competitive constraint exerted on the undertaking in question. Dominance entails that these competitive constraints are not sufficiently effective and hence that the undertaking in question enjoys substantial market power over a period of time. This means that the undertaking's decisions are largely insensitive to the actions and reactions of competitors, customers and, ultimately, consumers. The Commission may consider that effective competitive constraints are absent even if some actual or potential competition remains. In general, a dominant position derives from a combination of several factors which, taken separately, are not necessarily determinative.

11. The Commission considers that an undertaking which is capable of profitably increasing prices above the competitive level for a significant period of time does not face sufficiently effective competitive constraints and can thus generally be regarded as dominant. In this Communication, the expression 'increase prices' includes the power to maintain prices above the competitive level and is used as shorthand for the various ways in which the parameters of competition—such as prices, output, innovation, the variety or quality of goods or services—can be influenced to the advantage of the dominant undertaking and to the detriment of consumers.

12. The assessment of dominance will take into account the competitive structure of the market, and in particular the following factors:
— constraints imposed by the existing supplies from, and the position on the market of, actual competitors (the market position of the dominant undertaking and its competitors),
— constraints imposed by the credible threat of future expansion by actual competitors or entry by potential competitors (expansion and entry),
— constraints imposed by the bargaining strength of the undertaking's customers (countervailing buyer power).

(a) Market position of the dominant undertaking and its competitors

13. Market shares provide a useful first indication for the Commission of the market structure and of the relative importance of the various undertakings active on the market. However, the Commission will interpret market shares in the light of the relevant market conditions, and in particular of the dynamics of the market and of the extent to which products are differentiated.

The trend or development of market shares over time may also be taken into account in volatile or bidding markets.

14. The Commission considers that low market shares are generally a good proxy for the absence of substantial market power. The Commission's experience suggests that dominance is not likely if the undertaking's market share is below 40% in the relevant market. However, there may be specific cases below that threshold where competitors are not in a position to constrain effectively the conduct of a dominant undertaking, for example where they face serious capacity limitations. Such cases may also deserve attention on the part of the Commission.

15. Experience suggests that the higher the market share and the longer the period of time over which it is held, the more likely it is that it constitutes an important preliminary indication of the existence of a dominant position and, in certain circumstances, of possible serious effects of abusive conduct, justifying an intervention by the Commission under Article 82. However, as a general rule, the Commission will not come to a final conclusion as to whether or not a case should be pursued without examining all the factors which may be sufficient to constrain the behaviour of the undertaking.

NOTE: The Commission Communication is an attempt to bring the enforcement of Article 82 EC into line with other aspects of EC competition law that adopt more of an economic and effects-based approach, although its limitations are clear from the statement in para. 3 that 'This document is not intended to constitute a statement of the law and is without prejudice to the interpretation of Article 82 by the European Court of Justice or the Court of First Instance.' The Communication also reflects the Commission's willingness to address some of the criticism of its 2005 Discussion Paper, which launched the public consultation relating to Article 82 EC. One clear example is the statement in para. 31 of the Discussion Paper that 'undertakings with market shares of no more than 25% are not likely to enjoy a (single) dominant position on the market concerned'. This sentence attracted criticism for needlessly creating a degree of uncertainty for undertakings with a market share above 25% but below 40%. The reference to 25% has been removed from the subsequent Commission Communication. Some commentators viewed the Article 82 EC review as an opportunity to explore the consequences of a more radical change to the way EC competition law addresses anti-competitive unilateral conduct.

Majumdar, A., 'Whither Dominance?'
[2006] ECLR 161, pp. 163–4 [footnotes omitted]

The relationship between market power and dominance

Broadly speaking, economists link the legal concept of "dominance" with the economic concept of substantial market power. Competition economists have a relatively well-developed concept of market power. A firm with market power does not face sufficient competitive pressure from any of the following sources: existing competitors, potential competitors and buyers in the relevant market. As a result, it can profitably sustain prices above (or hold quality below) competitive levels in the long run. This definition seems entirely consistent with the spirit of dominance—indeed in the DG Comp Discussion Paper dominance is equated with "substantial market power".

However, economists would criticise some of the case law on dominance. First, contrary to established precedent, dominance should not necessarily be presumed from a market share persistently in excess of 50 per cent. This is because focussing on market shares alone downplays the importance of product differentiation, the scope for new entry and buyer power.

Secondly, some would also argue that the "special responsibility" of a dominant firm is an unhelpful and unclear concept that at worst chills competition (because the dominant firm must at times refrain from pro-competitive strategies that would harm its rivals) or at best is a trite reminder to dominant firms that they should not break the law. According to this view, an advantage of losing the dominance test would be dropping the "special responsibility" tag that shackles certain beneficial behaviour.

In short, the argument that dominance should be retained so as to maintain legal certainty and to benefit from existing case law is relatively weak (at least from an economics perspective).

We should, however, retain an economic assessment of market power that is free from case law that surrounds the dominance test. For example, competition authorities could replace the dominance test with a commitment to conduct an economic assessment of market power as an integral part of an effects-based analysis. Since the concept of market power is well developed and relatively uncontroversial, there should not be great difficulty establishing robust guidance. Market share safe harbours can be retained (although presumptions of dominance based on market shares would not be desirable).

Discarding dominance leads to excess intervention

A better argument for retaining the dominance test *and an essential argument for retaining an assessment of market power* is that, without it, the doors are potentially open for excess intervention.

The success of an effects-based approach depends crucially on the strength of evidence that is required to establish harm to competition and consumers. If, for example, abusive behaviour need only to be "capable" of harming competition then at the very least there should be a market power hurdle to establish that anti-competitive effects are feasible.

Without the dominance hurdle—and given that direct tests of the effect of alleged abusive behaviour are usually not robust when employed without a prior consideration of market power—nearly *all* firms could face genuine uncertainty that would chill price competition. For example, discounts are *capable* of having an anticompetitive effect. Almost all firms offer discounts and, when they do, their rivals tend to suffer. Suppose an inefficient rival left the market as a result of a discount policy adopted by a firm that had no market power. In the short term at least, some customers of the inefficient firm would suffer. But this "consumer harm" is not a good case for intervention. If it were, firms without market power could reasonably fear that by delivering pro-competitive discounts, the authorities could erroneously infer that they have market power!

Even if abusive behaviour must be "likely" or even "very likely" to harm competition, we noted above that in establishing that likelihood an assessment of market power will usually be important. In particular, economists view dominance to be *substantial* market power. While in theory this leaves room for firms with a lower degree of market power to harm competition and consumers, in practice, it is sensible to focus only on those firms with substantial market power since the harm they may cause is correspondingly greater (some theories of harm do not work at all unless firms are near monopolists) and so the risk of chilling price competition by mistaken interventions is correspondingly lower.

The same principle should carry through to an effects-based approach. To infer dominance from direct evidence of competitive effects, should require demonstrating (to a high standard) *substantial* adverse harm to consumers. We should not infer dominance from relatively small adverse effects on consumers given the margin for error likely to be involved.

NOTE: The Commission Communication clearly supports the retention of the dominance test in the application of Article 82 EC, but attempts to assert an approach to enforcement that is more clearly tied to economic theory and analysis. A similar balancing act, of retaining pre-existing case law whilst endorsing a more accurate means of analysis, was undertaken when revising the ECMR (see Chapter 12). The task is more difficult with regards to Article 82 EC as the Commission is unable to layout a revised approach in Community legislation. In spite of the review of Article 82 EC it has always been clear that a study of market shares is insufficient for a determination of dominance, and that an assessment of barriers to entry and possibly also countervailing buyer power is required.

■ QUESTIONS

Discuss the extent to which the Commission Communication will lead to a change in assessing dominance under Article 82 EC.

Why might the weight placed on market shares in Community case law be regarded as controversial?

G: Barriers to entry

Market strength, as usually denoted by market share, does not in itself establish dominance. For an undertaking to have true market power, it must be in a position to protect that strength over time. If an undertaking has a high market share, it merely gives a snapshot of its current position and does not indicate its ability to maintain that position. Even if an undertaking has retained a high market share for a lengthy period, it does not mean that it is not effectively constrained by competition. One of the key aspects of establishing dominance is not the pressure from existing competitors, as that will be indicated by market share over time, but potential competition from undertakings that are not currently active on the market. If potential competitors could enter a market quickly, their potential competition would constrain the activities of the current market leader. Therefore, any barrier which makes entry to a market difficult is very important in establishing if an undertaking has true dominance.

The precise meaning of the term 'barriers to entry' has proved controversial. We will first examine the economic debate that began in the United States in the 1970s.

Bork, R.H., *The Antitrust Paradox*
New York, Free Press, 1993, pp. 310 and 328

We may begin by asking what a 'barrier to entry' is. There appears to be no precise definition, and in current usage a 'barrier' often seems to be anything that makes the entry of new firms into an industry more difficult. It is at once apparent that an ambiguity lurks in the concept, and it is this ambiguity that causes the trouble. When existing firms are efficient and possess valuable plants, equipment, knowledge, skill, and reputation, potential entrants will find it correspondingly more difficult to enter the industry, since they must acquire those things. It is harder to enter the steel industry than the business of retailing shoes or pizzas, and it is harder to enter either of these fields than to become a suburban handyman. But these difficulties are natural; they inhere in the nature of the tasks to be performed. There can be no objection to barriers of this sort. Their existence means only that when market power is achieved by means other than efficiency, entry will not dissipate the objectionable power instantaneously, and law may therefore have a role to play. If entry were instantaneous, market forces would break up cartels before a typist in the Antitrust Division could rap out a form complaint. Antitrust is valuable because in some cases it can achieve results more rapidly than can market forces. We need not suffer losses while waiting for the market to erode cartels and monopolistic mergers . . .

The concept of barriers to entry is badly misunderstood. We have seen that the confusion of natural barriers with artificial barriers has led to a number of mistaken decisions. It leads economists to suppose that ordinary market forces do not control the structure of industries, and hence to recommend governmental intervention or investigation. A final example—dozens could be chosen—is Mark Schupack's application of the ideas of Bain:

'Consider what a potential entrant to the automobile industry would have to face in order to successfully overcome the product differentiation barrier. It would have to undertake heavy advertising expenditures to woo consumers away from other firms where they have already established some brand loyalty. It would have to spend money to differentiate its product successfully from closely related automobiles. It would have to undertake annual model changes. And perhaps most important, it would have to build a large nationwide network of dealers who are pretty much committed to the new manufacturer's products.'

This catalogue is intended to suggest that competition would not necessarily shape the structure of the automobile industry, that something artificial, something other than the efficiency of existing firms, keeps potential entrants out. Schupack might just as well have said: the new entrant would have to make an automobile with appealing features, change models to keep up with competition, spend money to inform consumers of what it had to sell, and find people who thought the car would sell well enough to make it profitable to retail and service the product. He might, with equal pertinence, have added that the entrant would also have to build a plant, hire engineers, sales experts, designers, accountants, lawyers, and managers, buy steel and fabric and paint, and so on. He actually says nothing more than that a new entrant would have to do the things other companies have found essential to please consumers. In that respect, there is no difference whatever between advertising or finding dealers and building a plant.

This is true of any and all industries. Where the product and its service are complex and expensive, it is natural that the entrant will have to do many complex and expensive things, and do them well, in order to succeed. These are natural barriers or costs of entry. To identify them is merely to make a descriptive statement, one that does not imply the propriety of invoking law to alter the size or behavior of firms already in the market.

The argument of this chapter in no way suggests that there are no artificial barriers to entry. It does suggest that the only artificial barriers of interest to antitrust are those capable of creation by private parties, and that such barriers are always instances of deliberate predation. The next two chapters deal with types of predation that may be employed either to block entry or to injure existing rivals. Unlike the faulty theory of entry barriers now in vogue, however, the possibility of predation does not require or justify such steps as prohibiting mergers or outlawing the vertical division of dealer territories. Prophylactic rules for predation are not justified, as we have seen, and the law should concern itself with entry blocking only in those instances where a deliberate attempt to block entry by means other than efficiency is proved.

NOTE: As we can see from Bork's description of the difficulties facing entrants to markets he believes that these are natural requirements of efficiency that will have to be achieved if an undertaking wants to enter a market with any success. The school of thought to which Bork is linked would define barriers to entry very narrowly, and would only accept that a true barrier exists where a cost is borne by a new entrant that was not borne by the incumbent market players.

Posner, R., *Antitrust Law*
Chicago, CUP, 1976, p. 59

In discussing the relevance of new entry to the propensity to collude I have carefully avoided using that confusing term 'barrier to entry'. A barrier to entry is commonly used in a quite literal sense to mean anything which a new entrant must overcome in order to gain a foothold in the market, such as the capital costs of entering the market on an efficient scale. This is a meaningless usage, since it is obvious that a new entrant must incur costs to enter the market, just as his predecessors, the firms now occupying the market, did previously. A more precise definition has been offered by Stigler: a barrier to entry is a condition that imposes higher long-run costs of production on a new entrant than are borne by the firms already in the market. A barrier to entry in Stigler's sense has important policy implications: it implies the existence of a range within which the firms in the market can increase the market price above the competitive level without having to worry at all about losing sales to a new entrant. But, as we shall see in the next chapter, barriers to entry in this sense appear to be rare. Of greater practical importance are factors that do not create a barrier to entry but increase the length of time required for new entry to take place, by making the production process a complex one which requires substantial time to organize efficiently. Such factors include vertical integration and economies of scale, which increase the optimum size of the new entrant.

NOTE: Posner's view is similar to Bork's, but makes the distinction between a true barrier to entry, in his view, and other factors that make entry more difficult and lengthy. The views of both Bork and Posner can be described as being nearer the narrow definition of barriers to entry. By taking such a view they would favour a more limited role for the competition authorities. As entry is still possible any anti-competitive activity by a strong undertaking on a market would be constrained by the potential of entry, and therefore there would be no need for intervention by the competition authorities. Only where entry is restricted by a true barrier to entry should the authorities need to intervene. Given the different nature of US antitrust law, and the different political emphasis of these US scholars from that of the European Commission and the Court, it is not surprising that EC law has taken a very different approach.

Centre Belge d'Etudes de Marche-Telemarketing SA v Compagnie Luxembourgeoise de Telediffusion SA
(Case 311/84) [1985] ECR 3261, [1986] 2 CMLR 558

Centre Belge brought an action before the Luxembourg courts, seeking an injunction restraining CLT from refusing to sell it television time on its TV station for telephone marketing operations, using a telephone number other than that operated by CLT. Centre Belge advertised using a technique known as telemarketing whereby products were advertised with a telephone number where they could see further information. CLT had an effective statutory monopoly on the TV advertising for the market in question.

[11] In substance the first question asks whether Article 86 of the Treaty applies to an undertaking holding a dominant position on a particular market where that position is due not to the activities of the undertaking itself but to the fact that by reason of provisions laid down by law there can be no competition or only very limited competition on the market.

[12] The Centre Belge proposes that the Court should answer that question in the affirmative. It maintains that, according to the case law of the Court, an undertaking holding a monopoly in a particular service has a dominant position on the market in that service within the meaning of Article 86 and that that Article applies to the conduct of broadcasting organisations. Compagnie Luxembourgeoise cannot rely on the proviso in Article 90(2), since it is not an undertaking 'entrusted with the operation of services of general economic interest' for the purposes thereof.

[13] Compagnie Luxembourgeoise states that the Court held, in its judgment in Case 155/73 (*Sacchi*) ([1974] ECR 409, [1974] 2 CMLR 177) that a State may, for reasons of public interest of a non-economic nature, remove radio and television broadcasting from competition by conferring a monopoly on an undertaking. Extending the scope of the question put to the Court, Compagnie Luxembourgeoise proposes, therefore, that the Court should reply that it is not as such incompatible with Article 86 of the Treaty for an undertaking to which a State has granted exclusive rights within the meaning of Article 90 to enjoy a monopoly.

[14] Information Publicite does not agree with the abstract definition of a dominant position which in its opinion is suggested by the question. It maintains that it is not possible to disregard the product or service at issue or the extent of the relevant market. Further, to fall within the provisions of Article 86 the dominant position must affect trade between Member States and exist within a substantial part of the Common Market. Information Publicite therefore proposes that the Court should reply that the existence of a statutory monopoly does not in itself entail a dominant position within the meaning of Article 86.

[15] In the Commission's view, the notion of a dominant position, as defined by the Court, refers to a factual situation independent of the reasons giving rise to that situation. The question must therefore be answered in the affirmative.

[16] With regard to the first question, it must first of all be remembered that, according to the established case law of the Court most recently confirmed by the judgment in Case 322/81

(*Michelin* v *EC Commission* [1983] ECR 3461, [1985] 1 CMLR 282), an undertaking occupies a dominant position for the purposes of Article 86 where it enjoys a position of economic strength which enables it to hinder the maintenance of effective competition on the relevant market by allowing it to behave to an appreciable extent independently of its competitors and customers and ultimately of consumers. The fact that the absence of competition or its restriction on the relevant market is brought about or encouraged by provisions laid down by law in no way precludes the application of Article 86, as the Court has held, *inter alia*, in Case 26/75 (*General Motors* v *EC Commission* [1975] ECR 1367, [1976] 1 CMLR 95), Case 13/77 (*INNO* v *ATAB* [1977] ECR 2115, [1978] 1 CMLR 283) and most recently in its judgment of 20 March 1985 in Case 41/83 (*Italy* v *EC Commission* [1985] 2 CMLR 368).

[17] Although it is true, as Compagnie Luxembourgeoise has pointed out, that it is not incompatible with Article 86 for an undertaking to which a Member State has granted exclusive rights within the meaning of Article 90 of the Treaty to enjoy a monopoly, it is none the less apparent from the same Article that such undertakings remain subject to the Treaty rules on competition and in particular those contained in Article 86. In *Sacchi*, the Court also stressed that, if certain Member States treat undertakings entrusted with the operation of television, even as regards their commercial activities and in particular advertising, as undertakings entrusted with the operation of services of general economic interest, the prohibitions of Article 86 apply, as regards their behaviour within the market, by reason of Article 90(2), so long as it is not shown that the said prohibitions are incompatible with the performance of their tasks.

[18] The reply to the first question must therefore be that Article 86 of the EEC Treaty must be interpreted as applying to an undertaking holding a dominant position on a particular market, even where that position is due not to the activities of the undertaking itself but to the fact that by reason of provisions laid down by law there can be no competition or only very limited competition on that market.

NOTE: In this instance it was clear that there was no effective competition for CLT and such competition was unlikely to develop while they retained a statutory monopoly. This would be considered as a barrier to entry by Bork, Posner, and, obviously, by the Court. CLT's position was protected by law and therefore their activities were not constrained by potential competitors. This is one of the few areas where the US scholars and the European Court are of a similar view.

Hilti AG v *Commission*
(Case T-30/89) [1991] ECR II-1439, [1992] 4 CMLR 16

[89] The Commission has proved that Hilti holds a market share of around 70 per cent to 80 per cent in the relevant market for nails. That figure was supplied to the Commission by Hilti following a request by the Commission for information pursuant to Article 11 of Regulation 17. As the Commission has rightly emphasised, Hilti was therefore obliged to supply information which, to the best of its knowledge, was as accurate as possible. Hilti's subsequent assertion that the figures were unsound is not corroborated by any evidence or by any examples showing them to be unreliable. Moreover, Hilti has supplied no other figures to substantiate its assertion. This argument of the applicant must therefore be rejected.

[90] The Court of Justice has held (Case 27/76 *United Brands* v *EC Commission* [1978] ECR 207, [1978] 1 CMLR 429 and Case 85/76 *Hoffmann-La Roche* v *EC Commission* [1979] ECR 461, [1979] 3 CMLR 211) that the dominant position referred to in Article 86 EEC relates to a position of economic strength enjoyed by an undertaking which enables it to prevent effective competition being maintained on the relevant market by giving it the power to behave to an appreciable extent independently of its competitors, customers and ultimately of its consumers; the existence of a dominant position may derive from a combination of several factors which, taken separately, are not necessarily determinative but among which a highly important one is the existence of very large market shares.

[91] With particular reference to market shares, the Court of Justice has held (*Hoffmann-La Roche*, cited above, paragraph [41]) that very large shares are in themselves, and save in exceptional circumstances, evidence of a dominant position.

[92] In this case it is established that Hilti holds a share of between 70 per cent and 80 per cent in the relevant market. Such a share is, in itself, a clear indication of the existence of a dominant position in the relevant market (see the judgment of the Court of Justice in Case 62/86 *AKZO Chemie BV v EC Commission* [1991] ECR I-3359 para. [60]).

[93] Furthermore, as regards the other factors noted by the Commission as helping to maintain and reinforce Hilti's position in the market, it must be pointed out that the very fact that Hilti holds a patent and, in the United Kingdom, invokes copyright protection in relation to the cartridge strips designed for use in its own tools strengthens its position in the markets for Hilti-compatible consumables. Hilti's strong position in those markets was enhanced by the patents which it held at the time on certain elements of its DX 450 nail gun. It should be added that, as the Commission rightly contended, it is highly improbable in practice that a non-dominant supplier will act as Hilti did, since effective competition will normally ensure that the adverse consequences of such behaviour outweigh any benefits.

[94] On the basis of all those considerations, the Court holds that the Commission was entitled to take the view that Hilti held a dominant position in the market in nails for the nail guns which it manufactures.

NOTE: In this judgment, high market shares held by Hilti were clearly relevant, but the CFI also relied on other factors that helped 'maintain and reinforce' their position (para. 93). Those factors could also be described as barriers to entry. As they held patent rights over cartridge strips it made it very difficult for any other undertaking to produce such strips without breaching Hilti's patent. Their position in the market for nail guns was also protected to some extent by patent rights, but not as strongly as their position in the consumables market. The combination of the high market shares and the protective IP rights ensured Hilti's position.

Hoffmann-La Roche v *Commission*
(Case 85/76) [1979] ECR 461, [1979] 3 CMLR 211

Having defined the relevant vitamins markets and examined La Roche's market shares, the Court went on to look at other factors that indicated dominance.

[42] The contested decision has mentioned besides the market shares a number of other factors which together with Roche's market shares would secure for it in certain circumstances a dominant position. These factors which the decision classifies as additional criteria are as follows:
(a) Roche's market shares are not only large but there is also a big disparity between its shares and those of its next largest competitors (Recitals 5 and 21 to the decision);
(b) Roche produces a far wider range of vitamins than its competitors (Recital 21 to the decision);
(c) Roche is the world's largest vitamin manufacturer whose turnover exceeds that of all the other producers and is at the head of a multinational group which in terms of sales is the world's leading pharmaceuticals producer (Recitals 5, 6 and 21 to the decision);
(d) Although Roche's patents for the manufacture of vitamins have expired Roche, since it has played a leading role in this field, still enjoys technological advantages over its competitors of which the highly developed customer information and assistance service which it has is evidence (Recitals 7 and 8 to the decision);
(e) Roche has a very extensive and highly specialised sales network (Recital 21 to the decision);
(f) There is no potential competition (Recital 21 to the decision).
Furthermore during the proceedings before the Court the Commission adduced as a factor establishing Roche's dominant position the latter's ability, notwithstanding lively competition, to maintain its market shares substantially intact.

[43] Before considering whether the factors taken into account by the Commission can in fact be confirmed in Roche's case it is necessary to ascertain, since the applicant challenges their relevance, whether these factors, in the light of the special features of the relevant markets and of the market shares, are of such a kind as to disclose the existence of a dominant position.

[44] In this connexion it is necessary to reject the criterion based on retention of market shares, since this may just as well result from effective competitive behaviour as from a position which ensures that Roche can behave independently of competitors, and the Commission, while admitting that there is competition, has not mentioned the factors which may account for the stability of market shares where it has been found to exist. However, if there is a dominant position then retention of the market shares may be a factor disclosing that this position is being maintained, and, on the other hand, the methods adopted to maintain a dominant position may be an abuse within the meaning of Article 86 of the Treaty.

[45] The fact that Roche produces a far wider range of vitamins than its competitors must similarly be rejected as being immaterial. The Commission regards this as a factor establishing a dominant position and asserts that 'since the requirements of many users extend to several groups of vitamins, Roche is able to employ a sales and pricing strategy which is far less dependent than that of the other manufacturers on the conditions of competition in each market'.

[46] However, the Commission has itself found that each group of vitamins constitutes a specific market and is not, or at least not to any significant extent, interchangeable with any other group or with any other products (Recital 20 to the decision) so that the vitamins belonging to the various groups are as between themselves products just as different as the vitamins compared with other products of the pharmaceutical and food sector. Moreover, it is not disputed that Roche's competitors, in particular those in the chemical industry, market besides the vitamins which they manufacture themselves, other products which purchasers of vitamins also want, so that the fact that Roche is in a position to offer several groups of vitamins does not in itself give it any advantage over its competitors, who can offer, in addition to a less or much less wide range of vitamins, other products which are also required by the purchasers of these vitamins.

[47] Similar considerations lead also to the rejection as a relevant factor of the circumstance that Roche is the world's largest vitamin manufacturer, that its turnover exceeds that of all the other manufacturers and that it is at the head of the largest pharmaceuticals group in the world. In the view of the Commission these three considerations together are a factor showing that there is a dominant position, because 'it follows that the applicant occupies a preponderant position not only within the Common Market but also on the world market; it therefore enjoys very considerable freedom of action, since its position enables it to adapt itself easily to the developments of the different regional markets. An undertaking operating throughout the markets of the world and having a market share which leaves all its competitors far behind it does not have to concern itself unduly about any competitors within the Common Market.' Such reasoning based on the benefits reaped from economies of scale and on the possibility of adopting a strategy which varies according to the different regional markets is not conclusive, seeing that it is accepted that each group of vitamins constitutes a group of separate products which require their own particular plant and form a separate market, in that the volume of the overall production of products which are different as between themselves does not give Roche a competitive advantage over its competitors, especially over those in the chemical industry, who manufacture on a world scale other products as well as vitamins and have in principle the same opportunities to set off one market against the other as are offered by a large overall production of products which differ from each other as much as the various groups of vitamins do.

[48] On the other hand the relationship between the market shares of the undertaking concerned and of its competitors, especially those of the next largest, the technological lead of an undertaking over its competitors, the existence of a highly developed sales network and the absence of potential competition are relevant factors, the first because it enables the competitive strength of the undertaking in question to be assessed, the second and third because they represent in themselves technical and commercial advantages and the fourth because it is the consequence of the existence of obstacles preventing new competitors from having access to the market. As far as the existence or non-existence of potential competition is concerned it must, however, be observed

that, although it is true—and this applies to all the groups of vitamins in question—that because of the amount of capital investment required the capacity of the factories is determined according to the anticipated growth over a long period so that access to the market by new producers is not easy, account must also be taken of the fact that the existence of considerable unused manufacturing capacity creates potential competition between established manufacturers. Nevertheless Roche is in this respect in a privileged position because, as it admits itself, its own manufacturing capacity was, during the period covered by the contested decision, in itself sufficient to meet world demand without this surplus manufacturing capacity placing it in a difficult economic or financial situation.

[49] It is in the light of the preceding considerations that Roche's shares of each of the relevant markets, complemented by those factors which in conjunction with the market shares make it possible to show that there may be a dominant position, must be evaluated. Finally, it will also be necessary to consider whether Roche's submissions relating to the implication of its conduct on the market, mainly as far as concerns prices, are of such a kind as to alter the findings to which the examination of the market shares and the other factors taken into account might lead.

NOTE: A number of factors put forward by the Commission were rejected by the Court: retention of market share, the fact that La Roche produced a wide range of vitamins, and La Roche was the world's largest vitamin producer. These were largely discounted as their use would have been contrary to the reasoning used by the Commission to define the relevant markets. The Court did accept a number of factors as being important; first, the technical lead La Roche possessed over its rivals; second, the existence of a developed sales network; and, third, the absence of potential competition. The latter of these adds little to the previous two without the Court's further explanation that this is because of the capital investment required to enter the market and the market's existing overcapacity. In effect, the Court had utilized four separate barriers to entry to support its finding of dominance in *Hoffman-La Roche*. All of these barriers would fail to meet Bork and Posner's definition of a true barrier and fit into the category of factors that merely make it more difficult to enter a market. By adopting these barriers in their jurisprudence the Court clearly take a much wider stance than the US scholars. The Court takes the view that any factor that would discourage entry, no matter whether the incumbent faced the same problems, is a barrier that can be used to support a finding of dominance. Sometimes these barriers are known are 'strategic' or 'first-mover' advantages as they are related to advantages possessed by an undertaking that is first to develop experience in the industry. The fact that 'second movers' have to spend heavily to develop that experience to begin to compete with the incumbent is considered a barrier to their entry.

United Brands v Commission
(Case 27/76) [1978] ECR 207, [1978] 1 CMLR 429

Having defined the relevant market and examined United Brands' market share, the Court moved on to consider if there were any other factors that might indicate or reinforce their dominance.

[69] It is advisable to examine in turn UBC's resources for and methods of producing, packaging, transporting, selling and displaying its product.

[70] UBC is an undertaking vertically integrated to a high degree.

[71] This integration is evident at each of the stages from the plantation to the loading on wagons or lorries in the ports of delivery after those stages, as far as ripening and sale prices are concerned, UBC even extends its control to ripener/distributors and wholesalers by setting up a complete network of agents.

[72] At the production stage UBC owns large plantations in Central and South America.

[73] In so far as UBC's own production does not meet its requirements it can obtain supplies without any difficulty from independent planters since it is an established fact that unless circumstances are exceptional there is a production surplus.

[74] Furthermore several independent producers have links with UBC through contracts for the growing of bananas which have caused them to grow the varieties of bananas which UBC advised them to adopt.

[75] The effects of natural disasters which could jeopardise supplies are greatly reduced by the fact that the plantations are spread over a wide geographic area and by the selection of varieties not very susceptible to diseases.

[76] This situation was born out by the way in which UBC was able to react to the consequences of hurricane 'Fifi' in 1974.

[77] At the production stage UBC therefore knows that it can comply with all the requests which it receives.

[78] At the stage of packaging and presentation on its premises UBC has at its disposal factories, manpower, plant and material which enable it to handle the goods independently.

[79] The bananas are carried from the place of production to the port of shipment by its own means of transport including railways.

[80] At the carriage by sea stage it has been acknowledged that UBC is the only undertaking of its kind which is capable of carrying two thirds of its exports by means of its own banana fleet.

[81] Thus UBC knows that it is able to transport regularly, without running the risk of its own ships not being used and whatever the market situation may be, two thirds of its average volume of sales and is alone able to ensure that three regular consignments reach Europe each week, and all this guarantees it commercial stability and well being.

[82] In the field of technical knowledge and as a result of continual research UBC keeps on improving the productivity and yield of its plantations by improving the draining system, making good soil deficiencies and combating effectively plant disease.

[83] It has perfected new ripening methods in which its technicians instruct the distributor/ripeners of the 'Chiquita' banana.

[84] That is another factor to be borne in mind when considering UBC's position since competing firms cannot develop research at a comparable level and are in this respect at a disadvantage compared with the applicant.

[85] It is acknowledged that at the stage where the goods are given the final finish and undergo quality control UBC not only controls the distributor/ripeners which are direct customers but also those who work for the account of its important customers such as the Scipio group.

[86] Even if the object of the clause prohibiting the sale of green bananas was only strict quality control, it in fact gives UBC absolute control of all trade in its goods so long as they are marketable wholesale, that is to say before the ripening process begins which makes an immediate sale unavoidable.

...

[122] The particular barriers to competitors entering the market are the exceptionally large capital investments required for the creation and running of banana plantations, the need to increase sources of supply in order to avoid the effects of fruit diseases and bad weather (hurricanes, floods), the introduction of an essential system of logistics which the distribution of a very perishable product makes necessary, economies of scale from which newcomers to the market cannot derive any immediate benefit and the actual cost of entry made up *inter alia* of all the general expenses incurred in penetrating the market such as the setting up of an adequate commercial network, the mounting of very large-scale advertising campaigns, all those financial risks, the costs of which are irrecoverable if the attempt fails.

[123] Thus, although, as UBC has pointed out, it is true that competitors are able to use the same methods of production and distribution as the applicant, they come up against almost insuperable practical and financial obstacles.

[124] That is another factor peculiar to a dominant position.

NOTE: The Court sets out a number of barriers to entry that it considers important to United Brands' ability to retain its dominant position. The first of those was United Brands' vertical integration. It has control of every stage of production from research and development to final ripening and distribution to retailers. As the Court notes at para. 122, it would be very difficult and expensive for a market entrant to replicate all these facilities to enter the market with the same scope as United Brands. The second barrier to entry discussed by the Court was United Brands' expertise developed through its research and development facilities (paras 82–4). Again it would be very difficult for a competitor to replicate the R & D facilities and know-how. The third barrier to entry invoked by the Court is that of 'product differentiation' through advertising (paras 87–96, not reproduced above). By investing heavily in advertising their 'Chiquita' brand, United Brands had created a demand for that product in particular that would make customers less likely to switch their preference to bananas from competing suppliers. Again, it would be very costly for a potential competitor to invest heavily in brand promotion to compete with the established 'Chiquita' brand.

Some commentators would argue that such brand promotion is not a significant barrier to entry:

Paterson, L., 'The power of the puppy—does advertising deter entry'
[1997] ECLR 337, pp. 341–2 [footnotes omitted]

Brand loyalty and entry

Suppose that economic analysis does point to the existence of strong brand loyalty. Why does this matter? The Commission's response to date has been that brand loyalty makes entry harder, as entrants have to sink costs into advertising and promotion if they are to persuade brand loyal customers to try something new.

In some circumstances, however, brand loyalty may actually facilitate entry, albeit of a market-segmenting or 'niche' variety. On the other hand, if an entrant is to compete head-to-head with incumbents for brand loyal customers, then the Commission is probably right to assert that this will require some sinking of advertising and promotional costs. What is less clear is whether these costs will deter entry.

Brand loyalty and market segmentation

In some markets, brand loyalty can facilitate entry of the 'market segmenting' variety. This is probably best illustrated by way of a simple example.

Suppose that, in a given market, the incumbent's brand, Brand X, enjoys some brand loyalty. In particular, suppose that 70 per cent of Brand X's customers are brand loyal and would never consider switching to another brand. An entrant comes into the market, with Brand Y. Brand Y is priced below Brand X. Brand Y is effectively targeting the 30 per cent of Brand X's customers who are not brand loyal. In this case, Brand X's best response may not be to enter into direct competition with Brand Y. Instead, the incumbent could let Brand Y take the 30 per cent of its customers that are non-brand loyal, and charge a higher price to its brand loyal customers.

However, brand loyalty will only facilitate this 'market segmenting' type of entry in certain circumstances.

First, there need to be at least some people who are prepared to buy from an entrant (i.e. are not completely brand loyal to Brand X), otherwise market segmentation of this type can never occur.

Second, there needs to be a sufficient number of customers who will not switch away from the incumbent's brand in response to price changes. If many of Brand X's customers are not brand loyal, and switch to lower priced Brand Y, then Brand X may do better by entering into direct price competition with Brand Y for the non brand loyal customers.

Third, there needs to be no substantial cost advantage from being a large market player. Suppose that economies of scale are very important, implying that large companies have much lower unit costs than small companies. If Brand Y only targets a market segment, it may be unable to cover its average unit costs of supply. In this case, if Brand Y is to be successful, it may have to target Brand X's loyal customers, as discussed further below.

So, in certain circumstances, brand loyalty may facilitate entry as it can imply that post-entry price competition will be relatively soft. However, the type of entry that is facilitated tends to be of the 'market segmenting' variety. This type of entry may lead to an increase in sales and a reduction in the price paid by some customers, but does not constrain the incumbent's power over its brand loyal customers. From an antitrust perspective, this may be a matter of concern.

Brand loyalty and head-to-head competition

Now suppose that, perhaps because of a combination of customer preferences and economies of scale, potential entrants have to compete head-to-head with incumbents for their brand loyal customers. In this case, by the very definition of brand loyalty, an entrant will have to incur significant advertising and promotional costs if he is to persuade brand loyal customers to try a new product. So, in these circumstances, the Commission is right to assert that:

The establishment of a new brand would require heavy investment in advertising and promotion in order to persuade brand loyal consumers to switch away from their usual brand.

But even if entry necessitates the sinking of advertising and promotional costs to persuade brand loyal customers to try something new, it is not clear that entry is impossible, or even improbable. The probability of entry rests crucially upon whether these sunk costs are large or small in the context of the likely scale of entry, as well as the nature of post-entry price competition.

How would one begin to assess whether sunk entry costs were 'large' or 'small'? The first step is to estimate the absolute size of advertising and promotional sunk costs. In doing this it is imperative to distinguish between entry-related advertising and promotional costs (which obviously do not have to be incurred by incumbents) and day-to-day advertising and promotional costs which need to be incurred by incumbents and entrants alike. Only the former cost plays any role in entry decisions. In other words, a competition authority has to measure the additional costs that an entrant will have to incur over and above the normal costs of doing business incurred by the incumbent (including any ongoing expenditures incumbents need to incur to maintain brand loyalty). It is, for example, insufficient to estimate the costs that an entrant will have to incur in its first year of business (which was in fact the figure calculated by the Commission in the *KC/Scott* decision).

After having estimated the size of any sunk advertising and promotional costs an entrant may have to incur (and these are likely to be larger the stronger is the degree of incumbent brand loyalty), the next step is to put these costs into their market context. One way might be to ask, given the likely scale of entry, what would be the mark-up over the incumbent's unit cost that the entrant would need to earn to break even.

AKZO Chemie BV v Commission
(Case C-62/86) [1991] ECR I-3359, [1993] 5 CMLR 215

AKZO was a large Dutch chemicals group active on the market for flour additives. It was accused of abusing its position on the market to exclude a competitor, ECS. After defining the relevant market as the market for organic peroxides the Commission looked at various factors that might support a finding of dominance.

2. The dominant position

[55] The Commission considers that AKZO has a dominant position within the organic peroxides market. It bases its view on AKZO's market share and on the existence of a number of factors which, combined with that market share, is said to give it a marked predominance.

[56] The Commission describes these factors at paragraph 69 of the decision as follows:

    (i) AKZO's market share is not only large in itself but is equivalent to all the remaining producers put together;

    (ii) apart from Interox and Luperox the remaining producers have a limited product range and/or are of local significance only;

    (iii) AKZO's market share (as well as that of the second and third placed producers Interox and Luperox) has remained steady over the period under consideration and AKZO has always successfully repulsed any attacks on its position by smaller producers;

(iv) AKZO was able even during periods of economic downturn to maintain its overall margin by regular price increases and/or increases in sales volume;

(v) AKZO offers a far broader range of products than any rival, has the most highly developed commercial and technical marketing organisation, and possesses the leading knowledge in safety and toxicology;

(vi) AKZO has on its own account been able effectively to eliminate 'troublesome' competitors (besides ECS) from the market or weaken them substantially: the example of SCADO for one shows that AKZO is in a position, if it so wishes, to exclude a less powerful producer;

(vii) once such small but potentially dangerous competitors are neutralised, AKZO has been able to raise the price for the particular product in respect of which their competition was felt.

[61] Moreover, the Commission rightly pointed out that other factors confirmed AKZO's predominance in the market. In addition to the fact that AKZO regards itself as the world leader in the peroxides market, it should be observed that, as AKZO itself admits, it has the most highly developed marketing organisation, both commercially and technically, and wider knowledge than that of its competitors with regard to safety and toxicology (Annexes 2 and 4 to the statement of objections).

[62] The pleas put forward by AKZO in order to deny that it had a dominant position within the organic peroxides market as a whole must therefore be rejected.

NOTE: The judgment in *AKZO* refers to a number of factors that the Commission used to support its decision, but it is arguable that several of these were factors that properly should be considered as matters relating to market strength, for example, comparability of market shares and market share stability over time. Only two of the Commission's factors raised by the Court could be seen as being barriers to entry, even under the broad definition adopted by the Court. The first was that it has specialized know-how and experience that its competitors would find difficult to replicate (para. 59(v)). This is a well-established barrier that the Court has utilized on many occasions. The second barrier is far more controversial and is perhaps an example of the widest use of the concept within EC jurisprudence. The Commission suggests that AKZO's previous behaviour on the market may, in itself, have acted as a barrier to entry (para. 56(vi)–(vii)). This is problematic as such behaviour was also alleged to be the abuse in the instant case. Normally, one considers the dominance and abuse as separate issues but here they become increasingly intertwined. The Court does not specifically address that assertion but its inclusion is indicative that it garners some support. There is an argument that this reasoning is circular in nature and should not be used, but it does give a real indication of the European view of barriers to entry being broadly drawn. Any factor in the market structure or because of the previous behaviour of an undertaking on the market that would discourage potential competitors from entering the market may be considered as a barrier to entry by the Community authorities. The Commission's latest approach to barriers to entry is outlined in the Communication following the Article 82 EC review.

Commission Communication: Guidance on the Commission's enforcement priorities in applying Article 82 EC Treaty to abusive exclusionary conduct by dominant undertakings
OJ, 2009, C45/7, paras 16–18 [footnotes omitted]

(b) Expansion or entry

16. Competition is a dynamic process and an assessment of the competitive constraints on an undertaking cannot be based solely on the existing market situation. The potential impact of expansion by actual competitors or entry by potential competitors, including the threat of such expansion or entry, is also relevant. An undertaking can be deterred from increasing prices if expansion or entry is likely, timely and sufficient. For the Commission to consider expansion or entry

likely it must be sufficiently profitable for the competitor or entrant, taking into account factors such as the barriers to expansion or entry, the likely reactions of the allegedly dominant undertaking and other competitors, and the risks and costs of failure. For expansion or entry to be considered timely, it must be sufficiently swift to deter or defeat the exercise of substantial market power. For expansion or entry to be considered sufficient, it cannot be simply small-scale entry, for example into some market niche, but must be of such a magnitude as to be able to deter any attempt to increase prices by the putatively dominant undertaking in the relevant market.

17. Barriers to expansion or entry can take various forms. They may be legal barriers, such as tariffs or quotas, or they may take the form of advantages specifically enjoyed by the dominant undertaking, such as economies of scale and scope, privileged access to essential inputs or natural resources, important technologies or an established distribution and sales network. They may also include costs and other impediments, for instance resulting from network effects, faced by customers in switching to a new supplier. The dominant undertaking's own conduct may also create barriers to entry, for example where it has made significant investments which entrants or competitors would have to match, or where it has concluded long-term contracts with its customers that have appreciable foreclosing effects. Persistently high market shares may be indicative of the existence of barriers to entry and expansion.

(c) Countervailing buyer power

18. Competitive constraints may be exerted not only by actual or potential competitors but also by customers. Even an undertaking with a high market share may not be able to act to an appreciable extent independently of customers with sufficient bargaining strength. Such countervailing buying power may result from the customers' size or their commercial significance for the dominant undertaking, and their ability to switch quickly to competing suppliers, to promote new entry or to vertically integrate, and to credibly threaten to do so. If countervailing power is of a sufficient magnitude, it may deter or defeat an attempt by the undertaking to profitably increase prices. Buyer power may not, however, be considered a sufficiently effective constraint if it only ensures that a particular or limited segment of customers is shielded from the market power of the dominant undertaking.

NOTE: The Communication appears to endorse the broad approach to barriers to entry that has developed in EC competition law, and also comments on countervailing buyer power as one further factor that should be taken into account when determining whether dominance exists, before assessing whether an undertaking's conduct is abusive.

■ QUESTION

What is the purpose of considering barriers to entry in the application of Article 82 EC?

H: Abuse

Once it has been established that an undertaking has a dominant position, it is necessary to investigate whether their behaviour could be categorized as being abusive. The Treaty itself sets out an indicative list of behaviour that was envisaged as being abusive by the drafters of the Treaty.

Such abuse may, in particular, consist in:

(a) directly or indirectly imposing unfair purchase or selling prices or other unfair trading conditions;

(b) limiting production, markets or technical development to the prejudice of consumers;

(c) applying dissimilar conditions to equivalent transactions with other trading parties, thereby placing them at a competitive disadvantage;

(d) making the conclusion of contracts subject to acceptance by the other parties of supplementary obligations which, by their nature or according to commercial usage, have no connection with the subject of such contracts.

This list is only indicative and the Court has used its teleological style of reasoning to expand the categories of abuse to cover many differing types of behaviour, which harm the competitive process within the EC. For the purposes of categorization it is useful to split the different abuses into two, somewhat overlapping, categories: exploitative and exclusionary abuses. Each of the categories has different characteristics and the reason that competition law finds them harmful is different.

I: Exploitative abuses

Exploitative abuse would describe a situation in which a dominant undertaking uses its position of power to exploit the market and make a supra-competitive profit. This behaviour is suggested as being rational for a monopolist who wishes to maximize profits and its avoidance is therefore considered to be one of the main aims of any competition law system. A dominant undertaking may be able to raise the prices on its goods by creating an artificial scarcity of its product and prices will increase above the level at which they would be priced on a 'competitive' market, thus the prices, and the profits, gained are described as being supra-competitive. There are several different ways a dominant undertaking may try to exploit its position on the market and its customers.

(a) Excessive pricing

The most obvious manner in which a dominant undertaking may attempt to exploit its customers is to charge an excessive price through creating an artificial scarcity of the dominant product. The major problem for competition authorities and lawyers is deciding what is an excessive price.

General Motors v Commission
(Case 26/75) [1975] ECR 1367, [1976] 1 CMLR 95

Vehicles to be used in Belgium have to satisfy certain technical standards set out in a Royal Decree. Each type of vehicle manufactured in or imported into Belgium must be approved. Once a type of vehicle has been approved the manufacturer should issue a certificate of conformity for all vehicles of that type. Vehicles registered abroad and re-imported into Belgium had to gain a certificate of conformity from the manufacturer's agent. For all GM cars the manufacturer's agent was the appellant. They charged the same for approval checks on European imports as they did for the import of US models. This was challenged as being an excessive price.

The abuse

[11] It is possible that the holder of the exclusive position referred to above may abuse the market by fixing a price—for a service which it is alone in a position to provide—which is to the detriment of any person acquiring a motor vehicle imported from another Member State and subject to the approval procedure.

[12] Such an abuse might lie, *inter alia*, in the imposition of a price which is excessive in relation to the economic value of the service provided, and which has the effect of curbing parallel imports by neutralising the possibly more favourable level of prices applying in other sales areas in the Community, or by leading to unfair trade in the sense of Article 86(2)(a).

[13] However, the applicant maintains on this point that the conduct complained of did not constitute an 'abuse' within the meaning of Article 86.

[14] In order to demonstrate this point the applicant puts forward a number of arguments based on the actual circumstances in which the charge in question was imposed and, subsequently, largely refunded in the five cases referred to by the Commission.

NOTE: The Court decided that the excessive price was not abusive as GM had quickly realized the price was too high and reduced the charge. It had then of its own volition refunded the excess charge to importers before the Commission investigation had started. The judgment clarified that excessive pricing could be abusive but that not all excessive pricing was abusive.

United Brands v Commission
(Case 27/76) [1978] ECR 207, [1978] 1 CMLR 429

In its decision the Commission argued that UBC had abused its dominant position by charging excessive prices to its customers in Germany, Denmark, and the Netherlands when compared to the price it charged its customers in Ireland.

[248] The imposition by an undertaking in a dominant position directly or indirectly of unfair purchase or selling prices is an abuse to which exception can be taken under Article 86 of the Treaty.

[249] It is advisable therefore to ascertain whether the dominant undertaking has made use of the opportunities arising out of its dominant position in such a way as to reap trading benefits which it would not have reaped if there had been normal and sufficiently effective competition.

[250] In this case charging a price which is excessive because it has no reasonable relation to the economic value of the product supplied is such an abuse.

[251] This excess could, *inter alia*, be determined objectively if it were possible for it to be calculated by making a comparison between the selling price of the product in question and its cost of production, which would disclose the amount of the profit margin; however the Commission has not done this since it has not analysed UBC's costs structure.

[252] The question therefore to be determined is whether the difference between the costs actually incurred and the price actually charged is excessive and, if the answer to this question is in the affirmative, to consider whether a price has been imposed which is either unfair in itself or when compared to competing products.

[253] Other ways may be devised—and economic theorists have not failed to think up several—of selecting the rules for determining whether the price of a product is unfair.

[254] While appreciating the considerable and at times very great difficulties in working out production costs which may sometimes include a discretionary apportionment of indirect costs and general expenditure and which may vary significantly according to the size of the undertaking, its object, the complex nature of its set up, its territorial area of operations, whether it manufactures one or several products, the number of its subsidiaries and their relationship with each other, the production costs of the banana do not seem to present any insuperable problems.

NOTE: *United Brands* highlights the difficulties in proving the existence of excessive pricing. Ultimately, the Commission had not provided enough evidence to show that the price charged by United Brands was indeed excessive. The method the Court suggests that the Commission should use to support a finding of excessive pricing is a complex 'cost-plus' approach, which will be difficult and complex to utilize in practice. Such a 'cost-plus' approach was considered insufficient by the Commission in the following decision.

Scandlines Sverige AB v *Port of Helsingborg*
(Commission Decision COMP/A.36.568/D3) [2006] 4 CMLR 1224

The Commission investigated complaints that the Port of Helsingborg in Sweden was charging excessive prices for services provided to ferry operators. Most of the ferry traffic was on route to or from the Port of Elsinore in Denmark.

[220] According to Scandlines, finding that the difference between the price and the production costs exceeds what it considers as a reasonable margin (which would be a determined percentage of the production costs) would necessarily lead to the conclusion that the price is unfair (see section II.B.2.1.d) above).

[221] The Commission does not exclude that the question whether a price is unfair may be assessed within a cost-plus framework which encompasses the respective relations between the production costs, the price (or the profit margin) and the economic value of the product/service. However, in such an assessment, the economic value of the product/service cannot simply be determined by adding to the costs incurred in the provision of this product/service a profit margin which would be a pre-determined percentage of the production costs.

[222] First, it should be recalled that there are uncertainties, in this case, as regards the precise determination of the incurred costs (the production costs) that the Commission has taken into account. For the reasons explained above in Section II.B.2.1.b), the assessment of the incurred costs by the Commission is based on an approximate cost allocation. The Commission has proceeded based on assumptions (notably the key of repartition of the distributed costs), which naturally affect the level of the incurred costs by HHAB in providing services to the ferry-operators.

[223] Moreover, due to the fact that HHAB did not provide a realistic cost model for its pricing, the Commission had to refer to the data available in the audited financial reports. This approach adopted by the Commission is rather strict as regards the determination of the production costs. In particular, in the Commission's approximate cost allocation, the depreciation costs are based on the historical values of the assets (for the reasons developed in Section II.B.3.b) of the Article 6 letter, the replacement values provided by HHAB in its cost allocation could not be retained). However, a company that sets its prices on the basis of depreciated historical costs may—depending on how the production costs of the relevant assets have developed over the years—well find itself in a position that its return does not (i.e. no longer) allow it to finance future capital expenditures for the replacement of existing assets.

[224] In addition, when setting a price *a priori*, a company does not necessarily only refer to the incurred costs (production costs). For instance, it is legitimate that a company may want to cover the cost of capital. As explained in section 7 of Appendix 3.1, the cost of capital (which corresponds to the profit which would allow the company to remunerate its shareholders at the appropriate level) is not a cost accounted for as such in the audited financial reports and is therefore not counted in the approximate costs allocation made by the Commission for the purposes of this decision (in absence of any reliable information on what the capital market would expect as a remuneration for investments in HHAB). Such a cost can, however, be viewed a priori as a charge for a company when setting the price for a product/service.

[225] In any event, in the present case, there is no information on what a reasonable profit margin should be. The Commission explained in section II.B.2.1.d) that there would be insuperable difficulties in establishing valid benchmarks as concerns the profitability of ferry-operations in ports. A comparison, as suggested by Scandlines, between the yearly average ROCE derived by HHAB from the ferry-operations and the yearly average ROCE of the Swedish industry, provided it is made on a consistent basis, could in principle only be considered as an indication and not as sufficient evidence in itself in determining whether the port charges are unfair in themselves.

[226] Moreover, the "cost-plus approach" suggested by Scandlines only takes into account the conditions of supply of the product/service. The determination of the economic value of the product/service should also take account of other non-cost related factors, especially as regards the demand-side aspects of the product/service concerned.

[227] The demand-side is relevant mainly because customers are notably willing to pay more for something specific attached to the product/service that they consider valuable. This specific feature does not necessarily imply higher production costs for the provider. However it is valuable for the customer and also for the provider, and thereby increases the economic value of the product/service.

[228] As a consequence, even if it were to be assumed that there is a positive difference between the price and the production costs exceeding what Scandlines claims as being a reasonable margin (whatever that may be), the conclusion should not necessarily be drawn that the price is unfair, provided that this price has a reasonable relation to the economic value of the product/service supplied. The assessment of the reasonable relation between the price and the economic value of the product/service must also take into account the relative weight of non-cost related factors.

...

[232] In the present case, the economic value of the product/service cannot simply be determined by adding to the approximate costs incurred in the provision of this product/service as assessed by the Commission, a profit margin which would be a pre-determined percentage of the production costs. The economic value must be determined with regards to the particular circumstances of the case and take into account also non-cost related factors such as the demand for the product/service.

[233] As a consequence, finding a positive difference between the price and the approximate production costs exceeding what Scandlines claims as being a reasonable margin, would not necessarily lead to the conclusion that the price is unfair, provided that this price has a reasonable relation to the economic value of the product/service supplied.

NOTE: The Commission Decision highlights the difficulty of substantiating a charge of 'unfair' or excessive pricing, particularly as it now seems clear that non-cost factors can also influence the economic value of the product or service. It is for these reasons that the Commission has not brought many cases on the basis of excessive prices since the 1970s (cf. the approach of the OFT in the UK in *Napp*).

Merci Convenzionali Porto Genova SpA v *Siderurgica Gabrielli*
(Case C-179/90) [1991] ECR I-5889, [1994] 4 CMLR 422

The port of Genova is administered by a public authority that regulates work within the port. All dock work, including the loading and unloading of ships, was reserved to certain groups of enrolled dockworkers. Siderurgica imported a consignment of steel in a vessel that was capable of direct unloading; but that was not allowed as the work would not be performed by the reserved workers. A dispute arose following the delay caused by the ship's inability directly to unload quickly and because of strikes by dockworkers.

[18] According to Article 86(2)(a), (b) and (c) EEC, such abuse may in particular consist in imposing on the persons requiring the services in question unfair purchase prices or other unfair trading conditions, in limiting technical development, to the prejudice of consumers, or in the application of dissimilar conditions to equivalent transactions with other trading parties.

[19] In that respect it appears from the circumstances described by the national court and discussed before the Court of Justice that the undertakings enjoying exclusive rights in accordance with the procedures laid down by the national rules in question are, as a result, induced either to demand payment for services which have not been requested, to charge disproportionate prices, to refuse to have recourse to modern technology, which involves an increase in the cost of the operations and a prolongation of the time required for their performance, or to grant price reductions to certain consumers and at the same time to offset such reductions by an increase in the charges to other consumers.

...

[22] In the main proceedings it may be seen from the national court's findings that the unloading of the goods could have been effected at a lesser cost by the ship's crew, so that compulsory recourse to the services of the two undertakings enjoying exclusive rights involved extra expense and was therefore capable, by reason of its effect on the prices of the goods, of affecting imports.

NOTE: This judgment focuses on another form of exploitative abuse by which a dominant undertaking could exploit its customers. This phenomenon is sometimes known as 'x-inefficiency' and occurs when the dominant undertaking uses its dominance to relax and no longer strives to produce its products or deliver its service in the most efficient and cost-effective manner possible. It is also sometimes said that the dominant undertaking is 'enjoying the quiet life'. If that is the case the consumers of the undertaking's product or service will not benefit from the cost savings that you would expect the undertaking to make and will in time have to pay more than would have occurred if there was a competitive market. Here the port authorities employed inefficient techniques that incurred higher costs on those who used the facility. If there was a competitive market they would have been forced to adopt more efficient practices, but without that competition they could afford not to change their ways.

■ QUESTION

Why is it difficult for competition authorities to take action against excessive pricing by dominant firms?

J: Exclusionary abuses

Exclusionary abuses are problematic and can result in a dominant undertaking strengthening its position in the market. As it is already in a very strong position, this may be particularly damaging for competition. Many of the abuses that Community competition law focuses on can be described as being exclusionary in nature. This is because Community law has traditionally taken a particular focus on protecting the competitive structure of the market rather than just protecting the consumer. It is these types of abuses that have been the subject of the Commission's Article 82 EC review, culminating in the Commission Communication, which will be discussed further below alongside case law and other selected materials.

Nederlandsche Banden-Industrie Michelin NV v Commission
(Case 322/81) [1983] ECR 3461, [1985] 1 CMLR 282

The appellant manufactured new tyres for vans and lorries. The Commission took action against Michelin for, *inter alia*, operating a system of selective and discriminatory discounts.

[70] As regards the application of Article 86 to a system of discounts conditional upon the attainment of sales targets, such as described above, it must be stated first of all that in prohibiting any abuse of a dominant position on the market in so far as it may affect trade between Member-States Article 86 covers practices which are likely to affect the structure of a market where, as a direct result of the presence of the undertaking in question, competition has already been weakened and which, through recourse to methods different from those governing normal competition in products or services based on traders' performance, have the effect of hindering the maintenance or development of the level of competition still existing on the market.

NOTE: This approach by the Court has raised a number of questions about the Commission's focus in competition law terms. Is it Commission policy to protect consumers, the process of competition, or a dominant undertaking's competitors? See, Springer, U., 'Meeting Competition: Justification of Price Discrimination under EC and US Antitrust Law' [1997] ECLR 251 and Andrews, P., 'Is Meeting Competition a Defence to Predatory Pricing? The Irish Sugar Decision Suggests a New Approach' [1998] ECLR 49.

(a) Exclusionary pricing

Complaints about the pricing practices of dominant undertakings are common in competition law. The main concern here is not that the dominant undertaking is charging high prices to its customers, but that it is pricing in a way that is designed to drive its competitors out of the market or make it difficult for them to compete with the dominant player.

Commission Communication: Guidance on the Commission's enforcement priorities in applying Article 82 EC Treaty to abusive exclusionary conduct by dominant undertakings
OJ, 2009, C45/7, paras 23–7 [footnotes omitted]

C. Price-based exclusionary conduct

[23] The considerations in paragraphs 23 to 27 apply to price based exclusionary conduct. Vigorous price competition is generally beneficial to consumers. With a view to preventing anti-competitive foreclosure, the Commission will normally only intervene where the conduct concerned has already been or is capable of hampering competition from competitors which are considered to be as efficient as the dominant undertaking.

[24] However, the Commission recognises that in certain circumstances a less efficient competitor may also exert a constraint which should be taken into account when considering whether particular price-based conduct leads to anti-competitive foreclosure. The Commission will take a dynamic view of that constraint, given that in the absence of an abusive practice such a competitor may benefit from demand-related advantages, such as network and learning effects, which will tend to enhance its efficiency.

[25] In order to determine whether even a hypothetical competitor as efficient as the dominant undertaking would be likely to be foreclosed by the conduct in question, the Commission will examine economic data relating to cost and sales prices, and in particular whether the dominant undertaking is engaging in below-cost pricing. This will require that sufficiently reliable data be available. Where available, the Commission will use information on the costs of the dominant undertaking itself. If reliable information on those costs is not available, the Commission may decide to use the cost data of competitors or other comparable reliable data.

[26] The cost benchmarks that the Commission is likely to use are average avoidable cost (AAC) and long-run average incremental cost (LRAIC). Failure to cover AAC indicates that the dominant undertaking is sacrificing profits in the short term and that an equally efficient competitor cannot serve the targeted customers without incurring a loss. LRAIC is usually above AAC because, in contrast to AAC (which only includes fixed costs if incurred during the period under examination), LRAIC includes product specific fixed costs made before the period in which allegedly abusive conduct took place. Failure to cover LRAIC indicates that the dominant undertaking is not recovering all the (attributable) fixed costs of producing the good or service in question and that an equally efficient competitor could be foreclosed from the market.

[27] If the data clearly suggest that an equally efficient competitor can compete effectively with the pricing conduct of the dominant undertaking, the Commission will, in principle, infer that the dominant undertaking's pricing conduct is not likely to have an adverse impact on effective competition, and thus on consumers, and will therefore be unlikely to intervene. If, on the contrary, the

data suggest that the price charged by the dominant undertaking has the potential to foreclose equally efficient competitors, then the Commission will integrate this in the general assessment of anti-competitive foreclosure (see Section B above), taking into account other relevant quantitative and/or qualitative evidence.

NOTE: The Commission Communication established an approach to assessing a dominant undertaking's costs firmly rooted in economic theory and analysis, and the significance of this approach can be seen from the discussion of predatory pricing below, where a knowledge of an undertaking's costs, as well as its pricing strategy is crucial.

(b) Predatory pricing

One prominent example of exclusionary pricing is predation. Predatory pricing may appear to benefit consumers in the form of very low prices, but this is a short-term view. In the longer term competition law is concerned about predation where dominant undertakings price below cost and either force a competitor from the market or weaken its competitive constraints, with the ability to raise prices to a high level after the predatory pricing strategy.

AKZO Chemie BV v Commission
(Case C-62/86) [1991] ECR I-3359, [1993] 5 CMLR 215

Following an investigation, the Commission found that AKZO had adopted a course of conduct designed to secure ECS's withdrawal from the organic peroxides market. One of the abuses concerned systematically providing products to customers of ECS at unreasonably low prices, which were below AKZO's cost and designed to damage ECS.

[69] It should be observed that, as the Court held in Case 85/76, *Hoffmann-La Roche* v *EC Commission*, the concept of abuse is an objective concept relating to the behaviour of an undertaking in a dominant position which is such as to influence the structure of a market where, as a result of the very presence of the undertaking in question, the degree of competition is weakened and through recourse to methods which, different from those which condition normal competition in products or services on the basis of the transactions of commercial operations, has the effect of hindering the maintenance of the degree of competition still existing in the market or the growth of that competition.

[70] It follows that Article 86 prohibits a dominant undertaking from eliminating a competitor and thereby strengthening its position by using methods other than those which come within the scope of competition on the basis of quality. From that point of view, however, not all competition by means of price can be regarded as legitimate.

[71] Prices below average variable costs (that is to say, those which vary depending on the quantities produced) by means of which a dominant undertaking seeks to eliminate a competitor must be regarded as abusive. A dominant undertaking has no interest in applying such prices except that of eliminating competitors so as to enable it subsequently to raise its prices by taking advantage of its monopolistic position, since each sale generates a loss, namely the total amount of the fixed costs (that is to say, those which remain constant regardless of the quantities produced) and, at least, part of the variable costs relating to the unit produced.

[72] Moreover, prices below average total costs, that is to say, fixed costs plus variable costs, but above average variable costs, must be regarded as abusive if they are determined as part of a plan for eliminating a competitor. Such prices can drive from the market undertakings which are perhaps as efficient as the dominant undertaking but which, because of their smaller financial resources, are incapable of withstanding the competition waged against them.

[73] These are the criteria that must be applied to the situation in the present case.

[74] Since the criterion of legitimacy to be adopted is a criterion based on the costs and the strategy of the dominant undertaking itself, AKZO's allegation concerning the inadequacy of the Commission's investigation with regard to the cost structure and the pricing policy of its competitors must be rejected at the outset.

NOTE: The *AKZO* formula has been used on many subsequent occasions but has caused several problems, namely the difficulties in categorizing costs as either fixed or variable costs. The test for predatory pricing was extended in Case T-51/89 *Tetra Pak II* [1990] ECR II-309, [1991] 4 CMLR 334 to a situation whereby the dominant undertaking abused its strength on one market to undercut competition on another related market. Debate has also focused on whether recoupment—the ability to recoup losses suffered during below-cost pricing in the course of subsequent price increases—is a necessary element of finding predation.

France Télécom v Commission
(Case T-340/03) [2007] ECR II-107, [2007] 4 CMLR 21

France Télécom (formerly Wanadoo Interactive—'WIN') was fined by the Commission for engaging in predatory pricing in the French high-speed internet access market. The Court of First Instance considered whether the Commission must demonstrate the ability of France Télécom to recoup losses incurred during the below-cost pricing strategy.

[219] WIN submits that the recoupment of losses is entirely separate from the test of predation and the Commission must provide evidence of it. It takes the view that, if an undertaking in a dominant position cannot reasonably expect to reduce long-term competition with a view to recouping its losses, in particular because it is easy to enter the market in question, it is not rational for that undertaking to engage in a policy of predatory pricing. In that situation, the policy of low prices applied by the undertaking must be explained otherwise than by a strategy of predation.

[220] According to WIN, that view is supported by all the economic and legal literature as well as by a number of courts and competition authorities, including those of the United States and several Member States of the European Union. The need to prove this has never been ruled out under Community case-law.

[221] However, the conditions of competition on the market for high-speed internet access are completely different from those on which the Court of First Instance and the Court of Justice have had to rule in previous cases on predation. The barriers to entry on this market are low, growth is robust, the competitive situation is not frozen and there are numerous actual and potential new entrants. The Commission thus seriously errs in law in maintaining that it is not necessary to prove recoupment of losses.

[222] Furthermore, according to WIN, the Commission committed a further manifest error of assessment, coupled with an error of law, by considering that it had furnished evidence of a possibility to recoup losses.

[223] The Commission contends that proof of recoupment of losses is not a precondition to making a finding of predatory pricing contrary to Article 82 EC. It considers that the case-law is clear on this point. In the alternative, the Commission points out that the recoupment of losses in the present case is made plausible by the structure of the market and the related revenues which thus can be expected in the future.

Findings of the Court

[224] In *AKZO* v *Commission*, paragraph 100 above, paragraphs 71 and 72, the Court of Justice sanctioned the existence of two different methods of analysis for determining whether an undertaking has applied predatory pricing. First, prices below average variable costs must always be considered abusive. In such a case, there is no conceivable economic purpose other than the elimination of a competitor, since each item produced and sold entails a loss for the undertaking.

Secondly, prices below average total costs but above average variable costs are only to be considered abusive if an intention to eliminate can be shown (Case C-333/94 P *Tetra Pak* v *Commission*, paragraph 130 above, paragraph 41).

[225] In Case C-333/94 P *Tetra Pak* v *Commission*, paragraph 130 above, paragraphs 42 and 43, the Court of Justice held that in the judgment under appeal the Court of First Instance had applied the same reasoning, reasoning which the Court of Justice endorsed. The Court of Justice explained that:

'[42] For sales of non-aseptic cartons in Italy between 1976 and 1981, [the Court of First Instance] found that prices were considerably lower than average variable costs. Proof of intention to eliminate competitors was therefore not necessary. In 1982, prices for those cartons lay between average variable costs and average total costs. For that reason, in paragraph 151 of its judgment, the Court of First Instance was at pains to establish—and the appellant has not criticised it in that regard—that Tetra Pak intended to eliminate a competitor.

[43] The Court of First Instance was also right, at paragraphs 189 to 191 of the judgment under appeal, to apply exactly the same reasoning to sales of non-aseptic machines in the United Kingdom between 1981 and 1984.'

[226] In relation to the recoupment of losses, the Court of Justice added, in paragraph 44 of that judgment:

'[I]t would not be appropriate, in the circumstances of the present case, to require in addition proof that Tetra Pak had a realistic chance of recouping its losses. It must be possible to penalise predatory pricing whenever there is a risk that competitors will be eliminated. The Court of First Instance found, at paragraphs 151 and 191 of its judgment, that there was such a risk in this case. The aim pursued, which is to maintain undistorted competition, rules out waiting until such a strategy leads to the actual elimination of competitors.'

[227] In line with Community case-law, the Commission was therefore able to regard as abusive prices below average variable costs. In that case, the eliminatory nature of such pricing is presumed (see, to that effect, Case T-83/91 *Tetra Pak* v *Commission*, paragraph 130 above, paragraph 148). In relation to full costs, the Commission had also to provide evidence that WIN's predatory pricing formed part of a plan to 'pre-empt' the market. In the two situations, it was not necessary to establish in addition proof that WIN had a realistic chance of recouping its losses.

[228] The Commission was therefore right to take the view that proof of recoupment of losses was not a precondition to making a finding of predatory pricing.

NOTE: The issue of recoupment is subject to much debate. On appeal to the Court of Justice Advocate General Mazák issued his Opinion in the case arguing against the CFI position.

France Télécom v *Commission*
(Case C-202/07 P)

Advocate General Mazák's Opinion

[68] After referring to *Tetra Pak II*, the Court of First Instance concludes at paragraph 228 of the judgment under appeal that the Commission was right to take the view that proof of recoupment of losses was not a precondition to making a finding of predatory pricing.

[69] I consider that the Court of First Instance's, and for that matter the Commission's, interpretation of the Court's case-law is incorrect. In my view that case-law requires the possibility of recoupment of losses to be proven.

[70] I consider that, by using the qualifying words 'in the circumstances of the present case' in *Tetra Pak II*, the Court clearly intended to avoid making a general statement that would render it unnecessary to prove the possibility of recoupment in future predatory pricing cases.

[71] Indeed, as Advocate General Fennelly rightly pointed out in his Opinion in *Compagnie maritime belge transports and Others* v *Commission*, '[t]he Court would not appear to have gone as far as Advocate General Ruiz-Jarabo Colomer, who had recommended that the Court "should not lay down the prospect of recouping losses as a new prerequisite for establishing the existence of predatory pricing contrary to Article [82 EC]", inter alia, because, in [Advocate General Ruiz-Jarabo Colomer's] view, "recouping losses is the result sought by the dominant undertaking, but predatory pricing is in itself anti-competitive, regardless of whether it achieves that aim".'

[72] Moreover, in using such qualifying words, the Court clearly departed from the categorical declaration in the Court of First Instance's judgment in *Tetra Pak II* that 'it is not necessary to demonstrate specifically that the undertaking in question had a reasonable prospect of recouping losses so incurred.'

[73] In my view, it also follows from *Akzo* and *Hoffmann-La Roche* that proof of the possibility of recoupment is required in order to find predation pursuant to Article 82 EC. Unless there is a possibility of recoupment, the dominant undertaking is probably engaged in normal competition.

[74] In such a case, where there is no possibility of recouping losses, consumers and their interests should, in principle, not be harmed. I may note here that I share the view of Advocate General Jacobs who in his Opinion in *Oscar Bronner* stated that 'the primary purpose of Article [82 EC] is to prevent distortion of competition—and in particular to safeguard the interests of consumers—rather than to protect the position of particular competitors'.

[75] Finally, I will take this opportunity to point out that, apart from the above case-law, the importance of proof of the possibility of recoupment was brought to the fore inter alia by the Economic Advisory Group on Competition Policy (EAGCP), the Organisation for Economic Co-operation and Development and the European Regulators Group.

[76] In my concluding remarks on the question of proof of the possibility of recoupment I would like to point out that I am not convinced by the Commission's line of argument that in Europe and under Article 82 EC recoupment is implied by the dominance, not least because the determination of dominance is often based on historical market conditions, whilst as I explained above proof of the possibility of recoupment is inherently *ex ante* and forward-looking, assessing the market structure as it will be in the future.

NOTE: The Court of Justice delivered its ruling on 2 April 2009 and upheld the Commission Decision and CFI ruling, thereby rejecting AG Mazák's Opinion (see paras 110–11 of ECJ ruling). Nonetheless, Gal also argues in favour of a recoupment test, or at least the possibility of a lack of recoupment being a possible objective justification.

Gal, M.S., 'Below-cost price alignment: Meeting or beating competition? The France Télécom case'
[2007] ECLR 382, p. 383 [footnotes omitted]

Although the Commission's decision also dealt with the issue of recoupment, the CFI followed previous case law and did not require such proof as a condition for finding an abuse. This is a missed opportunity. As many commentators have already argued, the possibility of recoupment should be part of the offence or at least provide a valid defence. This is because the rationality of the predatory scheme hinges on the possibility of recoupment: that the predator's long run profitability from the scheme justifies the short-term losses in the first period. If recoupment is not deemed probable at the time the alleged predatory conduct was engaged in, then it must be assumed that the conduct was not predatory, otherwise the firm would not have engaged in it. Moreover, since the costs of a dominant firm usually cannot be measured with much accuracy, the recoupment requirement also serves as a surrogate for such an analysis, to further ensure that the predatory pricing allegations are a rational explanation of the dominant firm's conduct. As the US Supreme Court recently stated in its *Weyerhaeuser* decision, recoupment should be a necessary element in the predatory pricing offence because:

> "[t]he costs of erroneous findings of predatory-pricing liability are quite high because the mechanism by which a firm engages in predatory pricing—lowering prices—is the same

mechanism by which a firm stimulates competition, and therefore mistaken liability findings would chill the very conduct the antitrust laws are designed to protect".

In addition, if the predatory strategy was not rational since recoupment is not possible since the dominant firm would not be able to raise prices in the second stage, then the dominant firm's conduct actually benefits consumers, as they enjoy the low prices in the first period while not suffering from high ones in the second one. Such conduct should therefore not be prohibited. The recoupment requirement should thus form an inherent part of any assessment of alleged predatory pricing, at least as a possible defence.

NOTE: A test of recoupment would considerably raise the difficulty for the Commission and NCAs in reaching a finding of predation, and it is clear from the Commission Communication that it still considers it to be unnecessary to prove recoupment as part of predation.

Commission Communication: Guidance on the Commission's enforcement priorities in applying Article 82 EC Treaty to abusive exclusionary conduct by dominant undertakings
OJ, 2009, C45/7, paras 63–74 [footnotes omitted]

C. Predation

[63] In line with its enforcement priorities, the Commission will generally intervene where there is evidence showing that a dominant undertaking engages in predatory conduct by deliberately incurring losses or foregoing profits in the short term (referred to hereafter as 'sacrifice'), so as to foreclose or be likely to foreclose one or more of its actual or potential competitors with a view to strengthening or maintaining its market power, thereby causing consumer harm.

(a) *Sacrifice*

[64] Conduct will be viewed by the Commission as entailing a sacrifice if, by charging a lower price for all or a particular part of its output over the relevant time period, or by expanding its output over the relevant time period, the dominant undertaking incurred or is incurring losses that could have been avoided. The Commission will take AAC as the appropriate starting point for assessing whether the dominant undertaking incurred or is incurring avoidable losses. If a dominant undertaking charges a price below AAC for all or part of its output, it is not recovering the costs that could have been avoided by not producing that output: it is incurring a loss that could have been avoided. Pricing below AAC will thus in most cases be viewed by the Commission as a clear indication of sacrifice.

[65] However, the concept of sacrifice does not only include pricing below AAC. In order to show a predatory strategy, the Commission may also investigate whether the allegedly predatory conduct led in the short term to net revenues lower than could have been expected from a reasonable alternative conduct, that is to say, whether the dominant undertaking incurred a loss that it could have avoided. The Commission will not compare the actual conduct with hypothetical or theoretical alternatives that might have been more profitable. Only economically rational and practicable alternatives will be considered which, taking into account the market conditions and business realities facing the dominant undertaking, can realistically be expected to be more profitable.

[66] In some cases it will be possible to rely upon direct evidence consisting of documents from the dominant undertaking which clearly show a predatory strategy, such as a detailed plan to sacrifice in order to exclude a competitor, to prevent entry or to pre-empt the emergence of a market, or evidence of concrete threats of predatory action.

(b) *Anti-competitive foreclosure*

[67] If sufficient reliable data are available, the Commission will apply the equally efficient competitor analysis, described in paragraphs 25 to 27, to determine whether the conduct is capable of harming consumers. Normally only pricing below LRAIC is capable of foreclosing as efficient competitors from the market.

[68] In addition to the factors already mentioned in paragraph 20, the Commission will generally investigate whether and how the suspected conduct reduces the likelihood that competitors will compete. For instance, if the dominant undertaking is better informed about cost or other market conditions, or can distort market signals about profitability, it may engage in predatory conduct so as to influence the expectations of potential entrants and thereby deter entry. If the conduct and its likely effects are felt on multiple markets and/or in successive periods of possible entry, the dominant undertaking may be shown to be seeking a reputation for predatory conduct. If the targeted competitor is dependent on external financing, substantial price decreases or other predatory conduct by the dominant undertaking could adversely affect the competitor's performance so that its access to further financing may be seriously undermined.

[69] The Commission does not consider that it is necessary to show that competitors have exited the market in order to show that there has been anti-competitive foreclosure. The possibility cannot be excluded that the dominant undertaking may prefer to prevent the competitor from competing vigorously and have it follow the dominant undertaking's pricing, rather than eliminate it from the market altogether. Such disciplining avoids the risk inherent in eliminating competitors, in particular the risk that the assets of the competitor are sold at a low price and stay in the market, creating a new low cost entrant.

[70] Generally speaking, consumers are likely to be harmed if the dominant undertaking can reasonably expect its market power after the predatory conduct comes to an end to be greater than it would have been had the undertaking not engaged in that conduct in the first place, that is to say, if the undertaking is likely to be in a position to benefit from the sacrifice.

[71] This does not mean that the Commission will only intervene if the dominant undertaking would be likely to be able to increase its prices above the level persisting in the market before the conduct. It is sufficient, for instance, that the conduct would be likely to prevent or delay a decline in prices that would otherwise have occurred. Identifying consumer harm is not a mechanical calculation of profits and losses, and proof of overall profits is not required. Likely consumer harm may be demonstrated by assessing the likely foreclosure effect of the conduct, combined with consideration of other factors, such as entry barriers. In this context, the Commission will also consider possibilities of re-entry.

[72] It may be easier for the dominant undertaking to engage in predatory conduct if it selectively targets specific customers with low prices, as this will limit the losses incurred by the dominant undertaking.

[73] It is less likely that the dominant undertaking engages in predatory conduct if the conduct concerns a low price applied generally for a long period of time.

(c) Efficiencies

[74] In general it is considered unlikely that predatory conduct will create efficiencies. However, provided that the conditions set out in Section III D are fulfilled, the Commission will consider claims by a dominant undertaking that the low pricing enables it to achieve economies of scale or efficiencies related to expanding the market.

NOTE: Para. 71 demonstrates the Commission's view that proof of recoupment is unnecessary to substantiate a finding of predation, and also sets out a rigorous economic-orientated approach to dealing with predatory pricing cases. Para. 72 sets out the possibility that a dominant undertaking can engage in predatory conduct by adopting a strategy of selective pricing. This scenario can be seen from the *Irish Sugar* case.

Irish Sugar plc v EC Commission
(Case T-228/97) [1999] ECR II-2969, [1999] 5 CMLR 1300

Irish Sugar was the dominant supplier of white granulated sugar in the Republic of Ireland. One of the alleged abuses addressed by the Commission was Irish Sugar's policy of offering selective low prices to potential customers of rival sugar suppliers from Northern Ireland. Irish Sugar granted so-called 'border rebates' to its customers who may have been tempted to source supplies outside the Republic. In its Decision (*Irish Sugar plc*, Commission Decision 97/624/EC, OJ, 1997, L258/1), the Commission specifically referred to the Court's judgment in *AKZO* on a number of occasions, particularly at para. 134:

[134] There is no doubt that a firm in a dominant position is entitled to defend that position by competing with other firms on its market. However, the dominant firm must not deliberately attempt to effectively shut out competitors. It has a special responsibility not to diminish further the degree of competition remaining on the market. Firms which may be strong or even dominant on one geographic market are in a different position with respect to other geographic markets where they are confronted with a local dominant undertaking. The maintenance of a system of effective competition does, however, require that competition from undertakings which are only small competitors on the geographic market where dominance prevails, regardless of their position on geographic markets which are separate for the purpose of assessing dominance, be protected against behaviour by the dominant undertaking designed to exclude them from the market not by virtue of greater efficiency or superior performance but by an abuse of market power. In the Commission's final decision in *ECS/AKZO* it was held to be abusive for a company with a 50 per cent or more market share to offer selectively low prices to customers of a small competitor while maintaining substantially higher prices for its existing customers. This principle was upheld by the Court. In the period in which it sought to restrict imports, Irish Sugar had over 90 per cent of both the Irish industrial and retail sugar markets.

NOTE: This was important in that the prices charged by Irish Sugar were not below ATC and therefore they would not appear to fall within the traditional reading of the *AKZO* test. This was confirmed by the Court of First Instance.

[184] In the particular circumstances of the case, the applicant cannot rely, in order to show that the special rebates granted between 1986 and 1988 to certain retailers established in the border area with Northern Ireland were lawful, either on the pricing policy of operators on the British market, or on its financial situation, or on the defensive nature of its conduct, or on the alleged existence of an illegal trade.

[185] First of all, the influence of the pricing policy of operators active principally on a neighbouring market, in this case the British and Northern Ireland market, on that of operators active on another national market is of the very essence of a common market. Anything which restricts that influence must therefore be regarded as an obstacle to the achievement of that common market and prejudicial to the outcome of effective and undistorted competition, especially with regard to the interests of consumers. Therefore, where such obstacles are brought about by an undertaking holding a dominant position as extensive as that enjoyed by the applicant, that is an abuse incompatible with Article 86. The applicant has, moreover, nowhere argued that the prices charged by its competitors along the border with Northern Ireland were below the cost price of the product, or supplied any evidence to that effect.

[186] Secondly, the applicant cannot rely on the insufficiency of the financial resources at its disposal at the time to justify the selective and discriminatory granting of those border rebates and thereby escape the application of Article 86, without making a dead letter of the prohibition contained in that article. The circumstances in which an undertaking in a dominant position may be led to react to the limited competition which exists on the market, especially where that undertaking holds more than 88 per cent of the market as in this case, form part of the competitive process which Article 86 is precisely designed to protect. Moreover, the applicant has several times underlined the high level of retail sale prices in Ireland, explaining it by the influence of the high level of the guaranteed intervention price in the context of the common organisation of the market in sugar.

[187] Finally, the defensive nature of the practice complained of in this case cannot alter the fact that it constitutes an abuse for the purposes of Article 86(c).

[188] In this case, the applicant has been unable to establish an objective economic justification for the rebates. They were given to certain customers in the retail sugar market by reference solely to their exposure to competition resulting from cheap imports from another Member State and, in this case, by reference to their being established along the border with Northern Ireland. It also appears, according to the applicant's own statements, that it was able to practise such price rebates owing to the particular position it held on the Irish market. Thus it states that it was unable to practise such rebates over the whole of Irish territory owing to the financial losses it was making at the time. It follows that, by the applicant's own admission, its economic capacity to offer rebates in the region along the border with Northern Ireland depended on the stability of its prices in other regions, which amounts to recognition that it financed those rebates by means of its sales in the rest of Irish territory. By conducting itself in that way, the applicant abused its dominant position in the retail sugar market in Ireland, by preventing the development of free competition on that market and distorting its structures, in relation to both purchasers and consumers. The latter were not able to benefit, outside the region along the border with Northern Ireland, from the price reductions caused by the imports of sugar from Northern Ireland.

[189] Thus, even if the existence of a dominant position does not deprive an undertaking placed in that position of the right to protect its own commercial interests when they are threatened (see paragraph [112] above), the protection of the commercial position of an undertaking in a dominant position with the characteristics of that of the applicant at the time in question must, at the very least, in order to be lawful, be based on criteria of economic efficiency and consistent with the interests of consumers. In this case, the applicant has not shown that those conditions were fulfilled.

NOTE: Although the Court was not clear that this was a case of predatory pricing, it appears certain that where a dominant undertaking adopts a course of conduct reducing prices selectively and there is an intention to drive a competitor from the market, that behaviour will certainly be seen as abusive. The benefits of such an approach are discussed in Andrews, P., 'Is Meeting Competition a Defence to Predatory Pricing? The Irish Sugar Decision Suggests a New Approach' [1998] ECLR 49.

■ **QUESTION**

Why is predatory pricing detrimental to consumer welfare?

(c) Discounts and rebates

While consumers may feel that they benefit from the savings made through discounts and rebates, they can be used by dominant undertakings to 'tie' customers to them and stifle the development of true competition on a market. For that reason some discounting practices have been challenged in the EC, while others are seen as justifiable.

Hoffmann-La Roche v Commission
(Case 85/76) [1979] ECR 461, [1979] 3 CMLR 211

Hoffmann-La Roche were held to have a dominant position in the market for a number of vitamins. The Commission had challenged a number of discounts offered by Hoffmann-La Roche in its contracts with customers on the basis that they were abusive.

[89] An undertaking which is in a dominant position on a market and ties purchasers—even if it does so at their request—by an obligation or promise on their part to obtain all or most of their requirements exclusively from the said undertaking abuses its dominant position within the meaning of Article 86 of the Treaty, whether the obligation in question is stipulated without further qualification or whether it is undertaken in consideration of the grant of a rebate. The

same applies if the said undertaking, without tying the purchasers by a formal obligation, applies, either under the terms of agreements concluded with these purchasers or unilaterally, a system of fidelity rebates, that is to say discounts conditional on the customer's obtaining all or most of its requirements—whether the quantity of its purchases be large or small—from the undertaking in a dominant position.

[90] Obligations of this kind to obtain supplies exclusively from a particular undertaking, whether or not they are in consideration of rebates or of the granting of fidelity rebates intended to give the purchaser an incentive to obtain his supplies exclusively from the undertaking in a dominant position, are incompatible with the objective of undistorted competition within the Common Market, because—unless there are exceptional circumstances which may make an agreement between undertakings in the context of Article 85 and in particular of paragraph (3) of that Article, permissible—they are not based on an economic transaction which justifies this burden or benefit but are designed to deprive the purchaser of or restrict his possible choices of sources of supply and to deny other producers access to the market. The fidelity rebate, unlike quantity rebates exclusively linked with the volume of purchases from the producer concerned, is designed through the grant of a financial advantage to prevent customers from obtaining their supplies from competing producers. Furthermore, the effect of fidelity rebates is to apply dissimilar conditions to equivalent transactions with other trading parties in that two purchasers pay a different price for the same quantity of the same product depending on whether they obtain their supplies exclusively from the undertaking in a dominant position or have several sources of supply. Finally, these practices by an undertaking in a dominant position and especially on an expanding market tend to consolidate this position by means of a form of competition which is not based on the transactions effected and is therefore distorted.

[91] For the purpose of rejecting the finding that there has been an abuse of a dominant position the interpretation suggested by the applicant that an abuse implies that the use of the economic power bestowed by a dominant position is the means whereby the abuse has been brought about cannot be accepted. The concept of abuse is an objective concept relating to the behaviour of an undertaking in a dominant position which is such as to influence the structure of a market where, as a result of the very presence of the undertaking in question, the degree of competition is weakened and which, through recourse to methods different from those which condition normal competition in products or services on the basis of the transactions of commercial operators, has the effect of hindering the maintenance of the degree of competition still existing in the market or the growth of that competition.

Section 5: The English clause

[102] All the contracts in question except five (the Animedica International, Guyomarc'h, Merck B6, Protector and Upjohn contracts) contain a clause, called the English clause, under which the customer, if he obtains from competitors offers at prices which are more favourable than those under the contracts at issue may ask Roche to adjust its prices to the said offers; if Roche does not comply with this request, the customer, in derogation from his undertaking to obtain his requirements exclusively from Roche, is entitled to get his supplies from the said competitor without for that reason losing the benefit of the fidelity rebates provided for in the contracts in respect of the other purchases already effected or still to be effected by him from Roche.

[103] In the applicant's view this clause destroys the restrictive effect on competition both of the exclusivity agreements and of the fidelity rebates. In particular in the case of those contracts which do not contain an express undertaking by the purchaser to obtain his requirements exclusively from Roche the English clause eliminates 'the attractive effect' of the rebates at issue since the customer does not have to choose between acceptance of Roche's less attractive offers or losing the benefit of the fidelity rebates on all purchases which he has already effected from Roche.

[104] There is no doubt whatever that this clause makes it possible to remedy some of the unfair consequences which undertakings by purchasers to obtain their requirements exclusively from Roche or the provision for fidelity rebates on all purchases accepted for relatively long periods, might have in so far as those purchasers are concerned. Nevertheless it is necessary to point out

that the purchaser's opportunities for exploiting competition for his own benefit are more restricted than appears at first sight.

...

[107] It is particularly necessary to stress that, even in the most favourable circumstances, the English clause does not in fact remedy to a great extent the distortion of competition caused by the clauses obliging purchasers to obtain their requirements exclusively from Roche and by the fidelity rebates on a market where an undertaking in a dominant position is operating and where for this reason the structure of competition has already been weakened. In fact the English clause under which Roche's customers are obliged to inform it of more favourable offers made by competitors together with the particulars above mentioned—so that it will be easy for Roche to identify the competitor—owing to its very nature, places at the disposal of the applicant information about market conditions and also about the alternatives open to, and the actions of, its competitors which is of great value for the carrying out of its market strategy. The fact that an undertaking in a dominant position requires its customers or obtains their agreement under contract to notify it of its competitors' offers, whilst the said customers may have an obvious commercial interest in not disclosing them, is of such a kind as to aggravate the exploitation of the dominant position in an abusive way. Finally by virtue of the machinery of the English clause it is for Roche itself to decide whether, by adjusting its prices or not, it will permit competition.

[108] It is able in this way, owing to the information which its own customers supply, to vary its market strategy in so far as it affects them and its competitors. It follows from all these factors that the Commission's view that the English clauses incorporated in the contracts at issue were not of such a kind as to take them out of the category of abuse of a dominant position has been arrived at by means of a proper construction and application of Article 86 of the Treaty.

Nederlandsche Banden-Industrie Michelin NV v Commission
(Case 322/81) [1983] ECR 3461, [1985] 1 CMLR 282

Michelin NV were found to have a dominant position on the market for replacement tyres for lorries and buses. They were accused of abusing that dominant position by operating a series of abusive discounting schemes.

(b) The application of Article 86 to a system of target discounts

[70] As regards the application of Article 86 to a system of discounts conditional upon the attainment of sales targets, such as described above, it must be stated first of all that in prohibiting any abuse of a dominant position on the market in so far as it may affect trade between Member States Article 86 covers practices which are likely to affect the structure of a market where, as a direct result of the presence of the undertaking in question, competition has already been weakened and which, through recourse to methods different from those governing normal competition in products or services based on traders' performance, have the effect of hindering the maintenance or development of the level of competition still existing on the market.

[71] In the case more particularly of the grant by an undertaking in a dominant position of discounts to its customers the Court has held in its judgments of 16 December 1975 in Joined Cases 40–48/73 etc. *Cooperatieve Vereniging 'Suiker Unie' ua v EC Commission* and of 13 February 1979 in Case 85/76 *Hoffmann-La Roche v EC Commission* that in contrast to a quantity discount, which is linked solely to the volume of purchases from the manufacturer concerned, a loyalty rebate, which by offering customers financial advantages tends to prevent them from obtaining their supplies from competing manufacturers, amounts to an abuse within the meaning of Article 86 of the Treaty.

[72] As regards the system at issue in this case, which is characterised by the use of sales targets, it must be observed that this system does not amount to a mere quantity discount linked solely to the volume of goods purchased since the progressive scale of the previous year's turnover indicates only the limits within which the system applies. Michelin NV has moreover itself pointed

out that the majority of dealers who bought more than 3,000 tyres a year were in any case in the group receiving the highest rebates. On the other hand the system in question did not require dealers to enter into any exclusive dealing agreements or to obtain a specific proportion of their supplies from Michelin NV, and that this point distinguishes it from loyalty rebates of the type which the Court had to consider in its judgment of 13 February 1979 in *Hoffmann-La Roche*.

[73] In deciding whether Michelin NV abused its dominant position in applying its discount system it is therefore necessary to consider all the circumstances, particularly the criteria and rules for the grant of the discount, and to investigate whether, in providing an advantage not based on any economic service justifying it, the discount tends to remove or restrict the buyer's freedom to choose his sources of supply, to bar competitors from access to the market, to apply dissimilar conditions to equivalent transactions with other trading parties or to strengthen the dominant position by distorting competition.

NOTE: When comparing these cases, it is clear that although the discounting schemes were different in nature, the reason that they were considered as abusive was the tying effect that they had on a market already distorted by the presence of the dominant undertaking. In both cases, the undertakings operated discounting schemes that were not challenged as those schemes were linked to quantity of sales and therefore could be justified on the basis of savings made by the dominant undertaking.

British Airways v Commission
(Case C-95/04 P) [2007] ECR I-2331, [2007] 4 CMLR 22

British Airways had a reward scheme in place with certain travel agents which rewarded loyalty, including providing commission on sales of BA flight tickets, and the incentive of higher commission for improving upon sales in the same month of the previous year. The Commission found that the loyalty scheme abused BA's dominant position and BA appealed initially to the Court of First Instance, and then to the Court of Justice.

[57] Concerning, first, the plea that the Court of First Instance wrongly failed to base its argument on the criteria in subparagraph (b) of the second paragraph of Article 82 EC in assessing whether the bonus schemes at issue were abusive, the list of abusive practices contained in Article 82 EC is not exhaustive, so that the practices there mentioned are merely examples of abuses of a dominant position (see, to that effect, Case C-333/94 P *Tetra Pak* v *Commission* [1996] ECR I-5951, paragraph 37). According to consistent case-law, the list of abusive practices contained in that provision does not exhaust the methods of abusing a dominant position prohibited by the EC Treaty (Case 6/72 *Europemballage and Continental Can* v *Commission* [1973] ECR 215, paragraph 26; Joined Cases C-395/96 P and C-396/96 P *Compagnie maritime belge transports a.o.* v *Commission* [2000] ECR I-1365, paragraph 112).

[58] It follows that discounts and bonuses granted by undertakings in a dominant position may be contrary to Article 82 EC even where they do not correspond to any of the examples mentioned in the second paragraph of that article. Thus, in determining that fidelity discounts had an exclusionary effect, the Court based its argument in *Hoffmann-La Roche* and *Michelin* on Article 82 of the EEC Treaty (subsequently Article 86 of the EC Treaty, and then Article 82 EC) in its entirety, and not just on subparagraph (b) of its second paragraph. Moreover, in its judgment in Joined Cases 40/73 to 48/73, 50/73, 54/73 to 56/73, 111/73, 113/73 and 114/73 *Suiker Unie and Others* v *Commission* [1975] ECR 1663, paragraph 523, concerning fidelity rebates, the Court expressly referred to subparagraph (c) of the second paragraph of Article 86 of the EEC Treaty, according to which practices constituting abuse of a dominant position may consist, for example, in applying dissimilar conditions to equivalent transactions with other trading parties, thereby placing them at a competitive disadvantage.

[59] The plea that the Court of First Instance erred in law by not basing its argument on the criteria in subparagraph (b) of the second paragraph of Article 82 EC is therefore unfounded.

[60] Nor does it appear that the Court's assessment of the exclusionary effect of the bonus schemes in question was based on a misapplication of the case-law of the Court of Justice.

[61] In the *Hoffmann-La Roche* and *Michelin* judgments, the Court of Justice found that certain discounts granted by two undertakings in a dominant position were abusive in character.

[62] The first of those two judgments concerned discounts granted to undertakings whose business was the production or sale of vitamins, and the grant of which was, for most of the time, expressly linked to the condition that the co-contractor obtained its supplies over a given period entirely or mainly from Hoffmann-La Roche. The Court found such a discount system an abuse of a dominant position and stated that the granting of fidelity discounts in order to give the buyer an incentive to obtain its supplies exclusively from the undertaking in a dominant position was incompatible with the objective of undistorted competition within the common market (*Hoffmann-La Roche*, paragraph 90).

[63] In *Michelin*, unlike in *Hoffmann-La Roche*, Michelin's co-contractors were not obliged to obtain their supplies wholly or partially from Michelin. However, the variable annual discounts granted by that undertaking were linked to objectives in the sense that, in order to benefit from them, its co-contractors had to attain individualised sales results. In that case, the Court found a series of factors which led it to regard the discount system in question as an abuse of a dominant position. In particular, the system was based on a relatively long reference period, namely a year, its functioning was non-transparent for co-contractors, and the differences in market share between Michelin and its main competitors were significant (see, to that effect, *Michelin*, paragraphs 81 to 83).

[64] Contrary to BA's argument, it cannot be inferred from those two judgments that bonuses and discounts granted by undertakings in a dominant position are abusive only in the circumstances there described. As the Advocate General has stated in point 41 of her Opinion, the decisive factor is rather the underlying factors which have guided the previous case-law of the Court of Justice and which can also be transposed to a case such as the present.

[65] In that respect, *Michelin* is particularly relevant to the present case, since it concerns a discount system depending on the attainment of individual sales objectives which constituted neither discounts for quantity, linked exclusively to the volume of purchases, nor fidelity discounts within the meaning of the judgment in *Hoffmann-La Roche*, since the system established by Michelin did not contain any obligation on the part of resellers to obtain all or a given proportion of its supplies from the dominant undertaking.

[66] Concerning the application of Article 82 EC to a system of discounts dependent on sales objectives, paragraph 70 of the *Michelin* judgment shows that, in prohibiting the abuse of a dominant market position in so far as trade between Member States is capable of being affected, that article refers to conduct which is such as to influence the structure of a market where, as a result of the very presence of the undertaking in question, the degree of competition is already weakened and which, through recourse to methods different from those governing normal competition in products or services on the basis of the transactions of commercial operators, has the effect of hindering the maintenance of the degree of competition still existing in the market or the growth of that competition.

[67] In order to determine whether the undertaking in a dominant position has abused such a position by applying a system of discounts such as that described in paragraph 65 of this judgment, the Court has held that it is necessary to consider all the circumstances, particularly the criteria and rules governing the grant of the discount, and to investigate whether, in providing an advantage not based on any economic service justifying it, the discount tends to remove or restrict the buyer's freedom to choose his sources of supply, to bar competitors from access to the market, to apply dissimilar conditions to equivalent transactions with other trading parties or to strengthen the dominant position by distorting competition (*Michelin*, paragraph 73).

[68] It follows that in determining whether, on the part of an undertaking in a dominant position, a system of discounts or bonuses which constitute neither quantity discounts or bonuses

nor fidelity discounts or bonuses within the meaning of the judgment in *Hoffmann-La Roche* constitutes an abuse, it first has to be determined whether those discounts or bonuses can produce an exclusionary effect, that is to say whether they are capable, first, of making market entry very difficult or impossible for competitors of the undertaking in a dominant position and, secondly, of making it more difficult or impossible for its co-contractors to choose between various sources of supply or commercial partners.

[69] It then needs to be examined whether there is an objective economic justification for the discounts and bonuses granted. In accordance with the analysis carried out by the Court of First Instance in paragraphs 279 to 291 of the judgment under appeal, an undertaking is at liberty to demonstrate that its bonus system producing an exclusionary effect is economically justified.

[70] With regard to the first aspect, the case-law gives indications as to the cases in which discount or bonus schemes of an undertaking in a dominant position are not merely the expression of a particularly favourable offer on the market, but give rise to an exclusionary effect.

[71] First, an exclusionary effect may arise from goal-related discounts or bonuses, that is to say those the granting of which is linked to the attainment of sales objectives defined individually (*Michelin*, paragraphs 70 to 86).

[72] It is clear from the findings of the Court of First Instance in paragraphs 10 and 15 to 17 of the judgment under appeal that the bonus schemes at issue were drawn up by reference to individual sales objectives, since the rate of the bonuses depended on the evolution of the turnover arising from BA ticket sales by each travel agent during a given period.

[73] It is also apparent from the case-law that the commitment of co-contractors towards the undertaking in a dominant position and the pressure exerted upon them may be particularly strong where a discount or bonus does not relate solely to the growth in turnover in relation to purchases or sales of products of that undertaking made by those co-contractors during the period under consideration, but extends also to the whole of the turnover relating to those purchases or sales. In that way, relatively modest variations—whether upwards or downwards—in the turnover figures relating to the products of the dominant undertaking have disproportionate effects on co-contractors (see, to that effect, *Michelin*, paragraph 81).

[74] The Court of First Instance found that the bonus schemes at issue gave rise to a similar situation. Attainment of the sales progression objectives gave rise to an increase in the commission paid on all BA tickets sold by the travel agent concerned, and not just on those sold after those objectives had been attained (paragraph 23 of the judgment under appeal). It could therefore be of decisive importance for the commission income of a travel agent as a whole whether or not he sold a few extra BA tickets after achieving a certain turnover (paragraphs 29 and 30 of the grounds for the Commission's decision, reproduced in paragraph 23 of the judgment under appeal). The Court of First Instance, which describes that characteristic and its consequences in paragraphs 272 and 273 of the judgment under appeal, states that the progressive nature of the increased commission rates had a 'very noticeable effect at the margin' and emphasises the radical effects which a small reduction in sales of BA tickets could have on the rates of performance-related bonus.

[75] Finally, the Court took the view that the pressure exerted on resellers by an undertaking in a dominant position which granted bonuses with those characteristics is further strengthened where that undertaking holds a very much larger market share than its competitors (see, to that effect, *Michelin*, paragraph 82). It held that, in those circumstances, it is particularly difficult for competitors of that undertaking to outbid it in the face of discounts or bonuses based on overall sales volume. By reason of its significantly higher market share, the undertaking in a dominant position generally constitutes an unavoidable business partner in the market. Most often, discounts or bonuses granted by such an undertaking on the basis of overall turnover largely take precedence in absolute terms, even over more generous offers of its competitors. In order to attract the co-contractors of the undertaking in a dominant position, or to receive a sufficient volume of orders from them, those competitors would have to offer them significantly higher rates of discount or bonus.

[76] In the present case, the Court of First Instance held in paragraph 277 of the judgment under appeal that BA's market share was significantly higher than that of its five main competitors in the United Kingdom. It concluded, in paragraph 278 of that judgment, that the rival airlines were not

in a position to grant travel agents the same advantages as BA, since they were not capable of attaining in the United Kingdom a level of revenue capable of constituting a sufficiently broad financial base to allow them effectively to establish a reward scheme similar to BA's (paragraph 278 of the judgment under appeal).

[77] Therefore, the Court of First Instance was right to examine, in paragraphs 270 to 278 of the judgment under appeal, whether the bonus schemes at issue had a fidelity-building effect capable of producing an exclusionary effect.

NOTE: The Court of Justice endorsed the traditional approach to discounts and rebates under Article 82 EC, yet the Commission has highlighted this area as one requiring a significant shift towards an effects-based approach, and characterizes rebates as being either 'conditional' or 'unconditional', thereby moving away from the emphasis on 'fidelity' and 'quantity'.

Commission Communication: Guidance on the Commission's enforcement priorities in applying Article 82 EC Treaty to abusive exclusionary conduct by dominant undertakings
OJ, 2009, C45/7, paras 37–41, 46 [footnotes omitted]

(b) *Conditional rebates*

37. Conditional rebates are rebates granted to customers to reward them for a particular form of purchasing behaviour. The usual nature of a conditional rebate is that the customer is given a rebate if its purchases over a defined reference period exceed a certain threshold, the rebate being granted either on all purchases (retroactive rebates) or only on those made in excess of those required to achieve the threshold (incremental rebates). Conditional rebates are not an uncommon practice. Undertakings may offer such rebates in order to attract more demand, and as such they may stimulate demand and benefit consumers. However, such rebates—when granted by a dominant undertaking—can also have actual or potential foreclosure effects similar to exclusive purchasing obligations. Conditional rebates can have such effects without necessarily entailing a sacrifice for the dominant undertaking.

38. In addition to the factors already mentioned in paragraph 20, the following factors are of particular importance to the Commission in determining whether a given system of conditional rebates is liable to result in anti-competitive foreclosure and, consequently, will be part of the Commission's enforcement priorities.

39. As with exclusive purchasing obligations, the likelihood of anti-competitive foreclosure is higher where competitors are not able to compete on equal terms for the entire demand of each individual customer. A conditional rebate granted by a dominant undertaking may enable it to use the 'non contestable' portion of the demand of each customer (that is to say, the amount that would be purchased by the customer from the dominant undertaking in any event) as leverage to decrease the price to be paid for the 'contestable' portion of demand (that is to say, the amount for which the customer may prefer and be able to find substitutes).

40. In general terms, retroactive rebates may foreclose the market significantly, as they may make it less attractive for customers to switch small amounts of demand to an alternative supplier, if this would lead to loss of the retroactive rebates. The potential foreclosing effect of retroactive rebates is in principle strongest on the last purchased unit of the product before the threshold is exceeded. However, what is in the Commission's view relevant for an assessment of the loyalty enhancing effect of a rebate is not simply the effect on competition to provide the last individual unit, but the foreclosing effect of the rebate system on (actual or potential) competitors of the dominant supplier. The higher the rebate as a percentage of the total price and the higher the threshold, the greater the inducement below the threshold and, therefore, the stronger the likely foreclosure of actual or potential competitors.

41. When applying the methodology explained in paragraphs 23 to 27, the Commission intends to investigate, to the extent that the data are available and reliable, whether the rebate system is

capable of hindering expansion or entry even by competitors that are equally efficient by making it more difficult for them to supply part of the requirements of individual customers. In this context the Commission will estimate what price a competitor would have to offer in order to compensate the customer for the loss of the conditional rebate if the latter would switch part of its demand ('the relevant range') away from the dominant undertaking. The effective price that the competitor will have to match is not the average price of the dominant undertaking, but the normal (list) price less the rebate the customer loses by switching, calculated over the relevant range of sales and in the relevant period of time. The Commission will take into account the margin of error that may be caused by the uncertainties inherent in this kind of analysis.

...

(c) Efficiencies

46. Provided that the conditions set out in Section III D are fulfilled, the Commission will consider claims by dominant undertakings that rebate systems achieve cost or other advantages which are passed on to customers. Transaction-related cost advantages are often more likely to be achieved with standardised volume targets than with individualized volume targets. Similarly, incremental rebate schemes are in general more likely to give resellers an incentive to produce and resell a higher volume than retroactive rebate schemes. Under the same conditions, the Commission will consider evidence demonstrating that exclusive dealing arrangements result in advantages to particular customers if those arrangements are necessary for the dominant undertaking to make certain relationship specific investments in order to be able to supply those customers.

NOTE: The friction between the Commission's preferred approach and the established case law of the Community Courts is discussed in Faella, G., 'The antitrust assessment of loyalty discounts and rebates' (2008) J Comp Law & Econ 375.

■ QUESTION

When is offering a discount to a good customer anti-competitive?

(d) Refusal to supply and essential facilities doctrine

As a dominant undertaking is, by definition, in a powerful position with regard to a particular product it is of concern to those who desire such a product that they can gain supplies from the dominant undertaking. Thus, a refusal to supply a potential customer can be problematic in relation to dominant undertakings. A complication in this area stems from the basic legal tenet that an undertaking may choose to deal with any customers in the manner of their choosing. To compel an undertaking to trade with another is a breach of their basic freedom of contract. It has been vital for competition law to set out the exceptional circumstances in which the law will interfere with an undertaking's basic commercial freedom.

Istituto Chemioterapico Italiano SpA and Commercial Solvents Corporation v EC Commission
(Joined Cases 6–7/73) [1974] ECR 223, [1974] 1 CMLR 309

Istituto and Commercial Solvents were the dominant producers of a number of intermediate chemical products, including 'nitropropane' and 'aminobutanol'. Those chemicals were used for the manufacture of 'ethambutol', used as an anti-tuberculosis drug. A customer of Commercial Solvents, Zoja SpA, used the intermediary products to produce ethambutol. At the end of 1970 Zoja attempted to source further supplies of the intermediary but Commercial Solvents made it clear that none would be available.

[23] The applicants state that they ought not to be held responsible for ceasing to supply aminobutanol to Zoja for this was due to the fact that in the spring of 1970 Zoja itself informed Istituto that it was cancelling the purchase of large quantities of aminobutanol which had been provided for in a contract then in force between Istituto and Zoja. When at the end of 1970 Zoja again contacted Istituto to obtain this product, the latter was obliged to reply, after consulting Commercial Solvents Corp., that in the meantime Commercial Solvents Corp. had changed its commercial policy and that the product was no longer available. The change of policy by Commercial Solvents Corp. was, they claim, inspired by a legitimate consideration of the advantage that would accrue to it of expanding its production to include the manufacture of finished products and not limiting itself to that of raw material or intermediary products. In pursuance of this policy it decided to improve its product and no longer to supply aminobutanol save in respect of commitments already entered into by its distributors.

[24] It appears from the documents and from the hearing that the suppliers of raw material are limited, as regards the EEC, to Istituto, which, as stated in the claim by Commercial Solvents Corp., started in 1968 to develop its own specialities based on ethambutol, and in November 1969 obtained the approval of the Italian government necessary for the manufacture and in 1970 started manufacturing its own specialities. When Zoja sought to obtain further supplies of aminobutanol, it received a negative reply. Commercial Solvents Corp. had decided to limit, if not completely to cease, the supply of nitropropane and aminobutanol to certain parties in order to facilitate its own access to the market for the derivatives.

[25] However, an undertaking being in a dominant position as regards the production of raw material and therefore able to control the supply to manufacturers of derivatives cannot, just because it decides to start manufacturing these derivatives (in competition with its former customers), act in such a way as to eliminate their competition which, in the case in question, would have amounted to eliminating one of the principal manufacturers of ethambutol in the Common Market. Since such conduct is contrary to the objectives expressed in Article 3(f) of the Treaty and set out in greater detail in Articles 85 and 86, it follows that an undertaking which has a dominant position in the market in raw materials and which, with the object of reserving such raw material for manufacturing its own derivatives, refuses to supply a customer, which is itself a manufacturer of these derivatives, and therefore risks eliminating all competition on the part of this customer, is abusing its dominant position within the meaning of Article 86. In this context it does not matter that the undertaking ceased to supply in the spring of 1970 because of the cancellation of the purchases by Zoja, because it appears from the applicants' own statement that, when the supplies provided for in the contract had been completed, the sale of aminobutanol would have stopped in any case.

NOTE: While the judgment in *Commercial Solvents* made it clear that a refusal to supply a customer could be abusive, it was an extreme case whereby the refusal would result in the de facto elimination of a major competitor in a downstream market. One of the major questions raised by the judgment was the extent of this obligation to supply customers and competitors. Did it only cover existing customers, or could it be extended to supplying new customers to create a competitor?

Particular problems exist when a dominant undertaking can protect its position through the exclusivity granted to it via intellectual property rights. There is tension in the relationship between competition law and IP law. Competition law attempts to deal with the problems created by an undertaking's power over the market where there are no other providers of a product; IP law attempts to reward innovation by ensuring that an innovator can retain exclusivity for a period of time. If an innovator is forced to provide protected material to competitors surely that would remove the reward that their exclusivity was supposed to create, and over time would remove the incentives to innovate in the first place.

Radio Telefís Eireann and Independent Television
Publications Limited v Commission
(Joined Cases C-241–242/91 P) [1995] ECR I-743, [1995] 4 CMLR 718

Most households in Ireland and a sizeable minority in Northern Ireland can receive television programmes broadcast by RTE, ITV, and BBC. No comprehensive weekly television guide was available on the market in Ireland or in Northern Ireland. Each television station published a television guide covering its own programmes and claimed, under Irish and UK legislation, copyright protection for its own weekly programme listings in order to prevent their reproduction by third parties. The copyright holders provided their programme schedules free of charge, on request, to daily and periodical newspapers, accompanied by a licence for which no charge was made, setting out the conditions under which that information could be reproduced. Daily listings could thus be published in the press. Magill TV Guide Ltd attempted to publish a comprehensive weekly television guide but was prevented from doing so by RTE, ITP, and the BBC, which obtained injunctions prohibiting publication of weekly television listings. Magill lodged a complaint with the Commission, which adopted a decision against RTE, ITP, and the BBC. In that decision the Commission found that there had been a breach of Article 82 EC and ordered the three organizations to put an end to that breach.

[48] With regard to the issue of abuse, the arguments of the appellants and IPO wrongly presuppose that where the conduct of an undertaking in a dominant position consist of the exercise of a right classified by national law as 'copyright', such conduct can never be reviewed in relation to Article 86 of the Treaty.

[49] Admittedly, in the absence of Community standardisation or harmonisation of laws, determination of the conditions and procedures for granting protection of an intellectual property right is a matter for national rules. Further, the exclusive right of reproduction forms part of the author's rights, so that refusal to grant a licence, even if it is the act of an undertaking holding a dominant position, cannot in itself constitute abuse of a dominant position. (See *Volvo* v *Veng*, above, at paras [7] and [8].)

[50] However, it is also clear from that judgment (at para. 9) that the exercise of an exclusive right by the proprietor may, in exceptional circumstances, involve abusive conduct.

[51] In the present case, the conduct objected to is the appellants' reliance on copyright conferred by national legislation so as to prevent Magill—or any other undertaking having the same intention—from publishing on a weekly basis information (channel, day, time and title of programmes) together with commentaries and pictures obtained independently of the appellants.

[52] Among the circumstances taken into account by the Court of First Instance in concluding that such conduct was abusive was, first, the fact that there was, according to the findings of the Court of First Instance, no actual or potential substitute for a weekly television guide offering information on the programmes for the week ahead. On this point, the Court of First Instance confirmed the Commission's finding that the complete lists of programmes for a 24-hour period—and for a 48-hour period at weekends and before public holidays—published in certain daily and Sunday newspapers, and the television sections of certain magazines covering, in addition, 'highlights' of the week's programmes, were only to a limited extent substitutable for advance information to viewers on all the week's programmes. Only weekly television guides containing comprehensive listings for the week ahead would enable users to decide in advance which programmes they wished to follow and arrange their leisure activities for the week accordingly. The Court of First Instance also established that there was a specific, constant and regular potential demand on the part of consumers (see the *RTE* judgment, paragraph [62], and the *ITP* judgment, paragraph [48]).

[53] Thus the appellants—who were, by force of circumstance, the only sources of the basic information on programme scheduling which is the indispensable raw material for compiling a weekly television guide—gave viewers wishing to obtain information on the choice of programmes for the week ahead no choice but to buy the weekly guides for each station and draw from each of them the information they needed to make comparisons.

[54] The appellants' refusal to provide basic information by relying on national copyright provisions thus prevented the appearance of a new product, a comprehensive weekly guide to television programmes, which the appellants did not offer and for which there was a potential consumer demand. Such refusal constitutes an abuse under heading (b) of the second paragraph of Article 86 of the Treaty.

[55] Second, there was no justification for such refusal either in the activity of television broadcasting or in that of publishing television magazines (*RTE* judgment, paragraph [73], and *ITP* judgment, paragraph [58]).

[56] Third, and finally, as the Court of First Instance also held, the appellants, by their conduct, reserved to themselves the secondary market of weekly television guides by excluding all competition on that market (see 6/73 and 7/73, *Commercial Solvents* v *EC Commission* [1974] ECR 223, [1974] 1 CMLR 309, at para. [25]) since they denied access to the basic information which is the raw material indispensable for the compilation of such a guide.

[57] In the light of all those circumstances, the Court of First Instance did not err in law in holding that the appellants' conduct was an abuse of a dominant position within the meaning of Article 86 of the Treaty.

[58] It follows that the plea in law alleging misapplication by the Court of First Instance of the concept of abuse of a dominant position must be dismissed as unfounded.

NOTE: The *Magill* judgment, as this series of litigation is sometimes known, made it clear that the Court may require an undertaking to supply a new customer with a product or service, especially when that refusal to supply would stop the creation of a new product for which there is a demand, or deserve a secondary market to the supplier. But the Court also made clear this was an exceptional circumstance, particularly because of the complications introduced because the material in question was protected by copyright. Is the position the same where there are no IP rights in question?

Oscar Bronner GmbH & Co KG v *Mediaprint Zeitungs-und Zeitschriftenverlag GmbH & Co KG*
(Case C-7/97) [1998] ECR I-7791, [1999] 4 CMLR 112

Oscar Bronner published a daily newspaper in Austria. Its share of the market was 3.6 per cent of circulation. Mediaprint published two newspapers that had a combined market share of 46.8 per cent of circulation. In the domestic courts Bronner sought an order requiring Mediaprint to allow Bronner access to its nationwide home-delivery service for daily newspapers against payment of reasonable remuneration. Mediaprint refused such access to their network, which was the only nationwide network in Austria. The domestic court referred a number of questions to the Court of Justice under Article 234 EC.

[23] In its first question, the national court effectively asks whether the refusal by a press undertaking which holds a very large share of the daily newspaper market in a Member State and operates the only nationwide newspaper home-delivery scheme in that Member State to allow the publisher of a rival newspaper, which by reason of its small circulation is unable either alone or in co-operation with other publishers to set up and operate its own home-delivery scheme in economically reasonable conditions, to have access to that scheme for appropriate remuneration constitutes the abuse of a dominant position within the meaning of Article 86 of the Treaty.

[24] In that respect, Oscar Bronner argues that the supply of services consisting in the home delivery of daily newspapers constitutes a separate market, inasmuch as that service is normally offered and requested separately from other services. Oscar Bronner also argues that, under the doctrine of 'essential facilities' as established by the Court of Justice in Joined Cases, C 241 & 242/91 P, *RTE and ITP* v *EC Commission* ([1995] ECR I-743; [1995] 4 CMLR 418) (the 'Magill' judgment'), the service performed by placing a facility at the disposal of others and that supplied by using that facility in principle constitute separate markets. It therefore maintains that, as the owner of such an 'essential facility', in this case the only economically viable home-delivery scheme existing in Austria on a national scale, Mediaprint is obliged to allow access to the scheme by competing products on market conditions and at market prices.

[25] Oscar Bronner also refers in this context to Joined Cases 6 and 7/73, *Commercial Solvents* v *EC Commission*, ([1974] ECR 223; [1974] 1 CMLR 309, para. [25]) which, in its submission, demonstrates that the refusal by an undertaking in a dominant position to supply undertakings immediately down-stream is lawful only if objectively justifed. Referring to the judgment of the Court of Justice in Case 311/84, *CBEM* v *CLT and IPB*, ([1985] ECR 3261; [1986] 2 CMLR 558) in which it held that an abuse within the meaning of Article 86 is committed where, without any objective necessity, an undertaking hold-ing a dominant position on a particular market reserves to itself or to an undertaking belonging to the same group an ancillary activity which might be carried out by another undertaking as part of its activities on a neighbouring but separate market, with the possibility of eliminating all competition from such undertaking, Oscar Bronner maintains that that consideration applies equally to the case of an undertaking holding a dominant position in the market for a given supply of services, which is indispensable for the activity of another undertaking in a different market.

[26] Mediaprint objects that, in principle, undertakings in a dominant position are also entitled to the freedom to arrange their own affairs, in that they are normally entitled to decide freely to whom they wish to offer their services and, in particular, to whom they wish to allow access to their own facilities. Thus, as the Court expressly held in *Magill*, an obligation to contract, to which an undertaking holding a dominant position would be subject, can be based on Article 86 of the Treaty only in exceptional circumstances.

[27] In Mediaprint's submission, the judgments in *Commercial Solvents* v *EC Commission and CBEM*, (cited above) show that such exceptional circumstances exist only if the dominant under-taking's refusal to supply is likely to eliminate all competition in a downstream market, which is not the case in the main proceedings, where, in parallel with home delivery, other distribution systems enable Oscar Bronner to sell its daily newspapers in Austria.

[28] Mediaprint adds that, even if such exceptional circumstances did exist, a dominant under-taking's refusal to contract is not abusive if it is objectively justified. That would be the case in the main proceedings if the inclusion of Der Standard were likely to compromise the functioning of Mediaprint's home-delivery scheme or were to be shown to be impossible for reasons relating to the capacity of that scheme.

[29] The Commission points out that it is for the national court to assess whether the condi-tions for applying Article 86 of the Treaty are met, and maintains that it is only if a separate market in home-delivery schemes exists and Mediaprint holds a dominant position in that market that it needs to be examined whether its refusal to include Oscar Bronner in that network constitutes an abuse.

. . .

[37] Finally it would need to be determined whether the refusal by the owner of the only nationwide home-delivery scheme in the territory of a Member State, which uses that scheme to distribute its own daily newspapers, to allow the publisher of a rival daily newspaper access to it constitutes an abuse of a dominant position within the meaning of Article 86 of the Treaty, on the ground that such refusal deprives that competitor of a means of distribution judged essential for the sale of its newspaper.

[38] Although in *Commercial Solvents* v *EC Commission* and *CBEM*, (cited above) the Court of Justice held the refusal by an undertaking holding a dominant position in a given market to supply

an undertaking with which it was in competition in a neighbouring market with raw materials (*Commercial Solvents* v *EC Commission*, para. [25]) and services (*CBEM*, para. [26]) respectively, which were indispensable to carrying on the rival's business, to constitute an abuse, it should be noted, first, that the Court did so to the extent that the conduct in question was likely to eliminate all competition on the part of that undertaking.

[39] Secondly, in *Magill*, at paras [49] and [50], the Court held that refusal by the owner of an intellectual property right to grant a licence, even if it is the act of an undertaking holding a dominant position, cannot in itself constitute abuse of a dominant position, but that the exercise of an exclusive right by the proprietor may, in exceptional circumstances, involve an abuse.

[40] In *Magill*, the Court found such exceptional circumstances in the fact that the refusal in question concerned a product (information on the weekly schedules of certain television channels) the supply of which was indispensable for carrying on the business in question (the publishing of a general television guide), in that, without that information, the person wishing to produce such a guide would find it impossible to publish it and offer it for sale, (para. [53]) the fact that such refusal prevented the appearance of a new product for which there was a potential consumer demand, (para. [54]) the fact that it was not justified by objective considerations, (para. [55]) and that it was likely to exclude all competition in the secondary market of television guides (para. [56]).

[41] Therefore, even if that case law on the exercise of an intellectual property right were applicable to the exercise of any property right whatever, it would still be necessary, for the *Magill* judgment to be effectively relied upon in order to plead the existence of an abuse within the meaning of Article 86 of the Treaty in a situation such as that which forms the subject-matter of the first question, not only that the refusal of the service comprised in home delivery be likely to eliminate all competition in the daily newspaper market on the part of the person requesting the service and that such refusal be incapable of being objectively justified, but also that the service in itself be indispensable to carrying on that person's business, inasmuch as there is no actual or potential substitute in existence for that home-delivery scheme.

[42] That is certainly not the case even if, as in the case which is the subject of the main proceedings, there is only one nationwide home-delivery scheme in the territory of a Member State and, moreover, the owner of that scheme holds a dominant position in the market for services constituted by that scheme or of which it forms part.

[43] In the first place, it is undisputed that other methods of distributing daily newspapers, such as by post and through sale in shops and at kiosks, even though they may be less advantageous for the distribution of certain newspapers, exist and are used by the publishers of those daily newspapers.

[44] Moreover, it does not appear that there are any technical, legal or even economic obstacles capable of making it impossible, or even unreasonably difficult, for any other publishers of daily newspapers to establish, alone or in cooperation with other publishers, its own nationwide home-delivery scheme and use it to distribute its own daily newspapers.

[45] It should be emphasised in that respect that, in order to demonstrate that the creation of such a system is not a realistic potential alternative and that access to the existing system is therefore indispensable, it is not enough to argue that it is not economically viable by reason of the small circulation of the daily newspaper or newspapers to be distributed.

[46] For such access to be capable of being regarded as indispensable, it would be necessary at the very least to establish, as the Advocate General has pointed out at paragraph 68 of his Opinion, that it is not economically viable to create a second home-delivery scheme for the distribution of daily newspapers with a circulation comparable to that of the daily newspapers distributed by the existing scheme.

[47] In the light of the foregoing considerations, the answer to the first question must be that the refusal by a press undertaking which holds a very large share of the daily newspaper market in a Member State and operates the only nationwide newspaper home-delivery scheme in that Member State to allow the publisher of a rival newspaper, which by reason of its small circulation is unable either alone or in cooperation with other publishers to set up and operate its

own home-delivery scheme in economically reasonable conditions, to have access to that scheme for appropriate remuneration does not constitute abuse of a dominant position within the meaning of Article 86 of the Treaty.

NOTE: *Oscar Bronner* settled a number of questions regarding the extent of the 'essential facilities' doctrine whereby a competitor should be given access to a facility owned and operated by a dominant undertaking. It restricts the doctrine to a limited number of circumstances where it is not practicable to replicate the facility. This would tend to limit its application to situations where there is a 'natural' monopoly, in that the market will only bear one such facility and it does not make economic sense to require a competitor to invest in replicating that which is currently operated by the dominant undertaking.

The situation in which an 'essential facility' can become a problem is explained by Ridyard.

Ridyard, D., 'Essential Facilities and the Obligation to Supply Competitors Under the UK and EC Competition Law'

(1996) 17(8) ECLR 438, pp. 438–40 [footnotes omitted]

Introduction to the Essential Facilities Doctrine

In the *Sealink* decision, the Commission describes an essential facility as follows: 'a facility or infrastructure, without access to which competitors cannot provide services to their customers'. The decision goes on to assert that refusal to grant access to an essential facility without 'objective justification', or the granting of access to that facility on 'discriminatory terms' represents an infringement of Article 86. This suggests that there are two central issues to the evaluation of essential facilities problems:

— First, what are the circumstances in which an essential facility can be said to exist?
— Second, where an essential facility has been identified, what are the terms on which access to that facility by competitors should be granted?

Although there are many cases involving essential facility issues, it is remarkable how little light these cases shed on these two central questions. In a review of the US cases, Areeda sums up the problem with the essential facilities doctrine as follows:

You will not find any case that provides a consistent rationale for the doctrine that explores the social costs and benefits of the administration costs of requiring the creator of an asset to share it with a rival. It is less a doctrine than an epithet indicating some exceptions to the right to keep one's creations to oneself, but not telling us what those exceptions are.

Areeda's conclusion is that there is a need for a 'limiting principle' to inject some discipline into the application of essential facilities arguments. A similar conclusion can readily be reached on

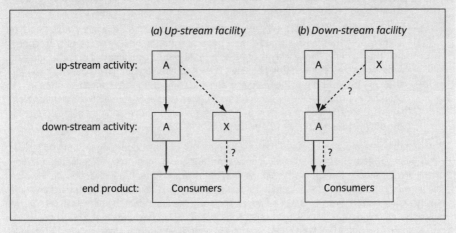

Figure 1 The Essential Facilities Problem

the UK and EC cases. Before discussing some of these cases in more detail, it may first be helpful to describe the essential facilities dilemma in terms of a simplified model into which most cases can be made to fit.

The market situation underlying the essential facilities problem is one involving two related activities, both of which form components of the product that is purchased by the end consumer. For convenience, these two components can be characterised as 'up-stream' and 'down-stream' activities, such as manufacture and distribution. The essential facilities problem might arise at either the up-stream or down-stream levels, and can be depicted as shown in Figure 1.

In the scenario of the up-stream facility, Firm A supplies consumers with its product, which is a combination or 'bundle' of the up-stream and down-stream activities. The question is, should firm X, which has a capability to perform the down-stream activity only, have access to the up-stream facility of firm A in order to supply consumers as well? Conceptually similar considerations apply in the case of the down-stream facility.

Since most products purchased by consumers go through a number of separate processing stages, almost any product market could in principle become subject to this kind of dispute. This explains why the concept of essential facility obligations is so threatening to business, and underlines the need for some form of discipline (or Areeda's 'limiting principle') to control its application. To illustrate, the up-stream/down-stream dichotomy depicted in Figure 1 can apply in the following cases:

'Up-stream'	'Down-stream'
Transport infrastructure (eg rail, port, airport)	Transport operator (eg train, ferry, airline)
Pipeline/Wire	Supply of water, gas, electricity, telephone services through pipe/wire
Manufacture	Retail/distribution
R & D	Manufacture
Raw material	Processing
Manufacture	Marketing/branding
Spare parts	Maintenance service

Whatever the precise context of the case, the basic arguments of both sides in an essential facilities case (firm 'X' the complainant, firm 'A' the defendant as depicted in Figure 1) are along the following lines:

— The complainant (firm X) typically argues that A's refusal to deal prevents firm X from entering the market, and that this reduces consumer choice, protects firm A's down-stream activity from competition and thus keeps prices for the product as a whole too high. It further argues that the costs of X establishing its own up-stream facility as an alternative to that of firm A would be prohibitive and would cancel out the potential advantages it is able to offer to consumers.

— The defendant (firm A) typically argues that there are intrinsic efficiency advantages in keeping both the up-stream and down-stream activities in-house ('economies of scope'); that the 'benefits' firm X claims to be able to deliver to consumers if only it could gain access to A's up-stream facility belong to firm A as a reward for having built up a sought-after up-stream facility in the first place; and that competition and consumer interests are adequately protected by the fact that firm A faces (actual or potential) competition from firms B, C, and D (not shown in Figure 1) who supply alternative 'bundles' of the up-stream and down-stream activities to consumers.

Without investigating the facts of the case, the merits of these opposing arguments cannot safely be prejudged. The inherent conflict between static and dynamic incentives for competition can clearly be seen in the above characterisation of the arguments. It will invariably be the case that denying supply to the complainant will stifle a potential short-term gain to consumers (in price, quality and/or choice terms). Equally, however, requiring the defendant to share its assets with a down-stream competitor will invariably affect the incentives and rewards in the market, and will thus to some extent dull the motivation for others to undertake similar investments in the future.'

NOTE: *Oscar Bronner* is seen by many as being the European Court's attempt to strike that balance by setting out the limited circumstances in which a dominant undertaking will be required to open up its 'facility' to competitors. Even though *Oscar Bronner* settles a number of important issues it still left a number of important issues unanswered, as Bergman explains.

Bergman, M.A., 'The Bronner Case—A Turning Point for the Essential Facilities Doctrine'

(2000) 21(2) ECLR 59, p. 61 [footnotes omitted]

A more restrictive view

If the new criterion set out in the *Bronner* case were to be used in other cases, without consideration of the specific circumstances, a Catch-22 situation may result. The criterion does not explicitly take into consideration that it may be impossible for the competitor to attain a market share of 50 per cent, even if in principle it would be possible to create and operate the required facility once that market share is reached. Furthermore, if this new criterion is applied generally, this will severely restrict the applicability of the essential facilities doctrine, i.e. to markets where only one firm has the possibility to be viable.

With such an interpretation, the essential facilities doctrine cannot be used to facilitate entry into markets with limited competition, as entry is only possible if more than one firm is expected to be economically viable in the long run. Instead, the doctrine will only be applicable to markets in which two or more firms can never be economically viable on their own unless the essential facilities doctrine is applied. Such markets are sometimes referred to as natural monopolies, although a more correct denomination may be 'inevitable monopolies'. In such markets, a second firm can only thrive on an artificial habitat created by the application of the doctrine. The effect of the doctrine is hence to serve as an instrument for indirect price regulation of markets that are 'inevitable monopolies'. In particular, the doctrine cannot create or preserve a market structure that will in turn stimulate competition and efficiency. The price-regulatory effect will follow because competitors will be granted access to the facility at non-discriminatory terms, which in turn will limit the dominant firm's ability to exploit customers on the related market. To favour the method of indirect price regulation over the method of creating structural conditions for competition stands in stark contrast to predominant views on competition policy. Normally, measures that prevent a firm from strengthening its dominance, e.g. by eliminating its rivals with predatory measures, are preferred over measures that prevent a firm from exploiting its customers, e.g. by abusively high prices.

That the essential facilities doctrine can only be applied towards 'inevitable monopolies' is not in accordance with earlier cases that are seen as applications of the doctrine, e.g. *Commercial Solvents*, and cases concerning airlines' computerised booking systems (so-called CRSs), e.g. *Sabena*. When it comes to CRSs, there do indeed exist a number of such systems. It appears unlikely that the chemical compound that Commercial Solvents produced could not even theoretically be profitably produced by more than one firm. When the doctrine has been applied and analysed earlier, it has been stressed that the prerequisite must not be that it is physically impossible for a competing firm to duplicate the facility, but that it should be economically unfeasible for competing firms. The *Bronner* case must also be interpreted along these lines. The statements of the Court could be read to imply that it must be economically impossible for every firm to duplicate the facility starting from any market share—unless it could simply replace the incumbent firm. In earlier cases, in contrast, it appears sometimes to have been sufficient that it was impossible for the concerned firm. A more reasonable interpretation is that the former condition was relevant in this particular case, although not necessarily in every case that concerns the essential facilities doctrine. Even so, the (preliminary) ruling has to some extent made the conditions for applying the doctrine stricter.

NOTE: It is clear that the concept of refusal to supply covers a wide range of conduct that can be abusive. Cases discussed above illustrate that refusals to supply both existing and new customers can be abusive, as well as a refusal to license intellectual property rights and refusal to grant access to an 'essential facility' in exceptional cases. One further circumstance of abuse is worthy of particular reference and has proven particularly controversial with the US antitrust authorities: the refusal to provide interface information.

Microsoft v *Commission*

(Case T-204/04) [2007] ECR II-3601, [2007] 5 CMLR 11

Microsoft was found to have abused the dominant position it held on the two operating system markets (the client PC market and work group server market). The prevalence of the Windows operating system afforded Mircosoft a very high degree of dominance, which it abused by refusing to supply its competitors with 'interoperability information' enabling the development of alternative software products in downstream markets. The Commission fined Mircosoft €497,196,304 for this conduct as well as abusively tying its media player with the purchase of the operating system, and Microsoft appealed the Decision to the Court of First Instance.

[317] At the hearing, the Commission, questioned on this issue by the Court, confirmed that it had considered in the contested decision that Microsoft's conduct presented three characteristics which allowed it to be characterised as abusive. The first consists in the fact that the information which Microsoft refuses to disclose to its competitors relates to interoperability in the software industry, a matter to which the Community legislature attaches particular importance. The second characteristic lies in the fact that Microsoft uses its extraordinary power on the client PC operating systems market to eliminate competition on the adjacent work group server operating systems market. The third characteristic is that the conduct in question involves disruption of previous levels of supply.

...

[331] It follows from the case-law cited above that the refusal by an undertaking holding a dominant position to license a third party to use a product covered by an intellectual property right cannot in itself constitute an abuse of a dominant position within the meaning of Article 82 EC. It is only in exceptional circumstances that the exercise of the exclusive right by the owner of the intellectual property right may give rise to such an abuse.

[332] It also follows from that case-law that the following circumstances, in particular, must be considered to be exceptional:
- – in the first place, the refusal relates to a product or service indispensable to the exercise of a particular activity on a neighbouring market;
- – in the second place, the refusal is of such a kind as to exclude any effective competition on that neighbouring market;
- – in the third place, the refusal prevents the appearance of a new product for which there is potential consumer demand.

[333] Once it is established that such circumstances are present, the refusal by the holder of a dominant position to grant a licence may infringe Article 82 EC unless the refusal is objectively justified.

[334] The Court notes that the circumstance that the refusal prevents the appearance of a new product for which there is potential consumer demand is found only in the case-law on the exercise of an intellectual property right.

[335] Finally, it is appropriate to add that, in order that a refusal to give access to a product or service indispensable to the exercise of a particular activity may be considered abusive, it is necessary to distinguish two markets, namely, a market constituted by that product or service and on which the undertaking refusing to supply holds a dominant position and a neighbouring market on which the product or service is used in the manufacture of another product or for the supply of another service. The fact that the indispensable product or service is not marketed separately does not exclude from the outset the possibility of identifying a separate market (see, to that effect, *IMS Health*, paragraph 107 above, paragraph 43). Thus, the Court of Justice held, at paragraph 44 of *IMS Health*, paragraph 107 above, that it was sufficient that a potential market or even a hypothetical

market could be identified and that such was the case where the products or services were indispensable to the conduct of a particular business activity and where there was an actual demand for them on the part of undertakings which sought to carry on that business. The Court of Justice concluded at the following paragraph of the judgment that it was decisive that two different stages of production were identified and that they were interconnected in that the upstream product was indispensable for supply of the downstream product.

...

[369] As already pointed out at paragraph 207 above, the Commission adopted a two-stage approach in determining whether the information at issue was indispensable, in that, first of all, it considered what degree of interoperability with the Windows domain architecture non-Microsoft work group server operating systems must achieve in order for its competitors to be able to remain viably on the market and, second, it appraised whether the interoperability that Microsoft refused to disclose was indispensable to the attainment of that degree of interoperability.

[370] Microsoft claims that that reasoning is incorrect in law and in fact.

The alleged error of law

[371] Microsoft's arguments concerning the Commission's supposed error of law relate to the first stage of its reasoning.

[372] Microsoft takes issue first of all with the degree of interoperability required by the Commission in the present case: it contends, in substance, that the Commission's position effectively requires that its competitors' work group server operating systems be able to communicate with Windows client PC and server operating systems in exactly the same way as Windows server operating systems do. The applicant reiterates that that degree of interoperability implies virtual identity between its systems and its competitors' systems.

[373] Those assertions must be rejected.

[374] The Court has already defined, at paragraphs 207 to 245 above, the degree of interoperability which the Commission required in the contested decision. The Court observed, in particular, that the Commission had concluded that, in order to be able to compete viably with Windows work group server operating systems, competitors' operating systems must be able to interoperate with the Windows domain architecture on an equal footing with those Windows systems (see paragraph 230 above). The Court has held that interoperability, as thus envisaged by the Commission, had two indissociable components, client/server interoperability and server/server interoperability and that it implied in particular that a server running a non-Microsoft work group server operating system could act as domain controller within a Windows domain using Active Directory and, consequently, would be able to participate in the multimaster replication mechanism with the other domain controllers (see paragraphs 231 and 233 above).

[375] The Court has also already found that, contrary to Microsoft's contention, by requiring such a degree of interoperability the Commission did not intend that non-Microsoft work group server operating systems should function in every respect as a Windows work group server operating system and, accordingly, that the applicant's competitors could develop work group server operating systems that were identical, or even 'virtually identical', to the applicant's (see paragraphs 234 to 242 above).

...

[619] The Commission had even more reason to conclude that there was a risk that competition would be eliminated on that market because the market has certain features which are likely to discourage organisations which have already taken up Windows for their work group servers from migrating to competing operating systems in the future. Thus, as the Commission correctly states at recital 523 to the contested decision, it follows from certain results of the third Mercer survey that the fact of having an 'established record as proven technology' is seen as a significant factor by the large majority of IT executives questioned. At the time of the adoption of the contested decision, Microsoft, at a conservative estimate, held a market share of at least 60% on the work group server operating systems market (recital 499 to the contested decision). Likewise,

certain results of that survey also establish that the factor 'available skill-sets and cost/availability of support (in-house or external)' is important for the majority of the IT executives questioned. As the Commission quite correctly states at recital 520 to the contested decision, '[that] means that the easier it is to find technicians skilled in using a given work group server operating system, the more customers are inclined to purchase that work group server operating system' and, '[i]n turn, however, the more popular a work group server operating system is among customers, the easier it is for technicians (and the more willing are technicians) to acquire skills related to that product'. Microsoft's very high market share on the work group server operating system market has the consequence that a very large number of technicians possess skills which are specific to Windows operating systems.

...

[647] The circumstance relating to the appearance of a new product, as envisaged in *Magill* and *IMS Health*, paragraph 107 above, cannot be the only parameter which determines whether a refusal to license an intellectual property right is capable of causing prejudice to consumers within the meaning of Article 82(b) EC. As that provision states, such prejudice may arise where there is a limitation not only of production or markets, but also of technical development.

[648] It was on that last hypothesis that the Commission based its finding in the contested decision. Thus, the Commission considered that Microsoft's refusal to supply the relevant information limited technical development to the prejudice of consumers within the meaning of Article 82(b) EC (recitals 693 to 701 and 782 to the contested decision) and it rejected Microsoft's assertion that it had not been demonstrated that its refusal caused prejudice to consumers (recitals 702 to 708 to the contested decision).

NOTE: The Court of First Instance systematically applied existing case law relating to refusal to supply in order to determine whether Microsoft's refusal to provide interoperability information was abusive under Article 82 EC. The Court considered the indispensability of the information sought, whether the refusal would lead to substantial elimination of competition in the secondary market, and whether the refusal would prevent the emergence of a 'new product', as well as whether there was any objective justification for Microsoft's behaviour: this last point will be considered further below. For a discussion of the *Microsoft* case see Howarth, D., and McMahon, K., 'Case Comment: "Windows has performed an illegal operation": the Court of First Instance's judgment in *Microsoft* v *Commission*' (2008) ECLR 117.

■ QUESTIONS

Why is treating a refusal to license intellectual property rights as abusive controversial?

Under what circumstances will a refusal to grant access to an essential facility be capable of being abusive?

K: Objective justification

As noted in the introduction, Article 82 EC does not explicitly allow for an undertaking to escape its prohibition by pointing to any pro-competitive aspects of its conduct, in sharp contrast to Article 81(3) EC. Nonetheless, it is widely accepted that conduct which is prima facie abusive is permissible if there is objective justification. There are many examples of undertakings unsuccessfully arguing the existence of objective justification, and one of the principal criticisms of Article 82 EC has been that its traditional form-based approach does not present a clear opportunity for pro-competitive effects to outweigh competition concerns about the conduct. The remainder of the discussion will focus on the extent to which 'meeting competition' and the existence of efficiencies can present objective justification for potentially abusive behaviour.

Irish Sugar plc v *EC Commission*
(Case T-228/97) [1999] ECR II-2969, [1999] 5 CMLR 1300

Irish Sugar was the dominant supplier of white granulated sugar in the Republic of Ireland. Irish Sugar contended that in offering rebates to its customers who could source supplies from Northern Ireland, its 'border rebates' were simply designed to 'meet competition' and were not abusive.

[112] Therefore, whilst the finding that a dominant position exists does not in itself imply any reproach to the undertaking concerned, it has a special responsibility, irrespective of the causes of that position, not to allow its conduct to impair genuine undistorted competition on the common market (*Michelin*, paragraph 57). Similarly, whilst the fact that an undertaking is in a dominant position cannot deprive it of its entitlement to protect its own commercial interests when they are attacked, and whilst such an undertaking must be allowed the right to take such reasonable steps as it deems appropriate to protect those interests, such behaviour cannot be allowed if its purpose is to strengthen that dominant position and thereby abuse it (*United Brands*, paragraph 189; *BPB Industries and British Gypsum*, paragraph 69; *Tetra Pak*, paragraph 147; *Compagnie Maritime Belge Transports*, paragraph 107).

NOTE: While the Court of First Instance accepted the possibility of objective justification, it did not believe it existed in this case. After launching the review of Article 82 EC in 2005, the Commission began applying a more effects-based approach to abuse as well as objective justification to a number of cases including *Telefónica*.

Wanadoo España v *Telefónica*
(Commission Decision Case COMP/38.784 of 4 July 2007)

Wanadoo España (now France Télécom) submitted a complaint to the European Commission alleging Telefónica was engaging in exclusionary pricing conduct in Spanish wholesale broadband access markets. The Commission considered whether Telefónica was engaging in margin squeezing. This involved assessing whether it was setting a high price for wholesale broadband access, which competitors needed to purchase in order to compete in the downstream retail market (offering broadband access to consumers), as well as setting a low price in that downstream market. This conduct thereby constrains the margins and economic viability of competing in the downstream market for dependent undertakings. The Commission Decision includes a detailed consideration of objective justification.

3 Meeting competition defence

[637] According to Telefónica, meeting competition represents an objective justification for margin squeeze allegations. Telefónica claims that it it has always reacted to its competitors' offers by aligning its prices to those charged by competitors and that it has never taken the initiative in price reductions and promotions on the retail market.

[638] The Community Courts have considered that defending own commercial and economic interests in the face of action taken by certain competitors may be a legitimate aim. A dominant operator is not strictly speaking prohibited from aligning its prices with those of competitors. However, the meeting competition defence may not legitimise a margin squeeze that enables the vertically integrated company to impose losses on its competitors that it does not incur itself. The

meeting competition defence may not legitimise a behaviour whose effect is to leverage and abuse an upstream dominance.

[639] However, the meeting competition defence will only apply if it is shown that the response is suitable, indispensable and proportionate. This requires that there are no other economically practicable and less anti-competitive alternatives, which is unlikely to be the case in a margin squeeze case. In the present case, Telefónica's conduct is certainly not indispensable because Telefónica could have lowered its wholesale prices without increasing its retail prices and still be profitable overall.

[640] Also in the present case, Telefónica's nominal retail prices are those which were defined by the company in its initial business plan and have not been changed since that date. A margin squeeze still exists if the costs relating to the promotions are excluded from the calculation. Therefore, it cannot be considered that the margin squeeze is a response to low pricing by competi-tors. Moreover, the mere fact that the initial business plan of the company shows that the net present value of its broadband business generates a positive net present value on an end-to-end basis while its downstream activity generates a negative present value (see section VI.D.2.1.2.3 above) is a strong evidence that the objective aim of Telefónica's conduct was to foreclose competitors.

NOTE: Para. 639 provides a useful discussion of when 'meeting competition' will be available as an objective justification for potentially abusive behaviour. The indispensible and proportional test sets a high standard. The Commission continued to discuss the availability of a so-called 'efficiency defence' that would objectively justify the conduct.

4 Efficiency defence

[641] In the present case, Telefónica alleged that its conduct has resulted in efficiencies, which have thus benefited consumers. Therefore, according to the company, its conduct as such is objectively justified and cannot constitute an infringement of Article 82 EC.

[642] Telefónica argued that its conduct must be assessed within the context of the market background in which it launched its retail products in 2001. A business strategy that kick-starts and increases the size of a market is welfare-enhancing. According to the company, its conduct seeks to achieve supply side efficiencies (economies of scale and learning effects) and demand side efficiencies (overcome market inertia, network effects, and incentives for the development of New Generation Networks).

[643] According to Telefónica, its conduct was indispensable to realise these efficiencies. Firstly, higher retail prices would have created less market-expanding efficiencies and would have resulted in a direct consumer-welfare loss. Secondly, lower wholesale prices would not have been an economically viable or realistic alternative because (i) Telefónica sold at a loss its wholesale products until 2005, (ii) a reduction of wholesale prices would have distorted the company's incentives to invest in its infrastructure and (iii) would have resulted in a transfer from Telefónica to its wholesale customers allowing them to free-ride on its infrastructure investments and (iv) a lowering of wholesale prices would have reduced the incentives of competitors to invest in their own infrastructure.

[644] Telefónica further alleged that the attained efficiencies have directly benefited consumers, in particular the economies of scale and learning effects attained by Telefónica have enabled it to upgrade its services at no cost.

[645] Lastly, Telefónica argued that its conduct has not been and is not liable to result in an elimination of competition and stressed, on the contrary, that the efficiencies realized as a result of its conduct have benefited to all broadband operators.

4.1 Lack of justification in the form of positive externalities on the demand side

[646] Telefónica claimed that stimulating demand by attractive pricing has a particular benefit on a market for a new technology. In particular, Telefónica suggests that its pricing policy was indispensable to increase awareness of broadband and thereby stimulate demand, which would in turn have benefited its competitors and the market in general.

[647] Telefónica's argument is deficient in one essential respect: there is no proof that the margin squeeze would alone have made it possible to attain the desired objective of increased

broadband use in Spain. The positive effects linked to market growth could have been brought about had the market developed under competitive conditions. If it had really been Telefónica's intention to develop the broadband market, Telefónica could have priced all its wholesale products at low levels encouraging the entry of competitors (avoiding a margin squeeze while still being profitable). Telefónica chose instead to oblige its retail competitors to incur losses, thereby diverting the market growth to its advantage. It cannot therefore cogently be maintained that Telefónica was guided by a desire to develop the market for the benefit of all stakeholders.

[648] Above all, Telefónica's argument is invalidated by the fact that, as already established, its conduct allowed it to sustain the highest retail prices in Europe, thereby negatively affecting consumers and the market as a whole, with a below EU average rate of penetration.

4.2 Lack of justification in the form of economies of scale and learning effects

[649] Telefónica argued that its investments will only be profitable if it can reach a minimum scale of operations. An attractive retail price attracts users to the service and thereby enables Telefónica to achieve economies of scale faster than if the price was set so as to cover costs already at the outset. Telefónica also explains that all companies operate on a "learning curve" and the company's effectiveness will increase as it becomes more experienced, i.e. as the number of customers increases. By attracting more customers at an early stage with attractive prices, a company is able to run down the learning curve faster than would otherwise be possible.

[650] In case of significant economies of scale or strong learning effects, in exceptional cases there could be reasons which could justify temporary prices below LRAIC. However, Telefónica's downstream losses cannot be regarded as temporary or aimed at searching scale economies and learning effects because Telefónica's downstream activity still generates losses more than 5 years after its start.

[651] Telefónica's argument, instead of objectively legitimising a margin squeeze, highlights on the contrary one of the rational objectives thereof. One of the objectives of a margin squeeze conduct may be to reserve for the company engaging in the practice the benefit of economies of scale on the downstream market and to delay accordingly for downstream competitors their arrival at the same volume threshold allowing the economies of scale. Moreover, a combination of being at a higher point on the learning curve than competitors and having higher output thanks to below-cost pricing may have exclusion effects capable of consolidating the dominant company's hegemony.

[652] Thus, while the search for scale economies and learning effects may be included among the rational justifications for below cost pricing, it may not serve to legitimize a margin squeeze that enables the vertically integrated company to impose losses upon its competitors that it does not incur itself.

[653] In addition, Telefónica would in fact have benefited from higher economies of scale if it had lowered its wholesale prices, as this would have allowed it to increase its sales at the wholesale level.

[654] Finally, and in any event, contrary to Telefónica's statements, the economies of scale attained by Telefónica have never benefited its wholesale customers by way of improvements to the regulated wholesale products because the prices of the relevant wholesale products have not changed until the CMT decision of 21 December 2006.

4.3 It is highly unlikely that in the long run the supply side efficiencies invoked by Telefónica would be passed on to the customers and that these benefits outweigh the restriction of competition brought about by the margin squeeze

[655] For an argument based on efficiency gains to be admissible, the dominant company must show that efficiencies brought about by the conduct concerned outweigh the likely negative effects on competition that the conduct might otherwise have. The greater the effects on competition, the more one must be sure that the claimed efficiencies are substantial, likely to be realised, and to be passed on, to a sufficient degree, to consumers.

[656] The incentive on the part of the dominant company to pass cost efficiencies on to consumers is often related to the existence of competitive pressure from the remaining firms in the market and from potential entry.

[657] An efficiency defence must be rejected if the short-term efficiency gains (if any) are weighed by longer-term losses stemming *inter alia* from expenditures incurred by the dominant company to maintain or reinforce its position (rent seeking), misallocation of resources, reduced innovation and higher prices. This is consistent with the fact that rivalry between undertakings is an essential driver of economic efficiency, including dynamic efficiencies in the shape of innovation. Ultimately, the protection of rivalry and the competitive process is given priority over possible short-term efficiency gains.

[658] In the present case, Telefónica's conduct consists in preventing its downstream rivals from replicating profitably its retail prices. Given Telefónica's market power at the retail level (see Section V.C.3 above) the incumbent is not forced to pass on the alleged efficiencies, if any, to the consumers. Moreover, the fact that Telefónica's retail prices are among the highest in the EU is a strong indication that Telefónica has rather profited from the alleged efficiencies in order to increase its profitability. It is therefore highly unlikely that the present exclusionary conduct that consists in raising rivals' costs can be justified on the ground that efficiency gains would be sufficient to outweigh its actual or likely anti-competitive effects and would benefit consumers.

NOTE: The so-called 'efficiency defence' was unsuccessful in this case but signifies the effect-based approach that the Commission is trying to introduce to the enforcement of Article 82 EC. Telefónica has filed an appeal against the Commission Decision, Case T-336/07 *Telefónica and Telefónica de España* v *Commission* (pending).

Commission Communication: Guidance on the Commission's enforcement priorities in applying Article 82 EC Treaty to abusive exclusionary conduct by dominant undertakings
OJ, 2009, C45/7, paras 28–31 [footnotes omitted]

D. Objective necessity and efficiencies

[28] In the enforcement of Article 82, the Commission will also examine claims put forward by a dominant undertaking that its conduct is justified. A dominant undertaking may do so either by demonstrating that its conduct is objectively necessary or by demonstrating that its conduct produces substantial efficiencies which outweigh any anticompetitive effects on consumers. In this context, the Commission will assess whether the conduct in question is indispensable and proportionate to the goal allegedly pursued by the dominant undertaking.

[29] The question of whether conduct is objectively necessary and proportionate must be determined on the basis of factors external to the dominant undertaking. Exclusionary conduct may, for example, be considered objectively necessary for health or safety reasons related to the nature of the product in question. However, proof of whether conduct of this kind is objectively necessary must take into account that it is normally the task of public authorities to set and enforce public health and safety standards. It is not the task of a dominant undertaking to take steps on its own initiative to exclude products which it regards, rightly or wrongly, as dangerous or inferior to its own product.

[30] The Commission considers that a dominant undertaking may also justify conduct leading to foreclosure of competitors on the ground of efficiencies that are sufficient to guarantee that no net harm to consumers is likely to arise. In this context, the dominant undertaking will generally be expected to demonstrate, with a sufficient degree of probability, and on the basis of verifiable evidence, that the following cumulative conditions are fulfilled:
- the efficiencies have been, or are likely to be, realised as a result of the conduct. They may, for example, include technical improvements in the quality of goods, or a reduction in the cost of production or distribution,
- the conduct is indispensable to the realisation of those efficiencies: there must be no less anti-competitive alternatives to the conduct that are capable of producing the same efficiencies,

- the likely efficiencies brought about by the conduct outweigh any likely negative effects on competition and consumer welfare in the affected markets,
- the conduct does not eliminate effective competition, by removing all or most existing sources of actual or potential competition. Rivalry between undertakings is an essential driver of economic efficiency, including dynamic efficiencies in the form of innovation. In its absence the dominant undertaking will lack adequate incentives to continue to create and pass on efficiency gains. Where there is no residual competition and no foreseeable threat of entry, the protection of rivalry and the competitive process outweighs possible efficiency gains. In the Commission's view, exclusionary conduct which maintains, creates or strengthens a market position approaching that of a monopoly can normally not be justified on the grounds that it also creates efficiency gains.

[31] It is incumbent upon the dominant undertaking to provide all the evidence necessary to demonstrate that the conduct concerned is objectively justified. It then falls to the Commission to make the ultimate assessment of whether the conduct concerned is not objectively necessary and, based on a weighing-up of any apparent anti-competitive effects against any advanced and substantiated efficiencies, is likely to result in consumer harm.

NOTE: The Commission continues to adopt a strict approach when applying the concept of objective justification, in line with established case law of the Community Courts, but has clarified the basis and circumstances under which objective justification may be possible. The issue of burden of proof with regards to objective justification is considered by the Commission in para. 31 of its Communication, and it has also been considered by the Court of First Instance in *Microsoft*.

Microsoft v *Commission*
(Case T-204/04) [2007] ECR II-3601, [2007] 5 CMLR 11

[688] The Court notes, as a preliminary point, that although the burden of proof of the existence of the circumstances that constitute an infringement of Article 82 EC is borne by the Commission, it is for the dominant undertaking concerned, and not for the Commission, before the end of the administrative procedure, to raise any plea of objective justification and to support it with arguments and evidence. It then falls to the Commission, where it proposes to make a finding of an abuse of a dominant position, to show that the arguments and evidence relied on by the undertaking cannot prevail and, accordingly, that the justification put forward cannot be accepted.

NOTE: There is clearly an onus upon undertakings that are the subject of EC competition law investigations to raise potential objective justifications with the Commission or NCA. The CFI continued to consider Microsoft's plea of objective justification on the basis of intellectual property rights covering the interoperability information, and the suggestion that supplying full details to third parties would diminish the incentives for innovation in the future. The CFI dismissed Microsoft's argument and upheld the Commission finding against the existence of any objective justification.

FURTHER READING

Albors-Llorens, A., 'The role of objective justification and efficiencies in the application of Article 82 EC' [2007] CML Rev 1727.

Azevedo, J.P., and Walker, M., 'Dominance: meaning and measurement' [2002] ECLR 363.

Baker, S., and Wu, L., 'Applying the Market Definition Guidelines of the European Commission' [1998] ECLR 273.

Géradin, D., 'Limiting the scope of Article 82 EC: What can the EU learn from the US Supreme Court's judgment in *Trinko* in the wake of *Microsoft, IMS,* and *Deutsche Telekom*?' (2004) 41 CML Rev 1519.

Furse, M., 'Excessive prices, unfair prices and economic value: the law of excessive pricing under article 82 EC and the Chapter II prohibition.' [2008] European Competition Journal 59.

Heit, J., 'The justifiability of the ECJ's wide approach to the concept of "barriers to entry"' [2006] ECLR 117.

Jebsen, P., and Stevens, R., 'Assumptions, Goals and Dominant Undertakings: The Regulation of Competition under Article 86 of the European Union' (1995–6) 64 Antitrust LJ 143.

Niels, G., and Jenkins, H., 'Reform of Article 82: where the link between dominance and effects breaks down' [2005] ECLR 605.

O'Donoghue, R., and Padilla, A.J., *The Law and Economics of Article 82*, Oxford, Hart Publishing, 2006.

Sher, B., 'The Last of the Steam-Powered Trains: Modernising Article 82' [2004] ECLR 243.

11

UK 'monopoly' control

The control of 'monopoly' in the UK underwent an extensive transformation with the introduction of the Chapter II prohibition in the Competition Act 1998 ('CA 1998'). The Fair Trading Act 1973 ('FTA 1973'), and its public interest test for assessing market structure and conduct was also subsequently replaced by the provisions for market investigations contained in Part IV of the Enterprise Act 2002 ('EA 2002'). Nonetheless, it is clear that the new prohibition under the CA 1998 is to be the key competition law tool in the UK for dealing with issues of market power, and Section 2 of this chapter will focus on abuse of dominance under UK competition law. However, market investigations under the EA 2002 embody the traditional UK competition law approach and remain a crucial component in the armoury of the UK competition authorities, as discussed in Sections 3 and 4 of the chapter.

Whish, R., 'The Competition Act 1998 and the prior debate on reform', Chapter 1 in Rodger, B.J., and MacCulloch, A. (eds), *The UK Competition Act*: *A New Era for UK Competition Law*
Oxford, Hart Publishing, 2000, at pp. 1–4

The Competition Act 1998, which entered into force on 1 March 2000, radically reforms the domestic law of the United Kingdom on restrictive agreements and anti-competitive practices. To understand just how radical the 1998 Act is, it is interesting to review briefly the pragmatic growth of legislation on this subject in the United Kingdom over the preceding fifty years: much of the complexity of the law arose from the fact that there was an accretion of several layers of competition control in a number of different Acts of Parliament. The years 1948, 1973 and 1998 can be seen to have been particularly important in the evolution of the law. This would suggest that the next major piece of legislation can be expected in 2023, the end of the next cycle of twenty-five years; however it may be that further change will come much sooner than this if reform follows the European Commission's White Paper on Modernisation,[1] and in particular its proposal that the system of notification of agreements should be abandoned, necessitating amendment of the Competition Act 1998. A central feature of the Act is the procedure of notification for guidance and/or a decision, which was itself modelled on the system in Regulation 17/62 which the Commission now proposes to abandon.

A review of the period from 1948 to 1998 shows that competition law in the United Kingdom has been in a continual process of formation, with the legislature having extended the law in a pragmatic,

---

[1] On this issue, see further Barry Rodger, Chapter 3.

ad hoc, way. Competition law in the United Kingdom cannot be traced back to a 'Big Bang', as could be said of the Sherman Act of 1890 in the USA or Articles 81 and 82 in the EC Treaty. Instead there have been a series of explosions at intervals of, normally, about four or five years, some quite minor, with the more substantial ones tending to occur at twenty-five year intervals. The 1998 Act sweeps away much of the system that has formed over the preceding fifty years, while retaining the investigative system for mergers and monopolies that has its origins in the first modern statute, the Monopolies and Restrictive Practices (Inquiry and Control) Act 1948. The system of merger control is now itself the subject of a consultation procedure, pursuant to a Department of Trade and Industry document published in August 1999.[2]

The first twenty-five years

The Monopolies and Restrictive Practices (Inquiry and Control) Act 1948[3] established the Monopolies and Restrictive Practices Commission, a direct ancestor of the Competition Commission created by the 1998 Act. The 1948 Act can be traced back to the White Paper published during the Second World War on Employment Policy,[4] which considered that a policy of full employment was most likely to be successful in a competitive economy. The 1948 Act enabled monopolies and restrictive practices to be investigated. The President of the Board of Trade was given the power to instigate investigations and to determine the appropriate remedy in the event that the Commission found there to be a detriment to the public interest. The function of the Commission was simply to investigate and report: it did not have an original jurisdiction of its own and it did not make decisions or impose remedies itself. Although the Competition Commission's role is more complex under the legislation in force today, including regulatory Acts such as the Telecommunications Act 1984 and the Railways Act 1993, much of its current work conforms to the original model in 1948.

After the 1948 Act, there followed numerous additions to the domestic legislation: a review of the legislative history shows that it has taken a long time to 'form' a system of competition law in the United Kingdom. As we shall go on to see, it also took a long time to determine how best to 'reform' it. Certain dates stand out in the years after 1948. In 1955 the Monopolies and Restrictive Practices Commission published its *Report on Collective Discrimination*,[5] the minority opinion in which led to the adoption of the Restrictive Trade Practices Act 1956. It was at this point that the treatment of 'monopoly situations' and restrictive trade practices diverged, the latter being subject to a stricter regime, albeit not strict enough; much of the motivation behind the new legislation was the need for effective sanctions. A controversial issue as the recent Competition Bill passed through Parliament was whether the provisions for the investigation of monopoly situations should be retained after the introduction of the new prohibitions for restrictive agreements and abuse of dominance. This matter is discussed further below by Mark Furse, Chapter 7.

The next important date was 1964, when the Resale Prices Act was passed; that Act, prohibiting collective resale price maintenance and rendering individual resale price maintenance unlawful unless authorised by the Restrictive Practices Court according to specified criteria, was enormously controversial at the time. Some of this controversy resurfaced as the Competition Bill passed through Parliament, where considerable time was spent on the position of pharmacies, the authorisation granted by the court to price maintenance for medicaments and the position that would obtain under the new regime.[6]

In 1965 the Monopolies and Mergers Act introduced for the first time a system of merger control in the United Kingdom, as part of the new Labour Government's policy of encouraging rationalisation

---

[2] *Mergers: A Consultation Document on Proposals for Reform* (London, DTI, August 1999).

[3] On the background to this Act, see R. Whish, *Competition Law* (3rd edn, London, Butterworths, 1993) pp. 60–2; S. Wilks, 'The Prolonged Reform of UK Competition Policy' in G.B. Doern and S. Wilks (eds), *Comparative Competition Policy: National Institutions in a Global Market* (Oxford, Clarendon Press, 1996) pp. 139–84 at 141–3; T. Freyer, *Regulating Big Business* (Cambridge, Cambridge University Press, 1992), ch 7.

[4] Cm 6527 (1944).

[5] Cmd 9504 (1955).

[6] See discussion *infra*.

and consolidation of industry but not at the expense of creating firms with excessive market power. This Act used the model of 1948, including reference to the Monopolies and Mergers Commission and action by the Secretary of State following the Commission's investigation and adverse report. This system for the control of mergers has remained in place ever since, but is currently under review by the Department of Trade and Industry.[7] Three years later the Restrictive Trade Practices Act 1968 made various changes to the 1956 Act, including the provision of powers to extend the legislation to catch 'information agreements'[8] and the introduction of the notion that unregistered, registrable agreements would be void in respect of any 'relevant restrictions'. In the years that followed, obedience to the legislation was much more likely to be attributable to firms needing to ensure that their agreements were enforceable than to their fear of action being taken against them by the Registrar of Restrictive Trading Agreements or, after 1973, the Director General of Fair Trading. One of the most unsatisfactory features of the restrictive practices legislation was that serious cartels, which should be prohibited, continued because the legislation lacked the investigatory powers and the sanctions to make it bite, while innocuous agreements were often registrable as a result of the form-based and highly complex provisions on 'restrictions', in consequence of which it was necessary to 'furnish particulars' of them to the Office of Fair Trading in order to avoid the risk of unenforceability.

The second twenty-five years

The Fair Trading Act 1973 was of major importance. The significance of this Act lay not so much in the substantive law, although this was the legislation that gave the power to the Secretary of State to bring the services sector within the scope of the Restrictive Trade Practices Act[9] and also reduced the 'monopoly situation' threshold from 33 per cent to 25 per cent. What was more significant was that this Act created the role of the Director General of Fair Trading and radically revised the institutional structure of competition law in the United Kingdom. The creation of this role, and of the Office of Fair Trading, meant that there was now an institution which, among its other roles, had responsibility for competition policy. At last it was beginning to be possible to see that there was 'competition law' in the United Kingdom; the fact that this was also the year in which the United Kingdom joined the European Economic Community, as it then was, and therefore that Articles 85 and 86 of the EC Treaty, as they then were, became directly applicable, made this point even clearer. Competition law achieved early adulthood in the United Kingdom in 1973, a rare example in the modern world of minority being abandoned at the advanced age of twenty-five.

Following the Fair Trading Act, further competition legislation continued to come onto the statute book at fairly regular intervals. The Restrictive Trade Practices Act 1976 consolidated the legislation, and the Restrictive Trade Practices Act 1977 introduced complex new provisions on 'financing terms'. The legislation on resale price maintenance was consolidated in the Resale Prices Act 1976. The Competition Act 1980 arose out of two consultation documents known as the Liesner Reports, which began the long process of reform. These Reports, and many subsequent ones, are discussed *infra*. Numerous statutes in the 1980s and 1990s made additional changes to the system of competition law, for example the Financial Services Act 1986, the Channel Tunnel Act 1987, the Companies Act 1989, the Courts and Legal Services Act 1990, the Deregulation and Contracting Out Act 1994 and the Broadcasting Act 1996. However by the late 1980s it had become clear that a major reform of the law had become necessary, and the Conservative Government committed itself in a White Paper as early as July 1989 to radical reform of the legislation on restrictive trade practices. Its inability to find parliamentary time for a Bill in the eight subsequent years that it remained in office caused great frustration for many, not least the Director General of Fair Trading who lacked the powers to pursue cartels that should be prohibited, and yet whose office had to spend inordinate

---

[7] See *supra* n. 2.

[8] The power was exercised in 1969 by the Restrictive Trade Practices Act (Information Agreements) Order (SI 1969/1842).

[9] The power was exercised in 1976 by the Restrictive Trade Practices Act (Services) Order (SI 1976/98).

amounts of time registering innocuous agreements that were nevertheless caught by the complex restrictive practices legislation.

NOTE: The CA 1998 certainly marked a 'radical' change from the traditional public interest test model which had been developed in the UK. (See further Wilks, below.) The influence of the European tradition of competition law over the past 40 years on the UK reform process resulting in the introduction of the CA 1998 cannot be underestimated. Whish's prediction that further major reform was unlikely to await another 25 years was accurate and the EA 2002 made further radical reform to UK competition law, based largely on the DTI White Paper, *A World Class Competition Regime*, Cm 5233, July 2001.

This chapter will look in detail at the CA 1998 Chapter II prohibition and practice thereunder. Then the chapter will look at the provisions in the EA for market investigations. Those provisions, and the practice to date under the EA 2002, build on, to a great extent, the monopoly provisions of the Fair Trading Act 1973, and, accordingly, the development of policy and practice under the earlier legislation cannot simply be ignored in the new statutory context.

SECTION 2: THE COMPETITION ACT 1998 CHAPTER II PROHIBITION

In 1998, the UK's 25-year competition law cycle was maintained with the introduction of the CA 1998. The aims of the legislation were to enhance the deterrent effect of UK competition law and to harmonize the UK system with the Community provisions, Articles 81 and 82 EC. The Act introduced two new prohibitions, the Chapter II prohibition being modelled very closely on the prohibition on the abuse of a dominant position in Article 82 EC. Chapter III of the Act introduced important powers of investigation and enforcement of the new prohibitions (see Chapter 3).

Wilks, S., *In the Public Interest, Competition Policy and the Monopolies and Mergers Commission*
Manchester, MUP, 1999, pp. 322–4

The Competition Act 1998

With an elegant accident of symmetry the Act comes exactly fifty years after the Monopolies and Restrictive Practices Act 1948. It is potentially a revolutionary piece of legislation which has considerable implications for the institutions of British capitalism. As explored in the concluding chapter, the 1948 Act catered to the voluntarism, the self-regulation and the accommodative arm's-length relationship between government and industry which permeated the political economy of the 1940s. The 1998 Act creates a more formal and legally objective framework for industry. It provides didactic guidance rather than the co-operative exploration which underlay its 1948 predecessor. The formal provisions of the Act are briefly reviewed in chapter 10.

Despite its European provenance, the new Act is a piece of British legislation although it builds in novel provisions to employ European jurisprudence. It is designed to dovetail with the European regime and doubtless many hope that this new, more effective, Act will increase the element of real subsidiarity. It represents something of a compromise, as can be seen if it is considered in the context of the debates reviewed above. In respect of the first debate it almost certainly represents a more active British competition policy, and one that stresses 'competition' as a principle rather than 'the public interest'. In respect of the second debate it adopts the European stance of prohibition and an effects doctrine, and does so for monopolies as well as restrictive practices. ... The European blueprint does indeed involve some major shifts in the regime of monopoly control. In order to evaluate the extent of change consider the following:

- the shift from agnostic investigation to prohibition
- the replacement of the 'public interest' test by an 'effect on competition' test
- the exclusion of the Secretary of State from the administrative process as regards actions and remedies
- the incorporation of the principles of European competition law jurisprudence into British administration
- hence the likely growth of legal involvement through defence, appeal and third-party action
- the empowerment of third parties through rights of appeal and the potential to pursue damages in the courts
- the imposition of substantial penalties.

Change of this magnitude is potentially of extraordinary significance and it is curious that press coverage of the Act was relatively subdued.

NOTE: As Wilks notes, the CA 1998 is certainly more legalistic than its predecessors. Wilks discusses the main changes, the key issue being the 'Europeanization' of domestic competition policy.

■ QUESTION

Is it appropriate that control of 'monopolies' under UK competition law has become more legalistic and harmonized with European competition law?

A: The prohibition

Section 18 provides:

COMPETITION ACT 1998 [S. 18]

Abuse of dominant position

18.—(1) Subject to section 19, any conduct on the part of one or more undertakings which amounts to the abuse of a dominant position in a market is prohibited if it may affect trade within the United Kingdom.

(2) Conduct may, in particular, constitute such an abuse if it consists in—
   (a) directly or indirectly imposing unfair purchase or selling prices or other unfair trading conditions;
   (b) limiting production, markets or technical development to the prejudice of consumers;
   (c) applying dissimilar conditions to equivalent transactions with other trading parties, thereby placing them at a competitive disadvantage;
   (d) making the conclusion of contracts subject to acceptance by the other parties of supplementary obligations which, by their nature or according to commercial usage, have no connection with the subject of the contracts.

(3) In this section—
   'dominant position' means a dominant position within the United Kingdom; and
   'the United Kingdom' means the United Kingdom or any part of it.

(4) The prohibition imposed by subsection (1) is referred to in this Act as 'the Chapter II prohibition'.

NOTE: This basically replicates Article 82 EC but places the provision in a UK context. As discussed more fully in Chapter 3 the OFT has been afforded a similar role to that of the

Commission under Community law with powers to investigate and fine companies for breaching the prohibition. This was a crucial change in the direction of UK competition policy and one would have anticipated extensive Parliamentary debates on the nature and likely impact of the prohibition.

Sufrin, B., 'The Chapter II prohibition', Chapter 6 in Rodger, B.J., and MacCulloch, A. (eds), *The UK Competition Act: A New Era for UK Competition Law*
Oxford, Hart Publishing, 2000, at pp. 120–1 and pp. 146–7

The effect of the Competition Act 1998 and in particular section 60, however, is that the adoption of the Chapter II, and Chapter I, prohibition is unlike other radical innovations in UK law.[1] The Chapter II prohibition is born trailing clouds, if not of glory, then at least of three decades of case law, and comes with the stipulation that UK courts are to follow future developments in its interpretation fashioned in Luxembourg and, to a lesser extent, in Brussels. The fact that the Competition Act brings into domestic law not only an Article 82-type system but also the substantive content of Article 82 as developed by the European Court was deliberate and was presented by the Government as a positively beneficial feature of the new law in that UK companies will no longer be subject to 'differing approaches and potentially differing judgments on the same competition issues'.[2]

There was little debate during the progress of the Competition Bill about what makes undertakings 'dominant', and therefore subject to the Chapter II prohibition, or about what conduct it prohibits, partly because the discussion was repeatedly side-tracked on to the issue of predatory pricing in the newspaper industry. In the Second Reading in the Commons John Redwood, the Shadow Secretary of State, asked the President of the Board of Trade 'what current legal business practices she hopes and expects the Bill to make illegal?' but was told this was a 'vague and wandering question' and that 'no one can be expected to give case-by-case definitions, especially not a Minister', these things being matters for the Director General of Fair Trading.[3] Parliament was assured that two cases called *AKZO*[4] and *Tetra Pak*[5] would take care of predatory pricing in newspapers. Although, in that context, the Minister of State did describe what dominance meant in European jurisprudence,[6] the scope and philosophy of the Community rules which were being brought into domestic law were not subjected to any detailed examination. This was 'a Bill for consumers, for business and for jobs...another step in the creation of strong markets that will make Britain a more competitive economy'[7] but exactly *how* the Chapter II prohibition would do this in terms of substantive law was not described.

Conclusion

The Chapter II prohibition cannot be expected to solve all problems concerning the abuse of market power by firms in the United Kingdom. We have bought Article 82 with all its complexities and uncertainties 'off the peg' so to speak, aware of its shortcomings, but its attractions are that it provides for the deterrence, enforcement and penalties which UK law on monopolies lacked before, and it produces harmony with Community law.

---

[1] There is a tempting analogy with the Human Rights Act 1998, ss. 2 and 3, but the interpretation provisions there are significantly different from the Competition Act 1998, s. 60. See S. Marshall, 'Interpreting Interpretation in the Human Rights Bill' [1998] *PL* 197 and D. Feldman, 'The Human Rights Act 1998 and Constitutional Principles' (1999) 19 *Legal Studies* 165.

[2] See Margaret Beckett, Second Reading, Hansard, HC, 11 May 1998, col 25.

[3] Hansard, HC, 11 May 1998, cols 23 and 24.

[4] See *infra*, n. 79.

[5] See *infra*, n. 80.

[6] Hansard, HC, 11 May 1998, col 118.

[7] Ibid., col 23.

The latter feature has been widely welcomed, in that undertakings have only to comply with one set of rules rather than two, but that argument is fallacious. If rules are unsatisfactory or imperfect, subjecting undertakings to them twice over is not necessarily an advantage, and subjecting undertakings which operate only domestically to those rules because it is supposedly easier for undertakings who must already comply with Article 82 in their inter-Member State dealings is unacceptable. If Article 82 is to be applied as domestic law it should be because Parliament believes that its substantive content provides the rules which should govern the conduct of dominant undertakings in the United Kingdom in order to promote consumer welfare. The fact that many UK undertakings already have to take account of Article 82 itself should be no reason for failing to subject the law introduced by section 18 of the 1998 Act to proper scrutiny.

Article 82 EC, in the name of competition, subjects dominant undertakings to a high degree of regulation but, despite section 60 of the 1998 Act, the nature of the issues raised in the control of market power inevitably gives a considerable margin of appreciation to the UK competition authorities. It is the way in which the Director General exercises that discretion which will determine how far the Chapter II prohibition really promotes competition.

NOTE: Sufrin points out that in fact there was very little debate on the substance of the prohibition. Indeed, one of the principal criticisms of Article 82 EC is the lack of certainty it allows for parties to determine what constitutes legitimate competitive behaviour as opposed to illegal and abusive conduct which is prohibited. One of the key debates during the passage of the Bill was whether to include a specific rule on predatory pricing in the newspaper industry, but ultimately this was rejected.

As Sufrin notes, ascertaining the impact of the new prohibition will be facilitated by the development of practice and case law, noted below, and also by the guidelines issued by the OFT under s. 52(1) of the Act, for example the Chapter II prohibition guideline (OFT 402).

B : Harmonization

The key to understanding the Chapter II prohibition and its impact is the basic rule that it should be interpreted consistently with Community law. This is provided through the operation of s. 60 of the CA 1998, otherwise known as the governing principles provision or 'Euro-clause'. The objective, set out in s. 60(1), is enshrined in s. 60(2) which seeks to ensure that the UK authorities and courts must interpret the prohibition in accordance with European Court jurisprudence. They are also required under s. 60(3) to have regard to relevant decisions or statements by the Commission. Section 60(1) permits departure from Community law where there are relevant differences. See generally Chapter 7 and specifically, Middleton, K., 'Harmonisation with Community Law; The Euro Clause', Chapter 3 in Rodger, B.J., and MacCulloch, A. (eds), *The UK Competition Act: A New Era for UK Competition Law*, Oxford, Hart Publishing, 2000 at pp. 21–3, 26–9, and 33–9. The OFT and CAT have clearly utilized s. 60 and relied on Community law in interpreting and applying the Chapter II prohibition in the case law to date, as exemplified by the CAT's detailed analysis of all prior Community predatory pricing jurisprudence in its first substantive judgment in *Napp Pharmaceutical* v *DGFT* [2002] CAT 1:

Napp Pharmaceutical Holdings Limited and Subsidiaries v DGFT
[2002] CAT 1, paras 228–30

228. On the basis of *AKZO* and *Tetra Pak II*, and having regard to our duty under section 60(2) of the Act to secure, so far as compatible with Part I of the Act, that there is no inconsistency between the principles we apply and the principles laid down by the Court of Justice, in our

judgment it follows, on the foregoing facts alone, that Napp has abused its dominant position in offering prices below average variable costs to hospitals contrary to the Chapter II prohibition, as the Director found in the Decision, without it being necessary to find that Napp had a specific intention to eliminate competition. In view of the fact that the *AKZO* approach was laid down in a case where the dominant undertaking had only 50 per cent of the market, it seems to us that it is only in the most exceptional of circumstances that a similar approach should not be applied in cases of 'superdominance' where the undertaking concerned has around 95 per cent of the market.

229. It is true, however, that in paragraph 127 of his opinion in *Compagnie Maritime Belge*, Advocate General Fennelly stated that while sales below average variable costs (for which in this case direct costs are considered to be a proxy) are 'in effect presumed to be abusive', he went on to say that 'a dominant firm, would be permitted to rebut this presumption by showing that such pricing was not part of a plan to eliminate its competitor'. In view of the remarks at paragraphs 132 and 137 of his opinion, we doubt whether Mr Fennelly would necessarily have taken the same approach on this point had he been considering a case, such as the present, of a virtual monopolist selling well below direct costs. Nonetheless, as a precaution we consider in this judgment whether it is shown that Napp had no plan or intention to eliminate competition, so as to bring itself within the exception to the *AKZO* test envisaged by Mr Fennelly.

230. In that connection we begin by considering Napp's fundamental argument that the *AKZO* and *Tetra Pak II* approach is not the right starting point in this case because, properly understood, Napp's hospital sales did not 'generate a loss' because of the 'follow-on effects'. That issue has to be considered also in the light of *Compagnie Maritime Belge* and *Irish Sugar*, cited above, which show that even if the prices of a dominant firm remain above costs, and simply match the price of a competitor, there may still be an abuse, at least where a superdominant firm is concerned, if the reduced prices in question are made on a selective basis and have no economic rationale other than the elimination of competition.

NOTE: This judgment is an excellent example of the application of Community law jurisprudence, following closely case law such as Case T-228/97 *Irish Sugar plc* v *Commission* [1999] ECR II-2969 and Joined Cases C-395/96 P and 396/96 P *Compagnie Maritime Belge* v *Commission* [2000] ECR I-1442, and the Community concept of 'superdominance'. The Tribunal went on to reject the 'net revenue' defence to the predatory pricing abuse.

C : Practice to date

From the emphasis placed on education and compliance, it was considered that the Chapter II prohibition was likely to have a significant impact on business practice. Nonetheless, there have been relatively few cases to date involving the Chapter II prohibition, although there has been some practice developed by the OFT, CAT, and the courts, as considered here in relation to excessive pricing, predatory pricing, and refusal to supply.

Rodger, B.J., 'Early Steps to a Mature Competition Law System: Case Law Developments in the First 18 Months of the Competition Act 1998'
[2002] ECLR 52

Introduction

The Competition Act 1998 has introduced a sea change in the way competition law is dealt with in the United Kingdom at a time when competition law has been developing a considerably higher profile. With the notable exceptions of the House of Lords debates regarding newspaper pricing and over-the-counter medicine pricing/community pharmacies, analysis of the likely impact of particular provisions during the passage of the Bill through Parliament, particularly in relation to section 18 and the Chapter II prohibition, was limited, and the Competition Act did not attract the attention of the broader public. However, the impact of the prohibitions on business practice, and the requirement for effective compliance strategies to be set up, is already becoming clearer.

In the space of a little over 18 months, there have been a considerable number of decisions taken under the Act by the Director General of Fair Trading (DGFT) and the Competition Commission has delivered one final judgment and a number of interim judgments. A wide range of issues have been dealt with in a short space of time, from excessive pricing to predatory pricing (*Napp*, *Aberdeen Journals*), the application of the Chapter I prohibition to self-regulation in the insurance industry (*GISC*), the grant of block exemptions (*travel cards*) and individual exemptions, and the acceptance of voluntary assurances in lieu of the imposition of interim measures, to the procedures and process of appeal against decision by the DGFT (as explored in *Napp*). The importance of section 60 of the Act and the role for Community jurisprudence in interpreting and applying the prohibitions has been clearly demonstrated (*Napp*, *Claritas*, etc.). The range of issues has varied from the small and localised, notably the warning about price-fixing to members of the Bury Private Hire Association, to the £27 billion insurance industry in the United Kingdom and the competitive strategy of BSkyB, demonstrating the importance of compliance with the Act across the whole spectrum of industry in the United Kingdom.

NOTE: The EA 2002 made no substantive reform to the Chapter II prohibition, although it altered the institutional structure by replacing the DGFT with the OFT, and it provided for parties damaged by an infringement of either prohibition to claim damages from the Competition Appeal Tribunal: see, for example, *Healthcare at Home Ltd* v *Genzyme Ltd* [2006] CAT 29. These issues were discussed in Chapter 3 on UK enforcement.

(a) Excessive pricing

Napp Pharmaceutical Holdings Limited and Subsidiaries v *DGFT*
[2002] CAT 1, paras 400–3

Napp sells sustained release morphine tablets and capsules in the UK. It was alleged that Napp had abused its dominant position by predatory discounting of drugs to hospitals and charged excessive prices to other customers. Its prices for the same product on the follow-on community market, where GPs followed the prescription practices of hospital consultants, were considerably higher.

400. It is therefore established, on the facts of this case, that during the period of infringement, Napp charged significantly higher prices in the community segment than in other markets or segments where it faced competition, and has significantly higher margins in the community segment than its most profitable competitor. In addition, Napp faced no competitive pressure on its prices in the community segment, had no patent protection, and enjoyed a market share of 96 per cent throughout.

401. The fact that the Director has not chosen to rely on other comparators such as international price comparisons or returns on capital does not in our view lessen the force of the comparators upon which he does rely. Napp itself has not, in the notice of appeal, put forward any other comparators.

402. On those facts we are satisfied that Napp "has made use of the opportunities arising out of its dominant position in such a way as to reap trading benefits which it would not have reaped if there had been normal and sufficiently effective competition", so as to satisfy the test of abuse as laid down by the Court of Justice in *United Brands* at paragraph 249 of its judgment.

403. To put the matter in terms of the principle set out at paragraph 203 of the Decision, in our view the above facts demonstrate (i) that, during the period of the infringement, Napp's prices in the community segment were significantly higher than would be expected in a competitive market;

and (ii) that, during the period of the infringement, there was no significant competitive pressure to bring them down to competitive levels, nor was there likely to be over any reasonable time scale.

NOTE: In *AttheRaces Ltd* v *British Horseracing Board* [2007] EWCA Civ 38, CA, the claimant, which supplied websites, TV channels, and other media relating to British horse racing, alleged that the defendant, which had a central role in the organization and promotion of British horse racing and which kept a computerized database of pre-race data, had abused a dominant position and infringed the Chapter II prohibition (and Article 82) by charging excessive, unfair, and discriminatory pricing. The Court of Appeal rejected this claim and held that the value of the data to ATR was relevant in determining whether the price was excessive. For a more recent judgment by the CAT determining the excessive nature of an access price in the water industry, see *Albion Water Limited* v *Water Services Regulation Authority* [2008] CAT 31. See also Furse, M., 'Excessive Prices, Unfair Prices and Economic Value: The Law of Excessive Pricing Under Article 82 EC and the Chapter II Prohibition' [2008] European Competition Journal 59.

■ QUESTION

Why do the authorities and courts appear to be reluctant to find high prices by dominant undertakings to be abusive?

(b) Predatory pricing

The first CAT judgment under the 1998 Act concerned predatory pricing by *Napp*, as outlined above, in which the CAT followed the developed body of ECJ jurisprudence, notably the cost and intention based tests set out in *AKZO*. The next case also concerned predatory pricing. The *Aberdeen & District Independent* newspaper complained that Aberdeen Journals Ltd was predating in the pricing of advertising space in its *Herald & Post*. Aberdeen Journals was owned by Northcliffe Newspapers Group Ltd, itself part of the Daily Mail & General Trust group. Aberdeen Journals was held by the DGFT to be dominant in the market for the supply of advertising space in local newspapers (paid-for and free) within the Aberdeen area, and that it had deliberately incurred losses on the *Herald & Post* in an attempt to expel the *Aberdeen & District Independent*, its only rival in the relevant market. Aberdeen Journals had therefore infringed the Chapter II prohibition by predating and a penalty of £1,328,040 was imposed. Aberdeen Journals appealed and the Tribunal considered that the relevant product market had not been assessed in sufficient detail. The DGFT subsequently restated and confirmed the earlier decision on the basis of an expanded treatment of the issue of the relevant market (No CA98/14/2002, 16 September 2002), and this decision was appealed to the CAT. The CAT upheld the finding that Aberdeen Journals had abused its dominant position by predatory pricing. The CAT did have to deal with a particularly complex argument regarding the assessment of costs for the purposes of determining whether a price was predatory:

Aberdeen Journals v DGFT
[2003] CAT 11, paras 378–80

378. Thirdly, and more fundamentally, the argument presented by Aberdeen Journals is, in effect, that a dominant firm, using its spare capacity, is entitled to price against a competitor on a marginal basis and that, so long as its marginal revenues exceed its marginal costs (for which average variable costs are a proxy) it is acting lawfully, and does not need to allocate any costs, other than marginal costs, to the particular activity in question.

379. This argument has not, so far as we know, yet been considered by the Court of Justice, or the Court of First Instance. The Tribunal has not heard submissions on this issue, and it is not necessary for the Tribunal to rule on it for the purpose of deciding the present case. Nonetheless, it does seem to us that if a dominant undertaking is able to exclude from its computations significant elements of cost which have to be borne one way or another, and which any equally efficient competitor would have to bear, there is a risk that the dominant firm will always be able, sooner or later, to undercut an equally efficient competitor and drive it from the market. That, in our view, is a particular risk where the marginal cost of a particular strategy, such as use of a "fighting title" (as in this case) or a "fighting ship" (as in *Compagnie Maritime Belge*, cited above) may well be very low.

380. In our view, the cost-based rules set out in *AKZO* and *Tetra Pak II*, while providing guidance, are not an end in themselves and should not be applied mechanistically. The ultimate aim of the 1998 Act is to secure conditions of undistorted and effective competition. With that primary aim in view, a principal role of the Chapter II prohibition is to prevent dominant firms from defending or strengthening their dominant position in ways that are unreasonable and disproportionate, particularly by using methods different from those found under normal competitive conditions. In our view, the decision of the Court of Justice in *Compagnie Maritime Belge* itself shows that the guidance available in *AKZO* and *Tetra Pak II* is open to further development.

NOTE: The CAT emphasized that a mechanistic approach should not be adopted in determining whether behaviour was abusive, despite the importance accorded to earlier Court jurisprudence. The CAT also noted that the authorities did not require to demonstrate the feasibility of 'recoupment' to establish predation and that caution should be exercised in seeking to transpose American and Australian decisions where the conceptual basis of the legislation is not the same. A subsequent case involving a margin squeeze abuse by Genzyme Ltd (*Genzyme Ltd v OFT* [2004] CAT 4; on margin squeezing, see Parker, J, 'Case Comment: *Dwr Cymru v Albion Water Ltd*: a consideration of margin squeeze in the UK' (2008) 7 Comp LJ 237) was the last finding of abusive behaviour by the OFT under the Chapter II prohibition for a period of five years until November 2008 and the OFT's finding that Cardiff Bus engaged in predatory conduct to eliminate a competitor.

Cardiff Bus
OFT Press Release, 133/08, 18 November 2008

Transport operator Cardiff Bus engaged in predatory conduct intended to eliminate a competitor, 2 Travel, the OFT decided today.

The OFT's decision relates to Cardiff Bus' behaviour between April 2004 and February 2005. Cardiff Bus responded to the introduction of a new no-frills bus service by another bus company, 2 Travel, by introducing its own no-frills bus services which ran on the same routes, at similar times as 2 Travel's services and made a loss for Cardiff Bus. Shortly after 2 Travel's exit from the market Cardiff Bus withdrew its own no-frills services.

Before 2 Travel's entry, Cardiff Bus, which is owned by Cardiff Council, was carrying 80,000 people each weekday, and was the only significant provider of urban commercial bus services in the County with a very substantial share of the relevant market.

Predatory behaviour occurs when a dominant company sustains losses in the short run in order to eliminate a competitor. Such behaviour is in breach of the Competition Act 1998.

John Fingleton, OFT Chief Executive, said:

'Predation by a dominant firm to eliminate a rival is a major distortion of competition that harms consumers. This type of behaviour can seriously affect the competitive process by weakening the incentives of efficient competitors to challenge dominant firms and bring greater choice and lower prices to consumers.

Our decision should send a clear signal to firms that may be dominant, whether on national markets or smaller local markets, that predatory behaviour is a serious infringement of the law.'

The OFT has not levied a financial penalty in this case. Cardiff Bus benefits from a limited immunity from penalties because the company's turnover did not exceed £50 million at the time of the conduct.

■ QUESTION

Is it possible to distinguish between competitive and anti-competitive pricing activity?

(c) Refusal to supply

There have been decisions by the OFT and the courts in which no infringement has been found, for instance in *Claritas (UK) Ltd* v *The Post Office and Postal Preference Service Ltd* [2001] UKCLR 2, Ch). A decision by the OFT to reject a compliant can be appealed to the CAT, as evidenced by the following case:

Burgess v OFT
[2005] CAT 25, paras 316–19 and 332

This case involved an alleged abuse of a dominant position consisting in the refusal by a firm of funeral directors in Stevenage to allow access to a crematorium owned by them to Burgess, a competing firm of funeral directors. The OFT rejected the substance of the complaint by Burgess, who appealed to the CAT. After reiterating the Community jurisprudence on determining what constitutes an abusive refusal to supply, the CAT applied the case law to the facts of the case as follows:

316. For the reasons already given, we accept that Burgess' Knebworth branch, situated only a short distance from Harwood Park, is unlikely to be viable without access to that crematorium. In our judgment, continued refusal of access to Harwood Park will inevitably lead to the closure of Burgess' Knebworth branch, probably sooner rather than later. On any view, Burgess' ability to compete effectively in the market for funeral directing services in the Stevenage/Knebworth area is likely to be significantly weakened by a refusal of access to Harwood Park. Indeed, in our judgment it is unlikely that a funeral director in the area of Stevenage/Knebworth could compete effectively in that local market without access to Harwood Park.

317. Austins, the owners of Harwood Park, already have a dominant position in the market for funeral directing services in the Stevenage/Knebworth area. It follows in our judgment that the elimination of Burgess as an effective competitor in the Stevenage/Knebworth area would inevitably tend to have the effect of strengthening Austins' dominant position in funeral directing services in that area, and weakening effective competition in that local market. For the reasons given below, we do not consider new entry to be a likely compensating factor.

318. In our judgment, the refusal of access to Burgess by a crematorium in the position of Harwood Park may fairly be described as "recourse to methods different from those which condition normal competition" within the meaning of paragraph 91 of *Hoffman La Roche*, cited above. We are unaware of any circumstances in which it could be suggested that it was normal practice in this industry for crematoria to discriminate against particular local funeral directors, without objective justification. Mr Nethercott's view, in his letter of 24 December 2003, was that Burgess' exclusion from Harwood Park was "unprecedented".

319. It follows that the protecting or strengthening of Austins' dominant position in the market for funeral directing services in the Stevenage/Knebworth area, which inevitably tends to follow from the elimination or serious weakening of Burgess in that area, is not the result of competition "on the merits", but of Austins' refusal to allow Burgess access to Harwood Park. ....

332. We accept therefore that the OFT is correct, up to a point, in submitting that the aim of the Chapter II prohibition is not to protect competitors, but to protect competition. On the other hand,

where effective competition is already weak through the presence of a dominant firm, there are circumstances in which competition can be protected and fostered only by imposing on the dominant firm a special responsibility under the Chapter II prohibition not to behave in certain ways vis-à-vis its remaining competitors, particularly where barriers to entry are high. In such circumstances the enforcement of the Chapter II prohibition may in a sense "protect" a competitor, by shielding the competitor from the otherwise abusive conduct of the dominant firm. However, that is the necessary consequence of taking action in order to protect effective competition. In a case such as the present, intervention under the Chapter II prohibition should not therefore be seen, as the OFT seemed to suggest, as merely "protecting a competitor", but from the point of view of the wider interest of preserving effective competition for the ultimate benefit of consumers. While Burgess is not entitled to be protected against normal market forces, it is in our view entitled under the Act not to be eliminated as an efficient operator in the market by the abusive practices of a dominant firm.

NOTE: The CAT applied the *Tetra Pak II* associative links doctrine to hold that there was an abuse in the related funeral directing services market. The CAT's discussion of the scope of the abuse prohibition and the rationale for intervention in the competition process at para. 332 is notable.

SECTION 3: FAIR TRADING ACT 1973

The Monopolies and Restrictive Trade Practices (Inquiry and Control) Act 1948, following upon the White Paper on Employment policy in 1944, introduced the UK system for dealing with monopoly, which was adopted by the FTA 1973. The following passage by Wilks sets out the background to the FTA 1973:

Wilks, S., *In the Public Interest, Competition Policy and the Monopolies and Mergers Commission*
Manchester, MUP, 1999, pp. 172–3

The British vocabulary talked similarly of 'monopolies' and 'restrictive practices' but it did not regard them as unlawful and was not 'anti' anything. Indeed, although nowadays these terms have become pejorative, the normative coloration was more muted in the 1940s when both monopoly and restrictive practices had proved their worth in responding to depression and mobilising for war. The term 'monopoly' is an especially curious shorthand with which the MMC has had to live. Cases of true monopoly, where 100 per cent of production is concentrated in one undertaking, are extremely rare and in principle indefensible. The MMC has in practice dealt with oligopoly. The economic illiteracy of its title underlines the way in which the MMC has found 'monopoly' not to be harmful—in cases such as flat glass or soluble coffee, where a principled stress on competition would have indicated remedial action but where an efficiency defence has been accepted. Thus British policy came late to a wholehearted commitment to competition. The focus of competition policy on 'competition'; the high salience of competition policy within the mix of economic policies; and the insertion of principles of competition into a range of unrelated policies—all these are developments of the Thatcher years. It is therefore important to set aside the preconceptions of the 1990s in evaluating earlier and more agnostic views of competition, and to appreciate that the machinery of government was designed as much to restrict competition as to encourage it.

The complexity and ambiguity of British competition agencies and law, as they stood in 1997 ahead of the Labour reforms, therefore reflected peculiar policy dynamics. The policies did not grow from a clear design or a policy vision. They were not forged in a furnace of public outrage (as in the United States); they were not imposed as part of the fruits of victory (as in Japan and, partially, Germany); neither were they conceived as part of a vision of political and economic integration (as with the European Economic Community (EEC)). Instead British policy emerged incrementally and piecemeal as a product of consensus building by a powerful civil service, heavily influenced by business lobbying, increasingly responding to developments in economic thought, and operating under a benign and exceptional mantle of political bi-partisanship.

NOTE: Wilks has provided an excellent account of the history of the Monopolies and Mergers Commission and the development of the institution of competition policy in the UK. This passage, which is set out in Chapter 7 of his book, focused on the 'unique and idiosyncratic model' of British competition policy. The 1973 Act provisions allowed markets to be investigated where there was market failure but not necessarily any anti-competitive activity confined to one undertaking. These provisions were particularly useful in relation to oligopolistic markets (see Rodger, B.J., 'Oligopolistic Market Failure, Collective Dominance v Complex Monopoly' [1995] ECLR 21) and the appropriateness for dealing with such markets under the FTA 1973 where it is difficult to attach blame was one of the reasons noted for the retention of these provisions when the CA 1998 was introduced.

Of particular interest in the genesis of the 1973 Act is the bi-partisan character of policy development and his critique of the 'shotgun marriage' between consumerism and competition law embedded in the 1973 Act due to a lack of Parliamentary time.

Under the 1973 Act, the Competition Commission was required to conduct its investigation and produce a report to the Secretary of State in which it would consider the public interest implications of the monopoly situation and make appropriate recommendations in order to remedy any adverse effects identified.

DGFT Annual Report, 1999

Introduction

'Rip-off Britain'

The issue of high prices has always been an important one, but has been an especially major theme in the media throughout 1999. Reckless talk of high prices can itself begin to erode consumer confidence. It may even reduce the attractiveness of the UK as a place to visit, or distort patterns of investment. The headlines and debate on 'rip-off Britain' are therefore something I have taken very seriously.

The UK has not operated a policy of general price control for many years. Nor have most other nations of the developed world. They, and increasingly also the former managed economies of Eastern Europe and the third world countries, have all concluded that a free market in which there is vigorous and genuine competition both rewards efficient businesses and gives the best deal to consumers. This is because entrepreneurs can enter new markets without encountering artificial barriers. They can study consumer needs and endeavour to increase their profits and market share by competing on price, quality, convenience or innovation. In an ideal market the consumer is in the driving seat and the supply of the right products at the right price matches the requirements of a discerning demand.

Unfortunately, we do not yet live in a perfect world and market failures occur. The task of making competition policy a success falls on enforcers such as the Competition Policy Division of my Office. My competition powers enable me to act on behalf of consumers in a direct way and many of the consumer issues which have featured so strongly in the headlines have, in fact, related to issues of competition policy. The view, sometimes expressed, that the consumer affairs and competition policy roles in regulation should be separated is, in my view, mistaken and would be a disservice to consumer welfare. Our system is mirrored by those of the United States, Canada, Australia and France.

Market failures occur because some businesses would prefer to make profits by preventing competition through abuse of dominant positions, or by adopting anti-competitive agreements which, under the new Competition Act, are now prohibited by law. High prices can sometimes be a symptom of such anti-competitive activity. My power to act under the Competition Act 1998 will depend on the ability to establish a breach of law. As with any other investigative process, it is dangerous to start with a presumption of guilt. Investigation must be fair and impartial. In such a case the Act provides the strong safeguard of a swift appeal system through the Competition Commission. In monopoly cases, which will continue to be investigated under the provisions of the Fair Trading Act, I must be satisfied that one or more companies may be involved in a monopoly situation. While there is no question of financial penalties, the disruption, expense and uncertainty of a monopoly reference to the Competition Commission should not be underestimated, nor should the threat of an imposed remedy by the Secretary of State. The stakes are high for all parties but the OFT will implement the law with vigour.

NOTE: The OFT has traditionally combined two roles: supervising competition policy and championing the rights of the consumer. Pricing policies, where a monopoly situation exists, would appear to be a clear concern of the competition authorities. This has not always been the case but the cyclical nature of competition law and its concerns was demonstrated by the 'rip-off Britain' strategy in the late 1990s, including in particular the Competition Commission report on new car pricing (Cm 4660, 2000). The position of the consumer was further facilitated by the EA 2002 provision to allow consumer bodies to bring super-complaints to the OFT involving a fast-track procedure. The close relationship between consumer and competition policy has been further demonstrated by the focus in the Competition Commission's work under the EA 2002 on the impact of market failures on consumers.

The following are merely selected examples of issues that the Commission has looked at under the monopoly provisions of the FTA 1973. The Commission was required to assess whether the monopoly position itself operated against the public interest. This was established in very few reports, partly because the obvious remedy of divestiture—breaking up the monopoly—is fairly radical.

The Supply of Beer
Cm 651, 1989, paras 1.9–1.10, 1.18–1.20, and 1.25

> 1.9. One of the most prominent features of the United Kingdom beer industry is the extent of vertical integration. Brewing companies differ greatly in size, but the majority of them brew beer *and* wholesale it *and* retail it. In order to retail beer, brewing companies own a substantial proportion of the public houses. We estimate that brewers own about 75 per cent of the public houses in Great Britain. Brewer-owned houses fall into two categories—managed, in which the publican and, as a rule, the staff are employees of the brewing company; and tenanted, where the publican is not an employee of the brewer-landlord, but pays the brewer a rent for the premises and earns his living from the retail profit made by the outlet. In both categories, the brewer specifies what beers may be sold in the public house, and where they must be bought (usually from the brewer himself). In the case of managed public houses, the brewer sets retail prices as well.

> 1.10. The on-licensed trade available outside brewer-owned outlets is usually described as the 'free trade'. Here, too, brewer influence is strong through the mechanism of the loan tie. In order to secure either exclusivity for his own products in a 'free house', or a minimum throughput, a brewer will offer a loan to the owner(s) of the house at below market rates of interest. It is open to the owners of free houses to have one loan, more than one, or none at all, but loan-tying is a widespread practice throughout the United Kingdom. We estimate that half of the 25 per cent of public houses that are not owned by brewers are tied to them by loans. About half of members' clubs are loan-tied as well. About two-thirds of all the beer that brewers sell, including that supplied for consumption at home, is sold to premises that they either own or tie by a loan.

> ...

Our view

> 1.18. Eloquently though the industry's case has been put, we are not persuaded that all is well. We have confirmed our provisional finding that a complex monopoly situation exists in favour of the brewers with tied estates and loan ties.

1.19. This complex monopoly restricts competition at all levels. Brewers are protected from competition in supplying their managed and tenanted estates because other brewers do not have access to them. Even in the free trade many brewers prefer to compete by offering low-interest loans, which then tie the outlet to them, rather than by offering beer at lower prices. Wholesale prices are higher than they would be in the absence of the tie. This inevitably feeds through into high retail prices.

1.20. The ownership and loan ties also give little opportunity for an independent wholesaling sector to prosper and offer competition to the brewers' wholesaling activities, for example by offering a mix of products from different producers.

Our recommendations

The property tie

1.25. It has been put to us repeatedly that smaller brewers in particular need their tied estates to stay in business. In present circumstances, if the tie were to be abolished altogether we believe that many regional and local brewers would withdraw from brewing, concentrate on retailing, and leave the market to domination by national and international brand owners. This would substantially reduce consumer choice. We therefore recommend, not the complete abolition of the tie, but a ceiling of 2,000 on the number of on-licensed premises, whether public houses, hotels or any other type of on-licensed outlet, which any brewing company or group may own. This ceiling will require the divestment of some 22,000 premises by United Kingdom national brewers. (No regional or local brewer currently reaches the 2,000 ceiling we recommend.) We do not believe that United Kingdom property or capital markets will have any difficulty in absorbing the change; we are recommending a maximum of three years for the divestments to take place.

NOTE: The Secretary of State subsequently made significant Orders, including The Supply of Beer (Tied Estate) Order 1989 (SI 1989/2390). Following a review, the limitations on ownership were subsequently removed due to changes in the beer market. Divestiture was also recommended in *Gas and British Gas plc* (Cm 2317, 1993), the Supply of Raw Milk report (Cm 4286, 1999), and most recently, in March 2009, in the Commission report on the Supply of Airport Services by BAA in the UK.

More commonly, the Commission proceeded to report upon aspects of the conduct of parties within a market under investigation, in particular pricing policies. A number of Commission reports have investigated the issues of excessive and oligopolistic pricing as demonstrated in their classic report on the drugs valium and librium:

Chlordiazepoxide and Diazepam
(1972–73) HCP 197 at paras 229–35 and 237

Profits

229. Roche Products does not accept that profitability should be, or in any realistic terms can be, examined in terms of individual drugs...We accept that the profitability of the Roche Group's drug business as a whole would be a factor to take into account if we had been afforded any precise information on the subject. But in the present context we have to reach conclusions about the prices for particular drugs; and it is at least clear that the prices charged for these drugs, in the United Kingdom and elsewhere, must play a major part in determining the profitability of the Group's drug business as a whole.

230. It is arguable that the pharmaceutical industry could not be expected to invest in speculative research of the kind that leads to innovations unless it were offered the prospect of an above average level of reward when it successfully introduces a new drug. If it were our task to determine a fair price for a recently introduced drug we would regard this as an argument to take seriously into account. But, for reasons which we explain in paragraphs 231 and 232, the level of profit which might have been allowed for in determining what should have been fair prices for the reference drugs up to the present is barely relevant to our present problem. For purposes of illustration only we have, as indicated in paragraphs

165 to 170, estimated the effect of adding a profit of 25 per cent on capital to the cost figures as set out in appendix 5, table 2 and arrived at notional prices of £421 and £964 per
kilo of Librium and Valium respectively (as compared with the actual average prices in 1970
of £734 and £1,962 respectively). But we regard these figures only as providing a starting
point for arriving at fair current and future prices.

Effects of past excessive prices

231. Successful patented drugs, whose sales as in the present case exceed the conservative
estimates on which the innovator's pricing policy is likely to have been based, often give a
high return (in terms of recovery of research costs and profit), particularly if there is no price
reduction. The public interest issues involved have been considered in principle many times
over the years, both in relation to the patent law generally and also with particular regard to
the situation in the pharmaceutical industry. There is a continuing conflict between the needs
on the one hand to provide pharmaceutical manufacturers with an incentive (in the form of attractive profit potential) to produce innovations, and on the other hand to set limits to the exploitation of successful innovations through excessively high prices under patent protection.

232. In considering what would be a reasonable limit to exploitation in a particular case, regard
must be had to the profitability of the drug over its patent life as a whole. Thus after a few
years, during which sales have increased and very high rates of profit indeed may have
been achieved, exploitation could be kept within reasonable limits by adequate, regular
price reductions. Where, as in the present case, no such reduction has been made over
two-thirds or more of the patent life, a more drastic price cut may therefore be required
thereafter. Accordingly, in determining what are the maximum prices that should be
charged for the reference drugs in future, we need to take into account, so far as this is
possible, the return the Roche Group has obtained from them over their patent lives up to
the present. It is quite clear that since the introduction of the reference drugs the Group
must have earned very high levels of profit indeed from the sale of these drugs in the United
Kingdom, besides recovering increasingly large contributions to its current expenditure on
research, the scale of which it was able, as one consequence of such profits in this country
and elsewhere, to expand with a view to developing future product innovations. Because of
the conflict of factors affecting the public interest to which we have referred, it can only be
a matter of judgment at what stage undue exploitation of success can be said to begin. But
we have no doubt that in the present exceptional case this stage has long been passed.

233. On the basis of cost figures which, as we have shown, we regard as higher than are acceptable for the purpose of arriving at fair prices, we have estimated the Group profit on the sale
of Librium and Valium in the United Kingdom in 1970 at about £4m after allowing for a Group
research contribution of about £1m from those two drugs. . . . More approximately but on the
same conservative basis, we have estimated that the total Group profits for the sale of all reference drugs in the United Kingdom in the seven years from 1966 to the end of 1972 were in
the region of £25m, out of which the Group repaid to DHSS, in response to pressure from the
Department, about £1m in respect of reference goods trading up to the end of 1969. . . . These
profits are calculated after allowing for recovery of research expenditure as a charge against
sales of the reference goods amounting probably to some £6m to £7m over the seven years.

234. In the light of these facts, the question of what rate of profit should be allowed in determining a fair price becomes, as we have said in paragraph 230, barely relevant to our problem,
since the Roche Group has already obtained from the sale of these drugs in this country
profits far in excess of what is justifiable.

Recommendations

235. Among the points we bear in mind in reaching a conclusion on the appropriate level of
prices in future are the following:
   (a) Even if we could accept the cost figures in appendix 5, table 2, fair prices based upon
   these costs might have been lower than those actually charged in 1970 by at least 40 per
   cent for Librium and at least 50 per cent for Valium (paragraph 230).

(b) For reasons we have given in detail (paragraphs 219 to 227) we are satisfied that some of the cost figures referred to—in particular those for research and promotion costs—grossly exceed the levels that should be taken into account to arrive at fair prices. It follows that fair prices should in any case be substantially below the levels indicated in (a).

(c) There are no grounds for maintaining the particular price differential between Valium and Librium which existed in 1970 (paragraph 228).

(d) The excessive prices charged up to the present have already produced excessive profits on a very large scale (paragraph 234).

Although we have made a number of calculations in an attempt to quantify the effects of (b) and (c) above, none has proved entirely satisfactory having regard to our incomplete knowledge of the business of the Roche Group. But in the event this scarcely matters in the light of (d).

...

237. We recommend that Roche Products' selling prices for the reference drugs should be reduced (i) as regards Librium, to not more than 40 per cent of the selling prices in 1970, (ii) as regards Valium, to not more than 25 per cent of the selling prices in 1970, (iii) as regards other drugs covered by the reference, by corresponding proportions as may be determined by DHSS.

NOTE: During the 1970s a number of reports focused on excessive pricing and price monitoring was considered an appropriate remedy, for instance by undertakings not to increase prices without government approval (following *Ready Cooked Breakfast Cereal Foods* (1972–73) HCP 2). During the 1980s and 1990s price regulation became less a feature of the monopoly controls as attitudes to the operation of the market changed. (See also the report, *Supply of Recorded Music*, Cm 2599, 1994 where the Commission did not find the pricing of CDs in the UK, higher in comparison with the US and EC, to be against the public interest.) The rip-off Britain campaign instituted in the late 1990s again placed pricing for consumers at the forefront of the FTA's concerns, although not all Commission reports have been critical of pricing strategies. (See Supply of New Cars, Cm 4660, 2000 and cf. Supermarket pricing, Cm 4842, 2000.)

Following a Commission report, if it concluded that there were specific public interest detriments, most commonly, the Secretary of State would request the DGFT to negotiate and obtain appropriate undertakings from parties in order to remedy the public interest effects specified by the Commission.

If undertakings are considered to be inappropriate, are not given, or are breached, the Secretary of State could resort to his Order-making powers in Sch. 8. These powers included the power to control prices, order the publication of prices, and prohibit discriminatory practices.

For instance, the Restriction on Agreements and Conduct (Specified Domestic Electrical Goods) Order 1998 (SI 1998/1271) was introduced in response to the Commission reports, *Domestic Electrical Goods: I* and *II* (Cm 3676, 1997) in order to increase price competition in a range of electrical goods.

SECTION 4: THE ENTERPRISE ACT 2002 AND MARKET INVESTIGATIONS

During the late 1980s and 1990s the existing UK provisions for the control of monopoly, including the provisions on anti-competitive practices contained in the Competition Act 1980, were the subject of numerous criticisms and proposals for reform. Notable in this regard was the DTI Green Paper, *Abuse of Market Power* (November 1992, Cm 2100: see particularly paras 4.3, 4.7, 4.12–13). Legislation was not introduced following these proposals although ultimately the CA 1998 adopted a version of model 3 in the Green Paper which stressed the versatility of the FTA provisions but recommended adoption of a new set of rules in harmony with the main Community competition rules, Article 82 EC in this context. However, shortly after the entry into force of the CA 1998 prohibitions, the DTI produced proposals to reform the monopoly provisions of the FTA 1973 and replace them with a new scheme for investigating markets.

DTI, *A World Class Competition Regime*
Cm 5233, July 2001, paras 6.12–6.15 and 6.21–6.24

The new regime for investigating markets

6.12 The new regime for investigating markets will have a similar scope to the existing monopoly provisions, but will operate along the same lines as the new merger regime. It will be used for market wide inquiries. It is not Government's intention that it will be used to deal with scale monopoly problems except in exceptional circumstances (see paragraphs 6.58 to 6.59 below).
   • The OFT will work pro-actively to keep markets under review—where it appears that markets may not be working well, it will be able to refer them to the Competition Commission for further investigation.
   • The Competition Commission will carry out a full investigation—assessing the market against a new competition-based test.
   • The Competition Commission will itself determine what remedies are necessary. If appropriate, it will ask the OFT to negotiate undertakings on its behalf.
   • Occasionally, even though there are adverse competition effects, the way a market operates may bring countervailing benefits to consumers. If this is the case, then the Competition Commission may decide to take no action or modify its remedies.
   • Ministers will retain the power to decide the very small minority of cases where clearly defined exceptional public interest issues arise.
   • There may be a case for Ministers retaining a limited role in relation to divestment remedies recommended by the Competition Commission.

Making references

6.13 The Fair Trading Act enables a reference to the Competition Commission to address complex monopoly questions when:
   • it can name or define companies in a market who collectively have a share of supply of 25 per cent more; and
   • it appears that the companies, whether voluntarily or not, and whether by agreement or not, so conduct their affairs as in any way to prevent, restrict or distort competition.

6.14 The Government believes that this test should be changed. The first limb is of little value—as in almost every market, it is possible to name or define companies who collectively have a share of supply of 25 per cent or more. The second limb is also problematic, as it asks the OFT to make an assessment that is not directly related to the substantive test applied by the Competition Commission in its subsequent inquiry.

A new reference test

6.15 For the new regime for investigating markets, the Government will develop a more flexible reference test—which allows the OFT to refer markets when it believes that conduct, or circumstances surrounding the operation of a market, suggest a Competition Commission investigation would be merited. The Government invites views on the following replacement test:

The OFT believes (or has a reasonable suspicion) that a market may operate in a manner which adversely affects competition.

Or, alternatively, and closer to the proposed merger test:

The OFT believes (or has a reasonable suspicion) that the market may operate in a manner which substantially lessens competition.

...

A new competition-based test

6.21 When a market is referred for investigation, a key question that the Competition Commission needs to answer is whether any facts found by the Commission during their investigations operate, or may be expected to operate, against the public interest. The test is concerned with the public interest rather than competition issues.

6.22 With the advent of the Competition Act 1998, monopolies and restrictive agreements are considered against a competition test. The continued presence of the public interest test in the Fair Trading Act now looks anomalous and outdated.

6.23 The Government intends to replace the public interest test with a narrower, more focused competition test.

6.24 In a merger case, the Competition Commission will assess whether a merger will lead to a substantial lessening of competition. A similar analysis may be applicable in a market-wide investigation (ie whether the conduct or performance of any firm or any other aspect of the market has the effect of substantially lessening competition). Alternatively, the test may be based on adverse effects (ie whether the conduct or performance of any firm or any other aspect of the market means that the market operates in a manner which adversely affects competition). The Government invites views on these two approaches. One issue is whether the test should include some degree of appreciability such as 'substantial'.

NOTE: Part IV of the EA 2002 contains a complicated set of provisions to implement these proposals. The Act has many novel features which distinguish the process of market investigations from their predecessor: the role of the OFT in referring markets, often following a 'super-complaint' by a representative consumer body; the abandonment of the public interest test in favour of a new competition test; and the wider role for the Competition Commission in fashioning remedies to deal with any competition concerns arising from an investigation. Nonetheless, the fundamental purpose and outcome of market investigations undertaken under the EA 2002 are similar in nature to those which were carried out under the 1973 Act.

A: Initiation and referral

To emphasize the importance of the consumer interest in the context of market investigations, the EA 2002 introduced a 'super-complaints' process under s. 11 of the Act as follows:

ENTERPRISE ACT 2002 [S. 11]

Super-complaints to OFT

11.— (1) This section applies where a designated consumer body makes a complaint to the OFT that any feature, or combination of features, of a market in the United Kingdom for goods or services is or appears to be significantly harming the interests of consumers.

(2) The OFT must, within 90 days after the day on which it receives the complaint, publish a response stating how it proposes to deal with the complaint, and in particular—

    (a) whether it has decided to take any action, or to take no action, in response to the complaint, and

    (b) if it has decided to take action, what action it proposes to take.

(3) The response must state the OFT's reasons for its proposals.

(4) The Secretary of State may by order amend subsection (2) by substituting any period for the period for the time being specified there.

(5) "Designated consumer body" means a body designated by the Secretary of State by order.

NOTE: The OFT has referred a number of markets to the Competition Commission following a super-complaint, for example in relation to *Payment Protection Insurance* and *Northern Ireland Banking*. Furthermore, following a super-complaint in relation to the *Scottish legal profession*, key rules of the Scottish Faculty of Advocates were revised, although no reference to the Competition Commission was made.

The reference test was dramatically reformed, and the 25 per cent market share threshold required for a reference under the FTA 1973 has disappeared. The test now focuses directly on markets where the OFT suspects that competition may be prevented, restricted, or distorted.

ENTERPRISE ACT 2002 [S. 131(1) AND (2)]

Power of OFT to make references

131.— (1) The OFT may, subject to subsection (4), make a reference to the Commission if the OFT has reasonable grounds for suspecting that any feature, or combination of features, of a market in the United Kingdom for goods or services prevents, restricts or distorts competition in connection with the supply or acquisition of any goods or services in the United Kingdom or a part of the United Kingdom.

(2) For the purposes of this Part any reference to a feature of a market in the United Kingdom for goods or services shall be construed as a reference to—
   (a) the structure of the market concerned or any aspect of that structure;
   (b) any conduct (whether or not in the market concerned) of one or more than one person who supplies or acquires goods or services in the market concerned; or
   (c) any conduct relating to the market concerned of customers of any person who supplies or acquires goods or services.

NOTE: A feature of a market can include both conduct and structural issues. Note in particular that the Secretary of State, in addition to the role in relation to exceptional public interest issues, has a power, under s. 132, to make a reference where not satisfied with the OFT decision not to refer a market. The following is the text of the reference made by the OFT under the EA 2002 in relation to *BAA Airports*:

BAA: The OFT's reference to the Competition Commission
April 2007

The OFT, in exercise of its powers under sections 131 and 133 of the Enterprise Act 2002 (the Act), hereby makes a reference to the Competition Commission for an investigation into the supply of airport services in the United Kingdom. In accordance with section 133(2) and (3)(b) of the Act the Competition Commission shall confine its investigation to the effects of features of such market or markets for airport services in the United Kingdom as exist in connection with the supply of airport services by BAA. The OFT has reasonable grounds for suspecting that a feature or a combination of features of the market or markets in which airport services are supplied by BAA prevents, restricts or distorts competition in connection with the supply of airport services in the United Kingdom.

   For the purposes of this reference:
   'airport services' means all airport services whether they are supplied to airlines, ground handlers, passengers or any other person and includes all or any of the following:
   (a) the provision of airport infrastructure services (including the development, maintenance, use and provision of access roads, runway facilities, fuelling facilities, taxiways, aprons, stands, loading bridges, piers and gaterooms, check-in and arrivals concourses, check-in desks, customs and immigration halls, baggage facilities, passenger care facilities, lifts, escalators, passenger conveyors, terminal offices, ramps, and other airport structures);

(b) the co-ordination and control of the activities performed on or in airport infrastructure and the provision of associated services including security services; and

(c) the provision (including the provision by persons other than BAA under arrangements made with BAA) of associated commercial services (including catering services, retail services, car rental services, the sale of advertising space, the provision of car parking, and activities relating to commercial property).

'BAA' means the group of interconnected bodies corporate directly or indirectly owned or controlled (including by way of material influence) by Airport Development and Investment Limited which (from time to time) own and/or operate Heathrow, Gatwick, Stansted, Southampton, Edinburgh, Glasgow and Aberdeen airports, the World Duty Free business, and the BAA Lynton business, and which (from time to time) own and/or operate any other business providing airport services in the UK;

'control' and 'material influence' shall be construed in accordance with section 26 of the Act; and

'group of interconnected bodies corporate' shall be construed in accordance with section 129(2) of the Act.

NOTE: The Commission's Final Report, published in March 2009, required BAA to sell three airports, Gatwick and Stanstend, and either Edinburgh or Glasgow, within two years.

B: The reporting stage: the Competition Commission

The Competition Commission has responsibility for conducting market investigations and finalizing reports, within a period of two years. A key feature of Part IV of the EA 2002 is the competition test to be applied by the Competition Commission, as opposed to the public interest test under the FTA 1973.

ENTERPRISE ACT 2002 [S. 134]

Questions to be decided on market investigation references

134.—(1) The Commission shall, on a market investigation reference, decide whether any feature, or combination of features, of each relevant market prevents, restricts or distorts competition in connection with the supply or acquisition of goods or services in the United Kingdom or part of the United Kingdom.

NOTE: The term 'adverse effect on competition' is used here as a shorthand for the test to be employed by the Commission. In line with the general pro-consumer ethos in the Act, sub-s. (4) allows the Commission to take action either to remedy the adverse effect on competition or any detrimental effect on customers arising from such adverse effect. In addition, the Commission can take into account any countervailing consumer benefits of the market features concerned.

The 'public interest' has not disappeared altogether although it has been retained in a very limited fashion. Chapter 2 of Part IV introduces a particularly complex set of provisions in relation to public interest intervention notices by the Secretary of State. (ss. 139–40) There was considerable debate in Parliament on the scope of these fall-back provisions, and Government Ministers stressed that they would be used rarely.

The Commission undertakes a detailed and time-consuming investigation of the market under reference. There are various stages in the process, including the publication of an introductory issues statement, a subsequent emerging thinking report, a provisional findings report, and the final report. The following are excerpts from the various stages in relation to certain recent inquiries to give a flavour of the Commission's investigation process:

Issues Statement, *Payment Protection Insurance*
12 April 2007, paras 1–7

1. On 7 February 2007, the Office of Fair Trading (OFT) referred the UK supply of payment protection insurance (PPI) to non-business customers to the Competition Commission (CC) for

investigation. The reference followed an initial OFT study into the sector, which was undertaken in response to a super-complaint from Citizens Advice.

2. PPI is defined in our terms of reference as: insurance services supplied for the purpose of protecting a borrower's ability to maintain credit repayments in the event that the borrower becomes unable to maintain the repayments due to accident and/or sickness and/or unemployment and, under some policies, death.

3. Store card PPI services have been excluded from the terms of reference. These services were covered by an earlier CC inquiry, with remedies not taking effect until 1 May 2007. It was the view of the OFT that it would be disproportionate to include store card PPI in the terms of another reference.

4. The CC is required to determine whether any feature, or combination of features, of the PPI market or markets prevents, restricts or distorts competition. If this is so, there will be an 'adverse effect on competition' and we will seek to answer the following additional questions:

(a) whether action should be taken to remedy, mitigate or prevent the adverse effect on competition concerned or any detrimental effect on customers, and if so what those actions should be; and

(b) whether it should recommend the taking of action by others for the same purpose and if so, what those recommendations should be.

5. We must distinguish competition issues from other issues of public concern associated with the supply of PPI which we have no power to investigate. While we can consider issues, such as mis-selling, where they have competition implications, we cannot, for example, either decide the merits of individual cases or indeed make decisions on wider issues such as responsible lending. Public concern about these issues may interact with competition issues and provide background and context for our investigation, but our focus must be on the competition issues.

6. This issues statement is based on our consideration of the OFT's decision document, and on our initial consideration of the issues we propose to investigate. We are publishing this statement before we have received main submissions from interested parties in order to assist those submitting evidence to focus on the issues we envisage being central to this investigation. If parties consider that there are additional issues which we should consider, they are invited to identify them and to explain why these are relevant to our statutory questions. We recognize that other issues may arise in the course of our investigation; we will consider these carefully and will pursue substantive issues which bear on competition.

7. We plan to hold hearings with interested parties during the period May to July 2007. Following these hearings, we expect to publish an 'emerging thinking' document for consultation. We may then hold further hearings before publishing our provisional findings.

Emerging Thinking Report, *BAA*
22 April 2008, para. 274

274. On the evidence that we have seen so far, our assessment of the potential features adversely affecting competition between airports and airlines is as follows:

(a) Our current view is that there is potential for competition between Edinburgh and Glasgow airports (see paragraph 145) (although we are still unclear of the strength of the potential competition between them) but such competition is prevented by common ownership of those two airports. Common ownership of Edinburgh and Glasgow is therefore a feature which adversely affects competition between the two airports.

(b) Our current view is also that there is potential competition between Aberdeen and the other two BAA airports in Scotland, although we need to consider further the evidence on Aberdeen, which is less strong. We also have to consider further therefore the extent to which the evidence that we have seen that cash generated at Aberdeen is used elsewhere in the group rather than being invested in the facilities at Aberdeen is attributable to the AEC of BAA's common ownership. However, these aspects of its performance could in turn adversely affect competition between airlines (see paragraph 82).

(c) Our current view is that the three BAA London airports are not subject to any material competitive pressure from other airports. However, we do believe that there is a real possibility of competition between them given the willingness of passengers to switch between them (see paragraph 167). While the three airports are in common ownership they will not compete, and common ownership of the three BAA London airports is therefore a potential feature of the market adversely affecting competition between them.

(d) We also see potential competition from Heathrow and Gatwick to Southampton (though not vice versa) and currently, under common ownership, these airports do not compete with each other: BAA's common ownership of the BAA London airports and Southampton is also therefore a potential feature of the market adversely affecting competition.

(e) The scope for competition between the BAA London airports is also restricted, at least in the short term, by capacity constraints. Capacity constraints are a further potential feature adversely affecting competition (see paragraph 182). However, notwithstanding these constraints, there is in our view some scope for competition between the three airports in the short term. In the longer term, even if capacity constraints are alleviated, common ownership will continue to prevent competition between BAA's London airports. Separate ownership would itself create a greater incentive to expand capacity at the three airports (see paragraph 245).

(f) These capacity constraints result in part from planning restrictions and aspects of government policy which may well also be features which prevent, restrict and distort competition (see paragraphs 242 and 244). However, BAA's conduct and approach to the operation of the planning system may also have contributed to the capacity constraints and thereby adversely affected competition between airports (see paragraph 245).

(g) The BAA south-east airports show a lack of responsiveness to the interests of airlines that may both result from an absence of competition, and itself (as shown in the concerns about the HET development) adversely effect competition between airlines (see paragraph 83).

(h) Economic regulation of airports in itself may well be a feature which prevents, restricts or distorts competition through its impact on the level of prices and other dimensions such as investment and quality of service. However, it is not yet clear to us precisely how either the system or the way in which it is conducted prevent, restrict or distort competition. It does appear to us, however, that both the regulatory system and/or the way it operates may facilitate, reinforce or exacerbate some of the other characteristics of the market (see paragraph 271). At the same time, BAA's ownership of the designated airports in turn exacerbates the inadequacies of the regulatory system, reducing the benefit of regulation, including by reducing the ability of the regulator to compare the performance of different airports, and thus ultimately affecting competition between airlines.

Provisional Findings Report, *Northern Ireland Personal Banking*
20 October 2006, paras 57–60

57. In many cases these findings are indicators or outcomes of a lack of competition in the market. The banks as a whole continue to be able to impose higher charges or levels of debit interest, pay lower levels of credit interest, and/or offer lower levels of service and innovation, in particular to existing customers, than might be the case if switching were more prevalent. Although the findings are caused by market-wide features, the findings may differ among individual banks depending, for example, on the bank's business model, ownership or strategy.

58. We provisionally found that the features within the meaning of the Act which prevent, restrict or distort competition in the PCA market in Northern Ireland are as follows:
(a) banks have unduly complex charging structures and practices;
(b) banks do not fully or sufficiently explain their charging structures and practices; and
(c) customers generally do not actively search for alternative PCAs or switch provider.

59. The first two of these features lead to difficulties in customers making properly informed choices. This applies both to new-to-banking customers in searching for an appropriate PCA, and to existing customers who might otherwise switch to a bank that might provide a PCA to meet their needs at lower cost. This is exacerbated by the third feature: the perception and, to some extent, experience of difficulties in switching, as well as by customer indifference.

60. We therefore provisionally found that, on the statutory questions that we have to decide pursuant to section 134(1) of the Act, there are features of the relevant market, either alone or in combination with each other, that prevent, restrict or distort competition in connection with the supply of PCAs in Northern Ireland, and hence that there is an adverse effect on competition within the meaning of section 134(2).

Final Report, *Store Cards*
7 March 2006, paras 25–7

25. The following are the features of the relevant market which we have concluded, when taken in combination, have the effects specified in paragraph 24 above:
   (a) providers and retailers structure the store card offer in such a way that many store cardholders take out such cards to obtain the retail benefits they offer rather than the credit available on them;
   (b) most retailers offering store cards do not exert competitive pressure on store card APRs;
   (c) most retailers' customers do not exert competitive pressure on store card APRs (either at the take up stage or when they take credit) because their sensitivity to them is low;
   (d) most retailers offering store cards do not exert competitive pressure on the level of, or the provider's policy in relation to the levying of, late payment fees;
   (e) most retailers' customers do not exert competitive pressure on the level of late payment fees levied on store cards because their sensitivity to them is low;
   (f) many providers combine different insurance products into packages (that is, payment protection insurance with one or both of purchase protection insurance and price protection insurance) which they sell in association with store cards;
   (g) most retailers offering store cards do not exert competitive pressure on providers to lower their insurance premiums to cardholders, or to offer the components of their insurance package separately;
   (h) most retailers' customers do not exert competitive pressure on premiums for insurance purchased in association with the provision and use of store cards because their sensitivity to the price of such insurance cover is low and they have a poor understanding of the terms of the cover they are purchasing; and
   (i) providers do not include sufficient information on their store card statements, leading to a lack of transparency in the provision of store card credit and card-related insurance.

Detrimental effects on customers

26. We identified the following detrimental effects on customers which have resulted from or may be expected to result from the adverse effect on competition identified in paragraph 24 above:
   (a) most store cardholders who take credit pay higher prices for that credit than would be expected in a competitive market;
   (b) most store cardholders have less choice in relation to the individual elements of insurance cover sold in association with the provision and use of store cards than would be expected in a competitive market;
   (c) some customers who revolve their store card balance will continue to pay for elements of the insurance package (purchase and/or price protection) that they no longer require or which no longer provide them with cover; and
   (d) lack of transparency in the provision of store card credit and insurance leads to cardholders taking credit or insurance on terms which are not clear to them.

> 27. We sought to estimate in broad terms the scale of the consumer detriment. Based on all the evidence, we found that the detriment to customers in terms of the excess prices paid has been substantial: over the period since 1999, the customer detriment has been at least £55 million a year and possibly significantly more.

NOTE: Protection of the consumer interest was a key factor in the work of the Commission under the FTA 1973 and this has clearly been continued and enhanced under the market investigation provisions of the EA 2002, as demonstrated by these excerpts. In particular there have been a number of inquiries in relation to the financial services sector with an emphasis on increasing transparency and awareness by consumers and thereby reducing prices/interest rates. This is exemplified by the reports on *Store Cards, Home Credit, Northern Irish Banking,* and *Payment Protection Insurance.*

■ QUESTION

Is competition law merely consumer law in a different guise? Is consumer protection the sole, or main, purpose of competition law enforcement?

C: Remedies following market investigations

In relation to market investigations, the role of the Competition Commission has been dramatically increased. Under the FTA 1973 the Commission simply submitted its final Report to the Secretary of State, who would take enforcement action, acting upon the advice of the DGFT. Prior to finalization of a Report, the Commission will now publish, where appropriate, a notice of its proposed remedies. The finalized remedies are incorporated in the final Report and thereafter the Commission can accept undertakings, or introduce Orders to remedy the anticompetitive outcomes. The following is an excerpt from the *Store Cards Market Investigation Order*:

Store Cards Market Investigation Order
27 July 2006

1. Citation and commencement

1. This Order may be cited as the 'Store Cards Market Investigation Order'.
2. *(a)* The date of commencement of this Order shall be 1 May 2007 when the provisions of this Order come into force.
   (b) The provisions of Article 4 of, and Schedule 1 to, this Order shall remain in force for a period of three years and continue in force thereafter unless, following a review of the operation of the said provisions by the Office of Fair Trading, they are superseded, varied or revoked by the Competition Commission.

2. Interpretation

In this Order:

...

'**store card**' means a payment card issued with respect to the purchase of the goods, services or facilities of (i) only one retailer or (ii) retailers who are members of a single group of interconnected bodies corporate or (iii) retailers who belong to a store card network or (iv) retailers who trade under a common name and which (in each case) has both associated retail benefits and permits the holder of the payment card under his contract with the issuer of the card to discharge less than the whole of any outstanding balance on his payment card account on or before the expiry of a specified period (subject to any contractual requirements with respect to minimum or fixed amounts of payment); ...

3. Full information on store card statements

A store card provider shall ensure that any store card statement contains:
   (a) the prescribed information; and
   (b) where applicable, the prescribed information in the prescribed form.

4. APR warning

A store card provider shall ensure that any relevant store card statement contains the APR warning.

5. Direct debit facility

When offering to provide a store card to a customer a store card provider shall ensure:
   1. there is an option to pay all the monies owing on the store card account by direct debit; and
   2. *(a)* direct debit provision is made available to the customer with the application form; or
      (b) direct debit provision is made available after an application for a store card is made, provided that the application form contains a direct debit notice for completion by the customer; and
         (i) contains the information that direct debit provision will be sent to the customer subsequently; or
         (ii) informs the customer that they can establish a direct debit facility by telephone; and
   3. any direct debit mandate provided to the customer is supplied with the minimum payment warning; and
   4. where an application to establish a direct debit facility is made by a customer by telephone, the oral minimum payment warning is given to the said customer.

6. Insurance

   1. Where a store card provider offers a package of insurance containing payment protection, price protection and purchase protection, the store card provider shall also offer, at the same time, payment protection as a separate insurance and also, and separately from the said payment protection alone, a package of insurance containing price protection and purchase protection or each of price protection and purchase protection as separate insurances.

   2. Where a store card provider offers a package of insurance containing payment protection and price protection or a package of insurance containing payment protection and purchase protection, the store card provider shall also offer, at the same time, payment protection alone as a separate insurance.

NOTE: The provisions on remedies are inevitably more detailed than this simplistic out-line. Undertakings may still be given in lieu of a reference. The key feature is the role of the Competition Commission to accept final undertakings (s. 159) and make appropriate orders (s. 160), although the Secretary of State has also retained an enforcement role under these provisions where there is a public interest consideration and an intervention notice has been given. The OFT is entrusted with monitoring undertakings and orders. Section 179 provides for judicial review by the CAT of decisions taken under Part IV of the EA 2002. For example, Tesco successfully challenged the Commission's decision to recommend the introduction of a new competition test for the assessment of planning applications in relation to large grocery stores (*Tesco plc* v *Competition Commission* [2009] CAT 6) following the Commission's Groceries report.

■ QUESTION

Are market investigations an unnecessary burden for businesses? Should the authorities focus solely on abusive conduct under the CA 1998?

FURTHER READING

Wilks, S., *In the Public Interest*, MUP, Manchester, 1999.

Rodger, B.J., and MacCulloch, A. (eds), *The UK Competition Act: A New Era for UK Competition Law*, Hart Publishing, Oxford, 2000.

Kon, S., and Turnbull, S., 'Pricing and the Dominant Firm: Implications of the Competition Appeal Tribunal's Judgment in the Napp Case' (2003) 24 ECLR 70.

12

EC merger control

Merger Control in the EC is one of the most politicized areas of competition law. The political importance of decisions taken by the Commission in the merger field is one of the reasons that EC competition law lacked explicit merger control provisions until 1990. Prior to 1990 Article 81 EC and particularly Article 82 EC provided some means of control but were generally regarded as inadequate. Once the political deadlock was broken, the Council adopted the first European Community Merger Control Regulation ('ECMR'), Regulation 4064/89 (OJ, 1997, L180/1), which came into force in 1990. This has now been replaced by Regulation 139/2004 (OJ, 2004, L24/1). It is important to appreciate in general terms why the introduction of the first ECMR was controversial. As a general rule with few exceptions, a merger (or 'concentration' to use the language of the ECMR) scrutinized by the Commission on the basis of the ECMR with a so-called 'Community dimension' cannot also be investigated by Member State competition authorities under domestic merger control rules. When the Commission has the competence to investigate a 'concentration', it has exclusive competence. The ECMR acts as a 'one-stop shop', which provides a 'level playing field', i.e. concentrations are treated in a fair and non-discriminatory manner. The one-stop shop provides a considerable degree of legal certainty for business and reduces the compliance costs that may otherwise be incurred as a result of notifications submitted to numerous Member States' competition authorities.

Sir Leon Brittan, *Hersch Lauterpacht Memorial Lectures: Competition Policy and Merger Control in the Single European Market,*
Cambridge, Grotius, 1991, at pp. 35, 38

The future of the major players in European business who are involved in mergers is now in [the Commission's] hands... They will benefit from a one stop shop, where there is one analysis by one authority on the basis of competition criteria which takes one month and is binding throughout the European Community. If there are serious doubts about a concentration compatibility with the Common Market, a further analysis becomes necessary... And, once again, subject to only two exceptions, the Commission's decision is final throughout the Community and is reviewable only by the Community's courts.

NOTE: Former Competition Commissioner, Sir Leon Brittan, alludes to the two circumstances where there is a permitted exception to the Commission's exclusive competence. Firstly, where the concentration only appears to affect a market within a Member State that has all the characteristics of a distinct market, it may be referred to the relevant competition authority of a Member State to be assessed under domestic merger control rules under Article 4(4) or Article 9 of the ECMR. Secondly, a Member State can act to protect 'legitimate interests' other than those covered by the ECMR in certain specified conditions as a result of Article 21(4) ECMR. These issues will be discussed further below but demonstrate the narrow approach to permitting exceptions to the Commission's exclusive competence. While the one-stop shop is beneficial for the business community seeking to minimize compliance costs and uncertainty, it was initially regarded as controversial by several Member States. Their reluctance was due to concerns from ceding oversight responsibility to the Commission over such a sensitive area of commercial practice, which can often impact on a country's economy and industrial policy.

■ QUESTION

Should there be a one-stop shop for merger clearance within the EC?

SECTION 2: REFORM OF THE MERGER REGULATION

The first ECMR was significantly amended in 1998 as a result of a review initiated in 1996, and the principal effect was a lowering of the thresholds that trigger the requirement for concentrations to be notified to the Commission. This move may initially have seemed to impose an additional burden on parties to those concentrations not initially caught under the ECMR regime, but it allowed more concentrations to benefit from the one-stop shop and avoid multiple filings to Member States in order to gain clearance. The Commission reviewed the changes in 2000 and concluded that they were ineffective.

Report from the Commission to the Council on the application of Merger Regulation thresholds
COM(2000) 399 final, paras 80–1

> 80...an important number of transactions with significant cross-border effects, and therefore a Community interest, remain outside the Community rules on merger control. There are also indications from the European business community that this is considered as problematic, and that it acts as a constraint on the investment decisions of European firms.
>
> 81. On that basis the Commission believes that a more in-depth analysis of the appropriate mechanism for establishing Community jurisdiction in merger cases is necessary. At this stage it would also appear that any change to the Merger Regulation that would remove this unbalance is likely to require:
>
> • To significantly change the existing system of case allocation (work distribution) between the Commission and the NCA's.
> • The attribution of significant additional Commission resources dedicated to treating all mergers with significant European cross-border effects.
> • A more thorough review, not only of the existing turnover thresholds, but also of other substantive and procedural rules relating to the control of concentrations.

NOTE: The Commission subsequently embarked on a more thorough review of the operation of the ECMR and published a Green Paper in 2001.

Green Paper, *Review of Council Regulation (EEC) No 4064/89*
COM(2001) 745/6 final [footnotes omitted]

2. Over its first 10 years of application, the Merger Regulation has received much acclaim for its ability to provide effective merger control at the European level. The introduction of short, strict legal deadlines was and remains one of the key aspects of the Regulation. The Commission believes that the Regulation continues to form an appropriate regulatory approach towards the continuing integration of markets across Europe, and in particular that it is capable of constant adaptation to new economic, legal and political developments—both within Europe and more widely.

3. The Merger Regulation was based on an understanding that the establishment of the internal market would lead to major cross-border corporate reorganisation, and that a *level playing field* was necessary to ensure that such transactions would not result in lasting damage to competition. The level playing field should ensure that the same notification requirements, procedure and legal standards apply to all concentrations with significant cross-border effects.

4. For this purpose the Merger Regulation conferred exclusive jurisdiction on the Commission over "concentrations with a Community dimension". This "one-stop shop" principle serves a dual purpose. First, in the spirit of *subsidiarity*, it builds on the realisation that merger control at Community level is justified in view of the inability of any single Member State to deal comprehensively with the cross-border scale and effects of such transactions. In addition, the single "stop" of the Regulation simplifies administrative procedures, thereby enabling both competition authorities and companies to minimise the costs of merger control.

5. Since the adoption of the Merger Regulation, the European Union has expanded from 12 to 15 Member States, whose markets are becoming increasingly integrated. Moreover, following the entry into force of the 1994 Agreement on the European Economic Area (EEA), the European Commission's exclusive competence for concentrations meeting the thresholds has been extended to cover the whole EEA territory. European cross-border corporate reorganisation has received further impetus from the introduction of Monetary Union in 1999.

6. We are now facing the prospect of a European Union with significantly more Member States as of 2004, and the completion of the monetary union with the final phase of the introduction of the Euro due to take place in 2002. At the same time the trend towards internationalisation, or even globalisation, of companies and markets is continuing at an increasing pace.

7. In a parallel development, an ever-greater number of pre-merger control regimes are being introduced across the globe (currently, about 60), with a consequent increase in the costs associated with multiple filing requirements.

8. Since 1990, some 1800 concentrations have been notified to the Commission (by July 2001). Still, that figure represents only a fraction of the total number of transactions that were notified to the EU's national competition authorities during the same period. Since 1990, many Member States as well as Candidate countries have introduced merger control rules (or amended previous existing ones). As a consequence many national merger control systems largely follow the principles of the Merger Regulation. Despite this "soft harmonisation", various degrees of discrepancy persist, notably in terms of procedure.

NOTE: The Commission highlights the key strengths of the ECMR based on Community competence when the extent of geographic effects justify a one-stop shop, on a non-discriminatory basis, before building the argument for further extending its competence (as will be seen by lowering the notification thresholds) in light of the enlargement of the EU when concentrations may have to be notified to a number of Member States if it falls below the ECMR notification thresholds. This remains a live issue with EU membership standing at 27 Member States in 2009 with three official Candidate States.

9. All of these factors point to the desirability of revising the overall system of European merger control, so that the Commission and each national authority, individually and together, can utilise their resources in the optimal way for protecting competition in the Community, while at the same

time reducing any unnecessary burden on industry, in terms of compliance costs and increasing legal certainty. This is particularly true for medium-sized companies which, owing to their limited size, fail to meet the current thresholds of the Merger Regulation, but who still remain subject to the burden of multiple national filings.

10. The experience gained over the first ten years of applying the Merger Regulation also indicates that certain improvements may be possible in both the scope and the functioning of the Regulation. As regards its scope, one of the basic concepts, namely that of a "concentration" has been re-assessed from a number of different perspectives. Similarly, the procedural setting of the Regulation has been re-examined and a number of options appear to exist for further improving both the effectiveness of the rules and legal certainty for those concerned by them.

11. Since its adoption in 1989, the Merger Regulation has been based on a principle by which concentrations are appraised in accordance with a criterion of market *dominance*: concentrations that create or strengthen such dominance should be declared incompatible with the common market (and therefore unlawful). Overall, this appraisal criterion has proved effective in averting potential competition problems. Indeed, many other jurisdictions have followed suit, introducing the same appraisal criterion into their rules. The main alternative merger control test, used in a number of major jurisdictions and currently contemplated in some Member States, is that of *substantial lessening of competition*. According to certain commentators, the lack of global harmonisation of the appraisal criteria for mergers is problematic. Therefore, and as significant experience has now been acquired in applying the dominance criterion, the Commission considers this an appropriate opportunity to open up a wider debate on the respective merits of the two tests, particularly in view of the acknowledged desirability of striving towards a greater degree of global convergence in merger control standards.

...

17. Experience has confirmed that the Commission generally is better placed to deal with concentrations where the merging parties are active on markets that are wider than national. For cases involving global or European wide markets, the Commission's powers of investigation and remedial and enforcement action are clearly more appropriate than the more limited means available to the Member States. The same often also holds true for cases which generate competition concern spreading across various Member States. Such cases may have significant competitive repercussions in other parts of the Community, for example by impeding entry by competitors from other Member States into the affected countries.

18. A particular feature of the creation of the internal market within the EU is that a number of markets may be seen as being in a transitional state. *Pirelli-BICC*, illustrates the result of a process where European deregulation and harmonisation effectively led to a widening of the relevant anti-trust markets. In this case the market was indeed confirmed to be EEA-wide on the basis that customers increasingly source power cables at a European level on the basis, *inter alia,* of the procedures provided for in the Community public procurement directives. The Pirelli case contrasted with earlier cases involving the same industry: in 1992, the same markets were still considered to be national in scope. The Commission is normally particularly well placed to handle cases where such a transition is occurring, as it is able to fully consider all effects at both national and European levels.

19. Although each Member State may be able to address issues such as these in so far as they relate to its own territory, the Commission is clearly better placed to address the totality of such concerns throughout the Community. Community competence in such cases would therefore be in line with the subsidiarity principle as it represents the most effective means of avoiding the creation of obstacles to further European integration. In addition, reasons of efficiency militate against parallel treatment of the same issues in a number of Member States.

20. Conversely, Member States are generally better placed to deal with cases which, owing to the activities of the companies involved, produce their effects within a Member State, that is where for instance no significant foreclosure or spillover effects occur. The effective treatment of such cases does not require access to the broader powers of the Commission, and the national authorities are normally better placed when it comes to gathering the relevant market information.

...

NOTE: The Commission is building the case for greater flexibility within the ECMR to allow referrals of concentrations between competition authorities, ensuring that the authority which reviews a merger is the most appropriate given the likely geographic effects of the transaction.

22. In the course of its review, the Commission has re-assessed the continued appropriateness of the turnover thresholds in Article 1 in the light, not only of their effectiveness, but also of their predictability and transparency. It should be pointed out that failure to attain the jurisdictional criteria in Article 1 normally means that the transaction will be subject to mandatory notification requirements in one or more Member States.

23. As to the functioning of the current thresholds, the review has not, as set out in further detail in Annex 1, indicated any urgent need to amend Article 1(2). This Article continues to provide results that are generally in line with subsidiarity, and a revision of the threshold levels set out therein would not be well suited to dealing with the multiple filing problem. Nor has the review brought to light any urgent need to modify the level of the 2/3-rule. The rule, which adopts a centre of gravity approach to the division of competence, appears to provide results that are generally in line with subsidiarity. Furthermore, to the limited extent that the 2/3-rule leads to multiple filings, it is very rare for this to go beyond notifications to two national authorities.

24. On the other hand, it must be concluded that Article 1(3) has fallen short of achieving its underlying objective. At the time of its adoption in 1997, this provision was intended to confer Commission competence over cases that affect three or more Member States. While the review broadly supports the validity of this objective on the grounds that these are generally cases with a Community interest, the provision has not lived up to expectations. Only a small proportion of such cases have fallen within the Merger Regulation. In 2000, only 20 cases were notified under Article 1(3), compared to 75 multiple notifications to three or more Member States. The failure of Article 1(3) is also shown by the fact that in 2000 only some 5% of all notifications were made under this Article, representing a significant decrease from the already low level in 1999.

...

32. At this stage, the Commission is therefore of the opinion that the desired results could best be achieved through the introduction of amendments that might be described as effects-oriented. They would seek directly to ensure a result where cases that typically involve a potentially significant cross-border effect would fall under the Commission's jurisdiction. The Commission seeks comments on the possibility of Article 1(3) being replaced by a provision whereby notification to three Member States can be seen as providing a reliable indication of the manifestly cross-border nature of a concentration. This possibility is built upon the ideas underlying the Commission's proposal in its 1996 Green Paper.

...

III. SUBSTANTIVE ISSUES

A. The substantive test

159. The substantive test according to which notified concentrations are appraised is set out in Article 2 of the Merger Regulation. In the course of this review it has been suggested that the Commission should use this opportunity to discuss the merits of the dominance test contained therein. Both procedural and substantive reasons have been advanced for a re-evaluation of the appropriateness of this test.

160. From a procedural viewpoint, the main reason proposed in favour of such a re-evaluation is that it could allow an alignment of the Merger Regulation's appraisal criteria with those applied in other major jurisdictions, such as the US, Canada and Australia, which rely on a concept of *substantial lessening of competition* ("the SLC test"). Such an alignment towards a global standard for merger assessment holds certain attractions. It would, for example, facilitate merging parties' global assessment of possible competition issues arising from contemplated transactions, by obviating the current need to argue their case according to differently formulated tests. This would in turn provide competition agencies with a better basis on which to build effective cooperation in cases that are notified in several jurisdictions. Moreover, as a common test would tend to highlight

the actual application of the test, rather than the test itself, it would provide for better bench-marking of the activities of competition authorities and courts, as well as facilitating the development of competition-oriented research and modelling.

161. It should nevertheless be pointed out that an amendment of the test in the Merger Regulation could also involve some drawbacks. Although this effect should not be exaggerated, interested parties may, at least for an initial period following such a reform, face greater difficulties in forecasting the likely outcome of merger control proceedings in Europe. The reason for this would be that the existing body of caselaw (emanating from both the Commission and the courts) has been built up under the Regulation's dominance test. Another possible complication relates to the fact that most Member States (as well as the Candidate Countries) have aligned their merger control provisions to the current dominance test. Thus, unless national rules were also amended, changing the Merger Regulation's competition test could have the awkward effect of creating greater alignment internationally, while leading to greater disparity within the Community.

NOTE: The Commission clearly wanted to take the opportunity, within the ambit of a significant review of the ECMR, to reconsider the appropriate substantive test applied when considering whether concentrations are compatible with the Common Market or not, i.e. whether to provide clearance to the transaction, or not. A significant disadvantage of introducing any new test would be the resulting doubt as to the status of case law of the Community courts that had built up over the preceding 11 years, and resultant legal uncertainty for the Commission and the business community. Note also, shortly after the Commission published this Green Paper, the UK adopted the substantial lessening of competition test in Part III of the Enterprise Act 2002: see Chapter 13.

162. From a substantive viewpoint it should be noted that there are many similarities between the dominance test and the SLC-test. Both types of test, will, for example, involve an investigation into the scope of the relevant market as well as an assessment of how the market(s) will be affected by the proposed concentration and which competitive constraints would be faced by the merged entity. It should also be noted that, despite the current difference in legal tests, the vast majority of cases dealt with by the Commission and other major jurisdictions using the SLC-test have revealed a significant degree of convergence in the approach to merger analysis.

163. Since the adoption of the Merger Regulation in 1989, the application of the notion of dominance has evolved, allowing it to be adapted both to developments in economic theory and to refinements of the now available econometric tools to measure market power. This implies that merger assessment today can be less reliant on the rather blunt and imprecise market share test than it was 10 years ago. The fact that the dominance test has undergone such an evolution is natural, and Article 2 has so far proved sufficiently flexible to accommodate an effects analysis made on the basis of more sophisticated micro-economic tools, instruments and models developed by econometric and industrial organisation research.

164. The perhaps most well-known example of this evolution is the European courts' interpretation of the Merger Regulation's competition test as applying to situations of collective dominance, in the judgments of the Court of Justice and the Court of First Instance in the *Kali und Salz* and *Gencor* cases.

165. It has nevertheless been suggested that the SLC-test might be closer to the spirit of the economically-based analysis undertaken in merger control and less (legally) rigid than the dominance test. As such, some consider it better adapted to an effective merger control, in particular in the context of growing industrial concentration. At the same time, it has also been suggested that adopting the more open-ended SLC test would lead to a greater degree of legal uncertainty.

166. One of the more specific hypothetical questions that has occasionally been raised about the reach of the dominance test in the Merger Regulation is the extent to which it would allow for effective control in some specific situations where firms unilaterally may be able to raise price and

thus exercise market power. The type of example that tends to be cited is of a merger between the second and third largest players in a market, where these firms are the closest substitutes. In such a scenario the merging firms may remain smaller than the existing market leader. The argument goes that the SLC-test would be better adapted to addressing such a situation, in particular if the market characteristics would not be conducive to a finding of collective dominance. While interesting as a hypothetical discussion, the Commission has so far not encountered a situation of this kind.

167. In conclusion, experience in applying the dominance test has not revealed major loopholes in the scope of the test. Nor has it frequently led to different results from SLC-test approaches in other jurisdictions. Still, in view in particular of the increasingly international scope of merger activity, the Commission believes that the time is right to initiate a thorough debate on the respective merits of the two tests for merger control.

NOTE: The theoretical 'gap' in the applicability of the dominance test, in that it may be unable to address a non-collusive oligopoly post-merger, was one of the strongest arguments favouring a revision of the substantive test.

Ysewyn, J., 'The New World of the Merger Task Force'
[2002] ECLR 207, pp. 208–9

Finally, the Commission has put forward for debate the substantive test that it applies for clearing—or blocking—mergers. Today, this test is based on 'dominance', but as the Green Paper suggests, it may be replaced by the US-inspired 'substantial lessening of competition' test (SLC for short). In addition, the Commission is also exploring ways of considering the efficiencies generated by the merger in its review process.

This debate could determine the future of EC merger control. Will the introduction of SLC alter the Commission's appraisal procedure, improving the outcome of its merger control review? In particular, will SLC align the European and US procedures in a way that really addresses the issue? And, to use an oversimplification, would *GE/Honeywell* have been decided differently, had the Commission toiled away with SLC?

One cannot get away from the simple truth: the underlying test in merger control is one of single-firm and multi-firm market power. In Europe, this led to a test based on 'dominance'. In the United States, the same test was baptised as reviewing the 'substantial lessening of competition'. Both tests wield the familiar instruments of market definition, the calculation of market shares, and the determination of concentration ratios. More sophisticated economics may increase the strength of the reasoning (especially in the United States) but why then does the Green Paper hide behind a semantic discussion of whether 'dominance' or 'substantial lessening of competition' is the better test? On both sides of the Atlantic the issue should be market power to the detriment of consumers. Once the dust settles and the contributions are counted, the Commission should acknowledge that introducing SLC would merely be a 'subtle language confusion'.

It has been suggested that the dominance test does not allow for a proper consideration of efficiencies that may result from mergers. It is true that, to date, the issue of efficiencies has only been raised in a limited number of decisions under the ECMR and, as the Commission acknowledges, the precise scope for taking such considerations into account may not have been fully developed. The US system, by contrast, expressly provides for an efficiency defence to rebut a finding of anti-competitive effects. The Green Paper indicates that the Commission is willing to debate how, and the extent to which, efficiencies should be taken into account in the merger analysis, but has not taken any sides.

NOTE: As will be discussed in Section 6 below, the dominance test was replaced by a new 'significant impediment to effective competition' ('SIEC') test in Regulation 139/2004, but the wording of the provision retains elements of the original dominance test, and protects the status of existing case law. The role of efficiencies is also explored in Section 6(C).

The Commission adopted a reform package in December 2002, one year after publishing its Green Paper and engaging in a consultation exercise, proposing a new EC Merger Regulation and accompanying guidelines. The aim was for a new ECMR to be approved in time to take effect with the enlargement of the EU on 1 May 2004, the same point at which Regulation 1/2003 would enter into force. The Commission's Director-General for Competition, Philip Lowe, has written on the aim of the reform package.

Lowe, P., 'The Future of EU Merger Control'
[2002] 1 Comp LJ 310 [footnotes omitted]

The ECMR has served Europe well. However, like all systems it is in need of constant revision, so as to ensure that it is able to grapple with the evolving challenges that it faces. Now it is time for reform, but we are also conscious of the need not to undermine the very real merits inherent in the current system. What the EC Commission is proposing, therefore, are significant improvements to the current system, transforming what is already a very good system into an even better one. In a nutshell, the key rationale underlying the reform is two-fold: on the one hand, it is designed to enhance the transparency and consistency of the EC Commission's policy with regard to merger control analysis; and, secondly, it seeks to improve the EC Commission's decision-making process, making sure that its investigations of proposed mergers are more thorough, more focused, and—most importantly—more firmly grounded in sound economic reasoning, with due regard for the rights of the merging parties and of third parties.

...

The EC Commission believe that the dominance test, if properly interpreted, is capable of dealing with the full range of anti-competitive scenarios which mergers may engender. However, some commentators are of the view that there may be a gap in the coverage of the test. Therefore, with a view to ensuring legal certainty regarding the scope of the current standard, the EC Commission is proposing to clarify the substantive test (by the addition of an additional paragraph in Art 2 of, and of additional recitals to, the ECMR) so as to make it particularly clear that the test applies where a merger results in 'unilateral effects' in situations of non-collusive oligopoly, the potential 'gap' to which some commentators have pointed.

...

One of the main objectives of the review is to optimise the allocation of merger cases between the EC Commission and national competition authorities in the light of the principle of subsidiarity, while at the same time tackling the phenomenon of 'multiple filing', i.e. notification to various competition authorities within the EU. The EC Commission is therefore proposing to simplify and add more flexibility to the ECMR's provisions concerning referral of cases for investigation from the EC Commission to Member States and vice versa.

NOTE: The Commission's proposals for reform of EC merger control were far broader than revising the substantive test and jurisdictional thresholds. The reform package also involved revising the time periods involved in merger review, the appointment of a Chief Competition Economist and an internal restructuring of DG Comp, including disbanding the Merger Task Force and placing the personnel into separate sector teams. Part of this was due to the Green Paper and the natural reform process, but it was also partly due to the disastrous merger control setbacks suffered by the Commission in 2002, when the Court of First Instance annulled the Commission's Decision in three separate cases: Case T-342/99 *Airtours* v *Commission* [2002] ECR II-2585; Case T-310/01 *Schneider Electric SA* v *Commission* [2002] ECR II-4071; and Case T-5/02 *Tetra Laval* v *Commission* [2002] ECR II-4381. See Section 7 below.

■ QUESTION

Why did the Commission propose significant reform of EC Merger Regulation 4064/89?

SECTION 3: THE EC MERGER REGULATION

The revised ECMR, Merger Regulation 139/2004, applied to concentrations from 1 May 2004 and implemented significant changes proposed in the Commission's 2001 reform package. The Commission also adopted the Implementing Regulation in 2004 (Commission Regulation 802/2004, OJ, 2004, L133/1, as amended by Regulation 1033/2008, OJ, 2008, L279/3), which sets out rules regarding the notification of concentrations under the ECMR, time limits for merger review, and the rights of parties to the proposed concentration, including hearings. The Implementing Regulation also provides for undertakings to offer commitments to the Commission to address any anti-competitive concerns that may arise from the proposed concentration, and allows for the appointment of an independent trustee to assist the Commission monitor compliance with commitments.

The Commission has also issued a series of Notices providing substantive and procedural guidance on the operation of the ECMR, including those covering the relevant market definition (OJ, 1997, C372/5), assessment of horizontal mergers (OJ, 2004, C31/5), non-horizontal mergers (OJ, 2008, C265/6), case referrals (OJ, 2005, C56/2), the Consolidated Jurisdictional Notice (OJ, 2008, C95/1), and remedies (OJ, 2008, C267/1).

All Notices can be accessed via the DG Comp website: http://ec.europa.eu/competition/mergers/legislation/legislation.html.

Council Regulation (EC) 139/2004 of 20 January 2004 on the control of concentrations between undertakings
OJ, 2004, L24/1, recitals 9, 13–16, 24–6, Articles 1–26 [footnotes omitted]

(9) The scope of application of this Regulation should be defined according to the geographical area of activity of the undertakings concerned and be limited by quantitative thresholds in order to cover those concentrations which have a Community dimension. The Commission should report to the Council on the implementation of the applicable thresholds and criteria so that the Council, acting in accordance with Article 202 of the Treaty, is in a position to review them regularly, as well as the rules regarding pre-notification referral, in the light of the experience gained; this requires statistical data to be provided by the Member States to the Commission to enable it to prepare such reports and possible proposals for amendments. The Commission's reports and proposals should be based on relevant information regularly provided by the Member States.

NOTE: EC Merger Regulation 139/2004 introduced revised thresholds in Article 1 (below) to be able to provide the benefits of a one-stop shop to a greater number of parties to proposed concentrations, but also required that the Commission regularly report on the operation of the thresholds. The Commission had to report to the Council of Ministers by July 2009, and opened a consultation exercise to enable it to do so (see Commission Press Release of 28 October 2008, IP/08/1591).

...

(13) The Commission should act in close and constant liaison with the competent authorities of the Member States from which it obtains comments and information.

(14) The Commission and the competent authorities of the Member States should together form a network of public authorities, applying their respective competences in close cooperation, using efficient arrangements for information-sharing and consultation, with a view to ensuring that a case is dealt with by the most appropriate authority, in the light of the principle of subsidiarity

and with a view to ensuring that multiple notifications of a given concentration are avoided to the greatest extent possible. Referrals of concentrations from the Commission to Member States and from Member States to the Commission should be made in an efficient manner avoiding, to the greatest extent possible, situations where a concentration is subject to a referral both before and after its notification.

(15) The Commission should be able to refer to a Member State notified concentrations with a Community dimension which threaten significantly to affect competition in a market within that Member State presenting all the characteristics of a distinct market. Where the concentration affects competition on such a market, which does not constitute a substantial part of the common market, the Commission should be obliged, upon request, to refer the whole or part of the case to the Member State concerned. A Member State should be able to refer to the Commission a concentration which does not have a Community dimension but which affects trade between Member States and threatens to significantly affect competition within its territory. Other Member States which are also competent to review the concentration should be able to join the request. In such a situation, in order to ensure the efficiency and predictability of the system, national time limits should be suspended until a decision has been reached as to the referral of the case. The Commission should have the power to examine and deal with a concentration on behalf of a requesting Member State or requesting Member States.

(16) The undertakings concerned should be granted the possibility of requesting referrals to or from the Commission before a concentration is notified so as to further improve the efficiency of the system for the control of concentrations within the Community. In such situations, the Commission and national competition authorities should decide within short, clearly defined time limits whether a referral to or from the Commission ought to be made, thereby ensuring the efficiency of the system. Upon request by the undertakings concerned, the Commission should be able to refer to a Member State a concentration with a Community dimension which may significantly affect competition in a market within that Member State presenting all the characteristics of a distinct market; the undertakings concerned should not, however, be required to demonstrate that the effects of the concentration would be detrimental to competition. A concentration should not be referred from the Commission to a Member State which has expressed its disagreement to such a referral. Before notification to national authorities, the undertakings concerned should also be able to request that a concentration without a Community dimension which is capable of being reviewed under the national competition laws of at least three Member States be referred to the Commission. Such requests for pre-notification referrals to the Commission would be particularly pertinent in situations where the concentration would affect competition beyond the territory of one Member State. Where a concentration capable of being reviewed under the competition laws of three or more Member States is referred to the Commission prior to any national notification, and no Member State competent to review the case expresses its disagreement, the Commission should acquire exclusive competence to review the concentration and such a concentration should be deemed to have a Community dimension. Such pre-notification referrals from Member States to the Commission should not, however, be made where at least one Member State competent to review the case has expressed its disagreement with such a referral.

NOTE: The recitals set out the principles of close cooperation that should guide the Commission and Member States' competition authorities when considering case referrals so that a proposed concentration is reviewed by the most appropriate authority, taking the extent of geographic effects into account. These principles are given effect through Articles 2, 4(4)–(5), and 19. Close cooperation between authorities is also required for the operation of the other referral mechanisms in place as a result of Articles 9, 21(4), and 22.

...

(24) In order to ensure a system of undistorted competition in the common market, in furtherance of a policy conducted in accordance with the principle of an open market economy with free competition, this Regulation must permit effective control of all concentrations from the point of view of their effect on competition in the Community. Accordingly, Regulation (EEC) No 4064/89

established the principle that a concentration with a Community dimension which creates or strengthens a dominant position as a result of which effective competition in the common market or in a substantial part of it would be significantly impeded should be declared incompatible with the common market.

(25) In view of the consequences that concentrations in oligopolistic market structures may have, it is all the more necessary to maintain effective competition in such markets. Many oligopolistic markets exhibit a healthy degree of competition. However, under certain circumstances, concentrations involving the elimination of important competitive constraints that the merging parties had exerted upon each other, as well as a reduction of competitive pressure on the remaining competitors, may, even in the absence of a likelihood of coordination between the members of the oligopoly, result in a significant impediment to effective competition. The Community courts have, however, not to date expressly interpreted Regulation (EEC) No 4064/89 as requiring concentrations giving rise to such non-coordinated effects to be declared incompatible with the common market. Therefore, in the interests of legal certainty, it should be made clear that this Regulation permits effective control of all such concentrations by providing that any concentration which would significantly impede effective competition, in the common market or in a substantial part of it, should be declared incompatible with the common market. The notion of "significant impediment to effective competition" in Article 2(2) and (3) should be interpreted as extending, beyond the concept of dominance, only to the anti-competitive effects of a concentration resulting from the non-coordinated behaviour of undertakings which would not have a dominant position on the market concerned.

(26) A significant impediment to effective competition generally results from the creation or strengthening of a dominant position. With a view to preserving the guidance that may be drawn from past judgments of the European courts and Commission decisions pursuant to Regulation (EEC) No 4064/89, while at the same time maintaining consistency with the standards of competitive harm which have been applied by the Commission and the Community courts regarding the compatibility of a concentration with the common market, this Regulation should accordingly establish the principle that a concentration with a Community dimension which would significantly impede effective competition, in the common market or in a substantial part thereof, in particular as a result of the creation or strengthening of a dominant position, is to be declared incompatible with the common market.

NOTE: Following on from Lowe's comments in Section 2, the above recitals are explicit in stating that the revised substantive test will cover all anti-competitive effects that may derive from proposed concentrations, including situations of non-collusive oligopoly, whilst also retaining the status of case law from the Community courts under the first ECMR. In light of the significance of the ECMR the substantive provisions are reproduced in full.

Article 1 Scope

1. Without prejudice to Article 4(5) and Article 22, this Regulation shall apply to all concentrations with a Community dimension as defined in this Article.

2. A concentration has a Community dimension where:
   (a) the combined aggregate worldwide turnover of all the undertakings concerned is more than EUR 5000 million; and
   (b) the aggregate Community-wide turnover of each of at least two of the undertakings concerned is more than EUR 250 million,

unless each of the undertakings concerned achieves more than two-thirds of its aggregate Community-wide turnover within one and the same Member State.

3. A concentration that does not meet the thresholds laid down in paragraph 2 has a Community dimension where:
   (a) the combined aggregate worldwide turnover of all the undertakings concerned is more than EUR 2500 million;
   (b) in each of at least three Member States, the combined aggregate turnover of all the undertakings concerned is more than EUR 100 million;

(c) in each of at least three Member States included for the purpose of point (b), the aggregate turnover of each of at least two of the undertakings concerned is more than EUR 25 million; and

(d) the aggregate Community-wide turnover of each of at least two of the undertakings concerned is more than EUR 100 million,

unless each of the undertakings concerned achieves more than two-thirds of its aggregate Community-wide turnover within one and the same Member State.

4. On the basis of statistical data that may be regularly provided by the Member States, the Commission shall report to the Council on the operation of the thresholds and criteria set out in paragraphs 2 and 3 by 1 July 2009 and may present proposals pursuant to paragraph 5.

5. Following the report referred to in paragraph 4 and on a proposal from the Commission, the Council, acting by a qualified majority, may revise the thresholds and criteria mentioned in paragraph 3.

Article 2 Appraisal of concentrations

1. Concentrations within the scope of this Regulation shall be appraised in accordance with the objectives of this Regulation and the following provisions with a view to establishing whether or not they are compatible with the common market.

In making this appraisal, the Commission shall take into account:
(a) the need to maintain and develop effective competition within the common market in view of, among other things, the structure of all the markets concerned and the actual or potential competition from undertakings located either within or outwith the Community;
(b) the market position of the undertakings concerned and their economic and financial power, the alternatives available to suppliers and users, their access to supplies or markets, any legal or other barriers to entry, supply and demand trends for the relevant goods and services, the interests of the intermediate and ultimate consumers, and the development of technical and economic progress provided that it is to consumers' advantage and does not form an obstacle to competition.

2. A concentration which would not significantly impede effective competition in the common market or in a substantial part of it, in particular as a result of the creation or strengthening of a dominant position, shall be declared compatible with the common market.

3. A concentration which would significantly impede effective competition, in the common market or in a substantial part of it, in particular as a result of the creation or strengthening of a dominant position, shall be declared incompatible with the common market.

4. To the extent that the creation of a joint venture constituting a concentration pursuant to Article 3 has as its object or effect the coordination of the competitive behaviour of undertakings that remain independent, such coordination shall be appraised in accordance with the criteria of Article 81(1) and (3) of the Treaty, with a view to establishing whether or not the operation is compatible with the common market.

5. In making this appraisal, the Commission shall take into account in particular:
— whether two or more parent companies retain, to a significant extent, activities in the same market as the joint venture or in a market which is downstream or upstream from that of the joint venture or in a neighbouring market closely related to this market,
— whether the coordination which is the direct consequence of the creation of the joint venture affords the undertakings concerned the possibility of eliminating competition in respect of a substantial part of the products or services in question.

Article 3 Definition of concentration

1. A concentration shall be deemed to arise where a change of control on a lasting basis results from:
(a) the merger of two or more previously independent undertakings or parts of undertakings, or

    (b) the acquisition, by one or more persons already controlling at least one undertaking, or by one or more undertakings, whether by purchase of securities or assets, by contract or by any other means, of direct or indirect control of the whole or parts of one or more other undertakings.

2. Control shall be constituted by rights, contracts or any other means which, either separately or in combination and having regard to the considerations of fact or law involved, confer the possibility of exercising decisive influence on an undertaking, in particular by:

    (a) ownership or the right to use all or part of the assets of an undertaking;

    (b) rights or contracts which confer decisive influence on the composition, voting or decisions of the organs of an undertaking.

3. Control is acquired by persons or undertakings which:

    (a) are holders of the rights or entitled to rights under the contracts concerned; or

    (b) while not being holders of such rights or entitled to rights under such contracts, have the power to exercise the rights deriving therefrom.

4. The creation of a joint venture performing on a lasting basis all the functions of an autonomous economic entity shall constitute a concentration within the meaning of paragraph 1(b).

5. A concentration shall not be deemed to arise where:

    (a) credit institutions or other financial institutions or insurance companies, the normal activities of which include transactions and dealing in securities for their own account or for the account of others, hold on a temporary basis securities which they have acquired in an undertaking with a view to reselling them, provided that they do not exercise voting rights in respect of those securities with a view to determining the competitive behaviour of that undertaking or provided that they exercise such voting rights only with a view to preparing the disposal of all or part of that undertaking or of its assets or the disposal of those securities and that any such disposal takes place within one year of the date of acquisition; that period may be extended by the Commission on request where such institutions or companies can show that the disposal was not reasonably possible within the period set;

    (b) control is acquired by an office-holder according to the law of a Member State relating to liquidation, winding up, insolvency, cessation of payments, compositions or analogous proceedings;

    (c) the operations referred to in paragraph 1(b) are carried out by the financial holding companies referred to in Article 5(3) of Fourth Council Directive 78/660/EEC of 25 July 1978 based on Article 54(3)(g) of the Treaty on the annual accounts of certain types of companies provided however that the voting rights in respect of the holding are exercised, in particular in relation to the appointment of members of the management and supervisory bodies of the undertakings in which they have holdings, only to maintain the full value of those investments and not to determine directly or indirectly the competitive conduct of those undertakings.

Article 4 Prior notification of concentrations and pre-notification referral at the request of the notifying parties

1. Concentrations with a Community dimension defined in this Regulation shall be notified to the Commission prior to their implementation and following the conclusion of the agreement, the announcement of the public bid, or the acquisition of a controlling interest.

Notification may also be made where the undertakings concerned demonstrate to the Commission a good faith intention to conclude an agreement or, in the case of a public bid, where they have publicly announced an intention to make such a bid, provided that the intended agreement or bid would result in a concentration with a Community dimension.

For the purposes of this Regulation, the term "notified concentration" shall also cover intended concentrations notified pursuant to the second subparagraph. For the purposes of paragraphs 4 and 5 of this Article, the term "concentration" includes intended concentrations within the meaning of the second subparagraph.

2. A concentration which consists of a merger within the meaning of Article 3(1)(a) or in the acquisition of joint control within the meaning of Article 3(1)(b) shall be notified jointly by the parties

to the merger or by those acquiring joint control as the case may be. In all other cases, the notification shall be effected by the person or undertaking acquiring control of the whole or parts of one or more undertakings.

3. Where the Commission finds that a notified concentration falls within the scope of this Regulation, it shall publish the fact of the notification, at the same time indicating the names of the undertakings concerned, their country of origin, the nature of the concentration and the economic sectors involved. The Commission shall take account of the legitimate interest of undertakings in the protection of their business secrets.

4. Prior to the notification of a concentration within the meaning of paragraph 1, the persons or undertakings referred to in paragraph 2 may inform the Commission, by means of a reasoned submission, that the concentration may significantly affect competition in a market within a Member State which presents all the characteristics of a distinct market and should therefore be examined, in whole or in part, by that Member State.

The Commission shall transmit this submission to all Member States without delay. The Member State referred to in the reasoned submission shall, within 15 working days of receiving the submission, express its agreement or disagreement as regards the request to refer the case. Where that Member State takes no such decision within this period, it shall be deemed to have agreed.

Unless that Member State disagrees, the Commission, where it considers that such a distinct market exists, and that competition in that market may be significantly affected by the concentration, may decide to refer the whole or part of the case to the competent authorities of that Member State with a view to the application of that State's national competition law.

The decision whether or not to refer the case in accordance with the third subparagraph shall be taken within 25 working days starting from the receipt of the reasoned submission by the Commission. The Commission shall inform the other Member States and the persons or undertakings concerned of its decision. If the Commission does not take a decision within this period, it shall be deemed to have adopted a decision to refer the case in accordance with the submission made by the persons or undertakings concerned.

If the Commission decides, or is deemed to have decided, pursuant to the third and fourth subparagraphs, to refer the whole of the case, no notification shall be made pursuant to paragraph 1 and national competition law shall apply. Article 9(6) to (9) shall apply mutatis mutandis.

5. With regard to a concentration as defined in Article 3 which does not have a Community dimension within the meaning of Article 1 and which is capable of being reviewed under the national competition laws of at least three Member States, the persons or undertakings referred to in paragraph 2 may, before any notification to the competent authorities, inform the Commission by means of a reasoned submission that the concentration should be examined by the Commission.

The Commission shall transmit this submission to all Member States without delay.

Any Member State competent to examine the concentration under its national competition law may, within 15 working days of receiving the reasoned submission, express its disagreement as regards the request to refer the case.

Where at least one such Member State has expressed its disagreement in accordance with the third subparagraph within the period of 15 working days, the case shall not be referred. The Commission shall, without delay, inform all Member States and the persons or undertakings concerned of any such expression of disagreement.

Where no Member State has expressed its disagreement in accordance with the third subparagraph within the period of 15 working days, the concentration shall be deemed to have a Community dimension and shall be notified to the Commission in accordance with paragraphs 1 and 2. In such situations, no Member State shall apply its national competition law to the concentration.

6. The Commission shall report to the Council on the operation of paragraphs 4 and 5 by 1 July 2009. Following this report and on a proposal from the Commission, the Council, acting by a qualified majority, may revise paragraphs 4 and 5.

Article 5 Calculation of turnover

1. Aggregate turnover within the meaning of this Regulation shall comprise the amounts derived by the undertakings concerned in the preceding financial year from the sale of products and

the provision of services falling within the undertakings' ordinary activities after deduction of sales rebates and of value added tax and other taxes directly related to turnover. The aggregate turnover of an undertaking concerned shall not include the sale of products or the provision of services between any of the undertakings referred to in paragraph 4.

Turnover, in the Community or in a Member State, shall comprise products sold and services provided to undertakings or consumers, in the Community or in that Member State as the case may be.

2. By way of derogation from paragraph 1, where the concentration consists of the acquisition of parts, whether or not constituted as legal entities, of one or more undertakings, only the turnover relating to the parts which are the subject of the concentration shall be taken into account with regard to the seller or sellers.

However, two or more transactions within the meaning of the first subparagraph which take place within a two-year period between the same persons or undertakings shall be treated as one and the same concentration arising on the date of the last transaction.

3. In place of turnover the following shall be used:
   (a) for credit institutions and other financial institutions, the sum of the following income items as defined in Council Directive 86/635/EEC, after deduction of value added tax and other taxes directly related to those items, where appropriate:
   (i) interest income and similar income;
   (ii) income from securities:
   — income from shares and other variable yield securities,
   — income from participating interests,
   — income from shares in affiliated undertakings;
   (iii) commissions receivable;
   (iv) net profit on financial operations;
   (v) other operating income.

The turnover of a credit or financial institution in the Community or in a Member State shall comprise the income items, as defined above, which are received by the branch or division of that institution established in the Community or in the Member State in question, as the case may be;

   (b) for insurance undertakings, the value of gross premiums written which shall comprise all amounts received and receivable in respect of insurance contracts issued by or on behalf of the insurance undertakings, including also outgoing reinsurance premiums, and after deduction of taxes and parafiscal contributions or levies charged by reference to the amounts of individual premiums or the total volume of premiums; as regards Article 1(2)(b) and (3)(b), (c) and (d) and the final part of Article 1(2) and (3), gross premiums received from Community residents and from residents of one Member State respectively shall be taken into account.

4. Without prejudice to paragraph 2, the aggregate turnover of an undertaking concerned within the meaning of this Regulation shall be calculated by adding together the respective turnovers of the following:
   (a) the undertaking concerned;
   (b) those undertakings in which the undertaking concerned, directly or indirectly:
   (i) owns more than half the capital or business assets, or
   (ii) has the power to exercise more than half the voting rights, or
   (iii) has the power to appoint more than half the members of the supervisory board, the administrative board or bodies legally representing the undertakings, or
   (iv) has the right to manage the undertakings' affairs;
   (c) those undertakings which have in the undertaking concerned the rights or powers listed in (b);
   (d) those undertakings in which an undertaking as referred to in (c) has the rights or powers listed in (b);
   (e) those undertakings in which two or more undertakings as referred to in (a) to (d) jointly have the rights or powers listed in (b).

5. Where undertakings concerned by the concentration jointly have the rights or powers listed in paragraph 4(b), in calculating the aggregate turnover of the undertakings concerned for the purposes of this Regulation:

(a) no account shall be taken of the turnover resulting from the sale of products or the provision of services between the joint undertaking and each of the undertakings concerned or any other undertaking connected with any one of them, as set out in paragraph 4(b) to (e);

(b) account shall be taken of the turnover resulting from the sale of products and the provision of services between the joint undertaking and any third undertakings. This turnover shall be apportioned equally amongst the undertakings concerned.

Article 6 Examination of the notification and initiation of proceedings

1. The Commission shall examine the notification as soon as it is received.

(a) Where it concludes that the concentration notified does not fall within the scope of this Regulation, it shall record that finding by means of a decision.

(b) Where it finds that the concentration notified, although falling within the scope of this Regulation, does not raise serious doubts as to its compatibility with the common market, it shall decide not to oppose it and shall declare that it is compatible with the common market.
A decision declaring a concentration compatible shall be deemed to cover restrictions directly related and necessary to the implementation of the concentration.

(c) Without prejudice to paragraph 2, where the Commission finds that the concentration notified falls within the scope of this Regulation and raises serious doubts as to its compatibility with the common market, it shall decide to initiate proceedings. Without prejudice to Article 9, such proceedings shall be closed by means of a decision as provided for in Article 8(1) to (4), unless the undertakings concerned have demonstrated to the satisfaction of the Commission that they have abandoned the concentration.

2. Where the Commission finds that, following modification by the undertakings concerned, a notified concentration no longer raises serious doubts within the meaning of paragraph 1(c), it shall declare the concentration compatible with the common market pursuant to paragraph 1(b).

The Commission may attach to its decision under paragraph 1(b) conditions and obligations intended to ensure that the undertakings concerned comply with the commitments they have entered into vis-à-vis the Commission with a view to rendering the concentration compatible with the common market.

3. The Commission may revoke the decision it took pursuant to paragraph 1(a) or (b) where:

(a) the decision is based on incorrect information for which one of the undertakings is responsible or where it has been obtained by deceit,
or

(b) the undertakings concerned commit a breach of an obligation attached to the decision.

4. In the cases referred to in paragraph 3, the Commission may take a decision under paragraph 1, without being bound by the time limits referred to in Article 10(1).

5. The Commission shall notify its decision to the undertakings concerned and the competent authorities of the Member States without delay.

Article 7 Suspension of concentrations

1. A concentration with a Community dimension as defined in Article 1, or which is to be examined by the Commission pursuant to Article 4(5), shall not be implemented either before its notification or until it has been declared compatible with the common market pursuant to a decision under Articles 6(1)(b), 8(1) or 8(2), or on the basis of a presumption according to Article 10(6).

2. Paragraph 1 shall not prevent the implementation of a public bid or of a series of transactions in securities including those convertible into other securities admitted to trading on a market such as a stock exchange, by which control within the meaning of Article 3 is acquired from various sellers, provided that:

(a) the concentration is notified to the Commission pursuant to Article 4 without delay; and

(b) the acquirer does not exercise the voting rights attached to the securities in question or does so only to maintain the full value of its investments based on a derogation granted by the Commission under paragraph 3.

3. The Commission may, on request, grant a derogation from the obligations imposed in paragraphs 1 or 2. The request to grant a derogation must be reasoned. In deciding on the request, the Commission shall take into account *inter alia* the effects of the suspension on one or more undertakings concerned by the concentration or on a third party and the threat to competition posed by the concentration. Such a derogation may be made subject to conditions and obligations in order to ensure conditions of effective competition. A derogation may be applied for and granted at any time, be it before notification or after the transaction.

4. The validity of any transaction carried out in contravention of paragraph 1 shall be dependent on a decision pursuant to Article 6(1)(b) or Article 8(1), (2) or (3) or on a presumption pursuant to Article 10(6).

This Article shall, however, have no effect on the validity of transactions in securities including those convertible into other securities admitted to trading on a market such as a stock exchange, unless the buyer and seller knew or ought to have known that the transaction was carried out in contravention of paragraph 1.

Article 8 Powers of decision of the Commission

1. Where the Commission finds that a notified concentration fulfils the criterion laid down in Article 2(2) and, in the cases referred to in Article 2(4), the criteria laid down in Article 81(3) of the Treaty, it shall issue a decision declaring the concentration compatible with the common market.

A decision declaring a concentration compatible shall be deemed to cover restrictions directly related and necessary to the implementation of the concentration.

2. Where the Commission finds that, following modification by the undertakings concerned, a notified concentration fulfils the criterion laid down in Article 2(2) and, in the cases referred to in Article 2(4), the criteria laid down in Article 81(3) of the Treaty, it shall issue a decision declaring the concentration compatible with the common market.

The Commission may attach to its decision conditions and obligations intended to ensure that the undertakings concerned comply with the commitments they have entered into vis-à-vis the Commission with a view to rendering the concentration compatible with the common market.

A decision declaring a concentration compatible shall be deemed to cover restrictions directly related and necessary to the implementation of the concentration.

3. Where the Commission finds that a concentration fulfils the criterion defined in Article 2(3) or, in the cases referred to in Article 2(4), does not fulfil the criteria laid down in Article 81(3) of the Treaty, it shall issue a decision declaring that the concentration is incompatible with the common market.

4. Where the Commission finds that a concentration:

(a) has already been implemented and that concentration has been declared incompatible with the common market, or

(b) has been implemented in contravention of a condition attached to a decision taken under paragraph 2, which has found that, in the absence of the condition, the concentration would fulfil the criterion laid down in Article 2(3) or, in the cases referred to in Article 2(4), would not fulfil the criteria laid down in Article 81(3) of the Treaty, the Commission may:

— require the undertakings concerned to dissolve the concentration, in particular through the dissolution of the merger or the disposal of all the shares or assets acquired, so as to restore the situation prevailing prior to the implementation of the concentration; in circumstances where restoration of the situation prevailing before the implementation of the concentration is not possible through dissolution of the concentration, the Commission may take any other measure appropriate to achieve such restoration as far as possible,

— order any other appropriate measure to ensure that the undertakings concerned dissolve the concentration or take other restorative measures as required in its decision.

In cases falling within point (a) of the first subparagraph, the measures referred to in that subparagraph may be imposed either in a decision pursuant to paragraph 3 or by separate decision.

5. The Commission may take interim measures appropriate to restore or maintain conditions of effective competition where a concentration:
    (a) has been implemented in contravention of Article 7, and a decision as to the compatibility of the concentration with the common market has not yet been taken;
    (b) has been implemented in contravention of a condition attached to a decision under Article 6(1)(b) or paragraph 2 of this Article;
    (c) has already been implemented and is declared incompatible with the common market.

6. The Commission may revoke the decision it has taken pursuant to paragraphs 1 or 2 where:
    (a) the declaration of compatibility is based on incorrect information for which one of the undertakings is responsible or where it has been obtained by deceit; or
    (b) the undertakings concerned commit a breach of an obligation attached to the decision.

7. The Commission may take a decision pursuant to paragraphs 1 to 3 without being bound by the time limits referred to in Article 10(3), in cases where:
    (a) it finds that a concentration has been implemented
        (i) in contravention of a condition attached to a decision under Article 6(1)(b), or
        (ii) in contravention of a condition attached to a decision taken under paragraph 2 and in accordance with Article 10(2), which has found that, in the absence of the condition, the concentration would raise serious doubts as to its compatibility with the common market; or
    (b) a decision has been revoked pursuant to paragraph 6.

8. The Commission shall notify its decision to the undertakings concerned and the competent authorities of the Member States without delay.

Article 9 Referral to the competent authorities of the Member States

1. The Commission may, by means of a decision notified without delay to the undertakings concerned and the competent authorities of the other Member States, refer a notified concentration to the competent authorities of the Member State concerned in the following circumstances.

2. Within 15 working days of the date of receipt of the copy of the notification, a Member State, on its own initiative or upon the invitation of the Commission, may inform the Commission, which shall inform the undertakings concerned, that:
    (a) a concentration threatens to affect significantly competition in a market within that Member State, which presents all the characteristics of a distinct market, or
    (b) a concentration affects competition in a market within that Member State, which presents all the characteristics of a distinct market and which does not constitute a substantial part of the common market.

3. If the Commission considers that, having regard to the market for the products or services in question and the geographical reference market within the meaning of paragraph 7, there is such a distinct market and that such a threat exists, either:
    (a) it shall itself deal with the case in accordance with this Regulation; or
    (b) it shall refer the whole or part of the case to the competent authorities of the Member State concerned with a view to the application of that State's national competition law.

If, however, the Commission considers that such a distinct market or threat does not exist, it shall adopt a decision to that effect which it shall address to the Member State concerned, and shall itself deal with the case in accordance with this Regulation.

In cases where a Member State informs the Commission pursuant to paragraph 2(b) that a concentration affects competition in a distinct market within its territory that does not form a substantial part of the common market, the Commission shall refer the whole or part of the case relating to the distinct market concerned, if it considers that such a distinct market is affected.

4. A decision to refer or not to refer pursuant to paragraph 3 shall be taken:
    (a) as a general rule within the period provided for in Article 10(1), second subparagraph, where the Commission, pursuant to Article 6(1)(b), has not initiated proceedings; or

(b) within 65 working days at most of the notification of the concentration concerned where the Commission has initiated proceedings under Article 6(1)(c), without taking the preparatory steps in order to adopt the necessary measures under Article 8(2), (3) or (4) to maintain or restore effective competition on the market concerned.

5. If within the 65 working days referred to in paragraph 4(b) the Commission, despite a reminder from the Member State concerned, has not taken a decision on referral in accordance with paragraph 3 nor has taken the preparatory steps referred to in paragraph 4(b), it shall be deemed to have taken a decision to refer the case to the Member State concerned in accordance with paragraph 3(b).

6. The competent authority of the Member State concerned shall decide upon the case without undue delay.

Within 45 working days after the Commission's referral, the competent authority of the Member State concerned shall inform the undertakings concerned of the result of the preliminary competition assessment and what further action, if any, it proposes to take. The Member State concerned may exceptionally suspend this time limit where necessary information has not been provided to it by the undertakings concerned as provided for by its national competition law.

Where a notification is requested under national law, the period of 45 working days shall begin on the working day following that of the receipt of a complete notification by the competent authority of that Member State.

7. The geographical reference market shall consist of the area in which the undertakings concerned are involved in the supply and demand of products or services, in which the conditions of competition are sufficiently homogeneous and which can be distinguished from neighbouring areas because, in particular, conditions of competition are appreciably different in those areas. This assessment should take account in particular of the nature and characteristics of the products or services concerned, of the existence of entry barriers or of consumer preferences, of appreciable differences of the undertakings' market shares between the area concerned and neighbouring areas or of substantial price differences.

8. In applying the provisions of this Article, the Member State concerned may take only the measures strictly necessary to safeguard or restore effective competition on the market concerned.

9. In accordance with the relevant provisions of the Treaty, any Member State may appeal to the Court of Justice, and in particular request the application of Article 243 of the Treaty, for the purpose of applying its national competition law.

Article 10 Time limits for initiating proceedings and for decisions

1. Without prejudice to Article 6(4), the decisions referred to in Article 6(1) shall be taken within 25 working days at most. That period shall begin on the working day following that of the receipt of a notification or, if the information to be supplied with the notification is incomplete, on the working day following that of the receipt of the complete information.

That period shall be increased to 35 working days where the Commission receives a request from a Member State in accordance with Article 9(2) or where, the undertakings concerned offer commitments pursuant to Article 6(2) with a view to rendering the concentration compatible with the common market.

2. Decisions pursuant to Article 8(1) or (2) concerning notified concentrations shall be taken as soon as it appears that the serious doubts referred to in Article 6(1)(c) have been removed, particularly as a result of modifications made by the undertakings concerned, and at the latest by the time limit laid down in paragraph 3.

3. Without prejudice to Article 8(7), decisions pursuant to Article 8(1) to (3) concerning notified concentrations shall be taken within not more than 90 working days of the date on which the proceedings are initiated. That period shall be increased to 105 working days where the undertakings concerned offer commitments pursuant to Article 8(2), second subparagraph, with a view to rendering the concentration compatible with the common market, unless these commitments have been offered less than 55 working days after the initiation of proceedings.

The periods set by the first subparagraph shall likewise be extended if the notifying parties make a request to that effect not later than 15 working days after the initiation of proceedings pursuant to Article 6(1)(c). The notifying parties may make only one such request. Likewise, at any time following the initiation of proceedings, the periods set by the first subparagraph may be extended by the Commission with the agreement of the notifying parties. The total duration of any extension or extensions effected pursuant to this subparagraph shall not exceed 20 working days.

4. The periods set by paragraphs 1 and 3 shall exceptionally be suspended where, owing to circumstances for which one of the undertakings involved in the concentration is responsible, the Commission has had to request information by decision pursuant to Article 11 or to order an inspection by decision pursuant to Article 13.

The first subparagraph shall also apply to the period referred to in Article 9(4)(b).

5. Where the Court of Justice gives a judgment which annuls the whole or part of a Commission decision which is subject to a time limit set by this Article, the concentration shall be re-examined by the Commission with a view to adopting a decision pursuant to Article 6(1).

The concentration shall be re-examined in the light of current market conditions.

The notifying parties shall submit a new notification or supplement the original notification, without delay, where the original notification becomes incomplete by reason of intervening changes in market conditions or in the information provided. Where there are no such changes, the parties shall certify this fact without delay.

The periods laid down in paragraph 1 shall start on the working day following that of the receipt of complete information in a new notification, a supplemented notification, or a certification within the meaning of the third subparagraph.

The second and third subparagraphs shall also apply in the cases referred to in Article 6(4) and Article 8(7).

6. Where the Commission has not taken a decision in accordance with Article 6(1)(b), (c), 8(1), (2) or (3) within the time limits set in paragraphs 1 and 3 respectively, the concentration shall be deemed to have been declared compatible with the common market, without prejudice to Article 9.

Article 11 Requests for information

1. In order to carry out the duties assigned to it by this Regulation, the Commission may, by simple request or by decision, require the persons referred to in Article 3(1)(b), as well as undertakings and associations of undertakings, to provide all necessary information.

2. When sending a simple request for information to a person, an undertaking or an association of undertakings, the Commission shall state the legal basis and the purpose of the request, specify what information is required and fix the time limit within which the information is to be provided, as well as the penalties provided for in Article 14 for supplying incorrect or misleading information.

3. Where the Commission requires a person, an undertaking or an association of undertakings to supply information by decision, it shall state the legal basis and the purpose of the request, specify what information is required and fix the time limit within which it is to be provided. It shall also indicate the penalties provided for in Article 14 and indicate or impose the penalties provided for in Article 15. It shall further indicate the right to have the decision reviewed by the Court of Justice.

4. The owners of the undertakings or their representatives and, in the case of legal persons, companies or firms, or associations having no legal personality, the persons authorised to represent them by law or by their constitution, shall supply the information requested on behalf of the undertaking concerned. Persons duly authorised to act may supply the information on behalf of their clients. The latter shall remain fully responsible if the information supplied is incomplete, incorrect or misleading.

5. The Commission shall without delay forward a copy of any decision taken pursuant to paragraph 3 to the competent authorities of the Member State in whose territory the residence of the person or the seat of the undertaking or association of undertakings is situated, and to the competent authority of the Member State whose territory is affected. At the specific request of the competent authority of a Member State, the Commission shall also forward to that authority copies of simple requests for information relating to a notified concentration.

6. At the request of the Commission, the governments and competent authorities of the Member States shall provide the Commission with all necessary information to carry out the duties assigned to it by this Regulation.

7. In order to carry out the duties assigned to it by this Regulation, the Commission may interview any natural or legal person who consents to be interviewed for the purpose of collecting information relating to the subject matter of an investigation. At the beginning of the interview, which may be conducted by telephone or other electronic means, the Commission shall state the legal basis and the purpose of the interview.

Where an interview is not conducted on the premises of the Commission or by telephone or other electronic means, the Commission shall inform in advance the competent authority of the Member State in whose territory the interview takes place. If the competent authority of that Member State so requests, officials of that authority may assist the officials and other persons authorised by the Commission to conduct the interview.

Article 12 Inspections by the authorities of the Member States

1. At the request of the Commission, the competent authorities of the Member States shall undertake the inspections which the Commission considers to be necessary under Article 13(1), or which it has ordered by decision pursuant to Article 13(4). The officials of the competent authorities of the Member States who are responsible for conducting these inspections as well as those authorised or appointed by them shall exercise their powers in accordance with their national law.

2. If so requested by the Commission or by the competent authority of the Member State within whose territory the inspection is to be conducted, officials and other accompanying persons authorised by the Commission may assist the officials of the authority concerned.

Article 13 The Commission's powers of inspection

1. In order to carry out the duties assigned to it by this Regulation, the Commission may conduct all necessary inspections of undertakings and associations of undertakings.

2. The officials and other accompanying persons authorised by the Commission to conduct an inspection shall have the power:
   (a) to enter any premises, land and means of transport of undertakings and associations of undertakings;
   (b) to examine the books and other records related to the business, irrespective of the medium on which they are stored;
   (c) to take or obtain in any form copies of or extracts from such books or records;
   (d) to seal any business premises and books or records for the period and to the extent necessary for the inspection;
   (e) to ask any representative or member of staff of the undertaking or association of undertakings for explanations on facts or documents relating to the subject matter and purpose of the inspection and to record the answers.

3. Officials and other accompanying persons authorised by the Commission to conduct an inspection shall exercise their powers upon production of a written authorisation specifying the subject matter and purpose of the inspection and the penalties provided for in Article 14, in the production of the required books or other records related to the business which is incomplete or where answers to questions asked under paragraph 2 of this Article are incorrect or misleading. In good time before the inspection, the Commission shall give notice of the inspection to the competent authority of the Member State in whose territory the inspection is to be conducted.

4. Undertakings and associations of undertakings are required to submit to inspections ordered by decision of the Commission. The decision shall specify the subject matter and purpose of the inspection, appoint the date on which it is to begin and indicate the penalties provided for in Articles 14 and 15 and the right to have the decision reviewed by the Court of Justice. The Commission shall take such decisions after consulting the competent authority of the Member State in whose territory the inspection is to be conducted.

5. Officials of, and those authorised or appointed by, the competent authority of the Member State in whose territory the inspection is to be conducted shall, at the request of that authority or of the Commission, actively assist the officials and other accompanying persons authorised by the Commission. To this end, they shall enjoy the powers specified in paragraph 2.

6. Where the officials and other accompanying persons authorised by the Commission find that an undertaking opposes an inspection, including the sealing of business premises, books or records, ordered pursuant to this Article, the Member State concerned shall afford them the necessary assistance, requesting where appropriate the assistance of the police or of an equivalent enforcement authority, so as to enable them to conduct their inspection.

7. If the assistance provided for in paragraph 6 requires authorisation from a judicial authority according to national rules, such authorisation shall be applied for. Such authorisation may also be applied for as a precautionary measure.

8. Where authorisation as referred to in paragraph 7 is applied for, the national judicial authority shall ensure that the Commission decision is authentic and that the coercive measures envisaged are neither arbitrary nor excessive having regard to the subject matter of the inspection. In its control of proportionality of the coercive measures, the national judicial authority may ask the Commission, directly or through the competent authority of that Member State, for detailed explanations relating to the subject matter of the inspection. However, the national judicial authority may not call into question the necessity for the inspection nor demand that it be provided with the information in the Commission's file. The lawfulness of the Commission's decision shall be subject to review only by the Court of Justice.

Article 14 Fines

1. The Commission may by decision impose on the persons referred to in Article 3(1)b, undertakings or associations of undertakings, fines not exceeding 1% of the aggregate turnover of the undertaking or association of undertakings concerned within the meaning of Article 5 where, intentionally or negligently:

(a) they supply incorrect or misleading information in a submission, certification, notification or supplement thereto, pursuant to Article 4, Article 10(5) or Article 22(3);

(b) they supply incorrect or misleading information in response to a request made pursuant to Article 11(2);

(c) in response to a request made by decision adopted pursuant to Article 11(3), they supply incorrect, incomplete or misleading information or do not supply information within the required time limit;

(d) they produce the required books or other records related to the business in incomplete form during inspections under Article 13, or refuse to submit to an inspection ordered by decision taken pursuant to Article 13(4);

(e) in response to a question asked in accordance with Article 13(2)(e),
  — they give an incorrect or misleading answer,
  — they fail to rectify within a time limit set by the Commission an incorrect, incomplete or misleading answer given by a member of staff, or
  — they fail or refuse to provide a complete answer on facts relating to the subject matter and purpose of an inspection ordered by a decision adopted pursuant to Article 13(4);

(f) seals affixed by officials or other accompanying persons authorised by the Commission in accordance with Article 13(2)(d) have been broken.

2. The Commission may by decision impose fines not exceeding 10% of the aggregate turnover of the undertaking concerned within the meaning of Article 5 on the persons referred to in Article 3(1)b or the undertakings concerned where, either intentionally or negligently, they:

(a) fail to notify a concentration in accordance with Articles 4 or 22(3) prior to its implementation, unless they are expressly authorised to do so by Article 7(2) or by a decision taken pursuant to Article 7(3);

(b) implement a concentration in breach of Article 7;

(c) implement a concentration declared incompatible with the common market by decision pursuant to Article 8(3) or do not comply with any measure ordered by decision pursuant to Article 8(4) or (5);

(d) fail to comply with a condition or an obligation imposed by decision pursuant to Articles 6(1)(b), Article 7(3) or Article 8(2), second subparagraph.

3. In fixing the amount of the fine, regard shall be had to the nature, gravity and duration of the infringement.

4. Decisions taken pursuant to paragraphs 1, 2 and 3 shall not be of a criminal law nature.

Article 15 Periodic penalty payments

1. The Commission may by decision impose on the persons referred to in Article 3(1)b, undertakings or associations of undertakings, periodic penalty payments not exceeding 5% of the average daily aggregate turnover of the undertaking or association of undertakings concerned within the meaning of Article 5 for each working day of delay, calculated from the date set in the decision, in order to compel them:

(a) to supply complete and correct information which it has requested by decision taken pursuant to Article 11(3);

(b) to submit to an inspection which it has ordered by decision taken pursuant to Article 13(4);

(c) to comply with an obligation imposed by decision pursuant to Article 6(1)(b), Article 7(3) or Article 8(2), second subparagraph; or;

(d) to comply with any measures ordered by decision pursuant to Article 8(4) or (5).

2. Where the persons referred to in Article 3(1)(b), undertakings or associations of undertakings have satisfied the obligation which the periodic penalty payment was intended to enforce, the Commission may fix the definitive amount of the periodic penalty payments at a figure lower than that which would arise under the original decision.

Article 16 Review by the Court of Justice

The Court of Justice shall have unlimited jurisdiction within the meaning of Article 229 of the Treaty to review decisions whereby the Commission has fixed a fine or periodic penalty payments; it may cancel, reduce or increase the fine or periodic penalty payment imposed.

Article 17 Professional secrecy

1. Information acquired as a result of the application of this Regulation shall be used only for the purposes of the relevant request, investigation or hearing.

2. Without prejudice to Article 4(3), Articles 18 and 20, the Commission and the competent authorities of the Member States, their officials and other servants and other persons working under the supervision of these authorities as well as officials and civil servants of other authorities of the Member States shall not disclose information they have acquired through the application of this Regulation of the kind covered by the obligation of professional secrecy.

3. Paragraphs 1 and 2 shall not prevent publication of general information or of surveys which do not contain information relating to particular undertakings or associations of undertakings.

Article 18 Hearing of the parties and of third persons

1. Before taking any decision provided for in Article 6(3), Article 7(3), Article 8(2) to (6), and Articles 14 and 15, the Commission shall give the persons, undertakings and associations of undertakings concerned the opportunity, at every stage of the procedure up to the consultation of the Advisory Committee, of making known their views on the objections against them.

2. By way of derogation from paragraph 1, a decision pursuant to Articles 7(3) and 8(5) may be taken provisionally, without the persons, undertakings or associations of undertakings concerned being given the opportunity to make known their views beforehand, provided that the Commission gives them that opportunity as soon as possible after having taken its decision.

3. The Commission shall base its decision only on objections on which the parties have been able to submit their observations. The rights of the defence shall be fully respected in the proceedings. Access to the file shall be open at least to the parties directly involved, subject to the legitimate interest of undertakings in the protection of their business secrets.

4. In so far as the Commission or the competent authorities of the Member States deem it necessary, they may also hear other natural or legal persons. Natural or legal persons showing

a sufficient interest and especially members of the administrative or management bodies of the undertakings concerned or the recognised representatives of their employees shall be entitled, upon application, to be heard.

Article 19 Liaison with the authorities of the Member States

1. The Commission shall transmit to the competent authorities of the Member States copies of notifications within three working days and, as soon as possible, copies of the most important documents lodged with or issued by the Commission pursuant to this Regulation. Such documents shall include commitments offered by the undertakings concerned vis-à-vis the Commission with a view to rendering the concentration compatible with the common market pursuant to Article 6(2) or Article 8(2), second subparagraph.

2. The Commission shall carry out the procedures set out in this Regulation in close and constant liaison with the competent authorities of the Member States, which may express their views upon those procedures. For the purposes of Article 9 it shall obtain information from the competent authority of the Member State as referred to in paragraph 2 of that Article and give it the opportunity to make known its views at every stage of the procedure up to the adoption of a decision pursuant to paragraph 3 of that Article; to that end it shall give it access to the file.

3. An Advisory Committee on concentrations shall be consulted before any decision is taken pursuant to Article 8(1) to (6), Articles 14 or 15 with the exception of provisional decisions taken in accordance with Article 18(2).

4. The Advisory Committee shall consist of representatives of the competent authorities of the Member States. Each Member State shall appoint one or two representatives; if unable to attend, they may be replaced by other representatives. At least one of the representatives of a Member State shall be competent in matters of restrictive practices and dominant positions.

5. Consultation shall take place at a joint meeting convened at the invitation of and chaired by the Commission. A summary of the case, together with an indication of the most important documents and a preliminary draft of the decision to be taken for each case considered, shall be sent with the invitation. The meeting shall take place not less than 10 working days after the invitation has been sent. The Commission may in exceptional cases shorten that period as appropriate in order to avoid serious harm to one or more of the undertakings concerned by a concentration.

6. The Advisory Committee shall deliver an opinion on the Commission's draft decision, if necessary by taking a vote. The Advisory Committee may deliver an opinion even if some members are absent and unrepresented. The opinion shall be delivered in writing and appended to the draft decision. The Commission shall take the utmost account of the opinion delivered by the Committee. It shall inform the Committee of the manner in which its opinion has been taken into account.

7. The Commission shall communicate the opinion of the Advisory Committee, together with the decision, to the addressees of the decision. It shall make the opinion public together with the decision, having regard to the legitimate interest of undertakings in the protection of their business secrets.

Article 20 Publication of decisions

1. The Commission shall publish the decisions which it takes pursuant to Article 8(1) to (6), Articles 14 and 15 with the exception of provisional decisions taken in accordance with Article 18(2) together with the opinion of the Advisory Committee in the Official Journal of the European Union.

2. The publication shall state the names of the parties and the main content of the decision; it shall have regard to the legitimate interest of undertakings in the protection of their business secrets.

Article 21 Application of the Regulation and jurisdiction

1. This Regulation alone shall apply to concentrations as defined in Article 3, and Council Regulations (EC) No 1/2003, (EEC) No 1017/68, (EEC) No 4056/86 and (EEC) No 3975/87 shall not apply, except in relation to joint ventures that do not have a Community dimension and which have as their object or effect the coordination of the competitive behaviour of undertakings that remain independent.

2. Subject to review by the Court of Justice, the Commission shall have sole jurisdiction to take the decisions provided for in this Regulation.

3. No Member State shall apply its national legislation on competition to any concentration that has a Community dimension.

The first subparagraph shall be without prejudice to any Member State's power to carry out any enquiries necessary for the application of Articles 4(4), 9(2) or after referral, pursuant to Article 9(3), first subparagraph, indent (b), or Article 9(5), to take the measures strictly necessary for the application of Article 9(8).

4. Notwithstanding paragraphs 2 and 3, Member States may take appropriate measures to protect legitimate interests other than those taken into consideration by this Regulation and compatible with the general principles and other provisions of Community law.

Public security, plurality of the media and prudential rules shall be regarded as legitimate interests within the meaning of the first subparagraph.

Any other public interest must be communicated to the Commission by the Member State concerned and shall be recognised by the Commission after an assessment of its compatibility with the general principles and other provisions of Community law before the measures referred to above may be taken. The Commission shall inform the Member State concerned of its decision within 25 working days of that communication.

Article 22 Referral to the Commission

1. One or more Member States may request the Commission to examine any concentration as defined in Article 3 that does not have a Community dimension within the meaning of Article 1 but affects trade between Member States and threatens to significantly affect competition within the territory of the Member State or States making the request.

Such a request shall be made at most within 15 working days of the date on which the concentration was notified, or if no notification is required, otherwise made known to the Member State concerned.

2. The Commission shall inform the competent authorities of the Member States and the undertakings concerned of any request received pursuant to paragraph 1 without delay.

Any other Member State shall have the right to join the initial request within a period of 15 working days of being informed by the Commission of the initial request.

All national time limits relating to the concentration shall be suspended until, in accordance with the procedure set out in this Article, it has been decided where the concentration shall be examined. As soon as a Member State has informed the Commission and the undertakings concerned that it does not wish to join the request, the suspension of its national time limits shall end.

3. The Commission may, at the latest 10 working days after the expiry of the period set in paragraph 2, decide to examine, the concentration where it considers that it affects trade between Member States and threatens to significantly affect competition within the territory of the Member State or States making the request. If the Commission does not take a decision within this period, it shall be deemed to have adopted a decision to examine the concentration in accordance with the request.

The Commission shall inform all Member States and the undertakings concerned of its decision. It may request the submission of a notification pursuant to Article 4.

The Member State or States having made the request shall no longer apply their national legislation on competition to the concentration.

4. Article 2, Article 4(2) to (3), Articles 5, 6, and 8 to 21 shall apply where the Commission examines a concentration pursuant to paragraph 3. Article 7 shall apply to the extent that the concentration has not been implemented on the date on which the Commission informs the undertakings concerned that a request has been made.

Where a notification pursuant to Article 4 is not required, the period set in Article 10(1) within which proceedings may be initiated shall begin on the working day following that on which the Commission informs the undertakings concerned that it has decided to examine the concentration pursuant to paragraph 3.

5. The Commission may inform one or several Member States that it considers a concentration fulfils the criteria in paragraph 1. In such cases, the Commission may invite that Member State or those Member States to make a request pursuant to paragraph 1.

Article 23 Implementing provisions

1. The Commission shall have the power to lay down in accordance with the procedure referred to in paragraph 2:
  (a) implementing provisions concerning the form, content and other details of notifications and submissions pursuant to Article 4;
  (b) implementing provisions concerning time limits pursuant to Article 4(4), (5) Articles 7, 9, 10 and 22;
  (c) the procedure and time limits for the submission and implementation of commitments pursuant to Article 6(2) and Article 8(2);
  (d) implementing provisions concerning hearings pursuant to Article 18.

2. The Commission shall be assisted by an Advisory Committee, composed of representatives of the Member States.
  (a) Before publishing draft implementing provisions and before adopting such provisions, the Commission shall consult the Advisory Committee.
  (b) Consultation shall take place at a meeting convened at the invitation of and chaired by the Commission. A draft of the implementing provisions to be taken shall be sent with the invitation. The meeting shall take place not less than 10 working days after the invitation has been sent.
  (c) The Advisory Committee shall deliver an opinion on the draft implementing provisions, if necessary by taking a vote. The Commission shall take the utmost account of the opinion delivered by the Committee.

Article 24 Relations with third countries

1. The Member States shall inform the Commission of any general difficulties encountered by their undertakings with concentrations as defined in Article 3 in a third country.

2. Initially not more than one year after the entry into force of this Regulation and, thereafter periodically, the Commission shall draw up a report examining the treatment accorded to undertakings having their seat or their principal fields of activity in the Community, in the terms referred to in paragraphs 3 and 4, as regards concentrations in third countries. The Commission shall submit those reports to the Council, together with any recommendations.

3. Whenever it appears to the Commission, either on the basis of the reports referred to in paragraph 2 or on the basis of other information, that a third country does not grant undertakings having their seat or their principal fields of activity in the Community, treatment comparable to that granted by the Community to undertakings from that country, the Commission may submit proposals to the Council for an appropriate mandate for negotiation with a view to obtaining comparable treatment for undertakings having their seat or their principal fields of activity in the Community.

4. Measures taken under this Article shall comply with the obligations of the Community or of the Member States, without prejudice to Article 307 of the Treaty, under international agreements, whether bilateral or multilateral.

Article 25 Repeal

1. Without prejudice to Article 26(2), Regulations (EEC) No 4064/89 and (EC) No 1310/97 shall be repealed with effect from 1 May 2004.

2. References to the repealed Regulations shall be construed as references to this Regulation and shall be read in accordance with the correlation table in the Annex.

Article 26 Entry into force and transitional provisions

1. This Regulation shall enter into force on the 20th day following that of its publication in the Official Journal of the European Union.
  It shall apply from 1 May 2004.

> 2. Regulation (EEC) No 4064/89 shall continue to apply to any concentration which was the subject of an agreement or announcement or where control was acquired within the meaning of Article 4(1) of that Regulation before the date of application of this Regulation, subject, in particular, to the provisions governing applicability set out in Article 25(2) and (3) of Regulation (EEC) No 4064/89 and Article 2 of Regulation (EEC) No 1310/97.
>
> 3. As regards concentrations to which this Regulation applies by virtue of accession, the date of accession shall be substituted for the date of application of this Regulation.
>
> This Regulation shall be binding in its entirety and directly applicable in all Member States.

NOTE: The ECMR operates an *ex ante* review mechanism with mandatory notification within the EC, in that the Commission investigates a merger *before* the transaction is completed (cf with an *ex post* system where scrutiny is applied *after* completion of the merger—this is possible in the UK: see Chapter 13). Further, if a concentration exists (Article 3: see Section 4(A) below), and has a 'Community dimension', the parties must notify the Commission (Article 1: see Section 4(B) below), and cannot complete the merger until it has been cleared by the Commission (Article 7). Article 14 provides the Commission with the power to impose financial penalties on parties to a concentration who supply incorrect or misleading information (up to 1 per cent aggregate turnover), or who fail to notify a concentration to the Commission when the thresholds have been satisfied, or complete the merger without clearance (up to 10 per cent aggregate turnover).

SECTION 4: JURISDICTION

The issue of jurisdiction under the ECMR covers several distinct and very important matters including: the concept of a concentration and which commercial activities are caught by the definition in Article 3; the Community dimension test in Article 1, which sets the turnover thresholds to determine whether parties to a proposed concentration must notify the Commission; and flexibility arrangements in Articles 4, 9, and 22 facilitating case referrals between the Commission and national competition authorities when appropriate. These matters will be considered below.

A: The concept of a concentration

The ECMR does not distinguish between the commercial concepts of a merger (e.g. firm A and firm B combining to create firm C) and acquisition (e.g. firm A acquires firm B), but Article 3 applies to include the concentration of direct or indirect control in the one undertaking or person after a transaction has been completed. The question of whether there has been a change of control is therefore critical to whether a concentration exists.

Commission Consolidated Jurisdictional Notice under Council Regulation (EC) No 139/2004 on the control of concentrations between undertakings
OJ, 2008, C95/1, paras 7–35 [footnotes omitted]

B. THE CONCEPT OF CONCENTRATION

(7) According to Article 3(1) of the Merger Regulation, a concentration only covers operations where a change of control in the undertakings concerned occurs on a lasting basis. Recital 20 in the

preamble to the Merger Regulation further explains that the concept of concentration is intended to relate to operations which bring about a lasting change in the structure of the market. Because the test in Article 3 is centred on the concept of control, the existence of a concentration is to a great extent determined by qualitative rather than quantitative criteria.

(8) Article 3(1) of the Merger Regulation defines two categories of concentrations:
— those arising from a merger between previously independent undertakings (point (a));
— those arising from an acquisition of control (point (b)).

These are treated respectively in Sections I and II below.

I. Mergers between previously independent undertakings

(9) A merger within the meaning of Article 3(1)(a) of the Merger Regulation occurs when two or more independent undertakings amalgamate into a new undertaking and cease to exist as separate legal entities. A merger may also occur when an undertaking is absorbed by another, the latter retaining its legal identity while the former ceases to exist as a legal entity.

(10) A merger within the meaning of Article 3(1)(a) may also occur where, in the absence of a legal merger, the combining of the activities of previously independent undertakings results in the creation of a single economic unit. This may arise in particular where two or more undertakings, while retaining their individual legal personalities, establish contractually a common economic management or the structure of a dual listed company. If this leads to a *de facto* amalgamation of the undertakings concerned into a single economic unit, the operation is considered to be a merger. A prerequisite for the determination of such a *de facto* merger is the existence of a permanent, single economic management. Other relevant factors may include internal profit and loss compensation or a revenue distribution as between the various entities within the group, and their joint liability or external risk sharing. The *de facto* amalgamation may be solely based on contractual arrangements, but it can also be reinforced by cross-shareholdings between the undertakings forming the economic unit.

II. Acquisition of control

1. Concept of control

1.1. Person or undertaking acquiring control

(11) Article 3 (1)(b) provides that a concentration occurs in the case of an acquisition of control. Such control may be acquired by one undertaking acting alone or by several undertakings acting jointly.

Person controlling another undertaking

(12) Control may also be acquired by a person in circumstances where that person already controls (whether solely or jointly) at least one other undertaking or, alternatively, by a combination of persons (which control another undertaking) and undertakings. The term 'person' in this context extends to public bodies and private entities, as well as natural persons. Acquisitions of control by natural persons are only considered to bring about a lasting change in the structure of the undertakings concerned if those natural persons carry out further economic activities on their own account or if they control at least one other undertaking.

Acquirer of control

(13) Control is normally acquired by persons or undertakings which are the holders of the rights or are entitled to rights conferring control under the contracts concerned (Article 3(3)(a)). However, there are also situations where the formal holder of a controlling interest differs from the person or undertaking having in fact the real power to exercise the rights resulting from this interest. This may be the case, for example, where an undertaking uses another person or undertaking for the acquisition of a controlling interest and has the power to exercise the rights conferring control through this person or undertaking, i.e. the latter is formally the holder of the rights, but acts only as a vehicle. In such a situation, control is acquired by the undertaking which in reality is behind the operation and in fact enjoys the power to control the target undertaking (Article 3(3)(b)). The Court of First Instance concluded from this provision that control held by commercial companies can be attributed to their exclusive shareholder, their majority shareholders or to those jointly controlling

the companies since these companies comply in any event with the decisions of those shareholders. A controlling shareholding which is held by different entities in a group is normally attributed to the undertaking exercising control over the different formal holders of the rights. In other cases, the evidence needed to establish this type of indirect control may include, either separately or in combination and to be assessed on a case-by-case basis, factors such as shareholdings, contractual relations, source of financing or family links.

Acquisition of control by investment funds

(14) Specific issues may arise in the case of acquisitions of control by investment funds. The Commission will analyse structures involving investment funds on a case-by-case basis, but some general features of such structures can be set out on the basis of the Commission's past experience.

(15) Investment funds are often set up in the legal form of limited partnerships, in which the investors participate as limited partners and normally do not exercise control, either individually or collectively. The investment funds usually acquire the shares and voting rights which confer control over the portfolio companies. Depending on the circumstances, control is normally exercised by the investment company which has set up the fund as the fund itself is typically a mere investment vehicle; in more exceptional circumstances, control may be exercised by the fund itself. The investment company usually exercises control by means of the organisational structure, *e.g.* by controlling the general partner of fund partnerships, or by contractual arrangements, such as advisory agreements, or by a combination of both. This may be the case even if the investment company itself does not own the company acting as a general partner, but their shares are held by natural persons (who may be linked to the investment company) or by a trust. Contractual arrangements with the investment company, in particular advisory agreements, will become even more important if the general partner does not have any own resources and personnel for the management of the portfolio companies, but only constitutes a company structure whose acts are performed by persons linked to the investment company. In these circumstances, the investment company normally acquires indirect control within the meaning of Article 3(1)(b) and 3(3)(b) of the Merger Regulation, and has the power to exercise the rights which are directly held by the investment fund.

1.2 Means of control

(16) Control is defined by Article 3(2) of the Merger Regulation as the possibility of exercising decisive influence on an undertaking. It is therefore not necessary to show that the decisive influence is or will be actually exercised. However, the possibility of exercising that influence must be effective. Article 3(2) further provides that the possibility of exercising decisive influence on an undertaking can exist on the basis of rights, contracts or any other means, either separately or in combination, and having regard to the considerations of fact and law involved. A concentration therefore may occur on a legal or a *de facto* basis, may take the form of sole or joint control, and extend to the whole or parts of one or more undertakings (cf. Article 3(1)(b)).

Control by the acquisition of shares or assets

(17) Whether an operation gives rise to an acquisition of control therefore depends on a number of legal and/or factual elements. The most common means for the acquisition of control is the acquisition of shares, possibly combined with a shareholders' agreement in cases of joint control, or the acquisition of assets.

Control on a contractual basis

(18) Control can also be acquired on a contractual basis. In order to confer control, the contract must lead to a similar control of the management and the resources of the other undertaking as in the case of acquisition of shares or assets. In addition to transferring control over the management and the resources, such contracts must be characterised by a very long duration (ordinarily without a possibility of early termination for the party granting the contractual rights). Only such contracts can result in a structural change in the market. Examples of such contracts are organisational contracts under national company law or other types of contracts, *e.g.* in the form of agreements for the lease of the business, giving the acquirer control over the management and the resources despite the fact that property rights or shares are not transferred. In this respect, Article 3(2)(a) specifies that control may also be constituted by a right to use the assets of an undertaking. Such

contracts may also lead to a situation of joint control if both the owner of the assets as well as the undertaking controlling the management enjoy veto rights over strategic business decisions.

Control by other means

(19) In line with these considerations, franchising agreements as such do not normally confer control over the franchisee's business on the franchisor. The franchisee usually exploits the entrepreneurial resources on its own account even if essential parts of the assets may belong to the franchisor. Furthermore, purely financial agreements, such as sale-and-lease-back transactions with arrangements for a buyback of the assets at the end of the term, do not normally constitute a concentration as they do not change control over the management and the resources.

(20) Furthermore, control can also be established by any other means. Purely economic relationships may play a decisive role for the acquisition of control. In exceptional circumstances, a situation of economic dependence may lead to control on a *de facto* basis where, for example, very important long-term supply agreements or credits provided by suppliers or customers, coupled with structural links, confer decisive influence. In such a situation, the Commission will carefully analyse whether such economic links, combined with other links, are sufficient to lead to a change of control on a lasting basis.

(21) There may be an acquisition of control even if it is not the declared intention of the parties or if the acquirer is only passive and the acquisition of control is triggered by action of third parties. Examples are situations where the change of control results from the inheritance of a shareholder or where the exit of a shareholder triggers a change of control, in particular a change from joint to sole control. Article 3(1)(b) covers such scenarios in specifying that control may also be acquired 'by any other means'.

Control and national company law

(22) National legislation within a Member State may provide specific rules on the structure of bodies representing the organization of decision-making within an undertaking. While such legislation may confer some power of control upon persons other than the shareholders, in particular on representatives of employees, the concept of control under the Merger Regulation is not related to such a means of influence as the Merger Regulation focuses on decisive influence enjoyed on the basis of rights, assets or contracts or equivalent *de facto* means. Restrictions in the articles of association or in general law concerning the persons eligible to sit on the board, such as a provisions requiring the appointment of independent members or excluding persons holding office or employment in the parent companies, do not exclude the existence of control as long as the shareholders decide the composition of the decision making bodies. Similarly, despite provisions of national law foreseeing that decisions of a company must be taken by its company organs in its interests, those persons holding the voting rights have the power to adopt those decisions and therefore have the possibility to exercise decisive influence on the company.

Control in other areas of legislation

(23) The concept of control under the Merger Regulation may be different from that applied in specific areas of Community and national legislation concerning, for example, prudential rules, taxation, air transport or the media. The interpretation of 'control' in other areas is therefore not necessarily decisive for the concept of control under the Merger Regulation

1.3. Object of control

(24) The Merger Regulation provides in Article 3(1)(b), (2) that the object of control can be one or more, or also parts of, undertakings which constitute legal entities, or the assets of such entities, or only some of these assets. The acquisition of control over assets can only be considered a concentration if those assets constitute the whole or a part of an undertaking, *i.e.* a business with a market presence, to which a market turnover can be clearly attributed. The transfer of the client base of a business can fulfil these criteria if this is sufficient to transfer a business with a market turnover. A transaction confined to intangible assets such as brands, patents or copyrights may also be considered to be a concentration if those assets constitute a business with a market turnover. In any case, the transfer of licences for brands, patents or copyrights, without additional assets, can only fulfil these criteria if the licences are exclusive at least in a certain territory and the transfer of such licences will transfer the turnover-generating activity. For non-exclusive licences it can be excluded that they may constitute on their own a business to which a market turnover is attached.

(25) Specific issues arise in cases where an undertaking outsources in-house activities, such as the provision of services or the manufacturing of products, to a service provider. Typical cases are the outsourcing of IT services to specialised IT companies. Outsourcing contracts can take several forms; their common characteristic is that the outsourcing service supplier shall provide those services to the customer which the latter has performed in-house before. Cases of simple outsourcing do not involve any transfer of assets or employees to the outsourcing service suppliers, but it is usually the case that any assets or employees are retained by the customer. Such an outsourcing contract is akin to a normal service contract and even if the outsourcing service supplier acquires a right to direct those assets and employees of the customer, no concentration arises if the assets and employees will be used exclusively to service the customer.

(26) The situation may be different if the outsourcing service supplier, in addition to taking over a certain activity which was previously provided internally, is transferred the associated assets and/or personnel. A concentration only arises in these circumstances if the assets constitute the whole or part of an undertaking, i.e. a business with access to the market. This requires that the assets previously dedicated to in-house activities of the seller will enable the outsourcing service supplier to provide services not only to the outsourcing customer but also to third parties, either immediately or within a short period after the transfer. This will be the case if the transfer relates to an internal business unit or a subsidiary already engaged in the provision of services to third parties. If third parties are not yet supplied, the assets transferred in the case of manufacturing should contain production facilities, the product know-how (it is sufficient if the assets transferred allow the build-up of such capabilities in the near future) and, if there is no existing market access, the means for the purchaser to develop a market access within a short period of time (e.g. including existing contracts or brands). As regards the provision of services, the assets transferred should include the required know-how (e.g. the relevant personnel and intellectual property) and those facilities which allow market access (such as, e.g., marketing facilities). The assets transferred therefore have to include at least those core elements that would allow an acquirer to build up a market presence in a time-frame similar to the start-up period for joint ventures as set out below under paragraphs 97, 100. As in the case of joint ventures, the Commission will take account of substantiated business plans and general market features for assessing this.

(27) If the assets transferred do not allow the purchaser to at least develop a market presence, it is likely that they will be used only for providing services to the outsourcing customer. In such circumstances, the transaction will not result in a lasting change in the market structure and the outsourcing contract is again similar to a service contract. The transaction will not constitute a concentration. The specific requirements under which a joint venture for the provision of outsourcing services is qualified as a concentration are assessed in the present Notice in the section on full-function joint ventures.

1.4. Change of control on a lasting basis

(28) Article 3(1) of the Merger Regulation defines the concept of a concentration in such a manner as to cover operations only if they bring about a lasting change in the control of the undertakings concerned and, as recital 20 adds, in the structure of the market. The Merger Regulation therefore does not deal with transactions resulting only in a temporary change of control. However, a change of control on a lasting basis is not excluded by the fact that the underlying agreements are entered into for a definite period of time, provided those agreements are renewable. A concentration may arise even in cases in which agreements envisage a definite end-date, if the period envisaged is sufficiently long to lead to a lasting change in the control of the undertakings concerned.

(29) The question whether an operation results in a lasting change in the market structure is also relevant for the assessment of several operations occurring in succession, where the first transaction is only transitory in nature. Several scenarios can be distinguished in this respect.

(30) In one scenario, several undertakings come together solely for the purpose of acquiring another company on the basis of an agreement to divide up the acquired assets according to a pre-existing plan immediately upon completion of the transaction. In such circumstances, in a first step, the acquisition of the entire target company is carried out by one or several undertakings. In a second step, the acquired assets are divided among several undertakings. The question is

then whether the first transaction is to be considered as a separate concentration, involving an acquisition of sole control (in the case of a single purchaser) or of joint control (in the case of a joint purchase) of the entire target undertaking, or whether only the acquisitions in the second step constitute concentrations, whereby each of the acquiring undertakings acquires its relevant part of the target undertaking.

(31) The Commission considers that the first transaction does not constitute a concentration, and examines the acquisitions of control by the ultimate acquirers, provided a number of conditions are met: First, the subsequent break-up must be agreed between the different purchasers in a legally binding way. Second, there must not be any uncertainty that the second step, the division of the acquired assets, will take place within a short time period after the first acquisition. The Commission considers that normally the maximum time-frame for the division of the assets should be one year.

(32) If both conditions are met, the first acquisition does not result in a structural change on a lasting basis. There is no effective concentration of economic power between the acquirer(s) and the target company as a whole since the acquired assets are not held in an undivided way on a lasting basis, but only for the time necessary to carry out the immediate split-up of the acquired assets. In those circumstances, only the acquisitions of the different parts of the undertaking in the second step will constitute concentrations, whereby each of these acquisitions by different purchasers will constitute a separate concentration. This is irrespective of whether the first acquisition is carried out by only one undertaking or jointly by the undertakings which are also involved in the second step. In any case, it must be noted that the scope of a clearance decision will only allow for a takeover of the entire target if the break-up can proceed within a short time-frame afterwards and the different parts of the target undertaking are directly sold on to the respective ultimate buyer.

(33) However, if these conditions are not fulfilled, in particular if it is not certain that the second step will proceed within a short time-frame after the first acquisition, the Commission will consider the first transaction as a separate concentration, involving the entire target undertaking. This, *e.g.*, is the case if the first transaction may also proceed independently of the second transaction or if a longer transitory period is needed to divide up the target undertaking.

(34) A second scenario is an operation leading to joint control for a starting-up period but, according to legally binding agreements, this joint control will be converted to sole control by one of the shareholders. As the joint control situation may not constitute a lasting change of control, the whole operation may be considered to be an acquisition of sole control. In the past, the Commission accepted that such a start-up period could last up to three years. Such a period seems to be too long to exclude that the joint control scenario has an impact on the structure of the market. The period therefore should, in general, not exceed one year and the joint control period should be only transitory in nature. Only such a relatively short period will make it unlikely that the joint control period will have a distinct impact on the market structure and can therefore be considered as not leading to a change in control on a lasting basis.

(35) In a third scenario, an undertaking is 'parked' with an interim buyer, often a bank, on the basis of an agreement on the future onward sale of the business to an ultimate acquirer. The interim buyer generally acquires shares 'on behalf' of the ultimate acquirer, which often bears the major part of the economic risks and may also be granted specific rights. In such circumstances, the first transaction is only undertaken to facilitate the second transaction and the first buyer is directly linked to the ultimate acquirer. Contrary to the situation described in the first scenario in paragraphs 30–33, no other ultimate acquirer is involved, the target business remains unchanged, and the sequence of transactions is initiated alone by the sole ultimate acquirer. From the date of the adoption of this Notice, the Commission will examine the acquisition of control by the ultimate acquirer, as provided for in the agreements entered into by the parties. The Commission will consider the transaction by which the interim buyer acquires control in such circumstances as the first step of a single concentration comprising the lasting acquisition of control by the ultimate buyer.

NOTE: The number of ways in which the management and relationships between undertakings can change is infinite, but the Notice attempts to put some concepts at the fore of the

ECMR. Where entirely new undertakings are created from others the position is generally clear, but it is much more difficult to ascertain in situations in which there is a gradual shift of control. In that situation the attainment of a 'decisive influence' is key. It should also be borne in mind that such influence does not have to be formal, but must be able to be exercised in practice. That influence can be achieved either solely, by one undertaking, or jointly, by more than one undertaking working together. The Commission Notice provides detailed guidance on the issue of control as this is essential to the determination of whether a concentration exists. A particular problem in this area is the acquisition of minority shareholdings and under what circumstances that can be held to amount to a concentration: see Leupold, H., and Haans, J., 'Minority Shareholdings and Merger Control after Ryanair/Aer Lingus—"No worries, mate?"' [2008] ECLR 624.

B: Concentrations having a Community dimension

Article 1 sets out two alternative turnover thresholds, and if either one is satisfied, the proposed concentration has a Community dimension. Article 5 provides details on how parties to concentrations should calculate their turnover from the previous financial year. In order to determine whether the turnover thresholds are satisfied, it is necessary to first establish which undertakings' turnover should be taken into account, and then calculate the turnover according to the provisions of the ECMR and relevant Commission Notice.

Christensen, P., Fountoukakos, K., and Sjöblom, D., Chapter 5, 'Mergers', in Faull, J., and Nikpay, A. (eds), *The EC law of Competition*
2nd edn, OUP, 2007, at paras 5.80–5.86 [footnotes omitted] By permission of Oxford University Press

(2) Concept of a Community Dimension

5.80 The Merger Regulation is intended to apply to concentrations of a significant size, the basic assumption being that such operations have a cross border impact across more than one Member State and therefore can be more effectively assessed at a European level.

5.81 After having established that a particular transaction constitutes a concentration within the meaning of Article 3 of the Merger Regulation, the second part of the jurisdictional test assesses whether the concentration has a 'Community dimension'. This analysis requires, first, the identification of the 'undertakings concerned' and secondly, establishment of the fact that the turnover attributable to these undertakings meets the thresholds laid down in Article 1 of the Merger Regulation.

(a) Identifying the Undertakings Concerned (Article 1)

5.82 As an introductory remark it should be noted that the purpose of this Article is to measure the total amount of turnover being combined through a concentration. It follows from this that the seller of a business will not be considered as an undertaking concerned, unless it retains a jointly controlling interest in the divested business. Consequently, the turnover of the seller (and its group) is only of interest if it retains such joint control.

5.83 (i) **Mergers** In the most straightforward scenario, the undertakings concerned will be each of the merging entities.

5.84 (ii) **Acquisition of Sole Control** Here, the undertakings concerned will be the company acquiring control and the target of the acquisition...

5.86 (iii) **Acquisition of Joint Control** When a new joint venture is created, the undertakings concerned will be each of its controlling parent companies. The joint venture, which at the time of the transaction does not exist, will not be considered as an undertaking concerned...

NOTE: The concise excerpt above discusses the most common scenarios and which undertakings should be taken into account in those situations. In addition to the Commission Consolidated Jurisdictional Notice, they discuss a far wider range of scenarios to provide guidance to parties to concentrations. The Commission Notice also provides guidance on whether the turnover thresholds in Article 1 have been satisfied.

Commission Consolidated Jurisdictional Notice under Council Regulation (EC) No 139/2004 on the control of concentrations between undertakings
OJ, 2008, C95/1, paras 124–8 [footnotes omitted]

C. COMMUNITY DIMENSION

I. Thresholds

(124) A two fold test defines the operations to which the Merger Regulation applies. The first test is that the operation must be a concentration within the meaning of Article 3. The second comprises the turnover thresholds contained in Article 1, designed to identify those operations which have an impact upon the Community and can be deemed to be of 'Community dimension'. Turnover is used as a proxy for the economic resources being combined in a concentration, and is allocated geographically in order to reflect the geographic distribution of those resources.

(125) Two sets of thresholds are set out in Article 1 to establish whether the operation has a Community dimension. Article 1(2) establishes three different criteria: The worldwide turnover threshold is intended to measure the overall dimension of the undertakings concerned; the Community turnover threshold seek to determine whether the concentration involves a minimum level of activities in the Community; and the two-thirds rule aims to exclude purely domestic transactions from Community jurisdiction.

(126) This second set of thresholds, contained in Article 1(3), is designed to tackle those concentrations which fall short of achieving Community dimension under Article 1(2), but would have a substantial impact in at least three Member States leading to multiple notifications under national competition rules of those Member States. For this purpose, Article 1(3) provides for lower turnover thresholds, both worldwide and Community-wide, and for a minimum level of activities of the undertakings concerned, jointly and individually, in at least three Member States. Similarly to Article 1(2), Article 1(3) also contains a two-thirds rule excluding predominantly domestic concentrations.

(127) The thresholds as such are designed to govern jurisdiction and not to assess the market position of the parties to the concentration nor the impact of the operation. In so doing they include turnover derived from, and thus the resources devoted to, all areas of activity of the parties, and not just those directly involved in the concentration. The thresholds are purely quantitative, since they are only based on turnover calculation instead of market share or other criteria. They pursue the objective to provide a simple and objective mechanism that can be easily handled by the companies involved in a merger in order to determine if their transaction has a Community dimension and is therefore notifiable.

(128) Whereas Article 1 sets out the numerical thresholds to establish jurisdiction, the purpose of Article 5 is to explain how turnover should be calculated to ensure that the resulting figures are a true representation of economic reality.

NOTE: Turnover thresholds provide the primary means of determining whether the Commission has jurisdiction under the ECMR, but Regulation 139/2004 provides even more flexibility than Regulation 4064/89 to try to ensure that the most appropriate competition authority reviews the proposed concentration, irrespective of whether the Community dimension test is satisfied or not. These are referred to as pre-notification and post-notification referral mechanisms.

■ QUESTION

When does the Commission have exclusive competence to assess a proposed concentration?

C: Flexibility and case referrals

Jurisdiction to investigate a proposed concentration would ideally be based entirely on geographic effects, yet the turnover thresholds within the Community dimension test in Article 1 are an attempt to formulate an efficient means of allocating jurisdiction. The turnover thresholds therefore must be supplemented by mechanisms allowing for flexibility when circumstances mean that the Commission would be the most appropriate reviewing authority in spite of the turnover thresholds not being satisfied, or where a national competition authority would be most appropriate in spite of the turnover thresholds being satisfied.

Budzinski, O., 'An economic perspective on the jurisdictional reform of the European merger control system'
(2006) 2 Euro CJ 119, at p 131 [footnotes omitted]

Turnover thresholds possess a considerable advantage in terms of efficiency: turnovers of enterprises can be calculated and determined comparably easy and unambiguous. Thus, turnover thresholds serve as a cost-saving proxy for "geographic relevant markets", which would be the theoretical paragon from an economic perspective. However, the delineation of relevant markets is a difficult, costly, and often controversial issue, which cannot sensibly be done before the competent jurisdiction(s) is (are) chosen, and thus cannot serve as an instrument for competence allocation.

A one-stop shop is always created by the EU turnover thresholds and, consequently, is exclusively allocated to the EU level. However, the one-stop shop principle falls short if a specific merger does not meet the thresholds but, nevertheless, is forced to be notified (according to national law) to more than one Member State authority. In such cases, multiple parallel proceedings occur, causing an inefficient increase in transaction and administration costs. The extent of multiple reviews on the Member State level depends (i) on the figures of the vertical threshold and (ii) on the figures of the horizontal threshold. The first aspect highlights how many cases are allocated to the Member State level in general, whereas the second aspect contributes to determining how many Member States are competent for a given case. The vertical threshold in the EU Merger Control System is theoretically designed to support the one-stop shop. In particular, the two-thirds rule (assigning competence to the most impacted Member State) represents an element which considers that the one-stop shop principle does not necessarily imply centralisation but, instead, can include an important role for decentralised competences. However, without horizontal thresholds, the problem of multiple reviews is likely to be considerable, causing an inefficiently high burden on businesses and taxpayers, because it is not ensured that only a substantial impact on domestic markets constitutes jurisdiction over a specific Member State. An ambitious and harmonised horizontal threshold would significantly reduce this problem, albeit not to zero.

The European Merger Control System implements another element in order to alleviate the deficiencies of turnover threshold-based competence allocation. The post-notification referral system re-allocates the competences to review and control a given merger. This could improve the one-stop shop principle, in particular regarding joint upward referrals. However, the non-mandatory character of upward referrals, leaving them at the discretion of the NCAs, generates a conflict...

NOTE: Budzinski highlights the post-notification referral mechanisms in Article 9, the so-called 'German clause', and Article 22, the so-called 'Dutch clause'. There are also pre-notification referral mechanisms in Article 4(4)–(5). In discussing the 'non-mandatory character of upward referrals' Budzinski is referring to Article 22 and the possibility of a Member State's competition authority referring a case to the Commission, even in the absence of a Community dimension, but he also highlights the conflict between improving the performance and reach of the ECMR one-stop shop and protecting the competence of national competition authorities. A similar tension is highlighted in the pre-notification referral system for 'upward referrals' under Article 4(5), where parties to a proposed concentration can submit a 'reasoned submission' to the Commission for it to investigate the concentration if it could be reviewed by the competition authorities of at least three Member States. Clearly this mechanism is designed to offer the benefit of the one-stop shop to a larger number of concentrations that do not satisfy the turnover thresholds in the Community dimension test, yet the discretionary nature of the provision, in that any one national competition authority can block the upward referral, diminishes its potential significance.

Commission Notice on Case Referral in respect of concentrations
OJ, 2005, C56/2, paras 1–45 [footnotes omitted]

1. The purpose of this Notice is to describe in a general way the rationale underlying the case referral system in Article 4(4) and (5), Article 9 and Article 22 of Council Regulation (EC) No 139/2004 of 20 January 2004 on the control of concentrations between undertakings (the EC Merger Regulation) (hereinafter "the Merger Regulation"), including the recent changes made to the system, to catalogue the legal criteria that must be fulfilled in order for referrals to be possible, and to set out the factors which may be taken into consideration when referrals are decided upon. The Notice also provides practical guidance regarding the mechanics of the referral system, in particular regarding the pre-notification referral mechanism provided for in Article 4(4) and (5) of the Merger Regulation. The guidance provided in this notice applies, *mutatis mutandis*, to the referral rules contained in the EEA Agreement.

I. INTRODUCTION

2. Community jurisdiction in the field of merger control is defined by the application of the turnover-related criteria contained in Articles 1(2) and 1(3) of the Merger Regulation. When dealing with concentrations, the Commission and Member States do not have concurrent jurisdiction. Rather, the Merger Regulation establishes a clear division of competence. Concentrations with a "Community dimension", i.e. those above the turnover thresholds in Article 1 of the Merger Regulation, fall within the exclusive jurisdiction of the Commission; Member States are precluded from applying national competition law to such concentrations by virtue of Article 21 of the Merger Regulation. Concentrations falling below the thresholds remain within the competence of the Member States; the Commission has no jurisdiction to deal with them under the Merger Regulation.

3. Determining jurisdiction exclusively by reference to fixed turnover-related criteria provides legal certainty for merging companies. While the financial criteria generally serve as effective proxies for the category of transactions for which the Commission is the more appropriate authority, Regulation (EEC) No 4064/89 complemented this "bright-line" jurisdictional scheme with a possibility for cases to be re-attributed by the Commission to Member States and vice versa, upon request and provided certain criteria were fulfilled.

4. When Regulation (EEC) No 4064/89 was first introduced, it was envisaged by the Council and Commission that case referrals would only be resorted to in "exceptional circumstances" and where "the interests in respect of competition of the Member State concerned could not be adequately protected in any other way". There have, however, been a number of developments since the adoption of Regulation (EEC) No 4064/89. First, merger control laws have been introduced in almost all Member States. Second, the Commission has exercised its discretion to refer a number of cases to Member States pursuant to Article 9 in circumstances where it was felt that the Member State in question was in a better position to carry out the investigation than the Commission. Likewise, in a number of cases, several Member States decided to make a joint referral of a case pursuant to Article 22 in circumstances where it was felt that the Commission was the authority in a better position to carry out the investigation. Third, there has been an increase in the number of transactions not meeting the thresholds in Article 1 of the Merger Regulation which must be filed in multiple Member State jurisdictions, a trend which is likely to continue in line with the Community's growing membership. Many of these transactions affect competition beyond the territories of individual Member States.

5. The revisions made to the referral system in the Merger Regulation are designed to facilitate the re-attribution of cases between the Commission and Member States, consistent with the

principle of subsidiarity, so that the more appropriate authority or authorities for carrying out a particular merger investigation should in principle deal with the case. At the same time, the revisions are intended to preserve the basic features of the Community merger control system introduced in 1989, in particular the provision of a "one-stop-shop" for the competition scrutiny of mergers with a cross-border impact and an alternative to multiple merger control notifications within the Community. Such multiple filings often entail considerable cost for competition authorities and businesses alike.

6. The case re-attribution system now provides that a referral may also be triggered before a formal filing has been made in any Member State jurisdiction, thereby affording merging companies the possibility of ascertaining, at as early as possible a stage, where jurisdiction for scrutiny of their transaction will ultimately lie. Such pre-notification referrals have the advantage of alleviating the additional cost, notably in terms of time delay, associated with post-filing referral.

7. The revisions made to the referral system in Regulation (EC) No. 139/2004 were motivated by a desire that it should operate as a jurisdictional mechanism which is flexible but which at the same time ensures effective protection of competition and limits the scope for "forum shopping" to the greatest extent possible. However, having regard in particular to the importance of legal certainty, it should be stressed that referrals remain a derogation from the general rules which determine jurisdiction based upon objectively determinable turnover thresholds. Moreover, the Commission and Member States retain a considerable margin of discretion in deciding whether to refer cases falling within their "original jurisdiction", or whether to accept to deal with cases not falling within their "original jurisdiction", pursuant to Article 4(4) and (5), Article 9(2)(a) and Article 22. To that extent, the current Notice is intended to provide no more than general guidance regarding the appropriateness of particular cases or categories of cases for referral.

II. REFERRAL OF CASES

Guiding principles

8. The system of merger control established by the Merger Regulation, including the mechanism for re-attributing cases between the Commission and Member States contained therein, is consistent with the principle of subsidiarity enshrined in the EC Treaty. Decisions taken with regard to the referral of cases should accordingly take due account of all aspects of the application of the principle of subsidiarity in this context, in particular which is the authority more appropriate for carrying out the investigation, the benefits inherent in a "one-stop-shop" system, and the importance of legal certainty with regard to jurisdiction. These factors are inter-linked and the respective weight placed upon each of them will depend upon the specificities of a particular case. Above all, in considering whether or not to exercise their discretion to make or accede to a referral, the Commission and Member States should bear in mind the need to ensure effective protection of competition in all markets affected by the transaction.

More appropriate authority

9. In principle, jurisdiction should only be re-attributed to another competition authority in circumstances where the latter is the more appropriate for dealing with a merger, having regard to the specific characteristics of the case as well as the tools and expertise available to the authority. Particular regard should be had to the likely locus of any impact on competition resulting from the merger. Regard may also be had to the implications, in terms of administrative effort, of any contemplated referral.

10. The case for re-attributing jurisdiction is likely to be more compelling where it appears that a particular transaction may have a significant impact on competition and thus may deserve careful scrutiny.

One-stop-shop

11. Decisions on the referral of cases should also have regard to the benefits inherent in a "one-stop-shop", which is at the core of the Merger Regulation. The provision of a one-stop-shop is beneficial to competition authorities and businesses alike. The handling of a merger by a single competition authority normally increases administrative efficiency, avoiding duplication and

fragmentation of enforcement effort as well as potentially incoherent treatment (regarding investigation, assessment and possible remedies) by multiple authorities. It normally also brings advantages to businesses, in particular to merging firms, by reducing the costs and burdens arising from multiple filing obligations and by eliminating the risk of conflicting decisions resulting from the concurrent assessment of the same transaction by a number of competition authorities under diverse legal regimes.

12. Fragmentation of cases through referral should therefore be avoided where possible, unless it appears that multiple authorities would be in a better position to ensure that competition in all markets affected by the transaction is effectively protected. Accordingly, while partial referrals are possible under Article 4(4) and Article 9, it would normally be appropriate for the whole of a case (or at least all connected parts thereof) to be dealt with by a single authority.

Legal certainty

13. Due account should also be taken of the importance of legal certainty regarding jurisdiction over a particular concentration, from the perspective of all concerned. Accordingly, referral should normally only be made when there is a compelling reason for departing from "original jurisdiction" over the case in question, particularly at the post-notification stage. Similarly, if a referral has been made prior to notification, a post-notification referral in the same case should be avoided to the greatest extent possible.

14. The importance of legal certainty should also be borne in mind with regard to the legal criteria for referral, and particularly—given the tight deadlines—at the pre-notification stage. Accordingly, pre-filing referrals should in principle be confined to those cases where it is relatively straightforward to establish, from the outset, the scope of the geographic market and/or the existence of a possible competitive impact, so as to be able to promptly decide upon such requests

Case referrals: legal requirements and other factors to be considered
Pre-notification referrals

15. The system of pre-notification referrals is triggered by a reasoned submission lodged by the parties to the concentration. When contemplating such a request, the parties to the concentration are required, first, to verify whether the relevant legal requirements set out in the Merger Regulation are fulfilled, and second, whether a pre-notification referral would be consistent with the guiding principles outlined above.

Referral of cases by the Commission to Member States under Article 4(4)
Legal requirements

16. In order for a referral to be made by the Commission to one or more Member States pursuant to Articles 4(4), two legal requirements must be fulfilled:

   (i) there must be indications that the concentration may significantly affect competition in a market or markets;

   (ii) the market(s) in question must be within a Member State and present all the characteristics of a distinct market.

17. As regards the first criterion, the requesting parties are in essence required to demonstrate that the transaction is liable to have a potential impact on competition on a distinct market in a Member State, which may prove to be significant, thus deserving close scrutiny. Such indications may be no more than preliminary in nature, and would be without prejudice to the outcome of the investigation. While the parties are not required to demonstrate that the effect on competition is likely to be an adverse one, they should point to indicators which are generally suggestive of the existence of some competitive effects stemming from the transaction.

18. As regards the second criterion, the requesting parties are required to show that a geographic market in which competition is affected by the transaction in the manner just described (paragraph 17) is national, or narrower than national in scope.

Other factors to be considered

19. Other than verification of the legal requirements, in order to anticipate to the greatest extent possible the likely outcome of a referral request, merging parties contemplating a request should

also consider whether referral of the case is likely to be considered appropriate. This will involve an examination of the application of the guiding principles referred to above (paragraphs 8 to 14), and in particular whether the competition authority or authorities to which they are contemplating requesting the referral of the case is the most appropriate authority for dealing with the case. To this end, consideration should be given in turn both to the likely locus of the competitive effects of the transaction and to how appropriate the national competition authority (NCA) would be for scrutinising the operation.

20. Concentrations with a Community dimension which are likely to affect competition in markets that have a national or narrower than national scope, and the effects of which are likely to be confined to, or have their main economic impact in, a single Member State, are the most appropriate candidate cases for referral to that Member State. This applies in particular to cases where the impact would occur on a distinct market which does not constitute a substantial part of the common market. To the extent that referral is made to one Member State only, the benefit of a "one-stop-shop" is also preserved.

21. The extent to which a concentration with a Community dimension which, despite having a potentially significant impact on competition in a nation-wide market, nonetheless potentially engenders substantial cross-border effects (e.g. because the effects of the concentration in one geographic market may have significant repercussions in geographic markets in other Member States, or because it may involve potential foreclosure effects and consequent fragmentation of the common market), may be an appropriate candidate for referral will depend on the specific circumstances of the case. As both the Commission and Member States may be equally well equipped or be in an equally good position to deal with such cases, a considerable margin of discretion should be retained in deciding whether or not to refer such cases.

22. The extent to which concentrations with a Community dimension, and potentially affecting competition in a series of national or narrower than national markets in more than one Member State, may be appropriate candidates for referral to Member States will depend on factors specific to each individual case, such as the number of national markets likely to be significantly affected, the prospect of addressing any possible concerns by way of proportionate, non-conflicting remedies, and the investigative efforts that the case may require. To the extent that a case may engender competition concerns in a number of Member States, and require coordinated investigations and remedial action, this may militate in favour of the Commission retaining jurisdiction over the entirety of the case in question. On the other hand, to the extent that the case gives rise to competition concerns which, despite involving national markets in more than one Member State, do not appear to require coordinated investigation and/or remedial action, a referral may be appropriate. In a limited number of cases, the Commission has even found it appropriate to refer a concentration to more than one Member State, in view of the significant differences in competitive conditions that characterised the affected markets in the Member States concerned. While fragmentation of the treatment of a case deprives the merging parties of the benefit of a one-stop-shop in such cases, this consideration is less pertinent at the pre-notification stage, given that the referral is triggered by a voluntary request from the merging parties.

23. Consideration should also, to the extent possible, be given to whether the NCA(s) to which referral of the case is contemplated may possess specific expertise concerning local markets, or be examining, or about to examine, another transaction in the sector concerned.

Referral of cases from Member States to the Commission under Article 4(5)

Legal requirements

24. Under Article 4(5), only two legal requirements must be met in order for the parties to the transaction to request the referral of the case to the Commission: the transaction must be a concentration within the meaning of Article 3 of the Merger Regulation, and the concentration must be *capable of being reviewed under the national competition laws for the control of mergers of at least three Member States* (see also paragraphs 65 et seq and 70 et seq).

Other factors to be considered

25. Other than verification of the legal requirements, in order to anticipate to the greatest extent possible the likely outcome of a referral request, merging parties contemplating a request should

also consider whether referral of the case is likely to be considered appropriate. This will involve an examination of the application of the guiding principles referred to above, and in particular whether the Commission is the more appropriate authority for dealing with the case.

26. In this regard, Recital 16 to the Merger Regulation states that "requests for pre-notification referrals to the Commission would be particularly pertinent in situations where the concentration would affect competition beyond the territory of one Member State." Particular consideration should therefore be given to the likely locus of any competitive effects resulting from the transaction, and to how appropriate it would be for the Commission to scrutinise the operation.

27. It should in particular be assessed whether the case is genuinely cross-border in nature, having regard to elements such as its likely effects on competition and the investigative and enforcement powers likely to be required to address any such effects. In this regard, particular consideration should be given to whether the case is liable to have a potential impact on competition in one or more markets affected by the concentration. In any case, indications of possible competitive impact may be no more than preliminary in nature, and would be without prejudice to the outcome of the investigation. Nor would it be necessary for the parties to demonstrate that the effect on competition is likely to be an adverse one.

28. Cases where the market(s) in which there may be a potential impact on competition is/are wider than national in geographic scope, or where some of the potentially affected markets are wider than national and the main economic impact of the concentration is connected to such markets, are the most appropriate candidate cases for referral to the Commission. In such cases, as the competitive dynamics extend over territories reaching beyond national boundaries, and may consequently require investigative efforts in several countries as well as appropriate enforcement powers, the Commission is likely to be in the best position to carry out the investigation.

29. The Commission may be more appropriately placed to treat cases (including investigation, assessment and possible remedial action) that give rise to potential competition concerns in a series of national or narrower than national markets located in a number of different Member States. The Commission is likely to be in the best position to carry out the investigation in such cases, given the desirability of ensuring consistent and efficient scrutiny across the different countries, of employing appropriate investigative powers, and of addressing any competition concerns by way of coherent remedies.

30. Similarly to what has been said above in relation to Article 4(4), the appropriateness of referring concentrations which, despite having a potentially significant impact on competition in a nation-wide market, nonetheless potentially engender substantial cross-border effects, will depend on the specific circumstances of the case. As both the Commission and Member States may be in an equally good position to deal with such cases, a considerable margin of discretion should be retained in deciding whether or not to refer such cases.

31. Consideration should also, to the extent possible, be given to whether the Commission is particularly well equipped to properly scrutinise the case, in particular having regard to factors such as specific expertise, or past experience in the sector concerned. The greater a merger's potential to affect competition beyond the territory of one Member State, the more likely it is that the Commission will be better equipped to conduct the investigation, particularly in terms of fact finding and enforcement powers.

32. Finally, the parties to the concentration might submit that, despite the apparent absence of an effect on competition, there is a compelling case for having the operation treated by the Commission, having regard in particular to factors such as the cost and time delay involved in submitting multiple Member State filings.

Post-notification referrals

Referrals from the Commission to Member States pursuant to Article 9

33. Under Article 9 there are two options for a Member State wishing to request referral of a case following its notification to the Commission: Articles 9(2)(a) and 9(2)(b) respectively.

Article 9(2)(a)

Legal requirements

34. In order for a referral to be made to a Member State or States pursuant to Article 9(2)(a), the following legal requirements must be fulfilled:

   (i) the concentration must threaten to affect significantly competition in a market; and

   (ii) the market in question must be within the requesting Member State, and present all the characteristics of a distinct market.

35. As regards the first criterion, in essence a requesting Member State is required to demonstrate that, based on a preliminary analysis, there is a real risk that the transaction may have a significant adverse impact on competition, and thus that it deserves close scrutiny. Such preliminary indications may be in the nature of prima facie evidence of such a possible significant adverse impact, but would be without prejudice to the outcome of a full investigation.

36. As regards the second criterion, the Member State is required to show that a geographic market(s) in which competition is affected by the transaction in the manner just described (paragraph 35) is/are national, or narrower than national in scope.

Other factors to be considered

37. Other than verification of the legal requirements, other factors should also be considered in assessing whether referral of a case is likely to be considered appropriate. This will involve an examination of the application of the guiding principles referred to above, and in particular whether the competition authority or authorities requesting the referral of the case is/are in the best position to deal with the case. To this end, consideration should be given in turn both to the likely locus of the competitive effects of the transaction and to how well equipped the NCA would be to scrutinise the operation (see above at paragraphs 19–23)

Article 9(2)(b)

Legal requirements

38. In order for a referral to be made to a Member State or States pursuant to Article 9(2)(b), the following legal requirements must be fulfilled:

   (i) the concentration must affect competition in a market; and

   (ii) the market in question must be within the requesting Member State, present all the characteristics of a distinct market, and must not constitute a substantial part of the common market.

39. As regards the first criterion, a requesting Member State is required to show, based on a preliminary analysis, that the concentration is liable to have an impact on competition in a market. Such preliminary indications may be in the nature of prima facie evidence of a possible adverse impact, but would be without prejudice to the outcome of a full investigation.

40. As to the second criterion, a requesting Member State is required to show not only that the market in which competition is affected by the operation in the manner just described (paragraph 38) constitutes a distinct market within a Member State, but also that the market in question does not constitute a substantial part of the common market. In this respect, based on the past practice and case-law, it appears that such situations are generally limited to markets with a narrow geographic scope, within a Member State.

41. If these conditions are met, the Commission has an obligation to refer the case.

Referrals from Member States to the Commission pursuant to Article 22

Legal requirements

42. In order for a referral to be made by one or more Member States to the Commission pursuant to Article 22, two legal requirements must be fulfilled:

   (i) the concentration must affect trade between Member States; and

   (ii) it must threaten to significantly affect competition within the territory of the Member State or States making the request.

43. As to the first criterion, a concentration fulfils this requirement to the extent that it is liable to have some discernible influence on the pattern of trade between Member States.

44. As to the second criterion, as under Article 9(2)(a), a referring Member State or States is/are required in essence to demonstrate that, based on a preliminary analysis, there is a real risk that the transaction may have a significant adverse impact on competition, and thus that it deserves close scrutiny. Such preliminary indications may be in the nature of prima facie evidence of such a possible significant adverse impact, but would be without prejudice to the outcome of a full investigation.

Other factors to be considered

45. As post-notification referrals to the Commission may entail additional cost and time delay for the merging parties, they should normally be limited to those cases which appear to present a real risk of negative effects on competition and trade between Member States, and where it appears that these would be best addressed at the Community level. The categories of cases normally most appropriate for referral to the Commission pursuant to Article 22 are accordingly the following:

— cases which give rise to serious competition concerns in one or more markets which are wider than national in geographic scope, or where some of the potentially affected markets are wider than national, and where the main economic impact of the concentration is connected to such markets,

— cases which give rise to serious competition concerns in a series of national or narrower than national markets located in a number of Member States, in circumstances where coherent treatment of the case (regarding possible remedies, but also, in appropriate cases, the investigative efforts as such) is considered desirable, and where the main economic impact of the concentration is connected to such markets.

NOTE: The Commission Notice also provides detailed guidance on the mechanics of the referral system, and in particular it attempts to establish strict time limits for referrals to avoid a situation whereby proposed concentrations are unduly delayed as a result of referrals between different competition authorities. There appears to be particular interest in the operation of the mechanisms for pre-notification referrals under Article 4(4) and (5).

Krajewska, T., 'Referrals under the new EC Merger Regulation regime: a UK perspective'
[2008] ECLR 279 [footnotes omitted]

Under Art.4(5), parties to a merger may inform the Commission by a "reasoned submission" (Form RS), before any notification to the national competent authorities, that it should examine a merger which, although it does not have a Community dimension, is capable of being reviewed by at least three Member States. Any Member State competent to examine the merger may, within 15 working days of receiving the reasoned submission from the Commission, disagree with the referral request. If no disagreement is expressed, the merger is deemed to have a Community dimension and benefits from the Commission's "one-stop-shop" assessment, rather than be subject to multiple national filings.

Since Art.4(5) came into force, 136 requests have been made to the Commission...

...

By making an Art.4(4) referral request at the pre-notification stage, parties to a merger affecting national or sub-national markets requiring a more detailed examination can avoid the administrative burden and potentially negative connotations attached to an Art.9 referral request by a Member State...

Unless the Member State disagrees, the Commission shall, within 25 working days, decide whether or not to make the referral in accordance with the request.

Since Art.4(4) came into force, the Commission has made 32 referral decisions, eight of which were to the United Kingdom.

...

Despite key differences between the United Kingdom and EC merger control regime—in particular, regarding the United Kingdom's voluntary notification system—the new referral mechanisms of Regulation 139/2004 have worked effectively for adjustment of jurisdiction and merger control of cases between the Commission and the United Kingdom. The relatively large number of Art.4(5) referrals made suggests that this mechanism is appreciated by business, as it enables parties to a merger to benefit from the Commission's "one-stop-shop" and to avoid the burden of multiple filings. It has also increased the Commission's workload appreciably. The United Kingdom exercised its veto on a pre-notification referral request under Art.4(5) only once, upon the principle of "best placed authority" to examine a merger.

The "best placed authority" to examine principle has also been applied in referrals made under Arts 4(4), 9 and 22. Over a quarter of Art.4(4) referrals from the Commission to a Member State have been made to the United Kingdom, perhaps reflecting the United Kingdom's more liberal business environment. The mergers concerned sub-national or very local markets and mostly those ones the OFT was familiar with from past examinations.

NOTE: The operation of the Article 4(4) and (5) pre-notification referral mechanisms is one of the issues that the Commission will report on to the Council of Ministers in 2009.

■ **QUESTION**

In what way does the revised ECMR provide flexibility for case referrals between the Commission and national competition authorities (and vice versa), and why is this important?

SECTION 5: PROCEDURE UNDER THE ECMR

The procedural rules that apply to application of the ECMR are balanced to provide a streamlined route for concentrations that are unlikely to raise competition concerns. While parties to a concentration must normally notify the Commission using a so-called 'Form CO', with requisite information provided, there is also a so-called 'Short Form' used for concentrations that satisfy specified conditions where there are unlikely to be competition concerns (both forms are annexed to the Implementation Regulation, No 802/2004, OJ, 2004, L133/1). Furthermore, proposed concentrations are normally initially investigated in a Phase I investigation, and if serious doubts are raised and an Article 6(1)(c) decision is adopted, then they must undergo a longer and far more detailed Phase II investigation. Yet for those specified concentrations that use the 'Short Form' for notification, the Commission also tends to operate a simplified procedure for the investigation; they are only subjected to a full Phase I investigation if a 'closer investigation' is required.

Commission Notice on a simplified procedure for treatment of certain concentrations
OJ, 2005, C56/32, paras 1–9 and 15 [footnotes omitted]

I. INTRODUCTION

1. This Notice sets out a simplified procedure under which the Commission intends to treat certain concentrations pursuant to Council Regulation (EC) No 139/2004 of 20 January 2004, on the control of concentrations between undertakings (the EC Merger Regulation) on the basis that they do not raise competition concerns. This Notice replaces the Notice on a simplified procedure for

treatment of certain concentrations under Council Regulation (EEC) No 4064/89. The Commission's experience gained in applying Council Regulation (EEC) No 4064/89 of 21 December 1989 on the control of concentrations between undertakings has shown that certain categories of notified concentrations are normally cleared without having raised any substantive doubts, provided that there were no special circumstances.

2. The purpose of this Notice is to set out the conditions under which the Commission usually adopts a short-form decision declaring a concentration compatible with the common market pursuant to the simplified procedure and to provide guidance in respect of the procedure itself. When all necessary conditions set forth at point 5 of this Notice are met and provided there are no special circumstances, the Commission adopts a short-form clearance decision within 25 working days from the date of notification, pursuant to Article 6(1)(b) of the EC Merger Regulation.

3. However, if the safeguards or exclusions set forth at points 6 to 11 of this Notice are applicable, the Commission may launch an investigation and/or adopt a full decision under the EC Merger Regulation.

4. By following the procedure outlined in the following sections, the Commission aims to make Community merger control more focused and effective.

II. CATEGORIES OF CONCENTRATIONS SUITABLE FOR TREATMENT UNDER THE SIMPLIFIED PROCEDURE

Eligible concentrations

5. The Commission will apply the simplified procedure to the following categories of concentrations:

(a) two or more undertakings acquire joint control of a joint venture, provided that the joint venture has no, or negligible, actual or foreseen activities within the territory of the European Economic Area (EEA). Such cases occur where:

(i) the turnover of the joint venture and/or the turnover of the contributed activities is less than EUR 100 million in the EEA territory; and

(ii) the total value of assets transferred to the joint venture is less than EUR 100 million in the EEA territory;

(b) two or more undertakings merge, or one or more undertakings acquire sole or joint control of another undertaking, provided that none of the parties to the concentration are engaged in business activities in the same product and geographical market, or in a product market which is upstream or downstream of a product market in which any other party to the concentration is engaged;

(c) two or more undertakings merge, or one or more undertakings acquire sole or joint control of another undertaking and:

(i) two or more of the parties to the concentration are engaged in business activities in the same product and geographical market (horizontal relationships) provided that their combined market share is less than 15%; or

(ii) one or more of the parties to the concentration are engaged in business activities in a product market which is upstream or downstream of a product market in which any other party to the concentration is engaged (vertical relationships), provided that none of their individual or combined market shares is at either level 25% or more;

(d) a party is to acquire sole control of an undertaking over which it already has joint control.

Safeguards and exclusions

6. In assessing whether a concentration falls into one of the categories referred to in point 5, the Commission will ensure that all relevant circumstances are established with sufficient clarity. Given that market definitions are likely to be a key element in this assessment, the parties should provide information on all plausible alternative market definitions during the pre-notification phase (see point 15). Notifying parties are responsible for describing all alternative relevant product and geographic markets on which the notified concentration could have an impact and for providing data and information relating to the definition of such markets. The Commission retains the

discretion to take the ultimate decision on market definition, basing its decision on an analysis of the facts of the case. Where it is difficult to define the relevant markets or to determine the parties' market shares, the Commission will not apply the simplified procedure. In addition, to the extent that concentrations involve novel legal issues of a general interest, the Commission would normally abstain from adopting short-form decisions, and would normally revert to a normal first phase merger procedure.

7. While it can normally be assumed that concentrations falling into the categories referred to in point 5 will not raise serious doubts as to their compatibility with the common market, there may nonetheless be certain situations, which exceptionally require a closer investigation and/or a full decision. In such cases, the Commission may revert to a normal first phase merger procedure.

8. The following are indicative examples of types of cases which may be excluded from the simplified procedure. Certain types of concentrations may increase the parties' market power, for instance by combining technological, financial or other resources, even if the parties to the concentration do not operate in the same market. Concentrations where at least two parties to the concentration are present in closely related neighbouring markets may also be unsuitable for the simplified procedure, in particular, where one or more of the parties to the concentration holds individually a market share of 25% or more in any product market in which there is no horizontal or vertical relationship between the parties but which is a neighbouring market to a market where another party is active. In other cases, it may not be possible to determine the parties' precise market shares. This is often the case when the parties operate in new or little developed markets. Concentrations in markets with high entry barriers, with a high degree of concentration or other known competition problems may also be unsuitable.

9. The Commission's experience to date has shown that a change from joint to sole control may exceptionally require closer investigation and/or a full decision. A particular competition concern could arise in circumstances where the former joint venture is integrated into the group or network of its remaining single controlling shareholder, whereby the disciplining constraints exercised by the potentially diverging incentives of the different controlling shareholders are removed and its strategic market position could be strengthened. For example, in a scenario in which undertaking A and undertaking B jointly control a joint venture C, a concentration pursuant to which A acquires sole control of C may give rise to competition concerns in circumstances in which C is a direct competitor of A and where C and A will hold a substantial combined market position and where this removes a degree of independence previously held by C. In cases where such scenarios require a closer analysis, the Commission may revert to a normal first phase merger procedure.

...

15. The Commission has found pre-notification contacts between notifying parties and the Commission beneficial even in seemingly unproblematic cases. The Commission's experience of the simplified procedure has shown that candidate cases for the simplified procedure may raise complex issues for instance, of market definition (see point 6) which should preferably be resolved prior to notification. Such contacts allow the Commission and the notifying parties to determine the precise amount of information to be provided in a notification. Pre-notification contacts should be initiated at least two weeks prior to the expected date of notification. Notifying parties are therefore advised to engage in pre-notification contacts, particularly where they request the Commission to waive full-form notification in accordance with Article 3(1) of Commission Regulation (EC) No 802/2004 of 7 April 2004 implementing Council Regulation (EC) No 139/2004 on the control of concentrations between undertakings on the grounds that the operation to be notified will not raise competition concerns.

NOTE: The adoption of this procedure allows the Commission to dispose of several well-known categories of case without needing to go through the full procedure. This obviously reduces the administrative burden on the Commission and will allow it to focus on more important cases. It also gives a degree of certainty to undertakings involved in such a concentration that the concentration is very likely to be approved.

SECTION 6: SUBSTANTIVE APPRAISAL

The Commission appraisal of concentrations, i.e. the substantive legal test applied to determine the legality of a merger under the ECMR, is one of the key changes in the revised ECMR and is based on the 'significant impediment to effective competition' ('SIEC') test found in Article 2. The jurisprudence of the Community courts under Article 82 EC was instructive in the 'creation or strengthening of a dominant position' test (i.e. the 'dominance test') under the first ECMR, and it is interesting to note the means by which the Commission has been able to retain the previous case law developed under Regulation 4064/89, effectively by including the wording of the dominance test in the second part of the sentence in both Article 2(2) and 2(3).

A: Significant impediment to effective competition

The change from a dominance based test in Regulation 4064/89 to the SIEC test in Regulation 139/2004 has already been explored in Section 2 while discussing the reform process. The SIEC test has already been demonstrated to cover a more complete set of anti-competitive effects post-merger, including 'unilateral effects' stemming from a non-collusive oligopoly post-merger. In applying the SIEC test, the Commission must identify the relevant markets in a similar fashion to that already discussed in relation to Article 82 EC in Chapter 10, and those aspects will not be repeated again here. The Commission has identified the key elements involved in applying the SIEC test in its Guidelines on the assessment of horizontal mergers.

Commission Notice on the assessment of horizontal mergers under the Council Regulation on the control of concentrations between undertakings
OJ, 2004, C31/5, paras 8–13, 22–5 [footnotes omitted]

II. OVERVIEW

8. Effective competition brings benefits to consumers, such as low prices, high quality products, a wide selection of goods and services, and innovation. Through its control of mergers, the Commission prevents mergers that would be likely to deprive customers of these benefits by significantly increasing the market power of firms. By "increased market power" is meant the ability of one or more firms to profitably increase prices, reduce output, choice or quality of goods and services, diminish innovation, or otherwise influence parameters of competition. In this notice, the expression "increased prices" is often used as shorthand for these various ways in which a merger may result in competitive harm. Both suppliers and buyers can have market power. However, for clarity, market power will usually refer here to a supplier's market power. Where a buyer's market power is the issue, the term "buyer power" is employed.

9. In assessing the competitive effects of a merger, the Commission compares the competitive conditions that would result from the notified merger with the conditions that would have prevailed without the merger. In most cases the competitive conditions existing at the time of the merger constitute the relevant comparison for evaluating the effects of a merger. However, in some circumstances, the Commission may take into account future changes to the market that can reasonably be predicted. It may, in particular, take account of the likely entry or exit of firms if the merger did not take place when considering what constitutes the relevant comparison.

10. The Commission's assessment of mergers normally entails:
   (a) definition of the relevant product and geographic markets;
   (b) competitive assessment of the merger.

The main purpose of market definition is to identify in a systematic way the immediate competitive constraints facing the merged entity. Guidance on this issue can be found in the Commission's Notice on the definition of the relevant market for the purposes of Community competition law. Various considerations leading to the delineation of the relevant markets may also be of importance for the competitive assessment of the merger.

11. This notice is structured around the following elements:
   (a) The approach of the Commission to market shares and concentration thresholds (Section III).
   (b) The likelihood that a merger would have anti-competitive effects in the relevant markets, in the absence of countervailing factors (Section IV).
   (c) The likelihood that buyer power would act as a countervailing factor to an increase in market power resulting from the merger (Section V).
   (d) The likelihood that entry would maintain effective competition in the relevant markets (Section VI).
   (e) The likelihood that efficiencies would act as a factor counteracting the harmful effects on competition which might otherwise result from the merger (Section VII).
   (f) The conditions for a failing firm defence (Section VIII).

12. In order to assess the foreseeable impact of a merger on the relevant markets, the Commission analyses its possible anti-competitive effects and the relevant countervailing factors such as buyer power, the extent of entry barriers and possible efficiencies put forward by the parties. In exceptional circumstances, the Commission considers whether the conditions for a failing firm defence are met.

13. In the light of these elements, the Commission determines, pursuant to Article 2 of the Merger Regulation, whether the merger would significantly impede effective competition, in particular through the creation or the strengthening of a dominant position, and should therefore be declared incompatible with the common market. It should be stressed that these factors are not a "checklist" to be mechanically applied in each and every case. Rather, the competitive analysis in a particular case will be based on an overall assessment of the foreseeable impact of the merger in the light of the relevant factors and conditions. Not all the elements will always be relevant to each and every horizontal merger, and it may not be necessary to analyse all the elements of a case in the same detail.

...

IV. POSSIBLE ANTI-COMPETITIVE EFFECTS OF HORIZONTAL MERGERS

22. There are two main ways in which horizontal mergers may significantly impede effective competition, in particular by creating or strengthening a dominant position:
   (a) by eliminating important competitive constraints on one or more firms, which consequently would have increased market power, without resorting to coordinated behaviour (non-coordinated effects);
   (b) by changing the nature of competition in such a way that firms that previously were not coordinating their behaviour, are now significantly more likely to coordinate and raise prices or otherwise harm effective competition. A merger may also make coordination easier, more stable or more effective for firms which were coordinating prior to the merger (coordinated effects).

23. The Commission assesses whether the changes brought about by the merger would result in any of these effects. Both instances mentioned above may be relevant when assessing a particular transaction.

Non-coordinated effects

24. A merger may significantly impede effective competition in a market by removing important competitive constraints on one or more sellers, who consequently have increased market power.

The most direct effect of the merger will be the loss of competition between the merging firms. For example, if prior to the merger one of the merging firms had raised its price, it would have lost some sales to the other merging firm. The merger removes this particular constraint. Non-merging firms in the same market can also benefit from the reduction of competitive pressure that results from the merger, since the merging firms' price increase may switch some demand to the rival firms, which, in turn, may find it profitable to increase their prices. The reduction in these competitive constraints could lead to significant price increases in the relevant market.

25. Generally, a merger giving rise to such non-coordinated effects would significantly impede effective competition by creating or strengthening the dominant position of a single firm, one which, typically, would have an appreciably larger market share than the next competitor post-merger. Furthermore, mergers in oligopolistic markets involving the elimination of important competitive constraints that the merging parties previously exerted upon each other together with a reduction of competitive pressure on the remaining competitors may, even where there is little likelihood of coordination between the members of the oligopoly, also result in a significant impediment to competition. The Merger Regulation clarifies that all mergers giving rise to such non-coordinated effects shall also be declared incompatible with the common market.

NOTE: The Commission Notice highlights the key issues likely to arise in relation to horizontal mergers that could give rise to 'non-coordinated effects' or 'coordinated effects'. The Commission's approach to assessing coordinated effects has been subject to scrutiny by the Court of First Instance and Court of Justice.

Bertelsmann AG and Sony Corp of America v Independent Music Publishers and Labels Association (Impala)
(Case C-413/06 P), [2008] 5 CMLR 17

The Commission approved the merger of the music industry recording activities of two international companies, Bertelsmann and Sony, to create Sony BMG, in spite of having initial concerns about coordinated effects that may derive from the concentration. Impala is an independent music publishers' group and lodged a third party challenge to the Commission's decision that the concentration was compatible with the Common Market. One of the key issues for the Court of First Instance to consider was whether the Commission had conducted a sufficiently rigorous analysis of the level of transparency in the market place, a crucial element in any finding of coordinated effects. The CFI was critical of the Commission's level of analysis and annulled its decision. On appeal against the CFI ruling, the Court of Justice outlined elements to consider when scrutinizing coordinated effects in a merger setting.

120 In the case of an alleged creation or strengthening of a collective dominant position, the Commission is obliged to assess, using a prospective analysis of the reference market, whether the concentration which has been referred to it will lead to a situation in which effective competition in the relevant market is significantly impeded by the undertakings which are parties to the concentration and one or more other undertakings which together, in particular because of correlative factors which exist between them, are able to adopt a common policy on the market (see Kali & Salz, paragraph 221) in order to profit from a situation of collective economic strength, without actual or potential competitors, let alone customers or consumers, being able to react effectively.

121 Such correlative factors include, in particular, the relationship of interdependence existing between the parties to a tight oligopoly within which, on a market with the appropriate characteristics, in particular in terms of market concentration, transparency and product homogeneity, those parties are in a position to anticipate one another's behaviour and are therefore strongly encouraged to align their conduct on the market in such a way as to maximise their joint profits by increasing prices, reducing output, the choice or quality of goods and services, diminishing

innovation or otherwise influencing parameters of competition. In such a context, each operator is aware that highly competitive action on its part would provoke a reaction on the part of the others, so that it would derive no benefit from its initiative.

122 A collective dominant position significantly impeding effective competition in the common market or a substantial part of it may thus arise as the result of a concentration where, in view of the actual characteristics of the relevant market and of the alteration to those characteristics that the concentration would entail, the latter would make each member of the oligopoly in question, as it becomes aware of common interests, consider it possible, economically rational, and hence preferable, to adopt on a lasting basis a common policy on the market with the aim of selling at above competitive prices, without having to enter into an agreement or resort to a concerted practice within the meaning of Article 81 EC and without any actual or potential competitors, let alone customers or consumers, being able to react effectively.

123 Such tacit coordination is more likely to emerge if competitors can easily arrive at a common perception as to how the coordination should work, and, in particular, of the parameters that lend themselves to being a focal point of the proposed coordination. Unless they can form a shared tacit understanding of the terms of the coordination, competitors might resort to practices that are prohibited by Article 81 EC in order to be able to adopt a common policy on the market. Moreover, having regard to the temptation which may exist for each participant in a tacit coordination to depart from it in order to increase its short-term profit, it is necessary to determine whether such coordination is sustainable. In that regard, the coordinating undertakings must be able to monitor to a sufficient degree whether the terms of the coordination are being adhered to. There must therefore be sufficient market transparency for each undertaking concerned to be aware, sufficiently precisely and quickly, of the way in which the market conduct of each of the other participants in the coordination is evolving. Furthermore, discipline requires that there be some form of credible deterrent mechanism that can come into play if deviation is detected. In addition, the reactions of outsiders, such as current or future competitors, and also the reactions of customers, should not be such as to jeopardise the results expected from the coordination.

NOTE: After the CFI annulled the original clearance decision, thereby requiring the Commission to reassess the proposed concentration, the Commission again cleared the concentration: *Sony/BMG* COMP/M.333. Impala has appealed the second clearance decision (Case T-229/08 *Impala* v *Commission*, pending). Bertelsmann and Sony's successful appeal against the CFI ruling in Case C-413/06 failed to provide finality for the parties as the ECJ referred the case back to the CFI to complete the latter's assessment of the Commission's original decision (Case T-464/04 is pending for a second time). For discussion see Szilagyi, P., 'Case Comment: The ECJ has spoken: where do we stand with standard of proof in merger control?' [2008] ECLR 726.

The Commission also provides guidance on the assessment of non-horizontal mergers, comparable to that discussed above with regards to horizontal mergers.

Commission Notice on the assessment of non-horizontal mergers under the Council Regulation on the control of concentrations between undertakings
OJ, 2008, C265/6, paras 11–22 [footnotes omitted]

11. Non-horizontal mergers are generally less likely to significantly impede effective competition than horizontal mergers.

12. First, unlike horizontal mergers, vertical or conglomerate mergers do not entail the loss of direct competition between the merging firms in the same relevant market. As a result, the main source of anti-competitive effect in horizontal mergers is absent from vertical and conglomerate mergers.

13. Second, vertical and conglomerate mergers provide substantial scope for efficiencies. A characteristic of vertical mergers and certain conglomerate mergers is that the activities and/or the products of the companies involved are complementary to each other. The integration of

complementary activities or products within a single firm may produce significant efficiencies and be pro-competitive. In vertical relationships for instance, as a result of the complementarity, a decrease in mark-ups downstream will lead to higher demand also upstream. A part of the benefit of this increase in demand will accrue to the upstream suppliers. An integrated firm will take this benefit into account. Vertical integration may thus provide an increased incentive to seek to decrease prices and increase output because the integrated firm can capture a larger fraction of the benefits. This is often referred to as the "internalisation of double mark-ups". Similarly, other efforts to increase sales at one level (e.g. improve service or stepping up innovation) may provide a greater reward for an integrated firm that will take into account the benefits accruing at other levels.

14. Integration may also decrease transaction costs and allow for a better co-ordination in terms of product design, the organisation of the production process, and the way in which the products are sold. Similarly, mergers which involve products belonging to a range or portfolio of products that are generally sold to the same set of customers (be they complementary products or not) may give rise to customer benefits such as one-stop-shopping.

15. However, there are circumstances in which non-horizontal mergers may significantly impede effective competition, in particular as a result of the creation or strengthening of a dominant position. This is essentially because a non-horizontal merger may change the ability and incentive to compete on the part of the merging companies and their competitors in ways that cause harm to consumers.

16. In the context of competition law, the concept of "consumers" encompasses intermediate and ultimate consumers. When intermediate customers are actual or potential competitors of the parties to the merger, the Commission focuses on the effects of the merger on the customers to which the merged entity and those competitors are selling. Consequently, the fact that a merger affects competitors is not in itself a problem. It is the impact on effective competition that matters, not the mere impact on competitors at some level of the supply chain. In particular, the fact that rivals may be harmed because a merger creates efficiencies cannot in itself give rise to competition concerns.

17. There are two main ways in which non-horizontal mergers may significantly impede effective competition: non-coordinated effects and coordinated effects.

18. Non-coordinated effects may principally arise when non-horizontal mergers give rise to foreclosure. In this document, the term "foreclosure" will be used to describe any instance where actual or potential rivals' access to supplies or markets is hampered or eliminated as a result of the merger, thereby reducing these companies' ability and/or incentive to compete. As a result of such foreclosure, the merging companies—and, possibly, some of its competitors as well—may be able to profitably increase the price charged to consumers. These instances give rise to a significant impediment to effective competition and are therefore referred to hereafter as "anticompetitive foreclosure".

19. Coordinated effects arise where the merger changes the nature of competition in such a way that firms that previously were not coordinating their behaviour, are now significantly more likely to coordinate to raise prices or otherwise harm effective competition. A merger may also make coordination easier, more stable or more effective for firms which were coordinating prior to the merger.

20. In assessing the competitive effects of a merger, the Commission compares the competitive conditions that would result from the notified merger with the conditions that would have prevailed without the merger. In most cases the competitive conditions existing at the time of the merger constitute the relevant comparison for evaluating the effects of a merger. However, in some circumstances, the Commission will take into account future changes to the market that can reasonably be predicted. It may, in particular, take account of the likely entry or exit of firms if the merger did not take place when considering what constitutes the relevant comparison. The Commission may take into account future market developments that result from impending regulatory changes.

21. In its assessment, the Commission will consider both the possible anti-competitive effects arising from the merger and the possible pro-competitive effects stemming from substantiated

efficiencies benefiting consumers. The Commission examines the various chains of cause and effect with a view to ascertaining which of them is the most likely. The more immediate and direct the perceived anti-competitive effects of a merger, the more likely the Commission is to raise competition concerns. Likewise, the more immediate and direct the pro-competitive effects of a merger, the more likely the Commission is to find that they counteract any anti-competitive effects.

22. This document describes the main scenarios of competitive harm and sources of efficiencies in the context of vertical mergers and, subsequently, in the context of conglomerate mergers.

NOTE: As should be expected, the Commission recognizes that non-horizontal mergers are far less likely to give rise to competition concerns than horizontal mergers, and notes the considerable efficiencies that can be generated by vertical integration achieved as a result of a concentration. Vertical mergers can nonetheless give rise to significant competition concerns in certain situations, such as where the concentration would lead to market foreclosure. Several of these issues are also explored in Chapter 8 in relation to the efficiencies and competition concerns that can arise as a result of vertical restraints. Röller and de la Mano discuss some of the implications of the shift away from the dominance test in the first ECMR.

Röller, L.H., and de la Mano, M., 'The Impact of the New Substantive Test in European Merger Control'
(2006) 2 Euro CJ 9

the primary justification for reformulating the test is to eliminate the requirement to show dominance to challenge a merger. This is expected to reduce false negatives, i.e. clear anti-competitive mergers, because the test can take full account of the equilibrium effects of the merger.

Oligopoly theory is used, either implicitly or explicitly, to make this assessment. Oligopoly theory examines situations in which a market is supplied by a small and fixed number of players. Each firm chooses its price (or quantity or other variable in which competition occurs), given the prices of its rivals. This gives a best response function, which is the set of prices that a firm would charge in response to any price configuration set by rivals. Equilibrium occurs where these best response functions intersect. In other words, each firm's price is a best reaction to the prices that the others are setting.

When two firms merge, their best response reaction function shifts upward: in other words, even if rivals did not change their prices, the merged firm would find it profitable to set a higher price. The size of this price rise will depend upon a variety of factors, including the number of firms in the market, relative efficiency, demand elasticity and substitutability of products.

...

The new test focuses on the merger-induced changes to the competitive environment, not on whether the merged entity reaches an intolerable level of market power. Put another way, the SIEC test directly measures the "delta", i.e. the degree of change in the dynamics of competition posed by a merger, while the dominance requirement in the old test in essence measures how much competition is left over, as opposed to how much has been lost. SIEC was also a condition under the old test but, as discussed above, problems of interpretation and the central role played by dominance meant that in practice mergers could be challenged on structural indicators alone. By eliminating dominance as a necessary condition, the new test focuses more directly on the principal economic question raised by a merger, namely whether competition is likely to be reduced. Such an effects-based approach should lead to a reduction in the number of false positives, i.e. the prohibition of pro-competitive mergers.

NOTE: Röller and de la Mano adopt an economic approach to consider the effectiveness of the SIEC test with favourable results, indicating a likely reduction in both Type I and Type II errors, i.e. false negatives—incorrectly approving a concentration, and false positives—incorrectly blocking a concentration.

■ **QUESTION**

What are the likely consequences of the change from a predominantly 'dominance' based appraisal test in EC Merger Regulation 4064/89 to a predominantly 'SIEC' test in EC Merger Regulation 139/2004?

B: Collective dominance

Collective dominance is a situation whereby two or more distinct undertakings act in a coordinated or unified fashion on the market, but generally without the degree of coordination required in order for Article 81 EC to be applicable. The markets in question are of an oligopolistic nature and are inherently difficult for competition law to deal with. The issue of collective dominance can arise under Article 82 EC as well as under the ECMR, but it is only considered at this point. The most significant recent case law concerning collective dominance has arisen in the context of EC merger control.

France v Commission ('Kali & Salz')
(Joined Cases C-68/94 and C-30/95) [1998] ECR I-1375

In 1993, the Commission approved a merger between the German potash producers Kali & Salz (subsidiary of BASF) and MdK. The Commission's investigation found that the combined undertaking would have a collective dominant position with the French undertaking SCPA as the undertakings had long-standing commercial links and the remaining competition was too fragmented to be effective competition to their combined market share of 60 per cent. These concerns were remedied however, by commitments offered by Kali & Salz and MdK relating to how they would act with SCPA post-merger. SCPA and France challenged the Commission decision giving effect to the commitments. The use of the ECMR to prohibit the creation or strengthening of a collective dominant position, as well as the legal elements involved in a finding of collective dominance, were challenged before the Court of Justice.

[165] The Court finds, first of all, that the applicants' submission, to the effect that the choice of legal bases in itself militates in favour of the argument that the Regulation does not apply to collective dominant positions, cannot be accepted. As the Advocate General observes in point 83 of the Opinion, Articles 87 and 235 of the Treaty can in principle be used as the legal bases of a regulation permitting preventive action with respect to concentrations which create or strengthen a collective dominant position liable to have a significant effect on competition.

[166] Second, it cannot be deduced from the wording of Article 2 of the Regulation that only concentrations which create or strengthen an individual dominant position, that is, a dominant position held by the parties to the concentration, come within the scope of the Regulation. Article 2, in referring to 'a concentration which creates or strengthens a dominant position', does not in itself exclude the possibility of applying the Regulation to cases where concentrations lead to the creation or strengthening of a collective dominant position, that is, a dominant position held by the parties to the concentration together with an entity not a party thereto.

[167] Third, with respect to the *travaux preparatoires*, it appears from the documents in the case that they cannot be regarded as expressing clearly the intention of the authors of the Regulation as to the scope of the term 'dominant position'. In those circumstances, the *travaux preparatoires* provide no assistance for the interpretation of the disputed concept (see, to that effect, Case 15/60 *Simon* v *Court of Justice* [1961] ECR 115).

[168] Since the textual and historical interpretations of the Regulation, and in particular Article 2 thereof, do not permit its precise scope to be assessed as regards the type of dominant position concerned, the provision in question must be interpreted by reference to its purpose and general structure (see, to that effect, Case 11/76 *Netherlands* v *EC Commission* [1979] ECR 245, para. [6]).

[169] As may be seen from the 1st and 2nd recitals in its preamble, the Regulation is founded on the premiss that the objective of instituting a system to ensure that competition in the Common Market is not distorted is essential for the achievement of the internal market by 1992 and for its future development.

[170] It follows from the 6th, 7th, 10th and 11th recitals in the preamble that the Regulation, unlike Articles 85 and 86 of the Treaty, is intended to apply to all concentrations with a Community dimension in so far as they are likely, because of their effect on the structure of competition within the Community, to prove incompatible with the system of undistorted competition envisaged by the Treaty.

[171] A concentration which creates or strengthens a dominant position on the part of the parties concerned with an entity not involved in the concentration is liable to prove incompatible with the system of undistorted competition which the Treaty seeks to secure. Consequently, if it were accepted that only concentrations creating or strengthening a dominant position on the part of the parties to the concentration were covered by the Regulation, its purpose as indicated in particular by the above mentioned recitals would be partially frustrated. The Regulation would thus be deprived of a not insignificant aspect of its effectiveness, without that being necessary from the perspective of the general structure of the Community system of control of concentrations.

[172] Neither the argument based on the lack of procedural safeguards nor the argument based on the 15th recital in the preamble to the Regulation can cast doubt on its applicability to cases where a collective dominant position is the result of a concentration.

[173] As to the first argument, it is true that the Regulation does not expressly provide that undertakings, not involved in the concentration, which are regarded as the external members of the dominant oligopoly must be given an opportunity to make their views known effectively where the Commission intends to attach to the 'authorisation' of the concentration conditions or obligations specifically affecting them. The same applies in a situation where the Commission intends to attach conditions or obligations affecting third parties to a concentration which will lead simply to the creation or strengthening of an individual dominant position.

[174] In any event, even on the assumption that a finding by the Commission that the proposed concentration creates or strengthens a collective dominant position involving the undertakings concerned on the one hand and a third party on the other may in itself adversely affect that third party, it must be borne in mind that observance of the right to be heard is, in all proceedings liable to culminate in a measure adversely affecting a particular person, a fundamental principle of Community law which must be guaranteed even in the absence of any rules governing the procedure (see, to that effect, Case 85/76 *Hoffmann-La Roche* v *EC Commission* [1979] ECR 461; [1979] 3 CMLR 211] and Case C-32/95 P *EC Commission* v *Lisrestal and Others* [1996] ECR I-5373; [1997] 2 CMLR 1, para. [21]).

[175] Given the existence of that principle, and the purpose of the Regulation as explained above, the fact that the Community legislature did not expressly provide in the Regulation for a procedure safeguarding the right to be heard of third party undertakings alleged to hold a collective dominant position together with the undertakings involved in the concentration cannot be regarded as decisive evidence of the Regulation's inapplicability to collective dominant positions.

[176] As to the second argument, the presumption that concentrations are compatible with the Common Market if the undertakings concerned have a combined market share of less than 25 per cent, as stated in the 15th recital in the preamble, is not developed in any way in the operative part of the Regulation.

[177] The 15th recital in the preamble to the Regulation must, having regard in particular to the realities of the market underlying this recital, be interpreted as meaning that a concentration which does not give the undertakings concerned a combined share of at least 25 per cent of the reference

market is presumed not to create or strengthen an anti-competitive dominant position on the part of those undertakings.

[178] It follows from the foregoing that collective dominant positions do not fall outside the scope of the Regulation.

NOTE: It is not surprising that the Court confirmed that the concept of dominance found under Article 82 EC is the same as the concept used in the first ECMR, and retained in the revised ECMR due to the language of the provisions in Article 2(2) and 2(3). Therefore the EC Merger Regulation can be used to prevent the creation or strengthening of a collective dominant position. The inclusion of the concept means that the Commission has an important structural tool to prevent the concentration of a market into a potentially uncompetitive oligopoly.

Gencor Ltd v *Commission*
(Case T-102/96) [1999] ECR II-753

The Commission had declared a proposed concentration between two South African-based platinum producers as incompatible with the Common Market as it believed the merger would create a duopoly with the Anglo American Corporation of South Africa.

[163] In assessing whether there is a collective dominant position, the Commission is therefore obliged to establish, using a prospective analysis of the relevant market, whether the concentration in question would lead to a situation in which effective competition in the relevant market would be significantly impeded by the undertakings involved in the concentration and one or more other undertakings which together, in particular because of factors giving rise to a connection between them, are able to adopt a common policy on the market and act to a considerable extent independently of their competitors, their customers and, ultimately, of consumers *France and Others* v *EC Commission*, para. (221).

...

[276] Furthermore, there is no reason whatsoever in legal or economic terms to exclude from the notion of economic links the relationship of interdependence existing between the parties to a tight oligopoly within which, in a market with the appropriate characteristics, in particular in terms of market concentration, transparency and product homogeneity, those parties are in a position to anticipate one another's behaviour and are therefore strongly encouraged to align their conduct in the market, in particular in such a way as to maximise their joint profits by restricting production with a view to increasing prices. In such a context, each trader is aware that highly competitive action on its part designed to increase its market share (for example a price cut) would provoke identical action by the others, so that it would derive no benefit from its initiative. All the traders would thus be affected by the reduction in price levels.

[277] That conclusion is all the more pertinent with regard to the control of concentrations, whose objective is to prevent anti-competitive market structures from arising or being strengthened. Those structures may result from the existence of economic links in the strict sense argued by the applicant or from market structures of an oligopolistic kind where each undertaking may become aware of common interests and, in particular, cause prices to increase without having to enter into an agreement or resort to a concerted practice.

[278] In the [present] case, therefore, the applicant's ground of challenge alleging that the Commission failed to establish the existence of structural links is misplaced.

[279] The Commission was entitled to conclude, relying on the envisaged alteration in the structure of the market and on the similarity of the costs of Amplats and Implats/LPD, that the proposed transaction would create a collective dominant position and lead in actual fact to a duopoly constituted by those two undertakings.

NOTE: The *Gencor* judgment was important for the development of the doctrine of collective dominance under both merger control and Article 82 EC. The importance of economic links between the combined undertaking and the other potential members of the collectively dominant position is an important part of the doctrine but will, in many cases, be very difficult to establish with sufficient evidence.

Airtours plc v *Commission*
(Case T-342/99) [2002] ECR II-2585

The Commission prohibited the proposed concentration between two UK package holiday providers, Airtours and First Choice, on the basis that post-merger a collectively dominant position would be held with Thomson and Thomas Cook. In the first of three highly critical rulings against the Commission in 2002, the CFI annulled the Commission decision.

58. Where, for the purposes of applying Regulation No 4064/89, the Commission examines a possible collective dominant position, it must ascertain whether the concentration would have the direct and immediate effect of creating or strengthening a position of that kind, which is such as significantly and lastingly to impede competition in the relevant market (see, to that effect, *Gencor* v *Commission*, paragraph 94). If there is no substantial alteration to competition as it stands, the merger must be approved (see, to that effect, Case T-2/93 *Air France* v *Commission* [1994] ECR II-323, paragraphs 78 and 79, and *Gencor* v *Commission*, paragraph 170, 180 and 193).

59. It is apparent from the case law that 'in the case of an alleged collective dominant position, the Commission is ... obliged to assess, using a prospective analysis of the reference market, whether the concentration which has been referred to it leads to a situation in which effective competition in the relevant market is significantly impeded by the undertakings involved in the concentration and one or more other undertakings which together, in particular because of factors giving rise to a connection between them, are able to adopt a common policy on the market and act to a considerable extent independently of their competitors, their customers, and also of consumers' (*Kali & Salz*, cited above, paragraph 221, and *Gencor* v *Commission*, paragraph 163).

60. The Court of First Instance has held that: 'There is no reason whatsoever in legal or economic terms to exclude from the notion of economic links the relationship of interdependence existing between the parties to a tight oligopoly within which, in a market with the appropriate characteristics, in particular in terms of market concentration, transparency and product homogeneity, those parties are in a position to anticipate one another's behaviour and are therefore strongly encouraged to align their conduct in the market, in particular in such a way as to maximise their joint profits by restricting production with a view to increasing prices. In such a context, each trader is aware that highly competitive action on its part designed to increase its market share (for example a price cut) would provoke identical action by the others, so that it would derive no benefit from its initiative. All the traders would thus be affected by the reduction in price levels.' (*Gencor* v *Commission*, paragraph 276).

61. A collective dominant position significantly impeding effective competition in the common market or a substantial part of it may thus arise as the result of a concentration where, in view of the actual characteristics of the relevant market and of the alteration in its structure that the transaction would entail, the latter would make each member of the dominant oligopoly, as it becomes aware of common interests, consider it possible, economically rational, and hence preferable, to adopt on a lasting basis a common policy on the market with the aim of selling at above competitive prices, without having to enter into an agreement or resort to a concerted practice within the meaning of Article 81 EC (see, to that effect, *Gencor* v *Commission*, paragraph 277) and without any actual or potential competitors, let alone customers or consumers, being able to react effectively.

62. As the applicant has argued and as the Commission has accepted in its pleadings, three conditions are necessary for a finding of collective dominance as defined:
   — first, each member of the dominant oligopoly must have the ability to know how the other members are behaving in order to monitor whether or not they are adopting the common policy. As the Commission specifically acknowledges, it is not enough for each member of the dominant oligopoly to be aware that interdependent market conduct is profitable for all of them but each member must also have a means of knowing whether

the other operators are adopting the same strategy and whether they are maintaining it. There must, therefore, be sufficient market transparency for all members of the dominant oligopoly to be aware, sufficiently precisely and quickly, of the way in which the other members' market conduct is evolving;

— second, the situation of tacit coordination must be sustainable over time, that is to say, there must be an incentive not to depart from the common policy on the market. As the Commission observes, it is only if all the members of the dominant oligopoly maintain the parallel conduct that all can benefit. The notion of retaliation in respect of conduct deviating from the common policy is thus inherent in this condition. In this instance, the parties concur that, for a situation of collective dominance to be viable, there must be adequate deterrents to ensure that there is a long-term incentive in not departing from the common policy, which means that each member of the dominant oligopoly must be aware that highly competitive action on its part designed to increase its market share would provoke identical action by the others, so that it would derive no benefit from its initiative (see, to that effect, *Gencor* v *Commission*, paragraph 276);

— third, to prove the existence of a collective dominant position to the requisite legal standard, the Commission must also establish that the foreseeable reaction of current and future competitors, as well as of consumers, would not jeopardise the results expected from the common policy.

63. The prospective analysis which the Commission has to carry out in its review of concentrations involving collective dominance calls for close examination in particular of the circumstances which, in each individual case, are relevant for assessing the effects of the concentration on competition in the reference market (*Kali & Salz*, paragraph 222). As the Commission itself has emphasised, at paragraph 104 of its decision of 20 May 1998 *Price Waterhouse/Coopers & Lybrand* (Case IV/M.1016) (OJ 1999 L 50, p. 27), it is also apparent from the judgment in *Kali and Salz* that, where the Commission takes the view that a merger should be prohibited because it will create a situation of collective dominance, it is incumbent upon it to produce convincing evidence thereof. The evidence must concern, in particular, factors playing a significant role in the assessment of whether a situation of collective dominance exists, such as, for example, the lack of effective competition between the operators alleged to be members of the dominant oligopoly and the weakness of any competitive pressure that might be exerted by other operators.

NOTE: In its examination of the case, the CFI rejected the Commission's argument on practically every point on the basis that the evidence did not support the Commission's findings. The CFI therefore annulled the Commission Decision (*Airtours/First Choice*, Case IV/M1524, OJ, 2000, L93/1). The Commission did not produce sufficient economic evidence to support its finding that the market would operate in an uncompetitive manner following the merger. This is a clear example of a Type II error, the likelihood of which Röller and de la Mano argue has been reduced by the introduction of the SIEC test (above). For further discussion of the development of collective dominance see Baxter, S., and Dethmers, F., 'Collective dominance under EC merger control—after Airtours and the introduction of unilateral effects is there still a future for collective dominance?' [2006] ECLR 148, and Kokkoris, I., 'The development of the concept of collective dominance in the ECMR. From its inception to its current status' (2007) 30 World Comp 419.

■ **QUESTION**

What are the conditions for a finding of collective dominance, and why have these cases often proven problematic for the Commission?

C: Efficiency defence

It has already been discussed in Section 2 above that the revised ECMR enhances the role of efficiencies under the ECMR process. Even before the revised ECMR however, it is clear that the Commission has taken a positive approach to considering countervailing efficiencies within EC merger control.

Camesasca, P.D., 'The Explicit Efficiency Defence in Merger Control: Does it Make the Difference?'
[1999] ECLR 14, pp. 25–6 [footnotes omitted]

Alcatel/Telettra, Mannesmann/Valourec/Ilva, Mercedes-Benz/Kässbohrer, ABB/Daimler-Benz and *Agfa-Gevaert/DuPont* show, however, that the Commission is ready to rely on efficiencies to clear a merger. The public dispute accompanying these mergers also exemplified the main problem with the Commission's approach—by handling efficiencies in between lines, the Commission has no fallback line to defend itself against accusations of industrial policy considerations, or paying attention to the competition from undertakings located outside the Community. To avoid this criticism, the Commission seems to insert efficiencies during the evaluative process of the merger at hand and in doing so, avoids a final finding of dominance. Market shares thus represent an important factor of evidence of a dominant position 'provided they not only reflect current conditions but are also a reliable indicator of future conditions'. The dynamic aspects of a market, as indicated by entry and exit, fluctuations of market share, and the pace of technological change and innovation, clearly have come to play a prominent part in the Commission's approach, pointing towards the necessity to make some sort of prediction about future developments when assessing mergers. This is probably what the Commission implied when it stated that 'the test of dominance is to be understood as an appreciable freedom of action uncontrolled by actual or potential competition'. Quite instructive for the Commission's willingness to take efficiencies into account implicitly while shaping its decision is the principle formulated in *Cyanamid/Shell*, where a finding of dominance was avoided as '[a]n analysis focusing on market share alone is not particularly probative in a dynamic and R&D-intensive industry'. As a result, the Commission has been prepared to approve very high market shares, especially in innovative markets. Most indicative, efficiencies move to the centre of the stage in *ABB/Daimler-Benz*, leading the Commission to conclude after assessing the purported synergies, that on the competitive conditions in general, the transaction will not worsen the situation; structurally speaking it will tend to improve it.

The Commission Notice on assessing horizontal mergers provides guidance on the role of efficiencies in the operation of the ECMR.

Commission Notice on the assessment of horizontal mergers under the Council Regulation on the control of concentrations between undertakings
OJ, 2004, C31/5, paras 76–88 [footnotes omitted]

VII. EFFICIENCIES

76. Corporate reorganisations in the form of mergers may be in line with the requirements of dynamic competition and are capable of increasing the competitiveness of industry, thereby improving the conditions of growth and raising the standard of living in the Community. It is possible that efficiencies brought about by a merger counteract the effects on competition and in particular the potential harm to consumers that it might otherwise have. In order to assess whether a merger would significantly impede effective competition, in particular through the creation or the strengthening of a dominant position, within the meaning of Article 2(2) and (3) of the Merger Regulation, the Commission performs an overall competitive appraisal of the merger. In making this appraisal, the Commission takes into account the factors mentioned in Article 2(1), including the development of technical and economic progress provided that it is to the consumers' advantage and does not form an obstacle to competition.

77. The Commission considers any substantiated efficiency claim in the overall assessment of the merger. It may decide that, as a consequence of the efficiencies that the merger brings about,

there are no grounds for declaring the merger incompatible with the common market pursuant to Article 2(3) of the Merger Regulation. This will be the case when the Commission is in a position to conclude on the basis of sufficient evidence that the efficiencies generated by the merger are likely to enhance the ability and incentive of the merged entity to act pro-competitively for the benefit of consumers, thereby counteracting the adverse effects on competition which the merger might otherwise have.

78. For the Commission to take account of efficiency claims in its assessment of the merger and be in a position to reach the conclusion that as a consequence of efficiencies, there are no grounds for declaring the merger to be incompatible with the common market, the efficiencies have to benefit consumers, be merger-specific and be verifiable. These conditions are cumulative.

Benefit to consumers

79. The relevant benchmark in assessing efficiency claims is that consumers will not be worse off as a result of the merger. For that purpose, efficiencies should be substantial and timely, and should, in principle, benefit consumers in those relevant markets where it is otherwise likely that competition concerns would occur.

80. Mergers may bring about various types of efficiency gains that can lead to lower prices or other benefits to consumers. For example, cost savings in production or distribution may give the merged entity the ability and incentive to charge lower prices following the merger. In line with the need to ascertain whether efficiencies will lead to a net benefit to consumers, cost efficiencies that lead to reductions in variable or marginal costs are more likely to be relevant to the assessment of efficiencies than reductions in fixed costs; the former are, in principle, more likely to result in lower prices for consumers. Cost reductions, which merely result from anti-competitive reductions in output, cannot be considered as efficiencies benefiting consumers.

81. Consumers may also benefit from new or improved products or services, for instance resulting from efficiency gains in the sphere of R & D and innovation. A joint venture company set up in order to develop a new product may bring about the type of efficiencies that the Commission can take into account.

82. In the context of coordinated effects, efficiencies may increase the merged entity's incentive to increase production and reduce prices, and thereby reduce its incentive to coordinate its market behaviour with other firms in the market. Efficiencies may therefore lead to a lower risk of coordinated effects in the relevant market.

83. In general, the later the efficiencies are expected to materialise in the future, the less weight the Commission can assign to them. This implies that, in order to be considered as a counteracting factor, the efficiencies must be timely.

84. The incentive on the part of the merged entity to pass efficiency gains on to consumers is often related to the existence of competitive pressure from the remaining firms in the market and from potential entry. The greater the possible negative effects on competition, the more the Commission has to be sure that the claimed efficiencies are substantial, likely to be realised, and to be passed on, to a sufficient degree, to the consumer. It is highly unlikely that a merger leading to a market position approaching that of a monopoly, or leading to a similar level of market power, can be declared compatible with the common market on the ground that efficiency gains would be sufficient to counteract its potential anti-competitive effects.

Merger specificity

85. Efficiencies are relevant to the competitive assessment when they are a direct consequence of the notified merger and cannot be achieved to a similar extent by less anticompetitive alternatives. In these circumstances, the efficiencies are deemed to be caused by the merger and thus, merger-specific. It is for the merging parties to provide in due time all the relevant information necessary to demonstrate that there are no less anti-competitive, realistic and attainable alternatives of a non-concentrative nature (e.g. a licensing agreement, or a cooperative joint venture) or of a concentrative nature (e.g. a concentrative joint venture, or a differently structured merger) than the notified merger which preserve the claimed efficiencies. The Commission only considers

alternatives that are reasonably practical in the business situation faced by the merging parties having regard to established business practices in the industry concerned.

Verifiability

86. Efficiencies have to be verifiable such that the Commission can be reasonably certain that the efficiencies are likely to materialise, and be substantial enough to counteract a merger's potential harm to consumers. The more precise and convincing the efficiency claims are, the better the Commission can evaluate the claims. Where reasonably possible, efficiencies and the resulting benefit to consumers should therefore be quantified. When the necessary data are not available to allow for a precise quantitative analysis, it must be possible to foresee a clearly identifiable positive impact on consumers, not a marginal one. In general, the longer the start of the efficiencies is projected into the future, the less probability the Commission may be able to assign to the efficiencies actually being brought about.

87. Most of the information, allowing the Commission to assess whether the merger will bring about the sort of efficiencies that would enable it to clear a merger, is solely in the possession of the merging parties. It is, therefore, incumbent upon the notifying parties to provide in due time all the relevant information necessary to demonstrate that the claimed efficiencies are merger-specific and likely to be realised. Similarly, it is for the notifying parties to show to what extent the efficiencies are likely to counteract any adverse effects on competition that might otherwise result from the merger, and therefore benefit consumers.

88. Evidence relevant to the assessment of efficiency claims includes, in particular, internal documents that were used by the management to decide on the merger, statements from the management to the owners and financial markets about the expected efficiencies, historical examples of efficiencies and consumer benefit, and pre-merger external experts' studies on the type and size of efficiency gains, and on the extent to which consumers are likely to benefit.

NOTE: There is also discussion of the role of efficiencies within the Commission Notice on the assessment of non-horizontal mergers (see above) as would be expected in the case of vertical and conglomerate mergers.

■ QUESTION

What is the role of an efficiency analysis under the revised ECMR?

D: Failing firm defence

The Commission has also demonstrated a willingness to take the financial status of a party to a concentration into account when applying the ECMR. The basic argument would be that a 'failing firm' no longer holds economic power and therefore the merger would be unlikely to have any anti-competitive effects.

France v Commission ('Kali & Salz')
(Joined Cases C-68/94 and C-30/95), [1998] ECR I-1375, [1998] 4 CMLR 829

The merger between Kali and Salz and MdK was approved as the Commission was of the view that MdK would have gone out of business in any event and Kali & Salz would have acquired their market share as there were no other competitors on the market. There was also no prospect of any other undertaking acquiring MdK. The use of such a 'failing firm defence' was, *inter alia,* challenged.

[90] The French Government criticises the Commission for applying the Regulation incorrectly by authorising, through the use of the 'failing company defence' and without imposing any conditions, a concentration leading to the creation of a monopoly on the German potash market.

[91] As regards the incorrect use of the 'failing company defence', the French Government notes that this defence is derived from United States antitrust legislation, under which a concentration may not be regarded as causing a dominant position to come into being or strengthening it if the following conditions are met:

(a) one of the parties to the concentration is in a position such that it will be unable to meet its obligations in the near future;

(b) it is unable to reorganise successfully under Chapter 11 of the Bankruptcy Act;

(c) there are no other solutions which are less anti-competitive than the concentration; and

(d) the failing undertaking would be forced out of the market if the concentration were not implemented.

[92] The Commission, it is submitted, referred to the 'failing company defence' without taking into account all the criteria used in the United States antitrust legislation, in particular those mentioned at (a) and (b), whereas only application of the United States criteria in full ensures that a derogating mechanism is established whose application does not have the effect of aggravating a competitive situation already in decline.

[93] The French Government submits that the Commission, which considered that K + S would take over MdK's market share in Germany in any case, arbitrarily introduced the criterion of the absorption of market shares.

[94] It submits that the absorption by K + S of MdK's market share if MdK is forced out proves that the German market is impermeable to competition, but does not mean that the anti-competitive nature of the concentration can be dismissed.

[95] In addition, it submits that the Commission did not show that the criteria it adopted concerning the undertaking's elimination from the market and the absence of a less anti-competitive alternative were in fact satisfied in this case.

[96] As regards the allegation that MdK would be forced out if the concentration did not take place, the French Government states that the Commission completely ignored the possibility that MdK might become viable again following an autonomous restructuring operation carried out with financial assistance from Treuhand compatible with Articles 92 and 93 EC.

[97] Finally, it considers that the Commission has not shown that there was no other way of carrying out the acquisition which was less harmful to competition. It observes in this respect that the MdK trade unions had stated that there was a lack of transparency in the tendering procedure.

[98] As regards the absence of conditions for authorisation of the concentration on the German market, the French Government submits that in any event the contested decision is vitiated by a manifest error of assessment, inasmuch as it authorises without any conditions the concentration on the German market where the joint undertaking will have a market share of 98 per cent, and is contrary to Article 2(3) of the Regulation. The concentration will clearly strengthen K + S's dominant position in Germany, with the result that competition will be significantly impeded in a substantial part of the Common Market.

[99] On this point, the Government observes that while the objective of economic and social cohesion mentioned in Articles 2 and 3(j) EC and also referred to in the thirteenth recital in the preamble to the Regulation, which the Commission referred to in its decision, must be taken into account in assessing concentrations, it cannot in any case justify an authorisation which frustrates the essential aim of Community control of concentrations, namely the protection of competition. Ultimately, the Commission could authorise the concentration by reference to the objective of economic and social cohesion only if the notifying undertakings had entered into precise and adequate commitments to open the relevant market to competition, as Nestlé did in Commission Decision 92/553 relating to a proceeding under Council Regulation 4064/89 (Case No IV/M.190—*Nestlé/Perrier*) (hereinafter 'the *Nestlé/Perrier* decision' [[1992] OJ L356/1]).

[100] The Commission concedes that in the contested decision it did not adopt the American 'failing company defence' in its entirety. However, it fails to see how that could affect the lawfulness of its decision.

[101] It considers, moreover, that it has shown to the necessary legal standard that the criteria it used for the application of the 'failing company defence' were indeed satisfied in the present case.

[102] With respect to the likelihood that MdK would soon be forced out unless it was acquired by another operator, the Commission observes that in points 76 and 77 of the contested decision it stated that Treuhand could not be expected to use public funds to cover the long-term debts of an undertaking which was no longer economically viable, and that even if it does not happen immediately, for social, regional and general policy reasons, it is very probable that MdK will close down in the near future.

[103] It is also not disputed that MdK's share of the market in Germany will in all probability be absorbed by K + S.

[104] As regards the condition that there should be no less anti-competitive alternative to the acquisition of MdK, the Commission refers to points 81 to 90 of the contested decision. It considers, moreover, that the French Government has not shown how the criticisms of the MdK trade unions could call into question its assessment. After all, the Commission was not satisfied with the finding that the tendering procedure had not permitted another purchaser to be found, but had itself carried out a further inquiry.

[105] With respect to the absence of conditions for authorisation of the concentration on the German market, the Commission observes that the French Government does not specify what commitments K + S and MdK could have entered into in order to open the German market to competition. The argument which the French Government attempts to base on the *Nestlé/Perrier* decision is immaterial. In that decision, according to the Commission, it was possible to authorise the concentration in view of certain commitments relating to the structure of competition in the relevant product market. In the present case, however, in order to open the German market to competition, it would be necessary to attack not the structure of competition but the behaviour of buyers. In the Commission's opinion, even if the means to open the German market could have been structural, no solution to the acquisition of MdK with a lesser effect on competition was available.

[106] The German Government submits that, under Article 2(3) of the Regulation, a concentration may be prohibited only if it will worsen conditions of competition. There is no causal link between the concentration and its effect on competition where the identical worsening of conditions of competition is to be expected even without the concentration. That will be the case when the three conditions applied by the Commission are satisfied.

[107] The German Government submits that, contrary to the French Government's contention, the Commission has shown to the necessary legal standard that the conditions it laid down were satisfied. First, MdK is not viable on its own, that is to say, it is not possible to restructure the undertaking while preserving its autonomy in the market. In point 76 of the contested decision, the Commission gave solid reasons for considering that with Treuhand's 100 per cent ownership being maintained MdK was not likely to be rescued in the long term. Second, there is no doubt that MdK's market share would automatically be absorbed by K + S, since K + S would be alone on the relevant market after MdK had been forced out, and that is an essential condition in this context. Third, the German Government submits that the Commission gave exhaustive reasons as to why no alternative means of acquiring MdK was available.

[108] As to the approval of the concentration on the German market without conditions or obligations, the German Government observes that in the absence of a causal link between the concentration and the strengthening of a dominant position, one of the conditions for imposing a prohibition under Article 2(3) of the Regulation was not fulfilled. The concentration therefore had to be authorised without obligations or conditions.

[109] The Court observes at the outset that under Article 2(2) of the Regulation, a 'concentration which does not create or strengthen a dominant position as a result of which effective competition would be significantly impeded in the Common Market or in a substantial part of it shall be declared compatible with the Common Market'.

[110] Thus if a concentration is not the cause of the creation or strengthening of a dominant position which has a significant impact on the competitive situation on the relevant market, it must be declared compatible with the Common Market.

[111] It appears from point 71 of the contested decision that, in the Commission's opinion, a concentration which would normally be considered as leading to the creation or reinforcement of a dominant position on the part of the acquiring undertaking may be regarded as not being the cause of it if, even in the event of the concentration being prohibited, that undertaking would inevitably achieve or reinforce a dominant position. Point 71 goes on to state that, as a general matter, a concentration is not the cause of the deterioration of the competitive structure if it is clear that:

— the acquired undertaking would in the near future be forced out of the market if not taken over by another undertaking,

— the acquiring undertaking would gain the market share of the acquired undertaking if it were forced out of the market,

— there is no less anti-competitive alternative purchase.

[112] It must be observed, first of all, that the fact that the conditions set by the Commission for concluding that there was no causal link between the concentration and the deterioration of the competitive structure do not entirely coincide with the conditions applied in connection with the United States 'failing company defence' is not in itself a ground of invalidity of the contested decision. Solely the fact that the conditions set by the Commission were not capable of excluding the possibility that a concentration might be the cause of the deterioration in the competitive structure of the market could constitute a ground of invalidity of the decision.

[113] In the present case, the French Government disputes the relevance of the criterion that it must be verified that the acquiring undertaking would in any event obtain the acquired undertaking's share of the market if the latter were to be forced out of the market.

[114] However, in the absence of that criterion, a concentration could, provided the other criteria were satisfied, be considered as not being the cause of the deterioration of the competitive structure of the market even though it appeared that, in the event of the concentration not proceeding, the acquiring undertaking would not gain the entire market share of the acquired undertaking. Thus, it would be possible to deny the existence of a causal link between the concentration and the deterioration of the competitive structure of the market even though the competitive structure of the market would deteriorate to a lesser extent if the concentration did not proceed.

[115] The introduction of that criterion is intended to ensure that the existence of a causal link between the concentration and the deterioration of the competitive structure of the market can be excluded only if the competitive structure resulting from the concentration would deteriorate in similar fashion even if the concentration did not proceed.

[116] The criterion of absorption of market shares, although not considered by the Commission as sufficient in itself to preclude any adverse effect of the concentration on competition, therefore helps to ensure the neutral effects of the concentration as regards the deterioration of the competitive structure of the market. This is consistent with the concept of causal connection set out in Article 2(2) of the Regulation.

NOTE: The argument in this case was not so much about the existence of a 'failing firm defence' under the Merger Regulation, but more about the exact nature and extent of the defence. In this case the merger was allowed to go ahead even though Kali & Salz would effectively gain a 98 per cent market share in Germany. While that was the case the Commission, and the Court, were of the view that Kali & Salz would have gained that share without the merger going ahead. Thus the necessary causal connection between the merger and the significant impediment to competition was not present. For a merger to benefit from the defence, it must meet the three conditions approved by the Court: (1) the acquired undertaking would in the near future be forced out of the market if not taken over by another undertaking, (2) the acquiring undertaking would gain the market share of the acquired undertaking if it were forced out of the market, and (3) there is no less anti-competitive alternative purchase. Although the interveners in the above case argued for a stricter application of the failing firm defence, the Commission and Court have not utilized it in many subsequent cases, even though it has been strongly argued by the parties. The Commission Notice on assessing horizontal mergers under the revised ECMR contains guidance on the use of the failing firm defence.

Commission Notice on the assessment of horizontal mergers under the Council Regulation on the control of concentrations between undertakings
OJ, 2004, C31/5, paras 89–91 [footnotes omitted]

VIII. FAILING FIRM

89. The Commission may decide that an otherwise problematic merger is nevertheless compatible with the common market if one of the merging parties is a failing firm. The basic requirement is that the deterioration of the competitive structure that follows the merger cannot be said to be caused by the merger. This will arise where the competitive structure of the market would deteriorate to at least the same extent in the absence of the merger.

90. The Commission considers the following three criteria to be especially relevant for the application of a "failing firm defence". First, the allegedly failing firm would in the near future be forced out of the market because of financial difficulties if not taken over by another undertaking. Second, there is no less anti-competitive alternative purchase than the notified merger. Third, in the absence of a merger, the assets of the failing firm would inevitably exit the market.

91. It is for the notifying parties to provide in due time all the relevant information necessary to demonstrate that the deterioration of the competitive structure that follows the merger is not caused by the merger.

SECTION 7: JUDICIAL REVIEW

Appeals against Commission decisions are to the Court of First Instance under Article 230 EC, and then to the European Court of Justice on points of law. Any doubts as to the rigour of the CFI's judicial review of Commission decisions in the field of merger control were dispelled in 2002, when three separate Commission decisions prohibiting proposed concentrations were annulled.

Ahlborn, C., and Ysewyn, J., 'EC Merger Control Regulation—Problems and Solutions'
[2002] Comp LJ 301 [footnotes omitted]

The European Court of First Instance in Luxembourg (CFI) has recently overturned three EC Commission decisions prohibiting the mergers of Airtours/First Choice, Schneider/Legrand and Tetra Laval/Sidel. The CFI's severe criticism of the EC Commission's approach has highlighted a number of important deficiencies in the EC merger control process...

'Losing one case may be regarded as a misfortune...losing two looks like carelessness', losing three reveals fundamental problems

...

...a number of significant problems identified by the CFI were recurring themes in the three cases.

Lack of procedural fairness
First, and most importantly, the CFI repeatedly criticised the EC Commission for its lack of procedural fairness and due process, highlighting the EC Commission's difficulties in combining its role as prosecutor and judge. In both Airtours/First Choice and Scheider/Legrand the EC Commission's prosecutorial instincts affected the process.

In *Airtours*, the EC Commission partly based its prohibition on a report of which it had seen only a summary. The full report did not support the EC Commission's conclusions and the CFI criticised the EC Commission's handling of the evidence, stating that 'the EC Commission construed the document without having regard to its actual wording and overall purpose'.

In *Schneider*, the EC Commission significantly changed the nature of its concerns relatively late in the proceedings, following its Statement of Objections. The CFI pointed out that, as a result, the merging parties were not given an adequate opportunity to address the new concerns raised by the EC Commission.

Failure to meet the burden of proof

The most consistent criticism given by the CFI in its three judgments was that the EC Commission's conclusions were based on assumptions rather than hard evidence, in other words, that the Commission failed to satisfy the requisite standard of proof.

In *Airtours*, the CFI emphasised that the burden of proof in EC merger cases lies with the EC Commission. The judgment stresses that by merely relying on assumptions without establishing 'cogent evidence', the EC Commission failed to '[prove] to the requisite legal standard that the concentration would give rise to a collective dominant position...'

...

Lack of predictability—deficient analytical framework

Finally, the CFI's judgments have also cast doubt on the EC Commission's analytical framework, particularly in areas other than straightforward horizontal issues, for example in relation to collective dominance and conglomerate issues.

NOTE: As Ahlborn and Ysewyn also point out in the full article, the Commission addressed several of these shortcomings in the reform package it published in December 2002, which resulted in the revised ECMR and the series of Notices discussed in this chapter. Nonetheless, it is clear that the CFI is prepared to conduct a rigorous review of Commission merger control decisions, no matter whether it is a prohibition decision or a clearance (see *Impala* above).

Commission v *Tetra Laval*
(Case C-12/03 P) [2005] ECR I-987

The Commission prohibited the proposed concentration between two undertakings, Tetra Laval and Sidel, involved in different levels of manufacturing carton packaging for liquid food. The CFI annulled the Commission decision. On appeal the Commission argued that the CFI committed an error of law as to the standard of proof that the Commission is required to satisfy and as to the scope of the CFI's power of judicial review.

19 By its first ground of appeal, the Commission complains that the Court of First Instance, whilst claiming to apply the test of manifest error of assessment, in fact applied a different test requiring the production of 'convincing evidence'. In doing so, the Court of First Instance infringed Article 230 EC by failing to take account of the discretion conferred on the Commission with regard to complex factual and economic matters. It also infringed Article 2(2) and (3) of the Regulation in that it applied a presumption of legality in respect of concentrations with conglomerate effect. Taking the example of the review of the Commission's forecast of significant growth in the use of PET packaging for sensitive products, the Commission claims that the Court of First Instance distorted the facts, failed to give adequate reasons for the rejection of its arguments and failed to take account of factors, arguments and evidence put forward by it in the contested decision and in its defence, and even refrained from referring to that defence.

...

25 The Commission claims that the Court of First Instance departed from principles laid down by the Court in its judgment in *Kali & Salz* in terms of both the nature of the judicial review carried

out by it and the standard of proof which it required the Commission to satisfy. It submits that the following paragraphs of that judgment are relevant in this regard:

'220 As stated above, under Article 2(3) of the Regulation, concentrations which create or strengthen a dominant position as a result of which effective competition would be significantly impeded in the common market or in a substantial part of it must be declared incompatible with the common market.

221 In the case of an alleged collective dominant position, the Commission is therefore obliged to assess, using a prospective analysis of the reference market, whether the concentration which has been referred to it leads to a situation in which effective competition in the relevant market is significantly impeded by the undertakings involved in the concentration and one or more other undertakings which together, in particular because of correlative factors which exist between them, are able to adopt a common policy on the market and act to a considerable extent independently of their competitors, their customers, and also of consumers.

222 Such an approach warrants close examination in particular of the circumstances which, in each individual case, are relevant for assessing the effects of the concentration on competition in the reference market.

223 In this respect, however, the basic provisions of the Regulation, in particular Article 2 thereof, confer on the Commission a certain discretion, especially with respect to assessments of an economic nature.

224 Consequently, review by the Community judicature of the exercise of that discretion, which is essential for defining the rules on concentrations, must take account of the discretionary margin implicit in the provisions of an economic nature which form part of the rules on concentrations.'

26 The Commission concludes from the principles referred to in *Kali & Salz* and from the review carried out by the Court in that case that it is required to examine the relevant market closely, weigh up all the relevant factors, and base its assessment on evidence which is factually accurate, is not clearly insignificant and is capable of substantiating the conclusions drawn from it and that it must reach its conclusions on the basis of consistent reasoning.

27 The Commission takes the view, first of all, that the standard of 'convincing evidence' differs substantially, in degree and in nature, both from the obligation to produce 'cogent and consistent' evidence, established in *Kali & Salz*, and from the principle that the Commission's assessment must be accepted unless it is shown to be manifestly wrong. The standard is different in degree because, unlike the standard of 'convincing evidence', that of cogent and consistent evidence does not rule out the possibility that another body might reach a different conclusion if it were competent to give a decision on the matter. The standard required is likewise different in nature inasmuch as it transforms the role of the Community Courts into that of a different body which is competent to rule on the matter in all its complexity and which is entitled to substitute its views for those of the Commission. The Court of First Instance was inconsistent in that it referred to the test of manifest error of assessment yet applied a very different test.

28 Next, the Commission submits that a margin of discretion is inherent in any prospective analysis. The likelihood of certain market developments within a foreseeable time-frame must be determined on the basis of the current market situation, observable trends and other appropriate indicators. To require that the Commission's assessment be, in effect, based on undisputed or virtually unequivocal evidence, irrespective of its merit, would deprive the Commission of its function of evaluating the evidence and attaching, for justifiable reasons, more weight to some sources than to others.

29 Finally, the Commission submits that the standard of proof required by the Court of First Instance means that it is placed under an obligation to authorise the transaction in cases in which the evidence does not meet the requisite standard, which is tantamount to a general, de facto presumption of the legality of certain concentrations or, at the very least, to the establishment of a bias in their favour. However, Article 2(3) and (3) imposes on the Commission a double obligation, namely either to prohibit a concentration if it creates or strengthens a dominant position or,

as a symmetrical but opposite obligation, to approve it if it neither creates nor strengthens such a position. That obligation reflects the intention of the Community legislature to protect equally the private interests of the parties to the concentration and the public interest in maintaining effective competition and in consumer protection. This symmetrical double obligation calls for the application of a symmetrical test in relation to the standard of proof required of the Commission since it must prove the merits of its assessment equally in both cases.

Findings of the Court as to the first ground of appeal

37 By its first ground of appeal, the Commission contests the judgment under appeal in so far as the Court of First Instance required it, when adopting a decision declaring a concentration incompatible with the common market, to satisfy a standard of proof and to provide a quality of evidence in support of its line of argument which are incompatible with the wide discretion which it enjoys in assessing economic matters. It thus complains that the Court of First Instance infringed Article 230 EC by exceeding the limits of its power of review established by case-law and, as a result, misapplied Article 2(2) and (3) of the Regulation by creating a presumption of legality in respect of certain concentrations.

38 It should be observed that, in paragraph 119 of the judgment under appeal, the Court of First Instance correctly set out the tests to be applied when carrying out judicial review of a Commission decision on a concentration as laid down in the judgment in *Kali & Salz*. In paragraphs 223 and 224 of that judgment, the Court stated that the basic provisions of the Regulation, in particular Article 2, confer on the Commission a certain discretion, especially with respect to assessments of an economic nature, and that, consequently, review by the Community Courts of the exercise of that discretion, which is essential for defining the rules on concentrations, must take account of the margin of discretion implicit in the provisions of an economic nature which form part of the rules on concentrations.

39 Whilst the Court recognises that the Commission has a margin of discretion with regard to economic matters, that does not mean that the Community Courts must refrain from reviewing the Commission's interpretation of information of an economic nature. Not only must the Community Courts, inter alia, establish whether the evidence relied on is factually accurate, reliable and consistent but also whether that evidence contains all the information which must be taken into account in order to assess a complex situation and whether it is capable of substantiating the conclusions drawn from it. Such a review is all the more necessary in the case of a prospective analysis required when examining a planned merger with conglomerate effect.

40 Thus, the Court of First Instance was right to find, in paragraph 155 of the judgment under appeal, in reliance on, in particular, the judgment in *Kali & Salz*, that the Commission's analysis of a merger producing a conglomerate effect is subject to requirements similar to those defined by the Court with regard to the creation of a situation of collective dominance and that it calls for a close examination of the circumstances which are relevant for an assessment of that effect on the conditions of competition on the reference market.

41 Although the Court of First Instance stated, in paragraph 155, that proof of anti-competitive conglomerate effects of a merger of the kind notified calls for a precise examination, supported by convincing evidence, of the circumstances which allegedly produce those effects, it by no means added a condition relating to the requisite standard of proof but merely drew attention to the essential function of evidence, which is to establish convincingly the merits of an argument or, as in the present case, of a decision on a merger.

42 A prospective analysis of the kind necessary in merger control must be carried out with great care since it does not entail the examination of past events—for which often many items of evidence are available which make it possible to understand the causes—or of current events, but rather a prediction of events which are more or less likely to occur in future if a decision prohibiting the planned concentration or laying down the conditions for it is not adopted.

43 Thus, the prospective analysis consists of an examination of how a concentration might alter the factors determining the state of competition on a given market in order to establish whether it would give rise to a serious impediment to effective competition. Such an analysis makes it necessary to envisage various chains of cause and effect with a view to ascertaining which of them are the most likely.

44 The analysis of a 'conglomerate-type' concentration is a prospective analysis in which, first, the consideration of a lengthy period of time in the future and, secondly, the leveraging necessary to give rise to a significant impediment to effective competition mean that the chains of cause and effect are dimly discernible, uncertain and difficult to establish. That being so, the quality of the evidence produced by the Commission in order to establish that it is necessary to adopt a decision declaring the concentration incompatible with the common market is particularly important, since that evidence must support the Commission's conclusion that, if such a decision were not adopted, the economic development envisaged by it would be plausible.

45 It follows from those various factors that the Court of First Instance did not err in law when it set out the tests to be applied in the exercise of its power of judicial review or when it specified the quality of the evidence which the Commission is required to produce in order to demonstrate that the requirements of Article 2(3) of the Regulation are satisfied.

46 With respect to the particular case of judicial review exercised by the Court of First Instance in the judgment under appeal, it is not apparent from the example given by the Commission, which relates to the growth in the use of PET packaging for sensitive products, that the Court of First Instance exceeded the limits applicable to the review of an administrative decision by the Community Courts. Contrary to what the Commission claims, paragraph 211 of the judgment under appeal merely restates more concisely, in the form of a finding by the Court of First Instance, the admission made by the Commission at the hearing, which is summarised in paragraph 210 of the judgment, that its forecast in the contested decision with regard to the increase in the use of PET for packaging UHT milk was exaggerated. In paragraph 212 of the judgment under appeal, the Court of First Instance gave the reasons for its finding that the evidence produced by the Commission was unfounded by stating that, of the three independent reports cited by the Commission, only the PCI report contained information on the use of PET for milk packaging. It went on, in that paragraph, to show that the evidence produced by the Commission was unconvincing by pointing out that the increase forecast in the PCI report was of little significance and that the Commission's forecast was inconsistent with the undisputed figures on the use of HDPE contained in the other reports. In paragraph 213 of the judgment under appeal, the Court of First Instance merely stated that the Commission's analysis was incomplete, which made it impossible to confirm its forecasts, given the differences between those forecasts and the forecasts made in the other reports.

47 Amongst the other examples given by it, the Commission challenges the Court of First Instance's finding, in paragraph 289 of the judgment under appeal, that 'fresh milk is not a product for which the marketing advantages offered by PET have any particular importance' and its conclusions as to the cost of PET in comparison to that of carton, which are set out in paragraphs 288 and 328 of the judgment under appeal. It should be noted that these are findings of fact, which are not subject to review by the Court in appeal proceedings. It is therefore unnecessary to give a ruling on the merits of those findings by the Court of First Instance and it need be stated only that the Court of First Instance was able to base those findings on various items in the contested decision.

48 It follows from these examples that the Court of First Instance carried out its review in the manner required of it, as set out in paragraph 39 of this judgment. It explained and set out the reasons why the Commission's conclusions seemed to it to be inaccurate in that they were based on insufficient, incomplete, insignificant and inconsistent evidence.

49 In doing so, the Court of First Instance observed the criteria to be applied in exercising the Community Courts' power of judicial review and, accordingly, complied with Article 230 EC.

NOTE: The ECJ therefore endorsed the CFI's more rigorous approach to judicial review whilst also confirming that the Commission does indeed have a 'margin of discretion' in exercising its powers, particularly with regard to conducting economic assessments. Nonetheless the ECJ held that it is for the Community Courts to ensure that the information relied on by the Commission is 'accurate, reliable and consistent' and whether it is 'capable of substantiating the conclusions drawn from it'. The CFI requirement for 'convincing evidence' therefore appears to be an acceptable standard for the Community Courts with regards to reviewing Commission evidence.

Weinberg, J., Chapter 6, 'Judicial review of mergers in Europe: Tetra Laval, GE/Honeywell and the convergence toward US standards', in Marsden, P. (ed.), *Handbook of Research in Trans-Atlantic Antitrust*

Cheltenham, Edward Elgar, 2006, at pp 166–7 [footnotes omitted]

The Commission's complaint with the Court of First Instance was of course broader than just the differing interpretations of the 2005 milk-market numbers. It was the very principle of the judiciary overturning what the competition regulators thought was a well-settled and reasonable administrative determination (well within its margin of discretion) that the Tetra Laval/Sidel combination created a dangerous risk of dominance in the drinks packaging market. In a variation on the 'judicial activism' criticism sometimes leveled at US judges, the Commission's first ground of appeal complained that the CFI had changed the very nature of EC judicial review of mergers. The use of a 'convincing evidence' standard of proof, which the Commission saw as tougher than 'cogent and consistent evidence', had the effect of 'transform[ing] the role of the Community Courts into that of a different body which is competent to rule on the matter in all its complexity and which is entitled to *substitute its view* for those of the Commission', the merger regulators complained...

With respect to the *Tetra Laval* case, however, Advocate General Tizzano, while agreeing with the standard to be used, differs with its application and with Judge Vesterdorf's potentially self-serving spin. Discussing the Commission's objection to the CFI's finding that use of plastic bottling would not increase for long-life milk, Tizzano writes that 'I agree with the Commission that with that terse statement...the Court of First Instance incorrectly *substituted its own point of view* for the Commission's, formulating its own autonomous prediction of future developments in the market'.

...compared with its judgments in earlier years, the CFI in 2002 took a more robust approach to its review, and in doing so found the Commission's denials of merger approval in *Airtours*, *Schneider* and *Tetra Laval* to be insufficiently supported. The critical language the Court used and the cumulative effect of the three judgments made their impact more powerful than a single, more neutral-sounding case such as *Kali & Salz*. On the other hand, it is quite possible that by 2002 the Commission simply had grown careless and/or overconfident in its merger review and, in at least these three cases, merited judicial rebuke and reversal. The Competition Directorate's internal overhaul and intensified focus on sophisticated economic analysis in the wake of the decisions implies at least a modicum of fault. Judicial review may well have been performing the function for which it was intended.

NOTE: Weinberg provides a balanced assessment of the implications stemming from the well-known annulment decisions in 2002, but particularly from the ECJ's endorsement of the CFI's general approach in *Tetra Laval*. Interestingly, the Commission's arguments in the case imply that the CFI is moving towards a model of judicial review adopted by the UK Competition Appeal Tribunal, whereby the CAT can substitute its own decision for that of the OFT under certain conditions. This movement by the CFI may well have stopped in light of its own rebuke from the ECJ in Case C-413/06 *Impala* [2008] 5 CMLR 17. For comparative purposes see Rayment, B., 'Powers of the Competition Appeal Tribunal' (2005) 4 Comp LJ 273.

■ QUESTION

What is the role of the Court of First Instance in EC merger control?

SECTION 8: INTERNATIONAL APPLICATION OF THE ECMR

Gencor Ltd* v *Commission

(Case T-102/96) [1999] ECR II-753, [1999] 4 CMLR 971

The Commission had declared a proposed concentration between two South African-based platinum producers as incompatible with the Common Market, and one of the grounds of appeal challenged the Commission's decision on the basis that the ECMR could not control a concentration where both parties were established outside the EC.

[78] The Regulation, in accordance with Article 1 thereof, applies to all concentrations with a Community dimension, that is to say to all concentrations between undertakings which do not each achieve more than two-thirds of their aggregate Community-wide turnover within one and the same Member State, where the combined aggregate worldwide turnover of those undertakings is more than 5,000 million ECUs and the aggregate Community-wide turnover of at least two of them is more than 250 million ECUs.

[79] Article 1 does not require that, in order for a concentration to be regarded as having a Community dimension, the undertakings in question must be established in the Community or that the production activities covered by the concentration must be carried out within Community territory.

[80] With regard to the criterion of turnover, it must be stated that, as set out in paragraph (13) of the contested Decision, the concentration at issue has a Community dimension within the meaning of Article 1(2) of the Regulation. The undertakings concerned have an aggregate worldwide turnover of more than 10,000 million ECUs, above the 5,000 million ECUs threshold laid down by the Regulation. Gencor and Lonrho each had a Community-wide turnover of more than 250 million ECUs in the last financial year. Finally, they do not each achieve more than two-thirds of their aggregate Community-wide turnover within one and the same Member State.

[81] The applicant's arguments to the effect that the legal bases for the Regulation and the wording of its preamble and substantive provisions preclude its application to the concentration at issue cannot be accepted.

[82] The legal bases for the Regulation, namely Articles 87 and 235 of the Treaty, and more particularly the provisions to which they are intended to give effect, that is to say Articles 3(g) and 85 and 86 of the Treaty, as well as paragraphs (1) to (5) and (9) to (11) in the preamble to the Regulation, merely point to the need to ensure that competition is not distorted in the Common Market, in particular by concentrations which result in the creation or strengthening of a dominant position. They in no way exclude from the Regulation's field of application concentrations which, while relating to mining and/or production activities outside the Community, have the effect of creating or strengthening a dominant position as a result of which effective competition in the Common Market is significantly impeded.

[83] In particular, the applicant's view cannot be founded on the closing words of paragraph (11) in the preamble to the Regulation.

[84] That paragraph states that:

> a concentration with a Community dimension exists . . . where the concentrations are effected by undertakings which do not have their principal fields of activities in the Community but which have substantial operations there.

[85] By that reference, in general terms, to the concept of substantial operations, the Regulation does not, for the purpose of defining its territorial scope, ascribe greater importance to production operations than to sales operations. On the contrary, by setting quantitative thresholds in Article 1 which are based on the worldwide and Community turnover of the undertakings concerned, it rather ascribes greater importance to sales operations within the Common Market as a factor linking the concentration to the Community. It is common ground that Gencor and Lonrho each carry out significant sales in the Community (valued in excess of 250 million ECUs).

[86] Nor is it borne out by either paragraph (30) in the preamble to the Regulation or Article 24 thereof that the criterion based on the location of production activities is well founded. Far from laying down a criterion for defining the territorial scope of the Regulation, Article 24 merely regulates the procedures to be followed in order to deal with situations in which non-member countries do not grant Community undertakings treatment comparable to that accorded by the Community to undertakings from those non-member countries in relation to the control of concentrations.

[87] The applicant cannot, by reference to the judgment in *Wood Pulp*, rely on the criterion as to the implementation of an agreement to support its interpretation of the territorial scope of the Regulation. Far from supporting the applicant's view, that criterion for assessing the link between an agreement and Community territory in fact precludes it. According to *Wood Pulp*, the criterion as to the implementation of an agreement is satisfied by mere sale within the Community, irrespective of the location of the sources of supply and the production plant. It is not disputed that Gencor and Lonrho carried out sales in the Community before the concentration and would have continued to do so thereafter.

[88] Accordingly, the Commission did not err in its assessment of the territorial scope of the Regulation by applying it in this case to a proposed concentration notified by undertakings whose registered offices and mining and production operations are outside the Community.

B Compatibility of the contested decision with public international law

[89] Following the concentration agreement, the previously existing competitive relationship between Implats and LPD, in particular so far as concerns their sales in the Community, would have come to an end. That would have altered the competitive structure within the Common Market since, instead of three South African PGM suppliers, there would have remained only two. The implementation of the proposed concentration would have led to the merger not only of the parties' PGM mining and production operations in South Africa but also of their marketing operations throughout the world, particularly in the Community where Implats and LPD achieved significant sales.

[90] Application of the Regulation is justified under public international law when it is foreseeable that a proposed concentration will have an immediate and substantial effect in the Community.

[91] In that regard, the concentration would, according to the contested Decision, have led to the creation of a dominant duopoly on the part of Amplats and Implats/LPD in the platinum and rhodium markets, as a result of which effective competition would have been significantly impeded in the Common Market within the meaning of Article 2(3) of the Regulation.

[92] It is therefore necessary to verify the three criteria of immediate, substantial and foreseeable effect are satisfied in this case.

NOTE: In *Gencor*, the CFI followed the position adopted by the Court of Justice under Articles 81 and 82 and applied the ECMR with extraterritorial effect. The Court affirmed the 'implementation' test set out in *Wood Pulp* (Joined Cases C-89/85, C-104/85, C-114/85, C-116/85, C-117/85, C-125/85, and C-129/85) [1998] ECR 5193, but goes somewhat further and refers to what is known as the 'effects' doctrine in para. 90. This means that the ECMR may be utilized even if there was no direct trading inside the EC, but the merger would in some way disturb the Community market. See Fox, E.M., 'The Merger Regulation and its Territorial Reach: *Gencor Ltd v Commission*' [1999] ECLR 334. Because of the increasing number of globally important mergers, the necessity for extraterritorial application of the ECMR is increasingly important, but it also raises the potential for increasing conflict between different competition authorities that seek to deal with a global merger under several different regulatory systems at the same time. See, e.g. Case IV/M877 *Boeing/McDonnel Douglas* OJ, 1997, L336/16 and Case IV/M1845 *AOL/Time Warner* OJ, 2001, L268/28 and Chapter 5 generally.

FURTHER READING

Baxter, S., and Dethmers, F., 'Collective dominance under EC merger control—after Airtours and the introduction of unilateral effects is there still a future for collective dominance?' [2006] ECLR 148.

Cook, J., and Kerse, C., *EC Merger Control*, 5th edn, London, Sweet & Maxwell, 2009.

Diaz, G., 'The Reform of European Merger Control: *Quid Novi Sub Sole?*' (2004) 27 World Competition 177.

Kokkoris, I., 'The development of the concept of collective dominance in the ECMR. From its inception to its current status' (2007) 30 World Comp 419.

Navarro, E., Font, A., Folguera, J., and Briones, J., *Merger Control in the EU*, 2nd edn, Oxford, OUP, 2005.

Thompson, R., 'Goodbye to "The Dominance Test"? Substantive Appraisal under the New UK and EC Merger Regimes' (2003) 2 Comp LJ 332.

Weinberg, J., Chapter 6, 'Judicial review of mergers in Europe: *Tetra Laval, GE/ Honeywell* and the convergence toward US standards', in Marsden, P. (ed.), *Handbook of Research in Trans-Atlantic Antitrust*, Cheltenham, Edward Elgar, 2006.

13

UK merger control

SECTION 1: INTRODUCTION

Merger policy is probably the most politically sensitive aspect of UK competition policy. The question of the appropriate degree of merger control and the form it should take have been widely debated, notably in relation to the reform of UK merger control introduced by Part III of the Enterprise Act 2002 ('EA 2002'). Furthermore, there was recently frenzied media debate and legal dispute in relation to the LloydsTSB/HBOS merger, which raised clear competition concerns, but was approved under UK merger controls on the basis of the perceived need to maintain the financial stability of the financial sector in a recessionary climate.

Section 1 will give an historical introduction to merger control in the UK and Section 2 will outline merger control as developed under the Fair Trading Act 1973 ('FTA 1973'). Section 3 addresses the debate on reform of the merger control provisions in the FTA 1973 and Section 4 will involve a detailed consideration of the current merger law, policy, and practice under Part III of the EA 2002.

Rodger, B.J., 'Reinforcing the Scottish "Ring-fence": A Critique of UK Mergers Policy vis-à-vis the Scottish Economy'
[1996] ECLR 104

Two views predominate on the exercise of control that may be deemed to be most appropriate. On the one hand, some argue that such intervention can only be justified if the merger is likely to have an adverse effect on the competitive formation of the industry, otherwise decisions ought to be left in the capable hands of the entrepreneurs. Protagonists of the second view would argue that a more interventionist stance is required, since mergers have generally been found not to produce the expected benefits, and 'so that various socio-political considerations, such as the effect of mergers upon unemployment and regional policy, can also be taken into account'.

Of all the arguments raised against mergers, that of the reduction in competition which may arise is viewed as the most prominent. The controversial issue is whether any other detrimental effects of mergers ought to be within the competition authorities' remit. It is widely believed that the effect on competition ought to be the sole consideration to be excluded from the market's determination as to the desirability of a particular merger. However the valid assumption may also be drawn that the interests of shareholders do not, at least necessarily, coincide with the public interest. This, in itself, may be viewed as the greatest justification for the existence of a control system which incorporates extraneous issues.

Various other specific detriments connected with mergers include objections as to the size and power of the merged firm, the possible detrimental effect on the balance of payments and transfer of control of a UK company into foreign hands, thus negating any economic advantages to be gained by the merger.

NOTE: The arguments that mergers are driven by efficiency gains and are beneficial for the economy in terms of enhanced R & D and innovation are not supported by any conclusive empirical data.

Sharpe, T., 'Merger Control in the United Kingdom'
[1983] ECLR 171

The most striking feature of merger policy in the United Kingdom has been its failure. The growth of concentration in manufacturing industry has continued unabated, and most of this increase can be attributed to mergers. There is little or no evidence to suggest any corresponding increase in efficiency associated with the increase in concentration. This is predictable because it is fundamental to this article that there is a clear connection between industrial *structure* and *behaviour* in the market. The more concentrated the market, the more opportunity exists for exploiting market power. Exploitation can take many forms. Traditionally, market power is regarded as the capacity to control price and output, to extract significant profits and thereby to reduce the real incomes of consumers. But market power can be enjoyed as well as exploited. Inefficiencies can be tolerated, there is less need to be responsive to consumers' wishes. Managers working in such an environment would be less than human if they did not award each other generous salaries and agreeable benefits, all of which could be justified to the inquisitive shareholder by reference to past growth and profits.

Moreover, the more concentrated a market becomes the greater is the capacity, if not for *express* collusion, at least for *tacit* collusion. There are so few players in the market. Their behaviour becomes interdependent: prices change in unison, new products are introduced in an orderly way, quality changes take place across an industry and mutually high levels of advertising expenditure maintain market shares. Technology, for some writers the source of violent discontinuities and dislocation, is, in fact, managed and directed. The stasis is confirmed and the textbook promiscuity of the market disappears. In short, mergers lead to increased market power, lower efficiency, lower real incomes and a diminishing of the sense of rivalry necessary for the market to work. The market becomes sclerotic.

NOTE: Sharpe was sceptical as to the merits of mergers and any gains for the economy, a view that has not always predominated.

Merger controls were first introduced into UK competition law in the Monopolies and Mergers Act 1965, based on the Board of Trade White Paper of 1964, *Monopolies, Mergers and Restrictive Practices* (Cmnd 2299, London, HMSO, March 1964).

Board of Trade White Paper of 1964, *Monopolies, Mergers and Restrictive Practices*
Cmnd 2299, London, HMSO, March 1964, paras 21–7

21. The Government recognise and welcome the contribution which mergers can make to the well-being of the economy. Mergers often enable better use to be made of resources, and result in units large enough both to finance desirable research and development and to produce economies of scale. Where this is so, mergers are clearly advantageous. They contribute to the strength of the economy, and put British industry in a better position to compete in international trade.

22. There is, however, a small minority of mergers which may have harmful results. The Government think it desirable that it should be made possible to have such cases investigated.

23. For this purpose, the Government propose that the new Monopolies Commission should be empowered at the direction of the Board of Trade, to inquire into any proposed or recently completed merger which would result in a monopoly or would increase the power of an

existing monopoly. It is expected that in practice an inquiry would seldom be necessary. It would always be possible for firms contemplating a merger to consult the Board of Trade about the proposals. The Board would welcome such consultations.

24. The Government contemplate directing the Commission's attention to certain considerations to which it should have regard in particular cases in assessing where the public interest lay. They have in mind such considerations as efficiency, technical and technological advance, industrial growth and competitive power in international trade.

25. The Government do not intend to seek powers to hold up a proposed merger while it is being investigated. This could well frustrate desirable mergers.

26. When the Commission had completed an inquiry, its function would be, as in the case of monopolies, to report on whether the merger was against the public interest, and if so in what respects. It would have to evaluate the evidence available on such questions as the extent to which competition would be reduced and the benefits to be expected from the larger scale of operation which the merger would permit.

27. In the light of the Commission's Report it would then be for the Government to take such action as they believed to be necessary. In a situation requiring such action a completed merger would be treated as a monopoly and the proposed powers for dealing with monopolies would be appropriate. Where a merger had not been completed, power would be required to prohibit it or to attach conditions to its completion. The exercise of this power would in each case be subject to Parliamentary approval.

NOTE: Tightening one area of competition law may lead to different forms of anti-competitive response by industry. It has been noted that the introduction of the Restrictive Trade Practices Act 1956, which laid down a registration system for restrictive practices, reduced the scope for British industry to employ price-fixing and market-sharing cartels that had become commonplace. (See Mercer, H., *Constructing a Competitive Order, The Hidden History of British Antitrust Policies*, Cambridge, CUP, 1995.) The introduction of the 1956 legislation resulted in a 'merger boom' as industry sought alternative ways to form cartels as a means of maximizing their profits. The 1965 legislation can be viewed, at least partially, as a response to the wave of mergers that could threaten competition in the UK.

Wilks, S., *In The Public Interest, Competition Policy and the Monopolies and Mergers Commission*
Manchester, MUP, 1999, pp. 204–5

The debates over the introduction of merger control in the UK were largely about detail and emphasis, they were not marked by fundamental disagreements and were bi-partisan (indeed, tri-partisan, with Liberal support). This allowed an incremental development of policy with much of the running being made by officials in the BoT. It follows that the principles and the core arguments about merger control were not fully exposed and debated. The outcome was, first, that merger control squeezed into competition policy largely unannounced; and second, that the model of control adopted was based on the methods of monopoly control. Charles Rowley was able to observe that 'perhaps the most important post-war extension of the power of the executive in the affairs of the private sector was legislated with scarce a suspicion of public anxiety'. Rowley's view seems initially to smack of hyperbole but, in historical perspective, the interventionist preoccupations of the Labour Government have melted like early morning mist, leaving intact an apparatus of merger control that has become a more and more dominant feature of the regulatory landscape.

This low key series of policy innovations incorporated a series of principles which have continued to influence merger policy. There are six principles to be emphasised:

- mergers are regarded with favour
- merger control is administrative, not judicial
- the American model of prohibition is rejected

- the economic impact of mergers is subject to a 'monopoly' test
- the procedures and the ultimate criteria are politically controlled
- the main discipline is business self-regulation.

NOTE: Wilks, *In the Public Interest*, provides a thought-provoking analysis of the history of the MMC, the precursor to the Competition Commission, and the parallel development of British competition policy. The introduction of merger control in 1965, he notes, regenerated the Commission although this crucial development 'sneaked in with little debate'. For further reading, see Pickering, J.F., 'The Implementation of British Competition Policy on Mergers' [1980] ECLR 177.

The Competition Act 1998 ('CA 1998'), outlined in earlier chapters, did not affect the existing system of merger control in the UK, set out in Part V of the FTA 1973, involving the traditional tripartite system of enforcement, with the DGFT, Secretary of State for Trade and Industry and the Competition Commission each playing a key role. The EA 2002 revised this system and the substantive test for assessing mergers. Nonetheless, it is important to understand the development of policy and practice under the FTA 1973 in order to appreciate the similarities in approach with the system introduced by the EA 2002 which may lead to similar outcomes, in addition to awareness of differences in the legal provision and role of the bodies involved.

■ QUESTION

What benefits and/or disadvantages may result from a merger or takeover?

SECTION 2: **THE FAIR TRADING ACT 1973**

A distinctive feature of the FTA 1973 was that only the Secretary of State could make a merger reference to the Competition Commission. In practice, merger references were normally made on the advice of the DGFT although the Secretary of State was not bound by the DGFT's advice.

Given the limited number of qualifying mergers actually referred to the Competition Commission, ascertaining the policy on referrals was important. The following passage suggests that the referral process lacked transparency:

Rodger, B.J., 'Reinforcing the Scottish "Ring-fence": A Critique of UK Mergers Policy vis-à-vis the Scottish Economy'
[1996] ECLR 104, pp. 111–12

The failure of current merger policy[56]

This section seeks to examine the nature and effect of prevailing government policy on the administration of the merger provisions. This will be investigated together with an insight into their practical effect in relation to the recent 'takeovers' of Distillers, Britoil and William Low.

The decision to refer is effectively taken by the Director General and the internal Merger Panel, whose discussions and reasoning need not be made public. The Office of Fair Trading has pointed out that although the section 84 guidelines were not addressed to the Director General they were factors taken into account by him in his advice to the Secretary of State.[57] This randomness of

[56] See Ashcroft and Love, Note 10 above, Chapters 6 and 7.
[57] See, for example, Office of Fair Trading booklet, *Mergers: A Guide to Procedures under the Fair Trading Act 1973*.

selection for referral has been one of the main criticisms of the operation of the Act. It was generally believed both that the referral process needed to be more visible and that the reasons for referral ought to be more easily discernible. One view is that UK merger policy had failed because of the wide-ranging public interest criteria and 'the authorities ceased to be interested in competition',[58] and most observers thought that non-competition issues ought to be left to the market or taken from the Commission and 'given to the Secretary of State in a more politically responsible way'.[59] It is considered that this separation of competition and non-competition issues would render the whole process more consistent. This indicates a belief that the law in these areas was initiated with the concern solely for the promotion of competition.[60]

The Liesner Report in May 1978 recognised that 'Governments have not adopted the promotion of competition in all circumstances as an overriding objective'.[61] To this end, they recommended the retention of the 'case by case' basis of merger control, and no alterations were made to the law as a result of the Report.[62] This issue of any prospective changes to the merger controls was dealt with admirably in a prophetic article by David Simpson early in 1983.[63] A change in the set of public interest guidelines was considered appropriate, although his concern was that such a move to redefine the public interest would be instituted by a government committed to free market forces. Simpson also harboured fears that the Government's tactics may result in policy changes being introduced by a 'quiet backdoor method'.

The dominant influence on merger control policy of recent years is undoubtedly the statement by Mr Norman Tebbit, the then Secretary of State for Trade and Industry, issued in July 1984 and often referred to as the 'Tebbit Doctrine'.[64] This confirmed that, save for the two tests in section 64, there were no statutory criteria for referral to the Commission. The 'Tebbit Doctrine' was spelled out as a means of bridging this inherent gap in the legislation, or perhaps as a 'backdoor method' to amend the public interest. 'I regard mergers policy as an important part of the Government's general policy of promoting competition...Accordingly my policy has been and will continue to be to make references primarily on competition grounds.'

The justification to designate this statement as an underhand method of restricting the public interest derives from the all-important position which the referral process occupies within the UK system. Under present arrangements, merger policy is made at least as much at the referral stage as by the Commission itself. With such a small percentage of mergers being selected for investigation by the Commission in accordance with the public interest, the chosen few will inevitably depend to a great extent on the prevalence, if any, of a particular government priority. This approach is consistent with the Conservative ethos that consumers' best interests are served by ensuring maximum competition and choice. There is no fault in this purest strand of theory, namely that the promotion of competition is to be ensured to the ultimate advantage of the consumer. Thus, mergers resulting in excessive concentration within a particular market should be considered sceptically. However, the underlying rationale to merger control may be neglected as a result of the non-interventionist stance adopted in tandem with the promotion of competition. It

[58] Sharpe, 'Merger Control in the United Kingdom' [1983] FCLR 171, at 171.

[59] *The Economist*, 5 February 1983. See also Hall, 'Merger Control: The Persistence of an Illusion' [1982] ECLR 347. For parallel views at the European Community level, see Ehlermann, 'Reflections on a European Cartel Office' [1995] CMLR 471.

[60] See Ellis, 'A Survey of the Government Control of Mergers in the United Kingdom' [1971] NILQ Volume 22, 251. This issue is particularly topical given the recent comments of Sir Bryan Carlsberg in the OFT Annual Report 1994 and the House of Commons Trade and Industry Select Committee Report on Competition Policy which will be considered below.

[61] 'A Review of Monopolies and Mergers Policy', Cmnd 7198 (1978), at paragraph 2.1.

[62] The Report recommended that a more critical stance together with a neutral stance ought to be adopted, in contrast with the existing presumption that mergers are beneficial.

[63] Simpson, 'Be it Marriage or Merger, Any Change in the Ceremony Calls for Deep Thought', *Financial Guardian*, 8 February 1983.

[64] DTI Press Notice, 5 July 1984.

is, considered that mergers raising non-competition issues should generally be left to the adjudication of the free market, considering it to be a better arbiter of what constitutes a good merger than the Government. It is, though, decidedly unlikely for the decision-makers in the market to forego an intended takeover of a competitive Scottish company for what would be deemed as parochial concerns over the loss of control and resultant effects on the Scottish economy.

The justification which the Secretary of State obviously had in mind was 'the desire of companies for stability and predictability in this field of policy'. However, in areas where the law and economic policy coincide, greater consistency may be achieved at the expense of an even more important principle or policy goals.[65]

NOTE: This critique of the merger referral process is set in the context of a discussion on merger control and regional policy. In the article the author noted that a previous series of reports on the public interest implications of takeovers of strategically important Scottish companies could effectively be ignored by the Secretary of State. Indeed, the FTA 1973 provided no legal basis upon which references were to be made and did not even require the Secretary of State to refer to the public interest test in s. 84 of the Act. The Tebbitt doctrine on referral policy was in effect given statutory effect when the EA 2002 was enacted and, indeed, a key cornerstone of the new regime was to remove ministerial involvement, and hence politics, from the merger control process. The key issue for the Competition Commission was to report on whether the merger was expected to operate against the public interest. The public interest test was set out in s. 84 of the Act.

THE FAIR TRADING ACT 1973 [S. 84]

Public interest

84.—(1) In determining for any purposes to which this section applies whether any particular matter operates, or may be expected to operate, against the public interest, the Commission shall take into account all matters which appear to them in the particular circumstances to be relevant and, among other things, shall have regard to the desirability—

   (a) of maintaining and promoting effective competition between persons supplying goods and services in the United Kingdom;

   (b) of promoting the interests of consumers, purchasers and other users of goods and services in the United Kingdom in respect of the prices charged for them and in respect of their quality and the variety of goods and services supplied;

   (c) of promoting, through competition, the reduction of costs and the development and use of new techniques and new products, and of facilitating the entry of new competitors into existing markets;

   (d) of maintaining and promoting the balanced distribution of industry and employment in the United Kingdom; and

   (e) of maintaining and promoting competitive activity in markets outside the United Kingdom on the part of producers of goods, and of suppliers of goods and services, in the United Kingdom.

NOTE: The public interest test was notable for its breadth. 'Competition' was a key issue but paras (a)–(e) were guidelines to be taken into account, together with any other relevant considerations. There was no presumption that promoting competition was the sole test as this would be incompatible with the other guidelines in the section, for instance the reference to 'regional policy' in sub-s. (d). See Sharpe, T., 'Merger Control in the UK' [1983] ECLR 171, and Rodger, B.J., 'Reinforcing the Scottish "Ring-fence": A Critique of UK Mergers Policy vis-à-vis the Scottish Economy' [1996] ECLR 104. Given the wide scope of the public interest test, it is

---

[65] See Brent and Lever, Note 8 above. For the debate at the EC level, see for instance, Frazer, 'Competition Policy after 1992: The Next Step' [1990] MLR 609 and Ehlermann, Note 59 above.

inevitable that there were criticisms of the Commission for its lack of consistency and predictability, and the following passage discusses the extent to which the Commission's reports can be based on precedent.

Wilks, S., *In The Public Interest, Competition Policy and the Monopolies and Mergers Commission*
Manchester, MUP, 1999, pp. 220–1

The third aspect is the question of precedents. This is a general issue running through all MMC cases and is discussed in chapter 5. It has been a constant source of criticism in merger cases and has been a matter of sustained concern for the Commission. From Sutherland's study in 1969 to the TIC investigation in 1991, analysts have searched for consistency across the various merger cases and complained that it was not to be found. Different critics stress different aspects of consistency. Certainly the procedures are consistent but what about the reasoning, the economic analysis and the findings? Fairburn's influential discussion is fairly typical. He concludes that 'it is hard to trace the Commission's reasoning from report to report, or even to perceive that it regards such continuity as an important matter'. This may reflect a difference of perception between economists and lawyers. While lawyers are concerned with regularity and precedent they are less concerned with universal economic principles. They tend to understand that legally precedent does not bind the Commission and that each case is different. Economists might accept that the cases are different but insist that the principles are the same. Curiously it has therefore been the economists who have been most agitated about precedent, lawyers have been more forgiving.

The Commission's concern about precedent in the late 1980s was fuelled by Peter Lilley's speech in June 1991 in which he declared, 'I welcome the emphasis Sir Sydney Lipworth...has given to maintaining consistency and developing the greater use of precedent in the MMC's work'. A *Precedents Handbook* was prepared in 1988 and is regularly updated and circulated to team managers and Chairmen. Similarly when Graeme Odgers was appointed in 1993 his creation of the Deputy Chairman's group was explicitly orientated towards maintaining consistency over time and between cases. Every meeting included briefings on current cases. But, despite all this attention, the fact remains that each case is different; the public interest test cannot be reduced to a formula. Moreover, each group is different. Chairmen have different mixes of skills and priorities and a group considering a particular precedent might well feel that it would not have come to the same conclusion. In honesty most members would concede this reality. One recently retired member observed in his valedictory note to the Chairman that, 'I am suspicious of resort to precedents in looking at cases. The facts of every case are different, and the application of similar principles might well lead to different conclusions in cases which might look similar on superficial investigation...I look upon the MMC very much as an economic jury, making individual judgements'. The precedents issue also has a temporal dimension. A case from 1976 may provide poor precedent in 1999, where industrial context, the stress on competition and evolution of economic theory would all bring new perspectives to bear. With the Commission constituted on its present basis it has put its emphasis on consistency of approach. Not only would binding precedents be of doubtful legality, they would contradict the whole essence of the Commission concept.

NOTE: Wilks correctly emphasizes that Commission merger reports cannot be precedent based. Each merger should be looked at on its own facts, given the particular characteristics of the parties and the industrial sector involved. These comments apply equally to the Commission's reporting function under the EA 2002. Where the Commission considered that a merger could be expected to operate against the public interest, it was required to consider what action should be taken in order to remedy or prevent the adverse effects. In addition, the Commission could, and routinely did, make recommendations as to the appropriate action to be taken.

The Secretary of State was required to publish the Commission's report and lay it before Parliament. If the report was not adverse, or less than two-thirds of the group supported any adverse findings, no formal enforcement action could be taken. Otherwise, the Secretary of State was empowered to make orders under Sch. 8 to the Act. The Secretary of State was not required to act upon any Competition Commission conclusion and recommendation. In *Bass/ Carlsberg/Tetley* (Cm 3662, 1997) he disregarded the recommendation that a sale of assets would be a sufficient remedy and effectively blocked the merger. Conversely, following an earlier report, *Charter Consolidated/Anderson Strathclyde* (Cmnd 8711, 1982) the Secretary of State allowed a takeover bid to proceed although the Commission had concluded, by a 4–2 majority, that it should be blocked as against the public interest. Judicial review of the Secretary of State's decision was subsequently unsuccessful in *R* v *Secretary of State for Trade and Industry, ex parte Anderson Strathclyde plc* [1983] 2 All ER 233, although there was a successful judicial review under the merger control provisions of the 1973 Act in 2001 in *Interbrew SA/Interbrew Holdings UK Ltd* v *Competition Commission/Secretary of State for Trade and Industry* (CO/402/2001, 25 May 2001, QBD, Moses J).

■ QUESTION

Was it appropriate for the Secretary of State to be provided with so much discretion under the 1973 Act merger control system?

SECTION 3: REFORM OF MERGER CONTROL

The CA 1998 beckoned a new era in UK competition law with a new institutional and regulatory framework and substantive competition law principles. The Act did not set out to reform merger control in any way, but the DTI made proposals for reform of the system not long after its enactment. In August 1999 the DTI published *Mergers: A Consultation Document on Proposals for Reform* and this was followed by *Mergers: The Response to the Consultation on Proposals for Reform* in October 2000.

Rodger, B.J., 'UK Merger Control: Politics, the Public Interest and Reform'
[2000] ECLR 24 at p. 25 and pp. 28–9 [footnotes omitted]

Aims of the reform

Although the DTI document stresses the 'overarching aim' of reform as promoting competitiveness, the consumer interest, effectiveness and efficiency, the key principles reflect the main underlying concerns:

— clarity, transparency and consistency, which in turn promote predictability, fairness and accountability;
— responsiveness to the needs of business and other users of the system, imposing only the minimum necessary burdens;
— effective and proportionate control of mergers which have harmful effects.

These clearly prioritise the interests of business as 'consumers' of competition law and resembles the European Merger Regulation intention to facilitate mergers by reducing regulatory burdens.
  The two main tenets of the proposals which seek to achieve these aims are to:

— focus decisions more clearly on competition; and
— minimise Ministerial involvement in decision-making.

These two tenets are, however, untenable if one considers competition policy, especially mergers policy, to be particularly politically sensitive. One can legitimately argue that competition law should serve the public interest which should therefore form the cornerstone of competition policy. The document indeed reflects the fairly empty debate on aims and goals of competition law undertaken during the passage of the Competition Bill, with the limited exceptions of the Parliamentary debates on resale price maintenance ('RPM') for over-the-counter medicines and newspaper pricing. The key issue of stakeholders in merger policy, it is suggested, has been skewed in favour of potentially merging companies.

Although understated in the DTI document, it is clear that the international dimension and the Community merger regime form an important aspect of the reform proposals. The Document notes the increasing extent of cross-border and global mergers and the concerns over duplication and multiplication of regulatory requirements. It is accepted that there is scope for procedural harmonisation, including notification forms, timetables, etc., but it is not clear that substantive harmonisation is necessary: this would proceed on the basis that facilitating international mergers is a goal of merger policy. Indeed, as the DTI notes, the arguments for harmonisation with the EC Merger Regulation are weak given the exclusive competence of the Commission where the Regulation applies and the lack of jurisdiction overlap.

Conclusions

The United Kingdom's distinctive merger control tradition with the public interest as its cornerstone has been under attack for a number of years and this Document is a culmination of that informal process. It is submitted that merger policy reform should be based on the promotion of the broad interests of the economy and it must be sceptical of the perceived benefits of mergers, given the lack of any compelling evidence of general benefits derived from them. The reforms are driven by the relentless pressure by practitioners and business for greater certainty and predictability in the law. There has been within that community growing unease over public interest competition enquiries and pejorative allegations of 'intervention on non-competition grounds'. This pressure is at the expense of a proper debate on the goals of merger policy, and the inevitable element of uncertainty in prediction involved in merger control has been ignored. The system of UK merger control has, in any event, already been informally altered to resemble the focus of the present proposals, notably by the Tebbit doctrine. Despite this, Stephen Byers, the Trade and Industry Secretary, has stressed that 'business is entitled to know that important merger decisions will not be influenced by short-term political considerations'. For instance, there were concerns expressed over the potential influence of certain Ministers in relation to the proposed BSkyB/Manchester United merger. However, 'political' and 'non-competition' considerations will inevitably be involved in some mergers and if we accept the need for a broad-based stakeholder basis for competition policy where business is not the 'consumer', then concerns regarding resort to short-term politics could be alleviated by the imposition of a duty on the Secretary of State, or alternatively the Director General, to comply with the public interest criteria in section 84 in their decision-making. It is submitted that reform of the assessment of merger situations should not focus purely on competition and that the wider public interest must be recognised. A competition and economic analysis is crucial but there are many other factors which should not be ignored. Geoffrey Howe, as the Minister for Trade Affairs, in the aftermath of the passing of the 1973 Act, summed up accurately the value of a public interest test in merger control:

> If a merger seemed likely to cause significant redundancies or to be incompatible with the Government's regional policies, the case for full investigation would be fully strengthened... What I have deliberately not attempted to do is to say what weight is to be attributed, for all time, to any particular aspects. Our national priorities change. The Government's powers must be sufficiently flexible to reflect these changing priorities.

The writer has a particular interest in regional policy and the public interest, and the concern over migration of company headquarters from Scotland following external takeovers. Interestingly, in the week following the DTI proposals there was speculation concerning the proposed takeover of Highland Distillers, a major Scottish whisky producing company, by another Glasgow-based company. As the *Herald* noted:

> Bids for large Scottish companies invariably mean a raider from south of the Border or overseas taking control. However many new jobs are created at the lower end of the scale, corporate Scotland is invariably left the poorer as the centre of decision making shifts elsewhere. Happily this is not the case with Highland Distillers.

In response to the DTI Document, similar sentiments were expressed by Unison in urging the retention of community and social interests within UK merger policy. The CBI has commented that there is little pressure for change—no doubt based on familiarity with the post-Tebbit doctrine system. In any event, it is thought that legislation is unlikely before the next General Election as the Government is likely to consider how the Competition Act 1998 'beds in', but there is the possibility that stricter time-tabling for the merger control process may be introduced in the interim.

NOTE: This critique is aimed at the initial proposals in the DTI 1999 document that were generally followed in the October 2000 document subject to minor modifications. For instance the October 2000 document proposed that the new focused competition test should be that of a 'substantial lessening of competition' in order to avoid some of the difficulties encountered under the EC Merger Regulation 4064/89 with its dominance-based test, particularly in relation to collective dominance. The 'modernizing' of the UK merger regime based on these proposals was taken forward in the DTI White Paper, 'A World Class Competition Regime' in July 2001 (Cm 5233, 2001).

DTI White Paper, *World Class Competition Regime*
Cm 5233, London, HMSO, July 2001, at pp. 23–5

- The Government is committed to introducing a new merger regime—with final decisions taken by independent competition authorities on the basis of a competition test.
- There will also be procedural and other improvements, building greater transparency into the process.
- The Government has now finalised the few remaining areas of policy—the conclusions are set out in this chapter.

5.1 The Government announced in 1999 its intention to reform the merger regime by taking most decisions out of the political arena. In October 2000, following a wide ranging consultation exercise, the Government announced its main conclusions on the way ahead. It also triggered further consultation on certain points of detail. This covered such matters as the treatment of consumer benefits in a competition-focused regime, and the development of the Competition Commission's procedures for identifying remedies. Following this consultation, the Government has taken a number of further decisions—set out below.

5.2 Government policy in recent years has been to take merger decisions primarily on competition grounds. Practice has also been for the Government to follow the advice of the competition authorities in most cases. The reform proposals build on these developments. They have two central elements. Firstly, decisions on the vast majority of mergers will be transferred from Ministers to the OFT and the Competition Commission. Secondly, the test against which mergers are assessed will be changed from a broad-based 'public interest' test to a new competition-based test. The Government is also committed to procedural and other improvements, such as the introduction of maximum statutory timetables for investigations, and building more transparency into the process.

Removing Ministers from the decision-making process

5.3 Removing Ministers from most decisions will bring the UK's merger regime into line with best practice in other countries. Decisions will be taken by those best qualified to make them— namely the expert competition authorities—in line with one of the Government's principles for competition policy.

5.4 This change will clarify arrangements and make decision-making more predictable. Business will no longer need to factor in the possibility that decisions will be influenced by political considerations.

Exceptional public interest cases

5.5 The new regime will, however, allow Ministers to continue to take final decisions on the small minority of mergers raising defined exceptional public interest issues. National security, covering essential defence interests and other public security concerns, will be defined as an exceptional public interest from the outset. Ministers will be able to define further criteria subsequently, but only by statutory instrument subject to the affirmative resolution procedure in both Houses of Parliament.

....

The competition test and the treatment of consumer benefits

5.8 In the new regime, mergers will be assessed against a test of whether they will result in a substantial lessening of competition. Making competition the focus of the assessment will ensure that the underlying economic arguments can be brought to bear on the analysis of a merger in a clear and straightforward manner.

5.9 The Government recognises, however, that there will occasionally be circumstances where a merger which results in a substantial lessening of competition can, nonetheless, bring overall benefits to consumers. The challenge is to identify a framework which allows such benefits—which will arise only infrequently—to be taken into account without undermining the central importance of the competition analysis.

5.10 In October, the Government sought views on how to take this issue forward. In the light of comments received, the Government has decided to proceed as follows:
- The competition test will be at the heart of the assessment carried out by the competition authorities. The authorities will be required to reach a clear view on the competition

---

Box 5.1: How will the new merger regime work?

- Final decisions on most mergers will be taken by independent competition authorities rather than Ministers.

- The test they will apply will be to determine whether the merger results in a substantial lessening of competition rather than the current public interest test.

- Exceptionally, where competition considerations point the other way, it will be possible for the authorities to clear a merger or allow it to proceed with less stringent competition remedies where they believe it will bring overall consumer benefits.

- The Secretary of State for Trade and Industry will continue to decide the small minority of mergers which raise defined exceptional public interest issues.

- National security will be defined at the outset as an exceptional public interest issue. It will be possible to define further exceptional public interest issues by statutory instrument using the affirmative resolution procedure.

- The new regime will retain a two-stage approach to merger investigations. The OFT will carry out first stage investigations which will be sufficient to decide most cases. The Competition Commission will continue to carry out second stage, in depth investigations where necessary.

- There will be statutory maximum timetables for both first and second stage investigations by the competition authorities. There will also continue to be the option of an administrative timetable at stage one.

- The criteria used to determine which mergers qualify for investigation will be modernised to focus more efficiently on cases that may raise concerns.

- The UK's system of voluntary rather than compulsory pre-notification of mergers will be retained.

aspects of each case. A merger will be cleared unless the authorities expect it would result in a substantial lessening of competition in any UK market.

- Where a merger fails the competition test, the authorities will have to take steps to remedy the competition problem.
- However, the authorities will—exceptionally—be able to clear a merger or allow it to proceed with less stringent competition remedies than would otherwise be the case where they believe that the merger will bring overall benefits to UK consumers affected by the merger.
- The authorities will be able to take account of consumer benefits which take the form of lower prices, or greater innovation, choice or quality of products or services. They must expect such benefits to materialise within a reasonable period and be satisfied they would be unlikely to happen without the merger.
- Consumer benefits will cover benefits to end-consumers, but will also extend to customer benefits in upstream markets where the immediate beneficiaries of a merger are other businesses.

NOTE: These proposals sought to effectively depoliticize merger control law by removing ministerial involvement and the public interest test, although there would remain scope for the introduction of exceptional public interest criteria. The insertion of a new consumer benefit test in relation to merger control is notable.

■ QUESTION

Do you agree that the 1973 Act merger control system was outdated and that the public interest test needed to be replaced?

SECTION 4: **ENTERPRISE ACT 2002, PART 3**

UK merger control is now set out in Part 3 of the EA 2002. This part of the Act is immensely complicated and only the key features will be outlined in this section. We shall focus on the main institutions and processes, and outline some of the practice to date. Essentially there are two institutions and two key processes. Initial investigation and referral is undertaken by the Office of Fair Trading, and the fuller inquiry and reporting stage is undertaken by the Competition Commission. This stage and the role of the Competition Commission also now incorporates enforcement and the appropriate remedies that may be required.

A: The referral stage

The new system seeks to remove politicians from the merger control process, except in certain defined cases, both at the stage of referral and subsequent enforcement.

DTI, *Government Response to Consultation*
December 2001, p. 5

Removing Ministers from merger decisions [paragraphs 5.3–5.7]

10. The White Paper re-iterated the Government's decision to remove Ministers from all merger decisions, other than those raising defined exceptional public interest issues.

11. There continues to be almost unanimous support for the principle of removing Ministers from the vast majority of merger decisions. Some respondents said that if the Competition Commission (CC) was to be given the final decision-making role on remedies both here and following market investigations, its procedures and composition needed to be improved and its accountability enhanced.

Government's response

The Government intends to press ahead with the removal of all but a tiny minority of merger decisions from Ministers. Decisions will be taken by those best qualified to make them—namely the expert competition authorities.

The Government intends to enhance the accountability of the competition authorities. There will be greater transparency in the operation of the new regime, and a new statutory right of appeal against certain decisions. The OFT and CC will be required to publish reasons for their important decisions, building on recent trends towards greater transparency. The CC Chairman will be required to set procedural rules for CC reporting groups so there will be greater certainty about how enquiries will be handled. The Government is also inviting Parliament through its Select Committees to play an active role in the scrutiny of the competition regime.

NOTE: This aspect was keenly debated in Parliament, and, although there were some concerns regarding the lack of democratic accountability in relation to mergers that may have serious repercussions on the economy, the greater independence of the competition authorities was generally supported. There are particular provisions for public interest mergers and special public interest mergers that we shall discuss briefly below. Accordingly, generally it will be for the OFT to decide whether to refer a merger to the Competition Commission. There are a number of stages in determining whether a merger qualifies for referral. First, if a merger has a Community dimension, thereby falling within the scope of Merger Regulation 139/2004, as discussed in Chapter 12, the European Commission has sole competence under Article 21(3) of the Regulation to assess the merger. The UK authorities are precluded from using national merger controls unless they seek resort to Articles 9 or 21(4) of the Regulation. Second, a merger situation must be established.

ENTERPRISE ACT 2002 [S. 23]

Relevant merger situations

23.—(1) For the purposes of this Part, a relevant merger situation has been created if—

    (a) two or more enterprises have ceased to be distinct enterprises at a time or in circumstances falling within section 24; and

    (b) the value of the turnover in the United Kingdom of the enterprise being taken over exceeds £70 million.

(2) For the purposes of this Part, a relevant merger situation has also been created if—

    (a) two or more enterprises have ceased to be distinct enterprises at a time or in circumstances falling within section 24; and

    (b) as a result, one or both of the conditions mentioned in subsections (3) and (4) below prevails or prevails to a greater extent.

(3) The condition mentioned in this subsection is that, in relation to the supply of goods of any description, at least one-quarter of all the goods of that description which are supplied in the United Kingdom, or in a substantial part of the United Kingdom—

    (a) are supplied by one and the same person or are supplied to one and the same person; or

    (b) are supplied by the persons by whom the enterprises concerned are carried on, or are supplied to those persons.

(4) The condition mentioned in this subsection is that, in relation to the supply of services of any description, the supply of services of that description in the United Kingdom, or in a substantial part of the United Kingdom, is to the extent of at least one-quarter—

    (a) supply by one and the same person, or supply for one and the same person; or

    (b) supply by the persons by whom the enterprises concerned are carried on, or supply for those persons.

(5) For the purpose of deciding whether the proportion of one-quarter mentioned in subsection (3) or (4) is fulfilled with respect to goods or (as the case may be) services of any description, the decision-making authority shall apply such criterion (whether value, cost, price, quantity, capacity, number of workers employed or some other criterion, of whatever nature), or such combination of criteria, as the decision-making authority considers appropriate.

(6) References in subsections (3) and (4) to the supply of goods or (as the case may be) services shall, in relation to goods or services of any description which are the subject of different forms of supply, be construed in whichever of the following ways the decision-making authority considers appropriate—
   (a) as references to any of those forms of supply taken separately;
   (b) as references to all those forms of supply taken together; or
   (c) as references to any of those forms of supply taken in groups.

(7) For the purposes of subsection (6) the decision-making authority may treat goods or services as being the subject of different forms of supply whenever—
   (a) the transactions concerned differ as to their nature, their parties, their terms or their surrounding circumstances; and
   (b) the difference is one which, in the opinion of the decision-making authority, ought for the purposes of that subsection to be treated as a material difference.

(8) The criteria for deciding when goods or services can be treated, for the purposes of this section, as goods or services of a separate description shall be such as in any particular case the decision-making authority considers appropriate in the circumstances of that case.

(9) For the purposes of this Chapter, the question whether a relevant merger situation has been created shall be determined as at—
   (a) in the case of a reference which is treated as having been made under section 22 by virtue of section 37(2), such time as the Commission may determine; and
   (b) in any other case, immediately before the time when the reference has been, or is to be, made.

NOTE: As under the FTA 1973, this requires that the enterprises have ceased to be distinct, as determined by ss. 26 and 27 (and s. 29 re obtaining control by stages). It is important to understand that common ownership or control does not only arise where 100 per cent of a company's shares are acquired. Effective control may be derived from the acquisition of a lesser shareholding, even where this does not include a majority of the shares and voting rights, partly dependent on the spread of ownership of the remainder of the shares. In addition, the merger must satisfy one of two additional tests. The key change here is the replacement of the assets value test with a turnover test, calculated in accordance with s. 28. The alternative, market-share, test reflects the competition concern regarding increased concentration in the market following the merger, but is less commonly resorted to at the referral stage. The Act requires the 25 per cent market share to be held in the UK, or in a substantial part of the UK. In *R* v *Monopolies and Mergers Commission, ex parte South Yorkshire Transport Ltd* [1993] 1 All ER 289 it was noted that 'the reference area must be … of such size, character and importance as to make it worth consideration for the purposes of the Act' (at p. 297). This test was subsequently applied in *Stagecoach Holdings plc* v *Secretary of State for Trade and Industry* 1997 SLT 940, OH.

The key changes in approach under the EA 2002 are set out in s. 22 (and s. 33 for anticipated mergers), which provides the OFT with formal referral criteria.

ENTERPRISE ACT 2002 [S. 22(1)–(2)]

Duty to make references in relation to completed mergers

22.—(1) The OFT shall, subject to subsections (2) and (3), make a reference to the Commission if the OFT believes that it is or may be the case that—
   (a) a relevant merger situation has been created; and

(b) the creation of that situation has resulted, or may be expected to result, in a substantial lessening of competition within any market or markets in the United Kingdom for goods or services.

(2) The OFT may decide not to make a reference under this section if it believes that—

(a) the market concerned is not, or the markets concerned are not, of sufficient importance to justify the making of a reference to the Commission; or

(b) any relevant customer benefits in relation to the creation of the relevant merger situation concerned outweigh the substantial lessening of competition concerned and any adverse effects of the substantial lessening of competition concerned.

NOTE: The key reform is that the OFT is under a duty to refer a merger, provided it believes that the merger will result in a substantial lessening of competition. The OFT's role and duty in making references was considered by the CAT and the Court of Appeal in *IBA Healthcare Ltd* v *Office of Fair Trading* [2003] CAT 27, [2004] 4 All ER 1103.

IBA Healthcare Ltd v *Office of Fair Trading*
[2003] CAT 27, [2004] 4 All ER 1103

IBA Health, a third-party competitor, challenged the OFT's decision not to refer the proposed acquisition by iSOFT Group plc of Torex plc to the Competition Commission. Both parties were involved in the supply of software and IT systems to the healthcare industry with fairly high combined market shares. The CAT stressed the differing roles of the OFT and Competition Commission, and held that the OFT was obliged to refer where there was a credible alternative view of the competitive impact of the merger. This decision was criticized as likely to significantly increase the number of references and have implications for the level of merger activity in the UK. The Court of Appeal overturned the CAT's interpretation of the statutory reference provision. (In this case s. 33, as opposed to s. 22, as it was an anticipated merger.)

Scott, A., 'The cutting of teeth, IBA Health v Office of Fair Trading'
[2004] Journal of Business Law at 672 and pp. 681–2 [footnotes omitted]

The *IBA Health* case involved two central themes: that which centred on the interpretation of s.33(1), and that regarding the extent of the duty of the OFT to provide sufficient reasons in substantiation of its findings. The latter point has been conclusively determined, and on the facts of the case saw the iSOFT/Torex merger remitted to the OFT. In contrast, on the former issue the judgment of the Court of Appeal left some uncertainty.

The CAT had sought to impose what was in effect an objective standard for the review of the merger assessments conducted by the OFT, and ruminated on the degree of credibility that would be required of alternative arguments before they should be taken into account. The Court of Appeal rejected the two-limb test that introduced the objective standard. Both substantive judgments included musings, however, on the degree of credibility that a hypothesis as to impact on competition must evince before being countenanced by the OFT. Like the CAT, the Court was happy to "exclude the purely fanciful because the OFT acting reasonably is not going to believe that the fanciful may be the case". Beyond this, the court left a "wide margin in which the OFT is required to exercise its judgment". It deemed it inappropriate "to attempt any more exact mathematical formulation of the degree of likelihood which OFT acting reasonably must require", but indicated that 50 per cent credibility would certainly be enough while even something less than that might be. On this basis Sir Andrew Morritt V.C. and Carnwath L.J. agreed that the reference to "significance" in guidance published by the OFT "tends to put the requisite likelihood too far up the scale of probability".

NOTE: Subsequently, the OFT revised its Guidance on when the reference test would be met (see also Parr, N., 'Merger control in the Wake of IBA Health' [2007] Comp LJ 282). The OFT and Competition commission are consulting on draft joint merger guidelines.

Mergers: Substantive assessment guidance
OFT 516, amended by OFT 516a, October 2004 [footnotes omitted]

3.2 The test for reference will be met if the OFT has a reasonable belief, objectively justified by relevant facts, that there is a realistic prospect that the merger will lessen competition substantially. By the term 'realistic prospect', the OFT means not only a prospect that has more than a 50 per cent chance of occurring, but also a prospect that is not fanciful but has less than a 50 per cent chance of occurring.

- This test differs from that used by the CC in its merger enquiries, reflecting the fact that the OFT is a first screen while the CC is determinative. Hence the threshold applied by the OFT for making a merger reference imports a lower degree of likelihood than the CC's threshold for *deciding* that a merger may be expected to lessen competition substantially.
- The OFT's test will be met where the OFT believes that there is more than a 50 per cent chance of a merger resulting in a substantial lessening of competition, because the OFT's view of such a merger is that it is 'more likely than not' to result in a substantial lessening of competition. In such cases, the degree of likelihood required for reference is necessarily met since the OFT believes that it is the case the merger may be expected to result in a substantial lessening of competition.
- The OFT's test may be met in other cases where the OFT believes that there is less than a 50 per cent chance of a merger resulting in a substantial lessening of competition. However, in such cases there is no exact mathematical formulation of the degree of likelihood which the OFT acting reasonably must require in order to make a merger reference. Between the fanciful and a degree of likelihood less than 50 per cent there is a wide margin in which the OFT must exercise its judgment as to whether it may be the case that the merger may be expected to result in a substantial lessening of competition.
- Merger review involves assessment of uncertain future prospects, often on the basis of imperfect information and in a limited time frame. The degree of uncertainty may vary from case to case depending on the subject-matter of the merger and the nature and scope of evidence available to the OFT. Whilst the OFT will seek information of its own initiative, the more comprehensive the information available to the OFT, the more confident it will be as to the possible effect of the merger. So, where the information available to the OFT is full and extensive, the degree of likelihood that the OFT must require to believe that it may be the case that a merger may be expected to result in a substantial lessening of competition may be higher up the scale of probability (albeit less than 50 per cent) than compared to when there is less information available, particularly as regards central points in the analysis. Merging parties and third parties are therefore encouraged to provide relevant information on a timely basis, whether or not it is expressly sought by the OFT.

NOTE: Section 22(2) contains a *de minimis* provision and also allows the OFT not to refer a merger where the consumer benefits outweigh the adverse competition consequences of the merger. In addition, the OFT may not refer a merger where the 'failing firm' defence has been satisfied, as demonstrated by the OFT clearance of the acquisition of Zavvi Stores by HMV in April 2009. There are similar provisions in relation to anticipated mergers (s. 33). Note also that the EA2002 contains provisions, similar to those under the FTA 1973, for avoiding references by giving undertakings to the OFT to alleviate the OFT's concerns about the merger. These can be structural undertakings, such as to divest assets or brands from the merged enterprise, or they can be behavioural undertakings, entailing a commitment to modify behaviour post-merger regarding issues such as pricing and service levels. Like the FTA 1973, the EA 2002 provides for references of mergers that have already taken place and for proposed (anticipated) mergers. In respect of the latter, although there is no compulsory pre-notification, there is the possibility for parties to seek confidential guidance as to whether their proposed merger is likely to be referred, although the guidance is not binding. In addition there exists the more formal mechanism of statutory pre-notification of the merger under ss. 96 and 97 of the Act where a final, formal decision is guaranteed within 30 days, failing which the merger cannot be referred to the Competition Commission.

The following is the text of the reference made by the OFT under the EA 2002 in relation to *Heinz/HP Foods Group*.

Heinz/HP Foods Group

CR/170/05

Completed Acquisition by HJ Heinz of HP Foods Limited, HP Food Holdings Limited and HP Foods International Limited

Terms of reference

1. Whereas in exercise of its duty under section 22(1) of the Enterprise Act 2002 ("the Act") to make a reference to the Competition Commission ("the Commission") in relation to a completed merger the Office of Fair Trading ("the OFT") believes that it is or may be the case that-

(a) a relevant merger situation has been created in that:

(i) enterprises carried on by or under the control of HJ Heinz Company will cease to be distinct form enterprises carried on by or under the control of HP Foods Holdings Limited and HP Foods International Limited; and

(ii) the value of the turnover in the United Kingdom of the enterprises carried on by or under the control of HP Foods Limited, HP Foods Holdings Limited and HP Foods International Limited exceeds £70 million; and

(b) the creation of that situation has resulted, or may be expected to result, in a substantial lessening of competition within any market or markets in the United Kingdom for goods or services, namely the markets for the supply of tomato ketchup, the supply of brown sauce, the supply of barbecue sauce, and the supply of tinned baked beans and tinned pasta products to retail customers in the United Kingdom.

2. Now therefore the OFT in exercise of its duty under section 22 of the Act, hereby refers to the Commission, for investigation and report within a period ending on 11 April 2006, the following questions in accordance with section 35 of the Act -

(a) whether a relevant merger situation has been created; and

(b) if so, whether the creation of that situation has resulted, or may be expected to result in a substantial lessening of competition within any market or markets in the United Kingdom for goods or services.

3. In relation to the question whether a relevant merger situation will be created, the Commission shall exclude from consideration one of the subsections (1) and (2) of section 23 of the Act if they find that the other is satisfied.

Vincent Smith
Director of Competition Enforcement, Office of Fair Trading
26 October 2005

■ QUESTION

How has the OFT's task in relation to merger control become more onerous under the EA 2002?

B: The Competition Commission inquiry

Introduction

The two main differences from the FTA 1973 are the introduction of a competition test at the core of the Competition Commission's inquiry, and the role for the Commission in deciding upon remedies. The Commission is first required to be satisfied that the statutory criteria for investigating the merger are met. The Commission is then required to determine whether the merger situation has resulted, or may be expected to result, in a substantial lessening of competition, as set out in ss. 35(1) and 36(1) of the Act, in relation to completed and anticipated mergers respectively.

The appropriate competition test was the subject of considerable debate following the White Paper, *World Class Competition Regime*, 2001.

DTI Government Response to Consultation
December 2001, p. 6, paras 5.8–5.10

The competition test and treatment of consumer benefits [paragraphs 5.8–5.10]

12. The White Paper re-iterated the Government's intention to replace the current public interest test for assessing mergers with a test based on whether mergers will result in a substantial lessening of competition. The White Paper set out the circumstances in which the authorities will be able to take account of consumer benefits in deciding what remedies to apply to a merger that has failed the competition test.

13. Responses to the White Paper showed continuing strong support for the decision to adopt a test focused on a substantial lessening of competition. A small minority of respondents continued to prefer the 'dominance' test that is applied under the European Community Merger Regulation. They felt that this would avoid creating a divergence with EU arrangements, and that the proposed domestic test represented a more stringent standard for assessing mergers. A number of respondents said that there would need to be a clear understanding of how the authorities would apply the new test.

14. There was strong support, particularly from business, for the Government's decision announced in the White Paper, that the competition authorities should be able to take account of customer benefits in upstream markets where the immediate beneficiaries were other businesses, as well as benefits to end-consumers.

15. Three respondents objected to the narrow competition focus of the new test. These respondents considered that other issues such as employment, the environment and the impact on local communities should be capable of being taken into account.

16. Two respondents connected with the water sector asked about the Government's plans regarding the future of the special regime for assessing water company mergers.

Government's response

The Government intends to replace the current public interest test with a substantial lessening of competition test. This will allow the competition authorities to take action whenever there is an increase of sole, joint or collective market power as a result of a merger. The competition authorities will publish guidance on the way the competition test will be applied in referring and assessing mergers.

NOTE: Ultimately, the American model of 'substantial lessening of competition' ('SLC') was adopted. The SLC test would avoid the difficulties evidenced by the application of the collective dominance test under the Merger Regulation, before it was revised in Regulation 139/2004. Sections 35 and 36 use the term 'anti-competitive outcome' as shorthand for satisfaction of the SLC test.

In order to discharge its functions, the Competition Commission has developed a set of procedures for the investigation of a merger situation. At the beginning of an inquiry the Competition Commission identifies parties that are likely to have an interest in the matter, such as the companies most directly involved, customers and consumer bodies and it will approach these parties for evidence. In addition, press advertisements are used to invite other interested persons to give their views. Questionnaires are often sent to the companies involved in a merger. After it has collected this initial evidence and information the Commission will publish an issues statement, and it will subsequently consider responses to that statement before publishing its provisional findings and proposed remedies for a further round of consultation, prior to publication of the final report. It is clear that the Commission group dealing with a merger inquiry must gain an understanding of the position in the relevant industry in a relatively short period of time. Although the merger control provisions have been criticized in the past for the delays they produce in commercial and strategic business planning, given the complexity of many of the industries under investigation, such as brewing and banking, a maximum period of 32 weeks (including a possible eight-week extension) does not appear to be particularly long.

The following are excerpts from the two key stages in the inquiry process in relation to recent inquiries to give a flavour of the Commission's investigation process.

Issues Statement, *HMV Group plc/Waterstone's plc/Ottakar's plc*
25 January 2006

The issues that the CC intends to consider are:

Assessment of the competitive effects of the proposed merger
The inquiry group (the Group) would like to explore the competitive effects of the proposed merger within any relevant market compared with what would be likely to occur in the absence of the merger (the counterfactual). In particular, the Group will consider:

Underlying factors
  (a) whether there are identifiable trends in the market which have had, or are likely to have, a significant effect on competition in any relevant market in the short to medium term;
  (b) whether new technologies (eg e-books, print-on-demand) might significantly affect competition in any relevant market in the short to medium term;

Competitive effects
  (c) whether, and if so to what extent, Waterstone's and Ottakar's have competed with each other historically, currently compete, or are likely to compete in the future;
  (d) whether, and if so to what extent, Waterstone's and Ottakar's have faced in the past, currently face, or are likely to face actual and/or potential competition from other 'bricks and mortar' book retailers (eg WHSmiths, Borders/Books etc, independent book retailers);
  (e) whether, and if so to what extent, Waterstone's and Ottakar's have faced in the past, currently face, or are likely to face actual and/or potential competition from other retailers including supermarkets, Internet retailers, book clubs etc;
  (f) whether any competition between 'bricks and mortar' retailers is primarily local, regional or national in nature;
  (g) whether any competition between Waterstone's, Ottakar's, and other retailers is competition on price and/or on non-price factors;
  (h) whether publishers' Recommended Retail Prices (RRPs) act as effective ceilings for retail prices and how the RRPs, and associated discounts negotiated between publishers and retailers, affect retail competition;

(i) whether the proposed merger might be expected to create or increase the exercise of market power by the merged entity in any relevant market at a local, regional or national level, and lead to

   (i) an increase in price (ie reduction in the level of discount off RRP offered to customers); and/or

   (ii) a reduction in range of books; and/or

   (iii) a reduction in quality of service; and/or

   (iv) a reduction in innovation;

and if so which customers would be affected and in what ways;

(j) whether the proposed merger might be expected to create or increase the exercise of market power by the merged entity in any relevant market and lead to a reduction in the number of independent book retailers, and if so what effect this might have on customers;

(k) whether, and if so to what extent, the proposed merger would reduce the opportunities for publishers to get their books stocked, and if so whether this would lead to a reduction in the range of books available to customers;

(l) whether, and if so to what extent, the proposed merger would result in fewer promotions of new titles by book retailers considered by customers as specialists, leading to:

   (i) fewer opportunities for the creation of 'bestsellers'; and/or

   (ii) fewer opportunities for other books to achieve a reasonable volume of sales;

(m) whether, and if so to what extent, the proposed merger might increase the bargaining power of retailers with respect to publishers which might be expected to cause authors and/or publishers to:

   (i) reduce the numbers of books published; and/or

   (ii) increase the RRP of certain books; and/or

   (iii) exit the market; ...

NOTE: Subsequently, the Commission considered that this merger would not result in a substantial lessening of competition and it was cleared.

Provisional findings report, *Somerfield/Morrisons Store Mergers Inquiry*
July 2005, paras 3–4 and 9–10

3. The focus of the 2003 Safeway inquiry was on larger stores. In contrast, in this inquiry the vast majority of the acquired stores are 'mid-range' stores and Somerfield, in particular, argued that a fresh look should be taken at the methodology previously used. Against this background we examined the methodology used in previous CC inquiries into mid-range stores; and considered the evidence from Somerfield and others on whether and, if so, how mid-range stores might be assessed on a different basis from that used in previous inquiries. We then determined a methodology appropriate to this inquiry.

4. We had no concerns that the merger would adversely affect competition at a national level. At a local level, as is apparent in much of the evidence we received, there is a considerable diversity in the particular characteristics of mid-range stores and the local markets they serve. We therefore adopted a two-stage approach. In Stage 1 we identified relevant product and geographic markets, and a rule that could be applied to identify those possible problem markets in which there may be some initial concern that the transaction may result in a substantial lessening of competition (SLC). We deliberately adopted an inclusive approach to ensure we captured all of the acquired stores where there may be a potential competition problem. In Stage 2 we then carried out a detailed competitive assessment of each of the local markets thus identified ....

9. We identified 14 stores, whose acquisition, in our view, had significantly reduced competition. They included three acquired stores where, following the merger, Somerfield had closed its existing stores, located close to the acquired stores, but where Somerfield still retains its interest in them. We did not feel we could rely upon the prospect of new entry to resolve any lessening of competition in any of these 14 areas. One of those stores, about which we were concerned, was a convenience store, at Filey; in the particular circumstances of that town, we considered that we could not rely on new entry from the opening of either a new convenience store, or of a larger store.

10. We therefore concluded that the acquisition may be expected to result in an SLC in each of the local markets served by those 14 stores, resulting in higher prices, or reduction in quality,

range or service. In addition, we concluded there would be the adverse effects on customers in those markets from a reduction of choice between competing stores, for example between different prices available for particular products, or between different quality or range of goods on offer or service provided.

NOTE: Subsequently, the Commission considered that this merger would result in a substantial lessening of competition and required 12 stores to be divested to allow the merger to proceed. This was the subject of an unsuccessful judicial review challenge at the CAT, as discussed below.

Merger inquiry practice to date

The following excerpts are from high-profile Commission reports in the latter years of the FTA 1973. Even though the process and substantive tests as laid out in the relevant legislation have been revised, it is instructive to look at these older reports as they provide a flavour of the merger control process and demonstrate a focus on competition issues such that the outcome is likely to have been identical under the EA 2002 provisions.

Competition Commission Summary of Ladbroke/Coral Report
Cm 4030, 1998

The Secretary of State for Trade and Industry asked us to investigate the implications for the public interest of the acquisition by Ladbroke Group PLC (Ladbroke) on 31 December 1997 of the Coral betting business from Bass PLC (Bass) (see Appendix 1.1 for our terms of reference).

Ladbroke is the largest firm in the UK off-course betting industry with a chain of some 1,900 licensed betting offices (LBOs). Its total turnover from LBOs and from its telephone betting business in 1997 was some £1.75 billion. Coral was number three in the industry, with a UK chain of 833 LBOs and a total turnover in 1996/97 of nearly £900 million. The only other national chain of LBOs is that of the William Hill Organization Limited (William Hill).

There are a number of distinctive features to the off-course betting market. Regulation of the industry on public policy grounds plays an important role, and has taken a form which has restrained competition. Moreover most bets are placed at prices (odds) which are not set in the off-course market but are determined in the on-course market at horse and greyhound race meetings in the form of board prices and starting prices.

We received submissions from about 90 third parties and held a larger than usual number of hearings. Many (but not all) of the third party submissions were, to a greater or lesser degree, hostile to the merger in its entirety or to major aspects of it.

For its part, Ladbroke argued that its acquisition of Coral did not present problems for the public interest for the following reasons:

- In keeping with the main thrust of our predecessors' report in 1989 on the Mecca/William Hill merger, competition among LBO operators was essentially a local matter; in this fundamental respect, the market had not changed;
- Since most racing betting was at prices determined by the operation of on-course markets, there was little scope for price variation in off-course LBOs;
- Punters' choice of LBOs was determined primarily by convenience of location, but secondarily by the quality of outlet and the service provided;
- Possession of a well-known brand name brought little competitive advantage; and
- Independent firms were fully capable of providing effective competition to outlets of the national chains.

Ladbroke said that in order to address the situation where, in local markets defined in terms of a 400 metre radius as used in our predecessors' report, the merger would eliminate competition, it had entered into a conditional agreement to sell 134 LBOs to Tote Bookmakers Limited (Tote

Bookmakers). During the course of the inquiry, Ladbroke also proposed to dispose of two more tranches, of 98 and 69 LBOs respectively, the two Coral greyhound race tracks, and the Coral telephone betting business together with the Coral brand.

In our view there is an important national component to competition in the provision of off-course betting services through pricing and through branding and quality of outlet. We believe this could be enhanced in an appropriate competitive environment. In particular, there is scope for price competition in the provision of early prices for racing bets, in the odds offered on other sports and numbers betting and in the terms of betting offered by different firms and outlets. The steps taken since 1989 to deregulate some aspects of the industry and its relations with customers, together with the effect of the National Lottery on public attitudes to gambling, have led us to the view that the further development of competition is both practicable and to be encouraged.

The merger increases Ladbroke's share of LBOs from 21 to 30 per cent and its share of off-course betting turnover from 26 to 38 per cent (these figures do not take account of the—relatively small—effect of the conditional sale of LBOs to Tote Bookmakers). As a consequence, Ladbroke has markedly increased its lead in the national retail betting market and its size in that market relative to William Hill. The merger also has the effect of removing Coral, which we consider to have been an important third national competitive force in this market. The structural effects of the merger are therefore quite different from those addressed in the 1989 report. That report, moreover, warned of the future risks of growing concentration of the market at national level.

The effect of this merger would, in our view, be to lead to a weakening of price competition, actual and potential, at national level to the detriment of punters. We also believe the merger would have a dampening effect on innovation and reduce punters' choice of major LBO chains. Prices and standards of service in telephone betting may be expected to be less favourable to punters.

As in much of retailing, the preservation of consumer choice at the local level is important. As national chains become more influential and market concentration increases in the provision of LBO services, so competition for sites in individual localities becomes an important element of the search for market share. In our view this merger will have significant adverse effects in reducing local choice and these effects go beyond the 134 local markets where Ladbroke has entered into a conditional agreement to dispose of outlets to Tote Bookmakers.

There are a number of other aspects on which the merger has consequences which, to a greater or lesser extent, we regard as undesirable, although as a Group we have made no formal findings with respect to them. These concern Satellite Information Services (Holdings) Limited, which supplies a televised information service to LBOs; Bookmakers' Afternoon Greyhound Services Limited (BAGS), which arranges for greyhound meetings to be held at times suitable for LBO punters to bet on; the betting industry's relationship with horse racing; and employment. However, two of us believe that the strengthening of Ladbroke's position in BAGS and in the ownership of greyhound tracks would have adverse effects on the public interest, additional to those described in paragraphs 1.8 to 1.10.

The adverse effects of the merger described in paragraphs 1.8 to 1.10 are not, in our view, offset by benefits and we conclude that the merger is against the public interest. We consider that the adverse effects can only effectively be remedied by restoring an industry structure which is conducive to the development of competition. This would best be achieved by Ladbroke divesting, as a single business, the entirety of Coral's UK business which it acquired from Bass, including those Coral LBOs which are part of Ladbroke's conditional agreement with Tote Bookmakers. We would not, however, rule out the possibility of its sale in more than one part if that seemed likely to lead to a more robust competitive environment. We therefore recommend that Ladbroke be required to divest the Coral business in a manner approved by the Director General of Fair Trading within six months of the publication of our report.

Competition Commission Summary of BSkyB/Man Utd Report
Cm 4305, 1999

On 29 October 1998 the Secretary of State referred to us the proposed acquisition by British Sky Broadcasting Group plc (BSkyB) of Manchester United PLC (Manchester United). Our terms of reference are in Appendix 1.1. We have concluded that arrangements are in progress or in contemplation which, if carried into effect, will result in the creation of a merger situation qualifying for investigation.

BSkyB is a vertically integrated broadcaster which buys TV rights, including those for sporting events, makes some of its own programmes, packages programmes from a range of sources into various channels, and distributes and retails these channels to its subscribers using its direct-to-home satellite platform as well as selling them wholesale to other retailers using different distribution platforms.

On all relevant measures, Manchester United is the strongest English football club. Its football-related activities include the supply of TV rights for its matches. At present the rights to Manchester United's Premier League matches, together with those of other Premier League clubs, are sold collectively by the Premier League itself. This arrangement is currently the subject of a Restrictive Practices Court (RPC) case brought by the Director General of Fair Trading.

We have concluded that the relevant football market in which Manchester United operates is no wider than the matches of Premier League clubs. We considered whether the broadcasting market in which BSkyB operates ought to compromise both pay TV and free-to-air TV and concluded that it was more appropriate to treat pay TV as a separate market. Based primarily on considerations of substitutability, we concluded that the relevant market for our purposes was for sports premium TV channels.

Except for small niche channels, BSkyB is currently the only provider of sports premium channels. Entry into this market depends crucially upon the ability of a channel provider to obtain the appropriate live sports rights. We think it unlikely that there are enough such rights to sustain many sports premium channels and BSkyB currently provides three. BSkyB's very high market share together with the difficulties of entry lead us to conclude that BSkyB has market power in the sports premium channel market.

In considering the public interest consequences of the merger, we looked primarily at its effect on competition among broadcasters for live Premier League rights. Because of uncertainties about the outcome of the RPC case on the collective selling of Premier League rights, we considered four scenarios, one or other of which may be expected to occur.

Our first scenario involved the continuation of existing collective selling arrangements and no other mergers between broadcasters and Premier League clubs. We have concluded that under this scenario, BSkyB would, as a result of the merger, gain influence over and information about the Premier League's selling of rights that would not be available to its competitors. It would also benefit from its ownership stake in Premier League rights, providing a further advantage in the bidding process.

Taken together, these factors would significantly improve BSkyB's chances of securing the Premier League's rights. We would expect this to influence the behaviour of BSkyB's competitors causing them to bid more cautiously than would otherwise be the case and, in some cases, even not to bid at all. This would enhance BSkyB's already strong position arising from its market power as a sports premium channel provider and from being the incumbent broadcaster of Premier League football. The effect would be to reduce competition for Premier League rights leading to less choice for the Premier League and less scope for innovation in the broadcasting of Premier League football.

Under our other scenarios we have concluded that:

(a) If the live rights of Premier League clubs were to be sold on an individual basis and there were no other mergers between broadcasters and clubs, BSkyB would, as a result of the merger, have substantial advantages over other broadcasters competing for the rights. This would have adverse effects for competition similar to those we identified under our first scenario.

(b) If existing selling arrangements continued and the BSkyB/Manchester United merger were to precipitate a further merger between a broadcaster and a Premier League club, the effects would be broadly similar to those of our first scenario. If there were several mergers between broadcasters and Premier League clubs precipitated by the BSkyB/Manchester United merger, then we believe that collective selling would continue only if broadcasters agreed among themselves to share the rights, which would have at least as adverse an effect on competition as our first scenario.

If rights were sold on an individual basis and there were several mergers between broadcasters and Premier League clubs precipitated by the BSkyB/Manchester United merger, all of the feasible outcomes would be less competitive than the situation in which rights were individually sold and no broadcaster/Premier League club mergers had occurred.

In most of the situations described in paragraphs 1.7 to 1.9, the merger would enhance BSkyB's ability to secure the Premier League rights in the future. We would expect this further to restrict entry into the sports premium channel market by new channel providers, causing the prices of BSkyB's sports channels to be higher and choice and innovation less than they otherwise would be. Reduced entry by sports premium channel providers would feed through into reduced competition in the wider pay TV market.

We conclude that, under all of the scenarios described in paragraphs 1.7 to 1.9, the merger may be expected to reduce competition for Premier League rights with the consequential adverse effects we have identified.

We have based our public interest conclusions mainly on the effects of the merger on competition among broadcasters. However, we also think that the merger would adversely affect football in two ways. Firstly, it would reinforce the existing trend towards greater inequality of wealth between clubs, thus weakening the smaller ones. Second, it would give BSkyB additional influence over Premier League decisions relating to the organisation of football, leading to some decisions which did not reflect the long-term interests of football. On both counts the merger may be expected to have the adverse effect of damaging the quality of British football. This adverse effect would be more pronounced if the merger precipitated other mergers between broadcasters and Premier League clubs.

We were unable to identify any public interest benefits from the proposed merger. We therefore conclude that the proposed merger between BSkyB and Manchester United may be expected to operate against the public interest.

We considered whether the adverse effects we have identified could be remedied by undertakings by BSkyB. We did not find any that we regarded as effective. We think that the adverse effects are sufficiently serious that prohibiting the merger is both an appropriate and a proportionate remedy. Accordingly, we recommend that the acquisition of Manchester United by BSkyB should be prohibited.

NOTE: These reports demonstrate that the merger control provisions may impact upon many aspects of our lives. For instance, if Ladbroke had been allowed to proceed with their merger with Coral, there would have been one fewer 'big' bookmaker in the market and it was likely that competition would have been reduced, resulting in lower odds, and less winnings for 'punters'. The Commission report on the competition consequences of the BSkyB/Man Utd merger, perhaps the most contentious merger in the last 20 years, was not favourable. In addition, the Commission highlighted the problems stemming from exacerbating inequality between football clubs and demonstrated its concern over the long-term effects on English football. Both of these mergers were blocked on the basis of the Commission's report.

There has also been considerable practice under the new provisions. The following are excerpts of the Report following the first full inquiry under the EA 2002, *Stena/P&O*, and also from the *Stagecoach/Scottish Citylink* Report.

Competition Commission Summary of Stena/P&O Report
Feb 2004

1. On 22 August 2003, the Office of Fair Trading (OFT) referred the proposed acquisition by Stena of certain assets operated by P&O on the Irish Sea to the Competition Commission (CC) for investigation and report. The reference was made under section 33(1) of the Enterprise Act 2002 (the Act). We are required to publish our final report by 5 February 2004.

...

14. We expected Stena to focus price increases, post-merger, on its Liverpool–Dublin route. In addition, there would be less incentive for Stena to reduce prices at Holyhead to attract additional

traffic to fill some of its spare capacity, since Stena's Holyhead–Dublin route would capture some of the displaced traffic from Mostyn and Liverpool. We thought it unlikely that either Norse Merchant Ferries or Irish Ferries would seek to increase capacity on the central corridor to deter Stena from exercising its market power, and that the most likely independent reaction of the two main competitors would be to view any price increase by Stena as an opportunity to raise prices themselves, albeit possibly by a little less.

16. We concluded that entry was not intrinsically difficult, and that potential entrants existed who might be prepared to come into the central corridor under appropriate market conditions. However, it would be particularly important for an entrant to have access to suitable berths and sufficient surrounding land available at peak times. Further, an entrant would need to attract and retain an economically viable customer base. We therefore concluded that entry or the threat of entry within the next two to three years would not offset the possible substantial lessening of competition in the central corridor.

17. We therefore concluded that, as a result of the proposed merger, we did not expect there to be a substantial lessening of competition on the northern corridor, but we did expect there to be a substantial lessening of competition on the central corridor.

18. We did not expect relevant customer benefits as defined under the Act. We considered possible remedies which might be imposed to address the substantial lessening of competition identified.

19. We concluded that prohibiting the transfer of P&O's Liverpool–Dublin route to Stena would be an effective remedy. The second remedy that we put forward related to facilitating access to berths at Dublin port or more generally on the central corridor. Stena proposed an enhanced package of behavioural remedies, aimed at addressing the substantial lessening of competition more comprehensively.

20. We concluded that the second possible remedy related to facilitating access to berths would not in itself enable us to form an expectation of entry occurring in a reasonable timescale and on a sufficient scale to act as a competitive constraint to Stena and hence remedy the substantial lessening of competition identified. We also concluded that the enhanced package of remedies put forward by Stena would not be effective in promoting entry that would act as a sufficient competitive constraint.

21. We therefore concluded that the action that should be taken for the purpose of remedying, mitigating or preventing the substantial lessening of competition was the prohibition of the transfer of the assets used on the Liverpool–Dublin route from P&O to Stena. Given that this would prevent the expected SLC, we did not recommend any action to be taken by others.

Competition Commission Summary of Stagecoach/Scottish Citylink Report
23 October 2006

1. On 15 March 2006, the Office of Fair Trading (OFT) referred the completed joint venture between Stagecoach Bus Holdings Limited (Stagecoach Bus) and Braddell plc (Braddell) in relation to the Scottish bus and coach businesses operating under the megabus.com, Motorvator and Scottish Citylink brands (the joint venture) to the Competition Commission (CC) for investigation and report under the Enterprise Act 2002 (the Act). We were asked to investigate whether one or more 'relevant merger situations' had been created and, if so, whether the creation of that situation or those situations had resulted, or might be expected to result, in a substantial lessening of competition (SLC) within any market or markets in the UK or parts of the UK for goods or services. We published our provisional findings on 16 August 2006. Following an extension to the original inquiry period ending on 29 August 2006, we are required to publish our final report by 24 October 2006.

...

28. Regardless of whether Scottish Citylink services on the Saltire Cross were reconfigured or withdrawn (followed by franchising), or whether Scottish Citylink was sold in its entirety as a going concern to a new owner, we expected that, under the counterfactual, binding constraints would

have remained on Stagecoach from actual competition to its Saltire Cross services from another network operator on that route group.

29. We found that, following the joint venture, competitive constraints on joint venture services on the remaining ten flows of concern on the Saltire Cross from rail services, the car, third party coach services and the threat of entry were weak. Using our profitability model, we also found that there was an incentive as a result of the joint venture for the joint venture to raise megabus fares on these flows and an incentive, although less of one, for fare increases on Scottish-Citylink-branded services. We found evidence of actual megabus fare increases following the joint venture above the level that could be explained by increases in costs, and there was insufficient evidence that increases over and above cost inflation were entirely due to a requirement for fare sustainability. There was also, according to our profitability model, an incentive for the joint venture to decrease service levels on both megabus and Scottish Citylink services.

30. We therefore found that binding constraints on fares and service levels on both megabus and Scottish Citylink services from actual competition had been lost as a result of the joint venture. As a result, we expected that the effect of the joint venture on the Saltire Cross route group would be to lead to prices being higher than would otherwise have been the case and to service levels being lower. We did not consider that there would be efficiency gains as a result of the joint venture that enhanced rivalry in the relevant markets.

31. For these reasons, we concluded that the joint venture has resulted, and may be expected to result, in an SLC in relation to the supply of scheduled coach services on the Saltire Cross route group.

NOTE: It is clear that not all Competition Commission inquiries result in a finding that there is, or is likely to be, a substantial lessening of competition. The *HMV/Ottakar's* Report concluded that the SLC test was not satisfied. Similarly, in the *Heinz/HP* inquiry, discussed above, the Commission concluded that although this merger combined the largest branded sauce suppliers in the UK, and that in the tomato ketchup market there would be very little competition, in fact the Daddies Brand, owned by HP, provided little competitive constraint on the leading Heinz brand prior to the merger, and therefore the merger would not alter the competitive situation on the market.

■ QUESTION

To what extent has the substantive analysis of the effects of mergers by the Competition Commission been affected by the introduction of the new competition-based test?

C: Enforcement

The Secretary of State no longer has any general role in relation to enforcement although the OFT has various powers to accept undertakings and make orders prior to or in lieu of references. However, the main reform has been to enhance the role of the Commission, which will no longer merely recommend remedial action following a negative report. The Commission is now under a duty to remedy the negative consequences of completed or anticipated mergers. The Commission has to decide what action needs to be taken to remedy the anti-competitive outcome of a merger or any adverse effects arising from it (ss. 35(3)–(4) and 36(2)–(3) respectively). The Commission, as with the OFT at the referral stage, is required to consider 'the effect of any action on any relevant customer benefits in relation to the creation of the relevant merger situation concerned' (ss. 35(5) and 36(4)). Customer benefits, for OFT and Commission purposes, are defined in s. 30 as follows:

ENTERPRISE ACT 2002 [S. 30]

Relevant customer benefits

30.—(1) For the purposes of this Part a benefit is a relevant customer benefit if—
  (a) it is a benefit to relevant customers in the form of—
    (i) lower prices, higher quality or greater choice of goods or services in any market in the United Kingdom (whether or not the market or markets in which the substantial lessening of competition concerned has, or may have, occurred or (as the case may be) may occur); or
    (ii) greater innovation in relation to such goods or services; and
  (b) the decision-making authority believes—
    (i) in the case of a reference or possible reference under section 22 or 45(2), as mentioned in subsection (2); and
    (ii) in the case of a reference or possible reference under section 33 or 45(2), as mentioned in subsection (3).

(2) The belief, in the case of a reference or possible reference under section 22 or section 45(2), is that—
  (a) the benefit has accrued as a result of the creation of the relevant merger situation concerned or may be expected to accrue within a reasonable period as a result of the creation of that situation; and
  (b) the benefit was, or is, unlikely to accrue without the creation of that situation or a similar lessening of competition.

(3) The belief, in the case of a reference or possible reference under section 33 or 45(4) is that—
  (a) the benefit may be expected to accrue within a reasonable period as a result of the creation of the relevant merger situation concerned; and
  (b) the benefit is unlikely to accrue without the creation of that situation or a similar lessening of competition.

(4) In subsection (1) 'relevant customers' means—
  (a) customers of any person carrying on an enterprise which, in the creation of the relevant merger situation concerned, has ceased to be, or (as the case may be) will cease to be, a distinct enterprise;
  (b) customers of such customers; and
  (c) any other customers in a chain of customers beginning with the customers mentioned in paragraph (a);
and in this subsection 'customers' includes future customers.

NOTE: Customer benefits are defined fairly narrowly for both referral and remedial purposes and are restricted to the creation of merger-specific efficiencies.

ENTERPRISE ACT 2002 [S. 41]

Duty to remedy effects of completed or anticipated mergers

41.—(1) Subsection (2) applies where a report of the Commission has been prepared and published under section 38 within the period permitted by section 39 and contains the decision that there is an anti-competitive outcome.

(2) The Commission shall take such action under section 82 or 84 as it considers to be reasonable and practicable—
  (a) to remedy, mitigate or prevent the substantial lessening of competition concerned; and
  (b) to remedy, mitigate or prevent any adverse effects which have resulted from, or may be expected to result from, the substantial lessening of competition.

(3) The decision of the Commission under subsection (2) shall be consistent with its decisions as included in its report by virtue of section 35(3) or (as the case may be) 36(2) unless there has been a material change of circumstances since the preparation of the report or the Commission otherwise has a special reason for deciding differently.

(4) In making a decision under subsection (2), the Commission shall, in particular, have regard to the need to achieve as comprehensive a solution as is reasonable and practicable to the substantial lessening of competition and any adverse effects resulting from it.

(5) In making a decision under subsection (2), the Commission may, in particular, have regard to the effect of any action on any relevant customer benefits in relation to the creation of the relevant merger situation concerned.

NOTE: The logical conclusion to a finding that a merger will have an anti-competitive outcome is to prohibit the merger. See the following press release issued under the FTA 1973 as an example:

DTI Press Release P/98/713
23 September 1998, re *Ladbroke/Coral*

Peter Mandelson, Secretary of State for Trade and Industry, announced today that he has decided not to permit the acquisition by Ladbroke of the Coral betting business. Mr Mandelson accepted the findings and recommendations of the Monopolies and Mergers Commission (MMC), and the advice of the Director General of Fair Trading (DGFT), that the merger may be expected to operate against the public interest and that it should be prohibited.
Publishing the MMC's report today, Mr Mandelson said:

'I accept the MMC's unanimous conclusions that the merger would lead to a weakening of price competition at national level to the detriment of punters, have a dampening effect on innovation and reduce punters' choice of major chains of betting shops, as well as reducing their local choice of betting shops in many areas. I also accept their conclusion that as a result of the merger, prices and standards of service in telephone betting would be less favourable to punters.

'I agree with the MMC's recommendation that these adverse effects could only effectively be remedied by requiring Ladbroke to divest the whole of Coral's UK business in order to restore an industry structure conducive to the development of competition.

'Before the merger, Ladbroke was already the largest firm in the UK off-course betting industry with a chain of some 1,900 licensed betting offices (LBOs). With its acquisition of the Coral business, Ladbroke increased its share of all LBOs from 21 to 30 per cent, and its share of off-course betting turnover rose from 26 to 38 per cent. The only other national chain is that of the William Hill Organisation, which has around 1,500 LBOs.

'I accept the MMC's view that there is an important national component to competition in off-course betting services through pricing (particularly in early prices for racing bets, in the odds offered on other sports and numbers betting, and in the terms of betting) and through branding and quality of outlet. The MMC believe this could be enhanced in an appropriate competitive environment and that further development of competition is both practicable and to be encouraged. They noted that as a result of the merger Ladbroke had markedly increased its lead in the national retail betting market and its size relative to William Hill, and that the merger also had the effect of removing Coral, which they consider to have been an important third national competitive force.

'Taking all these factors into account, I have decided to prohibit this merger, and to ask the DGFT to seek undertakings from Ladbroke that within a period of six months they will divest the whole of Coral's UK betting business in a manner approved by the DGFT and which he considers will restore an industry structure which is conducive to the development of competition.

'If satisfactory undertakings cannot be obtained by 23 December 1998 I would then have to consider using my powers to make an Order to enforce these remedies.'

The Competition Commission has been given power to accept final undertakings (s. 82) and make such orders (ss. 83 and 84) as are permitted by Sch. 8 to the Act. This includes divestment whereby the parties must find an 'up-front buyer' for a part of a business, or the sale of certain assets or brands. It is clear that the imposition of structural as opposed to behavioural remedies is the preferred option under UK merger control. (For a fuller discussion, see Hoehn, T., and Rab, S., 'UK Merger Remedies: Convergence or Conflict with Europe? A Comparative Assessment of Remedies in UK Mergers' [2009] ECLR 74.) For remedial action to be taken, two-thirds of the Commission panel must have decided that there is an anti-competitive outcome.

The following is an excerpt of the undertakings given to the Commission following its Report on Stagecoach/Scottish CityLink.

Notice of Acceptance of Undertakings, Stagecoach/Scottish Citylink
29 May 2007

NOTICE OF ACCEPTANCE OF UNDERTAKINGS

The completed joint venture between Stagecoach Bus Holdings Limited and Braddell PLC in relation to megabus.com, Motorvator and Scottish Citylink

Competition Commission acceptance of final undertakings pursuant to

section 82 of and Schedule 10 to the Enterprise Act 2002

Whereas on 23 October 2006 the Competition Commission (CC) published its report on the joint venture between Stagecoach Bus Holdings Limited and Braddell PLC concluding (i) that the joint venture has given rise to an anti-competitive outcome as defined in section 35(2) Enterprise Act 2002 and (ii) that for the purpose of remedying mitigating or preventing the anti-competitive outcome Scottish Citylink Coaches Limited should divest either its 'Scottish Citylink' or its 'Megabus' branded operations on the Saltire Cross route group.

And whereas on 31 January 2007 the CC gave for public consultation notice of the undertakings that it proposed to accept for the purposes of bringing about that divestment

And whereas on 10 May 2007 the CC published a decision stating that having considered the responses to public consultation it proposed to accept the undertakings without amendment

And whereas Stagecoach Group PLC, Braddell PLC and Scottish Citylink Coaches Limited have now offered the undertakings for the purpose of remedying, mitigating or preventing the anti-competitive outcome identified

Now the CC pursuant to section 82 of the Enterprise Act 2002 accepts the undertakings, a copy of which is in the attached annex, and accordingly the reference is finally determined and the undertakings come into force in accordance with section 82.

Signed under the authority of the group

John Baillie

Group Chair

29 May 2007

Note: The undertakings were published following a consultation process on the draft undertakings. This is a typical example of an adverse report followed by divestment undertakings, which are fairly standardized. The undertakings tend to be very technical and legalistic, requiring sale of a 'disposal business' to an 'approved purchaser', with the involvement of a divestment and/or monitoring trustee. The OFT is required to monitor undertakings and orders following a merger investigation report.

D: Public interest cases

The public interest has not disappeared altogether from UK merger control but has been retained in a restricted format, although the furore surrounding the

LloydsTSB/HBOS merger demonstrates its ongoing significance in certain cases. There are 'exceptional' types of mergers in which there are modifications to the general merger control scheme and in relation to which the Secretary of State will continue to play a role, albeit limited. The provisions are complex, even by the EA 2002 standards. In the first place, the Secretary of State may make an intervention notice, under s. 42, to the OFT where there is a relevant merger situation involving a public interest consideration. Following an OFT report, the merger may be referred under s. 45 to the Competition Commission directly by the Secretary of State. Following a Competition Commission report (s. 50), the Secretary of State can decide whether to make an adverse public interest finding (s. 54) and thereafter exercise the enforcement powers available to him under Sch. 7 to the Act. (s. 55). Public interest considerations are specified in s. 58 as follows:

ENTERPRISE ACT 2002 [S. 58]

Specified considerations

58.—(1) The interests of national security are specified in this section.

(2) In subsection (1) 'national security' includes public security; and in this subsection 'public security' has the same meaning as in article 21(4) of the EC Merger Regulations.

(2A) The need for—
(a) accurate presentation of news; and
(b) free expression of opinion;
in newspapers is specified in this section.

(2B) The need for, to the extent that it is reasonable and practicable, a sufficient plurality of views in newspapers in each market for newspapers in the United Kingdom or a part of the United Kingdom is specified in this section.

(2C) The following are specified in this section—
(a) the need, in relation to every different audience in the United Kingdom or in a particular area or locality of the United Kingdom, for there to be a sufficient plurality of persons with control of the media enterprises serving that audience;
(b) the need for the availability throughout the United Kingdom of a wide range of broadcasting which (taken as a whole) is both of high quality and calculated to appeal to a wide variety of tastes and interests; and
(c) the need for persons carrying on media enterprises, and for those with control of such enterprises, to have a genuine commitment to the attainment in relation to broadcasting of the standards objectives set out in section 319 of the Communications Act 2003.

(2D) The interest of maintaining the stability of the UK financial system is specified in this section (other than for the purposes of sections 67 and 68 or references made, or deemed to be made, by the European Commission to the OFT under article 4(4) or 9 of the EC Merger Regulation).

(3) The Secretary of State may by order modify this section for the purpose of specifying in this section a new consideration or removing or amending any consideration which is for the time being specified in this section.

(4) An order under this section may, in particular—
(a) provide for a consideration to be specified in this section for a particular purpose or purposes or for all purposes;
(b) apply in relation to cases under consideration by the OFT, OFCOM, the Commission or the Secretary of State before the making of the order as well as cases under consideration on or after the making of the order.

NOTE: Public interest considerations are currently restricted to national security issues. This section was vigorously debated in Parliament and at that stage the only public interest consideration was 'national security' in addition to 'special public interest cases' where an enterprise involved in a merger is a relevant government contractor, due to concerns over the UK's essential national security interests. Subsections (2A)–(2C) were added by the Communications Act 2003 to deal with freedom of expression and plurality of the media to deal with media mergers. (See, for instance, the Competition Commission Report into *BSkyB/ITV*, December 2007.) Subsection (2D) was added controversially in October 2008 to deal with the stability of the UK financial system during the protracted takeover of HBoS by LloydsTSB. The OFT considered that there was a significant prospect of a substantial lessening of competition in certain banking markets should the merger proceed but the Secretary of State refused to refer the merger to the Commission. In addition there was public concern that the merger would have a devastating effect on the Scottish economy, an issue that had been significant at one stage in the development of UK merger control.

Rodger, B.J., 'Reinforcing the Scottish "Ring-fence": A Critique of UK Mergers Policy vis-à-vis the Scottish Economy'
[1996] ECLR 104, pp. 109–10

The Commission and the magic ring around Scotland

'It is not the function of the Commission merely to promote competition; it is there to ensure market forces do not operate against the public interest'.[35] This section seeks to recount the passing of an era in which considerable weight was given to the regional policy issue as expressed within section 84(d) Fair Trading Act 1973 ('FTA'). There will be an examination of the series of important Commission reports on Scottish takeovers in which the consideration of singularly Scottish effects inherent in the aftermath of such takeovers brought issues such as the loss of employment and autonomous decision-making to the forefront of public debate. Sceptics believed the Commission in particular, and the referring agencies, to be constructing an artificial 'ring-fence' around Scottish companies, thus preventing predator takeovers. This belief was ultimately confounded, although this section will seek to analyse the reasons for the creation of this perception, its veracity and possible consequences.

Most commentators perceive the Highland Distilleries Report by the Commission as the starting point for discussion on this topic.[36] In August 1980 the Commission reported on the proposed merger between Hiram Walker, a Canadian company with an existing Scottish subsidiary (Hiram Walker Scotland), and Highland Distilleries, a Scottish whisky distilling company employing 1,600 people. Fears were expressed over the possibility of reduced investment in the Scottish company following a merger, especially since it was 'inherently unlikely that investment decisions, taken in the Canadian Head Office of a worldwide group with most of its assets and interests outside the United Kingdom, would favour Scotland'.[37] The Commission appreciated the concern of the SDA as to the removal of decision-making centres and, in particular, in this case the loss of marketing functions. They concluded, despite Hiram Walker's avowed intention of maintaining Highland Distilleries' autonomy, that 'the merger is likely to have an adverse effect on career opportunities in Scotland since Highland's top management will be deprived of the opportunity to take strategic decisions'. This admittedly limited effect on career opportunities was important in the Commission's ultimate refusal to allow the merger to proceed, although they indicated that their major concern was the increasing concentration of distillery ownership which would have resulted.[38]

The Royal Bank of Scotland's Board considered in the early 1980s that a merger with a suitable partner was required to enable the group to expand internationally. The Royal Bank's preferred means of expansion was with Standard Chartered, in defiance of a hostile bid by the Hong Kong and

---

[35] MacQueen, 'The Monopolies Commission and the Scottish Factor' [1982] JBL 316.
[36] Hiram Walker/Highland Distilleries HCP (1979/80) 743. Although the issue was earlier recognised in Lonrho/Suits/House of Fraser HCP (1978/79) 261.
[37] Hiram Walker/Highland Distilleries HCP, Note 36 above, at paragraph 6.14.
[38] See Ashcroft and Love, Note 10 above, Chapter 5.

Shanghai Banking Corp., registered in Hong Kong. However, both bids were referred together to the Commission by the Secretary of State amidst a strong Scottish lobby in opposition to any merger or takeover. Evidence was submitted by such organisations as the SDA, Strathclyde University's Fraser of Allander Institute, the Edinburgh Chamber of Commerce and the Bank of Scotland pointing to the possible damage to the Scottish industrial and financial communities if the Royal Bank lost its independence.

The Commission accepted the general arguments that the process of external control via acquisitions had accentuated 'the economic difficulties of regions such as Scotland'.[39] In depicting Scotland as becoming a 'branch economy',[40] they recognised that this could reduce the responsiveness of the local business to local needs. They also realised, importantly, the wider implications of the resulting reduction in local career opportunities.

> Functions such as marketing or product development may be removed from Scotland. Bright young Scots have less opportunity to develop their talents, or realise their potential by leaving. The harm done by such loss or failure to develop their skills goes wider than the direct effect on them and their businesses and to the vigour of a local economy affected by the general level of professional and business skills available there . . . and the effect of losing good people from Scotland or failing to develop their talents adequately, is fundamental.[41]

It was indicated that the impact of these general arguments would vary with each merger, depending 'on the nature of the company and its importance for the economy of Scotland'.[42]

In the instant case, the Commission foresaw 'a detriment to the public interest in Scotland arising from the removal of ultimate control from Edinburgh'[43] owing to the size of the company, the degree of control exercised from Edinburgh and the importance of it and its industry in Scotland. They upheld this objection in the face of assurances from both bidders that control would remain in Edinburgh as it was thought that in practice these were unlikely to be complied with in the long run.[44] The lower priority attached to the decision-making in Scotland would also result in reduced career opportunities and in many able Scots leaving the country. Loss of Scottish control of the Royal Bank of Scotland would be seen as a significant step in the long process of centralisation and of weakening local control over economic affairs. It would reinforce the impression of a 'branch economy' and diminish confidence and morale in Scottish business.[45]

MacQueen recognises this report as simultaneously the high and low point of the supremacy of regional considerations over purely commercial ones. Following this report, as Baur indicated, a theory was emerging that Scottish companies were becoming almost bid-proof and that 'a magic political ring-fence [had] been erected to protect them from predators'.[46] The present writer believes neither view to be a proper analysis, nor for that matter can either of the two extremes be of benefit to the Scottish economy. An absolute and artificial 'ring-fence' would inhibit takeovers of ailing Scottish companies in need of a boost for various reasons,[47] yet an exceptional protection would appear rather haphazard in the light of the literature on the expectation of detrimental effects from takeovers on the Scottish economy.

---

[39] The Hong Kong and Shanghai Banking Corp./Standard Chartered Bank/The Royal Bank of Scotland Group, Cmnd 8472 (1982), at paragraph 12.7. See also the earlier report, Lonrho/House of Fraser HCP (1981/82) 73.

[40] Ibid., at paragraph 12.8.

[41] Ibid., at paragraph 12.9.

[42] Ibid., at paragraph 12.11.

[43] Ibid., at paragraph 12.16.

[44] Compare later events in the Guinness/Distillers and BP/Britoil takeovers.

[45] The report contained two dissentient speeches by Mr Smethurst and Sir Alan Neale. See the views of MacQueen, Note 35 above, particularly at 318. It is interesting to note that there have been recent reports of further purported hostile bids for the Royal Bank.

[46] Baur, Note 34 above.

[47] See for instance Ashcroft and Love, Note 10 above, and the findings in their study that many of the acquisitions were actively sought after by the acquiree.

These reports created neither a 'ring-fence' nor an exceptional circumstance.[48] It highlighted at the time, and in the circumstances, the precedence attached by the Commission to 'regional policy' implications under section 84(d), albeit in the case of an exceptionally significant Scottish company. However, the mythical existence of an artificial 'ring-fence' around Scottish companies displeased both the City and 'free-marketeers', who were keen on restricting the grounds on which mergers could be declared against the public interest.

NOTE: This article demonstrated the importance of a particular non-competition-related issue in a series of Commission inquiries under the FTA 1973 prior to the application of the Tebbitt doctrine in referral policy where the public interest concern was the balanced distribution of employment and wealth in the UK. The great irony is that the financial stability public interest ground was used as a justification for the non-referral of the LLoydsTSB/HBoS merger in 2008 when that merger raised concerns about competition and the Scottish economy public interest.

■ QUESTIONS

Do you agree that ministerial involvement in the merger control process should be removed?

To what extent does the retention of a more limited role support the view that merger control raises important issues concerning democratic accountability and that the mantra 'removing politics from UK merger control' is unachievable?

E: Review

Any decision by the OFT or Competition Commission (or Secretary of State) is subject to judicial review by the Competition Appeal Tribunal ('CAT') and thereafter appeal to the Court of Appeal in England and Wales or the Court of Session in Scotland. The CAT has been involved in a number of challenges by third parties, unsatisfied about the non-referral of a merger by the OFT (e.g. *IBA Health Ltd* v *OFT* [2003 CAT 27]) and by the Secretary of State (*Merger Action Group* v *Secretary of State for BERR* [2008] CAT 34 or the acceptance of undertakings in lieu of reference (*Celesio* v *OFT* [2006] CAT 9). In addition, parties involved in a merger have challenged the OFT's remedies (*Cooperative Group (CWS) Ltd* v *OFT* [2007] CAT 24) or the outcome of a Commission merger report, including the remedies imposed (see, e.g. *Somerfield plc* v *Competition Commission* [2006] CAT 4; *Stericycle International LLC* v *Competition Commission* [2006] CAT 21; *BSkyB* v *Competition Commission/Secretary of State for BERR* [2008] CAT 25).

■ QUESTION

To what extent do you agree with Goodman's view that the EA 2002 simply charts a 'familiar course' for UK merger control?

FURTHER READING

Wilks, S., *In the Public Interest, Competition Policy and the Monopolies and Mergers Commission*, Manchester, MUP, 1999.

---

[48] On the one hand, owing to the recognised significance of such a major Scottish company as the Royal Bank, and on the other, owing to the awareness by the Commission of wider external effects of such takeovers.

Scott, A., Hviid, A., and Lyons, B., *Merger Control in the UK*, Oxford, OUP, 2006.

Goodman, S., 'Steady as she Goes: the Enterprise Act charts a familiar course for UK merger control' [2003] ECR 331.

Went, D., 'Recent Developments in UK Merger Control—Establishment of Solid Foundations for the New Regime' [2007] ECLR 627.

Hoehn, T., and Rab, S., 'UK Merger Remedies: Convergence or Conflict with Europe? A Comparative Assessment of Remedies in UK Mergers' [2009] ECLR 74.

14

State aid

SECTION 1: INTRODUCTION

One of the principal objectives of the Community competition law rules is to introduce a level playing field throughout the Community. However, this could be distorted if Member States were able to influence the competitive process in the Community by providing their companies with financial assistance in order for them to 'beat competition' from other Member States. The State aid rules seek to limit the extent to which this is possible. This is a controversial area of law and policy, particularly in a recessionary climate, as Governments tend to protectionism in order to support businesses and protect national jobs. This has been dramatically evidenced by the Commission approval of a raft of Member State measures to support the banking sector in the wake of the financial crisis late in 2008.

European Commission, State aid action plan—Less and better targeted state aid : a roadmap for state aid reform 2005–2009 (Consultation document)
Brussels, 7 June 2005 COM/2005/0107 final, paras 5–11

I. A MODERNISED STATE AID POLICY IN THE CONTEXT OF THE LISBON STRATEGY FOR GROWTH AND JOBS

I.1 Rationale for state aid policy: why does the EU need a state aid policy?

5. Ever since the signing of the Treaty of Rome in 1957, state aid policy has been an integral part of competition policy and the European Commission has been in charge of preventing that aid granted by Member States unduly distorts competition.

6. **Competition policy** rests upon the idea that a market-based economy provides the best guarantee for raising living conditions in the EU to the benefit of citizens, one of the primary objectives of the EU Treaty. Functioning markets are an essential element in providing consumers with the products they wish to obtain, at low prices. Competition is furthermore essential to enhance the competitiveness of the European economy, as it creates an environment in which efficient and innovative companies are rewarded properly.

7. State aid control comes from the need to **maintain a level playing field** for all undertakings active in the Single European Market, no matter in which Member State they are established. There is a particular need to be concerned with those state aid measures, which provide unwarranted selective advantages to some firms, preventing or delaying the market forces from rewarding the most competitive firms, thereby decreasing overall European competitiveness. It may also lead to a build-up of market power in the hands of some firms, for instance when companies that do not

receive state aid (e.g. non-domestic firms) have to cut down on their market presence, or where state aid is used to erect entry barriers. As a result of such distortions of competition, customers may be faced with higher prices, lower quality goods and less innovation.

8. Further, it is important to realise that **state aid does not come for free**. Nor is state aid a miracle solution that can instantly cure all problems. Tax payers in the end have to finance state aid and there are opportunity costs to it. Giving aid to undertakings means taking funding away from other policy areas. State resources are limited and they are needed for many essential purposes, such as the educational system, the health system, national security, social protection and others. It is therefore necessary for Member States to make choices transparently and to prioritise action.

9. Article 87 of **the EC Treaty** prohibits any aid granted by a Member State or through State resources in any form whatsoever which distorts or threatens to distort competition by favouring certain firms or the production of certain goods in so far as it affects trade between Member States. The Treaty has given the Commission the task to monitor proposed and existing state aid measures by Member States to ensure that they do not distort intra-community competition and trade to an extent contrary to the common interest. It falls under its responsibility to make sure that the level playing field would be maintained between Member States, no matter their different levels of resources and their different traditions of state intervention in the markets.

10. The Treaty explicitly allows exceptions to the ban on state aid where the proposed aid schemes may have a beneficial impact in overall Union terms. State aid may be declared compatible with the Treaty provided it fulfils clearly defined **objectives of common interest** and does not distort intra-community competition and trade to an extent contrary to the common interest. State aid measures can sometimes be effective tools for achieving objectives of common interest. They can correct market failures, thereby improving the functioning of markets and enhancing European competitiveness. They can also help promote e.g. social and regional cohesion, sustainable development and cultural diversity, irrespective of the correction of market failures.

11. However, state aid should only be used when it is an appropriate instrument for meeting a well defined objective, when it creates the right incentives, is proportionate and when it distorts competition to the least possible extent. For that reason, appreciating the compatibility of state aid is fundamentally about balancing the negative effects of aid on competition with its positive effects in terms of common interest.

NOTE: This excerpt from the Commission's State Aid Action Plan of 2005 highlights that the system is unique because domestic competition systems do not require an equivalent protection against 'beggar thy neighbour' governmental subsidies. The application of the State aid rules is the most contentious area of EU competition policy and has led to political tensions in the past, notably where State aid has been granted to national flag-carrying airlines where they have been uncompetitive and under threat of going out of business. See Soames, T., and Ryan, A., 'State Aid and Air Transport' [1995] ECLR 290. It is clear that a 'neutral referee' is required to supervise the State aid rules and that this role has to be carried out centrally by the Commission. Unlike Articles 81 and 82, there is very limited scope for decentralized enforcement of the State aid rules. See further, Ross, M., 'State Aids and National Courts: Definitions and Other problems—A Case of Premature Emancipation?' (2000) 37 CML Rev, pp. 401–23, below. As indicated above, the State aid rules and their application become potentially problematic during an economic crisis or recessionary period, when Member States are particularly concerned about the viability of their financial institutions and also sensitive to political pressures regarding unemployment should a significant number of major businesses come under threat. Following this brief introduction to the State aid rules, the following section will examine a range of issues related to the prohibition contained in Article 87 of the Treaty. The following two sections will deal respectively with exemptions from the prohibition, focusing on the impact of the General Block Exemption Regulation, and procedure and remedies respectively. The final section will consider recent State aid developments in relation to the ongoing economic crisis.

SECTION 2: THE PROHIBITION

The basic prohibition is contained in Article 87(1) EC. Articles 87(2) and 87(3) EC provide for exemptions from the prohibition.

ARTICLE 87(1) EC

1. Save as otherwise provided in this Treaty, any aid granted by a Member State or through State resources in any form whatsoever which distorts or threatens to distort competition by favouring certain undertakings or the production of certain goods shall, insofar as it affects trade between Member States, be incompatible with the common market.

NOTE: The terms of this prohibition can be broken down into the following constituent elements: advantage; state resources; selectivity; affect trade; and distortion of competition. This should allow parties to ascertain whether a measure constitutes State aid under Article 87(1) EC which would thereby require notification to the Commission under Article 88(3) EC. It should be noted that the introduction of a Regulation on State Aid procedures in 1999 (Council Regulation (EC) No 659/1999 of 22 March 1999 laying down detailed rules for the application of Article 93 EC of the EC Treaty, OJ, 1999, L 83/1) did not further clarify the scope of Article 87(1) EC, and it is the case law of the Court which sheds light on each of these issues.

A: Advantage

Article 87(1) EC refers to aid in any form whatsoever and therefore the Commission and Court have sought to ascertain how wide this phrase ought to be interpreted. The first point to note is that the concept of aid is objective, irrespective of its purpose.

France v Commission
(Case C-241/94) [1996] ECR I-4551

French legislation provided for contributions by the French Government through the *Fonds National d'Emploi* ('FNE'), a state body, to redundancy and redeployment costs involved in a social plan required to be drawn up by the undertaking following a restructuring. Did this amount to aid within Article 87(1)?

[19] It must be borne in mind that Article 92(1) of the Treaty provides that any aid granted by a Member State, or through State resources in any form whatsoever, which distorts or threatens to distort competition by favouring certain undertakings or the production of certain goods is incompatible with the common market.

[20] According to settled case-law, Article 92(1) does not distinguish between measures of State intervention by reference to their causes or aims but defines them in relation to their effects (Case 173/73 *Italy v Commission* [1974] ECR 709, paragraph 13).

[21] The social character of the FNE assistance is not therefore sufficient to exclude it outright from being categorized as aid for the purposes of Article 92 of the Treaty.

[22] It must also be noted that FNE intervention is not limited sectorially or territorially or by reference to a restricted category of undertakings.

[23] However, as the Commission has rightly pointed out, the FNE enjoys a degree of latitude which enables it to adjust its financial assistance having regard to a number of considerations such

as, in particular, the choice of beneficiaries, the amount of the financial assistance and the conditions under which it is provided. The French Government itself concedes that the administration may depart from its own guidelines where particular circumstances justify that course of action.

[24] In those circumstances, it must be held that, by virtue of its aim and general scheme, the system under which the FNE contributes to measures accompanying social plans is liable to place certain undertakings in a more favourable situation than others and thus to meet the conditions for classification as aid within the meaning of Article 92(1) of the Treaty.

NOTE: There may be scope in some situations for parties to argue that the state was not the source of funding. See Joined Cases C-52–54/97 *Viscido* v *Ente Poste Italiane* [1998] ECR I-2629.

More recently the Court has been required to consider the extent to which a party has been favoured by a state measure.

Demenagements-Manutention Transport SA (DMT)
(Case C-256/97) [1999] ECR I-3913, [1999] All ER (EC) 601

A Belgian undertaking facing insolvency was found to have been granted an exceptionally long period of grace for payment of mandatory employees' contributions by the national security office. By sustaining artificially the business of an insolvent undertaking did this constitute State aid?

[17] In order to reply to the first question, it is necessary to determine whether the various components of the definition of State aid in Article 92(1) of the Treaty are present.

[18] It is common ground that in the case in the main proceedings the payment facilities which the ONSS granted DMT were granted through State resources for the purposes of Article 92(1) of the Treaty, inasmuch as the ONSS is a public body established by the Belgian State which has been made responsible, under State supervision, for collecting mandatory employers' and workers' social security contributions and managing the social security system (see, to that effect, Joined Cases C-72/91 and C-73/91 *Sloman Neptun* [1993] ECR I-887, paragraph 19).

[19] As regards the concept of aid, it is settled case-law that that concept is wider than that of a subsidy because it embraces not only positive benefits, such as subsidies themselves, but also measures which, in various forms, mitigate the charges which are normally included in the budget of an undertaking (see Case C-387/92 *Banco Exterior de España* v *Ayuntamiento de Valencia* [1994] ECR I-877, paragraph 13). Where a public body with responsibility for collecting social security contributions tolerates late payment of such contributions, its conduct undoubtedly gives the recipient undertaking a significant commercial advantage by mitigating, for that undertaking, the burden associated with normal application of the social security system.

[20] However, DMT and the Belgian, French and Spanish Governments essentially argue that, where payment facilities are granted for a limited period, the advantage gained is offset in economic terms by the increase in the amounts payable in the form of interest and penalties for late payment, and it is therefore not possible to conclude that there is State aid.

[21] However, it should be noted that any interest or penalties for late payment which an undertaking experiencing very serious financial difficulties might have to pay in return for generous payment facilities, such as those which, according to the order for reference, the ONSS granted to DMT over a period of eight years, cannot wholly undo the advantage gained by that undertaking.

[22] Secondly, it is settled case-law that in order to determine whether a State measure constitutes aid for the purposes of Article 92 of the Treaty, it is necessary to establish whether the recipient undertaking receives an economic advantage which it would not have obtained under normal market conditions (Case C-342/96 *Spain* v *Commission* [1999] ECR I-2459, paragraph 41).

[23] The Commission contends that the payment facilities accorded to DNT amount to a contributions credit and that, in the light of the economic information provided in the order for reference,

it seems highly unlikely that, having regard to its situation, DMT would have been able to finance itself on the market by obtaining a loan from a private investor.

[24] It should be noted in that connection that the ONSS did not, in granting the payment facilities in question, act as a public investor whose conduct must, in accordance with settled case-law (see, in particular, Case C-42/93 *Spain* v *Commission* [1994] ECR I-4175, paragraph 14), be compared to the conduct of a private investor pursuing a structural policy—whether general or sectoral—guided by the longer term prospects of profitability of the capital invested. Indeed, as the Advocate General has pointed out in points 34 to 36 of his Opinion, the ONSS must be held to have acted, *vis-à-vis* DMT, as a public creditor which, like a private creditor, is seeking to obtain payment of sums owed to it by a debtor in financial difficulties (see, to that effect, the judgment in *Spain* v *Commission*, cited above, paragraph 46).

[25] It is for the national court to determine whether the payment facilities granted by the ONSS to DMT are manifestly more generous than those which a private creditor would have granted. To that end, the ONSS must be compared with a hypothetical private creditor which, so far as possible, is in the same position *vis-à-vis* its debtor as the ONSS and is seeking to recover the sums owed to it.

[26] The French Government argues that payment facilities in relation to social security contributions do not constitute State aid if they are granted in identical circumstances to any undertaking experiencing financial difficulties. That would seem to be the case under the regime established by the Belgian legislation. The Commission, however, claims that the ONSS has a discretionary power in regard to the grant of payment facilities.

[27] It follows from the wording of Article 92(1) of the Treaty that general measures which do not favour only certain undertakings or the production of only certain goods do not fall within that provision. By contrast, where the body granting financial assistance enjoys a degree of latitude which enables it to choose the beneficiaries or the conditions under which the financial assistance is provided, that assistance cannot be considered to be general in nature (see, to that effect, Case C-241/94 *France* v *Commission* [1996] ECR I-4551, paragraphs 23 and 24).

[28] It is for the national court in the main proceedings to determine whether the ONSS's power to grant payment facilities is discretionary or not and, if it is not, to establish whether the payment facilities granted by the ONSS are general in nature or whether they favour certain undertakings.

[29] It should also be pointed out that, if payment facilities such as those in the case in the main proceedings constitute aid, they may distort or threaten to distort competition under Article 92(1) of the Treaty by favouring certain undertakings and affecting trade between Member States, especially where the recipient undertaking will, as in DMT's case, be carrying on a cross-border activity.

[30] Consequently, the answer to the first question must be that payment facilities in respect of social security contributions granted in a discretionary manner to an undertaking by the body responsible for collecting such contributions constitute State aid for the purposes of Article 92(1) of the Treaty if, having regard to the size of the economic advantage so conferred, the undertaking would manifestly have been unable to obtain comparable facilities from a private creditor in the same situation *vis-à-vis* that undertaking as the collecting body.

NOTE: This case is a clear application of the various aspects of Article 87(1) EC to the problem. The reference to the term 'manifest' appears similar to the appreciability requirement under Article 81(1) EC. See Ross, M., pp. 439–40, above. See also the discussion of Services of General Economic Interest *infra* and the *Altmark* case in particular.

B: State source of funding

The rationale behind the State aid rules is to prevent companies being subsidized by the state. The first difficulty lies in determining what constitutes an organ of the state for these purposes. It is clear that it extends to local authorities but to what extent does it cover the activity of private bodies acting with state authority?

Compagnie Nationale Air France v Commission (Air France)
(Case T-358/94) [1996] ECR II-2112, [1997] 1 CMLR 492

Air France had been in severe financial difficulties for a number of years and in October 1992 drew up a second restructuring plan aimed at reducing costs. It approached the CDC-P, a wholly-owned subsidiary of the Caisse, a special public body established by statute to assist it in certain financing transactions. Subsequently the Commission adopted a decision declaring that the assistance constituted State aid and was incompatible with the Treaty.

[55] The issue to be examined is whether the investment in question by the CDC-P could properly be regarded by the Commission as arising from conduct imputable to the French State (Case C-303/88 *Italy* v *Commission*, cited above, paragraph 11).

[56] Article 92(1) of the Treaty and Article 61(1) of the EEA Agreement refer to aid granted by the States or through State resources 'in any form whatsoever'. Consequently, those provisions must be interpreted not on the basis of formal criteria but rather by reference to their purpose, which, according to Article 3(g) of the Treaty, is to ensure that competition is not distorted. It follows that all subsidies from the public sector threatening the play of competition are caught by the above-mentioned provisions, it being unnecessary for those subsidies to be granted by the government or by a central administrative authority of a Member State (see, to that effect, Case C-305/89 *Italy* v *Commission* [1991] ECR I-1603, paragraph 13, and *Sloman Neptun*, cited above, paragraph 19).

[57] In the present case, the Court may restrict its examination to the statute of the Caisse. Even though the subscription to the securities in question was formally carried out by the CDC-P, a limited company governed by private law, the applicant has expressly accepted (reply, paragraph 12) that this 'investment was carried out at the decisive instigation of its majority shareholder [the Caisse] and with the funds which the Caisse placed at its disposal'. It follows that, on any view, the subscription in question is imputable to the Caisse. Consequently, the applicant's argument that the CDC-P is independent is irrelevant.

[58] The Caisse was established by the Finance Law of 1816 as an '*établissement spécial*' placed 'under the supervision and guarantee of the legislature'. Its tasks—including in particular the administration of public and private funds composed of compulsory deposits—are governed by statutory and regulatory rules and its Director-General is appointed by the President of the Republic, the appointment of its other directors being a matter for the government.

[59] Those factors are sufficient for it to be held that the Caisse belongs to the public sector. Although it is subject only to the 'legislature', the legislative power is one of the constitutional powers of a State, and thus conduct of the legislature is necessarily imputable to the State.

[60] This reasoning is confirmed by the case-law of the Court of Justice concerning Member States' failure to fulfil their obligations under Article 169 of the Treaty. Under that case-law, a Member State incurs liability whatever the agency of the State whose action or inaction caused the failure to fulfil its obligations, 'even in the case of a constitutionally independent institution' (Case 77/69 *Commission* v *Belgium* [1970] ECR 237, paragraph 15). That assessment also applies in relation to control of State aid, since the Court of Justice has held that the means of redress provided for by the second subparagraph of Article 93(2) of the Treaty is merely a variant of the action for a declaration of failure to fulfil Treaty obligations, specifically adapted to the special problems which State aid poses for competition within the common market (Case C-301/87 *France* v *Commission* [1990] ECR I-307, paragraph 23).

[61] The Commission was accordingly entitled to treat the Caisse as a public-sector body whose conduct is attributable to the French State.

[62] That conclusion is not undermined by the arguments to the effect that the Caisse enjoys legal autonomy from the political authorities of the State, that the appointment of its Director-General, who is subject solely to supervision by an independent supervisory commission, is irrevocable, that the Caisse has a special statute in relation to the *Cour des Comptes*, and that it has

a particular accounting and fiscal regime. Those arrangements are part of the internal organization of the public sector, and the existence of rules for ensuring that a public body remains independent of other authorities does not call into question the principle itself of the public nature of that body. Community law cannot permit the rules on State aid to be circumvented merely through the creation of autonomous institutions charged with allocating aid.

[63] In so far as the applicant then contests the characterization of the investment in question as State aid by pointing to the private source of the funds managed by the Caisse and to the fact that the depositors of those funds may require their repayment at any time, the Court of Justice has held (*Van Tiggele*, cited above, paragraph 25, and Joined Cases 213/81, 214/81 and 215/81 *Norddeutsches Vieh-und Fleischkontor* v *BALM* [1982] ECR 3583, paragraph 22) that in order for the investment in question to be regarded as State aid, it must amount to an advantage granted directly or indirectly through State resources, which presupposes that 'the resources from which the aid is granted come from the Member State'.

[64] The applicant claims that, because they are reimbursable, the funds deposited with the Caisse are not identical to the 'compulsory contributions' considered in Case 173/73 *Italy* v *Commission*, cited above, because it is only the latter contributions which are permanently at the State's disposal. In that regard, it should be observed that in that judgment (paragraphs 15 and 16) the Court of Justice held that the partial reduction of social charges on undertakings in a particular industrial sector was aid within the meaning of Article 92 of the Treaty, since the loss of revenue resulting from it was made good by resources accruing from obligations made compulsory by the State's legislation.

[65] It is true that the present case differs from Case 173/73 *Italy* v *Commission* in that the sums deposited with the Caisse are not non-repayable but may be withdrawn by depositors. Consequently, unlike revenue from taxation or compulsory contributions, those sums are not permanently at the disposal of the public sector. Nevertheless, it is necessary to consider the extent to which the legal status of the funds managed by the Caisse is reflected by economic reality, having regard in particular to the fact that Community law applies to aid granted through State resources 'in any form whatsoever'.

[66] It is to be observed here that deposits with, and withdrawals from, the Caisse produce a constant balance which the Caisse is able to use as if the funds represented by that balance were permanently at its disposal. In that regard, the Caisse may therefore, as the applicant itself observed, 'act as an investor responding to developments on the markets' (application, paragraph 11) by using that available balance, at its own risk.

[67] The Court considers that the investment in question, financed by the balance available to the Caisse, is liable to distort competition within the meaning of Article 92(1) of the Treaty in the same way as if that investment had been financed by means of revenue from taxation or compulsory contributions. That provision therefore covers all the financial means by which the public sector may actually support undertakings, irrespective of whether or not those means are permanent assets of the public sector. Consequently, it is irrelevant that the funds used by the Caisse were repayable. Moreover, there is nothing in the documents before the Court to suggest that the realization of the investment in question was hampered by the refundability of the funds used.

[68] Finally, this conclusion is not undermined by the judgment of the Court of Justice in Case 290/83 *Commission* v *France* [1985] ECR 439, paragraph 15, in which it held that 'Article 92 of the Treaty covers aid which . . . was decided and financed by a public body and the implementation of which is subject to the approval of the public authorities . . .'. That judgment is not to be interpreted as meaning that a finding of State aid always presupposes the existence of approval of the public authorities, even where the financial transaction in question was decided upon and financed by a body which is itself part of the public sector. The Court was merely listing all the factors actually existing in the case before it and went on to conclude from them that, on any view, those factors, taken together, were caught by Article 92(1) of the Treaty. Consequently, even if the investment made by the Caisse in this case was not the subject of approval by the French Government, the fact that the Caisse, belonging to the public sector, used for that investment funds which were at its disposal is sufficient, as explained above, to characterize the investment as State action which may constitute aid within the meaning of Article 92(1) of the Treaty.

NOTE: The Court adopted a wide interpretation of what constitutes state action and therefore was not required to distinguish the apparent requirement set out by the Court in Case 290/83 *Commission* v *France*, [1985] ECR 439, for the existence of approval by a public authority.

The second difficulty is in ascertaining whether the advantage is granted from state resources.

Sloman Neptun Schiffahrts AG v Seebetriebstrat Bodo Ziesemer der Sloman Neptun Schiffahrts AG
(Joined Cases C-72 and 73/91) [1993] ECR I-887

National shipping legislation in the Federal Republic of Germany provided for the employment of foreign seafarers without a permanent abode or residence in the FRG on working conditions and rates of pay less favourable than those of German seafarers.

[18] It is important to note that, under Article 92(1) of the EEC Treaty, any aid granted by a Member State or through State resources in any form whatsoever which distorts or threatens to distort competition by favouring certain undertakings or the production of certain goods is, in so far as it affects trade between Member States, incompatible with the Common Market.

[19] As the Court held in its judgment in Case 82/77 *Openbaar Ministerie of the Netherlands* v *Van Tiggele* ([1978] ECR 25, paragraphs 23–25), only advantages which are granted directly or indirectly through State resources are to be regarded as State aid within the meaning of Article 92(1) of the EEC Treaty. The wording of this provision itself and the procedural rules laid down in Article 93 of the EEC Treaty show that advantages granted from resources other than those of the State do not fall within the scope of the provisions in question. The distinction between aid granted by the State and aid granted through State resources serves to bring within the definition of aid not only aid granted directly by the State, but also aid granted by public or private bodies designated or established by the State.

[20] Therefore it is necessary to determine whether or not the advantages arising from a system such as that applicable to the ISR are to be viewed as being granted through State resources.

[21] The system at issue does not seek, through its object and general structure, to create an advantage which would constitute an additional burden for the State or the abovementioned bodies, but only to alter in favour of shipping undertakings the framework within which contractual relations are formed between those undertakings and their employees. The consequences arising from this, in so far as they relate to the difference in the basis for the calculation of social security contributions, mentioned by the national court, and to the potential loss of tax revenue because of the low rates of pay, referred to by the Commission, are inherent in the system and are not a means of granting a particular advantage to the undertakings concerned.

[22] It follows that a system such as that applicable to the ISR is not a State aid within the meaning of Article 92(1) of the EEC Treaty.

NOTE: The Court here placed significance on the need for a measure to involve charges on public funds in order to constitute State aid. See Slotboom, M., 'State Aid in Community Law: A broad or narrow definition?' [1998] EL Rev 289. The Court is obviously concerned to limit the application of State aid where national legal regimes are involved. The Court confirmed, in Joined Cases C-52–54/97 *Viscido* v *Ente Poste Italiane* [1998] ECR I-2629 that national labour law regimes are excluded from the prohibition as they do not involve any direct or indirect transfer of state resources.

Rodger, B.J., 'State Aid—A Fully Level Playing Field?'
[1999] ECLR 251 at 254–5

Conclusions

The wider significance of this case concerns the coverage and extent of the state aid rules and Community competition law in general. This case merely highlights the problems faced in competition law enforcement by the lack of any clear dividing line between competition law and 'non-competition' law. For instance, industrial policy, environmental policy and other policy sectors have a role in competition policy assessment and, looking specifically at state aid, the goal of the level competitive playing field across the Community would appear to intersect with a whole range of policies at the Community and national level. In response to the earlier cases, *Sloman Neptun Schiffahrts* and *Kirsammer-Hack*, Davies, an eminent labour lawyer, discussed the difficulties involved in the interplay between the state aid rules and labour law in the context of the relationship generally between market integration and social policy.[21] That article noted the different position taken by A.G. Darmon from that adopted by the ECJ in both cases,[22] but its general theme was that in the areas, including state aid policy, where Community law conflicted with national labour policies either any attempt at balancing was avoided by the Court or the reasoning of the Court was hidden. It was suggested that subsidiarity considerations as provided for in Article 3b of the Treaty would be more clearly articulated by the Court.[23]

This acceptance of the broadened potential scope for competition law inevitably has significant effects on the relationship between competition policies and other Community policies and also as between national and Community policies and law. In competition law generally, and particularly under Article 85, the problem of diagonal conflicts arising between the application of Community competition law and national policies such as cultural policy has been evidenced, for instance in the treatment by the ECJ of national systems of resale price maintenance for books.[24] Perhaps it might have been anticipated, given the Advocate General's opinion in the two earlier cases and the developing notions both of what may constitute state aid and of the role of subsidiarity, that the European Court may have revised its earlier pronouncements. However, it appears that at least national labour and social policies will not be subject to state aid scrutiny. This exclusion itself may reflect subsidiarity concerns or more likely the acceptance that Community state aid control has practical limitations, as was noted by A.G. Jacobs in the present case: 'The answer is perhaps essentially a pragmatic one: to investigate all such regimes would entail an enquiry on the basis of the Treaty alone into the entire social and economic life of a member state'.[25]

NOTE: The Advocate General's comments are self-explanatory as to the perceived limits of the State aid prohibition.

C: Selectivity

This aspect requires one to differentiate between general economic measures and those measures which are more selective and benefit certain industries or undertakings therein. This provides similar difficulties to those encountered in ascertaining what constitutes state resources. General tax measures would not constitute State aid but specific and targeted tax reductions and differential rates of taxation may.

[21] P. Davies, 'Market Integration and Social Policy in the Court of Justice', [1995] I.L.J., Vol. 24, 49.

[22] He noted for instance that 'The Court was from the outset in favour of the solution which involved no further broadening of Article 92 and thus the exclusion of the labour law provisions *in limine*. The Advocate General..., by contrast, was in favour of bringing the labour law provisions into the net and subjecting them to Community law evaluation' (at pp. 59–60).

[23] See generally Joerges, for instance, 'The Impact of European Integration on Private Law: Reductionist Perceptions, True Conflicts and a New Constitutionalist Perspective', 1997 3 ELJ 378.

[24] Schmid, 'Diagonal Conflicts: Europeanised Competition Law with National Law', paper presented at Private Law Adjudication in the European Multi-level System, a workshop at the EUI, Florence, October 2–3, 1998, as yet unpublished.

[25] at para. 16.

Industrie Aeronautiche E Meccaniche Rinaldo Piaggio SpA v *International Factors Italia SpA (Ifitalia), Dornier Luftfahrt GmbH and Ministero della Difesa*
(Case C-295/97) [1999] ECR I-3735, [2000] 3 CMLR 825

Piaggio bought three aircraft for the Italian armed forces from the German company Dornier. In 1994, Piaggio was placed under special administration under Italian legislation for large companies in difficulties. In these circumstances the legislation provided, *inter alia,* for payments by insolvent undertakings in the two years prior to the decree of insolvency to be set aside for the benefit of the body of creditors and for the state to guarantee certain debts. On the basis of these provisions, Piaggio sought to recover the sums paid to Dornier, which claimed in its defence that the provisions in question were contrary to the Community rules on State aid.

[34] As the Court has already held, the concept of aid is wider than that of a subsidy because it embraces not only positive benefits, such as subsidies themselves, but also measures which, in various forms, mitigate the charges which are normally included in the budget of an undertaking and which, without therefore being subsidies in the strict meaning of the word, are similar in character and have the same effect (Case C-387/92 *Banco Exterior de España* v *Ayuntamiento de Valencia* [1994] ECR I-877, paragraph 13; *Ecotrade*, paragraph 34).

[35] The expression 'aid', within the meaning of Article 92(1) of the Treaty, necessarily implies advantages granted directly or indirectly through State resources or constituting an additional charge for the State or for bodies designated or established by the State for that purpose (see, in particular, Joined Cases C-52/97 to C-54/97 *Viscido and Others* v *Ente Poste Italiane* [1998] ECR I-2629, paragraph 13).

[36] By analogy with what the Court held in *Ecotrade* concerning Article 4c of the ECSC Treaty, several characteristics of the system established by Law No 95/79, particularly in the light of the facts in the main proceedings, might, if the significance attributed to them below were to be confirmed by the national court, make it possible to establish the existence of aid within the meaning of Article 92(1) of the Treaty.

[37] First, it is apparent from the documents before the Court that Law No 95/79 is intended to apply selectively for the benefit of large industrial undertakings in difficulties which owe particularly large debts to certain, mainly public, classes of creditors. As the Court held in paragraph 38 of its judgment in *Ecotrade*, it is even highly probable that the State or public bodies will be among the principal creditors of the undertaking in question.

[38] It is also important to note that, even if the decisions of the Minister for Industry to place the undertaking in difficulties under special administration and to allow it to continue trading are taken with regard, as far as possible, to the interests of the creditors and, in particular, to the prospects for increasing the value of the undertaking's assets, they are also influenced, as the Court held in paragraph 39 of its judgment in *Ecotrade* and as the national court has confirmed, by the concern to maintain the undertaking's economic activity in the light of national industrial policy considerations.

[39] In those circumstances, having regard to the class of undertakings covered by the legislation in issue and the scope of the discretion enjoyed by the minister when authorising, in particular, an insolvent undertaking under special administration to continue trading, that legislation meets the condition that it should relate to a specific undertaking, which is one of the defining features of State aid (see, to that effect, Case C-241/94 *France* v *Commission* [1996] ECR I-4551, paragraphs 23 and 24).

[40] Next, whatever the objective pursued by the national legislature, it would seem that the legislation in question is liable to place the undertakings to which it applies in a more favourable situation than others, inasmuch as it allows them to continue trading in circumstances in which that would not be allowed if the ordinary insolvency rules were applied, since under those rules

protection of creditors' interests is the determining factor. In view of the priority accorded to debts connected with the pursuit of economic activity, authorisation to continue to pursue that activity might, in those circumstances, involve an additional burden for the public authorities if it were in fact established that the State or public bodies were among the principal creditors of the undertaking in difficulties, all the more so because, by definition, that undertaking owes debts of considerable value.

[41] Furthermore, apart from the grant of a State guarantee under Article 2a of Law No 95/79 which the Italian authorities agreed to notify to the Commission in advance, placing an undertaking under special administration entails extension of the prohibition and suspension of all individual actions for enforcement to tax debts and penalties, interest and increases for belated payment of corporation tax, release from the obligation to pay fines and pecuniary penalties in the case of failure to pay social security contributions, and application of a preferential rate where all or part of the undertaking is transferred, the transfer being subject to a flat-rate registration duty of ITL 1 million, whereas the ordinary rate of registration duty is 3 per cent of the value of the property sold.

[42] Those advantages, conferred by the national legislature, could also entail an additional burden for the public authorities in the form of a State guarantee, a *de facto* waiver of public debts, exemption from the obligation to pay fines or other pecuniary penalties, or a reduced rate of tax. It could be otherwise only if it were established that placing the undertaking under special administration and allowing it to continue trading did not in fact entail or should not entail an additional burden for the State, compared to the situation that would have arisen had the ordinary insolvency provisions been applied. It is for the national court to verify those matters, after seeking clarification from the Commission if need be.

[43] In the light of the foregoing, it must be concluded that application to an undertaking of a system of the kind introduced by Law No 95/79, and derogating from the rules of ordinary law relating to insolvency, is to be regarded as giving rise to the grant of State aid, within the meaning of Article 92(1) of the Treaty, where it is established that the undertaking

— has been permitted to continue trading in circumstances in which it would not have been permitted to do so if the rules of ordinary law relating to insolvency had been applied, or

— has enjoyed one or more advantages, such as a State guarantee, a reduced rate of tax, exemption from the obligation to pay fines and other pecuniary penalties or *de facto* waiver of public debts wholly or in part, which could not have been claimed by another insolvent undertaking under the application of the rules of ordinary law relating to insolvency.

NOTE: Despite the underlying problems in ascertaining what constitutes State aid, this case suggests that it is becoming more difficult to argue that a state measure is general rather than selective. In particular, even where measures are of general application, they are more likely to constitute State aid where there exists some discretion in their application. Furthermore, the *Adria-Wien* case ((Case C-143/99) [2002] ECR I-8365) confirmed that the logic of the tax scheme must be transparent and coherent and that there will be selectivity and hence State aid where similar undertakings in a comparable situation are disproportionately affected by a tax measure.

Golfionopoulos, C., 'Concept of Selectivity Criterion in State Aid Definition Following the *Adria-Wien* Judgment-Measures Justified by the "Nature of the General System"'
[2003] ECLR 543 at pp. 548–9 [footnotes omitted]

The general rule emerging from the *Adria-Wien* judgment is that all relevant provisions of a piece of legislation providing for derogations from the general scheme should be justified on the same principle that dictates the application of the measure itself. Such derogations cannot escape being characterised as state aid if they aim at addressing shortcomings or undesirable side effects to a specific sector or industry, especially when linked to the competitiveness of that economic sector at an EU level. The logic of the scheme should be apparent throughout the scheme—all provisions should comply with the basic principle which should be clear and unambiguous. When the legislating authority faces difficulties in justifying its choices under one coherent principle (i.e. especially when this principle changes between publication of the first draft and finalisation and introduction of the relevant legislation), it will be hard to avoid the application of state aid rules based on an argument on the non-selective nature of the measure. It will then have to be assessed under Art 87(3) EC and the relevant state aid rules and guidelines available. In that way, Member States will be obliged to be transparent and consistent, rather than trying to promote their policy decisions when legislating on energy saving and environmental taxes, in line with Community objectives.

Effectively, in the *Adria-Wien* judgment the ECJ confirmed that the criteria comprising the definition of state aid according to Art. 87(1) must be defined strictly. We can see a trend in the latest case law developing towards elaborating and "simplifying" the definition of state aids. In addition to the *PreussenElektra* judgment, where the ECJ interpreted the "transfer of State resources" criterion, and the *Ferring* judgment, where it concluded that measures which may be regarded as compensation for the provision of public services may not be state aid within the meaning of Article 87(1), the ECJ has now provided guidance on the main types of assistance that escape being aid. We should expect the debate to continue, as these issues have not apparently been resolved.... Whilst it is not workable to establish a fixed test on what constitutes state aid, especially in cases of fiscal aid, the effort to establish a definition that is based as clearly as possible on the principles established by the Court's case law, rather than any motivation behind Member States' policy and industry considerations, is to be welcomed.

D: Affect intra-community trade/distortion of competition

The first aspect is fairly straightforward to satisfy as the granting of State aid will almost inevitably strengthen the competitive position of the aided undertaking(s) in relation to undertakings from other Member States, and thereby affect the flow of trade in the Community. See Case C-173/73 *Italy* v *Commission* [1974] ECR 709, [1974] 2 CMLR 593. Similarly the Court has confirmed that it is sufficient for the Commission to demonstrate the existence of the State aid as indicative of a distortion or potential distortion of competition: Case 730/79 *Phillip Morris Holland BV* v *Commission* [1980] ECR 2671, [1981] 2 CMLR 321. The mere strengthening of the competitive position of the aided undertaking distorts competition. See Case 173/73 *Italy* v *Commission (Textiles)* [1974] ECR 709, [1974] 2 CMLR 593.

Phillip Morris Holland BV v *Commission*
(Case 730/79) [1980] ECR 2671, [1981] 2 CMLR 321

The applicant was the Dutch subsidiary of a major tobacco manufacturer. It requested the Court to annul a Commission decision in respect of proposed government assistance to increase its production capacity. The aim of the aid in question was to help the applicant to concentrate and develop its production of cigarettes by closing one of the two factories which it owned in the Netherlands and by raising the annual production capacity of the second.

[9] The applicant maintains, that, in order to decide to what extent specific aid is incompatible with the Common Market, it is appropriate to apply first of all the criteria for deciding whether there are any restrictions on competition under Articles 85 and 86 of the Treaty. The Commission must therefore first determine the 'relevant market' and in order to do so must take account of the product, the territory and the period of time in question. It must then consider the pattern of the

market in question in order to be able to assess how far the aid in question in a given case affects relations between competitors. But these essential aspects of the matter are not found in the disputed decision. The decision does not define the relevant market either from the standpoint of the product or in point of time. The market pattern and moreover for that matter, the relations between competitors resulting therefrom which might in a given case be distorted by the disputed aid, have not been specified at all.

[10] It is common ground that when the applicant has completed its planned investment it will account for nearly 50 per cent of cigarette production in the Netherlands and that it expects to export over 80 per cent of its production to other Member States. The 'additional premium for major schemes' which the Dutch Government proposed to grant the applicant amounted to Hfl 6.2 million (2.3 million EUA) which is 3.8 per cent of the capital invested.

[11] When State financial aid strengthens the position of an undertaking compared with other undertakings competing in intra-Community trade the latter must be regarded as affected by that aid. In this case the aid which the Dutch Government proposed to grant was for an undertaking organised for international trade and this is proved by the high percentage of its production which it intends to export to other Member States. The aid in question was to help to enlarge its production capacity and consequently to increase its capacity to maintain the flow of trade including that between Member States. On the other hand the aid is said to have reduced the cost of converting the production facilities and has thereby given the applicant a competitive advantage over manufacturers who have completed or intend to complete at their own expense a similar increase in the production capacity of their plant.

[12] These circumstances, which have been mentioned in the recitals in the preamble to the disputed decision and which the applicant has not challenged, justify the Commission's deciding that the proposed aid would be likely to affect trade between Member States and would threaten to distort competition between undertakings established in different Member States.

NOTE: This demonstrates that both of these requirements for a measure to constitute State aid are easily satisfied. The Commission does not have to quantify any actual advantage gained and the Court is unlikely to interfere with the Commission's discretion in making complex economic and social assessment of the issues. See Joined Cases T-132/96 and T-143/96 *Freistaat Sachsen* v *Commission* [1999] ECR II-3663.

However, what is the position if the aid granted is minimal? In this case, the State aid may be regarded as *de minimis*, in a similar way to agreements that are not appreciable under Article 81(1) EC, where it satisfies the following test.

REGULATION 1998/2006
OJ, 2006, L379/5

Article 2 De minimis aid

1. Aid measures shall be deemed not to meet all the criteria of Article 87(1) of the Treaty and shall therefore be exempt from the notification requirement of Article 88(3) of the Treaty, if they fulfil the conditions laid down in paragraphs 2 to 5 of this Article.

2. The total de minimis aid granted to any one undertaking shall not exceed EUR 200000 over any period of three fiscal years. The total de minimis aid granted to any one undertaking active in the road transport sector shall not exceed EUR 100000 over any period of three fiscal years. These ceilings shall apply irrespective of the form of the de minimis aid or the objective pursued and regardless of whether the aid granted by the Member State is financed entirely or partly by resources of Community origin. The period shall be determined by reference to the fiscal years used by the undertaking in the Member State concerned.

When an overall aid amount provided under an aid measure exceeds this ceiling, that aid amount cannot benefit from this Regulation, even for a fraction not exceeding that ceiling. In such a case, the benefit of this Regulation cannot be claimed for this aid measure either at the time the aid is granted or at any subsequent time.

> 3. The ceiling laid down in paragraph 2 shall be expressed as a cash grant. All figures used shall be gross, that is, before any deduction of tax or other charge. Where aid is awarded in a form other than a grant, the aid amount shall be the gross grant equivalent of the aid.
>
> Aid payable in several instalments shall be discounted to its value at the moment of its being granted. The interest rate to be used for discounting purposes and to calculate the gross grant equivalent shall be the reference rate applicable at the time of grant.

NOTE: The Commission was empowered to introduce a Regulation on *de minimis* by Article 2 of Regulation 944/98. Regulation 1998/2006 revised the earlier Commission policy set out in Regulation 69/2001.

E: The market economy investor principle

Throughout the European Union there exists great disparity in the extent to which Member States are involved in public ownership or control of undertakings and the extent to which they also invest in private undertakings. This poses the difficulty that any investment by a Member State in an undertaking would prima facie appear to constitute State aid. The State aid rules seek to avoid this problem by applying the market economy investor principle ('MEIP') to distinguish between investment that would also have been acceptable to a private investor, which is not State aid, and conversely aid that would not have been acceptable to a private investor in a market economy, which is State aid. The following passage indicates the rationale and application of the MEIP.

Abbamonte, G.B., 'Market Economy Investor Principles:
A Legal Analysis of an Economic Problem'
[1996] ECLR 258 at pp. 259–60

> For the purpose of establishing whether a financial transaction between a Member State and an undertaking involves state aid the Commission applies the market economy investor principle ('MEIP'). According to the MEIP the transaction involves state aid if it takes place in circumstances that would not be acceptable to a private investor operating under normal market economy conditions. The MEIP is also used by the Commission to determine the amount of aid involved in the transaction (see below).
>
> Application of the MEIP safeguards the principle of neutrality of the Treaty with regard to the system of property ownership and the principle of equal treatment as between public and private undertakings. The MEIP strikes a balance between the Member States' interest in owning and running individual firms or entire economic sectors and the common interest in safeguarding a system of undistorted competition. The MEIP is a very blunt test; political, social or philanthropic considerations are extraneous to the principle. In treating the State as a venture capital investor and assessing the aid element as the difference between the preferential conditions and market ones, public and private firms are put on an equal footing.
>
> The MEIP has been devised by the Commission and endorsed by the Council. On several occasions the Court of Justice has confirmed the validity of the principle, by stating that in order to determine if the public investment amounts to state aid the criterion is that of the possibility for the undertaking 'of raising finance on the private capital market'. In its first judgments the Court appeared to compare the behaviour of the State to that of an ordinary private investor who normally seeks to maximise profits. According to the Court, 'the test is, in particular, whether in similar circumstances a private shareholder, having regard to the foreseeability of obtaining a return and leaving aside all social, regional-policy and sectoral considerations, would have subscribed to the capital in question.' ...

In the *Alfa Romeo* case the Court stated that

'In order to determine whether such measures are in the nature of State aid, it is necessary to consider whether in similar circumstances a private investor of a size comparable to that of the bodies administering the public sector might have provided capital of such an amount.'

In the *ENI-Lanerossi* case the Court noted that:

'when injections of capital by a public investor disregard any prospect of profitability, even in the long term, such provision of capital must be regarded as aid within the meaning of Article 92 of the Treaty...'

NOTE: As Abbamonte notes, this is a particularly difficult exercise for the Commission. The task has been facilitated to an extent by Commission Directive 2006/111/EC of 16 November 2006 on the transparency of financial relations between Member States and public undertakings as well as on financial transparency between certain undertakings OJ, 2006, L381/17. The comparison with a private investor must take into account the future prospects of profitability, even if this is not necessary in the short term. The next case demonstrates how the Commission applies the MEIP.

Neue Maxhutte Stahlwerke v Commission

(Joined Cases T-129/95, T-2/95, and T-97/96) [1999] ECR II-17, [1999] 3 CMLR 366 at paras 104–9 and 116

NMS, a German steel production company, sought annulment of a decision by the Commission that State aid had been granted to it by German authorities.

[104] It is common ground that the financial contributions provided for in the context of the privatisation of NMS and the loans granted by Bavaria constitute a transfer of public resources to a steel undertaking. In order to determine whether such a transfer constitutes state aid within the meaning of Article 4(c) of the ECSC Treaty, it is necessary to consider whether in similar circumstances a private investor of a size comparable to that of the bodies administering the public sector might have provided capital of such an amount (see the judgments in *Alfa Romeo*, cited in paragraph 75 above, paragraph 19, and in *Hytasa*, cited in paragraph 75 above, paragraph 21).

[105] The private investor test emanates from the principle that the public and private sectors are to be treated equally. Pursuant to that principle, capital placed directly or indirectly at the disposal of an undertaking by the State in circumstances which correspond to normal market conditions cannot be regarded as state aid (judgments in *ENI-Lanerossi*, cited in paragraph 76 above, paragraph 20, and in Case T-358/94 *Air France* v *Commission* [1996] ECR II-2109, paragraph 70).

[106] The Court of Justice has held, in the context of the application of Article 92(1) of the EC Treaty, that the consideration by the Commission of the question whether a particular measure may be regarded as aid, where the State had allegedly not acted 'as an ordinary economic agent', involves a complex economic appraisal (see the judgment in Case C-56/93 *Belgium* v *Commission* [1996] ECR I-723, paragraphs 10 and 11; see also the judgment in *Air France*, cited in the preceding paragraph, paragraph 71). The consideration of this same question in the context of the application of Article 4(c) of the ECSC Treaty requires equally complex appraisals of the same kind.

[107] It is in the light of the above considerations that the arguments put forward in the case must be assessed.

[108] While acknowledging that the private investor test is the essential point of reference, the applicants strive to demonstrate that the defendant's interpretation of this criterion is too narrow in the present case and consequently incorrect.

[109] In this regard, it is clear that although the conduct of a private investor with which that of a public investor pursuing economic policy aims must be compared need not be the conduct of an ordinary investor laying out capital with a view to realising a profit in the relatively short term, it must at least be the conduct of a private holding company or a private group of undertakings

pursuing a structural policy—whether general or sectoral—and guided by prospects of profitability in the longer term (judgment in *Alfa Romeo*, cited in paragraph 75 above, paragraph 20).

[116] Contrary to what is maintained by the applicants in Case T-129/95, when injections of capital by a public investor disregard any prospect of profitability, even in the long term, such provision of capital constitutes state aid (judgment in *ENI-Lanerossi*, cited in paragraph 76 above, paragraph 22). A redirection of the activities of the recipient undertaking can justify an injection of capital only if there is a reasonable likelihood that the assisted undertaking will become profitable again.

NOTE: This issue arose under the relevant provisions of the ECSC Treaty but the Court noted that the principles were the same as those under the EC Treaty. There is a wide range of scenarios in which the MEIP will be applied to ascertain whether State aid has been granted. The most obvious are by direct capital and equity injections by the state and in these circumstances the Commission will normally require the existence of a viable restructuring plan as the basis for investment in a loss-making undertaking. The Court has confirmed that review of the Commission's assessment of the MEIP would be limited to the grounds of procedural irregularity, manifest error, or misuse of powers: see Case T-358/94 *Air France* v *Commission* [1996] ECR II-2109, [1997] 1 CMLR 492. State aid comprises more than mere cash subsidies or loans and also extends, *inter alia*, to loan guarantees, where the undertaking would not have been given a loan, or would have faced a higher interest repayment rate, without the guarantee of repayment by the state in the event of default. See Commission Notice on the application of Articles 87 and 88 of the EC Treaty to State Aids in the form of Guarantees, OJ, 2000, C71/7.

■ QUESTION

Do you consider the application of the MEIP to be justified or too restrictive of state investment in industry?

F: Services of general economic interest

Sometimes referred to as 'public service obligations', services of general economic interest ('SGEI') are economic activities of particular significance to citizens that would not be supplied if there were no public intervention. These are essentially public services, such as public service broadcasting, or the provision of rural mail delivery services, which are not profitable, and would not exist but for a state subsidy. The relationship between the State aid rules and the State subsidy is a complex issue, considered by the court in the *Altmark* case as follows.

Altmark Trans GmbH v *Nahverkehrsgesellschaft Altmark GmbH*
(Case C-280/00) [2003] ECR I-7747, [2003] 3 CMLR 12 at paras 74–95 [footnotes omitted]

The case concerned the provision of transport services in Germany. Two companies sought to offer local road transport services in Germany, entailing compliance with specified public service obligations. The service was not capable of running without subsidy, although Altmark—the existing service provider—only required a low subsidy. N, which sought to break into the market but was not awarded the requisite licences, contested the award of licences to Altmark, alleging the subsidy amounted to unlawful aid.

74 To answer the first part of the question, the various elements of the concept of State aid in Art.92(1) of the Treaty must be considered. It is settled case law that classification as aid requires that all the conditions set out in that provision are fulfilled.

75 Article 92(1) of the Treaty lays down the following conditions. First, there must be an intervention by the State or through State resources. Secondly, the intervention must be liable to affect trade between Member States. Thirdly, it must confer an advantage on the recipient. Fourthly, it must distort or threaten to distort competition.

76 The national court's question concerns more particularly the second of those conditions.

77 In this respect, it must be observed, first, that it is not impossible that a public subsidy granted to an undertaking which provides only local or regional transport services and does not provide any transport services outside its State of origin may none the less have an effect on trade between Member States.

78 Where a Member State grants a public subsidy to an undertaking, the supply of transport services by that undertaking may for that reason be maintained or increased with the result that undertakings established in other Member States have less chance of providing their transport services in the market in that Member State.

79 In the present case, that finding is not merely hypothetical, since, as appears in particular from the observations of the Commission, several Member States have since 1995 started to open certain transport markets to competition from undertakings established in other Member States, so that a number of undertakings are already offering their urban, suburban or regional transport services in Member States other than their State of origin.

80 Next, the Commission notice of March 6, 1996 on the *de minimis* rule for State aid, as its fourth paragraph states, does not concern transport. Similarly, Commission Regulation 69/2001 of January 12, 2001 on the application of Arts 87 and 88 of the EC Treaty to *de minimis* aid, in accordance with the third recital in the preamble and Art.1(a), does not apply to that sector.

81 Finally, according to the Court's case law, there is no threshold or percentage below which it may be considered that trade between Member States is not affected. The relatively small amount of aid or the relatively small size of the undertaking which receives it does not as such exclude the possibility that trade between Member States might be affected.

82 The second condition for the application of Art.92(1) of the Treaty, namely that the aid must be capable of affecting trade between Member States, does not therefore depend on the local or regional character of the transport services supplied or on the scale of the field of activity concerned.

83 However, for a State measure to be able to come under Art.92(1) of the Treaty, it must also, as stated in para. [75] above, be capable of being regarded as an advantage conferred on the recipient undertaking.

84 Measures which, whatever their form, are likely directly or indirectly to favour certain undertakings or are to be regarded as an economic advantage which the recipient undertaking would not have obtained under normal market conditions are regarded as aid.

85 Mention should, however, be made of the Court's decision in a case concerning an indemnity provided for by Council Directive 75/439 of June 16, 1975 on the disposal of waste oils. That indemnity was able to be granted to waste oil collection and/or disposal undertakings as compensation for the collection and/or disposal obligations imposed on them by the Member State, provided that it did not exceed the annual uncovered costs actually recorded by the undertakings taking into account a reasonable profit. The Court held that an indemnity of that type did not constitute aid within the meaning of Arts 92 et seq. of the Treaty, but rather consideration for the services performed by the collection or disposal undertakings.

86 Similarly, the Court has held that, provided that a tax on direct sales imposed on pharmaceutical laboratories corresponds to the additional costs actually incurred by wholesale distributors in discharging their public service obligations, not assessing wholesale distributors to the tax may be regarded as compensation for the services they provide and hence not State aid within the meaning of Art.92 of the Treaty. The Court said that, provided there was the necessary equivalence between the exemption and the additional costs incurred, wholesale distributors would not be enjoying any real advantage for the purposes of Art.92(1) of the Treaty, because the only effect of the tax would be to put distributors and laboratories on an equal competitive footing.

87 It follows from those judgments that, where a State measure must be regarded as compensation for the services provided by the recipient undertakings in order to discharge public service obligations, so that those undertakings do not enjoy a real financial advantage and the measure thus does not have the effect of putting them in a more favourable competitive position than the undertakings competing with them, such a measure is not caught by Art.92(1) of the Treaty.

88 However, for such compensation to escape classification as State aid in a particular case, a number of conditions must be satisfied.

89 First, the recipient undertaking must actually have public service obligations to discharge, and the obligations must be clearly defined. In the main proceedings, the national court will therefore have to examine whether the public service obligations which were imposed on Altmark Trans are clear from the national legislation and/or the licences at issue in the main proceedings.

90 Secondly, the parameters on the basis of which the compensation is calculated must be established in advance in an objective and transparent manner, to avoid it conferring an economic advantage which may favour the recipient undertaking over competing undertakings.

91 Payment by a Member State of compensation for the loss incurred by an undertaking without the parameters of such compensation having been established beforehand, where it turns out after the event that the operation of certain services in connection with the discharge of public service obligations was not economically viable, therefore constitutes a financial measure which falls within the concept of State aid within the meaning of Art.92(1) of the Treaty.

92 Thirdly, the compensation cannot exceed what is necessary to cover all or part of the costs incurred in the discharge of public service obligations, taking into account the relevant receipts and a reasonable profit for discharging those obligations. Compliance with such a condition is essential to ensure that the recipient undertaking is not given any advantage which distorts or threatens to distort competition by strengthening that undertaking's competitive position.

93 Fourthly, where the undertaking which is to discharge public service obligations, in a specific case, is not chosen pursuant to a public procurement procedure which would allow for the selection of the tenderer capable of providing those services at the least cost to the community, the level of compensation needed must be determined on the basis of an analysis of the costs which a typical undertaking, well run and adequately provided with means of transport so as to be able to meet the necessary public service requirements, would have incurred in discharging those obligations, taking into account the relevant receipts and a reasonable profit for discharging the obligations.

94 It follows from the above considerations that, where public subsidies granted to undertakings expressly required to discharge public service obligations in order to compensate for the costs incurred in discharging those obligations comply with the conditions set out in paras [89] to [93] above, such subsidies do not fall within Art.92(1) of the Treaty. Conversely, a State measure which does not comply with one or more of those conditions must be regarded as State aid within the meaning of that provision.

95 The answer to the first part of the question referred for a preliminary ruling must therefore be that the condition for the application of Art.92(1) of the Treaty that the aid must be such as to affect trade between Member States does not depend on the local or regional character of the transport services supplied or on the scale of the field of activity concerned.

However, public subsidies intended to enable the operation of urban, suburban or regional scheduled transport services are not caught by that provision where such subsidies are to be regarded as compensation for the services provided by the recipient undertakings in order to discharge public service obligations. For the purpose of applying that criterion, it is for the national court to ascertain that the following conditions are satisfied:

— first, the recipient undertaking is actually required to discharge public service obligations and those obligations have been clearly defined;

— secondly, the parameters on the basis of which the compensation is calculated have been established beforehand in an objective and transparent manner;

— thirdly, the compensation does not exceed what is necessary to cover all or part of the costs incurred in discharging the public service obligations, taking into account the relevant receipts and a reasonable profit for discharging those obligations;

> — fourthly, where the undertaking which is to discharge public service obligations is not chosen in a public procurement procedure, the level of compensation needed has been determined on the basis of an analysis of the costs which a typical undertaking, well run and adequately provided with means of transport so as to be able to meet the necessary public service requirements, would have incurred in discharging those obligations, taking into account the relevant receipts and a reasonable profit for discharging the obligations.

NOTE: The Court noted its preference for public procurement procedures in the awarding of contracts for the provision of public service obligations, and the difficulties in satisfying the *Altmark* conditions were subsequently demonstrated in Joined Cases C-34–38/01 *Enirisorse SpA* v *Ministero delle Finanze* [2003] ECR I-14243. The Commission has also published a Framework and Decision on the general issue of public service compensation. (See OJ, 2005, C297/4 and OJ, 2005 L312/67 respectively).

SECTION 3: EXEMPTIONS

There are two types of exemption in respect of the State aid prohibition: mandatory and discretionary.

A: Mandatory exemptions

Article 87(2) EC sets out the mandatory exemptions:

> (2) The following shall be compatible with the common market:
> (a) aid having a social character, granted to individual consumers, provided that such aid is granted without discrimination related to the origin of the products concerned;
> (b) aid to make good the damage caused by natural disasters or exceptional occurrences;
> (c) aid granted to the economy of certain areas of the Federal Republic of Germany affected by the division of Germany, insofar as such aid is required in order to compensate for the economic disadvantages caused by that division.

B: Discretionary exemptions

Article 87(3) sets out the range of discretionary exemptions from the State aid prohibition on the basis that the State aid may contribute to the achievement of Community objectives:

> 3. The following may be considered to be compatible with the common market:
> (a) aid to promote the economic development of areas where the standard of living is abnormally low or where there is serious underemployment;
> (b) aid to promote the execution of an important project of common European interest or to remedy a serious disturbance in the economy of a Member State;
> (c) aid to facilitate the development of certain economic activities or of certain economic areas, where such aid does not adversely affect trading conditions to an extent contrary to the common interest;
> (d) aid to promote culture and heritage conservation where such aid does not affect trading conditions and competition in the Community to an extent that is contrary to the common interest;
> (e) such other categories of aid as may be specified by decision of the Council acting by a qualified majority on a proposal from the Commission.

NOTE: Aid falling within Article 87(3) EC requires to be notified for approval by the Commission. In order to increase transparency in its application of the discretionary rules, the Commission has over the years adopted a range of frameworks and guidelines clarifying how it will assess certain types of aid, in relation to forms of 'horizontal aid' (such as employment aid and regional aid), aid for restructuring of undertakings in difficulty, and also for particular industries, e.g. shipbuilding, transport, etc.

(a) The State aid action plan and the GBER

The Commission launched a comprehensive review of the procedures and rules in relation to State aid in 2005 with a view to reducing the overall amount of State aid under the mantra 'less and better targeted State aid'. A core objective of the Plan was to provide a coherent set of rules. Accordingly in 2008 a General Block Exemption Regulation ('GBER') was adopted which consolidated existing block exemption Regulations into one instrument, covering existing block-exempted types of horizontal aid and including, *inter alia*, environmental aid.

COMMISSION REGULATION (EC) NO 800/2008 OF 6 AUGUST 2008 DECLARING CERTAIN CATEGORIES OF AID COMPATIBLE WITH THE COMMON MARKET IN APPLICATION OF ARTICLES 87 AND 88 OF THE TREATY (GENERAL BLOCK EXEMPTION REGULATION)
OJ, 2008, L214, Preamble, paras 1–7

(1) Regulation (EC) No 994/98 empowers the Commission to declare, in accordance with Article 87 of the Treaty that under certain conditions aid to small and medium-sized enterprises ("SMEs"), aid in favour of research and development, aid in favour of environmental protection, employment and training aid, and aid that complies with the map approved by the Commission for each Member State for the grant of regional aid is compatible with the common market and not subject to the notification requirement of Article 88(3) of the Treaty.

(2) The Commission has applied Articles 87 and 88 of the Treaty in numerous decisions and gained sufficient experience to define general compatibility criteria as regards aid in favour of SMEs, in the form of investment aid in and outside assisted areas, in the form of risk capital schemes and in the area of research, development and innovation, in particular in the context of the implementation of Commission Regulation (EC) No 70/2001 of 12 January 2001 on the application of Articles 87 and 88 of the EC Treaty to State aid to small and medium-sized enterprises, and as regards the extension of the scope of that Regulation to include aid for research and development, the implementation of Commission Regulation (EC) No 364/2004 of 25 February 2004 amending Regulation (EC) No 70/2001, the implementation of the Commission communication on State aid and risk capital and the Community guidelines on State aid to promote risk capital investments in small and medium-sized enterprises, as well as the implementation of the Community framework for State aid for research and development and innovation.

(3) The Commission has also gained sufficient experience in the application of Articles 87 and 88 of the Treaty in the fields of training aid, employment aid, environmental aid, research and development and innovation aid and regional aid with respect to both SMEs and large enterprises, in particular in the context of the implementation of Commission Regulation (EC) No 68/2001 of 12 January 2001 on the application of Articles 87 and 88 of the EC Treaty to training aid, Commission Regulation (EC) No 2204/2002 of 12 December 2002 on the application of Articles 87 and 88 of the EC Treaty to State aid for employment, Commission Regulation (EC) No 1628/2006 of 24 October 2006 on the application of Articles 87 and 88 of the Treaty to national regional investment aid the Community framework for State aid for research and development, the Community Framework for State aid for research and development and innovation, the 2001 Community guidelines on State for environmental protection, the 2008 Community guidelines on State aid for environmental protection and the Guidelines on national regional aid for 2007–2013.

(4) In the light of this experience, it is necessary to adapt some of the conditions laid down in Regulations (EC) Nos 68/2001, 70/2001, 2204/2002 and 1628/2006. For reasons of simplification and to ensure more efficient monitoring of aid by the Commission, those Regulations should be replaced by a single Regulation. Simplification should result from, amongst other things, a set of common harmonised definitions and common horizontal provisions laid down in Chapter I of this Regulation. In order to ensure the coherence of State aid legislation, the definitions of aid and aid scheme should be identical to the definitions provided for these concepts in Council Regulation (EC) No 659/1999 of 22 March 1999 laying down detailed rules for the application of Article 93 of the EC Treaty. Such simplification is essential in order to ensure that the Lisbon Strategy for Growth and Jobs yields results, especially for SMEs.

(5) This Regulation should exempt any aid that fulfils all the relevant conditions of this Regulation, and any aid scheme, provided that any individual aid that could be granted under such scheme fulfils all the relevant conditions of this Regulation. In order to ensure transparency, as well as more efficient monitoring of aid, any individual aid measure granted under this Regulation should contain an express reference to the applicable provision of Chapter II and to the national law on which the individual aid is based.

(6) In order to monitor the implementation of this Regulation, the Commission should also be in a position to obtain all necessary information from Member States concerning the measures implemented under this Regulation. A failure of the Member State to provide information within a reasonable deadline on these aid measures may therefore be considered to be an indication that the conditions of this Regulation are not being respected. Such failure may therefore lead the Commission to decide that this Regulation, or the relevant part of this Regulation, should be withdrawn, for the future, as regards the Member State concerned and that all subsequent aid measures, including new individual aid measures granted on the basis of aid schemes previously covered by this Regulation, need to be notified to the Commission in accordance with Article 88 of the Treaty. As soon as the Member State has provided correct and complete information, the Commission should allow the Regulation to be fully applicable again.

(7) State aid within the meaning of Article 87(1) of the Treaty not covered by this Regulation should remain subject to the notification requirement of Article 88(3) of the Treaty. This Regulation should be without prejudice to the possibility for Member States to notify aid the objectives of which correspond to objectives covered by this Regulation. Such aid will be assessed by the Commission in particular on the basis of the conditions set out in this Regulation and in accordance with the criteria laid down in specific guidelines or frameworks adopted by the Commission wherever the aid measure at stake falls within the scope of application of such specific instrument.

NOTE: The GBER provides the legal rules for exemption in relation to a range of types of permitted horizontal aid. The Commission has set out its policy in relation to a number of types of horizontal aid in Guidelines, and the following are two particular types of aid that have been prominent in practice.

(b) Regional aid

Regional aid can fall within Article 87(3)(a) and 87(3)(c) EC.

GENERAL BLOCK EXEMPTION REGULATION
OJ, 2008, L214, Article 13 [footnotes omitted]

CHAPTER II

SPECIFIC PROVISIONS FOR THE DIFFERENT CATEGORIES OF AID

SECTION 1

Regional aid

Article 13

Regional investment and employment aid

1. Regional investment and employment aid schemes shall be compatible with the common market within the meaning of Article 87(3) of the Treaty and shall be exempt from the notification

requirement of Article 88(3) of the Treaty, provided that the conditions laid down in this Article are fulfilled.

Ad hoc aid which is only used to supplement aid granted on the basis of regional investment and employment aid schemes and which does not exceed 50% of the total aid to be granted for the investment, shall be compatible with the common market within the meaning of Article 87(3) of the Treaty and shall be exempt from the notification requirement of Article 88(3) of the Treaty provided that the ad hoc aid awarded fulfils all the conditions of this Regulation.

2. The aid shall be granted in regions eligible for regional aid, as determined in the approved regional aid map for the Member State concerned for the period 2007–2013. The investment must be maintained in the recipient region for at least five years, or three years in the case of SMEs, after the whole investment has been completed. This shall not prevent the replacement of plant or equipment which has become out-dated due to rapid technological change, provided that the economic activity is retained in the region concerned for the minimum period.

3. The aid intensity in present gross grant equivalent shall not exceed the regional aid threshold which is in force at the time the aid is granted in the assisted region concerned.

4. With the exception of aid granted in favour of large investment projects and regional aid for the transport sector, the thresholds fixed in paragraph 3 may be increased by 20 percentage points for aid awarded to small enterprises and by 10 percentage points for aid awarded to medium-sized enterprises.

5. The thresholds fixed in paragraph 3 shall apply to the intensity of the aid calculated either as a percentage of the investment's eligible tangible and intangible costs or as a percentage of the estimated wage costs of the person hired, calculated over a period of two years, for employment directly created by the investment project or a combination thereof, provided that the aid does not exceed the most favourable amount resulting from the application of either calculation.

6. Where the aid is calculated on the basis of tangible or intangible investment costs, or of acquisition costs in case of takeovers, the beneficiary must provide a financial contribution of at least 25% of the eligible costs, either through its own resources or by external financing, in a form which is free of any public support. However, where the maximum aid intensity approved under the national regional aid map for the Member State concerned, increased in accordance with paragraph 4, exceeds 75%, the financial contribution of the beneficiary is reduced accordingly. If the aid is calculated on the basis of tangible or intangible investment costs, the conditions set out in paragraph 7 shall also apply.

7. In the case of acquisition of an establishment, only the costs of buying assets from third parties shall be taken into consideration, provided that the transaction has taken place under market conditions. Where the acquisition is accompanied by other investment, the costs relating to the latter shall be added to the cost of the purchase.

Costs related to the acquisition of assets under lease, other than land and buildings, shall be taken into consideration only if the lease takes the form of financial leasing and contains an obligation to purchase the asset at the expiry of the term of the lease. For the lease of land and buildings, the lease must continue for at least five years after the anticipated date of the completion of the investment project or three years in the case of SMEs.

Except in the case of SMEs and takeovers, the assets acquired shall be new. In the case of takeovers, assets for the acquisition of which aid has already been granted prior to the purchase shall be deducted. For SMEs, the full costs of investments in intangible assets may also be taken into consideration. For large enterprises, such costs are eligible only up to a limit of 50% of the total eligible investment costs for the project.

8. Where the aid is calculated on the basis of wage costs, the employment shall be directly created by the investment project.

9. By way of derogation from paragraphs 3 and 4, the maximum aid intensities for investments in the processing and marketing of agricultural products may be set at:

(a) 50% of eligible investments in regions eligible under Article 87(3)(a) of the Treaty and 40% of eligible investments in other regions eligible for regional aid, as determined in the regional aid map approved for the Member States concerned for the period 2007–2013, if the beneficiary is an SME;

(b) 25% of eligible investments in regions eligible under Article 87(3)(a) of the Treaty and 20% of eligible investments in other regions eligible for regional aid, as determined in the regional aid map approved for the Member States concerned for the period 2007–2013, if the beneficiary has less than 750 employees and/or less than EUR 200 million turnover, calculated in accordance with Annex I to this Regulation.

10. In order to prevent a large investment being artificially divided into sub-projects, a large investment project shall be considered to be a single investment project when the investment is undertaken within a period of three years by the same undertaking or undertakings and consists of fixed assets combined in an economically indivisible way.

The Commission has set out its policy on when national regional aid is exemptible in Guidelines.

Guidelines on National Regional Aid for 2007–2013
OJ, 2006, C54/13, paras 1–7

---

1. Introduction

1. On the basis of Article 87(3)(a) and (c) of the Treaty, State aid granted to promote the economic development of certain disadvantaged areas within the European Union may be considered to be compatible with the common market by the Commission. This kind of State aid is known as national regional aid. National regional aid consists of aid for investment granted to large companies, or in certain limited circumstances, operating aid, which in both cases are targeted on specific regions in order to redress regional disparities. Increased levels of investment aid granted to small and medium-sized enterprises located within the disadvantaged regions over and above what is allowed in other areas are also considered as regional aid.

2. By addressing the handicaps of the disadvantaged regions, national regional aid promotes the economic, social and territorial cohesion of Member States and the European Union as a whole. This geographical specificity distinguishes regional aid from other forms of horizontal aid, such as aid for research, development and innovation, employment, training or the environment, which pursue other objectives of common interest in accordance with Article 87(3) of the Treaty, albeit sometimes with higher rates of aid in the disadvantaged areas in recognition of the specific difficulties which they face.

3. National regional investment aid is designed to assist the development of the most disadvantaged regions by supporting investment and job creation. It promotes the expansion and diversification of the economic activities of enterprises located in the less-favoured regions, in particular by encouraging firms to set up new establishments there.

4. The criteria applied by the Commission when examining the compatibility of national regional aid with the common market under Articles 87(3)(a) and 87(3)(c) of the EC Treaty have been codified in the 1998 guidelines on national regional aid which cover the period 2000–2006. The specific rules governing aid for large investment projects have been codified in the 2002 Multisectoral Framework. However, important political and economic developments since 1998, including the enlargement of the European Union on 1 May 2004, the anticipated accession of Bulgaria and Romania and the accelerated process of integration following the introduction of the single currency, have created the need for a comprehensive review in order to prepare new guidelines which will apply from 2007 to 2013.

5. Regional aid can only play an effective role if it is used sparingly and proportionately and is concentrated on the most disadvantaged regions of the European Union. In particular the permissible aid ceilings should reflect the relative seriousness of the problems affecting the development of the regions concerned. Furthermore, the advantages of the aid in terms of the development of a less-favoured region must outweigh the resulting distortions of competition. The weight given to the advantages of the aid is likely to vary according to the derogation applied, so that a greater distortion of competition can be accepted in the case of the most disadvantaged regions covered by Article 87(3)(a) than in those covered by Article 87(3)(c).

6. In certain very limited, well-defined cases, the structural handicaps of a region may be so severe that regional investment aid, together with a comprehensive horizontal aid regime may not be sufficient to trigger a process of regional development. Only in such cases may regional investment aid be supplemented by regional operating aid.

7. An increasing body of evidence suggests that there are significant barriers to the formation of new enterprises in the Community which are more acute inside the disadvantaged regions. The Commission has therefore decided to introduce a new aid instrument in these guidelines to encourage small business start-ups in disadvantaged regions with differentiated aid ceilings according to the regions concerned.

NOTE: These guidelines replaced the earlier Commission Communication on regional aid in 1998, OJ, 1998, C74/6. The Guidelines demonstrate the possibility of seeking exemption under either Article 87(3)(a) or 87(3)(c) EC. This type of aid is distinguishable from other forms of permissible horizontal aid as it is based on geographical specificity, and the Commission has determined appropriate aid ceilings for different regions according to the relative weakness of their economies. Exemption will not be granted if the assistance is directed at one undertaking: see Commission Decision (94/696/EC) *Olympic Airways*, OJ, 1994, 1273/22. The State aid exemption for regional aid demonstrates the cohesion between the State aid rules and the broader objective of the Community in reducing economic disparities between the regions of the Community.

(c) Sectoral aid—rescue and restructuring aid

Assistance from government is often sought and granted on the basis that there are circumstances in which State aid for rescuing firms in difficulty and helping them to restructure may be justified. The Commission has issued the following revised Guidelines:

Community guidelines on State aid for rescuing and restructuring firms in difficulty
OJ, 2004, C244/02, paras 24–48

---

3. GENERAL CONDITIONS FOR THE AUTHORISATION OF RESCUE AND/OR RESTRUCTURING AID NOTIFIED INDIVIDUALLY TO THE COMMISSION

24. This Chapter deals exclusively with aid measures that are notified individually to the Commission. Under certain conditions, the Commission may authorise rescue or restructuring aid schemes: those conditions are set out in Chapter 4.

3.1. Rescue aid

3.1.1. Conditions

25. In order to be approved by the Commission, rescue aid as defined in point 15 must:
    (a) consist of liquidity support in the form of loan guarantees or loans; in both cases, the loan must be granted at an interest rate at least comparable to those observed for loans to healthy firms, and in particular the reference rates adopted by the Commission; any loan must be reimbursed and any guarantee must come to an end within a period of not more than six months after the disbursement of the first instalment to the firm;
    (b) be warranted on the grounds of serious social difficulties and have no unduly adverse spillover effects on other Member States;
    (c) be accompanied, on notification, by an undertaking given by the Member State concerned to communicate to the Commission, not later than six months after the rescue aid measure has been authorised, a restructuring plan or a liquidation plan or proof that the loan has been reimbursed in full and/or that the guarantee has been terminated;

in the case of non-notified aid the Member State must communicate, no later than six months after the first implementation of a rescue aid measure, a restructuring plan or a liquidation plan or proof that the loan has been reimbursed in full and /or that the guarantee has been terminated;

(d) be restricted to the amount needed to keep the firm in business for the period during which the aid is authorised; such an amount may include aid for urgent structural measures in accordance with point 16; the amount necessary should be based on the liquidity needs of the company stemming from losses; in determining that amount regard will be had to the outcome of the application of the formula set out in the Annex; any rescue aid exceeding the result of that calculation will need to be duly explained;

(e) respect the condition set out in section 3.3 (one time, last time).

26. Where the Member State has submitted a restructuring plan within six months of the date of authorisation or, in the case of non-notified aid, of implementation of the measure, the deadline for reimbursing the loan or for putting an end to the guarantee is extended until the Commission reaches its decision on the plan, unless the Commission decides that such an extension is not justified.

27. Without prejudice to Article 23 of Regulation (EC) No 659/1999 and to the possibility of an action before the Court of Justice, in accordance with the second subparagraph of Article 88 (2) of the Treaty, the Commission will initiate proceedings under Article 88(2) of the Treaty if the Member State fails to communicate:

(a) a credible and substantiated restructuring plan or a liquidation plan, or

(b) proof that the loan has been reimbursed in full and/or that the guarantee has been terminated before the six-month deadline has expired,

28. In any event, the Commission may decide to initiate such proceedings, without prejudice to Article 23 of Regulation (EC) No 659/1999 and to the possibility of an action before the Court of Justice in accordance with the second subparagraph of Article 88(2) of the Treaty, if it considers that the loan or the guarantee has been misused, or that, after the six-month deadline has expired, the failure to reimburse the aid is no longer justified.

29. The approval of rescue aid does not necessarily mean that aid under a restructuring plan will subsequently be approved; such aid will have to be assessed on its own merits.

3.1.2. Simplified procedure

30. The Commission will as far as possible endeavour to take a decision within a period of one month in respect of rescue aids fulfilling all conditions set out in section 3.1.1 and the following cumulative requirements:

(a) the firm concerned satisfies at least one of the three criteria set out in point 10;

(b) the rescue aid is limited to the amount resulting from the application of the formula set out in the Annex and does not exceed EUR 10 million.

3.2. Restructuring aid

3.2.1. Basic principle

31. Aid for restructuring raises particular competition concerns as it can shift an unfair share of the burden of structural adjustment and the attendant social and economic problems onto other producers who are managing without aid, and to other Member States. The general principle should therefore be to allow the grant of restructuring aid only in circumstances in which it can be demonstrated that it does not run counter to the Community interest. This will only be possible if strict criteria are met, and if it is certain that any distortions of competition will be offset by the benefits flowing from the firm's survival (for instance, where it is clear that the net effect of redundancies resulting from the firm's going out of business, combined with the effects on its suppliers, would exacerbate employment problems or, exceptionally, where the firm's disappearance would result in a monopoly or tight oligopolistic situation) and that, in principle, there are adequate compensatory measures in favour of competitors.

3.2.2. Conditions for the authorisation of aid

32. Subject to the special provisions for assisted areas, SMEs and the agricultural sector (see points 55, 56, 57, 59 and Chapter 5), the Commission will approve aid only under the following conditions:

Eligibility of the firm

33. The firm must qualify as a firm in difficulty within the meaning of these Guidelines (see points 9 to 13).

Restoration of long-term viability

34. The grant of the aid must be conditional on implementation of the restructuring plan which must be endorsed by the Commission in all cases of individual aid, except in the case of SMEs, as laid down in section 3.2.5.

35. The restructuring plan, the duration of which must be as short as possible, must restore the long-term viability of the firm within a reasonable timescale and on the basis of realistic assumptions as to future operating conditions. Restructuring aid must therefore be linked to a viable restructuring plan to which the Member State concerned commits itself. The plan must be submitted in all relevant detail to the Commission and include, in particular, a market survey. The improvement in viability must derive mainly from internal measures contained in the restructuring plan; it may be based on external factors such as variations in prices and demand over which the company has no great influence, but only if the market assumptions made are generally acknowledged. Restructuring must involve the abandonment of activities which would remain structurally loss-making even after restructuring.

36. The restructuring plan must describe the circumstances that led to the company's difficulties, thereby providing a basis for assessing whether the proposed measures are appropriate. It must take account, *inter alia*, of the present state of and future prospects for supply and demand on the relevant product market, with scenarios reflecting best-case, worst-case and intermediate assumptions and the firm's specific strengths and weaknesses. It must enable the firm to progress towards a new structure that offers it prospects for long-term viability and enables it to stand on its own feet.

37. The plan must provide for a turnaround that will enable the company, after completing its restructuring, to cover all its costs including depreciation and financial charges. The expected return on capital must be enough to enable the restructured firm to compete in the marketplace on its own merits. Where the firm's difficulties stem from flaws in its corporate governance system, appropriate adaptations will have to be introduced.

Avoidance of undue distortions of competition

38. In order to ensure that the adverse effects on trading conditions are minimized as much as possible, so that the positive effects pursued outweigh the adverse ones, compensatory measures must be taken. Otherwise, the aid will be regarded as "contrary to the common interest" and therefore incompatible with the common market. The Commission will have regard to the objective of restoring the long-term viability in determining the adequacy of the compensatory measures.

39. These measures may comprise divestment of assets, reductions in capacity or market presence and reduction of entry barriers on the markets concerned. When assessing whether the compensatory measures are appropriate the Commission will take account of the market structure and the conditions of competition to ensure that any such measure does not lead to a deterioration in the structure of the market, for example by having the indirect effect of creating a monopoly or a tight oligopolistic situation. If a Member State is able to prove that such a situation would arise, the compensatory measures should be construed in such a way to avoid this situation.

40. The measures must be in proportion to the distortive effects of the aid and, in particular, to the size and the relative importance of the firm on its market or markets. They should take place in particular in the market(s) where the firm will have a significant market position after restructuring. The degree of reduction must be established on a case-by-case basis. The Commission will determine the extent of the measures necessary on the basis of the market survey attached to the restructuring plan and, where appropriate on the basis of any other information at the disposal of the Commission including that supplied by interested parties. The reduction must be an integral

part of the restructuring as laid down in the restructuring plan. This principle applies irrespective of whether the divestitures take place before or after the granting of the State aid, as long as they are part of the same restructuring. Write-offs and closure of loss-making activities which would at any rate be necessary to restore viability will not be considered reduction of capacity or market presence for the purpose of the assessment of the compensatory measures. Such an assessment will take account of any rescue aid granted beforehand.

41. However, this condition will not normally apply to small enterprises, since it can be assumed that ad hoc aid to small enterprises does not normally distort competition to an extent contrary to the common interest, except where otherwise provided by rules on State aid in a particular sector or when the beneficiary is active in a market suffering from long-term overcapacity.

42. When the beneficiary is active in a market suffering from long-term structural overcapacity, as defined in the context of the Multisectoral framework on regional aid for large investments, the reduction in the company's capacity or market presence may have to be as high as 100%.

Aid limited to the minimum: real contribution, free of aid

43. The amount and intensity of the aid must be limited to the strict minimum of the restructuring costs necessary to enable restructuring to be undertaken in the light of the existing financial resources of the company, its shareholders or the business group to which it belongs. Such assessment will take account of any rescue aid granted beforehand. Aid beneficiaries will be expected to make a significant contribution to the restructuring plan from their own resources, including the sale of assets that are not essential to the firm's survival, or from external financing at market conditions. Such contribution is a sign that the markets believe in the feasibility of the return to viability. Such contribution must be real, i.e., actual, excluding all future expected profits such as cash flow, and must be as high as possible.

44. The Commission will normally consider the following contributions to the restructuring to be appropriate: at least 25% in the case of small enterprises, at least 40%, for medium-sized enterprises and at least 50% for large firms. In exceptional circumstances and in cases of particular hardship, which must be demonstrated by the Member State, the Commission may accept a lower contribution.

45. To limit the distortive effect, the amount of the aid or the form in which it is granted must be such as to avoid providing the company with surplus cash which could be used for aggressive, market-distorting activities not linked to the restructuring process. The Commission will accordingly examine the level of the firm's liabilities after restructuring, including the situation after any postponement or reduction of its debts, particularly in the context of its continuation in business following collective insolvency proceedings brought against it under national law. None of the aid should go to finance new investment that is not essential for restoring the firm's viability.

Specific conditions attached to the authorisation of aid

46. In addition to the compensatory measures described in points 38 to 42, the Commission may impose any conditions and obligations it considers necessary in order to ensure that the aid does not distort competition to an extent contrary to the common interest, in the event that the Member State concerned has not given a commitment that it will adopt such provisions. For example, it may require the Member State:

    (a) to take certain measures itself (for example, to open up certain markets directly or indirectly linked to the company's activities to other Community operators with due respect to Community law);

    (b) to impose certain obligations on the recipient firm;

    (c) to refrain from granting other types of aid to the recipient firm during the restructuring period.

Full implementation of restructuring plan and observance of conditions

47. The company must fully implement the restructuring plan and must discharge any other obligations laid down in the Commission decision authorising the aid. The Commission will regard any failure to implement the plan or to fulfil the other obligations as misuse of the aid, without prejudice to Article 23 of Regulation (EC) No 659/1999 and to the possibility of an action before the Court of Justice in accordance with the second subparagraph of Article 88(2) of the Treaty.

48. Where restructuring operations cover several years and involve substantial amounts of aid, the Commission may require payment of the restructuring aid to be split into instalments and may make payment of each instalment subject to:
    (i) confirmation, prior to each payment, of the satisfactory implementation of each stage in the restructuring plan, in accordance with the planned timetable; or
    (ii) its approval, prior to each payment, after verification that the plan is being satisfactorily implemented.

NOTE: These guidelines revised the earlier 1999 guidelines, but it should be noted that there are specific policies for certain sectors including agriculture, fisheries, and steel. Rescue aid is intended to provide temporary respite from financial problems in order for a longer-term solution to be determined. Restructuring is intended to restore the long-term viability of the undertaking, and requires a viable restructuring plan. The need for submission of a credible restructuring plan, particularly regarding the recipient's long-term profitability, was emphasized by the Court in Case C-17/99 *France* v *Commission* [2001] ECR I-2481. There had been criticism in the past that the Commission had approved aid on this basis to the same company on more than one occasion, for instance in relation to financial assistance given to Air France. See, e.g. Commission Decision (94/653/EC) OJ, 1994, L254/73. Given the more recent focus on potentially beneficial forms of horizontal aid, the Guidelines demonstrate a willingness by the Commission to scrutinize rescue and restructuring aid more closely.

SECTION 4: PROCEDURE AND REMEDIES

The State aid rules are principally enforced by the Commission but the enforcement mechanisms are different from those under Articles 81 and 82 EC. Until 1999 there was no equivalent of Regulation 17/62, the precursor to Regulation 1/2003, in relation to the State aid rules. In order to enhance transparency and legal certainty, the Commission used its powers under Article 89 EC to introduce Regulation 659/99 to codify and modify existing practice in relation to the enforcement of the State aid rules (Council Regulation 659/99/EC laying down detailed rules for the application of Article 93 of the EC Treaty, OJ, 1999, L83/1).

Sinnaeve, A., and Slot, P.J., 'The New Regulation on State Aid Procedures'
(1999) 36 CML Rev, 1153 at 1153–7

1. Introduction: the context and objectives of the procedural regulation

On 22 March 1999, the Council adopted a 'Regulation laying down detailed rules for the application of Article 93 of the Treaty'. This Regulation is long overdue as, in 40 years of State aid policy, the procedural rules had never been codified. While in the anti-trust field, the implementation of Articles 81 and 82 (ex 85 and 86) of the EC Treaty, had taken place very early with Regulation no 17/62 and subsequent rules, Articles 87 and 88 (ex 92 and 93) had, until recently, not been properly implemented by means of a regulation adopted by the Council on the basis of Article 89 (ex 94) EC.

The Regulation was formally adopted by the Council on 22 March 1999, and entered into force on 16 April 1999.

The first objective of the Regulation was to integrate the procedural rules into one coherent and binding legal text. In the absence of a regulation, those rules had been developed over the years through the case law of the Court of Justice and the Commission's practice. Where important procedural issues had arisen or needed to be clarified, the Commission had also issued notices and communications, normally published in the Official Journal. These had provided some clarification, but from a legal point of view, they had contained no more than an interpretation by the Commission of certain procedural questions and did not provide legal certainty. Moreover, the piecemeal fashion in which procedures developed gradually resulted in a fragmentation of rules, which had reduced the clarity of the system provided for in the Treaty. A codification was necessary.

The second and equally important objective of the procedural Regulation was to strengthen the control of aid. Where aspects of the existing system could be considered as hampering the proper functioning and effective enforcement of the rules, the efficiency of the procedural system had to be reinforced, in particular with regard to unlawful aid and its recovery, and in relation to the monitoring of Commission decisions. The Regulation thus also sought to expand the system with some new instruments and to tighten the rules on those points where the current system was not entirely satisfactory.

NOTE: The main aspect of the Regulation concerns the requirement to notify new aid and the subsequent procedure involved. The Regulation gives the Commission powers to monitor and supervise the State aid rules and also introduces a new power under Article 22 to undertake site inspections in relation to its State aid duties. For a fuller discussion of the impact of the Regulation see Sinnaeve and Slot op. cit.

(a) Notification of new aid

Article 88(3) EC of the Treaty provides:

ARTICLE 88(3) EC

3. The Commission shall be informed, in sufficient time to enable it to submit its comments, of any plans to grant or alter aid. If it considers that any such plan is not compatible with the common market having regard to Article 87, it shall without delay initiate the procedure provided for in paragraph 2. The Member State concerned shall not put its proposed measures into effect until this procedure has resulted in a final decision.

NOTE: This is known as the 'standstill' provision and provides that aid cannot be paid until notified and approved by the Commission under Article 88(2) EC. The notification requirement has been codified in Article 2(1) of Regulation 659/99. The Regulation provides no definition of State aid and one is referred back to Article 87(1) EC and the existing body of Court jurisprudence. Notification is not required where the aid is *de minimis* or if it is existing aid already authorized and not exceeded by 20 per cent. The Regulation codifies existing Commission practice in relation to its decision making by providing for a preliminary examination phase and a formal investigation procedure in accordance with Article 88(2) EC of the Treaty (*per* Article 6). See Sinnaeve and Slot op. cit. for a fuller discussion. The recipient of State aid that is subject to a Commission decision has standing to bring an action under Article 230 EC challenging the Commission decision. See Case 332/82 *Intermills* v *Commission* [1984] ECR 3809, [1986] 1 CMLR 614.

Aid which has been implemented prior to notification and approval by the Commission is known as unlawful or illegal aid. What are the consequences of the grant of unlawful legal aid? This question was examined in the following case:

France v *Commission ('Boussac')*
(Case C-301/87) [1990] ECR I-307, paras 9–19

The French Government sought annulment of a Commission decision on aid granted to a producer of textiles, clothing, and paper products—Boussac Saint Frères. The financial assistance was provided without prior notification to and approval by the Commission. The Commission found that it had not been notified in advance of plans to grant the aid and for that reason considered it to be unlawful.

[9] It is necessary, as a preliminary point, to consider a problem raised by the Commission. It takes the view that, since the Court has already recognized the direct effect of the final sentence of Article 93(3) of the Treaty, a clear, binding provision involving public policy, failure to comply with

that provision is in itself sufficient to render that aid unlawful. Such illegality, it contends, makes it unnecessary to examine the matter in detail and entitles the Commission to order recovery of the aid. For that reason, the Commission believes that the Court should refuse to entertain the objections raised by the French Government against that part of the contested decision in which the Commission concludes that the aid in question is incompatible with Article 92 of the Treaty.

[10] The French Government contends that a possible failure to comply with the procedural rules in Article 93(3) of the Treaty cannot by itself render the financial assistance illegal and justify recovery of the aid. The Commission ought, in any case, to have carried out a detailed examination of the disputed contributions.

[11] It must be observed that each of these two arguments is liable to give rise to major practical difficulties. On the one hand, the argument put forward by the Commission implies that aid which is compatible with the common market may be declared unlawful because of procedural irregularities. On the other hand, it is not possible to accept the French Government's argument to the effect that the Commission, when faced with aid which has been granted or altered by a Member State in breach of the procedure laid down in Article 93(3) of the Treaty, has only the same rights and obligations as those which it has in the case of aid duly notified at the planning stage. Such an interpretation would in effect encourage the Member State concerned not to comply with Article 93(3) and would deprive that paragraph of its effectiveness.

[12] In the light of those arguments, it is necessary to examine the problem by analysing the powers and responsibilities which the Commission and the Member States have in cases where aid has been granted or altered.

[13] In the first place, it should be noted that Articles 92, 93 and 94, which form part of Section 3 of the Treaty entitled 'Aids granted by States', lay down procedures which imply that the Commission is in a position to determine, on the basis of the material at its disposal, whether the disputed financial assistance constitutes aid within the meaning of those articles.

[14] Secondly, it should be noted that the Council has not as yet adopted any recommendation under Article 94 of the Treaty for the application of Articles 92 and 93 thereof.

[15] Furthermore, it is necessary to bear in mind the established case-law of the Court. In its judgment of 22 March 1977 in Case 78/76 *Steinike und Weinlig* v *Germany* [1977] ECR 595, the Court held that the prohibition contained in Article 92(1) of the Treaty is neither absolute nor unconditional, since paragraph (3) in particular of that article confers on the Commission a wide discretion to admit aid by way of derogation from the general prohibition in Article 92(1). The assessment in such cases of whether a State aid is or is not compatible with the common market raises problems which presuppose the examination and appraisal of economic facts and conditions which may be both complex and liable to change rapidly.

[16] That was the reason for which the Treaty provided in Article 93 for a special procedure under which the Commission would monitor aid schemes and keep them under constant review. With regard to new aid which Member States might be intending to grant, a preliminary procedure was established; if this procedure was not followed, the aid could not be regarded as having been properly granted. By providing under Article 93 for the Commission to monitor and keep under constant review all aid schemes, the Treaty intended that any finding that aid might be incompatible with the common market should, subject to review by the Court, be the outcome of an appropriate procedure for the implementation of which the Commission was responsible.

[17] The Court has also held (see the judgment of 9 October 1984 in Joined Cases 91/83 and 127/83 *Heineken Brouwerijen BV* v *Inspecteurs der Vennootschapsbelasting, Amsterdam and Utrecht* [1984] ECR 3435) that the purpose of the first sentence of Article 93(3) of the Treaty is to provide the Commission with the opportunity to review, in sufficient time and in the general interest of the Communities, any plan to grant or alter aid. The final sentence of Article 93(3) of the Treaty constitutes the means of safeguarding the machinery for review laid down by that article, which, in turn, is essential for ensuring the proper functioning of the common market. The prohibition laid down in that article on putting any proposed measures into effect is designed to ensure that a system of aid cannot become operational before the Commission has had a reasonable period in which to study the proposed measures in detail and, if necessary, to initiate the procedure provided for in Article 93(2).

[18] In order for it to be effective, the system analysed above presupposes that measures may be taken to counteract any infringement of the rules laid down in Article 93(3) of the Treaty and that such measures may, with a view to protecting the legitimate interests of the Member States, form the subject of an action. With regard to this system, there can be no dispute as to the need to introduce conservatory measures in cases where the effect of practices engaged in by certain Member States with regard to aid is to render nugatory the system established by Articles 92 and 93 of the Treaty.

[19] Once it has established that aid has been granted or altered without notification, the Commission therefore has the power, after giving the Member State in question an opportunity to submit its comments on the matter, to issue an interim decision requiring it to suspend immediately the payment of such aid pending the outcome of the examination of the aid and to provide the Commission, within such period as it may specify, with all such documentation, information and data as are necessary in order that it may examine the compatibility of the aid with the common market.

NOTE: This emphasizes the importance of notification of any proposed new aid schemes. The Regulation codified existing powers to requir e information (Article 10(3)), order suspension of unlawful aid (Article 11(1)), and take provisional action (Article 11(2)). Article 14 confirms the Commission's powers to order recovery of aid except where it is contrary to a general principle of Community law, or recovery is beyond a 10-year limitation period. Earlier Court jurisprudence confirmed that recovery is only limited where it is impossible or would contravene the recipient's legitimate expectations.

Belgium v Commission
(Case C-142/87) [1990] ECR I-959, [1991] 3 CMLR 213, paras 61–3

This was an application for annulment of a Commission decision that aid granted, in various forms, by the Belgian State to a steel pipe and tube manufacturer was illegal, and incompatible with the common market and ordering its recovery.

[61] In principle the recovery of aid unlawfully paid must take place in accordance with the relevant procedural provisions of national law, subject however to the proviso that those provisions are to be applied in such a way that the recovery required by Community law is not rendered practically impossible (see the judgment of 2 February 1989 in Case 94/87 *Commission v Federal Republic of Germany* [1989] ECR 175).

[62] Moreover, that is the reason why the Commission stated at the hearing that the Belgian Government had fulfilled its obligations under the contested measure in regard to the recovery of the aid since, after the dismissal of its application for interim measures by the President of the Court, the Belgian Government sought to have its debt registered as one of Tubemeuse's unsecured liabilities and lodged an appeal against the judgment rejecting that application.

[63] It should be added that any procedural or other difficulties in regard to the implementation of the contested measure cannot have any influence on the lawfulness of the measure.

NOTE: This issue was confirmed in Case C-261/99 *France v Commission* [2001] ECR I-6557. The limitation based on 'legitimate expectations' is interpreted very strictly and is likely to be available only when the Commission was responsible for the recipient's 'legitimate expectations'. See Case C-5/89 *Commission v Germany* [1990] ECR I-3437, [1992] 1 CMLR 117.

Article 88(3) EC has direct effect and therefore an action may be raised before a national court which is required to take appropriate measures to ensure suspension and recovery of any unlawful/illegal aid.

(b) Competitor remedies

Regulation 659/99 gives competitors, who were aggrieved at the granting of State aid, certain rights in relation to the Commission investigation procedure.

REGULATION 659/99

Article 20 Rights of interested parties

1. Any interested party may submit comments pursuant to Article 6 following a Commission decision to initiate the formal investigation procedure. Any interested party which has submitted such comments and any beneficiary of individual aid shall be sent a copy of the decision taken by the Commission pursuant to Article 7.

2. Any interested party may inform the Commission of any alleged unlawful aid and any alleged misuse of aid. Where the Commission considers that on the basis of the information in its possession there are insufficient grounds for taking a view on the case, it shall inform the interested party thereof. Where the Commission takes a decision on a case concerning the subject matter of the information supplied, it shall send a copy of that decision to the interested party.

3. At its request, any interested party shall obtain a copy of any decision pursuant to Articles 4 and 7, Article 10(3) and Article 11.

NOTE: This provision largely codified existing practice, see, e.g. Case T-95/94 *Sytraval v Commission* [1995] ECR II-2651, although it does not afford the same rights as aggrieved competitors in relation to Articles 81 EC and 82 EC.

Competitors can also take proceedings to the Court under Articles 230 and 232 EC in order to challenge a Commission decision approving a State aid measure or a failure to act upon a complaint. One potential problem under Article 230 EC is in determining whether a contested decision is of 'direct and individual concern' to the party. This was discussed by the Court of First Instance in the following case:

British Airways v *Commission*
(Joined Cases T-371/94 and T-394/94) [1998] ECR II-2405, para. 83

British Airways and others challenged a Commission decision to approve a plan by the French authorities to inject FF 20 billion into Air France on the basis that the plan could restore the economic and financial viability of Air France and a genuine restructuring would enhance the competitiveness of the European air industry.

[83] In these contentions, the applicants and the interveners supporting them claim that the Commission authorised aid in an amount exceeding the restructuring requirements of Air France. These contentions are based essentially on the judgment in *Philip Morris* v *Commission* (paragraph 17, cited above in paragraph 79), in which the Court of Justice ruled that Member States could not be permitted to make payments which would improve the financial situation of the recipient undertaking 'although they were not necessary for the attainment of the objectives specified in Article 92(3)'.

NOTE: The Court annulled the Commission decision on the basis of inadequate legal reasoning for approving Air France's purchase of 17 new aircraft, and for failing to analyze the competitive effect the subsidy would have on business on routes outside the EEA in satisfying the conditions of Article 87(3)(c) EC. In relation to the question of admissibility, redress under Article 232 EC is similarly not restricted to potential addressees of a decision. In Case T-95/96 *Gestevision Telecino SA* v *Commission* [1998] ECR II-3407, the Court of First Instance noted, at para. 65, that redress could be sought by those 'whose interests might be affected by the grant of the aid, in particular competing undertakings and trade associations'. See also Case 323/82 *Intermills* v *Commission* [1984] ECR 3809, para. 16. Nonetheless, a works council and trade union representing the sector were not held to be individually concerned in Case C-106/98 *Comité d'entreprise de la Société française de production* v *Commission* [2000] ECR I-833.

As noted above, the notification obligation and standstill clause of Article 88(3) EC have direct effect and competitors may seek a decision in the national courts to prohibit the grant of illegal aid. In addition, where State aid is granted illegally, the Court has confirmed that individuals can seek redress in the national courts.

Syndicat Francais de l'Express International v La Poste ('La Poste')
(Case C-39/94) [1996] ECR I-3547, [1996] 3 CMLR 369, paras 72–6

SFEI and other companies brought an action before the Tribunal de Commerce, Paris, on 16 June 1993 against the Post Office and other parties. They sought a declaration that the logistical and commercial assistance afforded by the Post Office to other parties constituted State aid and had been implemented without prior notification to the Commission. They sought an order, *inter alia*, seeking repayment of State aid and also claimed damages of FF216 million from the defendants.

[72] By its third and fourth questions, the national court asks in essence whether the recipient of aid who does not verify that the aid has been notified to the Commission in accordance with Article 93(3) of the Treaty may incur liability on the basis of Community law.

[73] The machinery for reviewing and examining State aids established by Article 93 of the Treaty does not impose any specific obligation on the recipient of aid. First, the notification requirement and the prior prohibition on implementing planned aid laid down in Article 93(3) are directed to the Member State. Second, the Member State is also the addressee of the decision by which the Commission finds that aid is incompatible with the common market and requests the Member State to abolish the aid within the period determined by the Commission.

[74] That being so, Community law does not provide a sufficient basis for the recipient to incur liability where he has failed to verify that the aid received was duly notified to the Commission.

[75] That does not, however, prejudice the possible application of national law concerning non-contractual liability. If, according to national law, the acceptance by an economic operator of unlawful assistance of a nature such as to occasion damage to other economic operators may in certain circumstances cause him to incur liability, the principle of non-discrimination may lead the national court to find the recipient of aid paid in breach of Article 93(3) of the Treaty liable.

[76] In the light of the foregoing considerations, the answer to the third and fourth questions must be that a recipient of aid who does not verify that the aid has been notified to the Commission in accordance with Article 93(3) of the Treaty cannot incur liability solely on the basis of Community law.

NOTE: This case confirmed that damages may be sought from the relevant State on the basis of the non-contractual liability of Member States for breaches of Community law. See, for example, Case C-46/93 *Brasserie du Pêcheur SA-Factortame III* [1996] ECR I-1029, [1996] 1 CMLR 889 and Hernandez, A.G., 'The principle of non-contractual liability for breaches of EC law and its application to State aids' [1996] ECLR 355. The Court also pointed out that remedies may be sought from the recipient of the aid where provided by the rules of national law. In the legal systems of the UK, this may be possible under the rules on unjust enrichment, although there has been no case law to date. For a fuller discussion, see Rodger, B.J., 'The Interface between State Aid, Unjust Enrichment and Private International Law', in Schrage, E.J.H. (ed.), *Unjust Enrichment and the Law of Contract*, The Hague, Kluwer, 2001. In order to assist the national courts in their limited role in relation to the State aid rules, the Commission has issued guidelines to assist Member States' courts in applying the State aid rules: see http://ec.europa. eu/competition/state_aid/reform/reform.html.

■ QUESTION

To what extent is there scope for decentralization of State aid enforcement in line with the modernization of enforcement of Articles 81 and 82 EC?

SECTION 5: RECENT DEVELOPMENTS: STATE AID AND THE ECONOMIC CRISIS

In the late 1990s the Commission decided that the system of enforcement of the State aid rules required modernization. It introduced Regulation 994/98, which enabled the Commission to introduce Regulations for categories of horizontal aid, thereby exempting them from the requirement of notification. The Commission's policy, following the State Aid Action Plan, has shifted from supporting individual companies to focusing on exempting aid where it contributes to Community 'horizontal' objectives, under the mantra 'less and better targeted State aid'. The adoption of the GBER in 2008 has further consolidated and extended this process. Nonetheless, although the rationale of the State aid rules is the limitation of State 'beggar thy neighbour' subsidies partly due to a concern with State protectionist policies, in the midst of the global economic crisis there has been a recent temporary relaxation of the rules. The financial crisis has resulted in a credit squeeze and this has impacted on the real economy, and in particular SME's, and accordingly the Commission has recognized, in the context of this difficult economic and political climate, the need for well-targeted additional State measures, both in relation to the financial sector and the real economy.

Communication from the Commission, *The application of State aid rules to measures taken in relation to financial institutions in the context of the current global financial crisis*
OJ, 2008, C270/8, paras 1–16

1. INTRODUCTION

1. The global financial crisis has intensified markedly and has now impacted heavily on the EU banking sector. Over and above specific problems related in particular to the US mortgage market and mortgage-backed assets or linked to losses stemming from excessively risky strategies of individual banks, there has been a general erosion of confidence in the past weeks within the banking sector. The pervasive uncertainty about the credit risk of individual financial institutions has dried up the market of interbank lending and has consequently made access to liquidity progressively more difficult for financial institutions across the board.

2. The current situation threatens the existence of individual financial institutions with problems that are a result of their particular business model or business practices whose weaknesses are exposed and exacerbated by the crisis in the financial markets. If such institutions are to be returned to long-term viability rather than liquidated, a far reaching restructuring of their operations will be required. Under the prevailing circumstances, the crisis equally affects financial institutions that are fundamentally sound and whose difficulties stem exclusively from the general market conditions which have severely restricted access to liquidity. Long-term viability of these institutions may require less substantial restructuring. In any case however, measures taken by a Member State to support (certain) institutions operating within its national financial market may favour these institutions to the detriment of others operating within that Member State or in other Member States.

3. The ECOFIN Council on 7 October 2008 adopted Conclusions committing to take all necessary measures to enhance the soundness and stability of the banking system in order to restore confidence and the proper functioning of the financial sector. The recapitalisation of vulnerable systemically relevant financial institutions was recognized as one means, among others, of appropriately protecting the depositors' interests and the stability of the system. It was further agreed

that public intervention has to be decided on at national level but within a coordinated framework and on the basis of a number of EU common principles. On the same occasion the Commission offered to shortly issue guidance as to the broad framework within which the State aid compatibility of recapitalisation and guarantee schemes, and cases of application of such schemes, could be rapidly assessed.

4. Given the scale of the crisis, now also endangering fundamentally sound banks, the high degree of integration and interdependence of European financial markets, and the drastic repercussions of the potential failure of a systemically relevant financial institution further exacerbating the crisis, the Commission recognises that Member States may consider it necessary to adopt appropriate measures to safeguard the stability of the financial system. Due to the particular nature of the current problems in the financial sector such measures may have to extend beyond the stabilisation of individual financial institutions and include general schemes.

5. While the exceptional circumstances prevailing at the moment have to be duly taken into account when applying the State aid rules to measures addressing the crisis in the financial markets the Commission has to ensure that such measures do not generate unnecessary distortions of competitions between financial institutions operating in the market or negative spillover effects on other Member States. It is the purpose of this Communication to provide guidance on the criteria relevant for the compatibility with the Treaty of general schemes as well as individual cases of application of such schemes and ad hoc cases of systemic relevance. In applying these criteria to measures taken by Member States, the Commission will proceed with the swiftness that is necessary to ensure legal certainty and to restore confidence in financial markets.

2. GENERAL PRINCIPLES

6. State aid to individual undertakings in difficulties is normally assessed under Article 87(3)(c) of the Treaty and the Community Guidelines on State aid for rescuing and restructuring firms in difficulty (hereinafter "R&R guidelines") which articulate the Commission's understanding of Article 87(3)(c) of the Treaty for this type of aid. The R&R guidelines are of general application, while foreseeing certain specific criteria for the financial sector.

7. In addition, under Article 87(3)(b) of the Treaty the Commission may allow State aid "to remedy a serious disturbance in the economy of a Member State".

8. The Commission reaffirms that, in line with the case law and its decision making practice, Article 87(3)(b) of the Treaty necessitates a restrictive interpretation of what can be considered a serious disturbance of a Member State's economy.

9. In the light of the level of seriousness that the current crisis in the financial markets has reached and of its possible impact on the overall economy of Member States, the Commission considers that Article 87(3)(b) is, in the present circumstances, available as a legal basis for aid measures undertaken to address this systemic crisis. This applies, in particular, to aid that is granted by way of a general scheme available to several or all financial institutions in a Member State. Should the Member State's authorities responsible for financial stability declare to the Commission that there is a risk of such a serious disturbance, this shall be of particular relevance for the Commission's assessment.

10. Ad hoc interventions by Member States are not excluded in circumstances fulfilling the criteria of Article 87(3)(b). In the case of both schemes and ad hoc interventions, while the assessment of the aid should follow the general principles laid down in the R&R guidelines adopted pursuant to Article 87(3)(c) of the Treaty, the current circumstances may allow the approval of exceptional measures such as structural emergency interventions, protection of rights of third parties such as creditors, and rescue measures potentially going beyond 6 months.

11. It needs to be emphasised, however, that the above considerations imply that the use of Article 87(3)(b) cannot be envisaged as a matter of principle in crisis situations in other individual sectors in the absence of a comparable risk that they have an immediate impact on the economy of a Member State as a whole. As regards the financial sector, invoking this provision is possible only in genuinely exceptional circumstances where the entire functioning of financial markets is jeopardised.

12. Where there is a serious disturbance of a Member State's economy along the lines set out above, recourse to Article 87(3)(b) is possible not on an open-ended basis but only as long as the crisis situation justifies its application.

13. This entails the need for all general schemes set up on this basis, e.g. in the form of a guarantee or recapitalization scheme, to be reviewed on a regular basis and terminated as soon as the economic situation of the Member State in question so permits. While acknowledging that it is currently impossible to predict the duration of the current extraordinary problems in the financial markets and that it may be indispensable in order to restore confidence to signal that a measure will be extended as long as the crisis continues, the Commission considers it a necessary element for the compatibility of any general scheme that the Member State carries out a review at least every six months and reports back to the Commission on the result of such review.

14. Furthermore, the Commission considers that the treatment of illiquid but otherwise fundamentally sound financial institutions in the absence of the current exceptional circumstances should be distinguished from the treatment of financial institutions characterized by endogenous problems. In the first case, viability problems are inherently exogenous and have to do with the present extreme situation in the financial market rather than with inefficiency or excessive risk-taking. As a result distortions of competition resulting from schemes supporting the viability of such institutions will normally be more limited and require less substantial restructuring. By contrast, other financial institutions, likely to be particularly affected by losses stemming for instance from inefficiencies, poor asset-liability management or risky strategies, would fit with the normal framework of rescue aid, and in particular need a far-reaching restructuring, as well as compensatory measures to limit distortions of competition. In all cases, however, in the absence of appropriate safeguards, distortions of competition may be substantial from the implementation of guarantee and recapitalization schemes, as they could unduly favour the beneficiaries to the detriment of their competitors or may aggravate the liquidity problems for financial institutions located in other Member States.

15. Moreover, in line with the general principles underlying the State aid rules of the Treaty, which require that the aid granted does not exceed what is strictly necessary to achieve its legitimate purpose and that distortions of competition are avoided or minimized as far as possible, and taking due account of the current circumstances, all general support measures have to be:
— well-targeted in order to be able to achieve effectively the objective of remedying a serious disturbance in the economy,
— proportionate to the challenge faced, not going beyond what is required to attain this effect, and
— designed in such a way as to minimize negative spill-over effects on competitors, other sectors and other Member States.

16. The observance of these criteria in compliance with the State aid rules and the fundamental freedoms enshrined in the Treaty, including the principle of non-discrimination, is necessary for the preservation of the proper functioning of the internal market. In its assessment, the Commission will take into account the following criteria to decide upon the compatibility of the State aid measures enumerated below.

NOTE: The guidance is based in Article 87(3)(b) allowing for aid to remedy a serious disturbance in the economy of a Member State, and allows Member States to put in place co-ordinated measures to restore confidence in financial markets. A number of such measures have been adopted throughout the EU, including the measures necessary to salvage the Northern Rock bank in the UK in late 2008 and more generally the UK Recapitalisation and Guarantee Schemes introduced to rescue the UK banking sector in October 2008.

In addition, the Commission has extended this more relaxed approach to the crisis in the real economy, by the introduction of a Temporary Community Framework, for measures introduced between 17 December 2008 and 31 December 2010, designed to facilitate access to finance and thereby allow businesses to continue their activities and invest in a sustainable growth economy.

Communication from the Commission, *Temporary Community Framework for State aid measures to support access to finance in the current financial and economic crisis (as amended on 25 February 2009)*
OJ, 2009, C16/01, paras 1.1 and 4.1–4.2.2 [footnotes omitted]

1. THE FINANCIAL CRISIS, ITS IMPACT ON THE REAL ECONOMY AND THE NEED FOR TEMPORARY MEASURES

1.1. The financial crisis and its impact on the real economy

On 26 November 2008, the Commission adopted the Communication 'A European Economic Recovery Plan' ('the Recovery Plan') to drive Europe's recovery from the current financial crisis. The Recovery Plan is based on two mutually reinforcing main elements. Firstly, short-term measures to boost demand, save jobs and help restore confidence and, secondly, 'smart investment' to yield higher growth and sustainable prosperity in the longer term. The Recovery Plan will intensify and accelerate reforms already underway under the Lisbon Strategy.

In this context, the challenge for the Community is avoiding public intervention which would undermine the objective of less and better targeted State aid. Nevertheless, under certain conditions, there is a need for new temporary State aid.

The Recovery Plan also includes further initiatives to apply State aid rules in a way that achieves maximum flexibility for tackling the crisis while maintaining a level playing field and avoiding undue restrictions of competition. This Communication gives details of a number of additional temporary openings for Member States to grant State aid.

First, the financial crisis has a hard impact on the banking sector in the Community. The Council has stressed that, although public intervention has to be decided at national level, this needs to be done within a coordinated framework and on the basis of a number of common Community principles. The Commission reacted immediately with various measures including the adoption of the Communication on the application of State aid rules to measures taken in relation to financial institutions in the context of the current global financial crisis and of a number of decisions authorising rescue aid to financial institutions.

Sufficient and affordable access to finance is a precondition for investment, growth and job creation by the private sector. Member States need to use the leverage they have acquired as a result of providing substantial financial support to the banking sector to ensure that this support does not lead merely to an improvement in the financial situation of the banks without any benefit to the economy at large. Support for the financial sector should therefore be well targeted to guarantee that banks resume their normal lending activities. The Commission will take this into account when reviewing State aid to banks.

While the situation on financial markets appears to be improving, the full impact of the financial crisis on the real economy is now being felt. A very serious downturn is affecting the wider economy and hitting households, businesses and jobs. In particular, as a consequence of the crisis on financial markets, banks are deleveraging and becoming much more risk averse than in previous years, leading to a credit squeeze. This financial crisis could trigger credit rationing, a drop in demand and recession.

Such difficulties could affect not only weak companies without solvency buffers, but also healthy companies which will find themselves facing a sudden shortage or even unavailability of credit. This will be particularly true for small and medium-sized undertakings ('SMEs'), which in any event face greater difficulties with access to finance than larger companies. This situation could not only seriously affect the economic situation of many healthy companies and their employees in the short and medium term but also have longer-lasting negative effects since all Community investments in the future—in particular, towards sustainable growth and other objectives of the Lisbon Strategy—could be delayed or even abandoned.

4. APPLICABILITY OF ARTICLE 87(3)(b)

4.1. General principles

Pursuant to Article 87(3)(b) of the Treaty the Commission may declare compatible with the common market aid 'to remedy a serious disturbance in the economy of a Member State'. In this context, the

Court of First Instance of the European Communities has ruled that the disturbance must affect the whole of the economy of the Member State concerned, and not merely that of one of its regions or parts of its territory. This, moreover, is in line with the need to interpret strictly any derogating provision such as Article 87(3)(b) of the Treaty.

This strict interpretation has been consistently applied by the Commission in its decision-making.

In this context, the Commission considers that, beyond emergency support for the financial system, the current global crisis requires exceptional policy responses.

All Member States will be affected by this crisis, albeit in different ways and to different degrees, and it is likely that unemployment will increase, demand fall and fiscal positions deteriorate.

In the light of the seriousness of the current financial crisis and its impact on the overall economy of the Member States, the Commission considers that certain categories of State aid are justified, for a limited period, to remedy those difficulties and that they may be declared compatible with the common market on the basis of Article 87(3)(b) of the Treaty.

4.2. Compatible limited amount of aid

4.2.1. *Existing framework*

Article 2 of the *de minimis* Regulation, states that:

'Aid measures shall be deemed not to meet all the criteria of Article 87(1) of the Treaty and shall therefore be exempt from the notification requirement of Article 88(3) of the Treaty, if they fulfil the conditions laid down in paragraphs 2 to 5 of this Article. The total *de minimis* aid granted to any one undertaking shall not exceed EUR 200 000 over any period of three fiscal years. The total *de minimis* aid granted to any one undertaking active in the road transport sector shall not exceed EUR 100 000 over any period of three fiscal years. These ceilings shall apply irrespective of the form of the *de minimis* aid or the objective pursued and regardless of whether the aid granted by the Member State is financed entirely or partly by resources of Community origin. The period shall be determined by reference to the fiscal years used by the undertaking in the Member State concerned.'

4.2.2. *New measure*

The financial crisis is affecting not only structurally weak companies but also companies which will find themselves facing a sudden shortage or even unavailability of credit. An improvement in the financial situation of those companies will have positive effects for the whole European economy.

Therefore, in view of the current economic situation, it is considered necessary to temporarily allow the granting of a limited amount of aid that will nevertheless fall within the scope of Article 87(1) of the Treaty, since it exceeds the threshold indicated in the *de minimis* Regulation.

The Commission will consider such State aid compatible with the common market on the basis of Article 87(3)(b) of the Treaty, provided all the following conditions are met:

(a) the aid does not exceed a cash grant of EUR 500 000 per undertaking; all figures used must be gross, that is, before any deduction of tax or other charge; where aid is awarded in a form other than a grant, the aid amount is the gross grant equivalent of the aid;

(b) the aid is granted in the form of a scheme;

(c) the aid is granted to firms which were not in difficulty on 1 July 2008; it may be granted to firms that were not in difficulty at that date but entered in difficulty thereafter as a result of the global financial and economic crisis;

(d) the aid scheme does not apply to firms active in the fisheries sector;

(e) the aid is not export aid or aid favouring domestic over imported products;

(f) the aid is granted no later than 31 December 2010;

(g) prior to granting the aid, the Member State obtains a declaration from the undertaking concerned, in written or electronic form, about any other *de minimis* aid and aid pursuant to this measure received during the current fiscal year and checks that the aid will not raise the total amount of aid received by the undertaking during the period from 1 January 2008 to 31 December 2010, to a level above the ceiling of EUR 500 000;

> (h) the aid scheme does not apply to undertakings active in the primary production of agricultural products ; it may apply to undertakings active in the processing and marketing of agricultural products unless the amount of the aid is fixed on the basis of the price or quantity of such products purchased from primary producers or put on the market by the undertakings concerned, or the aid is conditional on being partly or entirely passed on to primary producers.

NOTE: This temporary framework is also based on Article 87(3)(b) allowing for aid to remedy a serious disturbance in the economy of a Member State. The framework is limited in time to the end of 2010 but extends to all sectors. In addition to the compatible limited amounts of aid (in relation to which the *de minimis* aid ceiling is increased to 500,000 euros per undertaking) it also makes provision for aid in relation to guarantees, aid in the form of subsidized interest rates and aid for the production of green products, although the measures are limited to undertakings that were 'not in difficulty' on 1 July 2008. Any measures require notification and approval although the Commission are seeking to ensure the process is expedited. A number of Member State measures adopted in relation to the real economy under this Temporary Framework have already been approved by the Commission.

■ QUESTION

To what extent do you agree with the accusation that with the adoption of these measures Europe is bribing multinationals and stealing jobs from neighbouring countries by using taxpayers' money to support businesses hit by the economic turmoil—i.e. are strict controls on State aid only feasible in expanding economies?

FURTHER READING

Abbamonte, G., 'Market Economy Investor Principle: A Legal Analysis of an Economic Problem' (1996) 4 ECLR 258.

Hancher, L., et al, *EC State Aids,* 3rd edn, London, Sweet and Maxwell, 2006.

Louis, F., and Vallery, A., 'Ferring Revisited, the Altmark case and State Financing of Public Services Obligations' (2004) 57 World Competition 53.

INDEX